AF819880

Recommended by **Teachers**
Trusted by **Toppers**

All in One

MATHEMATICS

Class 12

EVERYTHING YOU NEED TO SCORE

- Simplified NCERT Theory
- Topic & Chapter Exercises
- CBQs; MCQs, A-R, Case Based
- Board Questions Upto 2025
- Sample Question Papers

CBSE Exams 2026

Author
Er. Prem Kumar

Co-authors
Jitender Gupta, Brijesh Dwivedi

arihant
SUCCESS AND NOTHING LESS

ARIHANT PRAKASHAN
(School Division Series)

卐 ADMINISTRATIVE & PRODUCTION OFFICES

Regd. Office

'Ramchhaya' 4577/15, Agarwal Road, Darya Ganj, New Delhi -110002
Tele: 011- 47630600, 43518550; Fax: 011- 23280316

卐 Head Office

Kalindi, TP Nagar, Meerut (UP) - 250002, Tel: 0121-7156203, 7156204

卐 SALES & SUPPORT OFFICES

Agra, Ahmedabad, Bengaluru, Bareilly, Chennai, Delhi, Guwahati, Hyderabad, Jaipur, Jhansi, Kolkata, Lucknow, Nagpur & Pune.

PO No : TXT-XX-XXXXXXX-X-XX

Published By Arihant Publications (India) Ltd.

For further information about the books published by Arihant, log on to www.arihantbooks.com or e-mail at info@arihantbooks.com

Follow us on

卐 PRICE ₹ 500.00

PRODUCTION TEAM

Publishing Managers	Cover Designer	Inner Designer
Mahendra Singh Rawat & Keshav Mohan	Salman Shaikh	Ankit Tyagi
Project Head	**Page Layouting**	**Proof Reader**
Ashwani	Shivam Prajapati	Mukul Kaushik

Index *cum* Study Planner

	Page	Studied	Revised	Exam ready
1. Relations and Functions	**1-21**			
Relations	1-2	☐	☐	☐
Types of Relations	2	☐	☐	☐
Equivalence Classes	3-5	☐	☐	☐
Functions	6	☐	☐	☐
Types of Functions	6-9	☐	☐	☐
Exam Pattern Questions	11-20	☐	☐	☐
Mind Map	21	☐	☐	☐
2. Inverse Trigonometric Functions	**22-39**			
Domain, Range and Principal Value Branch of Inverse Trigonometric Functions	22-25	☐	☐	☐
Elementary Properties of Inverse Trigonometric Functions	26-28	☐	☐	☐
Exam Pattern Questions	29-38	☐	☐	☐
Mind Map	39	☐	☐	☐
3. Matrices	**40-70**			
Matrices	40-41	☐	☐	☐
Operations on Matrices	41-43	☐	☐	☐
Multiplication of Matrices	44-47	☐	☐	☐
Transpose of Matrices	48	☐	☐	☐
Invertible Matrices	48-50	☐	☐	☐
Exam Pattern Questions	52-69	☐	☐	☐
Mind Map	70	☐	☐	☐
4. Determinants	**71-104**			
Determinants	71-72	☐	☐	☐
Area of Triangles	72-75	☐	☐	☐
Minors and Cofactors	76-77	☐	☐	☐
Adjoint of a Matrix	78	☐	☐	☐
Singular and Non Singular Matrices	78	☐	☐	☐
Inverse of a Square Matrix	78-83	☐	☐	☐
Consistent and Inconsistent System	84	☐	☐	☐
Solution of System of Linear Equations Using Inverse of a Matrix	84-87	☐	☐	☐
Exam Pattern Questions	89-103	☐	☐	☐
Mind Map	104	☐	☐	☐
5. Continuity and Differentiability	**105-153**			
Continuity	105-109	☐	☐	☐
Differentiability (Derivability)	110	☐	☐	☐
Differentiation	110	☐	☐	☐

		Studied	Revised	Exam ready
Derivatives of Composite Functions	111	☐	☐	☐
Derivatives of Implicit Functions	111-114	☐	☐	☐
Derivatives of Inverse Trigonometric Functions	115-117	☐	☐	☐
Differentiation of Exponential and Logarithmic Functions	118-122	☐	☐	☐
Differentiation of Parametric Functions	123	☐	☐	☐
Differentiation of a Function w.r.t. Another Function	123-126	☐	☐	☐
Second Order Derivative	126-129	☐	☐	☐
Exam Pattern Questions	130-152	☐	☐	☐
Mind Map	153	☐	☐	☐
6. Application of Derivatives	**154-187**			
Rate of Change of Quantities	154	☐	☐	☐
Marginal Cost and Marginal Revenue	155-156	☐	☐	☐
Increasing and Decreasing Functions	157-159	☐	☐	☐
Maxima and Minima	160-165	☐	☐	☐
Exam Pattern Questions	166-186	☐	☐	☐
Mind Map	187	☐	☐	☐
7. Integrals	**188-236**			
Integration	188-190	☐	☐	☐
Integration by Substitution	191-194	☐	☐	☐
Some Special Integrals	195-200	☐	☐	☐
Integral by Partial Fractions	201-203	☐	☐	☐
Integration by Parts	204-207	☐	☐	☐
Definite Integral	208-212	☐	☐	☐
Exam Pattern Questions	214-235	☐	☐	☐
Mind Map	236	☐	☐	☐
8. Application of Integrals	**237-256**			
Area of a Curve Between Two Ordinates	237	☐	☐	☐
Area of a Curve Between Two Abscissae	238-242	☐	☐	☐
Exam Pattern Questions	243-255	☐	☐	☐
Mind Map	256	☐	☐	☐
9. Differential Equations	**257-290**			
Differential Equations	257-260	☐	☐	☐
Methods of Solving First Order and First Degree Differential Equations	261-263	☐	☐	☐
Homogeneous Differential Equations	264-267	☐	☐	☐
Linear Differential Equations	268-269	☐	☐	☐
Exam Pattern Questions	271-289	☐	☐	☐
Mind Map	290	☐	☐	☐

	Pages	Studied	Revised	Exam ready
10. Vector Algebra	**291-326**			
Scalars and Vectors	291-292	☐	☐	☐
Algebra of Vectors	291-293	☐	☐	☐
Components of a Vector	293	☐	☐	☐
Direction Cosines and Direction Ratios of a Vector	293-294	☐	☐	☐
Vector Joining Two Points	294	☐	☐	☐
Section Formula	294-297	☐	☐	☐
Scalar(or Dot) Product of Two Vectors	298-302	☐	☐	☐
Vector (or Cross) Product of Two Vectors	303-306	☐	☐	☐
Exam Pattern Questions	308-325	☐	☐	☐
Mind Map	326	☐	☐	☐
11. Three-Dimensional Geometry	**327-358**			
Direction Cosines of a Line	327-328	☐	☐	☐
Direction Ratios of a Line	328-329	☐	☐	☐
Lines in Space	330-331	☐	☐	☐
Angle between two lines	330-331	☐	☐	☐
Shortest Distance between Two Lines	332-337	☐	☐	☐
Exam Pattern Questions	339-357	☐	☐	☐
Mind Map	358	☐	☐	☐
12. Linear Programming	**359-383**			
Mathematical Form of LPP	359-360	☐	☐	☐
Graphical Method For Solving Linear Programming Problem	360	☐	☐	☐
Exam Pattern Questions	366-382	☐	☐	☐
Mind Map	383	☐	☐	☐
13. Probability	**384-419**			
Conditional Probability	385-389	☐	☐	☐
Multiplication Theorem	390-393	☐	☐	☐
Theorem of Total Probability	393	☐	☐	☐
Bayes' Theorem	393-396	☐	☐	☐
Exam Pattern Questions	397-418	☐	☐	☐
Mind Map	419	☐	☐	☐
Periodic Tests	**420-425**			
Activities	**426-438**			
3 Sample Question Paper	**439-451**			
CBSE Examination Paper 2025	**453-467**			

One Book- Endless Features

to Help you Succeed

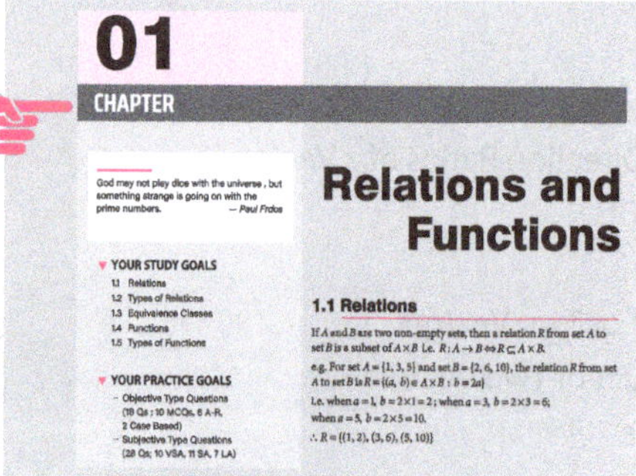

Chapter Intro

A quick information about the coverage of the chapter to explain students about what they are going to study.

1.1 Relations

If A and B are two non-empty sets, then a relation R from set A to set B is a subset of $A \times B$ i.e. $R: A \to B \Leftrightarrow R \subseteq A \times B$.

e.g. For set $A = \{1, 3, 5\}$ and set $B = \{2, 6, 10\}$, the relation R from set A to set B is $R = \{(a, b) \in A \times B : b = 2a\}$

i.e. when $a = 1$, $b = 2 \times 1 = 2$; when $a = 3$, $b = 2 \times 3 = 6$;

when $a = 5$, $b = 2 \times 5 = 10$.

$\therefore R = \{(1, 2), (3, 6), (5, 10)\}$

Domain, Range and Codomain of Relation

Suppose, a relation R from set A to set B is defined as $R = \{(a, b) \in A \times B\}$. Then,

Simplified Theory

It contains the necessary study material well supported by Definitions, Facts, Figures, Flow Charts, etc.

TEACHER TIPS

Empty relation and universal relation on a set A are respectively, the smallest and largest relations on set A. They are sometimes called trivial relations.

Teacher Tips

Important Points related to given concept to bring to help students focus on important points.

Quick Test 1

1. Find the domain and range of the following relations.
   (i) $R = \{(-3, 2), (-2, 4), (0, 5), (2, 6)\}$
   (ii) $S = \{(x, y) : 2x + y = 7, x, y \in N\}$
   (iii) $R = \{(a, a^2) : a$ is a prime number less than $8\}$
2. Let $A = \{0, 1, 2, 3\}$ and define a relation R on A as $R = \{(0, 0), (0, 1), (0, 3), (1, 0), (1, 1), (2, 2), (3, 0), (3, 3)\}$. Is R reflexive, symmetric and transitive? *NCERT Exemplar*
3. Check if the relation R in the set R of real numbers defined as $R = \{(a, b) : a < b\}$ is
   (i) symmetric (ii) transitive *CBSE 2020*
4. Check whether the relation S in the set of all real numbers (R) defined by $S = \{(a, b) : a \le b^3\}$ is reflexive, symmetric or transitive. *CBSE 2024 C*
5. A relation R is defined on a set of real numbers R as $R = \{(x, y) = x \cdot y$ is an irrational number$\}$. Check whether R is reflexive, symmetric and transitive or not. *CBSE 2023*
6. Let R be a relation defined on the set of natural numbers N as $R = \{(x, y): x \in N, y \in N$ and $2x + y = 24\}$. Then, find the domain and range of the relation R. Also, find whether R is an equivalence relation or not. *Competency Based Que*
7. Let $A = \{1, 2, 3, \ldots, 9\}$ and R be the relation in $A \times A$ defined by $(a, b) R (c, d)$, if $a + d = b + c$ for $(a, b), (c, d)$ in $A \times A$. Prove that R is an equivalence relation and also obtain the equivalence class $[(2, 5)]$. *CBSE 2014; NCERT Exemplar*
8. Show that the number of equivalence relation in set $\{1, 2, 3\}$ containing $(1, 2)$ and $(2, 1)$ is two. *NCERT*

Answers

1. (i) Domain $= \{-3, -2, 0, 2\}$, Range $= \{2, 4, 5, 6\}$
   (ii) Domain $= \{1, 2, 3\}$, Range $= \{5, 3, 1\}$
   (iii) Domain $= \{2, 3, 5, 7\}$, Range $= \{4, 9, 25, 49\}$
2. Reflexive, symmetric and not transitive.
3. (i) R is not symmetric. (ii) R is transitive.
4. Neither reflexive nor symmetric nor transitive.
5. Symmetric but neither reflexive nor transitive.
6. Domain $= \{1, 2, 3, 4, 5, 6, 7, 8, 9, 10, 11\}$ and range $= \{22, 20, 18, 16, 14, 12, 10, 8, 6, 4, 2\}$. R is not an equivalence relation.
7. $\{(1, 4), (2, 5), (3, 6), (4, 7), (5, 8), (6, 9)\}$

For Solutions, See QR Code on Pg. 20

Topical Exercises

To make students understand the chapter in a smooth part-by-part manner, Topical Exercises have been given in each chapter. These Exercises help students to assess the understanding of related concepts at regular interval.

One Book- Endless Features

to Help you Succeed

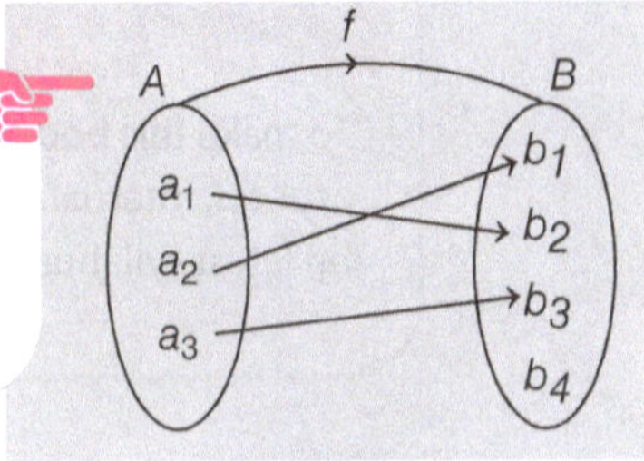

Illustrative Figures

To make the concepts completely visible, illustrative diagrams have been given at various place.

Example 3 Check whether the relation R defined in the set $A = \{1, 2, 3, 4, 5, 6\}$ as $R = \{(x, y) : y$ is divisible by $x\}$ is reflexive, symmetric and transitive. *CBSE 2020; NCERT*

Sol. Given, $R = \{(x, y) : y$ is divisible by $x\}$

and $A = \{1, 2, 3, 4, 5, 6\}$

Reflexive Let $x \in A$ be any arbitrary element.

We know that x is divisible by x.

[$\because$ every real number except zero is divisible by itself]

$\Rightarrow \quad (x, x) \in R$

So, R is reflexive.

Symmetric Clearly, $2, 4 \in A$ and 4 is divisible by 2 but 2 is not divisible by 4.

$\therefore \quad (2, 4) \in R$ but $(4, 2) \notin R$

So, R is not symmetric.

Transitive Let $x, y, z \in A$ such that $(x, y) \in R$ and $(y, z) \in R$.

Now, as $(x, y) \in R$, therefore y is divisible by x

i.e. $\frac{y}{x} = k_1$ (say) ...(i)

1. If the relation R is defined on the set $A = \{1, 2, 3, 4, 5\}$ by $R = \{(a, b) : |a^2 - b^2| < 8\}$. Then, find the relation R. **NCERT Exemplar**

NCERT Exemplar Problems

NCERT Exemplar Problems are considered to be the best problem books for School/Board Examinations. To make students practice of exemplary questions given in this book, each chapter has selected problems from NCERT Exemplar

NCERT Questions

To make students completely understand NCERT books, solutions of selected NCERT questions have been given in each chapter.

Exam Pattern Questions

To make students completely prepared for examination, this Exercise contains Exam Pattern Questions. This exercise covers all types of questions, like; MCQs, Case Based Questions, Assertion-Reason, VSA, SA & LA Type Questions. All the questions have hints and answers.

EXAM PATTERN QUESTIONS

Objective Type Questions

Multiple Choice Questions

1. Select the correct option out of the four given options. Let R be a relation in the set N given by $R = \{(a, b) : a = b - 2, b > 6\}$. Then, **CBSE 2023**
   (a) $(8, 7) \in R$ (b) $(6, 8) \in R$
   (c) $(3, 8) \in R$ (d) $(2, 4) \in R$
2. Let R be a relation from R to R, the set of real numbers defined by $R = \{(x, y) : x, y \in R$ and $x - y + \sqrt{3}$ is an irrational number$\}$. Then, R is
   (a) reflexive (b) transitive
   (c) symmetric (d) an equivalence relation

9. The function $f : R \to R$ defined as $f(x) = x^3$ is **CBSE Sample Paper 2022 (Term I)**
   (a) one-one but not onto
   (b) not one-one but onto
   (c) neither one-one nor onto
   (d) both one-one and onto
10. Let $A = \{1, 2, 3\}$, $B = \{4, 5, 6, 7\}$ and let $f = \{(1, 4), (2, 5), (3, 6)\}$ be a function from A to B. Based on the given information, f is best defined as **CBSE Sample Paper 2022 (Term I)**
    (a) surjective function (b) injective function
    (c) bijective function (d) None of these

One Book- Endless Features

to Help you Succeed

Internal Assessment of Practical Work

To make this book complete in all aspects, Internal Assessment based on latest syllabus is also given.

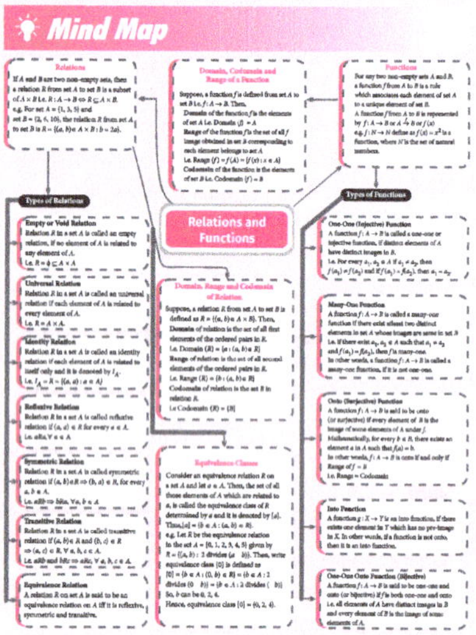

Mind Map

A quick revision visual tool for the complete chapter.

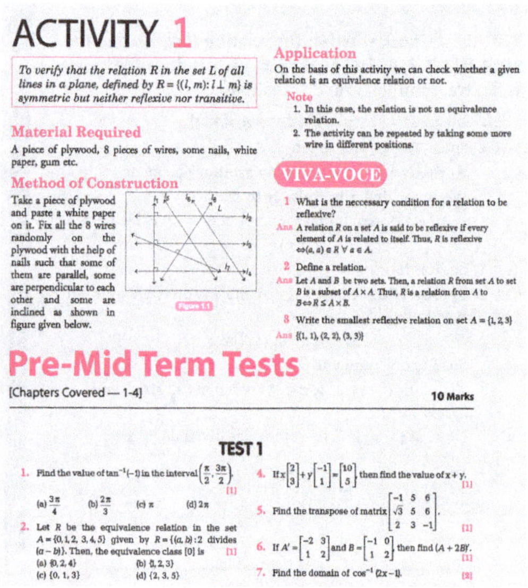

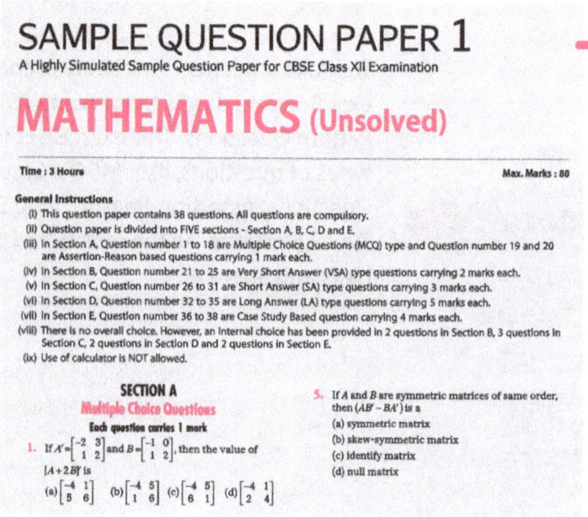

Sample Papers

To make students practice of examination in real sense, there are 3 Sample Question Papers at the end. All these Sample Questions Papers are exactly prepared on the latest syllabus & pattern of examination.

Latest Course Structure

Time : 3 Hrs | Max. Marks : 80

Unit		No. of Periods	Marks
I	Relations and Functions	30	08
II	Algebra	50	10
III	Calculus	80	35
IV	Vectors and Three-Dimensional Geometry	30	14
V	Linear Programming	20	05
VI	Probability	30	08
	Total	240	80
	Internal Assessment		20

UNIT I Relations and Functions

Chapter 1 : Relations and Functions **15 Periods**

Types of relations—reflexive, symmetric, transitive and equivalence relations.
One-one and onto functions.

Chapter 2 : Inverse Trigonometric Functions **15 Periods**

Definition, range, domain, principal value branch. Graphs of inverse trigonometric functions.

UNIT II Algebra

Chapter 3 : Matrices **25 Periods**

Concept, notation, order, equality, types of matrices, zero and identity matrix, transpose of a matrix, symmetric and skew-symmetric matrices. Operation on Matrices: Addition, multiplication and multiplication with a scalar, Simple properties of addition, multiplication and scalar multiplication. Non-commutativity of multiplication of matrices and existence of non-zero matrices whose product is the zero matrix (restrict to square matrices of order 2). Invertible matrices and proof of the uniqueness of inverse, if it exists; (Here all matrices will have real entries).

Chapter 4 : Determinants **25 Periods**

Determinant of a square matrix (upto 3×3 matrices), minors, co-factors and applications of determinants in finding the area of a triangle. Adjoint and inverse of a square matrix. Consistency, inconsistency and number of solutions of system of linear equations by examples, solving system of linear equations in two or three variables (having unique solution) using inverse of a matrix.

UNIT III Calculus

Chapter 5 : Continuity and Differentiability — 20 Periods

Continuity and differentiability, chain rule, derivatives of composite function, derivatives of inverse trigonometric functions, derivative of implicit functions. Concept of exponential and logarithmic functions.

Derivatives of logarithmic and exponential functions. Logarithmic differentiation, derivative of functions expressed in parametric forms. Second order derivatives.

Chapter 6 : Applications of Derivatives — 10 Periods

Applications of derivatives- rate of change of bodies, increasing/decreasing functions, maxima and minima (first derivative test motivated geometrically and second derivative test given as a provable tool). Simple problems (that illustrate basic principles and understanding of the subject as well as real life situations).

Chapter 7 : Integrals — 20 Periods

Integration as inverse process of differentiation. Integration of a variety of functions by substitution, by partial fractions and by parts, Evaluation of simple integrals of the following type and problems on them.

$$\int \frac{dx}{x^2 \pm a^2}, \int \frac{dx}{\sqrt{x^2 \pm a^2}}, \int \frac{dx}{\sqrt{a^2 - x^2}}, \int \frac{dx}{ax^2 + bx + c}, \int \frac{dx}{\sqrt{ax^2 + bx + c}},$$

$$\int \frac{px + q}{ax^2 + bx + c}\, dx, \int \frac{px + q}{\sqrt{ax^2 + bx + c}}\, dx, \int \sqrt{a^2 \pm x^2}\, dx, \int \sqrt{x^2 - a^2}\, dx,$$

$$\int \sqrt{ax^2 + bx + c}\, dx$$

Fundamental theorem of calculus (without proof). Basic properties of definite integrals and evaluation of definite integrals.

Chapter 8 : Applications of Integrals — 15 Periods

Applications in finding the area under simple curves, especially lines, circles/parabolas/ellipses (in standard form only).

Chapter 9 : Differential Equations — 15 Periods

Definition, order and degree, general and particular solutions of a differential equation. Solution of differential equations by method of separation of variables, Solution of homogeneous differential equations of first order and first degree. Solutions of linear differential equation of the type

$\frac{dy}{dx} + py = q$, where p and q are functions of x or constants.

$\frac{dx}{dy} + px = q$, where p and q are functions of y or constants.

UNIT IV

Vectors and Three-Dimensional Geometry

Chapter 10 : Vectors — 15 Periods

Vectors and scalars, magnitude and direction of a vector. Direction cosines and direction ratios of a vector. Types of vectors (equal, unit, zero, parallel and collinear vectors), position vector of a point, negative of a vector, components of a vector, addition of vectors, multiplication of a vector by a scalar, position vector of a point dividing a line segment in a given ratio. Definition, Geometrical, Interpretation, Properties and application of scalar (dot) product of vectors, Vector (cross) product of vectors.

Chapter 11 : Three-Dimensional Geometry — 15 Periods

Direction cosines and direction ratios of a line joining two points. Cartesian and vector equations of a line, skew-lines, Angle between two lines shortest distance between two lines.

UNIT V Linear Programming

Chapter 12 : Linear Programming — 20 Periods

Introduction, related terminology such as constraints, objective function, optimisation, graphical method of solution for problems in two variables, feasible and infeasible regions (bounded and unbounded), feasible and infeasible solutions, optimal feasible solutions (upto three non-trivial constraints).

UNIT VI Probability

Chapter 13 : Probability — 30 Periods

Conditional probability, multiplication theorem on probability, independent events, total probability, Baye's theorem.

01

CHAPTER

> God may not play dice with the universe , but something strange is going on with the prime numbers. — Paul Frdos

▼ YOUR STUDY GOALS

1.1 Relations
1.2 Types of Relations
1.3 Equivalence Classes
1.4 Functions
1.5 Types of Functions

▼ YOUR PRACTICE GOALS

- Objective Type Questions (18 Qs ; 10 MCQs, 6 A-R, 2 Case Based)
- Subjective Type Questions (28 Qs; 10 VSA, 11 SA, 7 LA)

Relations and Functions

1.1 Relations

If A and B are two non-empty sets, then a relation R from set A to set B is a subset of $A\times B$ i.e. $R: A\to B \Leftrightarrow R\subseteq A\times B$.

e.g. For set $A=\{1, 3, 5\}$ and set $B=\{2, 6, 10\}$, the relation R from set A to set B is $R=\{(a,\ b)\in A\times B:\ b=2a\}$

i.e. when $a=1,\ b=2\times 1=2$; when $a=3,\ b=2\times 3=6$;

when $a=5,\ b=2\times 5=10$.

$\therefore\ R=\{(1, 2), (3, 6), (5, 10)\}$

Domain, Range and Codomain of Relation

Suppose, a relation R from set A to set B is defined as $R=\{(a,\ b)\in A\times B\}$. Then,

- **Domain** of relation is the set of all first elements of the ordered pairs in R.
  i.e. Domain $(R)=\{a:(a,b)\in R\}$
- **Range** of relation is the set of all second elements of the ordered pairs in R.
  i.e. Range $(R)=\{b:(a,b)\in R\}$
- **Codomain** of relation is the set B in relation R.
  i.e Codomain $(R)=\{B\}$

e.g. For set $A=\{1, 3, 4, 5, 6\}$ to set $B=\{2, 4, 6, 9\}$, a relation R is given as $R=\{(1, 2), (3, 6), (4, 9)\}$.

Here, domain (R) = {set of first elements of all ordered pairs}
$=\{1, 3, 4\}$

Range (R) = {set of second elements of all ordered pairs}
$=\{2, 6, 9\}$

Codomain (R) = set $B=\{2, 4, 6, 9\}$

1.2 Types of Relations

Empty or Void Relation

Relation R in a set A is called an empty relation, if no element of A is related to any element of A.

i.e. $R=\phi \subset A \times A$

e.g. Let set $A=\{1, 2, 3, 8, 10, 11\}$ and R be a relation in A, given by $R=\{(a, b): a-b=4\}$. Then, R is an empty relation. Since, no element $(a, b) \in A \times A$ satisfy the property $a-b=4$.

Universal Relation

Relation R in a set A is called an universal relation, if each element of A is related to every element of A i.e. $R=A \times A$.

e.g. Let set $A=\{1, 2, 3, 4\}$ and relation R is given by $R=\{(a, b): |a-b| \geq 0\}$. Then, R is a universal relation. Since, all ordered pairs $(a, b) \in A \times A$ satisfy the property $|a-b| \geq 0$.

TEACHER TIPS

Empty relation and universal relation on a set A are respectively, the smallest and largest relations on set A. They are sometimes called trivial relations.

Identity Relation

Relation R in a set A is called an identity relation, if each element of A is related to itself only and it is denoted by I_A i.e. $I_A=R=\{(a, a): a \in A\}$

e.g. Let set $A=\{1, 2\}$, then the identity relation R on A is given by $R=\{(1, 1), (2, 2)\}$.

But the relation

$R_1=\{(1, 1), (2, 2), (1, 2)\}$ is not an identity relation on A because element 1 is related to elements 1 and 2.

Reflexive Relation

Relation R in a set A is called reflexive relation, if $(a, a) \in R$, for every $a \in A$.

i.e. $aRa, \forall a \in A$

e.g. Let $A=\{11, 12, 15\}$ and relation on it is defined as
$R=\{(11, 11), (12, 12), (11, 12), (15, 15), (11, 15), (12, 15)\}$

Here, we see that for every element 11, 12 and 15 of A, there exist (11, 11), (12, 12) and $(15, 15) \in R$, so R is a reflexive relation.

Symmetric Relation

Relation R in a set A is called symmetric relation, if $(a, b) \in R \Rightarrow (b, a) \in R$, for every $a, b \in A$.

i.e. $aRb \Rightarrow bRa, \forall a, b \in A$.

e.g. Let $A=\{11, 12, 13\}$ and relation on it is defined as $R=\{(11, 11), (11, 12), (12, 12), (12, 11)\}$. Here, we see that $(11, 12) \in R \Rightarrow (12, 11) \in R$, therefore R is a symmetric relation.

Transitive Relation

Relation R in a set A is called transitive relation, if $(a, b) \in R$ and $(b, c) \in R \Rightarrow (a, c) \in R, \forall a, b, c \in A$

i.e. aRb and $bRc \Rightarrow aRc, \forall a, b, c \in A$

e.g. Let $A=\{11, 12, 14\}$ and relation on it is defined as
$R=\{(11, 11), (11, 12), (12, 14), (12, 12), (11, 14)\}$.

Here, we see that

$(11, 11) \in R$ and $(11, 12) \in R \Rightarrow (11, 12) \in R$,

$(11, 11) \in R$ and $(11, 14) \in R \Rightarrow (11, 14) \in R$,

$(11, 12) \in R$ and $(12, 14) \in R \Rightarrow (11, 14) \in R$,

$(11, 12) \in R$ and $(12, 12) \in R \Rightarrow (11, 12) \in R$

and $(12, 12) \in R$ and $(12, 14) \in R \Rightarrow (12, 14) \in R$.

Then, it is a transitive relation.

Equivalence Relation

A relation R on set A is said to be an equivalence relation on A iff it is reflexive, symmetric and transitive.

e.g. Let $A=\{a, b, c\}$ and relation on it is defined as
$R=\{(a, a), (b, b), (c, c), (a, b), (b, a)\}$.

Here, R is reflexive, symmetric and transitive.

Thus, R is an equivalence relation.

1.3 Equivalence Classes

Consider an equivalence relation R on a set A and let $a \in A$, then the set of all those elements of A which are related to a, is called the equivalence class of R determined by a and it is denoted by $[a]$. Thus, $[a] = \{b \in A : (a, b) \in R\}$.

e.g. Consider R be the equivalence relation in the set $A = \{0, 1, 2, 3, 4, 5\}$ given by $R = \{(a, b) : 2 \text{ divides } (a - b)\}$. Then, write equivalence class [0] is defined as

$$[0] = \{b \in A : (0, b) \in R\} = \{b \in A : 2 \text{ divides } (0 - b)\}$$
$$= \{b \in A : 2 \text{ divides } (-b)\}.$$

So, b can be 0, 2, 4.

Hence, equivalence class $[0] = \{0, 2, 4\}$.

TEACHER TIPS

(i) A relation R on set A is not reflexive, if there exists an element $a \in A$ such that $(a, a) \notin R$.
(ii) Identity relation is always reflexive, symmetric and transitive.
(iii) Two equivalence classes are either disjoint or identical. The union of all equivalence classes gives the whole set.

Example 1 **If $R = \{(x, y) : x + 2y = 8\}$ is a relation on a set of natural numbers (N), then write the domain, range and codomain of R.** CBSE 2014

Sol. Given, $R = \{(x, y) : x + 2y = 8\}$ on a set of natural numbers

Consider $x + 2y = 8$, which can be rewritten as $y = \dfrac{8 - x}{2}$.

Now, as $x, y \in N$, therefore substitute values of x from natural numbers such that $y \in N$.

On putting $x = 2$, we get $y = \dfrac{8 - 2}{2} = 3$

On putting $x = 4$, we get $y = \dfrac{8 - 4}{2} = 2$

On putting $x = 6$, we get $y = \dfrac{8 - 6}{2} = 1$

Thus, $R = \{(2, 3), (4, 2), (6, 1)\}$

[$\because$ there is no other value of x, for which $y \in N$]

$\therefore$ Domain of $R = \{2, 4, 6\}$, codomain of $R = N$

and range of $R = \{3, 2, 1\}$.

Example 2 **Show that the relation R in the set $\{1, 2, 3\}$ given by $R = \{(1, 1), (2, 2), (3, 3), (1, 2), (2, 3)\}$ is reflexive but neither symmetric nor transitive.**

Sol. Let the given set be $A = \{1, 2, 3\}$

and $R = \{(1, 1), (2, 2), (3, 3), (1, 2), (2, 3)\}$

Reflexive Here, $1, 2, 3 \in A$ and $(1, 1), (2, 2), (3, 3) \in R$

i.e. for all $a \in A$, $(a, a) \in R$.

So, R is reflexive.

Symmetric Here, $(1, 2) \in R$ but $(2, 1) \notin R$.

So, R is not symmetric.

Transitive Here, $(1, 2) \in R$ and $(2, 3) \in R$ but $(1, 3) \notin R$.

So, R is not transitive. **Hence proved.**

Example 3 **Check whether the relation R defined in the set $A = \{1, 2, 3, 4, 5, 6\}$ as $R = \{(x, y) : y \text{ is divisible by } x\}$ is reflexive, symmetric and transitive.** CBSE 2020; NCERT

Sol. Given, $R = \{(x, y) : y \text{ is divisible by } x\}$

and $A = \{1, 2, 3, 4, 5, 6\}$

Reflexive Let $x \in A$ be any arbitrary element.

We know that x is divisible by x.

[$\because$ every real number except zero is divisible by itself]

$\Rightarrow \quad (x, x) \in R$

So, R is reflexive.

Symmetric Clearly, $2, 4 \in A$ and 4 is divisible by 2 but 2 is not divisible by 4.

$\therefore \quad (2, 4) \in R$ but $(4, 2) \notin R$

So, R is not symmetric.

Transitive Let $x, y, z \in A$ such that $(x, y) \in R$ and $(y, z) \in R$.

Now, as $(x, y) \in R$, therefore y is divisible by x

i.e. $\dfrac{y}{x} = k_1$ (say) ...(i)

where k_1 is a natural number.

and as $(y, z) \in R$, therefore z is divisible by y

i.e. $\dfrac{z}{y} = k_2$ (say) ...(ii)

where k_2 is a natural number.

On multiplying Eqs. (i) and (ii), we get

$$\frac{y}{x} \times \frac{z}{y} = k_1 k_2 \Rightarrow \frac{z}{x} = k_1 k_2$$

where $k_1 k_2$ is a natural number.

$\therefore$ z is divisible by x.

Thus, $(x, z) \in R$, for $(x, y), (y, z) \in R$

i.e. $(x, y) \in R, (y, z) \in R \Rightarrow (x, z) \in R$

Hence, R is transitive.

Example 4 **Show that the relation R on IR defined as $R = \{(a, b) : (a \leq b)\}$, is reflexive and transitive but not symmetric.** CBSE 2019

Sol. Given, a relation $R = \{(a, b) : a \leq b\}$ on IR (the set of real numbers)

Reflexivity Since, $a \leq a$ is true for all values of $a \in IR$.

$\therefore \quad (a, a) \in R, \forall a \in IR$

Hence, the given relation is reflexive.

Transitivity Let $(a, b) \in R$ and $(b, c) \in R$ be any arbitrary elements.

Then, we have $a \leq b$ and $b \leq c$

$\Rightarrow \quad a \leq b \leq c \Rightarrow a \leq c$

$\Rightarrow \quad (a, c) \in R$

Hence, the given relation is transitive.

Symmetricity Note that $(2,3) \in R$ as $2 < 3$ but $(3, 2) \notin R$ as $3 \not< 2$.

Hence, the given relation is not symmetric.

Hence proved.

Example 5 Let a relation R on the set A of real numbers be defined as $(a, b) \in R \Rightarrow 1 + ab > 0, \forall a, b \in A$. Show that R is reflexive and symmetric but not transitive.

Sol. Given, A = Set of real numbers

and $R = \{(a, b) : 1 + ab > 0\}$.

Reflexive Let a be any real number.

Then, $1 + aa = 1 + a^2 > 0$ $[\because a^2 \geq 0, \forall a \in A]$

$\Rightarrow (a, a) \in R, \forall a \in A$

So, R is reflexive.

Symmetric Let $(a, b) \in R$, then

$(1 + ab) > 0 \Rightarrow 1 + ba > 0$ $[\because ab = ba, \forall a, b \in A]$

$\Rightarrow (b, a) \in R$

Thus, $(a, b) \in R \Rightarrow (b, a) \in R, \forall a, b \in A$

So, R is symmetric.

Transitive We observe that $\left(1, \frac{1}{2}\right) \in R$ as

$$1 + 1 \cdot \frac{1}{2} = 1 + \frac{1}{2} > 0$$

and $\left(\frac{1}{2}, -1\right) \in R$ as $1 + (-1)\left(\frac{1}{2}\right) = 1 - \frac{1}{2} > 0$

But $(1, -1) \notin R$

Because $1 + 1 \times (-1) = 0 \not> 0$

So, R is not transitive. **Hence proved.**

Example 6 Let a relation R on the set N of natural number be defined as

$$R = \{(x, y) : 3x^2 - 7xy + 4y^2 = 0;\ x, y \in N\}.$$

Then, show that relation R is reflexive but neither symmetric nor transitive. *Competency Based Que*

Sol. Given, $R = \{(x, y) : 3x^2 - 7xy + 4y^2 = 0; x, y \in N\}$

$= \{(x, y) : 3x^2 - 3xy - 4xy + 4y^2 = 0; x, y \in N\}$

$= \{(x, y) : 3x(x - y) - 4y(x - y) = 0; x, y \in N\}$

$= \{(x, y) : (x - y)(3x - 4y) = 0; x, y \in N\}$

Here, we get those ordered pairs (x, y) which satisfy the equation defined in R.

Reflexive Since, $xRx \Rightarrow (x - x)(3x - 4x) = 0$

$\Rightarrow 0 = 0$, which is true, so R is reflexive.

Symmetric Now, $xRy \Rightarrow (x - y)(3x - 4y) = 0$

and $yRx \Rightarrow (y - x)(3y - 4x) = 0$

Clearly, $xRy \not\Rightarrow yRx$

So, R is not symmetric.

Transitive Now, $xRy \Rightarrow (x - y)(3x - 4y) = 0$,

$yRz \Rightarrow (y - z)(3y - 4z) = 0$

and $xRz \Rightarrow (x - z)(3x - 4z) = 0$

Here, $(x - y)(3x - 4y) = 0$ and $(y - z)(3y - 4z) = 0$

$\not\Rightarrow (x - z)(3x - 4z) = 0$

So, R is not transitive.

Example 7 Prove that the relation R on Z, defined by $R = \{(x, y) : (x - y)$ is divisible by $5\}$ is an equivalence relation. *Competency Based Que*

Sol. Given, $R = \{(a, b) : 5 \text{ divides } (a - b)\}$

and Z = Set of integers

Reflexive Let $a \in Z$ be any arbitrary element.

Now, if $(a, a) \in R$, then 5 divides $a - a$, which is true.

So, R is reflexive.

Symmetric Let $a, b \in Z$ such that

$(a, b) \in R \Rightarrow 5$ divides $(a - b)$

$\Rightarrow$ 5 divides $[-(a - b)]$

$\Rightarrow$ 5 divides $(b - a) \Rightarrow (b, a) \in R$

So, R is symmetric.

Transitive Let $a, b, c \in Z$ such that $(a, b) \in R$ and $(b, c) \in R$

$\Rightarrow a - b$ and $b - c$ both are divisible by 5

$\Rightarrow a - b + b - c$ is divisible by 5

$\Rightarrow (a - c)$ is divisible by 5

$\Rightarrow (a, c) \in R$

So, R is transitive.

Thus, R is reflexive, symmetric and transitive.

Hence, R is an equivalence relation. **Hence proved.**

Example 8 If N denotes the set of all natural numbers and R be the relation on $N \times N$ defined by $(a, b)\, R\, (c, d)$, if $ad(b + c) = bc(a + d)$. Show that R is an equivalence relation. *CBSE 2023, 15*

Sol. We have, a relation R on $N \times N$ defined by $(a, b) R (c, d)$, if $ad(b + c) = bc(a + d)$.

Reflexive Let $(a, b) \in N \times N$ be any arbitrary element. We have to show $(a, b)\, R\, (a, b)$ i.e. to show $ab(b + a) = ba(a + b)$ which is trivially true as natural numbers are commutative under usual multiplication and addition.

Since, $(a, b) \in N \times N$ was arbitrary, therefore R is reflexive.

Symmetric Let $(a, b), (c, d) \in N \times N$ such that $(a, b)\, R\, (c, d)$ i.e. $ad(b + c) = bc(a + d)$ ...(i)

To show, $(c, d)\, R\, (a, b)$

i.e. to show $cb(d + a) = da(c + b)$

From Eq.(i), we get

$ad(b + c) = bc(a + d) \Rightarrow da(c + b) = cb(d + a)$

[$\because$ natural numbers are commutative under usual addition and multiplication]

$\Rightarrow cb(d + a) = da(c + b) \Rightarrow (c, d)\, R\, (a, b)$

Thus, R is symmetric.

Transitive Let $(a, b), (c, d)$ and $(e, f) \in N \times N$ such that $(a, b)\, R\, (c, d)$ and $(c, d)\, R\, (e, f)$.

Now, $(a, b)\, R\, (c, d) \Rightarrow ad(b + c) = bc(a + d)$

$$\Rightarrow \quad \frac{b+c}{bc} = \frac{a+d}{ad} \Rightarrow \frac{1}{b} + \frac{1}{c} = \frac{1}{a} + \frac{1}{d} \quad \text{...(ii)}$$

and $\quad (c, d)\, R\, (e, f) \Rightarrow cf(d + e) = de(c + f)$

$$\Rightarrow \quad \frac{d+e}{de} = \frac{c+f}{cf} \Rightarrow \frac{1}{d} + \frac{1}{e} = \frac{1}{c} + \frac{1}{f} \quad \text{...(iii)}$$

On adding Eqs. (ii) and (iii), we get

$$\left(\frac{1}{b} + \frac{1}{c}\right) + \left(\frac{1}{d} + \frac{1}{e}\right) = \left(\frac{1}{a} + \frac{1}{d}\right) + \left(\frac{1}{c} + \frac{1}{f}\right)$$

$$\Rightarrow \quad \frac{1}{b} + \frac{1}{e} = \frac{1}{a} + \frac{1}{f} \Rightarrow \frac{e+b}{be} = \frac{f+a}{af}$$

$$\Rightarrow \quad af(e + b) = be(f + a)$$

$$\Rightarrow \quad af(b + e) = be(a + f) \Rightarrow (a, b)\, R\, (e, f)$$

$\Rightarrow$ R is transitive.

Thus, R is reflexive, symmetric and transitive. Hence, R is an equivalence relation.

Example 9 **Let N be the set of all natural numbers and R be a relation on $N \times N$ defined by $(a, b) R (c, d) \Leftrightarrow ad = bc$ for all $(a, b), (c, d) \in N \times N$. Show that R is an equivalence relation on $N \times N$. Also, find the equivalence class of (2, 6) i.e. [(2, 6)].**
CBSE Sample Paper 2024

Sol. We know that a relation R is an equivalence relation if it is reflexive, symmetric and transitive.

For reflexive

For any $(a, b) \in N \times N$,

$$ab = ba \quad [\because \text{ multiplication is commutative on } N]$$

$\Rightarrow (a, b)\, R\, (a, b)$ [from definition of relation R on $N \times N$]

Thus, R is reflexive.

For symmetric

Let $(a, b), (c, d)$ be arbitrary elements of $N \times N$

$$(a, b)\, R\, (c, d)$$

$$\Rightarrow \quad ad = bc \Rightarrow bc = ad$$

$\Rightarrow \quad cb = da$ [as $a, b, c, d \in N$ and multiplication is commutative on N]

$$\Rightarrow \quad (c, d)\, R\, (a, b)$$

$\therefore$ R is symmetric.

For transitive

Let $(a, b), (c, d), (e, f)$ be arbitrary elements of $N \times N$ such that $(a, b)\, R (c, d)$ and $(c, d)\, R (e, f)$.

Then, $\quad ad = bc$ and $cf = de$

$\Rightarrow (ad)(cf) = (bc)(de) \Rightarrow af = be \Rightarrow (a, b)\, R\, (e, f)$

$\therefore$ R is transitive.

Hence, R is an equivalence relation.

Now, $[(2, 6)] = \{(x, y) \in N \times N : (x, y)\, R (2, 6)\}$

$$\Rightarrow \quad 6x = 2y \Rightarrow 3x = y$$

$$\therefore \quad [(2, 6)] = \{(x, y) \in N \times N : 3x = y\}$$
$$= \{(x, 3x) : x \in N\} = \{(1, 3), (2, 6), (3, 9) \ldots\}$$

Quick Test 1

1. Find the domain and range of the following relations.
   (i) $R = \{(-3, 2), (-2, 4), (0, 5), (2, 6)\}$
   (ii) $S = \{(x, y) : 2x + y = 7,\ x, y \in N\}$
   (iii) $R = \{(a, a^2) : a$ is a prime number less than 8$\}$
2. Let $A = \{0, 1, 2, 3\}$ and define a relation R on A as $R = \{(0, 0), (0, 1), (0, 3), (1, 0), (1, 1), (2, 2), (3, 0), (3, 3)\}$. Is R reflexive, symmetric and transitive? *NCERT Exemplar*
3. Check if the relation R in the set R of real numbers defined as $R = \{(a, b) : a < b\}$ is
   (i) symmetric (ii) transitive *CBSE 2020*
4. Check whether the relation S in the set of all real numbers (R) defined by $S = \{(a, b) : a \leq b^3\}$ is reflexive, symmetric or transitive. *CBSE 2024 C*
5. A relation R is defined on a set of real numbers R as $R = \{(x, y) = x \cdot y$ is an irrational number$\}$. Check whether R is reflexive, symmetric and transitive or not. *CBSE 2023*
6. Let R be a relation defined on the set of natural numbers N as $R = \{(x, y) : x \in N, y \in N$ and $2x + y = 24\}$. Then, find the domain and range of the relation R. Also, find whether R is an equivalence relation or not. *Competency Based Que*
7. Let $A = \{1, 2, 3, \ldots, 9\}$ and R be the relation in $A \times A$ defined by $(a, b) R (c, d)$, if $a + d = b + c$ for $(a, b), (c, d)$ in $A \times A$. Prove that R is an equivalence relation and also obtain the equivalence class $[(2, 5)]$. *CBSE 2014; NCERT Exemplar*
8. Show that the number of equivalence relation in set $\{1, 2, 3\}$ containing $(1, 2)$ and $(2, 1)$ is two. *NCERT*

For Solutions, See QR Code on Pg. 20

Answers

1. (i) Domain $= \{-3, -2, 0, 2\}$, Range $= \{2, 4, 5, 6\}$
   (ii) Domain $= \{1, 2, 3\}$, Range $= \{5, 3, 1\}$
   (iii) Domain $= \{2, 3, 5, 7\}$, Range $= \{4, 9, 25, 49\}$
2. Reflexive, symmetric and not transitive.
3. (i) R is not symmetric. (ii) R is transitive.
4. Neither reflexive nor symmetric nor transitive.
5. Symmetric but neither reflexive nor transitive.
6. Domain $= \{1, 2, 3, 4, 5, 6, 7, 8, 9, 10, 11\}$ and range $= \{22, 20, 18, 16, 14, 12, 10, 8, 6, 4, 2\}$. R is not an equivalence relation.
7. $\{(1, 4), (2, 5), (3, 6), (4, 7), (5, 8), (6, 9)\}$

1.4 Functions

For any two non-empty sets A and B, a function f from A to B is a rule which associates each element of set A to a unique element of set B.

A function f from A to B is represented by

$$f: A \to B \text{ or } A \xrightarrow{f} B \text{ or } f(x)$$

e.g. $f: N \to N$ define as $f(x) = x^2$ is a function, where N is the set of natural numbers.

Domain, Codomain and Range of a Function

Suppose a function f is defined from set A to set B i.e. $f: A \to B$. Then,

- **Domain** of the function f is the elements of set A
  i.e. Domain $(f) = A$
- **Range** of the function f is the set of all f image obtained in set B corresponding to each element belongs to set A
  i.e. Range $(f) = f(A) = \{f(x): x \in A\}$
- **Codomain** of the function is the elements of set B
  i.e. Codomain $(f) = B$

1.5 Types of Functions

One-One (Injective) Function

A function $f: A \to B$ is called a one-one or injective function, if distinct elements of A have distinct images in B.

i.e. For every $a_1, a_2 \in A$, if $a_1 \neq a_2$, then $f(a_1) \neq f(a_2)$ and if $f(a_1) = f(a_2)$, then $a_1 = a_2$.

e.g. Let $f: A \to B$ be a function represented by the following diagram.

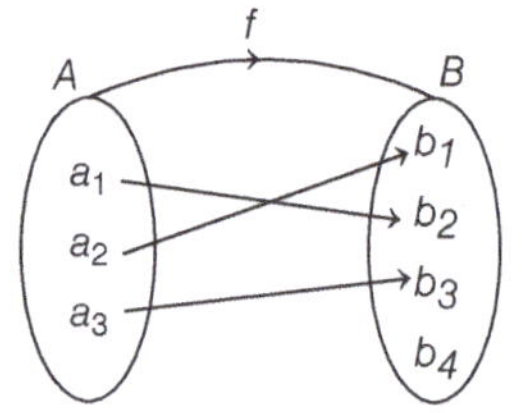

Here, f is a one-one function because each element of set A has distinct image in set B.

Many-One Function

A function $f: A \to B$ is called a many-one function, if there exist atleast two distinct elements in set A, whose images are same in set B

i.e. if there exist $a_1, a_2 \in A$ such that $a_1 \neq a_2$ and $f(a_1) = f(a_2)$, then f is many-one.

In other words, a function $f: A \to B$ is called a many-one function, if it is not one-one.

e.g. Let $f: A \to B$ be a function represented by the following diagram.

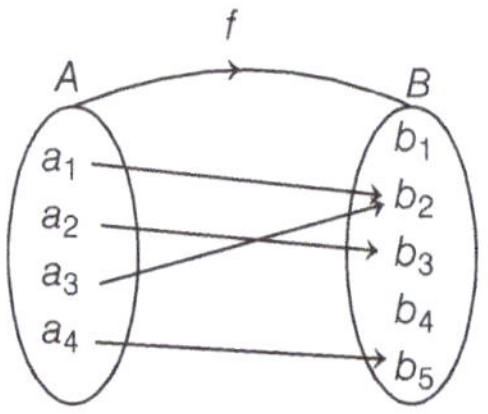

Here, f is many-one function because a_1 and a_3 have same image b_2.

Onto (Surjective) Function

A function $f: A \to B$ is said to be **onto** (or surjective), if every element of B is the image of some elements of A under f.

Mathematically, for every $b \in B$, there exists an element a in A such that $f(a) = b$.

In other words, $f: A \to B$ is onto if and only if

$$\text{Range of } f = B$$

i.e. $$\text{Range} = \text{Codomain}$$

e.g. Let $f: A \to B$ be a function represented by the following diagram.

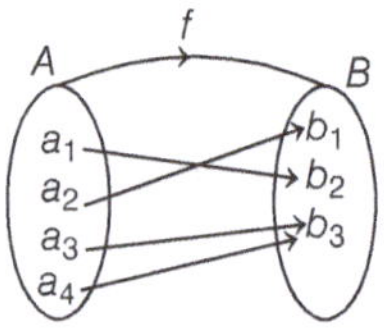

Here, f is an onto function.

Into Function

A function $g: X \to Y$ is an **into function**, if there exists one element in Y, which has no pre-image in X.

In other words, if a function is not onto, then it is an into function.

e.g. Let $g: X \to Y$ be a function represented by the following diagram.

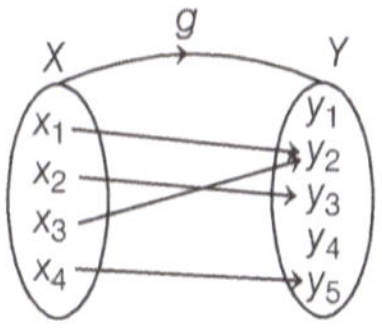

Here, g is an into function because y_1 and y_4 are the elements of Y, which have no pre-image in X.

5. One-One and Onto Function (Bijective)

A function $f: A \to B$ is said to be one-one and onto (or bijective), if f is both one-one and onto i.e. All elements of A have distinct images in B and every element of B is the image of some elements of A.

e.g. Let $f: A \to B$ be a function represented by the following diagram.

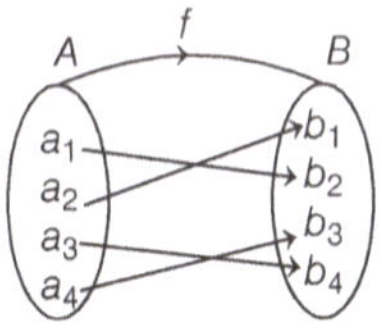

Here, f is bijective function because each element of set A has distinct image in set B and every element of B has pre-image in set A.

TEACHER TIPS

(i) For each $a \in A$, there exists $b \in B$ such that $(a, b) \in f$.

(ii) $(a,b) \in f$ and $(a, c) \in f \Rightarrow b = c$.
Here, b is called f-image or image of a under f and a is called pre-image of b under f.

(iii) If $n(A) = n$, then total number of bijective function $f: A \to A = n!$

(iv) If A is a finite set, then any one-one function $f: A \to A$ must be onto function.

(v) If A is a finite set, then any onto function $f: A \to A$ must be one-one.

(vi) If A is an infinite set, then any one-one function $f: A \to A$, not necessarily onto function and *vice-versa*.

(vii) If A and B are two finite sets having m and n elements respectively, then the number of functions from A to B is n^m.

Example 1 **Let $A = \{1, 2, 3\}$ and $B = \{2, 4, 6, 8\}$. Consider the rule $f: A \to B$, defined as $f(x) = 2x, \forall x \in A$. Find the domain, codomain and range of f.**

Sol. Given, $f(x) = 2x, \forall x \in A$

Value of function at $x = 1$, $f(1) = 2(1) = 2$

Value of function at $x = 2$, $f(2) = 2(2) = 4$

Value of function at $x = 3$, $f(3) = 2(3) = 6$

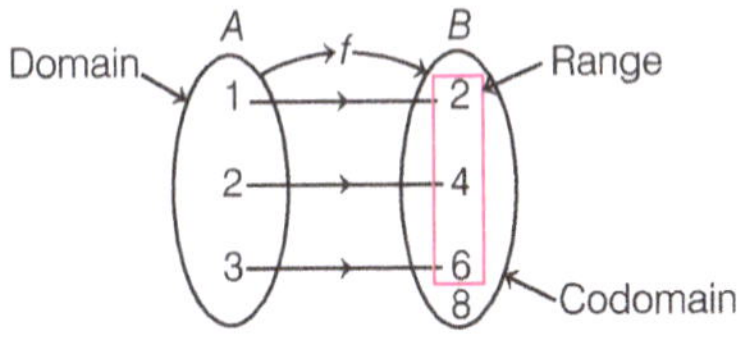

We can write it as $f = \{(1, 2), (2, 4), (3, 6)\}$

$\therefore$ Domain of $f = \{1, 2, 3\}$,

codomain of $f = \{2, 4, 6, 8\}$ and range of $f = \{2, 4, 6\}$

Example 2 **Find the domain and range of the following real functions.**

(i) $f(x) = |x - 3|$ (ii) $g(x) = \log(x + 2)$

Sol. (i) We have, $f(x) = |x - 3|$

It is a modulus function, which is define for all real values of x and the values of $f(x)$ is always non-negative.

$\therefore$ Domain $= R$ and range $= [0, \infty)$

(ii) We have, $g(x) = \log(x + 2)$

It is a logarithm function, which is defined for positive value.

$$\therefore \quad x + 2 > 0 \Rightarrow x > -2$$

and the values of logarithm function are always lie between $(-\infty, \infty)$.

$\therefore$ Domain $= (-2, \infty)$ and range $= (-\infty, \infty)$

Example 3 **Determine whether the following functions are one-one.**

(i) $f: R \to R$ defined by $f(x) = 4x + 7$.

(ii) $g: Z \to Z$ defined by $f(x) = x^2 + 5$.

Sol. (i) Given, $f: R \to R$ defined by $f(x) = 4x + 7$

Let $x_1, x_2 \in R$ such that $f(x_1) = f(x_2)$

$\Rightarrow \quad 4x_1 + 7 = 4x_2 + 7$

$\Rightarrow \quad 4x_1 = 4x_2 \Rightarrow x_1 = x_2$

So, f is one-one function.

(ii) Let $x_1, x_2 \in Z$ such that $f(x_1) = f(x_2)$

$\Rightarrow \quad x_1^2 + 5 = x_2^2 + 5$

$\Rightarrow \quad x_1^2 = x_2^2 \Rightarrow x_1 = \pm x_2$

$\therefore f$ is not a one-one function, as if we take $x_1 = 1$ and $x_2 = -1$, then $f(1) = 6 = f(-1)$ but $1 \neq -1$.

Example 4 **Show that the signum function $f: R \to R$, given by $f(x)=\begin{cases}1, \text{ if } x>0\\ 0, \text{ if } x=0\\ -1, \text{ if } x<0\end{cases}$ is many-one.**

Competency Based Que

Sol. Given, $f: R \to R$ defined by $f(x)=\begin{cases}1, \text{ if } x>0\\ 0, \text{ if } x=0\\ -1, \text{ if } x<0\end{cases}$

Clearly, $f(1)=f(2)=f(3)=1$, where $1, 2, 3 \in R$

$f(0)=0$, where $0 \in R$

and $f(-1)=f(-2)=f(-3)=-1$, where $-1, -2, -3 \in R$

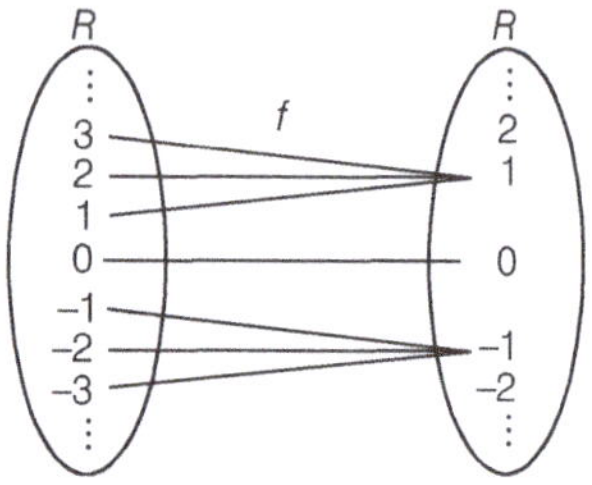

We can observe that all positive real numbers have same image 1 and all negative real numbers have same image −1.

Hence, it is a many-one function.

Example 5 **Let $f: R-\left\{\frac{-4}{3}\right\} \to R$ be a function defined as $f(x)=\frac{4x}{3x+4}$. Show that f is one-one function. Also, check whether f is an onto function or not.**

CBSE 2023

Sol. Given, $f(x)=\frac{4x}{3x+4}$

For one-one

Let $x_1, x_2 \in R-\left\{-\frac{4}{3}\right\}$ such that

$$f(x_1)=f(x_2)$$

$$\Rightarrow \quad \frac{4x_1}{3x_1+4}=\frac{4x_2}{3x_2+4}$$

$$\Rightarrow \quad 12x_1x_2+16x_1=12x_1x_2+16x_2$$

$$\Rightarrow \quad 16x_1=16x_2$$

$$\Rightarrow \quad x_1=x_2$$

So, f is one-one.

For onto

Let $y \in R$ be any arbitrary element.

Then, $y=f(x) \Rightarrow y=\frac{4x}{3x+4}$

$$\Rightarrow \quad 3xy+4y=4x$$

$$\Rightarrow x(4-3y)=4y \Rightarrow x=\frac{4y}{4-3y}$$

It is clear that for every $y \in R$ (codomain), $x \in R-\left\{\frac{-4}{3}\right\}$.

Thus, for each $y \in R$ (codomain), there exists

$x=\frac{4y}{4-3y} \in R-\left\{\frac{-4}{3}\right\}$ (domain) such that

$$f(x)=f\left(\frac{4y}{4-3y}\right)=\frac{4\left(\frac{4y}{4-3y}\right)}{3\left(\frac{4y}{4-3y}\right)+4}$$

$$=\frac{\frac{16y}{4-3y}}{\frac{12y+16-12y}{4-3y}}=\frac{16y}{16}=y$$

[i.e. every element of codomain has pre-image in domain]

So, f is onto.

Example 6 **Show that a function $f: R \to R$ defined as $f(x)=\frac{5x-3}{4}$ is both one-one and onto.**

CBSE 2023

Sol. Given, $f: R \to R$ defined as $f(x)=\frac{5x-3}{4}$

For one-one

Let $x_1, x_2 \in R$ such that $f(x_1)=f(x_2)$

$$\Rightarrow \quad \frac{5x_1-3}{4}=\frac{5x_2-3}{4}$$

$$\Rightarrow \quad 5x_1-3=5x_2-3$$

$$\Rightarrow \quad 5x_1=5x_2$$

$$\Rightarrow \quad x_1=x_2$$

So, f is one-one.

For onto

Let $y \in R$ (codomain) be any arbitrary element.

Then, $y=f(x)$

$$\Rightarrow \quad y=\frac{5x-3}{4} \Rightarrow 4y=5x-3$$

$$\Rightarrow \quad 5x=4y+3 \Rightarrow x=\frac{4y+3}{5}$$

Thus, for each $y \in R$, there exists

$$x=\frac{4y+3}{5} \in R$$

such that $f(x)=f\left(\frac{4y+3}{5}\right)$

$$=\frac{5\left(\frac{4y+3}{5}\right)-3}{4}=\frac{4y+3-3}{4}=y$$

[i.e. every element of codomain has pre-image in domain]

So, f is onto.

Example 7 **Show that the function $f: R \to R$ defined by $f(x) = \dfrac{x}{x^2+1}$, is neither one-one nor onto.**

CBSE 2023, 20, 18

Sol. Given, $f: R \to R$, defined by $f(x) = \dfrac{x}{x^2+1}, \forall x \in R$

Let $x_1, x_2 \in R$ such that $f(x_1) = f(x_2)$

$$\Rightarrow \frac{x_1}{x_1^2+1} = \frac{x_2}{x_2^2+1}$$

$$\Rightarrow x_1 x_2^2 + x_1 = x_2 x_1^2 + x_2$$

$$\Rightarrow x_1 x_2^2 - x_2 x_1^2 + x_1 - x_2 = 0$$

$$\Rightarrow x_1 x_2 (x_2 - x_1) - 1(x_2 - x_1) = 0$$

$$\Rightarrow (x_2 - x_1)(x_1 x_2 - 1) = 0$$

$$\Rightarrow x_2 = x_1 \text{ or } x_1 x_2 = 1$$

$$\Rightarrow x_1 = x_2 \text{ or } x_1 = \frac{1}{x_2}$$

$\therefore f$ is not one-one, as if we take $x_1 = 3$ and $x_2 = \dfrac{1}{3}$, then

$$f(3) = \frac{3}{10} = f\left(\frac{1}{3}\right) \text{ but } 3 \neq \frac{1}{3}$$

Now, let $k \in R$ be any arbitrary element

and let $f(x) = k$

$$\Rightarrow \frac{x}{x^2+1} = k \quad \left[\because f(x) = \frac{x}{x^2+1}\right]$$

$$\Rightarrow kx^2 + k = x \Rightarrow kx^2 - x + k = 0$$

$$\Rightarrow x = \frac{1 \pm \sqrt{1-4k^2}}{2k} \notin R, \text{ if } 1 - 4k^2 < 0$$

or $(1-2k)(1+2k) < 0$ i.e. $k > 1/2$ or $k < -1/2$

So, f is not onto.

Hence, f is neither one-one nor onto.

Example 8 **Show that the function $f: R \to \{x \in R: -1 < x < 1\}$ defined by $f(x) = \dfrac{x}{1+|x|}$, $x \in R$ is one-one and onto function.**

CBSE Sample Paper 2024, Competency Based Que

Sol. We have, $f(x) = \begin{cases} \dfrac{x}{1+x}, & x > 0 \\ \dfrac{x}{1-x}, & x < 0 \end{cases}$

Case I When $x \geq 0$, we have

$$f(x) = \frac{x}{1+x}$$

Checking one-one

$$f(x_1) = \frac{x_1}{1+x_1} \text{ (let } x_1 \in R)$$

and $$f(x_2) = \frac{x_2}{1+x_2} \text{ (let } x_2 \in R)$$

On putting $f(x_1) = f(x_2)$, $\dfrac{x_1}{1+x_1} = \dfrac{x_2}{1+x_2}$

$$\Rightarrow x_1 + x_1 x_2 = x_2 + x_1 x_2 \Rightarrow x_1 = x_2$$

$\therefore f(x)$ is one-one.

Checking onto

Let $f(x) = y$ such that $y \in (-1, 1)$

$$\therefore y = \frac{x}{1+x}$$

$$\Rightarrow y + xy = x \Rightarrow x - xy = y \Rightarrow x(1-y) = y$$

$$\Rightarrow x = \frac{y}{1-y}$$

Thus, for each $y \in R$, there exists

$$x = \frac{y}{1-y} \in R$$

such that $f(x) = f\left(\dfrac{y}{1-y}\right)$

$$= \frac{\left(\dfrac{y}{1-y}\right)}{1+\left(\dfrac{y}{1-y}\right)} = \frac{\dfrac{y}{1-y}}{\dfrac{1-y+y}{1-y}} = \frac{\dfrac{y}{1-y}}{\dfrac{1}{1-y}} = y$$

So, f is onto.

Case II When $x < 0$, we have

$$f(x) = \frac{x}{1-x}$$

Checking one-one

Let $x_1, x_2 \in R$

$$f(x_1) = f(x_2)$$

$$\Rightarrow \frac{x_1}{1-x_1} = \frac{x_2}{1-x_2}$$

$$\Rightarrow x_1 - x_2 x_1 = x_2 - x_2 x_1 \Rightarrow x_1 = x_2$$

$\therefore f(x)$ is one-one.

Checking onto

Let $y = f(x)$ such that $y \in (-1, 1)$

$$\Rightarrow y = \frac{x}{1-x} \Rightarrow y - yx = x \Rightarrow x = \frac{y}{1+y}$$

Thus, for each $y \in R$, there exists

$$x = \frac{y}{1+y} \in R$$

such that $f(x) = f\left(\dfrac{y}{1+y}\right)$

$$= \frac{\dfrac{y}{1+y}}{1-\left(\dfrac{y}{1+y}\right)} = \frac{\dfrac{y}{1+y}}{\dfrac{1+y-y}{1+y}} = \frac{\dfrac{y}{1+y}}{\dfrac{1}{1+y}} = y$$

So, f is onto.

Hence, $f(x)$ is one-one and onto function.

Quick Test 2

1. Suppose two sets A and B are defined as $A=\{2, 3, 4\}$, $B=\{6, 9, 12, 15\}$. The rule between two sets is defined as $f: A \rightarrow B$ such that $f(x)=3x, \forall\ x \in A$. Find the domain, codomain and range of f.

2. Find the domain and range of the following functions.

(i) $f(x)=|x-2|$

(ii) $f(x)=\log(x-2)$

(iii) $h(x)=e^{x-3}$

3. Check whether the function $f: R \rightarrow R$ defined as $f(x)=x^3$ is one-one or not. *CBSE Sample Paper 2021*

4. Let $f: N \rightarrow N$ be defined by

$$f(n)=\begin{cases}\dfrac{n+1}{2}, \text{ if } n \text{ is odd}\\ \dfrac{n}{2}, \text{if } n \text{ is even}\end{cases}.$$

Show that f is many-one and onto function. *NCERT, CBSE Sample Paper 2023*

5. For any real number x, we define the greatest integer as $[x]$ = greatest integer less than or equal to x. Prove that the greatest integer function $f: R \rightarrow R$ such that $f(x)=[x]$ is neither one-one nor onto. *Competency Based Que*

For Solutions, See QR Code on Pg. 20

6. Show that $f: N \rightarrow N$, given by

$$f(x)=\begin{cases}x+1, \text{ if } x \text{ is odd}\\ x-1, \text{if } x \text{ is even}\end{cases}$$ is bijective (both one-one and onto). *Competency Based Que*

7. Let A and B be sets. Show that $f: A \times B \rightarrow B \times A$ such that $f(a, b)=(b, a)$ is bijective function. *NCERT*

8. If $A=R-\{3\}$ and $B=R-\{1\}$. Consider the function $f: A \rightarrow B$ defined by $f(x)=\dfrac{x-2}{x-3}$, for all $x \in A$. Then, show that f is bijective. *CBSE 2025, 14C, 12*

Answers

1. Domain $(f)=\{2, 3, 4\}$,
Codomain $(f)=\{6, 9, 12, 15\}$
and range $(f)=\{6, 9, 12\}$

2. (i) Domain $= R$, Range $=[0, \infty)$
(ii) Domain $=(2, \infty)$, Range $=(-\infty, \infty)$
(iii) Domain $=(-\infty, \infty)$, Range $=(0, \infty)$

3. $f(x)$ is one-one function.

EXAM PATTERN QUESTIONS

Objective Type Questions

Multiple Choice Questions

1. Select the correct option out of the four given options.
Let R be a relation in the set N given by
$R = \{(a,b): a = b-2, b > 6\}$. Then, **CBSE 2023**

(a) $(8,7) \in R$ (b) $(6,8) \in R$
(c) $(3,8) \in R$ (d) $(2,4) \in R$

2. Let R be a relation from R to R, the set of real numbers defined by $R = \{(x, y): x, y \in R$ and $x - y + \sqrt{3}$ is an irrational number$\}$. Then, R is

(a) reflexive (b) transitive
(c) symmetric (d) an equivalence relation

3. Let $A = \{3, 5\}$. Then, number of reflexive relations on A is **CBSE 2023**

(a) 2 (b) 4 (c) 0 (d) 8

4. The maximum number of equivalence relations on the set $A = \{1, 2, 3\}$ are **NCERT Exemplar**

(a) 1 (b) 2 (c) 3 (d) 5

5. A relation R in set $A = \{1, 2, 3\}$ is defined as $R = \{(1, 1), (1, 2), (2, 2), (3, 3)\}$. Which of the following ordered pair in R shall be removed to make it an equivalence relation in A? **CBSE 2022 (Term I)**

(a) (1, 1) (b) (1, 2)
(c) (2, 2) (d) (3, 3)

6. Let the relation R in the set $A = \{x \in Z : 0 \le x \le 12\}$, given by $R = \{(a,b): |a-b|$ is a multiple of $4\}$. Then [1], the equivalence class containing 1, is

CBSE Sample Paper 2022 (Term I)

(a) $\{1, 5, 9\}$ (b) $\{0, 1, 2, 5\}$
(c) ϕ (d) A

7. Let $f : R \to R$ be defined as $f(x) = x^4$. Then, the correct option is **NCERT**

(a) f is one-one onto
(b) f is many-one onto
(c) f is one-one but not onto
(d) f is neither one-one nor onto

8. A function $f : R \to R$ defined as $f(x) = x^2 - 4x + 5$ is **CBSE 2024**

(a) injective but not surjective.
(b) surjective but not injective.
(c) both injective and surjective.
(d) neither injective nor surjective.

9. The function $f : R \to R$ defined as $f(x) = x^3$ is **CBSE Sample Paper 2022 (Term I)**

(a) one-one but not onto
(b) not one-one but onto
(c) neither one-one nor onto
(d) both one-one and onto

10. Let $A = \{1, 2, 3\}$, $B = \{4, 5, 6, 7\}$ and let $f = \{(1, 4), (2, 5), (3, 6)\}$ be a function from A to B. Based on the given information, f is best defined as **CBSE Sample Paper 2022 (Term I)**

(a) surjective function (b) injective function
(c) bijective function (d) None of these

Assertion-Reason Based Questions

Directions (Q. Nos. 11-16) *In the questions given below are two statements labelled as Assertion (A) and Reason (R). In the context of the two statements, which one of the following is correct?*

(a) Both A and R are correct; R is the correct explanation of A.
(b) Both A and R are correct; R is not the correct explanation of A.
(c) A is correct; R is incorrect.
(d) R is correct; A is incorrect.

11. **Assertion** (A) The relation R in the set $A = \{1, 2, 3, 4, 5, 6\}$ defined as $R = \{(x, y) : y$ is divisible by $x\}$ is not an equivalence relation.

Reason (R) The relation R will be an equivalence relation, if it is reflexive, symmetric and transitive.

12. **Assertion** (A) The relation R on the set $A = \{1, 2, 3, 4, 5\}$ given by $R = \{(a, b) : |a - b|$ is multiple of $4\}$ is an equivalence relation.

Reason (R) A relation R on set A is said to be equivalence if it is reflexive, symmetric and transitive.

13. **Assertion** (A) The function $f : R \to R$ given by $f(x) = x^3$ is injective.

Reason (R) The function $f : X \to Y$ is injective, if $f(x) = f(y) \Rightarrow x = y$ for all $x, y \in X$.

14. **Assertion** (A) The relation $f : \{1, 2, 3, 4\} \to \{x, y, z, p\}$ defined by $f = \{(1, x), (2, y), (3, z)\}$ is a bijective function.

Reason (R) The function $f : \{1, 2, 3\} \to \{x, y, z, p\}$ such that $f = \{(1, x), (2, y), (3, z)\}$ is one-one. **CBSE Sample Paper 2023**

15. **Assertion** (A) A function $f: R-\{0\} \to R-\{0\}$ defined by $f(x)=\frac{1}{x}$ is one-one and onto.

Reason (R) A function $f: N \to R-\{0\}$ defined by $f(x)=\frac{1}{x}$ is one-one and onto. **CBSE QB**

16. $f: X \to X$ is a function on the finite set X.

Assertion (A) If f is onto, then f is one-one and if f is one-one, then f is onto.

Reason (R) Every one-one function is always onto and every onto function is always one-one. **CBSE QB**

Case Study Based Questions

17. In a school, madam Sunita take lecture in Class XII. In this class, students divided into two groups A and B. Group A has 20 students and group B has 25 students.

Group A Group B

The relation between students of these groups are defined as R: group $A \to$ group B or $R: A \to B$

$R=\{(x, y): x \in A \text{ and } y \in B\}$.

(i) Find the number of elements in codomain of $R: A \to B$.

(ii) Find the type of relation of the set of all identity elements.

(iii) Find the total number of relations that can be formed from set A to B.

Or

Suppose the relation defined from set A to set B is $R_1=\{(a_1, b_1), (a_2, b_3), (a_3, b_4)\}$, then find the inverse relation.

18. Students of a school are taken to a railway museum to learn about railways heritage and its history.

An exhibit in the museum depicted many rail lines on the track near the railway station. Let L be the set of all rail lines on the railway track and R be the relation on L defined by $R=\{(l_1, l_2): l_1 \text{ is parallel to } l_2\}$.

On the basis of the above information, answer the following questions.

(i) Find whether the relation R is symmetric or not.

(ii) Find whether the relation R is transitive or not.

(iii) If one of the rail lines on the railway track is represented by the equation $y=3x+2$, then find the set of rail lines in R related to it.

Or

Let S be the relation defined by $S=\{(l_1, l_2): l_1 \text{ is perpendicular to } l_2\}$. Check whether the relation S is symmetric or transitive. **CBSE 2024**

Subjective Questions

Very Short Answer Type Questions

1. If the relation R is defined on the set $A=\{1, 2, 3, 4, 5\}$ by $R=\{(a, b): |a^2-b^2|<8\}$. Then, find the relation R. **NCERT Exemplar**

2. Find the domain and range of the following relation $R=\{(c, d): d=|c-1|, c \in Z \text{ and } |c|<4\}$.

3. Let $R=\{(a, a^3): a \text{ is a prime number less than } 5\}$ be a relation. Then, find the range of R. **Competency Based Que**

4. Check whether the relation R defined in set $A=\{4, 5, 6\}$ as $R=\{(4, 4), (4, 5), (5, 4), (4, 6), (6, 4)\}$ is reflexive, symmetric or transitive.

5. An equivalence relation R in A divides it into equivalence classes A_1, A_2, A_3. What is the value of $A_1 \cup A_2 \cup A_3$ and $A_1 \cap A_2 \cap A_3$? **Competency Based Que**

6. Let R be the equivalence relation in the set $A=\{0, 1, 2, 3, 4, 5\}$ given by $R=\{(a, b): 2 \text{ divides } (a-b)\}$. Write the equivalence class $[0]$. **CBSE 2014C**

7. A relation R in the set of real numbers R defined as $R = \{(a, b) : \sqrt{a} = b\}$ is a function or not. Justify. **CBSE Sample Paper 2021**

8. Let $A = \{1, 2, 3\}$, $B = \{4, 5, 6, 7\}$ and f be a function from set A to set B is $f = \{(1, 4), (2, 5), (3, 6)\}$. Then, check whether $f(x)$ is one-to-one or not.

9. Let $A = \{-3, -2, 1, 2\}$ and $B = \{1, 4, 9\}$, then function f is defined from set A to set B such that $f(x) = x^2$. Show that f is many-one function. **CBSE QB**

10. Show that the function $f: R \to R$ defined by $f(x) = 3x - 4$ is bijective. **Diksha App**

Short Answer Type Questions

11. Show that relation R in the set of real numbers, defined as $R = \{(a, b) : a \le b^2\}$ is neither reflexive nor symmetric nor transitive. **NCERT**

12. Check whether the relation R in the set Z of integers defined as $R = \{(a,b): a + b$ is 'divisible by 2'$\}$ is reflexive, symmetric or transitive. Write the equivalence class containing 0 i.e. $[0]$. **CBSE Sample Paper 2021**

13. Show that the relation R on the set $A = \{1, 2, 3, 4, 5\}$ given by $R = \{(a, b) : |a - b|$ is even$\}$ is an equivalence relation.

14. Let T be the set of all triangles in a plane with R, a relation in T given by $R = \{(T_1, T_2): T_1 \cong T_2\}$. Show that R is an equivalence relation. **NCERT**

15. Show that the function $f: N \to N$, given by $f(1) = f(2) = 1$ and $f(x) = x - 1$ for every $x > 2$, is onto but not one-one.

16. Let $A = R - \{3\}$, $B = R - \{1\}$. If $f: A \to B$ is the function defined by $f(x) = \dfrac{x-2}{x-3}$, $\forall\, x \in A$. Then, show that f is bijective. **NCERT Exemplar**

17. Let $A = R - \{2\}$ and $B = R - \{1\}$. If $f: A \to B$ is a function defined by $f(x) = \dfrac{x-1}{x-2}$, show that f is one-one and onto. **Competency Based Que**

18. Show that the modulus function $f: R \to R$ given by $f(x) = |x|$, is neither one-one nor onto, where $|x|$ is x, if x is positive or 0 and $|x|$ is $-x$, if x is negative. **Competency Based Que**

19. $A = \{1, 3, 5, 7, \ldots\}$ and $B = \{2, 4, 6, 8, \ldots\}$. Define a function from A to B that is neither one-one nor onto. **CBSE QB**

20. Show that the function $f: R \to R$ defined by $f(x) = 4x^3 - 5, \forall\, x \in R$ is one-one and onto. **CBSE 2025**

21. Suppose $A = B = \{x \in R: -1 \le x \le 1\}$. Show that $f: A \to B$ given by $f(x) = x|x|$ is a bijection.

Long Answer Type Questions

22. Check whether the relation R in the set N of natural numbers given by $R = \{(a, b) : a$ is divisor of $b\}$ is reflexive, symmetric or transitive. Also, determine whether R is an equivalence relation. **CBSE 2020**

23. Given, a non-empty set X, define the relation R in $P(X)$ as follows

For $A, B \in P(X)$, $(A, B) \in R$ iff $A \subset B$. Prove that R is reflexive, transitive but not symmetric. **CBSE Sample Paper 2023**

24. Show that the relation R on the set Z of all integers defined by $(x, y) \in R \Leftrightarrow (x - y)$ is divisible by 3 is an equivalence relation.

25. Prove that function $f: [0, \infty) \to [-5, \infty)$ defined as $f(x) = 4x^2 + 4x - 5$ is both one-one and onto. **CBSE 2023**

26. A function $f: [-4, 4] \to [0, 4]$ is given by $f(x) = \sqrt{16 - x^2}$. Show that f is an onto function but not a one-one function. Further, find all possible values of a for which $f(a) = \sqrt{7}$. **CBSE 2023**

27. Consider $f: R_+ \to [-9, \infty)$ given by $f(x) = 5x^2 + 6x - 9$. Show that f is bijective.

28. Show that the function $f: N \to N$ given by $f(n) = n - (-1)^n, \forall\, n \in N$ is a bijection.

Hints & Solutions

Objective Type Questions

1. (b) Given, $R = \{(a,b): a = b - 2, b > 6\}$

Since, $b > 6$

When $b = 7$, then $a = 7 - 2 = 5$

When $b = 8$, then $a = 8 - 2 = 6$

So, $(5,7) \in R$ and $(6,8) \in R$

2. (a) **Hint** Given, $R = \{(x,y): x, y \in R$ and $x - y + \sqrt{3}$ is an irrational number$\}$

Then, $x R x \Rightarrow x - x + \sqrt{3} = \sqrt{3}$, which is an irrational number.

So, R is reflexive.

Now, $2 R \sqrt{3} \Rightarrow 2 - \sqrt{3} + \sqrt{3} = 2$, which is not irrational.

Also, $\sqrt{3} R 2 \Rightarrow \sqrt{3} - 2 + \sqrt{3} = 2\sqrt{3} - 2$ which is an irrational number.

$\therefore 2 \not R \sqrt{3}$ but $\sqrt{3} R 2$

$\Rightarrow R$ is not symmetric.

Now, $-\sqrt{3} R \sqrt{5}$ and $\sqrt{5} R 2$

Here, $-\sqrt{3}$ is not related with 2.

$\Rightarrow R$ is not transitive.

3. (b) Here, $n(A) = 2$

The number of reflexive relations $= 2^{n^2 - n}$,

where n is the number of elements in the set

$$= 2^{2^2 - 2} = 2^{4-2} = 2^2 = 4$$

4. (d) We have, set $A = \{1, 2, 3\}$

Now, the possible equivalence relations are as follows

$R_1 = \{(1, 1), (2, 2), (3, 3)\}$,

$R_2 = \{(1, 1), (2, 2), (3, 3), (1, 2), (2, 1)\}$,

$R_3 = \{(1, 1), (2, 2), (3, 3), (1, 3), (3, 1)\}$,

$R_4 = \{(1, 1), (2, 2), (3, 3), (2, 3), (3, 2)\}$

and $R_5 = \{(1, 1), (2, 2), (3, 3), (1, 2), (1, 3), (2, 1), (2, 3), (3, 1), (3, 2)\}$

Thus, maximum number of equivalence relations is 5.

5. (b) We have, $A = \{1,2,3\}$

$$R = \{(1,1),(1,2),(2,2),(3,3)\}$$

R is an equivalence relation in A, if $(1,2)$ is removed from R.

6. (a) $A = \{0,1,2,3,\ldots.12\}$

$R = \{(a,b): |a - b|$ is multiple of $4\}$

The equivalence class containing 1 is $\{1, 5, 9\}$.

7. (d) Given, $f(x) = x^4$

Let $x, y \in R$ such that $f(x) = f(y)$

$\Rightarrow \quad x^4 = y^4$

$\Rightarrow \quad x = \pm y$

Therefore, $f(x_1) = f(x_2)$ does not imply that $x_1 = x_2$.

Also, there does not exist any x in domain R such that $f(x) = 2$.

Here, $f(x)$ is neither one-one nor onto.

8. (d) Given, $f(x) = x^2 - 4x + 5$

Consider two points x_1 and x_2 on R such that

$$f(x_1) = f(x_2)$$

This gives $x_1 \neq x_2$.

So, f is not one-one.

Now, let $y = x^2 - 4x + 5$

$\Rightarrow x^2 - 4x + 5 - y = 0$

Discriminant $(D) = 4^2 - 4(5 - y) \geq 0 \Rightarrow y \geq 1$

So, range $\in [1, \infty)$

Since, codomain $\neq$ range

$\therefore f$ is not onto.

Hence, $f(x)$ is neither one-one nor onto.

9. (d) We have, $f(x) = x^3$

For one-one, $f(x_1) = f(x_2)$

$\Rightarrow \quad x_1 = x_2$

Let $x_1, x_2 \in R$

$$f(x_1) = f(x_2)$$

$\Rightarrow \quad x_1^3 = x_2^3$

$\Rightarrow \quad x_1^3 - x_2^3 = 0$

$\Rightarrow \quad (x_1 - x_2)(x_1^2 + x_1x_2 + x_2^2) = 0$

$\Rightarrow \quad x_1 = x_2$ and $x_1^2 + x_1x_2 + x_2^2 \neq 0$

$\therefore f(x)$ is one-one function.

Range of $f(x) = (-\infty, \infty)$

$\Rightarrow \quad$ Range = Codomain

$\therefore f(x)$ is also onto function.

Hence, $f(x)$ is both one-one and onto.

10. (b) We have, $A = \{1,2,3\}, B = \{4,5,6,7\}$

Function $f = \{(1,4),(2,5),(3,6)\}$

Clearly, f is injective function.

Now, range of $f = \{4,5,6\}$

Codomain $= \{4,5,6,7\}$

Here, Range $\neq$ Codomain

$\therefore f$ is not surjective function.

11. (a) **For reflexive** We know that x is divisible by x, which is true for all $x \in A$.

$\therefore \quad (x,x) \in R$ for all $x \in A$.

So, R is reflexive.

For symmetry We observe that 6 is divisible by 2. This means that $(2,6) \in R$ but $(6,2) \notin R$. So, R is not symmetric.

For transitivity Let $(x,y) \in R$ and $(y,z) \in R$

$\Rightarrow y$ is divisible by x and z is divisible by y

$\Rightarrow z$ is divisible by x

$\Rightarrow (x, z) \in R$

e.g. 2 is divisible by 1 and 4 is divisible by 2.

So, 4 is divisible by 1. So, R is transitive.

Clearly, R is reflexive and transitive but not symmetric.

$\therefore$ R is not an equivalence relation.

Hence, both Assertion and Reason are correct and Reason is correct explanation of Assertion.

12. (a) A relation is said to equivalence relation, when relation is reflexive, symmetric and transitive.

$\therefore$ Reason is correct.

We have, $A = \{1, 2, 3, 4, 5\}$

$R = \{(a, b) : |a - b| \text{ is a multiple of } 4\}$, where $a, b \in A$

For Reflexive

Since, $|a - a| = |0| = 0$ and 0 is a multiple of 4.

$\Rightarrow$ $|a - a|$ is a multiple of 4.

$\Rightarrow$ $(a, a) \in R$.

$\therefore$ R is reflexive.

For Symmetric

We know that $|a - b| = |b - a|$

Hence, if $|a - b|$ is a multiple of 4, then $|b - a|$ is also a multiple of 4.

Hence, if $(a, b) \in R$, then $(b, a) \in R$.

$\therefore$ R is symmetric.

For Transitive If $|a - b|$ is a multiple of 4, then $(a - b)$ is multiple of 4.

Similarly, if $|b - c|$ is a multiple of 4, then $(b - c)$ is a multiple of 4.

Now, $(a - b + b - c)$ is also a multiple of 4

$\Rightarrow$ $(a - c)$ is a multiple of 4

Hence, $|a - c|$ is a multiple of 4

i.e. If $(a, b) \in R$ and $(b, c) \in R$, then $(a, c) \in R$

$\therefore$ R is transitive.

Since, R is an equivalence relation.

Hence, both Assertion and Reason are correct and Reason is the correct explanation of Assertion.

13. (a) Here, $f : R \to R$ is given as $f(x) = x^3$.

Suppose $f(x) = f(y)$ where $x, y \in R$

$\Rightarrow \quad x^3 = y^3 \quad \ldots(i)$

Now, we try to show that $x = y$.

Suppose $x \neq y$, their cubes will also be not equal.

$x^3 \neq y^3$

However, this will be a contradiction to Eq. (i).

Therefore, $x = y$.

Hence, f is injective.

Hence, both Assertion and Reason are correct and Reason is the correct explanation of Assertion.

14. (d) Given relation, $f : \{1, 2, 3, 4\} \to \{x, y, z, p\}$

and $f = \{(1, x), (2, y), (3, z)\}$

Since, 4 has no image under f, so relation f is not a function.

$\therefore$ Assertion is incorrect.

Now, $f : \{1, 2, 3\} \to \{x, y, z, p\}$

and $f = \{(1, x), (2, y), (3, z)\}$

Since, every element of {1, 2, 3} has different image in $\{x, y, z, p\}$ under f, so the given relation f is one-one.

$\therefore$ Reason is correct.

15. (c) $f : R - \{0\} \to R - \{0\}$

$$f(x) = \frac{1}{x}$$

For one-one $f(x_1) = f(x_2)$

$$\Rightarrow \quad \frac{1}{x_1} = \frac{1}{x_2}$$

$$\Rightarrow \quad x_1 = x_2 \quad [\because x_1, x_2 \neq 0]$$

$f(x)$ is one-one.

For onto let $y = \frac{1}{x}$

$\Rightarrow \quad x = \frac{1}{y}$ exists for all values of y except 0.

Range $= R - \{0\}$

Clearly, we can see that Codomain = Range

$\therefore$ $f(x)$ is onto.

Assertion is correct.

Now, $f : N \to R - \{0\}$

For one-one $f(x_1) = f(x_2)$

$$\Rightarrow \quad \frac{1}{x_1} = \frac{1}{x_2} \Rightarrow x_1 = x_2 \quad [\because x_1, x_2 \neq 0]$$

For onto If $x \in N$, then $\frac{1}{x} \in (0, 1]$

So, all numbers other than (0, 1] will not have pre-image.

Hence, f is not onto.

Reason is incorrect.

16. (c) $f : X \to X$ is a function on the finite set X.

For f to be onto, every element in the set X must be mapped to some elements in X.

Since, f maps from X to X, if every element is covered, there cannot be duplicate.

Hence, f must be one-one.

Also, f is one-one, then f is onto.

For f to be one-one, every element in X must map to a unique element in X.

Since, X is infinite, so f is onto.

Therefore, Assertion is correct for a function $f : X \to X$ on a finite set X.

Reason For function on finite sets, a one-one function implies onto and *vice-versa*. This is not necessarily true for infinite sets.

So, Reason is incorrect in this context.

17. (i) Given that number of students in group $A = 20$

i.e. $n(A) = 20$

Number of students in group $B = 25$

i.e. $n(B) = 25$

Hence, the number of elements in codomain is 25.

(ii) The set of all identity elements is equivalence.

(iii) **Hint** Total number of relations that can be formed from set A to set B is 2^{mn}. **Ans.** 2^{500}

or

Hint An inverse relation is a relation where the elements of each ordered pair are swapped.

Ans. $\{(b_1, a_1), (b_3, a_2), (b_4, a_3)\}$

18. We have, $R = \{(l_1, l_2) : l_1$ is parallel to $l_2\}$

(i) If l_1 is parallel to l_2, then l_2 is parallel to l_1.

So, if $(l_1, l_2) \in R$, then $(l_2, l_1) \in R$

$\therefore$ R is symmetric.

(ii) If l_1 is parallel to l_2 and l_2 is parallel to l_3, then l_1 is parallel to l_3.

So, if $(l_1, l_2) \in R$, $(l_2, l_3) \in R$, then $(l_1, l_3) \in R$

$\therefore$ R is transitive.

(iii) Let equation of line parallel to $y = 3x + 2$ be $y = mx + c$, where m is the slope of line.

Since, $y = 3x + 2$ and $y = mx + c$ are parallel.

Slope of $(y = 3x + 2)$ = Slope of $(y = mx + c)$

$\Rightarrow 3 = m$ i.e. $m = 3$

Hence, the required line is $y = 3x + c$, where $c \in R$.

or

We have, $S = \{(l_1, l_2) : l_1$ is perpendicular to $l_2\}$

For symmetric If l_1 is perpendicular to l_2, then l_2 is perpendicular to l_1.

So, if $(l_1, l_2) \in S$, then $(l_2, l_1) \in S$

$\therefore$ S is symmetric.

For transitive If l_1 is perpendicular to l_2 and l_2 is perpendicular to l_3, then l_1 is not perpendicular to l_3, it is parallel to l_3.

So, if $(l_1, l_2) \in S$, $(l_2, l_3) \in S$, then $(l_1, l_3) \notin S$.

$\therefore$ S is not transitive.

Subjective Questions

1. We have, set $A = \{1, 2, 3, 4, 5\}$

and relation $R = \{(a, b) : |a^2 - b^2| < 8\}$

This means we need to find pairs (a, b) such that the product $|(a - b)(a + b)|$ is less than 8.

Pairs for $a = 1$: (1, 1), (1, 2)

$a = 2$: (2, 1), (2, 2), (2, 3)

$a = 3$: (3, 2), (3, 3), (3, 4)

$a = 4$: (4, 3), (4, 4)

$a = 5$: (5, 5)

Thus, the relation is

$R = \{(1, 1), (1, 2), (2, 1), (2, 2), (2, 3), (3, 2), (3, 3), (3, 4), (4, 3), (4, 4), (5, 5)\}$

2. Since, $|c| < 4$ and $c \in Z$.

$\therefore$ $c = \{-3, -2, -1, 0, 1, 2, 3\}$

$\therefore$ $(-3, |-3-1|) = (-3, 4)$

$(-2, |-2-1|) = (-2, 3)$

$(-1, |-1-1|) = (-1, 2)$

$(0, |0-1|) = (0, 1)$

$(1, |1-1|) = (1, 0)$

$(2, |2-1|) = (2, 1)$

$(3, |3-1|) = (3, 2)$

Domain $= \{-3, -2, -1, 0, 1, 2, 3\}$

Range $= \{0, 1, 2, 3, 4\}$

3. Given, $R = \{(a, a^3) : a$ is a prime number less than $5\}$.

We know that 2 and 3 are the prime numbers less than 5.

So, a can take values 2 and 3.

Thus, $R = \{(2, 2^3), (3, 3^3)\} = \{(2, 8), (3, 27)\}$

Hence, the range of R is $\{8, 27\}$.

4. We have, $R = \{(4, 4), (4, 5), (5, 4), (4, 6), (6, 4)\}$

Reflexive Here, $(5, 5), (6, 6) \notin R$, so R is not reflexive.

Symmetric Here, $(5, 4) \in R$ and $(4, 5) \in R$, so R is symmetric.

Transitive Here, $(6, 4), (4, 6) \in R$ but $(6, 6) \notin R$, so R is not transitive.

5. As we know that an equivalence relation R defined on a set A partitions the set A into pairwise disjoint subsets and collection of all equivalence classes form set A.

$\therefore A_1 \cup A_2 \cup A_3 = A$ and $A_1 \cap A_2 \cap A_3 = \phi$

6. Given, $R = \{(a, b) : 2$ divides $(a - b)\}$ and $A = \{0, 1, 2, 3, 4, 5\}$

Clearly, $[0] = \{b \in A : (0, b) \in R\}$

$= \{b \in A : 2$ divides $(0 - b)\}$

$= \{b \in A : 2$ divides $(-b)\} = \{0, 2, 4\}$

Hence, the equivalence class of $[0] = \{0, 2, 4\}$.

7. Since, $\sqrt{a}$ is not defined for $a \in (-\infty, 0)$.

$\therefore R = \{(a, b) : \sqrt{a} = b\}$ is not a function.

8. We have, $f = \{(1, 4), (2, 5), (3, 6)\}$

Here, we see that every element of set A has unique image.

Hence, f is one-one.

9. We have, $A = \{-3, -2, 1, 2\}$, $B = \{1, 4, 9\}$ and $f(x) = x^2$

Now, $f(-2) = (-2)^2 = 4$ and $f(2) = (2)^2 = 4$

Here, we see that for different values of x, we get the same value of f. Hence, f is many-one function.

10. Given, $f(x) = 3x - 4$

One-one Let $x_1, x_2 \in R$ such that $f(x_1) = f(x_2)$

$\therefore$ $3x_1 - 4 = 3x_2 - 4$

$\Rightarrow$ $3x_1 = 3x_2 \Rightarrow x_1 = x_2$

So, $f(x)$ is one-one.

Onto Let $f(x) = y$ such that $y \in R$

$\therefore$ $y = 3x - 4$

$\Rightarrow$ $x = \dfrac{y + 4}{3}$

Thus, for each $y \in R$, there exists

$$x = \frac{y+4}{3} \in R$$

such that $f(x) = f\left(\frac{y+4}{3}\right) = 3 \times \left(\frac{y+4}{3}\right) - 4 = y + 4 - 4 = y$

Thus, $f(x)$ is onto.

Hence, $f(x)$ is bijective function.

11. We have, $R = \{(a, b) : a \le b^2\}$, where $a, b \in R$

For reflexivity We observe that $\frac{1}{2} \le \left(\frac{1}{2}\right)^2$ is not true.

So, R is not reflexive as $\left(\frac{1}{2}, \frac{1}{2}\right) \notin R$.

For symmetry We observe that

$$-1 \le 3^2 \text{ but } 3 \not\le (-1)^2$$

$\therefore$ $(-1, 3) \in R$ but $(3, -1) \notin R$

So, R is not symmetric.

For transitivity We observe that

$2 \le (-3)^2$ and $-3 \le (1)^2$ but $2 \not\le (1)^2$.

$\therefore$ $(2, -3) \in R$ and $(-3, 1) \in R$ but $(2, 1) \notin R$.

So, R is not transitive.

Hence, R is neither reflexive nor symmetric nor transitive.

12. We have, $R = \{(a,b): a + b$ is 'divisible by 2'$\}$

Reflexivity For any $a \in Z$, we have

$a + a = 2a$, which is divisible by 2.

$\Rightarrow$ $(a, a) \in R$

Thus, $(a, a) \in R$ for all $a \in Z$.

So, R is reflexive.

Symmetry Let $(a, b) \in R$.

Then, $(a + b)$ is divisible by 2.

$\Rightarrow$ $(b + a)$ is divisible by 2.

$\Rightarrow$ $(b, a) \in R$

So, R is symmetric.

Transitivity Let $(a, b) \in R$ and $(b, c) \in R$. Then,

$(a + b)$ is divisible by 2 and $(b + c)$ is divisible by 2

$\Rightarrow$ $a + b = 2\lambda$ ...(i)

and $b + c = 2\mu$ ...(ii)

On adding Eqs. (i) and (ii), we get

$$a + 2b + c = 2(\lambda + \mu)$$

$\Rightarrow$ $a + c = 2(\lambda + \mu - b)$

$\Rightarrow$ $a + c = 2k$, where $k = \lambda + \mu - b$

$\therefore$ $a + c$ is divisible by 2.

$\Rightarrow (a, c) \in R$

So, R is transitive.

Since, R is reflexive, symmetric and transitive, so R is equivalence relation.

Equivalence class of 0

Let $b \in Z$ such that $(0, b) \in R$

$\Rightarrow$ $0 + b$ is divisible by 2.

$\therefore$ $b = \{\ldots -6, -4, -2, 0, 2, 4, 6 \ldots\}$

13. **For reflexive** We know that $|a - a| = 0$ and zero is divisible by even number, so $(a, a) \in R, \forall a \in A$.

Hence, relation is reflexive.

For symmetric If $|a - b|$ is multiple of 2, then $|b - a|$ is also multiple of 2 because $|a - b| = |b - a|$.

Hence, if $(a, b) \in R$, then $(b, a) \in R, \forall a, b \in A$

Hence, relation is symmetric.

For transitive If $|a - b|$ is multiple of 2 (say $|a - b| = 2k$) and $|b - c|$ is also multiple of 2 (say $|b - c| = 2m$), then

$$|a - c| = |(a - b) + (b - c)|$$
$$= |2k + 2m| = 2|k + m|$$

Hence, $|a - c|$ is also multiple of 2.

So, $(a, b) \in R$ and $(b, c) \in R$, then $(a, c) \in R, \forall a, b, c \in A$.

Hence, it is transitive.

14. Given, $R = \{(T_1, T_2) \in T \times T : T_1 \cong T_2\}$

For reflexive $(T_1, T_1) \in R$ is true as $T_1 \cong T_1$ for all $T_1 \in T$ (i.e. triangle is congruent to itself).

Hence, R is reflexive.

For symmetric $(T_1, T_2) \in R$

$\Rightarrow$ $T_1 \cong T_2 \Rightarrow T_2 \cong T_1$

$\Rightarrow$ $(T_2, T_1) \in R$.

Hence, R is symmetric.

For transitive Let $(T_1, T_2) \in R$ and $(T_2, T_3) \in R$

$\Rightarrow$ $T_1 \cong T_2$ and $T_2 \cong T_3$

$\Rightarrow$ $T_1 \cong T_3 \Rightarrow (T_1, T_3) \in R$.

Hence, R is transitive.

Since, R is reflexive symmetric and transitive.

Hence, R is an equivalence relation.

15. We have, a function $f : N \to N$, defined as

$$f(1) = f(2) = 1 \text{ and } f(x) = x - 1, \text{ for every } x > 2$$

For one-one Since, $f(1) = f(2) = 1$, therefore 1 and 2 have same image, namely 1. So, f is not one-one.

For onto Note that $y = 1$ has two pre-images, namely 1 and 2. Now, let $y \in N$, $y \ne 1$ be any arbitrary element.

Then, $y = f(x) \Rightarrow y = x - 1$

$\Rightarrow$ $x = y + 1 > 2$ for every $y \in N, y \ne 1$.

Thus, for every $y \in N, y \ne 1$, there exists $x = y + 1$ such that

$$f(x) = f(y + 1) = y + 1 - 1 = y$$

Hence, f is onto.

16. Given that $A = R - \{3\}, B = R - \{1\}$.

$$f : A \to B \text{ is defined by } f(x) = \frac{x - 2}{x - 3}, \forall x \in A$$

For injectivity

Let $f(x_1) = f(x_2) \Rightarrow \frac{x_1 - 2}{x_1 - 3} = \frac{x_2 - 2}{x_2 - 3}$

$\Rightarrow$ $(x_1 - 2)(x_2 - 3) = (x_2 - 2)(x_1 - 3)$

$\Rightarrow x_1x_2 - 3x_1 - 2x_2 + 6 = x_1x_2 - 3x_2 - 2x_1 + 6$

$\Rightarrow \quad -3x_1 - 2x_2 = -3x_2 - 2x_1$

$\Rightarrow \quad -x_1 = -x_2 \Rightarrow x_1 = x_2$

So, $f(x)$ is an injective function.

For surjectivity

Let $\quad y = \dfrac{x-2}{x-3} \Rightarrow x - 2 = xy - 3y$

$\Rightarrow x(1-y) = 2 - 3y$

$\Rightarrow \quad x = \dfrac{2-3y}{1-y}$

$\Rightarrow \quad x = \dfrac{3y-2}{y-1} \in A, \forall\, y \in B \quad$ [codomain]

So, $f(x)$ is surjective function.

Hence, $f(x)$ is a bijective function.

17. Let $x_1, x_2 \in R - \{2\}$ such that

$$f(x_1) = f(x_2)$$

$\Rightarrow \quad \dfrac{x_1 - 1}{x_1 - 2} = \dfrac{x_2 - 1}{x_2 - 2}$

$\Rightarrow \quad x_1x_2 - 2x_1 - x_2 + 2 = x_1x_2 - 2x_2 - x_1 + 2$

$\Rightarrow \quad x_1 = x_2$

So, f is one-one.

For range Let $f(x) = y$

$$\frac{x-1}{x-2} = y \Rightarrow x = \frac{2y-1}{y-1}$$

Range of $f = R - \{1\} =$ codomain (B)

$\Rightarrow f$ is onto.

18. $f(x) = |x| = \begin{cases} x, \text{if } x \ge 0 \\ -x, \text{if } x < 0 \end{cases}$

One-one Let $x_1 = 1, x_2 = -1$ be two elements belong to R

$f(x_1) = f(1) = |1|$ and $f(x_2) = f(-1) = -(-1) = 1$

$\Rightarrow \quad f(x_1) = f(x_2)$, for $x_1 \ne x_2$

$\Rightarrow f(x)$ is not one-one.

Onto Let $f(x) = -1$

$\Rightarrow |x| = -1 \in R$, which is not possible.

$\Rightarrow f(x)$ is not onto.

Hence, f is neither one-one nor onto function.

19. Given, $A = \{1, 3, 5, 7, \ldots\}$ and $B = \{2, 4, 6, 8, \ldots\}$

To define a function $f : A \to B$, which is neither one-one nor onto.

$\therefore \quad f(x) = 2, \forall\, x \in A$

Here, all elements of A are mapped to the same element in B, the function is not one-one and only element $2 \in B$ is the image of elements in A.

The other elements in B are not images of any elements in A.

Hence, the function is not onto.

Thus, $f(x) = 2, \forall\, x \in A$ is neither one-one nor onto.

20. The given function is $f : R \to R$ such that

$$f(x) = 4x^3 - 5$$

One-one function Let $x_1, x_2 \in R$ such that $f(x_1) = f(x_2)$

$\Rightarrow \quad 4x_1^3 - 5 = 4x_2^3 - 5$

$\Rightarrow \quad 4x_1^3 = 4x_2^3$

$\Rightarrow \quad x_1^3 - x_2^3 = 0$

$\Rightarrow \quad (x_1 - x_2)(x_1^2 + x_1x_2 + x_2^2) = 0$

$[\because a^3 - b^3 = (a-b)(a^2 + ab + b^2)]$

$\Rightarrow \quad (x_1 - x_2)\left[\left(x_1 + \dfrac{x_2}{2}\right)^2 + \dfrac{3}{4}x_2^2\right] = 0$

$\Rightarrow$ Either $x_1 - x_2 = 0 \quad \ldots$(i)

or $\quad \left(x_1 + \dfrac{x_2}{2}\right)^2 + \dfrac{3}{4}x_2^2 = 0 \quad \ldots$(ii)

But Eq. (ii) gives complex roots as $x_1, x_2 \in R$.

$\therefore$ From Eq. (i), $x_1 - x_2 = 0 \Rightarrow x_1 = x_2$

Thus, $\quad f(x_1) = f(x_2) \Rightarrow x_1 = x_2, \ \forall\, x_1, x_2 \in R$

Therefore, $f(x)$ is a one-one function.

Onto function Let $y \in R$ (codomain) be any arbitrary number.

Then, $\quad f(x) = y$

$\Rightarrow \quad 4x^3 - 5 = y$

$\Rightarrow \quad 4x^3 = y + 5$

$\Rightarrow \quad x^3 = \dfrac{y+5}{4}$

$\Rightarrow \quad x = \left(\dfrac{y+5}{4}\right)^{1/3}$,

which is a real number. $\quad [\because y \in R]$

Thus, for every $y \in R$ (codomain), there exists

$$x = \left(\frac{y+5}{4}\right)^{1/3} \in R \text{ (domain) such that}$$

$$f(x) = f\left[\left(\frac{y+5}{4}\right)^{1/3}\right] = 4\left[\left(\frac{y+5}{4}\right)^{1/3}\right]^3 - 5$$

$$= 4\left(\frac{y+5}{4}\right) - 5 = y + 5 - 5 = y$$

Therefore, $f(x)$ is an onto function.

21. We have, $A = B = \{x \in R : -1 \le x \le 1\}$

Let x and y be any two distinct elements in set A.

Then, $x \ne y \Rightarrow x|x| \ne y|y| \Rightarrow f(x) \ne f(y)$

So, f is one-one function.

We have, $f(x) = x|x| = \begin{cases} x^2, & \text{if } x \ge 0 \\ -x^2, & \text{if } x < 0 \end{cases}$

If $0 \le x \le 1$, then $f(x) = x^2$ take all values of x from 0 to 1.

Also, if $-1 \le x < 0$, then $f(x) = -x^2$ take all values between -1 and 0 with including -1.

So, range of f is same as its codomain.

Thus, $f : A \to B$ is an onto function.

Hence, f is both one-one and onto, so it is a bijection.

22. Given relation R on the set N of natural numbers is given by $R=\{(a,b): a \text{ is divisor of } b\}$

Reflexive Let $a \in N$

We have, a is divisible by itself.

$\therefore a R a$ i.e. $(a,a) \in R$

It is reflexive.

Symmetric Let $a, b \in N$

$\therefore a R b \Rightarrow a$ is divisor of b

$\Rightarrow \quad b = ka$, where k is any positive integer

$\Rightarrow \quad \frac{1}{k} = \frac{a}{b} \Rightarrow \frac{a}{b} = \frac{1}{k} \neq$ any integer

$\Rightarrow b$ is not divisor of a

$\Rightarrow (b,a) \notin R$

$\therefore$ It is not symmetric.

Transitive Let $a, b, c \in N$

$a R b \Rightarrow a$ is divisor of b

$\Rightarrow \quad b = k_1 a \quad \ldots(i)$

where k_1 is any positive integer

and $b R c \Rightarrow b$ is divisor of c

$\Rightarrow \quad c = k_2 b \quad \ldots(ii)$

where k_2 is positive integer.

From Eqs. (i) and (ii), we get

$c = k_2 \times k_1 a$

$\Rightarrow \quad c = k_1 k_2 a$

$\Rightarrow \quad \frac{c}{a} = k_1 k_2 =$ positive integer

$\Rightarrow \quad a$ is divisor of c

$\Rightarrow \quad (a,c) \in R$

$\Rightarrow \quad a R c$

$\therefore$ It is transitive.

Since, R is reflexive and transitive but not symmetric.

Hence, R is not an equivalence relation.

23. Given, a relation R in the set $P(X)$, where X is a non-empty set as $(A,B) \in R$ iff $A \subset B$.

Let $\quad A \in P(X)$

Then, $\quad A \subset A$

$\Rightarrow \quad (A,A) \in R$

Hence, R is reflexive.

Now, let $\phi, A \in P(X)$ such that $\phi \subset A$

$\therefore \quad (\phi, A) \in R$

But $A \not\subset \phi$

$\therefore \quad (A, \phi) \notin R$

Hence, R is not symmetric.

Let $A, B, C \in P(X)$ such that $(A,B), (B,C) \in R$

$\Rightarrow \quad A \subset B$ and $B \subset C$

$\Rightarrow \quad A \subset C \Rightarrow (A,C) \in R$

Hence, R is transitive.

24. The given relation is $R = \{(x,y): x, y \in Z \text{ and } x-y \text{ is divisible by } 3\}$.

To prove R is an equivalence relation, we have to prove R is reflexive, symmetric and transitive.

Reflexive As for any $x \in Z$, we have $x - x = 0$, which is divisible by 3.

$\Rightarrow (x-x)$ is divisible by 3

$\Rightarrow (x,x) \in R, \forall x \in Z$

Therefore, R is reflexive.

Symmetric Let $(x,y) \in R$, where $x, y \in Z$.

$\Rightarrow \quad (x-y)$ is divisible by 3. [by definition of R]

$\Rightarrow x - y = 3A$ for some $A \in Z$.

$\Rightarrow y - x = 3(-A)$

$\Rightarrow (y-x)$ is also divisible by 3 $\Rightarrow (y,x) \in R$

Therefore, R is symmetric.

Transitive Let $(x,y) \in R$, where $x, y \in Z$.

$\Rightarrow \quad (x-y)$ is divisible by 3.

$\Rightarrow \quad x - y = 3A$ for some $A \in Z$

Again, let $(y,z) \in R$, where $y, z \in Z$.

$\Rightarrow \quad (y-z)$ is divisible by 3.

$\Rightarrow \quad y - z = 3B$ for some $B \in Z$.

Now, $(x-y)+(y-z) = 3A + 3B$

$\Rightarrow \quad x - z = 3(A+B)$

$\Rightarrow \quad (x-z)$ is divisible by 3 for some $(A+B) \in Z$

$\Rightarrow \quad (x,z) \in R$

Therefore, R is transitive.

Thus, R is reflexive, symmetric and transitive. Hence, it is an equivalence relation.

25. Given function $f:[0,\infty) \to [-5,\infty)$ defined as

$$f(x) = 4x^2 + 4x - 5$$

One-one

Let $x_1, x_2 \in [0,\infty)$ such that $x_1 \neq x_2$

$\therefore \quad 4x_1 \neq 4x_2$

$\Rightarrow \quad 4x_1 - 5 \neq 4x_2 - 5 \Rightarrow 4x_1^2 + 4x_1 - 5 \neq 4x_2^2 + 4x_2 - 5$

$\Rightarrow \quad f(x_1) \neq f(x_2)$

$\therefore$ Function is one-one.

Onto

For $x \in [0,\infty)$,

$f(x) = 4x^2 + 4x - 5 \quad$ [given]

$\Rightarrow \quad f(x) \geq -5$

$\Rightarrow \quad R(f) = [-5,\infty)$

$\therefore$ Given function is onto.

Hence, function is both one-one and onto.

26. Given function, $f:[-4,4] \to [0,4]$

defined by $f(x) = \sqrt{16 - x^2}$

For one-one

Let $x_1, x_2 \in [-4,4]$

such that $f(x_1) = f(x_2)$

$\Rightarrow \quad \sqrt{16 - x_1^2} = \sqrt{16 - x_2^2}$

$\Rightarrow \quad 16 - x_1^2 = 16 - x_2^2$

$\Rightarrow \quad x_1^2 = x_2^2 \Rightarrow (x_1^2 - x_2^2) = 0$

$\Rightarrow \quad (x_1 - x_2)(x_1 + x_2) = 0$

$\Rightarrow \quad x_1 - x_2 = 0$ or $x_1 + x_2 = 0$

$\Rightarrow \quad x_1 = x_2$ or $x_1 = -x_2$

$\Rightarrow f(x)$ is not one-one function.

For onto

Let $y \in [0,4]$ (codomain) be any arbitrary element.

Then, $y = f(x)$

$\Rightarrow \quad y = \sqrt{16 - x^2} \Rightarrow y^2 = 16 - x^2$

$\Rightarrow \quad x^2 = 16 - y^2 \Rightarrow x = \sqrt{16 - y^2}$

Thus, for each $y \in [0,4]$, there exists

$x = \sqrt{16 - y^2} \in [-4,4]$ such that $f(x) = y$

So, $f(x)$ is onto.

Also given, $f(a) = \sqrt{7} \Rightarrow \sqrt{16 - a^2} = \sqrt{7}$

$\Rightarrow \quad 16 - a^2 = 7 \Rightarrow a^2 = 9 \Rightarrow a = \pm 3$

27. Given, $f : R_+ \to [-9, \infty)$ given by

$$f(x) = 5x^2 + 6x - 9$$

One-one Let $x_1, x_2 \in R_+$, then

$$f(x_1) = f(x_2)$$

$\Rightarrow 5x_1^2 + 6x_1 - 9 = 5x_2^2 + 6x_2 - 9$

$\Rightarrow \quad 5x_1^2 + 6x_1 - 5x_2^2 - 6x_2 = 0$

$\Rightarrow \quad 5(x_1^2 - x_2^2) + 6(x_1 - x_2) = 0$

$\Rightarrow 5(x_1 - x_2)(x_1 + x_2) + 6(x_1 - x_2) = 0$

$\Rightarrow \quad (x_1 - x_2)(5x_1 + 5x_2 + 6) = 0$

$\Rightarrow \quad x_1 - x_2 = 0 \quad [\because 5x_1 + 5x_2 + 6 \neq 0]$

$\Rightarrow \quad x_1 = x_2$

i.e. f is one-one function.

Onto $\because f(x) = 5x^2 + 6x - 9 = 5\left\{x^2 + 2 \times x \times \frac{3}{5} - \frac{9}{5}\right\}$

$$= 5\left\{x^2 + 2 \times x \times \frac{3}{5} + \left(\frac{3}{5}\right)^2 - \left(\frac{3}{5}\right)^2 - \frac{9}{5}\right\}$$

$$= 5\left\{\left(x + \frac{3}{5}\right)^2 - \frac{9}{25} - \frac{9}{5}\right\}$$

$$= 5\left\{\left(x + \frac{3}{5}\right)^2 - \frac{54}{25}\right\}$$

$\because \left(x + \frac{3}{5}\right)^2 \geq \frac{9}{25} \Rightarrow \left(x + \frac{3}{5}\right)^2 - \frac{54}{25} \geq \frac{9}{25} - \frac{54}{25} = -\frac{9}{5}$

$\Rightarrow \quad 5\left\{\left(x + \frac{3}{5}\right)^2 - \frac{54}{25}\right\} \geq -9$

$\Rightarrow \quad f(x) \geq -9$

$\Rightarrow R(f) = [-9, \infty) =$ codomain.

As f is both one-one and onto.

$\Rightarrow f$ is bijective

Hence, f is one-one onto function.

28. We have, $f(n) = n - (-1)^n, \forall n \in N$

$$f(n) = \begin{cases} n + 1, \text{if } n \text{ is odd} \\ n - 1, \text{if } n \text{ is even} \end{cases}$$

For one-one

Case I If n is odd.

Let $x_1, x_2 \in N$ such that $f(x_1) = f(x_2)$

As $f(x_1) = f(x_2)$

$\Rightarrow x_1 + 1 = x_2 + 1$

$\Rightarrow \quad x_1 = x_2$

Case II If n is even

Let $x_1, x_2 \in N$ such that $f(x_1) = f(x_2)$

As $f(x_1) = f(x_2)$

$\Rightarrow x_1 - 1 = x_2 - 1$

$\Rightarrow \quad x_1 = x_2$

So, f is one-one function.

For onto

Case I If n is odd

As for every $n \in N$, there exists $y = n - 1$ in N such that $f(y) = f(n-1) = n - 1 + 1 = n$

Case II If n is even

As for every $n \in N$, there exists $y = n + 1$ in N such that $f(y) = f(n+1) = n + 1 - 1 = n$

So, f is onto.

Hence, $f(n)$ is bijective function.

QR Code
for Quick Test 1

QR Code
for Quick Test 2

Mind Map

Relations and Functions

Relations

If A and B are two non-empty sets, then a relation R from set A to set B is a subset of $A \times B$ i.e. $R : A \to B \Leftrightarrow R \subseteq A \times B$.
e.g. For set $A = \{1, 3, 5\}$ and set $B = \{2, 6, 10\}$, the relation R from set A to set B is $R = \{(a, b) \in A \times B : b = 2a\}$.

Domain, Codomain and Range of a Function

Suppose, a function f is defined from set A to set B i.e. $f : A \to B$. Then,

- **Domain** of the function f is the elements of set A i.e. Domain $(f) = A$
- **Range** of the function f is the set of all f image obtained in set B corresponding to each element belongs to set A i.e. Range $(f) = f(A) = \{f(x) : x \in A\}$
- **Codomain** of the function is the elements of set B i.e. Codomain $(f) = B$

Functions

For any two non-empty sets A and B, a function f from A to B is a rule which associates each element of set A to a unique element of set B.
A function f from A to B is represented by $f : A \to B$ or $A \xrightarrow{f} B$ or $f(x)$
e.g. $f : N \to N$ define as $f(x) = x^2$ is a function, where N is the set of natural numbers.

Types of Relations

Empty or Void Relation
Relation R in a set A is called an empty relation, if no element of A is related to any element of A.
i.e. $R = \phi \subseteq A \times A$

Universal Relation
Relation R in a set A is called an universal relation if each element of A is related to every element of A.
i.e. $R = A \times A$.

Identity Relation
Relation R in a set A is called an identity relation if each element of A is related to itself only and it is denoted by I_A.
i.e. $I_A = R = \{(a, a) : a \in A\}$

Reflexive Relation
Relation R in a set A is called reflexive relation if $(a, a) \in R$ for every $a \in A$.
i.e. $aRa, \forall\, a \in A$

Symmetric Relation
Relation R in a set A is called symmetric relation if $(a, b) \in R \Rightarrow (b, a) \in R$, for every $a, b \in A$.
i.e. $aRb \Rightarrow bRa, \forall a, b \in A$

Transitive Relation
Relation R in a set A is called transitive relation if $(a, b) \in R$ and $(b, c) \in R \Rightarrow (a, c) \in R, \forall\, a, b, c \in A$.
i.e. aRb and $bRc \Rightarrow aRc, \forall\, a, b, c \in A$.

Equivalence Relation
A relation R on set A is said to be an equivalence relation on A iff it is reflexive, symmetric and transitive.

Domain, Range and Codomain of Relation

Suppose, a relation R from set A to set B is defined as $R = \{(a, b) \in A \times B\}$. Then,

- **Domain** of relation is the set of all first elements of the ordered pairs in R. i.e. Domain $(R) = \{a : (a, b) \in R\}$
- **Range** of relation is the set of all second elements of the ordered pairs in R. i.e. Range $(R) = \{b : (a, b) \in R\}$
- **Codomain** of relation is the set B in relation R. i.e Codomain $(R) = \{B\}$

Equivalence Classes

Consider an equivalence relation R on a set A and let $a \in A$. Then, the set of all those elements of A which are related to a, is called the equivalence class of R determined by a and it is denoted by $[a]$. Thus, $[a] = \{b \in A : (a, b) \in R\}$.
e.g. Let R be the equivalence relation in the set $A = \{0, 1, 2, 3, 4, 5\}$ given by $R = \{(a, b) :$ 2 divides $(a - b)\}$. Then, write equivalence class $[0]$ is defined as
$[0] = \{b \in A : (0, b) \in R\} = \{b \in A :$ 2 divides $(0 - b)\} = \{b \in A :$ 2 divides $(-b)\}$
So, b can be 0, 2, 4.
Hence, equivalence class $[0] = \{0, 2, 4\}$.

Types of Functions

One-One (Injective) Function
A function $f : A \to B$ is called a one-one or injective function, if distinct elements of A have distinct images in B.
i.e. For every $a_1, a_2 \in A$ if $a_1 \neq a_2$, then $f(a_1) \neq f(a_2)$ and if $f(a_1) = f(a_2)$, then $a_1 = a_2$.

Many-One Function
A function $f : A \to B$ is called a many-one function if there exist atleast two distinct elements in set A whose images are same in set B i.e. if there exist $a_1, a_2 \in A$ such that $a_1 \neq a_2$ and $f(a_1) = f(a_2)$, then f is many-one.
In other words, a function $f : A \to B$ is called a many-one function, if it is not one-one.

Onto (Surjective) Function
A function $f : A \to B$ is said to be onto (or surjective) if every element of B is the image of some elements of A under f.
Mathematically, for every $b \in B$, there exists an element a in A such that $f(a) = b$.
In other words, $f : A \to B$ is onto if and only if Range of $f = B$
i.e. Range = Codomain

Into Function
A function $g : X \to Y$ is an into function, if there exists one element in Y which has no pre-image in X. In other words, if a function is not onto, then it is an into function.

One-One Onto Function (Bijective)
A function $f : A \to B$ is said to be one-one and onto (or bijective) if f is both one-one and onto i.e. all elements of A have distinct images in B and every element of B is the image of some elements of A.

02

CHAPTER

Talent is important, but how one develops and nurtures it is even more so.

— *Terence Tao*

Inverse Trigonometric Functions

▼ **YOUR STUDY GOALS**

2.1 Domain and Range of Inverse Trigonometric Functions

2.2 Elementary Properties of Inverse Trigonometric Functions

▼ **YOUR PRACTICE GOALS**

- Objective Type Questions (32 Qs ; 20 MCQs, 10 A-R, 2 Case Based)
- Subjective Type Questions (25 Qs ; 9 VSA, 11 SA, 5 LA)

If $f : A \rightarrow B$ is a one-one onto (bijective) function from A to B, then its inverse function will be $f^{-1} : B \rightarrow A$.

i.e. **Domain of f^{-1} = Range of f** and **Range of f^{-1} = Domain of f.**

2.1 Domain and Range (Principal Value Branch) of Inverse Trigonometric Functions

The range of trigonometric functions become the domain of inverse trigonometric functions and restricted domain of trigonometric function becomes range or principal value branch.

Function	Domain	Range (Principal value branch)
$\sin^{-1} x$	$[-1, 1]$	$\left[-\frac{\pi}{2}, \frac{\pi}{2}\right]$
$\cos^{-1} x$	$[-1, 1]$	$[0, \pi]$
$\tan^{-1} x$	R	$\left(-\frac{\pi}{2}, \frac{\pi}{2}\right)$
$\cot^{-1} x$	R	$(0, \pi)$
$\sec^{-1} x$	$R-(-1,1)$	$[0, \pi]-\left\{\frac{\pi}{2}\right\}$
$\operatorname{cosec}^{-1} x$	$R-(-1,1)$	$\left[-\frac{\pi}{2}, \frac{\pi}{2}\right]-\{0\}$

Graphs of Inverse Trigonometric Functions

Functions	Graph
$y = \sin^{-1} x$	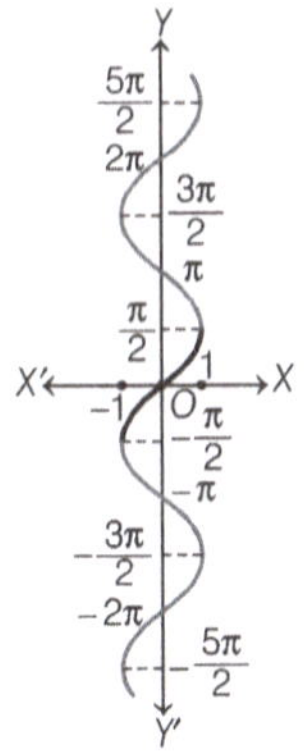
$y = \cos^{-1} x$	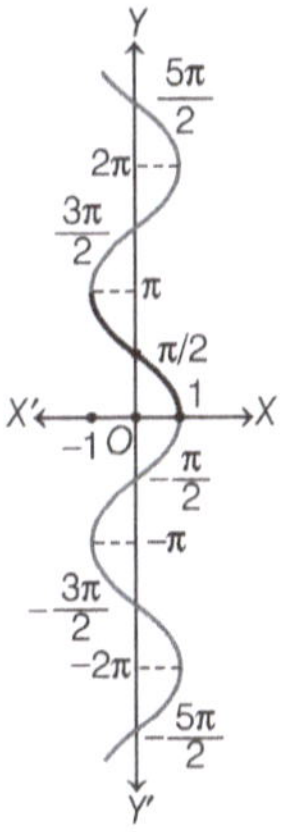
$y = \tan^{-1} x$	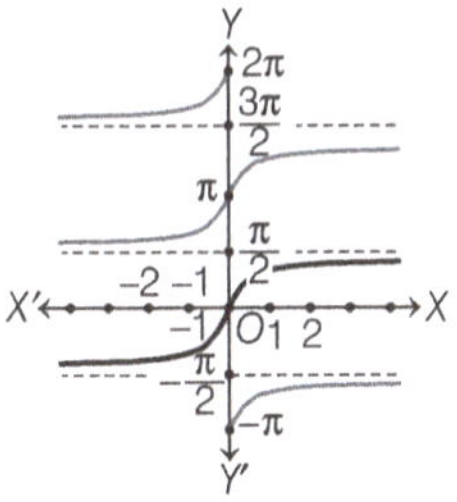
$y = \sec^{-1} x$	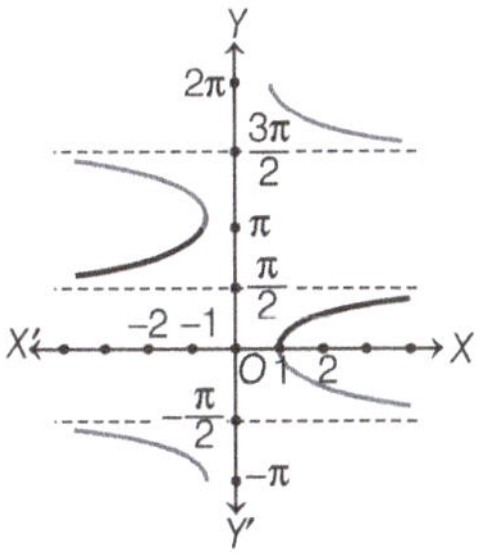

Functions	Graph
$y = \operatorname{cosec}^{-1} x$	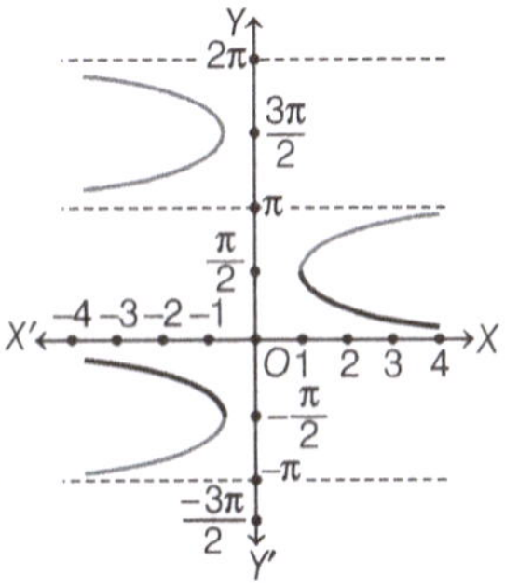
$y = \cot^{-1} x$	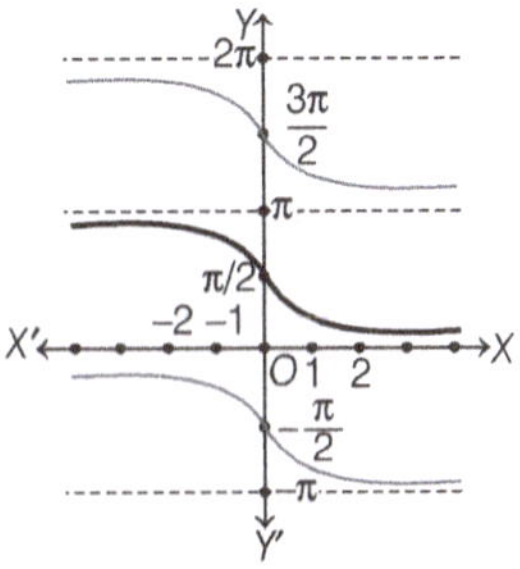

Note In the above graphs, dark line denotes the graph of inverse trigonometric functions in the principal value branch.

TEACHER TIPS

(i) $\sin^{-1} x$ should not be confused with $(\sin x)^{-1} = \dfrac{1}{\sin x}$ or $\sin x^{-1} = \sin \dfrac{1}{x}$. Similarly, for other inverse trigonometric functions.

(ii) When $y = f(x) = \sin x$, then $x = \sin^{-1} y$.

(iii) The value of an inverse trigonometric function which lies in its principal value branch is called the **Principal Value** of that inverse trigonometric function.

(iv) Whenever no branch of an inverse trigonometric function is mentioned, it means we have to consider the principal value branch of that function.

Example 1 **Find the domain of $\sin^{-1}(x^2 - 4)$.**

CBSE 2023, CBSE Sample Paper 2024

Sol. Let $y = \sin^{-1}(x^2 - 4) \Rightarrow \sin y = x^2 - 4$

i.e. $-1 \le x^2 - 4 \le 1$ $\quad [\because -1 \le \sin y \le 1]$

$\Rightarrow \quad 3 \le x^2 \le 5$

$\Rightarrow \quad \sqrt{3} \le |x| \le \sqrt{5}$

$\Rightarrow \quad x \in [-\sqrt{5}, -\sqrt{3}] \cup [\sqrt{3}, \sqrt{5}]$

Example 2 **Find the principal value of** $\cot^{-1}\left(-\frac{1}{\sqrt{3}}\right)$.

CBSE 2025, 20, NCERT Exemplar

Sol. Let $y = \cot^{-1}\left(\frac{-1}{\sqrt{3}}\right)$

$\Rightarrow \cot y = \frac{-1}{\sqrt{3}} \Rightarrow \cot y = -\cot\frac{\pi}{3} = \cot\left(\pi - \frac{\pi}{3}\right)$

$[\because \cot(\pi - \theta) = -\cot\theta]$

$\Rightarrow \cot y = \cot\left(\frac{2\pi}{3}\right)$

$\Rightarrow \quad y = \frac{2\pi}{3} \in (0, \pi)$

[$\because$ principal value branch of $\cot^{-1}$ is $(0, \pi)$]

Example 3 **Find the value of**

$$\tan^{-1}\left[2\cos\left(2\sin^{-1}\frac{1}{2}\right)\right] + \tan^{-1} 1.$$

CBSE 2023

Sol. **For principal value of** $\sin^{-1}\left(\frac{1}{2}\right)$

Let $\quad y = \sin^{-1}\frac{1}{2} \Rightarrow \sin y = \frac{1}{2}$

$\Rightarrow \sin y = \sin\frac{\pi}{6}$

$\Rightarrow \quad y = \frac{\pi}{6} \in \left[\frac{-\pi}{2}, \frac{\pi}{2}\right]$

For principal value of $\tan^{-1} 1$

Let $x = \tan^{-1} 1 \Rightarrow \tan x = 1$

$\Rightarrow \quad \tan x = \tan\frac{\pi}{4}$

$\Rightarrow \quad x = \frac{\pi}{4} \in \left(\frac{-\pi}{2}, \frac{\pi}{2}\right)$

Now, $\tan^{-1}\left[2\cos\left(2\sin^{-1}\frac{1}{2}\right)\right] + \tan^{-1} 1$

$= \tan^{-1}\left[2\cos\left(2 \times \frac{\pi}{6}\right)\right] + \frac{\pi}{4}$

$= \tan^{-1}\left[2\cos\frac{\pi}{3}\right] + \frac{\pi}{4} = \tan^{-1}\left[2 \times \frac{1}{2}\right] + \frac{\pi}{4}$

$= \tan^{-1} 1 + \frac{\pi}{4} = \frac{\pi}{4} + \frac{\pi}{4} = \frac{2\pi}{4} = \frac{\pi}{2}$

Example 4 **Find the value of**

$$\cos^{-1}\left(\frac{1}{2}\right) - \tan^{-1}\left(\frac{-1}{\sqrt{3}}\right) + \operatorname{cosec}^{-1}(-2).$$

CBSE 2024C

Sol. Let $x = \cos^{-1}\frac{1}{2}$

$\Rightarrow \cos x = \frac{1}{2} = \cos\frac{\pi}{3}$

$\Rightarrow \quad x = \frac{\pi}{3} \in [0, \pi]$

So, the principal value of $\cos^{-1}\left(\frac{1}{2}\right)$ is $\frac{\pi}{3}$.

Again, let $y = \tan^{-1}\left(\frac{-1}{\sqrt{3}}\right)$

$\Rightarrow \quad \tan y = \frac{-1}{\sqrt{3}} = -\tan\frac{\pi}{6}$

$\Rightarrow \quad \tan y = \tan\left(-\frac{\pi}{6}\right)$

$\Rightarrow \quad y = -\frac{\pi}{6} \in \left(-\frac{\pi}{2}, \frac{\pi}{2}\right)$

So, principal value of $\tan^{-1}\left(-\frac{1}{\sqrt{3}}\right)$ is $-\frac{\pi}{6}$.

And again, let $z = \operatorname{cosec}^{-1}(-2)$

$\Rightarrow \quad \operatorname{cosec} z = -2$

$\Rightarrow \quad \operatorname{cosec} z = -\operatorname{cosec}\frac{\pi}{6}$

$= \operatorname{cosec}\left(-\frac{\pi}{6}\right)$

$\Rightarrow \quad z = -\frac{\pi}{6} \in \left[-\frac{\pi}{2}, \frac{\pi}{2}\right] - \{0\}$

So, the principal value of $\operatorname{cosec}^{-1}(-2)$ is $-\frac{\pi}{6}$

$\therefore \quad \cos^{-1}\left(\frac{1}{2}\right) - \tan^{-1}\left(\frac{-1}{\sqrt{3}}\right) + \operatorname{cosec}^{-1}(-2)$

$= \frac{\pi}{3} - \left(-\frac{\pi}{6}\right) + \left(-\frac{\pi}{6}\right)$

$= \frac{\pi}{3} + \frac{\pi}{6} - \frac{\pi}{6}$

$= \frac{\pi}{3}$

Example 5 Find the value of k, if

$$\sin^{-1}\left[k\tan\left(2\cos^{-1}\frac{\sqrt{3}}{2}\right)\right]=\frac{\pi}{3}.$$

CBSE 2024

Sol. We have,

$$\sin^{-1}\left[k\tan\left(2\cos^{-1}\frac{\sqrt{3}}{2}\right)\right]=\frac{\pi}{3}$$

$$\Rightarrow \sin^{-1}\left[k\tan\left(2\times\frac{\pi}{6}\right)\right]=\frac{\pi}{3} \quad \left[\because \cos^{-1}\frac{\sqrt{3}}{2}=\frac{\pi}{6}\right]$$

$$\Rightarrow \sin^{-1}\left[k\tan\left(\frac{\pi}{3}\right)\right]=\frac{\pi}{3}$$

$$\Rightarrow \sin^{-1}(k\sqrt{3})=\frac{\pi}{3} \quad \left[\because \tan\frac{\pi}{3}=\sqrt{3}\right]$$

$$\Rightarrow k\sqrt{3}=\sin\frac{\pi}{3}$$

$$\Rightarrow k\sqrt{3}=\frac{\sqrt{3}}{2}$$

$$\Rightarrow k=\frac{1}{2}$$

Example 6 Draw the graph of $f(x)=\sin^{-1}x$, $x\in\left[-\frac{1}{\sqrt{2}},\frac{1}{\sqrt{2}}\right]$. Also, write range of $f(x)$.

CBSE 2023

Sol. Graph of $\sin^{-1}x$ is given below

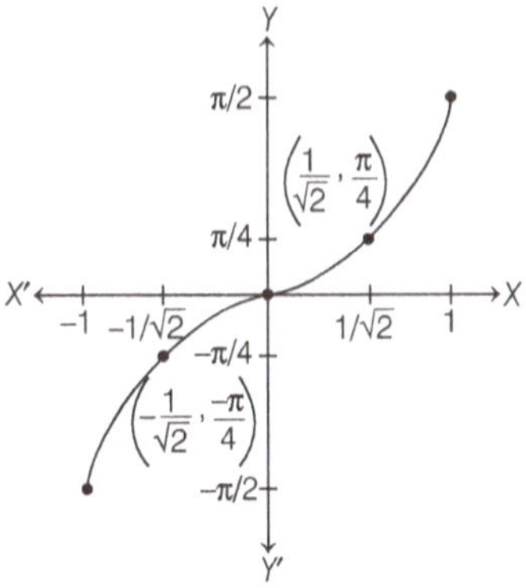

$$f(x)=\sin^{-1}x,\ x\in\left[-\frac{1}{\sqrt{2}},\frac{1}{\sqrt{2}}\right]$$

Range of $f(x)$ is $\left[-\frac{\pi}{4},\frac{\pi}{4}\right]$.

Quick Test 1

1. Find the domain of the following functions.
(i) $\sin^{-1}\sqrt{x-1}$ (ii) $\cos^{-1}(2x-1)$

2. Write the domain and range (principal value branch) of the following function $f(x)=\tan^{-1}x$. CBSE 2023

3. Find the principal value of the following
(i) $\operatorname{cosec}^{-1}(-\sqrt{2})$ (ii) $\cos^{-1}\left(-\frac{\sqrt{3}}{2}\right)$ NCERT

4. Evaluate $3\sin^{-1}\left(\frac{1}{\sqrt{2}}\right)+2\cos^{-1}\left(\frac{\sqrt{3}}{2}\right)+\cos^{-1}(0)$. CBSE 2023

5. Evaluate $\sin\left[\frac{\pi}{2}-\cos^{-1}\left(\frac{1}{\sqrt{2}}\right)\right]$.

6. Find the value of $\cos^{-1}\left(\frac{1}{2}\right)+2\sin^{-1}\left(\frac{1}{2}\right)$. CBSE 2025

7. Evaluate $\tan^{-1}\sqrt{3}-\cot^{-1}(-\sqrt{3})-\frac{\pi}{4}$. Competency Based Que

8. Find the value of $\operatorname{cosec}^{-1}\left(\frac{2}{\sqrt{3}}\right)-\cos^{-1}\left(-\frac{\sqrt{3}}{2}\right)$. Competency Based Que

9. Find the value of k, if $\tan^{-1}\left[k\sin\left(2\cos^{-1}\frac{\sqrt{3}}{2}\right)\right]=\frac{\pi}{3}$.

10. Draw the graph of $\cos^{-1}x$, where $x\in[-1,0]$. Also, write its range. CBSE 2023, Competency Based Que

Answers

1. (i) [1, 2] (ii) [0, 1]

2. Domain = R and Range (principal value branch) $=\left(-\frac{\pi}{2},\frac{\pi}{2}\right)$

3. (i) $\frac{-\pi}{4}$ (ii) $\frac{5\pi}{6}$ **4.** $\frac{19\pi}{12}$ **5.** $\frac{1}{\sqrt{2}}$

6. $\frac{2\pi}{3}$ **7.** $\frac{-3\pi}{4}$ **8.** $-\frac{\pi}{2}$ **9.** 2

10.

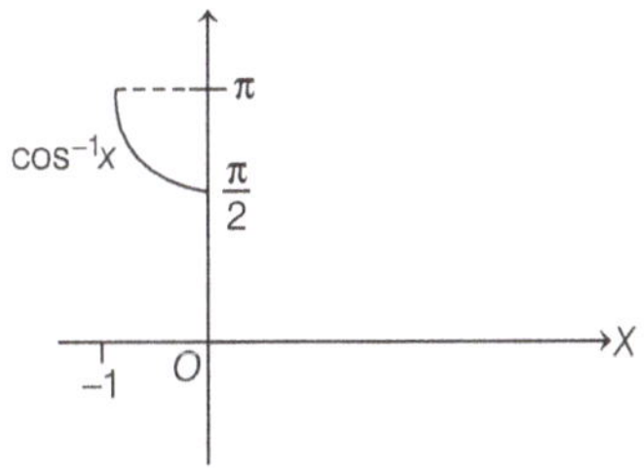

Range of $\cos^{-1}x$ is $\left[\frac{\pi}{2},\pi\right]$.

For Solutions, See QR Code on Pg. 38

2.2 Elementary Properties of Inverse Trigonometric Functions

Elementary properties of inverse trigonometric functions given are valid within the principal value branches of the corresponding inverse trigonometric function and wherever they are defined.

PROPERTY I

(i) $\sin^{-1}(\sin\theta) = \theta, \theta \in \left[-\frac{\pi}{2}, \frac{\pi}{2}\right]$

(ii) $\cos^{-1}(\cos\theta) = \theta, \theta \in [0, \pi]$

(iii) $\tan^{-1}(\tan\theta) = \theta, \theta \in \left(-\frac{\pi}{2}, \frac{\pi}{2}\right)$

(iv) $\cot^{-1}(\cot\theta) = \theta, \theta \in (0, \pi)$

(v) $\text{cosec}^{-1}(\text{cosec}\,\theta) = \theta, \theta \in \left[-\frac{\pi}{2}, \frac{\pi}{2}\right] - \{0\}$

(vi) $\sec^{-1}(\sec\theta) = \theta, \theta \in [0, \pi] - \left\{\frac{\pi}{2}\right\}$

PROPERTY II

(i) $\sin(\sin^{-1} x) = x, x \in [-1, 1]$

(ii) $\cos(\cos^{-1} x) = x, x \in [-1, 1]$

(iii) $\tan(\tan^{-1} x) = x, x \in R$

(iv) $\cot(\cot^{-1} x) = x, x \in R$

(v) $\text{cosec}(\text{cosec}^{-1} x) = x, x \in (-\infty, -1] \cup [1, \infty)$

(vi) $\sec(\sec^{-1} x) = x, x \in (-\infty, -1] \cup [1, \infty)$

Some Important Substitutions

Important substitutions to simplify trigonometrical expressions involving inverse trigonometrical functions are given below.

Expression	Substitution
$\sqrt{a^2 + x^2}$	$x = a\tan\theta$ or $x = a\cot\theta$
$\sqrt{a^2 - x^2}$	$x = a\sin\theta$ or $x = a\cos\theta$
$\sqrt{x^2 - a^2}$	$x = a\sec\theta$ or $x = a\,\text{cosec}\,\theta$
$\sqrt{a^2 + x^2} \pm \sqrt{a^2 - x^2}, \sqrt{\frac{a^2 + x^2}{a^2 - x^2}}, \sqrt{\frac{a^2 - x^2}{a^2 + x^2}}$	$x^2 = a^2\cos 2\theta$
$\sqrt{a + x} \pm \sqrt{a - x}, \sqrt{\frac{a + x}{a - x}}, \sqrt{\frac{a - x}{a + x}}$	$x = a\cos 2\theta$

Example 1 Evaluate $\cos^{-1}\left[\cos\left(-\frac{7\pi}{3}\right)\right]$. *CBSE 2023*

Sol. $\cos^{-1}\left[\cos\left(-\frac{7\pi}{3}\right)\right] = \cos^{-1}\left[\cos\frac{7\pi}{3}\right]$ $[\because \cos(-\theta) = \cos\theta]$

$= \cos^{-1}\left[\cos\left(2\pi + \frac{\pi}{3}\right)\right]$

$= \cos^{-1}\left(\cos\frac{\pi}{3}\right)$

$= \frac{\pi}{3} \in [0, \pi]$

$[\because \cos(2\pi + \theta) = \cos\theta \text{ and } \cos^{-1}(\cos\theta) = \theta]$

Example 2 Evaluate

$$\sin^{-1}\left(\sin\frac{3\pi}{4}\right) + \cos^{-1}\left(\cos\frac{3\pi}{4}\right) + \tan^{-1}(1)$$

CBSE 2023

Sol. We have, $\sin^{-1}\left(\sin\frac{3\pi}{4}\right) + \cos^{-1}\left(\cos\frac{3\pi}{4}\right) + \tan^{-1}(1)$

$= \sin^{-1}\left[\sin\left(\pi - \frac{\pi}{4}\right)\right] + \cos^{-1}\left[\cos\frac{3\pi}{4}\right] + \frac{\pi}{4}$

$= \sin^{-1}\left(\sin\frac{\pi}{4}\right) + \frac{3\pi}{4} + \frac{\pi}{4}$

$= \frac{\pi}{4} + \frac{3\pi}{4} + \frac{\pi}{4} = \frac{5\pi}{4}$

Example 3 Evaluate $\cos\left(\tan^{-1}\frac{3}{4}\right)$. *CBSE 2010*

Sol. We have, $\cos\left(\tan^{-1}\frac{3}{4}\right)$

Let $x = \tan^{-1}\frac{3}{4}$, then $\tan x = \frac{3}{4}$

$\because \sec x = \sqrt{1 + \tan^2 x} = \sqrt{1 + \left(\frac{3}{4}\right)^2}$

$= \sqrt{1 + \frac{9}{16}} = \sqrt{\frac{25}{16}} = \frac{5}{4}$

$\Rightarrow \cos x = \frac{4}{5}$ $\left[\because \cos x = \frac{1}{\sec x}\right]$

$\Rightarrow x = \cos^{-1}\left(\frac{4}{5}\right)$

$\therefore \tan^{-1}\left(\frac{3}{4}\right) = \cos^{-1}\left(\frac{4}{5}\right)$ $\left[\because x = \tan^{-1}\frac{3}{4}\right]$

Now, $\cos\left(\tan^{-1}\frac{3}{4}\right) = \cos\left(\cos^{-1}\frac{4}{5}\right) = \frac{4}{5}$

$[\because \cos(\cos^{-1} x) = x, \forall x \in [-1, 1]]$

Example 4 Find the value of $\tan(\cos^{-1} x)$ and hence evaluate $\tan\left(\cos^{-1}\dfrac{8}{17}\right)$.

NCERT Exemplar

Sol. Let $\cos^{-1} x = \theta \Rightarrow x = \cos\theta$

Now, $\sec\theta = \dfrac{1}{\cos\theta} = \dfrac{1}{x}$

$\therefore \quad \tan\theta = \sqrt{\sec^2\theta - 1} = \dfrac{\sqrt{1-x^2}}{x}$

Hence, $\tan(\cos^{-1} x) = \dfrac{\sqrt{1-x^2}}{x}$

Now, $\tan\left(\cos^{-1}\dfrac{8}{17}\right) = \dfrac{\sqrt{1-\left(\dfrac{8}{17}\right)^2}}{\dfrac{8}{17}}$

$= \dfrac{15}{8}$

Example 5 Write the value of $\tan\left(2\tan^{-1}\dfrac{1}{5}\right)$.

CBSE 2013

Sol. We have, $\tan\left(2\tan^{-1}\dfrac{1}{5}\right)$

Let $\tan^{-1}\left(\dfrac{1}{5}\right) = \theta \Rightarrow \tan\theta = \dfrac{1}{5}$

$\therefore \tan\left(2\tan^{-1}\dfrac{1}{5}\right) = \tan 2\theta = \dfrac{2\tan\theta}{1-\tan^2\theta}$

$= \dfrac{2\left(\dfrac{1}{5}\right)}{1-\left(\dfrac{1}{5}\right)^2} = \dfrac{\dfrac{2}{5}}{\dfrac{25-1}{25}}$

$= \dfrac{2}{5} \times \dfrac{25}{24} = \dfrac{5}{12}$

$\therefore \tan\left(2\tan^{-1}\dfrac{1}{5}\right) = \dfrac{5}{12}$

Example 6 Simplify $\cos^{-1} x + \cos^{-1}\left[\dfrac{x}{2} + \dfrac{\sqrt{3-3x^2}}{2}\right]$; $\dfrac{1}{2} \le x \le 1$.

CBSE 2024

Sol. We have, $\cos^{-1} x + \cos^{-1}\left[\dfrac{x}{2} + \dfrac{\sqrt{3-3x^2}}{2}\right]$

Let $\cos^{-1} x = \alpha \Rightarrow x = \cos\alpha$

$\therefore \quad \cos^{-1} x + \cos^{-1}\left[\dfrac{x}{2} + \dfrac{\sqrt{3-3x^2}}{2}\right]$

$= \alpha + \cos^{-1}\left[\cos\alpha \cdot \cos\dfrac{\pi}{3} + \dfrac{\sqrt{3}}{2}\sqrt{1-\cos^2\alpha}\right]$

$\left[\because \cos\dfrac{\pi}{3} = \dfrac{1}{2}\right]$

$= \alpha + \cos^{-1}\left[\cos\dfrac{\pi}{3}\cos\alpha + \sin\dfrac{\pi}{3}\sin\alpha\right]$

$\left[\because \sin\alpha = \sqrt{1-\cos^2\alpha} \text{ and } \sin\dfrac{\pi}{3} = \dfrac{\sqrt{3}}{2}\right]$

$= \alpha + \cos^{-1}\left[\cos\left(\dfrac{\pi}{3} - \alpha\right)\right]$

$[\because \cos(A-B) = \cos A \cos B + \sin A \sin B]$

$= \alpha + \dfrac{\pi}{3} - \alpha = \dfrac{\pi}{3}$ $\quad [\because \cos^{-1}(\cos\theta) = \theta]$

Example 7 Express $\tan^{-1}\left(\dfrac{\cos x}{1-\sin x}\right), \dfrac{-3\pi}{2} < x < \dfrac{\pi}{2}$ in the simplest form.

CBSE Sample Paper 2021

Sol. We have, $\tan^{-1}\left(\dfrac{\cos x}{1-\sin x}\right) = \tan^{-1}\left[\dfrac{\sin\left(\dfrac{\pi}{2}-x\right)}{1-\cos\left(\dfrac{\pi}{2}-x\right)}\right]$

$= \tan^{-1}\left[\dfrac{2\sin\left(\dfrac{\pi}{4}-\dfrac{x}{2}\right)\cos\left(\dfrac{\pi}{4}-\dfrac{x}{2}\right)}{2\sin^2\left(\dfrac{\pi}{4}-\dfrac{x}{2}\right)}\right]$

$= \tan^{-1}\cot\left(\dfrac{\pi}{4}-\dfrac{x}{2}\right) = \tan^{-1}\left[\tan\left(\dfrac{\pi}{2}-\left(\dfrac{\pi}{4}-\dfrac{x}{2}\right)\right)\right]$

$= \tan^{-1}\left[\tan\left(\dfrac{\pi}{4}+\dfrac{x}{2}\right)\right]$

Now, $-\dfrac{3\pi}{2} < x < \dfrac{\pi}{2}$

$\Rightarrow \quad -\dfrac{3\pi}{4} < \dfrac{x}{2} < \dfrac{\pi}{4} \Rightarrow -\dfrac{\pi}{2} < \dfrac{x}{2} + \dfrac{\pi}{4} < \dfrac{\pi}{2}$

$\therefore \tan^{-1}\left(\dfrac{\cos x}{1-\sin x}\right) = \tan^{-1}\tan\left(\dfrac{\pi}{4}+\dfrac{x}{2}\right) = \dfrac{\pi}{4}+\dfrac{x}{2}$

$\left[\because \tan^{-1}(\tan x) = x, x \in \left(-\dfrac{\pi}{2}, \dfrac{\pi}{2}\right)\right]$

Example 8 Prove that

$$\cos[\tan^{-1}\{\sin(\cot^{-1} x)\}] = \sqrt{\frac{1+x^2}{2+x^2}}.$$

CBSE 2010

Sol. LHS $= \cos[\tan^{-1}\{\sin(\cot^{-1} x)\}]$

Put $\cot^{-1} x = \theta \Rightarrow x = \cot\theta$

Then, LHS $= \cos[\tan^{-1}(\sin\theta)]$

$= \cos\left[\tan^{-1}\left(\dfrac{1}{\operatorname{cosec}\theta}\right)\right]$ $\left[\because \sin\theta = \dfrac{1}{\operatorname{cosec}\theta}\right]$

$$= \cos\left[\tan^{-1}\left(\frac{1}{\sqrt{1+\cot^2\theta}}\right)\right]$$

$[\because \text{cosec}^2\theta = 1+\cot^2\theta]$

$$= \cos\left[\tan^{-1}\left(\frac{1}{\sqrt{1+x^2}}\right)\right] \quad [\because \cot\theta = x]$$

$= \cos\phi$,

where $\tan^{-1}\left(\frac{1}{\sqrt{1+x^2}}\right) = \phi$ or $\tan\phi = \frac{1}{\sqrt{1+x^2}}$

Now, $\cos\phi = \frac{1}{\sec\phi}$ $\quad\left[\because \cos\theta = \frac{1}{\sec\theta}\right]$

$$= \frac{1}{\sqrt{1+\tan^2\phi}} \quad [\because \tan^2\theta + 1 = \sec^2\theta]$$

$$= \frac{1}{\sqrt{1+\frac{1}{1+x^2}}} \quad \left[\because \tan\phi = \frac{1}{\sqrt{1+x^2}}\right]$$

$$= \frac{1}{\sqrt{\frac{1+x^2+1}{1+x^2}}}$$

$$= \sqrt{\frac{1+x^2}{2+x^2}} = \text{RHS}$$

Hence proved.

Example 9 Show that

$$\tan^{-1}\sqrt{x} = \frac{1}{2}\cos^{-1}\left(\frac{1-x}{1+x}\right), x \in [0,1].$$

NCERT

Sol. RHS $= \frac{1}{2}\cos^{-1}\left(\frac{1-x}{1+x}\right)$

Let $x = \tan^2\theta \Rightarrow \sqrt{x} = \tan\theta \Rightarrow \tan^{-1}\sqrt{x} = \theta$

$$= \frac{1}{2}\cos^{-1}\left(\frac{1-\tan^2\theta}{1+\tan^2\theta}\right)$$

$$= \frac{1}{2}\cos^{-1}(\cos 2\theta) = \frac{1}{2}(2\theta) = \theta$$

$$= \tan^{-1}\sqrt{x} = \text{LHS}$$

Hence proved.

Example 10 **Find the real solutions of the equation $\tan^{-1}\sqrt{x(x+1)} + \sin^{-1}\sqrt{x^2+x+1} = \frac{\pi}{2}$.**

NCERT Exemplar

Sol. Given, $\tan^{-1}\sqrt{x(x+1)} + \sin^{-1}\sqrt{x^2+x+1} = \frac{\pi}{2}$

$$\Rightarrow \quad \tan^{-1}\sqrt{x^2+x} + \sin^{-1}\sqrt{x^2+x+1} = \frac{\pi}{2}$$

This equation holds, if

$$x^2 + x \ge 0 \text{ and } 0 \le x^2 + x + 1 \le 1$$

Now, $x^2 + x \ge 0$ and $0 \le x^2 + x + 1 \le 1$

$\Rightarrow \quad x^2 + x \ge 0$

and $x^2 + x + 1 \le 1$ $\quad [\because x^2 + x + 1 \ge 0, \forall\, x \in R]$

$\Rightarrow \quad x^2 + x \ge 0$

and $\quad x^2 + x \le 0$

$\therefore \quad x^2 + x = 0$

$\Rightarrow \quad x = 0, -1$

Clearly, these two values satisfy the given equation.
Hence, $x = 0, -1$ are the solutions of the given equation.

Quick Test 2

1. Evaluate $\sin^{-1}\left[\cos\left(\frac{33\pi}{5}\right)\right]$.
2. Find the value of $\cot\left(\frac{\pi}{2} - 2\cot^{-1}\sqrt{3}\right)$. *CBSE 2014*
3. Find the value of expression $\sin[\cot^{-1}\{\cos(\tan^{-1} 1)\}]$
4. Find the value of $\tan\frac{1}{2}\left[\sin^{-1}\frac{2x}{1+x^2} + \cos^{-1}\frac{1-y^2}{1+y^2}\right], |x| < 1, y > 0$ and $xy < 1$. *Competency Based Que, CBSE 2013*
5. Write the simplest form of $\sin^{-1}[x\sqrt{1-x} - \sqrt{x}\sqrt{1-x^2}]$. *Competency Based Que*
6. Solve the equation $2\tan^{-1}(\cos x) = \tan^{-1}(2\,\text{cosec}\, x)$. *NCERT*
7. Find the value of $\tan\left(\frac{1}{2}\sin^{-1}\frac{3}{4}\right)$. *Competency Based Que*
8. Find the value of x, if $\cos^{-1}\frac{12}{13} + \sin^{-1}\frac{3}{5} = \sin^{-1} x$.

For Solutions, See QR Code on Pg. 38

Answers

1. $\frac{-\pi}{10}$ 2. $\sqrt{3}$ 3. $\sqrt{\frac{2}{3}}$
4. $\frac{x+y}{1-xy}$ 5. $\sin^{-1} x - \sin^{-1}\sqrt{x}$
6. $\frac{\pi}{4}$ 7. $\frac{4 \pm \sqrt{7}}{3}$ 8. $\frac{56}{65}$

EXAM PATTERN QUESTIONS

Objective Type Questions

Multiple Choice Questions

1. The domain of function defined by $f(x) = \text{cosec}^{-1}(x)$ is

(a) $[-1, 1]$ (b) R
(c) $R-(-1, 1)$ (d) None of these

2. The range of function defined by $f(x) = \cot^{-1} x$ is

(a) $\left[-\frac{\pi}{2}, \frac{\pi}{2}\right]$ (b) $[0, \pi]$ (c) $(0, \pi)$ (d) $[0, \pi] - \left\{\frac{\pi}{2}\right\}$

3. If $\tan^{-1} x = y$, then **CBSE 2022 (Term I)**

(a) $-1 < y < 1$ (b) $-\frac{\pi}{2} \le y \le \frac{\pi}{2}$
(c) $-\frac{\pi}{2} < y < \frac{\pi}{2}$ (d) $y \in \left\{-\frac{\pi}{2}, \frac{\pi}{2}\right\}$

4. The domain of $\cos^{-1}(x^2 - 4)$ is **Competency Based Que**

(a) $[-1,1]$ (b) $[-2,2]$
(c) $[-\sqrt{5}, -\sqrt{3}] \cup [\sqrt{3}, \sqrt{5}]$ (d) $[0, \pi]$

5. The principal value of $\sin^{-1}\left[\sin \frac{13\pi}{7}\right]$ is

Competency Based Que

(a) $\frac{\pi}{6}$ (b) $-\frac{\pi}{7}$ (c) $\frac{\pi}{7}$ (d) $\frac{\pi}{3}$

6. $\sin^{-1}\left(\cos \frac{\pi}{6}\right)$ is

(a) $\frac{\pi}{4}$ (b) $\frac{\pi}{2}$ (c) $\frac{\pi}{3}$ (d) $\frac{\pi}{6}$

7. The value of $\cot(\sin^{-1} x)$ is

NCERT Exemplar, Competency Based Que

(a) $\frac{\sqrt{1+x^2}}{x}$ (b) $\frac{x}{\sqrt{1+x^2}}$ (c) $\frac{1}{x}$ (d) $\frac{\sqrt{1-x^2}}{x}$

8. The value of $\cot\left[\frac{1}{2} \sin^{-1} \frac{\sqrt{3}}{2}\right]$ is

(a) $\frac{1}{\sqrt{3}}$ (b) 1 (c) $\sqrt{3}$ (d) 0

9. $\sin\left[\frac{\pi}{3} + \sin^{-1}\left(\frac{1}{2}\right)\right]$ is equal to

CBSE 2023

(a) 1 (b) $\frac{1}{2}$ (c) $\frac{1}{3}$ (d) $\frac{1}{4}$

10. $\sin\left[\frac{\pi}{3} - \sin^{-1}\left(-\frac{1}{2}\right)\right]$ is equal to

CBSE Sample Paper 2022 (Term I)

(a) $\frac{1}{2}$ (b) $\frac{1}{3}$ (c) -1 (d) 1

11. The principal value of $\sec^{-1}(-2)$ is

(a) $\frac{\pi}{3}$ (b) $\frac{\pi}{6}$ (c) $\frac{3\pi}{4}$ (d) $\frac{2\pi}{3}$

12. $\tan^{-1}\left(\frac{1}{\sqrt{3}}\right) + \sec^{-1}(-\sqrt{2})$ is equal to

(a) $\frac{\pi}{12}$ (b) $\frac{11\pi}{12}$ (c) $\frac{7\pi}{12}$ (d) $\frac{3\pi}{4}$

13. If $\cos(\tan^{-1} x + \cot^{-1} \sqrt{3}) = 0$, then the value of x is

(a) 3 (b) $\frac{1}{\sqrt{3}}$ (c) $\frac{1}{3}$ (d) $\sqrt{3}$

14. $\sin\left[\frac{\pi}{2} - \sin^{-1}\left(-\frac{1}{2}\right)\right]$ is equal to

Competency Based Que, CBSE Sample Paper 2021

(a) $\frac{1}{2}$ (b) $\frac{1}{3}$ (c) -1 (d) $\frac{\sqrt{3}}{2}$

15. The value of $2\sin\left[\cot^{-1}\left(\frac{5}{12}\right)\right]$

(a) $\frac{24}{13}$ (b) $\frac{12}{13}$ (c) $\frac{13}{12}$ (d) $\frac{5}{13}$

16. $\sin(\tan^{-1} x)$, where $|x| < 1$ is equal to

CBSE Sample Paper 2022 (Term I)

(a) $\frac{x}{\sqrt{1-x^2}}$ (b) $\frac{1}{\sqrt{1-x^2}}$ (c) $\frac{1}{\sqrt{1+x^2}}$ (d) $\frac{x}{\sqrt{1+x^2}}$

17. If $\cos\left(\sin^{-1} \frac{3}{5} + \cos^{-1} x\right) = \frac{1}{\sqrt{2}}$, then x is equal to

Competency Based Que

(a) $\frac{1}{5}$ (b) $\frac{7}{5\sqrt{2}}$ (c) 0 (d) 1

18. The principal value of $\sin^{-1}\left(\cos \frac{43\pi}{5}\right)$ is

CBSE 2025

(a) $\frac{-7\pi}{5}$ (b) $\frac{-\pi}{10}$ (c) $\frac{\pi}{10}$ (d) $\frac{3\pi}{5}$

19. The value of $\cos^{-1}(2x^2 - 1)$, $0 \le x \le 1$ is equal to

Competency Based Que

(a) $2\cos^{-1} x$ (b) $2\sin^{-1} x$
(c) $\pi - 2\cos^{-1} x$ (d) $\pi + 2\cos^{-1} x$

20. Simplest form of

$$\tan^{-1}\left(\frac{\sqrt{1+\cos x} + \sqrt{1-\cos x}}{\sqrt{1+\cos x} - \sqrt{1-\cos x}}\right), \pi < x < \frac{3\pi}{2} \text{ is}$$

Competency Based Que, CBSE Sample Paper 2022 (Term I)

(a) $\frac{\pi}{4} - \frac{x}{2}$ (b) $\frac{3\pi}{2} - \frac{x}{2}$ (c) $-\frac{x}{2}$ (d) $\pi - \frac{x}{2}$

Assertion-Reason Based Questions

Directions (Q. Nos. 21-30) *In the questions given below are two statements labelled as Assertion (A) and Reason (R). In the context of the two statements, which one of the following is correct?*

(a) Both A and R are correct; R is the correct explanation of A.
(b) Both A and R are correct; R is not the correct explanation of A.
(c) A is correct; R is incorrect.
(d) R is correct; A is incorrect.

21. **Assertion** (A) The range of the function $f(x)=2\sin^{-1}x+\dfrac{3\pi}{2}$, where $x\in[-1,1]$ is $\left[\dfrac{\pi}{2},\dfrac{5\pi}{2}\right]$.

Reason (R) The range of the principal value branch of $\sin^{-1}x$ is $[0,\pi]$. **Competency Based Que, CBSE 2023**

22. **Assertion** (A) Maximum value of $(\cos^{-1}x)^2$ is π^2.

Reason (R) The principal value branch of $\cos^{-1}x$ is $\left[\dfrac{-\pi}{2},\dfrac{\pi}{2}\right]$. **CBSE 2023**

23. **Assertion** (A) All trigonometric functions have their inverses over their respective domains.

Reason (R) The inverse of $\tan^{-1}x$ exists for some $x\in R$. **Competency Based Que, CBSE 2023**

24. **Assertion** (A) Domain of $y=\cos^{-1}(x)$ is $[-1,1]$.

Reason (R) The range of the principal value branch of $y=\cos^{-1}(x)$ is $[0,\pi]-\left\{\dfrac{\pi}{2}\right\}$. **CBSE 2024**

25. **Assertion** (A) Range of $[2\cos^{-1}x]$ is $[0,\pi]$.

Reason (R) Principal value branch of $\sin^{-1}x$ has range $\left[-\dfrac{\pi}{2},\dfrac{\pi}{2}\right]$. **CBSE 2023**

26. **Assertion** (A) The domain of the function $\sec^{-1}2x$ is $\left(-\infty,-\dfrac{1}{2}\right]\cup\left[\dfrac{1}{2},\infty\right)$.

Reason (R) $\sec^{-1}(-2)=-\dfrac{\pi}{4}$.
Competency Based Que, CBSE Sample Paper 2023

27. **Assertion** (A) The value of $\sin^{-1}\left(\cos\dfrac{33\pi}{5}\right)$ is $-\dfrac{\pi}{10}$.

Reason (R) The principal value branch of $\sin^{-1}x$ is $[0,\pi]$.

28. **Assertion** (A) The value of $\sin\left(\tan^{-1}(-\sqrt{3})+\cos^{-1}\left(-\dfrac{\sqrt{3}}{2}\right)\right)$ is 1. **Competency Based Que**

Reason (R) $\tan^{-1}(-x)=\tan^{-1}x$ and $\cos^{-1}(-x)=\cos^{-1}x$.

29. **Assertion** (A) $\sin^{-1}\left(\dfrac{1}{2}\right)+\cot^{-1}\sqrt{3}=\dfrac{\pi}{3}$

Reason (R) Principal value branch of $\cos^{-1}x$ is $\left[-\dfrac{\pi}{2},\dfrac{\pi}{2}\right]$.

30. **Assertion** (A) $\sin(\tan^{-1}x), |x|<1$ is equal to $\dfrac{x}{\sqrt{1+x^2}}$.

Reason (R) Domain of $\tan^{-1}(x)$ is $(0,\pi)$.

Case Based Questions

31. Two men on either side of a temple of 30 m high observe its top at the angles of elevation α and β, respectively (as shown in the figure below).

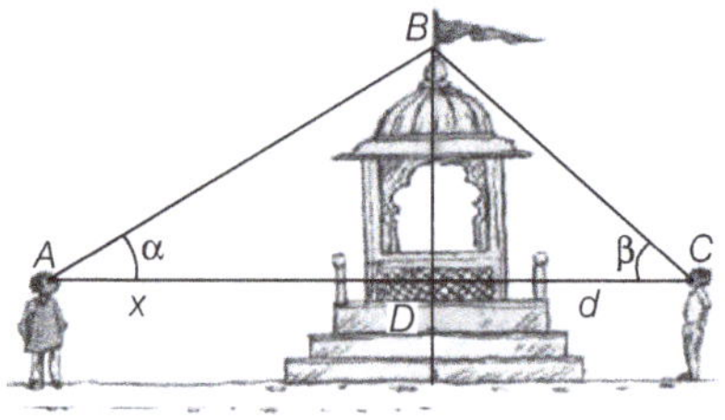

The distance between the two men is $40\sqrt{3}$ m and the distance between the first person A and the temple is $30\sqrt{3}$ m.

Based on the above information, answer the following questions. **CBSE QB**

(i) $\angle CAB=\alpha$ is
(a) $\sin^{-1}\left(\dfrac{2}{\sqrt{3}}\right)$ (b) $\sin^{-1}\left(\dfrac{1}{2}\right)$
(c) $\sin^{-1}(2)$ (d) $\sin^{-1}\left(\dfrac{\sqrt{3}}{2}\right)$

(ii) $\angle CAB=\alpha$ is
(a) $\cos^{-1}\left(\dfrac{1}{5}\right)$ (b) $\cos^{-1}\left(\dfrac{2}{5}\right)$
(c) $\cos^{-1}\left(\dfrac{\sqrt{3}}{2}\right)$ (d) $\cos^{-1}\left(\dfrac{4}{5}\right)$

(iii) $\angle BCA=\beta$ is
(a) $\tan^{-1}\left(\dfrac{1}{2}\right)$ (b) $\tan^{-1}(2)$
(c) $\tan^{-1}\left(\dfrac{1}{\sqrt{3}}\right)$ (d) $\tan^{-1}(\sqrt{3})$

(iv) $\angle ABC$ is
(a) $\dfrac{\pi}{4}$ (b) $\dfrac{\pi}{6}$ (c) $\dfrac{\pi}{2}$ (d) $\dfrac{\pi}{3}$

(v) Domain and range of $\cos^{-1}x$ is equal to
(a) $(-1,1),(0,\pi)$ (b) $[-1,1],(0,\pi)$
(c) $[-1,1],[0,\pi]$ (d) $(-1,1),\left[-\dfrac{\pi}{2},\dfrac{\pi}{2}\right]$

32. If $P = \tan^{-1}\left(\frac{\cos x}{1+\sin x}\right), x \in \left(-\frac{\pi}{2}, \frac{\pi}{2}\right)$,

$Q = \cot^{-1}\left(\frac{\sqrt{1+\sin x}+\sqrt{1-\sin x}}{\sqrt{1+\sin x}-\sqrt{1-\sin x}}\right), x \in \left(0, \frac{\pi}{4}\right)$

and $R = \tan\left[\frac{\pi}{4}+\frac{1}{2}\cos^{-1}\frac{a}{b}\right]+\tan\left[\frac{\pi}{4}-\frac{1}{2}\cos^{-1}\frac{a}{b}\right]$

Based on the above information, answer the following questions.

(i) Find the simplest form of P.

(ii) Find the simplest form of Q.

(iii) Find the simplest form of R.

(iv) If $P+Q=R$, then find the value of $\tan^{-1}\left(\frac{\pi a}{8b}\right)$.

Subjective Questions

Very Short Answer Type Questions

1. Write the domain and range (principal value branch) of the following function $f(x) = \sec^{-1} x$.

2. Find the principal value of $\cos^{-1}\left(-\frac{1}{2}\right)$.

3. Evaluate $\sin\left\{\pi - \cos^{-1}\left(\frac{1}{\sqrt{2}}\right)\right\}$.

4. Find the value of $\cot\left[\cos^{-1}\left(\frac{7}{25}\right)\right]$.

5. Evaluate $\cos\left[\cos^{-1}\left(\frac{-\sqrt{3}}{2}\right)+\frac{\pi}{6}\right]$. **Competency Based Que**

6. Find the value of x, if $\cos(2\sin^{-1} x) = \frac{1}{9}, x > 0$.

7. Write the simplest form of $\cot^{-1}\left(\frac{1}{\sqrt{x^2-1}}\right), |x| > 1$. **CBSE 2013**

8. Prove that $3\sin^{-1} x = \sin^{-1}(3x - 4x^3), x \in \left[-\frac{1}{2}, \frac{1}{2}\right]$. **Competency Based Que, CBSE 2018**

9. Write the simplest form of $\tan^{-1}\left[\sqrt{\frac{1-\cos x}{1+\cos x}}\right], x < \pi$. **NCERT**

Short Answer Type Questions

10. Find the domain of the following functions

(i) $\sin^{-1} 2x$ (ii) $\sin^{-1} x + \cos x$

11. If $a = \sin^{-1}\left(\frac{\sqrt{2}}{2}\right) + \cos^{-1}\left(-\frac{1}{2}\right)$ and $b = \tan^{-1}(\sqrt{3}) - \cot^{-1}\left(-\frac{1}{\sqrt{3}}\right)$, then find the value of $a+b$. **CBSE 2024**

12. Evaluate $\sin^{-1}\left(\sin\frac{13\pi}{6}\right) + \cos^{-1}\left(\cos\frac{\pi}{3}\right) + \tan^{-1}\sqrt{3}$ **CBSE 2024C**

13. Evaluate $\sin^{-1}\left[\cos\left(\sin^{-1}\left(\frac{\sqrt{3}}{2}\right)\right)\right]$.

14. Find the simplest form of $\sin^{-1}(2x\sqrt{1-x^2}), \frac{1}{\sqrt{2}} \le x \le 1$. **Competency Based Que**

15. If $\sin[\cot^{-1}(x+1)] = \cos(\tan^{-1} x)$, then find the value of x. **Competency Based Que**

16. Find the value of x, if $\tan^{-1}\left(\frac{1-x}{1+x}\right) = \frac{1}{2}\tan^{-1} x, x > 0$. **CBSE 2017**

17. Evaluate $\cos\left[\sin^{-1}\frac{1}{4} + \sec^{-1}\frac{4}{3}\right]$. **NCERT Exemplar**

18. Show that $\tan^{-1}\sqrt{x} = \frac{1}{2}\cos^{-1}\left(\frac{1-x}{1+x}\right), x \in [0, 1]$.

19. Express $\tan^{-1}\left[\frac{x}{a+\sqrt{a^2-x^2}}\right]$ in simplest form.

20. Express $\cos^{-1}\left(\frac{3}{5}\cos x + \frac{4}{5}\sin x\right)$ in simplest form. **Competency Based Que**

Long Answer Type Questions

21. $\cos^{-1}\frac{x}{a} + \cos^{-1}\frac{y}{b} = \theta$, then show that

$$\frac{x^2}{a^2} - \frac{2xy}{ab}\cos\theta + \frac{y^2}{b^2} = \sin^2\theta.$$

22. Show that $\tan^{-1}\left(\frac{6x-8x^3}{1-12x^2}\right) - \tan^{-1}\left(\frac{4x}{1-4x^2}\right) = \tan^{-1} 2x, |2x| < \frac{1}{\sqrt{3}}$. **Competency Based Que, CBSE 2016, 16C**

23. Prove that $\sin^{-1}\left(\frac{8}{17}\right) + \sin^{-1}\left(\frac{3}{5}\right) = \cos^{-1}\left(\frac{36}{85}\right)$ **CBSE 2014C, 12**

24. Solve the following.

$$3\sin^{-1}\frac{2x}{1+x^2} - 4\cos^{-1}\frac{1-x^2}{1+x^2} + 2\tan^{-1}\frac{2x}{1-x^2} = \frac{\pi}{3}$$

Competency Based Que

25. Prove that $\tan^{-1}\left(\frac{\sqrt{1+x^2}+\sqrt{1-x^2}}{\sqrt{1+x^2}-\sqrt{1-x^2}}\right) = \frac{\pi}{4} + \frac{1}{2}\cos^{-1} x^2$. **Competency Based Que, NCERT Exemplar**

Hints & Solutions

Objective Type Questions

1. (c) **Hint** Domain of $\text{cosec}^{-1}(x) = R - (-1, 1)$

2. (c) **Hint** Range of $\cot^{-1}(x) = (0, \pi)$

3. (c) **Hint** We know that if $\tan^{-1} x = \alpha$, then the principal range of α is $-\frac{\pi}{2} < \alpha < \frac{\pi}{2}$.

4. (c) Let $y = \cos^{-1}(x^2 - 4)$

$\Rightarrow \cos y = (x^2 - 4)$

i.e. $-1 \le x^2 - 4 \le 1$

$\Rightarrow 3 \le x^2 \le 5$

$\Rightarrow \sqrt{3} \le |x| \le \sqrt{5}$

$\Rightarrow x \in [-\sqrt{5}, -\sqrt{3}] \cup [\sqrt{3}, \sqrt{5}]$

5. (b) **Hint** $\sin^{-1}\left[\sin\left(\frac{13\pi}{7}\right)\right] = \sin^{-1}\left[\sin\left(2\pi - \frac{\pi}{7}\right)\right]$

$= \sin^{-1}\left[\sin\left(-\frac{\pi}{7}\right)\right] = -\frac{\pi}{7}$

$\left[\begin{array}{l}\because \sin(2\pi - \theta) = -\sin\theta \\ \text{and } -\sin\theta = \sin(-\theta)\end{array}\right]$

6. (c) We have, $\sin^{-1}\cos\frac{\pi}{6}$

$= \sin^{-1}\left(\frac{\sqrt{3}}{2}\right)$ $\left[\because \cos\frac{\pi}{6} = \frac{\sqrt{3}}{2}\right]$

$= \frac{\pi}{3}$ $\left[\because \sin\frac{\pi}{3} = \frac{\sqrt{3}}{2}\right]$

7. (d) **Hint** Let $\sin^{-1} x = \theta$.

Then, $\sin\theta = x$

$\Rightarrow \text{cosec}\,\theta = \frac{1}{x} \Rightarrow \text{cosec}^2\theta = \frac{1}{x^2}$

$\Rightarrow 1 + \cot^2\theta = \frac{1}{x^2} \Rightarrow \cot\theta = \frac{\sqrt{1-x^2}}{x}$

$\Rightarrow \cot(\sin^{-1} x) = \frac{\sqrt{1-x^2}}{x}$

8. (c) **Hint** $\cot\left[\frac{1}{2}\sin^{-1}\left(\frac{\sqrt{3}}{2}\right)\right] = \cot\left[\frac{1}{2} \times \frac{\pi}{3}\right] = \cot^{-1}\left(\frac{\pi}{6}\right) = \sqrt{3}$

9. (a) We have, $\sin\left[\frac{\pi}{3} + \sin^{-1}\left(\frac{1}{2}\right)\right] = \sin\left[\frac{\pi}{3} + \frac{\pi}{6}\right]$

$= \sin\frac{3\pi}{6} = \sin\frac{\pi}{2} = 1$

10. (d) We have, $\sin\left[\frac{\pi}{3} - \sin^{-1}\left(-\frac{1}{2}\right)\right]$

Let $\sin^{-1}\left(-\frac{1}{2}\right) = \theta \Rightarrow -\frac{1}{2} = \sin\theta$

$\Rightarrow \sin\left(-\frac{\pi}{6}\right) = \sin\theta \Rightarrow \theta = -\frac{\pi}{6}$

$\therefore \sin\left[\frac{\pi}{3} - \sin^{-1}\left(-\frac{1}{2}\right)\right] = \sin\left[\frac{\pi}{3} - \left(-\frac{\pi}{6}\right)\right] = \sin\frac{\pi}{2} = 1$

11. (d) Let $y = \sec^{-1}(-2)$

$\Rightarrow \sec y = -2$

$\Rightarrow \sec y = -\sec\frac{\pi}{3}$

$\Rightarrow \sec y = \sec\left(\pi - \frac{\pi}{3}\right)$

$\Rightarrow \sec y = \sec\left(\frac{2\pi}{3}\right)$

$\Rightarrow y = \frac{2\pi}{3}$

12. (b) Let $y = \sec^{-1}(-\sqrt{2})$

$\Rightarrow \sec y = -\sqrt{2}$

$\Rightarrow \sec y = -\sec\frac{\pi}{4}$

$\Rightarrow \sec y = \sec\left(\pi - \frac{\pi}{4}\right)$

$\Rightarrow \sec y = \sec\frac{3\pi}{4}$

$\Rightarrow y = \frac{3\pi}{4} \Rightarrow \sec^{-1}(-\sqrt{2}) = \frac{3\pi}{4}$

Now, $\tan^{-1}\left(\frac{1}{\sqrt{3}}\right) + \sec^{-1}(-\sqrt{2})$

$= \frac{\pi}{6} + \frac{3\pi}{4}$

$= \frac{2\pi + 9\pi}{12} = \frac{11\pi}{12}$

13. (d) Given, $\cos(\tan^{-1} x + \cot^{-1}\sqrt{3}) = 0$

$\Rightarrow \cos\left(\tan^{-1} x + \frac{\pi}{6}\right) = \cos\frac{\pi}{2}$

$\Rightarrow \tan^{-1} x = \frac{\pi}{2} - \frac{\pi}{6}$

$\Rightarrow \tan^{-1} x = \frac{\pi}{3}$

$\Rightarrow x = \tan\frac{\pi}{3}$

$\Rightarrow x = \sqrt{3}$

14. (d) **Hint** We have, $\sin\left[\frac{\pi}{2} - \sin^{-1}\left(-\frac{1}{2}\right)\right]$

$= \sin\left[\frac{\pi}{2} - \sin^{-1}\left(\sin\left(-\frac{\pi}{6}\right)\right)\right]$

$= \sin\left[\frac{\pi}{2} - \left(-\frac{\pi}{6}\right)\right]$

$= \sin\left[\frac{\pi}{2} + \frac{\pi}{6}\right] = \sin\frac{2\pi}{3} = \frac{\sqrt{3}}{2}$

15. (a) Let $\cot^{-1}\left(\frac{5}{12}\right)=x$

$\Rightarrow \quad \cot x=\frac{5}{12}$

$\therefore \quad \sin x=\frac{12}{13}$

$\Rightarrow \quad x=\sin^{-1}\left(\frac{12}{13}\right)$

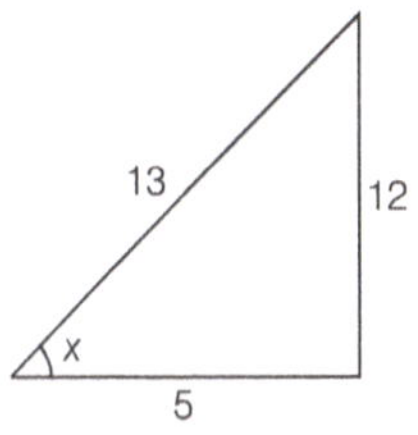

Now, $2\sin\left[\cot^{-1}\left(\frac{5}{12}\right)\right]=2\sin\left[\sin^{-1}\left(\frac{12}{13}\right)\right]$

$=2\times\frac{12}{13} \quad [\because \sin(\sin^{-1}y)=y]$

$=\frac{24}{13}$

16. (d) We have, $\sin(\tan^{-1}x)$, where $|x|<1$.

Let $\tan^{-1}x=\theta$. Then, $\tan\theta=x$

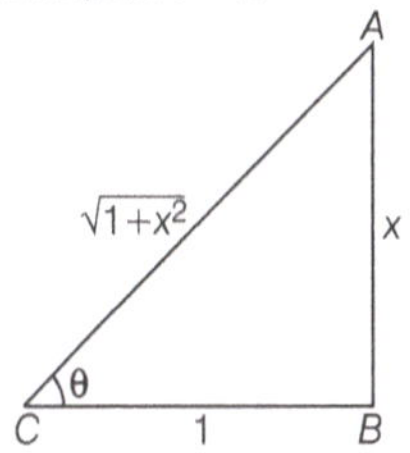

In ΔABC, $\sin\theta=\frac{x}{\sqrt{1+x^2}}$

$\therefore \sin(\tan^{-1}x)=\sin\theta=\frac{x}{\sqrt{1+x^2}}$

17. (b) $\cos\left(\sin^{-1}\frac{3}{5}+\cos^{-1}x\right)=\frac{1}{\sqrt{2}}$

$\Rightarrow \quad \sin^{-1}\frac{3}{5}+\cos^{-1}x=\cos^{-1}\frac{1}{\sqrt{2}}$

$\Rightarrow \quad \cos^{-1}x=\cos^{-1}\left(\frac{1}{\sqrt{2}}\right)-\sin^{-1}\frac{3}{5} \quad \ldots(\text{i})$

From RHS,

Let $\cos^{-1}\left(\frac{1}{\sqrt{2}}\right)=\alpha$ and $\sin^{-1}\left(\frac{3}{5}\right)=\beta$

$\Rightarrow \quad \cos\alpha=\frac{1}{\sqrt{2}}$ and $\sin\beta=\frac{3}{5}$

$\Rightarrow \quad \sin\alpha=\frac{1}{\sqrt{2}}$ and $\cos\beta=\frac{4}{5}$

Now, $\cos(\alpha-\beta)=\cos\alpha\cos\beta+\sin\alpha\sin\beta$

$=\frac{1}{\sqrt{2}}\times\frac{4}{5}+\frac{1}{\sqrt{2}}\times\frac{3}{5}$

$\Rightarrow \quad \cos(\alpha-\beta)=\frac{7}{5\sqrt{2}}$

$\Rightarrow \quad \alpha-\beta=\cos^{-1}\left(\frac{7}{5\sqrt{2}}\right)$

$\Rightarrow \quad \cos^{-1}\frac{1}{\sqrt{2}}-\sin^{-1}\frac{3}{5}=\cos^{-1}\frac{7}{5\sqrt{2}} \quad \ldots(\text{ii})$

From Eqs. (i) and (ii), we get

$\cos^{-1}x=\cos^{-1}\frac{7}{5\sqrt{2}}$

$\Rightarrow \quad x=\frac{7}{5\sqrt{2}}$

18. (b) **Hint** $\sin^{-1}\left(\cos\frac{40\pi+3\pi}{5}\right)$

$=\sin^{-1}\left(\cos\left(8\pi+\frac{3\pi}{5}\right)\right)=\sin^{-1}\left(\cos\frac{3\pi}{5}\right)$

$=\sin^{-1}\left(\sin\left(\frac{\pi}{2}-\frac{3\pi}{5}\right)\right)=\sin^{-1}\left(\sin\left(\frac{-\pi}{10}\right)\right)$

19. (a) **Hint** $\cos^{-1}(2x^2-1)$

Put $x=\cos\alpha$

$\Rightarrow \alpha=\cos^{-1}x=\cos^{-1}(2\cos^2\alpha-1)$

$=\cos^{-1}(\cos2\alpha)$

$=2\alpha=2\cos^{-1}x$

20. (a) We have,

$\tan^{-1}\left(\frac{\sqrt{1+\cos x}+\sqrt{1-\cos x}}{\sqrt{1+\cos x}-\sqrt{1-\cos x}}\right)$

$=\tan^{-1}\left(\frac{\sqrt{2}\left|\cos\frac{x}{2}\right|+\sqrt{2}\left|\sin\frac{x}{2}\right|}{\sqrt{2}\left|\cos\frac{x}{2}\right|-\sqrt{2}\left|\sin\frac{x}{2}\right|}\right)$

$=\tan^{-1}\left(\frac{-\cos\frac{x}{2}+\sin\frac{x}{2}}{-\cos\frac{x}{2}-\sin\frac{x}{2}}\right)$

$\left[\because \cos\frac{x}{2}<0, \quad x\in\left(\pi,\frac{3\pi}{2}\right) \text{ and } \sin\frac{x}{2}>0, \quad x\in\left(\pi,\frac{3\pi}{2}\right)\right]$

$=\tan^{-1}\left(\frac{\cos\frac{x}{2}-\sin\frac{x}{2}}{\cos\frac{x}{2}+\sin\frac{x}{2}}\right)$

$=\tan^{-1}\left(\frac{1-\tan\frac{x}{2}}{1+\tan\frac{x}{2}}\right)$

$=\tan^{-1}\left[\tan\left(\frac{\pi}{4}-\frac{x}{2}\right)\right]$

$=\frac{\pi}{4}-\frac{x}{2}$

21. (c) **Assertion** We know that $\frac{-\pi}{2} \le \sin^{-1} x \le \frac{\pi}{2}$

$$= -\pi \le 2\sin^{-1} x \le \pi$$
$$= -\pi + \frac{3\pi}{2} \le 2\sin^{-1} x + \frac{3\pi}{2} \le \pi + \frac{3\pi}{2}$$
$$= \frac{\pi}{2} \le 2\sin^{-1} x + \frac{3\pi}{2} \le \frac{5\pi}{2} = \frac{\pi}{2} \le f(x) \le \frac{5\pi}{2}$$

$\therefore$ The range of $f(x)$ is $\left[\frac{\pi}{2}, \frac{5\pi}{2}\right]$.

So, Assertion is correct.

Reason We know that $-\frac{\pi}{2} \le \sin^{-1} x \le \frac{\pi}{2}$

So, Reason is incorrect.

22. (c) **Assertion** Maximum value of $\cos^{-1} x$ is π, which occurs at $x = -1$.

$\therefore$ Maximum value of $(\cos^{-1} x)^2$ is π^2.

So, Assertion is correct.

Reason The principal value branch of $\cos^{-1} x$ is $[0, \pi]$.

So, Reason is incorrect.

23. (d) **Assertion** We know that all trigonometric functions have inverse over their restricted domains.

So, Assertion is incorrect.

Reason $\tan^{-1} x : R \to \left(\frac{-\pi}{2}, \frac{\pi}{2}\right)$.

i.e. $\tan^{-1} x$ exists for some $x \in R$.

So, Reason is correct.

24. (c) Given, $f(x) = y = \cos^{-1} x$

We know that the domain of $f(x)$ is equivalent to the range of value of x for which $f(x)$ exist.

Let $f(x) = \theta$

$\Rightarrow$ $\cos^{-1} x = \theta \Rightarrow x = \cos\theta$

Since, the range of $\cos\theta$ is $[-1, 1]$.

$\therefore$ The range of x is $[-1, 1]$.

Hence, the domain of $f(x)$ is $[-1, 1]$.

Thus, Assertion is correct.

The principal value branch of $\cos^{-1} x$ is $[0, \pi]$.

$\therefore$ Reason is incorrect.

25. (d) **Assertion** We know that $0 \le \cos^{-1} x \le \pi$

$$= 0 \le (2\cos^{-1} x) \le \pi \times 2$$
$$= 0 \le 2\cos^{-1} x \le 2\pi$$

So, Assertion is incorrect.

Reason We know that principal value branch of $\sin^{-1} x$ is $\left[-\frac{\pi}{2}, \frac{\pi}{2}\right]$.

So, Reason is correct.

26. (c) **Assertion** We know that

$\sec^{-1} x$ is defined, if $x \le -1$ or $x \ge 1$

Hence, $\sec^{-1} 2x$ will be defined, if $x \le \frac{-1}{2}$ or $x \ge \frac{1}{2}$.

So, Assertion is correct.

Now, $\sec^{-1}(-2) = \pi - \sec^{-1}(2) = \pi - \frac{\pi}{3} = \frac{2\pi}{3} \ne \frac{-\pi}{4}$

Hence, Reason is incorrect.

27. (c) **Hint** $\sin^{-1}\left(\cos\frac{33\pi}{5}\right) = \sin^{-1}\left[\cos\left(6\pi + \frac{3\pi}{5}\right)\right]$

$$= \sin^{-1}\left[\cos\left(\frac{\pi}{2} + \frac{\pi}{10}\right)\right]$$
$$= \sin^{-1}\left(-\sin\frac{\pi}{10}\right)$$
$$= -\frac{\pi}{10}$$

Also, principal branch value of $\sin^{-1} x$ is $\left[-\frac{\pi}{2}, \frac{\pi}{2}\right]$.

28. (c) We have, $\sin\left[\tan^{-1}(-\sqrt{3}) + \cos^{-1}\left(-\frac{\sqrt{3}}{2}\right)\right]$

$$= \sin\left[-\tan^{-1}\sqrt{3} + \pi - \cos^{-1}\frac{\sqrt{3}}{2}\right]$$

$[\because \tan^{-1}(-x) = -\tan^{-1} x \text{ and } \cos^{-1}(-x) = \pi - \cos^{-1} x]$

$$= \sin\left[-\frac{\pi}{3} + \pi - \frac{\pi}{6}\right] = \sin\frac{\pi}{2} = 1$$

Hence, Assertion is correct but Reason is incorrect.

29. (c) We have, $\sin^{-1}\frac{1}{2} + \cot^{-1}\sqrt{3} = \frac{\pi}{6} + \frac{\pi}{6} = \frac{2\pi}{6} = \frac{\pi}{3}$

Hence, Assertion is correct and Reason is incorrect.

30. (c) **Hint** Let $\tan^{-1} x = \theta \Rightarrow x = \tan\theta \Rightarrow \cot\theta = \frac{1}{x}$

$$\therefore \quad \sin\theta = \frac{1}{\operatorname{cosec}\theta} = \frac{1}{\sqrt{1+\cot^2\theta}} = \frac{1}{\sqrt{1+\frac{1}{x^2}}} = \frac{x}{\sqrt{1+x^2}}$$

Also, we know that domain of $\tan^{-1}(x) = R$.

Hence, Assertion is correct and Reason is incorrect.

31. Given figure,

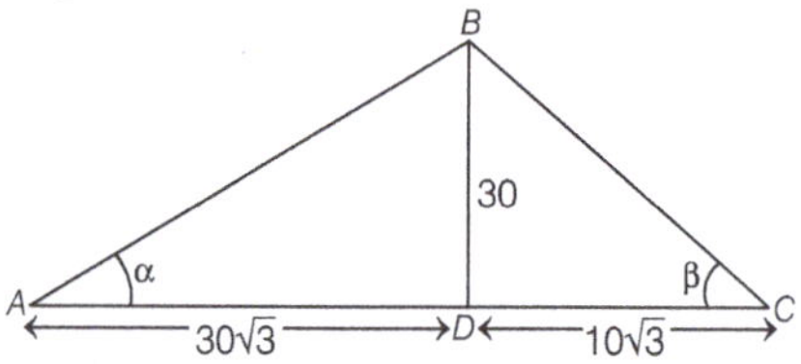

(i) (b) In ΔABD, $\tan\alpha = \frac{BD}{AD} = \frac{30}{30\sqrt{3}} = \frac{1}{\sqrt{3}}$

$\Rightarrow$ $\alpha = 30°$ $\left[\because \tan\frac{\pi}{6} = \frac{1}{\sqrt{3}}\right]$

$\therefore$ $\sin\alpha = \sin 30° = \frac{1}{2} \Rightarrow \alpha = \sin^{-1}\left(\frac{1}{2}\right)$

(ii) (c) $\cos\alpha = \cos 30° = \frac{\sqrt{3}}{2} \Rightarrow \alpha = \cos^{-1}\left(\frac{\sqrt{3}}{2}\right)$

(iii) (d) In ΔBDC, $\tan\beta = \frac{BD}{CD} = \frac{30}{10\sqrt{3}} = \sqrt{3}$

$\Rightarrow$ $\beta = \tan^{-1}(\sqrt{3})$

(iv) (c) Since, $\alpha = \sin^{-1}\left(\frac{1}{2}\right) = \frac{\pi}{6}$ and $\beta = \tan^{-1}(\sqrt{3}) = \frac{\pi}{3}$

$\therefore \quad \angle ABC = \pi - \left(\frac{\pi}{6} + \frac{\pi}{3}\right) = \pi - \frac{\pi}{2} = \frac{\pi}{2}$

(v) (c) We know that domain and range of $\cos^{-1} x$ are $[-1, 1]$ and $[0, \pi]$, respectively.

32. (i) **Hint** Use trigonometric identities,

$$\cos x = \cos^2\left(\frac{x}{2}\right) - \sin^2\left(\frac{x}{2}\right)$$

and $\sin x = 2\sin\left(\frac{x}{2}\right)\cos\left(\frac{x}{2}\right)$ and simplify. **Ans.** $\frac{\pi}{4} - \frac{x}{2}$

(ii) **Hint** $Q = \cot^{-1}\left(\frac{\sqrt{1+\sin x} + \sqrt{1-\sin x}}{\sqrt{1+\sin x} - \sqrt{1-\sin x}}\right)$

$$= \cot^{-1}\left(\frac{\sqrt{\cos^2\frac{x}{2} + \sin^2\frac{x}{2} + 2\sin\frac{x}{2}\cos\frac{x}{2}} + \sqrt{\sin^2\frac{x}{2} + \cos^2\frac{x}{2} - 2\sin\frac{x}{2}\cos\frac{x}{2}}}{\sqrt{\sin^2\frac{x}{2} + \cos^2\frac{x}{2} + 2\sin\frac{x}{2}\cos\frac{x}{2}} - \sqrt{\sin^2\frac{x}{2} + \cos^2\frac{x}{2} - 2\sin\frac{x}{2}\cos\frac{x}{2}}}\right)$$

Ans. $\frac{x}{2}$

(iii) $\tan\left(\frac{\pi}{4} + \frac{1}{2}\cos^{-1}\frac{a}{b}\right) + \tan\left(\frac{\pi}{4} - \frac{1}{2}\cos^{-1}\frac{a}{b}\right)$

$= \tan\left(\frac{\pi}{4} + x\right) + \tan\left(\frac{\pi}{4} - x\right)$, where $x = \frac{1}{2}\cos^{-1}\frac{a}{b}$

$$= \frac{\tan\frac{\pi}{4} + \tan x}{1 - \tan\frac{\pi}{4}\cdot\tan x} + \frac{\tan\frac{\pi}{4} - \tan x}{1 + \tan\frac{\pi}{4}\cdot\tan x}$$

$$= \frac{1+\tan x}{1-\tan x} + \frac{1-\tan x}{1+\tan x}$$

$$= \frac{(1+\tan x)^2 + (1-\tan x)^2}{1-\tan^2 x}$$

$$= \frac{1+\tan^2 x + 2\tan x + 1 + \tan^2 x - 2\tan x}{1-\tan^2 x}$$

$$= \frac{2(1+\tan^2 x)}{1-\tan^2 x} = \frac{2}{\cos 2x}$$

$$= \frac{2}{\cos 2\left(\frac{1}{2}\cos^{-1}\frac{a}{b}\right)}$$

$$= \frac{2}{\cos\left(\cos^{-1}\frac{a}{b}\right)}$$

$$= \frac{2}{\frac{a}{b}} = \frac{2b}{a}$$

[by property $\cos(\cos^{-1} x) = x$, if $x \in [-1, 1]$]

[here, $\frac{a}{b} \in [-1, 1]$]

(iv) **Hint** $P + Q = R$

$\Rightarrow \frac{\pi}{4} - \frac{x}{2} + \frac{x}{2} = \frac{2b}{a}$

$\Rightarrow \quad \frac{\pi}{4} = \frac{2b}{a} \Rightarrow \frac{b}{a} = \frac{\pi}{8}$

$\therefore \tan^{-1}\frac{\pi}{8}\left(\frac{a}{b}\right) = \tan^{-1}\frac{\pi}{8} \times \frac{8}{\pi} = \tan^{-1} 1 = \frac{\pi}{4}$

Ans. $\frac{\pi}{4}$

Subjective Questions

1. **Hint** For $f(x) = \sec^{-1} x$, domain $= R - (-1, 1)$

and $\quad$ range $= [0, \pi] - \left\{\frac{\pi}{2}\right\}$

2. **Hint** Let $\cos^{-1}\left(-\frac{1}{2}\right) = \theta$

$\Rightarrow \quad \cos\theta = -\frac{1}{2}$

$\therefore \quad \cos\theta = -\cos\frac{\pi}{3} = \cos\left(\pi - \frac{\pi}{3}\right)$ $[\because \cos(\pi - \theta) = -\cos\theta]$

$\Rightarrow \quad \theta = \pi - \frac{\pi}{3} = \frac{2\pi}{3} \in [0, \pi]$ **Ans.** $\frac{2\pi}{3}$

3. Let $\cos^{-1}\frac{1}{\sqrt{2}} = \theta$

$\Rightarrow \quad \cos\theta = \frac{1}{\sqrt{2}} = \cos\frac{\pi}{4}$

$\Rightarrow \quad \theta = \frac{\pi}{4} \in [0, \pi]$

$\therefore$ Given expression, $\sin\left[\pi - \cos^{-1}\left(\frac{1}{\sqrt{2}}\right)\right]$

$= \sin\left(\pi - \frac{\pi}{4}\right) = \sin\frac{3\pi}{4} = \frac{1}{\sqrt{2}}$

4. **Hint** Let $\cos^{-1}\frac{7}{25} = \theta$

$\Rightarrow \quad \cos\theta = \frac{7}{25}$

$\Rightarrow \quad \sin\theta = \frac{24}{25}$ $\quad [\because \sin\theta = \sqrt{1-\cos^2\theta}]$

$\Rightarrow \quad \cot\theta = \frac{7}{24}$ $\quad \left[\because \cot\theta = \frac{\cos\theta}{\sin\theta}\right]$

$\Rightarrow \quad \theta = \cos^{-1}\frac{7}{25} = \cot^{-1}\frac{7}{24}$

Now, $\cot\left[\cos^{-1}\left(\frac{7}{25}\right)\right] = \cot\left(\cot^{-1}\frac{7}{24}\right) = \frac{7}{24}$

5. We have, $\cos\left[\cos^{-1}\left(\frac{-\sqrt{3}}{2}\right) + \frac{\pi}{6}\right]$

$= \cos\left[\frac{5\pi}{6} + \frac{\pi}{6}\right]$

$= \cos\left[\frac{6\pi}{6}\right] = \cos\pi = -1$

6. Hint First, put $\sin^{-1} x = \theta \Rightarrow x = \sin\theta$

$\therefore \quad \cos 2\theta = \dfrac{1}{9}$

$\Rightarrow 1 - 2\sin^2\theta = \dfrac{1}{9} \Rightarrow 1 - 2x^2 = \dfrac{1}{9}$ **Ans.** $\dfrac{2}{3}$ $\quad [\because x > 0]$

7. Hint Let $x = \sec\theta$. Then, $\theta = \sec^{-1} x$.

$$\therefore \cot^{-1}\left(\frac{1}{\sqrt{x^2-1}}\right) = \cot^{-1}\left(\frac{1}{\sqrt{\sec^2\theta - 1}}\right)$$

$$= \cot^{-1}\left(\frac{1}{\tan\theta}\right) = \cot^{-1}(\cot\theta)$$

$$= \theta = \sec^{-1} x$$

8. Consider RHS $= \sin^{-1}(3x - 4x^3)$ ...(i)

Let $x = \sin\theta$

Then, $\theta = \sin^{-1} x$

Now, from Eq. (i), we get

RHS $= \sin^{-1}(3\sin\theta - 4\sin^3\theta)$

$= \sin^{-1}(\sin 3\theta)$ $\quad [\because \sin 3x = 3\sin x - 4\sin^3 x]$

$= 3\theta$ $\quad \left[\because \sin^{-1}(\sin\theta) = \theta, \forall \theta \in \left[\dfrac{-\pi}{2}, \dfrac{\pi}{2}\right] \text{ and here } -\dfrac{1}{2} \le x \le \dfrac{1}{2} \Rightarrow -\dfrac{\pi}{6} \le x \le \dfrac{\pi}{6}\right]$

$= 3\sin^{-1} x$ $\quad [\because \theta = \sin^{-1} x]$

= LHS **Hence proved.**

9. We have, $\tan^{-1}\left[\sqrt{\dfrac{1-\cos x}{1+\cos x}}\right] = \tan^{-1}\left[\sqrt{\dfrac{2\sin^2 x/2}{2\cos^2 x/2}}\right]$

$\left[\because 1 - \cos\theta = 2\sin^2\dfrac{\theta}{2}, 1 + \cos\theta = 2\cos^2\dfrac{\theta}{2}\right]$

$= \tan^{-1}[\sqrt{\tan^2 x/2}] = \tan^{-1}\left[\tan\dfrac{x}{2}\right] = \dfrac{x}{2}$

10. (i) **Hint** For domain of $\sin^{-1} 2x$, $-1 \le 2x \le 1$

$\Rightarrow -\dfrac{1}{2} \le x \le \dfrac{1}{2}$ $\quad \left[\therefore x \in \left[-\dfrac{1}{2}, \dfrac{1}{2}\right]\right]$

(ii) **Hint** The domain of $\sin^{-1} x$ is $[-1, 1]$ and domain of $\cos x$ is $(-\infty, \infty)$.

Therefore, domain of $f(x)$ will be $[-1, 1] \cap (-\infty, \infty)$ $= [-1, 1]$.

11. We have, $a = \sin^{-1}\left(\dfrac{\sqrt{2}}{2}\right) + \cos^{-1}\left(\dfrac{-1}{2}\right)$

$= \sin^{-1}\left(\dfrac{1}{\sqrt{2}}\right) + \cos^{-1}\left(-\cos\dfrac{\pi}{3}\right)$

$= \sin^{-1}\left(\dfrac{1}{\sqrt{2}}\right) + \cos^{-1}\left(\cos\left(\pi - \dfrac{\pi}{3}\right)\right)$

$= \dfrac{\pi}{4} + \pi - \dfrac{\pi}{3} = \dfrac{\pi}{4} + \dfrac{2\pi}{3}$

$= \dfrac{3\pi + 8\pi}{12} = \dfrac{11\pi}{12}$

and $\quad b = \tan^{-1}\sqrt{3} - \cot^{-1}\left(-\dfrac{1}{\sqrt{3}}\right)$

$= \dfrac{\pi}{3} - \dfrac{2\pi}{3} = \dfrac{\pi - 2\pi}{3} = -\dfrac{\pi}{3}$

$\therefore \quad a + b = \dfrac{11\pi}{12} - \dfrac{\pi}{3} = \dfrac{11\pi - 4\pi}{12} = \dfrac{7\pi}{12}$

12. We have, $\sin^{-1}\left(\sin\dfrac{13\pi}{6}\right) + \cos^{-1}\left(\cos\dfrac{\pi}{3}\right) + \tan^{-1}(\sqrt{3})$

$= \sin^{-1}\left[\sin\left(2\pi + \dfrac{\pi}{6}\right)\right] + \cos^{-1}\left(\cos\dfrac{\pi}{3}\right) + \tan^{-1}\left(\tan\dfrac{\pi}{3}\right)$ $\quad \left[\because \tan\dfrac{\pi}{3} = \sqrt{3}\right]$

$= \sin^{-1}\left(\sin\dfrac{\pi}{6}\right) + \dfrac{\pi}{3} + \dfrac{\pi}{3}$

$[\because \sin(2\pi + \theta) = \sin\theta, \cos^{-1}(\cos\theta) = \theta \text{ and } \tan^{-1}(\tan\theta) = \theta]$

$= \dfrac{\pi}{6} + \dfrac{2\pi}{3}$ $\quad [\because \sin^{-1}(\sin\theta) = \theta]$

$= \dfrac{5\pi}{6}$

13. Hint We have, $\sin^{-1}\left[\cos\left(\sin^{-1}\left(\dfrac{\sqrt{3}}{2}\right)\right)\right]$

$= \sin^{-1}\left[\cos\left(\sin^{-1}\left(\sin\dfrac{\pi}{3}\right)\right)\right]$

$= \sin^{-1}\left[\cos\dfrac{\pi}{3}\right] = \sin^{-1}\left[\sin\left(\dfrac{\pi}{2} - \dfrac{\pi}{3}\right)\right]$

Ans. $\dfrac{\pi}{6}$

14. LHS $= \sin^{-1}(2x\sqrt{1-x^2})$

Put $x = \cos\theta$, then $\cos^{-1} x = \theta$

$= \sin^{-1}(2\cos\theta\sqrt{1-\cos^2\theta})$

$= \sin^{-1}(2\cos\theta\sqrt{\sin^2\theta})$ $\quad [\because \sin^2\theta = 1 - \cos^2\theta]$

$= \sin^{-1}(2\cos\theta\sin\theta) = \sin^{-1}(\sin 2\theta) = 2\theta$

$= 2\cos^{-1} x$

15. Given, $\sin[\cot^{-1}(x+1)] = \cos(\tan^{-1} x)$ ...(i)

Let $\cot^{-1}(x+1) = \theta \Rightarrow \cot\theta = x + 1$

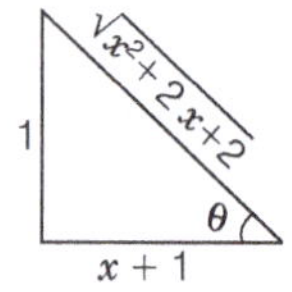

$\therefore \quad \sin\theta = \dfrac{1}{\sqrt{x^2+2x+2}}$

$\Rightarrow \quad \theta = \sin^{-1}\left(\dfrac{1}{\sqrt{x^2+2x+2}}\right)$

$\Rightarrow \quad \cot^{-1}(x+1) = \sin^{-1}\left(\dfrac{1}{\sqrt{x^2+2x+2}}\right)$

Let $\tan^{-1}x=\phi \Rightarrow \tan\phi = x$

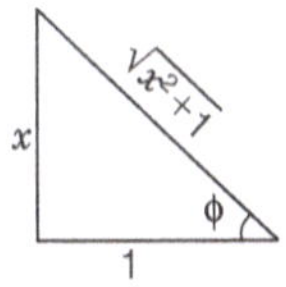

$\therefore \quad \cos\phi = \dfrac{1}{\sqrt{x^2+1}}$

$\Rightarrow \quad \phi = \cos^{-1}\left(\dfrac{1}{\sqrt{x^2+1}}\right)$

$\Rightarrow \quad \tan^{-1}x = \cos^{-1}\left(\dfrac{1}{\sqrt{x^2+1}}\right)$

Now, from Eq. (i), we get

$$\sin\left[\sin^{-1}\left(\frac{1}{\sqrt{x^2+2x+2}}\right)\right]=\cos\left[\cos^{-1}\left(\frac{1}{\sqrt{1+x^2}}\right)\right]$$

$\Rightarrow \quad \dfrac{1}{\sqrt{x^2+2x+2}}=\dfrac{1}{\sqrt{1+x^2}}$

$\Rightarrow \quad \sqrt{x^2+2x+2}=\sqrt{1+x^2}$

$\Rightarrow \quad x^2+2x+2=1+x^2$

$\Rightarrow \quad 2x+2=1$

$\Rightarrow \quad 2x=-1$

$\Rightarrow \quad x=-\dfrac{1}{2}$

16. We have, $\tan^{-1}\left(\dfrac{1-x}{1+x}\right)=\dfrac{1}{2}\tan^{-1}x, x>0$

Let $\quad \tan^{-1}\left(\dfrac{1-x}{1+x}\right)=\theta$

$\Rightarrow \quad \tan\theta=\dfrac{1-x}{1+x}$

$\therefore \quad \theta=\dfrac{1}{2}\tan^{-1}x$

$\Rightarrow \quad 2\theta=\tan^{-1}x$

$\Rightarrow \quad \tan2\theta=x$

$\Rightarrow \quad \dfrac{2\tan\theta}{1-\tan^2\theta}=x$

$\Rightarrow \quad \dfrac{2\left(\dfrac{1-x}{1+x}\right)}{1-\left(\dfrac{1-x}{1+x}\right)^2}=x$

$\Rightarrow \quad \dfrac{2(1-x)(1+x)}{(1+x)^2-(1-x)^2}=x \Rightarrow \dfrac{2-2x^2}{4x}=x$

$\Rightarrow \quad \dfrac{1-x^2}{2x}=x \Rightarrow 1-x^2=2x^2$

$\Rightarrow \quad 3x^2=1 \Rightarrow x=\pm\dfrac{1}{\sqrt{3}}$

$\because \quad x>0$

$\therefore \quad x=\dfrac{1}{\sqrt{3}}$

17. Hint We have, $\cos\left[\sin^{-1}\dfrac{1}{4}+\sec^{-1}\dfrac{4}{3}\right]$

$=\cos\left[\sin^{-1}\dfrac{1}{4}+\cos^{-1}\dfrac{3}{4}\right] \qquad \left[\because \sec^{-1}\dfrac{4}{3}=\cos^{-1}\dfrac{3}{4}\right]$

$=\cos\left(\sin^{-1}\dfrac{1}{4}\right)\cos\left(\cos^{-1}\dfrac{3}{4}\right)-\sin\left(\sin^{-1}\dfrac{1}{4}\right)\sin\left(\cos^{-1}\dfrac{3}{4}\right)$

$[\because \cos(A+B)=\cos A\cos B-\sin A\sin B]$

Ans. $\dfrac{3\sqrt{15}-\sqrt{7}}{16}$

18. RHS $=\dfrac{1}{2}\cos^{-1}\left(\dfrac{1-x}{1+x}\right)$

Let $x=\tan^2\theta \Rightarrow \sqrt{x}=\tan\theta \Rightarrow \tan^{-1}\sqrt{x}=\theta$

$=\dfrac{1}{2}\cos^{-1}\left(\dfrac{1-\tan^2\theta}{1+\tan^2\theta}\right)=\dfrac{1}{2}\cos^{-1}(\cos2\theta)$

$=\dfrac{1}{2}(2\theta)=\theta=\tan^{-1}\sqrt{x}=$ LHS **Hence proved.**

19. Let $y=\tan^{-1}\left[\dfrac{x}{a+\sqrt{a^2-x^2}}\right]$

Put $x=a\sin\theta$, then $\theta=\sin^{-1}\left(\dfrac{x}{a}\right)$

$\therefore \quad y=\tan^{-1}\left[\dfrac{a\sin\theta}{a+\sqrt{a^2-a^2\sin^2\theta}}\right]$

$=\tan^{-1}\left[\dfrac{a\sin\theta}{a+a\sqrt{1-\sin^2\theta}}\right]$

$=\tan^{-1}\left[\dfrac{a\sin\theta}{a(1+\cos\theta)}\right] \qquad [\because \sqrt{1-\sin^2\theta}=\sqrt{\cos^2\theta}=\cos\theta]$

$=\tan^{-1}\left[\dfrac{2\sin\dfrac{\theta}{2}\cos\dfrac{\theta}{2}}{2\cos^2\dfrac{\theta}{2}}\right] \qquad \left[\begin{array}{l}\because \sin2\theta=2\sin\theta\cos\theta \\ \text{and } 1+\cos2\theta=2\cos^2\theta\end{array}\right]$

$=\tan^{-1}\left(\tan\dfrac{\theta}{2}\right)=\dfrac{\theta}{2} \qquad [\because \tan^{-1}(\tan\theta)=\theta]$

$=\dfrac{1}{2}\sin^{-1}\left(\dfrac{x}{a}\right) \qquad$ [substituting the value of θ]

20. Hint Put $\dfrac{3}{5}=\cos\theta$, then $\sin\theta=\dfrac{4}{5}$

Then, solve and use formula

$\cos A\cos B+\sin A\sin B=\cos(A-B)$

Ans. $x-\tan^{-1}\dfrac{4}{3}$

21. Given, $\cos^{-1}\dfrac{x}{a}+\cos^{-1}\dfrac{y}{b}=\theta$

$\Rightarrow \quad \cos^{-1}\dfrac{x}{a}=\theta-\cos^{-1}\dfrac{y}{b}$

$$\Rightarrow \quad \frac{x}{a} = \cos\left(\theta - \cos^{-1}\frac{y}{b}\right)$$

$$\Rightarrow \quad \frac{x}{a} = \cos\theta\left[\cos\left(\cos^{-1}\frac{y}{b}\right)\right] + \sin\theta\left[\sin\left(\cos^{-1}\frac{y}{b}\right)\right]$$

$[\because \cos(A-B) = \cos A\cos B + \sin A \sin B]$

$$\Rightarrow \quad \frac{x}{a} = \frac{y}{b}\cos\theta + \sin\theta\left[\sin\left(\sin^{-1}\sqrt{1-\frac{y^2}{b^2}}\right)\right]$$

$$\left[\begin{array}{l} \because \text{let } z = \cos^{-1}\frac{y}{b}, \text{ then } \cos z = \frac{y}{b} \\ \text{Now}, \sin z = \sqrt{1-\cos^2 z} = \sqrt{1-\frac{y^2}{b^2}} \\ \Rightarrow \quad z = \sin^{-1}\sqrt{1-\frac{y^2}{b^2}} \\ \Rightarrow \cos^{-1}\frac{y}{b} = \sin^{-1}\sqrt{1-\frac{y^2}{b^2}} \end{array}\right]$$

$$\Rightarrow \quad \frac{x}{a} - \frac{y}{b}\cos\theta = \sin\theta\sqrt{1-\frac{y^2}{b^2}}$$

On squaring both sides, we get

$$\frac{x^2}{a^2} + \frac{y^2}{b^2}\cos^2\theta - \frac{2xy}{ab}\cos\theta = \sin^2\theta\left(1-\frac{y^2}{b^2}\right)$$

$$\Rightarrow \quad \frac{x^2}{a^2} - \frac{2xy}{ab}\cos\theta + \frac{y^2}{b^2}\cos^2\theta = \sin^2\theta - (\sin^2\theta)\frac{y^2}{b^2}$$

$$\Rightarrow \quad \frac{x^2}{a^2} - \frac{2xy}{ab}\cos\theta + \frac{y^2}{b^2}(\cos^2\theta + \sin^2\theta) = \sin^2\theta$$

$$\Rightarrow \quad \frac{x^2}{a^2} - \frac{2xy}{ab}\cos\theta + \frac{y^2}{b^2} = \sin^2\theta \qquad [\because \cos^2\theta + \sin^2\theta = 1]$$

Hence proved.

22. Hint Put $2x = \tan\theta$

$$\therefore \tan^{-1}\left(\frac{6x-8x^3}{1-12x^2}\right) - \tan^{-1}\left(\frac{4x}{1-4x^2}\right)$$

$$= \tan^{-1}\left(\frac{3\tan\theta - \tan^3\theta}{1-3\tan^2\theta}\right) - \tan^{-1}\left(\frac{2\tan\theta}{1-\tan^2\theta}\right)$$

$$= \tan^{-1}(\tan 3\theta) - \tan^{-1}(\tan 2\theta)$$

$$= 3\theta - 2\theta = \theta$$

$$= \tan^{-1} 2x$$

Hence proved.

23. Let $\sin^{-1}\left(\frac{8}{17}\right) = x$ and $\sin^{-1}\left(\frac{3}{5}\right) = y$

Then, $\sin x = \frac{8}{17}$ and $\sin y = \frac{3}{5}$

Now, $\cos(x+y) = \cos x \cos y - \sin x \sin y$

$$= \sqrt{1-\sin^2 x}\sqrt{1-\sin^2 y} - \sin x \sin y$$

$$= \sqrt{1-\left(\frac{8}{17}\right)^2}\sqrt{1-\left(\frac{3}{5}\right)^2} - \frac{8}{17}\times\frac{3}{5}$$

$$= \sqrt{1-\frac{64}{289}}\sqrt{1-\frac{9}{25}} - \frac{24}{85} = \sqrt{\frac{225}{289}}\sqrt{\frac{16}{25}} - \frac{24}{85}$$

$$= \frac{15}{17}\times\frac{4}{5} - \frac{24}{85}$$

$$\Rightarrow \quad x + y = \cos^{-1}\left(\frac{60}{85} - \frac{24}{85}\right)$$

$$\Rightarrow \sin^{-1}\left(\frac{8}{17}\right) + \sin^{-1}\left(\frac{3}{5}\right) = \cos^{-1}\left(\frac{36}{85}\right)$$

Hence proved.

24. We have, $3\sin^{-1}\left(\frac{2x}{1+x^2}\right) - 4\cos^{-1}\left(\frac{1-x^2}{1+x^2}\right) + 2\tan^{-1}\left(\frac{2x}{1-x^2}\right) = \frac{\pi}{3}$ ...(i)

On putting $x = \tan\theta$ in Eq. (i), we get

$$3\sin^{-1}\left(\frac{2\tan\theta}{1+\tan^2\theta}\right) - 4\cos^{-1}\left(\frac{1-\tan^2\theta}{1+\tan^2\theta}\right) + 2\tan^{-1}\left(\frac{2\tan\theta}{1-\tan^2\theta}\right) = \frac{\pi}{3} \quad \text{...(ii)}$$

Now, we know that

$$\sin 2\theta = \frac{2\tan\theta}{1+\tan^2\theta}, \cos 2\theta = \frac{1-\tan^2\theta}{1+\tan^2\theta} \text{ and } \tan 2\theta = \frac{2\tan\theta}{1-\tan^2\theta}$$

Using above formula in Eq. (ii), we get

$$3\times 2\theta - 4\times 2\theta + 2\times 2\theta = \frac{\pi}{3}$$

$$\Rightarrow \quad 6\theta - 8\theta + 4\theta = \frac{\pi}{3} \Rightarrow \theta = \frac{\pi}{6}$$

Recall, $\quad x = \tan\theta \Rightarrow x = \tan\frac{\pi}{6} \Rightarrow x = \frac{1}{\sqrt{3}}$

25. Hint Put $x^2 = \cos 2\theta$ and use formula

$1 + \cos 2\theta = 2\cos^2\theta$ and $1 - \cos 2\theta = 2\sin^2\theta$

QR Code for Quick Test 1

QR Code for Quick Test 2

Mind Map

Inverse Trigonometric Function

Domain and Range (Principle Branch Value)

The range of trigonometric functions become the domain of inverse trigonometric functions and restricted domain of trigonometric function becomes range or principal value branch.

Function	Domain	Range (Principal value branch)
$\sin^{-1} x$	$[-1, 1]$	$\left[-\frac{\pi}{2}, \frac{\pi}{2}\right]$
$\cos^{-1} x$	$[-1, 1]$	$[0, \pi]$
$\tan^{-1} x$	R	$\left(-\frac{\pi}{2}, \frac{\pi}{2}\right)$
$\cot^{-1} x$	R	$(0, \pi)$
$\sec^{-1} x$	$R - (-1, 1)$	$[0, \pi] - \left\{\frac{\pi}{2}\right\}$
$\text{cosec}^{-1} x$	$R - (-1, 1)$	$\left[-\frac{\pi}{2}, \frac{\pi}{2}\right] - \{0\}$

Graphs of Inverse Trigonometric Functions

Functions	Graphs
$\sin^{-1} x$	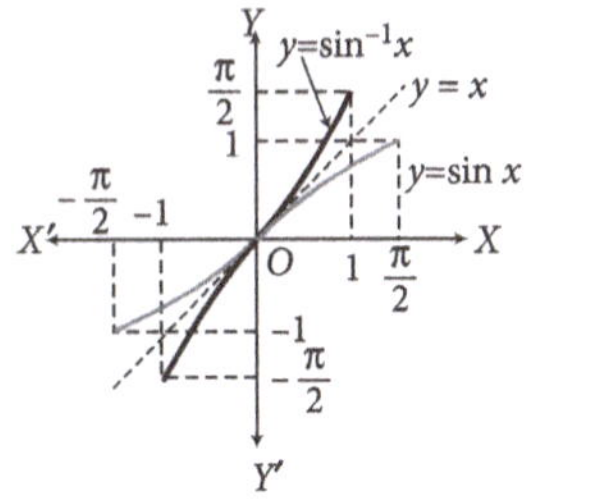
$\cos^{-1} x$	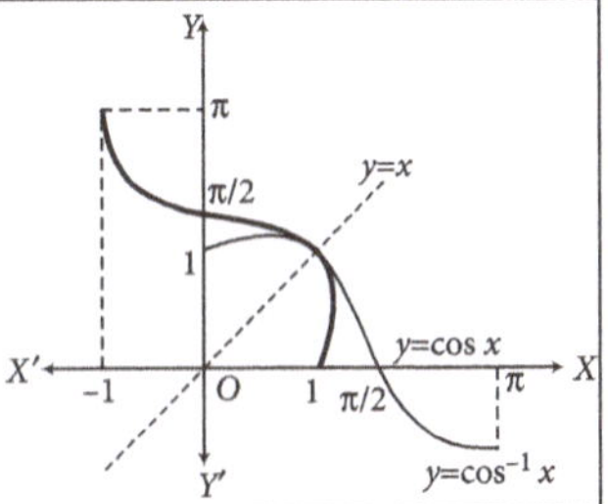
$\tan^{-1} x$	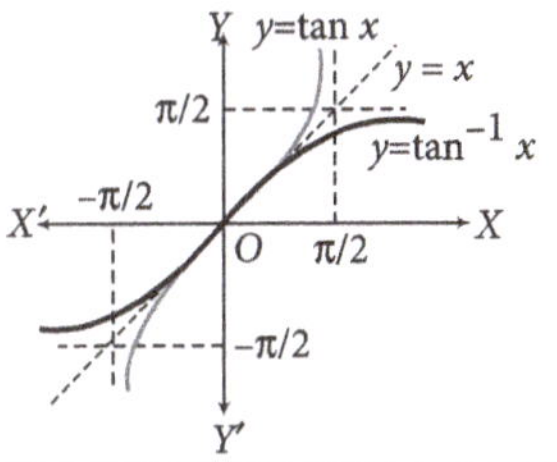
$\cot^{-1} x$	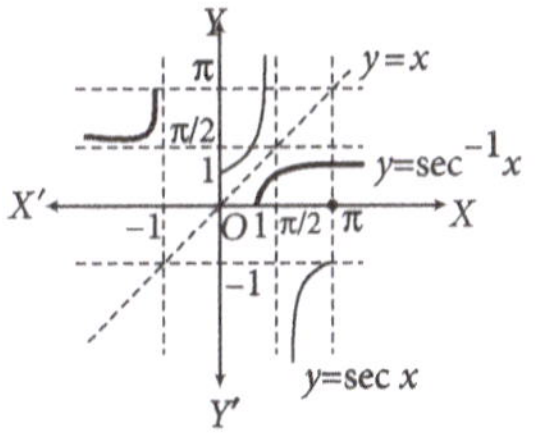
$\sec^{-1} x$	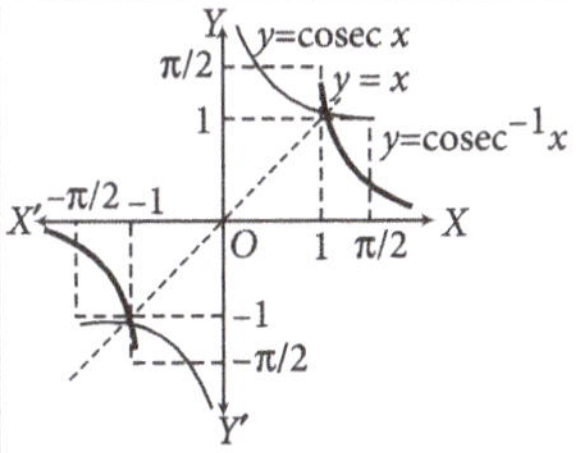
$\text{cosec}^{-1} x$	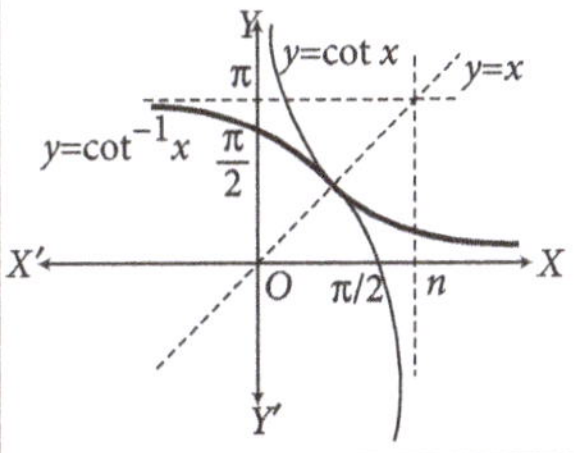

Elementary Properties

Elementary properties of inverse trigonometric functions given are valid within the principal value branches of the corresponding inverse trigonometric function and wherever they are defined.

Property 1

(i) $\sin^{-1}(\sin\theta) = \theta, \theta \in \left[-\frac{\pi}{2}, \frac{\pi}{2}\right]$

(ii) $\cos^{-1}(\cos\theta) = \theta, \theta \in [0, \pi]$

(iii) $\tan^{-1}(\tan\theta) = \theta, \theta \in \left(-\frac{\pi}{2}, \frac{\pi}{2}\right)$

(iv) $\cot^{-1}(\cot\theta) = \theta, \theta \in (0, \pi)$

(v) $\text{cosec}^{-1}(\text{cosec}\,\theta) = \theta, \theta \in \left[-\frac{\pi}{2}, \frac{\pi}{2}\right] - \{0\}$

(vi) $\sec^{-1}(\sec\theta) = \theta, \theta \in [0, \pi] - \left\{\frac{\pi}{2}\right\}$

Property 2

(i) $\sin^{-1}\frac{1}{x} = \text{cosec}^{-1} x, x \geq 1$ or $x \leq -1$

(ii) $\cos^{-1}\frac{1}{x} = \sec^{-1} x, x \geq 1$ or $x \leq -1$

(iii) $\tan^{-1}\frac{1}{x} = \cot^{-1} x, x \in R$

Property 3

$\sin(\sin^{-1} x) = x, x \in [-1, 1]$

$\cos(\cos^{-1} x) = x, x \in [-1, 1]$

$\tan(\tan^{-1} x) = x, x \in R$

$\cot(\cot^{-1} x) = x, x \in R$

$\text{cosec}(\text{cosec}^{-1} x) = x, x \in (-\infty, -1] \cup [1, \infty)$

$\sec(\sec^{-1} x) = x, x \in (-\infty, -1] \cup [1, \infty)$

03
CHAPTER

Matrices

Mathematicians are born, not made.
— *Henri Poincare*

▼ **YOUR STUDY GOALS**

3.1 Matrix
3.2 Operations on Matrices
3.3 Multiplication of Matrices
3.4 Transpose of Matrix
3.5 Invertible Matrix

▼ **YOUR PRACTICE GOALS**

- Objective Type Questions (37 Qs ; 25 MCQs, 10 A-R, 2 Case Based)
- Subjective Type Questions (49 Qs ; 20 VSA, 22 SA, 7 LA)

3.1 Matrix

A matrix is an ordered **rectangular array** of numbers or functions enclosed in [ ] or ( ). Each number (real or complex) or functions in a matrix is called an **element** or the **entry** of the matrix.

A matrix is represented by a single **capital letter** like A, B, X, Y, etc. and elements of a matrix are represented by the small letters $a, b, c, \ldots$ etc. In a matrix, horizontal lines are called **rows** and vertical lines are called **columns**.

e.g.
$$A = \begin{bmatrix} 2 & -5 \\ 7 & 0 \\ \sqrt{5} & 3 \end{bmatrix} \begin{matrix} \rightarrow \text{First row } (R_1) \\ \rightarrow \text{Second row } (R_2) \\ \rightarrow \text{Third row } (R_3) \end{matrix}$$

$\downarrow$ First column (C_1) $\downarrow$ Second column (C_2)

Order of a Matrix

A matrix having m rows and n columns is called a matrix of order $m \times n$ (read as m by n matrix) and it has mn elements.

In general, $m \times n$ matrix has the following rectangular array.

$$A = \begin{bmatrix} a_{11} & a_{12} & a_{13} & \cdots & a_{1n} \\ a_{21} & a_{22} & a_{23} & \cdots & a_{2n} \\ \vdots & \vdots & \vdots & \cdots & \vdots \\ a_{m1} & a_{m2} & a_{m3} & \cdots & a_{mn} \end{bmatrix}_{m \times n}$$

or $[a_{ij}]_{m \times n}$, where $1 \le i \le m, 1 \le j \le n; i, j \in N$

Here, ith row consists of the elements $a_{i1}, a_{i2}, a_{i3}, \ldots, a_{in}$, while jth column consists of the elements $a_{1j}, a_{2j}, a_{3j}, \ldots, a_{mj}$.

e.g. $A = \begin{bmatrix} 1 & 4 \\ -3 & 2 \\ 6 & -5 \end{bmatrix}$

Here, A has 3 rows and 2 columns. So, order of matrix is 3×2 and it has $3 \times 2 = 6$ elements.

Types of Matrices

	Type Name	Definition	Example
1.	Column Matrix	A matrix which has only one column is called a column matrix.	e.g. $A = \begin{bmatrix} 1 \\ -3 \\ 1 \end{bmatrix}$ is a column matrix of order 3×1.
2.	Row Matrix	A matrix which has only one row is called a row matrix.	e.g. $A = [2 \ \ 3 \ \ 6]$ is a row matrix of order 1×3.
3.	Zero or Null matrix	A matrix is said to be a zero or null matrix, if its all elements are zero and it is denoted by O.	e.g. $O = \begin{bmatrix} 0 & 0 \\ 0 & 0 \end{bmatrix}$ or $O = \begin{bmatrix} 0 & 0 & 0 \\ 0 & 0 & 0 \end{bmatrix}$
4.	Square matrix	A matrix which has equal number of rows and columns is called a square matrix.	e.g. $A = \begin{bmatrix} 3 & -1 \\ 5 & 2 \end{bmatrix}$ or $\begin{bmatrix} 4 & 3 & -1 \\ -2 & 3 & 0 \\ 1 & 2 & 3 \end{bmatrix}$
5.	Diagonal elements of a square matrix	If $A = [a_{ij}]$ is any square matrix of order n, then the elements $a_{11}, a_{22}, a_{33}, \ldots, a_{nn}$ are said to constitute the diagonal of the matrix A.	e.g. $A = \begin{bmatrix} 1 & -2 & 3 \\ 6 & 5 & 4 \\ 3 & -1 & 2 \end{bmatrix}$ Here, diagonal elements of square matrix A are 1, 5, 2.
6.	Diagonal matrix	A square matrix whose all the elements except the diagonal elements are zero, is called diagonal matrix.	e.g. $A = \begin{bmatrix} 3 & 0 & 0 \\ 0 & -3 & 0 \\ 0 & 0 & -8 \end{bmatrix}$ or $A = \text{diag.}(3, -3, -8)$
7.	Scalar matrix	A diagonal matrix whose all diagonal elements are equal (non-zero).	e.g. $A = \begin{bmatrix} -3 & 0 & 0 \\ 0 & -3 & 0 \\ 0 & 0 & -3 \end{bmatrix}$ or $B = \begin{bmatrix} 2 & 0 & 0 \\ 0 & 2 & 0 \\ 0 & 0 & 2 \end{bmatrix}$
8.	Unit or identity matrix	A diagonal matrix in which all diagonal elements are 1. It is denoted by I.	e.g. $I = \begin{bmatrix} 1 & 0 \\ 0 & 1 \end{bmatrix}$ or $I = \begin{bmatrix} 1 & 0 & 0 \\ 0 & 1 & 0 \\ 0 & 0 & 1 \end{bmatrix}$
9.	Equal Matrices	Two matrices A and B are said to be equal if their order are same and their corresponding elements are also equal.	e.g. $\begin{bmatrix} 1 & 3 \\ 0 & 5 \end{bmatrix}$ and $\begin{bmatrix} 1 & 3 \\ 0 & 5 \end{bmatrix}$ are equal matrices.

3.2 Operations on Matrices

Addition of Matrices

If A and B are two matrices of the same order $m \times n$, then their sum denoted by $A + B$ is also a matrix of the same order $m \times n$ and is obtained by adding the corresponding elements of A and B.

e.g. If $A = \begin{bmatrix} 6 & 7 \\ 4 & 3 \end{bmatrix}$ and $B = \begin{bmatrix} 1 & 3 \\ 2 & 9 \end{bmatrix}$, then

$$A + B = \begin{bmatrix} 7 & 10 \\ 6 & 12 \end{bmatrix}$$

Properties of Addition of Matrices

If $A = [a_{ij}]$ and $B = [b_{ij}]$ are any two matrices of same order say $m \times n$, then

(i) Addition of matrices is commutative
i.e. $\boldsymbol{A + B = B + A}$.

(ii) Addition of matrices is associative
i.e. $\boldsymbol{(A + B) + C = A + (B + C)}$.

(iii) **Existence of additive identity** Zero matrix is the additive identity of any matrix.
If A is any matrix of order $m \times n$ and O is a null matrix of order $m \times n$, then $\boldsymbol{A + O = O + A = A}$.
Here, O is the additive identity for matrix A.

(iv) If A is a any matrix, then the matrix $(-A)$ is called additive inverse of A.
i.e. $\boldsymbol{A + (-A) = O = (-A) + A}$

Multiplication of a Matrix by a Scalar

Let $A=[a_{ij}]_{m\times n}$ be a matrix and k is scalar. Then, kA is another matrix obtained by multiplying each element of A by the scalar k.

e.g. If $A=\begin{bmatrix}7 & 18\\ -1 & 3\end{bmatrix}$ and $k=3$, then

$$kA=3A=3\begin{bmatrix}7 & 18\\ -1 & 3\end{bmatrix}=\begin{bmatrix}3\times 7 & 3\times 18\\ 3\times(-1) & 3\times 3\end{bmatrix}=\begin{bmatrix}21 & 54\\ -3 & 9\end{bmatrix}$$

Properties of Scalar Multiplication of a Matrix

Let $A=[a_{ij}]$ and $B=[b_{ij}]$ be two matrices of the same order say $m\times n$, then

(i) $k(A+B)=kA+kB$, where k is a scalar.
(ii) $(k_1+k_2)A=k_1A+k_2A$, where k_1 and k_2 are scalars.
(iii) $(k_1k_2)A=k_1(k_2A)$, where k_1 and k_2 are scalars.
(iv) $(-k)A=-(kA)=k(-A)$, where k is a scalar.

Difference (or Subtraction) of Matrices

Difference of two matrices is simply the matrix whose elements are the difference of the corresponding elements of two matrices.

e.g. $A=\begin{bmatrix}1 & 2\\ 3 & 4\end{bmatrix}$ and $B=\begin{bmatrix}4 & 3\\ 2 & 1\end{bmatrix}$

Then, $B-A=\begin{bmatrix}4-1 & 3-2\\ 2-3 & 1-4\end{bmatrix}=\begin{bmatrix}3 & 1\\ -1 & -3\end{bmatrix}$

TEACHER TIPS

(i) In this chapter, we will consider only those matrices whose elements are real numbers or functions taking real values.
(ii) A matrix is an arrangement of number or functions and not a value.
(iii) To find all possible orders of a matrix with m elements, we will find all ordered pairs of natural numbers whose product is m.
(iv) If A and B are not of the same order, then $A+B$ is not defined.

Example 1 **If a matrix has 24 elements, then what are the possible orders it can have? What if it has 13 elements?** NCERT

Sol. The possible orders of a matrix having 24 elements are 1×24, 24×1, 2×12, 12×2, 3×8, 8×3, 4×6 and 6×4.

The possible orders of a matrix having 13 elements are 1×13 and 13×1.

Example 2 **What is the total number of possible matrices of order 3×3 with each entry $\sqrt{2}$ or $\sqrt{3}$.** CBSE 2025

Sol. Number of entries in 3×3 matrix is 9. Since, each entry has 2 choices, namely $\sqrt{2}$ or $\sqrt{3}$.

Therefore, number of possible matrices

$$=\underbrace{2\times 2\times 2\ldots\times 2}_{9\text{ times}}=2^9=512$$

Example 3 **Construct a matrix of order 3×2, whose elements are determined by $a_{ij}=\dfrac{2i-j}{3}$.**

Sol. Let A be a matrix of order 3×2.

Then, $$A=[a_{ij}]_{3\times 2}=\begin{bmatrix}a_{11} & a_{12}\\ a_{21} & a_{22}\\ a_{31} & a_{32}\end{bmatrix} \quad \ldots\text{(i)}$$

Given, $a_{ij}=\dfrac{2i-j}{3}$

$$\therefore \quad a_{11}=\frac{2(1)-1}{3}=\frac{1}{3},\ a_{12}=\frac{2(1)-2}{3}=0,$$
$$a_{21}=\frac{2(2)-1}{3}=1,\ a_{22}=\frac{2(2)-2}{3}=\frac{2}{3},$$
$$a_{31}=\frac{2(3)-1}{3}=\frac{5}{3} \text{ and } a_{32}=\frac{2(3)-2}{3}=\frac{4}{3}$$

On putting all above values in Eq. (i), we get

$$A=\begin{bmatrix}1/3 & 0\\ 1 & 2/3\\ 5/3 & 4/3\end{bmatrix},$$

which is the required 3×2 order matrix.

Example 4 **If $\begin{bmatrix}x-y & 2x+z\\ 2x-y & 3z+w\end{bmatrix}=\begin{bmatrix}-1 & 5\\ 0 & 13\end{bmatrix}$, then find x, y, z and w.**

Sol. Given, $\begin{bmatrix}x-y & 2x+z\\ 2x-y & 3z+w\end{bmatrix}=\begin{bmatrix}-1 & 5\\ 0 & 13\end{bmatrix}$

Here, both matrices are equal, so we equate the corresponding elements.

Now, $x-y=-1$ ...(i)
$2x+z=5$ ...(ii)
$2x-y=0$ ...(iii)
and $3z+w=13$ ...(iv)

On solving Eqs. (i) and (iii), we get

$$x=1 \text{ and } y=2$$

On putting the value of x in Eq. (ii), we get

$$2\times 1+z=5 \Rightarrow z=5-2=3$$

On putting the value of z in Eq. (iv), we get

$$3\times 3+w=13 \Rightarrow w=13-9=4$$

Hence, $x=1$, $y=2$, $z=3$ and $w=4$.

Example 5 **If $A = \begin{bmatrix} \cos\alpha & -\sin\alpha \\ \sin\alpha & \cos\alpha \end{bmatrix}$, then for what value of α, A is an identity matrix?**

Sol. Given, $A = \begin{bmatrix} \cos\alpha & -\sin\alpha \\ \sin\alpha & \cos\alpha \end{bmatrix}$

Also, given A is an identity matrix.

$$\therefore \begin{bmatrix} \cos\alpha & -\sin\alpha \\ \sin\alpha & \cos\alpha \end{bmatrix} = \begin{bmatrix} 1 & 0 \\ 0 & 1 \end{bmatrix}$$

On equating corresponding elements, we get

$$\Rightarrow \quad \cos\alpha = 1 \text{ and } \sin\alpha = 0$$

$$\therefore \quad \alpha = 0$$

Example 6 **If $A + B = \begin{bmatrix} 1 & 0 \\ 1 & 1 \end{bmatrix}$ and $A - 2B = \begin{bmatrix} -1 & 1 \\ 0 & -1 \end{bmatrix}$, then find the value of A.** *CBSE 2020*

Sol. We have, $A + B = \begin{bmatrix} 1 & 0 \\ 1 & 1 \end{bmatrix}$

$$\Rightarrow \quad B = \begin{bmatrix} 1 & 0 \\ 1 & 1 \end{bmatrix} - A$$

$$\because \quad A - 2B = \begin{bmatrix} -1 & 1 \\ 0 & -1 \end{bmatrix}$$

$$\therefore \quad A - 2\left(\begin{bmatrix} 1 & 0 \\ 1 & 1 \end{bmatrix} - A\right) = \begin{bmatrix} -1 & 1 \\ 0 & -1 \end{bmatrix}$$

$$\Rightarrow \quad 3A = \begin{bmatrix} -1 & 1 \\ 0 & -1 \end{bmatrix} + 2\begin{bmatrix} 1 & 0 \\ 1 & 1 \end{bmatrix} = \begin{bmatrix} 1 & 1 \\ 2 & 1 \end{bmatrix}$$

$$\therefore \quad A = \frac{1}{3}\begin{bmatrix} 1 & 1 \\ 2 & 1 \end{bmatrix} = \begin{bmatrix} 1/3 & 1/3 \\ 2/3 & 1/3 \end{bmatrix}$$

Example 7 **If $2\begin{bmatrix} 1 & 3 \\ 0 & x \end{bmatrix} + \begin{bmatrix} y & 0 \\ 1 & 2 \end{bmatrix} = \begin{bmatrix} 5 & 6 \\ 1 & 8 \end{bmatrix}$, then find the value of $x + y$.** *Delhi 2013C, 12*

Sol. Given, $2\begin{bmatrix} 1 & 3 \\ 0 & x \end{bmatrix} + \begin{bmatrix} y & 0 \\ 1 & 2 \end{bmatrix} = \begin{bmatrix} 5 & 6 \\ 1 & 8 \end{bmatrix}$

$$\Rightarrow \quad \begin{bmatrix} 2 & 6 \\ 0 & 2x \end{bmatrix} + \begin{bmatrix} y & 0 \\ 1 & 2 \end{bmatrix} = \begin{bmatrix} 5 & 6 \\ 1 & 8 \end{bmatrix}$$

$$\Rightarrow \quad \begin{bmatrix} 2 + y & 6 + 0 \\ 0 + 1 & 2x + 2 \end{bmatrix} = \begin{bmatrix} 5 & 6 \\ 1 & 8 \end{bmatrix}$$

On comparing the corresponding elements, we get

$$2 + y = 5$$

and $\quad 2x + 2 = 8$

$$\Rightarrow \quad y = 5 - 2 = 3$$

and $\quad 2x = 8 - 2$

$$\Rightarrow \quad y = 3 \text{ and } x = \frac{6}{2} = 3$$

$$\therefore \quad x + y = 3 + 3 = 6$$

Example 8 **If $A = \begin{bmatrix} 8 & 0 \\ 4 & -2 \\ 3 & 6 \end{bmatrix}$ and $B = \begin{bmatrix} 2 & -2 \\ 4 & 2 \\ -5 & 1 \end{bmatrix}$, then find the matrix X, such that $2A + 3X = 5B$.**

Sol. Given, $A = \begin{bmatrix} 8 & 0 \\ 4 & -2 \\ 3 & 6 \end{bmatrix}$ and $B = \begin{bmatrix} 2 & -2 \\ 4 & 2 \\ -5 & 1 \end{bmatrix}$

Also given, $2A + 3X = 5B$

$$\Rightarrow \quad 3X = 5B - 2A$$

$$\Rightarrow \quad X = \frac{1}{3}[5B - 2A] = \frac{1}{3}\left\{5\begin{bmatrix} 2 & -2 \\ 4 & 2 \\ -5 & 1 \end{bmatrix} - 2\begin{bmatrix} 8 & 0 \\ 4 & -2 \\ 3 & 6 \end{bmatrix}\right\}$$

$$= \frac{1}{3}\left\{\begin{bmatrix} 10 & -10 \\ 20 & 10 \\ -25 & 5 \end{bmatrix} + \begin{bmatrix} -16 & 0 \\ -8 & 4 \\ -6 & -12 \end{bmatrix}\right\}$$

$$= \frac{1}{3}\begin{bmatrix} 10 - 16 & -10 + 0 \\ 20 - 8 & 10 + 4 \\ -25 - 6 & 5 - 12 \end{bmatrix}$$

$$= \frac{1}{3}\begin{bmatrix} -6 & -10 \\ 12 & 14 \\ -31 & -7 \end{bmatrix}$$

$$\therefore \quad X = \begin{bmatrix} -2 & -\frac{10}{3} \\ 4 & \frac{14}{3} \\ -\frac{31}{3} & -\frac{7}{3} \end{bmatrix}$$, which is the required matrix X.

Example 9 **Find a matrix A such that $2A - 3B + 5C = O$, where $B = \begin{bmatrix} -2 & 2 & 0 \\ 3 & 1 & 4 \end{bmatrix}$ and $C = \begin{bmatrix} 2 & 0 & -2 \\ 7 & 1 & 6 \end{bmatrix}$.** *CBSE 2019*

Sol. Given, $2A - 3B + 5C = O$

$$\Rightarrow \quad 2A = 3B - 5C$$

$$\Rightarrow 2A = 3\begin{bmatrix} -2 & 2 & 0 \\ 3 & 1 & 4 \end{bmatrix} - 5\begin{bmatrix} 2 & 0 & -2 \\ 7 & 1 & 6 \end{bmatrix}$$

$$\Rightarrow 2A = \begin{bmatrix} -6 & 6 & 0 \\ 9 & 3 & 12 \end{bmatrix} - \begin{bmatrix} 10 & 0 & -10 \\ 35 & 5 & 30 \end{bmatrix}$$

$$\Rightarrow 2A = \begin{bmatrix} -6 - 10 & 6 - 0 & 0 - (-10) \\ 9 - 35 & 3 - 5 & 12 - 30 \end{bmatrix}$$

$$\Rightarrow \quad A = \frac{1}{2}\begin{bmatrix} -16 & 6 & 10 \\ -26 & -2 & -18 \end{bmatrix}$$

$$\therefore \quad A = \begin{bmatrix} -8 & 3 & 5 \\ -13 & -1 & -9 \end{bmatrix}$$

Quick Test 1

1. Write the number of all possible matrices of order 2×2 with each entry 1, 2 or 3. *Competency Based Que*
2. Write the element a_{23} of a 3×3 matrix $A = [a_{ij}]$, whose elements a_{ij} are given by $a_{ij} = \frac{|i-j|}{2}$. *CBSE 2015*
3. If a matrix has 5 elements, then write all possible orders it can have. *CBSE 2011*
4. Construct a 3×4 matrix, whose elements are given by $a_{ij} = \frac{1}{2}|-3i + j|$.
5. If $\begin{bmatrix} x+y & 7 \\ 9 & x-y \end{bmatrix} = \begin{bmatrix} 2 & 7 \\ 9 & 4 \end{bmatrix}$, then find $x \cdot y$. *CBSE 2020*
6. Find the values of a, b, c and d from the equation $\begin{bmatrix} 2a+b & a-2b \\ 5c-d & 4c+3d \end{bmatrix} = \begin{bmatrix} 4 & -3 \\ 11 & 24 \end{bmatrix}$. *Competency Based Que, NCERT*
7. Simplify : $\cos\theta \begin{bmatrix} \cos\theta & \sin\theta \\ -\sin\theta & \cos\theta \end{bmatrix} + \sin\theta \begin{bmatrix} \sin\theta & -\cos\theta \\ \cos\theta & \sin\theta \end{bmatrix}$. *NCERT; CBSE 2012*
8. Solve the matrix equation $\begin{bmatrix} x^2 \\ y^2 \end{bmatrix} - 3\begin{bmatrix} x \\ 2y \end{bmatrix} = \begin{bmatrix} -2 \\ 9 \end{bmatrix}$. *Competency Based Que*
9. Find X and Y, if $2X + 3Y = \begin{bmatrix} 2 & 3 \\ 4 & 0 \end{bmatrix}$ and $3X + 2Y = \begin{bmatrix} 2 & -2 \\ -1 & 5 \end{bmatrix}$. *NCERT*
10. If $A = \text{diag.}[2, -1, 3]$ and $B = \text{diag.}[3, 0, -1]$, then find $4A + 2B$. *Competency Based Que*

Answers

1. 81 2. $\frac{1}{2}$ 3. $5 \times 1, 1 \times 5$

4. $\begin{bmatrix} 1 & 1/2 & 0 & 1/2 \\ 5/2 & 2 & 3/2 & 1 \\ 4 & 7/2 & 3 & 5/2 \end{bmatrix}$ 5. -3

6. $a = 1, b = 2, c = 3, d = 4$ 7. I

8. $x = 1, 2$ and $y = 3 \pm 3\sqrt{2}$

9. $Y = \begin{bmatrix} \frac{2}{5} & \frac{13}{5} \\ \frac{14}{5} & -2 \end{bmatrix}, X = \begin{bmatrix} \frac{2}{5} & -\frac{12}{5} \\ -\frac{11}{5} & 3 \end{bmatrix}$

10. diag. $[14, -4, 10]$

For Solutions, See QR Code on Pg. 69

3.3 Multiplication of Matrices

The product AB of two matrices A and B is defined, if the number of columns of A is equal to the number of rows of B.

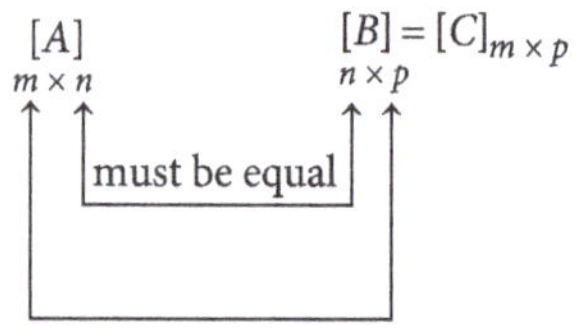

Order of product of matrix

Let A be the $m \times n$ matrix and B be the $n \times p$ matrix. Then, the product AB of the matrices A and B is matrix C of order $m \times p$.

e.g. $[1 \quad 4] \begin{bmatrix} 3 \\ 2 \end{bmatrix} = [(1 \times 3) + (4 \times 2)] = [3 + 8] = [11]$

[multiplying row by column]

Method of Multiplying Two Matrices

Suppose, we have two matrices $A = [a_{ij}]_{m \times n}$ and $B = [b_{jk}]_{n \times p}$, then to multiply them (i.e. for finding AB), we use the following steps

I. First, write the given two matrices (A and B), then find the number of columns of first matrix A and number of rows of second matrix B. If both are same, i.e. equal, then go to next step, otherwise product is not possible.

II. Multiply first row (R_1) of A with first column (C_1) of B element-wise and take the sum of all these products.

e.g. If $[a_{11} \quad a_{12} \quad a_{13}]$ is first row of A and $\begin{bmatrix} b_{11} \\ b_{21} \\ b_{31} \end{bmatrix}$ is first column of B, then their multiplication is $a_{11}b_{11} + a_{12}b_{21} + a_{13}b_{31}$.

Similarly, multiply first row (R_1) of A with second column (C_2) of B. Repeat this process to multiply each row of matrix A with each column of B.

III. From Step II, we get the elements of product matrix C, where c_{11} = Sum of products of elements of first row of A with corresponding elements of first column of B. In general,

$$c_{ik} = a_{i1}b_{1k} + a_{i2}b_{2k} + \ldots + a_{in}b_{nk} = \sum_{j=1}^{n} a_{ij}\, b_{jk}.$$

IV. Now, write the matrix $C = [c_{ik}]_{m \times p}$, whose elements are obtained in Step III.

Thus, we get the required product of A and B.

Properties of Multiplication of Matrices

(i) Matrix multiplication is not commutative

i.e. $AB \neq BA$

(ii) Matrix multiplication is associative

i.e. $(AB)C = A(BC)$

(iii) Matrix multiplication is distributive over matrix addition

i.e. $A(B+C) = AB + AC$

(iv) For every square matrix A, there exist an identity matrix I of same order such that

$$AI = A = IA$$

Here, I is the multiplicative identity for every square matrix A.

(v) The product of a matrix with a null or zero matrix is null or zero matrix

i.e. $AO = O = OA$

(vi) If the product of two non-zero matrices is a zero matrix, then it is not necessary that one of matrix is zero matrix.

Positive Integral Powers of a Square Matrix

If A be a square matrix, then we can define

(i) $A^{n+1} = A^n \cdot A$, where $n \in N$

(ii) $A^m \cdot A^n = A^{m+n}$, where $m, n \in N$

(iii) $(A^m)^n = A^{mn}\ \forall\ m, n \in N$

(iv) $I^n = I$ for any positive integer n, where I is the identity matrix.

Matrix Polynomial

Let $f(x) = a_0x^n + a_1x^{n-1} + a_2x^{n-2} + \ldots + a_{n-1}x + a_n$ be a polynomial and A be a square matrix. Then, $f(A) = a_0A^n + a_1A^{n-1} + a_2A^{n-2} + \ldots + a_{n-1}A + a_nI$

is called a matrix polynomial, where I is the identity matrix of order of A.

TEACHER TIPS

(i) If AB is defined, then BA need not to be defined.

(ii) If A and B are square matrices of the same order say m, then both the product AB and BA are defined and each is a square matrix of order n.

(iii) Multiplication of diagonal matrices of same order will be commutative.

Example 1 **Compute the product of** $\begin{bmatrix} 2 & 3 & 4 \\ 3 & 4 & 5 \\ 4 & 5 & 6 \end{bmatrix}$ **and** $\begin{bmatrix} 1 & -3 & 5 \\ 0 & 2 & 4 \\ 3 & 0 & 5 \end{bmatrix}$.

NCERT

Sol. Let $A = \begin{bmatrix} 2 & 3 & 4 \\ 3 & 4 & 5 \\ 4 & 5 & 6 \end{bmatrix}$ and $B = \begin{bmatrix} 1 & -3 & 5 \\ 0 & 2 & 4 \\ 3 & 0 & 5 \end{bmatrix}$.

Here, number of columns of A = number of rows of $B = 3$, so AB is defined.

Now, $AB = \begin{bmatrix} 2 & 3 & 4 \\ 3 & 4 & 5 \\ 4 & 5 & 6 \end{bmatrix}\begin{bmatrix} 1 & -3 & 5 \\ 0 & 2 & 4 \\ 3 & 0 & 5 \end{bmatrix}$

$$= \begin{bmatrix} 2+0+12 & -6+6+0 & 10+12+20 \\ 3+0+15 & -9+8+0 & 15+16+25 \\ 4+0+18 & -12+10+0 & 20+20+30 \end{bmatrix}$$

$$= \begin{bmatrix} 14 & 0 & 42 \\ 18 & -1 & 56 \\ 22 & -2 & 70 \end{bmatrix}$$

Example 2 **If** $A = [2\ \ -3\ \ 4]$, $B = \begin{bmatrix} 3 \\ 2 \\ 2 \end{bmatrix}$, $X = [1\ \ 2\ \ 3]$ **and** $Y = \begin{bmatrix} 2 \\ 3 \\ 4 \end{bmatrix}$, **then find** $AB + XY$.

CBSE 2023, 20

Sol. Given, $A = [2\ \ -3\ \ 4]$, $B = \begin{bmatrix} 3 \\ 2 \\ 2 \end{bmatrix}$, $X = [1\ \ 2\ \ 3]$ and $Y = \begin{bmatrix} 2 \\ 3 \\ 4 \end{bmatrix}$

Now, $AB = [2\ \ -3\ \ 4]\begin{bmatrix} 3 \\ 2 \\ 2 \end{bmatrix} = [6-6+8] = [8]$

and $XY = [1\ \ 2\ \ 3]\begin{bmatrix} 2 \\ 3 \\ 4 \end{bmatrix} = [2+6+12] = [20]$

$\therefore\ AB + XY = [8] + [20] = [28]$

Example 3 **Find the matrix** A **such that**

$$A\begin{bmatrix} 1 & 2 & 3 \\ 4 & 5 & 6 \end{bmatrix} = \begin{bmatrix} -7 & -8 & -9 \\ 2 & 4 & 6 \end{bmatrix}.$$

Competency Based Que

Sol. The right side of given matrix equation is of order 2×3, so left side of the given matrix equation should be of order 2×3. It is clear that the product of A with 2×3 matrix is a 2×3 matrix, therefore A is a 2×2 matrix.

Let $A = \begin{bmatrix} u & v \\ w & x \end{bmatrix}$.

Then, LHS $= \begin{bmatrix} u & v \\ w & x \end{bmatrix}\begin{bmatrix} 1 & 2 & 3 \\ 4 & 5 & 6 \end{bmatrix}$

$$= \begin{bmatrix} u+4v & 2u+5v & 3u+6v \\ w+4x & 2w+5x & 3w+6x \end{bmatrix}$$

$$\therefore \begin{bmatrix} u+4v & 2u+5v & 3u+6v \\ w+4x & 2w+5x & 3w+6x \end{bmatrix} = \begin{bmatrix} -7 & -8 & -9 \\ 2 & 4 & 6 \end{bmatrix}$$

On comparing the elements from both sides, we get

$$u+4v=-7,\ 2u+5v=-8,\ 3u+6v=-9,$$
$$w+4x=2,\ 2w+5x=4 \text{ and } 3w+6x=6$$

On solving, we get $u=1$, $v=-2$, $w=2$ and $x=0$

$$\therefore \quad A = \begin{bmatrix} 1 & -2 \\ 2 & 0 \end{bmatrix}$$

Example 4 If $f(\alpha) = \begin{bmatrix} \cos\alpha & -\sin\alpha & 0 \\ \sin\alpha & \cos\alpha & 0 \\ 0 & 0 & 1 \end{bmatrix}$, prove that $f(\alpha)\cdot f(-\beta) = f(\alpha-\beta)$. *CBSE 2023*

Sol. We have, $f(\alpha) = \begin{bmatrix} \cos\alpha & -\sin\alpha & 0 \\ \sin\alpha & \cos\alpha & 0 \\ 0 & 0 & 1 \end{bmatrix}$ ...(i)

For $f(-\beta)$, replace α in $f(\alpha)$ by $-\beta$

$$\therefore f(-\beta) = \begin{bmatrix} \cos(-\beta) & -\sin(-\beta) & 0 \\ \sin(-\beta) & \cos(-\beta) & 0 \\ 0 & 0 & 1 \end{bmatrix} = \begin{bmatrix} \cos\beta & \sin\beta & 0 \\ -\sin\beta & \cos\beta & 0 \\ 0 & 0 & 1 \end{bmatrix}$$

By LHS $= f(\alpha)f(-\beta)$

$$= \begin{bmatrix} \cos\alpha & -\sin\alpha & 0 \\ \sin\alpha & \cos\alpha & 0 \\ 0 & 0 & 1 \end{bmatrix} \begin{bmatrix} \cos\beta & \sin\beta & 0 \\ -\sin\beta & \cos\beta & 0 \\ 0 & 0 & 1 \end{bmatrix}$$

$$= \begin{bmatrix} \cos\alpha\cos\beta+\sin\alpha\sin\beta & \cos\alpha\sin\beta-\sin\alpha\cos\beta & 0 \\ \sin\alpha\cos\beta-\cos\alpha\sin\beta & \sin\alpha\sin\beta+\cos\alpha\cos\beta & 0 \\ 0 & 0 & 1 \end{bmatrix}$$

$$= \begin{bmatrix} \cos(\alpha-\beta) & -\sin(\alpha-\beta) & 0 \\ \sin(\alpha-\beta) & \cos(\alpha-\beta) & 0 \\ 0 & 0 & 1 \end{bmatrix} \quad \text{...(ii)}$$

RHS $= f(\alpha-\beta)$

Now, for $f(\alpha-\beta)$, replace α in $f(\alpha)$ by $(\alpha-\beta)$

$$\therefore f(\alpha-\beta) = \begin{bmatrix} \cos(\alpha-\beta) & -\sin(\alpha-\beta) & 0 \\ \sin(\alpha-\beta) & \cos(\alpha-\beta) & 0 \\ 0 & 0 & 1 \end{bmatrix} \quad \text{...(iii)}$$

From Eqs. (ii) and (iii), we get

LHS = RHS **Hence proved.**

Example 5 If $A = \begin{bmatrix} 0 & 1 \\ -1 & 0 \end{bmatrix}$, then find the real values x and y such that $(xI+yA)^2 = A$.

Sol. We have, $A = \begin{bmatrix} 0 & 1 \\ -1 & 0 \end{bmatrix}$

$$\therefore \quad xI+yA = x\begin{bmatrix} 1 & 0 \\ 0 & 1 \end{bmatrix} + y\begin{bmatrix} 0 & 1 \\ -1 & 0 \end{bmatrix}$$

$$= \begin{bmatrix} x & 0 \\ 0 & x \end{bmatrix} + \begin{bmatrix} 0 & y \\ -y & 0 \end{bmatrix} = \begin{bmatrix} x & y \\ -y & x \end{bmatrix}$$

Now, $(xI+yA)^2 = \begin{bmatrix} x & y \\ -y & x \end{bmatrix}^2 = \begin{bmatrix} x & y \\ -y & x \end{bmatrix}\begin{bmatrix} x & y \\ -y & x \end{bmatrix}$

$$= \begin{bmatrix} x^2-y^2 & 2xy \\ -2xy & x^2-y^2 \end{bmatrix}$$

Since, $(xI+yA)^2 = A$, therefore

$$\begin{bmatrix} x^2-y^2 & 2xy \\ -2xy & x^2-y^2 \end{bmatrix} = \begin{bmatrix} 0 & 1 \\ -1 & 0 \end{bmatrix}$$

On comparing the corresponding elements, we get

$\Rightarrow \quad x^2-y^2=0,\ 2xy=1,\ -2xy=-1$ and $x^2-y^2=0$

$\Rightarrow \quad x^2-y^2=0$ and $2xy=1$

$\Rightarrow \quad x=\pm y$ and $2xy=1$

Case I When $x=y$ and $2xy=1$.

In this case, $2x^2=1 \Rightarrow x=\pm\dfrac{1}{\sqrt{2}}$

Thus, $\left(x=\dfrac{1}{\sqrt{2}} \text{ and } y=\dfrac{1}{\sqrt{2}}\right)$ or $\left(x=-\dfrac{1}{\sqrt{2}} \text{ and } y=-\dfrac{1}{\sqrt{2}}\right)$

Case II When $x=-y$ and $2xy=1$.

In this case, $x^2=\dfrac{-1}{2} \Rightarrow x=\pm\dfrac{i}{\sqrt{2}}$, which is imaginary.

Hence, only real values of x and y are

$$x=\frac{1}{\sqrt{2}},\ y=\frac{1}{\sqrt{2}} \text{ or } x=-\frac{1}{\sqrt{2}},\ y=-\frac{1}{\sqrt{2}}$$

Example 6 If $A = \begin{bmatrix} 1 & -2 & 3 \\ -4 & 2 & 5 \end{bmatrix}$ and $B = \begin{bmatrix} 2 & 3 \\ 4 & 5 \\ 2 & 1 \end{bmatrix}$, then find AB and BA. Show that A and B are not commutative, i.e. $AB \neq BA$.

Sol. Here, order of matrix A is 2×3 and order of matrix B is 3×2. So, AB will be of order 2×2 and BA will be of order 3×3.

Now, $AB = \begin{bmatrix} 1 & -2 & 3 \\ -4 & 2 & 5 \end{bmatrix}\begin{bmatrix} 2 & 3 \\ 4 & 5 \\ 2 & 1 \end{bmatrix}$

$$= \begin{bmatrix} 2-8+6 & 3-10+3 \\ -8+8+10 & -12+10+5 \end{bmatrix}$$

[multiplying rows by columns]

$$AB = \begin{bmatrix} 0 & -4 \\ 10 & 3 \end{bmatrix}$$

and $BA = \begin{bmatrix} 2 & 3 \\ 4 & 5 \\ 2 & 1 \end{bmatrix}\begin{bmatrix} 1 & -2 & 3 \\ -4 & 2 & 5 \end{bmatrix}$

$$= \begin{bmatrix} 2-12 & -4+6 & 6+15 \\ 4-20 & -8+10 & 12+25 \\ 2-4 & -4+2 & 6+5 \end{bmatrix}$$

[multiplying rows by columns]

$$= \begin{bmatrix} -10 & 2 & 21 \\ -16 & 2 & 37 \\ -2 & -2 & 11 \end{bmatrix}$$

Clearly, $AB \neq BA$

Example 7 If A is a square matrix such that $A^2 = I$, then find the simplified value of $(A-I)^3+(A+I)^3-7A$. *CBSE 2016*

Sol. Given, $A^2 = I$ ...(i)

Now, $(A-I)^3+(A+I)^3-7A = (A^3-3A^2I+3AI^2-I^3)$
$+(A^3+3A^2I+3AI^2+I^3)-7A$
$=(A^3-3A^2+3AI-I)+(A^3+3A^2+3AI+I)-7A$
$[\because A^2I = A^2 \text{ and } I^3 = I^2 = I]$
$=2A^3+6AI-7A$
$=2A^2A+6A-7A$ $[\because AI = A]$
$=2IA-A$ [from Eq. (i)]
$=2A-A=A$ $[\because IA = A]$

Example 8 If $A=\begin{bmatrix}2 & 0 & 1\\ 2 & 1 & 3\\ 1 & -1 & 0\end{bmatrix}$, then find $A^2-5A+4I$ and hence find a matrix X, such that $A^2-5A+4I+X=O$. *CBSE 2015*

Sol. We have, $A=\begin{bmatrix}2 & 0 & 1\\ 2 & 1 & 3\\ 1 & -1 & 0\end{bmatrix}$

$$\therefore \quad A^2=\begin{bmatrix}2 & 0 & 1\\ 2 & 1 & 3\\ 1 & -1 & 0\end{bmatrix}\begin{bmatrix}2 & 0 & 1\\ 2 & 1 & 3\\ 1 & -1 & 0\end{bmatrix}$$
$$=\begin{bmatrix}4+0+1 & 0+0-1 & 2+0+0\\ 4+2+3 & 0+1-3 & 2+3+0\\ 2-2+0 & 0-1+0 & 1-3+0\end{bmatrix}$$
$$=\begin{bmatrix}5 & -1 & 2\\ 9 & -2 & 5\\ 0 & -1 & -2\end{bmatrix} \quad \text{[multiplying rows by columns]}$$

Now, consider $A^2-5A+4I$
$$=\begin{bmatrix}5 & -1 & 2\\ 9 & -2 & 5\\ 0 & -1 & -2\end{bmatrix}-5\begin{bmatrix}2 & 0 & 1\\ 2 & 1 & 3\\ 1 & -1 & 0\end{bmatrix}+4\begin{bmatrix}1 & 0 & 0\\ 0 & 1 & 0\\ 0 & 0 & 1\end{bmatrix}$$
$$=\begin{bmatrix}5 & -1 & 2\\ 9 & -2 & 5\\ 0 & -1 & -2\end{bmatrix}-\begin{bmatrix}10 & 0 & 5\\ 10 & 5 & 15\\ 5 & -5 & 0\end{bmatrix}+\begin{bmatrix}4 & 0 & 0\\ 0 & 4 & 0\\ 0 & 0 & 4\end{bmatrix}$$
$$=\begin{bmatrix}-5 & -1 & -3\\ -1 & -7 & -10\\ -5 & 4 & -2\end{bmatrix}+\begin{bmatrix}4 & 0 & 0\\ 0 & 4 & 0\\ 0 & 0 & 4\end{bmatrix}=\begin{bmatrix}-1 & -1 & -3\\ -1 & -3 & -10\\ -5 & 4 & 2\end{bmatrix}$$

Since, $A^2-5A+4I+X=O$
$\therefore A^2-5A+4I+X-X=O-X$
[subtracting matrix X from both sides]
$\Rightarrow A^2-5A+4I+O=-X$
$\Rightarrow \quad X=-(A^2-5A+4I)$
$$\Rightarrow \quad X=-\begin{bmatrix}-1 & -1 & -3\\ -1 & -3 & -10\\ -5 & 4 & 2\end{bmatrix}=\begin{bmatrix}1 & 1 & 3\\ 1 & 3 & 10\\ 5 & -4 & -2\end{bmatrix}$$

Quick Test 2

1. Evaluate AB and BA if possible

(i) $A=\begin{bmatrix}2 & 3\\ -1 & 0\end{bmatrix}, B=\begin{bmatrix}-2 & 1\\ 3 & -2\end{bmatrix}$ (ii) $A=[1\ -2\ 3], B=\begin{bmatrix}1 & 0\\ 2 & -1\\ 1 & 2\end{bmatrix}$

(iii) $A=\begin{bmatrix}2 & -1 & 3\\ -1 & 2 & 1\end{bmatrix}, B=\begin{bmatrix}1 & 3 & 2\\ 2 & -1 & 0\\ 3 & 1 & 2\end{bmatrix}$ (iv) $A=\begin{bmatrix}1 & 6 & -1\\ 2 & -3 & -9\\ 1 & 2 & 0\end{bmatrix}, B=\begin{bmatrix}6 & 2\\ 0 & 1\\ -1 & 3\end{bmatrix}$

2. If $[2x\ \ 3]\begin{bmatrix}1 & 2\\ -3 & 0\end{bmatrix}\begin{bmatrix}x\\ 3\end{bmatrix}=O$, then find x.

3. If $[1\ \ x\ \ 1]\begin{bmatrix}1 & 3 & 2\\ 2 & 5 & 1\\ 15 & 3 & 2\end{bmatrix}\begin{bmatrix}1\\ 2\\ x\end{bmatrix}=O$, then find the value of x. *Competency Based Que*

4. If $A=\begin{bmatrix}2 & -2\\ -2 & 2\end{bmatrix}$ and $A^2=pA$, then find the value of p. *CBSE 2013*

5. Let $A=\begin{bmatrix}2 & -1\\ 3 & 4\end{bmatrix}, B=\begin{bmatrix}5 & 2\\ 7 & 4\end{bmatrix}$ and $C=\begin{bmatrix}2 & 5\\ 3 & 8\end{bmatrix}$.
Find a matrix D such that $CD-AB=O$. *NCERT; CBSE 2017*

6. If $f(x)=\begin{bmatrix}\cos x & -\sin x & 0\\ \sin x & \cos x & 0\\ 0 & 0 & 1\end{bmatrix}$, then show that $f(x)\cdot f(y)=f(x+y)$. *NCERT*

7. If $A=\begin{bmatrix}0 & -\tan\alpha/2\\ \tan\alpha/2 & 0\end{bmatrix}$ and I is the identity matrix of order 2, then show that $I+A=(I-A)\begin{bmatrix}\cos\alpha & -\sin\alpha\\ \sin\alpha & \cos\alpha\end{bmatrix}$.

8. Find matrix A such that $\begin{bmatrix}2 & -1\\ 1 & 0\\ -3 & 4\end{bmatrix}A=\begin{bmatrix}-1 & -8\\ 1 & -2\\ 9 & 22\end{bmatrix}$ *Competency Based Que*

9. If A is a square matrix such that $A^2=A$, then write the value of $7A-(I+A)^3$, where I is an identity matrix. *Competency Based Que*

10. If $A=\begin{bmatrix}1 & 0 & 2\\ 0 & 2 & 1\\ 2 & 0 & 3\end{bmatrix}$ and $A^3-6A^2+7A+kI_3=O$, then find the value of k. *Competency Based Que, CBSE 2023, 16*

Answers

1. (i) $AB=\begin{bmatrix}5 & -4\\ 2 & -1\end{bmatrix}$, $BA=\begin{bmatrix}-5 & -6\\ 8 & 9\end{bmatrix}$

(ii) $AB=[0\ \ 8]$, BA does not exist.

(iii) $AB=\begin{bmatrix}9 & 10 & 10\\ 6 & -4 & 0\end{bmatrix}$, BA does not exist.

(iv) $AB=\begin{bmatrix}7 & 5\\ 21 & -26\\ 6 & 4\end{bmatrix}$, BA does not exist.

2. $x=0$ or $-\frac{3}{2}$ **3.** -14 or -2 **4.** 4 **5.** $\begin{bmatrix}-191 & -110\\ 77 & 44\end{bmatrix}$

8. $A=\begin{bmatrix}1 & -2\\ 3 & 4\end{bmatrix}$ **9.** $-I$ **10.** 2

For Solutions, See QR Code on Pg. 69

3.4 Transpose of Matrix

The matrix obtained by interchanging the rows and columns of matrix A is called the transpose of matrix A. The transpose of matrix A is represented by

$$A' \text{ or } A^c \text{ or } A^T$$

e.g. Let $A = \begin{bmatrix} 1 & 5 \\ \sqrt{2} & 1 \\ -1/5 & 0 \end{bmatrix}_{3\times 2}$. Then, $A' = \begin{bmatrix} 1 & \sqrt{2} & -1/5 \\ 5 & 1 & 0 \end{bmatrix}_{2\times 3}$

Properties of Transpose of Matrices

For any matrices A and B of suitable orders, we have

(i) $(A')' = A$

(ii) $(kA)' = kA'$, where k is any constant.

(iii) $(A \pm B)' = A' \pm B'$

(iv) $(AB)' = B'A'$ [reversal law]

(v) $(A^n)^T = (A^T)^n$, where n is a positive integer.

Symmetric and Skew-Symmetric Matrix

Symmetric Matrix

A square matrix A is called a symmetric matrix, if the transpose of matrix A is equal to the matrix A, i.e. $A' = A$.

e.g. $A = \begin{bmatrix} 2 & 1 & 5 \\ 1 & 2 & 7 \\ 5 & 7 & 3 \end{bmatrix}$

Then, $A' = \begin{bmatrix} 2 & 1 & 5 \\ 1 & 2 & 7 \\ 5 & 7 & 3 \end{bmatrix}' = \begin{bmatrix} 2 & 1 & 5 \\ 1 & 2 & 7 \\ 5 & 7 & 3 \end{bmatrix} = A$

[interchanging the elements of rows and columns]

Hence, A is a symmetric matrix.

Skew-Symmetric Matrix

A square matrix A is said to be skew-symmetric matrix, if the transpose of matrix A is equal to the negative of matrix A. i.e. $A' = -A$.

e.g. Let $A = \begin{bmatrix} 0 & 1 & 2 \\ -1 & 0 & 5 \\ -2 & -5 & 0 \end{bmatrix}$.

Then, $A' = \begin{bmatrix} 0 & -1 & -2 \\ 1 & 0 & -5 \\ 2 & 5 & 0 \end{bmatrix}$

[interchanging the elements of rows and columns]

$= -\begin{bmatrix} 0 & 1 & 2 \\ -1 & 0 & 5 \\ -2 & -5 & 0 \end{bmatrix}$

[taking (−1) common from the matrix]

$\Rightarrow \quad A' = -A$

Some Important Theorems

(i) For every square matrix A, $A + A'$ is a symmetric matrix and $A - A'$ is a skew-symmetric matrix.

(ii) Any square matrix can be expressed as the sum of a symmetric and a skew-symmetric matrices i.e.
Let A be a square matrix, then it can be written as
$$A = \frac{1}{2}(A + A') + \frac{1}{2}(A - A').$$

3.5 Invertible Matrices

Let A be a square matrix of order n, if there exist a square matrix B such that $AB = I_n = BA$, then B is called the inverse of A and is denoted by A^{-1}.

$\therefore AA^{-1} = I = A^{-1}A$

Some Important Theorems

(i) Inverse of a square matrix, if it exists, is unique.

(ii) If A and B are invertible matrices of the same order, then $(AB)^{-1} = B^{-1}A^{-1}$, where A and B are matrices of the same order.

TEACHER TIPS

- Diagonal elements of a skew-symmetric matrix are always zero.
- Only zero square matrix is both symmetric and skew-symmetric matrices.
- All positive integral powers of a symmetric matrix are symmetric.
- All odd positive integral powers of a skew-symmetric matrix are skew-symmetric.
- If B is the inverse of A, then A is also the inverse of B.

Example 1 For the matrices A and B, verify that $(AB)' = B'A'$, where $A = \begin{bmatrix} 1 \\ -4 \\ 3 \end{bmatrix}$ and $B = [-1 \quad 2 \quad 1]$. *NCERT*

Sol. Given, $A = \begin{bmatrix} 1 \\ -4 \\ 3 \end{bmatrix}_{3\times1}$ and $B = [-1 \quad 2 \quad 1]_{1\times3}$

$\therefore \quad A' = [1 \quad -4 \quad 3]_{1\times3}$

[interchanging the elements of rows and columns]

and $B' = \begin{bmatrix} -1 \\ 2 \\ 1 \end{bmatrix}_{3\times1}$

[interchanging the elements of rows and columns]

Now, $AB = \begin{bmatrix} 1 \\ -4 \\ 3 \end{bmatrix}_{3\times1} [-1 \quad 2 \quad 1]_{1\times3}$

Since, number of columns in A is equal to the number of rows in B. So, AB exists.

Thus, $AB = \begin{bmatrix} -1 & 2 & 1 \\ 4 & -8 & -4 \\ -3 & 6 & 3 \end{bmatrix}_{3\times3}$

[multiplying rows by columns]

$\Rightarrow \quad (AB)' = \begin{bmatrix} -1 & 4 & -3 \\ 2 & -8 & 6 \\ 1 & -4 & 3 \end{bmatrix}_{3\times3}$ ...(i)

[interchanging the elements of rows and columns]

Now, $B'A' = \begin{bmatrix} -1 \\ 2 \\ 1 \end{bmatrix}_{3\times1} [1 \quad -4 \quad 3]_{1\times3} = \begin{bmatrix} -1 & 4 & -3 \\ 2 & -8 & 6 \\ 1 & -4 & 3 \end{bmatrix}_{3\times3}$

[multiplying rows by columns] ...(ii)

From Eqs. (i) and (ii), we get

$\therefore \quad (AB)' = B'A'$ **Hence verified.**

Example 2 If A is 4×3 matrix and B is matrix such that $A'B$ and AB' are both defined, then find the order of B. *Competency Based Que*

Sol. Given, order of A is 4×3.

$\therefore$ Order of $A' = 3\times4$

Let the order of B be $m\times n$.

$\therefore$ Order of B' is $n\times m$

Since, $A'B$ is defined.

$\therefore$ Number of columns of A' is equal to the number of rows of B.

$\Rightarrow m = 4$

Similarly, AB' is defined.

$\therefore$ Number of columns of A is equal to the number of rows of B'.

$\Rightarrow n = 3$

$\therefore$ Order of matrix B is 4×3.

Example 3 If $A = \begin{bmatrix} \cos\alpha & \sin\alpha \\ -\sin\alpha & \cos\alpha \end{bmatrix}$, then find α satisfying $0 < \alpha < \frac{\pi}{2}$ when $A + A^T = \sqrt{2}\, I_2$, where A^T is transpose of A. *CBSE 2016*

Sol. Given, $A = \begin{bmatrix} \cos\alpha & \sin\alpha \\ -\sin\alpha & \cos\alpha \end{bmatrix}$

Also, given $A + A^T = \sqrt{2}\, I_2$

$\therefore \begin{bmatrix} \cos\alpha & \sin\alpha \\ -\sin\alpha & \cos\alpha \end{bmatrix} + \begin{bmatrix} \cos\alpha & \sin\alpha \\ -\sin\alpha & \cos\alpha \end{bmatrix}^T = \sqrt{2}\begin{bmatrix} 1 & 0 \\ 0 & 1 \end{bmatrix}$

$\Rightarrow \begin{bmatrix} \cos\alpha & \sin\alpha \\ -\sin\alpha & \cos\alpha \end{bmatrix} + \begin{bmatrix} \cos\alpha & -\sin\alpha \\ \sin\alpha & \cos\alpha \end{bmatrix} = \begin{bmatrix} \sqrt{2} & 0 \\ 0 & \sqrt{2} \end{bmatrix}$

$\Rightarrow \begin{bmatrix} \cos\alpha + \cos\alpha & \sin\alpha - \sin\alpha \\ -\sin\alpha + \sin\alpha & \cos\alpha + \cos\alpha \end{bmatrix} = \begin{bmatrix} \sqrt{2} & 0 \\ 0 & \sqrt{2} \end{bmatrix}$

$\Rightarrow \begin{bmatrix} 2\cos\alpha & 0 \\ 0 & 2\cos\alpha \end{bmatrix} = \begin{bmatrix} \sqrt{2} & 0 \\ 0 & \sqrt{2} \end{bmatrix}$

On equating the corresponding elements, we get

$2\cos\alpha = \sqrt{2} \Rightarrow \cos\alpha = \frac{\sqrt{2}}{2} \Rightarrow \cos\alpha = \frac{1}{\sqrt{2}} = \cos\frac{\pi}{4}$

$\therefore \alpha = \frac{\pi}{4}$, which is satisfying $0 < \alpha < \frac{\pi}{2}$.

Example 4 Show that all positive integral powers of a symmetric matrix are symmetric. *Competency Based Que*

Sol. Let A be a symmetric matrix and $n \in N$.

Then, $(A^n)^T = [A \cdot A \cdot A \ldots n \text{ times}]^T$

$= [A^T \cdot A^T \ldots n \text{ times}]$ $[\because (AB)^T = B^T A^T]$

$= [A\ A \ldots n \text{ times}] = (A)^n$

$[\because A$ is symmetric, therefore $A^T = A]$

Example 5 Matrix $A = \begin{bmatrix} 0 & 2b & -2 \\ 3 & 1 & 3 \\ 3a & 3 & -1 \end{bmatrix}$ is given to be symmetric, then find the value of a and b. *CBSE 2016*

Sol. Given, $A = \begin{bmatrix} 0 & 2b & -2 \\ 3 & 1 & 3 \\ 3a & 3 & -1 \end{bmatrix}$ is a symmetric matrix.

We know that a matrix A is symmetric, if $A' = A$.

$\therefore \begin{bmatrix} 0 & 2b & -2 \\ 3 & 1 & 3 \\ 3a & 3 & -1 \end{bmatrix}' = \begin{bmatrix} 0 & 2b & -2 \\ 3 & 1 & 3 \\ 3a & 3 & -1 \end{bmatrix}$

$\Rightarrow \begin{bmatrix} 0 & 3 & 3a \\ 2b & 1 & 3 \\ -2 & 3 & -1 \end{bmatrix} = \begin{bmatrix} 0 & 2b & -2 \\ 3 & 1 & 3 \\ 3a & 3 & -1 \end{bmatrix}$

On equating the corresponding elements, we get

$3 = 2b$ and $3a = -2$

$\therefore \quad b = \frac{3}{2}$ and $a = -\frac{2}{3}$

Example 6 **If the matrix $A = \begin{bmatrix} 0 & a & -3 \\ 2 & 0 & -1 \\ b & 1 & 0 \end{bmatrix}$ is skew-symmetric, then find the value of a and b.** *CBSE 2018*

Sol. Given, $A = \begin{bmatrix} 0 & a & -3 \\ 2 & 0 & -1 \\ b & 1 & 0 \end{bmatrix}$ is a skew-symmetric matrix.

$$\therefore \quad A^T = -A$$

$$\Rightarrow \quad \begin{bmatrix} 0 & a & -3 \\ 2 & 0 & -1 \\ b & 1 & 0 \end{bmatrix}^T = -\begin{bmatrix} 0 & a & -3 \\ 2 & 0 & -1 \\ b & 1 & 0 \end{bmatrix}$$

$$\Rightarrow \quad \begin{bmatrix} 0 & 2 & b \\ a & 0 & 1 \\ -3 & -1 & 0 \end{bmatrix} = \begin{bmatrix} 0 & -a & 3 \\ -2 & 0 & 1 \\ -b & -1 & 0 \end{bmatrix}$$

On equating the corresponding elements, we get

$$a = -2 \text{ and } b = 3$$

Example 7 **Show that all the diagonal elements of a skew-symmetric matrix are zero.** *Competency Based Que*

Sol. Let $A = [a_{ij}]$ be a skew-symmetric matrix.

Then, $a_{ji} = -a_{ij} \, \forall \, i, j$

Now, put $i = j$, we get

$\Rightarrow \quad a_{ii} = -a_{ii} \, \forall \, i$

$\Rightarrow \quad 2a_{ii} = 0$

$\Rightarrow \quad a_{ii} = 0 \, \forall \, i$

$\therefore \quad a_{11} = a_{22} = a_{33} = \ldots = a_{nn} = 0$

Hence, all the diagonal elements of a skew- symmetric matrix are zero. **Hence proved.**

Example 8 **Express the following matrix as a sum of a symmetric and a skew-symmetric matrix.**

$$\begin{bmatrix} 3 & -2 & -4 \\ 3 & -2 & -5 \\ -1 & 1 & 2 \end{bmatrix}$$

Sol. Let $A = \begin{bmatrix} 3 & -2 & -4 \\ 3 & -2 & -5 \\ -1 & 1 & 2 \end{bmatrix}$

$$\therefore \quad A' = \begin{bmatrix} 3 & 3 & -1 \\ -2 & -2 & 1 \\ -4 & -5 & 2 \end{bmatrix}$$

Now, let $P = \frac{1}{2}(A + A')$

$$= \frac{1}{2}\left\{\begin{bmatrix} 3 & -2 & -4 \\ 3 & -2 & -5 \\ -1 & 1 & 2 \end{bmatrix} + \begin{bmatrix} 3 & 3 & -1 \\ -2 & -2 & 1 \\ -4 & -5 & 2 \end{bmatrix}\right\}$$

$$= \frac{1}{2}\begin{bmatrix} 6 & 1 & -5 \\ 1 & -4 & -4 \\ -5 & -4 & 4 \end{bmatrix}$$

$$= \begin{bmatrix} 3 & 1/2 & -5/2 \\ 1/2 & -2 & -2 \\ -5/2 & -2 & 2 \end{bmatrix}$$

and $Q = \frac{1}{2}(A - A')$

$$= \frac{1}{2}\left\{\begin{bmatrix} 3 & -2 & -4 \\ 3 & -2 & -5 \\ -1 & 1 & 2 \end{bmatrix} - \begin{bmatrix} 3 & 3 & -1 \\ -2 & -2 & 1 \\ -4 & -5 & 2 \end{bmatrix}\right\}$$

$$= \frac{1}{2}\begin{bmatrix} 0 & -5 & -3 \\ 5 & 0 & -6 \\ 3 & 6 & 0 \end{bmatrix}$$

$$= \begin{bmatrix} 0 & -5/2 & -3/2 \\ 5/2 & 0 & -3 \\ 3/2 & 3 & 0 \end{bmatrix}$$

Clearly, here $P' = \begin{bmatrix} 3 & 1/2 & -5/2 \\ 1/2 & -2 & -2 \\ -5/2 & -2 & 2 \end{bmatrix} = P$

and $\quad Q' = \begin{bmatrix} 0 & 5/2 & 3/2 \\ -5/2 & 0 & 3 \\ -3/2 & -3 & 0 \end{bmatrix} = -Q$

So, P is a symmetric matrix and Q is a skew-symmetric matrix.

Now, $P + Q = \frac{1}{2}(A + A') + \frac{1}{2}(A - A')$

$$= \begin{bmatrix} 3 & 1/2 & -5/2 \\ 1/2 & -2 & -2 \\ -5/2 & -2 & 2 \end{bmatrix} + \begin{bmatrix} 0 & -5/2 & -3/2 \\ 5/2 & 0 & -3 \\ 3/2 & 3 & 0 \end{bmatrix}$$

$$= \begin{bmatrix} 3 & -2 & -4 \\ 3 & -2 & -5 \\ -1 & 1 & 2 \end{bmatrix} = A$$

Thus, given matrix is expressed as the sum of symmetric matrix and skew-symmetric matrix.

Example 9 **If $(AB)^{-1} = A^{-1}B^{-1}$, then prove that A^{-1} and B^{-1} satisfy commutative property with respect to multiplication.** *NCERT Exemplar*

Sol. Given, $(AB)^{-1} = A^{-1}B^{-1}$ ...(i)

Now, as $(AB)^{-1} = B^{-1}A^{-1}$ [by theorem 2]

$\therefore \quad A^{-1}B^{-1} = B^{-1}A^{-1}$ [from Eq. (i)]

Here, we see that A^{-1} and B^{-1} satisfy the property of commutative with respect to multiplication.

Quick Test 3

1. Find the transpose of the following matrix:

(i) $\begin{bmatrix} -1 & 5 & 6 \\ \sqrt{3} & 5 & 6 \\ 2 & 3 & -1 \end{bmatrix}$ (ii) $\begin{bmatrix} 5 \\ 1/2 \\ -1 \end{bmatrix}$

(iii) $\begin{bmatrix} -4 & 1 & -5 \\ 1 & 2 & 0 \\ 1 & 3 & 1 \end{bmatrix}$ (iv) $\begin{bmatrix} -1 & 2 & 3 \\ 5 & 7 & 9 \\ -2 & 1 & 1 \end{bmatrix}$

2. If $A' = \begin{bmatrix} 3 & 4 \\ -1 & 2 \\ 0 & 1 \end{bmatrix}$ and $B = \begin{bmatrix} -1 & 2 & 1 \\ 1 & 2 & 3 \end{bmatrix}$, then verify that $(A+B)' = A' + B'$. NCERT

3. If A is a matrix of order 2×3 and B is a matrix of order 3×5, what is the order of the matrix $(AB)^T$? Competency Based Que

4. Matrix $A = \begin{bmatrix} 0 & -b & -6 \\ 4 & 1 & 3 \\ 3a & 3 & 5 \end{bmatrix}$ is given to be symmetric, then find the values of a and b.

5. Show that $A'A$ and AA' are both symmetric matrices for any matrix A. NCERT Exemplar

6. If A is symmetric, then show that $B'AB$ is symmetric matrix. NCERT

7. If matrix $\begin{bmatrix} 0 & a & 3 \\ 2 & b & -1 \\ c & 1 & 0 \end{bmatrix}$ is a skew-symmetric matrix, then find the values of a, b and c. NCERT Exemplar

8. If A is a skew-symmetric matrix, then show that A^2 is a symmetric matrix. Competency Based Que, NCERT Exemplar

9. Express the matrix $A = \begin{bmatrix} 2 & 4 & -6 \\ 7 & 3 & 5 \\ 1 & -2 & 4 \end{bmatrix}$ as the sum of a symmetric and skew-symmetric matrix. Competency Based Que, CBSE 2015C

Answers

1. (i) $\begin{bmatrix} -1 & \sqrt{3} & 2 \\ 5 & 5 & 3 \\ 6 & 6 & -1 \end{bmatrix}$ (ii) $[5 \;\; 1/2 \;\; -1]$

(iii) $\begin{bmatrix} -4 & 1 & 1 \\ 1 & 2 & 3 \\ -5 & 0 & 1 \end{bmatrix}$ (iv) $\begin{bmatrix} -1 & 5 & -2 \\ 2 & 7 & 1 \\ 3 & 9 & 1 \end{bmatrix}$

3. 5×2

4. $a = -2, b = -4$

7. $a = -2, b = 0$ and $c = -3$

9. $A = \begin{bmatrix} 2 & 11/2 & -5/2 \\ 11/2 & 3 & 3/2 \\ -5/2 & 3/2 & 4 \end{bmatrix} + \begin{bmatrix} 0 & -3/2 & -7/2 \\ 3/2 & 0 & 7/2 \\ 7/2 & -7/2 & 0 \end{bmatrix}$

For Solutions, See QR Code on Pg. 69

EXAM PATTERN QUESTIONS

Objective Type Questions

Multiple Choice Questions

1. $A=[a_{ij}]_{m\times n}$ is a square matrix, if **NCERT**

(a) $m<n$ (b) $m>n$
(c) $m=n$ (d) None of these

2. If $A=[a_{ij}]$ is a square matrix of order 2 such that $a_{ij}=\begin{cases}1, & \text{when } i\neq j\\ 0, & \text{when } i=j\end{cases}$, then A^2 is **CBSE Sample Paper 2023**

(a) $\begin{bmatrix}1 & 0\\1 & 0\end{bmatrix}$ (b) $\begin{bmatrix}1 & 1\\0 & 0\end{bmatrix}$

(c) $\begin{bmatrix}1 & 1\\1 & 0\end{bmatrix}$ (d) $\begin{bmatrix}1 & 0\\0 & 1\end{bmatrix}$

3. A matrix $A=[a_{ij}]_{3\times 3}$ is defined by $a_{ij}=\begin{cases}2i+3j, & i<j\\ 5, & i=j\\ 3i-2j, & i>j\end{cases}$. The number of elements in A which are more than 5, is **CBSE 2022 (Term I)**

(a) 3 (b) 4 (c) 5 (d) 6

4. If product of rows and columns of matrix is 27, then the number of possible different ordered matrices are **Competency Based Que, Diksha App**

(a) 3 (b) 5 (c) 6 (d) 4

5. If $A=\begin{bmatrix}0 & 2\\3 & -4\end{bmatrix}$ and $kA=\begin{bmatrix}0 & 3a\\2b & 24\end{bmatrix}$, then the value of k, a and b respectively, are **CBSE 2022 (Term I)** **CBSE Sample Paper 2022 (Term I)**

(a) $-6,-12,-18$
(b) $-6,-4,-9$
(c) $-6,4,9$
(d) $-6,12,18$

6. If $\begin{bmatrix}2x+y & 4x\\5x-7 & 4x\end{bmatrix}=\begin{bmatrix}7 & 7y-13\\y & x+6\end{bmatrix}$, then **NCERT Exemplar**

(a) $x=3, y=1$
(b) $x=2, y=3$
(c) $x=2, y=4$
(d) $x=3, y=3$

7. If X, Y and XY are matrices of order 2×3, $m\times n$ and 2×5 respectively, then number of elements in matrix Y is **CBSE 2024C**

(a) 6 (b) 10 (c) 15 (d) 35

8. If $A=\frac{1}{\pi}\begin{bmatrix}\sin^{-1}x\pi & \tan^{-1}\frac{x}{\pi}\\ \sin^{-1}\frac{x}{\pi} & \cot^{-1}\pi x\end{bmatrix}$,

$B=\frac{1}{\pi}\begin{bmatrix}-\cos^{-1}x\pi & \tan^{-1}\frac{x}{\pi}\\ \sin^{-1}\frac{x}{\pi} & -\tan^{-1}\pi x\end{bmatrix}$, then $A-B$ is equal to **Diksha App**

(a) I (b) O (c) $2I$ (d) $\frac{1}{2}I$

9. If $A=\begin{bmatrix}0 & 1\\-1 & 0\end{bmatrix}$ and $(3I+4A)(3I-4A)=x^2I$, then the value(s) of x is/are **Competency Based Que, CBSE 2023**

(a) $\pm\sqrt{7}$ (b) 0 (c) ± 5 (d) 25

10. If $A=\begin{bmatrix}\alpha & \beta\\ \gamma & -\alpha\end{bmatrix}$ is such that $A^2=I$, then

(a) $1+\alpha^2+\beta\gamma=0$ (b) $1-\alpha^2+\beta\gamma=0$
(c) $1-\alpha^2-\beta\gamma=0$ (d) $1+\alpha^2-\beta\gamma=0$

11. If A is a square matrix and $A^2=A$, then $(I+A)^2-3A$ is equal to **Competency Based Que, CBSE 2023**

(a) I (b) A (c) $2A$ (d) $3I$

12. If $A=\begin{bmatrix}0 & 1\\0 & 0\end{bmatrix}$, then A^{2023} is equal to **CBSE 2023**

(a) $\begin{bmatrix}0 & 1\\0 & 0\end{bmatrix}$ (b) $\begin{bmatrix}0 & 2023\\0 & 0\end{bmatrix}$

(c) $\begin{bmatrix}0 & 0\\0 & 0\end{bmatrix}$ (d) $\begin{bmatrix}2023 & 0\\0 & 2023\end{bmatrix}$

13. If $A=\begin{bmatrix}x & 0\\1 & 1\end{bmatrix}$ and $B=\begin{bmatrix}4 & 0\\-1 & 1\end{bmatrix}$, then the value of x for which $A^2=B$ is **CBSE 2024**

(a) -2 (b) 2
(c) 2 or -2 (d) 4

14. Find the matrix A^2, where $A=[a_{ij}]$ is a 2×2 matrix whose elements are given by $a_{ij}=$ maximum (i,j) $-$ minimum (i,j) **Competency Based Que, CBSE 2024**

(a) $\begin{bmatrix}0 & 0\\0 & 0\end{bmatrix}$ (b) $\begin{bmatrix}0 & 1\\1 & 0\end{bmatrix}$

(c) $\begin{bmatrix}1 & 0\\0 & 1\end{bmatrix}$ (d) $\begin{bmatrix}1 & 1\\1 & 1\end{bmatrix}$

15. Given that $A = \begin{bmatrix} \alpha & \beta \\ \gamma & -\alpha \end{bmatrix}$ and $A^2 = 3I$, then

CBSE Sample Paper 2022 (Term I)

(a) $1 + \alpha^2 + \beta\gamma = 0$ (b) $1 - \alpha^2 - \beta\gamma = 0$
(c) $3 - \alpha^2 - \beta\gamma = 0$ (d) $3 + \alpha^2 + \beta\gamma = 0$

16. If $\begin{bmatrix} 1 & 1 & 1 \\ 0 & 1 & 1 \\ 0 & 0 & 1 \end{bmatrix} \begin{bmatrix} x \\ y \\ z \end{bmatrix} = \begin{bmatrix} 6 \\ 3 \\ 2 \end{bmatrix}$, then the value of $(2x + y - z)$ is **Competency Based Que, CBSE 2023**

(a) 1 (b) 2 (c) 3 (d) 5

17. If $\begin{bmatrix} 4 \\ 2 \\ 3 \end{bmatrix} [1 \;\; 3 \; -3] \begin{bmatrix} x \\ y \\ z \end{bmatrix} = O$, then $x + 3y - 3z$ is **Diksha App**

(a) 1 (b) 3 (c) 4 (d) 0

18. For what value of $x \in \left[0, \frac{\pi}{2}\right]$, is $A + A' = \sqrt{3}I$, where $A = \begin{bmatrix} \cos x & \sin x \\ -\sin x & \cos x \end{bmatrix}$? **Competency Based Que, CBSE 2023**

(a) $\frac{\pi}{3}$ (b) $\frac{\pi}{6}$ (c) 0 (d) $\frac{\pi}{2}$

19. If A and B are symmetric matrices, then $(BA)^T$ is

(a) AB (b) BA
(c) I (d) Null matrix

20. If $A = [a_{ij}]$ is a skew-symmetric matrix of order n, then

Competency Based Que, CBSE Sample Paper 2023

(a) $a_{ij} = \frac{1}{a_{ij}}, \forall i, j$ (b) $a_{ij} \neq 0, \forall i, j$
(c) $a_{ij} = 0$, where $i = j$ (d) $a_{ij} \neq 0$, where $i = j$

21. If a matrix A is both symmetric and skew- symmetric, then A is necessarily a

CBSE 2022 (Term I)

(a) diagonal matrix (b) zero square matrix
(c) square matrix (d) identity matrix

22. If $A = \begin{bmatrix} 0 & x & y \\ 2 & 0 & 5 \\ 6 & -5 & z \end{bmatrix}$ is skew-symmetric matrix, then the value of $x + y^2 + z$ is **Diksha App**

(a) -34 (b) 38 (c) 34 (d) 35

23. A and B are skew-symmetric matrices of same order. AB is symmetric, if **Competency Based Que, CBSE 2023**

(a) $AB = 0$ (b) $AB = -BA$
(c) $AB = BA$ (d) $BA = 0$

24. If for a square matrix A, $A^2 - 3A + I = O$ and $A^{-1} = xA + yI$, then the value of $x + y$ is

Competency Based Que, CBSE 2023

(a) -2 (b) 2 (c) 3 (d) -3

25. If for a square matrix A, $A^2 - A + I = O$, then A^{-1} is equal to **CBSE 2023**

(a) A (b) $A + I$
(c) $I - A$ (d) $A - I$

Assertion-Reason Based Questions

Directions (Q. Nos. 26-35) *In the questions given below are two statements labelled as Assertion (A) and Reason (R). In the context of the two statements, which one of the following is correct?*

(a) Both A and R are correct; R is the correct explanation of A.
(b) Both A and R are correct; R is not the correct explanation of A.
(c) A is correct; R is incorrect.
(d) R is correct; A is incorrect.

26. Assertion (A) $A =$ diag$[3 \;\; 5 \;\; 2]$ is a scalar matrix of order 3×3.

Reason (R) If a diagonal matrix has all non-zero elements equal, it is known as a scalar matrix. **CBSE 2025**

27. Assertion (A) $A = \begin{bmatrix} 1 & 0 \\ 0 & 1 \end{bmatrix}$ is an identity matrix.

Reason (R) $A = [a_{ij}]$ is a scalar matrix, if $a_{ij} = \begin{cases} k, & i = j \\ 0, & i \neq j \end{cases}$.

28. Assertion (A) If $\begin{bmatrix} xy & 4 \\ z + 5 & x + y \end{bmatrix} = \begin{bmatrix} 4 & w \\ 0 & 4 \end{bmatrix}$, then $x = 2, y = 2, z = -5$ and $w = 4$.

Reason (R) Two matrices are equal, if their orders are same and their corresponding elements are same.

29. Assertion (A) If $A = \begin{bmatrix} 2 & 4 \\ 3 & 2 \end{bmatrix}$ and $B = \begin{bmatrix} -2 & 5 \\ 3 & 4 \end{bmatrix}$, then $3A - B = \begin{bmatrix} 8 & 7 \\ 6 & 2 \end{bmatrix}$.

Reason (R) If the matrices A and B of same order, say $m \times n$ satisfy the commutative law, then $A + B = B + A$.

30. Assertion (A) The product of two matrices $\begin{bmatrix} 1 & 3 & 4 \\ -1 & 2 & 0 \\ 1 & 3 & 2 \end{bmatrix}$ and $\begin{bmatrix} -1 & 2 \\ 3 & 4 \\ -1 & 2 \end{bmatrix}$ is $\begin{bmatrix} 4 & 22 \\ 7 & 6 \\ 6 & 18 \end{bmatrix}$.

Reason (R) The product of two matrices A and B is defined, if the number of columns of A is equal to the number of rows of B.

31. **Assertion** (A) If $A=\begin{bmatrix}2 & 3 & -1\\1 & 4 & 2\end{bmatrix}$ and $B=\begin{bmatrix}2 & 5\\4 & -2\\2 & 1\end{bmatrix}$ and AB and BA both are defined.

Reason (R) For two matrices A and B, product AB is defined, if number of columns in A is equal to the number of rows in B.

32. Let A, B and C be three square matrices of same order. Now, consider the following statements. **Competency Based Que**

Assertion (A) If $A=B$, then $AC=BC$.

Reason (R) If $AC=BC$, then $A=B$.

33. **Assertion** (A) If $A=\begin{bmatrix}3 & -2\\4 & -2\end{bmatrix}$ and $I=\begin{bmatrix}1 & 0\\0 & 1\end{bmatrix}$, then value of K such that $A^2=KA-2I$ is -1.

Reason (R) If A and B are square matrices of the same order, then $(A+B)(A+B)=A^2+AB+BA+B^2$. **Competency Based Que**

34. **Assertion** (A) Matrix $A=\begin{bmatrix}1 & 2 & 4\\2 & 3 & -1\\4 & -1 & 5\end{bmatrix}$ is symmetric matrix.

Reason (R) Matrix $B=\begin{bmatrix}0 & 1 & -2\\-1 & 0 & 3\\2 & -3 & 0\end{bmatrix}$ is a skew-symmetric matrix.

35. **Assertion** (A) For any square matrix B with real number entries, $B+B'$ is a skew-symmetric matrix and $B-B'$ is a symmetric matrix.

Reason (R) A square matrix B can be expressed as the sum of a symmetric matrix and skew-symmetric matrix. **Competency Based Que**

Case Based Questions

36. Two distributors, of a chips company, distribute two varieties of chips packets Spicy Chips (SC) and Cheesy Chips (CC). At the beginning of a certain month, the number of chips packets available with the distributors is shown in matrix M.

The number of chips packets distributed during that month by them is shown in matrix N.

$$M=\begin{array}{c}\text{SC} \quad \text{CC}\\ \begin{bmatrix}965 & 498\\872 & 689\end{bmatrix}\end{array}\begin{array}{l}\longrightarrow \text{Distributor 1}\\ \longrightarrow \text{Distributor 2}\end{array}$$

$$N=\begin{array}{c}\text{SC} \quad \text{CC}\\ \begin{bmatrix}956 & 399\\650 & 511\end{bmatrix}\end{array}\begin{array}{l}\longrightarrow \text{Distributor 1}\\ \longrightarrow \text{Distributor 2}\end{array}$$

Based on the above information, answer the following questions.

(i) Find the number of chips packets remain with the distributors at the end of that month.

(ii) A packet of Spicy Chips and Cheesy Chips costs ₹ 10 and ₹ 20, respectively. Find the total cost of the chips distributed by each distributor that month using matrix multiplication.

Show your work and give your answer in the matrix form. **CBSE QB**

37. A company wanted to outsource the creation of its video and picture content for social media. They were approached by two firms offering the following rates per post (in ₹). **CBSE QB**

$$\begin{array}{c}\text{Video} \quad \text{Picture}\\ \begin{bmatrix}30 & 10\\25 & 15\end{bmatrix}\end{array}\begin{array}{l}\text{Firm 1}\\ \text{Firm 2}\end{array}$$

They gave the contract to both the firms for an equal number of posts. After 3 months, each firm created the following number of posts.

$$\begin{bmatrix}70\\100\end{bmatrix}\begin{array}{l}\text{Video}\\ \text{Picture}\end{array}$$

Each firm's posts created the following number of sales for the company.

$$\begin{array}{c}\text{Video} \quad \text{Picture}\\ \begin{bmatrix}500 & 200\\400 & 300\end{bmatrix}\end{array}\begin{array}{l}\text{Firm 1}\\ \text{Firm 2}\end{array}$$

Based on the above information, answer the following questions.

(i) Which firm cost more to the company?

(ii) If each sale was worth ₹ 300, which firm was more profitable for the company?

Show your work.

Subjective Questions

Very Short Answer Type Questions

1. If possible, then find the sum of the matrices A and B, where $A=\begin{bmatrix}\sqrt{3} & 1\\ 2 & 3\end{bmatrix}$ and $B=\begin{bmatrix}x & y & z\\ a & b & c\end{bmatrix}$.

Competency Based Que, NCERT Exemplar

2. Simplify $\begin{bmatrix}\cos^2 x & \sin^2 x\\ \sin^2 x & \cos^2 x\end{bmatrix}+\begin{bmatrix}\sin^2 x & \cos^2 x\\ \cos^2 x & \sin^2 x\end{bmatrix}$. **NCERT**

3. Find the value of $y-x$ from the following equation.

$$2\begin{bmatrix}x & 5\\ 7 & y-3\end{bmatrix}+\begin{bmatrix}3 & -4\\ 1 & 2\end{bmatrix}=\begin{bmatrix}7 & 6\\ 15 & 14\end{bmatrix}$$ **CBSE 2012**

4. Find non-zero values of x satisfying the matrix equation $x\begin{bmatrix}2x & 2\\ 3 & x\end{bmatrix}+2\begin{bmatrix}8 & 5x\\ 4 & 4x\end{bmatrix}=2\begin{bmatrix}x^2+8 & 24\\ 10 & 6x\end{bmatrix}$.

Competency Based Que, NCERT Exemplar

5. If $A=\begin{bmatrix}2 & 4\\ 3 & 2\end{bmatrix}$ and $B=\begin{bmatrix}1 & 3\\ -2 & 5\end{bmatrix}$, then find $A-B$.

6. If $\begin{bmatrix}9 & -1 & 4\\ -2 & 1 & 3\end{bmatrix}=A+\begin{bmatrix}1 & 2 & -1\\ 0 & 4 & 9\end{bmatrix}$, then find the matrix A. **CBSE 2013**

7. If $x\begin{bmatrix}1\\ 2\end{bmatrix}+y\begin{bmatrix}2\\ 5\end{bmatrix}=\begin{bmatrix}4\\ 9\end{bmatrix}$, then find the value of x.

8. If matrices A and B are of order $3\times n$ and $m\times 5$ respectively, then find the order of matrix $C=5A+3B$. **Competency Based Que**

9. Let $A=[a_{ij}]_{n\times n}$ be a diagonal matrix whose diagonal elements are different and $B=[b_{ij}]_{n\times n}$ is some another matrix. If $AB=[c_{ij}]_{n\times n}$, then find c_{ij}. **Competency Based Que**

10. Suppose $A=\begin{bmatrix}5 & 4\\ 2 & 3\end{bmatrix}$ and $B=\begin{bmatrix}3 & 5 & 1\\ 6 & 8 & 4\end{bmatrix}$, then find AB and BA, if they exist. **Competency Based Que**

11. Find x from the matrix equation $\begin{bmatrix}1 & 3\\ 4 & 5\end{bmatrix}\begin{bmatrix}x\\ 2\end{bmatrix}=\begin{bmatrix}5\\ 6\end{bmatrix}$.

12. If $\begin{bmatrix}1 & 0 & 0\\ 0 & y & 0\\ 0 & 0 & 1\end{bmatrix}\begin{bmatrix}x\\ -1\\ z\end{bmatrix}=\begin{bmatrix}1\\ 2\\ 1\end{bmatrix}$, find $x+y+z$. **CBSE 2016C**

13. If matrix $A=\begin{bmatrix}1 & -1\\ -1 & 1\end{bmatrix}$ and $A^2=kA$, then write the value of k. **CBSE 2013**

14. If $A=\begin{bmatrix}1 & 0\\ 2 & 1\end{bmatrix}$, $B=\begin{bmatrix}x & 0\\ 1 & 1\end{bmatrix}$ and $A=B^2$, then find the value of x.

15. If $A=[2\ -3\ \ 4]$, $B=\begin{bmatrix}3\\ 2\\ 2\end{bmatrix}$, $X=[1\ \ 2\ \ 3]$ and $Y=\begin{bmatrix}2\\ 3\\ 4\end{bmatrix}$, then find the value of $AB-XY$.

16. Find the product of $A=\begin{bmatrix}a & b\\ -b & a\end{bmatrix}$ and $B=\begin{bmatrix}a & -b\\ b & a\end{bmatrix}$.

17. If A is a 3×4 matrix and B is a matrix such that $A'B$ and AB' are both defined, then what is the order of matrix B? **Competency Based Que**

18. If a matrix $A=[1\ \ 2\ \ 3]$, then find the matrix AA' (where A' is the transpose of A).

19. For what value of x, is the matrix $A=\begin{bmatrix}0 & 1 & -4\\ -1 & 0 & 3\\ x & -3 & 0\end{bmatrix}$ a skew-symmetric matrix? **CBSE 2025**

20. If $A=\begin{bmatrix}a & c & -1\\ b & 0 & 5\\ 1 & -5 & 0\end{bmatrix}$ is a skew-symmetric matrix, then find the value of $2a-(b+c)$.

Short Answer Type Questions

21. If $\begin{bmatrix}x+3 & z+4 & 2y-7\\ -6 & a-1 & 0\\ b-3 & -21 & 0\end{bmatrix}=\begin{bmatrix}0 & 6 & 3y-2\\ -6 & -3 & 2c+2\\ 2b+4 & -21 & 0\end{bmatrix}$, then find the values of a, b, c and z. **NCERT**

22. Assume Y, W and P are the matrices of orders $3\times k$, $n\times 3$ and $p\times k$. Find the restrictions on n, k and p, so that $PY+WY$ will be defined. **Competency Based Que, NCERT**

23. If $A=\begin{bmatrix}3 & -4\\ 1 & 1\\ 2 & 0\end{bmatrix}$ and $B=\begin{bmatrix}2 & 1 & 2\\ 1 & 2 & 4\end{bmatrix}$, then verify that $(BA)^2\neq B^2A^2$. **NCERT Exemplar**

24. If $A=\begin{bmatrix}0 & 1\\ 1 & 1\end{bmatrix}$ and $B=\begin{bmatrix}0 & -1\\ 1 & 0\end{bmatrix}$, then show that $(A+B)\,(A-B)\neq A^2-B^2$. **NCERT Exemplar**

25. Solve the matrix $[x\ \ -5\ \ -1]\begin{bmatrix}1 & 0 & 2\\ 0 & 2 & 1\\ 2 & 0 & 3\end{bmatrix}\begin{bmatrix}x\\ 4\\ 1\end{bmatrix}=O$. **NCERT**

26. If $[2\ \ 1\ \ 3]\begin{bmatrix}-1 & 0 & -1\\ -1 & 1 & 0\\ 0 & 1 & 1\end{bmatrix}\begin{bmatrix}1\\0\\-1\end{bmatrix}=A$, then find the value of A.

27. If $A=\begin{bmatrix}4 & 0\\ 2k & 5k\end{bmatrix}$ and $B=\begin{bmatrix}k & 0\\ 3 & -1\end{bmatrix}$, such that $AB=BA$. Then, show that $2k^2+17k-12=0$.

28. Find the matrix A satisfying the matrix equation
$\begin{bmatrix}2 & 1\\ 3 & 2\end{bmatrix}A\begin{bmatrix}-3 & 2\\ 5 & -3\end{bmatrix}=\begin{bmatrix}1 & 0\\ 0 & 1\end{bmatrix}$. **NCERT Exemplar**

29. If $A=\begin{bmatrix}2 & 0 & 1\\ 2 & 1 & 3\\ 1 & -1 & 0\end{bmatrix}$, then find $A^2-5A+6I$.

30. For the matrix $A=\begin{bmatrix}3 & 1\\ 7 & 5\end{bmatrix}$, find a and b such that $A^2+aI=bA$, where I is a 2×2 identity matrix. **Competency Based Que**

31. If $A=\begin{bmatrix}2 & 3\\ 1 & 2\end{bmatrix}$, then prove that

$$A^3-4A^2+A=O.$$

32. If $A=\begin{bmatrix}1 & 0\\ -1 & 5\end{bmatrix}$, then find the value of k if $A^2=6A+KI_2$, where I_2 is an identity matrix. **CBSE 2025**

33. If $A=\text{diag }[a,b,c]$, then show that $A^n=\text{diag }[a^n,b^n,c^n], \forall\ n\in N$. **Competency Based Que**

34. In a legislative assembly election, a political group hired a public relations firm to promote its candidate in three ways: telephone, house calls and letters. The cost per contact (in paise) is given in matrix A as

Cost per contact

$$A=\begin{bmatrix}40\\100\\50\end{bmatrix}\begin{matrix}\text{Telephone}\\ \text{House call}\\ \text{Letter}\end{matrix}$$

The number of contacts of each type made in two cities X and Y is given by

$$\begin{matrix} & \text{Telephone} & \text{House call} & \text{Letter}\end{matrix}$$
$$B=\begin{bmatrix}1000 & 500 & 5000\\ 3000 & 1000 & 10000\end{bmatrix}\begin{matrix}\to X\\ \to Y\end{matrix}$$

Find the total amount spent by the group in the two cities X and Y.

35. If A and B are symmetric matrices of the same order, then show that AB is symmetric if and only if A and B commute, that is $AB=BA$. **Competency Based Que, NCERT**

36. If $A=\begin{bmatrix}-1 & 2 & 3\\ 5 & 7 & 9\\ -2 & 1 & 1\end{bmatrix}$ and $B=\begin{bmatrix}-4 & 1 & -5\\ 1 & 2 & 0\\ 1 & 3 & 1\end{bmatrix}$, then verify that

(i) $(A+B)'=A'+B'$ (ii) $(A-B)'=A'-B'$ **NCERT**

37. Find $\frac{1}{2}(A+A')$ and $\frac{1}{2}(A-A')$, where

$$A=\begin{bmatrix}0 & a & b\\ -a & 0 & c\\ -b & -c & 0\end{bmatrix}.$$ **NCERT**

38. If $A=\begin{bmatrix}3 & -4\\ 1 & -1\end{bmatrix}$, then show that $(A-A')$ is a skew-symmetric matrix, where A' is the transpose of matrix A. **NCERT Exemplar**

39. Show that the matrix B^TAB is skew-symmetric, if A is skew-symmetric. **Competency Based Que**

40. Give one example of skew-symmetric matrix of order 2 and order 3.

41. If A and B are symmetric matrices, then prove that $BA-2AB$ is neither a symmetric matrix nor skew-symmetric matrix. **NCERT Exemplar, Competency Based Que**

42. If $A=\begin{bmatrix}5 & 2\\ 3 & -6\end{bmatrix}$, then prove that A can be expressed as sum of symmetric and skew-symmetric matrices.

Long Answer Type Questions

43. Two farmers Ramkishan and Gurcharan Singh cultivates only three varieties of rice namely Basmati, Permal and Naura. The sale (in rupees) of these varieties of rice by both the farmers in the month of September and October are given by the following matrices A and B.

September sales (in rupees)

$$\begin{matrix} & \text{Basmati} & \text{Permal} & \text{Naura}\end{matrix}$$
$$A=\begin{bmatrix}10000 & 20000 & 30000\\ 50000 & 30000 & 10000\end{bmatrix}\begin{matrix}\text{Ramkishan}\\ \text{Gurcharan Singh}\end{matrix}$$

October sales (in rupees)

$$\begin{matrix} & \text{Basmati} & \text{Permal} & \text{Naura}\end{matrix}$$
$$B=\begin{bmatrix}5000 & 10000 & 6000\\ 20000 & 10000 & 10000\end{bmatrix}\begin{matrix}\text{Ramkishan}\\ \text{Gurcharan Singh}\end{matrix}$$

(i) Find the combined sales in September and October for each farmer in each variety.

(ii) Find the decrease in sales from September to October.

(iii) If both farmers receive 2% profit on gross sales, then compute the profit for each farmer and for each variety sold in October. **NCERT**

44. Find matrix A, if

$$\begin{bmatrix} 2 & -1 \\ 1 & 0 \\ -3 & 4 \end{bmatrix} A = \begin{bmatrix} -1 & -8 & -10 \\ 1 & -2 & -5 \\ 9 & 22 & 15 \end{bmatrix}.$$

CBSE 2017C

45. If $A = \begin{bmatrix} \cos\theta & \sin\theta \\ -\sin\theta & \cos\theta \end{bmatrix}$, then prove that

$A^n = \begin{bmatrix} \cos n\theta & \sin n\theta \\ -\sin n\theta & \cos n\theta \end{bmatrix}, n \in N.$ **NCERT, Competency Based Que**

46. If $A = \begin{bmatrix} 1 & 0 & 2 \\ 0 & 2 & 1 \\ 2 & 0 & 3 \end{bmatrix}$, then prove that A is a root of the polynomial $f(x) = x^3 - 6x^2 + 7x + 2$.

[**Hint** Prove that $f(A) = O$] **NCERT, Competency Based Que**

47. Let $A = \begin{bmatrix} 2 & 3 \\ -1 & 2 \end{bmatrix}$ and $f(x) = x^2 - 4x + 7$.

Show that $f(A) = O$. Use this result to find A^5.

48. A manufacturer sells the products x, y and z in two markets. Annual sales are indicated below

Market	Products		
	x	y	z
I	10000	2000	18000
II	6000	20000	8000

(i) If unit sale prices of x, y and z are ₹ 2.50, ₹ 1.50 and ₹ 1.00 respectively, then find the total revenue in each market with the help of matrix algebra.

(ii) If the unit cost of the above three commodities are ₹ 2.00, ₹ 1.00 and 50 paise, respectively. Find the gross profit. [**Hint** Profit = Revenue – Cost]

NCERT, Competency Based Que

49. A trust fund has ₹ 30000 that must be invested in two different types of bond. The first bond pays 5% interest per year and the second bond pays 7% interest per year. Using matrix multiplication, determine how to divide ₹ 30000 among the two type of bonds. If the trust fund must obtain an annual total interest of **Diksha App**

(a) ₹ 1800 (b) ₹ 2000

Hints & Solutions

Objective Type Questions

1. (c) We know that a matrix which has equal number of rows and columns is called a square matrix.

Therefore, $m = n$

2. (d) $A = [a_{ij}] = \begin{bmatrix} a_{11} & a_{12} \\ a_{21} & a_{22} \end{bmatrix} = \begin{bmatrix} 0 & 1 \\ 1 & 0 \end{bmatrix}$

$$A^2 = \begin{bmatrix} 0 & 1 \\ 1 & 0 \end{bmatrix}\begin{bmatrix} 0 & 1 \\ 1 & 0 \end{bmatrix} = \begin{bmatrix} 1 & 0 \\ 0 & 1 \end{bmatrix}$$

3. (b) Given, $A = [A_{ij}]_{3\times 3}$ and $a_{ij} = \begin{cases} 2i+3j, & i<j \\ 5, & i=j \\ 3i-2j, & i>j \end{cases}$

Let $A = \begin{bmatrix} a_{11} & a_{12} & a_{13} \\ a_{21} & a_{22} & a_{23} \\ a_{31} & a_{32} & a_{33} \end{bmatrix}$

$a_{11} = 5, a_{12} = 2+6 = 8, a_{13} = 2+9 = 11$

$a_{21} = 6-2 = 4, a_{22} = 5, a_{23} = 4+9 = 13$

$a_{31} = 9-2 = 7, a_{32} = 9-4 = 5, a_{33} = 5$

$$\therefore \; A = \begin{bmatrix} 5 & 8 & 11 \\ 4 & 5 & 13 \\ 7 & 5 & 5 \end{bmatrix}$$

$\therefore$ Number of elements in A which are more than 5 are 4.

4. (d) The possible different ordered matrices are $1\times 27, 3\times 9, 9\times 3$ and 27×1. Hence, number of possible ordered matrices are 4.

5. (b) We have, $A = \begin{bmatrix} 0 & 2 \\ 3 & -4 \end{bmatrix} \Rightarrow kA = \begin{bmatrix} 0 & 2k \\ 3k & -4k \end{bmatrix}$

Given, $kA = \begin{bmatrix} 0 & 3a \\ 2b & 24 \end{bmatrix} \Rightarrow \begin{bmatrix} 0 & 2k \\ 3k & -4k \end{bmatrix} = \begin{bmatrix} 0 & 3a \\ 2b & 24 \end{bmatrix}$

$\therefore \; 2k = 3a, 2b = 3k$ and $-4k = 24$

$\Rightarrow k = -6, a = -4$ and $b = -9$

6. (b) **Hint** On comparing the corresponding elements on both sides, we get

$$2x + y = 7 \quad \ldots(i)$$
$$7y - 13 = 4x \quad \ldots(ii)$$
$$5x - 7 = y \quad \ldots(iii)$$
and $$x + 6 = 4x \quad \ldots(iv)$$

On solving these equations, we get

$$x = 2, y = 3$$

7. (c) **Hint** Given, order of $X = 2\times 3$, order of $Y = m\times n$ and order of $XY = 2\times 5$

As we know that the product XY is defined, if the number of columns of X is equal to the number of rows of Y.

$\therefore$ Number of columns of X = Number of rows of Y

$\Rightarrow \quad 3 = m \Rightarrow m = 3$

Now, order of $XY = 2 \times n$

Also, order of $XY = 2 \times 5$ [given]

$\therefore \; n = 5$

Therefore, number of elements in matrix $Y = m \times n$

$= 3 \times 5 = 15$

8. (d) Given, $A = \frac{1}{\pi}\begin{bmatrix} \sin^{-1} x\pi & \tan^{-1}\frac{x}{\pi} \\ \sin^{-1}\frac{x}{\pi} & \cot^{-1}\pi x \end{bmatrix}$

and $B = \frac{1}{\pi}\begin{bmatrix} -\cos^{-1} x\pi & \tan^{-1}\frac{x}{\pi} \\ \sin^{-1}\frac{x}{\pi} & -\tan^{-1}\pi x \end{bmatrix}$

Now, $A - B = \frac{1}{\pi}\begin{bmatrix} \sin^{-1} x\pi & \tan^{-1}\frac{x}{\pi} \\ \sin^{-1}\frac{x}{\pi} & \cot^{-1}\pi x \end{bmatrix} - \frac{1}{\pi}\begin{bmatrix} -\cos^{-1} x\pi & \tan^{-1}\frac{x}{\pi} \\ \sin^{-1}\frac{x}{\pi} & -\tan^{-1}\pi x \end{bmatrix}$

$= \frac{1}{\pi}\begin{bmatrix} \sin^{-1} x\pi + \cos^{-1} x\pi & \tan^{-1}\frac{x}{\pi} - \tan^{-1}\frac{x}{\pi} \\ \sin^{-1}\frac{x}{\pi} - \sin^{-1}\frac{x}{\pi} & \cot^{-1}\pi x + \tan^{-1}\pi x \end{bmatrix}$

$= \frac{1}{\pi}\begin{bmatrix} \frac{\pi}{2} & 0 \\ 0 & \pi/2 \end{bmatrix}$ $\left[\because \sin^{-1}\theta + \cos^{-1}\theta = \frac{\pi}{2} \text{ and } \tan^{-1}\theta + \cot^{-1}\theta = \frac{\pi}{2}\right]$

$= \frac{1}{\pi} \times \frac{\pi}{2}\begin{bmatrix} 1 & 0 \\ 0 & 1 \end{bmatrix}$

$= \frac{1}{2}\begin{bmatrix} 1 & 0 \\ 0 & 1 \end{bmatrix} = \frac{1}{2}I$

9. (c) Given, $A = \begin{bmatrix} 0 & 1 \\ -1 & 0 \end{bmatrix}$ and $(3I + 4A)(3I - 4A) = x^2 I$

Now, $(3I + 4A)(3I - 4A) = x^2 I$

$\Rightarrow \left[3\begin{bmatrix} 1 & 0 \\ 0 & 1 \end{bmatrix} + 4\begin{bmatrix} 0 & 1 \\ -1 & 0 \end{bmatrix}\right]\left[3\begin{bmatrix} 1 & 0 \\ 0 & 1 \end{bmatrix} - 4\begin{bmatrix} 0 & 1 \\ -1 & 0 \end{bmatrix}\right] = x^2\begin{bmatrix} 1 & 0 \\ 0 & 1 \end{bmatrix}$

$\Rightarrow \begin{bmatrix} 3+0 & 0+4 \\ 0-4 & 3+0 \end{bmatrix}\begin{bmatrix} 3-0 & 0-4 \\ 0+4 & 3-0 \end{bmatrix} = \begin{bmatrix} x^2 & 0 \\ 0 & x^2 \end{bmatrix}$

$\Rightarrow \begin{bmatrix} 3 & 4 \\ -4 & 3 \end{bmatrix}\begin{bmatrix} 3 & -4 \\ 4 & 3 \end{bmatrix} = \begin{bmatrix} x^2 & 0 \\ 0 & x^2 \end{bmatrix}$

$\Rightarrow \begin{bmatrix} 25 & 0 \\ 0 & 25 \end{bmatrix} = \begin{bmatrix} x^2 & 0 \\ 0 & x^2 \end{bmatrix}$

On equating the corresponding elements, we get

$x^2 = 25$

$\therefore \; x = \pm 5$

10. (c) We have, $A^2 = I$

$\begin{bmatrix} \alpha & \beta \\ \gamma & -\alpha \end{bmatrix}\begin{bmatrix} \alpha & \beta \\ \gamma & -\alpha \end{bmatrix} = \begin{bmatrix} 1 & 0 \\ 0 & 1 \end{bmatrix}$

$\Rightarrow \begin{bmatrix} \alpha^2 + \beta\gamma & \alpha\beta - \alpha\beta \\ \gamma\alpha - \gamma\alpha & \gamma\beta + \alpha^2 \end{bmatrix} = \begin{bmatrix} 1 & 0 \\ 0 & 1 \end{bmatrix}$

On equating the corresponding elements of both the matrices, we get

$\alpha^2 + \beta\gamma = 1$ and $\gamma\beta + \alpha^2 = 1$

$\Rightarrow \; 1 - \alpha^2 - \beta\gamma = 0$

11. (a) Given, $A^2 = A$

$\therefore \; (I + A)^2 - 3A = I^2 + IA + AI + A^2 - 3A$

$= I + A + A + A - 3A$ $[\because A^2 = A]$

$= I + 3A - 3A = I$

12. (c) We have, $A = \begin{bmatrix} 0 & 1 \\ 0 & 0 \end{bmatrix}$

$\Rightarrow \; A^2 = A \cdot A = \begin{bmatrix} 0 & 1 \\ 0 & 0 \end{bmatrix}\begin{bmatrix} 0 & 1 \\ 0 & 0 \end{bmatrix} = \begin{bmatrix} 0 & 0 \\ 0 & 0 \end{bmatrix} = O$

Similarly, $A^3 = A^4 = A^5, \ldots = O$

$\therefore \; A^{2023} = O = \begin{bmatrix} 0 & 0 \\ 0 & 0 \end{bmatrix}$

13. (a) We have, $A = \begin{bmatrix} x & 0 \\ 1 & 1 \end{bmatrix}$

and $B = \begin{bmatrix} 4 & 0 \\ -1 & 1 \end{bmatrix}$

Now, $A^2 = A \cdot A = \begin{bmatrix} x & 0 \\ 1 & 1 \end{bmatrix}\begin{bmatrix} x & 0 \\ 1 & 1 \end{bmatrix} = \begin{bmatrix} x^2 + 0 & 0 + 0 \\ x + 1 & 0 + 1 \end{bmatrix}$

$= \begin{bmatrix} x^2 & 0 \\ x + 1 & 1 \end{bmatrix}$

Given, $A^2 = B$

$\Rightarrow \begin{bmatrix} x^2 & 0 \\ x + 1 & 1 \end{bmatrix} = \begin{bmatrix} 4 & 0 \\ -1 & 1 \end{bmatrix}$

$\Rightarrow \; x^2 = 4$ and $x + 1 = -1$

$\Rightarrow \; x = \pm 2$ and $x = -2$

Hence, $x = -2$

14. (b) $A = [a_{ij}]$ be 2×2 matrix whose elements are given by a_{ij} = maximum (i, j) – minimum (i, j).

Let $A = \begin{bmatrix} a_{11} & a_{12} \\ a_{21} & a_{22} \end{bmatrix}$

So, a_{11} = maximum (1, 1) – minimum (1, 1) $= 1 - 1 = 0$

a_{12} = maximum (1, 2) – minimum (1, 2) $= 2 - 1 = 1$

a_{21} = maximum (2, 1) – minimum (2, 1) $= 2 - 1 = 1$

a_{22} = maximum (2, 2) – minimum (2, 2) $= 2 - 2 = 0$

$\therefore \; A = \begin{bmatrix} 0 & 1 \\ 1 & 0 \end{bmatrix}$

15. (c) Given, $A=\begin{bmatrix}\alpha & \beta\\ \gamma & -\alpha\end{bmatrix}$

$$A^2=\begin{bmatrix}\alpha & \beta\\ \gamma & -\alpha\end{bmatrix}\begin{bmatrix}\alpha & \beta\\ \gamma & -\alpha\end{bmatrix}$$

$$\Rightarrow \quad A^2=\begin{bmatrix}\alpha^2+\beta\gamma & \alpha\beta-\alpha\beta\\ \alpha\gamma-\alpha\gamma & \beta\gamma+\alpha^2\end{bmatrix}$$

Given, $A^2=3I$

$$\therefore \begin{bmatrix}a^2+\beta\gamma & 0\\ 0 & \beta\gamma+\alpha^2\end{bmatrix}=\begin{bmatrix}3 & 0\\ 0 & 3\end{bmatrix} \qquad \left[\because I=\begin{bmatrix}1 & 0\\ 0 & 1\end{bmatrix}\right]$$

$$\Rightarrow \quad \alpha^2+\beta\gamma=3 \Rightarrow 3-\alpha^2-\beta\gamma=0$$

16. (d) We have, $\begin{bmatrix}1 & 1 & 1\\ 0 & 1 & 1\\ 0 & 0 & 1\end{bmatrix}\begin{bmatrix}x\\ y\\ z\end{bmatrix}=\begin{bmatrix}6\\ 3\\ 2\end{bmatrix}$

$$\Rightarrow \quad \begin{bmatrix}x+y+z\\ y+z\\ z\end{bmatrix}=\begin{bmatrix}6\\ 3\\ 2\end{bmatrix}$$

On equating the corresponding elements of both the matrices, we get

$$x+y+z=6,\ y+z=3 \text{ and } z=2$$

$\because \quad y+z=3$

$\therefore \quad y=3-2=1$

and $\quad x+y+z=6 \Rightarrow x=6-2-1=3$

Now, $2x+y-z=2\times 3+1-2=6+1-2=5$

17. (d) **Hint** We have, $\begin{bmatrix}4\\ 2\\ 3\end{bmatrix}[1\ \ 3\ \ -3]\begin{bmatrix}x\\ y\\ z\end{bmatrix}=O$

$$\begin{bmatrix}4 & 12 & -12\\ 2 & 6 & -6\\ 3 & 9 & -9\end{bmatrix}\begin{bmatrix}x\\ y\\ z\end{bmatrix}=O$$

$$\Rightarrow \quad \begin{bmatrix}4x+12y-12z\\ 2x+6y-6z\\ 3x+9y-9z\end{bmatrix}=\begin{bmatrix}0\\ 0\\ 0\end{bmatrix}$$

On comparing the corresponding elements of both sides, we get

$$4x+12y-12z=0 \quad \ldots\text{(i)}$$

$$2x+6y-6z=0 \quad \ldots\text{(ii)}$$

$$3x+9y-9z=0 \quad \ldots\text{(iii)}$$

On dividing by 4 both sides of Eq. (i), we get

$$x+3y-3z=0$$

18. (b) Given, $A=\begin{bmatrix}\cos x & \sin x\\ -\sin x & \cos x\end{bmatrix} \Rightarrow A'=\begin{bmatrix}\cos x & -\sin x\\ \sin x & \cos x\end{bmatrix}$

Since, $A+A'=\sqrt{3}I$

$$\Rightarrow \quad \begin{bmatrix}\cos x & \sin x\\ -\sin x & \cos x\end{bmatrix}+\begin{bmatrix}\cos x & -\sin x\\ \sin x & \cos x\end{bmatrix}=\sqrt{3}I$$

$$\Rightarrow \quad \begin{bmatrix}2\cos x & 0\\ 0 & 2\cos x\end{bmatrix}=\sqrt{3}\begin{bmatrix}1 & 0\\ 0 & 1\end{bmatrix}$$

$$\Rightarrow \quad \begin{bmatrix}2\cos x & 0\\ 0 & 2\cos x\end{bmatrix}=\begin{bmatrix}\sqrt{3} & 0\\ 0 & \sqrt{3}\end{bmatrix}$$

By equality of matrices, we have

$$2\cos x=\sqrt{3}$$

$$\Rightarrow \quad \cos x=\frac{\sqrt{3}}{2}=\cos\frac{\pi}{6} \Rightarrow x=\frac{\pi}{6}\in\left[0,\frac{\pi}{2}\right]$$

19. (a) Given, A and B are symmetric matrices.

$\therefore A'=A$ and $B'=B$

Now, $(BA)^T=A^TB^T \qquad [\because (AB)^T=B^TA^T]$

$=AB \qquad [\because A^T=A \text{ and } B^T=B]$

20. (c) In a skew-symmetric matrix, the (i,j)th element is negative of the (j,i)th element

i.e. $\quad a_{ij}=-a_{ji}$

For the element of ith row and ith column.

$$a_{ii}=-a_{ii} \Rightarrow 2a_{ii}=0 \Rightarrow a_{ii}=0$$

Hence, the (i,i)th element $=0$

21. (b) Since, A is a both symmetric and skew-symmetric matrix,

$$A'=A \text{ and } A'=-A$$

Comparing both equations,

$$A=-A \Rightarrow A+A=0 \Rightarrow 2A=0$$

Hence, A is a zero matrix.

22. (c) Given, $A=\begin{bmatrix}0 & x & y\\ 2 & 0 & 5\\ 6 & -5 & z\end{bmatrix}$ is a skew-symmetric matrix.

$\therefore \quad A'=-A$

$$\begin{bmatrix}0 & x & y\\ 2 & 0 & 5\\ 6 & -5 & z\end{bmatrix}'=-\begin{bmatrix}0 & x & y\\ 2 & 0 & 5\\ 6 & -5 & z\end{bmatrix}$$

$$\Rightarrow \begin{bmatrix}0 & 2 & 6\\ x & 0 & -5\\ y & 5 & z\end{bmatrix}=\begin{bmatrix}0 & -x & -y\\ -2 & 0 & -5\\ -6 & 5 & -z\end{bmatrix}$$

On comparing the corresponding elements of both sides, we get

$$x=-2,\ y=-6 \text{ and } z=0$$

Now, $x+y^2+z=(-2)+(-6)^2+0=-2+36=34$

23. (c) Given, A and B are skew-symmetric matrices of same order.

$\therefore A'=-A$ and $B'=-B$

Let AB be a symmetric matrix, then

$$(AB)'=AB$$

$$\Rightarrow \quad B'A'=AB$$

$$\Rightarrow \quad (-B)(-A)=AB$$

$$\therefore \quad BA=AB$$

24. (b) Given, $A^2 - 3A + I = O$ ...(i)

and $A^{-1} = xA + yI$ ...(ii)

From Eq. (i), $A^2 - 3A + I = O$

On post-multiply by A^{-1}, we get

$A(AA^{-1}) - 3AA^{-1} + IA^{-1} = O$

$\Rightarrow AI - 3I + A^{-1} = O$ $[\because AA^{-1} = I]$

$\Rightarrow A^{-1} = 3I - A$ ...(iii)

From Eqs. (ii) and (iii), we get

$3I - A = xA + yI$

$\therefore x = -1$ and $y = 3$

Thus, $x + y = -1 + 3 = 2$

25. (c) We have, $A^2 - A + I = O$

On pre-multiplying by A^{-1}, we get

$(A^{-1}A)A - A^{-1}A + A^{-1}I = O$

$\Rightarrow IA - I + A^{-1} = O$ $[\because A^{-1}A = I]$

$\Rightarrow A^{-1} = I - A$

26. (d) We know that a scalar matrix is a diagonal matrix where all diagonal elements are equal. In this case, the diagonal elements are 3, 5 and 2, which are not equal.

So, Assertion is incorrect but Reason is correct.

27. (b) **Hint** $A = \begin{bmatrix} 1 & 0 \\ 0 & 1 \end{bmatrix}$ = Identity matrix

and $A = \begin{bmatrix} k & 0 \\ 0 & k \end{bmatrix}$ = Scalar matrix

Assertion and Reason both are correct but Reason is not the correct explanation of Assertion.

28. (a) **Hint** $xy = 4$ ...(i)

$x + y = 4$ ...(ii)

$z + 5 = 0 \Rightarrow z = -5$

$4 = w \Rightarrow w = 4$

From Eqs. (i) and (ii), we get $x = 2$ and $y = 2$

29. (b) **Hint** $3A - B = 3\begin{bmatrix} 2 & 4 \\ 3 & 2 \end{bmatrix} - \begin{bmatrix} -2 & 5 \\ 3 & 4 \end{bmatrix} = \begin{bmatrix} 8 & 7 \\ 6 & 2 \end{bmatrix}$

So, Assertion is correct.

We know that addition of matrices is commutative, so Reason is correct but Reason is not the correct explanation of Assertion.

30. (a) Let $A = \begin{bmatrix} 1 & 3 & 4 \\ -1 & 2 & 0 \\ 1 & 3 & 2 \end{bmatrix}_{3 \times 3}$ and $B = \begin{bmatrix} -1 & 2 \\ 3 & 4 \\ -1 & 2 \end{bmatrix}_{3 \times 2}$

Here, number of columns in matrix A is equal to the number of rows in matrix B.

$\therefore AB$ is defined.

Now, $AB = \begin{bmatrix} 1 & 3 & 4 \\ -1 & 2 & 0 \\ 1 & 3 & 2 \end{bmatrix}\begin{bmatrix} -1 & 2 \\ 3 & 4 \\ -1 & 2 \end{bmatrix}$

$= \begin{bmatrix} -1+9-4 & 2+12+8 \\ 1+6+0 & -2+8+0 \\ -1+9-2 & 2+12+4 \end{bmatrix} = \begin{bmatrix} 4 & 22 \\ 7 & 6 \\ 6 & 18 \end{bmatrix}$

Hence, Assertion and Reason both are correct and Reason is the correct explanation of Assertion.

31. (a) Order of $A = 2 \times 3$

Order of $B = 3 \times 2$

For AB,

number of columns of A = number of rows of $B = 3$

So, AB is defined.

For BA,

number of columns of B = number of rows of $A = 2$

So, BA is defined.

So, Assertion is correct. Reason is also correct and Reason is the correct explanation of Assertion.

32. (c) **Hint** Clearly, if $A = B$

$\Rightarrow AC = BC$

But if $AC = BC$ it may be $A \neq B$

Let $A = \begin{bmatrix} 1 & 2 \\ 0 & 0 \end{bmatrix}$,

$B = \begin{bmatrix} 1 & 4 \\ 0 & 0 \end{bmatrix}$

and $C = \begin{bmatrix} 0 & 7 \\ 0 & 0 \end{bmatrix}$

Here, $AC = BC$

but $A \neq B$

So, Assertion is correct and Reason is incorrect.

33. (d) **Hint** : $A^2 = \begin{bmatrix} 3 & -2 \\ 4 & -2 \end{bmatrix}\begin{bmatrix} 3 & -2 \\ 4 & -2 \end{bmatrix} = \begin{bmatrix} 1 & -2 \\ 4 & -4 \end{bmatrix}$

$\because A^2 = KA - 2I$

$\Rightarrow \begin{bmatrix} 1 & -2 \\ 4 & -4 \end{bmatrix} = K\begin{bmatrix} 3 & -2 \\ 4 & -2 \end{bmatrix} - 2\begin{bmatrix} 1 & 0 \\ 0 & 1 \end{bmatrix}$

$= \begin{bmatrix} 3K-2 & -2K \\ 4K & -2K-2 \end{bmatrix}$

On comparing, $1 = 3K - 2$

$\Rightarrow K = 1$

So, Assertion is incorrect.

Now, by distributive law,

$(A+B)(A+B) = A^2 + AB + BA + B^2$

$\therefore$ Reason is correct.

34. (b) **Assertion** Given, $A=\begin{bmatrix}1 & 2 & 4\\ 2 & 3 & -1\\ 4 & -1 & 5\end{bmatrix}$

$$\therefore \quad A'=\begin{bmatrix}1 & 2 & 4\\ 2 & 3 & -1\\ 4 & -1 & 5\end{bmatrix}^T=\begin{bmatrix}1 & 2 & 4\\ 2 & 3 & -1\\ 4 & -1 & 5\end{bmatrix}=A$$

Thus, Assertion is correct.

Reason Given, $B=\begin{bmatrix}0 & 1 & -2\\ -1 & 0 & 3\\ 2 & -3 & 0\end{bmatrix}$

$$\therefore \quad B'=\begin{bmatrix}0 & 1 & -2\\ -1 & 0 & 3\\ 2 & -3 & 0\end{bmatrix}^T=\begin{bmatrix}0 & -1 & 2\\ 1 & 0 & -3\\ -2 & 3 & 0\end{bmatrix}=-\begin{bmatrix}0 & 1 & -2\\ -1 & 0 & 3\\ 2 & -3 & 0\end{bmatrix}=-B$$

Hence, Assertion and Reason both are correct but Reason is not the correct explanation of Assertion.

35. (d) For any square matrix B with real number entries, $B+B'$ is a symmetric matrix and $B-B'$ is a skew symmetric matrix.

So, Assertion is incorrect but Reason is correct.

36. Given, numbers of chips packets available with the distributors

$$M=\begin{matrix} & \text{sc} & \text{cc} & \\ & \begin{bmatrix}965 & 498\\ 872 & 689\end{bmatrix} & & \begin{matrix}\longrightarrow \text{Distributor 1}\\ \longrightarrow \text{Distributor 2}\end{matrix}\end{matrix}$$

Number of chips packets distributed

$$N=\begin{matrix} & \text{sc} & \text{cc} & \\ & \begin{bmatrix}956 & 399\\ 650 & 511\end{bmatrix} & & \begin{matrix}\longrightarrow \text{Distributor 1}\\ \longrightarrow \text{Distributor 2}\end{matrix}\end{matrix}$$

(i) Number of chips packets remain with the distributors at the end of month

$$=M-N=\begin{bmatrix}965 & 498\\ 872 & 689\end{bmatrix}-\begin{bmatrix}956 & 399\\ 650 & 511\end{bmatrix}$$

$$=\begin{matrix} \text{sc} \quad \text{cc} \\ \begin{bmatrix}9 & 99\\ 222 & 178\end{bmatrix}\end{matrix}\begin{matrix}\longrightarrow \text{Distributor 1}\\ \longrightarrow \text{Distributor 2}\end{matrix}$$

(ii) Let A denotes the matrix showing cost of spicy chips and cheesy chips.

We have, $A=\begin{bmatrix}10\\ 20\end{bmatrix}\begin{matrix}\text{sc}\\ \text{sc}\end{matrix}$

Cost of chips distributed by each distributor

$$=N\times A=\begin{matrix} \text{sc} \quad \text{cc} \\ \begin{bmatrix}956 & 399\\ 650 & 511\end{bmatrix}\end{matrix}\times\begin{bmatrix}10\\ 20\end{bmatrix}$$

$$=\begin{bmatrix}9560+7980\\ 6500+10220\end{bmatrix}=\begin{bmatrix}17540\\ 16720\end{bmatrix}\begin{matrix}\longrightarrow \text{Distributor 1}\\ \longrightarrow \text{Distributor 2}\end{matrix}$$

$\therefore$ Distributor 1 distributed chips of cost ₹ 17540 and distributor 2 distributed chips of cost ₹ 16720.

37. Given, matrix for rates per post (in ₹)

$$A=\begin{matrix}\text{Video} \quad \text{Picture}\\ \begin{bmatrix}30 & 10\\ 25 & 15\end{bmatrix}\end{matrix}$$

Matrix for the number of post created by the firm,

$$B=\begin{bmatrix}70\\ 100\end{bmatrix}\begin{matrix}\text{Video}\\ \text{Picture}\end{matrix}$$

Matrix for the number of sales for the company

$$C=\begin{matrix}\text{Video} \quad \text{Picture}\\ \begin{bmatrix}500 & 200\\ 400 & 300\end{bmatrix}\end{matrix}\begin{matrix}\text{Firm 1}\\ \text{Firm 2}\end{matrix}$$

(i) Cost of each firm $=A\times B$

$$=\begin{bmatrix}30 & 10\\ 25 & 15\end{bmatrix}\times\begin{bmatrix}70\\ 100\end{bmatrix}=\begin{bmatrix}2100+1000\\ 1750+1500\end{bmatrix}=\begin{bmatrix}3100\\ 3250\end{bmatrix}$$

$\therefore$ Cost for firm 1 = ₹ 3100

and cost for firm 2 = ₹ 3250

$\therefore$ Firm 2 cost more to the company.

(ii) Total revenue generated by each firm

$=300\times C$ [$\because$ given each sale worth ₹ 300]

$$=300\times\begin{bmatrix}500 & 200\\ 400 & 300\end{bmatrix}=\begin{bmatrix}150000 & 60000\\ 120000 & 90000\end{bmatrix}$$

$\therefore$ Revenue generated by firm 1

$=150000+60000=$ ₹ 210000

$\therefore$ Revenue generated by firm 2

$=120000+90000=$ ₹ 210000

Profit generated by firm 1 $=210000-3100$

= ₹ 206900

Profit generated by firm 2 $=210000-3250$

= ₹ 206750

$\therefore$ Firm 1 was more profitable for the company.

Subjective Questions

1. Given, $A=\begin{bmatrix}\sqrt{3} & 1\\ 2 & 3\end{bmatrix}$ and $B=\begin{bmatrix}x & y & z\\ a & b & c\end{bmatrix}$

Here, order of matrix $A=2\times 2$

and order of matrix $B=2\times 3$

Hence, the addition of given matrices is not possible because to add two matrices, the order of both the matrices will be same.

2. We have, $\begin{bmatrix}\cos^2 x & \sin^2 x\\ \sin^2 x & \cos^2 x\end{bmatrix}+\begin{bmatrix}\sin^2 x & \cos^2 x\\ \cos^2 x & \sin^2 x\end{bmatrix}$

$$=\begin{bmatrix}\cos^2 x+\sin^2 x & \sin^2 x+\cos^2 x\\ \sin^2 x+\cos^2 x & \cos^2 x+\sin^2 x\end{bmatrix}$$

$$=\begin{bmatrix}1 & 1\\ 1 & 1\end{bmatrix} \qquad [\because \sin^2 A+\cos^2 A=1]$$

3. We have, $2\begin{bmatrix}x & 5\\ 7 & y-3\end{bmatrix}+\begin{bmatrix}3 & -4\\ 1 & 2\end{bmatrix}=\begin{bmatrix}7 & 6\\ 15 & 14\end{bmatrix}$

$$\Rightarrow \begin{bmatrix}2x & 10\\ 14 & 2y-6\end{bmatrix}+\begin{bmatrix}3 & -4\\ 1 & 2\end{bmatrix}=\begin{bmatrix}7 & 6\\ 15 & 14\end{bmatrix}$$

$$\Rightarrow \begin{bmatrix}2x+3 & 6\\ 15 & 2y-4\end{bmatrix}=\begin{bmatrix}7 & 6\\ 15 & 14\end{bmatrix}$$

On equating the corresponding elements of both sides, we get

$$2x+3=7 \text{ and } 2y-4=14$$

$$\Rightarrow 2x=4 \text{ and } 2y=18$$

$$\Rightarrow x=2 \text{ and } y=9$$

Now, $y-x=9-2=7$

4. We have, $x\begin{bmatrix}2x & 2\\ 3 & x\end{bmatrix}+2\begin{bmatrix}8 & 5x\\ 4 & 4x\end{bmatrix}=2\begin{bmatrix}x^2+8 & 24\\ 10 & 6x\end{bmatrix}$

$$\Rightarrow \begin{bmatrix}2x^2 & 2x\\ 3x & x^2\end{bmatrix}+\begin{bmatrix}16 & 10x\\ 8 & 8x\end{bmatrix}=\begin{bmatrix}2x^2+16 & 48\\ 20 & 12x\end{bmatrix}$$

$$\Rightarrow \begin{bmatrix}2x^2+16 & 2x+10x\\ 3x+8 & x^2+8x\end{bmatrix}=\begin{bmatrix}2x^2+16 & 48\\ 20 & 12x\end{bmatrix}$$

On equating the corresponding element of both sides, we get

$$3x+8=20$$

$$\Rightarrow 3x=12 \Rightarrow x=4$$

5. Given, $A=\begin{bmatrix}2 & 4\\ 3 & 2\end{bmatrix}$ and $B=\begin{bmatrix}1 & 3\\ -2 & 5\end{bmatrix}$

Now, $A-B=\begin{bmatrix}2 & 4\\ 3 & 2\end{bmatrix}-\begin{bmatrix}1 & 3\\ -2 & 5\end{bmatrix}=\begin{bmatrix}2-1 & 4-3\\ 3-(-2) & 2-5\end{bmatrix}=\begin{bmatrix}1 & 1\\ 5 & -3\end{bmatrix}$

6. We have, $\begin{bmatrix}9 & -1 & 4\\ -2 & 1 & 3\end{bmatrix}=A+\begin{bmatrix}1 & 2 & -1\\ 0 & 4 & 9\end{bmatrix}$

$$\Rightarrow A=\begin{bmatrix}9 & -1 & 4\\ -2 & 1 & 3\end{bmatrix}-\begin{bmatrix}1 & 2 & -1\\ 0 & 4 & 9\end{bmatrix}$$

$$\Rightarrow A=\begin{bmatrix}9-1 & -1-2 & 4-(-1)\\ -2-0 & 1-4 & 3-9\end{bmatrix}$$

$$\Rightarrow A=\begin{bmatrix}8 & -3 & 5\\ -2 & -3 & -6\end{bmatrix}$$

7. We have, $x\begin{bmatrix}1\\ 2\end{bmatrix}+y\begin{bmatrix}2\\ 5\end{bmatrix}=\begin{bmatrix}4\\ 9\end{bmatrix}$

$$\begin{bmatrix}x\\ 2x\end{bmatrix}+\begin{bmatrix}2y\\ 5y\end{bmatrix}=\begin{bmatrix}4\\ 9\end{bmatrix}\Rightarrow\begin{bmatrix}x+2y\\ 2x+5y\end{bmatrix}=\begin{bmatrix}4\\ 9\end{bmatrix}$$

On equating the corresponding elements, we get

$$x+2y=4 \qquad \text{...(i)}$$

$$2x+5y=9 \qquad \text{...(ii)}$$

On solving Eqs. (i) and (ii), we get

$$x=2, y=1$$

8. Given, order of $A=3\times n$ and order of $B=m\times 5$

$$C=5A+3B$$

Two matrices are additive, if their orders are same.

$\therefore\quad 3\times n=m\times 5 \Rightarrow m=3$ and $n=5$

$\therefore$ Order of $C=3\times 5$

9. Here, $A=[a_{ij}]_{n\times n}$

$$=\begin{cases}0, \text{if } i\neq j\\ a_{ij}, \text{if } i=j\end{cases}$$

$$B=[b_{ij}]_{n\times n}$$

So, $c_{ij}=a_{ij}\cdot b_{ij}$

10. **Hint** Here, number of columns of A

$$= \text{number of rows of } B=2$$

and number of columns of $B\neq$ number of rows of A

So, product AB of matrices A and B is possible but product BA is not possible.

Ans. $AB=\begin{bmatrix}39 & 57 & 21\\ 24 & 34 & 14\end{bmatrix}$, BA does not exist.

11. We have, $\begin{bmatrix}1 & 3\\ 4 & 5\end{bmatrix}\begin{bmatrix}x\\ 2\end{bmatrix}=\begin{bmatrix}5\\ 6\end{bmatrix}$

$$\Rightarrow \begin{bmatrix}x+6\\ 4x+10\end{bmatrix}=\begin{bmatrix}5\\ 6\end{bmatrix}$$

On equating the corresponding element of both sides, we get

$$x+6=5$$

$$\therefore \quad x=-1$$

12. We have, $\begin{bmatrix}1 & 0 & 0\\ 0 & y & 0\\ 0 & 0 & 1\end{bmatrix}\begin{bmatrix}x\\ -1\\ z\end{bmatrix}=\begin{bmatrix}1\\ 2\\ 1\end{bmatrix}\Rightarrow\begin{bmatrix}x\\ -y\\ z\end{bmatrix}=\begin{bmatrix}1\\ 2\\ 1\end{bmatrix}$

On equating the corresponding elements of both the matrices, we get

$$x=1, y=-2 \text{ and } z=1$$

$$\therefore \quad x+y+z=1-2+1=0$$

13. Given, $A=\begin{bmatrix}1 & -1\\ -1 & 1\end{bmatrix}$ and $A^2=kA$

$$\therefore \begin{bmatrix}1 & -1\\ -1 & 1\end{bmatrix}\begin{bmatrix}1 & -1\\ -1 & 1\end{bmatrix}=k\begin{bmatrix}1 & -1\\ -1 & 1\end{bmatrix}$$

$$\Rightarrow \begin{bmatrix}1+1 & -1-1\\ -1-1 & 1+1\end{bmatrix}=\begin{bmatrix}k & -k\\ -k & k\end{bmatrix}$$

$$\Rightarrow \begin{bmatrix}2 & -2\\ -2 & 2\end{bmatrix}=\begin{bmatrix}k & -k\\ -k & k\end{bmatrix}$$

On equating the corresponding elements of both sides, we get

$$k=2$$

14. We have, $B=\begin{bmatrix}x & 0\\ 1 & 1\end{bmatrix}$

$$\therefore \quad B^2=B\cdot B=\begin{bmatrix}x & 0\\ 1 & 1\end{bmatrix}\begin{bmatrix}x & 0\\ 1 & 1\end{bmatrix}$$

$$=\begin{bmatrix}x^2+0 & 0+0\\ x+1 & 0+1\end{bmatrix}=\begin{bmatrix}x^2 & 0\\ x+1 & 1\end{bmatrix}$$

Since, $A=B^2 \Rightarrow \begin{bmatrix}1 & 0\\ 2 & 1\end{bmatrix}=\begin{bmatrix}x^2 & 0\\ x+1 & 1\end{bmatrix}$

By equality of matrices,

$$x^2=1, x+1=2$$

$$\Rightarrow \quad x=\pm 1, x=1 \Rightarrow x=1$$

15. Given, $A=[2 \quad -3 \quad 4]$, $B=\begin{bmatrix}3\\ 2\\ 2\end{bmatrix}$, $X=[1 \quad 2 \quad 3]$ and $Y=\begin{bmatrix}2\\ 3\\ 4\end{bmatrix}$

Now, $AB=[2 \quad -3 \quad 4]\begin{bmatrix}3\\ 2\\ 2\end{bmatrix}=[6-6+8]=[8]$

and $XY=[1 \quad 2 \quad 3]\begin{bmatrix}2\\ 3\\ 4\end{bmatrix}=[2+6+12]=[20]$

$\therefore \quad AB-XY=[8]-[20]=[-12]$

16. Hint $AB=\begin{bmatrix}a & b\\ -b & a\end{bmatrix}\begin{bmatrix}a & -b\\ b & a\end{bmatrix}=\begin{bmatrix}a^2+b^2 & -ab+ba\\ -ba+ab & b^2+a^2\end{bmatrix}$

$$=\begin{bmatrix}a^2+b^2 & 0\\ 0 & a^2+b^2\end{bmatrix}$$

17. Given, order of A is 3×4.

$\therefore$ Order of A' is 4×3.

Let order of B is $m\times n$

$\therefore$ Order of B' is $n\times m$

Since, $A'B$ is defined.

$\therefore$ Number of columns of A' = Number of rows of B.

$$m=3$$

Similarly, AB' is defined.

$\therefore$ Number of columns of A = Number of rows of B'.

$$n=4$$

$\therefore$ Order of the matrix B is 3×4.

18. Given, $A=[1 \ 2 \ 3]$

$$\therefore \quad A'=\begin{bmatrix}1\\ 2\\ 3\end{bmatrix}$$

Now, $AA'=[1 \ 2 \ 3]\begin{bmatrix}1\\ 2\\ 3\end{bmatrix}=[1+4+9]=[14]$

19. We have, $A=\begin{bmatrix}0 & 1 & -4\\ -1 & 0 & 3\\ x & -3 & 0\end{bmatrix}$

If matrix A is skew-symmetric, then $A'=-A$

$$\Rightarrow \begin{bmatrix}0 & 1 & -4\\ -1 & 0 & 3\\ x & -3 & 0\end{bmatrix}^T=-\begin{bmatrix}0 & 1 & -4\\ -1 & 0 & 3\\ x & -3 & 0\end{bmatrix}$$

$$\Rightarrow \begin{bmatrix}0 & -1 & x\\ 1 & 0 & -3\\ -4 & 3 & 0\end{bmatrix}=\begin{bmatrix}0 & -1 & 4\\ 1 & 0 & -3\\ -x & 3 & 0\end{bmatrix}$$

On comparing the corresponding element of both sides, we get

$$x=4$$

20. Given, $A=\begin{bmatrix}a & c & -1\\ b & 0 & 5\\ 1 & -5 & 0\end{bmatrix}$

Since, A is a skew-symmetric matrix.

$$\therefore \quad A^T=-A$$

$$\Rightarrow \begin{bmatrix}a & c & -1\\ b & 0 & 5\\ 1 & -5 & 0\end{bmatrix}^T=-\begin{bmatrix}a & c & -1\\ b & 0 & 5\\ 1 & -5 & 0\end{bmatrix}$$

$$\Rightarrow \begin{bmatrix}a & b & 1\\ c & 0 & -5\\ -1 & 5 & 0\end{bmatrix}=\begin{bmatrix}-a & -c & 1\\ -b & 0 & -5\\ -1 & 5 & 0\end{bmatrix}$$

On comparing the corresponding elements of both sides, we get

$$a=-a$$

$$\Rightarrow \quad a+a=0$$

$$\Rightarrow \quad 2a=0$$

$$\Rightarrow \quad a=0$$

and $\quad b=-c \Rightarrow b+c=0$

Thus, $\quad 2a-(b+c)=2(0)-0=0$

21. **Hint** Compare the corresponding elements of both the matrices and find the values of a, b, c and z.

Ans. $a = -2, b = -7, c = -1$ and $z = 2$

22. Given, matrices Y, W and P are the matrices of orders $3 \times k$, $n \times 3$ and $p \times k$.

$\because$ Order of $P = p \times k$ and order of $Y = 3 \times k$

$\therefore$ PY is possible, if $k = 3$.

$\Rightarrow$ Order of $PY = p \times 3$

$\because$ Order of $W = n \times 3$ and order of $Y = 3 \times k$

$\therefore$ Order of $WY = n \times 3$ $\quad [\because k = 3]$

Now, sum of PY and WY is possible only if both of them are of same order.

$\therefore$ $p \times 3 = n \times 3$

Hence, $PY + WY$ is defined if $p = n$ and $k = 3$.

23. Given, $A = \begin{bmatrix} 3 & -4 \\ 1 & 1 \\ 2 & 0 \end{bmatrix}$ and $B = \begin{bmatrix} 2 & 1 & 2 \\ 1 & 2 & 4 \end{bmatrix}$

Now, $BA = \begin{bmatrix} 2 & 1 & 2 \\ 1 & 2 & 4 \end{bmatrix} \begin{bmatrix} 3 & -4 \\ 1 & 1 \\ 2 & 0 \end{bmatrix} = \begin{bmatrix} 6+1+4 & -8+1+0 \\ 3+2+8 & -4+2+0 \end{bmatrix}$

$\Rightarrow \quad BA = \begin{bmatrix} 11 & -7 \\ 13 & -2 \end{bmatrix}$

and $\quad A^2 = A \cdot A = \begin{bmatrix} 3 & -4 \\ 1 & 1 \\ 2 & 0 \end{bmatrix} \begin{bmatrix} 3 & -4 \\ 1 & 1 \\ 2 & 0 \end{bmatrix}$

Here, number of columns of first matrix i.e. 2 is not equal to the number of rows of second matrix i.e. 3.

So, A^2 is not possible.

Similarly, B^2 is also not possible.

Hence, $(BA)^2 \neq B^2A^2$

24. Given, $A = \begin{bmatrix} 0 & 1 \\ 1 & 1 \end{bmatrix}$ and $B = \begin{bmatrix} 0 & -1 \\ 1 & 0 \end{bmatrix}$

Now, $A^2 = \begin{bmatrix} 0 & 1 \\ 1 & 1 \end{bmatrix} \begin{bmatrix} 0 & 1 \\ 1 & 1 \end{bmatrix} = \begin{bmatrix} 0+1 & 0+1 \\ 0+1 & 1+1 \end{bmatrix} = \begin{bmatrix} 1 & 1 \\ 1 & 2 \end{bmatrix}$ $\quad \ldots$(i)

$B^2 = \begin{bmatrix} 0 & -1 \\ 1 & 0 \end{bmatrix} \begin{bmatrix} 0 & -1 \\ 1 & 0 \end{bmatrix} = \begin{bmatrix} 0-1 & 0+0 \\ 0+0 & -1+0 \end{bmatrix} = \begin{bmatrix} -1 & 0 \\ 0 & -1 \end{bmatrix}$ $\quad \ldots$(ii)

$A + B = \begin{bmatrix} 0 & 1 \\ 1 & 1 \end{bmatrix} + \begin{bmatrix} 0 & -1 \\ 1 & 0 \end{bmatrix} = \begin{bmatrix} 0+0 & 1-1 \\ 1+1 & 1+0 \end{bmatrix} = \begin{bmatrix} 0 & 0 \\ 2 & 1 \end{bmatrix}$ $\quad \ldots$(iii)

$A - B = \begin{bmatrix} 0 & 1 \\ 1 & 1 \end{bmatrix} - \begin{bmatrix} 0 & -1 \\ 1 & 0 \end{bmatrix} = \begin{bmatrix} 0-0 & 1-(-1) \\ 1-1 & 1-0 \end{bmatrix} = \begin{bmatrix} 0 & 2 \\ 0 & 1 \end{bmatrix}$ $\quad \ldots$(iv)

From Eqs. (iii) and (iv), we get

$(A + B)(A - B) = \begin{bmatrix} 0 & 0 \\ 2 & 1 \end{bmatrix} \begin{bmatrix} 0 & 2 \\ 0 & 1 \end{bmatrix}$

$= \begin{bmatrix} 0+0 & 0+0 \\ 0+0 & 4+1 \end{bmatrix} = \begin{bmatrix} 0 & 0 \\ 0 & 5 \end{bmatrix}$ $\quad \ldots$(v)

From Eqs. (i) and (ii), we get

and $A^2 - B^2 = \begin{bmatrix} 1 & 1 \\ 1 & 2 \end{bmatrix} - \begin{bmatrix} -1 & 0 \\ 0 & -1 \end{bmatrix} = \begin{bmatrix} 2 & 1 \\ 1 & 3 \end{bmatrix}$ $\quad \ldots$(vi)

From Eqs. (v) and (vi), we get

$(A + B)(A - B) \neq A^2 - B^2$ **Hence proved.**

25. We have, $[x \;\; -5 \;\; -1] \begin{bmatrix} 1 & 0 & 2 \\ 0 & 2 & 1 \\ 2 & 0 & 3 \end{bmatrix} \begin{bmatrix} x \\ 4 \\ 1 \end{bmatrix} = O$

$\Rightarrow \quad [x-0-2 \;\; 0-10-0 \;\; 2x-5-3] \begin{bmatrix} x \\ 4 \\ 1 \end{bmatrix} = O$

$\Rightarrow \quad [x \;\; -2 \;\; -10 \;\; 2x-8] \begin{bmatrix} x \\ 4 \\ 1 \end{bmatrix} = O$

$\Rightarrow \quad [x^2 - 2x - 40 + 2x - 8] = [0]$

On comparing corresponding element, we get

$x^2 - 48 = 0$

$\Rightarrow \quad x^2 = 48$

$\therefore \quad x = \pm 4\sqrt{3}$

26. We have, $A = [2 \;\; 1 \;\; 3] \begin{bmatrix} -1 & 0 & -1 \\ -1 & 1 & 0 \\ 0 & 1 & 1 \end{bmatrix} \begin{bmatrix} 1 \\ 0 \\ -1 \end{bmatrix}$

$= [-2-1+0 \;\; 0+1+3 \;\; -2+0+3] \begin{bmatrix} 1 \\ 0 \\ -1 \end{bmatrix}$

$= [-3 \;\; 4 \;\; 1] \begin{bmatrix} 1 \\ 0 \\ -1 \end{bmatrix} = [-3+0-1] = [-4]$

27. Given, $A = \begin{bmatrix} 4 & 0 \\ 2k & 5k \end{bmatrix}$ and $B = \begin{bmatrix} k & 0 \\ 3 & -1 \end{bmatrix}$

Also given, $AB = BA$

$\therefore \quad \begin{bmatrix} 4 & 0 \\ 2k & 5k \end{bmatrix} \begin{bmatrix} k & 0 \\ 3 & -1 \end{bmatrix} = \begin{bmatrix} k & 0 \\ 3 & -1 \end{bmatrix} \begin{bmatrix} 4 & 0 \\ 2k & 5k \end{bmatrix}$

$\Rightarrow \quad \begin{bmatrix} 4k+0 & 0+0 \\ 2k^2+15k & 0-5k \end{bmatrix} = \begin{bmatrix} 4k+0 & 0+0 \\ 12-2k & 0-5k \end{bmatrix}$

$\Rightarrow \quad \begin{bmatrix} 4k & 0 \\ 2k^2+15k & -5k \end{bmatrix} = \begin{bmatrix} 4k & 0 \\ 12-2k & -5k \end{bmatrix}$

On equating the corresponding elements of both the matrices, we get

$2k^2 + 15k = 12 - 2k$

$\Rightarrow \quad 2k^2 + 15k + 2k - 12 = 0$

$\therefore \quad 2k^2 + 17k - 12 = 0$ **Hence proved.**

28. **Hint** Let $A=\begin{bmatrix} a & b \\ c & d \end{bmatrix}$ and find the value of A.

Ans. $\begin{bmatrix} 1 & 1 \\ 1 & 0 \end{bmatrix}$

29. Given, $A=\begin{bmatrix} 2 & 0 & 1 \\ 2 & 1 & 3 \\ 1 & -1 & 0 \end{bmatrix}$

Now, $A^2 - 5A + 6I$

$$=\begin{bmatrix} 2 & 0 & 1 \\ 2 & 1 & 3 \\ 1 & -1 & 0 \end{bmatrix}\begin{bmatrix} 2 & 0 & 1 \\ 2 & 1 & 3 \\ 1 & -1 & 0 \end{bmatrix} - 5\begin{bmatrix} 2 & 0 & 1 \\ 2 & 1 & 3 \\ 1 & -1 & 0 \end{bmatrix} + 6\begin{bmatrix} 1 & 0 & 0 \\ 0 & 1 & 0 \\ 0 & 0 & 1 \end{bmatrix}$$

$$=\begin{bmatrix} 5 & -1 & 2 \\ 9 & -2 & 5 \\ 0 & -1 & -2 \end{bmatrix} - \begin{bmatrix} 10 & 0 & 5 \\ 10 & 5 & 15 \\ 5 & -5 & 0 \end{bmatrix} + \begin{bmatrix} 6 & 0 & 0 \\ 0 & 6 & 0 \\ 0 & 0 & 6 \end{bmatrix}$$

$$=\begin{bmatrix} 5-10+6 & -1-0+0 & 2-5+0 \\ 9-10+0 & -2-5+6 & 5-15+0 \\ 0-5+0 & -1+5+0 & -2-0+6 \end{bmatrix}$$

$$=\begin{bmatrix} 1 & -1 & -3 \\ -1 & -1 & -10 \\ -5 & 4 & 4 \end{bmatrix}$$

30. Let $A=\begin{bmatrix} 3 & 1 \\ 7 & 5 \end{bmatrix}$

Now, $A^2 + aI = bA$

$$\begin{bmatrix} 3 & 1 \\ 7 & 5 \end{bmatrix}\begin{bmatrix} 3 & 1 \\ 7 & 5 \end{bmatrix} + a\begin{bmatrix} 1 & 0 \\ 0 & 1 \end{bmatrix} = b\begin{bmatrix} 3 & 1 \\ 7 & 5 \end{bmatrix}$$

$$\Rightarrow \begin{bmatrix} 16 & 8 \\ 56 & 32 \end{bmatrix} + \begin{bmatrix} a & 0 \\ 0 & a \end{bmatrix} = \begin{bmatrix} 3b & b \\ 7b & 5b \end{bmatrix}$$

$$\Rightarrow \begin{bmatrix} 16+a & 8 \\ 56 & 32+a \end{bmatrix} = \begin{bmatrix} 3b & b \\ 7b & 5b \end{bmatrix}$$

On comparing the corresponding elements of both matrices, we get

$16 + a = 3b$ and $b = 8$

$\Rightarrow \quad a = 3 \times 8 - 16$

$\Rightarrow \quad a = 8$

Hence, $a = 8$ and $b = 8$

31. Given, $A=\begin{bmatrix} 2 & 3 \\ 1 & 2 \end{bmatrix}$

$$A^2 = A \cdot A = \begin{bmatrix} 2 & 3 \\ 1 & 2 \end{bmatrix}\begin{bmatrix} 2 & 3 \\ 1 & 2 \end{bmatrix} = \begin{bmatrix} 7 & 12 \\ 4 & 7 \end{bmatrix}$$

$$A^3 = A^2 \cdot A = \begin{bmatrix} 7 & 12 \\ 4 & 7 \end{bmatrix}\begin{bmatrix} 2 & 3 \\ 1 & 2 \end{bmatrix} = \begin{bmatrix} 26 & 45 \\ 15 & 26 \end{bmatrix}$$

Now, LHS $= A^3 - 4A^2 + A$

$$=\begin{bmatrix} 26 & 45 \\ 15 & 26 \end{bmatrix} - 4\begin{bmatrix} 7 & 12 \\ 4 & 7 \end{bmatrix} + \begin{bmatrix} 2 & 3 \\ 1 & 2 \end{bmatrix}$$

$$=\begin{bmatrix} 26-28+2 & 45-48+3 \\ 15-16+1 & 26-28+2 \end{bmatrix}$$

$$=\begin{bmatrix} 0 & 0 \\ 0 & 0 \end{bmatrix} = O = \text{RHS}$$

Hence proved.

32. Given, $A=\begin{bmatrix} 1 & 0 \\ -1 & 5 \end{bmatrix}$ ...(i)

and $A^2 - 6A - KI_2 = O$ ...(ii)

Now, $A^2 = A \cdot A$

$$=\begin{bmatrix} 1 & 0 \\ -1 & 5 \end{bmatrix}\begin{bmatrix} 1 & 0 \\ -1 & 5 \end{bmatrix}$$

$$=\begin{bmatrix} 1+0 & 0+0 \\ -1-5 & 0+25 \end{bmatrix} = \begin{bmatrix} 1 & 0 \\ -6 & 25 \end{bmatrix} \quad \text{...(iii)}$$

From Eq. (ii), we get

$$A^2 - 6A + KI_2 = O$$

$$\begin{bmatrix} 1 & 0 \\ -6 & 25 \end{bmatrix} - 6\begin{bmatrix} 1 & 0 \\ -1 & 5 \end{bmatrix} - K\begin{bmatrix} 1 & 0 \\ 0 & 1 \end{bmatrix} = \begin{bmatrix} 0 & 0 \\ 0 & 0 \end{bmatrix}$$

$$\Rightarrow \begin{bmatrix} 1 & 0 \\ -6 & 25 \end{bmatrix} - \begin{bmatrix} 6 & 0 \\ -6 & 30 \end{bmatrix} - \begin{bmatrix} K & 0 \\ 0 & K \end{bmatrix} = \begin{bmatrix} 0 & 0 \\ 0 & 0 \end{bmatrix}$$

$$\Rightarrow \begin{bmatrix} 1-6 & 0-0 \\ -6+6 & 25-30 \end{bmatrix} - \begin{bmatrix} K & 0 \\ 0 & K \end{bmatrix} = \begin{bmatrix} 0 & 0 \\ 0 & 0 \end{bmatrix}$$

$$\Rightarrow \begin{bmatrix} -5 & 0 \\ 0 & -5 \end{bmatrix} - \begin{bmatrix} K & 0 \\ 0 & K \end{bmatrix} = \begin{bmatrix} 0 & 0 \\ 0 & 0 \end{bmatrix}$$

$$\Rightarrow \begin{bmatrix} -5-K & 0 \\ 0 & -5-K \end{bmatrix} = \begin{bmatrix} 0 & 0 \\ 0 & 0 \end{bmatrix}$$

On equating the corresponding element of both sides, we get

$$-5 - K = 0$$

$\therefore \quad K = -5$

33. Given, $A = \text{diag}\,[a, b, c]$

$$A^2 = A \cdot A = \begin{bmatrix} a & 0 & 0 \\ 0 & b & 0 \\ 0 & 0 & c \end{bmatrix}\begin{bmatrix} a & 0 & 0 \\ 0 & b & 0 \\ 0 & 0 & c \end{bmatrix}$$

$$=\begin{bmatrix} a^2 & 0 & 0 \\ 0 & b^2 & 0 \\ 0 & 0 & c^2 \end{bmatrix}$$

$= \text{diag}\,[a^2, b^2, c^2]$

Similarly, $A^3 = \text{diag}\,[a^3, b^3, c^3]$

and $A^4 = \text{diag}\,[a^4, b^4, c^4]$

Therefore, $A^n = \text{diag}\,[a^n, b^n, c^n]$

Hence proved.

34. **Hint** $BA=\begin{bmatrix}1000 & 500 & 5000\\3000 & 1000 & 10000\end{bmatrix}\begin{bmatrix}40\\100\\50\end{bmatrix}$

$$=\begin{bmatrix}1000\times 40+500\times 100+5000\times 50\\3000\times 40+1000\times 100+10000\times 50\end{bmatrix}$$

$$=\begin{bmatrix}40000+50000+250000\\120000+100000+500000\end{bmatrix}$$

$$=\begin{bmatrix}340000\\720000\end{bmatrix}$$

So, the total amount spent by the group in the two cities is 340000 paise and 720000 paise, i.e. ₹ 3400 and ₹ 7200, respectively.

35. Since, A and B both are symmetric matrices, therefore $A'=A$ and $B'=B$.

Let AB be symmetric, then $(AB)'=AB$

But $(AB)'=B'A'=BA$ $[\because B'=B \text{ and } A'=A]$

Therefore, $BA=AB$

Conversely, if $AB=BA$, then we shall show that AB is symmetric.

36. Given, $A=\begin{bmatrix}-1 & 2 & 3\\5 & 7 & 9\\-2 & 1 & 1\end{bmatrix}$ and $B=\begin{bmatrix}-4 & 1 & -5\\1 & 2 & 0\\1 & 3 & 1\end{bmatrix}$

Now, $A'=\begin{bmatrix}-1 & 2 & 3\\5 & 7 & 9\\-2 & 1 & 1\end{bmatrix}'=\begin{bmatrix}-1 & 5 & -2\\2 & 7 & 1\\3 & 9 & 1\end{bmatrix}$ ...(i)

$B'=\begin{bmatrix}-4 & 1 & -5\\1 & 2 & 0\\1 & 3 & 1\end{bmatrix}'=\begin{bmatrix}-4 & 1 & 1\\1 & 2 & 3\\-5 & 0 & 1\end{bmatrix}$ ... (ii)

$A+B=\begin{bmatrix}-1 & 2 & 3\\5 & 7 & 9\\-2 & 1 & 1\end{bmatrix}+\begin{bmatrix}-4 & 1 & -5\\1 & 2 & 0\\1 & 3 & 1\end{bmatrix}=\begin{bmatrix}-5 & 3 & -2\\6 & 9 & 9\\-1 & 4 & 2\end{bmatrix}$ ...(iii)

$(A+B)'=\begin{bmatrix}-5 & 3 & -2\\6 & 9 & 9\\-1 & 4 & 2\end{bmatrix}'=\begin{bmatrix}-5 & 6 & -1\\3 & 9 & 4\\-2 & 9 & 2\end{bmatrix}$ ...(iv)

$A-B=\begin{bmatrix}-1 & 2 & 3\\5 & 7 & 9\\-2 & 1 & 1\end{bmatrix}-\begin{bmatrix}-4 & 1 & -5\\1 & 2 & 0\\1 & 3 & 1\end{bmatrix}$

$=\begin{bmatrix}3 & 1 & 8\\4 & 5 & 9\\-3 & -2 & 0\end{bmatrix}$ ...(v)

$(A-B)'=\begin{bmatrix}3 & 1 & 8\\4 & 5 & 9\\-3 & -2 & 0\end{bmatrix}'=\begin{bmatrix}3 & 4 & -3\\1 & 5 & -2\\8 & 9 & 0\end{bmatrix}$ ...(vi)

(i) LHS $=(A+B)'=\begin{bmatrix}-5 & 6 & -1\\3 & 9 & 4\\-2 & 9 & 2\end{bmatrix}$ ...(vii) [using Eq. (iv)]

RHS $=A'+B'=\begin{bmatrix}-1 & 5 & -2\\2 & 7 & 1\\3 & 9 & 1\end{bmatrix}+\begin{bmatrix}-4 & 1 & 1\\1 & 2 & 3\\-5 & 0 & 1\end{bmatrix}$

[using Eqs. (i) and (ii)]

$=\begin{bmatrix}-5 & 6 & -1\\3 & 9 & 4\\-2 & 9 & 2\end{bmatrix}$ ...(viii)

From Eqs. (vii) and (viii), we get

LHS = RHS **Hence proved.**

(ii) LHS $=(A-B)'=\begin{bmatrix}3 & 4 & -3\\1 & 5 & -2\\8 & 9 & 0\end{bmatrix}$ ...(ix)

[using Eq. (vi)]

RHS $=A'-B'$

$=\begin{bmatrix}-1 & 5 & -2\\2 & 7 & 1\\3 & 9 & 1\end{bmatrix}-\begin{bmatrix}-4 & 1 & 1\\1 & 2 & 3\\-5 & 0 & 1\end{bmatrix}$

[using Eqs. (i) and (ii)]

$=\begin{bmatrix}3 & 4 & -3\\1 & 5 & -2\\8 & 9 & 0\end{bmatrix}$ ...(x)

From Eqs. (ix) and (x), we get

LHS = RHS **Hence proved.**

37. Given, $A=\begin{bmatrix}0 & a & b\\-a & 0 & c\\-b & -c & 0\end{bmatrix}$

Now, $\frac{1}{2}(A+A')=\frac{1}{2}\left[\begin{bmatrix}0 & a & b\\-a & 0 & c\\-b & -c & 0\end{bmatrix}+\begin{bmatrix}0 & a & b\\-a & 0 & c\\-b & -c & 0\end{bmatrix}'\right]$

$=\frac{1}{2}\left[\begin{bmatrix}0 & a & b\\-a & 0 & c\\-b & -c & 0\end{bmatrix}+\begin{bmatrix}0 & -a & -b\\a & 0 & -c\\b & c & 0\end{bmatrix}\right]$

$=\frac{1}{2}\begin{bmatrix}0+0 & a-a & b-b\\-a+a & 0+0 & c-c\\-b+b & -c+c & 0+0\end{bmatrix}=\frac{1}{2}\begin{bmatrix}0 & 0 & 0\\0 & 0 & 0\\0 & 0 & 0\end{bmatrix}$

$=\begin{bmatrix}0 & 0 & 0\\0 & 0 & 0\\0 & 0 & 0\end{bmatrix}$

and $\frac{1}{2}(A-A')=\frac{1}{2}\left[\begin{bmatrix}0 & a & b\\-a & 0 & c\\-b & -c & 0\end{bmatrix}-\begin{bmatrix}0 & a & b\\-a & 0 & c\\-b & -c & 0\end{bmatrix}'\right]$

$$=\frac{1}{2}\left[\begin{bmatrix}0 & a & b\\-a & 0 & c\\-b & -c & 0\end{bmatrix}-\begin{bmatrix}0 & -a & -b\\a & 0 & -c\\b & c & 0\end{bmatrix}\right]$$

$$=\frac{1}{2}\begin{bmatrix}0-0 & a-(-a) & b-(-b)\\-a-a & 0-0 & c-(-c)\\-b-b & -c-c & 0-0\end{bmatrix}$$

$$=\frac{1}{2}\begin{bmatrix}0 & 2a & 2b\\-2a & 0 & 2c\\-2b & -2c & 0\end{bmatrix}$$

$$=\begin{bmatrix}0 & a & b\\-a & 0 & c\\-b & -c & 0\end{bmatrix}$$

38. Given, $A=\begin{bmatrix}3 & -4\\1 & -1\end{bmatrix}$

Now, $A-A'=\begin{bmatrix}3 & -4\\1 & -1\end{bmatrix}-\begin{bmatrix}3 & -4\\1 & -1\end{bmatrix}'$

$$=\begin{bmatrix}3 & -4\\1 & -1\end{bmatrix}-\begin{bmatrix}3 & 1\\-4 & -1\end{bmatrix}=\begin{bmatrix}0 & -5\\5 & 0\end{bmatrix} \quad \ldots(i)$$

$\therefore \quad (A-A')'=\begin{bmatrix}0 & -5\\5 & 0\end{bmatrix}'$

$$=\begin{bmatrix}0 & 5\\-5 & 0\end{bmatrix}=-\begin{bmatrix}0 & -5\\5 & 0\end{bmatrix}$$

$\Rightarrow (A-A')'=-(A-A')$ [using Eq. (i)]

Hence, $(A-A')$ is a skew-symmetric matrix.

39. We have to prove,

B^TAB is a skew-symmetric if A is skew-symmetric.

Since, A is a skew-symmetric matrix, therefore $A^T=-A$.

Now, $(B^TAB)^T=(AB)^T(B^T)^T$ $[\because (AB)^T=B^TA^T]$

$=(AB)^TB$ $[\because (A^T)^T=A]$

$=B^TA^TB$

$=B^T(-A)B$ $[\because A^T=-A]$

$=-B^TAB$

Hence, B^TAB is a skew-symmetric matrix.

40. We know that the diagonal elements of skew-symmetric matrix are zero and $a_{ij}=-a_{ji}$.

Therefore, skew-symmetric matrices of order 2 and 3 are

$\begin{bmatrix}0 & 1\\-1 & 0\end{bmatrix}$ and $\begin{bmatrix}0 & 1 & -2\\-1 & 0 & -3\\2 & 3 & 0\end{bmatrix}$, respectively.

41. Given, A and B are symmetric matrices.

$\therefore A'=A$ and $B'=B$

Now, $(BA-2AB)'=(BA)'-(2AB)'=(A'B')-2(AB)'$

$[\because (kA)'=kA'$ and $(AB)'=B'A']$

$=A'B'-2B'A'$

$=AB-2BA$ $[\because A'=A$ and $B'=B]$

$=-(2BA-AB)$

Hence, $BA-2AB$ is neither a symmetric matrix nor skew-symmetric matrix.

42. Let $A=\begin{bmatrix}5 & 2\\3 & -6\end{bmatrix}$. Then, $A'=\begin{bmatrix}5 & 3\\2 & -6\end{bmatrix}$

[interchanging the elements of rows and columns]

Now, $A+A'=\begin{bmatrix}5 & 2\\3 & -6\end{bmatrix}+\begin{bmatrix}5 & 3\\2 & -6\end{bmatrix}$

$\Rightarrow \quad A+A'=\begin{bmatrix}5+5 & 2+3\\3+2 & -6-6\end{bmatrix}=\begin{bmatrix}10 & 5\\5 & -12\end{bmatrix}$

$\Rightarrow \frac{1}{2}(A+A')=\frac{1}{2}\begin{bmatrix}10 & 5\\5 & -12\end{bmatrix}$, which is symmetric. ...(i)

Also, $A-A'=\begin{bmatrix}5 & 2\\3 & -6\end{bmatrix}-\begin{bmatrix}5 & 3\\2 & -6\end{bmatrix}$

$$=\begin{bmatrix}5-5 & 2-3\\3-2 & -6+6\end{bmatrix}=\begin{bmatrix}0 & -1\\1 & 0\end{bmatrix}$$

$\Rightarrow \frac{1}{2}(A-A')=\frac{1}{2}\begin{bmatrix}0 & -1\\1 & 0\end{bmatrix}$,

which is skew-symmetric. ...(ii)

On adding Eqs. (i) and (ii), we get

$$\frac{1}{2}(A+A')+\frac{1}{2}(A-A')=\frac{1}{2}\begin{bmatrix}10 & 5\\5 & -12\end{bmatrix}+\frac{1}{2}\begin{bmatrix}0 & -1\\1 & 0\end{bmatrix}$$

$$=\frac{1}{2}\begin{bmatrix}10+0 & 5-1\\5+1 & -12+0\end{bmatrix}$$

$$=\frac{1}{2}\begin{bmatrix}10 & 4\\6 & -12\end{bmatrix}$$

$$=\begin{bmatrix}5 & 2\\3 & -6\end{bmatrix}=A$$ **Hence proved.**

43. (i) Combined sales in September and October for each farmer in each variety is given by

	Basmati	Permal	Naura	
$A+B=$	15000	30000	36000	Ramkishan
	70000	40000	20000	Gurcharan Singh

(ii) Change in sales from September to October is given by

	Basmati	Permal	Naura	
$A-B=$	5000	10000	24000	Ramkishan
	30000	20000	0	Gurcharan Singh

(iii) 2% of $B=\frac{2}{100}\times B=0.02\times B$

$$=0.02\begin{bmatrix}5000 & 10000 & 6000\\ 20000 & 10000 & 10000\end{bmatrix}\begin{matrix}\text{Ramkishan}\\ \text{Gurcharan Singh}\end{matrix}$$
(columns: Basmati, Permal, Naura)

$$=\begin{bmatrix}100 & 200 & 120\\ 400 & 200 & 200\end{bmatrix}\begin{matrix}\text{Ramkishan}\\ \text{Gurcharan Singh}\end{matrix}$$
(columns: Basmatri, Permal, Naura)

Thus, in October, Ramkishan receives ₹ 100, ₹ 200 and ₹ 120 as profit in the sale of each variety of rice, respectively and Gurcharan Singh receives profit of ₹ 400, ₹ 200 and ₹ 200 in the sale of each variety of rice, respectively.

44. **Hint** Let the order of A is $m\times n$.

$\therefore$ $m=2$ and $n=3$

So, order of matrix A is 2×3.

Let $A=\begin{bmatrix}a & b & c\\ d & e & f\end{bmatrix}$

Now, $\begin{bmatrix}2 & -1\\ 1 & 0\\ -3 & 4\end{bmatrix}\begin{bmatrix}a & b & c\\ d & e & f\end{bmatrix}=\begin{bmatrix}-1 & -8 & -10\\ 1 & -2 & -5\\ 9 & 22 & 15\end{bmatrix}$ and solve it.

Ans. $A=\begin{bmatrix}1 & -2 & -5\\ 3 & 4 & 0\end{bmatrix}$

45. We shall prove the result using principle of mathematical induction.

We have, $P(n)$: If $A=\begin{bmatrix}\cos\theta & \sin\theta\\ -\sin\theta & \cos\theta\end{bmatrix}$,

then $A^n=\begin{bmatrix}\cos n\theta & \sin n\theta\\ -\sin n\theta & \cos n\theta\end{bmatrix}, n\in N$

$P(1)$: If $A=\begin{bmatrix}\cos\theta & \sin\theta\\ -\sin\theta & \cos\theta\end{bmatrix}$,

so $A^1=\begin{bmatrix}\cos\theta & \sin\theta\\ -\sin\theta & \cos\theta\end{bmatrix}$

Therefore, the result is true for $n=1$.

Let the result be true for $n=k$.

So, $P(k)$: If $A=\begin{bmatrix}\cos\theta & \sin\theta\\ -\sin\theta & \cos\theta\end{bmatrix}$,

then $A^k=\begin{bmatrix}\cos k\theta & \sin k\theta\\ -\sin k\theta & \cos k\theta\end{bmatrix}$

Now, we prove that the result holds for $n=k+1$.

Now, $A^{k+1}=A\cdot A^k=\begin{bmatrix}\cos\theta & \sin\theta\\ -\sin\theta & \cos\theta\end{bmatrix}\begin{bmatrix}\cos k\theta & \sin k\theta\\ -\sin k\theta & \cos k\theta\end{bmatrix}$

$$=\begin{bmatrix}\cos\theta\cos k\theta-\sin\theta\sin k\theta & \cos\theta\sin k\theta+\sin\theta\cos k\theta\\ -\sin\theta\cos k\theta-\cos\theta\sin k\theta & -\sin\theta\sin k\theta+\cos\theta\cos k\theta\end{bmatrix}$$

$$=\begin{bmatrix}\cos(\theta+k\theta) & \sin(\theta+k\theta)\\ -\sin(\theta+k\theta) & \cos(\theta+k\theta)\end{bmatrix}$$

$$=\begin{bmatrix}\cos(k+1)\theta & \sin(k+1)\theta\\ -\sin(k+1)\theta & \cos(k+1)\theta\end{bmatrix}$$

Therefore, the result is true for $n=k+1$.

Thus, by principle of mathematical induction, we get

$A^n=\begin{bmatrix}\cos n\theta & \sin n\theta\\ -\sin n\theta & \cos n\theta\end{bmatrix}$, holds for all natural numbers.

46. **Hint** If A is a root of the polynomial

$$f(x)=x^3-6x^2+7x+2$$

Then, $f(A)=O$

i.e. $A^3-6A^2+7A+2I=O$

47. Given, $A=\begin{bmatrix}2 & 3\\ -1 & 2\end{bmatrix}$ and $f(x)=x^2-4x+7$

$\therefore f(A)=A^2-4A+7I$

Now, $A^2-4A+7I=\begin{bmatrix}2 & 3\\ -1 & 2\end{bmatrix}\begin{bmatrix}2 & 3\\ -1 & 2\end{bmatrix}-4\begin{bmatrix}2 & 3\\ -1 & 2\end{bmatrix}+7\begin{bmatrix}1 & 0\\ 0 & 1\end{bmatrix}$

$$=\begin{bmatrix}4-3 & 6+6\\ -2-2 & -3+4\end{bmatrix}-\begin{bmatrix}8 & 12\\ -4 & 8\end{bmatrix}+\begin{bmatrix}7 & 0\\ 0 & 7\end{bmatrix}$$

$$=\begin{bmatrix}1 & 12\\ -4 & 1\end{bmatrix}-\begin{bmatrix}8 & 12\\ -4 & 8\end{bmatrix}+\begin{bmatrix}7 & 0\\ 0 & 7\end{bmatrix}$$

$$=\begin{bmatrix}1-8 & 12-12\\ -4+4 & 1-8\end{bmatrix}+\begin{bmatrix}7 & 0\\ 0 & 7\end{bmatrix}$$

$$=\begin{bmatrix}-7 & 0\\ 0 & -7\end{bmatrix}+\begin{bmatrix}7 & 0\\ 0 & 7\end{bmatrix}=\begin{bmatrix}-7+7 & 0+0\\ 0+0 & -7+7\end{bmatrix}$$

$$=\begin{bmatrix}0 & 0\\ 0 & 0\end{bmatrix}=O$$ **Hence proved.**

We have, $A^2-4A+7I=O$

$$A^2=4A-7I$$

Thus, $A^3=A\cdot A^2=A(4A-7I)$

$=4A^2-7A=4(4A-7I)-7A$

$=16A-28I-7A=9A-28I$

and $A^5=A^3A^2$

$=(9A-28I)(4A-7I)$

$=36A^2-63A-112A+196I^2$

$=36(4A-7I)-175A+196I$

$=144A-252I-175A+196I=-31A-56I$

$=-31\begin{bmatrix}2 & 3\\ -1 & 2\end{bmatrix}-56\begin{bmatrix}1 & 0\\ 0 & 1\end{bmatrix}$

$=\begin{bmatrix}-62 & -93\\ 31 & -62\end{bmatrix}-\begin{bmatrix}56 & 0\\ 0 & 56\end{bmatrix}$

$=\begin{bmatrix}-62-56 & -93-0\\ 31-0 & -62-56\end{bmatrix}$

$=\begin{bmatrix}-118 & -93\\ 31 & -118\end{bmatrix}$

48. (i) Let the sales of products x, y and z per market be denoted by matrix A

$$\therefore\ A = \begin{array}{c} \\ \end{array}\begin{matrix} x & y & z \\ \end{matrix}$$

$$\therefore\ A = \begin{bmatrix} 10000 & 2000 & 18000 \\ 6000 & 20000 & 8000 \end{bmatrix} \begin{matrix} \text{Market I} \\ \text{Market II} \end{matrix}$$

(columns x, y, z)

and the unit sale price of products x, y and z be denoted by matrix B.

Unit sale price

$$\therefore\ B = \begin{bmatrix} 2.50 \\ 1.50 \\ 1.00 \end{bmatrix} \begin{matrix} x \\ y \\ z \end{matrix}$$

Now, total revenue = Total sales × Unit sales price

$$= AB$$

$$= \begin{bmatrix} 10000 & 2000 & 18000 \\ 6000 & 20000 & 8000 \end{bmatrix} \begin{bmatrix} 2.50 \\ 1.50 \\ 1.00 \end{bmatrix}$$

$$= \begin{bmatrix} 10000 \times 2.50 + 2000 \times 1.50 + 18000 \times 1.00 \\ 6000 \times 2.50 + 20000 \times 1.50 + 8000 \times 1.00 \end{bmatrix}$$

$$= \begin{bmatrix} 25000 + 3000 + 18000 \\ 15000 + 30000 + 8000 \end{bmatrix} = \begin{bmatrix} 46000 \\ 53000 \end{bmatrix} \quad \text{...(i)}$$

Hence, total revenue of Market I = ₹ 46000

and total revenue of Market II = ₹ 53000

(ii) Let the unit cost price of products x, y and z be denoted by matrix C.

Unit cost price

$$\therefore\quad C = \begin{bmatrix} 2.00 \\ 1.00 \\ 0.50 \end{bmatrix} \begin{matrix} x \\ y \\ z \end{matrix}$$

Now, total cost = Total sales × Unit cost price

$$= AC$$

$$= \begin{bmatrix} 10000 & 2000 & 18000 \\ 6000 & 20000 & 8000 \end{bmatrix} \begin{bmatrix} 2.00 \\ 1.00 \\ 0.50 \end{bmatrix}$$

$$= \begin{bmatrix} 10000 \times 2.00 + 2000 \times 1.00 + 18000 \times 0.50 \\ 6000 \times 2.00 + 20000 \times 1.00 + 8000 \times 0.50 \end{bmatrix}$$

$$= \begin{bmatrix} 20000 + 2000 + 9000 \\ 12000 + 20000 + 4000 \end{bmatrix} = \begin{bmatrix} 31000 \\ 36000 \end{bmatrix} \quad \text{...(ii)}$$

Now, Profit = Revenue − Cost

$$= \begin{bmatrix} 46000 \\ 53000 \end{bmatrix} - \begin{bmatrix} 31000 \\ 36000 \end{bmatrix} = \begin{bmatrix} 15000 \\ 17000 \end{bmatrix}$$

[from Eqs. (i) and (ii)]

Therefore, total profit of Market I = ₹ 15000

and total profit of Market II = 17000

Hence, gross profit = ₹ 15000 + ₹ 17000 = ₹ 32000

49. Let the amount invested in first bond = ₹ x

Therefore, the amount invested in second bond

= ₹ $(30000 - x)$

(a) If the total interest is ₹ 1800, then

Interest = Investment in bonds × Annual rate of interest

$$\Rightarrow [1800] = [x \quad 30000 - x] \begin{bmatrix} 5\% \\ 7\% \end{bmatrix}$$

$$\Rightarrow [1800] = [x \times 5\% + (30000 - x) \times 7\%]$$

On comparing the corresponding elements, we get

$$\frac{5x}{100} + \frac{7}{100}(30000 - x) = 1800$$

$$\Rightarrow \quad 5x + 210000 - 7x = 180000$$

$$\Rightarrow \quad -2x = -30000 \Rightarrow x = 15000$$

Therefore, the amount invested in first bond is ₹ 15000 and second bond is ₹ 15000.

(b) If the total interest is ₹ 2000, then

Interest = Investment in bonds × Annual rate of interest

$$\Rightarrow [2000] = [x \quad 30000 - x] \begin{bmatrix} 5\% \\ 7\% \end{bmatrix}$$

$$\Rightarrow [2000] = [x \times 5\% + (30000 - x) \times 7\%]$$

On comparing the corresponding elements, we get

$$\frac{5x}{100} + \frac{7}{100}(30000 - x) = 2000$$

$$\Rightarrow \quad 5x + 210000 - 7x = 200000$$

$$\Rightarrow \quad -2x = -10000$$

$$\Rightarrow \quad x = 5000$$

Therefore, the amount invested in first bond is ₹ 5000 and second bond is ₹ 25000.

QR Code for Quick Test 1	QR Code for Quick Test 2	QR Code for Quick Test 3

Mind Map

Matrices

A matrix is an ordered rectangular arry of numbers enclosed in [ ] or ( ).
Matrix is represented by a single capital letter.

e.g. $\begin{bmatrix} 0 & 8 & 3 \\ 4 & -1 & 5 \\ -7 & -3 & 0 \end{bmatrix}$

Order of Matrix

A matrix having m rows and n columns is called a matrix of order $m \times n$ and it has mn elements.

Operations on Matrices

Addition of Matrices

If A and B are two matrices of the same order $m \times n$, then their sum denoted by $A + B$ is also a matrix of the same order $m \times n$ and is obtained by adding the corresponding elements of A and B.

e.g. $\begin{bmatrix} 6 & 7 \\ 4 & 3 \end{bmatrix} + \begin{bmatrix} 1 & 3 \\ 2 & 9 \end{bmatrix} = \begin{bmatrix} 7 & 10 \\ 6 & 12 \end{bmatrix}$

Multiplication of a Matrix by a Scalar

If $A=[a_{ij}]_{m \times n}$ is a matrix and k is scalar. Then, kA is another matrix obtained by multiplying each element of A by the scalar k.

e.g. If $A = \begin{bmatrix} 7 & 18 \\ -1 & 3 \end{bmatrix}$ and $k = 3$, then $kA = \begin{bmatrix} 21 & 54 \\ -3 & 9 \end{bmatrix}$

Difference (or Subtraction) of Matrices

Difference of two matrices is simply the matrix whose elements are the difference of the corresponding elements of two matrices.

e.g. $\begin{bmatrix} 4 & 3 \\ 2 & 1 \end{bmatrix} - \begin{bmatrix} 1 & 2 \\ 3 & 4 \end{bmatrix} = \begin{bmatrix} 3 & 1 \\ -1 & -3 \end{bmatrix}$

Multiplication of Matrices

The product AB of two matrices A and B is defined, if the number of columns of A is equal to the number of rows of B.

$[A]_{m \times n} \; [B]_{n \times p} = [C]_{m \times p}$

must be equal

Order of product of matrix

Let A be the $m \times n$ matrix and B be the $n \times p$ matrix. Then, the product AB of the matrices A and B is matrix C of order $m \times p$.

e.g. $[1 \; 4]\begin{bmatrix} 3 \\ 2 \end{bmatrix} = [(1 \times 3) + (4 \times 2)] = [3 + 8] = [11]$

[multiplying row by column]

Positive Integral Powers of a Square Matrix

If A be a square matrix. Then, we can define

(i) $A^{n+1} = A^n \cdot A$, where $n \in N$

(ii) $A^m \cdot A^n = A^{m+n}$, where $m, n \in N$

(iii) $(A^m)^n = A^{mn} \; \forall m, n \in N$

(iv) $I^n = I$ for any positive integer n, where I is the identity matrix.

Matrix Polynomial

Let $f(x) = a_0x^n + a_1x^{n-1} + a_2x^{n-2} + \ldots + a_{n-1}a + a_n$ be a polynomial and A be a square matrix.

Then, $f(A) = a_0A^n + a_1A^{n-1} + a_2A^{n-2} + \ldots + a_{n-1}A + a_nI$ is called a matrix polynomial, where I is an identity matrix of order of A.

Transpose of Matrix

The matrix obtained by interchanging the rows and columns of matrix A is called the transpose of matrix A. The transpose of matrix A is represented by A' or A^c or A^T.

e.g. Let $A = \begin{bmatrix} 1 & 5 \\ \sqrt{2} & 1 \\ -1/5 & 0 \end{bmatrix}_{3 \times 2}$. Then, $A' = \begin{bmatrix} 1 & \sqrt{2} & -1/5 \\ 5 & 1 & 0 \end{bmatrix}_{2 \times 3}$

Some Important Theorems

(i) For every square matrix A, $A + A'$ is a symmetric matrix and $A - A'$ is a skew-symmetric matrix.

(ii) Any square matrix can be expressed as the sum of a symmetric and a skew-symmetric matrices i.e. let A be a square matrix. Then, it can be written as

$$A = \frac{1}{2}(A + A') + \frac{1}{2}(A - A')$$

(iii) Inverse of a matrix if it exists, is unique.

(iv) If A and B are invertible matrices of the same order, then

$$(AB)^{-1} = B^{-1}A^{-1},$$

where A and B are matrices of the same order.

Symmetric and Skew-Symmetric Matrix

Symmetric Matrix

A square matrix A is called a symmetric matrix, if the transpose of matrix A is equal to the matrix A, i.e. $A' = A$.

Skew-Symmetric Matrix

A square matrix A is said to be skew-symmetric matrix A, if the transpose of matrix A is equal to the negative of matrix A. i.e. $A' = -A$.

Invertible Matrices

Let A be a square matrix of order n, if there exist a square matrix B such that $AB = I_n = BA$, then B is called the inverse of A and is denoted by A^{-1}.

$\therefore \quad AA^{-1} = I = A^{-1}A$

04
CHAPTER

If you do not know the names of things, the knowledge of them is lost, too.

— *Carl Linnaeus*

Determinants

YOUR STUDY GOALS

4.1 Determinant
4.2 Area of Triangle
4.3 Minors and Cofactors
4.4 Adjoint of a Matrix
4.5 Singular and Non-singular Matrices
4.6 Inverse of a Square Matrix
4.7 Consistent and Inconsistent System
4.8 Solution of System of Linear Equations using Inverse of a Matrix

YOUR PRACTICE GOALS

- Objective Type Questions (33 Qs ; 21 MCQs, 8 A-R, 4 Case Based)
- Subjective Type Questions (29 Qs; 6 VSA, 11 SA, 12 LA)

4.1 Determinant

A square matrix A can be associate a number (real or complex) is called a determinant of the square matrix A.

It is denoted by det A or $|A|$.

Determinant of a Matrix of Order 1

Let $A=[a_{11}]$ be the matrix of order 1×1.

Then, det A is $|A|=|a_{11}|=a_{11}$.

Determinant of a Matrix of Order 2

Let $A=\begin{bmatrix} a_{11} & a_{12} \\ a_{21} & a_{22} \end{bmatrix}$ be a matrix of order 2×2.

Then, det A is $|A|=\begin{vmatrix} a_{11} & a_{12} \\ a_{21} & a_{22} \end{vmatrix}=a_{11}a_{22}-a_{21}a_{12}$

Determinant of a Matrix of Order 3

Determinant of a matrix of order 3 can be determined by expressing it in terms of second order determinants which is known as expansion of a determinant along row or column.

Let $A = \begin{bmatrix} a_{11} & a_{12} & a_{13} \\ a_{21} & a_{22} & a_{23} \\ a_{31} & a_{32} & a_{33} \end{bmatrix}$.

Then, $|A| = \begin{vmatrix} a_{11} & a_{12} & a_{13} \\ a_{21} & a_{22} & a_{23} \\ a_{31} & a_{32} & a_{33} \end{vmatrix}$

$$= a_{11} \begin{vmatrix} a_{22} & a_{23} \\ a_{32} & a_{33} \end{vmatrix} - a_{12} \begin{vmatrix} a_{21} & a_{23} \\ a_{31} & a_{33} \end{vmatrix} + a_{13} \begin{vmatrix} a_{21} & a_{22} \\ a_{31} & a_{32} \end{vmatrix} \quad \text{[expanding along } R_1]$$

Similarly, we can determine determinant value by expanding any row or column. Expanding a determinants along any row or column gives same value.

4.2 Area of Triangle

The area of triangle whose vertices are (x_1, y_1), (x_2, y_2) and (x_3, y_3) is given by

$$\Delta = \frac{1}{2} \begin{vmatrix} x_1 & y_1 & 1 \\ x_2 & y_2 & 1 \\ x_3 & y_3 & 1 \end{vmatrix}.$$

Collinearity of Three Points

Three points $(x_1, y_1)(x_2, y_2)$ and (x_3, y_3) are collinear if and only if the area of triangle formed by these three points is zero

i.e. $$\begin{vmatrix} x_1 & y_1 & 1 \\ x_2 & y_2 & 1 \\ x_3 & y_3 & 1 \end{vmatrix} = 0.$$

Equation of a Line Through Two Points

The equation of line joining two points (x_1, y_1) and (x_2, y_2) is given by

$$\begin{vmatrix} x & y & 1 \\ x_1 & y_1 & 1 \\ x_2 & y_2 & 1 \end{vmatrix} = 0.$$

TEACHER TIPS

(i) If we expand a determinant by any row or column, we attach following signs for a determinant of order three.

$$\begin{vmatrix} + & - & + \\ - & + & - \\ + & - & + \end{vmatrix}$$

For easier calculations, we should expand determinant along the row or column having maximum number of zeroes.

(ii) Only square matrices have determinants.

(iii) There are six ways of expanding a determinant of order 3 corresponding to each of three rows (R_1, R_2 and R_3) and each of three columns (C_1, C_2 and C_3).

(iv) For easier calculations, we will expand the determinant along that row (or column) which contains maximum number of zeroes.

(v) While expanding, instead of multiplying by $(-1)^{i+j}$, we can multiply by +1 or −1 according as $(i+j)$ is even or odd.

(vi) If $A = kB$ where A and B are square matrices of order n, then $|A| = k^n |B|$, where $n = 1, 2, 3$.

(vii) For any square matrix A, $|A'| = |A|$

(viii) For any square matrices A and B, $|AB| = |A||B|$.

(ix) Area is a positive quantity, so we take the absolute value of determinant.

(x) If area is given, then take both negative and positive values of determinant for calculation.

Example 1 **Evaluate the following determinants.**

(i) $|-12|$ (ii) $\begin{vmatrix} 3 & 5 \\ -2 & 4 \end{vmatrix}$

(iii) $\begin{vmatrix} x-1 & 1 \\ x^3 & x^2+x+1 \end{vmatrix}$ (iv) $\begin{vmatrix} \cos\theta & -\sin\theta \\ \sin\theta & \cos\theta \end{vmatrix}$

Sol. (i) Clearly, $|-12| = -12$ $[\because |-a| = -a]$

(ii) We have,

$$\begin{vmatrix} 3 & 5 \\ -2 & 4 \end{vmatrix} = 3 \times 4 - (-2) \times 5$$

$$\left[\because \begin{vmatrix} a_{11} & a_{12} \\ a_{21} & a_{22} \end{vmatrix} = a_{11}a_{22} - a_{21}a_{12}\right]$$

$$= 12 + 10 = 22$$

(iii) We have,

$$\begin{vmatrix} x-1 & 1 \\ x^3 & x^2+x+1 \end{vmatrix} = (x-1)(x^2+x+1) - x^3$$

$$\left[\because \begin{vmatrix} a_{11} & a_{12} \\ a_{21} & a_{22} \end{vmatrix} = a_{11}a_{22} - a_{21}a_{12}\right]$$

$$= (x^3 - 1) - x^3$$

$$[\because (a-b)(a^2+ab+b^2) = a^3 - b^3]$$

$$= -1$$

(iv) We have,

$$\begin{vmatrix} \cos\theta & -\sin\theta \\ \sin\theta & \cos\theta \end{vmatrix} = \cos\theta \times \cos\theta - (\sin\theta)(-\sin\theta)$$

$$\left[\because \begin{vmatrix} a_{11} & a_{12} \\ a_{21} & a_{22} \end{vmatrix} = a_{11}a_{22} - a_{21}a_{12}\right]$$

$$= \cos^2\theta + \sin^2\theta = 1$$

$$[\because \cos^2 x + \sin^2 x = 1]$$

Example 2 Evaluate the determinant of matrix $\begin{bmatrix} 3 & -4 & 5 \\ 1 & 1 & -2 \\ 2 & 3 & 1 \end{bmatrix}$.

Sol. Let $A = \begin{bmatrix} 3 & -4 & 5 \\ 1 & 1 & -2 \\ 2 & 3 & 1 \end{bmatrix}$.

Then, $|A| = \begin{vmatrix} 3 & -4 & 5 \\ 1 & 1 & -2 \\ 2 & 3 & 1 \end{vmatrix}$

On expanding along R_1, we get

$$|A| = 3\begin{vmatrix} 1 & -2 \\ 3 & 1 \end{vmatrix} - (-4)\begin{vmatrix} 1 & -2 \\ 2 & 1 \end{vmatrix} + 5\begin{vmatrix} 1 & 1 \\ 2 & 3 \end{vmatrix}$$

$$= 3(1+6) + 4(1+4) + 5(3-2)$$

$$= 21 + 20 + 5 = 46$$

Example 3 Find the maximum value of $\begin{vmatrix} 1 & 1 & 1 \\ 1 & 1+\sin\theta & 1 \\ 1 & 1 & 1+\cos\theta \end{vmatrix}$. *Competency Based Que*

Sol. Let $\Delta = \begin{vmatrix} 1 & 1 & 1 \\ 1 & 1+\sin\theta & 1 \\ 1 & 1 & 1+\cos\theta \end{vmatrix}$

On expanding along first row i.e. R_1, we get

$$\Delta = 1\begin{vmatrix} 1+\sin\theta & 1 \\ 1 & 1+\cos\theta \end{vmatrix} - 1\begin{vmatrix} 1 & 1 \\ 1 & 1+\cos\theta \end{vmatrix} + 1\begin{vmatrix} 1 & 1+\sin\theta \\ 1 & 1 \end{vmatrix}$$

$$= [(1+\sin\theta)(1+\cos\theta) - 1] - [1+\cos\theta - 1] + [1 - 1 - \sin\theta]$$

$$= 1 + \cos\theta + \sin\theta + \sin\theta\cos\theta - 1 - \cos\theta - \sin\theta$$

$$= \sin\theta\cos\theta$$

$$= \frac{1}{2}(2\sin\theta\cos\theta) = \frac{1}{2}\sin 2\theta$$

We know that maximum value of $\sin 2\theta$ is 1.

$$\therefore \quad \Delta = \frac{1}{2} \times 1 = \frac{1}{2}$$

Example 4 Prove that the determinant $\begin{vmatrix} x & \sin\theta & \cos\theta \\ -\sin\theta & -x & 1 \\ \cos\theta & 1 & x \end{vmatrix}$ is independent of θ.

CBSE 2023; NCERT

Sol. Let $\Delta = \begin{vmatrix} x & \sin\theta & \cos\theta \\ -\sin\theta & -x & 1 \\ \cos\theta & 1 & x \end{vmatrix}$

$$= x\begin{vmatrix} -x & 1 \\ 1 & x \end{vmatrix} - \sin\theta\begin{vmatrix} -\sin\theta & 1 \\ \cos\theta & x \end{vmatrix} + \cos\theta\begin{vmatrix} -\sin\theta & -x \\ \cos\theta & 1 \end{vmatrix}$$

$$= x(-x^2 - 1) - \sin\theta(-x\sin\theta - \cos\theta) + \cos\theta(-\sin\theta + x\cos\theta)$$

$$= -x^3 - x + x\sin^2\theta + \sin\theta\cos\theta - \sin\theta\cos\theta + x\cos^2\theta$$

$$= -x^3 - x + x(\sin^2\theta + \cos^2\theta)$$

$$= -x^3 - x + x = -x^3 \qquad [\because \sin^2 A + \cos^2 A = 1]$$

$\therefore$ Δ is independent of θ.

Example 5 If $(A+B+C) = \pi$, then find the value of $\begin{vmatrix} \sin(A+B+C) & \sin B & \cos C \\ -\sin B & 0 & \tan A \\ \cos(A+B) & -\tan A & 0 \end{vmatrix}$.

Competency Based Que, CBSE Sample Paper 2017

Sol. We have, $A + B + C = \pi$ ...(i)

Now, $\begin{vmatrix} \sin(A+B+C) & \sin B & \cos C \\ -\sin B & 0 & \tan A \\ \cos(A+B) & -\tan A & 0 \end{vmatrix}$

$$= \begin{vmatrix} \sin\pi & \sin B & \cos C \\ -\sin B & 0 & \tan A \\ \cos(\pi - C) & -\tan A & 0 \end{vmatrix}$$

$$= \begin{vmatrix} 0 & \sin B & \cos C \\ -\sin B & 0 & \tan A \\ -\cos C & -\tan A & 0 \end{vmatrix}$$

$$= 0 \times \begin{vmatrix} 0 & \tan A \\ -\tan A & 0 \end{vmatrix} - \sin B \times \begin{vmatrix} -\sin B & \tan A \\ -\cos C & 0 \end{vmatrix} + \cos C \times \begin{vmatrix} -\sin B & 0 \\ -\cos C & -\tan A \end{vmatrix}$$

[expanding along R_1]

$$= 0 - \sin B \tan A \cos C + \cos C \sin B \tan A = 0$$

Example 6 If $\begin{vmatrix} 2x & -9 \\ -2 & x \end{vmatrix} = \begin{vmatrix} -4 & 8 \\ 1 & -2 \end{vmatrix}$, then find the value of x.

CBSE 2020

Sol. We have, $\begin{vmatrix} 2x & -9 \\ -2 & x \end{vmatrix} = \begin{vmatrix} -4 & 8 \\ 1 & -2 \end{vmatrix}$

$$(2x)(x) - (-2)(-9) = (-4)(-2) - (1)(8)$$

$$\Rightarrow \quad 2x^2 - 18 = 8 - 8$$

$$\Rightarrow \quad 2x^2 = 18$$

$$\Rightarrow \quad x^2 = 9 \Rightarrow x = \pm 3$$

Example 7 If $A = \begin{bmatrix} 1 & 2 \\ 4 & 2 \end{bmatrix}$, then show that $|2A| = 4|A|$.

NCERT

Sol. We have, $A = \begin{bmatrix} 1 & 2 \\ 4 & 2 \end{bmatrix} \Rightarrow 2A = \begin{bmatrix} 2 & 4 \\ 8 & 4 \end{bmatrix}$

Now, $|A| = \begin{vmatrix} 1 & 2 \\ 4 & 2 \end{vmatrix} = (1)(2) - (4)(2) = 2 - 8 = -6$

and $|2A| = \begin{vmatrix} 2 & 4 \\ 8 & 4 \end{vmatrix} = (2)(4) - (8)(4) = 8 - 32 = -24$

$\therefore$ $|2A| = -24 = 4 \times (-6) = 4|A|$

Example 8 Find $|AB|$, if $A=\begin{bmatrix}0 & -1\\ 0 & 2\end{bmatrix}$ and $B=\begin{bmatrix}3 & 5\\ 0 & 0\end{bmatrix}$. *CBSE 2019*

Sol. Given, $A=\begin{bmatrix}0 & -1\\ 0 & 2\end{bmatrix}$ and $B=\begin{bmatrix}3 & 5\\ 0 & 0\end{bmatrix}$

Now, $AB=\begin{bmatrix}0 & -1\\ 0 & 2\end{bmatrix}\begin{bmatrix}3 & 5\\ 0 & 0\end{bmatrix}=\begin{bmatrix}0+0 & 0+0\\ 0+0 & 0+0\end{bmatrix}=\begin{bmatrix}0 & 0\\ 0 & 0\end{bmatrix}$

$\therefore \quad |AB|=0$

Example 9 A and B are square matrices of order 3 each, $|A|=2$ and $|B|=3$. Find $|3AB|$. *CBSE Sample Paper 2017*

Sol. Given, order of matrices A and B is 3, $|A|=2$ and $|B|=3$

Now, $|3AB|=3^3|A||B|$ $\quad [\because |kA|=k^n|A|]$

$=27\times 2\times 3=162$

Example 10 If A is a square matrix of order 3 such that $A^2=2A$, then find the value of $|A|$. *CBSE Sample Paper 2021*

Sol. We have, $A^2=2A$

$A\cdot A=2A$

$\Rightarrow \quad |A\cdot A|=|2A|$

$\Rightarrow |A|\cdot|A|=2^3|A|$

$[\because |AB|=|A||B| \text{ and } |kA|=k^n|A|]$

$\Rightarrow \quad |A|^2=8|A| \Rightarrow |A|^2-8|A|=0$

$\Rightarrow \quad |A|(|A|-8)=0\Rightarrow |A|=0 \text{ or } 8$

Example 11 If $A=\begin{bmatrix}p & 2\\ 2 & p\end{bmatrix}$ and $|A^3|=125$, then find the value of p. *CBSE 2019*

Sol. Given, $A=\begin{bmatrix}p & 2\\ 2 & p\end{bmatrix}$

$\therefore \quad |A|=\begin{vmatrix}p & 2\\ 2 & p\end{vmatrix}=p^2-4$

and $|A^3|=125\Rightarrow |A|^3=125$ $\quad [\because |A|^3=|A^3|]$

$\Rightarrow \quad (p^2-4)^3=125\Rightarrow p^2-4=5$

$\Rightarrow \quad p^2=9 \Rightarrow p=\pm 3$

Example 12 If A is symmetric matrix and B is a skew-symmetric matrix such that $A+B=\begin{bmatrix}4 & 6\\ 10 & -2\end{bmatrix}$, then find $|AB|$.

Sol. Given, A is symmetric matrix and B is skew-symmetric matrix.

$\therefore \quad A'=A$ and $B'=-B$

Also given, $A+B=\begin{bmatrix}4 & 6\\ 10 & -2\end{bmatrix}$ ...(i)

$(A+B)'=\begin{bmatrix}4 & 6\\ 10 & -2\end{bmatrix}' \Rightarrow A'+B'=\begin{bmatrix}4 & 10\\ 6 & -2\end{bmatrix}$

$\Rightarrow \quad A-B=\begin{bmatrix}4 & 10\\ 6 & -2\end{bmatrix}$ ...(ii)

On adding Eqs. (i) and (ii), we get

$2A=\begin{bmatrix}4 & 6\\ 10 & -2\end{bmatrix}+\begin{bmatrix}4 & 10\\ 6 & -2\end{bmatrix}=\begin{bmatrix}8 & 16\\ 16 & -4\end{bmatrix}$

$\Rightarrow \quad A=\begin{bmatrix}4 & 8\\ 8 & -2\end{bmatrix}$

From Eq. (i), $B=\begin{bmatrix}4 & 6\\ 10 & -2\end{bmatrix}-\begin{bmatrix}4 & 8\\ 8 & -2\end{bmatrix}=\begin{bmatrix}0 & -2\\ 2 & 0\end{bmatrix}$

Now, $AB=\begin{bmatrix}4 & 8\\ 8 & -2\end{bmatrix}\begin{bmatrix}0 & -2\\ 2 & 0\end{bmatrix}=\begin{bmatrix}16 & -8\\ -4 & -16\end{bmatrix}$

$\therefore \quad |AB|=\begin{vmatrix}16 & -8\\ -4 & -16\end{vmatrix}=16(-16)-(-8)(-4)$

$=-256-32=-288$

Example 13 Find the area of the triangle, whose vertices are (3, 8), (– 4, 2) and (5, 1).

Sol. Given vertices of a triangle are (3, 8), (– 4, 2) and (5, 1).

Let $(x_1, y_1)=(3, 8)$, $(x_2, y_2)=(-4, 2)$ and $(x_3, y_3)=(5, 1)$

Then, area of triangle $=\frac{1}{2}\begin{vmatrix}x_1 & y_1 & 1\\ x_2 & y_2 & 1\\ x_3 & y_3 & 1\end{vmatrix}=\frac{1}{2}\begin{vmatrix}3 & 8 & 1\\ -4 & 2 & 1\\ 5 & 1 & 1\end{vmatrix}$

$=\frac{1}{2}\left[3\begin{vmatrix}2 & 1\\ 1 & 1\end{vmatrix}-8\begin{vmatrix}-4 & 1\\ 5 & 1\end{vmatrix}+1\begin{vmatrix}-4 & 2\\ 5 & 1\end{vmatrix}\right]$

$=\frac{1}{2}[3(2-1)-8(-4-5)+1(-4-10)]$

$=\frac{1}{2}[3+72-14]=\frac{61}{2}$ sq units

Example 14 If the area of a triangle with vertices (–3, 0), (3, 0) and (0, k) is 9 sq units, then find the value(s) of k.

Sol. Given, area of a triangle with vertices (–3, 0), (3, 0) and (0, k) is 9 sq units.

We have, $\frac{1}{2}\begin{vmatrix}-3 & 0 & 1\\ 3 & 0 & 1\\ 0 & k & 1\end{vmatrix}=\pm 9$

$\begin{vmatrix}-3 & 0 & 1\\ 3 & 0 & 1\\ 0 & k & 1\end{vmatrix}=\pm 18$

$\Rightarrow \quad -3(0-k)-0+1(3k-0)=\pm 18$

$\Rightarrow \quad 3k+3k=\pm 18$

$\Rightarrow \quad 6k=\pm 18$

$\therefore \quad k=\pm 3$

Example 15 **If the points (2, – 3), (λ, – 1) and (0, 4) are collinear, then find the value of λ.**

Sol. Given points (2, – 3), (λ, – 1) and (0, 4) are collinear.

So, area of triangle formed by these three points will be zero.

$$\therefore \quad \begin{vmatrix} 2 & -3 & 1 \\ \lambda & -1 & 1 \\ 0 & 4 & 1 \end{vmatrix} = 0$$

Expanding along R_1, we get

$$2(-1-4)+3(\lambda-0)+1(4\lambda)=0$$

$$\Rightarrow \quad -10+3\lambda+4\lambda=0 \Rightarrow 7\lambda-10=0$$

$$\Rightarrow \quad \lambda=\frac{10}{7}$$

Hence, the required value of λ is $\frac{10}{7}$.

Example 16 **Find the equation of line joining (2, 3) and (–1, 2) using determinants.**

Sol. Given vertices are (2, 3) and (–1, 2).

Let $(x_1, y_1) = (2, 3)$ and $(x_2, y_2) = (-1, 2)$

Then, equation of line $\begin{vmatrix} x & y & 1 \\ x_1 & y_1 & 1 \\ x_2 & y_2 & 1 \end{vmatrix} = 0$

$$\therefore \quad \begin{vmatrix} x & y & 1 \\ 2 & 3 & 1 \\ -1 & 2 & 1 \end{vmatrix} = 0$$

$$\Rightarrow \quad x(3-2)-y(2+1)+1(4+3)=0$$

$$\therefore \quad x-3y+7=0$$

Quick Test 1

1. Write the value of the following determinants.

(i) $|-91|$

(ii) $\begin{vmatrix} 12 & 1 \\ 4 & 3 \end{vmatrix}$

(iii) $\begin{vmatrix} p & p+1 \\ p-1 & p \end{vmatrix}$ CBSE 2014C

(iv) $\begin{vmatrix} \sec\theta & -\tan\theta \\ -\tan\theta & \sec\theta \end{vmatrix}$ NCERT

(v) $\begin{vmatrix} \cos 15^\circ & \sin 15^\circ \\ \sin 75^\circ & \cos 75^\circ \end{vmatrix}$ CBSE 2011

2. Find the value of x.

(i) $\begin{vmatrix} 2x & x+3 \\ 2(x+1) & x+1 \end{vmatrix} = \begin{vmatrix} 1 & 5 \\ 3 & 3 \end{vmatrix}$ CBSE 2013C

(ii) $\begin{vmatrix} x+1 & x-1 \\ x-3 & x+2 \end{vmatrix} = \begin{vmatrix} 4 & -1 \\ 1 & 3 \end{vmatrix}$ CBSE 2013

3. If $A = \begin{bmatrix} 1 & 1 & -2 \\ 2 & 1 & -3 \\ 5 & 4 & -9 \end{bmatrix}$, then find $|A|$.

4. If $A = \begin{bmatrix} 1 & 2 \\ 3 & -1 \end{bmatrix}$ and $B = \begin{bmatrix} 1 & 3 \\ -1 & 1 \end{bmatrix}$, then write the value of $|AB|$. CBSE 2015C

5. If A is a 3×3 matrix, $|A| \neq 0$ and $|3A| = k|A|$, then find the value of k. Competency Based Que, CBSE 2016, 14

6. If A is a square matrix satisfying $A \cdot A^T = I$, then write the value of $|A|$. CBSE 2019

7. Find the area of the triangle whose vertices are

(i) (–2, –3), (3, 2) and (–1, –8)

(ii) (0, 0), (6, 0) and (4, 3)

8. If area of a triangle is 35 sq units with vertices (2, – 6), (5, 4) and (k, 4), then find the values of k. NCERT

9. Using determinants, show that the points (5, 5), (– 5, 1) and (10, 7) are collinear?

10. Find the equation of the line joining (1, 2) and (3, 6) using determinants. NCERT

Answers

1. (i) – 91 (ii) 32 (iii) 1 (iv) 1 (v) 0

2. (i) 1 (ii) 2

3. 0 **4.** – 28 **5.** 27 **6.** ± 1

7. (i) 15 sq units (ii) 9 sq units

8. 12 and – 2

10. $y = 2x$

For Solutions, See QR Code on Pg. 103

4.3 Minors and Cofactors

Minor

Minor of an element a_{ij} of a determinant A is a determinant obtained by deleting the ith row and jth column in which element a_{ij} lies. Minor of the element a_{ij} is denoted by M_{ij}.

Cofactor

Cofactor of the element a_{ij} of a determinant, denoted by A_{ij} or C_{ij}, is defined as $A_{ij} = (-1)^{i+j} M_{ij}$, where M_{ij} is a minor of the element a_{ij}.

Value of Determinant in Terms of Cofactors

The value of determinant corresponding to a square matrix is equal to the sum of products of elements in a row (or in a column) with their corresponding cofactors.

e.g. $$\Delta = \begin{vmatrix} a_{11} & a_{12} & a_{13} \\ a_{21} & a_{22} & a_{23} \\ a_{31} & a_{32} & a_{33} \end{vmatrix}$$

$$= a_{11}C_{11} + a_{12}C_{12} + a_{13}C_{13}$$

or

$$= a_{11}C_{11} + a_{21}C_{21} + a_{31}C_{31}$$

TEACHER TIPS

(i) Minor of an element of a determinant of order $n(n \geq 2)$ is a determinant of order $(n-1)$.

(ii) If elements of a row (or column) are multiplied with cofactors of any other row (or column), then their sum is zero.

Example 1 **Find minors and cofactors of all the elements of the determinant $\begin{vmatrix} 2 & -1 \\ 3 & 5 \end{vmatrix}$.**

Sol. Minors of elements of determinant $\begin{vmatrix} 2 & -1 \\ 3 & 5 \end{vmatrix}$ are

$M_{11} = 5$, [minor of an element a_{11}]

$M_{12} = 3$, [minor of an element a_{12}]

$M_{21} = -1$, [minor of an element a_{21}]

and $M_{22} = 2$ [minor of an element a_{22}]

Cofactors of elements of determinant $\begin{vmatrix} 2 & -1 \\ 3 & 5 \end{vmatrix}$ are

$C_{11} = (-1)^{1+1} M_{11} = (-1)^2 \times 5 = 5,$

[cofactor of element a_{11}]

$C_{12} = (-1)^{1+2} M_{12} = (-1)^3 \times 3 = -3,$

[cofactor of element a_{12}]

$C_{21} = (-1)^{2+1} M_{21} = (-1)^3 \times (-1) = 1$

[cofactor of element a_{21}]

and $C_{22} = (-1)^{2+2} M_{22} = (-1)^4 \times 2 = 2$

[cofactor of element a_{22}]

Example 2 **Find the minors and cofactors of the elements of first row of determinant $\begin{vmatrix} 1 & 2 & 0 \\ 3 & 5 & -1 \\ 4 & 7 & 8 \end{vmatrix}$.**

Sol. The minors and cofactors of the elements of first row of the determinant $\begin{vmatrix} 1 & 2 & 0 \\ 3 & 5 & -1 \\ 4 & 7 & 8 \end{vmatrix}$ are given below.

$M_{11} = \begin{vmatrix} 5 & -1 \\ 7 & 8 \end{vmatrix} = 40 + 7 = 47,$ [minor of an element a_{11}]

$M_{12} = \begin{vmatrix} 3 & -1 \\ 4 & 8 \end{vmatrix} = 24 + 4 = 28$ [minor of an element a_{12}]

and $M_{13} = \begin{vmatrix} 3 & 5 \\ 4 & 7 \end{vmatrix} = 21 - 20 = 1.$ [minor of an element a_{13}]

$C_{11} = (-1)^{1+1} M_{11} = (-1)^2 \times 47 = 47,$

[cofactor of an element a_{11}]

$C_{12} = (-1)^{1+2} M_{12} = (-1)^3 \times 28 = -28$

[cofactor of an element a_{12}]

and $C_{13} = (-1)^{1+3} M_{13} = (-1)^4 \times 1 = 1.$

[cofactor of an element a_{13}]

Example 3 **If A_{ij} is the cofactor of the element a_{ij} of the determinant $\begin{vmatrix} 2 & -3 & 5 \\ 6 & 0 & 4 \\ 1 & 4 & -7 \end{vmatrix}$, then write the value of $a_{32} \cdot A_{32}$.**

Competency Based Que

Sol. Let $\Delta = \begin{vmatrix} 2 & -3 & 5 \\ 6 & 0 & 4 \\ 1 & 4 & -7 \end{vmatrix}$

Here, $a_{32} = 4$ [element of third row and second column]

Given, A_{ij} is the cofactor of the element a_{ij}.

$\therefore$ $A_{32} = (-1)^{3+2} \begin{vmatrix} 2 & 5 \\ 6 & 4 \end{vmatrix}$

[removing 3rd row and 2nd column]

$= -1(8 - 30) = 22$

$\therefore$ $a_{32} \cdot A_{32} = 4 \times 22 = 88$

Example 4 **Find minors and cofactors of the elements of the determinant $\begin{vmatrix} 2 & -3 & 5 \\ 6 & 0 & 4 \\ 1 & 5 & -7 \end{vmatrix}$ and verify that $a_{11}C_{31} + a_{12}C_{32} + a_{13}C_{33} = 0$.**

NCERT

Sol. Given determinant, $\begin{vmatrix} 2 & -3 & 5 \\ 6 & 0 & 4 \\ 1 & 5 & -7 \end{vmatrix}$

Now,

$$M_{11} = \begin{vmatrix} 0 & 4 \\ 5 & -7 \end{vmatrix} = 0 - 20 = -20,$$

$$M_{12} = \begin{vmatrix} 6 & 4 \\ 1 & -7 \end{vmatrix} = -42 - 4 = -46,$$

$$M_{13} = \begin{vmatrix} 6 & 0 \\ 1 & 5 \end{vmatrix} = 30 - 0 = 30,$$

$$M_{21} = \begin{vmatrix} -3 & 5 \\ 5 & -7 \end{vmatrix} = 21 - 25 = -4,$$

$$M_{22} = \begin{vmatrix} 2 & 5 \\ 1 & -7 \end{vmatrix} = -14 - 5 = -19,$$

$$M_{23} = \begin{vmatrix} 2 & -3 \\ 1 & 5 \end{vmatrix} = 10 + 3 = 13,$$

$$M_{31} = \begin{vmatrix} -3 & 5 \\ 0 & 4 \end{vmatrix} = -12 - 0 = -12,$$

$$M_{32} = \begin{vmatrix} 2 & 5 \\ 6 & 4 \end{vmatrix} = 8 - 30 = -22$$

and $M_{33} = \begin{vmatrix} 2 & -3 \\ 6 & 0 \end{vmatrix} = 0 + 18 = 18.$

$C_{11} = (-1)^{1+1} M_{11} = (-20) = -20;$

$[\because \text{cofactor } C_{ij} = (-1)^{i+j} M_{ij}]$

$C_{12} = (-1)^{1+2} M_{12} = -(-46) = 46,$

$C_{13} = (-1)^{1+3} M_{13} = (30) = 30,$

$C_{21} = (-1)^{2+1} M_{21} = -(-4) = 4,$

$C_{22} = (-1)^{2+2} M_{22} = (-19) = -19,$

$C_{23} = (-1)^{2+3} M_{23} = -(13) = -13,$

$C_{31} = (-1)^{3+1} M_{31} = (-12) = -12,$

$C_{32} = (-1)^{3+2} M_{32} = -(-22) = 22$

and $C_{33} = (-1)^{3+3} M_{33} = (18) = 18.$

We have, $a_{11} = 2,$

$a_{12} = -3,$

$a_{13} = 5,$

$C_{31} = -12,$

$C_{32} = 22$

and $C_{33} = 18.$

$\therefore\ a_{11}C_{31} + a_{12}C_{32} + a_{13}C_{33}$

$= (2)(-12) + (-3)(22) + (5)(18)$

$= -24 - 66 + 90 = 0$

Quick Test 2

1. Write minors and cofactors of elements of following determinants.

(i) $\begin{vmatrix} 2 & -4 \\ 0 & 3 \end{vmatrix}$ (ii) $\begin{vmatrix} a & c \\ b & d \end{vmatrix}$ *NCERT* (iii) $\begin{vmatrix} 2 & -1 & 3 \\ 4 & 2 & 5 \\ 0 & 4 & -1 \end{vmatrix}$

2. If A is a matrix of order 3×3, then find the number of minors in determinant A. *NCERT Exemplar*

3. Find the minors of the diagonal elements of the determinant $\begin{vmatrix} 1 & i & -i \\ -i & 1 & i \\ 1 & -i & i \end{vmatrix}$. *Competency Based Que*

4. In the following cases, find the determinant using cofactors of indicated row or column.

(i) $\begin{vmatrix} 5 & 3 & 8 \\ 2 & 0 & 1 \\ 1 & 2 & 3 \end{vmatrix}$, second row *NCERT*

(ii) $\begin{vmatrix} 0 & 1 & -1 \\ 4 & -3 & 4 \\ 3 & -3 & 4 \end{vmatrix}$, first column (iii) $\begin{vmatrix} 1 & x & y+z \\ 1 & y & z+x \\ 1 & z & x+y \end{vmatrix}$, third row

(iv) $\begin{vmatrix} \sqrt{23}+\sqrt{3} & \sqrt{5} & \sqrt{5} \\ \sqrt{15}+\sqrt{46} & 5 & \sqrt{10} \\ 3+\sqrt{115} & \sqrt{15} & 5 \end{vmatrix}$, third row

5. If $A = [a_{ij}]$ is a matrix of order 2×2 such that $|A| = -15$ and C_{ij} represents the cofactor of a_{ij}, then find $a_{21}C_{21} + a_{22}C_{22}$.

Competency Based Que, CBSE Sample Paper 2018

Answers

1. (i) $M_{11} = 3, M_{12} = 0, M_{21} = -4, M_{22} = 2,$
$C_{11} = 3,\ C_{12} = 0,\ C_{21} = 4$ and $C_{22} = 2$

(ii) $M_{11} = d,\ M_{12} = b,\ M_{21} = c$ and $M_{22} = a,$
$C_{11} = d,\ C_{12} = -b, C_{21} = -c$ and $C_{22} = a$

(iii) $M_{11} = -22, M_{12} = -4, M_{13} = 16,$
$M_{21} = -11, M_{22} = -2, M_{23} = 8,$
$M_{31} = -11, M_{32} = -2, M_{33} = 8,$
$C_{11} = -22, C_{12} = 4, C_{13} = 16,$
$C_{21} = 11, C_{22} = -2, C_{23} = -8,$
$C_{31} = -11, C_{32} = 2$ and $C_{33} = 8$

2. 9 **3.** $i-1,\ 2i,\ 0$

4. (i) 7 (ii) -1 (iii) 0 (iv) 0 **5.** -15

For Solutions, See QR Code on Pg. 103

4.4 Adjoint of a Matrix

The adjoint of a square matrix $A=[a_{ij}]_{n\times n}$ is defined as the transpose of the matrix formed by corresponding A_{ij} or C_{ij} cofactors of the elements of $|A|$ and it is denoted by **adj*A*.**

$$\text{adj } A=[A_{ij} \text{ or } C_{ij}]^T_{n\times n}$$

Let $A=\begin{bmatrix} a_{11} & a_{12} & a_{13} \\ a_{21} & a_{22} & a_{23} \\ a_{31} & a_{32} & a_{33}\end{bmatrix}$. Then, adj A

$$=\text{Transpose of}\begin{bmatrix} A_{11} & A_{12} & A_{13} \\ A_{21} & A_{22} & A_{23} \\ A_{31} & A_{32} & A_{33}\end{bmatrix}=\begin{bmatrix} A_{11} & A_{21} & A_{31} \\ A_{12} & A_{22} & A_{32} \\ A_{13} & A_{23} & A_{33}\end{bmatrix}$$

Here, A_{ij} is the corresponding cofactor of a_{ij}.

Properties of Adjoint of a Matrix

Suppose, A and B are two matrices of same order n. Then,

- $\text{adj }(A^T)=[\text{adj }(A)]^T$
- $\text{adj }(kA)=k^{n-1}(\text{adj } A), k\in R$
- $\text{adj }(AB)=[\text{adj }(B)][\text{adj }(A)]$
- $|\text{adj } A|=|A|^{n-1}$
- $|\text{adj }[\text{adj }(A)]|=|A|^{(n-1)^2}$
- $\text{adj }(\text{adj } A)=|A|^{n-2}\cdot A$

4.5 Singular and Non-singular Matrices

A square matrix A is said to be a **singular matrix**, if $|A|=0$ and if $|A|\neq 0$, then matrix A is said to be **non-singular matrix**.

4.6 Inverse of a Square Matrix

A non-singular square matrix is said to be invertible, if there exists a square matrix B such that

$$AB=BA=I$$

Here, I is an identity matrix and matrix B is called the inverse of A.

If A is a non-singular matrix (i.e. $|A|\neq 0$), then

$$A^{-1}=\frac{1}{|A|}\text{adj }(A).$$

e.g. For non-singular matrix $A=\begin{bmatrix} a_{11} & a_{12} & a_{13} \\ a_{21} & a_{22} & a_{23} \\ a_{31} & a_{32} & a_{33}\end{bmatrix}$,

the inverse is $A^{-1}=\dfrac{[A_{ij}]^T}{|A|}=\dfrac{1}{|A|}\begin{bmatrix} A_{11} & A_{21} & A_{31} \\ A_{12} & A_{22} & A_{32} \\ A_{13} & A_{23} & A_{33}\end{bmatrix}$,

where A_{ij} is the cofactor of element a_{ij}.

Properties of Inverse of a Matrix

Let A and B be two square invertible matrices of same order. Then,

- $(A^{-1})^{-1}=A$
- $(AB)^{-1}=B^{-1}A^{-1}$
- $(A^T)^{-1}=(A^{-1})^T$
- $|A^{-1}|=|A|^{-1}$
- $AA^{-1}=A^{-1}A=I$
- $(kA)^{-1}=\frac{1}{k}A^{-1}, k\neq 0$

Some Important Theorems

Theorem 1 If A is any given square matrix of order n, then $A(\text{adj } A)=(\text{adj } A)A=|A|I_n$, where I is an identity matrix of order n.

Theorem 2 If A and B are non-singular matrices of the same order, then AB and BA are also non-singular matrices of the same order.

Theorem 3 The determinant of the product of matrices is equal to the product of their respective determinants

i.e. $$|AB|=|A||B|,$$

where A and B are square matrices of the same order.

Theorem 4 A square matrix A is invertible, if and only if A is non-singular matrix.

TEACHER TIPS

(i) For a square matrix of order 2, given by $A=\begin{bmatrix} a_{11} & a_{12} \\ a_{21} & a_{22} \end{bmatrix}$, the adj (A) can also be obtained by interchaning a_{11} and a_{22} and by changing signs of a_{12} and a_{21} i.e. adj $(A)=\begin{bmatrix} a_{22} & -a_{12} \\ -a_{21} & a_{11} \end{bmatrix}$.

(ii) If A, B and C are invertible matrices of the same order, then $(ABC)^{-1}=C^{-1}B^{-1}A^{-1}$.

(iii) Only square matrices have adjoint or inverse.

Example 1 Find adj (A), if $A=\begin{bmatrix} 2 & -1 \\ 4 & 3 \end{bmatrix}$. *CBSE 2020*

Sol. We have, $A=\begin{bmatrix} 2 & -1 \\ 4 & 3 \end{bmatrix}$

Cofactors of $|A|$ are

$A_{11}=3, A_{12}=-4, A_{21}=1$ and $A_{22}=2$

$\therefore \quad \text{adj}(A)=\begin{bmatrix} A_{11} & A_{21} \\ A_{12} & A_{22} \end{bmatrix}=\begin{bmatrix} 3 & 1 \\ -4 & 2 \end{bmatrix}$

Example 2 Find the adjoint of the matrix

$$\begin{bmatrix} 1 & -1 & 2 \\ 2 & 3 & 5 \\ -2 & 0 & 1 \end{bmatrix}$$ *NCERT*

Sol. Let $A=\begin{bmatrix} 1 & -1 & 2 \\ 2 & 3 & 5 \\ -2 & 0 & 1 \end{bmatrix}$.

Cofactors of elements of first row of $|A|$ are

$$C_{11}=\begin{vmatrix} 3 & 5 \\ 0 & 1 \end{vmatrix}=3-0=3,$$

$$C_{12}=-\begin{vmatrix} 2 & 5 \\ -2 & 1 \end{vmatrix}=-(2+10)=-12$$

and $$C_{13}=\begin{vmatrix} 2 & 3 \\ -2 & 0 \end{vmatrix}=0-(-6)=6$$

Cofactors of elements of second row of $|A|$ are

$$C_{21}=-\begin{vmatrix} -1 & 2 \\ 0 & 1 \end{vmatrix}=-(-1-0)=1,$$

$$C_{22}=\begin{vmatrix} 1 & 2 \\ -2 & 1 \end{vmatrix}=1+4=5$$

and $$C_{23}=-\begin{vmatrix} 1 & -1 \\ -2 & 0 \end{vmatrix}=-(0-2)=2$$

Cofactors of elements of third row of $|A|$ are

$$C_{31}=\begin{vmatrix} -1 & 2 \\ 3 & 5 \end{vmatrix}=-5-6=-11,$$

$$C_{32}=-\begin{vmatrix} 1 & 2 \\ 2 & 5 \end{vmatrix}=-(5-4)=-1$$

and $$C_{33}=\begin{vmatrix} 1 & -1 \\ 2 & 3 \end{vmatrix}=3+2=5$$

Hence, $$\text{adj } A=\begin{bmatrix} C_{11} & C_{12} & C_{13} \\ C_{21} & C_{22} & C_{23} \\ C_{31} & C_{32} & C_{33} \end{bmatrix}^T$$

$$=\begin{bmatrix} 3 & -12 & 6 \\ 1 & 5 & 2 \\ -11 & -1 & 5 \end{bmatrix}^T=\begin{bmatrix} 3 & 1 & -11 \\ -12 & 5 & -1 \\ 6 & 2 & 5 \end{bmatrix}$$

Example 3 Given that A is a square matrix of order 3×3 and $|A|=-4$. Find $|\text{adj } A|$. *Competency Based Que*

Sol. We know that $|\text{adj } A|=|A|^{n-1}$

$=(-4)^{3-1} \quad [\because |A|=-4, n=3]$

$=(-4)^2=16$

Example 4 If for any 2×2 square matrix A, $A(\text{adj } A)=\begin{bmatrix} -7 & 0 \\ 0 & -7 \end{bmatrix}$, then write the value of $|A|$.

Sol. Given, $A(\text{adj } A)=\begin{bmatrix} -7 & 0 \\ 0 & -7 \end{bmatrix}$

$\therefore \quad |A(\text{adj } A)|=\begin{vmatrix} -7 & 0 \\ 0 & -7 \end{vmatrix}=49-0=49$

$\Rightarrow \quad |A||\text{adj } A|=49 \quad [\because |AB|=|A||B|]$

$\Rightarrow \quad |A||A|^{2-1}=49 \quad [\because |\text{adj } A|=|A|^{n-1}]$

$\Rightarrow \quad |A||A|=49$

$\therefore \quad |A|=\pm 7$

Example 5 Verify $A(\text{adj } A)=(\text{adj } A)A=|A|I$ for matrix

$$A=\begin{bmatrix} 1 & -1 & 2 \\ 3 & 0 & -2 \\ 1 & 0 & 3 \end{bmatrix}.$$ *CBSE Sample Paper 2017*

Sol. Given, $A=\begin{bmatrix} 1 & -1 & 2 \\ 3 & 0 & -2 \\ 1 & 0 & 3 \end{bmatrix}$

Here, $|A|=\begin{vmatrix} 1 & -1 & 2 \\ 3 & 0 & -2 \\ 1 & 0 & 3 \end{vmatrix}$

$=1(0+0)+1(9+2)+2(0-0)=11$

Now, $|A|I=11I=\begin{bmatrix} 11 & 0 & 0 \\ 0 & 11 & 0 \\ 0 & 0 & 11 \end{bmatrix}$ ...(i)

Cofactors of $|A|$,

$$C_{11}=(-1)^{1+1}\begin{vmatrix} 0 & -2 \\ 0 & 3 \end{vmatrix}=0,$$

$$C_{12}=(-1)^{1+2}\begin{vmatrix} 3 & -2 \\ 1 & 3 \end{vmatrix}=-(9+2)=-11,$$

$$C_{13}=(-1)^{1+3}\begin{vmatrix} 3 & 0 \\ 1 & 0 \end{vmatrix}=0,$$

$$C_{21} = (-1)^{2+1}\begin{vmatrix} -1 & 2 \\ 0 & 3 \end{vmatrix} = -(-3-0) = 3,$$

$$C_{22} = (-1)^{2+2}\begin{vmatrix} 1 & 2 \\ 1 & 3 \end{vmatrix} = (3-2) = 1,$$

$$C_{23} = (-1)^{2+3}\begin{vmatrix} 1 & -1 \\ 1 & 0 \end{vmatrix} = -(0+1) = -1,$$

$$C_{31} = (-1)^{3+1}\begin{vmatrix} -1 & 2 \\ 0 & -2 \end{vmatrix} = (2-0) = 2,$$

$$C_{32} = (-1)^{3+2}\begin{vmatrix} 1 & 2 \\ 3 & -2 \end{vmatrix} = -(-2-6) = 8$$

and $$C_{33} = (-1)^{3+3}\begin{vmatrix} 1 & -1 \\ 3 & 0 \end{vmatrix} = (0+3) = 3$$

$$\text{adj } A = \begin{bmatrix} C_{11} & C_{21} & C_{31} \\ C_{12} & C_{22} & C_{32} \\ C_{13} & C_{23} & C_{33} \end{bmatrix} = \begin{bmatrix} 0 & 3 & 2 \\ -11 & 1 & 8 \\ 0 & -1 & 3 \end{bmatrix}$$

Now, $$A(\text{adj } A) = \begin{bmatrix} 1 & -1 & 2 \\ 3 & 0 & -2 \\ 1 & 0 & 3 \end{bmatrix}\begin{bmatrix} 0 & 3 & 2 \\ -11 & 1 & 8 \\ 0 & -1 & 3 \end{bmatrix}$$

$$= \begin{bmatrix} 0+11+0 & 3-1-2 & 2-8+6 \\ 0+0+0 & 9+0+2 & 6+0-6 \\ 0+0+0 & 3+0-3 & 2+0+9 \end{bmatrix}$$

$$= \begin{bmatrix} 11 & 0 & 0 \\ 0 & 11 & 0 \\ 0 & 0 & 11 \end{bmatrix}$$

and $$(\text{adj } A)\,A = \begin{bmatrix} 0 & 3 & 2 \\ -11 & 1 & 8 \\ 0 & -1 & 3 \end{bmatrix}\begin{bmatrix} 1 & -1 & 2 \\ 3 & 0 & -2 \\ 1 & 0 & 3 \end{bmatrix}$$

$$= \begin{bmatrix} 0+9+2 & 0+0+0 & 0-6+6 \\ -11+3+8 & 11+0+0 & -22-2+24 \\ 0-3+3 & 0+0+0 & 0+2+9 \end{bmatrix}$$

$$= \begin{bmatrix} 11 & 0 & 0 \\ 0 & 11 & 0 \\ 0 & 0 & 11 \end{bmatrix}$$

Thus, $A(\text{adj } A) = (\text{adj } A)A = |A|\,I$ **Hence proved.**

Example 6 **In the interval $\pi/2 < x < \pi$, find the value of x for which the matrix $\begin{bmatrix} 2\sin x & 3 \\ 1 & 2\sin x \end{bmatrix}$ is singular.**

Competency Based Que

Sol. Let $A = \begin{bmatrix} 2\sin x & 3 \\ 1 & 2\sin x \end{bmatrix}$

$\because$ A is a singular matrix.

$\therefore$ $|A| = 0 \Rightarrow \begin{vmatrix} 2\sin x & 3 \\ 1 & 2\sin x \end{vmatrix} = 0$

$\Rightarrow$ $4\sin^2 x - 3 = 0$

$\Rightarrow$ $\sin^2 x = \dfrac{3}{4}$

$\Rightarrow$ $\sin x = \dfrac{\sqrt{3}}{2}$ $\left[\text{taking positive square root because } \dfrac{\pi}{2} < x < \pi\right]$

$\therefore$ $x = \dfrac{2\pi}{3}$

Example 7 **For what value of x, the matrix $A = \begin{bmatrix} 1 & -2 & 3 \\ 1 & 2 & 1 \\ x & 2 & 3 \end{bmatrix}$ is singular?**

CBSE 2023

Sol. We know that A will be singular, iff $|A| = 0$

$\Rightarrow$ $\begin{vmatrix} 1 & -2 & 3 \\ 1 & 2 & 1 \\ x & 2 & 3 \end{vmatrix} = 0$

$\Rightarrow 1[6-2] - (-2)[3-x] + 3[2-2x] = 0$

$\Rightarrow$ $4 + 2(3-x) + 3(2-2x) = 0$

$\Rightarrow$ $4 + 6 - 2x + 6 - 6x = 0$

$\Rightarrow$ $16 - 8x = 0$

$\therefore$ $x = 2$

Example 8 **For $A = \begin{bmatrix} 3 & -4 \\ 1 & -1 \end{bmatrix}$, write A^{-1}.**

CBSE 2020

Sol. Given, $A = \begin{bmatrix} 3 & -4 \\ 1 & -1 \end{bmatrix}$

Then, $|A| = \begin{vmatrix} 3 & -4 \\ 1 & -1 \end{vmatrix} = -3 + 4 = 1 \neq 0$

So, A is not singular matrix and A^{-1} exists.

Now, cofactors of each element of $|A|$ are

$A_{11} = -1,\ A_{12} = -(1) = -1,\ A_{21} = -(-4) = 4$

and $A_{22} = 3$

Now, $\text{adj } A = \begin{bmatrix} -1 & 4 \\ -1 & 3 \end{bmatrix}$

$\therefore$ $A^{-1} = \dfrac{1}{|A|}\text{adj }(A) = \dfrac{1}{1}\begin{bmatrix} -1 & 4 \\ -1 & 3 \end{bmatrix} = \begin{bmatrix} -1 & 4 \\ -1 & 3 \end{bmatrix}$

Example 9 **Find the values of x, y and z, if $A = \begin{bmatrix} 0 & 2y & z \\ x & y & -z \\ x & -y & z \end{bmatrix}$ satisfies $A' = A^{-1}$.**

CBSE Sample Paper 2017

Sol. Given, $A = \begin{bmatrix} 0 & 2y & z \\ x & y & -z \\ x & -y & z \end{bmatrix}$

Then, $A' = \begin{bmatrix} 0 & x & x \\ 2y & y & -y \\ z & -z & z \end{bmatrix}$

Also, $A' = A^{-1}$

$\Rightarrow A'A = A^{-1}A = I$

Thus, $A'A = I$

$$\Rightarrow \begin{bmatrix} 0 & x & x \\ 2y & y & -y \\ z & -z & z \end{bmatrix}\begin{bmatrix} 0 & 2y & z \\ x & y & -z \\ x & -y & z \end{bmatrix} = \begin{bmatrix} 1 & 0 & 0 \\ 0 & 1 & 0 \\ 0 & 0 & 1 \end{bmatrix}$$

$$\Rightarrow \begin{bmatrix} 0+x^2+x^2 & 0+xy-xy & 0-xz+xz \\ 0+xy-xy & 4y^2+y^2+y^2 & 2yz-yz-yz \\ 0-zx+zx & 2yz-yz-yz & z^2+z^2+z^2 \end{bmatrix} = \begin{bmatrix} 1 & 0 & 0 \\ 0 & 1 & 0 \\ 0 & 0 & 1 \end{bmatrix}$$

$$\Rightarrow \begin{bmatrix} 2x^2 & 0 & 0 \\ 0 & 6y^2 & 0 \\ 0 & 0 & 3z^2 \end{bmatrix} = \begin{bmatrix} 1 & 0 & 0 \\ 0 & 1 & 0 \\ 0 & 0 & 1 \end{bmatrix}$$

On comparing both sides, we get

$$2x^2 = 1, 6y^2 = 1 \text{ and } 3z^2 = 1$$

$$\therefore \quad x = \pm\frac{1}{\sqrt{2}}, y = \pm\frac{1}{\sqrt{6}} \text{ and } z = \pm\frac{1}{\sqrt{3}}$$

Example 10 **If $A = \begin{bmatrix} 2 & 3 \\ 5 & -2 \end{bmatrix}$ be such that $A^{-1} = kA$, then find the value of k.** *CBSE 2025, 18C, 11*

Sol. We have, $A = \begin{bmatrix} 2 & 3 \\ 5 & -2 \end{bmatrix}$

Clearly, adj $A = \begin{bmatrix} -2 & -3 \\ -5 & 2 \end{bmatrix}$

and $|A| = \begin{vmatrix} 2 & 3 \\ 5 & -2 \end{vmatrix} = -4 - 15 = -19$

$$\therefore \quad A^{-1} = \frac{1}{|A|}\text{adj } A = \frac{1}{(-19)}\begin{bmatrix} -2 & -3 \\ -5 & 2 \end{bmatrix}$$

$$= \frac{1}{19}\begin{bmatrix} 2 & 3 \\ 5 & -2 \end{bmatrix} = \frac{1}{19}A$$

On comparing with $A^{-1} = kA$ (given), we get

$$k = \frac{1}{19}$$

Example 11 **Find the inverse of the matrix $\begin{bmatrix} -3 & 2 \\ 5 & -3 \end{bmatrix}$. Hence, find the matrix P satisfying the matrix equation $P\begin{bmatrix} -3 & 2 \\ 5 & -3 \end{bmatrix} = \begin{bmatrix} 1 & 2 \\ 2 & -1 \end{bmatrix}$.** *CBSE Sample Paper 2018*

Sol. Let $A = \begin{bmatrix} -3 & 2 \\ 5 & -3 \end{bmatrix}$ ...(i)

We know that

$$A^{-1} = \frac{1}{|A|}\begin{bmatrix} C_{11} & C_{12} \\ C_{21} & C_{22} \end{bmatrix}^T$$

Now, $|A| = \begin{vmatrix} -3 & 2 \\ 5 & -3 \end{vmatrix}$

$= (-3)(-3) - (2)(5)$

$= 9 - 10 = -1$

$\therefore$ $|A| = -1 \neq 0$, which shows that inverse of matrix exists.

$C_{11} = (-1)^{1+1}a_{22} = (-1)^2 a_{22} = a_{22} = -3,$

$C_{12} = (-1)^{1+2}a_{21} = (-1)^3 a_{21} = -5,$

$C_{21} = (-1)^{2+1}a_{12} = (-1)^3 a_{12} = -2$

and $C_{22} = (-1)^{2+2}a_{11} = (-1)^4 a_{11} = -3$

$$\therefore \quad A^{-1} = \frac{1}{(-1)}\begin{bmatrix} -3 & -5 \\ -2 & -3 \end{bmatrix}^T = \frac{1}{(-1)}\begin{bmatrix} -3 & -2 \\ -5 & -3 \end{bmatrix} = \begin{bmatrix} 3 & 2 \\ 5 & 3 \end{bmatrix}$$

Now, $P\begin{bmatrix} -3 & 2 \\ 5 & -3 \end{bmatrix} = \begin{bmatrix} 1 & 2 \\ 2 & -1 \end{bmatrix}$ [given]

$\Rightarrow \quad PA = \begin{bmatrix} 1 & 2 \\ 2 & -1 \end{bmatrix}$ [from Eq. (i)]

On post-multiplying both sides by A^{-1}, we get

$P = \begin{bmatrix} 1 & 2 \\ 2 & -1 \end{bmatrix}\begin{bmatrix} 3 & 2 \\ 5 & 3 \end{bmatrix}$ [$\because AA^{-1} = I$ and $PI = P$]

$$= \begin{bmatrix} 3+10 & 2+6 \\ 6-5 & 4-3 \end{bmatrix} = \begin{bmatrix} 13 & 8 \\ 1 & 1 \end{bmatrix}$$

Example 12 **If $A = \begin{bmatrix} 2 & 3 \\ 1 & -4 \end{bmatrix}$ and $B = \begin{bmatrix} 1 & -2 \\ -1 & 3 \end{bmatrix}$, then verify that $(AB)^{-1} = B^{-1}A^{-1}$.** *CBSE 2015C*

Sol. Given, $A = \begin{bmatrix} 2 & 3 \\ 1 & -4 \end{bmatrix}$ and $B = \begin{bmatrix} 1 & -2 \\ -1 & 3 \end{bmatrix}$

$$\therefore \quad AB = \begin{bmatrix} 2 & 3 \\ 1 & -4 \end{bmatrix}\begin{bmatrix} 1 & -2 \\ -1 & 3 \end{bmatrix}$$

$$= \begin{bmatrix} 2-3 & -4+9 \\ 1+4 & -2-12 \end{bmatrix} = \begin{bmatrix} -1 & 5 \\ 5 & -14 \end{bmatrix}$$

Now, $|A| = \begin{vmatrix} 2 & 3 \\ 1 & -4 \end{vmatrix} = -8 - 3 = -11 \neq 0,$

$|B| = \begin{vmatrix} 1 & -2 \\ -1 & 3 \end{vmatrix} = 3 - 2 = 1 \neq 0$

and $|AB| = \begin{vmatrix} -1 & 5 \\ 5 & -14 \end{vmatrix} = 14 - 25 = -11 \neq 0$

Thus, A, B and AB are non-singular matrices, so their inverse exist.

Now, adj$(A) = \begin{bmatrix} -4 & -3 \\ -1 & 2 \end{bmatrix}$, $\left[\because \text{adj}\begin{bmatrix} a & b \\ c & d \end{bmatrix} = \begin{bmatrix} d & -b \\ -c & a \end{bmatrix}\right]$

adj$(B) = \begin{bmatrix} 3 & 2 \\ 1 & 1 \end{bmatrix}$

and adj$(AB) = \begin{bmatrix} -14 & -5 \\ -5 & -1 \end{bmatrix}$

$$\therefore \quad (AB)^{-1} = \frac{1}{|AB|}\text{adj}(AB) = \frac{1}{-11}\begin{bmatrix} -14 & -5 \\ -5 & -1 \end{bmatrix}$$

$$= \frac{1}{11}\begin{bmatrix} 14 & 5 \\ 5 & 1 \end{bmatrix} \quad \text{...(i)}$$

$$A^{-1} = \frac{1}{|A|}\text{adj}(A) = \frac{1}{-11}\begin{bmatrix} -4 & -3 \\ -1 & 2 \end{bmatrix} = \frac{1}{11}\begin{bmatrix} 4 & 3 \\ 1 & -2 \end{bmatrix}$$

and $B^{-1} = \frac{1}{|B|}\text{adj}(B) = \frac{1}{1}\begin{bmatrix} 3 & 2 \\ 1 & 1 \end{bmatrix} = \begin{bmatrix} 3 & 2 \\ 1 & 1 \end{bmatrix}$

Now, $B^{-1}A^{-1} = \begin{bmatrix} 3 & 2 \\ 1 & 1 \end{bmatrix}\frac{1}{11}\begin{bmatrix} 4 & 3 \\ 1 & -2 \end{bmatrix}$

$$= \frac{1}{11}\begin{bmatrix} 3 & 2 \\ 1 & 1 \end{bmatrix}\begin{bmatrix} 4 & 3 \\ 1 & -2 \end{bmatrix} = \frac{1}{11}\begin{bmatrix} 12+2 & 9-4 \\ 4+1 & 3-2 \end{bmatrix} = \frac{1}{11}\begin{bmatrix} 14 & 5 \\ 5 & 1 \end{bmatrix}$$

$= (AB)^{-1}$ [from Eq. (i)]

Hence, $(AB)^{-1} = B^{-1}A^{-1}$.

Example 13 If $A = \begin{bmatrix} 1 & 2 & -2 \\ -1 & 3 & 0 \\ 0 & -2 & 1 \end{bmatrix}$ and $B^{-1} = \begin{bmatrix} 3 & -1 & 1 \\ -15 & 6 & -5 \\ 5 & -2 & 2 \end{bmatrix}$, find $(AB)^{-1}$.

CBSE 2023

Sol. We know that $(AB)^{-1} = B^{-1}A^{-1}$

Here, $A = \begin{bmatrix} 1 & 2 & -2 \\ -1 & 3 & 0 \\ 0 & -2 & 1 \end{bmatrix}$

$$|A| = 1(3+0) - 2(-1-0) - 2(2-0) = 3 + 2 - 4 = 1 \neq 0$$

So, A^{-1} exists.

$\therefore$ Cofactors of elements of $|A|$ are

$$A_{11} = (-1)^{1+1}\begin{vmatrix} 3 & 0 \\ -2 & 1 \end{vmatrix} = (3-0) = 3,$$

$$A_{12} = (-1)^{1+2}\begin{vmatrix} -1 & 0 \\ 0 & 1 \end{vmatrix} = -(-1-0) = 1,$$

$$A_{13} = (-1)^{1+3}\begin{vmatrix} -1 & 3 \\ 0 & -2 \end{vmatrix} = (2-0) = 2,$$

$$A_{21} = (-1)^{2+1}\begin{vmatrix} 2 & -2 \\ -2 & 1 \end{vmatrix} = -(2-4) = 2,$$

$$A_{22} = (-1)^{2+2}\begin{vmatrix} 1 & -2 \\ 0 & 1 \end{vmatrix} = 1 - 0 = 1,$$

$$A_{23} = (-1)^{2+3}\begin{vmatrix} 1 & 2 \\ 0 & -2 \end{vmatrix} = -(-2-0) = 2,$$

$$A_{31} = (-1)^{3+1}\begin{vmatrix} 2 & -2 \\ 3 & 0 \end{vmatrix} = (0+6) = 6,$$

$$A_{32} = (-1)^{3+2}\begin{vmatrix} 1 & -2 \\ -1 & 0 \end{vmatrix} = -(0-2) = 2$$

and $A_{33} = (-1)^{3+3}\begin{vmatrix} 1 & 2 \\ -1 & 3 \end{vmatrix} = (3+2) = 5$

$$\text{adj } A = \begin{bmatrix} A_{11} & A_{12} & A_{13} \\ A_{21} & A_{22} & A_{23} \\ A_{31} & A_{32} & A_{33} \end{bmatrix}^T = \begin{bmatrix} 3 & 1 & 2 \\ 2 & 1 & 2 \\ 6 & 2 & 5 \end{bmatrix}^T = \begin{bmatrix} 3 & 2 & 6 \\ 1 & 1 & 2 \\ 2 & 2 & 5 \end{bmatrix}$$

$\therefore \quad A^{-1} = \frac{1}{|A|}(\text{adj } A)$

$$= \frac{1}{1}\begin{bmatrix} 3 & 2 & 6 \\ 1 & 1 & 2 \\ 2 & 2 & 5 \end{bmatrix} = \begin{bmatrix} 3 & 2 & 6 \\ 1 & 1 & 2 \\ 2 & 2 & 5 \end{bmatrix}$$

Now, $(AB)^{-1} = B^{-1}A^{-1}$

$$= \begin{bmatrix} 3 & -1 & 1 \\ -15 & 6 & -5 \\ 5 & -2 & 2 \end{bmatrix}\begin{bmatrix} 3 & 2 & 6 \\ 1 & 1 & 2 \\ 2 & 2 & 5 \end{bmatrix}$$

$$= \begin{bmatrix} 9-1+2 & 6-1+2 & 18-2+5 \\ -45+6-10 & -30+6-10 & -90+12-25 \\ 15-2+4 & 10-2+4 & 30-4+10 \end{bmatrix}$$

$$= \begin{bmatrix} 10 & 7 & 21 \\ -49 & -34 & -103 \\ 17 & 12 & 36 \end{bmatrix}$$

Example 14 Show that for the matrix $A = \begin{bmatrix} 1 & 1 & 1 \\ 1 & 2 & -3 \\ 2 & -1 & 3 \end{bmatrix}$, $A^3 - 6A^2 + 5A + 11I = O$.

Hence, find A^{-1}.

CBSE 2019

Sol. We have, $A = \begin{bmatrix} 1 & 1 & 1 \\ 1 & 2 & -3 \\ 2 & -1 & 3 \end{bmatrix}$

$$\therefore \quad A^2 = AA = \begin{bmatrix} 1 & 1 & 1 \\ 1 & 2 & -3 \\ 2 & -1 & 3 \end{bmatrix}\begin{bmatrix} 1 & 1 & 1 \\ 1 & 2 & -3 \\ 2 & -1 & 3 \end{bmatrix} = \begin{bmatrix} 4 & 2 & 1 \\ -3 & 8 & -14 \\ 7 & -3 & 14 \end{bmatrix}$$

and $A^3 = A^2A = \begin{bmatrix} 4 & 2 & 1 \\ -3 & 8 & -14 \\ 7 & -3 & 14 \end{bmatrix}\begin{bmatrix} 1 & 1 & 1 \\ 1 & 2 & -3 \\ 2 & -1 & 3 \end{bmatrix}$

$$= \begin{bmatrix} 8 & 7 & 1 \\ -23 & 27 & -69 \\ 32 & -13 & 58 \end{bmatrix}$$

$\therefore\ A^3 - 6A^2 + 5A + 11I$

$$= \begin{bmatrix} 8 & 7 & 1 \\ -23 & 27 & -69 \\ 32 & -13 & 58 \end{bmatrix} - 6\begin{bmatrix} 4 & 2 & 1 \\ -3 & 8 & -14 \\ 7 & -3 & 14 \end{bmatrix} + 5\begin{bmatrix} 1 & 1 & 1 \\ 1 & 2 & -3 \\ 2 & -1 & 3 \end{bmatrix} + 11\begin{bmatrix} 1 & 0 & 0 \\ 0 & 1 & 0 \\ 0 & 0 & 1 \end{bmatrix}$$

$$= \begin{bmatrix} 8-24+5+11 & 7-12+5+0 & 1-6+5+0 \\ -23+18+5+0 & 27-48+10+11 & -69+84-15+0 \\ 32-42+10+0 & -13+18-5+0 & 58-84+15+11 \end{bmatrix}$$

$$= \begin{bmatrix} 0 & 0 & 0 \\ 0 & 0 & 0 \\ 0 & 0 & 0 \end{bmatrix} = O$$

Now, $A^3 - 6A^2 + 5A + 11I = O$

Now, on multiplying both sides by A^{-1}, we get

$A^{-1}(A^3 - 6A^2 + 5A + 11I) = A^{-1}O$

$\Rightarrow A^2 - 6A + 5I + 11A^{-1} = O$

$\Rightarrow 11A^{-1} = -A^2 + 6A - 5I$

$$\Rightarrow 11A^{-1} = -\begin{bmatrix} 4 & 2 & 1 \\ -3 & 8 & -14 \\ 7 & -3 & 14 \end{bmatrix} + 6\begin{bmatrix} 1 & 1 & 1 \\ 1 & 2 & -3 \\ 2 & -1 & 3 \end{bmatrix} - 5\begin{bmatrix} 1 & 0 & 0 \\ 0 & 1 & 0 \\ 0 & 0 & 1 \end{bmatrix}$$

$$\Rightarrow 11A^{-1} = \begin{bmatrix} -4+6-5 & -2+6+0 & -1+6+0 \\ 3+6+0 & -8+12-5 & 14-18+0 \\ -7+12+0 & 3-6+0 & -14+18-5 \end{bmatrix}$$

$$= \begin{bmatrix} -3 & 4 & 5 \\ 9 & -1 & -4 \\ 5 & -3 & -1 \end{bmatrix}$$

$$\therefore\ A^{-1} = \frac{1}{11}\begin{bmatrix} -3 & 4 & 5 \\ 9 & -1 & -4 \\ 5 & -3 & -1 \end{bmatrix}$$

Quick Test 3

1. Find the adjoint of the following matrices.

(i) $\begin{bmatrix} 3 & -5 \\ -1 & 2 \end{bmatrix}$ (ii) $\begin{bmatrix} 1 & 2 & 5 \\ 2 & 3 & 1 \\ -1 & 1 & 1 \end{bmatrix}$ (iii) $\begin{bmatrix} 4 & 5 & 3 \\ 1 & 0 & 6 \\ 2 & 7 & 9 \end{bmatrix}$

2. Find the adjoint of the following matrices and verify that $A(\text{adj}A) = |A|I$.

(i) $A = \begin{bmatrix} 1 & 2 \\ 3 & 4 \end{bmatrix}$ (ii) $A = \begin{bmatrix} -1 & -2 & -2 \\ 2 & 1 & -2 \\ 2 & -2 & 1 \end{bmatrix}$

3. If A is matrix of order 3 and $|A| = 4$, then find the value of $|\text{adj}A|$.

4. If A is a square matrix of order 3 such that $|\text{adj}(A)| = 64$, then find $|A|$. *CBSE 2013C*

5. For what value of λ, the matrix $\begin{bmatrix} 1 & \lambda & 0 \\ 3 & -1 & 2 \\ 4 & 1 & 5 \end{bmatrix}$ is singular?

6. Find the inverse of the following matrices, if exists.

(i) $\begin{bmatrix} 2 & -2 \\ 4 & 3 \end{bmatrix}$ (ii) $\begin{bmatrix} 1 & 0 & 0 \\ 0 & \cos\alpha & \sin\alpha \\ 0 & \sin\alpha & -\cos\alpha \end{bmatrix}$

7. If A is a matrix of order 3×3, then show that $(A^2)^{-1} = (A^{-1})^2$. *NCERT Exemplar*

8. Given $A = \begin{bmatrix} 2 & -3 \\ -4 & 7 \end{bmatrix}$, compute A^{-1} and show that $2A^{-1} = 9I - A$. *CBSE 2018*

9. If $A = \begin{bmatrix} 1 & 2 & -2 \\ -1 & 3 & 0 \\ 0 & -2 & 1 \end{bmatrix}$ and $B^{-1} = \begin{bmatrix} 3 & -1 & 1 \\ -15 & 6 & -5 \\ 5 & -2 & 2 \end{bmatrix}$, then find $(BA)^{-1}$.

10. If $A = \begin{bmatrix} 1 & 3 & 2 \\ 2 & 0 & -1 \\ 1 & 2 & 3 \end{bmatrix}$, then show that $A^3 - 4A^2 - 3A + 11I = O$. Hence, find A^{-1}. *CBSE 2020*

Answers

1. (i) $\begin{bmatrix} 2 & 5 \\ 1 & 3 \end{bmatrix}$ (ii) $\begin{bmatrix} 2 & 3 & -13 \\ -3 & 6 & 9 \\ 5 & -3 & -1 \end{bmatrix}$ (iii) $\begin{bmatrix} -42 & -24 & 30 \\ 3 & 30 & -21 \\ 7 & -18 & -5 \end{bmatrix}$

2. (i) $\begin{bmatrix} 4 & -2 \\ -3 & 1 \end{bmatrix}$ (ii) $\begin{bmatrix} -3 & 6 & 6 \\ -6 & 3 & -6 \\ -6 & -6 & 3 \end{bmatrix}$

3. 16 **4.** ± 8 **5.** -1

6. (i) $\frac{1}{14}\begin{bmatrix} 3 & 2 \\ -4 & 2 \end{bmatrix}$ (ii) $\begin{bmatrix} 1 & 0 & 0 \\ 0 & \cos\alpha & \sin\alpha \\ 0 & \sin\alpha & -\cos\alpha \end{bmatrix}$

8. $\frac{1}{2}\begin{bmatrix} 7 & 3 \\ 4 & 2 \end{bmatrix}$ **9.** $\begin{bmatrix} 9 & -3 & 5 \\ -2 & 1 & 0 \\ 1 & 0 & 2 \end{bmatrix}$ **10.** $\frac{1}{11}\begin{bmatrix} -2 & 5 & 3 \\ 7 & -1 & -5 \\ -4 & -1 & 6 \end{bmatrix}$

For Solutions, See QR Code on Pg. 103

4.7 Consistent and Inconsistent System

A system of equations is said to be **consistent**, if its solution (one or more) exists.

A system of equations is said to be **inconsistent**, if its solution does not exist i.e. no solution exist.

Here, we will study only those system of linear equations, which have unique solution only.

4.8 Solution of System of Linear Equations using Inverse of a Matrix

Let the system of linear equations be

$$a_1x + b_1y + c_1z = d_1,$$
$$a_2x + b_2y + c_2z = d_2$$
and $$a_3x + b_3y + c_3z = d_3.$$

Now, let $A = \begin{bmatrix} a_1 & b_1 & c_1 \\ a_2 & b_2 & c_2 \\ a_3 & b_3 & c_3 \end{bmatrix}, X = \begin{bmatrix} x \\ y \\ z \end{bmatrix}$ and $B = \begin{bmatrix} d_1 \\ d_2 \\ d_3 \end{bmatrix}$.

Then, the matrix representation of above system of linear equations is

$$AX = B \qquad \text{...(i)}$$

Now, some cases arise and discuss with the help of following flow chart

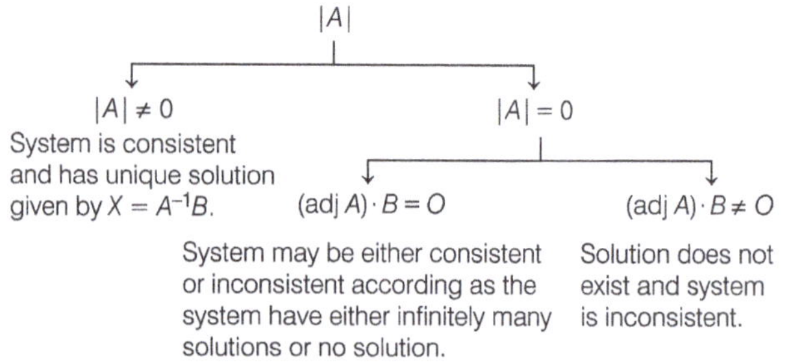

Example 1 **Show that the following system of equations is consistent.**

$$2x - y + 3z = 5, 3x + 2y + z = 7 \text{ and } 4x + 5y - 5z = 9.$$

Sol. Given equations can be written in matrix form as

$$AX = B,$$

where $A = \begin{bmatrix} 2 & -1 & 3 \\ 3 & 2 & 1 \\ 4 & 5 & -5 \end{bmatrix}, X = \begin{bmatrix} x \\ y \\ z \end{bmatrix}$ and $B = \begin{bmatrix} 5 \\ 7 \\ 9 \end{bmatrix}$

Now, $|A| = \begin{vmatrix} 2 & -1 & 3 \\ 3 & 2 & 1 \\ 4 & 5 & -5 \end{vmatrix}$

$$= 2(-10-5) + 1(-15-4) + 3(15-8)$$
$$= -30 - 19 + 21 = -28 \neq 0$$

Since, A is non-singular, so A^{-1} exists.

Hence, the given system of equations is consistent.

Example 2 **For what values of k, the system of linear equations**

$$x + y + z = 2$$
$$2x + y - z = 3$$
$$3x + 2y + kz = 4$$

has a unique solution? CBSE 2016

Sol. Given, system of linear equations is

$$x + y + z = 2$$
$$2x + y - z = 3$$
$$3x + 2y + kz = 4$$

It can be written in matrix form as

$$AX = B,$$

where $A = \begin{bmatrix} 1 & 1 & 1 \\ 2 & 1 & -1 \\ 3 & 2 & k \end{bmatrix}, X = \begin{bmatrix} x \\ y \\ z \end{bmatrix}$ and $B = \begin{bmatrix} 2 \\ 3 \\ 4 \end{bmatrix}$.

The condition for the system of linear equations has a unique solution, is $|A| \neq 0$.

$\therefore \quad \begin{vmatrix} 1 & 1 & 1 \\ 2 & 1 & -1 \\ 3 & 2 & k \end{vmatrix} \neq 0$

$\Rightarrow \quad 1(k+2) - 1(2k+3) + 1(4-3) \neq 0$

$\Rightarrow \quad k + 2 - 2k - 3 + 1 \neq 0 \Rightarrow -k \neq 0$

$\therefore \quad k \neq 0$

Hence, for a unique solution k should be a non-zero real number.

Example 3 **If $A = \begin{bmatrix} 3 & 2 \\ 5 & -7 \end{bmatrix}$, then find A^{-1} and use it to solve the following system of equations**

$$3x + 5y = 11 \text{ and } 2x - 7y = -3.$$ CBSE 2023

Sol. Given, $A = \begin{bmatrix} 3 & 2 \\ 5 & -7 \end{bmatrix}$

$$|A| = -21 - 10 = -31 \neq 0$$

Since, A is non-singular, so A^{-1} exists.

Now, cofactors of elements of $|A|$ are

$$A_{11} = (-1)^{1+1}(-7) = -7,$$
$$A_{12} = (-1)^{1+2}(5) = -5,$$
$$A_{21} = (-1)^{2+1}(2) = -2,$$
$$A_{22} = (-1)^{2+2}(3) = 3,$$

$$\therefore \quad \text{adj}A = \begin{bmatrix} A_{11} & A_{12} \\ A_{21} & A_{22} \end{bmatrix}^T$$

$$\Rightarrow \quad \text{adj } A = \begin{bmatrix} -7 & -5 \\ -2 & 3 \end{bmatrix}^T = \begin{bmatrix} -7 & -2 \\ -5 & 3 \end{bmatrix}$$

$$\therefore \quad A^{-1} = \frac{\text{adj } A}{|A|} = \frac{1}{(-31)}\begin{bmatrix} -7 & -2 \\ -5 & 3 \end{bmatrix} = \begin{bmatrix} \frac{7}{31} & \frac{2}{31} \\ \frac{5}{31} & -\frac{3}{31} \end{bmatrix}$$

Now, the given system of equations is expressible as

$$\begin{bmatrix} 3 & 5 \\ 2 & -7 \end{bmatrix}\begin{bmatrix} x \\ y \end{bmatrix} = \begin{bmatrix} 11 \\ -3 \end{bmatrix}$$

$$\Rightarrow \quad A^T X = B$$

$$\Rightarrow \quad X = (A^T)^{-1} B$$

$$\Rightarrow \quad X = (A^{-1})^T B \quad [\because |A^T| = |A| \neq 0]$$

$$\Rightarrow \begin{bmatrix} x \\ y \end{bmatrix} = \begin{bmatrix} \frac{7}{31} & \frac{2}{31} \\ \frac{5}{31} & -\frac{3}{31} \end{bmatrix}^T \begin{bmatrix} 11 \\ -3 \end{bmatrix} = \begin{bmatrix} \frac{7}{31} & \frac{5}{31} \\ \frac{2}{31} & -\frac{3}{31} \end{bmatrix}\begin{bmatrix} 11 \\ -3 \end{bmatrix}$$

$$= \begin{bmatrix} \frac{77}{31} - \frac{15}{31} \\ \frac{22}{31} + \frac{9}{31} \end{bmatrix} = \begin{bmatrix} \frac{62}{31} \\ \frac{31}{31} \end{bmatrix} = \begin{bmatrix} 2 \\ 1 \end{bmatrix} \Rightarrow x = 2 \text{ and } y = 1$$

Example 4 **Solve the following system of equations by matrix method** CBSE 2023

$$x + 2y + 3z = 6$$
$$2x - y + z = 2$$
$$3x + 2y - 2z = 3.$$

Sol. The given system of equation can be written as $AX = B$, where

$$A = \begin{bmatrix} 1 & 2 & 3 \\ 2 & -1 & 1 \\ 3 & 2 & -2 \end{bmatrix}, X = \begin{bmatrix} x \\ y \\ z \end{bmatrix} \text{ and } B = \begin{bmatrix} 6 \\ 2 \\ 3 \end{bmatrix}$$

Here, $|A| = 1(2-2) - 2(-4-3) + 3(4+3)$

$= 0 + 14 + 21 = 35 \neq 0$

So, A^{-1} exists.

$\therefore$ Cofactors of elements of $|A|$ are

$$A_{11} = (-1)^{1+1}\begin{vmatrix} -1 & 1 \\ 2 & -2 \end{vmatrix} = (2-2) = 0,$$

$$A_{12} = (-1)^{1+2}\begin{vmatrix} 2 & 1 \\ 3 & -2 \end{vmatrix} = -(-4-3) = 7,$$

$$A_{13} = (-1)^{1+3}\begin{vmatrix} 2 & -1 \\ 3 & 2 \end{vmatrix} = (4+3) = 7,$$

$$A_{21} = (-1)^{2+1}\begin{vmatrix} 2 & 3 \\ 2 & -2 \end{vmatrix} = -(-4-6) = 10,$$

$$A_{22} = (-1)^{2+2}\begin{vmatrix} 1 & 3 \\ 3 & -2 \end{vmatrix} = (-2-9) = -11,$$

$$A_{23} = (-1)^{2+3}\begin{vmatrix} 1 & 2 \\ 3 & 2 \end{vmatrix} = -(2-6) = 4,$$

$$A_{31} = (-1)^{3+1}\begin{vmatrix} 2 & 3 \\ -1 & 1 \end{vmatrix} = 2+3 = 5,$$

$$A_{32} = (-1)^{3+2}\begin{vmatrix} 1 & 3 \\ 2 & 1 \end{vmatrix} = -(1-6) = 5$$

$$\text{and } A_{33} = (-1)^{3+3}\begin{vmatrix} 1 & 2 \\ 2 & -1 \end{vmatrix} = (-1-4) = -5$$

$$\therefore \text{adj } A = \begin{bmatrix} A_{11} & A_{12} & A_{13} \\ A_{21} & A_{22} & A_{23} \\ A_{31} & A_{32} & A_{33} \end{bmatrix}^T$$

$$= \begin{bmatrix} 0 & 7 & 7 \\ 10 & -11 & 4 \\ 5 & 5 & -5 \end{bmatrix}^T = \begin{bmatrix} 0 & 10 & 5 \\ 7 & -11 & 5 \\ 7 & 4 & -5 \end{bmatrix}$$

$$\therefore \quad A^{-1} = \frac{1}{|A|}(\text{adj } A) = \frac{1}{35}\begin{bmatrix} 0 & 10 & 5 \\ 7 & -11 & 5 \\ 7 & 4 & -5 \end{bmatrix}$$

Now, $X = A^{-1}B$

$$\Rightarrow \begin{bmatrix} x \\ y \\ z \end{bmatrix} = \frac{1}{35}\begin{bmatrix} 0 & 10 & 5 \\ 7 & -11 & 5 \\ 7 & 4 & -5 \end{bmatrix}\begin{bmatrix} 6 \\ 2 \\ 3 \end{bmatrix}$$

$$= \frac{1}{35}\begin{bmatrix} 0 + 20 + 15 \\ 42 - 22 + 15 \\ 42 + 8 - 15 \end{bmatrix} = \frac{1}{35}\begin{bmatrix} 35 \\ 35 \\ 35 \end{bmatrix} = \begin{bmatrix} 1 \\ 1 \\ 1 \end{bmatrix}$$

$\therefore$ $x = 1$, $y = 1$ and $z = 1$

Example 5 **If** $A = \begin{bmatrix} 1 & 2 & -3 \\ 2 & 0 & -3 \\ 1 & 2 & 0 \end{bmatrix}$**, then find** A^{-1} **and hence solve the following system of equations**

$$x + 2y - 3z = 1, 2x - 3z = 2 \text{ and } x + 2y = 3.$$

CBSE 2024

Sol. Here, $|A| = \begin{vmatrix} 1 & 2 & -3 \\ 2 & 0 & -3 \\ 1 & 2 & 0 \end{vmatrix}$

$= 1(0+6) - 2(0+3) - 3(4)$

$= 6 - 6 - 12 = -12 \neq 0$

Thus, A is invertible.

Now, the cofactor of $|A|$ are

$C_{11} = 6, C_{12} = -3, C_{13} = 4$

$C_{21} = -6, C_{22} = 3, C_{23} = 0$

$C_{31} = -6, C_{32} = -3, C_{33} = -4$

$$\therefore \quad \text{adj } A = \begin{bmatrix} 6 & -3 & 4 \\ -6 & 3 & 0 \\ -6 & -3 & -4 \end{bmatrix}^T = \begin{bmatrix} 6 & -6 & -6 \\ -3 & 3 & -3 \\ 4 & 0 & -4 \end{bmatrix}$$

$$\text{So,} \quad A^{-1} = \frac{1}{|A|}\text{adj } A = \frac{1}{-12}\begin{bmatrix} 6 & -6 & -6 \\ -3 & 3 & -3 \\ 4 & 0 & -4 \end{bmatrix}$$

The given equations are

$x + 2y - 3z = 1$, $2x - 3z = 2$ and $x + 2y = 3$,

which can be written in matrix form as $AX = B$, where

$$A = \begin{bmatrix} 1 & 2 & -3 \\ 2 & 0 & -3 \\ 1 & 2 & 0 \end{bmatrix},$$

$$X = \begin{bmatrix} x \\ y \\ z \end{bmatrix}$$

and $$B = \begin{bmatrix} 1 \\ 2 \\ 3 \end{bmatrix}$$

$$\Rightarrow \begin{bmatrix} x \\ y \\ z \end{bmatrix} = \begin{bmatrix} 1 & 2 & -3 \\ 2 & 0 & -3 \\ 1 & 2 & 0 \end{bmatrix}^{-1} \begin{bmatrix} 1 \\ 2 \\ 3 \end{bmatrix}$$

$$= -\frac{1}{12} \begin{bmatrix} 6 & -6 & -6 \\ -3 & 3 & -3 \\ 4 & 0 & -4 \end{bmatrix} \begin{bmatrix} 1 \\ 2 \\ 3 \end{bmatrix}$$

$$= \frac{-1}{12} \begin{bmatrix} 6 - 12 - 18 \\ -3 + 6 - 9 \\ 4 + 0 - 12 \end{bmatrix}$$

$$= \frac{-1}{12} \begin{bmatrix} -24 \\ -6 \\ -8 \end{bmatrix}$$

$$\therefore \begin{bmatrix} x \\ y \\ z \end{bmatrix} = \begin{bmatrix} 2 \\ \frac{1}{2} \\ \frac{2}{3} \end{bmatrix}$$

$\therefore x = 2$, $y = \frac{1}{2}$ and $z = \frac{2}{3}$

Example 6 **Find the product of the matrices** $\begin{bmatrix} 1 & 2 & -3 \\ 2 & 3 & 2 \\ 3 & -3 & -4 \end{bmatrix} \begin{bmatrix} -6 & 17 & 13 \\ 14 & 5 & -8 \\ -15 & 9 & -1 \end{bmatrix}$ **and hence solve the system of linear equations** $x + 2y - 3z = -4$, $2x + 3y + 2z = 2$ **and** $3x - 3y - 4z = 11$.

Competency Based Que, CBSE 2024

Sol. Let $$B = \begin{bmatrix} 1 & 2 & -3 \\ 2 & 3 & 2 \\ 3 & -3 & -4 \end{bmatrix}$$

and $$A = \begin{bmatrix} -6 & 17 & 13 \\ 14 & 5 & -8 \\ -15 & 9 & -1 \end{bmatrix}$$

$$\therefore BA = \begin{bmatrix} 1 & 2 & -3 \\ 2 & 3 & 2 \\ 3 & -3 & -4 \end{bmatrix} \begin{bmatrix} -6 & 17 & 13 \\ 14 & 5 & -8 \\ -15 & 9 & -1 \end{bmatrix}$$

$$= \begin{bmatrix} -6 + 28 + 45 & 17 + 10 - 27 & 13 - 16 + 3 \\ -12 + 42 - 30 & 34 + 15 + 18 & 26 - 24 - 2 \\ -18 - 42 + 60 & 51 - 15 - 36 & 39 + 24 + 4 \end{bmatrix}$$

$$= \begin{bmatrix} 67 & 0 & 0 \\ 0 & 67 & 0 \\ 0 & 0 & 67 \end{bmatrix} = 67 \begin{bmatrix} 1 & 0 & 0 \\ 0 & 1 & 0 \\ 0 & 0 & 1 \end{bmatrix} = 67I$$

$\Rightarrow BA = 67I \Rightarrow B^{-1}BA = B^{-1}67$

[pre-multiplying both sides by B^{-1}]

$\Rightarrow A = B^{-1}67$ [$\because B^{-1}B = I$]

$$\Rightarrow B^{-1} = \frac{1}{67}A = \frac{1}{67} \begin{bmatrix} -6 & 17 & 13 \\ 14 & 5 & -8 \\ -15 & 9 & -1 \end{bmatrix}$$

Given system of equations can be written in matrix form as

$BX = C$

$\Rightarrow X = B^{-1}C$,

where, $B = \begin{bmatrix} 1 & 2 & -3 \\ 2 & 3 & 2 \\ 3 & -3 & -4 \end{bmatrix}$, $C = \begin{bmatrix} -4 \\ 2 \\ 11 \end{bmatrix}$ and $X = \begin{bmatrix} x \\ y \\ z \end{bmatrix}$

$$\therefore X = \frac{1}{67} \begin{bmatrix} -6 & 17 & 13 \\ 14 & 5 & -8 \\ 15 & 9 & -1 \end{bmatrix} \begin{bmatrix} -4 \\ 2 \\ 11 \end{bmatrix}$$

$$\begin{bmatrix} x \\ y \\ z \end{bmatrix} = \frac{1}{67} \begin{bmatrix} 24 + 34 + 143 \\ -56 + 10 - 88 \\ 60 + 18 - 11 \end{bmatrix}$$

$$= \frac{1}{67} \begin{bmatrix} 201 \\ -134 \\ 67 \end{bmatrix} = \begin{bmatrix} 3 \\ -2 \\ 1 \end{bmatrix}$$

On comparing corresponding elements, we get

$x = 3$, $y = -2$ and $z = 1$

Example 7 **Using matrix method, solve the following system of equations** $\frac{2}{x} + \frac{3}{y} + \frac{10}{z} = 4$, $\frac{4}{x} - \frac{6}{y} + \frac{5}{z} = 1$ **and** $\frac{6}{x} + \frac{9}{y} - \frac{20}{z} = 2$, $x, y, z \neq 0$.

Competency Based Que, CBSE Sample Paper 2023, CBSE 2011

Sol. The given system of equations is

$$\frac{2}{x} + \frac{3}{y} + \frac{10}{z} = 4, \ \frac{4}{x} - \frac{6}{y} + \frac{5}{z} = 1$$

and $$\frac{6}{x} + \frac{9}{y} - \frac{20}{z} = 2; \ x, y, z \neq 0$$

Let $\frac{1}{x} = u$, $\frac{1}{y} = v$ and $\frac{1}{z} = w$, then system of equations can be written as

$$\left.\begin{aligned} 2u + 3v + 10w &= 4 \\ 4u - 6v + 5w &= 1 \\ \text{and} \quad 6u + 9v - 20w &= 2 \end{aligned}\right\} \quad \text{...(i)}$$

Above system of Eqs. (i) can be written in matrix form as $AX = B$, where

$$A = \begin{bmatrix} 2 & 3 & 10 \\ 4 & -6 & 5 \\ 6 & 9 & -20 \end{bmatrix},$$

$$B = \begin{bmatrix} 4 \\ 1 \\ 2 \end{bmatrix} \text{ and } X = \begin{bmatrix} u \\ v \\ w \end{bmatrix}.$$

Its solution is given by

$$X = A^{-1}B \qquad \text{...(ii)}$$

Here, $|A| = 2(120-45) - 3(-80-30) + 10(36+36)$

$$= 2(75) - 3(-110) + 10(72)$$

$$= 150 + 330 + 720 = 1200$$

Since, $|A| \neq 0$, so A is non-singular and its inverse exists.

Now, cofactors of elements of $|A|$ are

$$A_{11} = (-1)^2 \begin{vmatrix} -6 & 5 \\ 9 & -20 \end{vmatrix} = 1(120-45) = 75,$$

$$A_{12} = (-1)^3 \begin{vmatrix} 4 & 5 \\ 6 & -20 \end{vmatrix} = -1(-80-30) = 110,$$

$$A_{13} = (-1)^4 \begin{vmatrix} 4 & -6 \\ 6 & 9 \end{vmatrix} = 1(36+36) = 72,$$

$$A_{21} = (-1)^3 \begin{vmatrix} 3 & 10 \\ 9 & -20 \end{vmatrix} = -1(-60-90) = 150,$$

$$A_{22} = (-1)^4 \begin{vmatrix} 2 & 10 \\ 6 & -20 \end{vmatrix} = 1(-40-60) = -100,$$

$$A_{23} = (-1)^5 \begin{vmatrix} 2 & 3 \\ 6 & 9 \end{vmatrix} = -1(18-18) = 0,$$

$$A_{31} = (-1)^4 \begin{vmatrix} 3 & 10 \\ -6 & 5 \end{vmatrix} = 1(15+60) = 75,$$

$$A_{32} = (-1)^5 \begin{vmatrix} 2 & 10 \\ 4 & 5 \end{vmatrix} = -1(10-40) = 30$$

and $A_{33} = (-1)^6 \begin{vmatrix} 2 & 3 \\ 4 & -6 \end{vmatrix} = 1(-12-12) = -24$

$$\therefore \text{adj}(A) = \begin{bmatrix} A_{11} & A_{12} & A_{13} \\ A_{21} & A_{22} & A_{23} \\ A_{31} & A_{32} & A_{33} \end{bmatrix}^T$$

$$= \begin{bmatrix} 75 & 110 & 72 \\ 150 & -100 & 0 \\ 75 & 30 & -24 \end{bmatrix}^T$$

$$= \begin{bmatrix} 75 & 150 & 75 \\ 110 & -100 & 30 \\ 72 & 0 & -24 \end{bmatrix}$$

and $A^{-1} = \dfrac{\text{adj}(A)}{|A|}$

$$= \frac{1}{1200} \begin{bmatrix} 75 & 150 & 75 \\ 110 & -100 & 30 \\ 72 & 0 & -24 \end{bmatrix}$$

On putting the values of X, A^{-1} and B in Eq. (ii), we get

$$\begin{bmatrix} u \\ v \\ w \end{bmatrix} = \frac{1}{1200} \begin{bmatrix} 75 & 150 & 75 \\ 110 & -100 & 30 \\ 72 & 0 & -24 \end{bmatrix} \begin{bmatrix} 4 \\ 1 \\ 2 \end{bmatrix}$$

$$= \frac{1}{1200} \begin{bmatrix} 300+150+150 \\ 440-100+60 \\ 288+0-48 \end{bmatrix}$$

$$\Rightarrow \begin{bmatrix} u \\ v \\ w \end{bmatrix} = \frac{1}{1200} \begin{bmatrix} 600 \\ 400 \\ 240 \end{bmatrix} = \begin{bmatrix} \frac{600}{1200} \\ \frac{400}{1200} \\ \frac{240}{1200} \end{bmatrix}$$

On comparing corresponding elements, we get

$$u = \frac{600}{1200},\ v = \frac{400}{1200} \text{ and } w = \frac{240}{1200}$$

$$\therefore \quad u = \frac{1}{2},\ v = \frac{1}{3} \text{ and } w = \frac{1}{5}$$

But $\quad \dfrac{1}{x} = u,\ \dfrac{1}{y} = v$ and $\dfrac{1}{z} = w$

$$\Rightarrow \quad \frac{1}{x} = \frac{1}{2},\ \frac{1}{y} = \frac{1}{3} \text{ and } \frac{1}{z} = \frac{1}{5}$$

$$\therefore \quad x = 2,\ y = 3 \text{ and } z = 5$$

Quick Test 4

1. Examine the consistency of the system of equations. NCERT

(i) $x+2y=2$ and $2x+3y=3$

(ii) $3x-y=5$ and $6x-2y=3$

(iii) $x+y+z=1, 2x+3y+2z=2$ and $bx+by+2bz=4$

2. Solve the following systems of linear equations using matrix method.

(i) $4x-3y=3$ and $3x-5y=7$

(ii) $2x+3y=-4$ and $-5x+4y=-13$

(iii) $5x+y-z=7, 4x-2y-3z=5$ and $7x+2y+2z=7$

(iv) $x-y+2z=7, 3x+4y-5z=-5$ and $2x-y+3z=12$

CBSE 2012

3. In the following cases, find A^{-1} and hence solve the system of equations.

(i) $A=\begin{bmatrix}1&-1&2\\0&2&-3\\3&-2&4\end{bmatrix}$ and system of linear equations

$x-y+2z=1, 2y-3z=1$ and $3x-2y+4z=3$. CBSE 2023

(ii) If $A=\begin{bmatrix}1&2&0\\-2&-1&-2\\0&-1&1\end{bmatrix}$ and system of equations; $x-2y=10$, $2x-y-z=8$ and $-2y+z=7$.

CBSE 2025, CBSE Sample Paper 2021

(iii) If $A=\begin{bmatrix}2&-3&5\\3&2&-4\\1&1&-2\end{bmatrix}$ and system of equations

$2x-3y+5z=11, 3x+2y-4z=-5$ and $x+y-2z=-3$.

CBSE Sample Paper 2023

4. If $A=\begin{bmatrix}2&3&10\\4&-6&5\\6&9&-20\end{bmatrix}$, then find A^{-1}. Using A^{-1} and solve the system of equations $\frac{2}{x}+\frac{3}{y}+\frac{10}{z}=2, \frac{4}{x}-\frac{6}{y}+\frac{5}{z}=5$ and $\frac{6}{x}+\frac{9}{y}-\frac{20}{z}=-4$.

Competency Based Que, CBSE 2017

5. If $A=\begin{bmatrix}-3&-2&-4\\2&1&2\\2&1&3\end{bmatrix}, B=\begin{bmatrix}1&2&0\\-2&-1&-2\\0&-1&1\end{bmatrix}$, then find AB and use it to solve the following system of equations CBSE 2023

$x-2y=3, 2x-y-z=2$ and $-2y+z=3$.

6. Given $A=\begin{bmatrix}-4&4&4\\-7&1&3\\5&-3&-1\end{bmatrix}$ and $B=\begin{bmatrix}1&-1&1\\1&-2&-2\\2&1&3\end{bmatrix}$, find AB.

Hence, solve the system of linear equations.

$$x-y+z=4$$
$$x-2y-2z=9$$
$$2x+y+3z=1$$

CBSE 2025

Answers

1. (i) Consistent

(ii) Inconsistent

(iii) Consistent

2. (i) $x=-\frac{6}{11}, y=\frac{-19}{11}$

(ii) $x=1, y=-2$

(iii) $x=1, y=1, z=-1$

(iv) $x=2, y=1, z=3$

3. (i) $A^{-1}=\begin{bmatrix}-2&0&1\\9&2&-3\\6&1&-2\end{bmatrix}$; $x=1, y=2$ and $z=1$

(ii) $A^{-1}=\begin{bmatrix}-3&-2&-4\\2&1&2\\2&1&3\end{bmatrix}$; $x=0, y=-5$ and $z=-3$

(iii) $A^{-1}=\begin{bmatrix}0&1&-2\\-2&9&-23\\-1&5&-13\end{bmatrix}$; $x=1, y=2$ and $z=3$

4. $A^{-1}=\frac{1}{1200}\begin{bmatrix}75&150&75\\110&-100&30\\72&0&-24\end{bmatrix}$; $x=2, y=-3$ and $z=5$

5. $AB=\begin{bmatrix}1&0&0\\0&1&0\\0&0&1\end{bmatrix}$; $x=1, y=-1, z=1$

6. $\begin{bmatrix}8&0&0\\0&8&0\\0&0&8\end{bmatrix}$; $x=3, y=-2, z=-1$

For Solutions, See QR Code on Pg. 103

EXAM PATTERN QUESTIONS

Objective Type Questions

Multiple Choice Questions

1. If $\begin{vmatrix} \alpha & 3 & 4 \\ 1 & 2 & 1 \\ 1 & 4 & 1 \end{vmatrix} = 0$, then the value of α is **CBSE 2023**

(a) 1 (b) 2 (c) 3 (d) 4

2. If A and B are two square matrices of order 2 and $|A| = 2$ and $|B| = 5$, then $|-3AB|$ is **CBSE 2024 C**

(a) -90 (b) -30 (c) 30 (d) 90

3. $\begin{vmatrix} 2 & 3 & 4 \\ 5 & 6 & 8 \\ 6x & 9x & 12x \end{vmatrix}$ is equal to

(a) 0 (b) $3x$ (c) $9x^2$ (d) None of these

4. If A is a square matrix of order 2 and $|A| = -2$, then value of $|5A'|$ is **CBSE 2024**

(a) -50 (b) -10 (c) 10 (d) 50

5. The value of $|A|$, if $A = \begin{bmatrix} 0 & 2x-1 & \sqrt{x} \\ 1-2x & 0 & 2\sqrt{x} \\ -\sqrt{x} & -2\sqrt{x} & 0 \end{bmatrix}$, where $x \in R^+$, is **CBSE Sample Paper 2022**

(a) $(2x+1)^2$ (b) 0
(c) $(2x+1)^3$ (d) None of these

6. Let P be a skew-symmetric matrix of order 3. If $\det(P) = \alpha$, then $(2025)^\alpha$ is **CBSE 2025**

(a) 0 (b) 1
(c) 2025 (d) $(2025)^3$

7. Let A be the area of a triangle having vertices $(x_1, y_1), (x_2, y_2)$ and (x_3, y_3). Which of the following is correct? **CBSE 2023**

(a) $\begin{vmatrix} x_1 & y_1 & 1 \\ x_2 & y_2 & 1 \\ x_3 & y_3 & 1 \end{vmatrix} = \pm A$ (b) $\begin{vmatrix} x_1 & y_1 & 1 \\ x_2 & y_2 & 1 \\ x_3 & y_3 & 1 \end{vmatrix} = \pm 2A$

(c) $\begin{vmatrix} x_1 & y_1 & 1 \\ x_2 & y_2 & 1 \\ x_3 & y_3 & 1 \end{vmatrix} = \pm \frac{A}{2}$ (d) $\begin{vmatrix} x_1 & y_1 & 1 \\ x_2 & y_2 & 1 \\ x_3 & y_3 & 1 \end{vmatrix}^2 = A^2$

8. The area of the triangle with vertices $(-1, 2), (4, 0)$ and $(3, 9)$ is

(a) $\frac{43}{2}$ sq units (b) $\frac{43}{4}$ sq units
(c) 21 sq units (d) 42 sq units

9. Given that $A = [a_{ij}]$ is a square matrix of order 3×3 and $|A| = -7$, then the value of $\sum_{i=1}^{3} a_{i2} A_{i2}$, where A_{ij} denotes the cofactor of element a_{ij} is **CBSE Sample Paper 2022 (Term I)**

(a) 7 (b) -7 (c) 0 (d) 49

10. The adjoint of the matrix $A = \begin{bmatrix} 1 & 2 \\ 3 & 4 \end{bmatrix}$ is

(a) $\begin{bmatrix} 4 & 2 \\ 3 & 1 \end{bmatrix}$ (b) $\begin{bmatrix} -4 & 2 \\ 3 & -1 \end{bmatrix}$ (c) $\begin{bmatrix} 4 & -2 \\ -3 & 1 \end{bmatrix}$ (d) $\begin{bmatrix} 1 & -2 \\ -3 & 4 \end{bmatrix}$

11. Let A be a 3×3 matrix such that $|\text{adj } A| = 81$. Then, $|A|$ is equal to

(a) 9 only (b) -9 only
(c) 81 (d) 9 or -9

12. If $A = \begin{bmatrix} a & 0 & 0 \\ 0 & a & 0 \\ 0 & 0 & a \end{bmatrix}$, then $|\text{adj } A|$ is equal to

(a) a^{27} (b) a^9 (c) a^6 (d) a^2

13. If A is a square matrix of order 3 such that the value of $|\text{adj } A| = 8$, then the value of $|A^T|$ is **CBSE 2024**

(a) $\sqrt{2}$ (b) $-\sqrt{2}$ (c) 8 (d) $2\sqrt{2}$

14. Let A be a square matrix of order 3. If $|A| = 5$, then $|\text{adj } A|$ is **CBSE 2025**

(a) 5 (b) 125 (c) 25 (d) -5

15. If $A = \begin{bmatrix} 0 & 1 & -1 \\ 1 & 2 & 1 \\ 0 & 3 & -2 \end{bmatrix}$, then the value of $|A \text{ adj } (A)|$ is **CBSE 2024 C**

(a) -1 (b) 1 (c) 2 (d) 3

16. If $\begin{bmatrix} 1 & 2 & 1 \\ 2 & 3 & 1 \\ 3 & a & 1 \end{bmatrix}$ is non-singular matrix and $a \in A$, then the set A is **CBSE 2023**

(a) R (b) $\{0\}$ (c) $\{4\}$ (d) $R - \{4\}$

17. If $A = \begin{bmatrix} 2 & \lambda & -3 \\ 0 & 2 & 5 \\ 1 & 1 & 3 \end{bmatrix}$, then A^{-1} exists, if **NCERT Exemplar**

(a) $\lambda = 2$ (b) $\lambda \neq 2$
(c) $\lambda \neq -2$ (d) None of these

18. If $|A|=2$, where A is a 2×2 matrix, then $|4A^{-1}|$ equal to **CBSE 2023**

(a) 4 (b) 2 (c) 8 (d) $\frac{1}{32}$

19. For the matrix $A=\begin{bmatrix}2 & -1 & 1\\ \lambda & 2 & 0\\ 1 & -2 & 3\end{bmatrix}$ to be invertible, the value of λ is **Competency Based Que, CBSE 2024**

(a) 0 (b) 10 (c) $R-\{10\}$ (d) $R-\{-10\}$

20. If A and B are invertible square matrices of the same order, then which of the following is not correct? **Competency Based Que, CBSE Sample Paper 2023**

(a) $\text{adj}A=|A|\cdot A^{-1}$ (b) $\det(A^{-1})=[\det(A)]^{-1}$
(c) $(AB)^{-1}=B^{-1}A^{-1}$ (d) $(A+B)^{-1}=B^{-1}+A^{-1}$

21. If for a square matrix A, $A^2-3A+I=O$ and $A^{-1}=xA+yI$, then the value of $x+y$ is **Competency Based Que, CBSE 2023**

(a) -2 (b) 2 (c) 3 (d) -3

Assertion-Reason Based Questions

Directions (Q. Nos. 22-29) *In the questions given below are two statements labelled as Assertion (A) and Reason (R). In the context of the two statements, which one of the following is correct?*

(a) Both A and R are correct; R is the correct explanation of A
(b) Both A and R are correct; R is not the correct explanation of A
(c) A is correct; R is incorrect
(d) R is correct; A is incorrect

22. **Assertion** (A) $\begin{vmatrix}0 & -1 & 2\\ 1 & 0 & 3\\ -2 & -3 & 0\end{vmatrix}=0$

Reason (R) Determinant of odd ordered skew-symmetric matrix is zero.

23. **Assertion** (A) Minor of the element 9 of $\begin{bmatrix}-2 & 0 & 1\\ 9 & 2 & -3\\ 6 & 1 & -2\end{bmatrix}$ is 1.

Reason (R) Minor of element a_{ij} is the value of determinant after deleting ith row and jth column.

24. **Assertion** (A) $\text{adj}(\text{adj}A)=|A|^{n-2}\cdot A$.

Reason (R) $|\quad A|=|A|^{n-1}$.

25. U and V are two non-singular matrices of order n and k is any scalar. **Competency Based Que, CBSE QB**

Assertion (A) $\det(kU)=k^n\times\det(U)$

Reason (R) If W is a matrix obtained by multiplying any one row or column of V by the scalar k, then $\det(W)=k\times\det(V)$.

26. **Assertion** (A) If A is a non-singular matrix, then A^{-1} exist.

Reason (R) Determinant of a non-singular matrix is zero.

27. **Assertion** (A) If $|A|=4$, then $|A^{-1}|=-4$.

Reason (R) $|A^{-1}|=\frac{1}{|A|}$.

28. **Assertion** (A) If A is invertible 3×3 matrix, then $|A^{-1}\,\text{adj}A|=|A|$.

Reason (R) If A and B are to invertible matrices such that B is the inverse of A, then $AB=BA=I$.

29. **Assertion** (A) If $A=\begin{bmatrix}p & 0 & 0\\ 0 & q & 0\\ 0 & 0 & r\end{bmatrix}$, then $A^{-1}=\begin{bmatrix}p^{-1} & 0 & 0\\ 0 & q^{-1} & 0\\ 0 & 0 & r^{-1}\end{bmatrix}$.

Reason (R) Inverse of a invertible diagonal matrix is always a diagonal matrix. **Competency Based Que**

Case Study Based Questions

30. Gautam buys 5 pens, 3 bags and 1 instrument box and pays a sum of ₹160. From the same shop, Vikram buys 2 pens, 1 bag and 3 instrument boxes and pays a sum of ₹ 190. Also, Ankur buys 1 pen, 2 bags and 4 instrument boxes and pays a sum of ₹ 250.

(i) Convert the given above situation into a matrix equation of the form $AX=B$.
(ii) Find $|A|$. **CBSE 2023**
(iii) Find A^{-1}.
Or Determine $P=A^2-5A$.

31. In an army camp, three teams Alpha, Beta and Charlie are located at the three corners of a triangular plot as shown below.

The area of the triangular plot is 37 sq units and the coordinates of team Charlie lie on the X-axis (positive direction). Team Charlie received a message from the camp head about a secret room as follows.

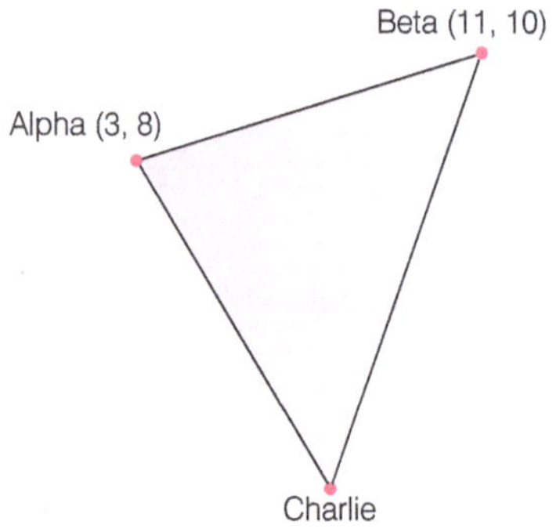

The coordinates of the secret room are (a_{12}, a_{21}) of the adjoint of the matrix $\begin{bmatrix} 3 & 8 \\ 11 & 10 \end{bmatrix}$.

Based on the above information, answer the following questions.

(i) Find the x-coordinate of the location of team Charlie. Use determinant method and show your steps.

(ii) The head of the camp plans to have a medical centre on the line joining the coordinates of teams Alpha and Beta such that its x-coordinate is 5.

Find the y-coordinate of the medical centre using the determinant method. Show your steps and give a valid reason. **CBSE QB**

32. A student in class XII is studying the concept of matrices. He comes across matrices A and B, defined as

$$A = \begin{bmatrix} 1 & -1 & 2 \\ 0 & 2 & -3 \\ 3 & -2 & 4 \end{bmatrix} \text{ and } B = \begin{bmatrix} -2 & 0 & 1 \\ 9 & 2 & -3 \\ 6 & 1 & -2 \end{bmatrix}$$

later on, he uses the product of AB in solving the system of equations $x + 3z = 9, -x + 2y - 2z = 4$ and $2x - 3y + 4z = -3$.

Based on the above information, answer the following question.

(i) Find the product AB.

(ii) Find the value of A^{-1}.

(iii) (a) What is the solution of given system of equation?

Or

(b) Find the value of $x + y + z$.

33. Two organisations, P and Q, plan to reward their selected individuals for demonstrating the value of Integrity, Diligence and Timeliness. Organisation P plans to award ₹x, ₹y and ₹z for each of the three respective values to 3, 2 and 1 individuals, respectively with a total award amount ₹ 2200. Organisation Q plan to spend ₹ 3100 to reward 4, 1 and 3 individuals for the same values respectively with the same award amounts (₹ x, ₹ y and ₹ z). Additionally, the total prize amount for one individual for all three values combined is ₹ 1200.

Based on the above information, answer the following questions.

(i) Write the system of linear equation in variables x, y and z.

(ii) Write the matrix equation represented by the above situation.

(iii) (a) Find the values of x, y and z.

Or

(b) Find the value of $\frac{x+y}{z}$.

Subjective Questions

Very Short Answer Type Questions

1. If $\begin{vmatrix} 3x & 7 \\ -2 & 4 \end{vmatrix} = \begin{vmatrix} 8 & 7 \\ 6 & 4 \end{vmatrix}$, then find the value of x. **CBSE 2014**

2. If $x \in N$ and $\begin{vmatrix} x+3 & -2 \\ -3x & 2x \end{vmatrix} = 8$, then find the value of x. **CBSE 2016C**

3. Find the area of triangle, whose vertices are (2, 7), (1, 1) and (10, 8).

4. If A_{ij} is the cofactor of the element a_{ij} of the determinant $\begin{vmatrix} 2 & -3 & 5 \\ 6 & 0 & 4 \\ 1 & 5 & -7 \end{vmatrix}$, then write the value of $a_{32} \cdot A_{32}$. **CBSE 2013**

5. For what value of x, $A = \begin{bmatrix} 2(x+1) & 2x \\ x & x-2 \end{bmatrix}$ is a singular matrix?

6. If A is an invertible matrix of order 2 and $\det A = 4$, then write the value of $\det(A^{-1})$. **CBSE 2017C**

Short Answer Type Questions

7. If $f(x) = \begin{vmatrix} 0 & x-a & x-b \\ x+a & 0 & x-c \\ x+b & x+c & 0 \end{vmatrix}$, then show that $f(0) = 0$. **Competency Based Que, NCERT Exemplar**

8. If A is skew-symmetric matrix of order 3, then prove that $\det A = 0$. **CBSE 2017**

9. Find the values of k, if the area of triangle is 4 sq units and vertices are (−2, 0), (0, 4) and (0, k). **NCERT**

10. Show that the points $(a+5, a-4)$, $(a-2, a+3)$ and (a, a) do not lie on a straight line for any value of a. **NCERT Exemplar**

11. If the value of a third order determinant is 12, then find the value of the determinant formed by replacing each element by its cofactor. **NCERT Exemplar**

12. Find the adjoint of the matrix $A = \begin{bmatrix} 1 & 4 & 5 \\ 3 & 2 & 6 \\ 0 & 1 & 0 \end{bmatrix}$ and hence show that $A(\text{adj } A) = |A| I_3$. **CBSE 2015**

13. If A is a non-singular symmetric matrix, then write whether A^{-1} is symmetric or skew-symmetric.

14. If $A = \begin{bmatrix} 1 & -2 & 3 \\ 0 & -1 & 4 \\ -2 & 2 & 1 \end{bmatrix}$, then find $(A')^{-1}$. **CBSE 2015**

15. If for the non-singular matrix A, $A^2 = I$, then find A^{-1}.

16. If $A = \begin{bmatrix} 3 & -2 \\ 4 & -2 \end{bmatrix}$, then find the value of λ so that $A^2 = \lambda A - 2I$. Hence, find A^{-1}.

17. If $A = \begin{bmatrix} 1 & 2 & 2 \\ 2 & 1 & 2 \\ 2 & 2 & 1 \end{bmatrix}$, then find A^{-1} and hence prove that $A^2 - 4A - 5I = O$.

Long Answer Type Questions

18. If $A = \begin{bmatrix} \cos\alpha & -\sin\alpha & 0 \\ \sin\alpha & \cos\alpha & 0 \\ 0 & 0 & 1 \end{bmatrix}$, then find adj A and verify that $A\,(\text{adj } A) = (\text{adj } A)\,A = |A|\,I_3$. **CBSE 2016**

19. Given, $A = \begin{bmatrix} 5 & 3 \\ -2 & 4 \end{bmatrix}$ and $B = \begin{bmatrix} 2 & -3 \\ 4 & -8 \end{bmatrix}$

Show that $(\text{adj } A) \times (\text{adj } B) = \text{adj}(BA)$ **CBSE QB**

20. If $A = \begin{pmatrix} 4 & -8 \\ 12 & 16 \end{pmatrix}$ and $B = \begin{pmatrix} -16 & -8 \\ 12 & -4 \end{pmatrix}$.

Identify what type of marix is $(\text{adj } A) \times (\text{adj } B)$.

Show your work. **CBSE QB**

21. If $A = \begin{bmatrix} 1 & \tan x \\ -\tan x & 1 \end{bmatrix}$, then show that

$A^T A^{-1} = \begin{bmatrix} \cos 2x & -\sin 2x \\ \sin 2x & \cos 2x \end{bmatrix}$.

22. If $A = \begin{bmatrix} 2 & -1 \\ -1 & 2 \end{bmatrix}$ and I is the identity matrix of order 2, then show that $A^2 = 4A - 3I$. Hence, find A^{-1} . **CBSE 2023, 15**

23. Find the matrix A satisfying the matrix equation

$\begin{bmatrix} 2 & 1 \\ 3 & 2 \end{bmatrix} A \begin{bmatrix} -3 & 2 \\ 5 & -3 \end{bmatrix} = \begin{bmatrix} 1 & 0 \\ 0 & 1 \end{bmatrix}$.

24. Let $A = \begin{bmatrix} 1 & -2 & 1 \\ -2 & 3 & 1 \\ 1 & 1 & 5 \end{bmatrix}$, verify that $(\text{adj } A)^{-1} = \text{adj}\,(A^{-1})$ **Diksha App**

25. Find matrix A, if

$$\begin{bmatrix} 2 & 4 \\ 1 & 3 \end{bmatrix} A \begin{bmatrix} 0 & 2 \\ 1 & 3 \end{bmatrix} = \begin{bmatrix} 1 & 6 \\ 3 & -2 \end{bmatrix}$$

Competency Based Que

26. If $A = \begin{bmatrix} 1 & 2 & -3 \\ 3 & 2 & -2 \\ 2 & -1 & -1 \end{bmatrix}$, then find A^{-1} and use it to solve the system $x + 3y + 2z = 6, 2x + 2y - z = 3$ and $-3x - 2y - z = 5$.

27. Evaluate the product AB, where

$$A = \begin{bmatrix} 1 & -1 & 0 \\ 2 & 3 & 4 \\ 0 & 1 & 2 \end{bmatrix} \text{ and } B = \begin{bmatrix} 2 & 2 & -4 \\ -4 & 2 & -4 \\ 2 & -1 & 5 \end{bmatrix}$$

Hence, solve the system of linear equations

$$x - y = 3,\ 2x + 3y + 4z = 17 \text{ and } y + 2z = 7.$$

Competency Based Que, CBSE Sample Paper 2021

28. If $A = \begin{bmatrix} 1 & 3 & 4 \\ 2 & 1 & 2 \\ 5 & 1 & 1 \end{bmatrix}$, then find A^{-1}.

Hence, solve the system of equations

$$x + 3y + 4z = 8,$$
$$2x + y + 2z = 5$$

and $$5x + y + z = 7$$ **CBSE 2019**

29. Using matrices, solve the system of equations

$$4x + 3y + 2z = 60,$$
$$x + 2y + 3z = 45$$

and $$6x + 2y + 3z = 70.$$ **CBSE 2011**

Hints & Solutions

Objective Type Questions

1. (d) Given, $\begin{vmatrix} \alpha & 3 & 4 \\ 1 & 2 & 1 \\ 1 & 4 & 1 \end{vmatrix} = 0$

On expanding along R_1, we get

$$\alpha(2-4) - 3(1-1) + 4(4-2) = 0$$
$$\Rightarrow \quad \alpha(-2) - 3(0) + 4(2) = 0$$
$$\Rightarrow \quad -2\alpha + 8 = 0$$
$$\Rightarrow \quad -2\alpha = -8$$
$$\therefore \quad \alpha = 4$$

2. (d) Given, $|A| = 2$ and $|B| = 5$

We know, $|AB| = |A||B|$

$\therefore \quad |AB| = 2 \cdot 5$

$|AB| = 10$

Now, $|-3AB| = (-3)^2 |AB| \quad [\because |kA| = k^n |A|]$

$= 9 \times 10$

$= 90$

3. (a) We have, $\begin{vmatrix} 2 & 3 & 4 \\ 5 & 6 & 8 \\ 6x & 9x & 12x \end{vmatrix}$

$= 2(72x - 72x) - 3(60x - 48x) + 4(45x - 36x)$ [expanding along R_1]

$= 2(0) - 36x + 36x$

$= 0$

4. (a) Given, $|A| = -2$

Now, $|5A'| = 25|A'| \quad [\because |kA| = k^n |A|]$

$= 25|A| \quad [\because |A'| = |A|]$

$= 25(-2) = -50$

5. (b) Given, $A = \begin{bmatrix} 0 & 2x-1 & \sqrt{x} \\ 1-2x & 0 & 2\sqrt{x} \\ -\sqrt{x} & -2\sqrt{x} & 0 \end{bmatrix}$

$\therefore \quad |A| = 0 - (2x-1)(0 + \sqrt{x}(2\sqrt{x})) + \sqrt{x}(-2\sqrt{x}(1-2x) - 0)$

$= -(2x-1)(2x) - 2x(1-2x) = 0$

6. (b) We know that the determinant of an odd order skew-symmetric matrix is zero.

$\therefore \quad |A| = 0 = \alpha$

$\therefore \quad (2023)^{\alpha} = (2023)^0 = 1$

7. (b) The area of a triangle whose vertices are (x_1, y_1), (x_2, y_2) and (x_3, y_3) is $\frac{1}{2}\begin{vmatrix} x_1 & y_1 & 1 \\ x_2 & y_2 & 1 \\ x_3 & y_3 & 1 \end{vmatrix}$.

According to the question,

$$\frac{1}{2}\begin{vmatrix} x_1 & y_1 & 1 \\ x_2 & y_2 & 1 \\ x_3 & y_3 & 1 \end{vmatrix} = \pm A \Rightarrow \begin{vmatrix} x_1 & y_1 & 1 \\ x_2 & y_2 & 1 \\ x_3 & y_3 & 1 \end{vmatrix} = \pm 2A$$

8. (a) The area of triangle with vertices (x_1, y_1), (x_2, y_2) and (x_3, y_3) is defined as

$$A = \frac{1}{2}\left\|\begin{matrix} x_1 & y_1 & 1 \\ x_2 & y_2 & 1 \\ x_3 & y_3 & 1 \end{matrix}\right\|$$

$$A = \frac{1}{2}\left\|\begin{matrix} -1 & 2 & 1 \\ 4 & 0 & 1 \\ 3 & 9 & 1 \end{matrix}\right\|$$

$$= \frac{1}{2}|-1(0-9) - 2(4-3) + 1(36-0)|$$

$$= \frac{1}{2}|9 - 2 + 36| = \frac{43}{2} \text{ sq. units}$$

9. (b) Let $A = \begin{bmatrix} a_{11} & a_{12} & a_{13} \\ a_{21} & a_{22} & a_{23} \\ a_{31} & a_{32} & a_{33} \end{bmatrix}$

On expanding along C_2, then

$$|A| = -a_{12}\begin{vmatrix} a_{21} & a_{23} \\ a_{31} & a_{33} \end{vmatrix} + a_{22}\begin{vmatrix} a_{11} & a_{13} \\ a_{31} & a_{33} \end{vmatrix} - a_{32}\begin{vmatrix} a_{11} & a_{13} \\ a_{21} & a_{23} \end{vmatrix}$$

$\Rightarrow \quad |A| = a_{12}A_{12} + a_{22}A_{22} + a_{32}A_{32}$

$\therefore \quad |A| = \sum_{i=1}^{3} a_{i2}A_{i2} = -7 \quad [\because |A| = -7]$

10. (c) We know that if $A = \begin{bmatrix} a & b \\ c & d \end{bmatrix}$, then $\text{adj}\,A = \begin{bmatrix} d & -b \\ -c & a \end{bmatrix}$

$\therefore$ If $A = \begin{bmatrix} 1 & 2 \\ 3 & 4 \end{bmatrix}$, then $\text{adj}\,A = \begin{bmatrix} 4 & -2 \\ -3 & 1 \end{bmatrix}$

11. (d) We know that, $|\text{adj}A| = |A|^{n-1}$, where n is the order of matrix A.

$\therefore \quad |\text{adj}A| = |A|^{3-1} \Rightarrow 81 = |A|^2$

$\therefore \quad |A| = \pm 9$

12. (c) Given, $A = \begin{bmatrix} a & 0 & 0 \\ 0 & a & 0 \\ 0 & 0 & a \end{bmatrix}$

$\therefore \quad |A| = \begin{vmatrix} a & 0 & 0 \\ 0 & a & 0 \\ 0 & 0 & a \end{vmatrix} = a^3 \neq 0$

Here, $n = 3$

Thus, we have

$|\text{adj}A| = |A|^{n-1} = (a^3)^2 = a^6$

13. (d) We know that $|\text{adj}A| = |A|^{n-1}$, where n is the order of the square matrix.

$\therefore \quad 8 = |A|^{3-1} \quad [\because |\text{adj}A| = 8]$

$\Rightarrow \quad |A|^2 = 8$

$\Rightarrow \quad |A| = \pm 2\sqrt{2}$

$\therefore \quad |A| = 2\sqrt{2}$ [consider positive value]

Hence, $|A^T| = |A| = 2\sqrt{2}$

14. (c) Given, $|A|=5$ and order of A is 3.
We know that $|\text{adj}A|=|A|^{n-1}$, where n is order of matrix.
$\therefore \quad |\text{adj}A|=|A|^2$
Hence, $|\text{adj}A|=(5)^2=25$

15. (a) Given, $A=\begin{bmatrix}0 & 1 & -1\\ 1 & 2 & 1\\ 0 & 3 & -2\end{bmatrix}$

$\therefore \quad |A|=0(-4-3)-1(-2-0)-1(3-0)$
$=2-3=-1$

Now, $|A \text{ adj } A|=|A|\,|\text{adj } A|$ $\quad [\because |AB|=|A||B|]$
$=|A||A|^{3-1}$ $\quad [\because |\text{adj } A|=A^{n-1}]$
$=-1\times|A|^2$
$=-1\times(-1)^2=-1$

16. (d) Given, $\begin{bmatrix}1 & 2 & 1\\ 2 & 3 & 1\\ 3 & a & 1\end{bmatrix}$ is non-singular matrix.

$\therefore \quad \begin{vmatrix}1 & 2 & 1\\ 2 & 3 & 1\\ 3 & a & 1\end{vmatrix}\neq 0$

$\Rightarrow \quad 1(3-a)-2(2-3)+1(2a-9)\neq 0$
$\Rightarrow \quad 3-a+2+2a-9\neq 0$
$\Rightarrow \quad -4+a\neq 0\Rightarrow a\neq 4$
$\therefore$ Set $A=R-\{4\}$

17. (d) We have, $A=\begin{bmatrix}2 & \lambda & -3\\ 0 & 2 & 5\\ 1 & 1 & 3\end{bmatrix}$

$\Rightarrow \quad |A|=\begin{vmatrix}2 & \lambda & -3\\ 0 & 2 & 5\\ 1 & 1 & 3\end{vmatrix}$
$=2(6-5)-\lambda(0-5)-3(0-2)$
$=2+5\lambda+6=8+5\lambda$

If A^{-1} exists, then $|A|\neq 0$.
$\therefore \quad 8+5\lambda\neq 0$
$\Rightarrow \quad \lambda\neq-\dfrac{8}{5}$

18. (c) We know that $|A^{-1}|=\dfrac{1}{|A|}$

Now, $|4A^{-1}|=(4)^2|A^{-1}|$
$=16\cdot\dfrac{1}{|A|}=16\times\dfrac{1}{2}$ $\quad [\because \text{given, } |A|=2]$
$=8$

19. (d) Given, $A=\begin{bmatrix}2 & -1 & 1\\ \lambda & 2 & 0\\ 1 & -2 & 3\end{bmatrix}$

A matrix A is invertible, if $|A|\neq 0$.

Here, $|A|=\begin{vmatrix}2 & -1 & 1\\ \lambda & 2 & 0\\ 1 & -2 & 3\end{vmatrix}\neq 0$

$\Rightarrow \quad 2(6-0)+1(3\lambda-0)+1(-2\lambda-2)\neq 0$
$\Rightarrow \quad 12+3\lambda-2\lambda-2\neq 0$
$\Rightarrow \quad \lambda+10\neq 0\Rightarrow\lambda\neq-10$
$\therefore \quad \lambda=R-\{-10\}$

20. (d) $(A+B)^{-1}=B^{-1}+A^{-1}$ is not true.

21. (b) Given, $A^2-3A+I=O$
$A^2-3A=-I$
$\Rightarrow \quad A\cdot A-3A=-I$
$\Rightarrow \quad A\cdot(A\cdot A^{-1})-3A\cdot A^{-1}=-I\cdot A^{-1}$
[post multiplying both sides by A^{-1}]
$\Rightarrow \quad A\cdot I-3I=-A^{-1}\Rightarrow A^{-1}=-A+3I$
On comparing with $A^{-1}=xA+yI$, we get
$x=-1$ and $y=3$
$\therefore \quad x+y=-1+3=2$

22. (a) Let $A=\begin{bmatrix}0 & -1 & 2\\ 1 & 0 & 3\\ -2 & -3 & 0\end{bmatrix}$

$=0(0+9)+1(0+6)+2(-3-0)$
$=0+6-6=0$

We know that determinant of odd ordered skew-symmetric matrix is zero.
Hence, Assertion and Reason both are correct and Reason is the correct explanation of Assertion.

23. (d) We have, $\begin{vmatrix}-2 & 0 & 1\\ 9 & 2 & -3\\ 6 & 1 & -2\end{vmatrix}$

9 is $a_{21}\Rightarrow M_{21}=-2\times 0-1\times 1=-1$
$\therefore$ Assertion is incorrect.

If we have, $\begin{vmatrix}a_{11} & a_{12} & a_{13}\\ a_{21} & a_{22} & a_{23}\\ a_{31} & a_{32} & a_{33}\end{vmatrix}$

Then, $M_{21}=\begin{vmatrix}a_{12} & a_{13}\\ a_{32} & a_{33}\end{vmatrix}$
$=a_{12}\cdot a_{33}-a_{13}\cdot a_{32}$
$\therefore$ Reason is correct.

24. (a) **Assertion** We know that
$$A^{-1}=\frac{1}{|A|}\text{adj}A \qquad \text{...(i)}$$
Also, $AA^{-1}=I\Rightarrow A^{-1}=\dfrac{I}{A}$ $\qquad$ ...(ii)
From Eqs. (i) and (ii), we get
$$\frac{\text{adj}A}{|A|}=\frac{I}{A}$$
$\Rightarrow \quad A(\text{adj}A)=|A|$ $\qquad$ ...(iii)
On replacing A by adj A in Eq. (iii), we get
$\text{adj}A(\text{adj}(\text{adj } A))=|\text{adj}A|$
$\Rightarrow \quad \text{adj}(\text{adj}A))=\dfrac{|\text{adj}A|}{\text{adj}A}$ $\qquad$ ...(iv)

From Eq. (iii), $\text{adj}A = \frac{|A|}{A}$

$\therefore \quad \text{adj}(\text{adj}A) = \frac{|\text{adj}A|A}{|A|}$

$= \frac{|A|^{n-1}A}{|A|} \quad [\because \text{adj}A = |A|^{n-1}]$

$= |A|^{n-2}A$

Hence, Assertion and Reason both are correct and Reason is the correct explanation of Assertion.

25. (a) **Assertion** The determinant of a matrix after multiplying each row by a scalar k is given by multiplying the determinant by k raised to the power of the number of rows.

Therefore, $\det(kU) = k^n \times \det(U)$

Assertion is correct.

Reason If W is a matrix obtained by multiplying any one row or column of V by the scalar k, then the determinant of W is $k \times \det(V)$.

Hence, Assertion and Reason both are correct and Reason is the correct explanation of Assertion.

26. (c) Here, Assertion is correct and Reason is incorrect.

27. (d) Given, $|A| = 4$

We know that $|A^{-1}| = \frac{1}{|A|}$

$\therefore \quad |A^{-1}| = \frac{1}{4}$

Hence, Assertion is incorrect but Reason is correct.

28. (b) Given, order of matrix A is 3.

Now, $|A^{-1}\text{adj}A| = |A^{-1}||\text{adj}A| \quad [\because |AB| = |A|\cdot|B|]$

$= \frac{1}{|A|}|A|^{3-1} \quad \left[\because |A^{-1}| = \frac{1}{|A|} \text{ and } |\text{adj}A| = |A|^{n-1}\right]$

$= \frac{|A|^2}{|A|} = |A|$

$\therefore$ Assertion is correct.

If B is inverse of A, then $AB = BA = I$

$\therefore$ Reason is also correct but Reason is not correct explanation of Assertion.

29. (b) Given, $A = \begin{bmatrix} p & 0 & 0 \\ 0 & q & 0 \\ 0 & 0 & r \end{bmatrix}$

Cofactors of elements of $|A|$ are $A_{11} = (-1)^{1+1}(qr - 0) = qr$,

$A_{12} = (-1)^{1+2}(0) = 0,$

$A_{13} = (-1)^{1+3}(0) = 0, A_{21} = (-1)^{1+2}(0) = 0,$

$A_{22} = (-1)^{2+2}(pr) = pr,$

$A_{23} = (-1)^{2+3}(0) = 0,$

$A_{31} = (-1)^{1+3}(0) = 0, A_{32} = (-1)^{3+2}(0) = 0$

$A_{33} = (-1)^{3+3}(pq) = pq$

and $|A| = a_{11}A_{11} + a_{12}A_{12} + a_{13}A_{13}$

$= pqr$

Now, $\text{adj}A = \begin{bmatrix} qr & 0 & 0 \\ 0 & pr & 0 \\ 0 & 0 & pq \end{bmatrix}^T = \begin{bmatrix} qr & 0 & 0 \\ 0 & pr & 0 \\ 0 & 0 & pq \end{bmatrix}$

and $A^{-1} = \frac{1}{|A|}(\text{adj}A) = \frac{1}{pqr}\begin{bmatrix} qr & 0 & 0 \\ 0 & pr & 0 \\ 0 & 0 & pq \end{bmatrix}$

$= \begin{bmatrix} \frac{qr}{pqr} & 0 & 0 \\ 0 & \frac{pr}{pqr} & 0 \\ 0 & 0 & \frac{pq}{pqr} \end{bmatrix} = \begin{bmatrix} \frac{1}{p} & 0 & 0 \\ 0 & \frac{1}{q} & 0 \\ 0 & 0 & \frac{1}{r} \end{bmatrix}$

$\Rightarrow \quad A^{-1} = \begin{bmatrix} p^{-1} & 0 & 0 \\ 0 & q^{-1} & 0 \\ 0 & 0 & r^{-1} \end{bmatrix}$

$\therefore$ Assertion is correct.

We know that inverse of invertible diagonal matrix is always diagonal.

So, Assertion and Reason both are correct but Reason is not the correct explanation of Assertion.

30. Let the price of a pen, a bag and a instrument box be ₹ x, ₹ y and ₹ z, respectively. Then

For Gautam,

$$5x + 3y + z = 160 \quad \ldots\text{(i)}$$

For Vikram,

$$2x + y + 3z = 190 \quad \ldots\text{(ii)}$$

For Ankur,

$$x + 2y + 4z = 250 \quad \ldots\text{(iii)}$$

(i) This system of equations can be written as $AX = B$, where

$A = \begin{bmatrix} 5 & 3 & 1 \\ 2 & 1 & 3 \\ 1 & 2 & 4 \end{bmatrix}$,

$X = \begin{bmatrix} x \\ y \\ z \end{bmatrix}$ and $B = \begin{bmatrix} 160 \\ 190 \\ 250 \end{bmatrix}$

(ii) $|A| = 5(4-6) - 3(8-3) + 1(4-1)$

$= 5(-2) - 3(5) + 1(3)$

$= -10 - 15 + 3 = -22 \neq 0$

(iii) Cofactors of elements of $|A|$ are

$A_{11} = (-1)^{1+1}\begin{vmatrix} 1 & 3 \\ 2 & 4 \end{vmatrix} = (4-6) = -2,$

$A_{12} = (-1)^{1+2}\begin{vmatrix} 2 & 3 \\ 1 & 4 \end{vmatrix} = -(8-3) = -5,$

$A_{13} = (-1)^{1+3}\begin{vmatrix} 2 & 1 \\ 1 & 2 \end{vmatrix} = 4 - 1 = 3,$

$A_{21}=(-1)^{2+1}\begin{vmatrix}3 & 1\\2 & 4\end{vmatrix}=-(12-2)=-10,$

$A_{22}=(-1)^{2+2}\begin{vmatrix}5 & 1\\1 & 4\end{vmatrix}=20-1=19,$

$A_{23}=(-1)^{2+3}\begin{vmatrix}5 & 3\\1 & 2\end{vmatrix}=-(10-3)=-7,$

$A_{31}=(-1)^{3+1}\begin{vmatrix}3 & 1\\1 & 3\end{vmatrix}=(9-1)=8,$

$A_{32}=(-1)^{3+2}\begin{vmatrix}5 & 1\\2 & 3\end{vmatrix}=-(15-2)=-13$

and $A_{33}=(-1)^{3+3}\begin{vmatrix}5 & 3\\2 & 1\end{vmatrix}=(5-6)=-1$

$$\therefore \text{ adj } A=\begin{bmatrix}A_{11} & A_{12} & A_{13}\\A_{21} & A_{22} & A_{23}\\A_{31} & A_{32} & A_{33}\end{bmatrix}^T$$

$$=\begin{bmatrix}-2 & -5 & 3\\-10 & 19 & -7\\8 & -13 & -1\end{bmatrix}^T$$

$$=\begin{bmatrix}-2 & -10 & 8\\-5 & 19 & -13\\3 & -7 & -1\end{bmatrix}$$

$$\therefore A^{-1}=\frac{\text{adj } A}{|A|}=-\frac{1}{22}\begin{bmatrix}-2 & -10 & 8\\-5 & 19 & -13\\3 & -7 & -1\end{bmatrix}$$

Or

(iii) $P=A^2-5A$

$$=\begin{bmatrix}5 & 3 & 1\\2 & 1 & 3\\1 & 2 & 4\end{bmatrix}\begin{bmatrix}5 & 3 & 1\\2 & 1 & 3\\1 & 2 & 4\end{bmatrix}-5\begin{bmatrix}5 & 3 & 1\\2 & 1 & 3\\1 & 2 & 4\end{bmatrix}$$

$$=\begin{bmatrix}25+6+1 & 15+3+2 & 5+9+4\\10+2+3 & 6+1+6 & 2+3+12\\5+4+4 & 3+2+8 & 1+6+16\end{bmatrix}-\begin{bmatrix}25 & 15 & 5\\10 & 5 & 15\\5 & 10 & 20\end{bmatrix}$$

$$=\begin{bmatrix}32 & 20 & 18\\15 & 13 & 17\\13 & 13 & 23\end{bmatrix}-\begin{bmatrix}25 & 15 & 5\\10 & 5 & 15\\5 & 10 & 20\end{bmatrix}$$

$$=\begin{bmatrix}7 & 5 & 13\\5 & 8 & 2\\8 & 3 & 3\end{bmatrix}$$

31. (i) Given, location of team Charlie lies on X-axis.

$\therefore$ y-coordinate i.e. $y=0$

Let the location of team Charlie $=(x, 0)$

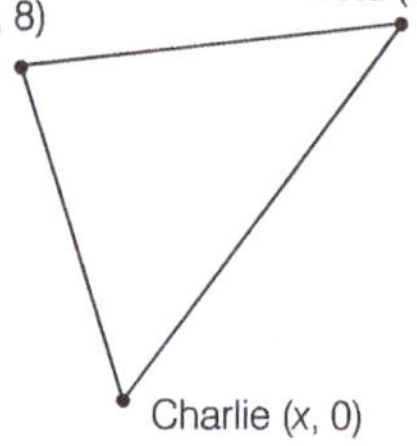

$\therefore$ Area of the triangle is

$$\pm 37=\frac{1}{2}\begin{vmatrix}3 & 8 & 1\\11 & 10 & 1\\x & 0 & 1\end{vmatrix}$$

$\Rightarrow \quad \pm 37=\frac{1}{2}[3(10-0)-8(11-x)+1(0-10x)]$

$\Rightarrow \quad \pm 37=\frac{1}{2}(30-88+8x-10x)$

$\Rightarrow \quad \pm 74=-58-2x \Rightarrow x=-66$ or 8

$\therefore \quad x=8$

(ii) The Alpha team, medical centre and Beta team are on the same line and hence area of the triangle formed by three collinear points will be zero.

$$\therefore \quad \frac{1}{2}\begin{vmatrix}3 & 8 & 1\\11 & 10 & 1\\5 & y & 1\end{vmatrix}=0$$

$\Rightarrow \frac{1}{2}[3(10-y)-8(11-5)+1(11y-50)]=0$

$\Rightarrow \quad 30-3y-88+40+11y-50=0$

$\Rightarrow \quad 8y=68$

$\therefore \quad y=\frac{68}{8}=8.5$ units

32. (i) $AB=\begin{bmatrix}1 & -1 & 2\\0 & 2 & -3\\3 & -2 & 4\end{bmatrix}\begin{bmatrix}-2 & 0 & 1\\9 & 2 & -3\\6 & 1 & -2\end{bmatrix}$

$$=\begin{bmatrix}-2-9+12 & 0-2+2 & 1+3-4\\0+18-18 & 0+4-3 & 0-6+6\\-6-18+24 & 0-4+4 & 3+6-8\end{bmatrix}$$

$$=\begin{bmatrix}1 & 0 & 0\\0 & 1 & 0\\0 & 0 & 1\end{bmatrix}=I$$

(ii) $|A|=\begin{vmatrix}1 & -1 & 2\\0 & 2 & -3\\3 & -2 & 4\end{vmatrix}$

$=1(8-6)+1(0+9)+2(0-6)=2+9-12=-1\neq 0$

So, A^{-1} exists.

Let A_{ij} be the cofactors of a_{ij} in $|A|$.

$A_{11}=(-1)^2(8-6)=2,$

$A_{21}=(-1)^3(-4+4)=0,$

$A_{31}=(-1)^4(3-4)=-1,$

$A_{12}=(-1)^3(0+9)=-9,$

$A_{22}=(-1)^4(4-6)=-2,$

$A_{32}=(-1)^5(-3-0)=3,$

$A_{13}=(-1)^4(0-6)=-6,$

$A_{23}=(-1)^5(-2+3)=-1$

and $\quad A_{33}=(-1)^6(2-0)=2$

$$\text{So, adj }(A)=\begin{bmatrix}2 & 0 & -1\\-9 & -2 & 3\\-6 & -1 & 2\end{bmatrix}$$

$$\therefore \quad A^{-1}=\frac{\text{adj}(A)}{|A|}=\begin{bmatrix}-2 & 0 & 1\\9 & 2 & -3\\6 & 1 & -2\end{bmatrix}$$

(iii) (a) The given system of equation is

$$x+3z=9$$
$$-x+2y-2z=4$$
$$2x-3y+4z=-3$$

In matrix form, $CX=D$, where

$$C=\begin{bmatrix}1&0&3\\-1&2&-2\\2&-3&4\end{bmatrix}, X=\begin{bmatrix}x\\y\\z\end{bmatrix} \text{ and } D=\begin{bmatrix}9\\4\\-3\end{bmatrix}$$

Now, $X=C^{-1}D$ ...(i)

But, $C=A^T$

$\therefore$ From Eq. (i),

$$X=(A^T)^{-1}D$$
$$\Rightarrow X=(A^{-1})^TD$$
$$\Rightarrow \begin{bmatrix}x\\y\\z\end{bmatrix}=\begin{bmatrix}-2&9&6\\0&2&1\\1&-3&-2\end{bmatrix}\begin{bmatrix}9\\4\\-3\end{bmatrix}$$
$$\Rightarrow \begin{bmatrix}x\\y\\z\end{bmatrix}=\begin{bmatrix}-18+36-18\\0+8-3\\9-12+6\end{bmatrix}=\begin{bmatrix}0\\5\\3\end{bmatrix}$$
$$\Rightarrow x=0, y=5 \text{ and } z=3$$

Or

(b) We have, $x=0, y=5$ and $z=3$

$\therefore x+y+z=0+5+3=8$

33. (i) The award money for Integrity, Diligence and Timeliness is ₹ x, ₹ y and ₹ z.

Now, Organisation P awarded a total of ₹ 2200 to 3, 2 and 1.

$$3x+2y+z=2200 \quad \text{...(i)}$$

Organisation Q awarded a total of ₹ 3100 to 4, 1 and 3.

$$4x+y+3z=3100 \quad \text{...(ii)}$$

Also, $x+y+z=1200$ ...(iii)

(ii) The above system of equation can be written in matrix form as $AX=B$

i.e. $$\begin{bmatrix}3&2&1\\4&1&3\\1&1&1\end{bmatrix}\begin{bmatrix}x\\y\\z\end{bmatrix}=\begin{bmatrix}2200\\3100\\1200\end{bmatrix}$$

When $$A=\begin{bmatrix}3&2&1\\4&1&3\\1&1&1\end{bmatrix}, X=\begin{bmatrix}x\\y\\z\end{bmatrix} \text{ and } B=\begin{bmatrix}2200\\3100\\1200\end{bmatrix}$$

(iii) (a) $$|A|=\begin{vmatrix}3&2&1\\4&1&3\\1&1&1\end{vmatrix}=3(1-3)-2(4-3)+1(4-1)$$
$$=-6-2+3=-5$$

Since, $|A|\neq 0$, so A^{-1} exists.

Let A_{ij} be the cofactors of a_{ij} in $|A|$.

$$A_{11}=(-1)^2(1-3)=-2,$$
$$A_{12}=(-1)^3(4-3)=-1,$$
$$A_{13}=(-1)^4(4-1)=3,$$
$$A_{21}=(-1)^3(2-1)=-1,$$
$$A_{22}=(-1)^4(3-1)=2,$$
$$A_{23}=(-1)^5(3-2)=-1,$$
$$A_{31}=(-1)^4(6-1)=5,$$
$$A_{32}=(-1)^5(9-4)=-5$$
and $$A_{33}=(-1)^6(3-8)=-5$$

So, $$\text{adj } A=\begin{bmatrix}-2&-1&5\\-1&2&-5\\3&-1&-5\end{bmatrix}$$

$$\therefore A^{-1}=\frac{\text{adj}(A)}{|A|}=\frac{-1}{5}\begin{bmatrix}-2&-1&5\\-1&2&-5\\3&-1&-5\end{bmatrix}$$

Now, $X=A^{-1}B$ ...(i)

$$\Rightarrow \begin{bmatrix}x\\y\\z\end{bmatrix}=\frac{-1}{5}\begin{bmatrix}-2&-1&5\\-1&2&-5\\3&-1&-5\end{bmatrix}\begin{bmatrix}2200\\3100\\1200\end{bmatrix}$$
$$\Rightarrow \begin{bmatrix}x\\y\\z\end{bmatrix}=\frac{-1}{5}\begin{bmatrix}-4400-3100+6000\\-2200+6200-6000\\6600-3100-6000\end{bmatrix}$$
$$=\begin{bmatrix}300\\400\\500\end{bmatrix}$$

$\therefore x=$ ₹ 300, $y=$ ₹ 400 and $z=$ ₹ 500

Or

(b) We have, $x=300$, $y=400$, $z=500$

Now, $$\frac{x+y}{z}=\frac{300+400}{500}=\frac{700}{500}=\frac{7}{5}$$

Subjective Questions

1. Given, $$\begin{vmatrix}3x&7\\-2&4\end{vmatrix}=\begin{vmatrix}8&7\\6&4\end{vmatrix}$$
$$\Rightarrow 12x+14=32-42$$
$$\Rightarrow 12x=-10-14$$
$$\Rightarrow 12x=-24$$
$$\therefore x=-2$$

2. We have, $$\begin{vmatrix}x+3&-2\\-3x&2x\end{vmatrix}=8$$
$$\Rightarrow 2x(x+3)-6x=8$$
$$\Rightarrow 2x^2+6x-6x=8$$
$$\Rightarrow 2x^2=8$$
$$\Rightarrow x^2=4$$
$$\Rightarrow x=\pm 2$$
$$\therefore x=2 \quad [\because x\in N]$$

3. Given, vertices of a triangle are (2, 7), (1, 1) and (10, 8).

Let $(x_1,y_1)=(2,7),(x_2,y_2)=(1,1)$ and $(x_3,y_3)=(10,8)$

Then, area of triangle $$=\frac{1}{2}\begin{vmatrix}x_1&y_1&1\\x_2&y_2&1\\x_3&y_3&1\end{vmatrix}$$
$$=\frac{1}{2}\begin{vmatrix}2&7&1\\1&1&1\\10&8&1\end{vmatrix}$$

$$= \frac{1}{2}[2(1-8) - 7(1-10) + 1(8-10)]$$
$$= \frac{1}{2}(-14 + 63 - 2) = \frac{1}{2}(47)$$
$$= 23.5 \text{ sq units}$$

4. Let $\Delta = \begin{vmatrix} 2 & -3 & 5 \\ 6 & 0 & 4 \\ 1 & 5 & -7 \end{vmatrix}$

Here, $a_{32} = 5$

Given, A_{ij} is the cofactor of the element a_{ij} of Δ.

$\because \quad A_{32} = (-1)^{3+2} \begin{vmatrix} 2 & 5 \\ 6 & 4 \end{vmatrix}$
$= -1(8 - 30) = 22$

$\therefore \quad a_{32} \cdot A_{32} = 5 \times 22 = 110$

5. We know that a matrix A is said to be singular, if $|A| = 0$.

$\because \quad \begin{vmatrix} 2x+2 & 2x \\ x & x-2 \end{vmatrix} = 0$

$(2x+2)(x-2) - 2x^2 = 0$

$\Rightarrow \quad 2x^2 - 2x - 4 - 2x^2 = 0$

$\Rightarrow \quad -2x = 4$

$\therefore \quad x = -2$

6. Given, $|A| = 4$

We know that $AA^{-1} = I$

$|AA^{-1}| = |I|$

$\Rightarrow \quad |A||A^{-1}| = |I| \quad [\because |AB| = |A||B|]$

$\Rightarrow \quad |A||A^{-1}| = 1 \quad [\because |I| = 1]$

$\Rightarrow \quad |A^{-1}| = \frac{1}{|A|}$

$\therefore \quad |A^{-1}| = \frac{1}{4}$

7. Given, $f(x) = \begin{vmatrix} 0 & x-a & x-b \\ x+a & 0 & x-c \\ x+b & x+c & 0 \end{vmatrix}$

$\therefore \quad f(0) = \begin{vmatrix} 0 & 0-a & 0-b \\ 0+a & 0 & 0-c \\ 0+b & 0+c & 0 \end{vmatrix}$

$= \begin{vmatrix} 0 & -a & -b \\ a & 0 & -c \\ b & c & 0 \end{vmatrix}$

$= a(bc) - b(ac) = 0$ **Hence proved.**

8. Given, A is skew-symmetric matrix.

$\therefore \quad A' = -A$

$\Rightarrow \quad |A'| = -|A|$

$\Rightarrow \quad |A| = -|A| \quad [\because |A| = |A'|]$

$\Rightarrow \quad 2|A| = 0$

$\therefore \quad |A| = 0$

9. Given area of a triangle with vertices $(-2, 0)$, $(0, 4)$ and $(0, k)$ is 4 sq units.

We have, $\frac{1}{2}\begin{vmatrix} -2 & 0 & 1 \\ 0 & 4 & 1 \\ 0 & k & 1 \end{vmatrix} = \pm 4$

$\Rightarrow \quad \begin{vmatrix} -2 & 0 & 1 \\ 0 & 4 & 1 \\ 0 & k & 1 \end{vmatrix} = \pm 8$

$\Rightarrow -2(4-k) - 0 + 1(0-0) = \pm 8$

$\Rightarrow \quad -8 + 2k = \pm 8$

$\Rightarrow \quad 2k = \pm 8 + 8$

$\Rightarrow \quad 2k = 16 \text{ or } 2k = 0$

$\therefore \quad k = 8 \text{ or } k = 0$

10. **Hint** We have to prove that these points form a triangle.

11. Given, $|A| = 12$

We know that if A is a square matrix of order n, then $|\text{adj}A| = |A|^{n-1}$.

$\therefore \quad |\text{adj}A| = |A|^{3-1} = |A|^2 = (12)^2 = 144$

12. **Hint** $\text{adj}A = \begin{bmatrix} C_{11} & C_{12} & C_{13} \\ C_{21} & C_{22} & C_{23} \\ C_{31} & C_{32} & C_{33} \end{bmatrix}^T$

and then show that $A(\text{adj}A) = |A|I_3$.

13. Let A be an invertible symmetric matrix.

Then, $|A| \neq 0$ and $A' = A$

Now, $(A^{-1})' = (A')^{-1}$

$\Rightarrow \quad (A^{-1})' = A^{-1} \quad [\because A = A']$

Thus, A^{-1} is symmetric matrix.

14. We have, $A = \begin{bmatrix} 1 & -2 & 3 \\ 0 & -1 & 4 \\ -2 & 2 & 1 \end{bmatrix}$

Now, $|A| = \begin{vmatrix} 1 & -2 & 3 \\ 0 & -1 & 4 \\ -2 & 2 & 1 \end{vmatrix}$

$= 1(-1-8) + 2(0+8) + 3(0-2)$ [expanding along R_1]

$= -9 + 16 - 6 = 1 \neq 0$

So, A is non-singular matrix and its inverse exists.

Cofactors of elements of $|A|$ are

$A_{11} = (-1)^{1+1}\begin{vmatrix} -1 & 4 \\ 2 & 1 \end{vmatrix} = (-1-8) = -9,$

$A_{12} = (-1)^{1+2}\begin{vmatrix} 0 & 4 \\ -2 & 1 \end{vmatrix} = -(0+8) = -8,$

$A_{13} = (-1)^{1+3}\begin{vmatrix} 0 & -1 \\ -2 & 2 \end{vmatrix} = (0-2) = -2,$

$A_{21} = (-1)^{2+1}\begin{vmatrix} -2 & 3 \\ 2 & 1 \end{vmatrix} = -(-2-6) = 8,$

$A_{22} = (-1)^{2+2}\begin{vmatrix} 1 & 3 \\ -2 & 1 \end{vmatrix} = (1+6) = 7,$

$$A_{23}=(-1)^{2+3}\begin{vmatrix}1 & -2\\ -2 & 2\end{vmatrix}=-(2-4)=2,$$

$$A_{31}=(-1)^{3+1}\begin{vmatrix}-2 & 3\\ -1 & 4\end{vmatrix}=(-8+3)=-5,$$

$$A_{32}=(-1)^{3+2}\begin{vmatrix}1 & 3\\ 0 & 4\end{vmatrix}=-(4-0)=-4$$

and $A_{33}=(-1)^{3+3}\begin{vmatrix}1 & -2\\ 0 & -1\end{vmatrix}=(-1+0)=-1$

Thus, $\text{adj}A=\begin{bmatrix}A_{11} & A_{21} & A_{31}\\ A_{12} & A_{22} & A_{32}\\ A_{13} & A_{23} & A_{33}\end{bmatrix}=\begin{bmatrix}-9 & 8 & -5\\ -8 & 7 & -4\\ -2 & 2 & -1\end{bmatrix}$

Hence, $A^{-1}=\frac{1}{|A|}\text{adj}A=\frac{1}{1}\begin{bmatrix}-9 & 8 & -5\\ -8 & 7 & -4\\ -2 & 2 & -1\end{bmatrix}$

Now, $(A')^{-1}=(A^{-1})'=\begin{bmatrix}-9 & 8 & -5\\ -8 & 7 & -4\\ -2 & 2 & -1\end{bmatrix}'=\begin{bmatrix}-9 & -8 & -2\\ 8 & 7 & 2\\ -5 & -4 & -1\end{bmatrix}$

15. Given, $A^2=I$ ...(i)

Since, A is non-singular matrix.

$\therefore$ $|A|\neq 0$, so A^{-1} exists.

On pre-multiplying both sides by A^{-1} in Eq. (i), we get

$$A^{-1}(A^2)=A^{-1}I$$

$\Rightarrow$ $(A^{-1}A)A=A^{-1}$

$\Rightarrow$ $IA=A^{-1}$ $[\because A^{-1}A=I]$

$\therefore$ $A^{-1}=A$

16. Given, $A=\begin{bmatrix}3 & -2\\ 4 & -2\end{bmatrix}$

Also given, $A^2=\lambda A-2I$

$\Rightarrow$ $\lambda A=A^2+2I$

$$=\begin{bmatrix}3 & -2\\ 4 & -2\end{bmatrix}\begin{bmatrix}3 & -2\\ 4 & -2\end{bmatrix}+2\begin{bmatrix}1 & 0\\ 0 & 1\end{bmatrix}$$

$\Rightarrow$ $\lambda\begin{bmatrix}3 & -2\\ 4 & -2\end{bmatrix}=\begin{bmatrix}1 & -2\\ 4 & -4\end{bmatrix}+\begin{bmatrix}2 & 0\\ 0 & 2\end{bmatrix}$

$\Rightarrow$ $\begin{bmatrix}3\lambda & -2\lambda\\ 4\lambda & -2\lambda\end{bmatrix}=\begin{bmatrix}3 & -2\\ 4 & -2\end{bmatrix}$

$\Rightarrow$ $3\lambda=3\Rightarrow\lambda=1$

So, $A^2=A-2I$

$\Rightarrow$ $A^{-1}(A^2)=A^{-1}A-2A^{-1}I$ [pre-multiplying by A^{-1}]

$\Rightarrow$ $(A^{-1}A)A=I-2A^{-1}$ $[\because A^{-1}A=I]$

$\Rightarrow$ $IA=I-2A^{-1}$

$\Rightarrow$ $2A^{-1}=I-A$

$\Rightarrow$ $2A^{-1}=\begin{bmatrix}1 & 0\\ 0 & 1\end{bmatrix}-\begin{bmatrix}3 & -2\\ 4 & -2\end{bmatrix}$

$\Rightarrow$ $2A^{-1}=\begin{bmatrix}-2 & 2\\ -4 & 3\end{bmatrix}$

$\therefore$ $A^{-1}=\frac{1}{2}\begin{bmatrix}-2 & 2\\ -4 & 3\end{bmatrix}$

17. $|A|=\begin{vmatrix}1 & 2 & 2\\ 2 & 1 & 2\\ 2 & 2 & 1\end{vmatrix}=1(1-4)-2(2-4)+2(4-2)$

$=-3+4+4=5\neq 0.$

Cofactors of elements of $|A|$ are

$A_{11}=+(1-4)=-3.$

$A_{12}=-(2-4)=2$

$A_{13}=+(4-2)=2$

$A_{21}=-(2-4)=2$

$A_{22}=+(1-4)=-3$

$A_{23}=-(2-4)=2$

$A_{31}=+(4-2)=2$

$A_{32}=-(2-4)=2$

$A_{33}=+(1-4)=-3$

$\therefore$ $\text{adj}\,A=\begin{bmatrix}A_{11} & A_{21} & A_{31}\\ A_{12} & A_{22} & A_{32}\\ A_{13} & A_{23} & A_{33}\end{bmatrix}=\begin{bmatrix}-3 & 2 & 2\\ 2 & -3 & 2\\ 2 & 2 & -3\end{bmatrix}$

$\therefore$ $A^{-1}=\frac{1}{|A|}\text{adj}\,A=\frac{1}{5}\begin{bmatrix}-3 & 2 & 2\\ 2 & -3 & 2\\ 2 & 2 & -3\end{bmatrix}$ ...(i)

Consider $A^2-4A-5I=O$

On pre-multiplying both sides by A^{-1}, we get

$A^{-1}(AA)-4A^{-1}A-5A^{-1}I=A^{-1}O$

$\Rightarrow$ $(A^{-1}A)A-4I-5A^{-1}=O$

$\Rightarrow$ $IA-4I-5A^{-1}=O$

$\Rightarrow$ $IA-4I=5A^{-1}$

$\Rightarrow$ $A-4I=5A^{-1}$

$$\text{LHS}=\begin{bmatrix}1 & 2 & 2\\ 2 & 1 & 2\\ 2 & 2 & 1\end{bmatrix}-4\begin{bmatrix}1 & 0 & 0\\ 0 & 1 & 0\\ 0 & 0 & 1\end{bmatrix}=\begin{bmatrix}1 & 2 & 2\\ 2 & 1 & 2\\ 2 & 2 & 1\end{bmatrix}-\begin{bmatrix}4 & 0 & 0\\ 0 & 4 & 0\\ 0 & 0 & 4\end{bmatrix}$$

$$=\begin{bmatrix}1-4 & 2-0 & 2-0\\ 2-0 & 1-4 & 2-0\\ 2-0 & 2-0 & 1-4\end{bmatrix}$$

$$=\begin{bmatrix}-3 & 2 & 2\\ 2 & -3 & 2\\ 2 & 2 & -3\end{bmatrix}=5\times\frac{1}{5}\begin{bmatrix}-3 & 2 & 2\\ 2 & -3 & 2\\ 2 & 2 & -3\end{bmatrix}$$

$=5A^{-1}=\text{RHS}$

Hence, $A^2-4A-5I=O$

18. We have, $A=\begin{bmatrix}\cos\alpha & -\sin\alpha & 0\\ \sin\alpha & \cos\alpha & 0\\ 0 & 0 & 1\end{bmatrix}$

Clearly, the cofactors of elements of $|A|$ are given by

$A_{11}=\cos\alpha$, $A_{12}=-\sin\alpha$, $A_{13}=0$,

$A_{21}=\sin\alpha$, $A_{22}=\cos\alpha$, $A_{23}=0$,

$A_{31}=0, A_{32}=0$ and $A_{33}=1$

$\therefore$ adj $(A) = \begin{bmatrix} A_{11} & A_{12} & A_{13} \\ A_{21} & A_{22} & A_{23} \\ A_{31} & A_{32} & A_{33} \end{bmatrix}^T$

$= \begin{bmatrix} \cos\alpha & -\sin\alpha & 0 \\ \sin\alpha & \cos\alpha & 0 \\ 0 & 0 & 1 \end{bmatrix}^T = \begin{bmatrix} \cos\alpha & \sin\alpha & 0 \\ -\sin\alpha & \cos\alpha & 0 \\ 0 & 0 & 1 \end{bmatrix}$

Now, $A(\text{adj}A)$

$= \begin{bmatrix} \cos\alpha & -\sin\alpha & 0 \\ \sin\alpha & \cos\alpha & 0 \\ 0 & 0 & 1 \end{bmatrix} \begin{bmatrix} \cos\alpha & \sin\alpha & 0 \\ -\sin\alpha & \cos\alpha & 0 \\ 0 & 0 & 1 \end{bmatrix}$

$= \begin{bmatrix} \cos^2\alpha + \sin^2\alpha & 0 & 0 \\ 0 & \sin^2\alpha + \cos^2\alpha & 0 \\ 0 & 0 & 1 \end{bmatrix} = \begin{bmatrix} 1 & 0 & 0 \\ 0 & 1 & 0 \\ 0 & 0 & 1 \end{bmatrix}$ ...(i)

$(\text{adj}A)\cdot(A) = \begin{bmatrix} \cos\alpha & \sin\alpha & 0 \\ -\sin\alpha & \cos\alpha & 0 \\ 0 & 0 & 1 \end{bmatrix} \begin{bmatrix} \cos\alpha & -\sin\alpha & 0 \\ \sin\alpha & \cos\alpha & 0 \\ 0 & 0 & 1 \end{bmatrix}$

$= \begin{bmatrix} \cos^2\alpha + \sin^2\alpha & 0 & 0 \\ 0 & \sin^2\alpha + \cos^2\alpha & 0 \\ 0 & 0 & 1 \end{bmatrix} = \begin{bmatrix} 1 & 0 & 0 \\ 0 & 1 & 0 \\ 0 & 0 & 1 \end{bmatrix}$ ...(ii)

and $|A| = \begin{vmatrix} \cos\alpha & -\sin\alpha & 0 \\ \sin\alpha & \cos\alpha & 0 \\ 0 & 0 & 1 \end{vmatrix} = 1\cdot(\cos^2\alpha + \sin^2\alpha) = 1$

[expanding along R_3]

$\therefore \quad |A| I_3 = \begin{bmatrix} 1 & 0 & 0 \\ 0 & 1 & 0 \\ 0 & 0 & 1 \end{bmatrix}$ ...(iii)

From Eqs. (i), (ii) and (iii), we get

$$A(\text{adj}A) = (\text{adj}A)\cdot A = |A| I_3$$

19. Given, $A = \begin{bmatrix} 5 & 3 \\ -2 & 4 \end{bmatrix}$ and $B = \begin{bmatrix} 2 & -3 \\ 4 & -8 \end{bmatrix}$

$\therefore$ adj $A = \begin{bmatrix} 4 & -3 \\ 2 & 5 \end{bmatrix}$ and adj $B = \begin{bmatrix} -8 & 3 \\ -4 & 2 \end{bmatrix}$

Now, $(\text{adj}A) \times (\text{adj}B) = \begin{bmatrix} 4 & -3 \\ 2 & 5 \end{bmatrix} \times \begin{bmatrix} -8 & 3 \\ -4 & 2 \end{bmatrix}$

$\Rightarrow \quad (\text{adj}A) \times (\text{adj}B) = \begin{bmatrix} -20 & 6 \\ -36 & 16 \end{bmatrix}$ ... (i)

and $\quad B \times A = \begin{bmatrix} 2 & -3 \\ 4 & -8 \end{bmatrix} \times \begin{bmatrix} 5 & 3 \\ -2 & 4 \end{bmatrix} = \begin{bmatrix} 16 & -6 \\ 36 & -20 \end{bmatrix}$

adj $(BA) = \begin{bmatrix} -20 & 6 \\ -36 & 16 \end{bmatrix}$ ... (ii)

From Eqs. (i) and (ii), we get

$(\text{adj}A) \times (\text{adj}B) = \text{adj}(BA)$ **Hence proved.**

20. Given, $A = \begin{bmatrix} 4 & -8 \\ 12 & 16 \end{bmatrix}$ and $B = \begin{bmatrix} -16 & -8 \\ 12 & -4 \end{bmatrix}$

Cofactors of elements of $|A|$,

$A_{11} = 16, A_{12} = -12, A_{21} = 8$ and $A_{22} = 4$

$\therefore \quad \text{adj}(A) = \begin{bmatrix} 16 & -12 \\ 8 & 4 \end{bmatrix}' = \begin{bmatrix} 16 & 8 \\ -12 & 4 \end{bmatrix}$

and cofactors of elements of $|B|$,

$B_{11} = -4, B_{12} = -12$

$B_{21} = 8$ and $B_{22} = -16$

$\therefore \quad \text{adj}(B) = \begin{bmatrix} -4 & -12 \\ 8 & -16 \end{bmatrix}' = \begin{bmatrix} -4 & 8 \\ -12 & -16 \end{bmatrix}$

Now, $\text{adj}(A) \times \text{adj}(B) = \begin{bmatrix} 16 & 8 \\ -12 & 4 \end{bmatrix} \begin{bmatrix} -4 & 8 \\ -12 & -16 \end{bmatrix}$

$= 16 \begin{bmatrix} 4 & 2 \\ -3 & 1 \end{bmatrix} \begin{bmatrix} -1 & 2 \\ -3 & -4 \end{bmatrix}$

$= 16 \begin{bmatrix} -4-6 & 8-8 \\ 3-3 & -6-4 \end{bmatrix}$

$= 16 \begin{bmatrix} -10 & 0 \\ 0 & -10 \end{bmatrix}$

$= \begin{bmatrix} -160 & 0 \\ 0 & -160 \end{bmatrix}$,

which is a diagonal matrix.

21. Clearly, $|A| = \begin{vmatrix} 1 & \tan x \\ -\tan x & 1 \end{vmatrix} = 1 + \tan^2 x \neq 0$

So, A is invertible.

Let C_{ij} be the cofactor of a_{ij} in $A = [a_{ij}]$.

Then, $C_{11} = 1, C_{12} = \tan x, C_{21} = -\tan x$ and $C_{22} = 1$

$\therefore \quad \text{adj}A = \begin{bmatrix} C_{11} & C_{12} \\ C_{21} & C_{22} \end{bmatrix}^T = \begin{bmatrix} 1 & \tan x \\ -\tan x & 1 \end{bmatrix}^T$

$= \begin{bmatrix} 1 & -\tan x \\ \tan x & 1 \end{bmatrix}$

Now, $A^{-1} = \dfrac{1}{|A|}\text{adj}A = \dfrac{1}{1+\tan^2 x} \begin{bmatrix} 1 & -\tan x \\ \tan x & 1 \end{bmatrix}$

$= \begin{bmatrix} \dfrac{1}{1+\tan^2 x} & \dfrac{-\tan x}{1+\tan^2 x} \\ \dfrac{\tan x}{1+\tan^2 x} & \dfrac{1}{1+\tan^2 x} \end{bmatrix}$

$\therefore \quad A^T A^{-1} = \begin{bmatrix} 1 & -\tan x \\ \tan x & 1 \end{bmatrix} \begin{bmatrix} \dfrac{1}{1+\tan^2 x} & \dfrac{-\tan x}{1+\tan^2 x} \\ \dfrac{\tan x}{1+\tan^2 x} & \dfrac{1}{1+\tan^2 x} \end{bmatrix}$

$= \begin{bmatrix} \dfrac{1}{1+\tan^2 x} - \dfrac{\tan^2 x}{1+\tan^2 x} & -\dfrac{\tan x}{1+\tan^2 x} - \dfrac{\tan x}{1+\tan^2 x} \\ \dfrac{\tan x}{1+\tan^2 x} + \dfrac{\tan x}{1+\tan^2 x} & -\dfrac{\tan^2 x}{1+\tan^2 x} + \dfrac{1}{1+\tan^2 x} \end{bmatrix}$

$= \begin{bmatrix} \dfrac{1-\tan^2 x}{1+\tan^2 x} & \dfrac{-2\tan x}{1+\tan^2 x} \\ \dfrac{2\tan x}{1+\tan^2 x} & \dfrac{1-\tan^2 x}{1+\tan^2 x} \end{bmatrix} = \begin{bmatrix} \cos 2x & -\sin 2x \\ \sin 2x & \cos 2x \end{bmatrix}$

22. Here, $A=\begin{bmatrix}2 & -1\\ -1 & 2\end{bmatrix}$.

Now, $A^2=A\cdot A=\begin{bmatrix}2 & -1\\ -1 & 2\end{bmatrix}\begin{bmatrix}2 & -1\\ -1 & 2\end{bmatrix}$

$$=\begin{bmatrix}4+1 & -2-2\\ -2-2 & 1+4\end{bmatrix}=\begin{bmatrix}5 & -4\\ -4 & 5\end{bmatrix}$$

[multiplying the rows by columns] ...(i)

Also, $4A-3I=4\begin{bmatrix}2 & -1\\ -1 & 2\end{bmatrix}-3\begin{bmatrix}1 & 0\\ 0 & 1\end{bmatrix}$

$$=\begin{bmatrix}8 & -4\\ -4 & 8\end{bmatrix}-\begin{bmatrix}3 & 0\\ 0 & 3\end{bmatrix}=\begin{bmatrix}5 & -4\\ -4 & 5\end{bmatrix} \quad \text{...(ii)}$$

From Eqs. (i) and (ii), we get

$$A^2=4A-3I \quad \text{...(iii)}$$

Now, $|A|=\begin{vmatrix}2 & -1\\ -1 & 2\end{vmatrix}=4-1=3\neq 0$

$\therefore$ A^{-1} exists.

Now, pre-multiplying both sides of Eq. (iii) by A^{-1}, we get

$$A^{-1}\cdot A^2=A^{-1}\cdot(4A-3I)$$

$\Rightarrow$ $(A^{-1}\cdot A)\cdot A=4A^{-1}\cdot A-3A^{-1}\cdot I$

$\Rightarrow$ $IA=4I-3A^{-1}$

$[\because A\cdot A^{-1}=I=A^{-1}A \text{ and } A^{-1}\cdot I=A^{-1}]$

$\Rightarrow$ $A=4I-3A^{-1}$ $[\because IA=A=AI]$

$\Rightarrow$ $3A^{-1}=4I-A$

$\therefore$ $A^{-1}=\dfrac{1}{3}\left(4\begin{bmatrix}1 & 0\\ 0 & 1\end{bmatrix}-\begin{bmatrix}2 & -1\\ -1 & 2\end{bmatrix}\right)$

$$=\frac{1}{3}\left(\begin{bmatrix}4 & 0\\ 0 & 4\end{bmatrix}-\begin{bmatrix}2 & -1\\ -1 & 2\end{bmatrix}\right)$$

$$=\frac{1}{3}\begin{bmatrix}2 & 1\\ 1 & 2\end{bmatrix}=\begin{bmatrix}2/3 & 1/3\\ 1/3 & 2/3\end{bmatrix}$$

23. Let $B=\begin{bmatrix}2 & 1\\ 3 & 2\end{bmatrix}$ and $C=\begin{bmatrix}-3 & 2\\ 5 & -3\end{bmatrix}$, then the given equation reduces to

$$BAC=I \quad \text{...(i)}$$

Now, as $|B|=\begin{vmatrix}2 & 1\\ 3 & 2\end{vmatrix}=4-3=1\neq 0$

and $|C|=\begin{vmatrix}-3 & 2\\ 5 & -3\end{vmatrix}=9-10=-1\neq 0$

$\therefore$ Both B^{-1} and C^{-1} exist.

Now, pre-multiplying both sides by B^{-1} in Eq. (i), we get

$$B^{-1}(BAC)=B^{-1}\cdot I \quad [\because B^{-1}I=B^{-1}]$$

$\Rightarrow$ $(B^{-1}B)(AC)=B^{-1}\Rightarrow I(AC)=B^{-1}$ $[\because B^{-1}B=I]$

$\Rightarrow$ $AC=B^{-1}$ ...(ii)

Now, post-multiplying both sides of Eq. (ii) by C^{-1}, we get

$$(AC)C^{-1}=B^{-1}C^{-1}$$

$\Rightarrow$ $A(CC^{-1})=B^{-1}C^{-1}$

$\Rightarrow$ $A\cdot I=B^{-1}C^{-1}$ $[\because CC^{-1}=I]$

$\Rightarrow$ $A=B^{-1}C^{-1}$ ...(iii)

Now, let us find B^{-1} and C^{-1}.

Clearly, $B^{-1}=\dfrac{1}{|B|}\text{adj}\,B=\dfrac{1}{1}\begin{bmatrix}2 & -1\\ -3 & 2\end{bmatrix}$

$$\left[\because \text{adj}\begin{bmatrix}a & b\\ c & d\end{bmatrix}=\begin{bmatrix}d & -b\\ -c & a\end{bmatrix}\right]$$

$$=\begin{bmatrix}2 & -1\\ -3 & 2\end{bmatrix}$$

and $C^{-1}=\dfrac{1}{|C|}\text{adj}\,C=\dfrac{1}{-1}\begin{bmatrix}-3 & -2\\ -5 & -3\end{bmatrix}=\begin{bmatrix}3 & 2\\ 5 & 3\end{bmatrix}$

$\therefore$ From Eq. (iii), we get

$$A=\begin{bmatrix}2 & -1\\ -3 & 2\end{bmatrix}\begin{bmatrix}3 & 2\\ 5 & 3\end{bmatrix}=\begin{bmatrix}6-5 & 4-3\\ -9+10 & -6+6\end{bmatrix}=\begin{bmatrix}1 & 1\\ 1 & 0\end{bmatrix}$$

24. Hint First of all find adj A and A^{-1} and then find $(\text{adj}\,A)^{-1}$ $=\dfrac{1}{|\text{adj}\,A|}$ adj (adj A) and adj A^{-1}.

25. Let $B=\begin{bmatrix}2 & 4\\ 1 & 3\end{bmatrix}$, $C=\begin{bmatrix}0 & 2\\ 1 & 3\end{bmatrix}$ and $D=\begin{bmatrix}1 & 6\\ 3 & -2\end{bmatrix}$

Then, $BAC=D\Rightarrow A=B^{-1}DC^{-1}$ ...(i)

Now, $B=\begin{bmatrix}2 & 4\\ 1 & 3\end{bmatrix}\Rightarrow|B|=\begin{vmatrix}2 & 4\\ 1 & 3\end{vmatrix}=6-4=2$

and adj $B=\begin{bmatrix}3 & -4\\ -1 & 2\end{bmatrix}$

$\therefore$ $B^{-1}=\dfrac{1}{|B|}\text{adj}\,B=\dfrac{1}{2}\begin{bmatrix}3 & -4\\ -1 & 2\end{bmatrix}$

Now, $C=\begin{bmatrix}0 & 2\\ 1 & 3\end{bmatrix}\Rightarrow|C|=\begin{vmatrix}0 & 2\\ 1 & 3\end{vmatrix}=0-2=-2$

and adj $C=\begin{bmatrix}3 & -2\\ -1 & 0\end{bmatrix}$

$\therefore$ $C^{-1}=\dfrac{1}{|C|}\text{adj}\,C=-\dfrac{1}{2}\begin{bmatrix}3 & -2\\ -1 & 0\end{bmatrix}$

From Eq. (i), $A=B^{-1}DC^{-1}$

$$=-\frac{1}{4}\begin{bmatrix}3 & -4\\ -1 & 2\end{bmatrix}\begin{bmatrix}1 & 6\\ 3 & -2\end{bmatrix}\begin{bmatrix}3 & -2\\ -1 & 0\end{bmatrix}$$

$$=-\frac{1}{4}\begin{bmatrix}3 & -4\\ -1 & 2\end{bmatrix}\begin{bmatrix}3-6 & -2+0\\ 9+2 & -6-0\end{bmatrix}$$

$$=-\frac{1}{4}\begin{bmatrix}3 & -4\\ -1 & 2\end{bmatrix}\begin{bmatrix}-3 & -2\\ 11 & -6\end{bmatrix}$$

$$=-\frac{1}{4}\begin{bmatrix}-9-44 & -6+24\\ 3+22 & 2-12\end{bmatrix}=-\frac{1}{4}\begin{bmatrix}-53 & 18\\ 25 & -10\end{bmatrix}$$

26. We have, $A=\begin{bmatrix}1 & 2 & -3\\ 3 & 2 & -2\\ 2 & -1 & -1\end{bmatrix}$

Cofactors of elements of determinant A

$$A_{11}=(-1)^{1+1}(-2-2)=-4,$$
$$A_{12}=(-1)^{1+2}(-3+4)=-1,$$
$$A_{13}=(-1)^{1+3}(-3-4)=-7,$$
$$A_{21}=(-1)^{2+1}(-2-3)=5,$$

$$A_{22}=(-1)^{2+2}(-1+6)=5,$$
$$A_{23}=(-1)^{2+3}(-1-4)=5,$$
$$A_{31}=(-1)^{3+1}(-4+6)=2,$$
$$A_{32}=(-1)^{3+2}(-2+9)=-7$$

and $A_{33}=(-1)^{3+3}(2-6)=-4$

$$\therefore \quad \text{adj}A=\begin{bmatrix}-4&-1&-7\\5&5&5\\2&-7&-4\end{bmatrix}^T=\begin{bmatrix}-4&5&2\\-1&5&-7\\-7&5&-4\end{bmatrix}$$

$$|A|=a_{11}A_{11}+a_{12}A_{12}+a_{13}A_{13}$$
$$=1\times(-4)+2\times(-1)+(-3)\times(-7)$$
$$=-4-2+21=15$$

and $$A^{-1}=\frac{1}{|A|}\text{adj}A=\frac{1}{15}\begin{bmatrix}-4&5&2\\-1&5&-7\\-7&5&-4\end{bmatrix}$$

Now, we have $x+3y+2z=6, 2x+2y-z=3$ and $-3x-2y-z=5$

$$\begin{bmatrix}1&3&2\\2&2&-1\\-3&-2&-1\end{bmatrix}\begin{bmatrix}x\\y\\z\end{bmatrix}=\begin{bmatrix}6\\3\\5\end{bmatrix}\Rightarrow\begin{bmatrix}x\\y\\z\end{bmatrix}=\begin{bmatrix}1&3&2\\2&2&-1\\-3&-2&-1\end{bmatrix}^{-1}\begin{bmatrix}6\\3\\5\end{bmatrix}$$

$$=\left(\begin{bmatrix}1&2&-3\\3&2&-2\\2&-1&-1\end{bmatrix}^T\right)^{-1}\begin{bmatrix}6\\3\\5\end{bmatrix}$$

$$=\left(\begin{bmatrix}1&2&-3\\3&2&-2\\2&-1&-1\end{bmatrix}^{-1}\right)'\begin{bmatrix}6\\3\\5\end{bmatrix}$$

$$[\because (A')^{-1}=(A^{-1})']$$

$$=\left(\frac{1}{15}\begin{bmatrix}-4&5&2\\-1&5&-7\\-7&5&-4\end{bmatrix}\right)'\begin{bmatrix}6\\3\\5\end{bmatrix}$$

$$=\frac{1}{15}\begin{bmatrix}-4&-1&-7\\5&5&5\\2&-7&-4\end{bmatrix}\begin{bmatrix}6\\3\\5\end{bmatrix}$$

$$\Rightarrow \begin{bmatrix}x\\y\\z\end{bmatrix}=\frac{1}{15}\begin{bmatrix}-24-3-35\\30+15+25\\12-21-20\end{bmatrix}=\frac{1}{15}\begin{bmatrix}-62\\70\\-29\end{bmatrix}$$

$$\therefore \quad x=-\frac{62}{15}, y=\frac{70}{15} \text{ and } z=-\frac{29}{15}$$

27. We have,

$$A=\begin{bmatrix}1&-1&0\\2&3&4\\0&1&2\end{bmatrix} \text{ and } B=\begin{bmatrix}2&2&-4\\-4&2&-4\\2&-1&5\end{bmatrix}$$

$$\therefore \quad AB=\begin{bmatrix}1&-1&0\\2&3&4\\0&1&2\end{bmatrix}\begin{bmatrix}2&2&-4\\-4&2&-4\\2&-1&5\end{bmatrix}$$

$$=\begin{bmatrix}2+4+0&2-2+0&-4+4+0\\4-12+8&4+6-4&-8-12+20\\0-4+4&0+2-2&0-4+10\end{bmatrix}$$

$$=\begin{bmatrix}6&0&0\\0&6&0\\0&0&6\end{bmatrix}=6I$$

$$\Rightarrow \quad A\left(\frac{1}{6}B\right)=I$$

$$\Rightarrow \quad A^{-1}=\frac{1}{6}B$$

$$=\frac{1}{6}\begin{bmatrix}2&2&-4\\-4&2&-4\\2&-1&5\end{bmatrix}$$

The given system of equations can be written in matrix form as, $\begin{bmatrix}1&-1&0\\2&3&4\\0&1&2\end{bmatrix}\begin{bmatrix}x\\y\\z\end{bmatrix}=\begin{bmatrix}3\\17\\7\end{bmatrix}$

or $AX=D$, where $A=\begin{bmatrix}1&-1&0\\2&3&4\\0&1&2\end{bmatrix}, X=\begin{bmatrix}x\\y\\z\end{bmatrix}$

and $D=\begin{bmatrix}3\\17\\7\end{bmatrix}\Rightarrow X=A^{-1}D$

$$=\frac{1}{6}\begin{bmatrix}2&2&-4\\-4&2&-4\\2&-1&5\end{bmatrix}\begin{bmatrix}3\\17\\7\end{bmatrix}$$

$$=\frac{1}{6}\begin{bmatrix}6+34-28\\-12+34-28\\6-17+35\end{bmatrix}=\frac{1}{6}\begin{bmatrix}12\\-6\\24\end{bmatrix}=\begin{bmatrix}2\\-1\\4\end{bmatrix}$$

$\therefore \ x=2, y=-1$ and $z=4$

28. Here, $|A|=\begin{vmatrix}1&3&4\\2&1&2\\5&1&1\end{vmatrix}$

$$=1(1-2)-3(2-10)+4(2-5)$$
$$=-1+24-12=11\neq 0$$

Thus, A is invertible.

Clearly, the system has a unique solution given by $X=A^{-1}B$

Now, the cofactors of elements of $|A|$ are

$$A_{11}=-1, A_{12}=8, A_{13}=-3,$$
$$A_{21}=1, A_{22}=-19, A_{23}=14,$$
$$A_{31}=2, A_{32}=6 \text{ and } A_{33}=-5$$

$$\therefore \ \text{adj}(A)=\begin{bmatrix}-1&8&-3\\1&-19&14\\2&6&-5\end{bmatrix}'=\begin{bmatrix}-1&1&2\\8&-19&6\\-3&14&-5\end{bmatrix}$$

So, $A^{-1}=\frac{1}{|A|}\cdot\text{adj}(A)$

$$=\frac{1}{11}\cdot\begin{bmatrix}-1&1&2\\8&-19&6\\-3&14&-5\end{bmatrix}=\begin{bmatrix}-\frac{1}{11}&\frac{1}{11}&\frac{2}{11}\\\frac{8}{11}&-\frac{19}{11}&\frac{6}{11}\\-\frac{3}{11}&\frac{14}{11}&\frac{-5}{11}\end{bmatrix}$$

$$= \frac{1}{11} \cdot \begin{bmatrix} -1 & 1 & 2 \\ 8 & -19 & 6 \\ -3 & 14 & -5 \end{bmatrix} = \begin{bmatrix} -\frac{1}{11} & \frac{1}{11} & \frac{2}{11} \\ \frac{8}{11} & -\frac{19}{11} & \frac{6}{11} \\ -\frac{3}{11} & \frac{14}{11} & \frac{-5}{11} \end{bmatrix}$$

The given equations are

$$x + 3y + 4z = 8 \quad \text{...(i)}$$

$$2x + y + 2z = 5 \quad \text{...(ii)}$$

$$5x + y + z = 7 \quad \text{...(iii)}$$

Which can be written in matrix form as $AX = B$,

where $A = \begin{bmatrix} 1 & 3 & 4 \\ 2 & 1 & 2 \\ 5 & 1 & 1 \end{bmatrix}, X = \begin{bmatrix} x \\ y \\ z \end{bmatrix}$ and $B = \begin{bmatrix} 8 \\ 5 \\ 7 \end{bmatrix}$

$$\Rightarrow \begin{bmatrix} x \\ y \\ z \end{bmatrix} = \begin{bmatrix} \frac{-1}{11} & \frac{1}{11} & \frac{2}{11} \\ \frac{8}{11} & \frac{-19}{11} & \frac{6}{11} \\ \frac{-3}{11} & \frac{14}{11} & \frac{-5}{11} \end{bmatrix} \begin{bmatrix} 8 \\ 5 \\ 7 \end{bmatrix} \quad [\because X = A^{-1}B]$$

$$= \begin{bmatrix} -\frac{8}{11} + \frac{5}{11} + \frac{14}{11} \\ \frac{64}{11} - \frac{95}{11} + \frac{42}{11} \\ -\frac{24}{11} + \frac{70}{11} - \frac{35}{11} \end{bmatrix} = \begin{bmatrix} \frac{11}{11} \\ \frac{11}{11} \\ \frac{11}{11} \end{bmatrix} \Rightarrow \begin{bmatrix} x \\ y \\ z \end{bmatrix} = \begin{bmatrix} 1 \\ 1 \\ 1 \end{bmatrix}$$

$\therefore \; x = 1, y = 1$ and $z = 1$

29. The given system of linear equations can be written in matrix form as

$$AX = B \quad \text{...(i)}$$

Where, $A = \begin{bmatrix} 4 & 3 & 2 \\ 1 & 2 & 3 \\ 6 & 2 & 3 \end{bmatrix}, X = \begin{bmatrix} x \\ y \\ z \end{bmatrix}$ and $B = \begin{bmatrix} 60 \\ 45 \\ 70 \end{bmatrix}$

Now, $|A| = \begin{vmatrix} 4 & 3 & 2 \\ 1 & 2 & 3 \\ 6 & 2 & 3 \end{vmatrix}$

$$= 4(6-6) - 3(3-18) + 2(2-12)$$

$$= 0 + 45 - 20 = 25 \neq 0$$

Thus, A is a non-singular matrix.

So, A^{-1} exits.

Cofactors of elements of $|A|$ are

$C_{11} = (-1)^{1+1}\begin{vmatrix} 2 & 3 \\ 2 & 3 \end{vmatrix} = 6 - 6 = 0,$

$C_{12} = (-1)^{1+2}\begin{vmatrix} 1 & 3 \\ 6 & 3 \end{vmatrix} = -(3-18) = 15,$

$C_{13} = (-1)^{1+3}\begin{vmatrix} 1 & 2 \\ 6 & 2 \end{vmatrix} = (2-12) = -10,$

$C_{21} = (-1)^{2+1}\begin{vmatrix} 3 & 2 \\ 2 & 3 \end{vmatrix} = -(9-4) = -5,$

$C_{22} = (-1)^{2+2}\begin{vmatrix} 4 & 2 \\ 6 & 3 \end{vmatrix} = (12-12) = 0,$

$C_{23} = (-1)^{2+3}\begin{vmatrix} 4 & 3 \\ 6 & 2 \end{vmatrix} = -(8-18) = 10,$

$C_{31} = (-1)^{3+1}\begin{vmatrix} 3 & 2 \\ 2 & 3 \end{vmatrix} = (9-4) = 5,$

$C_{32} = (-1)^{3+2}\begin{vmatrix} 4 & 2 \\ 1 & 3 \end{vmatrix} = -(12-2) = -10$

and $C_{33} = (-1)^{3+3}\begin{vmatrix} 4 & 3 \\ 1 & 2 \end{vmatrix} = (8-3) = 5$

Thus, adj $A = \begin{bmatrix} C_{11} & C_{12} & C_{13} \\ C_{21} & C_{22} & C_{23} \\ C_{31} & C_{32} & C_{33} \end{bmatrix}^T$

$$= \begin{bmatrix} 0 & 15 & -10 \\ -5 & 0 & 10 \\ 5 & -10 & 5 \end{bmatrix}^T = \begin{bmatrix} 0 & -5 & 5 \\ 15 & 0 & -10 \\ -10 & 10 & 5 \end{bmatrix}$$

Now, $A^{-1} = \frac{1}{|A|}\text{adj}|A| = \frac{1}{25}\begin{bmatrix} 0 & -5 & 5 \\ 15 & 0 & -10 \\ -10 & 10 & 5 \end{bmatrix}$

and the solution of Eq. (i) is given by $X = A^{-1}B$.

$$\therefore \quad \begin{bmatrix} x \\ y \\ z \end{bmatrix} = \frac{1}{25}\begin{bmatrix} 0 & -5 & 5 \\ 15 & 0 & -10 \\ -10 & 10 & 5 \end{bmatrix}\begin{bmatrix} 60 \\ 45 \\ 70 \end{bmatrix}$$

$$= \frac{1}{25}\begin{bmatrix} 125 \\ 200 \\ 200 \end{bmatrix}$$

$$\Rightarrow \quad \begin{bmatrix} x \\ y \\ z \end{bmatrix} = \begin{bmatrix} 5 \\ 8 \\ 8 \end{bmatrix}$$

On comparing corresponding elements, we get

$\therefore \quad x = 5, y = 8$ and $z = 8$

QR Code for Quick Test 1

QR Code for Quick Test 2

QR Code for Quick Test 3

QR Code for Quick Test 4

Mind Map

Determinant

Every square matrix can be associate a number, real or complex is called a determinant of the square matrix A. It is denoted by det A or $|A|$.

e.g. Let $A = \begin{bmatrix} a_{11} & a_{12} & a_{13} \\ a_{21} & a_{22} & a_{23} \\ a_{31} & a_{32} & a_{33} \end{bmatrix}$. Then,

$$|A| = a_{11}\begin{vmatrix} a_{22} & a_{23} \\ a_{32} & a_{33} \end{vmatrix} - a_{12}\begin{vmatrix} a_{21} & a_{23} \\ a_{31} & a_{33} \end{vmatrix} + a_{13}\begin{vmatrix} a_{21} & a_{22} \\ a_{31} & a_{32} \end{vmatrix}$$

Adjoint of a Matrix

The adjoint of a square matrix $A = [a_{ij}]_{n \times n}$ is defined as the transpose of the matrix formed by corresponding A_{ij} or C_{ij} cofactors of the elements $[A]$ and it denoted by **adj*A***.

Properties of Adjoint of a Matrix

Suppose, A and B are two matrices of same order n. Then,

- adj $(A^T) = [\text{adj}\,(A)]^T$
- adj $(kA) = k^{n-1}$ (adj A), $k \in R$
- adj $(AB) = [\text{adj}\,(B)]\,[\text{adj}\,(A)]$
- adj $|A| = |A|^{n-1}$
- $|\text{adj}\,[\text{adj}\,(A)]| = |A|^{(n-1)^2}$
- adj (adj A) $= |A|^{n-2} \cdot A$

Area of Triangle

The area of triangle whose vertices are (x_1, y_1), (x_2, y_2) and (x_3, y_3) is given by

$$\Delta = \frac{1}{2}\begin{vmatrix} x_1 & y_1 & 1 \\ x_2 & y_2 & 1 \\ x_3 & y_3 & 1 \end{vmatrix}$$

Collinearity of Three Points

Three points (x_1, y_1), (x_2, y_2) and (x_3, y_3) are collinear, if the area of triangle formed by these three points is zero.

i.e. $$\begin{vmatrix} x_1 & y_1 & 1 \\ x_2 & y_2 & 1 \\ x_3 & y_3 & 1 \end{vmatrix} = 0$$

Equation of Line Through Two Points

The equation of line joining two points (x_1, y_1) and (x_2, y_2) is given by

$$\begin{vmatrix} x & y & 1 \\ x_1 & y_1 & 1 \\ x_2 & y_2 & 1 \end{vmatrix} = 0$$

Minors and Cofactors

Minor

Minor of an element a_{ij} of a determinant A is a determinant obtained by deleting the ith row and jth column in which element a_{ij} lies. Minor of the element a_{ij} is denoted by M_{ij}.

Cofactor

Cofactor of the element a_{ij} of a determinant, denoted by A_{ij} or C_{ij}, is defined as $A_{ij} = (-1)^{i+j} M_{ij}$, where M_{ij} is a minor of the element a_{ij}.

Value of Determinant in Terms of Cofactors

e.g. $$\Delta = \begin{vmatrix} a_{11} & a_{12} & a_{13} \\ a_{21} & a_{22} & a_{23} \\ a_{31} & a_{32} & a_{33} \end{vmatrix}$$

$$= a_{11}C_{11} + a_{12}C_{12} + a_{13}C_{13} \text{ or } a_{11}C_{11} + a_{21}C_{21} + a_{31}C_{31}$$

Consistent and Inconsistent System

A system of equations is said to be **consistent**, if its solution (one or more) exists.

A system of equations is said to be **inconsistent**, if its solution does not exist i.e. no solution exist.

Solution of System of Linear Equations Using Inverse of a Matrix

Let the system of linear equations be

$$a_1x + b_1y + c_1z = d_1,$$
$$a_2x + b_2y + c_2z = d_2$$
and $$a_3x + b_3y + c_3z = d_3$$

Now, let $A = \begin{bmatrix} a_1 & b_1 & c_1 \\ a_2 & b_2 & c_2 \\ a_3 & b_3 & c_3 \end{bmatrix}$, $X = \begin{bmatrix} x \\ y \\ z \end{bmatrix}$ and $B = \begin{bmatrix} d_1 \\ d_2 \\ d_3 \end{bmatrix}$

Then, the matrix representation of above system of linear equations is

$$AX = B \qquad \text{...(i)}$$

Now, some cases arise

(i) When $|A| \neq 0$

System is consistent and has unique solution given by $X = A^{-1}B$.

(ii) When $|A| = 0$ and $(\text{adj } A) \cdot B = O$

System may be either consistent or inconsistent according as the system have either infinitely many solutions or no solution.

(iii) When $|A| = 0$ and $(\text{adj } A) \cdot B \neq O$

Solution does not exist and system is inconsistent.

Some Important Theorems

Theorem 1 If A is any given square matrix of order n, then

$$A(\text{adj } A) = (\text{adj } A)\,A = |A| I_n,$$

where I is an identity matrix of order n.

Theorem 2 If A and B are non-singular matrices of the same order, then AB and BA are also non-singular matrices of the same order.

Theorem 3 The determinant of the product of matrices is equal to the product of their respective determinants

i.e. $$|AB| = |A||B|,$$

where A and B are square matrices of the same order.

Theorem 4 A square matrix A is invertible, if and only if A is non-singular matrix.

Singular and Non-singular Matrices

A square matrix A is said to be a **singular matrix**, if $|A| = 0$ and if $|A| \neq 0$, then matrix A is said to be **non-singular matrix**.

Inverse of a Square Matrix

A non-singular square matrix is said to be invertible, if there exists a square matrix B such that

$$AB = BA = I$$

Here, I is an identity matrix and matrix B is called the inverse of A.

If A is a non-singular matrix (i.e. $|A| \neq 0$), then

$$A^{-1} = \frac{1}{|A|} \text{adj } (A)$$

Properties of Inverse of a Matrix

Let A and B be two square invertible matrices of same order. Then,

- $(A^{-1})^{-1} = A$
- $(AB)^{-1} = B^{-1}A^{-1}$ or $(ABC)^{-1} = C^{-1}B^{-1}A^{-1}$
- $(A^T)^{-1} = (A^{-1})^T$
- $|A^{-1}| = |A|^{-1}$
- $AA^{-1} = A^{-1}A = I$
- $(kA)^{-1} = \frac{1}{k}A^{-1}, k \neq 0$

05

CHAPTER

Mathematics is as much an aspect of culture as it is a collection of algorithms.
— *Carl Benjamin Boyer*

Continuity and Differentiability

▼ YOUR STUDY GOALS

5.1 Continuity
5.2 Differentiability
5.3 Differentiation
5.4 Derivatives of Implicit Functions
5.5 Derivatives of Inverse Trigonometric Functions
5.6 Differentiation of Exponential and Logarithmic Functions
5.7 Differentiation of Parametric Functions
5.8 Differentiation of a Function w.r.t. Another Function
5.9 Second Order Derivative

▼ YOUR PRACTICE GOALS

- Objective Type Questions 35 Qs ; 23 MCQs, 10 A-R, 2 Case Based)
- Subjective Type Questions (64 Qs ; 15 VSA, 13 SA, 36 LA)

5.1 Continuity

Continuity of a Function at a Point

A function $f(x)$ is said to be continuous at a point $x = a$,

if $\quad (\text{LHL})_{x=a} = (\text{RHL})_{x=a} = f(a) \;$ or $\; \lim_{x\to a} f(x) = f(a)$

where, $(\text{LHL})_{x=a} = \lim_{x\to a^-} f(x)$

and $\quad (\text{RHL})_{x=a} = \lim_{x\to a^+} f(x)$.

Discontinuity of a Function

A function $f(x)$ is said to be discontinuous at $x = a$, if it is not continuous at $x = a$ i.e. when any of the following cases arise :

(i) $\lim_{x\to a^+} f(x)$ or $\lim_{x\to a^-} f(x)$ or $\lim_{x\to a} f(x)$ does not exist.

(ii) $\lim_{x\to a^-} f(x) \neq \lim_{x\to a^+} f(x)$

(iii) $\lim_{x\to a^-} f(x) = \lim_{x\to a^+} f(x) \neq f(a)$ or $\lim_{x\to a} f(x) \neq f(a)$

Continuity of a Function in its Domain

A function $f(x)$ is said to be continuous in its domain, if it is continuous at every point in its domain.

(i) A function $f(x)$ is said to be continuous in open interval (a, b), if it is continuous for every value of x in the interval (a, b).

(ii) A function $f(x)$ is said to be continuous in closed interval $[a, b]$, if

- it is continuous for every value of x in the open interval (a, b).
- $f(x)$ is continuous at $x = a$ from right, i.e. $\lim_{x \to a^+} f(x) = f(a)$.
- $f(x)$ is continuous at $x = b$ from left, i.e. $\lim_{x \to b^-} f(x) = f(b)$.

Some important results

There are some functions which are always continuous in their respective domain.

e.g.

(i) Every constant function is continuous.

(ii) Every identity function is continuous.

(iii) Every rational function is continuous.

(iv) Every polynomial function is continuous.

(v) Modulus function $f(x) = |x|$ is continuous.

(vi) All trigonometric functions are continuous.

Algebra of Continuous Functions

We know that continuity of a function at a point is entirely dictated by the limit of the function at that point, so algebra of continuous function is similar to algebra of limits, as given below

Theorem 1 Let f and g be two real functions, continuous at a real number c, then

- $(f + g)$ is continuous at $x = c$.
- $(f - g)$ is continuous at $x = c$.
- $f \cdot g$ is continuous at $x = c$.
- $\dfrac{f}{g}$ is continuous at $x = c$, provided that $g(c) \neq 0$.

Theorem 2 Suppose f and g are real valued functions such that fog is defined at c. If g is continuous at c and if f is continuous at $g(c)$, then fog is continuous at c.

Standard Results of Limits

(i) $\lim_{x \to a} \dfrac{x^n - a^n}{x - a} = na^{n-1}$ (ii) $\lim_{x \to 0} \dfrac{\sin x}{x} = 1$

(iii) $\lim_{x \to 0} \dfrac{\tan x}{x} = 1$ (iv) $\lim_{x \to 0} \dfrac{e^x - 1}{x} = 1$

(v) $\lim_{x \to \infty} \dfrac{1}{x^p} = 0, p \in (0, \infty)$

Example 1 **Examine the continuity of the following functions at given points.**

(i) $f(x) = x^2$ at $x = -2$

(ii) $f(x) = |x - 5|$ at $x = 5$ NCERT

Sol. (i) Given, $f(x) = x^2$

At point $x = -2$, $f(-2) = (-2)^2 = 4$

Now, $\lim_{x \to -2} f(x) = \lim_{x \to -2} x^2 = (-2)^2 = 4$

Here, $f(-2) = \lim_{x \to -2} f(x)$

Hence, $f(x)$ is continuous at $x = -2$.

(ii) Given, $f(x) = |x - 5| = \begin{cases} x - 5, & \text{if } x \geq 5 \\ 5 - x, & \text{if } x < 5 \end{cases}$

At point $x = 5$, $f(5) = |5 - 5| = 0$

Now, LHL $= \lim_{x \to 5^-} f(x) = \lim_{x \to 5^-} (5 - x)$

$= \lim_{h \to 0} [5 - (5 - h)] = \lim_{h \to 0} h = 0$

[put $x = 5 - h$; when $x \to 5^-$, then $h \to 0$]

and RHL $= \lim_{x \to 5^+} f(x) = \lim_{x \to 5^+} (x - 5)$

$= \lim_{h \to 0} [(5 + h) - 5] = \lim_{h \to 0} h = 0$

[put $x = 5 + h$; when $x \to 5^+$, then $h \to 0$]

Thus, LHL $=$ RHL $= f(5) = 0$

Hence, $f(x)$ is continuous at $x = 5$.

Example 2 **Discuss the continuity of the function**

$$f(x) = \begin{cases} \dfrac{|x|}{x} & \text{if } x \neq 0 \\ 0 & \text{if } x = 0 \end{cases} \text{ at } x = 0.$$

NCERT

Sol. We have, $f(x) = \begin{cases} \dfrac{|x|}{x} & \text{if } x \neq 0 \\ 0 & \text{if } x = 0 \end{cases}$

At $x = 0$, LHL $= \lim_{x \to 0^-} f(x) = \lim_{x \to 0^-} \dfrac{|x|}{x} = \lim_{h \to 0} \dfrac{|0 - h|}{0 - h}$

[put $x = 0 - h$; when $x \to 0^-$, then $h \to 0$]

$= \lim_{h \to 0} \dfrac{h}{-h}$ [$\because |0 - h| = |-h| = h$]

$= \lim_{h \to 0} (-1) = -1$

and $\quad \text{RHL} = \lim_{x \to 0^+} f(x) = \lim_{x \to 0^+} \frac{|x|}{x} = \lim_{h \to 0} \frac{|0+h|}{0+h}$

[put $x = 0 + h$; when $x \to 0^+$, then $h \to 0$]

$= \lim_{h \to 0} \frac{h}{h} \qquad [\because |0+h| = |h| = h]$

$= \lim_{h \to 0} (1) = 1$

Thus, $\quad$ LHL $\neq$ RHL

Hence, $f(x)$ is not continuous at $x = 0$.

Example 3 **Verify whether the function f defined by**

$$f(x) = \begin{cases} x\sin\left(\frac{1}{x}\right), & x \neq 0 \\ 0, & x = 0 \end{cases}$$

is continuous at $x = 0$ or not. *CBSE 2024*

Sol. Given, $f(x) = \begin{cases} x\sin\left(\frac{1}{x}\right), & x \neq 0 \\ 0, & x = 0 \end{cases}$

For $x = 0$, we get $f(0) = 0$ ...(i)

$\text{LHL} = \lim_{x \to 0^-} x\sin\frac{1}{x} = \lim_{h \to 0} f(0-h)\sin\left(\frac{1}{0-h}\right)$

$= \lim_{h \to 0} (-h)\sin\left(\frac{1}{-h}\right) = \lim_{h \to 0} h\sin\left(\frac{1}{h}\right)$

$[\because \sin(-\theta) = -\sin\theta]$

$= 0$ ...(ii)

$\text{RHL} = \lim_{x \to 0^+} x\sin\frac{1}{x} = \lim_{h \to 0} (0+h)\sin\left(\frac{1}{0+h}\right)$

$= \lim_{h \to 0} h\sin\left(\frac{1}{h}\right) = 0$ ...(iii)

From Eqs. (i), (ii) and (iii), we get

LHL = RHL = $f(0)$

Hence, $f(x)$ is continuous at $x = 0$.

Example 4 **Find the relationship between a and b so that the function f defined by $f(x) = \begin{cases} ax+1, & \text{if } x \leq 3 \\ bx+3, & \text{if } x > 3 \end{cases}$**

is continuous at $x = 3$. *NCERT, CBSE 2011*

Sol. Given, $f(x) = \begin{cases} ax+1, & \text{if } x \leq 3 \\ bx+3, & \text{if } x > 3 \end{cases}$

and $f(x)$ is continuous at $x = 3$.

Here, a and b are two unknowns.

Now, at $x = 3$, $f(3) = a(3) + 1 = 3a + 1$

$\text{LHL} = \lim_{x \to 3^-} f(x) = \lim_{x \to 3^-} (ax+1) = \lim_{h \to 0} \{a(3-h)+1\}$

[put $x = 3 - h$; when $x \to 3^-$ then $h \to 0$]

$= \lim_{h \to 0} (3a - ah + 1) = 3a + 1$

and $\text{RHL} = \lim_{x \to 3^+} f(x) = \lim_{x \to 3^+} \{bx+3\}$

$= \lim_{h \to 0} \{b(3+h)+3\}$

[put $x = 3 + h$; when $x \to 3^+$, then $h \to 0$]

$= \lim_{h \to 0} \{3b + bh + 3\} = 3b + 3$

Since, $f(x)$ is continuous at $x = 3$.

$\therefore$ $f(3)$ = LHL = RHL

i.e. $\quad 3a + 1 = 3a + 1 = 3b + 3$

$\Rightarrow \quad 3a + 1 = 3b + 3 \Rightarrow 3a = 3b + 3 - 1$

$\Rightarrow \quad a = \frac{(3b+2)}{3} \Rightarrow a = b + \frac{2}{3}$,

which is the required relation between a and b.

Example 5 **Find the values of a and b such that the function defined by $f(x) = \begin{cases} 5, \text{if } x \leq 2 \\ ax+b, \text{if } 2 < x < 10 \\ 21, \text{if } x \geq 10 \end{cases}$**

is continuous function.

Competency Based Que, CBSE 2023, NCERT

Sol. Here, $f(x) = \begin{cases} 5 & \text{if } x \leq 2 \\ ax + b & \text{if } 2 < x < 10 \\ 21 & \text{if } x \geq 10 \end{cases}$

At $x = 2$, $\text{LHL} = \lim_{x \to 2^-} f(x) = \lim_{x \to 2^-} (5) = 5$

and $\quad \text{RHL} = \lim_{x \to 2^+} f(x) = \lim_{x \to 2^+} (ax+b)$

$\therefore \quad \text{RHL} = \lim_{h \to 0} [a(2+h)+b]$

[put $x = 2 + h$; when $x \to 2^+$, then $h \to 0$]

$= \lim_{h \to 0} (2a + ah + b) = 2a + b$

Also, $f(2) = 5$

Since, $f(x)$ is continuous at $x = 2$.

$\therefore$ LHL = RHL = $f(2)$

$\Rightarrow \quad 2a + b = 5$ ...(i)

Now, at $x = 10$,

$\text{LHL} = \lim_{x \to 10^-} f(x) = \lim_{x \to 10^-} (ax+b)$

$\therefore \quad \text{LHL} = \lim_{h \to 0} [a(10-h)+b] = \lim_{h \to 0} (10a - ah + b)$

[put $x = 10 - h$; when $x \to 10^-$, then $h \to 0$]

$= 10a + b$

$\text{RHL} = \lim_{x \to 10^+} f(x) = \lim_{x \to 10^+} (21) = 21$

Also, $f(10) = 21$.

Since, $f(x)$ is continuous at $x = 10$.

$\therefore \quad$ LHL = RHL = $f(10) \Rightarrow 10a + b = 21$ ...(ii)

On subtracting Eq. (i) from Eq. (ii), we get

$8a = 16 \Rightarrow a = 2$

On putting $a = 2$ in Eq. (i), we get $2 \times 2 + b = 5 \Rightarrow b = 1$

Hence, the values of a and b are 2 and 1, respectively.

Example 6 **Discuss the continuity of**

$$f(x) = |\sin x + \cos x| \text{ at } x = \pi.$$

Sol. Let $g(x) = \sin x + \cos x$ and $k(y) = |y|$

We shall first show that g is continuous at $x = \pi$ and k is continuous at $y = g(\pi)$.

Now, $\lim\limits_{x \to \pi} g(x) = \lim\limits_{x \to \pi} (\sin x + \cos x)$

$= \sin \pi + \cos \pi = -1$

Also, $g(\pi) = \sin \pi + \cos \pi = -1$

$\Rightarrow \lim\limits_{x \to \pi} g(x) = g(\pi)$

So, g is continuous at $x = \pi$.

Now, $g(\pi) = -1$

$\therefore k[g(\pi)] = k(-1) = |-1| = 1$

Now, $\lim\limits_{y \to (-1)^+} k(y) = \lim\limits_{y \to (-1)^+} |y| = \lim\limits_{h \to 0} |-1+h| = 1$

[put $y = -1 + h$; when $y \to -1^+$, then $h \to 0$]

and $\lim\limits_{y \to (-1)^-} k(y) = \lim\limits_{y \to (-1)^-} |y| = \lim\limits_{h \to 0} |-1-h| = 1$

[put $y = -1 - h$; when $y \to -1^-$, then $h \to 0$]

$\therefore k[g(\pi)] = \lim\limits_{y \to g(\pi)} k(y)$

This shows that k is continuous at $g(\pi)$.

Consequently, (kog) is continuous at $x = \pi$.

But $kog(x) = k[g(x)] = k(\sin x + \cos x)$

$= |\sin x + \cos x| = f(x)$

Hence, $f(x)$ is continuous at $x = \pi$.

Example 7 **Show that the function**

$$f(x) = \begin{cases} \dfrac{e^{1/x} - 1}{e^{1/x} + 1}, & \text{when } x \neq 0 \\ 0, & \text{when } x = 0 \end{cases}$$

is discontinuous at $x = 0$. *NCERT Exemplar*

Sol. We have, $\begin{cases} \dfrac{e^{1/x} - 1}{e^{1/x} + 1}, & \text{when } x \neq 0 \\ 0, & \text{when } x = 0 \end{cases}$

At $x = 0$, $f(0) = 0$

$$\text{LHL} = \lim_{x \to 0^-} f(x) = \lim_{x \to 0^-} \frac{(e^{1/x} - 1)}{(e^{1/x} + 1)}$$

$$= \lim_{h \to 0} \frac{e^{\frac{1}{0-h}} - 1}{e^{\frac{1}{0-h}} + 1} = \lim_{h \to 0} \frac{e^{-1/h} - 1}{e^{-1/h} + 1}$$

[put $x = 0 - h$; when $x \to 0^-$, then $h \to 0$]

$$= \lim_{h \to 0} \frac{\frac{1}{e^{1/h}} - 1}{\frac{1}{e^{1/h}} + 1} = \frac{0 - 1}{0 + 1} = -1 \quad \left[\because \lim_{h \to 0} \frac{1}{e^{1/h}} = 0\right]$$

$$\text{RHL} = \lim_{x \to 0^+} f(x) = \lim_{x \to 0^+} \frac{e^{1/x} - 1}{e^{1/x} + 1}$$

$$= \lim_{h \to 0} \frac{e^{\frac{1}{(0+h)}} - 1}{e^{\frac{1}{(0+h)}} + 1}$$

[put $x = 0 + h$; when $x \to 0^+$, then $h \to 0$]

$$= \lim_{h \to 0} \frac{e^{1/h} - 1}{e^{1/h} + 1}$$

On dividing numerator and denominator by $e^{1/h}$, we get

$$\text{RHL} = \lim_{h \to 0} \frac{\left(1 - \frac{1}{e^{1/h}}\right)}{\left(1 + \frac{1}{e^{1/h}}\right)} = \frac{1 - 0}{1 + 0} = 1 \quad \left[\because \lim_{h \to 0} \frac{1}{e^{1/h}} = 0\right]$$

Here, LHL $\neq$ RHL

Hence, $f(x)$ is not continuous at $x = 0$.

Example 8 **Find all points of discontinuity of f, where f is defined by** $f(x) = \begin{cases} |x| + 3 & \text{if } x \leq -3 \\ -2x & \text{if } -3 < x < 3 \\ 6x + 2 & \text{if } x \geq 3 \end{cases}$. *NCERT*

Sol. Given, $f(x) = \begin{cases} |x| + 3, & \text{if } x \leq -3 \\ -2x, & \text{if } -3 < x < 3 \\ 6x + 2, & \text{if } x \geq 3 \end{cases}$

Here, we have to check the continuity only at points $x = -3$ and $x = 3$.

[$\because$ functions defined in each interval is a polynomial, so it is continuous in each interval]

At $x = -3$,

$\text{LHL} = \lim\limits_{x \to -3^-} f(x) = \lim\limits_{x \to -3^-} \{|x| + 3\} = \lim\limits_{h \to 0} \{|-3 - h| + 3\}$

[put $x = -3 - h$; when $x \to -3^-$, then $h \to 0$]

$= \lim\limits_{h \to 0} (3 + h + 3) = \lim\limits_{h \to 0} (6 + h) = 6$

$\text{RHL} = \lim\limits_{x \to -3^+} f(x) = \lim\limits_{x \to -3^+} (-2x) = \lim\limits_{h \to 0} -2(-3 + h)$

[put $x = -3 + h$; when $x \to -3^+$, then $h \to 0$]

$= \lim\limits_{h \to 0} (6 - 2h) = 6$ and $f(-3) = |-3| + 3 = 6$

Thus, $f(-3) = \text{LHL} = \text{RHL}$.

So, $f(x)$ is continuous at $x = -3$.

At $x = 3$,

$\text{LHL} = \lim\limits_{x \to 3^-} f(x) = \lim\limits_{x \to 3^-} (-2x) = \lim\limits_{h \to 0} -2(3 - h)$

[put $x = 3 - h$; when $x \to 3^-$, then $h \to 0$]

$= \lim\limits_{h \to 0} (-6 + 2h) = -6$

$\text{RHL} = \lim\limits_{x \to 3^+} f(x) = \lim\limits_{x \to 3^+} (6x + 2) = \lim\limits_{h \to 0} \{6(3 + h) + 2\}$

[put $x = 3 + h$; when $x \to 3^+$, then $h \to 0$]

$= \lim\limits_{h \to 0} (18 + 6h + 2) = 20$

Thus, LHL $\neq$ RHL

So, $f(x)$ is not continuous at $x = 3$.

Hence, the point of discontinuity is $x = 3$.

Example 9 Find the number of points of discontinuity of f defined by $f(x) = |x| - |x+1|$. *CBSE 2020*

Sol. We have, $f(x) = |x| - |x+1|$

$$f(x) = \begin{cases} 1, & x < -1 \\ -2x - 1, & -1 \le x < 0 \\ -1, & x \ge 0 \end{cases}$$

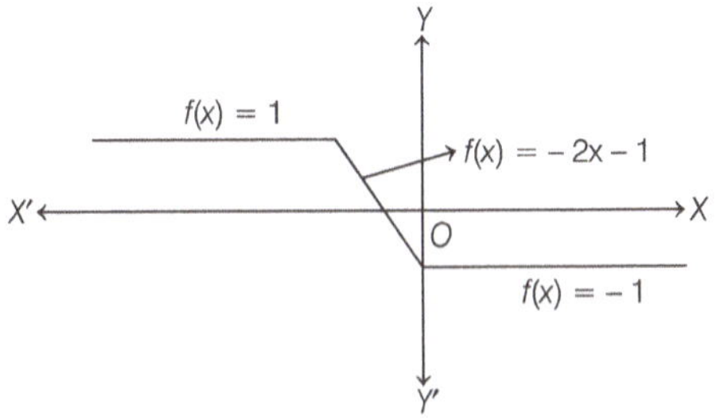

Clearly, $f(x)$ is continuous for all values of x.

Hence, no discontinuous point exist.

Quick Test 1

1. Examine the continuity of the following functions at the given points.

(i) $f(x) = 5x - 3$ at $x = -3$ *NCERT*

(ii) $f(x) = x^2 + 5$ at $x = -1$

(iii) $f(x) = |x - 2|$ at $x = 2$ *Competency Based Que*

2. Discuss the continuity of the following functions at the indicated points.

(i) $f(x) = \begin{cases} \dfrac{\sin 3x}{x}, & \text{if } x \neq 0 \\ 3, & \text{if } x = 0 \end{cases}$

(ii) $f(x) = \begin{cases} x^2 \sin\left(\dfrac{1}{x}\right), & \text{if } x \neq 0 \\ 0, & \text{if } x = 0 \end{cases}$

(iii) $f(x) = \begin{cases} 1, & \text{if } x \le -1 \\ -2x - 1, & \text{if } -1 < x < 0 \\ -1, & \text{if } x \ge 0 \end{cases}$

3. Show that the function

$$f(x) = \begin{cases} \dfrac{\sin x}{x} + \cos x, & \text{if } x \neq 0 \\ 2, & \text{if } x = 0 \end{cases}$$

is continuous at $x = 0$. *Competency Based Que*

4. Discuss the continuity of sine function. *Competency Based Que, NCERT*

5. Show that the function $f(x) = \begin{cases} |x| \cos\dfrac{1}{x}, & \text{if } x \neq 0 \\ 0, & \text{if } x = 0 \end{cases}$

is continuous at $x = 0$. *NCERT Exemplar*

6. Find the value(s) of λ, if the function

$$f(x) = \begin{cases} \dfrac{\sin^2 \lambda x}{x^2}, & x \neq 0 \\ 1, & x = 0 \end{cases}$$ is continuous at $x = 0$. *CBSE 2023*

7. Find the value of k for which the function given as

$$f(x) = \begin{cases} \dfrac{1 - \cos x}{2x^2}, & x \neq 0 \\ k, & x = 0 \end{cases}$$ is continuous at $x = 0$. *CBSE 2023*

8. If $f(x) = \begin{cases} \dfrac{1 - \cos 4x}{x^2}, & \text{if } x < 0 \\ a, & \text{if } x = 0 \\ \dfrac{\sqrt{x}}{\sqrt{16 + \sqrt{x}} - 4}, & \text{if } x > 0 \end{cases}$

is continuous at $x = 0$, then find the value of a.

Competency Based Que, NCERT Exemplar, CBSE 2013C

9. Find the values of a and b for which the function

$$f(x) = \begin{cases} x + 2, & \text{if } x \le 2 \\ ax + b, & \text{if } 2 < x < 5 \\ 3x - 2, & \text{if } x \ge 5 \end{cases}$$

is continuous. *CBSE 2010*

10. Find the point of discontinuity of the function

$$f(x) = \begin{cases} \dfrac{1}{2} - x, & \text{if } 0 \le x < \dfrac{1}{2} \\ 1, & \text{if } x = \dfrac{1}{2} \\ \dfrac{3}{2} - x, & \text{if } \dfrac{1}{2} < x \le 1 \end{cases}.$$

Answers

1. (i) Yes (ii) Yes (iii) Yes

2. (i) continuous at $x = 0$

(ii) continuous at $x = 0$

(iii) Everywhere continuous

6. ± 1 **7.** $\dfrac{1}{4}$ **8.** 8 **9.** $a = 3$ and $b = -2$ **10.** $x = \dfrac{1}{2}$

For Solutions, See QR Code on Pg. 152

5.2 Differentiability (Derivability)

A function $f(x)$ is said to be differentiable at a point $x = a$, if Left hand derivative at $x = a$ equals to Right hand derivative at $x = a$, provided both the derivatives exist.

i.e. LHD (at $x = a$) = RHD (at $x = a$),

where Right hand derivative,

$$Rf'(a) = \lim_{h \to 0} \frac{f(a+h) - f(a)}{h}$$

and Left hand derivative,

$$Lf'(a) = \lim_{h \to 0} \frac{f(a-h) - f(a)}{-h}$$

If $Rf'(a) \neq Lf'(a)$, the function is not differentiable at $x = a$.

Useful Results for Differentiability

(i) Every polynomial, exponential and constant functions are differentiable.

(ii) Logarithmic function is differentiable in their domain.

(iii) Trigonometric and inverse trigonometric functions are differentiable in their domain.

(iv) Modulus function is differentiable everywhere except at that point, where it is zero.

(v) Every differentiable function is continuous but every continuous function need not be differentiable.

5.3 Differentiation

The process of finding derivative of a function is called differentiation. The derivative of a function is also called the **differential coefficient** of the function.

Derivatives of some standard functions are given below

(i) $\frac{d}{dx}(\text{constant}) = 0$

(ii) $\frac{d}{dx}(x^n) = nx^{n-1}$

(iii) $\frac{d}{dx}(cx^n) = cnx^{n-1}$

(iv) $\frac{d}{dx}(\sin x) = \cos x$

(v) $\frac{d}{dx}(\cos x) = -\sin x$

(vi) $\frac{d}{dx}(\tan x) = \sec^2 x$

(vii) $\frac{d}{dx}(\text{cosec } x) = -\text{cosec } x \cot x$

(viii) $\frac{d}{dx}(\sec x) = \sec x \tan x$

(ix) $\frac{d}{dx}(\cot x) = -\text{cosec}^2 x$

(x) $\frac{d}{dx}(e^x) = e^x$

(xi) $\frac{d}{dx}(a^x) = a^x \log_e a, a > 0$

(xii) $\frac{d}{dx}(\log_e x) = \frac{1}{x}, x > 0$

(xiii) $\frac{d}{dx}(\log_a x) = \frac{1}{x \log_e a}, a > 0, a \neq 1$

(xiv) $\frac{d}{dx}(\sqrt{x}) = \frac{1}{2\sqrt{x}}, x > 0$

Rule of Derivatives

(i) **Sum and Difference Rule** Let $y = f(x) \pm g(x)$.

Then, its derivative is written as

$$\frac{dy}{dx} = \frac{d}{dx} f(x) \pm \frac{d}{dx} g(x).$$

(ii) **Product Rule** Let $y = f(x) \cdot g(x)$.

Then, its derivative is written as

$$\frac{dy}{dx} = \left[\frac{d}{dx} f(x)\right] g(x) + \left[\frac{d}{dx} g(x)\right] f(x).$$

(iii) **Quotient Rule** Let $y = \frac{f(x)}{g(x)}$; $g(x) \neq 0$.

Then, its derivative is written as

$$\frac{dy}{dx} = \frac{g(x) \times \frac{d}{dx}[f(x)] - f(x) \times \frac{d}{dx}[g(x)]}{[g(x)]^2}$$

(iv) **Chain Rule** Chain rule is applied when the given function is the function of function i.e. a function is in the form of $fog(x)$ or $f[g(x)]$.

Let $y = f(u)$ and $u = f(x)$, then by using chain rule, we may write $\frac{dy}{dx} = \frac{dy}{du} \cdot \frac{du}{dx}$, when $\frac{dy}{du}$ and $\frac{du}{dx}$ both exist.

5.4 Derivatives of Composite Functions

Derivative of a composite function can be found out by chain rule.

Chain Rule

Chain rule is applied when the given function is the function of function, i.e. a function is in the form of $fog(x)$ or $f[g(x)]$.

Let y be a real valued function which is a composite of two functions, say $y = f(u)$ and $u = g(x)$.

Then, $\frac{dy}{dx} = \frac{dy}{du} \cdot \frac{du}{dx} = f'(u) \cdot g'(x)$

i.e. $\frac{d}{dx}[f\{g(x)\}] = f'\{g(x)\} \cdot g'(x)$

Extension of Chain Rule

Extension of chain rule is applied when the given function (say y) is a composite of three functions.

e.g.

If $y = f(u), u = g(v)$ and $v = h(x)$, then

$\frac{dy}{dx} = \frac{dy}{du} \cdot \frac{du}{dv} \cdot \frac{dv}{dx} = f'(u) \cdot g'(v) \cdot h'(x)$

i.e. $\frac{d}{dx}[f(g(h(x)))] = f'[g(h(x)]. g'(h(x)) \cdot h'(x)$.

5.5 Derivatives of Implicit Functions

A function of the form $f(x, y) = 0$, where it is not possible to express y directly as a function of x, in the form of $y = \phi(x)$, is said to be an **implicit function** of x and y.

e.g. $x^2 + y^2 = xy, \cos(x + y) = \log(xy)$

Following steps are used to find $\frac{dy}{dx}$ of implicit functions.

I. Write the given equation in x and y and then differentiate both sides of the given equation w.r.t. x.

II. Take all terms involving $\frac{dy}{dx}$ on LHS and transfer the remaining terms on RHS to get equation in the form of $\frac{dy}{dx} f(x, y) = g(x, y)$.

III. Now, $\frac{dy}{dx} = \frac{g(x, y)}{f(x, y)}$.

Example 1 **Discuss the differentiability of $f(x) = x^2$ at $x = 1$.**

Sol. We have, $f(x) = x^2$

At $x = 1$,

$$\text{LHD} = \lim_{h \to 0} \frac{f(1-h) - f(1)}{-h} = \lim_{h \to 0} \frac{(1-h)^2 - 1^2}{-h}$$

$$= \lim_{h \to 0} \frac{1 + h^2 - 2h - 1}{-h} = \lim_{h \to 0}(-h + 2) = 2$$

$$\text{RHD} = \lim_{h \to 0} \frac{f(1+h) - f(1)}{h} = \lim_{h \to 0} \frac{(1+h)^2 - 1^2}{h}$$

$$= \lim_{h \to 0} \frac{h^2 + 2h + 1 - 1}{h} = \lim_{h \to 0}(h + 2) = 2$$

$\because$ LHD = RHD = 2

Hence, $f(x)$ is differentiable at $x = 1$.

Example 2 **If $f(x) = \begin{cases} ax + b, & 0 < x \le 1 \\ 2x^2 - x, & 1 < x < 2 \end{cases}$ is a differentiable function in $(0, 2)$, then find the values of a and b.**

Competency Based Que, 2023

Sol. Given, function

$f(x) = \begin{cases} ax + b, & 0 < x \le 1 \\ 2x^2 - x, & 1 < x < 2 \end{cases}$ is a differentiable function in $(0, 2)$.

If $f(x)$ is differentiable at $x = 1 \in (0, 2)$ then $f(x)$ will also be continuous at $x = 1$.

At $x = 1$, LHL $= \lim_{x \to 1^-} f(x) = \lim_{h \to 0} f(1-h)$

$$= \lim_{h \to 0}(a(1-h) + b) = \lim_{h \to 0}(a - ah + b)$$

$$= a + b$$

$$\text{RHL} = \lim_{x \to 1^+} f(x) = \lim_{h \to 0} f(1+h)$$

$$= \lim_{h \to 0}\{2(1+h)^2 - (1+h)\}$$

$$= \lim_{h \to 0}\{2(1 + h^2 + 2h) - (1+h)\}$$

$$= \lim_{h \to 0}(2 + 2h^2 + 4h - 1 - h)$$

$$= \lim_{h \to 0}(2h^2 + 3h + 1)$$

$$= 2 \times 0 + 3 \times 0 + 1 = 1 \text{ and } f(1) = a + b$$

Since, $f(x)$ is continuous at $x = 1$.

$\therefore$ LHL = RHL = $f(1)$

$\Rightarrow a + b = 1 = a + b \Rightarrow a + b = 1$ ...(i)

Now, $f(x)$ is differentiable at $x = 1$, we get

$$Lf'(1) = Rf'(1)$$

$$\Rightarrow \lim_{h \to 0} \frac{f(1-h) - f(1)}{-h} = \lim_{h \to 0} \frac{f(1+h) - f(1)}{h}$$

$$\Rightarrow \lim_{h \to 0} \frac{\{a(1-h) + b\} - (a + b)}{-h}$$

$$= \lim_{h \to 0} \frac{\{2(1+h)^2 - (1+h)\} - (a + b)}{h}$$

$$\Rightarrow \lim_{h\to 0}\frac{(a-ah+b-a-b)}{-h} = \lim_{h\to 0}\frac{(2+2h^2+4h-1-h-a-b)}{h}$$

$$\Rightarrow \quad \lim_{h\to 0}\left(\frac{-ah}{-h}\right) = \lim_{h\to 0}\frac{2h^2+3h+1-a-b}{h}$$

$$\Rightarrow \quad a = \lim_{h\to 0}\frac{2h^2+3h+1-1}{h} \quad \text{[from Eq. (i)]}$$

$$\Rightarrow \quad a = \lim_{h\to 0}\frac{h(2h+3)}{h} \Rightarrow a = \lim_{h\to 0}(2h+3)$$

$$\Rightarrow \quad a = 2\times 0+3 \Rightarrow a = 3$$

From Eq. (i), $3+b=1 \Rightarrow b=-2$

Example 3 **Show that the function $f(x)=|x-3|, x\in R$, is continuous but not differentiable at $x=3$.**

Competency Based Que

Sol. Given, $f(x)=|x-3|$

First, we check the continuity of $f(x)$ at $x=3$.

Here, $\text{LHL} = \lim_{x\to 3^-}|x-3| = \lim_{h\to 0}|3-h-3|$

[put $x=3-h$; when $x\to 3^-$, then $h\to 0$]

$= \lim_{h\to 0}|-h| = 0$

$\text{RHL} = \lim_{x\to 3^+}|x-3| = \lim_{h\to 0}|3+h-3| = \lim_{h\to 0}|h| = 0$

[put $x=3+h$; when $x\to 3^+$, then $h\to 0$]

and $f(3) = |3-3| = 0$

Thus, LHL = RHL = $f(3)$

Hence, f is continuous at $x=3$.

Now, let us check the differentiability of $f(x)$ at $x=3$.

$$\text{LHD} = Lf'(3^-) = \lim_{h\to 0}\frac{f(3-h)-f(3)}{-h}$$

$$\left[\because Lf'(a) = \lim_{h\to 0}\frac{f(a-h)-f(a)}{-h}\right]$$

$$= \lim_{h\to 0}\frac{|3-h-3|-|3-3|}{-h}$$

$$= \lim_{h\to 0}\frac{|-h|}{-h} = \lim_{h\to 0}\frac{h}{-h} = -1$$

$[\because |-x| = x, \text{ if } x>0]$

$$\text{RHD} = Rf'(3^+) = \lim_{h\to 0}\frac{f(3+h)-f(3)}{h}$$

$$\left[\because Rf'(a) = \lim_{h\to 0}\frac{f(a+h)-f(a)}{h}\right]$$

$$= \lim_{h\to 0}\frac{|3+h-3|-|3-3|}{h} = \lim_{h\to 0}\frac{|h|}{h} = \lim_{h\to 0}\frac{h}{h}$$

$= 1$ $\quad [\because |x| = x, \text{ if } x>0]$

Since, LHD $\neq$ RHD at $x=3$.

So, f is not differentiable at $x=3$. **Hence proved.**

Example 4 **Find the derivative of $x^4+3x^{5/3}+10x+7$.**

Sol. Let $y = x^4+3x^{5/3}+10x+7$

On differentiating both sides w.r.t. x, we get

$$\frac{dy}{dx} = \frac{d}{dx}(x^4+3x^{5/3}+10x+7)$$

$$= \frac{d}{dx}(x^4)+\frac{d}{dx}(3x^{5/3})+\frac{d}{dx}(10x)+\frac{d}{dx}(7)$$

[using sum and difference rule]

$$= 4x^{4-1}+3\left(\frac{5}{3}\right)x^{\frac{5}{3}-1}+10x^{1-1}+0$$

$$\left[\because \frac{d}{dx}x^n = nx^{n-1}; \frac{d}{dx}(cx^n) = cnx^{n-1} \text{ and } \frac{d}{dx}(\text{constant}) = 0\right]$$

$$= 4x^3+5x^{2/3}+10$$

Example 5 **Differentiate $\dfrac{\sec x-1}{\sec x+1}$ w.r.t. x.**

Sol. Let $y = \dfrac{\sec x-1}{\sec x+1} \Rightarrow y = \dfrac{\left(\dfrac{1}{\cos x}-1\right)}{\left(\dfrac{1}{\cos x}+1\right)}$ $\quad\left[\because \sec x = \dfrac{1}{\cos x}\right]$

$$\Rightarrow y = \frac{1-\cos x}{1+\cos x}$$

On differentiating both sides w.r.t. x, we get

$$\frac{dy}{dx} = \frac{\left[(1+\cos x)\frac{d}{dx}(1-\cos x)-(1-\cos x)\frac{d}{dx}(1+\cos x)\right]}{(1+\cos x)^2}$$

[using Quotient rule]

$$= \frac{[(1+\cos x)(0+\sin x)-(1-\cos x)(0-\sin x)]}{(1+\cos x)^2}$$

$$= \frac{[(1+\cos x)\sin x-(1-\cos x)(-\sin x)]}{(1+\cos x)^2}$$

$$= \frac{[\sin x+\cos x\cdot\sin x+\sin x-\cos x\cdot\sin x]}{(1+\cos x)^2}$$

$$= \frac{2\sin x}{(1+\cos x)^2}$$

Example 6 **If $y = \cos(\sqrt{3x})$, then find $\dfrac{dy}{dx}$.**

Sol. Given, $y = \cos(\sqrt{3x})$

On differentiating both sides w.r.t. x, we get

$$\frac{dy}{dx} = \frac{d}{dx}\{\cos(\sqrt{3x})\} = -\sin(\sqrt{3x})\cdot\frac{d}{dx}(\sqrt{3x})$$

$$= -\sin(\sqrt{3x})\cdot\frac{1}{2\sqrt{3x}}\cdot 3 = -\frac{3\sin\sqrt{3x}}{2\sqrt{3x}}$$

Example 7 **Differentiate $\sin(x^2+5)$ w.r.t. x.** [NCERT]

Sol. Let $y = \sin u$, where $u = x^2 + 5$. Using chain rule,

$$\frac{dy}{dx} = \frac{dy}{du}\cdot\frac{du}{dx} = \cos u \cdot \frac{du}{dx} = \cos(x^2+5)\frac{d}{dx}(x^2+5)$$
$$= \cos(x^2+5)\cdot(2x) = 2x\cdot\cos(x^2+5)$$

Example 8 **Differentiate $\sin^2(3x+1)$ w.r.t. x.**

Sol. Let $y = \sin^2(3x+1)$

Here, y is a composite of three functions.

Let $y = t^2$, where $t = \sin u$ and $u = 3x+1$.

Then, $\frac{dy}{dx} = \frac{dy}{dt}\cdot\frac{dt}{du}\cdot\frac{du}{dx}$ [by chain rule]

$$= \frac{d}{dt}[t^2]\cdot\frac{d}{du}(\sin u)\cdot\frac{d}{dx}(3x+1)$$
$$= 2t(\cos u)\cdot 3 = 6t\cos u$$
$$= 6\sin u\cos u \quad [\because t = \sin u]$$
$$= 3\sin 2u \quad [\because 2\sin\theta\cos\theta = \sin 2\theta]$$
$$= 3\sin 2(3x+1) = 3\sin(6x+2) \quad [\text{put } u = 3x+1]$$

Example 9 **If $y = (x+\sqrt{x^2-1})^2$, then show that $(x^2-1)\left(\frac{dy}{dx}\right)^2 = 4y^2$.** CBSE 2023

Sol. Given, $y = (x+\sqrt{x^2-1})^2$

On differentiating both sides w.r.t. x, we get

$$\frac{dy}{dx} = 2(x+\sqrt{x^2-1})\frac{d}{dx}(x+\sqrt{x^2-1})$$
$$\Rightarrow \frac{dy}{dx} = 2(x+\sqrt{x^2-1})\left(1+\frac{2x}{2\sqrt{x^2-1}}\right)$$
$$= 2(x+\sqrt{x^2-1})\left(\frac{\sqrt{x^2-1}+x}{\sqrt{x^2-1}}\right)$$
$$= \frac{2(x+\sqrt{x^2-1})^2}{\sqrt{x^2-1}} = \frac{2y}{\sqrt{x^2-1}}$$
$$[\because y = (x+\sqrt{x^2-1})^2]$$
$$\Rightarrow \left(\frac{dy}{dx}\right)^2 = \frac{4y^2}{x^2-1} \Rightarrow (x^2-1)\left(\frac{dy}{dx}\right)^2 = 4y^2$$

Hence proved.

Example 10 **Find $\frac{dy}{dx}$ at $x = 1$, $y = \frac{\pi}{4}$, if $\sin^2 y + \cos xy = K$.** CBSE 2017

Sol. We have, $\sin^2 y + \cos xy = K$

On differentiating both sides w.r.t. x, we get

$$\frac{d}{dx}(\sin^2 y + \cos xy) = \frac{d}{dx}(K)$$
$$\Rightarrow \frac{d}{dx}(\sin^2 y) + \frac{d}{dx}(\cos xy) = 0$$
$$\Rightarrow 2\sin y\cos y\frac{dy}{dx} + (-\sin xy)\frac{d}{dx}(xy) = 0$$
$$\Rightarrow \sin 2y\frac{dy}{dx} - \sin xy\left(x\frac{dy}{dx} + y\cdot 1\right) = 0$$
$$\Rightarrow \sin 2y\frac{dy}{dx} - x\sin xy\frac{dy}{dx} = y\sin xy$$
$$\Rightarrow \frac{dy}{dx} = \frac{y\sin(xy)}{\sin 2y - x\sin(xy)}$$
$$\therefore \left(\frac{dy}{dx}\right) \text{ at } x = 1,\ y = \frac{\pi}{4} = \frac{\frac{\pi}{4}\sin\left(1\cdot\frac{\pi}{4}\right)}{\sin\left(2\cdot\frac{\pi}{4}\right) - 1\sin\left(1\cdot\frac{\pi}{4}\right)}$$
$$= \frac{\frac{\pi}{4}\sin\left(\frac{\pi}{4}\right)}{\sin\left(\frac{\pi}{2}\right) - \sin\left(\frac{\pi}{4}\right)} = \frac{\frac{\pi}{4}\left(\frac{1}{\sqrt{2}}\right)}{1 - \frac{1}{\sqrt{2}}}$$
$$= \frac{\frac{\pi}{4\sqrt{2}}}{(\sqrt{2}-1)/\sqrt{2}} = \frac{\pi}{4\sqrt{2}}\times\frac{\sqrt{2}}{(\sqrt{2}-1)} = \frac{\pi}{4(\sqrt{2}-1)}$$

Example 11 **If $x + y = t + \frac{1}{t}$ and $x^3 + y^3 = t^3 + \frac{1}{t^3}$, then prove that $\frac{dy}{dx} = -\frac{1}{x^2}$.** Competency Based Que

Sol. Given, $(x+y) = t + \frac{1}{t}$

On cubing both sides, we get $(x+y)^3 = \left(t+\frac{1}{t}\right)^3$

$$\Rightarrow x^3 + y^3 + 3xy(x+y) = t^3 + \frac{1}{t^3} + 3\left(t+\frac{1}{t}\right)$$
$$[\because (a+b)^3 = a^3 + b^3 + 3ab(a+b)]$$
$$\Rightarrow x^3 + y^3 + 3xy(x+y) = x^3 + y^3 + 3(x+y)$$
$$\left[\because x^3 + y^3 = t^3 + \frac{1}{t^3} \text{ and } (x+y) = t + \frac{1}{t}\right]$$
$$\Rightarrow 3xy(x+y) = 3(x+y)$$
$$\Rightarrow xy = 1 \quad \text{...(i)}$$

On differentiating both sides w.r.t. x, we get

$$x\cdot\frac{dy}{dx} + y\cdot\frac{d}{dx}(x) = \frac{d}{dx}\cdot 1$$
[product rule of derivative]
$$\Rightarrow x\cdot\frac{dy}{dx} + y = 0 \Rightarrow x\frac{dy}{dx} = -y$$
$$\Rightarrow x\frac{dy}{dx} = -\frac{1}{x} \Rightarrow \frac{dy}{dx} = -\frac{1}{x^2}$$

Hence proved.

Quick Test 2

1. Examine the differentiability of the function

$$f(x)=\begin{cases} x[x] & \text{if } 0\le x<2 \\ (x-1)x & \text{if } 2\le x<3 \end{cases} \text{ at } x=2.$$

Competency Based Que, NCERT Exemplar

2. Show that a function $f(x)$ is defined as follows

$$f(x)=\begin{cases} x^2\sin\frac{1}{x}, & \text{if } x\ne 0 \\ 0, & \text{if } x=0 \end{cases}$$ is differentiable at $x=0$.

3. Differentiate the following functions with respect to x.

(i) $x^{20}+30$ (ii) $7x^6+\frac{5}{4}x^8$

(iii) $-3x^{-5}+\frac{1}{\sqrt{x}}$ (iv) $(ax^2+b)(px^{5/3}+q)$

(v) $\frac{x+\sin x}{x+\cos x}$ (vi) $x^2\sec x+\frac{x^2}{(1+\sin x)}$

4. Differentiate the following functions with respect to x.

Competency Based Que

(i) $\tan(x^2+5)$ (ii) $\cos(\sin x^3)$

(iii) $\sqrt{\cos(1+x^2)}$ (iv) $\text{cosec }(\sqrt{x^2+2})$

5. If $f(x)=\sin 2x-\cos 2x$, then find $f'\left(\frac{\pi}{6}\right)$. *CBSE 2017C*

6. If $y=[x+\sqrt{x^2+a^2}]^n$, then prove that $\frac{dy}{dx}=\frac{ny}{\sqrt{x^2+a^2}}$.

Competency Based Que

7. If $y=\sqrt{\frac{1-\sin 2x}{1+\sin 2x}}$, then show that

$$\frac{dy}{dx}+\sec^2\left(\frac{\pi}{4}-x\right)=0,\ x\in\left[0,\frac{\pi}{4}\right].$$

Competency Based Que

8. Find $\frac{dy}{dx}$ in each of the following.

(i) $xy=a^2$ (ii) $-2x^2-5xy+y^3=76$

(iii) $y=\tan(x+y)$ *CBSE 2025*

(iv) $(x^2+y^2)^2=xy$ *CBSE 2023; NCERT Exemplar*

(v) $y=\sqrt{\sin x+y}$ *Competency Based Que*

9. If $ax^2+2hxy+by^2+2gx+2fy+c=0$,

then show that $\frac{dy}{dx}\cdot\frac{dx}{dy}=1$. *NCERT Exemplar*

10. If $\tan(x+y)+\tan(x-y)=1$, then prove that

$$\frac{dy}{dx}=\frac{\sec^2(x+y)+\sec^2(x-y)}{\sec^2(x-y)-\sec^2(x+y)}.$$

Answers

1. not differentiable

3. (i) $20x^{19}$

(ii) $42x^5+10x^7$

(iii) $15x^{-6}-\frac{1}{2}x^{-3/2}$

(iv) $(ax^2+b)\left(\frac{5p}{3}x^{2/3}\right)+(2ax)(px^{5/3}+q)$

(v) $\frac{x(\cos x+\sin x)+(\cos x-\sin x)+1}{(x+\cos x)^2}$

(vi) $x^2\sec x\tan x+2x\sec x+\frac{[2x(1+\sin x)-x^2\cos x]}{(1+\sin x)^2}$

4. (i) $2x\sec^2(x^2+5)$ (ii) $-3x^2\sin(\sin x^3)\cos x^3$

(iii) $\frac{-x\sin(1+x^2)}{\sqrt{\cos(1+x^2)}}$

(iv) $-\text{cosec}\sqrt{x^2+2}\ \cot\sqrt{x^2+2}\times\frac{x}{\sqrt{x^2+2}}$

5. $1+\sqrt{3}$

8. (i) $-y/x$ (ii) $\frac{2y-x}{y-2x}$ (iii) $-\text{cosec}^2(x+y)$

(iv) $\frac{-[y-4x(x^2+y^2)]}{[x-4y(x^2+y^2)]}$ (v) $\frac{\cos x}{2y-1}$

For Solutions, See QR Code on Pg. 152

5.6 Derivatives of Inverse Trigonometric Functions

Derivatives of inverse trigonometric functions are given below

- $\frac{d}{dx}(\sin^{-1}x)=\frac{1}{\sqrt{1-x^2}}$
- $\frac{d}{dx}(\cos^{-1}x)=\frac{-1}{\sqrt{1-x^2}}$
- $\frac{d}{dx}(\tan^{-1}x)=\frac{1}{1+x^2}$
- $\frac{d}{dx}(\cot^{-1}x)=\frac{-1}{1+x^2}$
- $\frac{d}{dx}(\sec^{-1}x)=\frac{1}{x\sqrt{x^2-1}}$
- $\frac{d}{dx}(\text{cosec}^{-1}x)=\frac{-1}{x\sqrt{x^2-1}}$

Differentiation of Inverse Trigonometric Functions by Trigonometrical Transformations

Sometimes differentiation of inverse trigonometric functions becomes difficult by chain rule, then we can differentiate them easily by using trigonometrical transformation.

- $\sin 2x = 2\sin x\cos x$
- $\cos 2x=\cos^2 x-\sin^2 x=2\cos^2 x-1=1-2\sin^2 x$
- $\sin 2x=\frac{2\tan x}{1+\tan^2 x}$
- $\cos 2x=\frac{1-\tan^2 x}{1+\tan^2 x}$
- $\tan 2x=\frac{2\tan x}{1-\tan^2 x}$
- $\tan(x+y)=\frac{\tan x+\tan y}{1-\tan x\tan y}$
- $\tan(x-y)=\frac{\tan x-\tan y}{1+\tan x\tan y}$

Following are some substitutions useful in finding derivatives.

	Expressions	Substitutions
(i)	$\sqrt{a^2-x^2}$	$x=a\sin\theta$ or $x=a\cos\theta$
(ii)	$\sqrt{a^2+x^2}$ or a^2+x^2	$x=a\tan\theta$ or $x=a\cot\theta$
(iii)	$\sqrt{x^2-a^2}$	$x=a\sec\theta$ or $x=a\,\text{cosec}\,\theta$
(iv)	$\sqrt{\frac{a-x}{a+x}}$ or $\sqrt{\frac{a+x}{a-x}}$	$x=a\cos 2\theta$
(v)	$\sqrt{\frac{x}{a-x}}$ or $\sqrt{\frac{a-x}{x}}$	$x=a\sin^2\theta$
(vi)	$\sqrt{\frac{x}{a+x}}$ or $\sqrt{\frac{a+x}{x}}$	$x=a\tan^2\theta$
(vii)	$\sqrt{\frac{x}{x-a}}$ or $\sqrt{\frac{x-a}{x}}$	$x=a\sec^2\theta$
(viii)	$\sqrt{\frac{a^2-x^2}{a^2+x^2}}$ or $\sqrt{\frac{a^2+x^2}{a^2-x^2}}$	$x^2=a^2\cos 2\theta$

Example 1 **Differentiate the following with respect to x.**

(i) $\sin^{-1}7x$ **(ii) $\cos^{-1}(5x^2+4)$**

(iii) $\tan^{-1}(\cot x)$

Sol. (i) Let $y=\sin^{-1}7x$

Put $z=7x$. Then, $y=\sin^{-1}z$

On differentiating both sides w.r.t. x, we get

$$\frac{dy}{dx}=\frac{d}{dx}(\sin^{-1}z)=\frac{d}{dz}(\sin^{-1}z)\frac{dz}{dx}\quad\text{[by chain rule]}$$

$$=\frac{1}{\sqrt{1-z^2}}\frac{d}{dx}(7x)=\frac{7}{\sqrt{1-(7x)^2}}=\frac{7}{\sqrt{1-49x^2}}$$

$[\because z=7x]$

(ii) Let $y=\cos^{-1}(5x^2+4)$

Put $z=5x^2+4$

Then, $y=\cos^{-1}z$

On differentiating both sides w.r.t. x, we get

$$\frac{dy}{dx}=\frac{d}{dx}(\cos^{-1}z)=\frac{d}{dz}(\cos^{-1}z)\frac{dz}{dx}$$

[by chain rule]

$$= \frac{-1}{\sqrt{1-(5x^2+4)^2}} \frac{d}{dx}(5x^2+4) \text{ [put } z = 5x^2+4]$$

$$= -\frac{1}{\sqrt{1-(5x^2+4)^2}} \times [5 \times 2x + 0]$$

$$= -\frac{10x}{\sqrt{1-(5x^2+4)^2}}$$

(iii) Let $y = \tan^{-1}(\cot x)$

Put $z = \cot x$. Then, $y = \tan^{-1} z$

On differentiating both sides w.r.t. x, we get

$$\frac{dy}{dx} = \frac{d}{dx}(\tan^{-1} z) = \frac{d}{dz}(\tan^{-1} z)\frac{dz}{dx}$$

$$= \frac{1}{1+z^2} \frac{d}{dx}(\cot x) \quad \text{[by chain rule]}$$

$$= \frac{-\operatorname{cosec}^2 x}{1+\cot^2 x} \quad [\because z = \cot x]$$

$$= \frac{-\operatorname{cosec}\ x}{\operatorname{cosec}\ x} = -1$$

Example 2 **Differentiate $\tan^{-1}\left(\frac{1+\cos x}{\sin x}\right)$ w.r.t. x.** *CBSE 2018*

Sol. Let $y = \tan^{-1}\left(\frac{1+\cos x}{\sin x}\right) = \tan^{-1}\left(\frac{2\cos^2 \frac{x}{2}}{2\sin\frac{x}{2}\cos\frac{x}{2}}\right)$

$\left[\because 1+\cos A = 2\cos^2\frac{A}{2} \text{ and } \sin A = 2\sin\frac{A}{2}\cos\frac{A}{2}\right]$

$$= \tan^{-1}\left(\frac{\cos\frac{x}{2}}{\sin\frac{x}{2}}\right) = \tan^{-1}\left(\cot\frac{x}{2}\right)$$

$$= \tan^{-1}\left(\tan\left(\frac{\pi}{2}-\frac{x}{2}\right)\right)$$

$$= \frac{\pi}{2}-\frac{x}{2} \quad [\because \tan^{-1}(\tan\theta) = \theta]$$

Now, on differentiating both sides w.r.t. x, we get

$$\frac{dy}{dx} = 0 - \frac{1}{2} = -\frac{1}{2}$$

Example 3 **If $\sqrt{1-x^2} + \sqrt{1-y^2} = a(x-y)$, prove that $\frac{dy}{dx} = \sqrt{\frac{1-y^2}{1-x^2}}$.** *CBSE 2024*

Sol. Given, $\sqrt{1-x^2} + \sqrt{1-y^2} = a(x-y)$

Let $x = \sin A$, $y = \sin B$

$\Rightarrow \sqrt{1-\sin^2 A} + \sqrt{1-\sin^2 B} = a(\sin A - \sin B)$

$\Rightarrow \quad \cos A + \cos B = a(\sin A - \sin B)$

$[\because 1-\sin^2\theta = \cos^2\theta]$

$\Rightarrow \quad 2\cos\left(\frac{A+B}{2}\right)\cos\left(\frac{A-B}{2}\right) = a\left(2\sin\left(\frac{A-B}{2}\right)\cos\left(\frac{A+B}{2}\right)\right)$

$\Rightarrow \quad 2\cos\left(\frac{A-B}{2}\right) = 2a\sin\left(\frac{A-B}{2}\right)$

$\Rightarrow \quad \cot\left(\frac{A-B}{2}\right) = a \Rightarrow \frac{A-B}{2} = \cot^{-1}(a)$

$\Rightarrow \quad \sin^{-1} x - \sin^{-1} y = 2\cot^{-1}(a)$

On differentiating both sides, we get

$\Rightarrow \quad \frac{1}{\sqrt{1-x^2}} - \frac{1}{\sqrt{1-y^2}}\frac{dy}{dx} = 0 \Rightarrow \frac{dy}{dx} = \sqrt{\frac{1-y^2}{1-x^2}}$

Example 4 **If $y = \sin^{-1}(6x\sqrt{1-9x^2}), -\frac{1}{3\sqrt{2}} < x < \frac{1}{3\sqrt{2}}$, then find $\frac{dy}{dx}$.** *CBSE 2017*

Sol. Given, $y = \sin^{-1}(6x\sqrt{1-9x^2})$

$\Rightarrow \quad y = \sin^{-1}(2\cdot 3x\sqrt{1-(3x)^2})$

On putting $3x = \sin\theta$, then

$y = \sin^{-1}(2\sin\theta\sqrt{1-\sin^2\theta})$

$\Rightarrow \quad y = \sin^{-1}(2\sin\theta\cdot\cos\theta)$

$\Rightarrow \quad y = \sin^{-1}(\sin 2\theta) \Rightarrow y = 2\theta$

$\Rightarrow \quad y = 2\sin^{-1}(3x) \quad [\because \theta = \sin^{-1}(3x)]$

$\Rightarrow \quad \frac{dy}{dx} = \frac{2}{\sqrt{1-9x^2}}(3) \Rightarrow \frac{dy}{dx} = \frac{6}{\sqrt{1-9x^2}}$

Example 5 **If $y = \sin^{-1}\left(\frac{\sqrt{1+x}+\sqrt{1-x}}{2}\right)$, then show that $\frac{dy}{dx} = \frac{-1}{2\sqrt{1-x^2}}$.** *CBSE 2020*

Sol. We have, $y = \sin^{-1}\left(\frac{\sqrt{1+x}+\sqrt{1-x}}{2}\right)$

On putting $x = \sin\theta$, we get

$$y = \sin^{-1}\left(\frac{\sqrt{1+\sin\theta}+\sqrt{1-\sin\theta}}{2}\right)$$

$$\Rightarrow \quad y = \sin^{-1}\left[\frac{\cos\theta/2 + \sin\theta/2 + \cos\theta/2 - \sin\theta/2}{2}\right]$$

$[\because 1 \pm \sin\theta = (\cos\theta/2 \pm \sin\theta/2)^2]$

$$\Rightarrow \quad y = \sin^{-1}\left[\frac{2\cos\theta/2}{2}\right]$$

$$\Rightarrow \quad y = \sin^{-1}(\cos\theta/2) = \sin^{-1}\left(\sin\left(\frac{\pi}{2} - \frac{\theta}{2}\right)\right)$$

$$\Rightarrow \quad y = \frac{\pi}{2} - \frac{\theta}{2} \Rightarrow y = \frac{\pi}{2} - \frac{1}{2}\sin^{-1} x$$

On differentiating w.r.t. x, we get

$$\frac{dy}{dx} = -\frac{1}{2\sqrt{1-x^2}}$$

Hence proved.

EXAMPLE 6 **If $y = \tan^{-1}\left(\dfrac{\sqrt{1+x^2}+\sqrt{1-x^2}}{\sqrt{1+x^2}-\sqrt{1-x^2}}\right)$, $x^2 \le 1$, then find $\dfrac{dy}{dx}$.**

CBSE 2015

Sol. Given, $y = \tan^{-1}\left(\dfrac{\sqrt{1+x^2}+\sqrt{1-x^2}}{\sqrt{1+x^2}-\sqrt{1-x^2}}\right)$

On putting $x^2 = \sin\theta \Rightarrow \theta = \sin^{-1} x^2$

$$\therefore\ y = \tan^{-1}\left(\frac{\sqrt{1+\sin\theta}+\sqrt{1-\sin\theta}}{\sqrt{1+\sin\theta}-\sqrt{1-\sin\theta}}\right)$$

$$= \tan^{-1}\left(\frac{\sqrt{\cos^2\frac{\theta}{2}+\sin^2\frac{\theta}{2}+2\sin\frac{\theta}{2}\cos\frac{\theta}{2}}+\sqrt{\cos^2\frac{\theta}{2}+\sin^2\frac{\theta}{2}-2\sin\frac{\theta}{2}\cos\frac{\theta}{2}}}{\sqrt{\cos^2\frac{\theta}{2}+\sin^2\frac{\theta}{2}+2\sin\frac{\theta}{2}\cos\frac{\theta}{2}}-\sqrt{\cos^2\frac{\theta}{2}+\sin^2\frac{\theta}{2}-2\sin\frac{\theta}{2}\cos\frac{\theta}{2}}}\right)$$

$$= \tan^{-1}\left[\frac{\sqrt{\left(\cos\frac{\theta}{2}+\sin\frac{\theta}{2}\right)^2}+\sqrt{\left(\cos\frac{\theta}{2}-\sin\frac{\theta}{2}\right)^2}}{\sqrt{\left(\cos\frac{\theta}{2}+\sin\frac{\theta}{2}\right)^2}-\sqrt{\left(\cos\frac{\theta}{2}-\sin\frac{\theta}{2}\right)^2}}\right]$$

$$= \tan^{-1}\left[\frac{\left(\cos\frac{\theta}{2}+\sin\frac{\theta}{2}\right)+\left(\cos\frac{\theta}{2}-\sin\frac{\theta}{2}\right)}{\left(\cos\frac{\theta}{2}+\sin\frac{\theta}{2}\right)-\left(\cos\frac{\theta}{2}-\sin\frac{\theta}{2}\right)}\right]$$

$$= \tan^{-1}\left(\frac{2\cos\frac{\theta}{2}}{2\sin\frac{\theta}{2}}\right) = \tan^{-1}\left(\cot\frac{\theta}{2}\right)$$

$$= \tan^{-1}\left[\tan\left(\frac{\pi}{2}-\frac{\theta}{2}\right)\right] \qquad \left[\because \cot\theta = \tan\left(\frac{\pi}{2}-\theta\right)\right]$$

$$= \frac{\pi}{2} - \frac{\theta}{2} \qquad [\because \tan^{-1}(\tan\theta) = \theta]$$

$$\Rightarrow\ y = \frac{\pi}{2} - \frac{1}{2}\sin^{-1} x^2 \qquad [\because \theta = \sin^{-1} x^2]$$

On differentiating both sides w.r.t. x, we get

$$\frac{dy}{dx} = -\frac{1}{2}\frac{1}{\sqrt{1-(x^2)^2}}(2x)$$

$$= \frac{-x}{\sqrt{1-x^4}}$$

Example 7 **If $y = \sin^{-1}[x\sqrt{1-x} - \sqrt{x}\sqrt{1-x^2}]$ and $0 < x < 1$, then find $\dfrac{dy}{dx}$.**

Competency Based Que, CBSE 2014C, 10

Sol. Given, $y = \sin^{-1}[x\sqrt{1-x} - \sqrt{x}\sqrt{1-x^2}]$

Above equation can be rewritten as

$$y = \sin^{-1}[x\sqrt{1-(\sqrt{x})^2} - \sqrt{x}\sqrt{1-x^2}]$$

Now, put $\sqrt{x} = \sin\theta$ and $x = \sin\phi$ so that

$$y = \sin^{-1}[\sin\phi\sqrt{1-\sin^2\theta} - \sin\theta\sqrt{1-\sin^2\phi}]$$

$$\Rightarrow\quad y = \sin^{-1}[\sin\phi\cos\theta - \sin\theta\cos\phi]$$

$$[\because \sqrt{1-\sin^2 x} = \cos x]$$

$$\Rightarrow\quad y = \sin^{-1}\sin(\phi-\theta)$$

$$[\because \sin A\cos B - \cos A\sin B = \sin(A-B)]$$

$$\Rightarrow\quad y = \phi - \theta \qquad [\because \sin^{-1}\sin A = A]$$

$$\Rightarrow\quad y = \sin^{-1} x - \sin^{-1}\sqrt{x}$$

$$[\because \phi = \sin^{-1} x \text{ and } \theta = \sin^{-1}\sqrt{x}]$$

On differentiating both sides w.r.t. x, we get

$$\frac{dy}{dx} = \frac{1}{\sqrt{1-x^2}} - \frac{1}{\sqrt{1-(\sqrt{x})^2}} \times \frac{d}{dx}(\sqrt{x})$$

$$\left[\because \frac{d}{d\theta}(\sin^{-1}\theta) = \frac{1}{\sqrt{1-\theta^2}}\right]$$

$$\Rightarrow\quad \frac{dy}{dx} = \frac{1}{\sqrt{1-x^2}} - \frac{1}{\sqrt{1-x}}\cdot\frac{1}{2\sqrt{x}}$$

Hence, $$\frac{dy}{dx} = \frac{1}{\sqrt{1-x^2}} - \frac{1}{2\sqrt{x-x^2}}$$

Quick Test 3

1. Differentiate the following functions w.r.t. x.

(i) $\cos^{-1}5x$ (ii) $\sin^{-1}\left(\frac{x}{a}\right)$

(iii) $\sin^{-1}(x\sqrt{x})$ (iv) $[\sqrt{1-x^2}\sin^{-1}x - x]$

Competency Based Que

(v) $\sqrt{\cot^{-1}\sqrt{x}}$ (vi) $x\sec^{-1}x$

Directions (Q. Nos. 2-9) *Differentiate each of the following with respect to x.* NCERT

2. $\cot^{-1}\left(\frac{1-x}{1+x}\right)$

3. $\sin^{-1}(2x\sqrt{1-x^2}), -\frac{1}{\sqrt{2}} < x < \frac{1}{\sqrt{2}}$ NCERT

4. $\sin^{-1}\left(\sqrt{\frac{1+x}{2}}\right), x \neq 0$

5. $\cos^{-1}\left(\frac{1-x^2}{1+x^2}\right)$ NCERT

6. $\cos^{-1}\left[\frac{\sin x + \cos x}{\sqrt{2}}\right], \frac{-\pi}{4} < x < \frac{\pi}{4}$

Competency Based Que, NCERT

7. $\tan^{-1}\left(\frac{\sqrt{1+a^2x^2}-1}{ax}\right)$

8. $\tan^{-1}(\sqrt{1+x^2}+x)$

9. $\tan^{-1}\left(\frac{3a^2x-x^3}{a^3-3ax^2}\right), -\frac{1}{\sqrt{3}} < \frac{x}{a} < \frac{1}{\sqrt{3}}$

Competency Based Que, NCERT Exemplar

10. If $y = \frac{x\sin^{-1}x}{\sqrt{1-x^2}}$, then prove that

$$\frac{dy}{dx} = \frac{x(\sqrt{1-x^2}) + \sin^{-1}x}{(1-x^2)^{\frac{3}{2}}}.$$

Competency Based Que

Answers

1. (i) $\frac{-5}{\sqrt{1-25x^2}}$ (ii) $\frac{1}{\sqrt{a^2-x^2}}$ (iii) $\frac{3}{2}\frac{\sqrt{x}}{\sqrt{1-x^3}}$

(iv) $\frac{-x\sin^{-1}x}{\sqrt{1-x^2}}$ (v) $\frac{-1}{4(\sqrt{\cot^{-1}\sqrt{x}})(1+x)\sqrt{x}}$

(vi) $\frac{1}{\sqrt{x^2-1}} + \sec^{-1}x$

2. $\frac{1}{1+x^2}$ **3.** $\frac{2}{\sqrt{1-x^2}}$ **4.** $\frac{1}{2\sqrt{1-x^2}}$

5. $\frac{2}{1+x^2}$ **6.** -1 **7.** $\frac{a}{2(1+a^2x^2)}$

8. $\frac{1}{2(1+x^2)}$ **9.** $\frac{3a}{a^2+x^2}$

For Solutions, See QR Code on Pg. 152

5.7 Differentiation of Exponential and Logarithmic Functions

Exponential Function

The function defined as $y = f(x) = b^x$ with positive base $b > 0$, $b \neq 1$ is called the exponential function.

- If the base of an exponential function is e i.e. $b = e$, then it is called **natural exponential** function.
- If the base of an exponential function is 10 i.e. $b = 10$, then it is called the **common exponential function.**

Logarithmic Function

If b is any number such that $b > 0$ and $b \neq 1$ and $x > 0$, then $y = \log_b x$ is equivalent to $b^y = x$.

We usually read as 'log base b of x'.

Basic properties of logarithms are given below

(i) $\log_a(mn) = \log_a m + \log_a n, m > 0, n > 0, a > 0, a \neq 1$

(ii) $\log_a x = \log_a e \log_e x, a > 0, a \neq 1, x > 0$

(iii) $\log_a \frac{m}{n} = \log_a m - \log_a n, m > 0, n > 0, a > 0, a \neq 1$

(iv) $\log_a m^n = n\log_a m, m > 0, a > 0, a \neq 1$

(v) $e^{\log_e x} = x, x > 0$

(vi) $\log_a x = \frac{\log x}{\log a}, a > 0, a \neq 1, x > 0$

(vii) $\log_n m = \frac{1}{\log_m n}, m, n > 0$ and $m, n \neq 1$

(viii) $\log_{10} 10 = 1, \log_e e = 1$ and $\log_a 1 = 0, a > 0, a \neq 1$

Differentiation of Logarithmic Functions

When the given function is in the form $[f(x)]^{g(x)}$, where $f(x)$ and $g(x)$ are functions of x.

Then, we take logarithm both sides and use properties of logarithm to simplify it and then differentiate it. This process is known as **logarithmic differentiation**.

Let $\quad y=[f(x)]^{g(x)}$

On taking logarithm (to base e), we get

$$\log y = g(x)\log(f(x))$$

Using chain rule, we get

$$\frac{dy}{dx}=[f(x)]^{g(x)}\left[\frac{g(x)}{f(x)}f'(x)+g'(x)\log f(x)\right]$$

Here, functions should always be positive otherwise their logarithms are not defined.

Important Theorems

Theorem 1 The derivative of e^x w.r.t. x is e^x

i.e. $\quad \frac{d}{dx}(e^x)=e^x.$

Theorem 2 The derivative of $\log x$ w.r.t. x is $\frac{1}{x}$

i.e. $\quad \frac{d}{dx}(\log x)=\frac{1}{x}.$

Example 1 Differentiate the following w.r.t. x.

(i) e^{x^3}

(ii) $e^{\sqrt{\cot x}}$

(iii) $\log(\cos e^x)$ *NCERT*

(iv) $\log\tan\frac{x}{2}$

(v) a^x, **where a is a positive constant** *NCERT*

(vi) $x^{\frac{1}{x}}$

Sol. (i) Let $y=e^{x^3}$

On differentiating both sides w.r.t. x, we get

$$\frac{dy}{dx}=\frac{d}{dx}e^{x^3}$$

$$=e^{x^3}\cdot 3x^2=3x^2e^{x^3}$$

(ii) Let $y=e^{\sqrt{\cot x}}$

On taking log on both sides, we get

$$\log y=\sqrt{\cot x}\cdot\log e=\sqrt{\cot x} \qquad [\because \log_e e=1]$$

On differentiating both sides w.r.t. x, we get

$$\frac{1}{y}\frac{dy}{dx}=\frac{1}{2\sqrt{\cot x}}\frac{d}{dx}(\cot x)$$

$$\Rightarrow \frac{1}{y}\cdot\frac{dy}{dx}=\frac{1}{2\sqrt{\cot x}}\times(-\operatorname{cosec}^2 x)$$

$$\Rightarrow \frac{dy}{dx}=y\left[-\frac{\operatorname{cosec}^2 x}{2\sqrt{\cot x}}\right]$$

$$\Rightarrow \frac{dy}{dx}=-e^{\sqrt{\cot x}}\frac{\operatorname{cosec}^2 x}{2\sqrt{\cot x}}$$

(iii) Let $y=\log(\cos e^x)$, it is a composite function.

On differentiating both sides w.r.t. x, we get

$$\frac{dy}{dx}=\frac{1}{\cos e^x}\cdot\frac{d}{dx}(\cos e^x)$$

$$\left[\text{by chain rule and } \frac{d}{dx}(\log t)=\frac{1}{t}\right]$$

$$=\frac{1}{\cos e^x}(-\sin e^x)\frac{d}{dx}(e^x) \quad [\text{again by chain rule}]$$

$$=-\tan e^x\times e^x=-e^x\tan e^x$$

(iv) Let $y=\log\tan\frac{x}{2}$

On differentiating both sides w.r.t. x, we get

$$\frac{dy}{dx}=\frac{1}{\tan\frac{x}{2}}\frac{d}{dx}\left(\tan\frac{x}{2}\right)$$

$$=\frac{1}{\tan\frac{x}{2}}\times\sec^2\frac{x}{2}\times\frac{d}{dx}\left(\frac{x}{2}\right)$$

$$=\frac{\cos\frac{x}{2}}{\sin\frac{x}{2}}\times\frac{1}{\cos^2\frac{x}{2}}\times\frac{1}{2}=\frac{1}{2\sin\frac{x}{2}\cos\frac{x}{2}}$$

$$\Rightarrow \frac{dy}{dx}=\frac{1}{\sin x}=\operatorname{cosec} x$$

(v) Let $y=a^x$

On taking log both sides, we get

$$\log y=\log a^x \Rightarrow \log y=x\log a$$

On differentiating both sides w.r.t. x, we get

$$\frac{1}{y}\frac{dy}{dx}=\log a \Rightarrow \frac{dy}{dx}=y\log a$$

Thus, $\frac{d}{dx}(a^x)=a^x\log a$

(vi) Let $y=x^{\frac{1}{x}}$

On taking log both sides, we get

$$\log y=\log x^{\frac{1}{x}}$$

$$\Rightarrow \log y=\frac{1}{x}\log x=\frac{\log x}{x}$$

On differentiating both sides w.r.t. x, we get

$$\frac{1}{y}\frac{dy}{dx} = \frac{x\frac{d}{dx}(\log x) - \log x\frac{d}{dx}(x)}{x^2}$$

$$\Rightarrow \frac{1}{y}\frac{dy}{dx} = \frac{x\cdot\frac{1}{x} - \log x\cdot 1}{x^2} \Rightarrow \frac{dy}{dx} = \frac{y(1-\log x)}{x^2}$$

Thus, $$\frac{d}{dx}x^{\frac{1}{x}} = \frac{x^{\frac{1}{x}}(1-\log x)}{x^2}$$

Example 2 **If $y = \log\sqrt{\dfrac{1+\sin^2 x}{1-\sin x}}$, then find $\dfrac{dy}{dx}$.**

CBSE 2023

Sol. Given, $y = \log\sqrt{\dfrac{1+\sin^2 x}{1-\sin x}} \Rightarrow y = \log\left(\dfrac{1+\sin^2 x}{1-\sin x}\right)^{1/2}$

$$\Rightarrow y = \frac{1}{2}\log\left(\frac{1+\sin^2 x}{1-\sin x}\right) \quad [\because \log m^n = n\log m]$$

$$\Rightarrow y = \frac{1}{2}[\log(1+\sin^2 x) - \log(1-\sin x)]$$

$$\left[\because \log\left(\frac{m}{n}\right) = \log m - \log n\right]$$

On differentiating both sides w.r.t. x, we get

$$\frac{dy}{dx} = \frac{1}{2}\left[\frac{1}{1+\sin^2 x}\times(0+2\sin x\cdot\cos x) - \frac{1}{1-\sin x}(-\cos x)\right]$$

$$= \frac{1}{2}\left[\frac{\sin 2x}{1+\sin^2 x} + \frac{\cos x}{1-\sin x}\right]$$

Example 3 **If $\log(x^2+y^2) = 2\tan^{-1}\left(\dfrac{y}{x}\right)$, then show that $\dfrac{dy}{dx} = \dfrac{x+y}{x-y}$.**

CBSE 2019

Sol. $\log(x^2+y^2) = 2\tan^{-1}\left(\dfrac{y}{x}\right)$

On differentiating both sides w.r.t. x, we get

$$\frac{1}{x^2+y^2}\left(2x+2y\frac{dy}{dx}\right) = 2\cdot\frac{1}{1+\frac{y^2}{x^2}}\left(\frac{\frac{dy}{dx}x - y}{x^2}\right)$$

$$\Rightarrow \frac{2\left(x+y\frac{dy}{dx}\right)}{x^2+y^2} = \frac{2x^2}{x^2+y^2}\left(\frac{\frac{dy}{dx}x-y}{x^2}\right)$$

$$\Rightarrow x + y\cdot\frac{dy}{dx} = \frac{dy}{dx}x - y$$

$$\Rightarrow \frac{dy}{dx}(x-y) = x+y \Rightarrow \frac{dy}{dx} = \frac{x+y}{x-y}$$

Hence proved.

Example 4 **If $y = x^{\frac{1}{x}}$, then find $\dfrac{dy}{dx}$ at $x = 1$.**

CBSE 2023

Sol. Given,

$$y = x^{1/x}$$

On taking log both sides, we get

$$\log y = \frac{1}{x}\log x$$

On differentiating both sides, we get

$$\frac{1}{y}\frac{dy}{dx} = \frac{1}{x}\frac{d}{dx}(\log x) + \log x\frac{d}{dx}\left(\frac{1}{x}\right)$$

$$\Rightarrow \frac{1}{y}\frac{dy}{dx} = \frac{1}{x}\cdot\frac{1}{x} + \log x\left(\frac{-1}{x^2}\right)$$

$$\Rightarrow \frac{dy}{dx} = y\left(\frac{1}{x^2} - \frac{\log x}{x^2}\right)$$

$$\Rightarrow \frac{dy}{dx} = x^{1/x}\left(\frac{1-\log x}{x^2}\right)$$

$\therefore$ At $x = 1$,

$$\frac{dy}{dx} = 1\frac{(1-\log 1)}{1}$$

$$= 1 - 0 = 1 \quad [\because \log 1 = 0]$$

Example 5 **Differentiate $x^{\sin x} + (\sin x)^{\cos x}$ with respect to x.**

Competency Based Que, CBSE 2019

Sol. Let $y = x^{\sin x} + (\sin x)^{\cos x}$

$$\Rightarrow y = e^{\sin x\log x} + e^{\cos x\cdot\log\sin x} \quad [\because a^b = e^{\log a^b} = e^{b\log a}]$$

On differentiating both sides w.r.t. x, we get

$$\frac{dy}{dx} = e^{\sin x\cdot\log x}\frac{d}{dx}(\sin x\cdot\log x) + e^{\cos x\cdot\log\sin x}\frac{d}{dx}(\cos x\cdot\log\sin x)$$

$$= x^{\sin x}\left\{\log x\frac{d}{dx}(\sin x) + \sin x\frac{d}{dx}(\log x)\right\} + (\sin x)^{\cos x}\left\{\log\sin x\frac{d}{dx}(\cos x) + \cos x\cdot\frac{d}{dx}(\log\sin x)\right\}$$

$$= x^{\sin x}\left\{\cos x\cdot\log x + \frac{\sin x}{x}\right\} + (\sin x)^{\cos x}\left\{-\sin x\log(\sin x) + \cos x\times\frac{1}{\sin x}\times\cos x\right\}$$

$$= x^{\sin x}\left\{\cos x\cdot\log x + \frac{\sin x}{x}\right\} + (\sin x)^{\cos x}\left\{-\sin x\log(\sin x) + \frac{\cos^2 x}{\sin x}\right\}$$

Example 6 If $x^m y^n = (x+y)^{m+n}$, prove that $\frac{dy}{dx} = \frac{y}{x}$.

CBSE 2014

Sol. Given, $x^m y^n = (x+y)^{m+n}$

On taking log both sides, we get

$$\log(x^m y^n) = \log(x+y)^{m+n}$$

$$\Rightarrow \log(x^m) + \log(y^n) = (m+n)\log(x+y)$$

$$\Rightarrow m\log x + n\log y = (m+n)\log(x+y)$$

On differentiating both sides w.r.t. x, we get

$$\frac{m}{x} + \frac{n}{y}\frac{dy}{dx} = \frac{m+n}{x+y}\left(1+\frac{dy}{dx}\right)$$

$$\Rightarrow \frac{m}{x} + \frac{n}{y}\frac{dy}{dx} = \frac{m+n}{x+y} + \frac{m+n}{x+y}\frac{dy}{dx}$$

$$\Rightarrow \frac{m}{x} - \frac{(m+n)}{x+y} = \left(\frac{m+n}{x+y} - \frac{n}{y}\right)\frac{dy}{dx}$$

$$\Rightarrow \left[\frac{my+ny-nx-ny}{y(x+y)}\right]\frac{dy}{dx} = \frac{mx+my-mx-nx}{x(x+y)}$$

$$\Rightarrow \frac{dy}{dx}\left[\frac{my-nx}{y}\right] = \frac{my-nx}{x}$$

Hence, $\frac{dy}{dx} = \frac{y}{x}$ **Hence proved.**

Example 7 Find $\frac{dy}{dx}$, if $y = (\cos x)^x + \cos^{-1}\sqrt{x}$

CBSE 2024C

Sol. Given, $y = (\cos x)^x + \cos^{-1}\sqrt{x}$

Let $u = (\cos x)^x$

$\therefore \; y = u + \cos^{-1}\sqrt{x}$

On differentiating both sides w.r.t. x, we get

$$\frac{dy}{dx} = \frac{du}{dx} + \frac{-1}{\sqrt{1-(\sqrt{x})^2}}\frac{1}{2\sqrt{x}} \quad \text{....(i)}$$

$\because \quad u = (\cos x)^x$

On taking log both sides, we get

$$\log u = x\log\cos x$$

On differentiating both sides w.r.t. x, we get

$$\frac{1}{u}\frac{du}{dx} = \frac{x}{\cos x}(-\sin x) + \log\cos x$$

$$\Rightarrow \frac{du}{dx} = (\cos x)^x[\log\cos x - x\tan x]$$

On putting value of $\frac{du}{dx}$ in Eq. (i), we get

$$\frac{dy}{dx} = (\cos x)^x[\log\cos x - x\tan x]$$

$$-\frac{1}{\sqrt{1-x}}\cdot\frac{1}{2\sqrt{x}}$$

Example 8 If $x^y - y^x = a^b$, find $\frac{dy}{dx}$.

CBSE 2019

Sol. Given, $x^y - y^x = a^b$

Let $x^y = u$ and $y^x = v$

Then, $u - v = a^b \Rightarrow \frac{du}{dx} - \frac{dv}{dx} = 0$ ...(i)

Now, $u = x^y$

On taking log both sides, we get

$$\log u = y\log x$$

On differentiating both sides, we get

$$\Rightarrow \frac{1}{u}\frac{du}{dx} = \frac{y}{x} + \log x\frac{dy}{dx}$$

$$\Rightarrow \frac{du}{dx} = y\cdot x^{y-1} + x^y\cdot\log x\frac{dy}{dx} \quad \text{...(ii)}$$

Now, $v = y^x$

On taking log both sides, we get

$$\log v = x\log y$$

On differentiating both sides, we get

$$\Rightarrow \frac{1}{v}\cdot\frac{dv}{dx} = \frac{x}{y}\frac{dy}{dx} + \log y$$

$$\Rightarrow \frac{dv}{dx} = xy^{x-1}\frac{dy}{dx} + y^x\log y \quad \text{...(iii)}$$

From Eqs. (i), (ii) and (iii), we get

$$y\cdot x^{y-1} + x^y\cdot\log x\frac{dy}{dx} - xy^{x-1}\frac{dy}{dx} - y^x\log y = 0$$

$$\Rightarrow \frac{dy}{dx}(x^y\log x - xy^{x-1}) = y^x\log y - y\cdot x^{y-1}$$

$$\Rightarrow \frac{dy}{dx} = \frac{y^x\cdot\log y - y\cdot x^{y-1}}{x^y\cdot\log x - x\cdot y^{x-1}}$$

Example 9 If $(\cos x)^y = (\cos y)^x$, then find $\frac{dy}{dx}$.

CBSE 2024, 19, 12

Sol. Given, $(\cos x)^y = (\cos y)^x$

On taking log both sides, we get

$$\log(\cos x)^y = \log(\cos y)^x$$

$$\Rightarrow y\log(\cos x) = x\log(\cos y) \; [\because \log x^n = n\log x]$$

On differentiating both sides w.r.t. x, we get

$$y\cdot\frac{d}{dx}\log(\cos x) + \log\cos x\cdot\frac{d}{dx}(y)$$

$$= x\frac{d}{dx}\log(\cos y) + \log(\cos y)\frac{d}{dx}(x)$$

[using product rule of derivative]

$$\Rightarrow y\cdot\frac{1}{\cos x}\frac{d}{dx}(\cos x) + \log(\cos x)\frac{dy}{dx}$$

$$= x\cdot\frac{1}{\cos y}\frac{d}{dx}(\cos y) + \log\cos y\cdot 1$$

$$\Rightarrow y\cdot\frac{1}{\cos x}(-\sin x)+\log(\cos x)\cdot\frac{dy}{dx}$$

$$=x\frac{1}{\cos y}(-\sin y)\cdot\frac{dy}{dx}+\log(\cos y)\cdot 1$$

$$\Rightarrow -y\tan x+\log(\cos x)\frac{dy}{dx}=-x\tan y\frac{dy}{dx}+\log(\cos y)$$

$$\Rightarrow [x\tan y+\log(\cos x)]\frac{dy}{dx}=\log(\cos y)+y\tan x$$

$$\therefore \quad \frac{dy}{dx}=\frac{\log(\cos y)+y\tan x}{x\tan y+\log(\cos x)}$$

Example 10 **If $y=e^{x\sin^2 x}+(\sin x)^x$, find $\frac{dy}{dx}$.**

CBSE Sample Paper 2023

Sol. We have, $y=e^{x\sin^2 x}+(\sin x)^x$

Let $u=e^{x\sin^2 x}$ and $v=(\sin x)^x$

$\therefore \quad y=u+v$

$$\Rightarrow \frac{dy}{dx}=\frac{du}{dx}+\frac{dv}{dx} \quad \text{...(i)}$$

Now, $u=e^{x\sin^2 x}$

$$\Rightarrow \frac{du}{dx}=e^{x\sin^2 x}[1\cdot\sin^2 x+x(2\sin x\cos x)]$$

$$=e^{x\sin^2 x}[\sin^2 x+x\sin 2x] \quad \text{...(ii)}$$

Also, $v=(\sin x)^x$

On taking log both sides, we get

$\Rightarrow \quad \log v=\log(\sin x)^x=x\log\sin x$

On differentiating w.r.t. x, we get

$$\Rightarrow \frac{1}{v}\frac{dv}{dx}=1\cdot\log\sin x+x\cdot\left(\frac{1}{\sin x}\right)\cos x$$

$$\Rightarrow \frac{dv}{dx}=v[\log\sin x+x\cot x]$$

$$\Rightarrow \frac{dv}{dx}=(\sin x)^x[\log\sin x+x\cot x] \quad \text{...(iii)}$$

$\therefore$ From Eqs. (i), (ii) and (iii), we get

$$\frac{dy}{dx}=e^{x\sin^2 x}[\sin^2 x+x\sin 2x]+(\sin x)^x[\log\sin x+x\cot x]$$

Example 11 **Find $\frac{dy}{dx}$, if $y=e^{\sin^2 x}\left\{2\tan^{-1}\sqrt{\frac{1-x}{1+x}}\right\}$.**

Competency Based Que, CBSE Sample Paper 2017

Sol. We have, $y=e^{\sin^2 x}\left\{2\tan^{-1}\sqrt{\frac{1-x}{1+x}}\right\}$ ...(i)

On putting $x=\cos 2\theta$ in $\left\{2\tan^{-1}\sqrt{\frac{1-x}{1+x}}\right\}$, we get

$$2\tan^{-1}\sqrt{\frac{1-\cos 2\theta}{1+\cos 2\theta}}=2\tan^{-1}\sqrt{\frac{2\sin^2\theta}{2\cos^2\theta}}$$

$$=2\tan^{-1}(\tan\theta)=2\theta$$

$$=\cos^{-1}x$$

Then, from Eq. (i), we get

$$y=e^{\sin^2 x}\cos^{-1}x$$

On taking log both sides, we get

$$\log y=\sin^2 x+\log(\cos^{-1}x)$$

On differentiating both sides w.r.t. x, we get

$$\frac{1}{y}\times\frac{dy}{dx}=2\sin x\cos x+\frac{1}{\cos^{-1}x}\times\frac{-1}{\sqrt{1-x^2}}$$

$$=\sin 2x-\frac{1}{\cos^{-1}x\sqrt{1-x^2}}$$

$$\therefore \quad \frac{dy}{dx}=e^{\sin^2 x}\cos^{-1}x\left[\sin 2x-\frac{1}{\cos^{-1}x\sqrt{1-x^2}}\right]$$

Quick Test 4

1. Differentiate the following functions with respect to x.

(i) e^{-x} (ii) $e^{\sqrt{3x}}$ (iii) $e^{\cos 3x}$

(iv) $e^{\sin^{-1}x}$ (v) $x\cos x + e^x$ (vi) $xe^x \sin x$

(vii) $\log(\tan x)$ (viii) $\log(x+\sqrt{1+x^2})$ (ix) $\dfrac{\log x}{x}$

2. Differentiate each of the following functions w.r.t. x.

(i) x^x (ii) $\left(\dfrac{1}{x}\right)^x$ (iii) $x^{\cos^{-1}x}$ (iv) $(\tan x)^{\log x}$

Directions (Q. Nos. 3-8) *Find* $\dfrac{dy}{dx}$.

3. $y^x = x^y$ *CBSE 2024C, NCERT*

4. $y=(x+3)^2(x+4)^3(x+5)^4$ *NCERT*

5. $y=\cos x\cos 2x\cos 3x$ *Competency Based Que, NCERT*

6. $y=(\log x)^x + x^{\log x}$ *Competency Based Que, CBSE 2013*

7. $y = x^{\cot x} + \dfrac{2x^2-3}{x^2+x+2}$ *Competency Based Que, CBSE 2012*

8. $y = x^{\sin x - \cos x} + \dfrac{x^2-1}{x^2+1}$

9. If $xy = e^{x-y}$, then prove that $\dfrac{dy}{dx} = \dfrac{y(x-1)}{x(y+1)}$. *CBSE 2023*

10. If $y = \dfrac{ax^2}{(x-a)(x-b)(x-c)} + \dfrac{bx}{(x-b)(x-c)} + \dfrac{c}{(x-c)} + 1$, then prove that $\dfrac{1}{y}\dfrac{dy}{dx} = \dfrac{1}{x}\left[\dfrac{a}{a-x}+\dfrac{b}{b-x}+\dfrac{c}{c-x}\right]$. *Competency Based Que*

Answers

1. (i) $-e^{-x}$ (ii) $\dfrac{3e^{\sqrt{3x}}}{2\sqrt{3x}}$ (iii) $-3\sin 3x e^{\cos 3x}$

(iv) $\dfrac{e^{\sin^{-1}x}}{\sqrt{1-x^2}}$ (v) $-x\sin x + \cos x + e^x$

(vi) $xe^x \cos x + (x+1)e^x \sin x$

(vii) $\text{cosec}x \cdot \sec x$ (viii) $\dfrac{1}{\sqrt{1+x^2}}$ (ix) $\dfrac{1-\log x}{x^2}$

2. (i) $x^x(1+\log x)$ (ii) $-\left(\dfrac{1}{x}\right)^x(1+\log x)$

(iii) $x^{\cos^{-1}x}\left[\dfrac{\cos^{-1}x}{x} - \dfrac{\log x}{\sqrt{1-x^2}}\right]$

(iv) $(\tan x)^{\log x}\left[\dfrac{\log x}{\sin x\cos x} + \dfrac{\log(\tan x)}{x}\right]$

3. $\dfrac{y}{x}\left[\dfrac{y - x\log y}{x - y\log x}\right]$

4. $(x+3)(x+4)^2(x+5)^3\,[9x^2+70x+133]$

5. $-\cos x\cos 2x\cos 3x\,[\tan x + 2\tan 2x + 3\tan 3x]$

6. $(\log x)^{x-1}[1+\log x\log(\log x)] + 2x^{\log x - 1}\cdot\log x$

7. $x^{\cot x}\left(\dfrac{\cot x}{x} - \text{cosec}^2 x\cdot\log x\right) + \dfrac{2x^2+14x+3}{(x^2+x+2)^2}$

8. $x^{\sin x - \cos x}\left[\dfrac{\sin x - \cos x}{x} + \log x(\cos x + \sin x)\right] + \dfrac{4x}{(x^2+1)^2}$

For Solutions, See QR Code on Pg. 152

5.8 Differentiation of Parametric Functions

Sometimes, x and y are given as functions of one another variable, say $x = f(t)$ and $y = g(t)$ are two functions and t is a variable.

In such case, x and y are called **parametric functions** and t is called the **parameter**.

Let $x = f(t)$ and $y = g(t)$, where t is a parameter, then

$$\frac{dy}{dx} = \frac{\left(\frac{dy}{dt}\right)}{\left(\frac{dx}{dt}\right)}, \text{ whenever } \frac{dx}{dt} \neq 0$$

$\dfrac{dy}{dx}$ is expressed in terms of parameter only without directly involving the main variables x and y.

5.9 Differentiation of a Function w.r.t. Another Function

Suppose it is required to differentiate a function $f(x)$ with respect to another function $g(x)$.

Let $y = f(x)$ and $z = g(x)$.

Here, both functions are different but both are in same variable x. Then, to find the derivative of $f(x)$ with respect to $g(x)$ or derivative of $g(x)$ with respect to $f(x)$ i.e. to find $\dfrac{dy}{dz}$ or $\dfrac{dz}{dy}$.

First differentiate both functions $f(x)$ and $g(x)$ with respect to x separately and then put these values in the following formulae

$$\frac{dy}{dz}=\frac{dy/dx}{dz/dx} \text{ or } \frac{dz}{dy}=\frac{dz/dx}{dy/dx}$$

Example 1 **If $x=a\sin 2t$ and $y=a(\cos 2t+\log\tan t)$, then find $\frac{dy}{dx}$.** CBSE 2023

Sol. Given, $x=a\sin 2t$

On differentiating both sides w.r.t. t, we get

$$\frac{dx}{dt}=a\cos 2t(2)=2a\cos 2t$$

and $\quad y=a(\cos 2t+\log\tan t)$

On differentiating both sides w.r.t. t, we get

$$\frac{dy}{dt}=a\left(-2\sin 2t+\frac{1}{\tan t}\sec^2 t\right)$$

$$=a\left(-2\sin 2t+\frac{2}{2\sin t\cos t}\right)=a\left(-2\sin 2t+\frac{2}{\sin 2t}\right)$$

$$=2a\left(\frac{-\sin^2 2t+1}{\sin 2t}\right)=2a\frac{\cos^2 2t}{\sin 2t}$$

$$\therefore \quad \frac{dy}{dx}=\frac{dy/dt}{dx/dt}=\frac{2a\cos^2 2t/\sin 2t}{2a\cos 2t}=\cot 2t$$

Example 2 **Find the value of $\frac{dy}{dx}$ at $\theta=\frac{\pi}{3}$, if $x=\cos\theta-\cos 2\theta,\ y=\sin\theta-\sin 2\theta$.** CBSE 2020

Sol. We have, $x=\cos\theta-\cos 2\theta,\ y=\sin\theta-\sin 2\theta$

On differentiating both sides of x and y w.r.t. θ, we get

$$\frac{dx}{d\theta}=-\sin\theta+2\sin 2\theta,\ \frac{dy}{d\theta}=\cos\theta-2\cos 2\theta$$

$$\therefore \quad \frac{dy}{dx}=\frac{dy/d\theta}{dx/d\theta}=\frac{\cos\theta-2\cos 2\theta}{-\sin\theta+2\sin 2\theta}$$

$$\Rightarrow \quad \left(\frac{dy}{dx}\right)_{\theta=\frac{\pi}{3}}=\frac{\cos\pi/3-2\cos(2\pi/3)}{-\sin\frac{\pi}{3}+2\sin(2\pi/3)}$$

$$=\frac{\frac{1}{2}+2\left(\frac{1}{2}\right)}{-\frac{\sqrt{3}}{2}+2\left(\frac{\sqrt{3}}{2}\right)}=\frac{\frac{3}{2}}{\frac{\sqrt{3}}{2}}=\frac{3}{\sqrt{3}}=\sqrt{3}$$

Example 3 **If $x=2\cos\theta-\cos 2\theta$ and $y=2\sin\theta-\sin 2\theta$, then prove that $\frac{dy}{dx}=\tan\left(\frac{3\theta}{2}\right)$.** CBSE 2013C

Sol. Given, $x=2\cos\theta-\cos 2\theta$ and $y=2\sin\theta-\sin 2\theta$

On differentiating both sides of x and y w.r.t. θ, we get

$$\frac{dx}{d\theta}=-2\sin\theta+2\sin 2\theta \text{ and } \frac{dy}{d\theta}=2\cos\theta-2\cos 2\theta$$

$$\therefore \quad \frac{dy}{dx}=\frac{dy/d\theta}{dx/d\theta}=\frac{2(\cos\theta-\cos 2\theta)}{2(-\sin\theta+\sin 2\theta)}$$

$$=\frac{\left[2\sin\left(\frac{\theta+2\theta}{2}\right)\sin\left(\frac{2\theta-\theta}{2}\right)\right]}{\left[2\cos\left(\frac{2\theta+\theta}{2}\right)\sin\left(\frac{2\theta-\theta}{2}\right)\right]}$$

$$\left[\because \cos C-\cos D=2\sin\left(\frac{C+D}{2}\right)\sin\left(\frac{D-C}{2}\right) \quad \sin C-\sin D=2\cos\left(\frac{C+D}{2}\right)\sin\left(\frac{C-D}{2}\right)\right]$$

$$=\frac{\sin\left(\frac{3\theta}{2}\right)\sin\left(\frac{\theta}{2}\right)}{\cos\left(\frac{3\theta}{2}\right)\sin\left(\frac{\theta}{2}\right)}=\tan\left(\frac{3\theta}{2}\right)$$

Hence proved.

Example 4 **If $x=\sqrt{a^{\sin^{-1}t}}$ and $y=\sqrt{a^{\cos^{-1}t}}$, then show that $\frac{dy}{dx}=\frac{-y}{x}$.** NCERT, CBSE 2012

Sol. Given, $x=\sqrt{a^{\sin^{-1}t}}$ and $y=\sqrt{a^{\cos^{-1}t}}$

Consider $x=(a^{\sin^{-1}t})^{1/2}$

On differentiating both sides w.r.t. t, we get

$$\frac{dx}{dt}=\frac{1}{2}(a^{\sin^{-1}t})^{-1/2}\frac{d}{dt}(a^{\sin^{-1}t})$$

[using chain rule of derivative]

$$=\frac{1}{2}(a^{\sin^{-1}t})^{-1/2}a^{\sin^{-1}t}\log a\frac{d}{dt}(\sin^{-1}t)$$

$$\left[\because \frac{d}{dx}(a^x)=a^x\log a\right]$$

$$=\frac{1}{2}(a^{\sin^{-1}t})^{-1/2}a^{\sin^{-1}t}\log a\cdot\frac{1}{\sqrt{1-t^2}}$$

$$=\frac{1}{2}(a^{\sin^{-1}t})^{1/2}\log a\cdot\frac{1}{\sqrt{1-t^2}}$$

$$\Rightarrow \quad \frac{dx}{dt}=\frac{\frac{1}{2}\sqrt{a^{\sin^{-1}t}}\cdot\log a}{\sqrt{1-t^2}} \quad \text{...(i)}$$

Now, consider $y=(a^{\cos^{-1}t})^{1/2}$

On differentiating both sides w.r.t. t, we get

$$\frac{dy}{dt}=\frac{1}{2}(a^{\cos^{-1}t})^{-1/2}\frac{d}{dt}(a^{\cos^{-1}t})$$

[using chain rule of derivative]

$$=\frac{1}{2}(a^{\cos^{-1}t})^{-1/2}a^{\cos^{-1}t}\log a\frac{d}{dt}(\cos^{-1}t)$$

$$\left[\because \frac{d}{dx}(a^x)=a^x\log a\right]$$

$$= \frac{1}{2}(a^{\cos^{-1} t})^{1/2} \log a \cdot \frac{(-1)}{\sqrt{1-t^2}}$$

$$\Rightarrow \frac{dy}{dt} = \frac{-\frac{1}{2}\sqrt{a^{\cos^{-1} t}} \cdot \log a}{\sqrt{1-t^2}} \quad \text{...(ii)}$$

On dividing Eq. (ii) by Eq. (i), we get

$$\frac{dy}{dx} = \frac{\left(\frac{dy}{dt}\right)}{\left(\frac{dx}{dt}\right)} = \frac{\left(\frac{-\frac{1}{2}\sqrt{a^{\cos^{-1} t}} \log a}{\sqrt{1-t^2}}\right)}{\left(\frac{\frac{1}{2}\sqrt{a^{\sin^{-1} t}} \log a}{\sqrt{1-t^2}}\right)} = -\frac{\sqrt{a^{\cos^{-1} t}}}{\sqrt{a^{\sin^{-1} t}}} = -\frac{y}{x}$$

[given, $\sqrt{a^{\cos^{-1} t}} = y$ and $\sqrt{a^{\sin^{-1} t}} = x$]

Hence proved.

Example 5 **Find the differential of $\sin^2 x$ with respect to $e^{\cos x}$.**

NCERT, CBSE 2020

Sol. Let $y = \sin^2 x$ and $z = e^{\cos x}$.

On differentiating both sides of y and z w.r.t. x, we get

$$\frac{dy}{dx} = 2\sin x \cos x$$

and $$\frac{dz}{dx} = e^{\cos x}(-\sin x) = -(\sin x)\, e^{\cos x}$$

Now, $$\frac{dy}{dz} = \frac{dy/dx}{dz/dx} = \frac{2\sin x \cos x}{-(\sin x)\, e^{\cos x}} = \frac{-2\cos x}{e^{\cos x}}$$

Example 6 **Find the derivative of $x^{\log x}$ w.r.t. $\log x$.**

CBSE 2023, 20

Sol. Let $y = x^{\log x}$

On taking log both sides, we get

$$\log y = \log x \cdot \log x = (\log x)^2$$

On differentiating both sides w.r.t. x, we get

$$\frac{1}{y}\frac{dy}{dx} = 2\log x \frac{d}{dx}(\log x)$$

$$\Rightarrow \frac{1}{y}\frac{dy}{dx} = 2\log x\left(\frac{1}{x}\right) \Rightarrow \frac{dy}{dx} = y\left(\frac{2\log x}{x}\right)$$

$$\Rightarrow \frac{dy}{dx} = x^{\log x}\left(\frac{2\log x}{x}\right) = x^{\log x - 1}(2\log x)$$

Again, let $z = \log x$

On differentiating both sides w.r.t. x, we get

$$\frac{dz}{dx} = \frac{1}{x}$$

Now, $$\frac{dy}{dz} = \frac{\frac{dy}{dx}}{\frac{dz}{dx}} = \frac{x^{\log x - 1}(2\log x)}{\frac{1}{x}} = x^{\log x}(2\log x)$$

Example 7 **Differentiate $\sec^{-1}\left(\frac{1}{\sqrt{1-x^2}}\right)$ with respect to $\sin^{-1}[2x\sqrt{1-x^2}]$**

Competency Based Que, CBSE 2023

Sol. Let $u = \sec^{-1}\left(\frac{1}{\sqrt{1-x^2}}\right)$

On putting $x = \sin\theta$

$$\Rightarrow \theta = \sin^{-1} x$$

$$\therefore u = \sec^{-1}\left(\frac{1}{\sqrt{1-\sin^2\theta}}\right) = \sec^{-1}\left(\frac{1}{\sqrt{\cos^2\theta}}\right)$$

$$= \sec^{-1}(\sec\theta) = \theta = \sin^{-1} x$$

On differentiating both sides w.r.t. x, we get

$$\frac{du}{dx} = \frac{1}{\sqrt{1-x^2}}$$

Again, let $v = \sin^{-1}(2x\sqrt{1-x^2})$

On putting $x = \sin\theta$

$$\Rightarrow \theta = \sin^{-1} x$$

$$\therefore v = \sin^{-1}(2\sin\theta\sqrt{1-\sin^2\theta})$$

$$= \sin^{-1}(2\sin\theta.\cos\theta)$$

$$= \sin^{-1}(\sin 2\theta) = 2\theta = 2\sin^{-1} x$$

On differentiating both sides w.r.t. x, we get

$$\frac{dv}{dx} = \frac{d}{dx}(2\sin^{-1} x) = \frac{2}{\sqrt{1-x^2}}$$

$$\therefore \frac{du}{dv} = \frac{du/dx}{dv/dx} = \frac{1/\sqrt{1-x^2}}{2/\sqrt{1-x^2}} \Rightarrow \frac{du}{dv} = \frac{1}{2}$$

Example 8 **Differentiate $\tan^{-1}\left(\frac{\sqrt{1+x^2}-1}{x}\right)$ with respect to $\sin^{-1}\left(\frac{2x}{1+x^2}\right)$, when $x \neq 0$.**

CBSE 2016, 14

Sol. Let $u = \tan^{-1}\left(\frac{\sqrt{1+x^2}-1}{x}\right)$

Put $x = \tan\theta \Rightarrow \theta = \tan^{-1} x$, then

$$u = \tan^{-1}\left[\frac{\sqrt{1+\tan^2\theta}-1}{\tan\theta}\right] = \tan^{-1}\left[\frac{\sqrt{\sec^2\theta}-1}{\tan\theta}\right]$$

$$= \tan^{-1}\left[\frac{\sec\theta - 1}{\tan\theta}\right] = \tan^{-1}\left[\frac{1-\cos\theta}{\sin\theta}\right]$$

$$= \tan^{-1}\left[\frac{2\sin^2\theta/2}{2\sin\theta/2 \cdot \cos\theta/2}\right] = \tan^{-1}[\tan\theta/2]$$

$$\Rightarrow u = \frac{\theta}{2} = \frac{1}{2}\tan^{-1} x \qquad [\because \tan^{-1}(\tan\theta) = \theta]$$

On differentiating both sides w.r.t. x, we get

$$\frac{du}{dx} = \frac{1}{2(1+x^2)} \quad \left[\because \frac{d}{dx}(\tan^{-1} y) = \frac{1}{1+y^2}\right] \quad \text{...(i)}$$

Also, let $v = \sin^{-1}\left(\frac{2x}{1+x^2}\right)$

Put $x = \tan\theta \Rightarrow \theta = \tan^{-1} x$, then we get

$$v = \sin^{-1}\left[\frac{2\tan\theta}{1+\tan^2\theta}\right]$$

$\Rightarrow \quad v = \sin^{-1}[\sin 2\theta] \Rightarrow v = 2\theta \Rightarrow v = 2\tan^{-1} x$

On differentiating both sides w.r.t. x, we get

$$\frac{dv}{dx} = \frac{2}{1+x^2} \quad \text{...(ii)}$$

Now, $\frac{du}{dv} = \frac{du}{dx} \times \frac{dx}{dv} = \frac{1}{2(1+x^2)} \times \frac{(1+x^2)}{2}$

[from Eqs. (i) and (ii)]

$\therefore \quad \frac{du}{dv} = \frac{1}{4}$

Quick Test 5

Directions (Q. Nos. 1-5) *Find* $\frac{dy}{dx}$.

1. $x = a\cos\theta$ and $y = a\sin\theta$

2. $x = \frac{1-t^2}{1+t^2}$ and $y = \frac{2t}{1+t^2}$.

Competency Based Que

3. $x = \frac{\sin^3 t}{\sqrt{\cos 2t}}$ and $y = \frac{\cos^3 t}{\sqrt{\cos 2t}}$.

Competency Based Que, NCERT

4. $x = a(2\theta - \sin 2\theta)$ and $y = a(1 - \cos 2\theta)$, when $\theta = \frac{\pi}{3}$.

CBSE 2025

5. If $x = a\sec^3\theta$ and $y = a\tan^3\theta$ at $\theta = \frac{\pi}{3}$.

NCERT Exemplar

6. If $x = e^{\cos 2t}$ and $y = e^{\sin 2t}$, then prove that $\frac{dy}{dx} = \frac{-y\log x}{x\log y}$.

7. Differentiate $\sin x^2$ w.r.t. x^2.

8. Differentiate $\cos^{-1}(2x^2 - 1)$ w.r.t. $\cos^{-1} x$.

9. Differentiate $\tan^{-1}\left(\frac{\sqrt{1+x^2}-1}{x}\right)$ w.r.t. $\tan^{-1} x$, when $x \neq 0$.

Competency Based Que, NCERT Exemplar

10. Differentiate $\cos^{-1}(4x^3 - 3x)$ w.r.t. $\tan^{-1}\left(\frac{\sqrt{1-x^2}}{x}\right)$, if $\frac{1}{2} < x < 1$.

Competency Based Que

Answers

1. $-\cot\theta$ 2. $\frac{t^2-1}{2t}$ 3. $-\cot 3t$ 4. $\frac{1}{\sqrt{3}}$ 5. $\frac{\sqrt{3}}{2}$ 7. $\cos x^2$

8. 2 9. $\frac{1}{2}$ 10. 3

For Solutions, See QR Code on Pg. 152

5.9 Second Order Derivative

Second order derivative is the derivative of the first order derivative.

Let $\quad y = f(x) \quad$ ...(i)

Then, $\frac{dy}{dx} = f'(x)$ is called the **first derivative of** y or $f(x)$. It can also be written as y' or y_1.

Again, differentiating w.r.t. x, we get

$$\frac{d}{dx}\left(\frac{dy}{dx}\right) = \frac{d}{dx}[f'(x)]$$

$$\Rightarrow \quad \frac{d^2y}{dx^2} = f''(x),$$

where, $\frac{d}{dx}\left(\frac{dy}{dx}\right)$ is called the **second order derivative of** y w.r.t. x and it is denoted by

$$\frac{d^2y}{dx^2} \text{ or } f''(x) \text{ or } y'' \text{ or } D^2y \text{ or } y_2.$$

Other higher order derivatives may be defined similarly.

Example 1 **Find the second order derivative of**

(i) x^{20}

(ii) $\tan^{-1} x$

(iii) $\sin(\log x)$

Sol. (i) Let $y = x^{20}$

On differentiating both sides w.r.t. x, we get

$$\frac{dy}{dx} = 20x^{19}$$

Again, on differentiating both sides w.r.t. x, we get

$$\frac{d}{dx}\left(\frac{dy}{dx}\right) = (20 \times 19)\, x^{18}$$

$$\Rightarrow \quad \frac{d^2y}{dx^2} = 380x^{18}$$

(ii) Let $y = \tan^{-1} x$

On differentiating both sides w.r.t. x, we get

$$\frac{dy}{dx} = \frac{1}{1+x^2} = (1+x^2)^{-1}$$

Again, on differentiating both sides w.r.t. x, we get

$$\frac{d}{dx}\left(\frac{dy}{dx}\right) = \frac{d}{dx}(1+x^2)^{-1}$$

$$\Rightarrow \quad \frac{d^2y}{dx^2} = (-1)(1+x^2)^{-2}\frac{d}{dx}(1+x^2)$$

$$= (-1)(1+x^2)^{-2}(2x)$$

$$= \frac{-2x}{(1+x^2)^2}$$

(iii) Let $y = \sin(\log x)$

On differentiating both sides w.r.t. x, we get

$$\frac{dy}{dx} = \cos(\log x)\frac{d}{dx}(\log x)$$

$$\Rightarrow \quad \frac{dy}{dx} = \cos(\log x)\cdot\frac{1}{x}$$

$$\Rightarrow \quad x.\frac{dy}{dx} = \cos(\log x) \qquad \text{...(i)}$$

Again, on differentiating both sides w.r.t. x, we get

$$x\cdot\frac{d^2y}{dx^2} + \frac{dy}{dx} = -\frac{\sin(\log x)}{x}$$

$$\Rightarrow \quad x^2\frac{d^2y}{dx^2} + x\frac{dy}{dx} = -\sin(\log x)$$

$$\Rightarrow \quad x^2\frac{d^2y}{dx^2} + \cos(\log x) = -\sin(\log x) \quad \text{[from Eq. (i)]}$$

$$\Rightarrow \quad x^2\frac{d^2y}{dx^2} = -\sin(\log x) - \cos(\log x)$$

$$\therefore \quad \frac{d^2y}{dx^2} = -\frac{1}{x^2}[\sin(\log x) + \cos(\log x)]$$

Example 2 **If $x = a\sin^3\theta$, $y = b\cos^3\theta$, then find $\frac{d^2y}{dx^2}$ at $\theta = \frac{\pi}{4}$.**

CBSE 2024

Sol. Given, $x = a\sin^3\theta$ and $y = b\cos^3\theta$

$$\therefore \quad \frac{dx}{d\theta} = 3a\sin^2\theta\frac{d}{d\theta}(\sin\theta) = 3a\sin^2\theta\cos\theta$$

and

$$\frac{dy}{d\theta} = 3b\cos^2\theta\frac{d}{d\theta}(\cos\theta) = -3b\cos^2\theta\sin\theta$$

$$\therefore \quad \frac{dy}{dx} = \frac{\frac{dy}{d\theta}}{\frac{dx}{d\theta}} = \frac{-3b\cos^2\theta\sin\theta}{3a\sin^2\theta\cos\theta}$$

$$\Rightarrow \quad \frac{dy}{dx} = -\frac{b}{a}\cot\theta$$

Again,

$$\frac{d^2y}{dx^2} = -\frac{b}{a}(-\operatorname{cosec}^2\theta)\cdot\frac{d\theta}{dx}$$

$$= \frac{b}{a}\operatorname{cosec}^2\theta\cdot\frac{d\theta}{dx}$$

$$= \frac{b}{a}\operatorname{cosec}^2\theta\cdot\frac{1}{3a\sin^2\theta\cos\theta}$$

$$= \frac{b}{a}\cdot\frac{1}{\sin^2\theta}\cdot\frac{1}{3a\sin^2\theta\cos\theta}$$

$$= \frac{b}{3a^2}\times\frac{1}{\sin^4\theta\cos\theta}$$

$$\therefore \left(\frac{d^2y}{dx^2}\right)_{\theta=\frac{\pi}{4}} = \frac{b}{3a^2\left(\sin\frac{\pi}{4}\right)^4\left(\cos\frac{\pi}{4}\right)}$$

$$= \frac{b}{3a^2\cdot\left(\frac{1}{\sqrt{2}}\right)^4\cdot\left(\frac{1}{\sqrt{2}}\right)} = \frac{b}{3a^2\left(\frac{1}{4}\right)\left(\frac{1}{\sqrt{2}}\right)} = \frac{4\sqrt{2}b}{3a^2}$$

Example 3 **If $y = (\tan^{-1} x)^2$, show that**

$$(x^2+1)^2\frac{d^2y}{dx^2} + 2x(x^2+1)\frac{dy}{dx} = 2.$$

CBSE 2024

Sol. We have, $y = (\tan^{-1} x)^2$

On differentiating both sides w.r.t. x, we get

$$\frac{dy}{dx} = 2\tan^{-1}x \times \frac{1}{1+x^2} \Rightarrow (1+x^2)\frac{dy}{dx} = 2\tan^{-1}x$$

Again, on differentiating both sides w.r.t. x, we get

$$(1+x^2)\frac{d^2y}{dx^2} + 2x\cdot\frac{dy}{dx} = \frac{2}{1+x^2}$$

$$\Rightarrow (1+x^2)(1+x^2)\frac{d^2y}{dx^2} + 2x(1+x^2)\frac{dy}{dx} = 2$$

$$\therefore \quad (x^2+1)^2\frac{d^2y}{dx^2} + 2x(x^2+1)\frac{dy}{dx} = 2$$

Hence proved.

Example 4 **If $y=\tan x+\sec x$, then prove that**

$$\frac{d^2y}{dx^2}=\frac{\cos x}{(1-\sin x)^2}$$

CBSE 2023

Sol. Given, $y=\tan x+\sec x$

$$\Rightarrow \quad y=\frac{\sin x}{\cos x}+\frac{1}{\cos x}=\frac{\sin x+1}{\cos x}$$

On differentiating twice both sides w.r.t. x, we get

$$\frac{dy}{dx}=\frac{\cos x\frac{d}{dx}(\sin x+1)-(\sin x+1)\frac{d}{dx}(\cos x)}{(\cos x)^2}$$

$$=\frac{\cos x(\cos x)-(\sin x+1)(-\sin x)}{\cos^2 x}$$

$$=\frac{\cos^2 x+\sin^2 x+\sin x}{\cos^2 x}=\frac{1+\sin x}{\cos^2 x}$$

$$\Rightarrow \quad \frac{dy}{dx}=\frac{1+\sin x}{1-\sin^2 x}=\frac{1}{1-\sin x}$$

$$\Rightarrow \quad \frac{d^2y}{dx^2}=\frac{(1-\sin x)(0)-1(0-\cos x)}{(1-\sin x)^2}=\frac{\cos x}{(1-\sin x)^2}$$

Hence proved.

Example 5 **If $y=\sin(\sin x)$, prove that**

$$\frac{d^2y}{dx^2}+\tan x\frac{dy}{dx}+y\cos^2 x=0.$$

CBSE 2018

Sol. Given, $y=\sin(\sin x)$ ...(i)

On differentiating both sides w.r.t. x, we get

$$\frac{dy}{dx}=\cos(\sin x)\cdot\cos x \quad \text{...(ii)}$$

Again, on differentiating both sides w.r.t. x, we get

$$\frac{d^2y}{dx^2}=\cos(\sin x)\cdot(-\sin x)+\cos x(-\sin(\sin x))\cdot\cos x$$

$$\Rightarrow \quad \frac{d^2y}{dx^2}=\frac{1}{\cos x}\cdot\left(\frac{dy}{dx}\right)(-\sin x)-y\cos^2 x$$

[using Eqs. (i) and (ii)]

$$\Rightarrow \quad \frac{d^2y}{dx^2}=-\tan x\frac{dy}{dx}-y\cos^2 x$$

$$\therefore \quad \frac{d^2y}{dx^2}+\tan x\frac{dy}{dx}+y\cos^2 x=0$$

Hence proved.

Example 6 **If $(a+bx)e^{\frac{y}{x}}=x$, then prove that**

$$x\frac{d^2y}{dx^2}=\left(\frac{a}{a+bx}\right)^2.$$

Competency Based Que, CBSE 2023

Sol. Given, $(a+bx)e^{\frac{y}{x}}=x \Rightarrow e^{\frac{y}{x}}=\dfrac{x}{a+bx}$

On taking $\log_e$ both sides, we get

$$\log_e e^{\frac{y}{x}}=\log_e\left(\frac{x}{a+bx}\right)$$

$$\Rightarrow \quad \frac{y}{x}\log_e e=\log_e\left(\frac{x}{a+bx}\right)$$

$$\Rightarrow \quad \frac{y}{x}=\log_e\frac{x}{a+bx} \quad [\because \log_e e=1]$$

$$\Rightarrow \quad \frac{y}{x}=\log_e x-\log_e(a+bx)$$

On differentiating both sides w.r.t. x, we get

$$\frac{x\frac{dy}{dx}-y}{x^2}=\frac{1}{x}-\frac{b}{a+bx}$$

$$\Rightarrow \quad \frac{xdy}{dx}-y=x^2\left(\frac{1}{x}-\frac{b}{a+bx}\right)=\frac{ax}{a+bx}$$

On differentiating again w.r.t x, we get

$$\Rightarrow \frac{xd^2y}{dx^2}+\frac{dy}{dx}-\frac{dy}{dx}=\frac{(a+bx)a-ax(b)}{(a+bx)^2}$$

$$\Rightarrow \quad \frac{xd^2y}{dx^2}=\frac{a^2}{(a+bx)^2}=\left(\frac{a}{a+bx}\right)^2$$

Example 7 **If $y=x^x$, then prove that**

$$\frac{d^2y}{dx^2}-\frac{1}{y}\left(\frac{dy}{dx}\right)^2-\frac{y}{x}=0.$$

CBSE 2023, 16, 14

Sol. Given, $y=x^x$

On taking log both sides, we get

$$\log y=\log x^x \Rightarrow \log y=x\log x$$

On differentiating both sides w.r.t. x, we get

$$\frac{1}{y}\frac{dy}{dx}=x\frac{d}{dx}(\log x)+\log x\frac{d}{dx}(x)$$

[using product rule of derivative]

$$\Rightarrow \quad \frac{1}{y}\frac{dy}{dx}=x\times\frac{1}{x}+\log x\cdot 1$$

$$\Rightarrow \quad \frac{1}{y}\frac{dy}{dx}=(1+\log x)$$

$$\Rightarrow \quad \frac{dy}{dx}=y(1+\log x) \quad \text{...(i)}$$

Again, on differentiating both sides w.r.t. x, we get

$$\frac{d^2y}{dx^2}=y\frac{d}{dx}(1+\log x)+(1+\log x)\frac{dy}{dx}$$

[using product rule of derivative]

$$\Rightarrow \quad \frac{d^2y}{dx^2}=y\times\frac{1}{x}+(1+\log x)\frac{dy}{dx}$$

$$\Rightarrow \quad \frac{d^2y}{dx^2}=\frac{y}{x}+(1+\log x)\frac{dy}{dx}$$

$$\Rightarrow \quad \frac{d^2y}{dx^2}=\frac{y}{x}+\frac{1}{y}\left(\frac{dy}{dx}\right)\left(\frac{dy}{dx}\right) \quad \text{[using Eq. (i)]}$$

$$\therefore \quad \frac{d^2y}{dx^2}-\frac{1}{y}\left(\frac{dy}{dx}\right)^2-\frac{y}{x}=0$$

Hence proved.

Example 8 If $x = \cos t + \log\left(\tan\left(\frac{t}{2}\right)\right)$, $y = \sin t$, then find the values of $\frac{d^2y}{dt^2}$ and $\frac{d^2y}{dx^2}$ at $t = \frac{\pi}{4}$. CBSE 2019, 12 C

Sol. Given that $y = \sin t$

$$\Rightarrow \frac{dy}{dt} = \cos t \quad \text{[differentiate w.r.t. } t\text{]} \quad ...(i)$$

$$\Rightarrow \frac{d^2y}{dt^2} = -\sin t \quad \text{[differentiate w.r.t. } t\text{]}$$

$$\left[\frac{d^2y}{dt^2}\right]_{t=\frac{\pi}{4}} = -\sin\frac{\pi}{4} = -\frac{1}{\sqrt{2}}$$

Again, $x = \cos t + \log\left(\tan\left(\frac{t}{2}\right)\right)$

$$\Rightarrow \frac{dx}{dt} = -\sin t + \frac{1}{\tan\frac{t}{2}}\cdot\sec^2\frac{t}{2}\cdot\frac{1}{2}$$

[differentiate w.r.t. t]

$$= -\sin t + \frac{\cos\frac{t}{2}}{2\cdot\sin\frac{t}{2}}\cdot\frac{1}{\cos^2\frac{t}{2}}$$

$$= -\sin t + \frac{1}{\sin\left(2\times\frac{t}{2}\right)} \quad [\because 2\sin a\cos a = \sin 2a]$$

$$= -\sin t + \operatorname{cosec} t \quad ...(ii)$$

Now, $\frac{dy}{dx} = \frac{dy/dt}{dx/dt} = \frac{\cos t}{\operatorname{cosec} t - \sin t}$ [using Eqs.(i) and (ii)]

$$= \frac{\cos t}{1-\sin^2 t}\cdot\sin t = \frac{\sin t\cdot\cos t}{\cos^2 t}$$

$$\Rightarrow \frac{dy}{dx} = \tan t$$

$$\therefore \frac{d^2y}{dx^2} = \frac{d}{dx}\left(\frac{dy}{dx}\right) = \frac{\frac{d}{dt}\left(\frac{dy}{dx}\right)}{\frac{dx}{dt}} = \frac{\sec^2 t}{\operatorname{cosec} t - \sin t}$$

$$\left[\because \frac{d}{dx}\tan x = \sec^2 x\right]$$

$$= \frac{\sec^2 t\cdot\sin t}{\cos^2 t} = \sec^3 t\cdot\tan t$$

$$\Rightarrow \left[\frac{d^2y}{dx^2}\right]_{t=\frac{\pi}{4}} = \sec^3\frac{\pi}{4}\cdot\tan\frac{\pi}{4}$$

$$= 2\sqrt{2}\times 1 = 2\sqrt{2} \quad \left[\because \sec\frac{\pi}{4} = \sqrt{2}\right]$$

Quick Test 6

1. Find the second order derivative of the following.

(i) $x^3 - x^2 + 2$ (ii) e^{ax}

(iii) $x\cos 2x$ (iv) $\log(\log x)$

(v) $2\tan^{-1}x$

2. If $y = 5\cos x - 3\sin x$, then prove that $\frac{d^2y}{dx^2} + y = 0$. NCERT

3. If $y = \operatorname{cosec} x + \cot x$, then prove that $(\sin x)\frac{d^2y}{dx^2} - y^2 = 0$.

Competency Based Que

4. If $e^y(x+1) = 1$, then prove that $\frac{d^2y}{dx^2} = \left(\frac{dy}{dx}\right)^2$. CBSE 2017

5. If $y = x^3\log\left(\frac{1}{x}\right)$, then prove that $x\frac{d^2y}{dx^2} - 2\frac{dy}{dx} + 3x^2 = 0$.

Competency Based Que

6. If $y = (\sec^{-1}x)^2$, then prove that

$x^2(x^2-1)\frac{d^2y}{dx^2} + (2x^3 - x)\frac{dy}{dx} = 2$. CBSE 2017C

7. If $y = \log[x + \sqrt{x^2+1}]$, then prove that

$(x^2+1)\frac{d^2y}{dx^2} + x\frac{dy}{dx} = 0$. CBSE 2011

8. If $x^m y^n = (x+y)^{m+n}$, then prove that $\frac{d^2y}{dx^2} = 0$.

Competency Based Que, CBSE 2017

9. If $x = 3\cos t - 2\cos^3 t$ and $y = 3\sin t - 2\sin^3 t$, then find $\frac{d^2y}{dx^2}$. CBSE 2017C

10. If $x = a(\cos t + t\sin t)$ and $y = a(\sin t - t\cos t)$, then find $\frac{d^2y}{dx^2}$ at $t = \frac{\pi}{4}$. CBSE 2017C, 14C

Answers

1. (i) $6x - 2$ (ii) $a^2\cdot e^{ax}$ (iii) $-4x\cos 2x - 4\sin 2x$

(iv) $\frac{-(1+\log x)}{(x\log x)^2}$ (v) $\frac{-4x}{(1+x^2)^2}$

9. $\frac{-1}{3\sin^3 t\cos 2t}$ **10.** $\frac{8\sqrt{2}}{a\pi}$

For Solutions, See QR Code on Pg. 152

EXAM PATTERN QUESTIONS

Objective Type Questions

Multiple Choice Questions

1. The value of k for which $f(x)=\begin{cases}3x+5, & x\geq 2\\ kx^2, & x<2\end{cases}$ is a continuous function, is **CBSE 2023**

(a) $-\frac{11}{4}$ (b) $\frac{4}{11}$ (c) 11 (d) $\frac{11}{4}$

2. The value of k for which the function

$f(x)=\begin{cases}\frac{1-\cos 4x}{8x^2} & \text{if } x\neq 0\\ k & \text{if } x=0\end{cases}$ is continuous at $x=0$ is **CBSE Sample Paper 2023**

(a) 0 (b) -1 (c) 1 (d) 2

3. The function $f(x)=[x]$, where $[x]$ denotes the greatest integer less than or equal to x, is continuous at **Competency Based Que, CBSE 2023**

(a) $x=1$ (b) $x=1.5$
(c) $x=-2$ (d) $x=4$

4. The points, at which the function f given by

$f(x)=\begin{cases}\frac{x}{|x|}, & x<0\\ -1, & x\geq 0\end{cases}$ is continuous, is/are

Competency Based Que, CBSE Sample paper 2022 (Term I)

(a) $x\in R$ (b) $x=0$
(c) $x\in R-\{0\}$ (d) $x=-1$ and 1

5. For what value of x will the function,

$f(x)=\begin{cases}\frac{x+4}{x+4}, & x\neq -4\\ 1, & x=-4\end{cases}$ is discontinuous? **Diksha App**

(a) -4
(b) 4
(c) 1
(d) No point of discontinuity

6. If $f(x)=2|x|+3|\sin x|+6$, then the right hand derivative of $f(x)$ at $x=0$ is **CBSE 2023, 20**

(a) 6 (b) 5 (c) 3 (d) 2

7. The function $f(x)=x|x|$ is **Competency Based Que, CBSE 2023**

(a) continuous and differentiable at $x=0$.
(b) continuous but not differentiable at $x=0$.
(c) differentiable but not continuous at $x=0$.
(d) neither differentiable nor continuous at $x=0$.

8. The value of k for which function $f(x)=\begin{cases}x^2, & x\geq 0\\ kx, & x<0\end{cases}$ is differentiable at $x=0$ is **CBSE 2023**

(a) 1 (b) 2
(c) any real number (d) 0

9. The set of all points, where the function $f(x)=x+|x|$ is differentiable, is **Competency Based Que, CBSE Sample Paper 2023**

(a) $(0,\infty)$ (b) $(-\infty,0)$
(c) $(-\infty,0)\cup(0,\infty)$ (d) $(-\infty,\infty)$

10. The function $f(x)=|x|$ is **Competency Based Que, CBSE 2023**

(a) continuous and differentiable everywhere.
(b) continuous and differentiable nowhere.
(c) continuous everywhere but differentiable everywhere except at $x=0$.
(d) continuous everywhere but differentiable nowhere.

11. Let $f(x)=\begin{vmatrix}x^2 & \sin x\\ p & -1\end{vmatrix}$, where p is a constant. Then, the value of p for which $f'(0)=1$ is **CBSE 2024**

(a) R (b) 1 (c) 0 (d) -1

12. If $y=\frac{\cos x-\sin x}{\cos x+\sin x}$, then $\frac{dy}{dx}$ is **CBSE 2023**

(a) $-\sec^2\left(\frac{\pi}{4}-x\right)$ (b) $\sec^2\left(\frac{\pi}{4}-x\right)$
(c) $\log\left|\sec\left(\frac{\pi}{4}-x\right)\right|$ (d) $-\log\left|\sec\left(\frac{\pi}{4}-x\right)\right|$

13. If $y=\log\sqrt{\sec\sqrt{x}}$, then the value of $\frac{dy}{dx}$ at $x=\frac{\pi^2}{16}$ is **CBSE 2024 C**

(a) $\frac{1}{\pi}$ (b) π (c) $\frac{1}{2}$ (d) $\frac{1}{4}$

14. If $f(x)=|\cos x|$, then $f'\left(\frac{3\pi}{4}\right)$ is **Competency Based Que, CBSE 2023**

(a) 1 (b) -1 (c) $\frac{-1}{\sqrt{2}}$ (d) $\frac{1}{\sqrt{2}}$

15. If $xe^y=1$, then the value of $\frac{dy}{dx}$ at $x=1$ is **CBSE 2024**

(a) -1 (b) 1 (c) $-e$ (d) $-\frac{1}{e}$

16. If $\sin(xy) = 1$, then $\frac{dy}{dx}$ is equal to **CBSE 2024**

(a) $\frac{x}{y}$ (b) $-\frac{x}{y}$ (c) $\frac{y}{x}$ (d) $-\frac{y}{x}$

17. If $x = 3\cos\theta$ and $y = 5\sin\theta$, then $\frac{dy}{dx}$ is equal to **CBSE 2024C**

(a) $-\frac{3}{5}\tan\theta$ (b) $-\frac{5}{3}\cot\theta$

(c) $-\frac{5}{3}\tan\theta$ (d) $-\frac{3}{5}\cot\theta$

18. If $y = 10^{10^x}$, then $\frac{dy}{dx}$ is equal to **Diksha App**

(a) $10^{10^x}\log 10$ (b) $10^{10^x}(\log 10)^2$

(c) $10^{10^x}\cdot 10^x(\log 10)^2$ (d) $10^{10^x}\cdot 10^x\log 10$

19. Derivative of $e^{\sin^2 x}$ with respect to cos x is **CBSE 2024**

(a) $\sin x e^{\sin^2 x}$ (b) $\cos x e^{\sin^2 x}$

(c) $-2\cos x e^{\sin^2 x}$ (d) $-2\sin^2 x\cos x e^{\sin^2 x}$

20. If $x = at^2, y = 2at$, then $\frac{d^2y}{dx^2}$ is equal to **Diksha App**

(a) $-\frac{1}{t^2}$ (b) $\frac{1}{2at^3}$ (c) $-\frac{1}{t^3}$ (d) $-\frac{1}{2at^3}$

21. If $y = x\cos x$, then $\frac{d^2y}{dx^2}$ is **CBSE 2023**

(a) $-x\cos x - 2\sin x$ (b) $x\cos x + 2\sin x$

(c) $x\sin x + \cos x$ (d) None of these

22. If $y = \sin^{-1} x$, then $(1 - x^2)y_2$ is equal to **Competency Based Que, CBSE Sample Paper 2023**

(a) xy_1 (b) xy (c) xy_2 (d) x^2

23. If $y^{\frac{1}{m}} + y^{-\frac{1}{m}} = 2x$, then $(x^2 - 1)y_2 + xy_1$ is equal to **Competency Based Que, CBSE 2023**

(a) $\pm m^2 y$ (b) $m^2 y$ (c) $-m^2 y$ (d) $-my$

Assertion-Reason Based Questions

Directions (Q. Nos. 24-33) *In the questions given below are two statements labelled as Assertion (A) and Reason (R). In the context of the two statements, which one of the following is correct?*

(a) Both A and R are correct; R is the correct explanation of A.
(b) Both A and R are correct; R is not the correct explanation of A.
(c) A is correct; R is incorrect.
(d) R is correct; A is incorrect.

24. **Assertion** (A) $\sin^{-1} x$ is continuous on $[-1, 1]$.

Reason (R) $\cos x^2$ is discontinuous on $x \in R$.

25. **Assertion** (A) $|\sin x|$ is not a continuous function.

Reason (R) If $f(x)$ and $g(x)$ both are continuous functions, then $gof(x)$ is also a continuous function. **Competency Based Que**

26. **Assertion** (A) If $y = \cos x$, then $\left(\frac{dy}{dx}\right)_{\text{at } x = \frac{\pi}{2}}$ is 0.

Reason (R) $\frac{d}{dx}(\cos x) = -\sin x$.

27. **Assertion** (A) If $y = \cos^2 x^2$, then $\frac{dy}{dx} = -4x\cos x^2 \sin x^2$.

Reason (R) For the curve $\sqrt{x} + \sqrt{y} = 1$, $\frac{dy}{dx}$ at $\left(\frac{1}{4}, \frac{1}{4}\right)$ is -1.

28. **Assertion** (A) If $f(x) = \sqrt{1 + \cos^2(x^2)}$, then $f'\left(\frac{\sqrt{\pi}}{2}\right)$ is $\frac{\pi}{3}$.

Reason (R) If $f(x) = e^x$, $g(x) = \sin^{-1} x$ and $h(x) = f(g(x))$, then $\frac{h'(x)}{h(x)}$ is $\frac{1}{\sqrt{1 - x^2}}$. **Competency Based Que**

29. **Assertion** (A) If $e^{xy} + \log(xy) + \cos(xy) + 4 = 0$, then $\frac{dy}{dx} = -\frac{y}{x}$.

Reason (R) $\frac{d}{dx}(xy) = 0 \Rightarrow \frac{dy}{dx} = -\frac{y}{x}$. **Competency Based Que**

30. **Assertion** (A) If $f(x) = \sin^{-1} x + \cos^{-1} x + 4$, then $f'(4) = 0$

Reason (R) $\frac{d}{dx}(\cos x) = -\sin x$.

31. **Assertion** (A) If $f(x)$ is an odd function, then $f'(x)$ is an even function.

Reason (R) If $u = f(x), v = g(x)$, then the derivative of f with respect to g is $\frac{du}{dv} = \frac{du/dx}{dv/dx}$.

32. **Assertion** (A) If $y = \sin x + \cos x$, then $\left(\frac{dy}{dx}\right)_{\text{at } x = \pi/4} = 0$.

Reason (R) $\frac{d^2y}{dx^2} = \frac{d}{dx}\left(\frac{dy}{dx}\right)$.

33. **Assertion** (A) If $y = \tan^{-1} x$, then $\frac{dy}{dx} = \frac{1}{1 + x^2}$.

Reason (R) $\frac{d^2y}{dx^2} = \left(\frac{dy}{dx}\right)^2$.

Case Study Based Questions

34. Ambika, a mathematics teacher is conducting a practice session on calculus where she is discussing continuity and differentiability of several functions in their domains. Shown below are four cards that contain a function each along with their domains and graphs.

Competency Based Que, CBSE QB

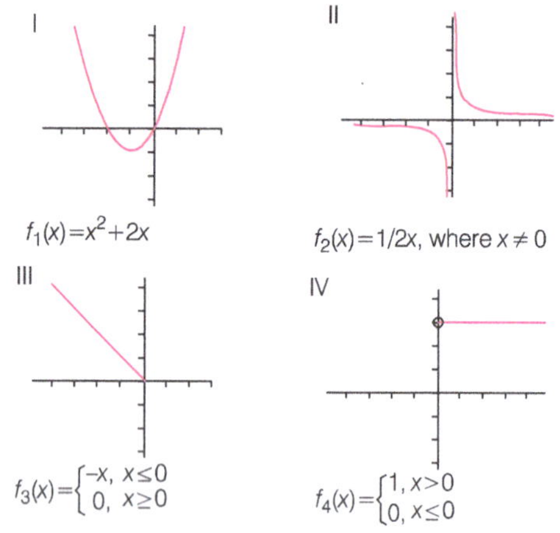

While discussing in the group, four students claimed as follows

Leela 'As the function on card I is both continuous and differentiable, we can say that every continuous function is differentiable.'

Irfan 'As the graph is not in one piece, the function on card II is discontinuous.'

Deepak 'The function on card III is continuous.'

Kiran 'The function on card IV is discontinuous.'

Based on above information, answer the following questions.

(i) Check whether Deepak and Kiran's claims are correct. Justify your answer.

(ii) Is Irfan's claim correct? Does the reason given by him support his claim? Justify.

(iii) Is Leela's claim true for all continuous functions? Justify with a valid reason or provide a counter example.

35. Let $f(x)$ be a real valued function. Then, its

Left Hand Derivative (LHD),

$$Lf'(a) = \lim_{h\to 0}\frac{f(a-h)-f(a)}{-h}$$

Right Hand Derivative (RHD),

$$Rf'(a) = \lim_{h\to 0}\frac{f(a+h)-f(a)}{h}$$

Also, a function $f(x)$ is said to be differentiable at $x=a$, if its LHD and RHD at $x=a$ exist and both are equal.

For the function $f(x)=\begin{cases}|x-3|, & x\geq 1\\ \dfrac{x^2}{4}-\dfrac{3x}{2}+\dfrac{13}{4}, & x<1\end{cases}$

CBSE 2023

On the basis of above information, answer the following questions.

(i) What is RHD of $f(x)$ at $x=1$?

(ii) What is LHD of $f(x)$ at $x=1$?

(iii) (a) Check if the function $f(x)$ is differentiable at $x=1$.

or

(b) Find $f'(2)$ and $f'(-1)$.

Subjective Questions

Very Short Answer Type Questions

1. If the following function $f(x)$ is continuous at $x=0$, then write the value of k.

$$f(x)=\begin{cases}\dfrac{\sin\frac{3x}{2}}{x}, & x\neq 0\\ k, & x=0\end{cases}$$

CBSE 2017C

2. Determine the value of the constant k, so that function $f(x)=\begin{cases}\dfrac{kx}{|x|} & \text{if } x<0\\ 3 & \text{if } x\geq 0\end{cases}$ is continuous at $x=0$.

CBSE 2017

3. If the function f defined as $f(x)=\begin{cases}\dfrac{x^2-9}{x-3}, & x\neq 3\\ k, & x=3\end{cases}$ is continuous at $x=3$, find the value of k.

CBSE 2020

4. Determine the value of k for which the following function is continuous at $x=3$

$$f(x)=\begin{cases}\dfrac{(x+3)^2-36}{x-3}, & x\neq 3\\ k, & x=3\end{cases}$$

Competency Based Que, CBSE 2017

5. Prove that the greatest integer function defined by $f(x)=[x]$, $0<x<2$ is not differentiable at $x=1$.

Competency Based Que, CBSE Sample Paper 2021

6. Find the derivative of $\cos(\sqrt{x})$.

NCERT

7. If $f(x)=x|x|$, then find $f'(x)$.

Competency Based Que, CBSE 2020

8. If $y = x|x|$, find $\frac{dy}{dx}$ for $x < 0$. **CBSE 2019**

9. Find $\frac{dy}{dx}$, when $2x + 3y = \sin y$.

10. Find the derivative of $\sin(\tan^{-1} x)$ w.r.t. x.

11. If $y\sqrt{1-x^2} + x\sqrt{1-y^2} = 1$, then prove that $\frac{dy}{dx} = -\sqrt{\frac{1-y^2}{1-x^2}}$.

Competency Based Que, CBSE Sample Paper 2023

12. Differentiate $e^{\sqrt{x}}$ w.r.t. x.

13. Differentiate $e^{3x} \cdot \cos 2x$ w.r.t. x.

14. Find the derivative of $\log \sin x$ w.r.t. x.

15. Find the second derivative of $\log x$. **NCERT**

Short Answer Type Questions

16. Discuss the continuity of secant. **NCERT**

17. Examine the continuity of the function

$$f(x) = \begin{cases} \frac{|\sin x|}{x}, & \text{if } x \neq 0 \\ 1, & \text{if } x = 0 \end{cases} \text{ at } x = 0.$$

18. If the function $f(x) = \begin{cases} 3ax + b, & \text{if } x > 1 \\ 11, & \text{if } x = 1 \\ 5ax - 2b, & \text{if } x < 1 \end{cases}$

is continuous at $x = 1$, then find the values of a and b. **CBSE 2011, 10**

19. Find the value of k, if the function,

$$f(x) = \begin{cases} \frac{1-\sin x}{(\pi - 2x)^2}, & \text{if } x \neq \frac{\pi}{2} \\ k, & \text{if } x = \frac{\pi}{2} \end{cases} \text{ is continuous at } x = \pi/2.$$

Competency Based Que

20. Find the value of k so that the function f is continuous at $x = \pi/2$, $f(x) = \begin{cases} \frac{k \cos x}{\pi - 2x}, & \text{if } x \neq \frac{\pi}{2} \\ 3, & \text{if } x = \frac{\pi}{2} \end{cases}$. **CBSE 2025, 12**

21. The function $f(x) = \begin{cases} \frac{x^2}{a}, & \text{if } 0 \le x < 1 \\ a, & \text{if } 1 \le x < \sqrt{2} \\ \frac{2b^2 - 4b}{x^2}, & \text{if } \sqrt{2} \le x < \infty \end{cases}$ is continuous on $[0, \infty)$. Find the most suitable values of a and b.

22. If the function $f(x)$ defined by

$$f(x) = \begin{cases} \frac{\log(1+ax) - \log(1-bx)}{x}, & \text{if } x \neq 0 \\ k, & \text{if } x = 0 \end{cases}$$

is continuous at $x = 0$, then find the value of k.

Competency Based Que

23. Determine the values of a and b such that the following function is continuous at $x = 0$.

$$f(x) = \begin{cases} \frac{x + \sin x}{\sin(a+1)x}, & \text{if } -\pi < x < 0 \\ 2, & \text{if } x = 0 \\ \frac{2(e^{\sin bx} - 1)}{bx}, & \text{if } x > 0 \end{cases}$$

Competency Based Que, CBSE Sample paper 2018

24. Find the value of k so that the function

$$f(x) = \begin{cases} \left(\frac{1-\cos 4x}{8x^2}\right), & \text{if } x \neq 0 \\ k, & \text{if } x = 0 \end{cases}$$

is continuous at $x = 0$. **CBSE 2014C**

25. Find the value of k, so that the following function is continuous at $x = 2$.

$$f(x) = \begin{cases} \frac{x^3 + x^2 - 16x + 20}{(x-2)^2}, & \text{if } x \neq 2 \\ k, & \text{if } x = 2 \end{cases}$$

CBSE 2012C

26. Examine the continuity of the following function

$$f(x) = \begin{cases} \frac{x}{2|x|}, & \text{if } x \neq 0 \\ \frac{1}{2}, & \text{if } x = 0 \end{cases} \text{ at } x = 0.$$

Competency Based Que

27. Find the point of discontinuity of the function

$$f(x) = \begin{cases} x^{10} - 1, & \text{if } x \le 1 \\ x^2, & \text{if } x > 1 \end{cases}$$

NCERT

28. Find the point of discontinuity of the function

$$f(x) = \begin{cases} \frac{\sin 2x}{x}, & \text{if } x < 0 \\ x + 2, & \text{if } x \ge 0 \end{cases}$$

Long Answer Type Questions

29. Find the value of a for which the function f is defined as

$$f(x) = \begin{cases} a \sin \frac{\pi}{2}(x+1), & x \le 0 \\ \frac{\tan x - \sin x}{x^3}, & x > 0 \end{cases}$$

is continuous at $x = 0$. **Competency Based Que, CBSE 2011**

30. Find the value of k so that the function f defined by $f(x)=\begin{cases} kx+1, \text{if } x\le\pi \\ \cos x, \text{if } x>\pi \end{cases}$ is continuous at $x=\pi$. **CBSE 2011**

31. For what values of λ, is the function

$$f(x)=\begin{cases} \lambda(x^2-2x), \text{if } x\le 0 \\ 4x+1, \text{if } x>0 \end{cases}$$

is continuous at $x=0$? **CBSE 2011**

32. Find the value of a, if the function $f(x)$ defined by

$$f(x)=\begin{cases} 2x-1, & x<2 \\ a, & x=2 \\ x+1, & x>2 \end{cases}$$

is continuous at $x=2$. Also, discuss the continuity of $f(x)$ at $x=3$. **CBSE 2011C**

33. If a function f is differentiable at a point c, then prove that it is also continuous at that point. **Competency Based Que**

34. Show that the function $f(x)=|x-3|, x\in R$ is continuous but not differentiable at $x=3$. **Competency Based Que**

35. Test the continuity and differentiability at $x=1$ of the function f defined by

$$f(x)=\begin{cases} 3^x, & -1\le x<1 \\ 4-x, & 1\le x<4 \end{cases}.$$

36. For what value of λ the function defined by $f(x)=\begin{cases} \lambda(x^2+2) \text{ if } x\le 0 \\ 4x+6 \quad \text{if } x>0 \end{cases}$ is continuous at $x=0$? Hence, check the differentiability of $f(x)$ at $x=0$. **CBSE 2015C**

37. Find the values of a and b so that the following function is differentiable for all values of x

$$f(x)=\begin{cases} ax+b, & x>-1 \\ bx^2-3, & x\le -1 \end{cases}$$

Competency Based Que, CBSE 2024

38. Find a and b, if the function given by $f(x)=\begin{cases} ax^2+b \text{ if } x<1 \\ 2x+1 \text{ if } x\ge 1 \end{cases}$ is differentiable at $x=1$. **CBSE Sample Paper 2018**

39. Find the values of a and b, if the function f defined by $f(x)=\begin{cases} x^2+3x+a, & x\le 1 \\ bx+2, & x>1 \end{cases}$ is differentiable at $x=1$. **Competency Based Que, CBSE 2016**

40. If $y=\dfrac{\sin(ax+b)}{\cos(cx+d)}$, then find $\dfrac{dy}{dx}$. **NCERT**

41. If $x\sqrt{1+y}+y\sqrt{1+x}=0, (x\ne y)$, then prove that $\dfrac{dy}{dx}=-\dfrac{1}{(1+x)^2}$. **Competency Based Que, CBSE 2025, 19, 12, 11C, Diksha App**

42. If $\sin y = x\cos(a+y)$, then show that $\dfrac{dy}{dx}=\dfrac{\cos^2(a+y)}{\cos a}$. Also, show that $\dfrac{dy}{dx}=\cos a$, when $x=0$. **Competency Based Que, CBSE 2018 C**

43. If $y=\tan^{-1}\left(\dfrac{a}{x}\right)+\log\sqrt{\dfrac{x-a}{x+a}}$, then prove that $\dfrac{dy}{dx}=\dfrac{2a^3}{x^4-a^4}$. **NCERT, CBSE 2012**

44. If $\log(\sqrt{1+x^2}-x)=y\sqrt{1+x^2}$, then show that

$$(1+x^2)\frac{dy}{dx}+xy+1=0.$$

CBSE 2011C

45. If $y=\cos^{-1}\left(\dfrac{3x+4\sqrt{1-x^2}}{5}\right)$, then find $\dfrac{dy}{dx}$. **Diksha App, Competency Based Que**

46. If $y=\tan^{-1}\left(\dfrac{\sqrt{1+x^2}-\sqrt{1-x^2}}{\sqrt{1+x^2}+\sqrt{1-x^2}}\right)$, then find $\dfrac{dy}{dx}$. **Diksha App**

47. Differentiate $\sin^{-1}\left[\dfrac{2^{x+1}\cdot 3^x}{1+(36)^x}\right]$ w.r.t. x. **Competency Based Que**

48. Differentiate $x^{\sin x}$ w.r.t. x. **NCERT**

49. Find the derivative of the following, function w.r.t. x at $x=1$.

$$\cos^{-1}\left[\sin\sqrt{\frac{1+x}{2}}\right]+x^x$$

Competency Based Que

50. If $y=(\sin x-\cos x)^{(\sin x-\cos x)}, \dfrac{\pi}{4}<x<\dfrac{3\pi}{4}$, then find $\dfrac{dy}{dx}$. **Competency Based Que**

51. If $x=\cos t\,(3-2\cos^2 t)$ and $y=\sin t\,(3-2\sin^2 t)$, then find the value of $\dfrac{dy}{dx}$ at $t=\dfrac{\pi}{4}$. **CBSE 2014**

52. If $x=a\sin 2t\,(1+\cos 2t)$ and $y=b\cos 2t\,(1-\cos 2t)$, then find the values of $\dfrac{dy}{dx}$ at $t=\dfrac{\pi}{4}$ and $t=\dfrac{\pi}{3}$. **CBSE 2016, 14**

53. If $x=ae^t(\sin t+\cos t)$ and $y=ae^t(\sin t-\cos t)$, then prove that $\dfrac{dy}{dx}=\dfrac{x+y}{x-y}$ **CBSE 2019**

54. Differentiate $\tan^{-1}\left(\dfrac{\sqrt{1+x^2}-\sqrt{1-x^2}}{\sqrt{1+x^2}+\sqrt{1-x^2}}\right)$ w.r.t. $\cos^{-1} x^2$.

Competency Based Que

55. Differentiate $\tan^{-1}\left(\dfrac{x}{1+\sqrt{1-x^2}}\right)$ w.r.t. $\sin\left(2\cot^{-1}\sqrt{\dfrac{1+x}{1-x}}\right)$.

56. Differentiate $\tan^{-1}\left(\dfrac{x}{\sqrt{1-x^2}}\right)$ with respect to $\sin^{-1}(2x\sqrt{1-x^2})$. **CBSE 2014**

57. If $x = a\cos t$ and $y = b\sin t$, then find $\dfrac{d^2y}{dx^2}$. **CBSE 2023**

58. If $x = a\cos^3\theta$ and $y = a\sin^3\theta$, then find the value of $\dfrac{d^2y}{dx^2}$ at $\theta=\dfrac{\pi}{6}$. **CBSE 2013**

59. If $(x-a)^2+(y-b)^2=c^2$, for some $c>0$, then prove that $\dfrac{\left[1+\left(\dfrac{dy}{dx}\right)^2\right]^{3/2}}{\dfrac{d^2y}{dx^2}}$ is a constant independent of a and b. **Competency Based Que, CBSE 2019**

60. If $y=\log\left(\sqrt{x}+\dfrac{1}{\sqrt{x}}\right)^2$, then prove that $x(x+1)^2y_2+(x+1)^2y_1=2$.

Competency Based Que, CBSE 2025, CBSE Sample Paper 2018

61. If $x\cos(a+y)=\cos y$, then prove that

$$\frac{dy}{dx}=\frac{\cos^2(a+y)}{\sin a}.$$

Hence, show that $\sin a\dfrac{d^2y}{dx^2}+\sin 2(a+y)\dfrac{dy}{dx}=0$.

Competency Based Que, CBSE 2016

62. If $y=(\sin^{-1}x)^2$, then find

$$(1-x^2)\frac{d^2y}{dx^2}-x\frac{dy}{dx}=2.$$

CBSE 2024C

63. If $x=a\sec^3\theta$ and $y=a\tan^3\theta$, then find

$$\frac{d^2y}{dx^2} \text{ at } \theta=\frac{\pi}{3}.$$

CBSE 2018 C

64. If $x=\sin t$ and $y=\sin pt$, then prove that

$$(1-x^2)\frac{d^2y}{dx^2}-x\frac{dy}{dx}+p^2y=0.$$

Competency Based Que, CBSE 2016

Hints & Solutions

Objective Type Questions

1. (d) **Hint** $\lim_{x\to 2^-} f(x)=\lim_{x\to 2^+} f(x)$

$\Rightarrow \lim_{x\to 2^-} kx^2=\lim_{x\to 2^+}(3x+5)$

$\Rightarrow k(2)^2=3(2)+5$

$\Rightarrow k=\dfrac{11}{4}$

2. (c) Given, $f(x)=\begin{cases}\dfrac{1-\cos 4x}{8x^2} & \text{if } x\neq 0\\ k & \text{if } x=0\end{cases}$

The function $f(x)$ is continuous at $x=0$

If $\lim_{x\to 0} f(x)=f(0)$ ...(i)

We have, $f(0)=k$ ...(ii)

Now, $\lim_{x\to 0} f(x)=\lim_{x\to 0}\left(\dfrac{1-\cos 4x}{8x^2}\right)$

$=\lim_{x\to 0}\left(\dfrac{2\sin^2 2x}{8x^2}\right)$

$=\lim_{x\to 0}\left(\dfrac{\sin^2 2x}{4x^2}\right)$

$=\lim_{x\to 0}\left(\dfrac{\sin 2x}{2x}\right)^2=1$ ...(iii)

Now, from Eqs. (i), (ii) and (iii), we get

$k=1$

3. (b) We know that the greatest integer function $[x]$ is continuous at all points except at integer points. So, $f(x)$ is continuous at $x=1.5$ only.

4. (a) We have, $f(x)=\begin{cases}\dfrac{x}{|x|}, & x<0\\ -1, & x\geq 0\end{cases}$

$=\begin{cases}\dfrac{x}{-x}, & x<0\\ -1, & x\geq 0\end{cases}=\begin{cases}-1, & x<0\\ -1, & x\geq 0\end{cases}$

$\Rightarrow f(x)=-1, \forall x\in R$

As we know that constant function is continuous, $\forall x\in R$.

Therefore, $f(x)$ is continuous, $\forall x\in R$.

5. (d) We have, $f(x)=\begin{cases}\dfrac{x+4}{x+4}, & \text{if } x\neq -4\\ 1, & \text{if } x=-4\end{cases}$

When $x\neq -4$, $f(x)=\dfrac{x+4}{x+4}=1$

As it is a constant function so, it will be continuous at $x\neq -4$

Now, for $x=-4$

$$\text{LHL}=\lim_{x\to -4^-} f(x)=\lim_{h\to 0} f(-4-h)$$
$$=\lim_{h\to 0}\frac{-4-h+4}{-4-h+4}=1$$
$$\text{RHL}=\lim_{x\to -4^+} f(x)=\lim_{h\to 0} f(-4+h)$$
$$=\lim_{h\to 0}\frac{-4+h+4}{-4+h+4}=1$$

$f(-4)=1$

So, LHL = RHL = $f(-4)$

Thus, $f(x)$ is continuous at $x=-4$

Hence, there is no point of discontinuity.

6. (b) Given, $f(x)=2|x|+3|\sin x|+6$

$$Rf'(0)=\lim_{h\to 0}\frac{f(0+h)-f(0)}{h}=\lim_{h\to 0}\frac{f(h)-f(0)}{h}$$
$$=\lim_{h\to 0}\frac{(2|h|+3|\sin h|+6)-(2|0|+3|\sin 0|+6)}{h}$$
$$=\lim_{h\to 0}\frac{(2h+3\sin h+6)-(6)}{h}$$
$$=\lim_{h\to 0}\frac{2h+3\sin h}{h}=\lim_{h\to 0}\left(2+3\frac{\sin h}{h}\right)$$
$$=2+\lim_{h\to 0}\left(\frac{3\sin h}{h}\right)=2+3=5$$

7. (a) Given, $f(x)=x|x|=\begin{cases}x^2, & x\geq 0\\ -x^2, & x<0\end{cases}$

$$Lf'(0)=\lim_{h\to 0}\frac{f(0-h)-f(0)}{-h}$$
$$=\lim_{h\to 0}\frac{f(-h)-f(0)}{-h}=\lim_{h\to 0}\left(\frac{-h^2-0}{-h}\right)$$
$$=\lim_{h\to 0}(h)=0$$
$$Rf'(0)=\lim_{h\to 0}\frac{f(0+h)-f(0)}{h}$$
$$=\lim_{h\to 0}\frac{f(h)-f(0)}{h}=\lim_{h\to 0}\left(\frac{h^2-0}{h}\right)$$
$$=\lim_{h\to 0}(h)=0$$

$\because$ LHD = RHD = 0

$\Rightarrow f(x)$ is differentiable at $x=0$.

As we know, every differentiable function is continuous.

$\therefore\ f(x)$ is also continuous at $x=0$.

8. (d) We have, $f(x)=\begin{cases}x^2, \text{if } x\geq 0\\ kx, \text{if } x<0\end{cases}$

$$Lf'(0)=\lim_{h\to 0}\frac{f(0-h)-f(0)}{-h}$$
$$=\lim_{h\to 0}\frac{f(-h)-f(0)}{-h}$$
$$=\lim_{h\to 0}\frac{k(-h)-0}{-h}=k \qquad \ldots\text{(i)}$$
$$Rf'(0)=\lim_{h\to 0}\frac{f(0+h)-f(0)}{h}$$
$$=\lim_{h\to 0}\frac{f(h)-f(0)}{h}$$
$$=\lim_{h\to 0}\frac{h^2-0}{h}=\lim_{h\to 0}(h)=0 \qquad \ldots\text{(ii)}$$

Since, $f(x)$ is differentiable at $x=0$.

$\therefore \qquad Lf'(0)=Rf'(0)$

$\Rightarrow \qquad k=0$ [using Eqs. (i) and (ii)]

9. (c) Given, $f(x)=x+|x|=\begin{cases}2x, & x\geq 0\\ 0, & x<0\end{cases}$

Now, (RHD at $x=0$) $=\dfrac{d}{dx}2x\Big|_{x=0}=2$

and (LHD at $x=0$) $\dfrac{d}{dx}0\Big|_{x=0}=0$

LHD at $x=0\neq$ RHD at $x=0$

$\therefore$ The function is not differentiable at $x=0$.

For $x\geq 0$, $f(x)=2x$ which is a linear function and when $x<0$, $f(x)=0$ which is a constant function.

$\therefore f(x)$ is differentiable when $x\in(-\infty,0)\cup(0,\infty)$.

10. (c)

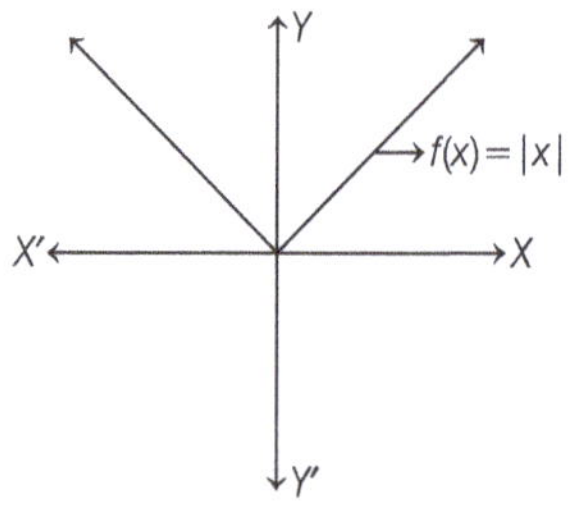

We know that modulus function is continuous everywhere.

Now, check differentiability of $f(x)$ at $x=0$.

$$Lf'(0)=\lim_{h\to 0}\frac{f(0-h)-f(0)}{-h}$$
$$=\lim_{h\to 0}\frac{f(-h)-f(0)}{-h}$$
$$=\lim_{h\to 0}\frac{|-h|-|0|}{-h}=\lim_{h\to 0}\frac{h}{-h}$$
$$=\lim_{h\to 0}(-1)=-1$$

and $Rf'(0)=\lim_{h\to 0}\frac{f(0+h)-f(0)}{h}$

$=\lim_{h\to 0}\frac{f(h)-f(0)}{h}$

$=\lim_{h\to 0}\frac{|h|-|0|}{h}$

$=\lim_{h\to 0}\frac{h}{h}=\lim_{h\to 0}(1)=1$

$\because Lf'(0)\neq Rf'(0)$

$\Rightarrow f$ is not differentiable at $x=0$.

11. (d) Given, $f(x)=\begin{vmatrix} x^2 & \sin x \\ p & -1 \end{vmatrix}$

$\Rightarrow \quad f(x)=-x^2-p\sin x$

$\Rightarrow \quad f'(x)=-2x-p\cos x$

Also, given that $f'(0)=1$

$\Rightarrow \quad -2(0)-p(\cos 0)=1$

$\Rightarrow \quad -p=1\Rightarrow p=-1$

12. (a) Given, $y=\frac{\cos x-\sin x}{\cos x+\sin x}$

$=\frac{1-\tan x}{1+\tan x}$ [divide each term by $\cos x$]

$=\frac{\tan\pi/4-\tan x}{1+\tan\pi/4\tan x}$

$\Rightarrow \quad y=\tan(\pi/4-x)$

On differentiating both sides w.r.t. x, we get

$\frac{dy}{dx}=\sec^2(\pi/4-x)(-1)$

$\Rightarrow \quad \frac{dy}{dx}=-\sec^2(\pi/4-x)$

13. (a) Given, $y=\log\sqrt{\sec\sqrt{x}}$

On differentiating both sides, w.r.t. x, we get

$\frac{dy}{dx}=\frac{1}{\sqrt{\sec\sqrt{x}}}\frac{d}{dx}\sqrt{\sec\sqrt{x}}$

$=\frac{1}{\sqrt{\sec\sqrt{x}}}\times\frac{1}{2\sqrt{\sec\sqrt{x}}}\sec\sqrt{x}\,\frac{\tan\sqrt{x}}{2\sqrt{x}}$

$=\frac{1}{4}\frac{\tan\sqrt{x}}{\sqrt{x}}$

Now, $\left(\frac{dy}{dx}\right)_{x=\frac{\pi^2}{16}}=\frac{1}{4}\times\frac{\tan\pi/4}{\pi/4}=\frac{1}{\pi}$

14. (d) Given, $f(x)=|\cos x|$

$\Rightarrow \quad f(x)=-\cos x$, if $\frac{\pi}{2}<x<\pi$

$\Rightarrow \quad f'(x)=\sin x$

$\therefore \quad f'\left(\frac{3\pi}{4}\right)=\sin\left(\frac{3\pi}{4}\right)$

$=\sin\left(\pi-\frac{\pi}{4}\right)=\sin\frac{\pi}{4}=\frac{1}{\sqrt{2}}$

15. (a) Given, $xe^y=1$

On differentiating both sides, w.r.t. x, we get

$x\cdot e^y\frac{dy}{dx}+e^y\cdot 1=0$

[using product rule of differentiation]

$\Rightarrow \quad xe^y\frac{dy}{dx}=-e^y$

$\Rightarrow \quad \frac{dy}{dx}=\frac{-e^y}{xe^y}=-\frac{1}{x}$

Now, $\left.\frac{dy}{dx}\right|_{x=1}=-\frac{1}{1}=-1$

16. (d) We have, $\sin(xy)=1$

On differentiating both sides w.r.t. x, we get

$\cos(xy)\cdot\left[x\frac{dy}{dx}+y\right]=0$

$\Rightarrow \quad x\frac{dy}{dx}+y=0$

$\Rightarrow \quad x\frac{dy}{dx}=-y$

$\Rightarrow \quad \frac{dy}{dx}=-\frac{y}{x}$

17. (b) We have, $x=3\cos\theta$ and $y=5\sin\theta$

On differentiating both sides of x and y w.r.t. θ, we get

$\frac{dx}{d\theta}=-3\sin\theta$ and $\frac{dy}{d\theta}=5\cos\theta$

Now, $\frac{dy}{dx}=\frac{dy/d\theta}{dx/d\theta}=\frac{5\cos\theta}{-3\sin\theta}=-\frac{5}{3}\cot\theta$

18. (c) Given, $y=10^{10^x}$

On differentiating both sides w.r.t. x, we get

$\frac{dy}{dx}=10^{10^x}\cdot\log 10\cdot\frac{d}{dx}(10^x)$

$=10^{10^x}\cdot\log 10\cdot 10^x\cdot\log 10$

$=10^{10^x}\cdot 10^x(\log 10)^2$

19. (c) Let $f(x)=e^{\sin^2 x}$ and $g(x)=\cos x$

On differentiating both sides w.r.t. x, we get

$f'(x)=e^{\sin^2 x}\cdot\frac{d}{dx}(\sin^2 x)$

$=e^{\sin^2 x}\cdot 2\sin x\cdot\cos x$

and $g'(x)=\frac{d}{dx}(\cos x)=-\sin x$

Thus, derivative of $e^{\sin^2 x}$ w.r.t. $\cos x$, we get

$\frac{f'(x)}{g'(x)}=\frac{e^{\sin^2 x}\cdot 2\sin x\cdot\cos x}{-\sin x}$

$=-2\cos x\,e^{\sin^2 x}$

20. (d) We have, $x = at^2$

On differentiating both sides w.r.t. t, we get

$$\frac{dx}{dt} = 2at \text{ and } y = 2at$$

On differentiating both sides w.r.t. t, we get

$$\frac{dy}{dt} = 2a$$

Now, $\frac{dy}{dx} = \frac{2a}{2at} = \frac{1}{t}$

Again, on differentiating both sides w.r.t. x, we get

$$\frac{d^2y}{dx^2} = \frac{d}{dx}\left(\frac{1}{t}\right) = \frac{-1}{t^2}\frac{dt}{dx}$$

$$= \frac{-1}{t^2}\frac{1}{2at} = -\frac{1}{2at^3}$$

21. (a) We have, $y = x\cos x$

$\therefore \quad \frac{dy}{dx} = x(-\sin x) + \cos x$

$$= -x\sin x + \cos x$$

and $\frac{d^2y}{dx^2} = -[x\cos x + \sin x] - \sin x$

$$= -x\cos x - \sin x - \sin x$$

$$= -x\cos x - 2\sin x$$

22. (a) We have, $y = \sin^{-1} x$

$\Rightarrow \quad \frac{dy}{dx} = \frac{1}{\sqrt{1-x^2}}$

$\Rightarrow \quad (\sqrt{1-x^2})\cdot\frac{dy}{dx} = 1$

Again, on differentiating both sides w.r.t. x, we get

$$(\sqrt{1-x^2})\frac{d}{dx}\left(\frac{dy}{dx}\right) + \frac{dy}{dx}\left(\frac{d}{dx}\sqrt{1-x^2}\right) = 0$$

$\Rightarrow \quad \sqrt{1-x^2}\frac{d^2y}{dx^2} + \frac{dy}{dx}\left(\frac{-2x}{2\sqrt{1-x^2}}\right) = 0$

$\Rightarrow \quad \sqrt{1-x^2}\frac{d^2y}{dx^2} - \frac{x}{\sqrt{1-x^2}}\left(\frac{dy}{dx}\right) = 0$

$\Rightarrow \quad (1-x^2)\frac{d^2y}{dx^2} - x\left(\frac{dy}{dx}\right) = 0$

$\Rightarrow \quad (1-x^2)\frac{d^2y}{dx^2} = x\frac{dy}{dx}$

or $\quad (1-x^2)y_2 = xy_1$

23. (b) We have, $y^{1/m} + y^{-1/m} = 2x$

On differentiating both sides w.r.t. x, we get

$$\left(\frac{1}{m}y^{\frac{1}{m}-1} - \frac{1}{m}y^{-\frac{1}{m}-1}\right)\frac{dy}{dx} = 2$$

$\Rightarrow \quad \frac{1}{m}y^{-1}[y^{1/m} - y^{-1/m}]\frac{dy}{dx} = 2$

$\Rightarrow \quad \frac{1}{my}[y^{1/m} - y^{-1/m}]\frac{dy}{dx} = 2$

$\Rightarrow \quad [y^{1/m} - y^{-1/m}]\frac{dy}{dx} = 2my$

On squaring both sides, we get

$$4m^2y^2 = [y^{2/m} + y^{-2/m} - 2]\left(\frac{dy}{dx}\right)^2 \quad \ldots(i)$$

Also, $y^{1/m} + y^{-1/m} = 2x$

On squaring both sides, we get

$$y^{2/m} + y^{-2/m} + 2 = 4x^2$$

$\Rightarrow \quad y^{2/m} + y^{-2/m} = 4x^2 - 2 \quad \ldots(ii)$

From Eqs. (i) and (ii), we get

$$4m^2y^2 = [4x^2 - 2 - 2]\left(\frac{dy}{dx}\right)^2$$

$\Rightarrow \quad 4m^2y^2 = [4x^2 - 4]\left(\frac{dy}{dx}\right)^2$

$\Rightarrow \quad m^2y^2 = (x^2 - 1)\left(\frac{dy}{dx}\right)^2$

On differentiating both sides w.r.t. x, we get

$$2m^2y\left(\frac{dy}{dx}\right) = 2\left(\frac{dy}{dx}\right)\left(\frac{d^2y}{dx^2}\right)(x^2-1) + 2x\left(\frac{dy}{dx}\right)^2$$

$\Rightarrow \quad m^2y = \left(\frac{d^2y}{dx^2}\right)(x^2-1) + x\left(\frac{dy}{dx}\right)$

$\therefore \quad (x^2-1)y_2 + xy_1 = m^2y$

24. (c) **Assertion** Let $a \in [-1, 1]$

and $y = \sin^{-1} x \Rightarrow x = \sin y$

When $x \to a$, then $\sin y \to a$

$\Rightarrow \quad y = \sin^{-1} a$

$\therefore \quad \lim_{x \to a} f(x) = \lim_{x \to a} \sin^{-1} x = \lim_{y \to \sin^{-1} a} y$

$$= \sin^{-1} a = f(a)$$

Reason Let $a \in R$

Then, $\lim_{x \to a^-} f(x) = \lim_{x \to a^+} f(x) = f(a)$

$\Rightarrow f(x)$ is continuous at $x = a$.

25. (d) Let, $f(x) = \sin x$ and $g(x) = |x|$

$\therefore \quad gof(x) = g(f(x)) = g(\sin x) = |\sin x|$

Here, $\sin x$ and $|x|$ both are continuous functions.

$\therefore$ $|\sin x|$ is also continuous function.

Hence, Assertion is incorrect and Reason is correct.

26. (d) We have, $y = \cos x$

$\therefore \quad \left(\frac{dy}{dx}\right) = -\sin x$

$\Rightarrow \quad \left(\frac{dy}{dx}\right)_{x=\frac{\pi}{2}} = -\sin\frac{\pi}{2} = -1$

Hence, Assertion is incorrect but Reason is correct.

27. (b) **Assertion** $y=\cos^2 x^2=(\cos x^2)^2$

$\therefore \quad \frac{dy}{dx}=-4x\cos x^2\sin x^2$ [using chain rule]

Assertion is correct.

Reason We have,

$$\sqrt{x}+\sqrt{y}=1$$

$$\Rightarrow \frac{1}{2\sqrt{x}}+\frac{1}{2\sqrt{y}}\frac{dy}{dx}=0 \Rightarrow \frac{dy}{dx}=-\frac{\sqrt{y}}{\sqrt{x}}$$

$$\therefore \left(\frac{dy}{dx}\right)_{\left(\frac{1}{4},\frac{1}{4}\right)}=\frac{-1/2}{1/2}=-1$$

Reason is also correct but Reason is not the correct explanation of Assertion.

28. (d) **Assertion**

Since, $f(x)=\sqrt{1+\cos^2(x^2)}$

$$\therefore \quad f'(x)=\frac{-2\sin x^2\cos x^2}{\sqrt{1+\cos^2 x^2}}(x)$$

$$\Rightarrow \quad f'(x)=\frac{-\sin 2x^2}{\sqrt{1+\cos^2 x^2}}(x)$$

$$\Rightarrow \quad f\left(\frac{\sqrt{\pi}}{2}\right)=-\sqrt{\frac{\pi}{6}}$$

$\therefore$ Assertion is incorrect.

Reason

Since, $h(x)=f(g(x)) \Rightarrow h(x)=f(\sin^{-1}x)=e^{\sin^{-1}x}$

$$\Rightarrow \quad h'(x)=e^{\sin^{-1}x}\frac{1}{\sqrt{1-x^2}}$$

$$\therefore \quad \frac{h'(x)}{h(x)}=\frac{1}{\sqrt{1-x^2}}$$

$\therefore$ Reason is correct.

29. (a) $e^{xy}+\log(xy)+\cos(xy)+4=0$

$$\Rightarrow e^{xy}\frac{d}{dx}(xy)+\frac{1}{xy}\frac{d}{dx}(xy)-\sin(xy)\frac{d}{dx}(xy)=0$$

$$\Rightarrow \frac{d}{dx}(xy)\left\{e^{xy}+\frac{1}{xy}-\sin(xy)\right\}=0$$

$$\because \quad e^{xy}+\frac{1}{xy}-\sin(xy)\neq 0$$

$$\therefore \quad \frac{d}{dx}(xy)=0$$

$$\Rightarrow \quad x\frac{dy}{dx}+y=0$$

$$\Rightarrow \quad \frac{dy}{dx}=\frac{-y}{x}$$

Hence, Assertion is correct and Reason is also correct; Reason is the correct explanation of Assertion.

30. (b) Given, $f(x)=\sin^{-1}x+\cos^{-1}x+4$

$$\therefore \quad f'(x)=\frac{1}{\sqrt{1-x^2}}-\frac{1}{\sqrt{1-x^2}}+0$$

$$\Rightarrow \quad f'(x)=0 \Rightarrow f'(4)=0$$

Hence, Assertion is correct and Reason is also correct but Reason is not the correct explanation of Assertion.

31. (b) Both Assertion and Reason are correct.

32. (b) Given, $y=\sin x+\cos x$

$$\therefore \quad \frac{dy}{dx}=\cos x-\sin x$$

$$\Rightarrow \left(\frac{dy}{dx}\right)_{x=\pi/4}=\cos\frac{\pi}{4}-\sin\frac{\pi}{4}=\frac{1}{\sqrt{2}}-\frac{1}{\sqrt{2}}=0$$

Hence, Assertion and Reason both are correct but Reason is not the correct explanation of Assertion.

33. (c) We have, $y=\tan^{-1}x$

$$\therefore \quad \frac{dy}{dx}=\frac{1}{1+x^2}$$

Hence, Assertion is correct but Reason is incorrect.

34. (i) **Deepak** 'The function on card III is continuous'.

$$f_3(x)=\begin{cases}-x, & x\le 0\\ 0, & x\ge 0\end{cases}$$

$\text{LHL}=\lim_{x\to 0^-}f(x)=\lim_{h\to 0}f(-h)=\lim_{h\to 0}-(-h)=0$

$\text{RHL}=\lim_{x\to 0^+}f(x)=\lim_{h\to 0}f(h)=\lim_{h\to 0}0=0$

At $x=0$, $f(x)=0$

$\text{LHL}=\text{RHL}=f(0)$.

So, the function on card III is continuous.

Therefore, Deepak is right and

Kiran 'The function on card IV is discontinuous'.

$$f_4(x)=\begin{cases}1, & x>0\\ 0 & x\le 0\end{cases}$$

Here, LHL = 0 and RHL = 1

LHL ≠ RHL

So, $f_4(x)$ is not continuous.

Hence, Deepak and Kiran's claims are correct.

(ii) **Irfan** 'As the function is not in one piece, the function on card II is discontinuous'.

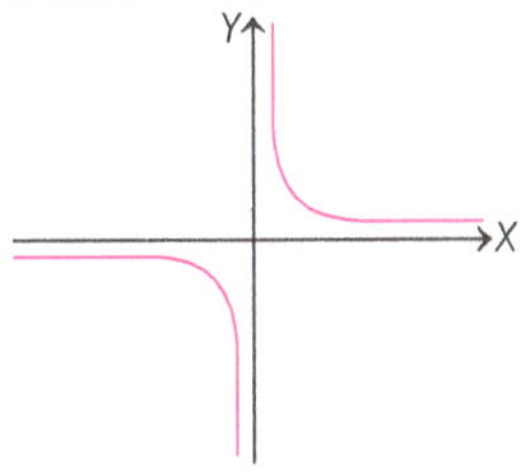

Here, $f_2(x)=\frac{1}{2x}, x\neq 0$

The function $f_2(x)=\frac{1}{2x}$ is continuous everywhere, except $x=0$ because at $x=0$ the function is undefined.

Hence, Irfan's reason does not support his claim.
Also, his claim is wrong.

(iii) **Leela** 'As the function on card I is both continuous and differentiable, we can say that every continuous function is differentiable'.

$$f_1(x) = x^2 + 2x.$$

As we know that

Every continuous function need not to be differentiable function i.e. a function can be continuous at a point but not differentiable.

e.g. $f(x) = |x|$.

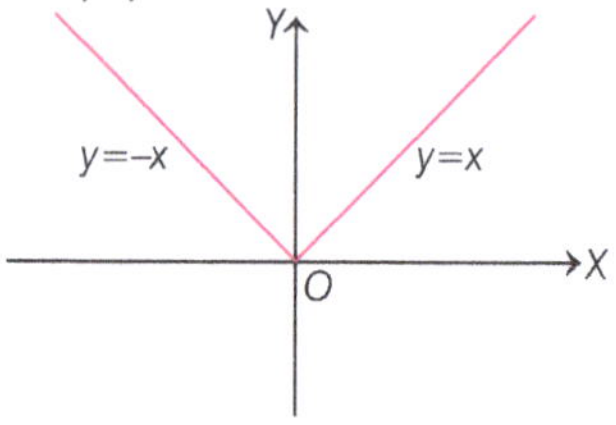

which is continuous but not differentiable at $x = 0$.

Hence, Leela's claim is not true for all continuous functions.

35. Given, $f(x) = \begin{cases} |x-3|, x \geq 1 \\ \frac{x^2}{4} - \frac{3x}{2} + \frac{13}{4}, x < 1 \end{cases}$

$$\Rightarrow \quad f(x) = \begin{cases} 3-x, 1 \leq x < 3 \\ \frac{x^2}{4} - \frac{3x}{2} + \frac{13}{4}, x < 1 \end{cases}$$

$$f'(x) = \begin{cases} -1, & 1 < x < 3 \\ \frac{x}{2} - \frac{3}{2}, & x < 1 \end{cases}$$

(i) $Rf'(1) = -1$

(ii) $Lf'(1) = \frac{1}{2} - \frac{3}{2} = \frac{-2}{2} = -1$

(iii) (a) Since, $Lf'(1) = Rf'(1) = -1$

$\Rightarrow f(x)$ is differentiable at $x = -1$

or (b) $f'(2) = -1, 1 \leq 2 < 3$

and $f'(-1) = \frac{-1}{2} - \frac{3}{2}, x < 1 = \frac{-4}{2} = -2$

Subjective Questions

1. Hint As $\lim_{x \to 0} \frac{\sin \frac{3x}{2}}{x} = \lim_{x \to 0} \frac{3}{2} \frac{\sin \frac{3x}{2}}{3x/2} = \frac{3}{2}$

Ans. $k = 3/2$

2. Since, the function is continuous at $x = 0$.

$$\therefore \quad \lim_{x \to 0^-} f(x) = \lim_{x \to 0^+} f(x) = f(0)$$

$$\Rightarrow \quad \lim_{x \to 0} \frac{-kx}{x} = \lim_{x \to 0} 3 = 3$$

$$\Rightarrow \quad -k = 3$$

$$\therefore \quad k = -3$$

3. Given, $f(x) = \begin{cases} \frac{x^2-9}{x-3}, & x \neq 3 \\ k, & x = 3 \end{cases}$

Since, $f(x)$ is continuous at $x = 3$.

$$\therefore \quad \lim_{x \to 3} f(x) = f(3)$$

$$\Rightarrow \quad \lim_{x \to 3} \frac{x^2-9}{x-3} = k$$

$$\Rightarrow \quad \lim_{x \to 3} \frac{(x-3)(x+3)}{(x-3)} = k$$

$$\Rightarrow \quad \lim_{x \to 3} (x+3) = k$$

$$\Rightarrow \quad 3+3 = k \Rightarrow k = 6$$

4. Given, $f(x) = \begin{cases} \frac{(x+3)^2 - 36}{x-3}, & x \neq 3 \\ k, & x = 3 \end{cases}$

Given, $f(x)$ is continuous at $x = 3$

Then, we have $\lim_{x \to 3} f(x) = f(3)$

$$\Rightarrow \quad \lim_{x \to 3} \frac{(x+3)^2 - 36}{x-3} = k \Rightarrow \lim_{x \to 3} \frac{(x+3)^2 - 6^2}{x-3} = k$$

$$\Rightarrow \quad \lim_{x \to 3} \frac{(x+3-6)(x+3+6)}{x-3} = k$$

$$\Rightarrow \quad \lim_{x \to 3} \frac{(x-3)(x+9)}{(x-3)} = k \Rightarrow \lim_{x \to 3} (x+9) = k$$

$$\Rightarrow \quad 3+9 = k \Rightarrow k = 12$$

5. We have, $f(x) = [x], 0 < x < 2$

$$\therefore \quad \text{LHL(at } x = 1) = \lim_{x \to 1^-} f(x)$$

$$= \lim_{x \to 1^-} [x] = \lim_{h \to 0} [1-h]$$

$$= \lim_{h \to 0} 0 = 0$$

$$\text{RHL (at } x = 1) = \lim_{x \to 1^+} f(x) = \lim_{x \to 1^+} [x]$$

$$= \lim_{h \to 0} [1+h] = \lim_{h \to 0} 1 = 1$$

and $f(1) = [1] = 1$

Since, LHL $\neq$ RHL

$\therefore f(x)$ is discontinuous at $x = 1$

Hence, $f(x)$ is not differentiable at $x = 1$.

6. Let $y = \cos(\sqrt{x})$

On differentiating both sides w.r.t. x, we get

$$\frac{dy}{dx} = \frac{d}{dx}(\cos\sqrt{x})$$

$$= -\sin\sqrt{x} \cdot \frac{d}{dx}(\sqrt{x})$$

$$= -\sin\sqrt{x} \cdot \frac{1}{2\sqrt{x}}$$

$$= \frac{-\sin\sqrt{x}}{2\sqrt{x}}$$

7. Given, $f(x)=x|x|$

$$f(x)=\begin{cases}-x^2, & x<0\\ x^2, & x\geq 0\end{cases}$$

$$f'(x)=\begin{cases}-2x, & x<0\\ 2x, & x>0\end{cases}$$

$\therefore \quad f'(x)=2|x|$

8. We have, $y=x|x|$

When, $x<0$, then $|x|=-x$

$\therefore \quad y=x(-x)=-x^2$

$\Rightarrow \quad \dfrac{dy}{dx}=-2x$

9. Given, $2x+3y=\sin y$

On differentiating both sides w.r.t. x, we get

$$2+\frac{3dy}{dx}=\cos y\left(\frac{dy}{dx}\right)$$

$\Rightarrow \dfrac{dy}{dx}(\cos y-3)=2$

$\Rightarrow \quad \dfrac{dy}{dx}=\dfrac{2}{\cos y-3}$

10. Let $y=\sin(\tan^{-1}x)$

On differentiating both sides w.r.t. x, we get

$$\frac{dy}{dx}=\cos(\tan^{-1}x)\cdot\frac{d}{dx}(\tan^{-1}x)$$

$$=\frac{\cos(\tan^{-1}x)}{1+x^2}$$

11. Given, $y\sqrt{1-x^2}+x\sqrt{1-y^2}=1$ ...(i)

On putting $x=\sin A$ and $y=\sin B$ in Eq. (i), we get

$\sin B\cos A+\sin A\cos B=1 \Rightarrow \sin(A+B)=1$

$\Rightarrow \quad A+B=\sin^{-1}(1)=\dfrac{\pi}{2}$

$\Rightarrow \quad \sin^{-1}x+\sin^{-1}y=\dfrac{\pi}{2}$ ...(ii)

Now, on differentiating both sides of Eq. (ii), we get

$$\frac{1}{\sqrt{1-x^2}}+\frac{1}{\sqrt{1-y^2}}\left(\frac{dy}{dx}\right)=0\Rightarrow\frac{dy}{dx}=-\sqrt{\frac{1-y^2}{1-x^2}}$$

12. Let $y=e^{\sqrt{x}}$

On differentiating both sides w.r.t. x, we get

$$\frac{dy}{dx}=\frac{d}{dx}(e^{\sqrt{x}})$$

$$=e^{\sqrt{x}}\frac{d}{dx}(\sqrt{x})=e^{\sqrt{x}}\cdot\frac{1}{2\sqrt{x}}=\frac{e^{\sqrt{x}}}{2\sqrt{x}}$$

13. Let $y=e^{3x}\cdot\cos 2x$

On differentiating both sides w.r.t. x, we get

$$\frac{dy}{dx}=\frac{d}{dx}(e^{3x}\cdot\cos 2x)$$

$$=e^{3x}\frac{d}{dx}(\cos 2x)+\cos 2x\frac{d}{dx}(e^{3x})$$

$$=e^{3x}(-2\sin 2x)+\cos 2x(3e^{3x})$$

$$=e^{3x}(-2\sin 2x+3\cos 2x)$$

14. Let $y=\log\sin x$

On differentiating both sides w.r.t. x, we get

$$\frac{dy}{dx}=\frac{d}{dx}(\log\sin x)$$

$$=\frac{1}{\sin x}\frac{d}{dx}(\sin x)=\frac{\cos x}{\sin x}=\cot x$$

15. Let $y=\log x$

On differentiating both sides w.r.t x, we get

$$\frac{dy}{dx}=\frac{1}{x}$$

Again, differentiating both sides w.r.t x, we get

$$\frac{d^2y}{dx^2}=\frac{-1}{x^2}$$

16. **Hint** Secant is continuous everywhere except $x=(2n+1)\dfrac{\pi}{2}$, $n\in I$.

17. **Hint** $\lim\limits_{x\to 0^-}f(x)=\lim\limits_{x\to 0^-}\dfrac{|\sin x|}{x}$

$$=\lim_{x\to 0^-}\frac{-\sin x}{x}=-1$$

and $\lim\limits_{x\to 0^+}f(x)=\lim\limits_{x\to 0^+}\dfrac{|\sin x|}{x}=\lim\limits_{x\to 0^+}\dfrac{\sin x}{x}=1$

Since, LHL $\neq$ RHL

$\therefore$ $f(x)$ is not continuous at $x=0$.

18. Given, $f(x)=\begin{cases}3ax+b & \text{if } x>1\\ 11 & \text{if } x=1\\ 5ax-2b & \text{if } x<1\end{cases}$

is continuous at $x=1$.

$\therefore \quad \text{LHL}=\text{RHL}=f(1)$ ...(i)

Now, $\text{LHL}=\lim\limits_{x\to 1^-}f(x)=\lim\limits_{x\to 1^-}(5ax-2b)$

$=\lim\limits_{h\to 0}[5a(1-h)-2b]$

[$\because x=1-h$; when $x\to 1^-$, then $h\to 0$]

$=\lim\limits_{h\to 0}(5a-5ah-2b)$

$=5a-2b$

and $\text{RHL}=\lim\limits_{x\to 1^+}(3ax+b)=\lim\limits_{h\to 0}[3a(1+h)+b]$

[$\because x=1+h$; when $x\to 1^+$, then $h\to 0$]

$=\lim\limits_{h\to 0}(3a+3ah+b)=3a+b$

Also, $f(1)=11$

On substituting these values in Eq. (i), we get

$$5a-2b=3a+b=11$$

$\Rightarrow \quad 3a+b=11$ ...(ii)

and $\quad 5a-2b=11$ ...(iii)

On multiplying Eq. (ii) by 5 and Eq. (iii) by 3 and then subtracting Eq. (iii) from Eq. (ii), we get

$$15a+5b-15a+6b=55-33$$
$$\Rightarrow \quad 11b=22$$
$$\Rightarrow \quad b=2$$

On putting the value of b in Eq. (ii), we get

$$3a+2=11 \Rightarrow 3a=9 \Rightarrow a=3$$

Hence, $a=3$ and $b=2$.

19. Hint $\lim_{x\to\frac{\pi}{2}^-} f(x)=\lim_{x\to\frac{\pi}{2}^+} f(x)=f\left(\frac{\pi}{2}\right)$

$$\Rightarrow \quad \lim_{h\to 0} f\left(\frac{\pi}{2}-h\right)=\lim_{h\to 0} f\left(\frac{\pi}{2}+h\right)=k$$

$$\Rightarrow \quad \lim_{h\to 0}\frac{1-\sin\left(\frac{\pi}{2}-h\right)}{\left\{\pi-2\left(\frac{\pi}{2}-h\right)\right\}^2}=\lim_{h\to 0}\frac{1-\sin\left(\frac{\pi}{2}+h\right)}{\left\{\pi-2\left(\frac{\pi}{2}+h\right)\right\}^2}=k$$

$$\Rightarrow \quad \lim_{h\to 0}\frac{1-\cos h}{(2h)^2}=\lim_{h\to 0}\frac{1-\cos h}{(-2h)^2}=k$$

$$\Rightarrow \quad \lim_{h\to 0}\frac{2\sin^2\frac{h}{2}}{4h^2}=\lim_{h\to 0}\frac{2\sin^2\frac{h}{2}}{4h^2}=k$$

$$\Rightarrow \quad \frac{1}{8}\lim_{h\to 0}\left(\frac{\sin\frac{h}{2}}{\frac{h}{2}}\right)^2=\frac{1}{8}\lim_{h\to 0}\left(\frac{\sin\frac{h}{2}}{\frac{h}{2}}\right)^2=k$$

Ans. $k=\frac{1}{8}$

20. Hint $\lim_{x\to\frac{\pi}{2}} f(x)=f\left(\frac{\pi}{2}\right)$

$$\Rightarrow \quad \lim_{h\to 0} f\left(\frac{\pi}{2}+h\right)=3$$

$$\Rightarrow \quad \lim_{h\to 0}\frac{k\cos\left(\frac{\pi}{2}+h\right)}{\pi-2\left(\frac{\pi}{2}+h\right)}=3$$

Ans. $k=6$

21. Hint $\lim_{x\to 1^-} f(x)=\lim_{x\to 1^+} f(x)=f(1)$

and $\lim_{x\to\sqrt{2}^-} f(x)=\lim_{x\to\sqrt{2}^+} f(x)=f(\sqrt{2})$

Ans. $a=-1, b=1$ or $a=1, b=1\pm\sqrt{2}$

22. Hint $\lim_{x\to 0} f(x)=f(0)$

$$\Rightarrow \quad \lim_{x\to 0}\frac{\log(1+ax)-\log(1-bx)}{x}=k$$

$$\Rightarrow \quad \lim_{x\to 0}\left\{\frac{\log(1+ax)}{x}-\frac{\log(1-bx)}{x}\right\}=k$$

$$\Rightarrow \quad a\lim_{x\to 0}\frac{\log(1+ax)}{ax}-(-b)\lim_{x\to 0}\frac{\log(1-bx)}{(-b)x}=k$$

$$\Rightarrow \quad a(1)-(-b)(1)=k$$

Ans. $k=a+b$

23. We have, $f(x)=\begin{cases}\frac{x+\sin x}{\sin(a+1)x} & \text{if } -\pi<x<0\\ 2 & \text{if } \quad x=0\\ \frac{2(e^{\sin bx}-1)}{bx} & \text{if } \quad x>0\end{cases}$

Now, LHL $=\lim_{x\to 0^-} f(x)=\lim_{x\to 0^-}\frac{x+\sin x}{\sin(a+1)x}$

On multiplying and dividing denominator by $(a+1)x$, we get

$$=\lim_{x\to 0^-}\frac{x+\sin x}{\sin[(a+1)x]}\times\frac{(a+1)x}{(a+1)x}$$

$$=\lim_{x\to 0^-}\frac{\frac{x+\sin x}{x}}{\frac{\sin(a+1)x}{(a+1)x}\cdot(a+1)}$$

$$=\lim_{x\to 0^-}\frac{1+\frac{\sin x}{x}}{\frac{\sin(a+1)x}{(a+1)x}\cdot(a+1)}$$

$$=\frac{1+1}{1\cdot(a+1)}=\frac{2}{a+1} \qquad \left[\because \lim_{x\to 0}\frac{\sin x}{x}=1\right]$$

Again, RHL $=\lim_{x\to 0^+} f(x)=\lim_{x\to 0^+}\frac{2(e^{\sin bx}-1)}{bx}$

On multiplying and dividing by $\sin bx$, we get

$$\lim_{x\to 0^+}\frac{2(e^{\sin bx}-1)}{\sin bx}\times\frac{\sin bx}{bx}=2\times 1\times 1=2 \quad \left[\because \lim_{x\to 0}\frac{e^{\sin x}-1}{\sin x}=1\right]$$

Since, function is continuous at $x=0$.

$$\therefore \quad \lim_{x\to 0^-} f(x)=\lim_{x\to 0^+} f(x)=f(0) \Rightarrow \frac{2}{a+1}=2$$

$$\Rightarrow \quad 2(a+1)=2 \Rightarrow a=0 \text{ and } b\in R, b\neq 0$$

24. Given, $f(x)=\begin{cases}\left(\frac{1-\cos 4x}{8x^2}\right) & \text{if } x\neq 0\\ k & \text{if } x=0\end{cases}$

is continuous at $x=0$.

Then, $(\text{LHL})_{x=0}=(\text{RHL})_{x=0}=f(0)$ ...(i)

Now, LHL $=\lim_{x\to 0^-} f(x)$

$$=\lim_{x\to 0^-}\frac{1-\cos 4x}{8x^2}=\lim_{h\to 0}\frac{1-\cos 4(0-h)}{8(0-h)^2}$$

$$[\because x=0-h; \text{ when } x\to 0^-, \text{then } h\to 0]$$

$$=\lim_{h\to 0}\frac{1-\cos 4h}{8h^2} \qquad [\because \cos(-\theta)=\cos\theta]$$

$$= \lim_{h \to 0} \frac{2\sin^2 2h}{8h^2} \qquad [\because 1 - \cos 2\theta = 2\sin^2\theta]$$

$$= \lim_{h \to 0} \frac{\sin^2 2h}{4h^2} = \lim_{h\to 0}\left(\frac{\sin 2h}{2h}\right)^2 = 1 \quad \left[\because \lim_{x \to 0} \frac{\sin x}{x} = 1\right]$$

On substituting this value in Eq. (i), we get

$$1 = f(0) \Rightarrow 1 = k \qquad [\text{given}, f(0) = k]$$

Hence, for $k = 1$, the given function $f(x)$ is continuous at $x = 0$.

25. Given, $f(x) = \begin{cases} \dfrac{x^3 + x^2 - 16x + 20}{(x-2)^2}, & x \neq 2 \\ k, & x = 2 \end{cases}$

is continuous at $x = 2$.

Now, we have $f(2) = k$

and $\lim_{x\to 2} f(x) = \lim_{x\to 2} \dfrac{x^3 + x^2 - 16x + 20}{(x-2)^2}$

$$= \lim_{x\to 2} \frac{(x-2)(x^2 + 3x - 10)}{(x-2)^2}$$

$$= \lim_{x\to 2} \frac{(x-2)(x+5)(x-2)}{(x-2)^2}$$

$$= \lim_{x\to 2} (x+5) = 2 + 5 = 7$$

Since, $f(x)$ is continuous at $x = 2$.

$\therefore \quad \lim_{x\to 2} f(x) = f(2) \Rightarrow 7 = k \Rightarrow k = 7$

26. Hint LHL $= \lim_{x \to 0^-} \dfrac{x}{2|x|}$

$$= \lim_{x \to 0^-} \frac{x}{2(-x)} = \frac{-1}{2}$$

and RHL $= \lim_{x \to 0^+} \dfrac{x}{2|x|} = \lim_{x \to 0^+} \dfrac{x}{2x} = \dfrac{1}{2}$

Since, LHL $\neq$ RHL

$\therefore f(x)$ is discontinuous at $x = 0$.

27. Hint LHL $= \lim_{x \to 1^-} f(x) = \lim_{x \to 1^-} (x^{10} - 1)$

$$= 1^{10} - 1 = 0$$

and RHL $= \lim_{x\to 1^+} f(x) = \lim_{x \to 1^+} x^2 = 1^2 = 1$

Since, LHL $\neq$ RHL

$\therefore f(x)$ is discontinuous at $x = 1$.

28. Hint LHL $= \lim_{x \to 0^-} f(x)$

$$= \lim_{h \to 0} f(0-h) = \lim_{h \to 0} \frac{\sin 2(0-h)}{(0-h)}$$

$$= \lim_{h \to 0} \frac{2(-\sin 2h)}{-2h} = 2$$

RHL $= \lim_{x \to 0^+} f(x) = \lim_{h \to 0} f(0+h)$

$$= \lim_{h \to 0} (0 + h + 2) = \lim_{h \to 0} h + 2 = 2$$

Now, $f(0) = 0 + 2 = 2$

Since, LHL = RHL = $f(0)$

$\therefore f(x)$ is continuous everywhere.

29. Let $f(x) = \begin{cases} a\sin\dfrac{\pi}{2}(x+1), & x \leq 0 \\ \dfrac{\tan x - \sin x}{x^3}, & x > 0 \end{cases}$

is continuous at $x = 0$.

Then, LHL = RHL = $f(0)$ ...(i)

Now, LHL $= \lim_{x \to 0^-} a\sin\dfrac{\pi}{2}(x+1)$

$\Rightarrow$ LHL $= \lim_{h \to 0} a\sin\dfrac{\pi}{2}(-h+1)$

[$\because x = 0 - h$; when $x \to 0^-$, then $h \to 0$]

$$= a\sin\frac{\pi}{2} = a \qquad \text{...(ii)}$$

$$f(0) = a\sin\frac{\pi}{2} = a \qquad \text{...(iii)}$$

Now, we need to evaluate RHL at $x = 0$.

[$\because$ LHL $= f(0) = a$ and from this, we can not find the value of a]

Here, RHL $= \lim_{x \to 0^+} \dfrac{\tan x - \sin x}{x^3}$

$\Rightarrow$ RHL $= \lim_{h \to 0} \dfrac{\tan h - \sin h}{h^3}$

[$\because x = 0 + h = h$; when $x \to 0^+$, then $h \to 0$]

$$= \lim_{h \to 0} \frac{\dfrac{\sin h}{\cos h} - \sin h}{h^3} = \lim_{h \to 0} \frac{\sin h - \sin h \cos h}{h^3 \cos h}$$

$$= \lim_{h \to 0} \frac{\sin h(1 - \cos h)}{h^3 \cos h}$$

$$= \lim_{h \to 0} \frac{\sin h}{h} \cdot \lim_{h \to 0} \frac{1 - \cos h}{h^2} \cdot \lim_{h \to 0} \frac{1}{\cos h}$$

$$= 1 \times \lim_{h \to 0} \frac{1 - \cos h}{h^2} \times 1$$

$$\left[\because \lim_{h \to 0} \frac{\sin h}{h} = 1 \text{ and } \lim_{h \to 0} \frac{1}{\cos h} = \frac{1}{\cos 0} = \frac{1}{1} = 1\right]$$

$$= \lim_{h \to 0} \frac{1 - \cos h}{h^2}$$

$$= \lim_{h \to 0} \frac{2\sin^2 \dfrac{h}{2}}{h^2} \qquad \left[\because 1 - \cos x = 2\sin^2\frac{x}{2}\right]$$

$$= \lim_{h \to 0} \frac{2 \times \sin^2 \dfrac{h}{2}}{\left(\dfrac{h^2}{4} \times 4\right)}$$

$$= \lim_{h\to 0} \frac{2}{4} \times \lim_{h\to 0} \frac{\sin^2 \frac{h}{2}}{\frac{h^2}{4}}$$

$$= \frac{1}{2} \times \lim_{h\to 0} \left(\frac{\sin\frac{h}{2}}{\frac{h}{2}}\right)^2 = \frac{1}{2}\times 1 \qquad \left[\because \lim_{x\to 0} \frac{\sin x}{x} = 1\right]$$

$\therefore$ RHL $= \frac{1}{2}$ ...(iv)

On substituting the values from Eqs. (ii), (iii) and (iv) to Eq. (i), we get

$$a = \frac{1}{2}$$

30. Given, $f(x) = \begin{cases} kx+1 & \text{if } x \le \pi \\ \cos x & \text{if } x > \pi \end{cases}$

is continuous at $x = \pi$.

Then, LHL = RHL = $f(\pi)$ ...(i)

Now, LHL $= \lim_{x\to\pi^-} f(x) = \lim_{x\to\pi^-} (kx+1)$

$= \lim_{h\to 0} [k(\pi - h) + 1]$ $[\because x = \pi - h;$ when $x \to \pi^-$, then $h \to 0]$

$= \lim_{h\to 0} (k\pi - kh + 1) = k\pi + 1$

and RHL $= \lim_{x\to\pi^+} f(x) = \lim_{x\to\pi^+} \cos x$

$= \lim_{h\to 0} \cos(\pi + h)$ $[\because x = \pi + h;$ when $x \to \pi^+$, then $h \to 0]$

$= \cos\pi = -1$ $[\because \cos\pi = -1]$

Now, from Eq. (i), we get

LHL = RHL

$\Rightarrow$ $k\pi + 1 = -1 \Rightarrow k\pi = -2$

$\therefore$ $k = -\frac{2}{\pi}$

31. Let $f(x) = \begin{cases} \lambda(x^2 - 2x) & \text{if } x \le 0 \\ 4x+1 & \text{if } x > 0 \end{cases}$

is continuous at $x = 0$.

Then, $(\text{LHL})_{x=0} = (\text{RHL})_{x=0} = f(0)$ ...(i)

Now, $f(0) = \lambda[0 - 0] = 0$,

LHL $= \lim_{x\to 0^-} f(x) = \lim_{h\to 0} f(0-h)$

$= \lambda \lim_{h\to 0} [(0-h)^2 - 2(0-h)]$

$= \lambda \times 0 = 0$

and RHL $= \lim_{x\to 0^+} f(x)$

$= \lim_{h\to 0} f(0+h)$

$= \lim_{h\to 0} 4(0+h) + 1 = 1$

$\because$ LHL $\ne$ RHL, which is a contradiction to Eq. (i).

$\therefore$ There is no value of λ for which $f(x)$ is continuous at $x = 0$.

32. Given, $f(x) = \begin{cases} 2x-1, & x<2 \\ a, & x=2 \\ x+1, & x>2 \end{cases}$ is continuous at $x = 2$.

$\therefore$ $(\text{LHL})_{x=2} = (\text{RHL})_{x=2} = f(2)$ ...(i)

Now, $f(2) = a$

and LHL $= \lim_{x\to 2^-} f(x) = \lim_{x\to 2^-} (2x-1)$

$= \lim_{h\to 0} [2(2-h) - 1] = 3$

$[\because x = 2 - h;$ when $x \to 2^-$, then $h \to 0]$

From Eq. (i), we get

LHL $= f(2) \Rightarrow a = 3$

Now, let us check the continuity at $x = 3$.

Consider, $\lim_{x\to 3} f(x) = \lim_{x\to 3}(x+1)$ $[\because f(x) = x+1$ for $x > 2]$

$= 4 = f(3)$ $[\because f(3) = 3+1 = 4]$

$\therefore$ $f(x)$ is continuous at $x = 3$.

33. Given, f is a differentiable at c.

$$\therefore \quad \lim_{x\to c} \frac{f(x) - f(c)}{x - c} = f'(c)$$

Now, $\lim_{x\to c} [f(x) - f(c)] = \lim_{x\to c} \left[\frac{f(x) - f(c)}{x-c}(x-c)\right]$

$$= \lim_{x\to c} \frac{f(x) - f(c)}{x - c} \cdot \lim_{x\to c} (x - c) = 0$$

$\Rightarrow$ $\lim_{x\to c} f(x) = f(c)$

34. Given, $f(x) = |x - 3|$

$$\Rightarrow \quad f(x) = \begin{cases} -(x-3), & x<3 \\ 0, & x=3 \\ (x-3), & x>3 \end{cases}$$

For continuity

LHL $= \lim_{x\to 3^-} f(x) = \lim_{h\to 0} f(3-h)$

$= \lim_{h\to 0} -(3-h-3) = \lim_{h\to 0} h = 0$

RHL $= \lim_{x\to 3^+} f(x) = \lim_{h\to 0} f(3+h)$

$= \lim_{h\to 0} (3+h-3)$

$= \lim_{h\to 0} h = 0$

Also, $f(3) = 0$

Since, LHL = RHL = $f(3)$

$\therefore f(x)$ is continuous at $x = 3$.

For differentiability

$$\text{LHD} = \lim_{h\to 0} \frac{f(3-h) - f(3)}{-h}$$

$$= \lim_{h\to 0} \frac{-(3-h-3) - 0}{-h}$$

$$= \lim_{h\to 0} \frac{h}{-h} = -1$$

$$\text{RHD} = \lim_{h \to 0} \frac{f(3+h) - f(3)}{h}$$
$$= \lim_{h \to 0} \frac{(3+h-3) - 0}{h}$$
$$= \lim_{h \to 0} \frac{h}{h} = 1$$

Since, LHD $\neq$ RHD

$\therefore f(x)$ is not differentiable at $x = 3$.

35. **Hint** For continuity at $x = 1$.

$$\lim_{x \to 1^-} f(x) = \lim_{x \to 1^+} f(x) = f(1)$$

For differentiability at $x = 1$,

$$Lf'(1) = Rf'(1)$$

Continuous at $x = 1$ but not differentiable at $x = 1$

36. **Hint** $\text{LHL} = \lim_{x \to 0^-} f(x) = 2\lambda$

$$\text{RHL} = \lim_{x \to 0^+} f(x) = 6$$

and $f(0) = 2\lambda$

As given function is continuous at $x = 0$.

$\therefore \quad 2\lambda = 6$

$\Rightarrow \quad \lambda = 3$

For differentiability

$$\text{LHD} = \lim_{h \to 0} \frac{f(0-h) - f(0)}{-h} = 0$$

$$\text{RHD} = \lim_{h \to 0} \frac{f(0+h) - f(0)}{h} = 4$$

LHD $\neq$ RHD

$\therefore f(x)$ is not differentiable at $x = 0$.

37. Given, $f(x) = \begin{cases} ax + b, & x > -1 \\ bx^2 - 3, & x \le -1 \end{cases}$

is differentiable at $x = -1$

$\therefore \quad Lf'(-1) = Rf'(-1) = f'(-1) \quad \ldots$(i)

Here, $Lf'(-1) = \lim_{h \to 0} \frac{f(-1-h) - f(-1)}{-h}$

$$= \lim_{h \to 0} \frac{[b(-1-h)^2 - 3] - [b(-1)^2 - 3]}{-h}$$
$$= \lim_{h \to 0} \frac{[b(1+h^2+2h) - 3] - [b-3]}{-h}$$
$$= \lim_{h \to 0} \frac{b + bh^2 + 2bh - 3 - b + 3}{-h}$$
$$= \lim_{h \to 0} \frac{h(bh + 2b)}{-h}$$
$$= -\lim_{h \to 0} (2b + bh)$$
$$= -2b$$

and $Rf'(-1) = \lim_{h \to 0} \frac{f(-1+h) - f(-1)}{h}$

$$= \lim_{h \to 0} \frac{[a(-1+h) + b] - (b-3)}{h}$$
$$= \lim_{h \to 0} \frac{[-a + ah + b - b + 3]}{h}$$
$$= \lim_{h \to 0} \frac{-a + ah + 3}{h} = \lim_{h \to 0} \frac{ah - a + 3}{h}$$

Clearly, for $Rf'(-1)$ to be exist $(-a+3)$ should be equal to 0.

i.e. $\quad -a + 3 = 0 \Rightarrow a = 3 \quad \ldots$(ii)

Now, $Rf'(-1) = \lim_{h \to 0} \frac{ah}{h} = a$

From Eq. (i), we get

$$Lf'(1) = Rf'(1) \Rightarrow -2b = a$$

$\Rightarrow \quad b = \frac{-a}{2} \Rightarrow b = \frac{-3}{2}$ [from Eq. (ii)]

Hence, $a = 3$ and $b = \frac{-3}{2}$

38. We have, $f(x) = \begin{cases} ax^2 + b, & \text{if } x < 1 \\ 2x + 1, & \text{if } x \ge 1 \end{cases}$ is differentiable at $x = 1$.

$\therefore \quad f(x)$ is also continuous at $x = 1$.

Hence, $\lim_{x \to 1^+} f(x) = \lim_{x \to 1^+} (2x+1) = 2(1) + 1 = 3$

and $\quad \lim_{x \to 1^-} f(x) = \lim_{x \to 1^-} (ax^2 + b) = a(1)^2 + b = a + b$

Thus, $\quad f(1) = 3$

As, $f(x)$ is continuous at $x = 1$.

$\therefore \quad a + b = 3 \quad \ldots$(i)

$$Lf'(1) = \lim_{h \to 0^-} \frac{f(1-h) - f(1)}{-h}$$
$$= \lim_{h \to 0^-} \frac{a(1-h)^2 + b - 3}{-h}$$
$$= \lim_{h \to 0^-} \frac{a + ah^2 - 2ah + b - 3}{-h}$$
$$= \lim_{h \to 0^-} (-ah + 2a) = 2a \quad \text{[from Eq. (i)]}$$

$$Rf'(1) = \lim_{h \to 0^+} \frac{f(1+h) - f(1)}{h}$$
$$= \lim_{h \to 0^+} \frac{2(1+h) + 1 - 3}{h}$$
$$= \frac{2(1+h) - 2}{h} = \frac{2(1+h-1)}{h} = \frac{2h}{h} = 2$$

As, $f(x)$ is differentiable at $x = 1$, so $Lf'(1) = Rf'(1)$.

So, we get

$$2a = 2 \Rightarrow a = 1.$$

$\therefore \quad a = 1$ and $b = 2$ [from Eq. (i)]

39. Given, $f(x)=\begin{cases} x^2+3x+a, & x\le 1 \\ bx+2 & , x>1 \end{cases}$ is differentiable at $x=1$.

$\therefore \quad Lf'(1)=Rf'(1) \quad \ldots(i)$

Here, $Lf'(1)=\lim_{h\to 0}\dfrac{f(1-h)-f(1)}{-h}$

$$=\lim_{h\to 0}\frac{(1-h)^2+3(1-h)+a-(4+a)}{-h}$$

$$=\lim_{h\to 0}\frac{1+h^2-2h+3-3h+a-4-a}{-h}$$

$$=\lim_{h\to 0}\frac{h^2-5h}{-h}$$

$$=\lim_{h\to 0}5-h=5$$

and $Rf'(1)=\lim_{h\to 0}\dfrac{f(1+h)-f(1)}{h}$

$$=\lim_{h\to 0}\frac{b(1+h)+2-(4+a)}{h}$$

$$=\lim_{h\to 0}\frac{b+bh+2-4-a}{h}$$

$$=\lim_{h\to 0}\frac{bh+b-a-2}{h}$$

Clearly, for $Rf'(1)$ to be exist $b-a-2$ should be equal to 0 i.e.

$$b-a-2=0 \quad \ldots(ii)$$

Now, $\quad Rf'(1)=\lim_{h\to 0}\dfrac{bh}{h}=\lim_{h\to 0}b=b$

From Eq. (i), we get

$$Lf'(1)=Rf'(1)$$

$\Rightarrow \quad 5=b \Rightarrow b=5$

Now, on substituting $b=5$ in Eq. (ii), we get

$$5-a-2=0\Rightarrow a=3$$

Hence, $a=3$ and $b=5$.

40. Given, $y=\dfrac{\sin(ax+b)}{\cos(cx+d)}$

On differentiating both sides, w.r.t. x, we get

$$\frac{dy}{dx}=\frac{\cos(cx+d)\dfrac{d}{dx}\sin(ax+b)-\sin(ax+b)\dfrac{d}{dx}\cos(cx+d)}{\{\cos(cx+d)\}^2}$$

[by quotient rule]

$$=\frac{\cos(cx+d)\cos(ax+b)(a+0)+\sin(ax+b)\sin(cx+d)(c+0)}{\cos^2(cx+d)}$$

$$=\frac{a\cos(cx+d)\cos(ax+b)+c\sin(ax+b)\sin(cx+d)}{\cos^2(cx+d)}$$

41. Given equation is $x\sqrt{1+y}+y\sqrt{1+x}=0$, where $x\ne y$,

we first convert the given equation into $y=f(x)$ form.

Clearly, $\quad x\sqrt{1+y}=-y\sqrt{1+x}$

On squaring both sides, we get

$$x^2(1+y)=y^2(1+x)$$

$\Rightarrow \quad x^2+x^2y=y^2+y^2x$

$\Rightarrow \quad x^2-y^2=y^2x-x^2y$

$\Rightarrow \quad (x-y)(x+y)=-xy(x-y)$

$[\because a^2-b^2=(a-b)(a+b)]$

$\Rightarrow \quad (x-y)(x+y)+xy(x-y)=0$

$\Rightarrow \quad (x-y)(x+y+xy)=0$

$\therefore$ Either $\quad x-y=0$ or $x+y+xy=0$

Now, $\quad x-y=0\Rightarrow x=y$

But it is given that $x\ne y$.

So, $y+xy+x=0$

$\Rightarrow \quad y(1+x)=-x$

$\Rightarrow \quad y=\dfrac{-x}{1+x} \quad \ldots(i)$

On differentiating both sides w.r.t. x, we get

$$\frac{dy}{dx}=\frac{(1+x)\times\dfrac{d}{dx}(-x)-(-x)\times\dfrac{d}{dx}(1+x)}{(1+x)^2}$$

[using quotient rule of derivative]

$\Rightarrow \quad \dfrac{dy}{dx}=\dfrac{(1+x)(-1)+x(1)}{(1+x)^2}$

$\Rightarrow \quad \dfrac{dy}{dx}=\dfrac{-1-x+x}{(1+x)^2}$

$\therefore \quad \dfrac{dy}{dx}=\dfrac{-1}{(1+x)^2}$ **Hence proved.**

42. Given, $\sin y=x\cos(a+y) \quad \ldots(i)$

$\Rightarrow \quad x=\dfrac{\sin y}{\cos(a+y)}$

On differentiating both sides w.r.t. y, we get

$$\frac{dx}{dy}=\frac{\cos(a+y)\dfrac{d}{dy}(\sin y)-\sin y\dfrac{d}{dy}\cos(a+y)}{\cos^2(a+y)}$$

[using quotient rule of derivative]

$\Rightarrow \dfrac{dx}{dy}=\dfrac{\cos(a+y)\cos y+\sin y\sin(a+y)}{\cos^2(a+y)}$

$=\dfrac{\cos(a+y-y)}{\cos^2(a+y)}$ $[\because \cos A\cos B+\sin A\sin B=\cos(A-B)]$

$\Rightarrow \dfrac{dx}{dy}=\dfrac{\cos a}{\cos^2(a+y)}$

$\Rightarrow \dfrac{dy}{dx}=\dfrac{\cos^2(a+y)}{\cos a}$

Put $x=0$ in Eq. (i), we get

$$y=0$$

Now, $\dfrac{dy}{dx}=\dfrac{\cos^2(a+0)}{\cos a}=\dfrac{\cos^2 a}{\cos a}=\cos a$ **Hence proved.**

43. Given, $y = \tan^{-1}\left(\frac{a}{x}\right) + \log\sqrt{\frac{x-a}{x+a}}$

$$= \tan^{-1}\left(\frac{a}{x}\right) + \frac{1}{2}[\log(x-a) - \log(x+a)]$$

$$\therefore \quad \frac{dy}{dx} = \frac{1}{1+\frac{a^2}{x^2}}\left(\frac{-a}{x^2}\right) + \frac{1}{2}\left[\frac{1}{x-a} - \frac{1}{x+a}\right]$$

$$= \frac{-a}{x^2+a^2} + \frac{1}{2}\left[\frac{x+a-x+a}{(x-a)(x+a)}\right]$$

$$= \frac{-a}{x^2+a^2} + \frac{a}{x^2-a^2} = \frac{2a^3}{x^4-a^4}$$

44. Given, $\log(\sqrt{1+x^2} - x) = y\sqrt{1+x^2}$

On differentiating both sides w.r.t. x, we get

$$\frac{1}{\sqrt{1+x^2}-x}\frac{d}{dx}(\sqrt{1+x^2}-x)$$

$$= y\frac{d}{dx}\sqrt{1+x^2} + \sqrt{1+x^2}\frac{dy}{dx}$$

$$\Rightarrow \frac{1}{\sqrt{1+x^2}-x}\left[\frac{1}{2\sqrt{1+x^2}}\frac{d}{dx}(1+x^2) - 1\right]$$

$$= \frac{y}{2\sqrt{1+x^2}}\frac{d}{dx}(1+x^2) + \sqrt{1+x^2}\frac{dy}{dx}$$

$$\Rightarrow \frac{1}{\sqrt{1+x^2}-x}\left[\frac{2x}{2\sqrt{1+x^2}} - 1\right]$$

$$= y \times \frac{2x}{2\sqrt{1+x^2}} + \sqrt{1+x^2}\frac{dy}{dx}$$

$$\Rightarrow \frac{1}{\sqrt{1+x^2}-x}\left[\frac{x-\sqrt{1+x^2}}{\sqrt{1+x^2}}\right] = \frac{xy}{\sqrt{1+x^2}} + \sqrt{1+x^2}\frac{dy}{dx}$$

$$\Rightarrow \frac{-1}{\sqrt{1+x^2}} = \frac{xy + (1+x^2)\frac{dy}{dx}}{\sqrt{1+x^2}}$$

$$\Rightarrow -1 = xy + (1+x^2)\frac{dy}{dx}$$

$$\Rightarrow (1+x^2)\frac{dy}{dx} + xy + 1 = 0$$

45. We have, $y = \cos^{-1}\left(\frac{3x + 4\sqrt{1-x^2}}{5}\right)$

Let $x = \cos\theta \Rightarrow \theta = \cos^{-1}x$

$$y = \cos^{-1}\left[\frac{3\cos\theta + 4\sqrt{1-\cos^2\theta}}{5}\right]$$

$$= \cos^{-1}\left[\frac{3}{5}\cos\theta + \frac{4}{5}\sin\theta\right] \qquad [\because 1-\cos^2\beta = \sin^2\beta]$$

Let us assume a right angled triangle with base 3 and perpendicular 4.

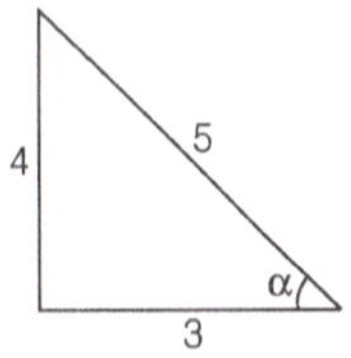

Then, $\frac{3}{5} = \cos\alpha$ $\qquad \left[\because \cos\alpha = \frac{\text{base}}{\text{hypotenuse}}\right]$

and $\frac{4}{5} = \sin\alpha$ $\qquad \left[\because \sin\alpha = \frac{\text{perpendicular}}{\text{hypotenuse}}\right]$

$$\therefore \quad y = \cos^{-1}[\cos\alpha\cos\theta + \sin\alpha\sin\theta]$$

$$\Rightarrow \quad y = \cos^{-1}[\cos(\theta-\alpha)] = \theta - \alpha$$

$$\Rightarrow \quad y = \cos^{-1}x - \cos^{-1}\frac{3}{5}$$

$$\therefore \quad \frac{dy}{dx} = \frac{-1}{\sqrt{1-x^2}}$$

46. We have, $\quad y = \tan^{-1}\left[\frac{\sqrt{1+x^2} - \sqrt{1-x^2}}{\sqrt{1+x^2} + \sqrt{1-x^2}}\right]$

Let us assume, $x^2 = \cos\theta \Rightarrow \theta = \cos^{-1}x^2$

$$y = \tan^{-1}\left[\frac{\sqrt{1+\cos\theta} - \sqrt{1-\cos\theta}}{\sqrt{1+\cos\theta} + \sqrt{1-\cos\theta}}\right]$$

$$= \tan^{-1}\left[\frac{\sqrt{2\cos^2\frac{\theta}{2}} - \sqrt{2\sin^2\frac{\theta}{2}}}{\sqrt{2\cos^2\frac{\theta}{2}} + \sqrt{2\sin^2\frac{\theta}{2}}}\right]$$

$$\left[\because 1-\cos\alpha = 2\sin^2\frac{\alpha}{2} \text{ and } 1+\cos\alpha = 2\cos^2\frac{\alpha}{2}\right]$$

$$= \tan^{-1}\left[\frac{\sqrt{2}\cos\frac{\theta}{2} - \sqrt{2}\sin\frac{\theta}{2}}{\sqrt{2}\cos\frac{\theta}{2} + \sqrt{2}\sin\frac{\theta}{2}}\right]$$

On dividing numerator and denominator by $\sqrt{2}\cos\frac{\theta}{2}$, we get

$$\tan^{-1}\left[\frac{1-\tan\frac{\theta}{2}}{1+\tan\frac{\theta}{2}}\right]$$

$$= \tan^{-1}\left(\tan\left(\frac{\pi}{4} - \frac{\theta}{2}\right)\right)$$

$$\left[\because \frac{1-\tan\alpha}{1+\tan\alpha} = \tan\left(\frac{\pi}{4} - \alpha\right)\right]$$

$$= \frac{\pi}{4} - \frac{\theta}{2}$$

$$y = \frac{\pi}{4} - \frac{1}{2}\cos^{-1}x^2$$

$$\frac{dy}{dx}=0-\frac{1}{2}\frac{(-1)}{\sqrt{1-(x^2)^2}}\frac{d}{dx}(x^2) \quad \text{[by chain rule]}$$

$$=\frac{1(2x)}{2\sqrt{1-x^4}}$$

$$=\frac{x}{\sqrt{1-x^4}}$$

47. Let $y=\sin^{-1}\left[\frac{2^{x+1}\cdot 3^x}{1+(36)^x}\right]=\sin^{-1}\left[\frac{2\cdot 2^x\cdot 3^x}{1+(6^x)^2}\right]$

$$=\sin^{-1}\left[\frac{2\cdot 6^x}{1+(6^x)^2}\right]=\sin^{-1}\left(\frac{2\tan\theta}{1+\tan^2\theta}\right) \quad [\text{put } 6^x=\tan\theta]$$

$$=\sin^{-1}(\sin 2\theta)=2\theta=2\tan^{-1}(6^x)$$

On differentiating both sides w.r.t. x, we get

$$\frac{dy}{dx}=2\frac{d}{dx}\tan^{-1}(6^x)$$

$$=\frac{2}{1+(6^x)^2}\cdot 6^x\log 6$$

$$=\frac{2\cdot 6^x\log 6}{1+(36)^x}$$

$$=\left[\frac{2\cdot 2^x\cdot 3^x}{1+(36)^x}\right]\log 6$$

$$=\left[\frac{2^{x+1}\cdot 3^x}{1+(36)^x}\right]\log 6$$

48. Let $y=x^{\sin x}$

On taking log both sides, we get

$$\log y=\sin x(\log x)$$

On differentiating both sides w.r.t. x, we get

$$\frac{1}{y}\frac{dy}{dx}=\sin x\frac{d}{dx}(\log x)+\log x\frac{d}{dx}(\sin x)$$

$$\Rightarrow \frac{dy}{dx}=x^{\sin x}\left[\frac{\sin x}{x}+\log x\cos x\right]$$

49. Hint Let $y=\cos^{-1}\left[\sin\sqrt{\frac{1+x}{2}}\right]+x^x$

$$y=\cos^{-1}\left[\cos\left(\frac{\pi}{2}-\sqrt{\frac{1+x}{2}}\right)\right]+x^x=\frac{\pi}{2}-\sqrt{\frac{1+x}{2}}+x^x$$

$$\therefore \frac{dy}{dx}=-\frac{1}{2\sqrt{\frac{1+x}{2}}}\left(\frac{1}{2}\right)+x^x(1+\log x)$$

$$\left[\because \frac{d}{dx}x^x=x^x(1+\log x)\right]$$

$\therefore$ At $x=1$,

$$\frac{dy}{dx}=-\frac{1}{2\sqrt{\frac{1+1}{2}}}\left(\frac{1}{2}\right)+1(1+\log 1)=-\frac{1}{4}+1=\frac{3}{4}$$

50. Let $y=(\sin x-\cos x)^{\sin x-\cos x}$

On taking log both sides, we get

$\log y=(\sin x-\cos x)\log(\sin x-\cos x)$

On differentiating both sides w.r.t. x, we get

$$\frac{1}{y}\frac{dy}{dx}=\frac{\sin x-\cos x}{\sin x-\cos x}(\cos x+\sin x)+(\cos x+\sin x)\log(\sin x-\cos x)$$

$$\Rightarrow \frac{dy}{dx}=y[(\cos x+\sin x)+(\cos x+\sin x)\log(\sin x-\cos x)]$$

$$=(\sin x-\cos x)^{\sin x-\cos x}\times(\cos x+\sin x)[1+\log(\sin x-\cos x)]$$

51. Given, $x=\cos t(3-2\cos^2 t)$

$\Rightarrow \quad x=3\cos t-2\cos^3 t$

On differentiating both sides w.r.t. t, we get

$$\frac{dx}{dt}=3(-\sin t)-2(3)\cos^2 t(-\sin t)$$

$$\Rightarrow \frac{dx}{dt}=-3\sin t+6\cos^2 t\sin t \quad \text{...(i)}$$

Also, $y=\sin t(3-2\sin^2 t)\Rightarrow y=3\sin t-2\sin^3 t$

On differentiating both sides w.r.t. t, we get

$$\frac{dy}{dt}=3\cos t-2\times 3\times\sin^2 t\cos t$$

$$\Rightarrow \frac{dy}{dt}=3\cos t-6\sin^2 t\cos t \quad \text{...(ii)}$$

Now, $\frac{dy}{dx}=\frac{dy}{dt}\times\frac{dt}{dx}=\frac{3\cos t-6\cos t\sin^2 t}{-3\sin t+6\cos^2 t\sin t}$

[from Eqs. (i) and (ii)]

$$=\frac{\cos t-2\cos t\sin^2 t}{-\sin t+2\cos^2 t\sin t}$$

$$=\frac{\cos t(1-2\sin^2 t)}{\sin t(2\cos^2 t-1)}$$

$$=\frac{\cos t\cdot\cos 2t}{\sin t\cdot\cos 2t}$$

$$=\cot(t)$$

$$\therefore \left.\frac{dy}{dx}\right|_{\text{at } t=\frac{\pi}{4}}=\cot\left(\frac{\pi}{4}\right)=1$$

52. Given, $x=a\sin 2t(1+\cos 2t)$

and $y=b\cos 2t(1-\cos 2t)$

On differentiating x and y separately w.r.t. t, we get

$$\frac{dx}{dt}=a\left[\sin 2t\frac{d}{dt}(1+\cos 2t)+(1+\cos 2t)\frac{d}{dt}(\sin 2t)\right]$$

[using product rule of derivative]

$$=a[\sin 2t\times(0-2\sin 2t)+(1+\cos 2t)(2\cos 2t)]$$

$$=a(-2\sin^2 2t+2\cos 2t+2\cos^2 2t)$$

$$=a[2(\cos^2 2t-\sin^2 2t)+2\cos 2t]$$

$$=a(2\cos 4t+2\cos 2t)=2a(\cos 4t+\cos 2t)$$

$$[\because \cos^2 2\theta-\sin^2 2\theta=\cos 4\theta]$$

$$= 2a\left[2\cos\left(\frac{4t+2t}{2}\right)\cdot\cos\left(\frac{4t-2t}{2}\right)\right]$$

$$\left[\because \cos x + \cos y = 2\cos\left(\frac{x+y}{2}\right)\cdot\cos\left(\frac{x-y}{2}\right)\right]$$

$$= 4a\cos 3t\cos t$$

and $\dfrac{dy}{dt} = b\left[\cos 2t\dfrac{d}{dt}(1-\cos 2t) + (1-\cos 2t)\dfrac{d}{dt}(\cos 2t)\right]$

[using product rule of derivative]

$$= b[\cos 2t \times (0 + 2\sin 2t) + (1-\cos 2t)(-2\sin 2t)]$$

$$= b(2\sin 2t\cos 2t - 2\sin 2t + 2\sin 2t\cos 2t)$$

$$= 2b(2\sin 2t\cos 2t - \sin 2t)$$

$$= 2b(\sin 4t - \sin 2t) \quad [\because 2\sin 2\theta\cos 2\theta = \sin 4\theta]$$

$$= 2b\left[2\cos\left(\frac{4t+2t}{2}\right)\sin\left(\frac{4t-2t}{2}\right)\right]$$

$$\left[\because \sin x - \sin y = 2\cos\left(\frac{x+y}{2}\right)\cdot\sin\left(\frac{x-y}{2}\right)\right]$$

$$= 4b\cos 3t\sin t$$

Now, $\dfrac{dy}{dx} = \dfrac{dy/dt}{dx/dt}$

$$= \frac{4b\cos 3t\sin t}{4a\cos 3t\cdot\cos t} = \frac{b}{a}\tan t$$

At $t = \dfrac{\pi}{4}, \dfrac{dy}{dx} = \dfrac{b}{a}\tan\dfrac{\pi}{4} = \dfrac{b}{a}$

At $t = \dfrac{\pi}{3}, \dfrac{dy}{dx} = \dfrac{b}{a}\tan\dfrac{\pi}{3} = \dfrac{\sqrt{3}b}{a}$

53. Given, $x = ae^t(\sin t + \cos t)$

and $y = ae^t(\sin t - \cos t)$

$\therefore \dfrac{dx}{dt} = a[e^t(\cos t - \sin t) + e^t(\sin t + \cos t)]$

$$= -y + x = x - y$$

and $\dfrac{dy}{dt} = a[e^t(\sin t - \cos t) + e^t(\sin t + \cos t)]$

$$= y + x = x + y$$

Now, $\dfrac{dy}{dx} = \dfrac{dy/dt}{dx/dt}$

$\Rightarrow \dfrac{dy}{dx} = \dfrac{x+y}{x-y}$ **Hence proved.**

54. Hint Let $u = \tan^{-1}\left(\dfrac{\sqrt{1+x^2} - \sqrt{1-x^2}}{\sqrt{1+x^2} + \sqrt{1-x^2}}\right)$

and $v = \cos^{-1}x^2 \Rightarrow x^2 = \cos v$

$\therefore u = \tan^{-1}\left(\dfrac{\sqrt{1+\cos v} - \sqrt{1-\cos v}}{\sqrt{1+\cos v} + \sqrt{1-\cos v}}\right)$

$$= \tan^{-1}\left(\frac{\cos\left(\frac{v}{2}\right) - \sin\left(\frac{v}{2}\right)}{\cos\left(\frac{v}{2}\right) + \sin\left(\frac{v}{2}\right)}\right)$$

$$= \tan^{-1}\left\{\tan\left(\frac{\pi}{4} - \frac{v}{2}\right)\right\} = \frac{\pi}{4} - \frac{v}{2}$$

Ans. $\dfrac{du}{dv} = -\dfrac{1}{2}$

55. Hint Put $x = \sin\theta$ in first function and $x = \cos\theta$ in second function. **Ans.** $\dfrac{-1}{2x}$

56. Let $u = \tan^{-1}\left(\dfrac{x}{\sqrt{1-x^2}}\right)$

On putting $x = \sin\theta \Rightarrow \theta = \sin^{-1}x$, then

$$u = \tan^{-1}\left[\frac{\sin\theta}{\sqrt{1-\sin^2\theta}}\right]$$

$\Rightarrow u = \tan^{-1}\left[\dfrac{\sin\theta}{\cos\theta}\right]$ $\left[\begin{array}{l}\because \sin^2 A + \cos^2 A = 1 \\ \Rightarrow \cos A = \sqrt{(1-\sin^2 A)}\end{array}\right]$

$\Rightarrow u = \tan^{-1}(\tan\theta)$

$\Rightarrow u = \theta \Rightarrow u = \sin^{-1}x$

On differentiating both sides w.r.t. x, we get

$$\frac{du}{dx} = \frac{1}{\sqrt{1-x^2}} \quad \text{...(i)}$$

Again, let $v = \sin^{-1}(2x\sqrt{1-x^2})$

On putting $x = \sin\theta \Rightarrow \theta = \sin^{-1}x$, then

$$v = \sin^{-1}(2\sin\theta\sqrt{1-\sin^2\theta})$$

$\Rightarrow v = \sin^{-1}(2\sin\theta\cos\theta)$

$\Rightarrow v = \sin^{-1}(\sin 2\theta) \Rightarrow v = 2\theta \Rightarrow v = 2\sin^{-1}x$

On differentiating both sides w.r.t. x, we get

$$\frac{dv}{dx} = \frac{2}{\sqrt{1-x^2}} \quad \text{...(ii)}$$

Now, $\dfrac{du}{dv} = \dfrac{du}{dx} \times \dfrac{dx}{dv}$

$\Rightarrow \dfrac{du}{dv} = \dfrac{1}{\sqrt{1-x^2}} \times \dfrac{\sqrt{1-x^2}}{2}$

$\therefore \dfrac{du}{dv} = \dfrac{1}{2}$

57. Given, $x = a\cos t$

$\therefore \dfrac{dx}{dt} = a(-\sin t) = -a\sin t$

and $y = b\sin t$

$\therefore \dfrac{dy}{dt} = b\cos t$

$\therefore \dfrac{dy}{dx} = \dfrac{dy/dt}{dx/dt} = \dfrac{b\cos t}{-a\sin t}$

$$= \frac{-b}{a}\cot t$$

Now, $\frac{d^2y}{dx^2}=\frac{-b}{a}(-\text{cosec}^2 t)\cdot\frac{dt}{dx}$

$$=\frac{b}{a}\text{cosec}^2 t\,\frac{-1}{a\sin t}$$

$$=\frac{-b}{a^2}\text{cosec}^3 t$$

58. **Hint** Given, $x=a\cos^3\theta$ and $y=a\sin^3\theta$

$$\therefore \quad \frac{dx}{d\theta}=3a\cos^2\theta\frac{d}{d\theta}(\cos\theta)$$

$$=3a\cos^2\theta(-\sin\theta)$$

$$\frac{dy}{d\theta}=3a\sin^2\theta\frac{d}{d\theta}(\sin\theta)$$

$$=3a\sin^2\theta(\cos\theta)$$

$$\therefore \quad \frac{dy}{dx}=-\tan\theta$$

Again, $\frac{d^2y}{dx^2}=\frac{d}{dx}(-\tan\theta)=-\sec^2\theta\frac{d\theta}{dx}$

$$=-\sec^2\theta\left(-\frac{1}{3a\cos^2\theta\sin\theta}\right)$$

$$=\frac{1}{3a\cos^4\theta\sin\theta}$$

$$\therefore \left(\frac{d^2y}{dx^2}\right)_{\theta=\frac{\pi}{6}}=\frac{1}{3a\left(\cos\frac{\pi}{6}\right)^4\left(\sin\frac{\pi}{6}\right)}$$

Ans. $\frac{32}{27a}$

59. Given, $(x-a)^2+(y-b)^2=c^2$

On differentiating both sides w.r.t. x, we get

$$\frac{d\{(x-a)^2+(y-b)^2\}}{dx}=\frac{d(c^2)}{dx}$$

$$\Rightarrow \quad \frac{d\{(x-a)^2\}}{dx}+\frac{d\{(y-b)^2\}}{dx}=0$$

$$\Rightarrow \quad 2(x-a)\cdot\frac{d(x-a)}{dx}+2(y-b)\cdot\frac{d(y-b)}{dx}=0$$

$$\Rightarrow \quad 2(x-a)\cdot(1-0)+2(y-b)\cdot\left(\frac{dy}{dx}-0\right)=0$$

$$\Rightarrow \quad 2(x-a)+2(y-b)\cdot\left(\frac{dy}{dx}\right)=0$$

$$\Rightarrow \quad 2(y-b)\cdot\frac{dy}{dx}=-2(x-a)$$

$$\Rightarrow \quad \frac{dy}{dx}=-\frac{(x-a)}{(y-b)}$$

Again, on differentiating both sides w.r.t. x, we get

$$\frac{d}{dx}\left(\frac{dy}{dx}\right)=\frac{d}{dx}\left\{-\frac{(x-a)}{(y-b)}\right\}$$

$$\frac{d^2y}{dx^2}=-\frac{\left\{(y-b)\frac{d(x-a)}{dx}-(x-a)\frac{d(y-b)}{dx}\right\}}{(y-b)^2}$$

$$=-\frac{\left\{(y-b)\cdot(1-0)-(x-a)\left(\frac{dy}{dx}-0\right)\right\}}{(y-b)^2}$$

$$=-\frac{\left\{(y-b)-\frac{dy}{dx}(x-a)\right\}}{(y-b)^2}$$

$$=-\frac{\left\{(y-b)+\frac{(x-a)}{(y-b)}(x-a)\right\}}{(y-b)^2}$$

$$=-\frac{\{(y-b)^2+(x-a)^2\}}{(y-b)^3}$$

$$=-\frac{c^2}{(y-b)^3} \qquad [\because (x-a)^2+(y-b)^2=c^2]$$

Now, $\frac{\left[1+\left(\frac{dy}{dx}\right)^2\right]^{3/2}}{\frac{d^2y}{dx^2}}=\frac{\left[1+\left\{-\frac{(x-a)}{(y-b)}\right\}^2\right]^{3/2}}{\frac{-c^2}{(y-b)^3}}$

$$=-\frac{\left[\frac{(y-b)^2+(x-a)^2}{(y-b)^2}\right]^{3/2}}{\frac{c^2}{(y-b)^3}}=-\frac{\left[\frac{c^2}{(y-b)^2}\right]^{3/2}}{\frac{c^2}{(y-b)^3}}$$

$$=-\left[\frac{c^2}{(y-b)^2}\right]^{3/2}\times\frac{(y-b)^3}{c^2}$$

$$=-\left(\frac{c}{y-b}\right)^{2\times\frac{3}{2}}\times\frac{(y-b)^3}{c^2}$$

$$=-\frac{c^3}{c^2}\times\frac{(y-b)^3}{(y-b)^3}=-c$$

which is constant and independent of a and b.

Hence proved.

60. We have,

$$y=\log\left(\sqrt{x}+\frac{1}{\sqrt{x}}\right)^2=2\log\left(\frac{x+1}{\sqrt{x}}\right)$$

$$=2[\log(x+1)-\log\sqrt{x}]$$

$$=2\left[\log(x+1)-\frac{1}{2}\log x\right]$$

$$\Rightarrow \quad y=2\log(x+1)-\log x$$

On differentiating both sides w.r.t. x, we get

$$y_1=\frac{2}{x+1}\cdot\frac{d}{dx}(x+1)-\frac{1}{x}$$

$$\Rightarrow \quad y_1=\frac{2}{x+1}-\frac{1}{x}$$

$$\Rightarrow \quad y_1=\frac{2x-(x+1)}{x(x+1)}$$

$$=\frac{x-1}{x(x+1)} \quad \ldots(\text{i})$$

Again, on differentiating both sides w.r.t. x, we get

$$y_2=\frac{x(x+1)\frac{d}{dx}(x-1)-(x-1)\frac{d}{dx}[x(x+1)]}{[x(x+1)]^2}$$

$$=\frac{(x^2+x)\times 1-(x-1)\left[x\frac{d}{dx}(x+1)+(x+1)\frac{d}{dx}x\right]}{x^2(x+1)^2}$$

$$=\frac{x^2+x-(x-1)[x\times 1+(x+1)\times 1]}{x^2(x+1)^2}$$

$$=\frac{x^2+x-(x-1)(2x+1)}{x^2(x+1)^2}$$

$$=\frac{x^2+x-(2x^2+x-2x-1)}{x^2(x+1)^2}$$

$$=\frac{x^2+x-(2x^2-x-1)}{x^2(x+1)^2}$$

$$=\frac{x^2+x-2x^2+x+1}{x^2(x+1)^2}$$

$$\Rightarrow y_2=\frac{-x^2+2x+1}{x^2(x+1)^2}$$

$$\Rightarrow x(x+1)^2y_2=\frac{-x^2+2x+1}{x}$$

$$=\frac{2x-(x+1)(x-1)}{x}$$

$$=2-\frac{(x+1)(x-1)}{x}$$

$$\Rightarrow x(x+1)^2y_2=2-(x+1)^2y_1 \quad \text{[from Eq. (i)]}$$

$$\Rightarrow x(x+1)^2y_2+(x+1)^2y_1=2$$ **Hence proved.**

61. Given, $x\cos(a+y)=\cos y \Rightarrow x=\dfrac{\cos y}{\cos(a+y)}$

On differentiating both sides w.r.t. y, we get

$$\frac{dx}{dy}=\frac{\cos(a+y)\frac{d}{dy}\cos y-\cos y\frac{d}{dy}\cos(a+y)}{\cos^2(a+y)}$$

[using quotient rule of derivative]

$$=\frac{\cos(a+y)\times(-\sin y)+\cos y\times\sin(a+y)}{\cos^2(a+y)}$$

$$=\frac{\sin(a+y)\cos y-\cos(a+y)\sin y}{\cos^2(a+y)}$$

$$\Rightarrow \frac{dx}{dy}=\frac{\sin(a+y-y)}{\cos^2(a+y)}$$

$$=\frac{\sin a}{\cos^2(a+y)}$$

$[\because \sin A\cos B-\cos A\sin B=\sin(A-B)]$

$$\Rightarrow \frac{dy}{dx}=\frac{\cos^2(a+y)}{\sin a} \quad \ldots(\text{i})$$

Again, on differentiating both sides of Eq. (i) w.r.t. x, we get

$$\frac{d^2y}{dx^2}=\frac{1}{\sin a}\frac{d}{dx}\cos^2(a+y)$$

$$=\frac{1}{\sin a}\times 2\cos(a+y)[-\sin(a+y)]\times\frac{dy}{dx}$$

$$=-\frac{2\sin(a+y)\cos(a+y)}{\sin a}\times\frac{dy}{dx}$$

$$\Rightarrow \frac{d^2y}{dx^2}=-\frac{\sin 2(a+y)}{\sin a}\frac{dy}{dx} \quad [\because 2\sin\theta\cos\theta=\sin 2\theta]$$

$$\therefore \sin a\frac{d^2y}{dx^2}+\sin 2(a+y)\frac{dy}{dx}=0$$ **Hence proved.**

62. Given, $y=(\sin^{-1}x)^2$ ...(i)

On differentiating w.r.t. x, we get

$$\frac{dy}{dx}=2\sin^{-1}x\cdot\frac{1}{\sqrt{1-x^2}} \quad \ldots(\text{ii})$$

Again, on differentiating w.r.t. x, we get

$$\frac{d^2y}{dx^2}=\frac{(\sqrt{1-x^2})\left(\frac{2}{\sqrt{1-x^2}}\right)-\left(\frac{\frac{1}{2}(-2x)}{\sqrt{1-x^2}}\right)\cdot(2\sin^{-1}x)}{(\sqrt{1-x^2})^2}$$

$$=\frac{2+\frac{2x\sin^{-1}x}{\sqrt{1-x^2}}}{1-x^2}$$

$$\Rightarrow \quad (1-x^2)\frac{d^2y}{dx^2}=2+\frac{2\sin^{-1}x}{\sqrt{1-x^2}}\cdot x$$

$$\Rightarrow \quad (1-x^2)\frac{d^2y}{dx^2}=2+x\frac{dy}{dx} \quad \text{[from Eq. (ii)]}$$

$$\Rightarrow (1-x^2)\frac{d^2y}{dx^2}-x\frac{dy}{dx}=2$$

63. Given, $y=a\tan^3\theta$ and $x=a\sec^3\theta$

On differentiating w.r.t. θ, we get

$$\frac{dy}{d\theta}=3a\tan^2\theta\frac{d}{d\theta}(\tan\theta)$$

and $$\frac{dx}{d\theta}=3a\sec^2\theta\frac{d}{d\theta}(\sec\theta)$$

$$\Rightarrow \quad \frac{dy}{d\theta} = 3a\tan^2\theta\sec^2\theta$$

and $\dfrac{dx}{d\theta} = 3a\sec^2\theta\sec\theta\tan\theta$

$$\therefore \quad \frac{dy}{dx} = \frac{dy/d\theta}{dx/d\theta} = \frac{3a\tan^2\theta\sec^2\theta}{3a\sec^2\theta\sec\theta\tan\theta}$$

$$\Rightarrow \frac{dy}{dx} = \frac{\tan\theta}{\sec\theta} = \sin\theta$$

Again, on differentiating both sides w.r.t. x, we get

$$\frac{d}{dx}\left(\frac{dy}{dx}\right) = \frac{d}{dx}(\sin\theta)$$

$$= \frac{d}{d\theta}(\sin\theta)\frac{d\theta}{dx}$$

$$= \frac{\cos\theta}{3a\sec^3\theta\tan\theta} = \frac{\cos^5\theta}{3a\sin\theta}$$

At $\theta = \dfrac{\pi}{3}$,

$$\frac{d^2y}{dx^2} = \frac{\cos^5\frac{\pi}{3}}{3a\sin\frac{\pi}{3}} = \frac{\left(\frac{1}{2}\right)^5}{3a\left(\frac{\sqrt{3}}{2}\right)}$$

$$= \frac{1\times 2}{2^5\times 3a\sqrt{3}} = \frac{1}{48\sqrt{3}a}$$

64. Given, $x = \sin t$ and $y = \sin pt$

On differentiating x and y separately w.r.t. t, we get

$$\frac{dx}{dt} = \cos t \text{ and } \frac{dy}{dt} = \cos pt \cdot p$$

$$\Rightarrow \quad \frac{dy}{dx} = \frac{\frac{dy}{dt}}{\frac{dx}{dt}} = \frac{\cos pt \cdot p}{\cos t}$$

Now, on differentiating both sides w.r.t. x, we get

$$\frac{d^2y}{dx^2} = p\frac{[\cos t(-\sin pt\cdot p) - \cos pt(-\sin t)]}{\cos^2 t}\cdot\frac{dt}{dx}$$

$$\Rightarrow \quad \frac{d^2y}{dx^2} = \frac{p[\cos pt\cdot\sin t - \cos t\sin pt\cdot p]}{\cos^2 t}\cdot\frac{1}{\cos t}$$

$$\Rightarrow \quad \cos^2 t\frac{d^2y}{dx^2} = \frac{p\cos pt\cdot\sin t - p^2\cos t\sin pt}{\cos t}$$

$$\Rightarrow \quad (1-\sin^2 t)\frac{d^2y}{dx^2} = \frac{p\cos pt}{\cos t}\cdot\sin t - p^2\sin pt$$

$$\Rightarrow \quad (1-x^2)\frac{d^2y}{dx^2} = \frac{dy}{dx}\cdot x - p^2y$$

$$\left[\because \frac{dy}{dx} = \frac{p\cos pt}{\cos t}, x = \sin t \text{ and } y = \sin pt\right]$$

$$\therefore \quad (1-x^2)\frac{d^2y}{dx^2} - x\frac{dy}{dx} + p^2y = 0$$ **Hence proved.**

QR Code for Quick Test 1 | QR Code for Quick Test 2 | QR Code for Quick Test 3 | QR Code for Quick Test 4 | QR Code for Quick Test 5 | QR Code for Quick Test 6

Mind Map

Continuity and Differentiability

Continuity

Continuity of a Function at a Point
A function $f(x)$ is said to be continuous at a point $x = a$,
if $(LHL)_{x=a} = (RHL)_{x=a} = f(a)$ or $\lim_{x\to a} f(x) = f(a)$
where, $(LHL)_{x=a} = \lim_{x\to a^-} f(x)$ and $(RHL)_{x=a} = \lim_{x\to a^+} f(x)$

Discontinuity of a Function
A function $f(x)$ is said to be discontinuous at $x = a$, if it is not continuous at $x = a$ i.e. when any of the following cases arise :

(i) $\lim_{x\to a^+} f(x)$ or $\lim_{x\to a^-} f(x)$ or $\lim_{x\to a} f(x)$ does not exist.

(ii) $\lim_{x\to a^-} f(x) \neq \lim_{x\to a^+} f(x)$

(iii) $\lim_{x\to a^-} f(x) = \lim_{x\to a^+} f(x) \neq f(a)$ or $\lim_{x\to a} f(x) \neq f(a)$

Algebra of Continuous Functions
Theorem 1 Let f and g be two real functions, continuous at a real number c, then
(i) $(f+g)$ is continuous at $x = c$.
(ii) $(f-g)$ is continuous at $x = c$.
(iii) fg is continuous at $x = c$.
(iv) $\frac{f}{g}$ is continuous at $x = c$, provided that $g(c) \neq 0$.

Theorem 2 Suppose f and g are real valued functions such that fog is defined at c. If g is continuous at c and if f is continuous at $g(c)$, then fog is continuous at c.

Continuity of a Function in its Domain
A function $f(x)$ is said to be continuous in its domain, if it is continuous at every point in its domain.
(i) A function $f(x)$ is said to be continuous in open interval (a, b), if it is continuous for every value of x in the interval (a, b).
(ii) A function $f(x)$ is said to be continuous in closed interval $[a, b]$, if
(a) it is continuous for every value of x in the open interval (a, b).
(b) $f(x)$ is continuous at $x = a$ from right, i.e. $\lim_{x\to a^+} f(x) = f(a)$.
(c) $f(x)$ is continuous at $x = b$ from left, i.e. $\lim_{x\to b^-} f(x) = f(b)$.

Differentiability
A function $f(x)$ is said to be differentiable at a point $x = a$, if Left hand derivative at $x = a$ equals to Right hand derivative at $x = a$, provided both the derivatives exist. i.e. LHD (at $x = a$) = RHD (at $x = a$), where Right hand derivative,

$$Rf'(a) = \lim_{h\to 0} \frac{f(a+h) - f(a)}{h}$$

and Left hand derivative,

$$Lf'(a) = \lim_{h\to 0} \frac{f(a-h) - f(a)}{-h}$$

If $Rf'(a) \neq Lf'(a)$, the function is not differentiable at $x = a$.

Differentiation
The process of finding derivative of a function is called differentiation. The derivative of a function is also called the **differential coefficient** of the function.

Derivatives of some standard functions
(i) $\frac{d}{dx}(\text{constant}) = 0$
(ii) $\frac{d}{dx}(x^n) = nx^{n-1}$
(iii) $\frac{d}{dx}(\sin x) = \cos x$
(iv) $\frac{d}{dx}(\cos x) = -\sin x$
(v) $\frac{d}{dx}(\tan x) = \sec^2 x$
(vi) $\frac{d}{dx}(\text{cosec } x) = -\text{cosec } x \cot x$
(vii) $\frac{d}{dx}(\sec x) = \sec x \tan x$
(viii) $\frac{d}{dx}(\cot x) = -\text{cosec}^2 x$
(ix) $\frac{d}{dx}(e^x) = e^x$
(x) $\frac{d}{dx}(a^x) = a^x \log_e a, a > 0$
(xi) $\frac{d}{dx}(\log_e x) = \frac{1}{x}, x > 0$
(xii) $\frac{d}{dx}(\log_a x) = \frac{1}{x \log_e a}, a > 0, a \neq 1$

Rule of Derivatives
(i) **Sum and Difference Rule** Let $y = f(x) \pm g(x)$.
Then, $\frac{dy}{dx} = \frac{d}{dx} f(x) \pm \frac{d}{dx} g(x)$

(ii) **Product Rule** Let $y = f(x) \cdot g(x)$.
Then, $\frac{dy}{dx} = \left[\frac{d}{dx} f(x)\right] g(x) + \left[\frac{d}{dx} g(x)\right] f(x)$

(iii) **Quotient Rule** Let $y = \frac{f(x)}{g(x)}; g(x) \neq 0$
Then, $\frac{dy}{dx} = \frac{g(x) \times \frac{dy}{dx}[f(x)] - f(x) \times \frac{dy}{dx}[g(x)]}{[g(x)]^2}$

(iv) **Chain Rule** Let $y = f(u)$ and $u = f(x)$, then using chain rule, we may write $\frac{dy}{dx} = \frac{dy}{du} \cdot \frac{du}{dx}$, when $\frac{dy}{du}$ and $\frac{du}{dx}$ both exist.

Differentiation of Parametric Functions
Let $x = f(t)$ and $y = g(t)$, where t is a parameter.

Then, $\frac{dy}{dx} = \frac{\left(\frac{dy}{dt}\right)}{\left(\frac{dx}{dt}\right)}$, whenever $\frac{dx}{dt} \neq 0$

$\frac{dy}{dx}$ is expressed in terms of parameter only without directly involving the main variables x and y.

Differentiation of a Function w.r.t. Another Function
Let $y = f(x)$ and $z = g(x)$
First differentiate both functions $f(x)$ and $g(x)$ with respect to x separately and then put these values in the following formulae $\frac{dy}{dz} = \frac{dy/dx}{dz/dx}$ or $\frac{dz}{dy} = \frac{dz/dx}{dy/dx}$

Second order Derivative
Let $y = f(x)$ ...(i)
$\frac{d}{dx}\left(\frac{dy}{dx}\right)$ is called the **second order derivative of** y w.r.t. x and it is denoted by $\frac{d^2y}{dx^2}$ or $f''(x)$ or y'' or D^2y or y_2.

Derivatives of Inverse Trigonometric Functions
(i) $\frac{d}{dx}(\sin^{-1} x) = \frac{1}{\sqrt{1-x^2}}$
(ii) $\frac{d}{dx}(\cos^{-1} x) = \frac{-1}{\sqrt{1-x^2}}$
(iii) $\frac{d}{dx}(\tan^{-1} x) = \frac{1}{1+x^2}$
(iv) $\frac{d}{dx}(\cot^{-1} x) = \frac{-1}{1+x^2}$
(v) $\frac{d}{dx}(\sec^{-1} x) = \frac{1}{x\sqrt{x^2-1}}$
(vi) $\frac{d}{dx}(\text{cosec}^{-1} x) = -\frac{1}{x\sqrt{x^2-1}}$

Differentiation of Implicit Functions
A function of the form $f(x, y) = 0$, where it is not possible to express y directly as a function of x in the form of $y = \phi(x)$, is said to be an **implicit function** of x and y.
e.g. $x + y = xy$
On differentiating both sides w.r.t x, we get

$$1 + \frac{dy}{dx} = \frac{xdy}{dx} + y \Rightarrow 1 - y = \frac{dy}{dx}(x-1) \Rightarrow \frac{1-y}{x-1} = \frac{dy}{dx}$$

Differentiation of Logarithmic Functions
Let $y = [f(x)]^{g(x)}$
On taking logarithm (to base e), we get
$\log y = g(x) \log(f(x))$
Using chain rule, we get $\frac{dy}{dx} = [f(x)]^{g(x)}\left[\frac{g(x)}{f(x)} f'(x) + g'(x) \log f(x)\right]$
Here, functions should always be positive otherwise their logarithms are not defined.

06

CHAPTER

If you do not know the names of things, the knowledge of them is lost, too.

— *Carl Linnaeus*

Application of Derivatives

YOUR STUDY GOALS

6.1 Rate of Change of Quantities
6.2 Increasing and Decreasing Functions
6.3 Maxima and Minima

YOUR PRACTICE GOALS

- Objective Type Questions (31 Qs ; 15 MCQs, 10 A-R, 6 Case Based)
- Subjective Type Questions (51 Qs ; 15 VSA , 21 SA, 15 LA)

6.1 Rate of Change of Quantities

Let $y = f(x)$ be a function of x. Then, $\frac{dy}{dx}$ represents the rate of change of y with respect to x.

Also, $\left(\frac{dy}{dx}\right)_{\text{at } x=x_0}$ represents the rate of change of y with respect to x at $x = x_0$.

- Suppose two variables are varying with respect to another variable t

  i.e. $\quad y = f(t)$ and $x = g(t)$.

  Then, rate of change of y with respect to x is given by

  $$\frac{dy}{dx} = \frac{dy}{dt} \cdot \frac{dt}{dx}. \qquad \text{[by chain rule of derivative]}$$

- $\frac{dy}{dx}$ is positive, if y increases as x increases and $\frac{dy}{dx}$ is negative, if y decreases as x increases.

6.2 Marginal Cost and Marginal Revenue

Marginal Cost

If $C(x)$ represents the cost function for x units produced, then marginal cost denoted by MC, is given by

$$MC = \frac{d}{dx}\{C(x)\}$$

Marginal Revenue

If $R(x)$ represents the revenue function for x units sold, then marginal revenue denoted by MR, is given by

$$MR = \frac{d}{dx}\{R(x)\}$$

If fixed cost and variable cost of a commodity are given, then total cost can be determined by the relation.

Total cost = Fixed cost + Variable cost

i.e. $C(x) = f(c) + v(x)$

Example 1 **The area of the circle is increasing at a uniform rate of 2 cm^2/sec. How fast is the circumference of the circle increasing when the radius $r = 5$ cm?** CBSE 2024

Sol. Let r be the radius, A be the area and C be the circumference of the circle at any time t.

Then, $A = \pi r^2$ and $C = 2\pi r$

It is given that $\frac{dA}{dt} = 2\ cm^2/s$

$$\Rightarrow \quad \frac{d}{dt}(\pi r^2) = 2$$

$$\Rightarrow \quad 2\pi r \cdot \frac{dr}{dt} = 2$$

$$\Rightarrow \quad \frac{dr}{dt} = \frac{1}{\pi r}$$

Now, $C = 2\pi r$

$$\Rightarrow \quad \frac{dC}{dt} = 2\pi \cdot \frac{dr}{dt} = 2\pi \times \frac{1}{\pi r}$$

$$\Rightarrow \quad \frac{dC}{dt} = \frac{2}{r}$$

$$\therefore \quad \left(\frac{dC}{dt}\right)_{r=5} = \frac{2}{5}\ cm/s$$

Example 2 **The volume of a cube is increasing at the rate of 8 cm^3/s. How fast is the surface area increasing when the length of its edge is 12 cm?** CBSE 2019

Sol. Let x be the length of an edge of the cube, V be the volume and S be the surface area at any time t.

Then, $V = x^3$ and $S = 6x^2$.

It is given that

$$\frac{dV}{dt} = 8\ cm^3/s$$

$$\Rightarrow \quad \frac{d}{dt}(x^3) = 8$$

$$\Rightarrow \quad 3x^2\frac{dx}{dt} = 8 \Rightarrow \frac{dx}{dt} = \frac{8}{3x^2}$$

Now, $S = 6x^2$

$$\Rightarrow \quad \frac{dS}{dt} = 12x\frac{dx}{dt} \Rightarrow \frac{dS}{dt} = 12x \times \frac{8}{3x^2}$$

$$\Rightarrow \quad \frac{dS}{dt} = \frac{32}{x}$$

$$\Rightarrow \quad \left(\frac{dS}{dt}\right)_{x=12} = \frac{32}{12}\ cm^2/s = \frac{8}{3}\ cm^2/s$$

Example 3 **Find the point on the curve $y^2 = 8x$ for which the abscissa and ordinate change at the same rate.** CBSE 2023

Sol. Let the required point be (x, y).

Given, $\frac{dy}{dt} = \frac{dx}{dt}$ ...(i)

and $y^2 = 8x$ ...(ii)

On differentiating both sides of Eq. (ii) w.r.t. t, we get

$$2y\frac{dy}{dt} = 8 \cdot \frac{dx}{dt}$$

$\Rightarrow \quad 2y = 8$ [from Eq. (i)]

$$\Rightarrow \quad y = 4$$

On putting $y = 4$ in Eq. (ii), we get

$$8x = 16$$

$$\Rightarrow \quad x = 2$$

Hence, the required point is (2, 4).

Example 4 **The radius r of a right circular cone is decreasing at the rate of 3 cm/min and the height h is increasing at the rate of 2 cm/min. When $r = 9$ cm and $h = 6$ cm, then find the rate of change of its volume.** CBSE 2017C

Sol. We have, $\frac{dr}{dt} = -3$ cm/min ...(i)

and $\frac{dh}{dt} = 2$ cm/min ...(ii)

Let V be the volume of a cone. Then,

$$V = \frac{1}{3}\pi r^2 h$$

$$\Rightarrow \quad \frac{dV}{dt} = \frac{1}{3}\pi\left(r^2 \cdot \frac{dh}{dt} + h \cdot 2r\frac{dr}{dt}\right)$$

$$\Rightarrow \quad \frac{dV}{dt} = \frac{1}{3}\pi\,[2r^2 + 2rh(-3)]$$

[using Eqs. (i) and (ii)]

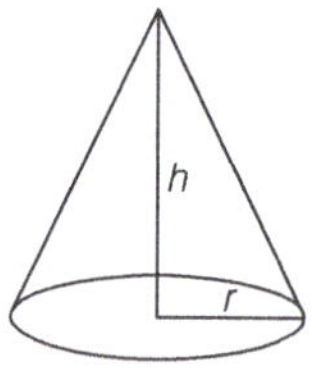

Now, $\frac{dV}{dt}$ when $r = 9$ and $h = 6$, is given by

$$\left(\frac{dV}{dt}\right)_{\text{at } r=9,\, h=6} = \frac{1}{3}\pi[2(9)^2 - 6(9)(6)]$$

$$= \frac{1}{3}\pi(162 - 324)$$

$$= \frac{1}{3}\pi(-162)$$

$$= -54\pi \text{ cm}^3/\text{min}$$

Thus, the volume is decreasing at the rate 54π cm^3/min.

Example 5 A man 1.6 m tall walks at the rate of 0.3 m/sec away from a street light that is 4 m above the ground. At what rate is the tip of his shadow moving? At what rate is his shadow lengthening?

CBSE Sample Paper 2023

Sol. Let AB represent the height of the street light from the ground.

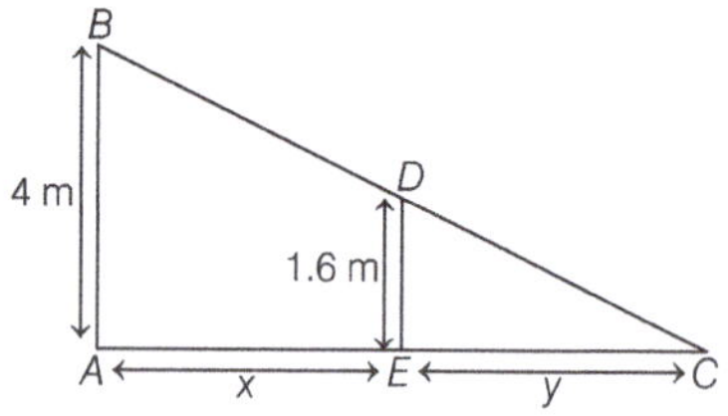

At any time t second, let the man represented as ED of height 1.6 m be at a distance of x metre from AB and the length of his shadow EC be y metre.

From similarity of ΔABC and ΔEDC, we get

$$\frac{4}{1.6} = \frac{x+y}{y}$$

$$\Rightarrow \quad 4y = 1.6x + 1.6y$$

$$\Rightarrow \quad 2.4y = 1.6x$$

$$\Rightarrow \quad 3y = 2x \quad \text{...(i)}$$

Now, on differentiating both sides of Eq. (i) w.r.t. t, we get

$$3\frac{dy}{dt} = 2\frac{dx}{dt}$$

$$\Rightarrow \quad \frac{dy}{dt} = \frac{2}{3} \times 0.3 \qquad \left[\because \frac{dx}{dt} = 0.3 \text{ m/s}\right]$$

$$\Rightarrow \quad \frac{dy}{dt} = 0.2$$

At any time t second, the tip of his shadow is at a distance of $(x + y)$ metre from AB.

$\therefore$ The rate at which the tip of his shadow is moving

$$= \left(\frac{dx}{dt} + \frac{dy}{dt}\right) = (0.3 + 0.2) = 0.5 \text{ m/s}$$

The rate at which his shadow is lengthening

$$= \frac{dy}{dt} = 0.2 \text{ m/s}$$

Example 6 The total cost $C(x)$ associated with the production of x units of an item is given by $C(x) = 0.005x^3 - 0.02x^2 + 30x + 5000$. Find the marginal cost when 3 units are produced, where by marginal cost, we mean the instantaneous rate of change of total cost at any level of output.

CBSE 2018

Sol. We have,

$$C(x) = 0.005x^3 - 0.02x^2 + 30x + 5000$$

Clearly, the marginal cost,

$$\text{MC}(x) = \frac{d}{dx}C(x)$$

$$= \frac{d}{dx}(0.005x^3 - 0.02x^2 + 30x + 5000)$$

$$= 0.005 \times 3x^2 - 0.02 \times 2x + 30 + 0$$

$$= 0.015x^2 - 0.04x + 30$$

Now, marginal cost when 3 units are produced,

$$\text{MC}(3) = 0.015(9) - 0.04(3) + 30$$

$$= 0.135 - 0.12 + 30$$

$$= 30.015 \text{ units}$$

Example 7 The total revenue (in ₹) received from the sale of x units of a product is given by $R(x) = 3x^2 + 6x + 5$. Find the marginal revenue, when $x = 5$.

NCERT

Sol. Given, $R(x) = 3x^2 + 6x + 5$

We know that marginal revenue is the rate of change of total revenue with respect to the number of units sold.

$\therefore$ Marginal revenue,

$$\text{MR} = \frac{dR}{dx} = 6x + 6$$

When $x = 5$, then

$$\text{MR} = 6(5) + 6 = 36$$

Hence, the required marginal revenue is ₹ 36.

Quick Test 1

1. The radius of an air bubble is increasing at the rate of $\frac{1}{2}$ cm/s. At what rate is the volume of bubble increasing, when the radius is 1 cm? NCERT
2. A balloon which always remains spherical on inflation is being inflated by pumping in 900 cu cm of gas per second. Find the rate at which the radius of the balloon increases, when the radius is 15 cm. NCERT
3. The length x of a rectangle is decreasing at the rate of 5 cm/min and the width y is increasing at the rate of 4 cm/min. When $x = 8$ cm and $y = 6$ cm, then find the rate of change of the area of rectangle. NCERT, CBSE 2017
4. The volume of a sphere is increasing at the rate of 8 cm^3/s. Find the rate at which its surface area is increasing when the radius of the sphere is 12 cm.
5. Sand is pouring from a pipe at the rate of 12 cm^3/s. The falling sand form a cone on the ground in such a way that the height of the cone is always one-sixth of the radius of the base. How fast is the height of the sand cone increasing when the height is 4 cm?
6. The volume of a cube is increasing at constant rate. Prove that the increase in surface area varies inversely as the length of the edge of the cube. Diksha App
7. A car starts from a point P at time $t = 0$ s and stops at Q. The distance x (in metres), covered by it in t seconds is given by $x = t^2\left(2 - \frac{t}{3}\right)$. Find the time taken by it to reach Q and also the distance P and Q.
8. Water is dripping out at a steady rate of 1 cm^3/s through a tiny hole at the vertex of the conical vessel, whose axis is vertical. When the slant height of water in the vessel is 4 cm, then find the rate of decrease of slant height, where the semi-vertical angle of the conical vessel is $\frac{\pi}{6}$.
9. If the total cost $C(x)$ (in ₹) associated with the production of x units of an item is given by $C(x) = 0.007x^3 - 0.003x^2 + 15x + 4000$, then find the marginal cost when 17 units are produced.
10. The total revenue in rupees received from the sale of x units of a product is given by $R(x) = 13x^2 + 26x + 15$. Find the marginal revenue, when $x = 7$.

Answers

1. 2π cm^3/s.	2. $\frac{1}{\pi}$ cm/sec	3. 2 cm^2/min
4. $\frac{4}{3}$ cm^2/sec	5. $\frac{1}{48\pi}$ cm/s	7. 4 sec, $\frac{32}{3}$ m
8. $\frac{1}{2\sqrt{3}\pi}$ cm/s	9. ₹ 20.967	10. ₹ 208

For Solutions, See QR Code on Pg. 186

6.3 Increasing and Decreasing Functions

Increasing Function

A function f is called a increasing function on interval I, if $x_1 < x_2$ in $I \Rightarrow f(x_1) \le f(x_2)$ for all $x_1, x_2 \in I$.

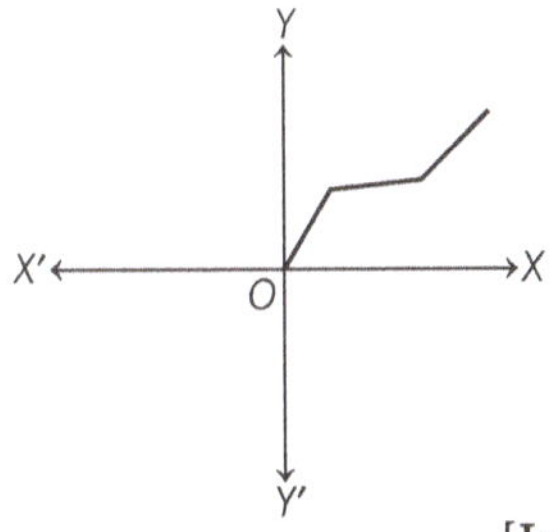

[Increasing curve]

Strictly Increasing Function

A function f is called a strictly increasing function on interval I, if $x_1 < x_2$ in I.

$\Rightarrow f(x_1) < f(x_2)$ for all $x_1, x_2 \in I$.

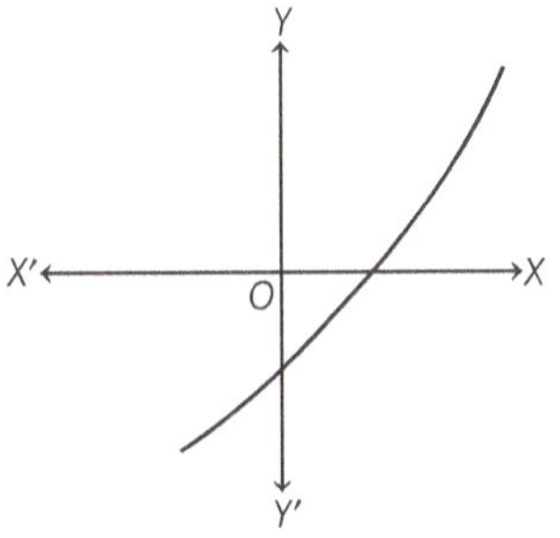

[Strictly increasing curve]

Decreasing Function

A function f is called a decreasing function on interval I, if $x_1 < x_2$ in I.

$\Rightarrow f(x_1) \ge f(x_2)$ for all $x_1, x_2 \in I$.

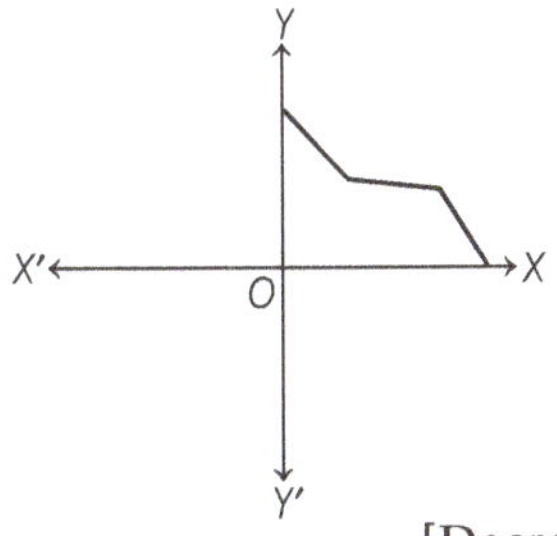

[Decreasing function]

Strictly Decreasing Function

A function f is called a strictly decreasing function on interval I, if $x_1 < x_2$ in I $\Rightarrow f(x_1) > f(x_2)$ for all $x_1, x_2 \in I$.

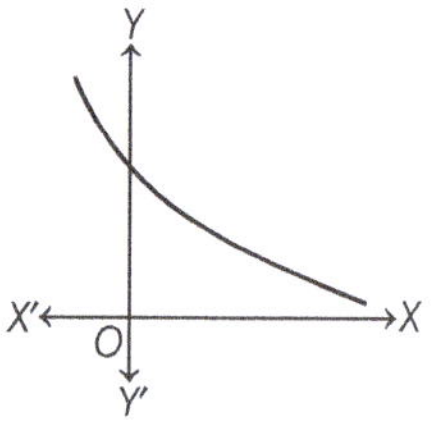

[Strictly decreasing function]

Theorem

Let f be continuous on $[a, b]$ and differentiable on the open interval (a, b).

Then,

- f is increasing function in $[a, b]$ if $f'(x) \geq 0$.
- f is strictly increasing in (a, b) if $f'(x) > 0$ for each $x \in (a, b)$.
- f is decreasing function in $[a, b]$ if $f'(x) \leq 0$.
- f is strictly decreasing in (a, b) if $f'(x) < 0$ for each $x \in (a, b)$.
- A function will be increasing (decreasing) in R, if it is so as even interval of R.

TEACHER TIPS

1. A function is increasing if its derivative is greater than zero, decreasing if its derivative is less than zero and constant if its derivative is zero.
2. An increasing function's graph goes upwards as you move from left to right along the X-axis, while a decreasing function's graph goes downward.
3. A strictly decreasing function is an decreasing function but a decreasing function may or may not be strictly decreasing (same is true for increasing function).

Example 1 Find the interval/s in which the function $f: R \rightarrow R$ defined by $f(x) = xe^x$, is increasing.

Sol. Given, $f(x) = xe^x$

On differentiating w.r.t. x, we get

$$f'(x) = xe^x + e^x = e^x(x+1)$$

For $f(x)$ to be increasing, we get

$$f'(x) = e^x(x+1) \geq 0$$

$$\Rightarrow \quad x \geq -1 \text{ as } e^x > 0, \forall\, x \in R$$

Hence, the required interval, where $f(x)$ increases is $[-1, \infty)$.

Example 2 Show that the function f defined by $f(x) = (x-1)e^x + 1$ is an increasing function for all $x > 0$. CBSE 2020

Sol. We have, $f(x) = (x-1)e^x + 1$

On differentiating w.r.t. x, we get

$$f'(x) = (x-1)e^x + e^x$$

$$\Rightarrow \quad f'(x) = xe^x, \forall\, x > 0$$

$$\Rightarrow \quad f'(x) > 0.$$

$\therefore f(x)$ is an increasing for all $x > 0$.

Example 3 Find whether the function $f(x) = \cos\left(2x + \frac{\pi}{4}\right)$ is increasing or decreasing in interval $\left(\frac{3\pi}{8}, \frac{5\pi}{8}\right)$. CBSE 2019

Sol. We have, $f(x) = \cos\left(2x + \frac{\pi}{4}\right)$

On differentiating w.r.t. x, we get

$$f'(x) = -2\sin\left(2x + \frac{\pi}{4}\right)$$

As $\quad \frac{3\pi}{8} < x < \frac{5\pi}{8}$

$$\Rightarrow \quad \frac{3\pi}{4} < 2x < \frac{5\pi}{4}$$

$$\Rightarrow \quad \pi < 2x + \frac{\pi}{4} < \frac{3\pi}{2}$$

$$\Rightarrow \quad \sin\left(2x + \frac{\pi}{4}\right) < 0 \Rightarrow f'(x) > 0$$

$\therefore f(x)$ is increasing in $\left(\frac{3\pi}{8}, \frac{5\pi}{8}\right)$.

Example 4 Show that the function $f(x) = 3x^2 - x + 1$ is neither increasing nor decreasing on (0, 1).

Sol. We have, $f(x) = 3x^2 - x + 1$

On differentiating w.r.t. x, we get

$$f'(x) = 6x - 1$$

Put $f'(x) = 0 \Rightarrow 6x - 1 = 0 \Rightarrow x = \frac{1}{6}$

Here, $f'(x) < 0$ when $x \in \left(0, \frac{1}{6}\right)$

and $\quad f'(x) > 0$ when $x \in \left(\frac{1}{6}, 1\right)$

Thus, $f(x)$ is decreasing in $\left(0, \frac{1}{6}\right)$ and increasing in $\left(\frac{1}{6}, 1\right)$.

Hence, the given function is neither increasing nor decreasing on (0, 1).

Example 5 **Find the interval in which the function $f(x) = 2x^3 - 3x$ is strictly increasing.** *CBSE 2023*

Sol. We have, $f(x) = 2x^3 - 3x$

$\therefore \quad f'(x) = 6x^2 - 3$

For strictly increasing,

put $\quad f'(x) > 0$

$\therefore \quad f'(x) = 6x^2 - 3 > 0$

$\Rightarrow \quad 6x^2 > 3$

$\Rightarrow \quad x^2 > \frac{1}{2}$

$\Rightarrow \quad |x| > \frac{1}{\sqrt{2}}$

$\Rightarrow \quad x \in R - \left[\frac{-1}{\sqrt{2}}, \frac{1}{\sqrt{2}}\right]$

So, $f(x)$ is strictly increasing in $R - \left[\frac{-1}{\sqrt{2}}, \frac{1}{\sqrt{2}}\right]$.

Example 6 **Show that the function $f(x) = \frac{16\sin x}{4 + \cos x} - x$, is strictly decreasing in $\left(\frac{\pi}{2}, \pi\right)$.** *CBSE 2023*

Sol. We have, $f(x) = \frac{16\sin x}{4 + \cos x} - x$

On differentiating both sides w.r.t. x, we get

$$f'(x) = \frac{(4 + \cos x)(16\cos x) - 16\sin x(-\sin x)}{(4 + \cos x)^2} - 1$$

$$= \frac{64\cos x + 16\cos^2 x + 16\sin^2 x}{(4 + \cos x)^2} - 1$$

$$= \frac{64\cos x + 16}{(4 + \cos x)^2} - 1 \qquad [\because \sin^2 x + \cos^2 x = 1]$$

$$= \frac{64\cos x + 16 - 16 - \cos^2 x - 8\cos x}{(4 + \cos x)^2}$$

$$= \frac{56\cos x - \cos^2 x}{(4 + \cos x)^2} = \frac{\cos x(56 - \cos x)}{(4 + \cos x)^2}$$

For all $x \in \left(\frac{\pi}{2}, \pi\right)$, $\frac{\cos x(56 - \cos x)}{(4 + \cos x)^2} < 0$

$\Rightarrow \quad f'(x) < 0, \forall x \in \left(\frac{\pi}{2}, \pi\right)$

$\therefore$ $f(x)$ is strictly decreasing in $\left(\frac{\pi}{2}, \pi\right)$.

Example 7 **Find the intervals in which the function f given by $f(x) = \tan x - 4x, x \in \left(0, \frac{\pi}{2}\right)$ is**

(i) strictly increasing

(ii) strictly decreasing *CBSE Sample Paper 2021*

Sol. We have, $f(x) = \tan x - 4x$

$\Rightarrow \quad f'(x) = \sec^2 x - 4$

(i) For $f(x)$ to be strictly increasing,

$f'(x) > 0$

$\Rightarrow \quad \sec^2 x - 4 > 0$

$\Rightarrow \quad \frac{1 - 4\cos^2 x}{\cos^2 x} > 0$

$\Rightarrow \quad \frac{(1 - 2\cos x)(1 + 2\cos x)}{\cos^2 x} > 0$

$\therefore \quad \cos x \in \left(-\frac{1}{2}, \frac{1}{2}\right)$

$\Rightarrow \quad x \in \left(\frac{\pi}{3}, \frac{\pi}{2}\right)$

$\therefore$ $f(x)$ is strictly increasing on $\left(\frac{\pi}{3}, \frac{\pi}{2}\right)$.

(ii) For $f(x)$ to be strictly decreasing,

$f'(x) < 0$

$\Rightarrow \quad \sec^2 x - 4 < 0$

$\Rightarrow \quad \frac{1 - 4\cos^2 x}{\cos^2 x} < 0$

$\Rightarrow \quad \frac{(1 - 2\cos x)(1 + 2\cos x)}{\cos^2 x} < 0$

$\Rightarrow \quad \cos x \in \left(-\infty, -\frac{1}{2}\right) \cup \left(\frac{1}{2}, \infty\right)$

$\Rightarrow \quad x \in \left(0, \frac{\pi}{3}\right) \qquad \left[\because x \in \left(0, \frac{\pi}{2}\right)\right]$

$\therefore$ $f(x)$ is strictly decreasing on $\left(0, \frac{\pi}{3}\right)$.

Quick Test 2

1. Find the interval in which the function $f(x)=2x^3+9x^2+12x+20$ is decreasing.

2. Find the interval in which the function $f(x)=x^x, x>0$ is increasing.

3. Find the intervals in which the function given by $f(x)=\sin 3x, x\in\left[0,\frac{\pi}{2}\right]$ is

(i) increasing (ii) decreasing

4. Show that the function $f(x)=\frac{x}{3}+\frac{3}{x}$ decrease in the interval $(-3,0)\cup(0,3)$. *CBSE 2020*

5. Show that the function given by $f(x)=e^{2x}$ is strictly increasing on R. *NCERT*

6. Find the interval in which the function $f(x)=2x^3+9x^2+12x-1$ is increasing or decreasing.

7. Determine for what values of x, the function $f(x)=x^3+\frac{1}{x^3}(x\neq 0)$ is strictly increasing or strictly decreasing? *CBSE Sample Paper 2017*

8. Find the intervals in which the function $f(x)=-3\log(1+x)+4\log(2+x)-\frac{4}{2+x}$ is strictly increasing or strictly decreasing. *CBSE Sample Paper 2018*

9. Find the intervals in which the function $f(x)=4\sin^3 x-6\sin^2 x+12\sin x+100$ is strictly decreasing in $\left(-\frac{\pi}{2},\pi\right)$.

10. Find the intervals in which $f(x)=\sin 3x-\cos 3x, 0<x<\pi$ is strictly increasing or strictly decreasing.

Answers

1. $(-2,-1)$ 2. $\left[\frac{1}{e},\infty\right)$

3. (i) Increasing in $\left[0,\frac{\pi}{6}\right)$ (ii) Decreasing in $\left(\frac{\pi}{6},\frac{\pi}{2}\right]$

6. Decreasing in $[-2,-1]$, Increasing in $(-\infty,-2]\cup[-1,\infty)$

7. $f(x)$ is strictly increasing for $x>1$ or $x<-1$ and strictly decreasing for $(-1,0)\cup(0,1)$.

8. Strictly increasing in $(0,\infty)$ and strictly decreasing in $(-1,0)$.

9. $\left(\frac{\pi}{2},\pi\right)$

10. f is strictly increasing in the intervals $\left(0,\frac{\pi}{4}\right)$ and $\left(\frac{7\pi}{12},\frac{11\pi}{12}\right)$ and f is strictly decreasing in the interval $\left(\frac{\pi}{4},\frac{7\pi}{12}\right)$ and $\left(\frac{11\pi}{12},\pi\right)$.

For Solutions, See QR Code on Pg. 186

6.4 Maxima and Minima

Maximum and Minimum Values in an Interval

Let f be a function defined in an interval I (i.e. I is the domain of f). Then,

(i) A function $f(x)$ is said to have a **maximum value** in I, if there exists a point c in interval I such that

$$f(c)>f(x),\ \forall\ x\in I$$

Here, the number $f(c)$ is called the maximum value of f in I and point c is called a **point of maximum value** of f in I.

(ii) A function $f(x)$ is said to have a **minimum value** in I, if there exists a point c in interval I such that

$$f(c)<f(x),\ \forall\ x\in I$$

Here, the number $f(c)$ is called the minimum value of f in I and the point c is called a **point of minimum value** of f in I.

(iii) f is said to have an **extreme value** in I, if there exists a point c in I such that $f(c)$ is either a maximum value or a minimum value of f in I. The number $f(c)$ is called an extreme value of f in I and the point c is called an **extreme point**.

Local Maxima and Local Minima

Let f be a real valued function and c be an interior point in the domain of f. Then,

- c is called a point of **local maxima**, if $h>0$ such that $f(c)>f(x),\ \forall\ x$ in $(c-h,c+h)$

  Here, value $f(c)$ is called the **local maximum value** (or relative maximum value) of f.

- c is called a point of **local minima**, if $h>0$ such that $f(c)<f(x),\ \forall\ x$ in $(c-h,c+h)$

  Here, value $f(c)$ is called the **local minimum value** (or relative minimum value) of f.

Geometrically, the graph of local maxima and local minima are shown below.

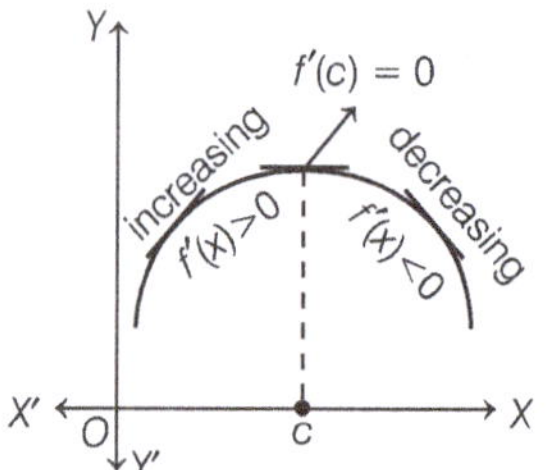

Local Maxima

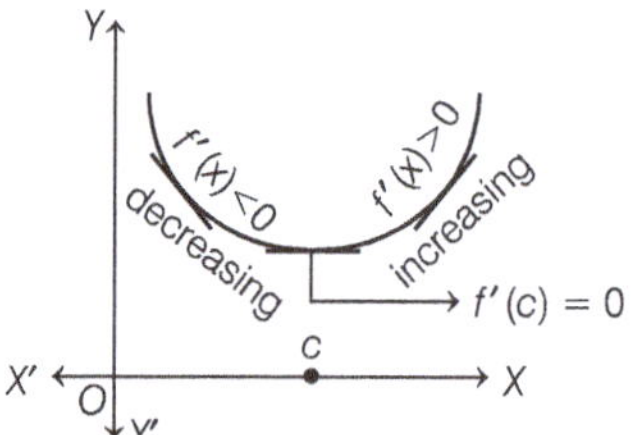

Local Minima

Some Important Theorems

Theorem 1 Let f be a function defined on an open interval I. Suppose $c \in I$ be any point. If f has a local maxima or a local minima at $x = c$, then either $f'(c) = 0$ or f is not differentiable at c.

The converse of above theorem need not be true.

e.g. If $f(x) = x^3$, then $f'(x) = 3x^2$ and so $f'(0) = 0$. But 0 is neither a point of local maxima nor a point of local minima.

Theorem 2 (First Derivative Test) Let f be a function defined on an open interval I and f be continuous at a critical point c in I.

(i) If $f'(x)$ changes sign from positive to negative as x increases through point c (i.e. $f'(x) > 0$ when $x \in (c-h, h)$ and $f'(x) < 0$ when $x \in (c, c+h)$, then c is a point of **local maxima.**

(ii) If $f'(x)$ changes sign from negative to positive as x increases through point c (i.e. $f'(x) < 0$, when $x \in (c-h, h)$ and $f'(x) > 0$, when $x \in (c, c+h)$, then c is a point of **local minima.**

Point of Inflection

If $f'(x)$ does not change sign as x increases through c, then c is neither a point of local maxima nor a point of local minima. Infact, such a point is called **point of inflection.**

Critical Point

A point c in the domain of a function f at which either $f'(c) = 0$ or f is not differentiable (i.e. $f'(c) = \infty$), is called a critical (stationary or turning) point of f.

Theorem 3 (Second Derivative Test)

Let f be a function defined on an interval I and $c \in I$ and f be twice differentiable at c. Then,

- $x = c$ is a point of local maxima, if
$$f'(c) = 0 \text{ and } f''(c) < 0$$
The value $f(c)$ is **local maximum value of f.**
- $x = c$ is a point of local minima, if $f'(c) = 0$ and $f''(c) > 0$.
The value $f(c)$ is **local minimum value of f.**
- The test fails, if $f'(c) = 0$ and $f''(c) = 0$. In this case, we go back to the first derivative test and find whether c is a point of local maxima, local minima or a point of inflection.

Maximum and Minimum Values of a Function in a Closed Interval

Theorem 4 Let f be a continuous function on an interval $I = [a, b]$. Then, f has the absolute maximum value and f attains it atleast once in I. Also, f has the absolute minimum value and attains it atleast once in I.

Theorem 5 Let f be a differentiable function on a closed interval I and c be any interior point of I. Then,

- $f'(c) = 0$, if f attains its absolute maximum value at c.
- $f'(c) = 0$, if f attains its absolute minimum value at c.

TEACHER TIPS

1. Every monotonic function i.e. either increasing or decreasing function assumes its maximum/minimum value at the end points of the domain of definition of the function.
2. Every continuous function on a closed interval has a maximum and a minimum value.
3. The highest point of a function within the entire domain is known as the absolute maximum of the function, whereas the lowest point of the function within the entire domain of the function, is known as the absolute minimum of the function.

Example 1 **Find the maximum and minimum values of the function $f(x) = |\cos(4x+5)|$.**

Sol. We have, $f(x) = |\cos(4x+5)|$

We know that maximum value of $|\cos\theta|$ is 1, so the maximum value of $|\cos(4x+5)|$ is 1.

As absolute value is non-negative. So, the minimum value of $|\cos(4x+5)|$ is 0.

Example 2 **Find the local maxima or local minima, if any, of the function $f(x) = \dfrac{1}{x^2+5}$.**

Sol. We have, $f(x) = \dfrac{1}{x^2+5} \Rightarrow f'(x) = \dfrac{-2x}{(x^2+5)^2}$

For a local maxima or local minima,

put $f'(x) = 0 \Rightarrow -\dfrac{2x}{(x^2+5)^2} = 0 \Rightarrow x = 0$

Now, when x is slightly less than 0, i.e. when x is negative, then $f'(x) = -\dfrac{2x}{(x^2+5)^2}$ is positive.

When x is slightly greater than 0, then

$f'(x) = -\dfrac{2x}{(x^2+5)^2}$ is negative.

Thus, $f'(x)$ changes sign from positive to negative.

So, $x = 0$ is a point of local maxima and local maximum value is $f(0) = \dfrac{1}{0+5} = \dfrac{1}{5}$.

Example 3 **Find all the points of local maxima and minima of the function**

$$f(x) = x^3 - 6x^2 + 9x - 8.$$

Sol. We have, $f(x) = x^3 - 6x^2 + 9x - 8$

On differentiating both sides w.r.t. x, we get

$$f'(x) = 3x^2 - 12x + 9$$

Put $f'(x) = 0$

$\Rightarrow \quad 3x^2 - 12x + 9 = 0$

$\Rightarrow \quad 3(x^2 - 4x + 3) = 0$

$\Rightarrow \quad 3(x-1)(x-3) = 0 \qquad ...(i)$

$\Rightarrow \quad x = 1, 3$

These are the critical points.

Now, for values close to 1 and to the right of 1, $f'(x) < 0$ and for values close to 1 and to the left of 1, $f'(x) > 0$.

$\therefore$ $x = 1$ is a point of local maxima.

For values close to 3 and to the right of 3, $f'(x) > 0$ and for values close to 3 and to the left of 3, $f'(x) < 0$.

$\therefore$ $x = 3$ is a point of local minima.

Hence, $x = 1$ is a point of local maxima and $x = 3$ is a point of local minima for given function.

Example 4 **Find the points of local maxima and local minima of the function $f(x) = (x-1)^3 (x+1)^2$. Also, find the local maximum and minimum values of $f(x)$.**

Sol. We have, $f(x) = (x-1)^3 (x+1)^2$

$\therefore$ $f'(x) = 3(x-1)^2 (x+1)^2 + (x-1)^3\, 2(x+1)$

$= (x-1)^2 (x+1)[3(x+1) + 2(x-1)]$

$= (x-1)^2 (x+1)(5x+1)$

For local maxima or local minima, put $f'(x) = 0$,

$(x-1)^2 (x+1)(5x+1) = 0$

$\Rightarrow \quad x = -\frac{1}{5}, -1, 1$

For $x = -1$, $f'(x) > 0$ to the left of $x = -1$ and $f'(x) < 0$ to the right of $x = -1$.

$\therefore$ $x = -1$ is a point of local maxima.

For $x = -\frac{1}{5}$, $f'(x) < 0$ to the left of $x = -\frac{1}{5}$ and $f'(x) > 0$ to the right of $x = -\frac{1}{5}$.

$\therefore$ $x = -\frac{1}{5}$ is a point of local minima.

For $x = 1$, $f'(x) > 0$ to the left of $x = 1$ and $f'(x) > 0$ to the right of $x = 1$.

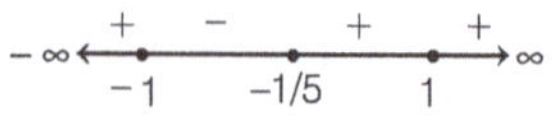

$\therefore$ $x = 1$ is neither a point of local maxima nor local minima.

Thus, we have the following table

Value of x		Sign of $f'(x)$	Nature of point
Close to -1	to the right of -1	< 0	Local maxima
	and to the left of -1	> 0	
Close to $\frac{-1}{5}$	to the right of $\frac{-1}{5}$	> 0	Local minima
	and to the left of $\frac{-1}{5}$	< 0	
Close to 1	to the right of 1	> 0	Neither local maxima nor local minima
	and to the left of 1	> 0	

At $x = \frac{-1}{5}$,

$$f\left(-\frac{1}{5}\right) = \left(-\frac{1}{5} - 1\right)^3 \left(-\frac{1}{5} + 1\right)^2 = \left(\frac{-6}{5}\right)^3 \left(\frac{4}{5}\right)^2 = -\frac{3456}{3125}$$

At $x = -1$, $f(-1) = (-1-1)^3 (-1+1)^2 = 0$

Hence, the point of local maxima is -1 and the local maximum value $= 0$ and the point of local minima is $-\frac{1}{5}$ and the local minimum value $= \frac{-3456}{3125}$.

Also, point $x = 1$ is the point of inflection.

Example 5 **If $f(x) = \frac{1}{4x^2 + 2x + 1}$, $x \in R$, then find the maximum value of $f(x)$.** *CBSE Sample Paper 2023*

Sol. $f(x) = \frac{1}{4x^2 + 2x + 1}$

On differentiating w.r.t. x, we get

$$f'(x) = \frac{-1(8x+2)}{(4x^2 + 2x + 1)^2} \qquad ...(i)$$

For maxima or minima, we put

$f'(x) = 0$

$\Rightarrow \quad 8x + 2 = 0 \Rightarrow x = -\frac{1}{4}$

Again, on differentiating Eq. (i) w.r.t. x, we get

$$f''(x) = \frac{-8(4x^2 + 2x + 1)^2 + (8x+2) \times 2(4x^2 + 2x + 1)(8x+2)}{(4x^2 + 2x + 1)^4}$$

At $x = \frac{-1}{4}$, $f''\left(\frac{-1}{4}\right) < 0$

$\Rightarrow f(x)$ is maximum at $x = \frac{-1}{4}$.

$\therefore$ Maximum value of $f(x)$ is

$$f\left(\frac{-1}{4}\right) = \frac{1}{4\left(\frac{-1}{4}\right)^2 + 2\left(\frac{-1}{4}\right) + 1} = \frac{1}{\frac{1}{4} + \frac{1}{2}} = \frac{4}{3}$$

Example 6 **Find the maximum profit that a company can make, if the profit function is given by $P(x) = 72 + 42x - x^2$, where x is the number of units and P is the profit in rupees.** *CBSE Sample Paper 2023*

Sol. Given, $P(x) = 72 + 42x - x^2$

On differentiating w.r.t. x, we get

$$P'(x) = 42 - 2x$$

For maximum profit, we put

$$P'(x) = 0$$

$$\Rightarrow \quad 42 - 2x = 0$$

$$\Rightarrow \quad x = 21$$

Now, $P''(x) = -2$

$\because P''(x) < 0.$

$\therefore P(x)$ is maximum at $x = 21$.

$\therefore$ The maximum value of $P(x)$ is at $x = 21$

$$\Rightarrow \quad P(21) = 72 + 42(21) - 21^2$$

$$= 72 + 882 - 441$$

$$= 513$$

Thus, the maximum profit is ₹ 513.

Example 7 **Find the dimensions of the rectangle of perimeter 36 cm which will sweep out a volume as large as possible, when revolved about one of its side. Also, find the maximum volume.** *CBSE 2020*

Sol. Here, $ABCD$ is a rectangle with length $AD = y$ cm and breadth $AB = x$ cm.

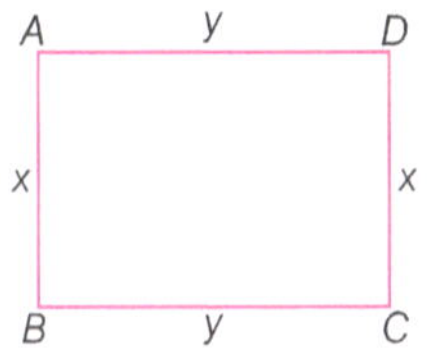

The rectangle is rotated about AD. Let V be the volume of the cylinder.

$$\therefore \quad V = \pi x^2 y \quad \text{...(i)}$$

Perimeter of rectangle $= 2(x + y)$

$$\Rightarrow \quad 36 = 2(x + y) \Rightarrow y = 18 - x$$

Now, $V = \pi x^2 (18 - x) \Rightarrow V = \pi(18x^2 - x^3)$

$$\Rightarrow \quad \frac{dV}{dx} = \pi(36x - 3x^2)$$

For maxima or minima, put $\frac{dV}{dx} = 0$

$$\Rightarrow \quad \pi(36x - 3x^2) = 0 \Rightarrow x = 12, x \neq 0$$

Now, $$\frac{d^2V}{dx^2} = \pi(36 - 6x)$$

$$\left(\frac{d^2V}{dx^2}\right)_{x=12} = \pi(36 - 72) = -36\pi < 0$$

$\therefore$ Volume is maximum when $x = 12$ cm.

$\therefore \; y = 18 - x = 18 - 12 = 6$ cm

Hence, the dimension of rectangle, which have maximum volume, when revolved about one of its side is $12 \text{ cm} \times 6 \text{ cm}$.

$\therefore$ Maximum volume of cylinder,

$$V_{x=12} = \pi[18(12)^2 - (12)^3]$$

$$= \pi(12)^2 \cdot [18 - 12]$$

$$= 864\pi \text{ cm}^3$$

Example 8 **All the closed right circular cylindrical cans of volume $128\pi \text{ cm}^3$, find the dimensions of the can which has minimum surface area.** *CBSE 2014*

Sol. Let r cm be the radius of the base and h cm be the height of the cylindrical can. Let its volume be V and S be its total surface area.

Then, $\quad V = 128\pi \text{ cm}^3$ [given]

$$\Rightarrow \quad \pi r^2 h = 128\pi$$

$$\Rightarrow \quad h = \frac{128}{r^2} \quad \text{...(i)}$$

Also, $\quad S = 2\pi r^2 + 2\pi r h$ ...(ii)

$$\Rightarrow \quad S = 2\pi r^2 + 2\pi r\left(\frac{128}{r^2}\right) \quad \text{[using Eq.(i)]}$$

$$\Rightarrow \quad S = 2\pi r^2 + \frac{256\pi}{r} \quad \text{...(iii)}$$

On differentiating both sides of Eq. (iii) w.r.t. r, we get

$$\frac{dS}{dr} = 4\pi r - \frac{256\pi}{r^2} \quad \text{...(iv)}$$

For maxima or minima, put $\frac{dS}{dr} = 0$

$$\Rightarrow \quad 4\pi r = \frac{256\pi}{r^2}$$

$$\Rightarrow \quad r^3 = 64$$

On taking cube root on both sides, we get

$$r = (64)^{1/3}$$

$$\Rightarrow \quad r = 4$$

Again, on differentiating Eq. (iv) w.r.t. r, we get

$$\frac{d^2S}{dr^2} = 4\pi + \frac{512\pi}{r^3}$$

At $r = 4$, $$\frac{d^2S}{dr^2} = \frac{512\pi}{64} + 4\pi$$

$$= 8\pi + 4\pi = 12\pi > 0$$

By second derivative test, the surface area is minimum, when the radius of cylinder is 4 cm.

On putting the value of r in Eq. (i), we get

$$h = \frac{128}{(4)^2} = \frac{128}{16} = 8 \text{ cm}$$

Hence, for the minimum surface area of can, the dimensions are $r = 4$ cm and $h = 8$ cm.

Example 9 **Find absolute maximum and minimum values of a function f given by**

$$f(x) = 12x^{4/3} - 6x^{1/3}, x \in [-1, 1].$$ NCERT

Sol. We have, $f(x) = 12x^{4/3} - 6x^{1/3}$

On differentiating both sides w.r.t. x, we get

$$f'(x) = 12 \times \frac{4}{3} x^{1/3} - 6 \times \frac{1}{3} x^{-2/3}$$

$$= 16x^{1/3} - \frac{2}{x^{2/3}} = \frac{2(8x-1)}{x^{2/3}}$$

For critical points, put $f'(x) = 0$

$$\Rightarrow \quad \frac{2(8x-1)}{x^{2/3}} = 0 \Rightarrow 8x - 1 = 0 \Rightarrow x = \frac{1}{8}$$

Also, $f'(x)$ is not defined at $x = 0$, so critical points are $x = 0$ and $x = \frac{1}{8}$ and end points of interval are -1 and 1.

Now, $f(-1) = 12(-1)^{4/3} - 6(-1)^{1/3} = 12 + 6 = 18$

$$f(0) = 12(0) - 6(0) = 0$$

$$f\left(\frac{1}{8}\right) = 12\left(\frac{1}{8}\right)^{4/3} - 6\left(\frac{1}{8}\right)^{1/3} = 12\left(\frac{1}{16}\right) - 6\left(\frac{1}{2}\right) = \frac{-9}{4}$$

and $\quad f(1) = 12(1)^{4/3} - 6(1)^{1/3} = 6$

Hence, absolute maximum value of function f is 18 at $x = -1$ and absolute minimum value of function f is $\frac{-9}{4}$ at $x = \frac{1}{8}$.

EXAMPLE 10 **Find the maximum and minimum values of $(x + \sin 2x)$ on $[0, \pi]$.**

Sol. Let $f(x) = x + \sin 2x$

On differentiating both sides w.r.t. x, we get

$$f'(x) = (1 + 2\cos 2x)$$

For critical points, put $f'(x) = 0$

$$\Rightarrow \quad \cos 2x = \frac{-1}{2}, \text{ where } x \in [0, \pi]$$

$$\Rightarrow \quad 2x = \frac{2\pi}{3}, \frac{4\pi}{3} \Rightarrow x = \frac{\pi}{3}, \frac{2\pi}{3}$$

Now, $f\left(\frac{\pi}{3}\right) = \frac{\pi}{3} + \sin\frac{2\pi}{3} = \frac{\pi}{3} + \frac{\sqrt{3}}{2} = \frac{2\pi + 3\sqrt{3}}{6}$,

$$f\left(\frac{2\pi}{3}\right) = \frac{2\pi}{3} + \sin\frac{4\pi}{3} = \frac{2\pi}{3} - \sin\frac{\pi}{3} = \frac{4\pi - 3\sqrt{3}}{6},$$

$$f(0) = 0 \text{ and } f(\pi) = \pi + \sin 2\pi = \pi$$

Hence, the minimum value of $f(x)$ is 0 at $x = 0$ and the maximum value of $f(x)$ is π at $x = \pi$.

EXAMPLE 11 **A wire of length 25 m is to be cut into two pieces. One of the wires is to be made into a square and the other into a circle. What should be the lengths of the two pieces so that the combined area of the square and the circle is minimum?**

Sol. Let x m and $(25 - x)$ m be the required lengths for square and circle, respectively.

Again, let a be the side of the square formed and r be the radius of the circle formed.

Then, $4a = x$ and $2\pi r = 25 - x \Rightarrow a = \frac{x}{4}$ and $r = \frac{25 - x}{2\pi}$

$\therefore$ Area of the square $= a^2 = \left(\frac{x^2}{16}\right)$ sq m

and area of the circle $= \pi r^2 = \pi\left(\frac{25-x}{2\pi}\right)^2 = \frac{(25-x)^2}{4\pi}$

Now, combined area, $A = \frac{x^2}{16} + \frac{(25-x)^2}{4\pi}$

On differentiating both sides w.r.t. x, we get

$$\frac{dA}{dx} = \frac{x}{8} - \frac{(25-x)}{2\pi} = \frac{(\pi+4)x - 100}{8\pi} \text{ and } \frac{d^2A}{dx^2} = \frac{(\pi+4)}{8\pi}$$

For maxima or minima, put $\frac{dA}{dx} = 0$

$$\Rightarrow \frac{(\pi+4)x - 100}{8\pi} = 0 \Rightarrow x = \frac{100}{(\pi+4)};$$

$$\frac{d^2A}{dx^2} = \frac{(\pi+4)}{8\pi} > 0$$

$\therefore$ Combined area of the square and the circle is minimum at $x = \frac{100}{\pi + 4}$.

$\therefore \quad x = \frac{100}{(\pi+4)}$ is a point of local minima.

Hence, the lengths of pieces are $\left(\frac{100}{\pi+4}\right)$ m and $\left(\frac{25\pi}{\pi+4}\right)$ m, respectively.

EXAMPLE 12 **Show that the height of the cylinder of maximum volume that can be inscribed in a sphere of radius R is $\frac{2R}{\sqrt{3}}$. Find the volume of the largest cylinder inscribed in a sphere of radius R.** CBSE 2019, NCERT

Sol. Let we have a sphere of radius R and a cylinder is inscribed in it. $EB = r$ be the radius of the cylinder and $BC = h$ be the height of cylinder.

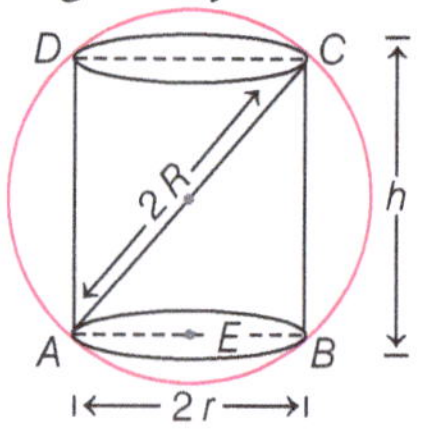

In right angled ΔABC, we get

$$(AC)^2 = (AB)^2 + (BC)^2 \quad \text{[using Pythagoras theorem]}$$

$$\Rightarrow \quad (2R)^2 = (2r)^2 + h^2$$

$$\Rightarrow \quad 4R^2 = 4r^2 + h^2$$

$$\Rightarrow \quad r^2 = \frac{1}{4}(4R^2 - h^2) \qquad \text{...(i)}$$

Volume of cylinder, $V = \pi r^2 h$

$$\Rightarrow \quad V = \pi\left[\frac{1}{4}(4R^2 - h^2)\right]h \quad \text{[from Eq. (i)]}$$

$$\Rightarrow \quad V = \frac{\pi}{4}(4R^2h - h^3) \qquad \text{...(ii)}$$

On differentiating V w.r.t. h, we get

$$\frac{dV}{dh} = \frac{\pi}{4}(4R^2 - 3h^2) \qquad \text{...(iii)}$$

For maxima or minima, put $\frac{dV}{dh} = 0$

$$\Rightarrow \frac{\pi}{4}(4R^2 - 3h^2) = 0 \Rightarrow 4R^2 = 3h^2$$

$$\Rightarrow \quad h = \frac{2R}{\sqrt{3}} \quad [\because \text{height cannot be negative}]$$

On differentiating both sides of Eq. (iii) w.r.t. h, we get

$$\frac{d^2V}{dh^2} = -\frac{3}{2}\pi h$$

At $h = \frac{2R}{\sqrt{3}}, \frac{d^2V}{dh^2} = -\frac{3}{2}\pi \times \frac{2R}{\sqrt{3}} = -\sqrt{3}\,\pi R < 0 \quad [\because R > 0]$

$\therefore$ Volume of cylinder is maximum at $h = \frac{2R}{\sqrt{3}}$.

From Eq. (i), we get $r^2 = \frac{1}{4}\left(4R^2 - \frac{4R^2}{3}\right) = \frac{2R^2}{3}$

$\therefore$ Volume of largest cylinder inscribed in a sphere,

$$V = \pi\left(\frac{2R^2}{3}\right) \times \frac{2R}{\sqrt{3}}$$

$$= \frac{1}{\sqrt{3}} \times \left(\frac{4}{3}\pi R^3\right)$$

$$= \frac{1}{\sqrt{3}} \times \text{Volume of sphere}$$

Hence, the height of the cylinder of maximum volume is $\frac{2R}{\sqrt{3}}$ and volume of largest cylinder inscribed in sphere is $\frac{1}{\sqrt{3}}$ times volume of sphere.

Quick Test 3

1. Find the maximum and minimum values of the function $f(x) = \frac{(x-1)(x-6)}{x-10}, x \neq 0.$
2. Find all the points of local maxima and local minima of the function
$$f(x) = -\frac{3}{4}x^4 - 8x^3 - \frac{45}{2}x^2 + 105.$$
NCERT Exemplar
3. Find the local maxima and local minima. Also, determine the local maximum and local minimum values of function $f(x) = \log(3x+8)$.
4. Find the least value of $f(x) = e^x + e^{-x}$.
5. Find the two positive numbers x and y such that $x + y = 60$ and xy^3 is maximum. *Competency Based Que*
6. The sum of the perimeter of a circle and square is k, where k is some constant. Prove that the sum of their areas is least, when the side of square is double the radius of the circle. *Competency Based Que*
7. Manufacturer can sell x items at a price of ₹$\left(5 - \frac{x}{100}\right)$ each. The cost price is ₹$\left(\frac{x}{5} + 500\right)$. Then, find the number of items, he should sell to earn maximum profit.
8. If the sum of the lengths of the hypotenuse and a side of a right triangle are given, then show that the area of the triangle is maximum, when the angle between them is $\frac{\pi}{3}$.
NCERT Exemplar, CBSE 2017, 14
9. Find the maximum and minimum values of $g(x) = 3x^4 - 8x^3 + 12x^2 - 48x + 25$ on $[0, 3]$.
Competency Based Que

Answers

1. Minimum value = 25, maximum value = 1
2. Local maxima at $x = 0, -5$
   Local minima at $x = -3$
3. No local maximum and local minimum values exist.
4. Least value = 2
5. Numbers are 15 and 45.
7. Required number of items = 240
9. Maximum value = 25, Minimum value = −39

For Solutions, See QR Code on Pg. 186

EXAM PATTERN QUESTIONS

Objective Type Questions

Multiple Choice Questions

1. Edge of a variable cube increases at the rate of 5cm/s. The rate at which the surface area of the cube increases when the edge is 2 cm long is **CBSE 2025**

(a) 24 cm^2/s (b) 120 cm^2/s
(c) 12 cm^2/s (d) 5 cm^2/s

2. For $0 < \theta < \frac{\pi}{2}$, the value of θ, if it increases twice as fast as its sine, is

(a) $\frac{\pi}{2}$ (b) $\frac{\pi}{3}$
(c) $\frac{\pi}{6}$ (d) None of these

3. Given a curve $y = 7x - x^3$ and x increases at the rate of 2 units per sec. The rate at which the slope of the curve is changing when $x = 5$ is **CBSE 2024**

(a) – 60 units/sec (b) 60 units/sec
(c) – 70 units/sec (d) – 140 units/sec

4. If the radius of a circle is increasing at the rate of 0.5 cm/s, then the rate of increase of its circumference is **CBSE 2024C**

(a) $\frac{2\pi}{3}$ cm/s (b) π cm/s
(c) $\frac{4\pi}{3}$ cm/s (d) 2π cm/s

5. The function $f(x) = x^3 + 3x$ is increasing in interval **CBSE 2023**

(a) $(-\infty, 0)$ (b) $(0, \infty)$ (c) R (d) (0, 1)

6. The interval in which the function $f(x) = 2x^3 + 9x^2 + 12x - 1$ is decreasing is **CBSE 2023**

(a) $(-1, \infty)$ (b) $(-2, -1)$
(c) $(-\infty, -2)$ (d) $(-1, 1)$

7. If $f : R \to R$ is defined as $f(x) = 2x - \sin x$, then f is **CBSE 2025**

(a) a decreasing function (b) an increasing function
(c) maximum at $x = \frac{\pi}{2}$ (d) maximum at $x = 0$

8. The real function $f(x) = 2x^3 - 3x^2 - 36x + 7$ is **CBSE 2022 (Term I)**

(a) strictly increasing in $(-\infty, -2)$ and strictly decreasing in $(-2, \infty)$
(b) strictly decreasing in $(-2, 3)$
(c) strictly decreasing in $(-\infty, 3)$ and strictly increasing in $(3, \infty)$
(d) strictly decreasing in $(-\infty, -2) \cup (3, \infty)$

9. The value of b for which the function $f(x) = x + \cos x + b$ is strictly decreasing over R is **CBSE 2022 (Term I)**

(a) $b < 1$
(b) no value of b exist
(c) $b \le 1$
(d) $b \ge 1$

10. The function $y = x^2 e^{-x}$ is decreasing in the interval **CBSE 2022 (Term I)**

(a) (0, 2)
(b) $(2, \infty)$
(c) $(-\infty, 0)$
(d) $(-\infty, 0) \cup (2, \infty)$

11. If the function $f(x) = 2x^2 - kx + 5$ is increasing on [1, 2], then k lies in the interval **Diksha App**

(a) $(-\infty, 4)$ (b) $(4, \infty)$
(c) $(-\infty, 8)$ (d) $(8, \infty)$

12. If the function f is given by $f(x) = x^3 - 3x^2 + 4x, x \in R$, then

(a) f is strictly increasing on R
(b) f is decreasing on R
(c) f is neither increasing nor decreasing on R
(d) f is strictly decreasing on R

13. The minimum value of $f(x) = x \log_e x$ is equal to **Diksha App**

(a) e (b) $\frac{1}{e}$ (c) $-\frac{1}{e}$ (d) $2e$

14. If the function f is given by $f(x) = x^3 - 3x + 3$, then

(a) $x = \pm 2$ are the only critical points for local maxima or local minima.
(b) $x = 3$ is a point of local minima.
(c) local minimum value is 2.
(d) local maximum value is 5.

15. The smallest value of polynomial $x^3 - 18x^2 + 96x$ in [0, 9] is

(a) 126 (b) 0
(c) 135 (d) 160

Assertion-Reason Based Questions

Directions (Q. Nos. 16-25) *In the questions given below are two statements labelled as Assertion (A) and Reason (R). In the context of the two statements, which one of the following is correct?*

(a) Both A and R are correct; R is the correct explanation of A.
(b) Both A and R are correct; R is not the correct explanation of A.
(c) A is correct; R is incorrect.
(d) R is correct; A is incorrect.

16. **Assertion** (A) The rate of change of area of a circle with respect to its radius r when $r = 3$ cm, is 6π cm^2/cm.

Reason (R) Rate of change of area of a circle with respect to its radius r is $\frac{dA}{dr}$, where A is the area of the circle.

17. **Assertion** (A) A balloon, which always remains spherical, has a variable radius. The rate, at which its volume is increasing with the radius when the radius is 10 cm, is 400 π cm^3/cm.

Reason (R) Rate of change of volume V of balloon with respect to radius r is $\frac{dV}{dr} = \left(\frac{2}{3}\pi\right) \cdot 3r^2$.

18. **Assertion** (A) The side of an equilateral triangle is increasing at the rate of 0.5 cm/s, then the rate of increase of its perimeter is 2.5 cm/s.

Reason (R) Rate of change in side of a triangle with side a is $\frac{da}{dt}$, then rate of change in the perimeter of triangle $= \frac{dP}{dt}$, where P = perimeter.

19. **Assertion** (A) If the total revenue (in rupees) received from the sale of x units of an article is given by $R(x) = 3x^2 + 36x + 5$, then the marginal revenue when $x = 15$ is ₹ 126.

Reason (R) If $R(x)$ is the revenue function for x units sold, then marginal revenue

$$\text{MR} = \frac{d}{dx}\{R(x)\}$$

20. **Assertion** (A) The function $f(x) = 4x + 3, x \in R$ is an increasing function.

Reason (R) Let $f(x)$ be a function. Then, $f(x)$ is increasing function, if $f'(x) > 0$.

21. **Assertion** (A) Function $f(x) = \tan x - x$ always increases.

Reason (R) Any function $y = f(x)$ is increasing, if $\frac{dy}{dx} < 0$.

22. **Assertion** (A) The function is given by $f(x) = x^4$ is decreasing in the interval $(0, \infty)$.

Reason (R) Any function $y = f(x)$ is decreasing, if $\frac{dy}{dx} < 0$.

23. **Assertion** (A) The function $f(x) = x^2 - 4x + 6$ is strictly increasing in the interval $(2, \infty)$.

Reason (R) The function $f(x) = x^2 - 4x + 6$ is strictly decreasing in the interval $(-\infty, 2)$.

24. Consider the information given below.
The function f is given by

$$f(x) = 2x^3 - 3x^2 - 36x + 7.$$

Assertion (A) The given function f is strictly increasing in intervals $(-\infty, +2)$ and $(-3, \infty)$.

Reason (R) The given function f is strictly decreasing in interval $(-2, 3)$.

25. **Assertion** (A) The slope of the curve $y = -x^3 + 3x^2 + 9x - 27$ is maximum at the point $(1, -16)$.

Reason (R) Let f be a function defined on an interval I and $c \in I$ and also, if f be twice differentiable at c, then $x = c$ is a point of local maxima if $f'(c) = 0$ and $f''(c) < 0$ and the value $f(c)$ is local maximum value of f.

Case Study Based Questions

26. A rectangular visiting card is to contain 24 sq cm of printed matter. The margins at the top and bottom of the card are to be 1 cm and the margins on the left and right are to be $1\frac{1}{2}$ cm as shown below.

CBSE 2024

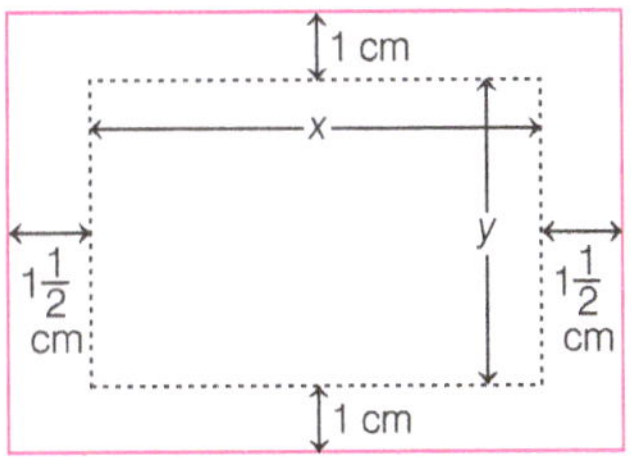

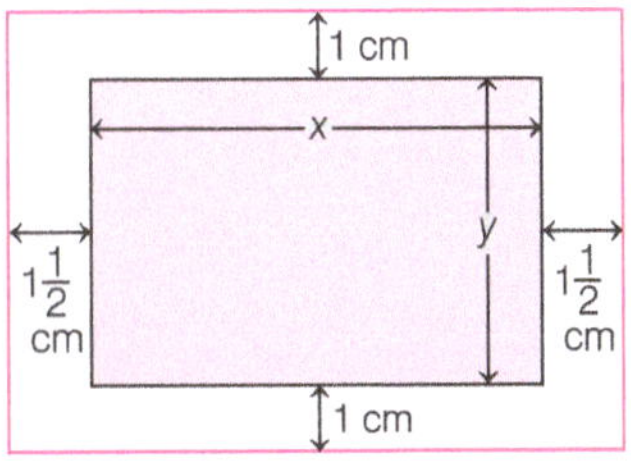

On the basis of the above information, answer the following questions.

(i) Write the expression for the area of the visiting card in terms of x.

(ii) Obtain the dimensions of the card of minimum area.

27. In order to set up a rainwater harvesting system, a tank to collect rainwater is to be dug. The tank should have a square base and a capacity of 250 m^3. The cost of land is ₹ 5000 per m^2 and cost of digging increases with depth and for the whole tank, it is $40000 h^2$, where h is the depth of the tank in metres. x is the side of the square base of the tank in metres.

Elements of a Typical Rainwater Harvesting System

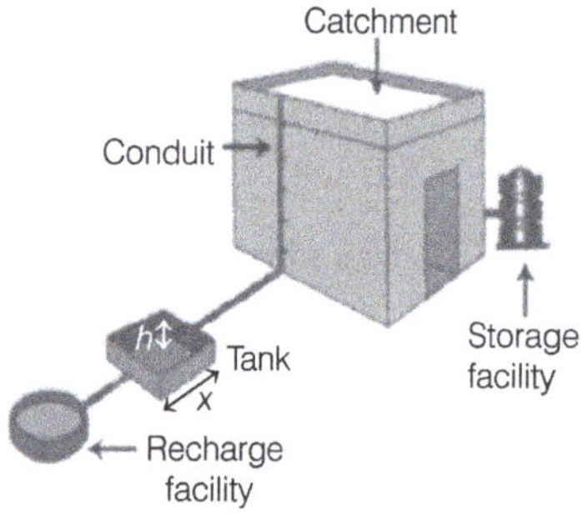

Based on the above information, answer the following questions.

(i) Find the total cost C of digging the tank in terms of x.

(ii) Find $\frac{dC}{dx}$.

(iii) (a) Find the value of x for which cost C is minimum.

Or

(b) Check whether the cost function $C(x)$ expressed in terms of x is increasing or not, where $x > 0$.

28. A channel company in a town has 500 subscribers on its list and collects fixed charges of ₹ 300 per subscriber per year. The company proposes to increase the annual subscription and it is believed that for every increase of one subscriber will discontinue the service. **CBSE QB**

Based on above information, answer the following questions.

(i) If x is the increment in annual subscription, then find the total revenue of the company after increment. (in terms of x).

(ii) How much fee the company should increase to have maximum revenue?

(iii) What will be the maximum revenue of the company?

(iv) How many subscriber will be there when revenue is maximum?

29. The petrol cost per hour for running a car is proportional to the square of the speed, it generates in km per hour. If the petrol cost ₹ 48 per hour at speed of 16 km/h and the fixed charges to run the car amounts to ₹ 1200 per hour.

Assume the speed of car as v km/h. **CBSE QB**

Based on above information, answer the following questions.

(i) If it is given that the petrol cost per hour is K times the square of the speed the car generates in km/h, then find the value of K.

(ii) If the car has travelled a distance of 1000 km, then find the function representing the total cost running the car.

(iii) Find the most economical speed to run the car.

(iv) Find the cost of petrol when car is running 1000 km at economical speed.

30. A tank with a rectangular base and rectangular sides, open at the top is to be constructed so that its height is 2 m and volume is 8 m^3. If building of tank cost ₹ 700 per square metre for the base and ₹ 450 per square metre for sides. Let x and y be the length and breadth of the least expensive tank. **CBSE QB**

(i) Find the total cost in terms of x and y.

(ii) Find the cost of constructing the tank depends on x only.

(iii) When cost is minimum, what will be the length?

(iv) Find the minimum cost of the tank in rupees.

31. The lifespan of a certain flowering plant is around 6 yr. After t years, the sapling is planted, the plant produces r grams of flowers each day.

The relation between r and t can be approximated as

$r = \frac{t^3}{3} - 6t^2 + 32t, 0 \le t \le 6.$ **CBSE QB**

(i) What will be the yield per day, 3 yr after planting the sapling?

(ii) When will the maximum yield per day?

Show your steps with valid reasons.

Subjective Questions

Very Short Answer Type Questions

1. The surface area of a cube increases at the rate of $72 \text{ cm}^2/\text{sec}$. Find the rate of change of its volume when the edge of the cube measures 3 cm. **CBSE 2024**

2. Find the points on the curve $6y = x^3 + 2$ at which ordinate is changing 8 times as fast as abscissa. **CBSE 2023**

3. A particle moves along the curve $3y = ax^3 + 1$ such that at a point with x-coordinate 1, y-coordinate is changing twice as fast at x-coordinate. Find the value of a. **CBSE 2023**

4. The radius of a circle increases at a rate of 0.2 cm/s. Calculate the rate of the increase of the area, when the radius is 5 cm.

5. The sides of an equilateral triangle are increasing at the rate of 2 cm/s. Find the rate at which the area increases, when the side is 10 cm. **CBSE 2014**

6. For the curve $y = 5x - 2x^3$, if x increase at the rate of 2 units/s, then find the rate of change of the slope of curve when $x = 3$. **CBSE 2017, NCERT Exemplar**

7. The radius of a circle is increasing at the rate of 0.7 cm/s. What is the rate of increase of its circumference? **NCERT**

8. Find the values of k for which $f(x) = kx^3 - 9kx^2 + 9x + 3$ is increasing on R. **Diksha App**

9. Find the interval in which the function $f(x) = \dfrac{x}{\sin x}$ is increasing.

10. Given that $f(x) = \dfrac{\log x}{x}$, find the point of local maximum of $f(x)$. **CBSE 2024C**

11. Find the local maximum and local minimum values of the function $f(x) = e^{x+2}$.

12. Find the stationary (critical) point of the function $f(x) = x^x$.

13. Prove that the maximum value of $\left(\dfrac{1}{x}\right)^x$ is $e^{1/e}$.

14. It is given that at $x = 1$, the function $x^4 - 62x^2 + ax + 9$ attains maximum value on the interval $(0, 2)$. Find the value of a. **NCERT**

15. Find the maximum slope of curve $y = -x^3 + 3x^2 + 9x - 27$.

Short Answer Type Questions

16. Sand is pouring from a pipe at the rate of $15 \text{ cm}^3/\text{min}$. The falling sand forms a cone on the ground such that the height of the cone is always one third of the radius of the base. How fast is the height of the sand cone increasing at the instant when the height is 4 cm ? **CBSE 2024**

17. A man is walking at the rate of 6.5 km/hr towards the foot of the tower 120 m high. At what rate is he approaching the top of the tower when he is 50m away from the tower? **Diksha App**

18. The volume of a sphere is increasing at the rate of $3 \text{ cm}^3/\text{s}$. Find the rate of increase of its surface area, when the radius is 2 cm. **CBSE 2017**

19. A balloon which always remains spherical has a variable radius, find the rate at which its volume is increasing with respect to its radius, when the radius is 7 cm.

20. The length x of a rectangle is decreasing at the rate of 6 cm/min and the width y is increasing at the rate of 5 cm/min. Find the rate of change of the perimeter and the area of the rectangle when $x = 10$ cm and $y = 8$ cm.

21. A balloon which always remains spherical has a variable diameter $\dfrac{3}{2}(2x + 1)$. Then, find the rate of change of its volume with respect to x. **CBSE 2017C**

22. A spherical ball of salt is dissolving in water in such a manner that the rate of decreasing of the volume at any instant is proportional to the surface. Prove that the radius is decreasing at a constant rate. **NCERT Exemplar**

23. A man 2 m tall, walks at a uniform speed of 6 km/h away from a lamp post 6 m high. Find the rate at which the length of his shadow increases.

24. Show that the function $f(x) = 4x^3 - 18x^2 + 27x - 7$ is always increasing on R. **CBSE 2017**

25. Find the interval in which the function $f(x) = -2x^3 - 9x^2 - 12x + 1$ is strictly increasing or strictly decreasing. **NCERT, CBSE 2011**

26. Find the value(s) of x for which $y = [x(x-2)]^2$ is an increasing function. **NCERT, CBSE 2014**

27. Show that $f(x) = 2x + \cot^{-1} x + \log(\sqrt{1 + x^2} - x)$ is increasing in R. **NCERT Exemplar**

28. Show that the function f given by $f(x) = \tan^{-1}(\sin x + \cos x)$, $x > 0$ is always an strictly increasing function in $\left(0, \dfrac{\pi}{4}\right)$. **NCERT**

29. Find the local maxima and local minima and the corresponding local maximum and local minimum values of the function $f(x) = \dfrac{2}{x} + \dfrac{x}{2}$, $x > 0$.

30. Find the maximum profit that a company can make, if the profit function is given by $P(x) = 51 + 42x - x^2$, where x is the number of units and P is the profit in rupees.

31. Check whether the function $f:R\to R$ defined by $f(x)=x^3+x$, has any critical point(s) or not? If yes, then find the point(s). **CBSE Sample Paper 2023**

32. Find the least value of the function

$$f(x)=ax+\frac{b}{x}(a>0,b>0,x>0).$$

CBSE 2020

33. Find the points of local maxima, local minima and the points of inflection of the function

$f(x)=x^5-5x^4+5x^3-1.$

Also, find the corresponding local maximum and local minimum values. **CBSE 2016C**

34. Prove that the largest rectangle with a given perimeter is a square.

35. Let AP and BQ be two vertical poles at points A and B, respectively. If $AP=16$ m, $BQ=22$ m and $AB=20$ m, then find the distance of a point R on AB from the point A such that RP^2+RQ^2 is minimum.

36. An Apache helicopter of enemy is flying along the curve given by $y=x^2+7$. A soldier placed at (3, 7) wants to shoot down the helicopter, when it is nearest to him. Find the nearest distance. **NCERT Exemplar**

Long Answer Type Questions

37. A swimming pool is to be drained for cleaning. If L represents the number of litres of water in the pool, t seconds after the pool has been plugged off to drain and $L=200(10-t)^2$. How fast is the water running out at the end of 5 s and what is the average rate at which the water flows out during the first 5 s? **NCERT Exemplar**

38. A kite is moving horizontally at a height of 151.5 m. If the speed of kite is 10 m/s, then how fast is the string being let out, when the kite is 250 m away from the boy who is flying the kite, if the height of boy is 1.5 m? **NCERT Exemplar**

39. Two men A and B start with velocity v at the same time from the junction of two roads inclined at 45° to each other. If they travel by different roads, then find the rate at which they are being separated. **NCERT Exemplar**

40. Water is running into a conical vessel, 15 cm deep and 5 cm in radius at the rate of 0.1 cm^3/s, when the water is 6 cm deep. Find at what rate is

(i) the water level rising?

(ii) the water surface area increasing?

(iii) the wetted surface of the vessel increasing?

41. A water tank has the shape of an inverted right circular cone with its axis vertical and vertex lowermost. Its semi-vertical angle is $\tan^{-1}(0.5)$. Water is poured into it at a constant rate of 5 m^3/h. Find the rate at which the level of the water is rising at the instant, when the depth of water in the tank is 4 m.

42. Show that for $a\ge 1$, $f(x)=\sqrt{3}\sin x-\cos x-2ax+b$ is decreasing in R. **NCERT Exemplar**

43. Find the intervals in which the function

$f(x)=\dfrac{x^4}{4}-x^3-5x^2+24x+12$ is

(a) strictly increasing

(b) strictly decreasing. **NCERT**

44. Prove that the function f defined by $f(x)=x^2-x+1$ is neither increasing nor decreasing in $(-1, 1)$. Hence, find the interval in which $f(x)$, is

(i) strictly increasing (ii) strictly decreasing

45. Prove that $y=\dfrac{4\sin\theta}{2+\cos\theta}-\theta$ is an increasing function of θ on $\left[0,\dfrac{\pi}{2}\right]$. **CBSE 2025, 16**

46. Find the maximum and minimum values of the function given by $f(x)=5+\sin 2x$. **CBSE 2023**

47. Show that the altitude of the right circular cone of maximum volume that can be inscribed in a sphere of radius r is $\dfrac{4r}{3}$. Also, find the maximum volume in terms of volume of the sphere. **CBSE 2019, 16**

48. AB is the diameter of a circle and C is any point on the circle. Show that the area of ΔABC is maximum, when it is an isosceles triangle. **CBSE 2017, 14C**

49. Show that the semi-vertical angle of the cone of the maximum volume and of given slant height is $\cos^{-1} 1/\sqrt{3}$. **CBSE 2016, 14**

50. If the length of three sides of a trapezium other than the base are each equal to 10 cm, then find the area of the trapezium, when it is maximum. **CBSE 2014C, 13C, 10**

51. Prove that the semi-vertical angle of the right circular cone of given volume and least curved surface area is $\cot^{-1}\sqrt{2}$. **CBSE 2014**

Hints & Solutions

Objective Type Questions

1. (b) Let x be the length of a side and S be the surface area of cube.

Then, $S = 6x^2$

On differentiating w.r.t. t, we get

$$\frac{dS}{dt} = 12x\frac{dx}{dt} \quad \ldots(i)$$

Given, $\frac{dx}{dt} = 5$ cm/s

From Eq. (i), $\frac{dS}{dt} = 12 \times x \times 5$

$\because \quad x = 2$ cm

$\therefore \quad \frac{ds}{dt} = 12 \times 2 \times 5 = 120 \text{ cm}^2/\text{s}$

2. (b) According to the given condition,

$$\frac{d\theta}{dt} = 2\frac{d}{dt}(\sin\theta)$$

$\Rightarrow \quad \frac{d\theta}{dt} = 2\cos\theta \cdot \frac{d\theta}{dt} \Rightarrow 1 = 2\cos\theta$

$\Rightarrow \quad \cos\theta = \frac{1}{2} \Rightarrow \cos\theta = \cos\frac{\pi}{3}$

$\therefore \quad \theta = \frac{\pi}{3}$

3. (a) Given, $y = 7x - x^3$

On differentiating both sides w.r.t. x, we get

$$\frac{dy}{dx} = 7 - 3x^2$$

Let s be the slope.

Then, $s = \frac{dy}{dx} = 7 - 3x^2$

Now, $\frac{ds}{dt} = \frac{d}{dt}(7 - 3x^2) = -6x\frac{dx}{dt}$

Since, it is given that $\frac{dx}{dt} = 2$ units/sec and $x = 5$,

$$\frac{ds}{dt} = -6(5)(2) = -60$$

$\therefore \quad \frac{ds}{dt} = -60$ units/sec

4. (b) Let r be the radius and C be the circumference of the circle. We know that circumference, $C = 2\pi r$

On differentiating both sides w.r.t t, we get

$$\frac{dc}{dt} = 2\pi\frac{dr}{dt}$$

$\Rightarrow \quad \frac{dc}{dt} = 2\pi \times 0.5 \quad \left[\because \frac{dr}{dt} = 0.5 \text{ cm / sec}\right]$

$\Rightarrow \quad \frac{dc}{dt} = \pi$ cm/s

5. (c) Given function, $f(x) = x^3 + 3x$

$\Rightarrow \quad f'(x) = 3x^2 + 3 = 3(x^2 + 1)$

For $x \in R$, $x^2 + 1 > 0 \Rightarrow 3(x^2 + 1) > 0$

$\Rightarrow \quad f'(x) > 0, \forall\, x \in R$

$\therefore f(x)$ is increasing on R.

6. (b) Given, $f(x) = 2x^3 + 9x^2 + 12x - 1$

$\Rightarrow \quad f'(x) = 6x^2 + 18x + 12$

For $f(x)$ to be decreasing, $f'(x) \leq 0$

$\therefore \quad (6x^2 + 18x + 12) \leq 0$

$\Rightarrow \quad 6(x^2 + 3x + 2) \leq 0$

$\Rightarrow \quad (x+2)(x+1) \leq 0 \Rightarrow -2 \leq x \leq -1$

7. (b) We have, $f(x) = 2x - \sin x$

On differentiating both sides w.r.t. x, we get

$$f'(x) = 2 - \cos x$$

$\because -1 \leq \cos x \leq 1$, then $1 \geq -\cos x \geq -1$

$\Rightarrow \quad 2 + 1 \geq (2 - \cos x) \geq 2 - 1$

$\Rightarrow \quad 3 \geq (2 - \cos x) \geq 1$

$\Rightarrow \quad 3 \geq f'(x) \geq 1$

$\therefore f'(x)$ is always positive.

So, $f(x)$ is an increasing function.

8. (b) Given, $f(x) = 2x^3 - 3x^2 - 36x + 7$

$$f'(x) = 6x^2 - 6x - 36 = 6(x-3)(x+2)$$

On putting $f'(x) = 0$, so $x = -2$ and $x = 3$

Plotting points on number line

Here, f is strictly increasing in $(-\infty, -2)$ and $(3, \infty)$.

$\therefore$ f is strictly decreasing in $(-2, 3)$.

9. (b) Given, $f(x) = x + \cos x + b$

Now, $f'(x) = 1 - \sin x$

Since, $f(x)$ is strictly decreasing over R.

$\therefore \quad f'(x) < 0 \Rightarrow 1 - \sin x < 0 \Rightarrow \sin x > 1$

Since, $-1 \leq \sin x \leq 1$

Thus, $\sin x > 1$ is not possible.

Thus, for no value of b, $f(x)$ is strictly decreasing.

10. (d) Given, $y = x^2 e^{-x}$

$$\frac{dy}{dx} = 2xe^{-x} - x^2 e^{-x} \Rightarrow \frac{dy}{dx} = e^{-x}(2x - x^2)$$

On putting $\frac{dy}{dx} = 0$, so $x = 0, 2$

Plotting points on number line

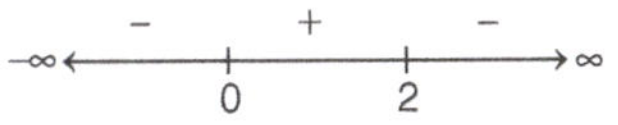

Here, y is decreasing in the interval $(-\infty, 0) \cup (2, \infty)$.

11. (a) Given, $f(x) = 2x^2 - kx + 5$

$\Rightarrow \quad f'(x) = 4x - k$

$f''(x) = 4$

Now, $f''(x) = 4 > 0, \forall x \in [1, 2]$

Thus, $f'(1)$ is the least value of $f(x)$.

Now, $f'(1) > 0$ gives $4 - k > 0$

$\Rightarrow \quad k < 4$

$\therefore \quad k \in (-\infty, 4)$

12. (a) Given function is

$$f(x) = x^3 - 3x^2 + 4x$$

On differentiating w.r.t. x, we get

$$f'(x) = 3x^2 - 6x + 4$$

$\Rightarrow \quad f'(x) = 3(x-1)^2 + 1$

Here, $f'(x) > 0$, for all $x \in R$.

Hence, $f(x)$ is strictly increasing on R.

13. (c) We have, $f(x) = x \log_e x$

On differentiating w.r.t. x, we get

$$f'(x) = x \frac{d}{dx} \log_e x + \log_e x \frac{d}{dx} x$$

[using product rule]

$\Rightarrow \quad f'(x) = x \cdot \frac{1}{x} + \log_e x \cdot 1$

$\Rightarrow \quad f'(x) = 1 + \log_e x$

For maxima and minima,

put $\quad f'(x) = 0$

$\Rightarrow \quad 1 + \log_e x = 0$

$\Rightarrow \quad \log_e x = -1$

$\Rightarrow \quad x = e^{-1} = \frac{1}{e}$

Now, $f''(x) = \frac{1}{x}$

$\Rightarrow \quad f''\left(\frac{1}{e}\right) = e > 0$

$\therefore \ x = \frac{1}{e}$ is a point of minima.

Minimum value $= f\left(\frac{1}{e}\right) = \frac{1}{e} \cdot \log_e \frac{1}{e}$

$= \frac{1}{e} \log_e e^{-1} = \frac{-1}{e} \quad [\because \log_e e = 1]$

14. (d) We have, $f(x) = x^3 - 3x + 3$

$\Rightarrow \quad f'(x) = 3x^2 - 3$

$= 3(x-1)(x+1)$

and $\quad f''(x) = 6x$

For maxima or minima, $f'(x) = 0$

$\therefore \quad 3(x-1)(x+1) = 0$

$\Rightarrow \quad x = 1$ and $x = -1$

Thus, $x = \pm 1$ are the only critical points.

Here, $x = 1$ is the point of local minima.

Local minimum value $= f(1) = 1 - 3 + 3 = 1$

and $x = -1$ is the point of local maxima.

Local maximum value $= f(-1) = (-1)^3 - 3(-1) + 3$

$= -1 + 3 + 3 = 5$

15. (b) Let $f(x) = x^3 - 18x^2 + 96x$

$\Rightarrow \quad f'(x) = 3x^2 - 36x + 96$

For local maxima or local minima, $f'(x) = 0$.

$\therefore \quad 3x^2 - 36x + 96 = 0$

$\Rightarrow \quad (x-8)(x-4) = 0$

$\therefore \quad x = 8, 4 \in [0, 9]$

So, $x = 4, 8$ are the points of local maxima or local minima.

Now, calculate the absolute maximum value or absolute minimum value at $x = 0, 4, 8, 9$.

$f(0) = 0$

$f(4) = 64 - 288 + 384 = 160$

$f(8) = 512 - 1152 + 768 = 128$

$f(9) = 729 - 1458 + 864 = 135$

Hence, the absolute minimum value of f is 0 at $x = 0$.

16. (a) We have, $\frac{dA}{dr} = \frac{d}{dr}(\pi r^2) = 2\pi r$

At $r = 3$ cm,

$$\left.\frac{dA}{dr}\right|_{r=3} = 2\pi \times 3 = 6\pi \text{ cm}^2/\text{cm}$$

Hence, Assertion and Reason both are correct and Reason is the correct explanation of Assertion.

17. (c) Let r be the radius of spherical balloon and V be its volume.

Then, $V = \frac{4}{3}\pi r^3$

Rate of change of volume w.r.t. radius r, $\frac{dV}{dr} = \left(\frac{4}{3}\pi\right) 3r^2$

[differentiating w.r.t. r]

$= 4\pi r^2 = 4\pi (10)^2 = 400\pi \text{ cm}^3/\text{cm}$

$[\because r = 10 \text{ cm}]$

Hence, Assertion is correct but Reason is incorrect.

18. (d) Let the side of the triangle be a. Then, $\frac{da}{dt} = 0.5$ cm/s

Perimeter of equilateral triangle $= 3a$

$\Rightarrow \quad \frac{dP}{dt} = 3\frac{da}{dt} = 3 \times 0.5 = 1.5$ cm/s

Hence, Assertion is incorrect but Reason is correct.

19. (a) We have, $\quad R(x) = 3x^2 + 36x + 5$

$\Rightarrow \quad \frac{d}{dx}(R(x)) = 6x + 36$

When $x = 15$,

$$\left.\frac{d}{dx}(R(x))\right|_{\text{at } x=15} = 6 \times 15 + 36$$

$= ₹\ 126$

Hence, Assertion and Reason both are correct and Reason is the correct explanation of Assertion.

20. (a) As, $f(x)=4x+3$

$\Rightarrow \quad f'(x)=4+0=4$

Since, $f'(x)>0, \forall\, x\in R$.

So, function $f(x)$ is increasing on R.

Hence, Assertion and Reason both are correct and Reason is the correct explanation of Assertion.

21. (c) We have, $f(x)=\tan x - x$

$$\Rightarrow \quad f'(x)=\sec^2 x - 1 = \tan^2 x \geq 0, \forall\, x\in R.$$

$\therefore$ $f(x)$ is increasing function.

Thus, Assertion is correct but Reason is incorrect.

22. (d) Given, $f(x)=x^4$

$\Rightarrow f'(x)=4x^3$

For decreasing function,

$$f'(x)<0 \Rightarrow 4x^3<0$$

$$\Rightarrow \quad x^3<0 \Rightarrow x<0$$

$$\Rightarrow \quad x\in(-\infty,0)$$

Clearly, Assertion is incorrect and Reason is correct.

23. (b) We have,

$$f(x)=x^2-4x+6$$

$$\therefore \quad f'(x)=2x-4$$

For increasing or decreasing, $f'(x)=0$ gives $x=2$.

Now, the point $x=2$ divides the real line into two disjoint intervals namely, $(-\infty,2)$ and $(2,\infty)$.

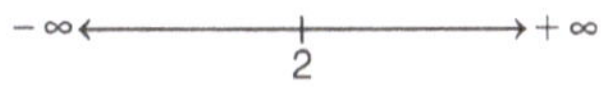

In the interval $(-\infty,2)$, $f'(x)=2x-4<0$.

Therefore, f is strictly decreasing in this interval. Also, in the interval $(2,\infty)$, $f'(x)>0$ and so the function f is strictly increasing in this interval.

Hence, Assertion and Reason both are correct but Reason is not the correct explanation of Assertion.

24. (d) Given, $f(x)=2x^3-3x^2-36x+7$

On differentiating w.r.t. x, we get

$$f'(x)=\frac{d}{dx}(2x^3-3x^2-36x+7)$$

$$=2\cdot3x^2-3\cdot2x-36\cdot1+0$$

$$=6x^2-6x-36$$

$$=6(x^2-x-6)$$

$$\Rightarrow \quad f'(x)=6(x-3)(x+2)$$

On putting $f'(x)=0$, we get

$$6(x-3)(x+2)=0$$

$$\Rightarrow \quad x=3 \text{ and } -2$$

which divides real line into three intervals namely $(-\infty,-2),(-2,3)$ and $(3,\infty)$.

Intervals	Sign of $f'(x)$	Nature of $f(x)$
$(-\infty,-2)$	$(-)(-)=+$ ve ($\because x<-2$ i.e. x is $-3,-4,-5$ ... for these values, $(x-3)$ and $(x+2)$ both will be negative)	Strictly increasing
$(-2,3)$	$(-)(+)=-$ ve ($\because -2<x<3$ i.e. x is 1, 2, 0, -1 ... for these values $(x-3)$ will be negative and $(x+2)$ will be positive)	Strictly decreasing
$(3,\infty)$	$(+)(+)=+$ ve ($\because x>3$ i.e. x is 4, 5, 6, ... for these values $(x-3)$ and $(x+2)$ both are positive)	Strictly increasing

Thus, the given function f is strictly increasing in intervals $(-\infty,-2)$ and $(3,\infty)$, while function f is strictly decreasing in the interval $(-2,3)$.

Hence, Assertion is incorrect but Reason is correct.

25. (a) We have,

Curve $y=-x^3+3x^2+9x-27$

$$\text{Slope}=\frac{dy}{dx}=-3x^2+6x+9=m \text{ (say)}$$

$$\Rightarrow \quad \frac{dm}{dx}=\frac{d^2y}{dx^2}=-6x+6$$

$$\text{Now, } \frac{dm}{dx}=0$$

$$\Rightarrow -6x+6=0$$

$$\Rightarrow \quad x=1$$

$$\text{Also, } \frac{d^2m}{dx^2}=-6<0 \text{ for } x=1.$$

$\therefore$ At $x=1$, slope is maximum.

At $x=1$, $y=-16$

Hence, the coordinates of the point are $(1,-16)$.

$\therefore$ Assertion is correct.

Reason is also correct and Reason is the correct explanation of Assertion.

26. (i) Let the length of the printed part be x cm and width of the printed part be y cm.

Given, area of printed part $=24$ cm^2

$$\Rightarrow \quad xy=24 \Rightarrow y=\frac{24}{x}$$

From given condition,

Length of the card $=(x+3)$ cm

and width of the card $=(y+2)$ cm

$$\therefore \text{ Area of card, } A=(x+3)(y+2)=(x+3)\left(\frac{24}{x}+2\right)$$

$$=24+2x+\frac{72}{x}+6=30+2x+\frac{72}{x}\text{ cm}^2$$

(ii) We have, $A = 30 + 2x + \frac{72}{x}$

$\therefore \quad \frac{dA}{dx} = 2 - \frac{72}{x^2}$

For maxima or minima,

$\frac{dA}{dx} = 0$

$\therefore \; 2x^2 - 72 = 0$

$\Rightarrow \quad x^2 = 36$

$\Rightarrow \quad x = \pm 6 \Rightarrow x = 6$ [$\because x$ cannot be negative]

Now, $\frac{d^2A}{dx^2} = \frac{144}{x^3}$

At $x = 6$, $\frac{d^2A}{dx^2} > 0$

$\therefore$ Area is minimum, when $x = 6$

$\Rightarrow \quad y = \frac{24}{6} = 4$

$\therefore$ Dimensions of the card are

length of the card $= x + 3 = 6 + 3 = 9$ cm

and width of the card $= y + 2 = 4 + 2 = 6$ cm

27. (i) We have, volume of the tank $= 250 \text{ m}^3$

$\Rightarrow \quad x^2 \times h = 250 \text{ m}^3 \Rightarrow h = \frac{250}{x^2}$

$\because$ Total cost of digging tank $= 40000h^2 + 5000x^2$

$\therefore \quad C(x) = 40000 \times \left(\frac{250}{x^2}\right)^2 + 5000x^2$

(ii) $\because C(x) = 40000 \times \left(\frac{250}{x^2}\right)^2 + 5000x^2$

$= 40000 \times \frac{62500}{x^4} + 5000x^2$

$\therefore \frac{dC(x)}{dx} = \frac{40000 \times 62500 \times (-4)}{x^5} + 10000x$

(iii) (a) For maximum or minimum cost $C(x)$,

$\frac{dC(x)}{dx} = 0$

$\Rightarrow \frac{-4 \times 40000 \times 62500}{x^5} + 10000x = 0$

$\Rightarrow \quad x^6 = 1000000$

$\Rightarrow \quad x^6 = (10)^6 \Rightarrow x = 10$

Now, $\frac{d^2C(x)}{dx^2} = 10000 + \frac{20 \times 40000 \times 62500}{x^6}$

$\Rightarrow \quad \left.\frac{d^2C(x)}{dx^2}\right|_{\text{at } x=10} > 0$

$\therefore C(x)$ is minimum at $x = 10$ m.

Or

(b) $\because \; C(x) = \frac{40000 \times 62500}{x^4} + 5000x^2$

$\Rightarrow \quad C'(x) = \frac{-(10)^{10}}{x^5} + 10000x$

For increasing, $C'(x) > 0$

$\Rightarrow \quad 10000x - \frac{(10)^{10}}{x^5} > 0$

$\Rightarrow \quad x^6 > 10^6$

$\therefore \quad x > 10$ [$\because x > 0$, a real number]

So, for $C(x)$ to be increasing, $x > 10$

and $C'(x) < 0, \forall \; x \in (0, 10)$.

Therefore, $C(x)$ is decreasing for $0 < x < 10$.

Hence, $C(x)$ is not increasing for $x > 0$.

28. Let x be the increment in annual subscription.

So, new subscription cost = ₹$(300 + x)$

According to question, if we increase subscription by ₹ x, x subscribers will reduce.

New number of subscribers $= (500 - x)$

(i) Total revenue after increment $= (300 + x)(500 - x)$

$= 150000 - 300x + 500x - x^2$

$\Rightarrow \quad R(x) = 150000 + 200x - x^2$

(ii) $\frac{dR}{dx} = 200 - 2x$

For critical points, $\frac{dR}{dx} = 0 \Rightarrow 200 - 2x = 0$

$x = 100$

$\therefore \quad \frac{d^2R}{dx^2} = -2 \, (-\text{ve})$

So, R is maximum at $x = 100$.

So, company should increase ₹ 100.

(iii) Maximum revenue,

$R(100) = 150000 + 200 \times 100 - (100)^2$

$= 150000 + 20000 - 10000 =$ ₹ 160000

(iv) New number of subscribers will be

$= 500 - x = 500 - 100 = 400$

29. Let f be the cost of petrol consumed by running the car for time t.

Then, $\frac{f}{t} \propto v^2 \Rightarrow \frac{f}{t} = K \cdot v^2$

(i) $f =$ ₹ 48, $v = 16$ km

$48 = K \cdot (16)^2 \Rightarrow K = \frac{48}{16 \times 16} = \frac{3}{16}$

(ii) Let x be the total cost of running the car.

Then, $\quad \frac{x}{t} = Kv^2 + 1200$

$\Rightarrow \quad x = K \cdot tv^2 + 1200t \quad \left[\text{put } K = \frac{3}{16}\right]$

$\Rightarrow \quad x = \frac{3tv^2}{16} + 1200t$

Car has travelled a distance of 1000 km.

$\therefore \quad v = \frac{1000}{t} \Rightarrow t = \frac{1000}{v}$

$\therefore \quad x = \frac{3}{16} \cdot \left(\frac{1000}{v}\right) \cdot v^2 + 1200\left(\frac{1000}{v}\right)$

$\Rightarrow \quad x = \frac{375}{2} \cdot v + \frac{1200000}{v}$

(iii) For minimum cost, $\frac{dx}{dv} = \frac{375}{2} - \frac{1200000}{v^2}$

For critical points, $\frac{dx}{dv} = 0$

$\Rightarrow \quad \frac{375}{2} - \frac{1200000}{v^2} = 0 \Rightarrow \frac{1200000}{v^2} = \frac{375}{2}$

$\Rightarrow \quad v^2 = 6400 = 80$ km/h

$\therefore \quad \frac{d^2x}{dv^2} = \frac{2400000}{v^3}$ (+ve)

So, x will be minimum.

(iv) We have, $\frac{f}{t} = \frac{3}{16}v^2$

$f = \frac{3}{16}v^2 t = \frac{3}{16}v^2\left(\frac{1000}{v}\right) \Rightarrow f = \frac{375}{2}v$

$f = \frac{375}{2}\cdot(80) = ₹\,15000 \qquad [\because v = 80 \text{ km/h}]$

30. Given, length $= x$ m, breadth $= y$ m and height $= 2$ m

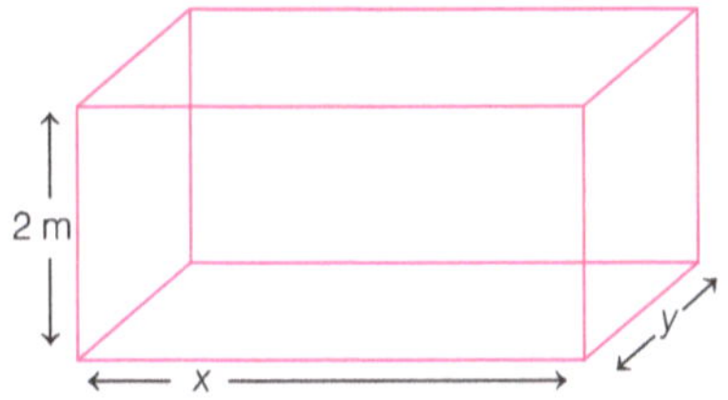

$\therefore$ Volume $= x\cdot y\cdot 2 = 8\text{ m}^3$ [given]

$\Rightarrow \quad xy = 4$

(i) Area of base $= x\cdot y\text{ m}^2$

Cost of base $= x\cdot y\cdot 700 = ₹\,700xy$

Area of four walls $= 2h(l+b) = 2\times 2(x+y) = 4(x+y)\text{ m}^2$

Cost of four walls $= 4(x+y)\,450 = ₹\,1800(x+y)$

$\therefore$ Total cost $= 700xy + 1800(x+y)$ ...(i)

(ii) We know that $x\cdot y = 4 \Rightarrow y = \frac{4}{x}$

On putting the value of y in Eq. (i), we get

Total cost $= 700x\left(\frac{4}{x}\right) + 1800\left(x + \frac{4}{x}\right)$

$\therefore \quad T = 2800 + 1800\left(x + \frac{4}{x}\right)$

(iii) We have, $T = 2800 + 1800\left(x + \frac{4}{x}\right)$

On differentiating w.r.t. x, we get

$\frac{dT}{dx} = 1800\left(1 - \frac{4}{x^2}\right)$

For critical points, $\frac{dT}{dx} = 0$

$\Rightarrow \quad 1800\left(1 - \frac{4}{x^2}\right) = 0 \Rightarrow x^2 = 4$

$\Rightarrow \quad x = 2$ [negative value will be rejected because length cannot be negative]

Now, $\frac{d^2T}{dx^2} = 1800\left(\frac{8}{x^3}\right)$,

which is positive when $x = 2$.

So, T is minimum at $x = 2$.

(iv) Minimum cost $= 2800 + 1800\left(2 + \frac{4}{2}\right) = 2800 + 1800(4)$

$= 2800 + 7200 = ₹\,10000$

31. Given, $r = \frac{t^3}{3} - 6t^2 + 32t,\ 0 \le t \le 6$ ...(i)

(i) After 3 years the yield per day of planting the sapling is,

$r = \frac{(3)^3}{3} - 6(3)^2 + 32(3) = 9 - 54 + 96$

$\Rightarrow \quad r = 51$ gm

(ii) We have, $r = \frac{t^3}{3} - 6t^2 + 32t$ ...(ii)

On differentiating w.r.t. t, we get

$\frac{dr}{dt} = t^2 - 12t + 32$

For critical points, $\frac{dr}{dt} = 0$

$\Rightarrow \quad t^2 - 12t + 32 = 0$

$\Rightarrow \quad t^2 - 8t - 4t + 32 = 0$

$\Rightarrow \quad t(t-8) - 4(t-8) = 0$

$\Rightarrow \quad (t-4)(t-8) = 0$

$\Rightarrow \quad t = 4$ or $t = 8$

Since, the lifespan of the plant is around 6 yr.

$\therefore \quad t = 4$

Again, on differentiating Eq. (i) w.r.t. t, we get

$\frac{d^2r}{dt^2} = 2t - 12$

$\therefore \quad \left.\frac{d^2r}{dt^2}\right|_{t=4} = (-4) < 0$

Hence, maximum yield per day is obtained 4 yr after planting the sapling.

Subjective Questions

1. Let a be the edge, S be the surface area and V be volume of cube.

Given, $\frac{dS}{dt} = 72\text{ cm}^2/\text{s}$ and $a = 3$ cm

Surface area of cube $= 6a^2$

$\Rightarrow \quad \frac{dS}{dt} = 12a\cdot\frac{da}{dt}$

$\Rightarrow \quad \frac{da}{dt} = \frac{72}{12a} = \frac{6}{a}$

Now, volume of cube, $V = a^3$

On differentiating w.r.t. t, we get

$\frac{dV}{dt} = 3a^2\cdot\frac{da}{dt} = 3a^2\cdot\frac{6}{a} \Rightarrow \frac{dV}{dt} = 18a$

$\Rightarrow \quad \left(\frac{dV}{dt}\right)_{a=3} = 18\times 3 = 54\text{ cm}^3/\text{s}$

2. Given, $6y = x^3 + 2$

$\Rightarrow \quad 6\frac{dy}{dt} = 3x^2\frac{dx}{dt}$

Also, given $\frac{dy}{dt} = 8\frac{dx}{dt}$

$\therefore \quad 6\left(8\frac{dx}{dt}\right) = 3x^2\frac{dx}{dt}$

$\Rightarrow \quad 48 = 3x^2 \Rightarrow x^2 = 16$

$\Rightarrow \quad x = \pm 4$

When $x = 4$, then $6y = (4)^3 + 2$

$\Rightarrow \quad 6y = 66$

$\Rightarrow \quad y = 11$

and when $x = -4$, then $6y = (-4)^3 + 2$

$\Rightarrow \quad 6y = -62$

$\Rightarrow \quad y = -\frac{31}{3}$

$\therefore$ Required points are $(4, 11)$ and $\left(-4, \frac{-31}{3}\right)$.

3. Given, $3y = ax^3 + 1$ ...(i)

and $\frac{dy}{dt} = 2\frac{dx}{dt}$ ...(ii)

Now, from Eq. (i), $3\frac{dy}{dt} = a(3x^2)\frac{dx}{dt}$

$\Rightarrow \quad 3\left(2\frac{dx}{dt}\right) = a(3x^2)\frac{dx}{dt}$ [using Eq. (ii)]

$\Rightarrow \quad 2 = ax^2$

When $x = 1$, then $a(1)^2 = 2 \Rightarrow a = 2$

4. Let x be the radius and y be the area of circle.

Then, $y = \pi x^2$ ...(i)

Also, rate of change of radius with respect to time is 0.2 cm/s.

$\therefore \quad \frac{dx}{dt} = 0.2$ ...(ii)

Now, on differentiating both sides of Eq. (i) w.r.t. t, we get

$\frac{dy}{dt} = \pi \cdot 2x \cdot \frac{dx}{dt}$ [by chain rule]

$= 2\pi x(0.2) = 0.4\pi x$ [using Eq. (ii)]

When radius $x = 5$ cm, then

$\left(\frac{dy}{dt}\right) = 0.4\,\pi \times 5 = 2\pi \text{ cm}^2/\text{s}$

Hence, the required rate of increase of the area is $2\pi \text{ cm}^2/\text{s}$.

5. Let the side of triangle be a.

Given, $\frac{da}{dt} = 2$ cm/s

Now, area of equilateral triangle having side a is given by

$A = \frac{\sqrt{3}a^2}{4}$

On differentiating both sides w.r.t. t, we get

$\frac{dA}{dt} = \frac{\sqrt{3}}{4} \cdot (2a)\frac{da}{dt}$

On putting $\frac{da}{dt} = 2$ cm/s and $a = 10$ cm, we get

$\frac{dA}{dt} = \frac{\sqrt{3}}{4} \times 2 \times 10 \times 2 = 10\sqrt{3} \text{ cm}^2/\text{s}$

6. Given curve is $y = 5x - 2x^3$ and $\frac{dx}{dt} = 2$ units/s ...(i)

Now, slope of the curve $\frac{dy}{dx} = 5 - 6x^2 = M$ (say)

Rate of change of the slope,

$\frac{dM}{dt} = -6\frac{d}{dt}(x^2) \Rightarrow \frac{dM}{dt} = -12x\frac{dx}{dt}$

When $x = 3$, then $\frac{dM}{dt} = -12 \times 3 \times 2 = -72$ unit/s

Thus, the slope is decreasing at the rate of 72 units/s.

7. Let r be the radius and C be the circumference of circle.

Given, $\frac{dr}{dt} = 0.7$ cm/s

Now, circumference of a circle, $C = 2\pi r$

On differentiating both sides w.r.t. t, we get

$\frac{dC}{dt} = 2\pi\frac{dr}{dt}$

$\Rightarrow \quad \frac{dC}{dt} = 2\,\pi \times 0.7 = 1.4\,\pi$ cm/s

Hence, the rate of increase of circumference is $1.4\,\pi$ cm/s.

8. We have, $f(x) = kx^3 - 9kx^2 + 9x + 3$

On differentiating w.r.t. x, we get

$f'(x) = 3kx^2 - 18kx + 9$

If $f(x)$ is increasing on R, then

$f'(x) \geq 0 \Rightarrow 3kx^2 - 18kx + 9 \geq 0$

When a quadratic $ax^2 + bx + c \geq 0$

Then, $a > 0$ and $D \leq 0$

So, $3k > 0$ and $(-18k)^2 - 4 \times 9 \times 3k \leq 0$

$\Rightarrow \quad k > 0$ and $324k^2 - 108k \leq 0$

$\Rightarrow \quad 108k(3k - 1) \leq 0$

$\Rightarrow \quad 0 \leq k \leq \frac{1}{3}$

So, $k \in \left[0, \frac{1}{3}\right]$

9. We have, $f(x) = \frac{x}{\sin x}$

$\Rightarrow \quad f'(x) = \frac{\sin x \cdot 1 - x \cdot \cos x}{\sin^2 x} = \frac{\sin x - x\cos x}{\sin^2 x}$

Clearly, $\sin^2 x > 0, \forall x \in \left(0, \frac{\pi}{2}\right]$.

Now, $f'(x) > 0 \Rightarrow \sin x - x\cos x > 0 \Rightarrow \sin x > x\cos x$

$\Rightarrow \quad \tan x > x$, which is true, $\forall x \in \left(0, \frac{\pi}{2}\right)$.

Thus, $f'(x) > 0, \forall\, x \in \left(0, \frac{\pi}{2}\right)$.

So, $f(x)$ is increasing on $\left(0, \frac{\pi}{2}\right)$.

10. Given, $f(x)=\frac{\log x}{x}$

On differentiating both sides w.r.t. x, we get

$$f'(x)=\frac{x\frac{d}{dx}(\log x)-\log x\frac{d}{dx}(x)}{x^2}\quad\left[\because\left(\frac{u}{v}\right)'=\frac{vu'-uv'}{v^2}\right]$$

$$\Rightarrow\quad f'(x)=\frac{x\cdot\frac{1}{x}-\log x}{x^2}=\frac{1-\log x}{x^2}\quad\ldots(i)$$

For local maxima, $f'(x)=0$

$$\Rightarrow\quad \frac{1-\log x}{x^2}=0\Rightarrow 1-\log x=0$$

$$\Rightarrow\quad \log x=1\Rightarrow x=e$$

Again, on differentiating Eq. (i) both sides w.r.t. x, we get

$$f''(x)=\frac{x^2\frac{d}{dx}(1-\log x)-(1-\log x)\frac{d}{dx}(x^2)}{(x^2)^2}$$

$$=\frac{x^2(-1/x)-2x(1-\log x)}{x^4}$$

$$=\frac{-x-2x(1-\log x)}{x^4}$$

$$=\frac{-1-2+2\log x}{x^3}=\frac{-3+2\log x}{x^3}$$

At $x=e$, $f''(x)=\frac{-3+2\log e}{e^3}=\frac{-1}{e^3}<0$

$\therefore$ $x=e$ is point of maxima.

Hence, $f(x)$ is maximum at $x=e$.

11. We have, $f(x)=e^{x+2}$

On differentiating both sides, we get

$$f'(x)=e^{x+2}$$

For local maximum or local minimum,

on putting $f'(x)=0\Rightarrow e^{x+2}=0\Rightarrow$ No value of x exist.

Hence, no local maximum and no local minimum value can be determined.

12. Hint We have, $f(x)=x^x$

Let $\quad y=x^x$

On taking log both sides, we get

$$\log y=\log x^x\Rightarrow\log y=x\log x$$

$$\therefore\quad \frac{1}{y}\cdot\frac{dy}{dx}=x\cdot\frac{1}{x}+\log x\cdot 1$$

$$\Rightarrow\quad \frac{dy}{dx}=(1+\log x)\cdot x^x\quad[\because y=x^x]$$

For local maxima or local minima,

$$\frac{dy}{dx}=0$$

$$\Rightarrow\ (1+\log x)\cdot x^x=0\Rightarrow\log x=-1$$

$$\Rightarrow\quad \log x=\log e^{-1}\Rightarrow x=e^{-1}\Rightarrow x=\frac{1}{e}$$

Ans. $f(x)$ has a stationary point at $x=\frac{1}{e}$.

13. Hint Let $y=x^{-x}\Rightarrow\frac{dy}{dx}=-x^{-x}(1+\log x)$

$$\Rightarrow\quad \frac{dy}{dx}=0\Rightarrow x=\frac{1}{e}$$

14. Hint $f'(x)=4x^3-124x+a$, put $f'(1)=0$ **Ans.** $a=120$

15. We have, $y=-x^3+3x^2+9x-27$

$$\therefore\quad \frac{dy}{dx}=-3x^2+6x+9=\text{ Slope of the curve}$$

and $\quad\frac{d^2y}{dx^2}=-6x+6=-6(x-1)$

For maxima or minima,

$$\frac{d^2y}{dx^2}=0\ \Rightarrow\ -6(x-1)=0$$

$$\Rightarrow\quad x=1$$

Now, $\quad\frac{d^3y}{dx^3}=-6<0$

So, the maximum slope of given curve is at $x=1$.

$$\therefore\quad\left(\frac{dy}{dx}\right)_{(x=1)}=-3\cdot1^2+6\cdot1+9=12$$

16. Let r be the radius, h be the height and V be the volume of the sand cone.

Given, $\frac{dV}{dt}=15\text{ cm}^3/\text{min}$ and $h=\frac{1}{3}r$

$$\Rightarrow\quad r=3h\text{ and }h=4\text{ cm}$$

Volume of sand cone, $V=\frac{1}{3}\pi r^2h$

$$\Rightarrow\quad V=\frac{1}{3}\pi(3h)^2h=\frac{1}{3}\pi\times9h^2\times h=3\pi h^3$$

On differentiating both sides w.r.t. t, we get

$$\frac{dV}{dt}=3\pi\times3h^2\cdot\frac{dh}{dt}=9\pi h^2\frac{dh}{dt}$$

$$\Rightarrow\quad 15=9\pi(4)^2\frac{dh}{dt}$$

$$\Rightarrow\quad \frac{dh}{dt}=\frac{15}{9\pi\times16}=\frac{5}{48\pi}\text{ cm/min}$$

Hence, the height of the sand cone is increasing at the rate of $\frac{5}{48\pi}$ cm/min, when the height is 4 cm.

17. Let AB be the tower and C is the man. Height of the man will be negligible as compare to the tower.

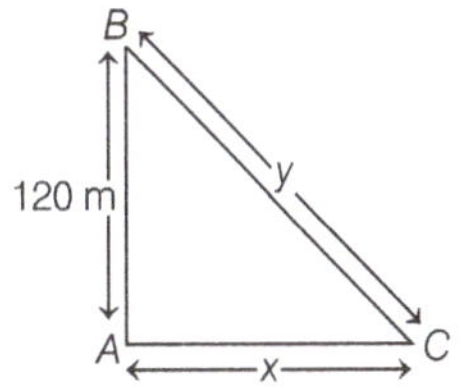

If man is walking towards tower than x is decreasing

$$\Rightarrow\quad \frac{dx}{dt}=-6.5\text{ km/hr.}$$

We have to find the rate of approaching the top of tower, so we have to find $\frac{dy}{dt}$.

Applying Pythagoras in ΔABC,

$$y^2 = (120)^2 + x^2 \Rightarrow y = \sqrt{(120)^2 + x^2}$$

On differentiating w.r.t. t, we get

$$\frac{dy}{dt} = \frac{1}{2\sqrt{(120)^2 + (x^2)}} \frac{d}{dt}((120)^2 + x^2)$$

$$= \frac{1}{2\sqrt{(120)^2 + x^2}} 2x \cdot \frac{dx}{dt} = \frac{x}{\sqrt{(120)^2 + x^2}} \frac{dx}{dt}$$

On putting $x = 50$ m and $\frac{dx}{dt} = -6.5$ km/hr, we get

$$\frac{dy}{dt} = \frac{50}{\sqrt{(120)^2 + (50)^2}}(-6.5) = \frac{50}{130} \times (-6.5) \text{ km/hr}$$

$$= -2.5 \text{ km/hr.}$$

18. Let r be the radius of sphere and V be its volume.

Then, $V = \frac{4}{3}\pi r^3$

Given, $\frac{dV}{dt} = 3 \text{ cm}^3 \text{ s}$

$\therefore \quad \frac{d}{dt}\left(\frac{4}{3}\pi r^3\right) = 3$

$\Rightarrow \quad \frac{4}{3}\pi(3r^2)\frac{dr}{dt} = 3$

$\Rightarrow \quad (4\pi r^2)\frac{dr}{dt} = 3$

$\Rightarrow \quad \frac{dr}{dt} = \frac{3}{4\pi r^2}$ ... (i)

Now, let S be the surface area of sphere.

Then, $S = 4\pi r^2$

$\Rightarrow \quad \frac{dS}{dt} = 4\pi(2r)\frac{dr}{dt}$

$\Rightarrow \quad \frac{dS}{dt} = 8\pi r\left(\frac{3}{4\pi r^2}\right)$ [using Eq. (i)]

$\Rightarrow \quad \left(\frac{dS}{dt}\right) = \frac{6}{r}$

When $r = 2$, then

$$\frac{dS}{dt} = \frac{6}{2} = 3 \text{ cm}^2/\text{s}$$

19. Here, we have to find rate of change of volume with respect to radius, so volume is dependent quantity and radius is independent quantity.

Let r be the radius and V be the volume of spherical balloon.

Then, $V = \frac{4}{3}\pi r^3$.

On differentiating both sides w.r.t. r, we get

$$\frac{dV}{dr} = \frac{4}{3}\pi(3r^2) = 4\pi r^2 \quad \text{...(i)}$$

Now, we have to find rate of change of volume, when radius is 7 cm. So, on putting $r = 7$ in Eq. (i), we get

$$\left(\frac{dV}{dr}\right)_{r=7} = 4\pi(7)^2 = 4\pi(49) = 196\pi \text{ cm}^3/\text{cm}$$

Hence, the volume is increasing with respect to its radius at the rate of 196π cm^3/cm, when the radius is 7 cm.

20. Given that $\frac{dx}{dt} = -6$ cm/min and $\frac{dy}{dt} = 5$ cm/min

Let P and A be the perimeter and area of rectangle.

Then, $P = 2(x + y)$

On differentiating w.r.t. t, we get

$$\frac{dP}{dt} = 2\left(\frac{dx}{dt} + \frac{dy}{dt}\right) = 2(-6 + 5) = -2 \text{ cm/min}$$

And $\quad A = xy$

On differentiating w.r.t. t, we get

$$\frac{dA}{dt} = \frac{dx}{dt}y + x \cdot \frac{dy}{dt}$$

$$= [-6 \times 8 + 10 \times 5]$$

$$= -48 + 50 = 2 \text{ cm}^2/\text{min}$$

Hence, the perimeter of a rectangle is decreasing at the rate of 2 cm/min and area of rectangle is increasing at the rate of 2 cm^2/min.

21. Given, diameter of the balloon $= \frac{3}{2}(2x + 1)$

$\therefore$ Radius of the balloon $= \frac{\text{Diameter}}{2}$

$$= \frac{1}{2}\left[\frac{3}{2}(2x+1)\right] = \frac{3}{4}(2x+1)$$

For the balloon, the volume V is given by

$$V = \frac{4}{3}\pi(\text{radius})^3 = \frac{4}{3}\pi\left[\frac{3}{4}(2x+1)\right]^3 = \frac{9\pi}{16}(2x+1)^3$$

For the rate of change of volume, differentiate w.r.t. x, we get

$$\frac{dV}{dx} = \frac{9\pi}{16} \times 3(2x+1)^2 \times 2 = \frac{27\pi}{8}(2x+1)^2$$

Thus, the rate of change of volume is $\frac{27\pi}{8}(2x+1)^2$.

22. Let the radius of spherical ball of the salt be r.

$\therefore$ Volume of the ball, $V = \frac{4}{3}\pi r^3$ and surface area, $S = 4\pi r^2$

$$\therefore \frac{dV}{dt} = \frac{d}{dt}\left(\frac{4}{3}\pi r^3\right) = -\frac{4}{3}\pi \cdot 3r^2 \frac{dr}{dt} = -4\pi r^2 \frac{dr}{dt}$$

[here, we take negative sign because salt is dissolving]

According to the given condition,

$$\frac{dV}{dt} \propto S \Rightarrow \frac{dV}{dt} = kS,$$

where k is proportionality constant.

$$\Rightarrow \quad -4\pi r^2 \frac{dr}{dt} = k \cdot 4\pi r^2 \Rightarrow \frac{dr}{dt} = -k$$

Hence proved.

23. Let AB be the lamp post and a man CD be at a distance x from the lamp post and let $CE = y$ be his shadow.

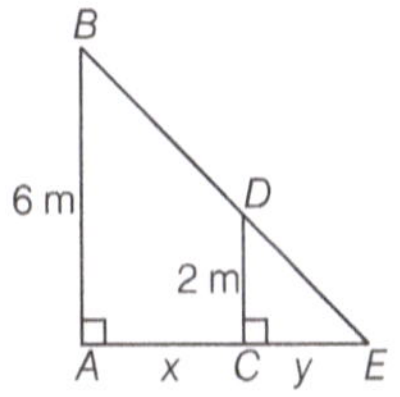

Given that $\frac{dx}{dt} = 6$ km / h, $AB = 6$ m $= \frac{6}{1000}$ km and

$CD = 2$ m $= \frac{2}{1000}$ km [$\because$ 1 km = 1000 m]

Here, $\Delta BAE \sim \Delta DCE$

$\therefore \quad \frac{AB}{CD} = \frac{AE}{CE}$ [by property of similar triangles]

$\Rightarrow \quad \frac{\frac{6}{1000}}{\frac{2}{1000}} = \frac{x+y}{y} \Rightarrow 3 = \frac{x+y}{y}$

$\Rightarrow \quad 3y = x + y \Rightarrow 3y - y = x \Rightarrow 2y = x$

On differentiating both sides w.r.t. t, we get

$$2\frac{dy}{dt} = \frac{dx}{dt}$$

$\Rightarrow \quad 2\frac{dy}{dt} = 6$ $\left[\because \frac{dx}{dt} = 6\right]$

$\Rightarrow \quad \frac{dy}{dt} = \frac{6}{2} = 3$ km/h

Hence, the shadow increases at the rate of 3 km/h.

24. We have, $f(x) = 4x^3 - 18x^2 + 27x - 7$

On differentiating both sides w.r.t. x, we get

$f'(x) = 12x^2 - 36x + 27$

$\Rightarrow \quad f'(x) = 3(4x^2 - 12x + 9)$

$\Rightarrow \quad f'(x) = 3(2x-3)^2$

$\Rightarrow$ For any $x \in R$,

$(2x-3)^2 \geq 0$

[since, a perfect square number cannot be negative.]

$\therefore \quad 3(2x-3)^2 \geq 0, \forall x \in R$

$\therefore \quad f'(x) \geq 0, \forall x \in R$

$\therefore$ Given function $f(x)$ is an increasing function on R.

25. Given, $f(x) = -2x^3 - 9x^2 - 12x + 1$

On differentiating both sides w.r.t. x, we get

$f'(x) = -6x^2 - 18x - 12$

$\Rightarrow \quad f'(x) = -6(x^2 + 3x + 2)$

$\Rightarrow \quad f'(x) = -6(x^2 + 2x + x + 2)$

$= -6[x(x+2) + 1(x+2)]$

$= -6(x+2)(x+1)$

Now, put $f'(x) = 0$

$\Rightarrow -6(x+2)(x+1) = 0 \Rightarrow x = -2, -1$

The points $x = -2$ and $x = -1$ divide the real line into three disjoint intervals $(-\infty, -2)$, $(-2, -1)$ and $(-1, \infty)$.

The nature of function in these intervals are given below.

Interval	Sign of $f'(x)$ $f'(x) = -6(x+2)(x+1)$	Nature of function
$(-\infty, -2)$	$(-)(-)(-) = (-) < 0$	Strictly decreasing
$(-2, -1)$	$(-)(+)(-) = (+) > 0$	Strictly increasing
$(-1, \infty)$	$(-)(+)(+) = (-) < 0$	Strictly decreasing

Hence, $f(x)$ is strictly increasing in the interval $(-2, -1)$ and $f(x)$ is strictly decreasing in the interval $(-\infty, -2) \cup (-1, \infty)$.

26. Given, $y = [x(x-2)]^2 = [x^2 - 2x]^2$

On differentiating both sides w.r.t. x, we get

$$\frac{dy}{dx} = 2(x^2 - 2x) \cdot \frac{d}{dx}(x^2 - 2x)$$

$= 2(x^2 - 2x)(2x - 2)$

$= 2[2x^3 - 6x^2 + 4x]$

$= 4x[x^2 - 3x + 2]$

$= 4x(x-2)(x-1)$

On putting $\frac{dy}{dx} = 0$, we get

$4x(x-2)(x-1) = 0 \Rightarrow x = 0, 1$ and 2

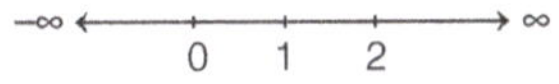

These values divide the real line into four disjoint intervals $(-\infty, 0)$, $(0, 1)$, $(1, 2)$ and $(2, \infty)$.

In each interval, nature of $y(x)$ is given below.

Interval	Sign of $f'(x)$	Nature of $y(x)$
$(-\infty, 0)$	$(-)(-)(-) = -$ve	Strictly decreasing
$(0, 1)$	$(+)(-)(-) = +$ ve	Strictly increasing
$(1, 2)$	$(+)(-)(+) = -$ ve	Strictly decreasing
$(2, \infty)$	$(+)(+)(+) = +$ve	Strictly increasing

Therefore, $y(x)$ is increasing in $(0, 1)$ and $(2, \infty)$.

$\Rightarrow \quad 0 < x < 1$ and $x > 2$.

27. Hint $f'(x) = \frac{1+2x^2}{1+x^2} - \frac{1}{\sqrt{1+x^2}} = \frac{1+2x^2 - \sqrt{1+x^2}}{1+x^2}$

Now, $f'(x) \geq 0$

$\Rightarrow \quad \frac{1+2x^2 - \sqrt{1+x^2}}{1+x^2} \geq 0 \Rightarrow 1 + 2x^2 \geq \sqrt{1+x^2}$

$\Rightarrow \quad 1 + 4x^4 + 4x^2 \geq 1 + x^2$

$\Rightarrow \quad 4x^4 + 3x^2 \geq 0$, which is true for all $x \in R$.

So, $f'(x) \geq 0, \forall x \in R$.

28. Here, $f'(x) = \frac{1}{1+(\sin x+\cos x)^2} \times (\cos x - \sin x)$

$= \frac{(\cos x - \sin x)}{1+(\sin x + \cos x)^2}$

In the interval $\left(0, \frac{\pi}{4}\right)$, $\cos x > \sin x > 0$

$\therefore$ $\cos x - \sin x > 0$ or $\frac{\cos x - \sin x}{1+(\sin x+\cos x)^2} > 0$

$\Rightarrow$ $f'(x) > 0, \forall\ x \in \left(0, \frac{\pi}{4}\right)$

Hence, $f(x)$ is strictly increasing in $\left(0, \frac{\pi}{4}\right)$.

29. Given, $f(x) = \frac{2}{x} + \frac{x}{2}$

On differentiating twice w.r.t. x, we get

$f'(x) = -\frac{2}{x^2} + \frac{1}{2}$

and $f''(x) = \frac{4}{x^3} + 0$

For local maxima or local minima, put $f'(x) = 0$

$\Rightarrow$ $-\frac{2}{x^2} + \frac{1}{2} = 0 \Rightarrow x^2 = 4 \Rightarrow x = \pm 2$

Since, it is given that $x > 0$, so we consider $x = 2$ only.

Now, $f''(2) = \frac{4}{2^3} = \frac{4}{8} = \frac{1}{2} > 0$

Thus, $f(x)$ is local minima at $x = 2$.

So, local minimum value of $f(x)$ at $x = 2$ is

$f(2) = \frac{2}{2} + \frac{2}{2} = 1 + 1 = 2.$

30. Given, $P(x) = 51 + 42x - x^2$

On differentiating w.r.t. x, we get

$P'(x) = 42 - 2x$

For maximum profit, we put $P'(x) = 0$

$\Rightarrow$ $42 - 2x = 0$

$\Rightarrow$ $x = 21$

Now, $P''(x) = -2$

$\because$ $P''(x) < 0$

$\therefore$ $P(x)$ is maximum at $x = 21$.

$\therefore$ The maximum value of $P(x)$ is at $x = 21$.

$\Rightarrow$ $P(21) = 51 + 42(21) - (21)^2$

$= 51 + 882 - 441 = 492$

Thus, the maximum profit is ₹ 492.

31. Given, $f(x) = x^3 + x, \forall\ x \in R$

On differentiating w.r.t. x, we get

$f'(x) = 3x^2 + 1$

$\because$ $x^2 > 0, \forall\ x \in R$

$\therefore$ $f'(x)$ can never be zero or undefined, $\forall\ x \in R$.

$\Rightarrow$ $f'(x) > 0$

Hence, no critical point exist.

32. We have, $f(x) = ax + \frac{b}{x} (a > 0, b > 0, x > 0)$

$\therefore$ $f'(x) = a - \frac{b}{x^2}$ and $f''(x) = \frac{2b}{x^3}$

For maxima or minima of $f(x)$, $f'(x) = 0$

$\Rightarrow$ $a - \frac{b}{x^2} = 0 \Rightarrow x^2 = \frac{b}{a}$

$\Rightarrow$ $x = \sqrt{\frac{b}{a}}$ $[\because x > 0 \text{ (given)}]$

Again, $f''\left(\sqrt{\frac{b}{a}}\right) = \frac{2b}{\left(\frac{b}{a}\right)^{3/2}} = \frac{2a^{3/2}}{\sqrt{b}} > 0$ $[\because a > 0, b > 0]$

So, $f(x)$ has least value at $x = \sqrt{\frac{b}{a}}$.

$\therefore$ Least value of $f(x) = f\left(\sqrt{\frac{b}{a}}\right) = a\sqrt{\frac{b}{a}} + \frac{b}{\sqrt{\frac{b}{a}}}$

$= \sqrt{ab} + \sqrt{ab} = 2\sqrt{ab}$

33. **Hint** $f'(x) = 5x^2(x-1)(x-3)$

Ans. $x = 1$ is point of local maxima,

$x = 3$ is point of local minima, $x = 0$ is point of inflection,

Local maximum value $= 0$,

Local minimum value $= -28$

34. **Hint** Let x be length and y be breadth of rectangle.

Given, $2(x + y) = p$, then $A = xy = x\left(\frac{p}{2} - x\right)$

$\because$ $\frac{dA}{dx} = 0$, we get $x = y$.

35. **Hint** Let $AR = x$. Then, $BR = 20 - x$

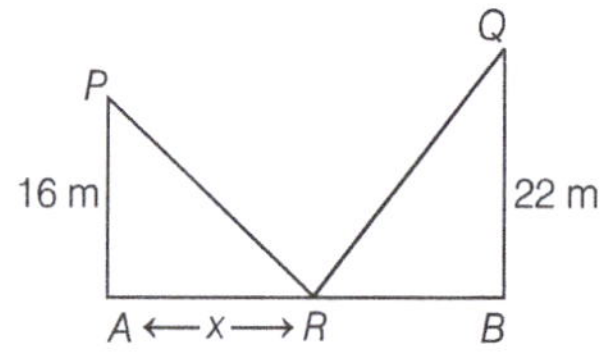

$\because$ $RP^2 + RQ^2 = x^2 + (20 - x)^2 + 740$

Ans. 10 m

36. **Hint** Let $A(h, k)$ be any point on the curve $y = x^2 + 7$ and $B(3, 7)$ be the given point.

$\therefore$ Distance between A and B is $AB = \sqrt{(h-3)^2 + (k-7)^2}$.

Since, the point $A(h, k)$ lies on the curve.

$\therefore$ $k = h^2 + 7 \Rightarrow AB = \sqrt{(h-3)^2 + (h^2 + 7 - 7)^2}$

or $AB^2 = (h-3)^2 + (h^2)^2$

Let $AB^2 = f(h)$, then AB is maximum or minimum accordingly as $f(h)$ is maximum or minimum.

$\therefore$ $f(h) = (h-3)^2 + h^4$ **Ans.** $\sqrt{5}$ units.

37. Given that L represents the number of litres of water in the pool, t seconds after the pool has been plugged off to drain, then

$$L = 200(10-t)^2$$

$\therefore$ Rate at which the water is running out,

$$\frac{dL}{dt} = -200 \cdot 2(10-t)\cdot(-1)$$

$$= 400(10-t)$$

[here, we take negative sign because the water is decreasing]

Rate at which the water is running out at the end of 5 s

$$= 400(10-5) = 2000 \text{ L/s} = \text{Final rate}$$

Initial rate (at $t = 0$) $= \left(\frac{dL}{dt}\right)_{t=0} = 4000$ L/s

$\therefore$ Average rate during 5 s $= \frac{\text{Initial rate} + \text{Final rate}}{2}$

$$= \frac{4000+2000}{2} = 3000 \text{ L/s}$$

Hence, the water flows out during the first 5 s with average rate of 3000 L/s.

38. Let CD be the height of kite and AB be the height of boy.

Then, height of kite $CD = h = 151.5$ m.

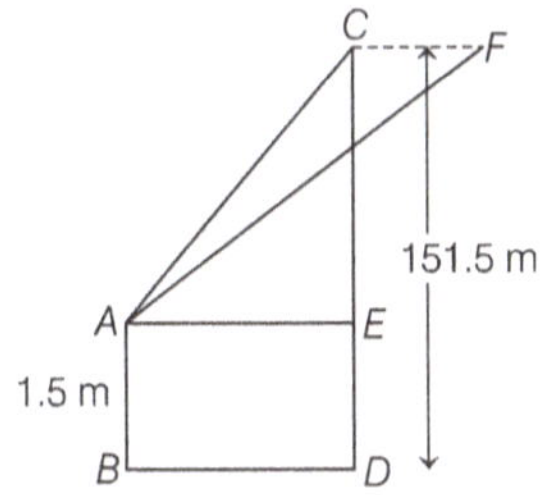

Let $DB = x \text{ m} = EA$

Since, the kite is 250 m away from the boy.

So, $AC = y = 250$ m

Speed of the kite, $v = \frac{dx}{dt} = 10$ m/s

From the figure, we get

$$EC = 151.5 - 1.5 = 150 \text{ m}$$

In right angled ΔCEA, we get

$$AE^2 + EC^2 = AC^2 \quad \text{[by Pythagoras theorem]}$$

$\Rightarrow \quad x^2 + (150)^2 = y^2 \quad$ ...(i)

$\Rightarrow \quad x^2 + (150)^2 = (250)^2$

$\Rightarrow \quad x^2 = (250)^2 - (150)^2$

$\Rightarrow \quad x^2 = (250+150)(250-150) = 400 \times 100$

$\Rightarrow \quad x = 20 \times 10 = 200$

On differentiating both sides of Eq. (i) w.r.t. t, we get

$$2x \cdot \frac{dx}{dt} + 0 = 2y\frac{dy}{dt}$$

$\Rightarrow \quad 2y \cdot \frac{dy}{dt} = 2x\frac{dx}{dt}$

$\Rightarrow \quad \frac{dy}{dt} = \frac{x}{y}\cdot\frac{dx}{dt} = \frac{200}{250}\cdot 10 = 8 \text{ m/s} \quad \left[\because \frac{dx}{dt} = 10 \text{ m/s}\right]$

Hence, the required rate at which the string is being let out is 8 m/s.

39. Let two men start from the point C with velocity v each at the same time.

Also, $\angle BCA = 45°$

Since, A and B are moving with same velocity v, so they will cover same distance in same time.

Therefore, ΔABC is an isosceles triangle with $AC = BC$.

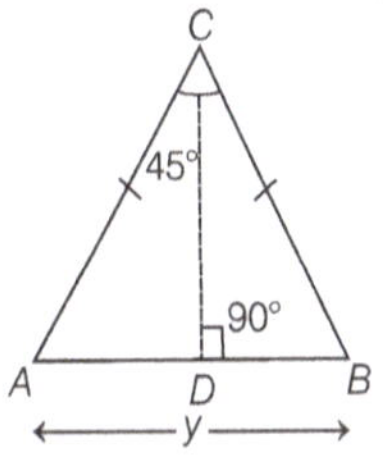

Now, draw $CD \perp AB$.

Let at any instant t, the distance between them is AB.

Let $AC = BC = x$ and $AB = y$

In ΔACD and ΔDCB, we get

$$\angle CAD = \angle CBD \quad [\because BC = AC \Rightarrow \angle A = \angle B]$$

[angles opposite to equal sides]

$$\angle CDA = \angle CDB = 90°$$

$\therefore \quad \angle ACD = \angle DCB$ or $\angle ACD = \frac{1}{2} \times \angle ACB$

$\Rightarrow \quad \angle ACD = \frac{1}{2} \times 45° \Rightarrow \angle ACD = 22.5°$

$\therefore \quad \sin 22.5° = \frac{AD}{AC} \Rightarrow \sin 22.5° = \frac{y/2}{x}$

$\Rightarrow \quad \frac{y}{2} = x\sin 22.5° \Rightarrow y = 2x \cdot \sin 22.5°$

On differentiating both sides w.r.t. t, we get

$$\frac{dy}{dt} = 2\cdot\sin 22.5°\frac{dx}{dt} = 2\cdot\sin 22.5° v \quad \left[\because v = \frac{dx}{dt}\right]$$

$$= 2v\cdot\frac{\sqrt{2-\sqrt{2}}}{2} = v\sqrt{2-\sqrt{2}} \quad \left[\because \sin 22.5° = \frac{\sqrt{2-\sqrt{2}}}{2}\right]$$

which is the required rate at which A and B are being separated.

40. (i) Let r be the radius, h be the height, α be the semi-vertical angle and V be the volume of the cone.

Given, $\frac{dV}{dt} = 0.1 \text{ cm}^3\text{/s}$

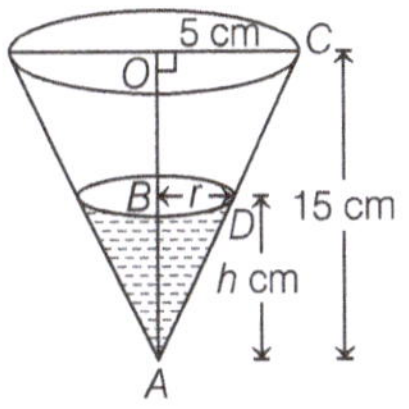

In $\Delta OAC, \tan\alpha = \frac{5}{15} = \frac{1}{3}$ ...(i)

Also, $\tan\alpha = \frac{BD}{AB} = \frac{r}{h}$ ...(ii)

From Eqs. (i) and (ii), we get

$$\frac{1}{3} = \frac{r}{h} \Rightarrow 3r = h$$

Now, $V = \frac{1}{3}\pi r^2 h = \frac{1}{3}\pi\left(\frac{h}{3}\right)^2 h = \frac{\pi}{27}h^3$ ...(iii)

On differentiating Eq. (i) w.r.t. t, we get

$$\frac{dV}{dt} = \frac{\pi}{27}\cdot 3h^2\frac{dh}{dt}$$

$$\Rightarrow \quad 0.1 = \frac{\pi}{9}h^2\frac{dh}{dt} = \frac{\pi\cdot 36}{9}\frac{dh}{dt} \quad [\because h = 6 \text{ cm (given)}]$$

$$\Rightarrow \quad \frac{dh}{dt} = \frac{0.1}{4\pi} = \frac{1}{40\pi} \text{ cm/s}$$

(ii) Water surface area (A) at any time $t = \pi r^2$

$$= \pi\frac{h^2}{9} \quad \left[\text{from part (i)}, \frac{5}{r} = \frac{15}{h} \Rightarrow r = \frac{h}{3}\right]$$

$$\Rightarrow \quad \frac{dA}{dt} = \frac{2\pi}{9}h\frac{dh}{dt}$$

Now, $\left(\frac{dA}{dt}\right)_{h=6} = \frac{2\pi}{9}\times 6\times\frac{1}{40\pi} = \frac{1}{30} \text{ cm}^2\text{/s}$

$$\left[\because \frac{dh}{dt} = \frac{1}{40\pi}, \text{ from part (i)}\right]$$

(iii) Wetted surface area (S) of the vessel at any time t

$$= \pi rl$$

$$= \pi\frac{h}{3}\sqrt{r^2 + h^2} = \pi\frac{h}{3}\sqrt{\frac{h^2}{9} + h^2}$$

$$= \pi\cdot\frac{h}{3}\cdot\frac{\sqrt{10}h}{3} = \frac{\pi}{9}\sqrt{10}h^2$$

Now, $\frac{dS}{dt} = \frac{2\pi\sqrt{10}}{9}h\frac{dh}{dt}$

$$\Rightarrow \quad \left(\frac{dS}{dt}\right)_{\text{at } h=6} = \frac{2\pi\sqrt{10}}{9}\times 6\times\frac{1}{40\pi}$$

$$= \frac{\sqrt{10}}{30} \text{ cm}^2\text{/s}$$

41. Hint Let r be the radius, h be the height, α be semi-vertical angle and V be the volume of the cone.

Given, $\frac{dV}{dt} = 5 \text{ m}^3\text{/h}$ and $h = 4$ m

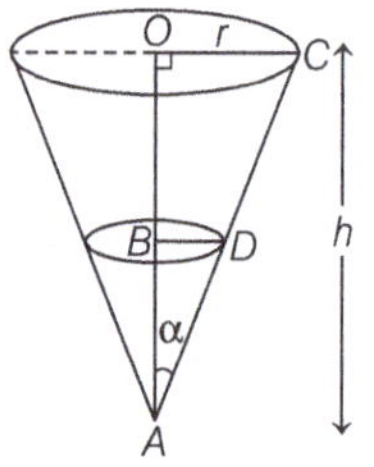

In ΔOAC, $\tan\alpha = \frac{r}{h}$

$$\Rightarrow \quad \alpha = \tan^{-1}\left(\frac{r}{h}\right)$$

But $\alpha = \tan^{-1}(0.5)$

$$\therefore \quad \tan^{-1}\left(\frac{r}{h}\right) = \tan^{-1}(0.5)$$

$$\Rightarrow \quad r = \frac{h}{2}$$

$\therefore$ Volume of the tank is

$$V = \frac{1}{3}\pi r^2 h$$

$$= \frac{1}{3}\pi\left(\frac{h}{2}\right)^2 h$$

Ans. $\frac{35}{88}$ m/h

42. Given, for $a \ge 1$, $f(x) = \sqrt{3}\sin x - \cos x - 2ax + b$

On differentiating both sides w.r.t. x, we get

$$f'(x) = \sqrt{3}\cos x - (-\sin x) - 2a$$

$$= \sqrt{3}\cos x + \sin x - 2a$$

$$= 2\left[\frac{\sqrt{3}}{2}\cdot\cos x + \frac{1}{2}\cdot\sin x\right] - 2a$$

[multiply and divide by 2]

$$= 2\left[\cos\frac{\pi}{6}\cdot\cos x + \sin\frac{\pi}{6}\cdot\sin x\right] - 2a$$

$$= 2\cos\left(\frac{\pi}{6} - x\right) - 2a$$

$$[\because \cos(A - B) = \cos A\cdot\cos B + \sin A\cdot\sin B]$$

$$= 2\left[\cos\left(\frac{\pi}{6} - x\right) - a\right]$$

We know that $\cos x \in [-1, 1]$ and $a \ge 1$.

So, $2\left[\cos\left(\frac{\pi}{6} - x\right) - a\right] \le 0 \Rightarrow f'(x) \le 0$

Hence, $f(x)$ is a decreasing function in R.

43. We have, $\quad f(x) = \frac{x^4}{4} - x^3 - 5x^2 + 24x + 12$

On differentiating both sides w.r.t. x, we get

$$f'(x) = x^3 - 3x^2 - 10x + 24$$

$$= (x - 2)(x^2 - x - 12)$$

$$= (x - 2)(x^2 - 4x + 3x - 12)$$

$$= (x - 2)[x(x - 4) + 3(x - 4)]$$

$$= (x - 2)(x - 4)(x + 3)$$

Now, put $f'(x) = 0$, which gives $x = 2, 4$ and -3.

The points $x = -3$, $x = 2$ and $x = 4$ divides the whole real line into four disjoint intervals namely, $(-\infty, -3), (-3, 2), (2, 4), (4, \infty)$.

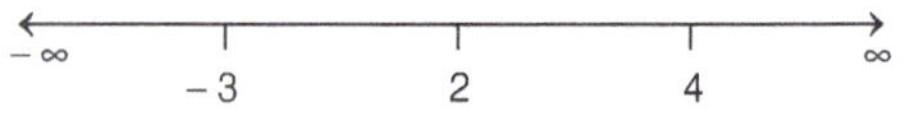

Note that

for $x \in (-\infty, -3)$, $f'(x) < 0$

for $x \in (-3, 2)$, $f'(x) > 0$

for $x \in (2, 4)$, $f'(x) < 0$

and for $x \in (4, \infty)$, $f'(x) > 0$

$\therefore$ $f(x)$ is strictly increasing in the intervals $(-3, 2)$ and $(4, \infty)$, and strictly decreasing in the intervals $(-\infty, -3)$ and $(2, 4)$.

44. Hint $f'(x) = 2x - 1$, which is both positive and negative in $(-1, 1)$.

Hence, $f(x)$ is neither increasing nor decreasing.

Ans. (i) $\left(\frac{1}{2}, 1\right)$ (ii) $\left(-1, \frac{1}{2}\right)$

45. Let $y = f(\theta) = \dfrac{4\sin\theta}{2 + \cos\theta} - \theta$

On differentiating both sides w.r.t. θ, we get

$$f'(\theta) = \frac{(2 + \cos\theta)(4\cos\theta) - 4\sin\theta\,(0 - \sin\theta)}{(2 + \cos\theta)^2} - 1$$

[by quotient rule of derivative]

$$= \frac{8\cos\theta + 4\cos^2\theta + 4\sin^2\theta}{(2 + \cos\theta)^2} - 1$$

$$= \frac{8\cos\theta + 4}{(2 + \cos\theta)^2} - 1 \qquad [\because \sin^2 A + \cos^2 A = 1]$$

$$= \frac{8\cos\theta + 4 - 4 - \cos^2\theta - 4\cos\theta}{(2 + \cos\theta)^2}$$

$$= \frac{4\cos\theta - \cos^2\theta}{(2 + \cos\theta)^2}$$

$$= \frac{\cos\theta\,(4 - \cos\theta)}{(2 + \cos\theta)^2}$$

For all $x \in \left(0, \frac{\pi}{2}\right)$, $\dfrac{\cos\theta\,(4 - \cos\theta)}{(2 + \cos\theta)^2} > 0$

$\Rightarrow$ $f'(\theta) > 0, \forall\, \theta \in \left(0, \frac{\pi}{2}\right)$

Therefore, $f(\theta)$ is strictly increasing in $\left(0, \frac{\pi}{2}\right)$.

Hence, $f(\theta)$ is increasing in $\left[0, \frac{\pi}{2}\right]$. **Hence proved.**

46. Given, $f(x) = 5 + \sin 2x$

$\Rightarrow$ $f'(x) = 2\cos 2x$

$\Rightarrow$ $f''(x) = -4\sin 2x$

For maxima or minima, put $f'(x) = 0$

$\Rightarrow$ $2\cos 2x = 0$

$\Rightarrow$ $\cos 2x = 0 = \cos\frac{\pi}{2}$ or $\cos\frac{3\pi}{2}$

$\Rightarrow$ $2x = \frac{\pi}{2}, \frac{3\pi}{2} \Rightarrow x = \frac{\pi}{4}, \frac{3\pi}{4}$

Now, $f''\left(\frac{\pi}{4}\right) = -4\sin\left(2 \times \frac{\pi}{4}\right)$

$= -4\sin\frac{\pi}{2} = -4 < 0$

So, $x = \frac{\pi}{4}$ is point of maxima.

and $f''\left(\frac{3\pi}{4}\right) = -4\sin\left(2 \times \frac{3\pi}{4}\right) = -4\sin\frac{3\pi}{2}$

$= -4\sin\left(2\pi - \frac{\pi}{2}\right) = 4\sin\frac{\pi}{2} = 4 > 0$

$\therefore$ $x = \frac{3\pi}{4}$ is the point of minima.

$\therefore$ Maximum value of $f(x)$ at $x = \frac{\pi}{4} = 5 + \sin\left(2 \times \frac{\pi}{4}\right)$

$= 5 + \sin\left(\frac{\pi}{2}\right) = 5 + 1 = 6$

and minimum value of $f(x)$ at $x = \frac{3\pi}{4}$

$= 5 + \sin\left(2 \times \frac{3\pi}{4}\right)$

$= 5 + \sin\frac{3\pi}{2} = 5 - \sin\frac{\pi}{2} = 5 - 1 = 4$

47. Let R be the radius and h be the height of the cone, which inscribed in a sphere of radius r.

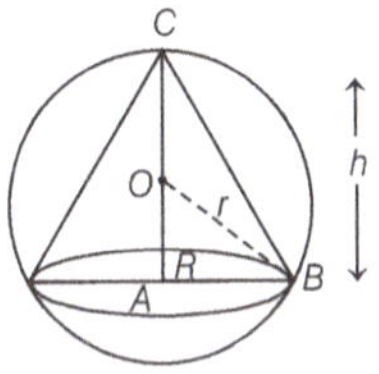

$\therefore$ $OA = h - r$

In ΔOAB, by Pythagoras theorem, we get

$$r^2 = R^2 + (h - r)^2$$

$\Rightarrow$ $r^2 = R^2 + h^2 + r^2 - 2rh$

$\Rightarrow$ $R^2 = 2rh - h^2$ ...(i)

The volume of sphere $= \frac{4}{3}\pi r^3$

and the volume V of the cone,

$$V = \frac{1}{3}\pi R^2 h$$

$\Rightarrow$ $V = \frac{1}{3}\pi h(2rh - h^2)$ [from Eq. (i)]

$\Rightarrow$ $V = \frac{1}{3}\pi(2rh^2 - h^3)$ ...(ii)

On differentiating both sides of Eq. (ii) w.r.t. h, we get

$$\frac{dV}{dh} = \frac{1}{3}\pi(4rh - 3h^2) \qquad \text{...(iii)}$$

For maxima or minima, put $\frac{dV}{dh} = 0$

$\Rightarrow$ $\frac{1}{3}\pi(4rh - 3h^2) = 0$

$\Rightarrow \quad 4rh = 3h^2 \Rightarrow 4r = 3h$

$\Rightarrow \quad h = \frac{4r}{3} \qquad [\because h \neq 0]$

Again, on differentiating Eq. (iii) w.r.t. h, we get

$$\frac{d^2V}{dh^2} = \frac{1}{3}\pi(4r - 6h)$$

At $h = \frac{4r}{3}$, $\left(\frac{d^2V}{dh^2}\right)_{h=\frac{4r}{3}} = \frac{1}{3}\pi\left(4r - 6 \times \frac{4r}{3}\right)$

$$= \frac{\pi}{3}(4r - 8r) = -\frac{4r\pi}{3} < 0$$

$\Rightarrow V$ is maximum at $h = \frac{4r}{3}$.

On putting the value of h in Eq. (ii), we get

$$V = \frac{1}{3}\pi\left[2r\left(\frac{4r}{3}\right)^2 - \left(\frac{4r}{3}\right)^3\right]$$

$$= \frac{1}{3}\pi\left[2r \times \frac{16}{9}r^2 - \frac{64r^3}{27}\right]$$

$$= \frac{1}{3}\pi\left[\frac{32r^3}{9} - \frac{64r^3}{27}\right]$$

$$= \frac{1}{3}\pi\frac{32r^3}{9}\left[1 - \frac{2}{3}\right] = \frac{32\pi}{27}r^3\left[\frac{1}{3}\right]$$

$$= \frac{8}{27} \times \frac{4\pi r^3}{3}$$

$$= \frac{8}{27} \times \text{Volume of sphere.}$$

Hence, the maximum volume of the cone is $\frac{8}{27}$ of the volume of the sphere.

48. Let $AC = x$, $BC = y$ and r be the radius of circle.

Also, $\angle C = 90°$ [$\because$ angle made in semi-circle is 90°]

In ΔABC, we have

$$AB^2 = AC^2 + BC^2$$

$\Rightarrow \quad (2r)^2 = (x)^2 + (y)^2$

$\Rightarrow \quad 4r^2 = x^2 + y^2 \qquad \ldots(i)$

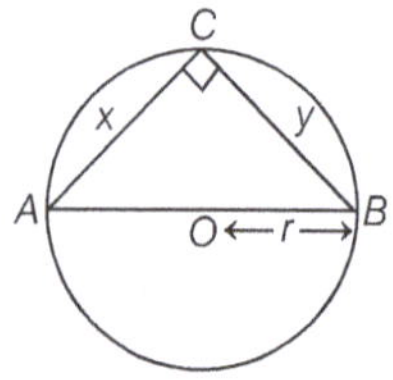

We know that area of ΔABC, $A = \frac{1}{2}x \cdot y$

On squaring both sides, we get

$$A^2 = \frac{1}{4}x^2y^2$$

Let $\quad A^2 = S$

Then, $\quad S = \frac{1}{4}x^2y^2$

$\Rightarrow \quad S = \frac{1}{4}x^2(4r^2 - x^2) \qquad$ [from Eq. (i)]

$\Rightarrow \quad S = \frac{1}{4}(4x^2r^2 - x^4)$

On differentiating both sides w.r.t. x, we get

$$\frac{dS}{dx} = \frac{1}{4}(8r^2x - 4x^3)$$

For maxima or minima, put $\frac{dS}{dx} = 0$

$\therefore \quad \frac{1}{4}(8r^2x - 4x^3) = 0$

$\Rightarrow \quad 8r^2x = 4x^3$

$\Rightarrow \quad 8r^2 = 4x^2 \Rightarrow x^2 = 2r^2$

$\Rightarrow \quad x = \sqrt{2}r$

From Eq. (i), we get

$$y^2 = 4r^2 - 2r^2 = 2r^2 \Rightarrow y = \sqrt{2}r$$

Here, $x = y$, so triangle is an isosceles.

Also, $\frac{d^2S}{dx^2} = \frac{d}{dx}\left[\frac{1}{4}(8r^2x - 4x^3)\right] = \frac{1}{4}(8r^2 - 12x^2)$

$$= 2r^2 - 3x^2$$

At $x = \sqrt{2}r$, $\frac{d^2S}{dx^2} = 2r^2 - 3(2r^2) < 0 = -4r^2 < 0$

Hence, the area is maximum when triangle is an isosceles.

49. Let θ be the semi-vertical angle of the cone.

It is clear that $\theta \in \left(0, \frac{\pi}{2}\right)$.

Let r, h and l be the radius, height and the slant height of the cone, respectively.

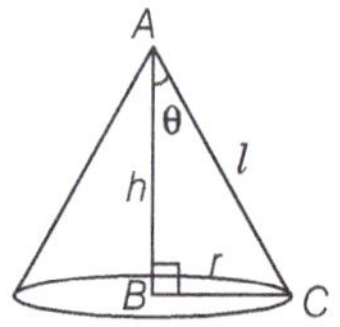

Since, slant height of the cone is given, so consider it as constant.

Now, in ΔABC, $r = l\sin\theta$ and $h = l\cos\theta$

Let V be the volume of the cone.

Then, $V = \frac{\pi}{3}r^2h \Rightarrow V = \frac{1}{3}\pi(l^2\sin^2\theta)(l\cos\theta)$

$\Rightarrow \quad V = \frac{1}{3}\pi l^3 \sin^2\theta\cos\theta$

On differentiating both sides w.r.t. θ two times, we get

$$\frac{dV}{d\theta} = \frac{l^3\pi}{3}[\sin^2\theta(-\sin\theta) + \cos\theta(2\sin\theta\cos\theta)]$$

$$= \frac{l^3\pi}{3}(-\sin^3\theta + 2\sin\theta\cos^2\theta)$$

and $\frac{d^2V}{d\theta^2} = \frac{l^3\pi}{3}(-3\sin^2\theta\cos\theta + 2\cos^3\theta - 4\sin^2\theta\cos\theta)$

$\Rightarrow \quad \frac{d^2V}{d\theta^2} = \frac{l^3\pi}{3}(2\cos^3\theta - 7\sin^2\theta\cos\theta)$

For maxima or minima, put $\frac{dV}{d\theta} = 0$

$\Rightarrow \quad \sin^3\theta = 2\sin\theta\cos^2\theta \Rightarrow \tan^2\theta = 2$

$\Rightarrow \quad \tan\theta = \sqrt{2} \quad \Rightarrow \quad \theta = \tan^{-1}\sqrt{2}$

Now, when $\theta = \tan^{-1}\sqrt{2}$, then $\tan^2\theta = 2$

$\Rightarrow \quad \sin^2\theta = 2\cos^2\theta$

Now, we have

$$\frac{d^2V}{d\theta^2} = \frac{l^3\pi}{3}(2\cos^3\theta - 14\cos^3\theta)$$

$$= -4\pi l^3\cos^3\theta < 0, \text{ for } \theta \in \left(0, \frac{\pi}{2}\right)$$

$\therefore V$ is maximum, when $\theta = \tan^{-1}\sqrt{2}$ or $\theta = \cos^{-1}\frac{1}{\sqrt{3}}$.

$$\left[\because \cos\theta = \frac{1}{\sqrt{1+\tan^2\theta}} = \frac{1}{\sqrt{1+2}} = \frac{1}{\sqrt{3}}\right]$$

Hence, for given slant height, the semi-vertical angle of the cone of maximum volume is $\cos^{-1}\frac{1}{\sqrt{3}}$. **Hence proved.**

50. Let $ABCD$ be the given trapezium in which $AD = BC = CD = 10$ cm.

Let $\quad AP = x$ cm

$\because \quad \Delta APD \cong \Delta BQC$

$\therefore \quad QB = x$ cm

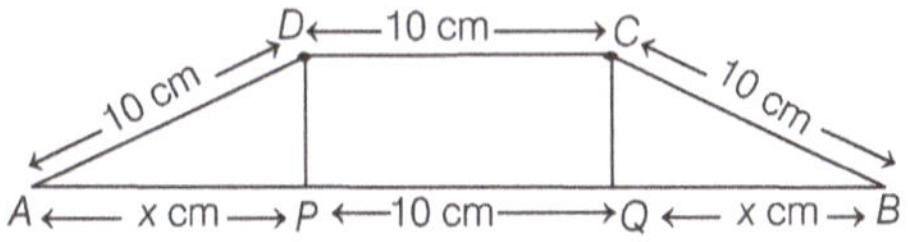

In ΔAPD,

$DP = \sqrt{10^2 - x^2}$ [by Pythagoras theorem]

Now, area of trapezium,

$$A = \frac{1}{2} \times \text{Sum of parallel sides} \times \text{Height}$$

$$= \frac{1}{2} \times (2x + 10 + 10) \times \sqrt{100 - x^2}$$

$$= (x + 10)\sqrt{100 - x^2} \quad \text{...(i)}$$

On differentiating both sides of Eq. (i) w.r.t. x, we get

$$\frac{dA}{dx} = (x + 10)\frac{(-2x)}{2\sqrt{100 - x^2}} + \sqrt{100 - x^2}$$

$$= \frac{-x^2 - 10x + 100 - x^2}{\sqrt{100 - x^2}}$$

$$= \frac{-2x^2 - 10x + 100}{\sqrt{100 - x^2}} \quad \text{...(ii)}$$

For maxima or minima, put $\frac{dA}{dx} = 0$,

$$-2x^2 - 10x + 100 = 0$$

$\Rightarrow \quad x^2 + 5x - 50 = 0$

$\Rightarrow \quad x^2 + 10x - 5x - 50 = 0$

$\Rightarrow \quad (x + 10)(x - 5) = 0$

$\Rightarrow \quad x = 5, -10$

$\Rightarrow \quad x = 5$

[$\because$ length cannot be negative]

$$\text{Now, } \frac{d^2A}{dx^2} = \frac{\sqrt{100 - x^2}[-4x - 10] - [-2x^2 - 10x + 100]\left[\frac{-2x}{2\sqrt{100 - x^2}}\right]}{100 - x^2}$$

$$= \frac{(100 - x^2)(-4x - 10) + (-2x^3 - 10x^2 + 100x)}{(100 - x^2)^{3/2}}$$

$$= \frac{-400x - 1000 + 4x^3 + 10x^2 - 2x^3 - 10x^2 + 100x}{(100 - x^2)^{3/2}}$$

$$= \frac{2x^3 - 300x - 1000}{(100 - x^2)^{3/2}}$$

$$\Rightarrow \left.\frac{d^2A}{dx^2}\right|_{x=5} = \frac{250 - 1500 - 1000}{(75)^{3/2}} \Rightarrow \frac{d^2A}{dx^2} < 0$$

$\therefore$ Area is maximum at $x = 5$.

Now, the maximum area of trapezium,

$$A_{max} = (5 + 10)\sqrt{100 - 25}$$

$$= 15\sqrt{75}$$

$$\Rightarrow \quad A_{max} = 75\sqrt{3} \text{ cm}^2$$

51. Let r be the radius of the base, h be the height, V be the volume, S be the surface area of the cone ABC and θ be the semi-vertical angle.

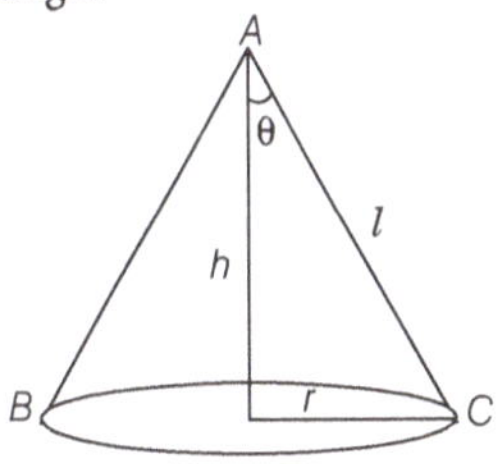

Then, $\quad V = \frac{1}{3}\pi r^2 h \Rightarrow 3V = \pi r^2 h$

$\Rightarrow \quad 9V^2 = \pi^2 r^4 h^2$ [squaring both sides]

$\Rightarrow \quad h^2 = \frac{9V^2}{\pi^2 r^4}$ ...(i)

and curved surface area, $S = \pi r l$

$\Rightarrow \quad S = \pi r\sqrt{r^2 + h^2}$ [$\because l = \sqrt{h^2 + r^2}$]

$\Rightarrow \quad S^2 = \pi^2 r^2(r^2 + h^2)$ [squaring both sides]

$\Rightarrow \quad S^2 = \pi^2 r^2\left(\frac{9V^2}{\pi^2 r^4} + r^2\right)$ [from Eq. (i)]

$\Rightarrow \quad S^2 = \frac{9V^2}{r^2} + \pi^2 r^4$ ...(ii)

When S is least, then S^2 is also least.

Since, volume is given, so it is consider as constant.

Now, $\frac{d}{dr}(S^2) = -\frac{18V^2}{r^3} + 4\pi^2 r^3$ ...(iii)

For maxima or minima, put $\frac{d}{dr}(S^2) = 0$

$$\Rightarrow \quad -\frac{18V^2}{r^3} + 4\pi^2 r^3 = 0$$

$$\Rightarrow \quad 18V^2 = 4\pi^2 r^6$$

$$\Rightarrow \quad 9V^2 = 2\pi^2 r^6 \quad \text{...(iv)}$$

Again, on differentiating Eq. (iii) w.r.t. r, we get

$$\frac{d^2}{dr^2}(S^2) = \frac{54V^2}{r^4} + 12\pi^2 r^2$$

At $r = \left(\frac{9V^2}{2\pi^2}\right)^{1/6}$, $\frac{d^2}{dr^2}(S^2) > 0$

So, S^2 or S is minimum, when

$$V^2 = \frac{2\pi^2 r^6}{9}$$

On putting $V^2 = \frac{2\pi^2 r^6}{9}$ in Eq. (i), we get

$$2\pi^2 r^6 = \pi^2 r^4 h^2$$

$$\Rightarrow \quad 2r^2 = h^2$$

$$\Rightarrow \quad h = \sqrt{2}\, r \Rightarrow \frac{h}{r} = \sqrt{2}$$

$$\Rightarrow \quad \cot\theta = \sqrt{2} \quad \left[\text{from the figure, } \cot\theta = \frac{h}{r}\right]$$

$$\therefore \quad \theta = \cot^{-1}\sqrt{2}$$

Hence, the semi-vertical angle of the right circular cone of given volume and least curved surface area is $\cot^{-1}\sqrt{2}$.

QR Code for Quick Test 1

QR Code for Quick Test 2

Mind Map

Application of Derivatives

Increasing and Decreasing Functions

Increasing Function

A function f is called an increasing function on interval I if $x_1 < x_2$ in $I \Rightarrow f(x_1) \le f(x_2)$ for all $x_1, x_2 \in I$

Strictly Increasing Function

A function f is called a strictly increasing function on interval I, if $x_1 < x_2$ in $I \Rightarrow f(x_1) \le f(x_2)$ for all $x_1, x_2 \in I$

Decreasing Function

A function f is called a decreasing function on interval I, if $x_1 < x_2$ in $I \Rightarrow f(x_1) \ge f(x_2)$ for all $x_1, x_2 \in I$

Strictly Decreasing Function

A function f is called a strictly decreasing function on interval I, if $x_1 < x_2$ in $I \Rightarrow f(x_1) > f(x_2)$ for all $x_2 \in I$.

Rate of Change of Quantities

Let $y = f(x)$ be a function of x. Then, $\frac{dy}{dx}$ represents the rate of change of y with respect to x.

Also, $\left(\frac{dy}{dx}\right)_{\text{at } x=x_0}$ represents the rate of change of with respect to x at $x = x_0$.

$\frac{dy}{dx}$ is positive, if y increases as x increases. $\frac{dy}{dx}$ is negative, if y decreases as x increases.

Theorem

Let f be continuous on $[a, b]$ and differentiable on the open interval (a, b). Then,

- f is increasing function in $[a, b]$ if $f'(x) \ge 0$.
- f is strictly increasing in (a, b) if $f'(x) > 0$ for each $x \in (a, b)$.
- f is decreasing function in $[a, b]$ if $f'(x) \le 0$.
- f is strictly decreasing in (a, b) if $f'(x) < 0$ for each $x \in (a, b)$.
- A function will be increasing (decreasing) in R, if it is so as even interval of R.

Marginal Cost and Marginal Revenue

Marginal Cost

If $C(x)$ represents the cost function for x units produced, then marginal cost denoted by MC, is given by

$$MC = \frac{d}{dx}\{C(x)\}$$

Marginal Revenue

If $R(x)$ represents the revenue function for x units sold, then marginal revenue denoted by MR, is given by

$$MR = \frac{d}{dx}\{R(x)\}$$

If fixed cost and variable cost of a commodity are given, then total cost can be determined by the relation.

Total cost = Fixed cost + Variable cost

i.e. $C(x) = f(c) + v(x)$

Maximum and Minimum Values of a Function in a Closed Interval

Theorem 4 Let f be a continuous function on an interval $I = [a, b]$.

Then, f has the absolute maximum value and f attains it atleast once in I.

Also, f has the absolute minimum value and attains it atleast once in I.

Theorem 5 Let f be a differentiable function on a closed interval I and c be any interior point of I. Then,

- $f'(c) = 0$, if f attains its absolute maximum value at c.
- $f'(c) = 0$, if f attains its absolute minimum value at c.

Test of Local Maxima and Local Minima

First Derivative Test

Let f be a function defined on an open interval I and f be continuous at a critical point c in I.

(i) If $f'(x)$ changes sign from positive to negative as x increases through point c (i.e. $f'(x) > 0$ when $x \in (c-h, h)$ and $f'(x) < 0$ when $x \in (c, c+h)$, then c is a point of local maxima.

(ii) If $f'(x)$ changes sign from negative to positive as x increases through point c (i.e. $f'(x) < 0$ when $x \in (c-h, h)$ and $f'(x) > 0$ when $x \in (c, c+h)$, then c is a point of local minima.

Point of Inflection

If $f'(x)$ does not change sign as x increases through c, then c is neither a point of local maxima nor a point of local minima. Infact, such a point is called point of inflection.

Critical Point

A point c in the domain of a function f at which either $f'(c) = 0$ or f is not differentiable (i.e. $f'(c) = -\infty$) is called a critical (stationary or turning) point of f.

Maxima and Minima

Maximum and Minimum Values in an Interval

- A function $f(x)$ is said to have a **maximum value** in I, if there exists a point c in interval I such that $f(c) > f(x), \forall x \in I$
- A function $f(x)$ is said to have a **minimum value** in I, if there exists a point c in interval I such that $f(c) < f(x), \forall x \in I$
- f is said to have an **extreme value** in I, if there exists a point c in I such that $f(c)$ is either a maximum value or a minimum value of f in I.

Local Maxima and Local Minima

Let f be a real valued function and c be an interior point in the domain of f. Then,

- c is called a point of local maxima, if $h > 0$ such that $f(c) > f(x), \forall x$ in $(c-h, c+h)$. Here, value $f(c)$ is called the local maximum value (or relative maximum value) of f.
- c is called a point of local minima, if $h > 0$ such that $f(c) < f(x), \forall x$ in $(c-h, c+h, c+h)$. Here, value $f(c)$ is called the local minimum value (or relative minimum value) of f.

Second Derivative Test

Let f be a function defined on an interval I and $c \in I$ and f be twice differentiable at c. Then,

- $x = c$ is a point of local maxima, if $f'(c) = 0$ and $f''(c) < 0$. The value $f(c)$ is local maximum value of f.
- $x = c$ is a point of local minima, if $f'(c) = 0$ and $f''(c) > 0$. The value $f(c)$ is local minimum value of f.
- The test fails, if $f'(c) = 0$ and $f''(c) = 0$. In this case, we go back to the first derivative test and find whether c is a point of local maxima, local minima or a point of inflection.

07

CHAPTER

If you do not know the names of things, the knowledge of them is lost, too.

— *Carl Linnaeus*

Integrals

YOUR STUDY GOALS

7.1 Integration
7.2 Integration by Substitution
7.3 Some Special Integrals
7.4 Integration by Partial Fractions
7.5 Integration by Parts
7.6 Definite Integral

YOUR PRACTICE GOALS

- Objective Type Questions (39 Qs ; 25 MCQs , 10 A-R , 4 Case Based)
- Subjective Type Questions (63 Qs ; 22 VSA , 28 SA , 13 LA)

7.1 Integration

Integration is reverse process of differentiation. If the derivative of $F(x)$ is $f(x)$, then we say that the integral (anti-derivative) of $f(x)$ is $F(x)$ and we write

$$\int f(x)\,dx = F(x) + C$$

where C is an arbitrary constant known as **constant of integration.**

Integration of some standard functions are given below.

	Functions	Integration
1.	$\int x^n dx$	$\frac{x^{n+1}}{n+1} + C, n \neq -1$
2.	$\int dx$	$x + C$
3.	$\int \cos x\, dx$	$\sin x + C$
4.	$\int \sin x\, dx$	$-\cos x + C$
5.	$\int \sec^2 x\, dx$	$\tan x + C$
6.	$\int \operatorname{cosec}^2 x\, dx$	$-\cot x + C$

	Functions	Integration
7.	$\int \sec x \cdot \tan x\, dx$	$\sec x + C$
8.	$\int \operatorname{cosec} x \cdot \cot x\, dx$	$-\operatorname{cosec} x + C$
9.	$\int \frac{dx}{\sqrt{1-x^2}}$	$\sin^{-1} x + C$
10.	$\int \frac{dx}{\sqrt{1-x^2}}$	$-\cos^{-1} x + C$
11.	$\int \frac{dx}{1+x^2}$	$\tan^{-1} x + C$
12.	$\int e^x\, dx$	$e^x + C$
13.	$\int \frac{1}{x}\, dx$	$\log\lvert x\rvert + C$
14.	$\int a^x\, dx$	$\frac{a^x}{\log a} + C, a > 0, a \neq 1$

Properties of Indefinite Integrals

(i) $\int \{f(x) \pm g(x)\} dx = \int f(x)\, dx \pm \int g(x)\, dx$

(ii) $\int k \cdot f(x)\, dx = k \cdot \int f(x)\, dx$, where k is any non-zero real number.

(iii) In general, if $f_1, f_2, \ldots, f_n$ are functions and $k_1, k_2, \ldots, k_n$ are non-zero real numbers, then

$$\int [k_1 f_1(x) + k_2 f_2(x) + \ldots + k_n f_n(x)]\, dx$$
$$= k_1 \int f_1(x)\, dx + k_2 \int f_2(x)\, dx + \ldots + k_n \int f_n(x)\, dx$$

Example 1 Evaluate $\int a^{3\log_a x}\, dx$.

Sol. Let $I = \int a^{3\log_a x} dx$

$$= \int a^{\log_a x^3} dx \qquad [\because m \log n = \log n^m]$$
$$= \int x^3 dx \qquad [\because a^{\log_a f(x)} = f(x)]$$
$$= \frac{x^4}{4} + C \qquad \left[\because \int x^n dx = \frac{x^{n+1}}{n+1} + C, n \neq -1\right]$$

Example 2 Evaluate $\int \frac{(1+x)^2}{\sqrt{x}} dx$.

Sol. Let $I = \int \frac{(1+x)^2}{\sqrt{x}} dx = \int \frac{(1+x^2+2x)}{\sqrt{x}} dx$

$$[\because (a+b)^2 = a^2 + b^2 + 2ab]$$

$$= \int \frac{1}{\sqrt{x}} dx + \int \frac{x^2}{\sqrt{x}} dx + 2\int \frac{x}{\sqrt{x}} dx$$
$$= \int x^{-\frac{1}{2}} dx + \int x^{2-\frac{1}{2}} dx + 2\int x^{1-\frac{1}{2}} dx$$
$$= \int x^{-1/2} dx + \int x^{3/2} dx + 2\int x^{1/2} dx$$
$$= \frac{x^{-\frac{1}{2}+1}}{-\frac{1}{2}+1} + \frac{x^{\frac{3}{2}+1}}{\frac{3}{2}+1} + \frac{2x^{\frac{1}{2}+1}}{\frac{1}{2}+1} + C$$
$$\left[\because \int x^n dx = \frac{x^{n+1}}{n+1} + C\right]$$
$$= \frac{x^{1/2}}{1/2} + \frac{x^{5/2}}{5/2} + \frac{2x^{3/2}}{3/2} + C$$
$$= 2x^{1/2} + \frac{2}{5}x^{5/2} + \frac{4}{3}x^{3/2} + C$$
$$= 2\sqrt{x} + \frac{2}{5}x^{5/2} + \frac{4}{3}x^{3/2} + C$$

Example 3 Evaluate $\int \frac{(2^x + 3^x)^2}{6^x} dx$.

Sol. Let $I = \int \frac{(2^x + 3^x)^2}{6^x} dx$

$$= \int \frac{(2^x)^2 + (3^x)^2 + 2 \cdot 2^x \cdot 3^x}{6^x} dx$$
$$= \int \frac{4^x + 9^x + 2 \cdot 6^x}{6^x} dx$$
$$= \int \left(\frac{4^x}{6^x} + \frac{9^x}{6^x} + 2\right) dx$$
$$= \int \left[\left(\frac{2}{3}\right)^x + \left(\frac{3}{2}\right)^x + 2\right] dx$$
$$= \int \left(\frac{2}{3}\right)^x dx + \int \left(\frac{3}{2}\right)^x dx + 2\int dx$$
$$= \frac{\left(\frac{2}{3}\right)^x}{\log\left(\frac{2}{3}\right)} + \frac{\left(\frac{3}{2}\right)^x}{\log\left(\frac{3}{2}\right)} + 2x + C$$
$$\left[\because \int a^x dx = \frac{a^x}{\log a} + C, a > 0, a \neq 1\right]$$

Example 4 Evaluate $\int \frac{1+\sin x}{1-\sin x}$.

Sol. Let $I = \int \frac{1+\sin x}{1-\sin x} \times \frac{1+\sin x}{1+\sin x} dx$

$$= \int \frac{(1+\sin x)^2}{1-\sin^2 x} dx = \int \frac{(1+\sin^2 x + 2\sin x)}{\cos^2 x} dx$$
$$= \int \left(\frac{1}{\cos^2 x} + \frac{\sin^2 x}{\cos^2 x} + \frac{2\sin x}{\cos^2 x}\right) dx$$

$$= \int (\sec^2 x + \tan^2 x + 2\sec x \tan x)dx$$

$$= \int (\sec^2 x + \sec^2 x - 1 + 2\sec x \tan x)dx \quad [\because \tan^2 x = \sec^2 x - 1]$$

$$= \int (2\sec^2 x - 1 + 2\sec x \tan x)dx$$

$$= 2\int \sec^2 x\, dx - \int 1 dx + 2\int \sec x \tan x\, dx$$

$$= 2\tan x - x + 2\sec x + C$$

Example 5 Find $\int \frac{\cos 2x - \cos 2\theta}{\cos x - \cos\theta} dx.$ CBSE 2025

Sol. Let $I = \int \frac{\cos 2x - \cos 2\theta}{\cos x - \cos\theta} dx$

$$= \int \frac{(2\cos^2 x - 1) - (2\cos^2\theta - 1)}{\cos x - \cos\theta} dx$$

$$= \int \frac{2(\cos^2 x - \cos^2\theta)}{\cos x - \cos\theta} dx = 2\int (\cos x + \cos\theta)\, dx$$

$$= 2\int \cos x\, dx + 2\cos\theta \int 1\, dx$$

$$= 2\sin x + 2x\cos\theta + C$$

Example 6 Evaluate the following

$$\int \sin^{-1}(\cos x)\, dx, 0 \le x \le \pi.$$

Sol. Let $I = \int \sin^{-1}(\cos x)\, dx$

$$= \int \sin^{-1}\left\{\sin\left(\frac{\pi}{2} - x\right)\right\} dx = \int \left(\frac{\pi}{2} - x\right) dx$$

$$= \frac{\pi}{2}\int 1\, dx - \int x\, dx = \frac{\pi}{2}x - \frac{x^2}{2} + C$$

Example 7 Evaluate

$$\int \tan^{-1}\left\{\sqrt{\frac{(1-\cos 2x)}{1+\cos 2x}}\right\} dx, 0 < x < \frac{\pi}{2}.$$

Sol. Let $I = \int \tan^{-1}\left\{\sqrt{\frac{1-\cos 2x}{1+\cos 2x}}\right\} dx$

$$= \int \tan^{-1}\left\{\sqrt{\frac{2\sin^2 x}{2\cos^2 x}}\right\} dx$$

$$= \int \tan^{-1}(\tan x)\, dx = \int x\, dx = \frac{x^2}{2} + C$$

Example 8 Evaluate the following integral

$$\int \tan^{-1}\left(\frac{\sin 2x}{1+\cos 2x}\right) dx.$$

Sol. Let $I = \int \tan^{-1}\left(\frac{\sin 2x}{1+\cos 2x}\right) dx$

$$= \int \tan^{-1}\left(\frac{2\sin x \cos x}{1 + 2\cos^2 x - 1}\right) dx$$

$$= \int \tan^{-1}\left(\frac{2\sin x \cos x}{2\cos^2 x}\right) dx$$

$$= \int \tan^{-1}(\tan x)\, dx = \int x\, dx = \frac{x^2}{2} + C$$

EXAMPLE 9 Find the anti-derivative of $3x^2 + 4x^3$.

Sol. Let us look for a function whose derivative is $3x^2 + 4x^3$.

Note that $\frac{d}{dx}(x^3 + x^4) = 3x^2 + 4x^3$

$\therefore$ An anti-derivative of $3x^2 + 4x^3$ is $x^3 + x^4$.

Quick Test 1

Direction (Q. Nos. 1-8) *Evaluate the following integrals.*

1. $\int \frac{1}{\sqrt[3]{x^2}} dx$
2. $\int \frac{e^{9\log x} - e^{8\log x}}{e^{6\log x} - e^{5\log x}} dx$ CBSE 2025
3. $\int \sqrt{x}(ax^2 + bx + c)\, dx$
4. $\int \left(x^2 - \frac{1}{x^2}\right)^3 dx$
5. $\int \frac{(x^3+8)(x-1)}{x^2 - 2x + 4} dx$
6. $\int \sec x(\sec x + \tan x)\, dx$
7. $\int \frac{\sin^2 x - \cos^2 x}{\sin^2 x \cos^2 x} dx$
8. $\int \sin^{-1}\left(\frac{2\tan x}{1+\tan^2 x}\right) dx$
9. If $\frac{d}{dx} f(x) = 4x^3 - \frac{3}{x^4}$ such that $f(2) = 0$, then find $f(x)$.
10. Find the anti-derivatives of the following functions.
    (i) $\sin 2x$ (ii) e^{2x} Competency Based Que

For Solutions, See QR Code on Pg. 235

Answers

1. $3(x)^{1/3} + C$
2. $\frac{x^3}{3} + C$
3. $\frac{2ax^{7/2}}{7} + \frac{2bx^{5/2}}{5} + \frac{2cx^{3/2}}{3} + C$
4. $\frac{x^7}{7} - x^3 - \frac{3}{x} + \frac{1}{5x^5} + C$
5. $\frac{x^3}{3} + \frac{x^2}{2} - 2x + C$
6. $\tan x + \sec x + C$
7. $\tan x + \cot x + C$
8. $x^2 + C$
9. $x^4 + \frac{1}{x^3} - \frac{129}{8}$
10. (i) $-\frac{1}{2}\cos 2x$ (ii) $\frac{1}{2}e^{2x}$

7.2 Integration by Substitution

The method of reducing a given integral into one of the standard integrals by a proper substitution is called method of substitution.

Suppose, in the integral $I = \int f(x)\,dx$, $f(x)$ is not in any standard form.

Now, $\int f(x)\,dx$ can be transformed to another form by changing the independent variable x to other variable t by substituting $x = g(t)$.

$\therefore \dfrac{dx}{dt} = g'(t)$ or $dx = g'(t)\,dt$

Now, putting the value of dx in the above integral, we get

$$\int f(x)\,dx = \int f(g(t))\,g'(t)\,dt$$

Some Important Results using Substitutions

(i) $\int (ax+b)^n\,dx = \dfrac{(ax+b)^{n+1}}{a(n+1)} + C, n \neq -1$ and n is a rational number.

(ii) $\int \sin(ax+b)\,dx = \dfrac{-\cos(ax+b)}{a} + C$

(iii) $\int \cos(ax+b)\,dx = \dfrac{\sin(ax+b)}{a} + C$

(iv) $\int \tan(ax+b)dx = -\dfrac{1}{a}\log|\cos(ax+b)| + C$

$= \dfrac{1}{a}\log|\sec(ax+b)| + C$

(v) $\int \cot(ax+b)\,dx = \dfrac{1}{a}\log|\sin(ax+b)| + C$

(vi) $\int \sec(ax+b)\,dx = \dfrac{1}{a}\log|\sec(ax+b) + \tan(ax+b)| + C$

(vii) $\int \operatorname{cosec}(ax+b)\,dx = \dfrac{1}{a}\log|\operatorname{cosec}(ax+b) - \cot(ax+b)| + C$

(viii) $\int \sec(ax+b)\tan(ax+b)\,dx = \dfrac{1}{a}\sec(ax+b) + C$

(ix) $\int \operatorname{cosec}(ax+b)\cot(ax+b)\,dx = -\dfrac{1}{a}\operatorname{cosec}(ax+b) + C$

(x) $\int \sec^2(ax+b)\,dx = \dfrac{1}{a}\tan(ax+b) + C$

(xi) $\int \operatorname{cosec}^2(ax+b)\,dx = -\dfrac{1}{a}\cot(ax+b) + C$

(xii) $\int e^{(ax+b)}\,dx = \dfrac{e^{(ax+b)}}{a} + C$

(xiii) $\int a^{mx+b}\,dx = \dfrac{a^{mx+b}}{m\log_e a} + C$

Note Above integral can be derived by substituting $ax + b = t$ and $dx = \dfrac{1}{a}dt$.

Integration Using Trigonometric Identities

Sometimes when the integrand involves some trigonometric functions, we use the following identities to find the integral.

1. $\sin 2x = 2\sin x\cos x = \dfrac{2\tan x}{1+\tan^2 x}$

2. $\cos 2x = \cos^2 x - \sin^2 x = 2\cos^2 x - 1$

   $= 1 - 2\sin^2 x = \dfrac{1-\tan^2 x}{1+\tan^2 x}$

3. $\tan 2x = \dfrac{2\tan x}{1-\tan^2 x}$

4. $\cot 2x = \dfrac{\cot^2 x - 1}{2\cot x}$

5. $\sin 3x = -\sin^3 x + 3\cos^2 x\sin x$

   $= -4\sin^3 x + 3\sin x$

6. $\cos 3x = \cos^3 x - 3\sin^2 x\cos x = 4\cos^3 x - 3\cos x$

7. $\tan 3x = \dfrac{3\tan x - \tan^3 x}{1 - 3\tan^2 x}$

8. $\cot 3x = \dfrac{3\cot x - \cot^3 x}{1 - 3\cot^2 x}$

9. $\tan\dfrac{x}{2} = \operatorname{cosec} x - \cot x = \sqrt{\dfrac{1-\cos x}{1+\cos x}}$

   $= \dfrac{\sin x}{1+\cos x} = \dfrac{1-\cos x}{\sin x}$

10. $\cot\frac{x}{2} = \operatorname{cosec} x + \cot x = \sqrt{\frac{1+\cos x}{1-\cos x}}$
$= \frac{\sin x}{1-\cos x} = \frac{1+\cos x}{\sin x}$

11. $\sin(x+y) = \sin x\cos y + \cos x\sin y$

12. $\sin(x-y) = \sin x\cos y - \cos x\sin y$

13. $\cos(x+y) = \cos x\cos y - \sin x\sin y$

14. $\cos(x-y) = \cos x\cos y + \sin x\sin y$

15. $\tan(x+y) = \frac{\tan x + \tan y}{1-\tan x\tan y}$

16. $\tan(x-y) = \frac{\tan x - \tan y}{1+\tan x\tan y}$

17. $2\sin A\cos B = \sin(A+B) + \sin(A-B)$

18. $2\cos A\sin B = \sin(A+B) - \sin(A-B)$

19. $2\cos A\cos B = \cos(A+B) + \cos(A-B)$

20. $2\sin A\sin B = \cos(A-B) - \cos(A+B)$

21. $\sin A + \sin B = 2\sin\frac{A+B}{2}\cdot\cos\frac{A-B}{2}$

22. $\sin A - \sin B = 2\cos\frac{A+B}{2}\cdot\sin\frac{A-B}{2}$

23. $\cos A + \cos B = 2\cos\frac{A+B}{2}\cdot\cos\frac{A-B}{2}$

24. $\cos A - \cos B = -2\sin\frac{A+B}{2}\cdot\sin\frac{A-B}{2}$

25. Inverse trigonometric functions

(i) $\sin^{-1}(\sin x) = x$ (ii) $\cos^{-1}(\cos x) = x$

(iii) $\tan^{-1}(\tan x) = x$ (iv) $\operatorname{cosec}^{-1}(\operatorname{cosec} x) = x$

(v) $\sec^{-1}(\sec x) = x$ (vi) $\cot^{-1}(\cot x) = x$

Some Standard Formulae

Some standard formulae for integrals involving trigonometric functions are given below. These formulae are obtained using substitution technique.

(i) $\int \tan x\,dx = -\log|\cos x| + C = \log|\sec x| + C$

(ii) $\int \cot x\,dx = \log|\sin x| + C$

(iii) $\int \sec x\,dx = \log|\sec x + \tan x| + C$

(iv) $\int \operatorname{cosec} x\,dx = \log|\operatorname{cosec} x - \cot x| + C$

TEACHER TIPS

(i) In integral of type $\int \frac{p(x)}{(ax+b)^n}dx, n \in N$, where $p(x)$ is a polynomial. First express this as proper fraction, then put $ax+b=t$ and then integrate.

(ii) In integral of type $\int (ax+b)\sqrt{cx+d}\,dx$ and $\int \frac{ax+b}{\sqrt{cx+d}}dx$, put $cx+d=t$ and then integrate.

(iii) If the numerator in an integral is the exact derivative of denominator, then its integral is logarithmic of denominator

i.e. $\int \frac{f'(x)}{f(x)}dx = \log|f(x)| + C$

(iv) In type of integral $\int (f(x))^n f'(x)\,dx$, put $f(x)=t$ and $f'(x)dx = dt$.

(v) In type of integral $\int \sin^m x\cdot\cos^n x\,dx$,

- if the exponent of $\sin x$ is an odd positive integer, then put $\cos x = t$.
- if the exponent of $\cos x$ is an odd integer, then put $\sin x = t$.
- If the exponents of both $\sin x$ and $\cos x$ are odd, then put either $\sin x = t$ or $\cos x = t$.

Example 1 Evaluate $\int e^{2x+5}\,dx$.

Sol. Let $I = \int e^{2x+5}dx$

Put $2x+5 = t \Rightarrow 2\,dx = dt$

$\Rightarrow \quad dx = \frac{1}{2}dt$

$\therefore \quad I = \frac{1}{2}\int e^t\,dt = \frac{1}{2}e^t + C = \frac{1}{2}e^{2x+5} + C$

Example 2 Evaluate $\int \frac{x+1}{\sqrt{2x+1}}dx$.

Sol. Let $I = \int \frac{x+1}{\sqrt{2x+1}}dx$

Put $2x+1 = t \Rightarrow 2dx = dt$

$\Rightarrow \quad dx = \frac{1}{2}dt$ and $x = \frac{t-1}{2}$

$\therefore \quad I = \frac{1}{2}\int \frac{\frac{t-1}{2}+1}{\sqrt{t}}dt = \frac{1}{4}\int \frac{t+1}{\sqrt{t}}dt$

$= \frac{1}{4}\int (t^{1/2} + t^{-1/2})\,dt = \frac{1}{4}\left[\frac{t^{3/2}}{\left(\frac{3}{2}\right)} + \frac{t^{1/2}}{\left(\frac{1}{2}\right)}\right] + C$

$= \frac{1}{6}(2x+1)^{3/2} + \frac{1}{2}(2x+1)^{1/2} + C$

Example 3 Find $\int \sin^5\left(\frac{x}{2}\right)\cdot\cos\frac{x}{2}\,dx.$ CBSE 2020

Sol. Let $I = \int \sin^5\left(\frac{x}{2}\right)\cos\left(\frac{x}{2}\right)dx$

Put $\sin\frac{x}{2} = t \Rightarrow \frac{1}{2}\cos\frac{x}{2}dx = dt$

$\therefore \quad I = 2\int t^5 dt$

$I = 2\cdot\frac{t^6}{6} + C$

$I = \frac{1}{3}\left(\sin^6\frac{x}{2}\right) + C$

Example 4 Evaluate $\int \frac{e^{\tan^{-1}x}}{1+x^2}dx.$

Sol. Let $I = \int \frac{e^{\tan^{-1}x}}{1+x^2}dx$

Put $\tan^{-1}x = t \Rightarrow \frac{1}{1+x^2}dx = dt$

Now, $I = \int e^t dt = e^t + C = e^{\tan^{-1}x} + C$

Example 5 $\int \frac{\tan^4\sqrt{x}\sec^2\sqrt{x}}{\sqrt{x}}dx$ NCERT

Sol. Let $I = \int \frac{\tan^4\sqrt{x}\sec^2\sqrt{x}}{\sqrt{x}}dx$

Put $\tan\sqrt{x} = t \Rightarrow \sec^2\sqrt{x}\cdot\frac{1}{2\sqrt{x}}dx = dt$

$\Rightarrow \quad \frac{\sec^2\sqrt{x}}{\sqrt{x}}dx = 2dt$

$\therefore \quad I = \int t^4(2dt) = 2\int t^4 dt$

$= 2\cdot\frac{t^5}{5} + C$

$= \frac{2}{5}\tan^5\sqrt{x} + C$

Example 6 Evaluate $\int \frac{1}{\sqrt{1+\sin 2x}}dx.$

Sol. Let $I = \int \frac{1}{\sqrt{1+\sin 2x}}dx$

$= \int \frac{1}{\sqrt{1-\cos\left(\frac{\pi}{2}+2x\right)}}dx$

$= \int \frac{1}{\sqrt{2\sin^2\left(\frac{\pi}{4}+x\right)}}dx$

$= \frac{1}{\sqrt{2}}\int \operatorname{cosec}\left(\frac{\pi}{4}+x\right)dx$

$= \frac{1}{\sqrt{2}}\log\left|\tan\left(\frac{\pi}{8}+\frac{x}{2}\right)\right| + C$

Example 7 Find the value of $\int \frac{\sin x + \cos x}{\sqrt{1+\sin 2x}}dx.$

Competency Based Que, NCERT Exemplar, CBSE 2013

Sol. Let $I = \int \frac{\sin x + \cos x}{\sqrt{1+\sin 2x}}dx$

$= \int \frac{(\sin x + \cos x)}{\sqrt{\sin^2 x + \cos^2 x + 2\sin x\cos x}}dx$

$[\because \sin^2\theta + \cos^2\theta = 1 \text{ and } \sin 2\theta = 2\sin\theta\cos\theta]$

$= \int \frac{\sin x + \cos x}{\sqrt{(\sin x + \cos x)^2}}dx \quad [\because (a+b)^2 = a^2 + b^2 + 2ab]$

$= \int \frac{\sin x + \cos x}{\sin x + \cos x}dx = \int dx = x + C$

Example 8 Evaluate the integral $\int \frac{\sin x}{\sin(x+a)}dx.$

Competency Based Que

Sol. Let $I = \int \frac{\sin x}{\sin(x+a)}dx$

Now, put $x + a = t \Rightarrow dx = dt$ and $x = t - a$

$\therefore \quad I = \int \frac{\sin(t-a)}{\sin t}dt = \int \frac{\sin t\cos a - \cos t\sin a}{\sin t}dt$

$[\because \sin(A-B) = \sin A\cos B - \cos A\sin B]$

$= \cos a\int dt - \sin a\int \cot t\,dt$

$= (\cos a)t - \sin a\log|\sin t| + C_1$

$= (x+a)\cos a - \sin a\log|\sin(x+a)| + C_1$

$[\because t = x + a]$

$= x\cos a - \sin a\log|\sin(x+a)| + C_1 + a\cos a$

$= x\cos a - \sin a\log|\sin(x+a) + C,$

where $C = C_1 + a\cos a$

Example 9 Evaluate $\int \tan^{-1}\left(\frac{1-\cos x}{\sin x}\right)dx.$

Sol. Let $I = \int \tan^{-1}\left(\frac{1-\cos x}{\sin x}\right)dx = \int \tan^{-1}\left(\frac{2\sin^2\frac{x}{2}}{2\sin\frac{x}{2}\cos\frac{x}{2}}\right)dx$

$\left[\because \sin^2\theta = \frac{1-\cos 2\theta}{2} \text{ and } \sin\theta = 2\sin\frac{\theta}{2}\cos\frac{\theta}{2}\right]$

$= \int \tan^{-1}\left(\tan\frac{x}{2}\right)dx = \int \frac{x}{2}dx \quad [\because \tan^{-1}(\tan\theta) = \theta]$

$= \frac{1}{2}\int x\,dx = \frac{1}{2}\cdot\frac{x^2}{2} + C = \frac{x^2}{4} + C$

Example 10 Evaluate $\int \tan^{-1}\left(\frac{\cos x - \sin x}{\cos x + \sin x}\right) dx.$

Sol. Let $I = \int \tan^{-1}\left(\frac{\cos x - \sin x}{\cos x + \sin x}\right) dx$

$$= \int \tan^{-1}\left(\frac{\frac{\cos x}{\cos x} - \frac{\sin x}{\cos x}}{\frac{\cos x}{\cos x} + \frac{\sin x}{\cos x}}\right) dx$$

[dividing numerator and denominator by cos x]

$$= \int \tan^{-1}\left(\frac{1 - \tan x}{1 + \tan x}\right) dx$$

$$= \int \tan^{-1}\left(\frac{\tan\frac{\pi}{4} - \tan x}{1 + \tan\frac{\pi}{4}\tan x}\right) dx \qquad \left[\because \tan\frac{\pi}{4} = 1\right]$$

$$= \int \tan^{-1}\left[\tan\left(\frac{\pi}{4} - x\right)\right] dx$$

$$\left[\because \tan(x - y) = \frac{\tan x - \tan y}{1 + \tan x \tan y}\right]$$

$$= \int \left(\frac{\pi}{4} - x\right) dx \qquad [\because \tan^{-1}(\tan\theta) = \theta]$$

$$= \int \frac{\pi}{4} dx - \int x\, dx$$

$$= \frac{\pi}{4}x - \frac{x^2}{2} + C$$

Example 11 Evaluate $\int \frac{1}{\cos(x - \alpha)\cos(x - \beta)} dx.$

Competency Based Que, CBSE 2023

Sol. Let $I = \int \frac{1}{\cos(x - \alpha)\cos(x - \beta)} dx$

$$= \int \frac{1}{\cos(x - \alpha)\cos(x - \beta)} \times \frac{\sin(\beta - \alpha)}{\sin(\beta - \alpha)} dx$$

[multiply numerator and denominator by sin $(\beta - \alpha)$]

$$= \frac{1}{\sin(\beta - \alpha)} \int \frac{\sin[(x - \alpha) - (x - \beta)]}{\cos(x - \alpha)\cos(x - \beta)} dx$$

[adding and subtracting x from numerator]

$$= \frac{1}{\sin(\beta - \alpha)} \int \frac{\sin(x - \alpha)\cos(x - \beta) - \cos(x - \alpha)\sin(x - \beta)}{\cos(x - \alpha)\cos(x - \beta)} dx$$

$[\because \sin(A - B) = \sin A \cos B - \cos A \sin B]$

$$= \frac{1}{\sin(\beta - \alpha)} \int \left[\frac{\sin(x - \alpha)\cos(x - \beta)}{\cos(x - \alpha)\cos(x - \beta)} - \frac{\cos(x - \alpha)\sin(x - \beta)}{\cos(x - \alpha)\cos(x - \beta)}\right] dx$$

$$= \frac{1}{\sin(\beta - \alpha)} \int [\tan(x - \alpha) - \tan(x - \beta)]\, dx$$

$$= \frac{1}{\sin(\beta - \alpha)} [-\log|\cos(x - \alpha)| + \log|\cos(x - \beta)|] + C$$

$[\because \int \tan x\, dx = -\log|\cos x|]$

$$= \frac{1}{\sin(\beta - \alpha)} \log\left|\frac{\cos(x - \beta)}{\cos(x - \alpha)}\right| + C$$

$\left[\because \log m - \log n = \log\frac{m}{n}\right]$

Example 12 Evaluate $\int \tan^2 x \sec^4 x\, dx.$

NCERT Exemplar

Sol. Let $I = \int \tan^2 x \sec^4 x\, dx$

$$= \int \tan^2 x \sec^2 x \sec^2 x\, dx$$

$$= \int \tan^2 x(1 + \tan^2 x)\sec^2 x\, dx \qquad [\because \sec^2\theta = 1 + \tan^2\theta]$$

Now, put $\tan x = t \Rightarrow \sec^2 x\, dx = dt$

$$\therefore \quad I = \int t^2(1 + t^2)\, dt = \int (t^2 + t^4) dt$$

$$= \frac{t^3}{3} + \frac{t^5}{5} + C = \frac{\tan^3 x}{3} + \frac{\tan^5 x}{5} + C \qquad [\because t = \tan x]$$

Example 13 Evaluate $\int \sec^{4/3} x \operatorname{cosec}^{8/3} x\, dx.$

Competency Based Que, CBSE 2023

Sol. Let $I = \int \sec^{4/3} x \operatorname{cosec}^{8/3} x\, dx$

$$= \int \frac{dx}{\cos^{4/3} x \cdot (\sin^{8/3} x)}$$

$$= \int \cos^{-4/3} x \sin^{-8/3} x\, dx$$

Here, $-\left(\frac{4}{3} + \frac{8}{3}\right) = -4$, which is a negative even integer.

So, multiply both numerator and denominator by $\cos^4 x$.

$$\therefore \quad I = \int \frac{\cos^4 x \cos^{-4/3} x \sin^{-8/3} x}{\cos^4 x} dx$$

$$= \int \frac{\cos^{8/3} x \sin^{-8/3} x}{\cos^4 x} dx$$

$$= \int \frac{\sec^4 x}{\tan^{8/3} x} dx$$

$$= \int \frac{\sec^2 x \cdot \sec^2 x}{\tan^{8/3} x} dx$$

$$= \int \frac{\sec^2 x \cdot (1 + \tan^2 x)}{\tan^{8/3} x} dx$$

Now, put $\tan x = t \Rightarrow \sec^2 x\, dx = dt$

$$\therefore \quad I = \int \frac{1 + t^2}{t^{8/3}} dt = \int (t^{-8/3} + t^{-2/3})\, dt$$

$$= -\frac{3}{5}t^{-5/3} + 3t^{1/3} + C$$

$$= -\frac{3}{5}\tan^{-5/3} x + 3\tan^{1/3} x + C$$

$[\because t = \tan x]$

Quick Test 2

Direction (Q. Nos. 1-9) *Evaluate the following integrals.*

1. $\int \frac{x^2+1}{(x+1)^2}dx$

2. $\int \text{cosec}^2(3x+2)\,dx$ NCERT

3. $\int \frac{1}{\sqrt{3x+4}-\sqrt{3x+1}}dx$ Competency Based Que

4. $\int \frac{\sin x - x\cos x}{x(x+\sin x)}dx$ Competency Based Que

5. $\frac{\cos 2x + x + 1}{x^2+\sin 2x+2x}dx$ CBSE 2015

6. (i) $\int \sqrt{\frac{1-\cos x}{1+\cos x}}dx$ (ii) $\int \frac{1+\sin x}{1+\cos x}dx$

7. $\int \frac{\cos 5x+\cos 4x}{1-2\cos 3x}dx$ NCERT Exemplar

8. $\int \cot^{-1}\left[\frac{\sqrt{1+\cos 2x}+\sqrt{1-\cos 2x}}{\sqrt{1+\cos 2x}-\sqrt{1-\cos 2x}}\right]dx$ Competency Based Que

9. $\int \tan^5 x\sec^4 x\,dx$

Answers

1. $x-2\log|x+1|-\frac{2}{x+1}+C$

2. $\frac{-1}{3}\cot(3x+2)+C$

3. $\frac{2}{27}[(3x+4)^{3/2}+(3x+1)^{3/2}]+C$

4. $\log x-\log(x+\sin x)+C$

5. $\frac{1}{2}\log|x^2+\sin 2x+2x|+C$

6. (i) $2\log\left|\sec\frac{x}{2}\right|+C$ (ii) $\tan\frac{x}{2}-2\log\left|\cos\frac{x}{2}\right|+C$

7. $-\frac{1}{2}\sin 2x-\sin x+C$

8. $\frac{\pi}{4}x-\frac{x^2}{2}+C$

9. $\frac{1}{6}\tan^6 x+\frac{1}{8}\tan^8 x+C$

For Solutions, See QR Code on Pg. 235

7.3 Some Special Integrals

Some standard formulae are given below. We can use them to solve the some standard integrals.

(i) $\int \frac{dx}{x^2-a^2}=\frac{1}{2a}\log\left|\frac{x-a}{x+a}\right|+C$

(ii) $\int \frac{dx}{a^2-x^2}=\frac{1}{2a}\log\left|\frac{a+x}{a-x}\right|+C$

(iii) $\int \frac{dx}{x^2+a^2}=\frac{1}{a}\tan^{-1}\frac{x}{a}+C$

(iv) $\int \frac{dx}{\sqrt{x^2-a^2}}=\log|x+\sqrt{x^2-a^2}|+C$

(v) $\int \frac{dx}{\sqrt{a^2-x^2}}=\sin^{-1}\frac{x}{a}+C$

(vi) $\int \frac{dx}{\sqrt{x^2+a^2}}=\log|x+\sqrt{x^2+a^2}|+C$

(vii) Integrals of the types

$$\int \frac{dx}{ax^2+bx+c} \text{ or } \int \frac{dx}{\sqrt{ax^2+bx+c}}$$

can be transformed into standard form by expressing $ax^2+bx+c=a\left[x^2+\frac{b}{a}x+\frac{c}{a}\right]$

$$=a\left[\left(x+\frac{b}{2a}\right)^2+\left(\frac{c}{a}-\frac{b^2}{4a^2}\right)\right]$$

(viii) Integrals of the types

$$\int \frac{px+q}{ax^2+bx+c}dx \text{ or } \int \frac{px+q}{\sqrt{ax^2+bx+c}}dx$$

can be transformed into standard form by expressing $px+q=A\frac{d}{dx}(ax^2+bx+c)+B$

$$=A(2ax+b)+B,$$

where A and B are determined by comparing coefficients on both sides.

Some Standard Integrals and Substitutions for Them

Integral	Substitution
$\int \frac{dx}{a \pm b\cos x}$	Put $\cos x = \frac{1-\tan^2 \frac{x}{2}}{1+\tan^2 \frac{x}{2}}$, then put $\tan \frac{x}{2} = t$
$\int \frac{dx}{a \pm b\sin x}$	Put $\sin x = \frac{2\tan \frac{x}{2}}{1+\tan^2 \frac{x}{2}}$, then put $\tan \frac{x}{2} = t$
$\int \frac{dx}{a\sin x + b\cos x}$, $\int \frac{dx}{a\sin x + b\cos x + c}$	Put $\sin x = \frac{2\tan \frac{x}{2}}{1+\tan^2 \frac{x}{2}}$ and $\cos x = \frac{1-\tan^2 \frac{x}{2}}{1+\tan^2 \frac{x}{2}}$, then put $\tan \frac{x}{2} = t$
$\int \frac{dx}{a\sin x + b\cos x}$	Put $a = r\cos\theta$ and $b = r\sin\theta$, where $r = \sqrt{a^2+b^2}$ and $\theta = \tan^{-1}\left(\frac{b}{a}\right)$
$\int \frac{dx}{(ax+b)\sqrt{px+q}}$, $\int \frac{dx}{(ax^2+bx+c)\sqrt{px+q}}$	Put $\sqrt{px+q} = t$
$\int \frac{dx}{(px+q)(\sqrt{ax^2+bx+c})}$	Put $px+q = \frac{1}{t}$
$\int \frac{dx}{(px^2+q)\sqrt{ax^2+b}}$	Put $x = \frac{1}{t}$ and then put $\sqrt{a+bt^2} = u$

Example 1 Find $\int \frac{1}{5+4x-x^2}\,dx$. *CBSE 2024*

Sol. Let $I = \int \frac{1}{5+4x-x^2}\,dx$

$$= \int \frac{1}{5+2\cdot 2x - x^2 - (2)^2 + (2)^2}\,dx$$

$$= \int \frac{1}{5+4-(x^2+(2)^2-2\cdot 2\cdot x)}\,dx$$

$$= \int \frac{1}{9-(x-2)^2}\,dx = \int \frac{1}{(3)^2-(x-2)^2}\,dx$$

$$= \frac{1}{2\times 3}\log\left|\frac{3+x-2}{3-x+2}\right| + C$$

$$\left[\because \int \frac{dx}{a^2-x^2} = \frac{1}{2a}\log\left|\frac{a+x}{a-x}\right| + C\right]$$

$$= \frac{1}{6}\log\left|\frac{1+x}{5-x}\right| + C$$

Example 2 Find $\int \frac{dx}{x^2-6x+13}$. *CBSE 2022 (Term II)*

Sol. Let $I = \int \frac{dx}{x^2-6x+13} = \int \frac{dx}{(x-3)^2+13-9}$

$$= \int \frac{dx}{(x-3)^2+4} = \int \frac{dx}{(x-3)^2+2^2} = \frac{1}{2}\tan^{-1}\frac{x-3}{2} + C$$

$$\left[\because \int \frac{dx}{x^2+a^2} = \frac{1}{a}\tan^{-1}\frac{x}{a} + C\right]$$

Example 3 Find $\int \frac{\sin 2x}{\sqrt{9-\cos^4 x}}\,dx$. *CBSE Sample Paper 2022 (Term II)*

Sol. Let $I = \int \frac{\sin 2x}{\sqrt{9-\cos^4 x}}\,dx = \int \frac{\sin 2x}{\sqrt{(3)^2-(\cos^2 x)^2}}\,dx$

Put $\cos^2 x = t \Rightarrow -2\cos x \sin x\,dx = dt$

$\Rightarrow \sin 2x\,dx = -dt$

$$\therefore \quad I = -\int \frac{dt}{\sqrt{3^2-t^2}} = -\sin^{-1}\left(\frac{t}{3}\right) + C$$

$$\left[\because \int \frac{dx}{\sqrt{a^2-x^2}} = \sin^{-1}\frac{x}{a} + C\right]$$

$$\Rightarrow \quad I = -\sin^{-1}\left(\frac{\cos^2 x}{3}\right) + C$$

Example 4 Evaluate $\int \frac{1}{9x^2+6x+5}\,dx$.

Sol. Let $I = \int \frac{1}{9x^2+6x+5}\,dx = \frac{1}{9}\int \frac{1}{x^2+\frac{2}{3}x+\frac{5}{9}}\,dx$

[take 9 common from denominator]

$$= \frac{1}{9}\int \frac{1}{x^2+2\cdot\frac{1}{3}\cdot x + \left(\frac{1}{3}\right)^2 + \frac{5}{9} - \left(\frac{1}{3}\right)^2}\,dx$$

$$\left[\text{adding and subtracting } \left(\frac{1}{3}\right)^2 \text{ in denominator}\right]$$

$$= \frac{1}{9}\int \frac{1}{x^2+\frac{2}{3}x+\left(\frac{1}{3}\right)^2+\frac{5}{9}-\frac{1}{9}}\,dx$$

$$= \frac{1}{9}\int \frac{1}{\left(x+\frac{1}{3}\right)^2+\left(\frac{2}{3}\right)^2}\,dx$$

$$= \frac{1}{9}\left(\frac{1}{2/3}\right)\tan^{-1}\left(\frac{x+1/3}{2/3}\right) + C$$

$$\left[\because \int \frac{dx}{x^2+a^2} = \frac{1}{a}\tan^{-1}\left(\frac{x}{a}\right) + C\right]$$

$$= \frac{1}{6}\tan^{-1}\left(\frac{3x+1}{2}\right) + C$$

Example 5 Evaluate $\int \frac{e^x}{e^{2x}+6e^x+5}\,dx.$

Sol. Let $I = \int \frac{e^x}{e^{2x}+6e^x+5}\,dx = \int \frac{e^x}{(e^x)^2+6(e^x)+5}\,dx$

Put $e^x = t \Rightarrow e^x\,dx = dt$

$\therefore \quad I = \int \frac{dt}{t^2+6t+5} = \int \frac{dt}{(t+3)^2-(2)^2}$

$= \frac{1}{2\times 2}\log\left|\frac{t+3-2}{t+3+2}\right| + C = \frac{1}{4}\log\left|\frac{e^x+1}{e^x+5}\right| + C$

$\left[\because \int \frac{dx}{x^2-a^2} = \frac{1}{2a}\log\left|\frac{x-a}{x+a}\right| + C\right]$

Example 6 Evaluate $\int \frac{dx}{\sqrt{3-x+x^2}}.$

Sol. Let $I = \int \frac{dx}{\sqrt{3-x+x^2}} = \int \frac{dx}{\sqrt{x^2-x+3}}$

$= \int \frac{dx}{\sqrt{x^2 - 2\times x\times\frac{1}{2} + \left(\frac{1}{2}\right)^2 - \left(\frac{1}{2}\right)^2 + 3}}$

$\left[\text{adding and subtracting } \left(\frac{1}{2}\right)^2 \text{ in denominator}\right]$

$= \int \frac{dx}{\sqrt{\left(x-\frac{1}{2}\right)^2 + 3 - \frac{1}{4}}} = \int \frac{dx}{\sqrt{\left(x-\frac{1}{2}\right)^2 + \frac{11}{4}}}$

Now, put $x - \frac{1}{2} = t \;\Rightarrow\; dx = dt$

$\therefore I = \int \frac{dt}{\sqrt{t^2 + \left(\frac{\sqrt{11}}{2}\right)^2}} = \log\left|t + \sqrt{t^2 + \left(\frac{\sqrt{11}}{2}\right)^2}\right| + C$

$\left[\because \int \frac{dx}{\sqrt{x^2+a^2}} = \log|x+\sqrt{x^2+a^2}| + C\right]$

$= \log\left|\left(x-\frac{1}{2}\right) + \sqrt{\left(x-\frac{1}{2}\right)^2 + \left(\frac{\sqrt{11}}{2}\right)^2}\right| + C \quad \left[\because t = x - \frac{1}{2}\right]$

Hence, $I = \log\left|\left(x-\frac{1}{2}\right) + \sqrt{3-x+x^2}\right| + C$

Example 7 Evaluate $\int \frac{e^x}{\sqrt{5-4e^x-e^{2x}}}\,dx.$ CBSE 2023

Sol. Let $I = \int \frac{e^x}{\sqrt{5-4e^x-e^{2x}}}\,dx$

Now, put $e^x = t \Rightarrow e^x dx = dt$

$\therefore \quad I = \int \frac{dt}{\sqrt{5-4t-t^2}} = \int \frac{dt}{\sqrt{-(t^2+4t-5)}}$

$= \int \frac{dt}{\sqrt{-[(t+2)^2-5-4]}}$

[adding and subtracting $(2)^2$ in denominator]

$= \int \frac{dt}{\sqrt{9-(t+2)^2}} = \int \frac{dt}{\sqrt{(3)^2-(t+2)^2}}$

$= \sin^{-1}\left(\frac{t+2}{3}\right) + C \quad \left[\because \int \frac{dx}{\sqrt{a^2-x^2}} = \sin^{-1}\frac{x}{a} + C\right]$

$= \sin^{-1}\left(\frac{e^x+2}{3}\right) + C \quad [\because t = e^x]$

Example 8 Evaluate $\int \frac{dx}{1-3\sin x}.$

Sol. Let $I = \int \frac{dx}{1-3\sin x}$

$= \int \frac{dx}{1 - 3\left(\frac{2\tan\frac{x}{2}}{1+\tan^2\frac{x}{2}}\right)} \quad \left[\because \sin\theta = \frac{2\tan\frac{\theta}{2}}{1+\tan^2\frac{\theta}{2}}\right]$

$= \int \frac{\left(1+\tan^2\frac{x}{2}\right)}{\left(\tan^2\frac{x}{2} - 6\tan\frac{x}{2} + 1\right)}dx = \int \frac{\sec^2\frac{x}{2}}{\tan^2\frac{x}{2} - 6\tan\frac{x}{2} + 1}dx$

$[\because \sec^2\theta = 1 + \tan^2\theta]$

Now, put $\tan\frac{x}{2} = t$

$\Rightarrow \quad \sec^2\frac{x}{2}\cdot\frac{1}{2}dx = dt$

$\Rightarrow \quad \sec^2\frac{x}{2}dx = 2dt$

$\therefore \quad I = \int \frac{2dt}{t^2-6t+1} = 2\int \frac{dt}{t^2-6t+9+1-9}$

[adding and subtracting 9 in denominator]

$= 2\int \frac{dt}{(t-3)^2-8} = 2\int \frac{dt}{(t-3)^2-(2\sqrt{2})^2}$

$= \frac{2\times 1}{2\times 2\sqrt{2}}\log\left|\frac{t-3-2\sqrt{2}}{t-3+2\sqrt{2}}\right| + C$

$\left[\because \int \frac{dx}{x^2-a^2} = \frac{1}{2a}\log\left|\frac{x-a}{x+a}\right| + C\right]$

$= \frac{1}{2\sqrt{2}}\log\left|\frac{\tan\frac{x}{2} - 3 - 2\sqrt{2}}{\tan\frac{x}{2} - 3 + 2\sqrt{2}}\right| + C \quad \left[\because \tan\frac{x}{2} = t\right]$

Example 9 Evaluate $\int \frac{dx}{\sqrt{3}\sin x + \cos x}$. *Competency Based Que*

Sol. Let $I = \int \frac{dx}{\sqrt{3}\sin x + \cos x}$

Now, put $\sqrt{3} = r\cos\theta$ and $1 = r\sin\theta$, then

$$r = \sqrt{(\sqrt{3})^2 + 1^2} = \sqrt{3+1} = 2$$

and $\theta = \tan^{-1}\left(\frac{1}{\sqrt{3}}\right) = \frac{\pi}{6}$

$\left[\because \text{ the type of integral } \int \frac{dx}{a\sin x + b\cos x}, \text{ put } a = r\cos\theta \text{ and } b = r\sin\theta, \text{ where } r = \sqrt{a^2+b^2} \text{ and } \theta = \tan^{-1}\left(\frac{b}{a}\right)\right]$

$$\therefore \quad I = \int \frac{dx}{r\cos\theta\sin x + r\sin\theta\cos x}$$

$$= \frac{1}{r}\int \frac{dx}{\sin(x+\theta)}$$

$$= \frac{1}{2}\int \operatorname{cosec}(x+\theta)\,dx \qquad [\because r = 2]$$

$$= \frac{1}{2}\log|\operatorname{cosec} x+\theta) - \cot(x+\theta)| + C$$

$$= \frac{1}{2}\log\left|\frac{1-\cos(x+\theta)}{\sin(x+\theta)}\right| + C$$

$$= \frac{1}{2}\log\left|\frac{2\sin^2\left(\frac{x+\theta}{2}\right)}{2\sin\left(\frac{x+\theta}{2}\right)\cos\left(\frac{x+\theta}{2}\right)}\right| + C$$

$\left[\because 1-\cos\theta = 2\sin^2\frac{\theta}{2} \text{ and } \sin\theta = 2\sin\frac{\theta}{2}\cos\frac{\theta}{2}\right]$

$$= \frac{1}{2}\log\left|\tan\left(\frac{x+\theta}{2}\right)\right| + C$$

$$= \frac{1}{2}\log\left|\tan\left(\frac{x}{2}+\frac{\pi}{12}\right)\right| + C \qquad \left[\because \theta = \frac{\pi}{6}\right]$$

Example 10 Evaluate $\int \frac{x^2-1}{x^4+x^2+1}dx$. *CBSE 2025*

Sol. Let $I = \int \frac{x^2-1}{x^4+x^2+1}dx$

$$\Rightarrow \quad I = \int \frac{1-\frac{1}{x^2}}{x^2+1+\frac{1}{x^2}}dx$$

[dividing numerator and denominator by x^2]

$$= \int \frac{\left(1-\frac{1}{x^2}\right)}{\left(x^2+\frac{1}{x^2}\right)+1}dx$$

$$= \int \frac{\left(1-\frac{1}{x^2}\right)dx}{\left(x^2+\frac{1}{x^2}+2\right)+1-2}$$

[adding and subtracting 2 in denominator]

$$= \int \frac{\left(1-\frac{1}{x^2}\right)dx}{\left(x+\frac{1}{x}\right)^2-1}$$

Now, put $x+\frac{1}{x} = t \Rightarrow \left(1-\frac{1}{x^2}\right)dx = dt$

$$\therefore \quad I = \int \frac{dt}{t^2-1^2} = \frac{1}{2}\log\left|\frac{t-1}{t+1}\right| + C$$

$\left[\because \int \frac{dx}{x^2-a^2} = \frac{1}{2a}\log\left|\frac{x-a}{x+a}\right| + C\right]$

$$\Rightarrow \quad I = \frac{1}{2}\log\left|\frac{x+\frac{1}{x}-1}{x+\frac{1}{x}+1}\right| + C = \frac{1}{2}\log\left|\frac{x^2+1-x}{x^2+1+x}\right| + C$$

$\left[\because t = x+\frac{1}{x}\right]$

Example 11 Evaluate $\int \frac{dx}{(x-1)\sqrt{2x+3}}$. *CBSE 2023*

Sol. Let $I = \int \frac{dx}{(x-1)\sqrt{2x+3}}$

Now, put $\sqrt{2x+3} = t$

$$\Rightarrow \quad 2x+3 = t^2$$

$$\Rightarrow \quad x = \frac{t^2-3}{2}$$

Then, $dx = \frac{(2t-0)}{2}dt = t\,dt$

$$\therefore \quad I = \int \frac{t\,dt}{\left(\frac{t^2-3}{2}-1\right)\cdot t}$$

$$= \int \frac{dt}{\frac{t^2-3-2}{2}}$$

$$= 2\int \frac{dt}{t^2-5} = 2\int \frac{dt}{t^2-(\sqrt{5})^2}$$

$$= 2\times\frac{1}{2\sqrt{5}}\log\left|\frac{t-\sqrt{5}}{t+\sqrt{5}}\right| + C$$

$\left[\because \int \frac{dx}{x^2-a^2} = \frac{1}{2a}\log\left|\frac{x-a}{x+a}\right| + C\right]$

$$= \frac{1}{\sqrt{5}}\log\left|\frac{\sqrt{2x+3}-\sqrt{5}}{\sqrt{2x+3}+\sqrt{5}}\right| + C \qquad [\because t = \sqrt{2x+3}]$$

Example 12 Evaluate $\int \frac{dx}{x\sqrt{ax - x^2}}$. *NCERT*

Sol. Let $I = \int \frac{dx}{x\sqrt{ax - x^2}}$

Now, put $x = \frac{1}{t} \Rightarrow dx = -\frac{1}{t^2} dt$

$$\therefore \quad I = \int \frac{\left(-\frac{1}{t^2}\right) dt}{\frac{1}{t}\sqrt{\frac{a}{t} - \frac{1}{t^2}}}$$

$$= \int \frac{-dt}{t^2 \cdot \frac{1}{t} \frac{\sqrt{at-1}}{t}} = \int \frac{-dt}{\sqrt{at-1}}$$

$$= -\int (at-1)^{-\frac{1}{2}} dt = -\frac{(at-1)^{-\frac{1}{2}+1}}{a \cdot \left(-\frac{1}{2}+1\right)} + C$$

$$= \frac{-2}{a}(at-1)^{\frac{1}{2}} + C$$

$$= -\frac{2}{a}\sqrt{a \cdot \frac{1}{x} - 1} + C \qquad \left[\because t = \frac{1}{x}\right]$$

$$= \frac{-2}{a}\sqrt{\frac{a-x}{x}} + C$$

Example 13 Evaluate $\int \frac{x+2}{2x^2 + 6x + 5} dx.$

Competency Based Que, CBSE 2015C

Sol. Let $(x + 2) = A \frac{d}{dx}(2x^2 + 6x + 5) + B$

$\Rightarrow \quad (x + 2) = A(4x + 6) + B$ ...(i)

$\Rightarrow \quad (x + 2) = 4Ax + (6A + B)$

On equating the coefficients of x and constant terms from both sides, we get

$1 = 4A$ and $6A + B = 2$

$\Rightarrow \quad A = \frac{1}{4}$ and $6 \cdot \frac{1}{4} + B = 2 \Rightarrow A = \frac{1}{4}$ and $B = 2 - \frac{3}{2}$

$\Rightarrow \quad A = \frac{1}{4}$ and $B = \frac{1}{2}$

$\therefore$ From Eq. (i), we get

$$(x + 2) = \frac{1}{4}(4x + 6) + \frac{1}{2}$$

Now, the given integral can be written as

$$I = \int \frac{(x+2)}{2x^2 + 6x + 5} = \int \frac{\frac{1}{4}(4x+6) + \frac{1}{2}}{2x^2 + 6x + 5} dx$$

$$= \frac{1}{4}\int \frac{4x+6}{2x^2+6x+5} dx + \frac{1}{2}\int \frac{dx}{2x^2+6x+5}$$

$$\Rightarrow \quad I = \frac{1}{4} I_1 + \frac{1}{2} I_2 \qquad \text{...(ii)}$$

where, $I_1 = \int \frac{4x+6}{2x^2+6x+5} dx$ and $I_2 = \int \frac{dx}{2x^2+6x+5}$

Now, consider $I_1 = \int \frac{4x+6}{2x^2+6x+5} dx$

Now, put $2x^2 + 6x + 5 = t \Rightarrow (4x + 6)\, dx = dt$

$$\therefore \quad I_1 = \int \frac{dt}{t} = \log|t| + C_1 = \log\left|2x^2 + 6x + 5\right| + C_1$$

and $I_2 = \int \frac{dx}{2x^2 + 6x + 5} = \frac{1}{2}\int \frac{dx}{x^2 + 3x + \frac{5}{2}}$

$$= \frac{1}{2}\int \frac{dx}{x^2 + 2 \cdot \frac{3}{2} \cdot x + \left(\frac{3}{2}\right)^2 - \left(\frac{3}{2}\right)^2 + \frac{5}{2}}$$

$\left[\text{adding and subtracting } \left(\frac{3}{2}\right)^2 \text{ in denominator}\right]$

$$= \frac{1}{2}\int \frac{dx}{\left(x + \frac{3}{2}\right)^2 + \left(\frac{1}{2}\right)^2} = \frac{1}{2} \cdot \frac{1}{\left(\frac{1}{2}\right)} \tan^{-1}\left(\frac{x + \frac{3}{2}}{\frac{1}{2}}\right) + C_2$$

$\left[\because \int \frac{dx}{x^2 + a^2} = \frac{1}{a}\tan^{-1}\left(\frac{x}{a}\right) + C\right]$

$$= \frac{1}{2} \cdot 2\tan^{-1}(2x + 3) + C_2 = \tan^{-1}(2x + 3) + C_2$$

Now, substitute the values of I_1 and I_2 in Eq. (ii).

Then, the given integral becomes

$$I = \frac{1}{4}\log|2x^2 + 6x + 5| + \frac{1}{2}\tan^{-1}(2x + 3) + \frac{1}{4}C_1 + \frac{1}{2}C_2$$

$$= \frac{1}{4}\log\left|2x^2 + 6x + 5\right| + \frac{1}{2}\tan^{-1}(2x + 3) + C,$$

where $C = \frac{1}{4}C_1 + \frac{1}{2}C_2$.

Example 14 Evaluate $\int \frac{x+3}{\sqrt{5 - 4x - 2x^2}} dx.$

Competency Based Que, CBSE 2015C

Sol. Let $\quad x + 3 = A\frac{d}{dx}(5 - 4x - 2x^2) + B$

$\Rightarrow \quad x + 3 = A(-4 - 4x) + B$ ...(i)

$\Rightarrow \quad x + 3 = -4A - 4Ax + B$

$\Rightarrow \quad x + 3 = -4Ax + (B - 4A)$

On equating the coefficients of x and constant term from both sides, we get

$1 = -4A$ and $3 = B - 4A$

$\Rightarrow \quad A = -\frac{1}{4}$ and $B = 3 + 4 \times \left(-\frac{1}{4}\right)$

$\Rightarrow \quad A = -\frac{1}{4}$ and $B = 2$

$\therefore$ From Eq. (i), we get

$$(x + 3) = -\frac{1}{4}(-4 - 4x) + 2$$

Now, the given integral can be written as

$$I=\int \frac{x+3}{\sqrt{5-4x-2x^2}}dx=\int \frac{-\frac{1}{4}(-4-4x)+2}{\sqrt{5-4x-2x^2}}dx$$

$$=-\frac{1}{4}\int \frac{(-4-4x)}{\sqrt{5-4x-2x^2}}dx+2\int \frac{dx}{\sqrt{5-4x-2x^2}}$$

$$=-\frac{1}{4}I_1+2I_2 \qquad \text{...(ii)}$$

where, $I_1=\int \frac{(-4-4x)}{\sqrt{5-4x-2x^2}}dx,\ I_2=\int \frac{dx}{\sqrt{5-4x-2x^2}}$

Consider $I_1=\int \frac{(-4-4x)}{\sqrt{5-4x-2x^2}}dx$

Now, put $5-4x-2x^2=t \Rightarrow (-4-4x)\,dx=dt$

$$\therefore I_1=\int \frac{dt}{\sqrt{t}}=\int t^{-\frac{1}{2}}dt=2\sqrt{t}+C_1=2\sqrt{5-4x-2x^2}+C_1$$

and $I_2=\int \frac{dx}{\sqrt{5-4x-2x^2}}=\int \frac{dx}{\sqrt{(-2)\left(x^2+2x-\frac{5}{2}\right)}}$

$$=\frac{1}{\sqrt{2}}\int \frac{dx}{\sqrt{-\left(x^2+2\cdot x\cdot 1+1^2-1^2-\frac{5}{2}\right)}}$$

[adding and subtracting $(1)^2$ in denominator]

$$=\frac{1}{\sqrt{2}}\int \frac{dx}{\sqrt{-\left[(x+1)^2-\left(\sqrt{\frac{7}{2}}\right)^2\right]}}$$

$$=\frac{1}{\sqrt{2}}\int \frac{dx}{\sqrt{\left(\sqrt{\frac{7}{2}}\right)^2-(x+1)^2}}$$

$$=\frac{1}{\sqrt{2}}\sin^{-1}\left(\frac{x+1}{\sqrt{7/2}}\right)+C_2$$

$$\left[\because \int \frac{dx}{\sqrt{a^2-x^2}}=\sin^{-1}\left(\frac{x}{a}\right)+C\right]$$

$$=\frac{1}{\sqrt{2}}\sin^{-1}\left[\frac{\sqrt{2}(x+1)}{\sqrt{7}}\right]+C_2$$

Now, on putting the values of I_1 and I_2 in Eq. (ii), we get

$$I=-\frac{1}{4}\times 2\sqrt{5-4x-2x^2}-\frac{1}{4}C_1+2\cdot\frac{1}{\sqrt{2}}\sin^{-1}\left[\frac{\sqrt{2}(x+1)}{\sqrt{7}}\right]+2C_2$$

$$=-\frac{1}{2}\sqrt{5-4x-2x^2}+\sqrt{2}\sin^{-1}\left[\frac{\sqrt{2}(x+1)}{\sqrt{7}}\right]+C,$$

where $C=-\frac{1}{4}C_1+2C_2$

Quick Test 3

Direction (Q. Nos. 1-9) *Evaluate the following integrals.*

1. $\int \frac{\cos x}{\sqrt{3+\cos^2 x}}dx$

2. $\int \frac{dx}{x^2+4x+8}$ CBSE 2017

3. $\int \frac{\sin x+\cos x}{9+16\sin 2x}dx$

4. $\int \frac{dx}{\sqrt{(x-\alpha)(\beta-x)}},\ \beta>\alpha$ NCERT Exemplar

5. $\int \frac{\sin 2x\cos 2x}{\sqrt{9-\cos^4 2x}}dx$ Competency Based Que, NCERT

6. $\int \frac{x+2}{\sqrt{x^2+5x+6}}dx$ CBSE 2014

7. $\int \frac{dx}{2\sin^2 x+5\cos^2 x}dx$ NCERT Exemplar

8. $\int \frac{1}{\cos^4 x+\sin^4 x}dx$ CBSE 2014

9. $\int \frac{1}{\sin^4 x+\sin^2 x\cos^2 x+\cos^4 x}dx$ Competency Based Que, CBSE 2014

For Solutions, See QR Code on Pg. 235

Answers

1. $\sin^{-1}\left(\frac{\sin x}{2}\right)+C$
2. $\frac{1}{2}\tan^{-1}\left(\frac{x+2}{2}\right)+C$
3. $\frac{1}{40}\log\left|\frac{5+4(\sin x-\cos x)}{5-4(\sin x-\cos x)}\right|+C$
4. $2\sin^{-1}\left(\sqrt{\frac{x-\alpha}{\beta-\alpha}}\right)+C$
5. $-\frac{1}{4}\sin^{-1}\left(\frac{\cos^2 2x}{3}\right)+C$
6. $\sqrt{x^2+5x+6}-\frac{1}{2}\log\left|\left(x+\frac{5}{2}\right)+\sqrt{x^2+5x+6}\right|+C$
7. $\frac{1}{\sqrt{10}}\tan^{-1}\left(\frac{\sqrt{2}\tan x}{\sqrt{5}}\right)+C$
8. $\frac{1}{\sqrt{2}}\tan^{-1}\left(\frac{\tan^2 x-1}{\sqrt{2}\tan x}\right)+C$
9. $\frac{1}{\sqrt{3}}\tan^{-1}\left(\frac{\tan^2 x-1}{\sqrt{3}\tan x}\right)+C$

7.4 Integration by Partial Fractions

A rational function is a ratio of two polynomials i.e. of the form $\frac{p(x)}{q(x)}$, where $p(x)$ and $q(x)$ are polynomials in x and $q(x) \neq 0$. If degree of $p(x) >$ degree of $q(x)$, then we may divide $p(x)$ by $q(x)$ so that $\frac{p(x)}{q(x)} = t(x) + \frac{p_1(x)}{q(x)}$, where $t(x)$ is a polynomial in x which can be integrated easily and degree of $p_1(x)$ is less than the degree of $q(x)$. Now, $\frac{p_1(x)}{q(x)}$ can be integrated by expressing $\frac{p_1(x)}{q(x)}$ as the sum of partial fractions of the following types :

S.No.	Form of the rational function	Form of the partial fraction
1.	$\frac{px+q}{(x-a)(x-b)}, a \neq b$	$\frac{A}{x-a} + \frac{B}{x-b}$
2.	$\frac{px+q}{(x-a)^2}$	$\frac{A}{(x-a)} + \frac{B}{(x-a)^2}$
3.	$\frac{px^2+qx+r}{(x-a)(x-b)(x-c)}$	$\frac{A}{(x-a)} + \frac{B}{(x-b)} + \frac{C}{(x-c)}$
4.	$\frac{px^2+qx+r}{(x-a)^2(x-b)}$	$\frac{A}{(x-a)} + \frac{B}{(x-a)^2} + \frac{C}{(x-b)}$
5.	$\frac{px^2+qx+r}{(x-a)(x^2+bx+c)}$	$\frac{A}{(x-a)} + \frac{Bx+C}{x^2+bx+c}$, where, x^2+bx+c cannot be factorised further.

Example 1 Find $\int \frac{5x}{(x+1)(x^2+9)} dx$ CBSE 2025

Sol. Let $I = \int \frac{5x}{(x+1)(x^2+9)} dx$

Again, let $\frac{5x}{(x+1)(x^2+9)} = \frac{A}{(x+1)} + \frac{Bx+C}{(x^2+9)}$ ...(i)

$\Rightarrow \quad 5x = A(x^2+9) + (Bx+C)(x+1)$

$\Rightarrow \quad 5x = Ax^2 + 9A + Bx^2 + Bx + Cx + C$ ...(ii)

On comparing the coefficients of x^2, x and constant term both sides of Eq. (ii), we get

$$A + B = 0,\ B + C = 5 \text{ and } 9A + C = 0$$

On solving these equations, we get

$$A = -\frac{1}{2},\ B = \frac{1}{2} \text{ and } C = \frac{9}{2}$$

On substituting the values of A, B and C in Eq. (i), we get

$$\frac{5x}{(x+1)(x^2+9)} = \frac{-1}{2(x+1)} + \frac{\frac{x}{2}+\frac{9}{2}}{(x^2+9)}$$

$$\therefore \quad I = \int \frac{5x}{(x+1)(x^2+9)} dx = \int \frac{-1}{2(x+1)} dx + \int \frac{x+9}{2(x^2+9)} dx$$

$$= \frac{-1}{2} \log|x+1| + \frac{1}{2}\int \frac{x}{x^2+9} dx + \frac{9}{2}\int \frac{1}{x^2+9} dx$$

$$= \frac{-1}{2} \log|x+1| + \frac{1}{4}\int \frac{2x}{x^2+9} dx + \frac{9}{2}\int \frac{1}{x^2+9} dx$$

$$= \frac{-1}{2} \log|x+1| + \frac{1}{4} \log|x^2+9| + \frac{9}{2} \cdot \frac{1}{3} \tan^{-1}\frac{x}{3} + C$$

$$= \frac{-1}{2} \log|x+1| + \frac{1}{4} \log|x^2+9| + \frac{3}{2} \tan^{-1}\frac{x}{3} + C$$

Example 2 Evaluate $\int \frac{2x-1}{(x-1)(x+2)(x-3)} dx.$

Sol. Let $I = \int \frac{2x-1}{(x-1)(x+2)(x-3)} dx$

Again, let $\frac{2x-1}{(x-1)(x+2)(x-3)} = \frac{A}{x-1} + \frac{B}{x+2} + \frac{C}{x-3}$ ...(i)

$\Rightarrow \quad 2x - 1 = A(x+2)(x-3) + B(x-1)(x-3) + C(x-1)(x+2)$ ...(ii)

$\Rightarrow \quad 2x - 1 = (A+B+C)x^2 + (-A-4B+C)x + (-6A+3B-2C)$

On comparing the coefficients of x^2, x and constant terms on both sides of Eq. (ii), we get

$$A + B + C = 0,\ -A - 4B + C = 2$$

and $-6A + 3B - 2C = -1$

$\Rightarrow \quad A = -\frac{1}{6},\ B = -\frac{1}{3}$ and $C = \frac{1}{2}$

On substituting the values of A, B and C in Eq. (i), we get

$$\frac{2x-1}{(x-1)(x+2)(x-3)} = -\frac{1}{6} \cdot \frac{1}{x-1} - \frac{1}{3} \cdot \frac{1}{x+2} + \frac{1}{2} \cdot \frac{1}{x-3}$$

$$\Rightarrow I = -\frac{1}{6}\int \frac{1}{x-1} dx - \frac{1}{3}\int \frac{1}{x+2} dx + \frac{1}{2}\int \frac{1}{x-3} dx$$

$$\Rightarrow I = -\frac{1}{6} \log|x-1| - \frac{1}{3} \log|x+2| + \frac{1}{2} \log|x-3| + C$$

Example 3 Find $\int \frac{2x+1}{(x+1)^2 (x-1)} dx.$ CBSE 2024

Sol. Let $I = \int \frac{2x+1}{(x+1)^2 (x-1)} dx$

Let $\frac{2x+1}{(x+1)^2(x-1)} = \frac{A}{(x+1)} + \frac{B}{(x+1)^2} + \frac{C}{(x-1)}$ ...(i)

$$\Rightarrow \frac{2x+1}{(x+1)^2(x-1)} = \frac{A(x+1)(x-1) + B(x-1) + C(x+1)^2}{(x+1)^2(x-1)}$$

$\Rightarrow 2x+1 = A(x+1)(x-1) + B(x-1) + C(x+1)^2$ ...(ii)

On putting $x=-1$ in Eq. (ii), we get

$2(-1)+1 = A(-1+1)(-1-1) + B(-1-1) + C(-1+1)^2$

$\Rightarrow \quad -1 = -2B \Rightarrow B = \frac{1}{2}$

On putting $x=1$ in Eq. (ii), we get

$2(1)+1 = A(1+1)(1-1) + B(1-1) + C(1+1)^2$

$\Rightarrow \quad 3 = C(4) \Rightarrow C = \frac{3}{4}$

On putting $x=0$ in Eq. (ii), we get

$2(0)+1 = A(0+1)(0-1) + B(0-1) + C(0+1)^2$

$\Rightarrow \quad 1 = -A - B + C \Rightarrow A = C - B - 1$

$\Rightarrow \quad A = \frac{3}{4} - \frac{1}{2} - 1 = -\frac{3}{4} \quad \left[\because C = \frac{3}{4}, B = \frac{1}{2}\right]$

Now, on putting the values of A, B and C in Eq. (i), we get

$$\frac{2x+1}{(x+1)^2(x-1)} = \frac{-\frac{3}{4}}{x+1} + \frac{\frac{1}{2}}{(x+1)^2} + \frac{\frac{3}{4}}{x-1}$$

$$\therefore I = \int \frac{2x+1}{(x+1)^2(x-1)} dx$$

$$= \frac{-3}{4}\int \frac{dx}{x+1} + \frac{1}{2}\int \frac{dx}{(x+1)^2} + \frac{3}{4}\int \frac{dx}{x-1}$$

$$= \frac{-3}{4}\log|x+1| + \frac{1}{2}\int (x+1)^{-2} dx + \frac{3}{4}\log|x-1| + C$$

$$= \frac{-3}{4}\log|x+1| + \frac{1}{2}\cdot\frac{(x+1)^{-1}}{(-1)} + \frac{3}{4}\log|x-1| + C$$

$$= \frac{-3}{4}\log|x+1| - \frac{1}{2(x+1)} + \frac{3}{4}\log|x-1| + C$$

$$= \frac{3}{4}[\log|x-1| - \log|x+1|] - \frac{1}{2(x+1)} + C$$

$$= \frac{3}{4}\log\left|\frac{x-1}{x+1}\right| - \frac{1}{2(x+1)} + C$$

Example 4 Find $\int \frac{2}{(1-x)(1+x^2)} dx.$

CBSE 2023

Sol. We have, $\int \frac{2}{(1-x)(1+x^2)} dx$

Let $\frac{2}{(1-x)(1+x^2)} = \frac{A}{1-x} + \frac{Bx+C}{1+x^2}$

$$\Rightarrow \frac{2}{(1-x)(1+x^2)} = \frac{A(1+x^2)+(Bx+C)(1-x)}{(1-x)(1+x^2)}$$

$\Rightarrow \quad 2 = A + Ax^2 + Bx - Bx^2 + C - Cx$

$\Rightarrow \quad 2 = (A+C) + x(B-C) + x^2(A-B)$

On equating coefficients of constant term, coefficient of x and coefficients of x^2, we get

$A + C = 2$ ...(i)

$B - C = 0$ ...(ii)

and $A - B = 0$ ...(iii)

On solving Eqs. (i), (ii) and (iii), we get

$A = 1, B = 1$ and $C = 1$

$$\therefore \frac{2}{(1-x)(1+x^2)} = \frac{1}{1-x} + \frac{x+1}{1+x^2}$$

$$\therefore \int \frac{2}{(1-x)(1+x^2)} dx = \int \frac{1}{1-x} dx + \int \frac{x+1}{1+x^2} dx$$

$$= -\log(1-x) + \frac{1}{2}\int \frac{2x}{1+x^2} dx + \int \frac{dx}{1+x^2}$$

$$= -\log(1-x) + \frac{1}{2}\log(1+x^2) + \tan^{-1}x + C$$

Example 5 Find $\int \frac{x^2+x+1}{(x+1)^2(x+2)} dx.$

CBSE 2023, 14C

Sol. We have, $\int \frac{x^2+x+1}{(x+1)^2(x+2)} dx$

Given integrand $\frac{x^2+x+1}{(x+1)^2(x+2)}$ is a proper rational function.

By partial fraction,

let $\frac{x^2+x+1}{(x+1)^2(x+2)} = \frac{A}{x+1} + \frac{B}{(x+1)^2} + \frac{C}{x+2}$ ...(i)

$\Rightarrow x^2+x+1 = A(x+1)(x+2) + B(x+2) + C(x+1)^2$

$\Rightarrow x^2+x+1 = (A+C)x^2 + (3A+B+2C)x + (2A+2B+C)$

On comparing the coefficients of like powers of x from both sides, we get

$A + C = 1, 3A + B + 2C = 1$ and $2A + 2B + C = 1$

On solving these equations, we get

$A = -2, B = 1$ and $C = 3$

From Eq. (i), we get

$$\frac{x^2+x+1}{(x+1)^2(x+2)} = \frac{-2}{x+1} + \frac{1}{(x+1)^2} + \frac{3}{x+2}$$

$$\therefore \int \frac{x^2+x+1}{(x+1)^2(x+2)} dx = -2\int \frac{1}{x+1} dx + \int \frac{dx}{(x+1)^2} + 3\int \frac{dx}{(x+2)}$$

$$= -2\log|x+1| - \frac{1}{x+1} + 3\log|x+2| + C$$

Example 6 Find $\int \frac{(x^3+x+1)}{(x^2-1)} dx.$

Competency Based Que, CBSE Sample Paper 2023

Sol. Let $I = \int \frac{(x^3+x+1)}{(x^2-1)} dx = \int \frac{x^3-x+x+x+1}{(x^2-1)} dx$

$$= \int \frac{x(x^2-1)+(2x+1)}{(x^2-1)} dx \Rightarrow I = \int \left(x + \frac{2x+1}{(x^2-1)}\right) dx$$

$\therefore \quad I = \int x\,dx + \int \frac{2x+1}{x^2-1} dx$ ...(i)

Now, resolving $\frac{2x+1}{x^2-1}$ into partial fraction as

$\frac{2x+1}{(x-1)(x+1)} = \frac{A}{x-1} + \frac{B}{x+1}$ ...(ii)

$\Rightarrow \quad 2x+1 = A(x+1) + B(x-1)$

$\Rightarrow \quad 2x+1 = x(A+B) + A - B$

On comparing the coefficients of x and constant terms both sides, we get

$A + B = 2$ and $A - B = 1$

On solving these equations, we get $A = \frac{3}{2}$ and $B = \frac{1}{2}$

On substituting the values of A and B in Eq. (ii), we get

$$\frac{2x+1}{(x-1)(x+1)} = \frac{3}{2(x-1)} + \frac{1}{2(x+1)}$$

From Eq. (i), we get

$$I = \int x\,dx + \frac{3}{2}\int \frac{1}{x-1}dx + \frac{1}{2}\int \frac{1}{x+1}dx$$

$$\Rightarrow I = \frac{x^2}{2} + \frac{3}{2}\log|x-1| + \frac{1}{2}\log|x+1| + C$$

$$\Rightarrow I = \frac{x^2}{2} + \frac{1}{2}\log|x-1|^3 + \frac{1}{2}\log|x+1| + C$$

$[\because n\log m = \log m^n]$

$$\Rightarrow I = \frac{x^2}{2} + \frac{1}{2}[\log|(x-1)^3(x+1)|] + C$$

$[\because \log m + \log n = \log mn]$

Example 7 **Find** $\int \frac{x^2}{(x^2+1)(3x^2+4)}dx.$ *CBSE 2022 (Term II)*

Sol. Let $I = \int \frac{x^2}{(x^2+1)(3x^2+4)}dx$

Again, let $\frac{x^2}{(x^2+1)(3x^2+4)} = \frac{Ax+B}{(x^2+1)} + \frac{Cx+D}{(3x^2+4)}$

$\Rightarrow \quad x^2 = (Ax+B)(3x^2+4) + (Cx+D)(x^2+1)$

$\Rightarrow \quad x^2 = (3A+C)x^3 + (3B+D)x^2 + (4A+C)x + 4B + D$

On equating similar terms, we get

$3A + C = 0,\ 3B + D = 1,\ 4A + C = 0$ and $4B + D = 0$

On solving, we get $A = 0,\ B = -1,\ C = 0$ and $D = 4$

Thus, $I = \int \frac{-dx}{(x^2+1)} + \int \frac{4dx}{(3x^2+4)}$

$$= \int -\frac{dx}{(x^2+1)} + \frac{4}{3}\int \frac{dx}{\left(x^2+\frac{4}{3}\right)}$$

$$= \int -\frac{dx}{x^2+1} + \frac{4}{3}\int \frac{dx}{x^2+\left(\frac{2}{\sqrt{3}}\right)^2}$$

$$= -\tan^{-1}x + \frac{4}{3}\cdot\frac{\sqrt{3}}{2}\tan^{-1}\left(\frac{\sqrt{3}x}{2}\right) + C$$

$$\left[\because \int \frac{dx}{x^2+a^2} = \frac{1}{a}\tan^{-1}\frac{x}{a} + C\right]$$

$$= \frac{2}{\sqrt{3}}\tan^{-1}\left(\frac{\sqrt{3}x}{2}\right) - \tan^{-1}x + C$$

Quick Test 4

Direction (Q. Nos. 1-10) *Evaluate the following integrals.*

1. $\int \frac{2x-3}{(x^2-1)(2x+3)}dx$

2. $\int \frac{e^x}{(1+e^x)(2+e^x)}dx$ *NCERT*

3. $\int \frac{dx}{\sin x + \sin 2x}$

4. $\int \frac{2\cos x}{(1-\sin x)(1+\sin^2 x)}dx$

5. $\int \frac{x+1}{(x^2+1)x}dx$ *CBSE Sample Paper 2022 (Term II)*

6. $\int \frac{1}{x(x^2+1)}dx$ *NCERT*

7. $\int \frac{x^4}{(x-1)(x^2+1)}dx$ *CBSE 2023, NCERT*

8. $\int \frac{x^2}{x^4-x^2-12}dx$ *Competency Based Que*

9. $\int \frac{x^2+x+1}{(x^2+1)(x+2)}dx$ *CBSE 2016, 15*

10. $\int \frac{\cos\theta}{(4+\sin^2\theta)(5-4\cos^2\theta)}d\theta$ *Competency Based Que, CBSE 2017*

Answers

1. $\frac{5}{2}\log|x+1| - \frac{1}{10}\log|x-1| - \frac{12}{5}\log|2x+3| + C$

2. $\log\left|\frac{1+e^x}{2+e^x}\right| + C$

3. $\frac{1}{6}\log|1-\cos x| + \frac{1}{2}\log|1+\cos x| - \frac{2}{3}\log|1+2\cos x| + C$

4. $\tan^{-1}(\sin x) + \log\left|\frac{\sqrt{1+\sin^2 x}}{1-\sin x}\right| + C$

5. $\frac{-1}{2}\log(x^2+1) + \tan^{-1}x + \log|x| + C$

6. $\log|x| - \frac{1}{2}\log(x^2+1) + C$

7. $\frac{x^2}{2} + x + \frac{1}{2}\log|x-1| - \frac{1}{4}\log|x^2+1| - \frac{1}{2}\tan^{-1}x + C$

8. $\frac{1}{7}\log\left|\frac{x-2}{x+2}\right| + \frac{\sqrt{3}}{7}\tan^{-1}\frac{x}{\sqrt{3}} + C$

9. $\frac{3}{5}\log|x+2| + \frac{1}{5}\log|x^2+1| + \frac{1}{5}\tan^{-1}x + C$

10. $\frac{-1}{30}\tan^{-1}\frac{\sin\theta}{2} + \frac{2}{15}\tan^{-1}2\cdot\sin\theta + C$

For Solutions, See QR Code on Pg. 235

7.5 Integration by Parts

Let u and v be two differentiable functions of x.

Then, $\int \underset{\text{I}}{u} \cdot \underset{\text{II}}{v}\, dx = u \int v\, dx - \int \left(\frac{d}{dx}(u) \int v\, dx \right) dx$

i.e. the integral of the product of these two functions

= Ist function × Integral of the IInd function

− Integral of [Derivatives of Ist function

× Integral of the IInd function]

Here, we can choose first function according to its position in ILATE, where

- **I** Inverse trigonometric function. e.g. $\sin^{-1} x$
- **L** Logarithmic function. e.g. $\log x$
- **A** Algebraic function. e.g. $1, x, x^2$
- **T** Trigonometric function. e.g. $\sin x, \cos x$
- **E** Exponential function. e.g. e^x

The function which comes first in ILATE should taken as first function and other as second function.

Integral of the Type $\int e^x [f(x) + f'(x)]\, dx$

In this type of integral, integrand is the product of two functions. One is in exponential form and second function is the sum of two functions in which one is derivative of other function. Then, to evaluate such integrals, we directly use the following formula

$$\int e^x [f(x) + f'(x)]\, dx = e^x f(x) + C$$

Some More Special Types of Integrals

Here, we will discuss some more special types of integrals, which can be proved using integration by parts and directly used to evaluate the given integrals.

(i) $\int \sqrt{x^2 - a^2}\, dx = \frac{x}{2}\sqrt{x^2 - a^2} - \frac{a^2}{2}\log|x + \sqrt{x^2 - a^2}| + C$

(ii) $\int \sqrt{x^2 + a^2}\, dx = \frac{x}{2}\sqrt{x^2 + a^2} + \frac{a^2}{2}\log|x + \sqrt{x^2 + a^2}| + C$

(iii) $\int \sqrt{a^2 - x^2}\, dx = \frac{x}{2}\sqrt{a^2 - x^2} + \frac{a^2}{2}\sin^{-1}\frac{x}{a} + C$

TEACHER TIPS

(i) If the integrand contains a logarithmic or an inverse trigonometric function and the second function is not given, then we take second function as 1.

e.g. In the integral of $\int \sin^{-1} x\, dx$, we take second function as unity (i.e. 1).

(ii) Integration by parts is not applicable in all cases.

e.g. The method does not work for $\int \sqrt{x} \sin x\, dx$.

The reason is that there does not exist any function whose derivative is $\sqrt{x} \sin x$.

Example 1 Evaluate $\int x \log x\, dx$.

Sol. Let $I = \int \underset{\text{II}}{x} \underset{\text{I}}{\log x}\, dx$

$$= \log x \int x\, dx - \int \left\{ \frac{d}{dx}(\log x) \times \int x\, dx \right\} dx$$

$$= (\log x) . \frac{x^2}{2} - \int \frac{1}{x} \times \frac{x^2}{2}\, dx$$

$$= \frac{1}{2} x^2 \log x - \frac{1}{2} \int x\, dx$$

$$= \frac{1}{2} x^2 \log x - \frac{1}{2}\left(\frac{x^2}{2}\right) + C$$

$$= \frac{1}{2} x^2 \log x - \frac{x^2}{4} + C$$

Example 2 Evaluate $\int x^2 \cos x\, dx$. NCERT

Sol. Let $I = \int \underset{\text{I}}{x^2} \underset{\text{II}}{\cos x}\, dx$

$$= x^2 \int \cos x\, dx - \int \left\{ \frac{d}{dx}(x^2) \int \cos x\, dx \right\} dx$$

$$= x^2 \sin x - \int 2x \sin x\, dx$$

$$= x^2 \sin x - 2\int \underset{\text{I}}{x} \underset{\text{II}}{\sin x}\, dx$$

$$= x^2 \sin x - 2\left[x \int \sin x\, dx - \int \left\{ \frac{d}{dx}(x) \int \sin x\, dx \right\} dx \right]$$

$$= x^2 \sin x - 2[x(-\cos x) - \int (-\cos x)\, dx]$$

$$= x^2 \sin x + 2x \cos x - 2\sin x + C$$

Example 3 Evaluate $\int \frac{\log x}{(x+1)^2}$. CBSE 2015

Sol. Let $I = \int \frac{\log x}{(x+1)^2}\, dx$

$$= \int \log x \cdot \frac{1}{(x+1)^2}\, dx$$

On applying integration by parts, we get

$$I = \log x \cdot \int \frac{dx}{(x+1)^2} - \int \left\{ \frac{d}{dx}(\log x) \cdot \left(\int \frac{dx}{(x+1)^2} \right) \right\} dx$$

$$\left[\because \int u \cdot v\, dx = u \int v\, dx - \int \left(\frac{d}{dx}(u) \int v\, dx \right) dx \right]$$

$$= \log x \cdot \frac{(-1)}{x+1} + \int \frac{1}{x(x+1)}\, dx$$

$$\left[\because \int \frac{1}{(x+1)^2}\, dx = -\frac{1}{(x+1)} \right]$$

$$= \frac{-\log x}{x+1} + I_1, \text{ where } I_1 = \int \frac{dx}{x(x+1)} \text{ (say)} \quad \ldots\text{(i)}$$

Now, using partial fraction method, consider

$$\frac{1}{x(x+1)} = \frac{A}{x} + \frac{B}{x+1}$$

$$\Rightarrow \quad 1 = A(x+1) + Bx$$

On putting $x = 0$, we get $A = 1$

Again, on putting $x = -1$, we get $B = -1$

$$\therefore \quad I_1 = \int \left(\frac{1}{x} - \frac{1}{x+1} \right) dx = \int \frac{1}{x}\, dx - \int \frac{dx}{x+1}$$

$$= \log|x| - \log|x+1| + C \quad \ldots\text{(ii)}$$

Now, from Eqs. (i) and (ii), we get

$$I = \frac{-\log x}{x+1} + \log|x| - \log|x+1| + C$$

$$= \frac{-\log x}{x+1} + \log\left|\frac{x}{x+1}\right| + C$$

$$\left[\because \log m - \log n = \log \frac{m}{n} \right]$$

Example 4 **Evaluate** $\int \frac{\sin^{-1} x}{(1-x^2)^{3/2}}\, dx.$

Sol. Let $I = \int \frac{\sin^{-1} x}{(1-x^2)^{3/2}}\, dx$

Put $x = \sin t \Rightarrow dx = \cos t\, dt$ and $t = \sin^{-1} x$

$$\therefore \quad I = \int \frac{t \cos t}{(1-\sin^2 t)^{3/2}}\, dt = \int \frac{t \cos t}{(\cos^2 t)^{3/2}}\, dt$$

$$= \int \frac{t \cos t}{\cos^3 t}\, dt$$

$$= \int \underset{\text{I}}{t} \underset{\text{II}}{\sec^2 t}\, dt$$

$$= t \cdot (\tan t) - \int 1 \cdot \tan t\, dt = t \tan t + \log|\cos t| + C$$

$$\left[\because \int \tan x\, dx = -\log|\cos x| + C \right]$$

$$= \sin^{-1} x \cdot \frac{x}{\sqrt{1-x^2}} + \log|\sqrt{1-x^2}| + C$$

$$= \frac{x \sin^{-1} x}{\sqrt{1-x^2}} + \frac{1}{2} \log|(1-x^2)| + C$$

Example 5 **Find the value of** $\int \frac{x + \sin x}{1 + \cos x}\, dx.$

NCERT Exemplar, CBSE 2023, 12

Sol. Let $I = \int \frac{x + \sin x}{1 + \cos x}\, dx$

$$= \int \frac{x + 2\sin\frac{x}{2}\cos\frac{x}{2}}{1 + \left(2\cos^2\frac{x}{2} - 1\right)}\, dx \quad \left[\because \sin\theta = 2\sin\frac{\theta}{2}\cos\frac{\theta}{2} \text{ and } \cos\theta = 2\cos^2\frac{\theta}{2} - 1 \right]$$

$$= \int \frac{x + 2\sin\frac{x}{2}\cos\frac{x}{2}}{2\cos^2\frac{x}{2}}\, dx$$

$$= \int \left(\frac{x}{2\cos^2\frac{x}{2}} + \frac{2\sin\frac{x}{2}\cos\frac{x}{2}}{2\cos^2\frac{x}{2}} \right) dx$$

$$= \int \left(\frac{1}{2} x \sec^2\frac{x}{2} + \tan\frac{x}{2} \right) dx$$

$$= \frac{1}{2} \int \underset{\text{I}}{x} \underset{\text{II}}{\sec^2} \frac{x}{2}\, dx + \int \tan\frac{x}{2}\, dx$$

$$= \frac{1}{2} \left[x \int \sec^2\frac{x}{2}\, dx - \int \left\{ \frac{d}{dx}(x) \int \sec^2\frac{x}{2}\, dx \right\} dx \right]$$

$$+ \int \tan\frac{x}{2}\, dx \quad \text{[using integration by parts]}$$

$$= \frac{1}{2} \left[x\left(2\tan\frac{x}{2}\right) - \int 1\left(2\tan\frac{x}{2}\right) dx \right] + \int \tan\frac{x}{2}\, dx$$

$$= x\tan\frac{x}{2} - \int \tan\frac{x}{2}\, dx + \int \tan\frac{x}{2}\, dx = x\tan\frac{x}{2} + C$$

Example 6 **Find the value of** $\int \frac{x \tan^{-1} x}{(1+x^2)^{3/2}}\, dx.$

Competency Based Que, CBSE 2015

Sol. Let $I = \int \frac{x \tan^{-1} x}{(1+x^2)^{3/2}}\, dx = \int \frac{x \tan^{-1} x\, dx}{\sqrt{1+x^2}\,(1+x^2)}$

Put $\tan^{-1} x = t \Rightarrow \frac{1}{1+x^2}\, dx = dt$ and $x = \tan t$

Then, $I = \int \frac{\tan t \cdot t\, dt}{\sqrt{1+\tan^2 t}} = \int \frac{\sin t}{\cos t} \cdot t \cdot \frac{1}{\sec t}\, dt$

$$[\because 1 + \tan^2\theta = \sec^2\theta]$$

$$= \int \underset{\text{I}}{t} \underset{\text{II}}{\sin t}\, dt = t(-\cos t) - \int 1(-\cos t)\, dt + C$$

[using integration by parts]

$$= -t\cos t + \int \cos t\, dt + C$$

$$= -t\cos t + \sin t + C = \sin t - t\cos t + C$$

$$= \frac{x}{\sqrt{1+x^2}} - \tan^{-1} x \cdot \frac{1}{\sqrt{1+x^2}} + C$$

$$\left[\because \tan t = x, \text{ then } \sin t = \frac{x}{\sqrt{1+x^2}} \text{ and } \cos t = \frac{1}{\sqrt{1+x^2}} \right]$$

$$= (1+x^2)^{-1/2}(x - \tan^{-1} x) + C$$

Example 7 $\int \frac{\sqrt{x^2+1}\{\log(x^2+1)-2\log x\}}{x^4}dx$

Competency Based Que, NCERT, CBSE 2012

Sol. Let $I = \int \frac{\sqrt{x^2+1}\,\{\log(x^2+1)-2\log x\}}{x^4}dx$

$\Rightarrow I = \int \frac{\sqrt{x^2+1}}{x^4}\{\log(x^2+1)-\log x^2\}\,dx$

$\Rightarrow I = \int \sqrt{1+\frac{1}{x^2}}\log\left(1+\frac{1}{x^2}\right)\frac{1}{x^3}dx$

Let $1+\frac{1}{x^2}=t$

Then, $\frac{d}{dx}\left(1+\frac{1}{x^2}\right)=\frac{dt}{dx}$

$\Rightarrow \quad -\frac{2}{x^3}dx = dt \Rightarrow \frac{1}{x^3}dx = -\frac{1}{2}dt$

$\therefore \quad I = -\frac{1}{2}\int \underset{\text{II}}{\sqrt{t}}\ \underset{\text{I}}{\log t}\ dt$

$\Rightarrow I = -\frac{1}{2}\left\{\frac{2}{3}(\log t)t^{3/2} - \frac{2}{3}\int\frac{1}{t}\times t^{3/2}dt\right\}$

$= -\frac{1}{2}\left\{\frac{2}{3}(\log t)t^{3/2} - \frac{4}{9}t^{3/2}\right\}+C$

$\Rightarrow I = -\frac{1}{3}t^{3/2}\left\{\log t - \frac{2}{3}\right\}+C$

$= -\frac{1}{3}\left(1+\frac{1}{x^2}\right)^{3/2}\left\{\log\left(1+\frac{1}{x^2}\right)-\frac{2}{3}\right\}+C$

Example 8 Prove that

$\int \sin^n x\,dx = -\frac{1}{n}\sin^{n-1}x\cos x + \frac{n-1}{n}\int \sin^{n-2}x\,dx.$

Competency Based Que, CBSE 2017

Sol. Let $I = \int \sin^n x\,dx = \int \sin^{n-1}x\cdot\sin x\,dx$

$= \sin^{n-1}x\cdot(-\cos x) - \int (n-1)\sin^{n-2}x\cos x$

$(-\cos x)\,dx$ [using integration by parts]

$= -\sin^{n-1}x\cdot\cos x + (n-1)\int \sin^{n-2}x\,(1-\sin^2 x)\,dx$

$= -\sin^{n-1}x\cdot\cos x + (n-1)\int\sin^{n-2}x\,dx - (n-1)\int\sin^n x\,dx$

$\Rightarrow I = -\sin^{n-1}x\cdot\cos x + (n-1)\int\sin^{n-2}x\,dx - (n-1)I$

$\Rightarrow nI = -\sin^{n-1}x\cos x + (n-1)\int \sin^{n-2}x\,dx$

$\Rightarrow \int \sin^n x\,dx = \frac{-\sin^{n-1}x\cos x}{n} + \frac{n-1}{n}\int\sin^{n-2}x\,dx$

Hence proved.

Example 9 Find $\int e^x \frac{\sqrt{1+\sin 2x}}{1+\cos 2x}dx.$

CBSE Sample Paper 2018

Sol. Let $I = \int e^x \frac{\sqrt{1+\sin 2x}}{1+\cos 2x}dx$

$= \int e^x \frac{\sqrt{\sin^2 x+\cos^2 x+2\sin x\cos x}}{1+\cos 2x}dx$

$[\because \sin^2\theta+\cos^2\theta=1 \text{ and } \sin 2\theta = 2\sin\theta\cos\theta]$

$= \int e^x \frac{\sqrt{(\sin x+\cos x)^2}}{2\cos^2 x}dx \quad [\because 1+\cos 2\theta = 2\cos^2\theta]$

$= \int e^x \frac{(\sin x+\cos x)}{2\cos^2 x}dx$

$= \frac{1}{2}\int e^x\left(\frac{\sin x}{\cos^2 x}+\frac{\cos x}{\cos^2 x}\right)dx$

$= \frac{1}{2}\int e^x(\sec x\tan x + \sec x)\,dx$

Let $f(x)=\sec x$, then $f'(x)=\sec x\tan x$

$\therefore \quad I = \frac{1}{2}e^x\sec x + C$

$[\because \int e^x(f(x)+f'(x))\,dx = e^x f(x)+C]$

Example 10 Evaluate $\int e^x(\sin x+\cos x)\,dx.$ *NCERT*

Sol. Let $I=\int e^x(\sin x+\cos x)\,dx$ and $f(x)=\sin x.$

Then, $f'(x)=\cos x$

So, the given integral is of the form

$I = \int e^x\,[f(x)+f'(x)]\,dx$

We know that $\int e^x[f(x)+f'(x)]\,dx = e^x f(x)+C$

$\therefore \quad I = e^x\sin x + C$

Example 11 Evaluate $\int\left(\log(\log x)+\frac{1}{(\log x)^2}\right)dx$

Competency Based Que, CBSE 2010

Sol. Let $I = \int\left(\log(\log x)+\frac{1}{(\log x)^2}\right)dx$

Put $\log x = t \Rightarrow x = e^t \Rightarrow dx = e^t dt$

$\therefore \quad I = \int\left(\log t+\frac{1}{t^2}\right)e^t dt = \int\left(\log t + \frac{1}{t}-\frac{1}{t}+\frac{1}{t^2}\right)e^t dt$

$= \int e^t\left(\log t+\frac{1}{t}\right)dt + \int e^t\left(-\frac{1}{t}+\frac{1}{t^2}\right)dt$

Let $f(t)=\log t$ and $g(t)=\frac{-1}{t}$, then $f'(t)=\frac{1}{t}$

and $g'(t)=\frac{1}{t^2}$

$\therefore \quad I = e^t\log t + e^t\left(-\frac{1}{t}\right)+C$

$= e^t\left(\log t - \frac{1}{t}\right)+C = x\left(\log(\log x)-\frac{1}{\log x}\right)+C$

Example 12 Evaluate $\int e^{-x} \cos x\, dx$

Sol. Let $I = \int \underset{\text{II}}{e^{-x}} \underset{\text{I}}{\cos x}\, dx$

$$\Rightarrow I = \cos x \int e^{-x} dx - \int \left\{ \frac{d}{dx}(\cos x) \int e^{-x} dx \right\} dx$$

$$\Rightarrow I = \cos x(-e^{-x}) - \int (-\sin x)(-e^{-x})\, dx$$

$$\Rightarrow I = -e^{-x} \cos x - \int \underset{\text{II}}{e^{-x}} \underset{\text{I}}{\sin x}\, dx$$

$$\Rightarrow I = -e^{-x} \cos x - \left[\sin x \int e^{-x} dx - \int \left\{ \frac{d}{dx}(\sin x) \int e^{-x} dx \right\} dx \right]$$

$$\Rightarrow I = -e^{-x} \cos x - \sin x(-e^{-x}) + \int \cos x(-e^{-x}) dx$$

$$\Rightarrow I = -e^{-x} \cos x + e^{-x} \sin x - I$$

$$\Rightarrow 2I = e^{-x}(-\cos x + \sin x)$$

$$\Rightarrow I = \frac{e^{-x}}{2}(-\cos x + \sin x) + C$$

Example 13 Evaluate $\int x \sin^{-1} x\, dx$ *CBSE 2025*

Sol. Let $I = \int \underset{\text{II}}{x} \underset{\text{I}}{\sin^{-1} x}\, dx$

$$= \sin^{-1} x \int x\, dx - \int \left[\frac{d}{dx}(\sin^{-1} x) \cdot \int x\, dx \right] dx$$

[using integration by parts]

$$= \frac{x^2}{2} \sin^{-1} x - \frac{1}{2} \int \frac{x^2}{\sqrt{1-x^2}} dx$$

$$= \frac{x^2}{2} \sin^{-1} x + \frac{1}{2} \int \frac{(-x^2 dx)}{\sqrt{1-x^2}}$$

$$= \frac{x^2}{2} \sin^{-1} x + \frac{1}{2} \int \frac{1-x^2-1}{\sqrt{1-x^2}} dx$$

$$= \frac{x^2}{2} \sin^{-1} x + \frac{1}{2} \int \sqrt{1-x^2}\, dx - \frac{1}{2} \int \frac{dx}{\sqrt{1-x^2}}$$

$$= \frac{x^2}{2} \sin^{-1} x + \frac{1}{2} \left[\frac{x}{2}\sqrt{1-x^2} + \frac{1}{2} \sin^{-1} x \right] - \frac{1}{2} \sin^{-1} x + C$$

$$\left[\because \int \sqrt{a^2 - x^2} dx = \frac{x}{2}\sqrt{a^2-x^2} + \frac{a^2}{2} \sin^{-1} \frac{x}{a};\ \int \frac{dx}{\sqrt{1-x^2}} = \sin^{-1} x \right]$$

$$= \frac{x^2}{2} \sin^{-1} x + \frac{1}{4} x\sqrt{1-x^2} + \frac{1}{4} \sin^{-1} x - \frac{1}{2} \sin^{-1} x + C$$

$$= \frac{x^2}{2} \sin^{-1} x + \frac{1}{4} x\sqrt{1-x^2} - \frac{1}{4} \sin^{-1} x + C$$

$$= \frac{\sin^{-1} x}{4}(2x^2 - 1) + \frac{1}{4} x\sqrt{1-x^2} + C$$

Quick Test 5

Direction (Q. Nos. 1-10) *Evaluate the following integrals.*

1. $\int x^2 \tan^{-1} x\, dx$

2. $\int \frac{x \sin^{-1} x}{\sqrt{1-x^2}} dx$

3. $\int \frac{x^2+1}{(x+1)^2} e^x dx$ *Competency Based Que, CBSE 2015 C*

4. $\int e^x \cos x\, dx$

5. $\int \frac{\log x}{2(x+1)^2} dx$

6. $\int \frac{\sqrt{1-\sin x}}{1+\cos x} e^{-x/2} dx$ *CBSE 2013*

7. $\int e^x \frac{\sqrt{1-x^2} \sin^{-1} x + 1}{\sqrt{1-x^2}} dx$ *Competency Based Que*

8. $\int e^x \cos^2 x\, dx$

9. $\int e^{\tan^{-1} x} \left(\frac{1+x+x^2}{1+x^2} \right) dx$ *Competency Based Que, CBSE 2012*

10. $\int \frac{x^2 - 3x + 1}{\sqrt{1-x^2}} dx$ *Competency Based Que, CBSE 2015*

Answers

1. $\frac{x^3}{3} \tan^{-1} x - \frac{x^2}{6} + \frac{1}{6} \log|x^2+1| + C$
2. $-\sin^{-1} x \sqrt{1-x^2} + x + C$
3. $e^x - 2\frac{e^x}{x+1} + C$
4. $\frac{e^x}{2}(\cos x + \sin x) + C$
5. $\frac{-\log x}{2x+2} + \frac{1}{2} \log\left| \frac{x}{x+1} \right| + C$
6. $-e^{-x/2} \sec \frac{x}{2} + C$
7. $e^x \sin^{-1} x + C$
8. $\frac{1}{2} e^x + \frac{1}{2} \left[\frac{e^x}{5}(\cos 2x + 2 \sin 2x) \right] + C$
9. $x e^{\tan^{-1} x} + C$
10. $\frac{3}{2} \sin^{-1} x - \frac{x}{2}\sqrt{1-x^2} + 3\sqrt{1-x^2} + C$

For Solutions, See QR Code on Pg. 235

7.6 Definite Integral

Let $f(x)$ be a continuous function defined on an interval $[a, b]$ and having anti-derivative $F(x)$.

Then, its definite integral over $[a, b]$ is denoted by $\int_a^b f(x)\,dx$, which is defined as

$$\int_a^b f(x)\,dx = [F(x)]_a^b = F(b) - F(a)$$

where, a and b are known as **lower limit** and **upper limit**, respectively.

Definite Integral by Substitution Method

To evaluate the definite integral, say $\int_a^b f(x)\,dx$ by substitution method, following steps are used.

I. Consider the integral without limits and substitute, $y = f(x)$ or $x = g(y)$ to reduce the given integral to a known form.

II. Integrate the new integrand with respect to the new variable without mentioning the constant of integration.

III. Resubstitute for the new variable and write the answer in terms of the original variable.

IV. Find the values of answers obtained in Step III at the given limits of integral and find the difference of the values at the upper and lower limits.

Properties of Definite Integral

There are following properties of definite integrals

(i) $\int_a^b f(x)\,dx = \int_a^b f(t)\,dt$

(ii) $\int_a^a f(x)\,dx = 0$

(iii) $\int_a^b f(x)\,dx = -\int_b^a f(x)\,dx$

(iv) $\int_a^b f(x)\,dx = \int_a^c f(x)\,dx + \int_c^b f(x)\,dx$, where $a < c < b$

(v) $\int_a^b f(x)\,dx = \int_a^b f(a+b-x)\,dx$

(vi) $\int_0^a f(x)\,dx = \int_0^a f(a-x)\,dx$

(vii) $\int_0^{2a} f(x)\,dx = \int_0^a f(x)\,dx + \int_0^a f(2a-x)\,dx$

(viii) $\int_{-a}^a f(x)\,dx$

$$= \begin{cases} 0, \text{if } f(x) \text{ is an odd function i.e. } f(-x) = -f(x) \\ 2\int_0^a f(x)\,dx, \text{ if } f(x) \text{ is an even function} \\ \qquad \text{i.e. } f(-x) = f(x) \end{cases}$$

(ix) $\int_0^{2a} f(x)\,dx = \begin{cases} 2\int_0^a f(x)\,dx, & \text{if } f(2a-x) = f(x) \\ 0, & \text{if } f(2a-x) = -f(x) \end{cases}$

TEACHER TIPS

(i) In $\int_a^b f(x)\,dx$, the function f needs to be well-defined and continuous in $[a, b]$.

e.g. Definite integral $\int_{-2}^3 x(x^2-1)^{1/2}\,dx$ is erroneous, since the function f expressed by $f(x) = x(x^2-1)^{1/2}$ is not defined in a portion $-1 < x < 1$ of the closed interval $[-2, 3]$.

(ii) The value of the definite integral of a function over any particular interval depends on the function and the interval but not on the variable of integration that we choose to represent the independent variable.

(iii) If the independent variable is denoted by t or u instead of x, then we simply write the integral as $\int_a^b f(t)\,dt$ or $\int_a^b f(u)\,du$ instead of $\int_a^b f(x)\,dx$. So, the variable of integration is a dummy variable.

Example 1 Evaluate $\int_0^1 \frac{e^{2x}+e^{4x}}{e^{3x}}\,dx.$

Sol. $\int_0^1 \frac{e^{2x}+e^{4x}}{e^{3x}}\,dx = \int_0^1 \left(\frac{e^{2x}}{e^{3x}} + \frac{e^{4x}}{e^{3x}}\right)dx = \int_0^1 (e^{-x} + e^x)\,dx$

$$= [-e^{-x} + e^x]_0^1$$

$$= [(-e^{-1} + e) - (-e^{-0} + e^0)]$$

$$= \left(-\frac{1}{e} + e\right) - (-1+1) \qquad [\because e^0 = e^{-0} = 1]$$

$$= e - \frac{1}{e} = \frac{e^2-1}{e}$$

Example 2 Evaluate $\int_1^2 (4x^3 - 5x^2 + 6x + 9)\,dx.$ *NCERT*

Sol. Let $I = \int_1^2 (4x^3 - 5x^2 + 6x + 9)\,dx$

$$= \left[\frac{4x^4}{4} - \frac{5x^3}{3} + \frac{6x^2}{2} + 9x\right]_1^2 = \left[x^4 - \frac{5}{3}x^3 + 3x^2 + 9x\right]_1^2$$

$$= \left[(2)^4 - \frac{5}{3}(2)^3 + 3(2)^2 + 9(2)\right] - \left[1 - \frac{5}{3}(1)^3 + 3(1)^2 + 9(1)\right]$$

$$= \left[16 - \frac{40}{3} + 12 + 18\right] - \left[1 - \frac{5}{3} + 3 + 9\right]$$

$$= \left[46 - \frac{40}{3}\right] - \left[13 - \frac{5}{3}\right] = \left[\frac{138 - 40}{3}\right] - \left[\frac{39 - 5}{3}\right]$$

$$= \frac{98}{3} - \frac{34}{3} = \frac{64}{3}$$

Example 3 Evaluate $\int_0^{\pi/2} \cos^2 x\, dx.$ *CBSE 2023*

Sol. Let $I = \int_0^{\pi/2} \cos^2 x\, dx$

$$= \int_0^{\pi/2} \left(\frac{\cos 2x + 1}{2}\right) dx \qquad [\because \cos 2x = 2\cos^2 x - 1]$$

$$= \frac{1}{2}\int_0^{\pi/2} \cos 2x\, dx + \frac{1}{2}\int_0^{\pi/2} 1\, dx$$

$$= \left\{\frac{1}{2}\left[\frac{\sin 2x}{2}\right] + \frac{1}{2}[x]\right\}_0^{\pi/2}$$

$$= \left[\frac{1}{4}\sin 2\left(\frac{\pi}{2}\right) + \frac{1}{2}\left(\frac{\pi}{2}\right)\right] - \left[\frac{1}{4}\sin(0) + \frac{1}{2}(0)\right]$$

$$= \left[\frac{1}{4}(0) + \frac{\pi}{4}\right] - [0 + 0] = \frac{\pi}{4}$$

Example 4 Evaluate $\int_0^{\sqrt{2}} \sqrt{2 - x^2}\, dx.$ *CBSE 2023*

Sol. Let $I = \int_0^{\sqrt{2}} \sqrt{2 - x^2}\, dx = \int_0^{\sqrt{2}} \sqrt{(\sqrt{2})^2 - x^2}\, dx$

$$= \left[\frac{x}{2}\sqrt{2 - x^2} + \frac{(\sqrt{2})^2}{2}\sin^{-1}\frac{x}{\sqrt{2}}\right]_0^{\sqrt{2}}$$

$$= (0 + \sin^{-1} 1) - (0 + \sin^{-1} 0)$$

$$= \frac{\pi}{2}$$

Example 5 Evaluate $\int_1^3 \frac{1}{x(1 + \log x)} dx.$

Sol. Let $I = \int_1^3 \frac{dx}{x(1 + \log x)}$

Now, on putting $\log x = t \Rightarrow \frac{1}{x} dx = dt$

Lower limit When $x = 1$, then $t = \log 1 \Rightarrow t = 0$

Upper limit When $x = 3$, then $t = \log 3$

Now, $I = \int_0^{\log 3} \frac{dt}{(1 + t)}$

$$= [\log|1 + t|]_0^{\log 3}$$

$$= \log|1 + \log 3| - \log|1 + 0|$$

$$= \log|1 + \log 3| - \log 1$$

$$= \log|1 + \log 3| - 0 \qquad [\because \log 1 = 0]$$

$$= \log|1 + \log 3|$$

Example 6 Evaluate $\int_0^{\pi/2} \frac{\sin x}{1 + \cos^2 x} dx.$ *NCERT*

Sol. Let $I = \int_0^{\pi/2} \frac{\sin x}{1 + \cos^2 x} dx$

Put $\cos x = t \Rightarrow -\sin x\, dx = dt$

Lower limit When $x = 0 \Rightarrow t = \cos 0 = 1$

Upper limit When $x = \pi/2 \Rightarrow t = \cos \pi/2 = 0$

Now, $I = -\int_1^0 \frac{dt}{1 + t^2} = -[\tan^{-1} t]_1^0$

$$= -[\tan^{-1} 0 - \tan^{-1} 1] = -[0 - \pi/4] = \pi/4$$

Example 7 Evaluate $\int_0^{\pi/2} \sqrt{\sin\phi}\cos^5\phi\, d\phi.$ *CBSE 2023*

Sol. Let $I = \int_0^{\pi/2} \sqrt{\sin\phi}\cos^5\phi\, d\phi$

$$= \int_0^{\pi/2} \sqrt{\sin\phi}\cos^4\phi\cos\phi\, d\phi$$

$$= \int_0^{\pi/2} \sqrt{\sin\phi}(1 - \sin^2\phi)^2\cos\phi\, d\phi$$

Now, put $\sin\phi = t \Rightarrow \cos\phi\, d\phi = dt$

Lower limit When $\phi = 0$, then $t = 0$

Upper limit When $\phi = \frac{\pi}{2}$, then $t = 1$

Now, $I = \int_0^1 \sqrt{t}(1 - t^2)^2\, dt = \int_0^1 \sqrt{t}(1 + t^4 - 2t^2)\, dt$

$$= \int_0^1 (t^{1/2} + t^{9/2} - 2t^{5/2})\, dt$$

$$= \left[\frac{t^{3/2}}{3/2} + \frac{t^{11/2}}{11/2} - \frac{2t^{7/2}}{7/2}\right]_0^1$$

$$= \left[\frac{2}{3}t^{3/2} + \frac{2}{11}t^{11/2} - \frac{4}{7}t^{7/2}\right]_0^1$$

$$= \frac{2}{3} + \frac{2}{11} - \frac{4}{7} = \frac{154 + 42 - 132}{11 \times 3 \times 7} = \frac{64}{231}$$

Example 8 Evaluate $\int_{1/3}^1 \frac{(x - x^3)^{1/3}}{x^4} dx$

Competency Based Que, CBSE 2023

Sol. Let $I = \int_{1/3}^1 \frac{(x - x^3)^{1/3}}{x^4} dx$

$$= \int_{1/3}^1 \frac{(x^3)^{1/3}\left(\frac{1}{x^2} - 1\right)^{1/3}}{x^4} dx$$

$$= \int_{1/3}^1 \frac{x\left(\frac{1}{x^2} - 1\right)^{1/3}}{x^4} dx$$

$$= \int_{1/3}^1 \frac{\left(\frac{1}{x^2} - 1\right)^{1/3}}{x^3} dx$$

On putting $\frac{1}{x^2} = t$, we get

$$\frac{-2}{x^3}\,dx = dt \Rightarrow \frac{dx}{x^3} = -\frac{dt}{2}$$

Lower limit When $x = \frac{1}{3}$, then $t = 9$

Upper limit When $x = 1$, then $t = 1$

$$\therefore \quad I = \int_9^1 \frac{(t-1)^{1/3}}{(-2)}\,dt$$

$$= -\frac{1}{2}\int_9^1 (t-1)^{1/3}\,dt$$

$$= -\frac{1}{2}\left[\frac{(t-1)^{1/3+1}}{\frac{1}{3}+1}\right]_9^1$$

$$= -\frac{1}{2}\times\frac{3}{4}\,[(t-1)^{4/3}]_9^1$$

$$= -\frac{3}{8}[(1-1)^{4/3} - (9-1)^{4/3}]$$

$$= -\frac{3}{8}(0 - 8^{4/3})$$

$$= -\frac{3}{8}(-16) = 6$$

Example 9 Prove that

$$\int_0^{\pi/2} \frac{d\theta}{a^2\cos^2\theta + b^2\sin^2\theta} = \frac{\pi}{2ab}.$$

CBSE 2013, 11

Sol. $\text{LHS} = \int_0^{\pi/2} \frac{d\theta}{a^2\cos^2\theta + b^2\sin^2\theta}$

On dividing the numerator and denominator by $\cos^2\theta$, we get

$$\text{LHS} = \int_0^{\pi/2} \frac{\sec^2\theta\,d\theta}{a^2 + b^2\tan^2\theta}$$

Let $\tan\theta = t \Rightarrow \sec^2\theta\,d\theta = dt$

Upper limit When $\theta = \frac{\pi}{2}$, then $t = \tan\frac{\pi}{2} = \infty$

Lower limit When $\theta = 0$, then $t = \tan 0 = 0$

$$\therefore \text{LHS} = \int_0^\infty \frac{dt}{a^2 + b^2t^2} = \frac{1}{b^2}\int_0^\infty \frac{dt}{\left(\frac{a}{b}\right)^2 + t^2}$$

$$= \frac{1}{b^2}\times\frac{1}{\left(\frac{a}{b}\right)}\tan^{-1}\left[\frac{t}{a/b}\right]_0^\infty = \frac{1}{ab}\tan^{-1}\left[\frac{bt}{a}\right]_0^\infty$$

$$= \frac{1}{ab}[\tan^{-1}(\infty) - \tan^{-1}(0)]$$

$$= \frac{1}{ab}\left[\frac{\pi}{2} - 0\right] = \frac{\pi}{2ab} = \text{RHS}$$

Hence proved.

Example 10 Find the value of $\int_0^\pi \frac{dx}{5 + 2\cos x}$. CBSE 2005

Sol. Let $I = \int_0^\pi \frac{dx}{5 + 2\cos x}$

$$= \int_0^\pi \frac{dx}{5 + 2\left(\frac{1-\tan^2\frac{x}{2}}{1+\tan^2\frac{x}{2}}\right)} \qquad \left[\because \cos\theta = \frac{1-\tan^2\frac{\theta}{2}}{1+\tan^2\frac{\theta}{2}}\right]$$

$$= \int_0^\pi \frac{\left(1+\tan^2\frac{x}{2}\right)dx}{5\left(1+\tan^2\frac{x}{2}\right) + 2\left(1-\tan^2\frac{x}{2}\right)} = \int_0^\pi \frac{\sec^2\frac{x}{2}\,dx}{7 + 3\tan^2\frac{x}{2}}$$

Put $\tan\frac{x}{2} = t \Rightarrow \sec^2\frac{x}{2}\times\frac{1}{2}dx = dt$

Lower limit When $x = 0$, then $t = \tan\frac{0}{2} = 0$

Upper limit When $x = \pi$, then $t = \tan\frac{\pi}{2} = \infty$

$$\therefore I = \int_0^\infty \frac{2dt}{3t^2 + 7} = \frac{2}{3}\int_0^\infty \frac{dt}{t^2 + \left(\sqrt{\frac{7}{3}}\right)^2}$$

$$= \frac{2}{3}\times\left[\frac{1}{\sqrt{7/3}}\tan^{-1}\left(\frac{t}{\sqrt{7/3}}\right)\right]_0^\infty \qquad \left[\because \int \frac{dx}{x^2 + a^2} = \frac{1}{a}\tan^{-1}\frac{x}{a}\right]$$

$$= \frac{2}{3}\times\frac{\sqrt{3}}{\sqrt{7}}[\tan^{-1}\infty - \tan^{-1}0]$$

$$= \frac{2}{\sqrt{21}}\left[\frac{\pi}{2} - 0\right] = \frac{\pi}{\sqrt{21}}$$

Example 11 Evaluate $\int_0^\pi |\cos x|\,dx$ Competency Based Que

Sol. Let $I = \int_0^\pi |\cos x|\,dx$

$$= \int_0^{\pi/2} |\cos x|\,dx + \int_{\pi/2}^\pi |\cos x|\,dx$$

$$= \int_0^{\pi/2} (\cos x)\,dx + \int_{\pi/2}^\pi (-\cos x)\,dx$$

$$= [\sin x]_0^{\pi/2} - [\sin x]_{\pi/2}^\pi$$

$$= \left(\sin\frac{\pi}{2} - \sin 0\right) - \left(\sin\pi - \sin\frac{\pi}{2}\right)$$

$$= (1 - 0) - (0 - 1) = 2$$

Example 12 Evaluate the following

$$\int_1^4 f(x)\,dx, \text{ where } f(x) = \begin{cases} 4x+3, & \text{if } 1 \le x \le 2 \\ 3x+5, & \text{if } 2 \le x \le 4 \end{cases}$$

Sol. We have, $f(x) = \begin{cases} 4x+3, & \text{if } 1 \le x \le 2 \\ 3x+5, & \text{if } 2 \le x \le 4 \end{cases}$

$$\therefore \quad \int_1^4 f(x)\,dx = \int_1^2 f(x)\,dx + \int_2^4 f(x)\,dx$$

$$= \int_1^2 (4x+3)dx + \int_2^4 (3x+5)\,dx$$

$$= [2x^2 + 3x]_1^2 + \left[\frac{3x^2}{2} + 5x\right]_2^4$$

$$= [(8+6)-(2+3)] + [(24+20)-(6+10)]$$

$$= 14 - 5 + 44 - 16$$

$$= 9 + 28$$

$$= 37$$

Example 13 Evaluate $\int_1^3 \{|(x-1)| + |(x-2)|\}\,dx$

Competency Based Que, CBSE 2023

Sol. Let $I = \int_1^3 \{|(x-1)| + |(x-2)|\}\,dx$

For $1 \le x \le 3, |x-1| = x-1$

$1 \le x < 2, |x-2| = 2-x$

$2 \le x \le 3, |x-2| = x-2$

$$\therefore \; I = \int_1^3 (x-1)\,dx + \int_1^2 (2-x)\,dx + \int_2^3 (x-2)\,dx$$

$$= \left(\frac{x^2}{2} - x\right)_1^3 + \left(2x - \frac{x^2}{2}\right)_1^2 + \left(\frac{x^2}{2} - 2x\right)_2^3$$

$$\Rightarrow I = \left(\frac{9}{2} - 3\right) - \left(\frac{1}{2} - 1\right) + \left(4 - \frac{4}{2}\right) - \left(2 - \frac{1}{2}\right) + \left(\frac{9}{2} - 6\right) - \left(\frac{4}{2} - 4\right)$$

$$= \frac{3}{2} + \frac{1}{2} + 2 - \frac{3}{2} - \frac{3}{2} + 2 = 4 - \frac{3}{2} + \frac{1}{2} = 3$$

Example 14 Evaluate $\int_1^3 \frac{\sqrt{4-x}}{\sqrt{x} + \sqrt{4-x}}\,dx$

CBSE 2023

Sol. Let $I = \int_1^3 \frac{\sqrt{4-x}}{\sqrt{x} + \sqrt{4-x}}\,dx$ ...(i)

$$= \int_1^3 \frac{\sqrt{4-(4-x)}}{\sqrt{4-x} + \sqrt{4-(4-x)}}\,dx$$

$$\left[\because \int_a^b f(x)\,dx = \int_a^b f(a+b-x)\,dx\right]$$

$$= \int_1^3 \frac{\sqrt{x}}{\sqrt{4-x} + \sqrt{x}}\,dx \quad \text{...(ii)}$$

On adding Eqs. (i) and (ii), we get

$$2I = \int_1^3 \left(\frac{\sqrt{4-x} + \sqrt{x}}{\sqrt{x} + \sqrt{4-x}}\right) dx$$

$$\Rightarrow 2I = \int_1^3 1\,dx = [x]_1^3$$

$$= 3 - 1 = 2$$

$$\Rightarrow \; I = 1$$

Example 15 $\int_{\pi/6}^{\pi/3} \frac{1}{1 + \sqrt{\cot x}}\,dx$

NCERT, CBSE 2014

Sol. Let $I = \int_{\pi/6}^{\pi/3} \frac{1}{1 + \sqrt{\cot x}}\,dx$

$$\Rightarrow \; I = \int_{\pi/6}^{\pi/3} \frac{\sqrt{\sin x}}{\sqrt{\sin x} + \sqrt{\cos x}}\,dx \quad \text{...(i)}$$

$$= \int_{\pi/6}^{\pi/3} \frac{\sqrt{\sin\left(\frac{\pi}{3} + \frac{\pi}{6} - x\right)}}{\sqrt{\sin\left(\frac{\pi}{3} + \frac{\pi}{6} - x\right)} + \sqrt{\cos\left(\frac{\pi}{3} + \frac{\pi}{6} - x\right)}}\,dx$$

$$\left[\because \int_a^b f(x)\,dx = \int_a^b f(a+b-x)\,dx\right]$$

$$= \int_{\pi/6}^{\pi/3} \frac{\sqrt{\sin\left(\frac{\pi}{2} - x\right)}}{\sqrt{\sin\left(\frac{\pi}{2} - x\right)} + \sqrt{\cos\left(\frac{\pi}{2} - x\right)}}\,dx$$

$$= \int_{\pi/6}^{\pi/3} \frac{\sqrt{\cos x}}{\sqrt{\cos x} + \sqrt{\sin x}}\,dx \quad \text{...(ii)}$$

On adding Eqs. (i) and (ii), we get

$$2I = \int_{\pi/6}^{\pi/3} \frac{\sqrt{\sin x} + \sqrt{\cos x}}{\sqrt{\sin x} + \sqrt{\cos x}}\,dx$$

$$= \int_{\pi/6}^{\pi/3} 1\,dx = [x]_{\pi/6}^{\pi/3} = \frac{\pi}{3} - \frac{\pi}{6} = \frac{\pi}{6}$$

$$\therefore \quad I = \frac{\pi}{12}$$

Example 16 Evaluate $\int_0^{\pi} \frac{e^{\cos x}}{e^{\cos x} + e^{-\cos x}}\,dx$

CBSE 2024

Sol. Let $I = \int_0^{\pi} \frac{e^{\cos x}}{e^{\cos x} + e^{-\cos x}}\,dx$ ...(i)

$$\Rightarrow \; I = \int_0^{\pi} \frac{e^{\cos(\pi - x)}}{e^{\cos(\pi - x)} + e^{-\cos(\pi - x)}}$$

$$\left[\because \int_0^a f(x)dx = \int_0^a f(a-x)dx\right]$$

$$= \int_0^{\pi} \frac{e^{-\cos x}}{e^{-\cos x} + e^{\cos x}}\,dx \quad \text{...(ii)}$$

On adding Eqs. (i) and (ii), we get

$$2I = \int_0^{\pi} \frac{e^{\cos x} + e^{-\cos x}}{e^{\cos x} + e^{-\cos x}}\,dx$$

$$= \int_0^{\pi} 1\,dx = [x]_0^{\pi} = \pi$$

$$\Rightarrow \; I = \frac{\pi}{2}$$

Example 17 $\int_0^{\pi/4} \log(1+\tan x)\,dx$

Diksha App, NCERT, CBSE 2023

Sol. Let $I = \int_0^{\pi/4} \log(1+\tan x)\,dx$ ...(i)

$\Rightarrow I = \int_0^{\pi/4} \log\left[1+\tan\left(\frac{\pi}{4}-x\right)\right]dx$

$\left[\because \int_0^a f(x)\,dx = \int_0^a f(a-x)\,dx\right]$

$= \int_0^{\pi/4} \log\left(1+\frac{1-\tan x}{1+\tan x}\right)dx$

$\left[\because \tan(A-B) = \frac{\tan A - \tan B}{1+\tan A \tan B}\right]$

$= \int_0^{\pi/4} \log\left(\frac{2}{1+\tan x}\right)dx$

$= \int_0^{\pi/4} \{\log 2 - \log(1+\tan x)\}\,dx$ ...(ii)

$\left[\because \log\left(\frac{m}{n}\right) = \log m - \log n\right]$

On adding Eqs. (i) and (ii), we get

$2I = \int_0^{\pi/4} \log 2\,dx = \log 2\int_0^{\pi/4} 1\,dx = \log 2\,[x]_0^{\pi/4}$

$= \log 2\left(\frac{\pi}{4}-0\right)$

$\Rightarrow 2I = \frac{\pi}{4}\log 2 \Rightarrow I = \frac{\pi}{8}\log 2$

Example 18 Evaluate $\int_0^{2\pi} \frac{1}{1+e^{\sin x}}\,dx.$

CBSE 2023

Sol. Let $I = \int_0^{2\pi} \frac{1}{1+e^{\sin x}}\,dx$

$\therefore I = \int_0^{\pi}\left[\frac{1}{1+e^{\sin x}} + \frac{1}{1+e^{\sin(2\pi-x)}}\right]dx$

$\left[\because \int_0^{2a} f(x)\,dx = \int_0^a \{f(x)+f(2a-x)\}\,dx\right]$

$= \int_0^{\pi}\left[\frac{1}{1+e^{\sin x}} + \frac{1}{1+e^{-\sin x}}\right]dx$

$[\because \sin(2\pi-x) = -\sin x]$

$= \int_0^{\pi}\left[\frac{1}{1+e^{\sin x}} + \frac{e^{\sin x}}{e^{\sin x}+1}\right]dx$

$= \int_0^{\pi}\frac{1+e^{\sin x}}{1+e^{\sin x}}\,dx = \int_0^{\pi} 1\,dx = [x]_0^{\pi} = \pi$

Example 19 Evaluate $\int_0^{4\pi} \cos^5 x\,dx.$

NCERT

Sol. Let $I = \int_0^{4\pi} \cos^5 x\,dx$

Here, $f(4\pi-x) = \cos^5(4\pi-x) = \cos^5 x$

$\therefore I = 2\int_0^{2\pi} \cos^5 x\,dx$

$\left[\because \int_0^{2a} f(x)dx = 2\int_0^a f(x)dx, \text{ if } f(2a-x) = f(x)\right]$

Here, $\cos^5(2\pi-x) = \cos^5 x$

$\therefore I = 4\int_0^{\pi} \cos^5 x\,dx$

$\left[\because \int_0^{2a} f(x)dx = 2\int_0^a f(x)\,dx, \text{ if } f(2a-x) = f(x)\right]$

Here, $\cos^5(\pi-x) = -\cos^5 x$

$\therefore I = 4\times 0 = 0 \left[\because \int_0^{2a} f(x) = 0, \text{ if } f(2a-x) = -f(x)\right]$

Example 20 Evaluate $\int_{-\frac{\pi}{2}}^{\frac{\pi}{2}} x\cos^2 x\,dx.$

CBSE 2020

Sol. Let $f(x) = x\cos^2 x$

$\therefore f(-x) = (-x)\cos^2(-x)$

$= -x(\cos(-x))^2 = -x(\cos x)^2$

$= -x\cos^2 x = -f(x)$

$\therefore f(x)$ is an odd function.

Hence, $\int_{-\pi/2}^{\pi/2} x\cos^2 x\,dx = 0$

Example 21 Evaluate the integral $\int_{-\pi/2}^{\pi/2} \sin^2 x\,dx.$

Competency Based Que, NCERT

Sol. Let $I = \int_{-\pi/2}^{\pi/2} \sin^2 x\,dx$

Again, let, $f(x) = \sin^2 x$

Now, $f(-x) = \sin^2(-x)$

$= [\sin(-x)]^2 = (-\sin x)^2$

$[\because \sin(-\theta) = -\sin\theta]$

$= \sin^2 x = f(x)$

So, $f(x)$ is an even function.

$\therefore I = \int_{-\pi/2}^{\pi/2} \sin^2 x\,dx = 2\int_0^{\pi/2} \sin^2 x\,dx$

[$\because \int_{-a}^{a} f(x)\,dx = 2\int_0^a f(x)\,dx$, if $f(x)$ is an even function.
And here $\sin^2 x$ is an even function.]

$= 2\int_0^{\pi/2}\left[\frac{1-\cos 2x}{2}\right]dx \quad [\because \cos 2\theta = 1-2\sin^2\theta]$

$= \int_0^{\pi/2}(1-\cos 2x)\,dx$

$= \left[x - \frac{\sin 2x}{2}\right]_0^{\pi/2}$

$= \left[\frac{\pi}{2} - \frac{\sin\pi}{2}\right] - [0-0]$

$= \frac{\pi}{2} - 0 = \frac{\pi}{2}$

Quick Test 6

Direction (Q. Nos. 1-10) *Evaluate the following integrals.*

1. $\int_0^{\pi/4} \cos 3x \cos 2x \, dx$

2. $\int_0^1 \left(xe^x + \sin \frac{\pi x}{4} \right) dx$ NCERT

3. $\int_0^{\pi/2} e^x (\sin x - \cos x) \, dx$ CBSE 2014

4. $\int_0^{\pi/2} \frac{\cos\theta}{(1+\sin\theta)(2+\sin\theta)} d\theta$ CBSE 2004

5. $\int_0^{\pi/2} \sin 2x \tan^{-1}(\sin x) \, dx$ NCERT, CBSE 2023

6. $\int_2^5 [|x-2| + |x-3| + |x-5|] \, dx$ Competency Based Que, CBSE 2013

7. $\int_{-\pi/2}^{\pi/2} \frac{x \sin x}{e^x + 1} dx$ Competency Based Que

8. $\int_0^{\pi/2} \log \left(\frac{4 + 3\sin x}{4 + 3\cos x} \right) dx$ NCERT

9. $\int_0^{\pi/2} \frac{x \sin x \cos x}{\sin^4 x + \cos^4 x} dx$ Competency Based Que, CBSE 2014, 11, 10 C

10. $\int_0^{\pi} \log(1 + \cos x) \, dx$ Competency Based Que

Answers

1. $\frac{\sqrt{2}}{5}$
2. $1 + \frac{4}{\pi} - \frac{2\sqrt{2}}{\pi}$
3. 1
4. $\log\left(\frac{4}{3}\right)$
5. $\frac{\pi}{2} - 1$
6. $\frac{23}{2}$
7. 1
8. 0
9. $\frac{\pi^2}{16}$
10. $-\pi \log 2$

For Solutions, See QR Code on Pg. 235

EXAM PATTERN QUESTIONS

Objective Type Questions

Multiple Choice Questions

1. $\int \frac{1}{x^{3/4}} dx$ is equal to

(a) $x^{1/4} + C$ (b) $4x^{1/4} + C$

(c) $\frac{x^{1/4}}{4} + C$ (d) $\frac{x^3}{4} + C$

2. $\int 5^x dx$ is equal to

(a) $\log 5 + C$ (b) $\frac{5^x}{\log x} + C$

(c) $\frac{5^x}{\log 5} + C$ (d) $5 \log x + C$

3. $\int e^{5 \log x} dx$ is equal to **Competency Based Que, CBSE 2023**

(a) $\frac{x^5}{5} + C$ (b) $\frac{x^6}{6} + C$

(c) $5x^4 + C$ (d) $6x^5 + C$

4. If $f'(x) = x + \frac{1}{x}$, then $f(x)$ is **CBSE Sample Paper 2023**

(a) $x^2 + \log|x| + C$ (b) $\frac{x^2}{2} + \log|x| + C$

(c) $\frac{x}{2} + \log|x| + C$ (d) $\frac{x}{2} - \log|x| + C$

5. $\int \frac{\sec x}{\sec x - \tan x} dx$ equals **Competency Based Que, CBSE 2023**

(a) $\sec x - \tan x + C$

(b) $\sec x + \tan x + C$

(c) $\tan x - \sec x + C$

(d) $-(\sec x + \tan x) + C$

6. $\int x^2 e^{x^3} dx$ is equal to **Competency Based Que**

(a) $\frac{1}{3} e^{x^3} + C$ (b) $\frac{1}{3} e^{x^2} + C$

(c) $\frac{1}{2} e^{x^3} + C$ (d) $\frac{1}{2} e^{x^2} + C$

7. $\int \frac{1}{x(\log x)^2} dx$ is equal to **CBSE 2024**

(a) $2 \log(\log x) + C$ (b) $-\frac{1}{\log x} + C$

(c) $\frac{(\log x)^3}{3} + C$ (d) $\frac{3}{(\log x)^3} + C$

8. $\int e^{3 \log x} (x^4 + 1)^{-1} dx$ is equal to **CBSE 2024C, Competency Based Que**

(a) $\frac{1}{4} \log(x^4 + 1) + C$ (b) $\frac{1}{4} \log\left(\frac{1}{x^4 + 1}\right) + C$

(c) $\frac{x^3}{x^4 + 1} + C$ (d) $\frac{e^x}{x^4 + 1} + C$

9. $\int \tan x \, dx$ is equal to

(a) $\sec x + C$ (b) $\sec^2 x + C$

(c) $\log|\sec x| + C$ (d) $\log|\cos x| + C$

10. The integral $\int \frac{dx}{\sqrt{9 - 4x^2}}$ is equal to **CBSE 2024**

(a) $\frac{1}{6} \sin^{-1}\left(\frac{2x}{3}\right) + C$ (b) $\frac{1}{2} \sin^{-1}\left(\frac{2x}{3}\right) + C$

(c) $\sin^{-1}\left(\frac{2x}{3}\right) + C$ (d) $\frac{3}{2} \sin^{-1}\left(\frac{2x}{3}\right) + C$

11. $\int \frac{dx}{x^2 - 16}$ is equal to

(a) $\frac{1}{4} \log\left|\frac{x-4}{x+4}\right| + C$ (b) $\frac{1}{8} \log\left|\frac{x-4}{x+4}\right| + C$

(c) $\frac{1}{16} \log\left|\frac{x-4}{x+4}\right| + C$ (d) $\frac{1}{2} \log\left|\frac{x-4}{x+4}\right| + C$

12. If $\frac{d}{dx} f(x) = \log x$, then $f(x)$ equals **Competency Based Que, CBSE 2023**

(a) $-\frac{1}{x} + C$ (b) $x(\log x - 1) + C$

(c) $x(\log x + x) + C$ (d) $\frac{1}{x} + C$

13. Find integration of $\tan^{-1} x$. **Diksha App**

(a) $x \tan^{-1} x - \frac{1}{2} \log(1 + x^2) + C$

(b) $x \tan^{-1} x + \frac{1}{2} \log(1 + x^2) + C$

(c) $\frac{x}{2} \tan^{-1} x - \frac{1}{2} \log(1 + x^2) + C$

(d) $\frac{x}{2} \tan^{-1} x + \frac{1}{2} \log(1 + x^2) + C$

14. $\int \frac{x-3}{(x-1)^3} e^x dx$ is equal to **CBSE 2024C**

(a) $\frac{2e^x}{(x-1)^3} + C$ (b) $\frac{-2e^x}{x-1} + C$ (c) $\frac{e^x}{(x-1)} + C$ (d) $\frac{e^x}{(x-1)^2} + C$

15. If $\int_0^a 3x^2\,dx = 8$, then the value of a is **CBSE 2023**

(a) 2 (b) 4 (c) 8 (d) 10

16. $\int_{-1}^{1} \frac{|x-2|}{x-2}\,dx$, $x \neq 2$ is equal to **Competency Based Que, CBSE 2023**

(a) 1 (b) -1 (c) 2 (d) -2

17. For any integer n, the value of $\int_0^{\pi} e^{\sin^2 x} \cos^3(2n+1)x\,dx$ is **Competency Based Que, CBSE 2023**

(a) -1 (b) 0 (c) 1 (d) 2

18. $\int_0^{\frac{\pi}{6}} \sec^2\left(x - \frac{\pi}{6}\right)dx$ is equal to **CBSE 2023**

(a) $\frac{1}{\sqrt{3}}$ (b) $-\frac{1}{\sqrt{3}}$ (c) $\sqrt{3}$ (d) $-\sqrt{3}$

19. Find value of $\int_{\frac{\pi}{4}}^{\frac{\pi}{2}} \cot\theta \operatorname{cosec}^2\theta\,d\theta$. **CBSE 2024**

(a) $\frac{1}{2}$ (b) $-\frac{1}{2}$ (c) 0 (d) $-\frac{\pi}{8}$

20. $\int_0^4 (e^{2x} + x)\,dx$ is equal to **CBSE 2023**

(a) $\frac{15+e^8}{2}$ (b) $\frac{16-e^8}{2}$ (c) $\frac{e^8-15}{2}$ (d) $\frac{-e^8-15}{2}$

21. The value of $\int_{-1}^{1} x|x|\,dx$ is **Competency Based Que, CBSE 2024**

(a) $\frac{1}{6}$ (b) $\frac{1}{3}$ (c) $-\frac{1}{6}$ (d) 0

22. Which of the expression is equal to $\int_0^{\frac{\pi}{2}} \log(\tan x)dx$? **Diksha App**

(a) $\int_0^{\frac{\pi}{2}} \log(\sin x)\,dx$ (b) $\int_0^{\frac{\pi}{2}} \log(\cos x)\,dx$

(c) $\int_0^{\frac{\pi}{2}} \log(\sec x)\,dx$ (d) $\int_0^{\frac{\pi}{2}} \log(\cot x)\,dx$

23. $\int_0^1 \log\left(\frac{1-x}{x}\right)dx$ **Competency Based Que, Diksha App**

(a) $\log 3 - \log 2$ (b) $\log 2 - \log 3$

(c) $\log 4 - \log 5$ (d) 0

24. If $\int_{-2}^{3} x^2 dx = k\int_0^2 x^2\,dx + \int_2^3 x^2 dx$, then the value of k is **Competency Based Que, CBSE 2024**

(a) 2 (b) 1 (c) 0 (d) $\frac{1}{2}$

25. The value of $\int_1^e \log x\,dx$ is **CBSE 2024**

(a) 0 (b) 1 (c) e (d) $e \log e$

Assertion-Reason Based Questions

Directions (Q. Nos. 26-35) *In the questions given below are two statements labelled as Assertion (A) and Reason (R). In the context of the two statements, which one of the following is correct?*

(a) Both A and R are correct; R is the correct explanation of A.

(b) Both A and R are correct; R is not the correct explanation of A.

(c) A is correct; R is incorrect.

(d) R is correct; A is incorrect.

26. **Assertion** (A) $\int \frac{1}{\sqrt[3]{x^5}}\,dx$ is equal to $-\frac{3}{2}x^{-2/3} + C$.

Reason (R) $\int x^n dx$ gives $\frac{x^{n+1}}{n+1} + C, n \neq -1$

27. **Assertion** (A) $\int (4-3x)^7\,dx$ is equal to $-\frac{1}{24}(4-3x)^8 + C$.

Reason (R) $\int (ax+b)^n dx = \frac{(ax+b)^{n+1}}{a(n+1)} + C, n \neq -1$

28. **Assertion** (A) $\int \frac{1}{\sqrt{1+\cos 2x}}\,dx = \frac{1}{\sqrt{2}}\log|\sec x + \tan x| + C$

Reason (R) $\int \cot x\,dx = \log|\sin x| + C$

Competency Based Que

29. **Assertion** (A) $\int \tan^3 x \sec^3 x\,dx = \frac{1}{5}\sec^5 x - \frac{1}{3}\sec^3 x + C$

Reason (R) $\int x^n dx$ gives $\frac{x^{n+1}}{n+1} + C, n \neq -1$ **Competency Based Que**

30. **Assertion** (A) $\int \frac{1}{9+4x^2}dx = \frac{1}{6}\tan^{-1}\frac{2x}{3} + C$

Reason (R) $\int \frac{1}{x^2+a^2}dx = \frac{1}{a}\tan^{-1}\frac{x}{a} + C$

31. **Assertion** (A) $\int \frac{1}{\sqrt{4-x^2}}\,dx = \sin^{-1}\frac{x}{2} + C$

Reason (R) $\int \frac{1}{\sqrt{a^2-x^2}}\,dx = \sin^{-1}\frac{x}{a} + C$

32. **Assertion** (A) $\int x\log x\,dx = \frac{1}{2}x^2\log x - \frac{x^2}{4} + C$

Reason (R) $\int u \cdot v\,dx = u\int v\,dx - \int\left(\frac{d}{dx}(u)\int v\,dx\right)dx$

33. **Assertion** (A) The value of $\int_0^1 \frac{dx}{1+x^2}$ is $\frac{3\pi}{4}$.

Reason (R) $\int_a^b f(x)\,dx$ is known as definite integral and is given by $\int_a^b f(x)\,dx = g(b) - g(a)$, $g(x)$ is anti-derivative of $f(x)$.

34. **Assertion** (A) $\int_{-\pi}^{\pi}(1-x^2)\sin x\cdot\cos^2 x\,dx = 0.$

Reason (R) $\int_{-a}^{a} f(x)\,dx = 0$, if $f(x)$ is an odd function.

Competency Based Que

35. **Assertion** (A) $\int_{2}^{8}\frac{\sqrt{10-x}}{\sqrt{x}+\sqrt{10-x}}\,dx = 3$

Reason (R) $\int_{a}^{b} f(x)\,dx = \int_{a}^{b} f(a+b-x)\,dx$ **CBSE 2023**

Case Study Based Questions

36. The derivative of the velocity function $v(t)$ with respect to time t, gives us the acceleration of the object.

This can be written as $\frac{dv}{dt} = a(t)$ (in m/s^2).

The derivative of the displacement function $x(t)$ with respect to time t, gives us the velocity of the object.

This can be written as $\frac{dx}{dt} = v(t)$ (in m/s).

A car is moving at a constant velocity of 15 m/s. It starts decelerating when it is about to reach its destination with acceleration, $a(t) = -\frac{t}{3}$ m/s^2, where t is the time (in seconds) for which it decelerated before coming to rest.

Based on the above information, answer the following questions.

(i) Find the velocity function of the car after it started decelerating. Show your steps.

(ii) Find the time it takes the car to stop after it starts decelerating. Show your work and give a valid reason.

(iii) Find the displacement function of the car and calculate its displacement from the moment it starts decelerating till it stops. Show your steps.

Competency Based Que, CBSE QB

37. We know that a given function $f(x)$ is said to be an even function, if $f(-x) = f(x)$ and an odd function when $f(-x) = -f(x)$, also

$$\int_{-a}^{a} f(x)dx = \begin{cases} 2\int_{0}^{a} f(x)\,dx, & \text{if } f(x) \text{ is even} \\ 0, & \text{if } f(x) \text{ is odd} \end{cases}$$

Based on the above information, answer the following questions.

(i) Find whether $f(x) = x^3\sin^{40} x$ is even or odd function.

(ii) Find whether $f(x) = \sin|x| + \cos|x|$ is even or odd function.

(iii) Find the value of $\int_{-\pi}^{\pi} x^{17}\cos^4 x\,dx.$

(iv) Find the value of $\int_{-2}^{2}(x^3 + x\cos x + \tan^5 x + 1)\,dx.$

38. Let $f(x)$ be a function and $f'(x)$ be its derivative. Now, teacher ask Raju, can you answer my question. Raju says, 'What is your question?'

Teacher wrote question on blackboard.

After reading the question, Raju gave the answer as $e^x f(x) + C$.

On the basis of above information, answer the following questions.

(i) If $\int e^x\left(\frac{1}{x^2} - \frac{2}{x^3}\right)dx = e^x f(x) + C$, then find the value of $f(x)$.

(ii) Find the value of $\int e^x \sec x(1+\tan x)dx.$

(iii) Find the value of $\int \frac{e^x}{x}\{x(\log x)^2 + 2\log x\}\,dx.$

Or

Find the value of $\int[\tan(\log x) + \sec^2(\log x)]dx.$

39. We have two properties of definite integration. First is $\int_0^a f(x)\,dx = \int_0^a f(a-x)\,dx$ and second is $\int_a^b f(x)\,dx = \int_a^b f(a+b-x)\,dx.$

Based on the above information, answer the following questions. **Competency Based Que**

(i) Find the value of $\int_0^{\pi/2}\sin^2 x\,dx.$

(ii) Find the value of $\int_0^{\pi/2}\frac{\sin x - \cos x}{1+\sin x\cos x}\,dx.$

(iii) Find the value of $\int_0^{\pi/4}\log(1+\tan x)\,dx.$

(iv) Find the value of $\int_{\pi/6}^{\pi/3}\log(\tan x)\,dx.$

Subjective Questions

Very Short Answer Type Questions

1. Find $\int \frac{2}{1-\cos 2x}\,dx$

2. Evaluate $\int \frac{\cos 2x + 2\sin^2 x}{\sin^2 x}\,dx$

3. Evaluate $\int \left(\frac{x^4+x^2+1}{x^2-x+1}\right)dx$ **Competency Based Que**

4. Evaluate $\sin x\left(\cot x + \frac{1}{\sin^3 x}\right)dx$

5. Evaluate $\int \frac{x^4}{x^2+1}\,dx$

6. Evaluate $\int \frac{\cos 2x + 2\sin^2 x}{\cos^2 x}\,dx$ **CBSE 2018**

7. Evaluate $\int \frac{1}{e^x+1}\,dx$ **Competency Based Que, 2003**

8. Evaluate $\int \sin^3 x \cos^5 x\,dx$ **Competency Based Que**

9. Find $\int \cos^3 x\, e^{\log \sin x}\,dx$ **CBSE 2024**

10. Evaluate $\int \tan^{-1}\sqrt{\frac{1+\cos x}{1-\cos x}}\,dx$

11. Find $\int \frac{dx}{\sqrt{9-25x^2}}$

12. Find $\int \frac{dx}{5-8x-x^2}$ **CBSE 2017**

13. Find $\int \frac{e^x}{\sqrt{9-e^{2x}}}\,dx$

14. Evaluate $\int x \sin 3x\,dx$

15. Evaluate $\int \frac{\log x}{x^2}\,dx$

16. Evaluate $\int x \tan^{-1} x\,dx$ **NCERT, CBSE 2019**

17. Find $\int e^x\left(\frac{2+\sin 2x}{1+\cos 2x}\right)dx$ **Competency Based Que, NCERT**

18. Evaluate $\int \sin^{-1} 2x\,dx$ **CBSE 2019**

19. Evaluate $\int_0^{\pi/2} \sin^2 x\,dx$ **Diksha App**

20. Evaluate $\int_0^3 \frac{dx}{9+x^2}$ **CBSE 2014**

21. Evaluate $\int_0^1 x e^{x^2}\,dx$ **CBSE 2014**

22. Evaluate $\int_{-1}^{2} \frac{|x|}{x}\,dx$ **Competency Based Que, CBSE 2019**

Short Answer Type Questions

23. Evaluate $\int \frac{x^3-x^2+x-1}{x-1}\,dx$

24. Find $\int \frac{3-5\sin x}{\cos^2 x}\,dx$ **CBSE 2018C**

25. Find $\int \frac{dx}{\cos x\sqrt{\cos 2x}}$ **CBSE 2024C**

26. Evaluate $\int \frac{x^3}{(x+2)^4}\,dx$

27. Evaluate $\int \frac{3x+1}{(3x^2+2x+1)^3}\,dx$

28. Evaluate $\int \cos 6x\sqrt{1+\sin 6x}\,dx$ **NCERT, Competency Based Que**

29. Evaluate $\int \sin 5x \cos 3x\,dx$ **Competency Based Que**

30. Evaluate $\int \frac{dx}{\sin^2 x \cos^2 x}$ **CBSE 2025**

31. Evaluate $\int \cos^{-1}(\sin x)\,dx$ **CBSE 2014C**

32. Evaluate $\int \frac{1}{\sqrt{x^2-4x}}\,dx$ **CBSE 2017C**

33. Find the value of $\int \frac{\tan^2 x \cdot \sec^2 x}{1-\tan^6 x}\,dx.$ **CBSE 2019**

34. Find the value of $\int \frac{\cos x}{(1+\sin x)(2+\sin x)}\,dx.$ **Competency Based Que, CBSE 2019**

35. Find $\int \frac{4}{(x-2)(x^2+4)}\,dx$ **CBSE 2018C**

36. Evaluate $\int x^3 \log 2x\,dx$

37. Evaluate $\int_0^{\pi/2} \frac{x}{\cos x + \sin x}\,dx$ **CBSE 2025**

38. Evaluate $\int_0^2 \frac{1}{\sqrt{x}+\sqrt{1+x}}\,dx$

39. Evaluate $\int_1^4 \frac{1}{\sqrt{2x+1}-\sqrt{2x-1}}\,dx$ **CBSE 2023**

40. Evaluate $\int_0^{\pi/4} \sqrt{1-\sin 2x}\,dx$ **CBSE 2004**

41. Evaluate $\int_0^1 \frac{2x+3}{5x^2+1}\,dx$ **Competency Based Que, NCERT**

42. Evaluate $\int_0^1 x\tan^{-1}(x)\,dx$ **CBSE 2016**

43. Evaluate $\int_{\pi/4}^{\pi/2} e^{2x}\left(\frac{1-\sin 2x}{1-\cos 2x}\right)dx$ **Competency Based Que, CBSE 2023**

44. Find $\int_0^1 \frac{\tan^{-1}x}{1+x^2}dx$ **Diksha App**

45. Evaluate $\int_{-4}^{0}|x+2|dx$ **CBSE 2024C**

46. Evaluate $\int_0^{\pi/4} \frac{\sin 2x}{\sin^4 x+\cos^4 x}\,dx$ **Competency Based Que**

47. Evaluate $\int_{-1}^{2}|x^3-x|\,dx$ **Competency Based Que, NCERT, CBSE 2016, 13, 12**

48. Evaluate $\int_{-\pi/3}^{\pi/3} \frac{1}{1+e^{\sin x}}\,dx$

49. Evaluate $\int_0^{\pi/2} \frac{\sin^3 x}{\sin^3 x+\cos^3 x}\,dx$

50. Evaluate $\int_0^{\pi/2} \frac{\tan^7 x}{\cot^7 x+\tan^7 x}\,dx.$ **Competency Based Que**

Long Answer Type Questions

51. Evaluate $\int \cos 2x\cos 4x\cos 6x\,dx$ **Competency Based Que, NCERT**

52. Evaluate $\int \frac{\sin^6 x+\cos^6 x}{\sin^2 x\cos^2 x}\,dx$ **Competency Based Que, NCERT Exemplar, CBSE 2014C**

53. Evaluate $\int \frac{dx}{a^2\sin^2 x+b^2\cos^2 x}$

54. Find $\int \frac{x^2+x+1}{(x+2)(x^2+1)}\,dx$ **CBSE 2019, 16, 15, 09C**

55. Evaluate $\int \frac{x}{(x^2+1)(x-1)}\,dx$ **NCERT, CBSE 2015C**

56. Find $\int \frac{\sec x}{1+\operatorname{cosec} x}dx$ **CBSE Sample Paper 2018**

57. Evaluate $\int e^{ax}\sin bx\,dx$ **Competency Based Que**

58. Evaluate $\int \frac{2x-5}{(2x-3)^3}e^{2x}\,dx$ **Competency Based Que, CBSE 2016**

59. Find $\int e^{2x}\cdot\sin(3x+1)\,dx$ **CBSE 2015**

60. Evaluate $\int_0^{\pi/4} \frac{dx}{\cos^3 x\sqrt{2\sin 2x}}$ **Competency Based Que, CBSE 2015**

61. Evaluate $\int_0^{\pi/4} \frac{\sin x+\cos x}{16+9\sin 2x}dx$ **Competency Based Que, CBSE 2018**

62. Evaluate $\int_0^{\pi} x\log|\sin x|\,dx$ **NCERT Exemplar**

63. Evaluate $\int_0^{\pi/2}\{2\log(\sin x)-\log(\sin 2x)\}dx$ **Competency Based Que, NCERT**

Hints & Solutions

Objective Type Questions

1. (b) Let $I=\int\left[\frac{1}{x^{3/4}}\right]dx=\int x^{-3/4}dx$

$$=\frac{x^{-\frac{3}{4}+1}}{-\frac{3}{4}+1}+C \qquad \left[\because \int x^n dx=\frac{x^{n+1}}{n+1}+C, n\neq -1\right]$$

$$=\frac{x^{1/4}}{1/4}+C=4x^{1/4}+C$$

2. (c) Let $I=\int 5^x dx=\frac{5^x}{\log 5}+C \qquad \left[\because \int a^x dx=\frac{a^x}{\log a}+C\right]$

3. (b) Given, $\int e^{5\log x}\,dx=\int e^{\log x^5}dx=\int x^5 dx \qquad [\because e^{\log p}=p]$

$$=\frac{x^6}{6}+C$$

4. (b) Given, $f'(x)=x+\frac{1}{x}$ ...(i)

On integrating both sides of Eq. (i), we get

$$\int f'(x)\,dx=\int\left(x+\frac{1}{x}\right)dx$$

$$\Rightarrow \quad f(x)=\int x\,dx+\int\frac{1}{x}dx$$

$$\Rightarrow \quad f(x)=\frac{x^2}{2}+\log|x|+C$$

5. (b) Let $I=\int \frac{\sec x}{\sec x-\tan x}dx$

Multiply $(\sec x+\tan x)$ in numerator and denominator, we get

$$I=\int \frac{\sec x(\sec x+\tan x)}{(\sec^2 x-\tan^2 x)}dx$$

$$=\frac{\int(\sec^2 x+\sec x\tan x)dx}{1} \quad [\because \sec^2\theta-\tan^2\theta=1]$$

$$=\int \sec^2 x\,dx+\int \sec x\tan x\,dx$$

$$=\tan x+\sec x+C$$

6. (a) Let $I=\int x^2 e^{x^3}dx$

Again, let $x^3=t$

$\Rightarrow \quad 3x^2dx=dt$

$\Rightarrow \quad x^2dx=\frac{1}{3}dt$

$\therefore \quad I=\int e^t\frac{dt}{3}$

$\Rightarrow \quad I=\frac{1}{3}e^t+C$

$\Rightarrow \quad I=\frac{1}{3}e^{x^3}+C$

7. (b) Given, $\int \frac{1}{x(\log x)^2}dx$

Let $\log x=t$

Then, $\frac{1}{x}dx=dt \quad \left[\because \frac{d}{dx}(\log x)=\frac{1}{x}\right]$

$\therefore \int \frac{1}{x(\log x)^2}dx=\int \frac{1}{t^2}dt$

$$=\int t^{-2}dt=\frac{-1}{t}+C,$$

where $C=$ constant of integration.

$\therefore \int \frac{1}{x(\log x)^2}dx=\frac{-1}{\log x}+C \quad [\because \log x=t]$

8. (a) Let $I=\int e^{3\log x}(x^4+1)^{-1}dx$

$$=\int \frac{e^{\log x^3}}{x^4+1}dx \quad [\because n\log m=\log m^n]$$

$$=\int \frac{x^3}{x^4+1}dx \quad [\because e^{\log x}=x]$$

Again, let $x^4+1=t$

$\Rightarrow \quad 4x^3dx=dt$

$\Rightarrow \quad x^3dx=\frac{dt}{4}$

$\therefore \quad I=\frac{1}{4}\int \frac{dt}{t}$

$$=\frac{1}{4}\log|t|+C \quad \left[\because \int \frac{dx}{x}=\log x+C\right]$$

$$=\frac{1}{4}\log|x^4+1|+C$$

9. (c) Let $I=\int \tan x\,dx=\int \frac{\sin x}{\cos x}dx$

Now, put $\cos x=t \Rightarrow -\sin x\,dx=dt$

$\Rightarrow \quad \sin x\,dx=-dt$

$\therefore \quad I=-\int \frac{1}{t}dt=-\log|t|+C$

$$=-\log|\cos x|+C \quad [\because t=\cos x]$$

$$=\log|(\cos x)^{-1}|+C$$

$$=\log|\sec x|+C \quad \left[\because \frac{1}{\cos x}=\sec x\right]$$

10. (b) Let $I=\int \frac{dx}{\sqrt{9-4x^2}}dx=\int \frac{dx}{\sqrt{9-(2x)^2}}$

Let $2x=t \Rightarrow dx=\frac{1}{2}dt$

$\therefore \quad I=\frac{1}{2}\int \frac{dt}{\sqrt{(3)^2-(t)^2}}=\frac{1}{2}\sin^{-1}\frac{t}{3}+C$

$$\left[\because \frac{dx}{\sqrt{a^2-x^2}}=\sin^{-1}\frac{x}{a}+C\right]$$

$$=\frac{1}{2}\sin^{-1}\frac{2x}{3}+C$$

11. (b) Let $I=\int \frac{dx}{x^2-16}=\int \frac{dx}{x^2-4^2}$

$$=\frac{1}{2(4)}\log\left|\frac{x-4}{x+4}\right|+C=\frac{1}{8}\log\left|\frac{x-4}{x+4}\right|+C$$

$$\left[\because \int \frac{dx}{x^2-a^2}=\frac{1}{2a}\log\left|\frac{x-a}{x+a}\right|+C\right]$$

12. (b) Given, $\frac{d}{dx}[f(x)]=\log x$

On integrating both sides, we get

$$f(x)=\int \underset{\text{I}}{\log x}\cdot \underset{\text{II}}{1}dx$$

$$=\log x\int dx-\int\left[\frac{d}{dx}(\log x)\int dx\right]dx$$

[integration by parts]

$\Rightarrow \quad f(x)=\log x\cdot x-\int \frac{1}{x}\cdot x\,dx$

$\Rightarrow \quad f(x)=\log x\cdot x-\int dx$

$\Rightarrow \quad f(x)=x\log x-x+C$

$\Rightarrow \quad f(x)=x(\log x-1)+C$

13. (a) Let $I=\int \tan^{-1}x\,dx=\int \tan^{-1}x\cdot 1dx$

$$=\tan^{-1}x\cdot x-\int \frac{1}{1+x^2}x\,dx \quad \text{[integration by parts]}$$

$$=x\tan^{-1}x-\frac{1}{2}\int \frac{2x}{1+x^2}dx$$

$$=x\tan^{-1}x-\frac{1}{2}\log(1+x^2)+C$$

$$\left[\because \int \frac{f'(x)}{f(x)}dx=\log f(x)+C\right]$$

14. (d) Let $I=\int e^x\left[\frac{x-1-2}{(x-1)^3}\right]dx$

$$=\int e^x\left[\frac{1}{(x-1)^2}-\frac{2}{(x-1)^3}\right]dx$$

Let $f(x)=\frac{1}{(x-1)^2}=(x-1)^{-2}$

Then, $f'(x)=\frac{-2}{(x-1)^3}$

$\therefore \quad I=e^x\frac{1}{(x-1)^2}+C$

$[\because \int e^x[f(x)+f'(x)]=e^x f(x)+C]$

15. (a) Given, $\int_0^a 3x^2\,dx=8 \Rightarrow 3\int_0^a x^2dx=8$

$\Rightarrow \quad 3\left(\frac{x^3}{3}\right)_0^a=8 \Rightarrow 3\left(\frac{a^3}{3}-0\right)=8$

$\Rightarrow \quad a^3=8 \Rightarrow a=2$

16. (d) $\int_{-1}^{1}\frac{|x-2|}{x-2}dx=\int_{-1}^{1}\frac{-(x-2)}{x-2}dx$

$$=\int_{-1}^{1}(-1)\,dx=-(x)_{-1}^{1}=-(1+1)=-2$$

17. (b) Let $I=\int_0^\pi e^{\sin^2 x}\cos^3(2n+1)x\,dx$ ...(i)

$$=\int_0^\pi e^{\sin^2(\pi-x)}\cos^3(2n+1)(\pi-x)\,dx$$

$[\because \int_0^a f(x)dx=\int_0^a f(a-x)\,dx]$

$$=\int_0^\pi e^{\sin^2 x}[\cos(2n+1)(\pi-x)]^3\,dx$$

$$=\int_0^\pi e^{\sin^2 x}[\cos\{(2n+1)\pi-(2n+1)x\}]^3\,dx$$

$$=\int_0^\pi e^{\sin^2 x}[-\cos(2n+1)x]^3\,dx$$

$\Rightarrow \quad I=-\int_0^\pi e^{\sin^2 x}\cos^3(2n+1)x\,dx$

$\Rightarrow \quad 2I=0 \Rightarrow I=0$ [using Eq. (i)]

18. (a) Let $I=\int_0^{\frac{\pi}{6}}\sec^2\left(x-\frac{\pi}{6}\right)dx$

$$=\left[\tan\left(x-\frac{\pi}{6}\right)\right]_0^{\pi/6}$$

$[\because \int \sec^2(ax+b)\,dx=\frac{1}{a}\tan(ax+b)+C]$

$$=\tan\left(\frac{\pi}{6}-\frac{\pi}{6}\right)-\tan\left(0-\frac{\pi}{6}\right)=0+\tan\frac{\pi}{6}=\frac{1}{\sqrt{3}}$$

19. (a) Let $I=\int_{\frac{\pi}{4}}^{\frac{\pi}{2}}\cot\theta\,\text{cosec}^2\,\theta\,d\theta$

On putting $\cot\theta=t$, we get

$\Rightarrow \quad -\text{cosec}^2\,\theta\,d\theta=dt \Rightarrow \text{cosec}^2\,\theta\,d\theta=-dt$

When $\theta=\frac{\pi}{4}$, then $t=1$

When $\theta=\frac{\pi}{2}$, then $t=0$

$\therefore \quad I=\int_1^0 t(-dt)=-\int_1^0 t\,dt=-\left(\frac{t^2}{2}\right)_1^0=-\left[0-\frac{1}{2}\right]=\frac{1}{2}$

20. (a) Let $I=\int_0^4(e^{2x}+x)\,dx=\int_0^4 e^{2x}dx+\int_0^4 x\,dx$

On putting $2x=t \Rightarrow 2dx=dt \Rightarrow dx=\frac{dt}{2}$

Lower limit When $x=0$, then $t=0$

Upper limit When $x=4$, then $t=8$

$\therefore \quad I=\int_0^8 e^t\frac{dt}{2}+\left(\frac{x^2}{2}\right)_0^4$

$$=\frac{1}{2}\int_0^8 e^t\,dt+\frac{1}{2}(x^2)_0^4$$

$$=\frac{1}{2}(e^t)_0^8+\frac{1}{2}(16-0)$$

$$=\frac{1}{2}(e^8-e^0)+\frac{1}{2}(16)$$

$$=\frac{1}{2}(e^8-1)+8$$

$$=\frac{e^8-1+16}{2}=\frac{e^8+15}{2}$$

21. (d) We know that

$$|x|=\begin{cases}-x, & x<0\\ x, & x\geq 0\end{cases}$$

$$\therefore \quad x|x|=\begin{cases}-x^2, & -1\leq x\leq 0\\ x^2, & 0\leq x\leq 1\end{cases}$$

Now, $\int_{-1}^1 x|x|\,dx=\int_{-1}^0 -x^2dx+\int_0^1 x^2dx$

$$=\left[\frac{-x^3}{3}\right]_{-1}^0+\left[\frac{x^3}{3}\right]_0^1$$

$$=\frac{-1}{3}[0^3-(-1)^3]+\frac{1}{3}[1^3-0^3]$$

$$=-\frac{1}{3}+\frac{1}{3}=0$$

$\therefore \quad \int_{-1}^1 x|x|\,dx=0$

22. (d) Let $I=\int_0^{\frac{\pi}{2}}\log(\tan x)\,dx$

$\Rightarrow I=\int_0^{\frac{\pi}{2}}\log\left[\tan\left(\frac{\pi}{2}-x\right)\right]dx \quad \left[\because \int_0^a f(x)\,dx=\int_0^a f(a-x)\,dx\right]$

$\Rightarrow I=\int_0^{\frac{\pi}{2}}\log[\cot x]\,dx \quad \left[\because \tan\left(\frac{\pi}{2}-\theta\right)=\cot\theta\right]$

23. (d) Let $I=\int_0^1 \log\left(\frac{1-x}{x}\right)dx$ ...(i)

$\Rightarrow \quad I=\int_0^1 \log\left[\frac{1-(1-x)}{1-x}\right]dx \quad \left[\because \int_0^a f(x)\,dx=\int_a^a f(a-x)\,dx\right]$

$=\int_0^1 \log\left(\frac{x}{1-x}\right)dx$ ...(ii)

On adding Eqs. (i) and (ii), we get

$2I=\int_0^1 \log\left(\frac{1-x}{x}\right)dx+\int_0^1 \log\left(\frac{x}{1-x}\right)dx$

$=\int_0^1 \log\left[\left(\frac{1-x}{x}\right)\left(\frac{x}{1-x}\right)\right]dx \quad [\because \log m+\log n=\log mn]$

$=\int_0^1 \log 1\,dx=\int_0^1 0\,dx \quad [\because \log 1=0]$

$=0$

24. (a) We have, $\int_{-2}^{3} x^2dx=k\int_0^2 x^2dx+\int_2^3 x^2dx$

$\Rightarrow \quad \left(\frac{x^3}{3}\right)_{-2}^{3}=k\left(\frac{x^3}{3}\right)_0^2+\left(\frac{x^3}{3}\right)_2^3$

$\Rightarrow \quad \left[\frac{27}{3}-\left(-\frac{8}{3}\right)\right]=k\left[\frac{8}{3}-0\right]+\left[\frac{27}{3}-\frac{8}{3}\right]$

$\Rightarrow \quad \left(\frac{27}{3}+\frac{8}{3}\right)=k\left(\frac{8}{3}\right)+\frac{19}{3}$

$\Rightarrow \quad \frac{35}{3}=k\left(\frac{8}{3}\right)+\frac{19}{3}$

$\Rightarrow \quad k\left(\frac{8}{3}\right)=\frac{35}{3}-\frac{19}{3}=\frac{16}{3}$

$\Rightarrow \quad k=\frac{16}{3}\times\frac{3}{8}\Rightarrow k=2$

25. (b) Let $I=\int_1^e \log x\,dx$

$=\int_1^e \underset{\text{I}}{\log x}\cdot \underset{\text{II}}{1}\,dx=(x\log x)_1^e-\int_1^e \frac{1}{x}x\,dx$

$=(e\log e-\log 1)-(x)_1^e=e\log e-0-(e-1)$

$=e-e+1=1$

26. (a) Let $I=\int \frac{1}{\sqrt[3]{x^5}}dx=\int \frac{1}{(x^{5/3})}dx$

$=\int x^{-5/3}dx=\frac{x^{-\frac{5}{3}+1}}{\frac{-5}{3}+1}+C$

$=\frac{x^{-2/3}}{\frac{-2}{3}}+C=-\frac{3}{2}x^{-2/3}+C$

Hence, Assertion and Reason both are correct and Reason is correct explanation of Assertion.

27. (a) Let $I=\int (4-3x)^7dx$

$\Rightarrow \quad I=\int (-3x+4)^7\,dx$ ...(i)

Now, we know that

$\int (ax+b)^n\,dx=\frac{(ax+b)^{n+1}}{a(n+1)}+C, n\neq -1$

Using above property in Eq. (i), we get

$I=\frac{(-3x+4)^{7+1}}{(-3)(7+1)}+C=\frac{-1}{24}(4-3x)^8+C$

Hence, Assertion and Reason both are correct and Reason is correct explanation of Assertion.

28. (b) Let $I=\int \frac{1}{\sqrt{1+\cos 2x}}dx=\int \frac{1}{\sqrt{2\cos^2 x}}dx$

$[\because \cos 2x=2\cos^2 x-1]$

$=\int \frac{1}{\sqrt{2}\cos x}dx=\frac{1}{\sqrt{2}}\int \sec x\,dx$

$=\frac{1}{\sqrt{2}}\log|\sec x+\tan x|+C$

Assertion is correct.

Also, we know that $\int \cot x\,dx=\log|\sin x|+C$

Hence, Assertion and Reason both are correct but Reason is not correct explanation of Assertion.

29. (a) Let $I=\int \tan^3 x\sec^3 x\,dx$

$=\int \tan^2 x\sec^2 x\cdot\tan x\sec x\,dx$

$=\int (\sec^2 x-1)\sec^2 x\cdot\tan x\sec x\,dx$

$[\because \tan^2 x=\sec^2 x-1]$

Now, put $\sec x=t \Rightarrow \sec x\tan x\,dx=dt$

$\therefore \quad I=\int (t^2-1)\,t^2\,dt$

$=\int (t^4-t^2)\,dt$

$=\frac{t^5}{5}-\frac{t^3}{3}+C$

$=\frac{1}{5}\sec^5 x-\frac{1}{3}\sec^3 x+C \quad [\because t=\sec x]$

$\therefore$ Assertion is correct.

Hence, Assertion and Reason both are correct and Reason is the correct explanation of Assertion.

30. (a) Let $I=\int \frac{1}{9+4x^2}dx$

$\Rightarrow \quad I=\frac{1}{4}\int \frac{dx}{\frac{9}{4}+x^2}$

$=\frac{1}{4}\int \frac{dx}{\left(\frac{3}{2}\right)^2+(x)^2}$ ...(i)

We know that

$\int \frac{dx}{a^2+x^2}=\frac{1}{a}\tan^{-1}\left(\frac{x}{a}\right)+C$

Then, from Eq. (i), we get

$$I=\frac{1}{4}\left[\frac{1}{\frac{3}{2}}\tan^{-1}\left(\frac{x}{\frac{3}{2}}\right)\right]+C$$

$$=\frac{1}{6}\tan^{-1}\left(\frac{2x}{3}\right)+C$$

Hence, Assertion and Reason both are correct and Reason is correct explanation of Assertion.

31. (a) We have, $\int\frac{1}{\sqrt{4-x^2}}dx$

We know that

$$\int\frac{1}{\sqrt{a^2-x^2}}dx=\sin^{-1}\frac{x}{a}+C$$

$$\therefore \int\frac{1}{\sqrt{(2)^2-(x)^2}}dx=\sin^{-1}\frac{x}{2}+C$$

Hence, Assertion and Reason both are correct and Reason is the correct explanation of Assertion.

32. (a) Let $I=\int \underset{\text{II}}{x}\,\underset{\text{I}}{\log x}\,dx$

$$=\log x\int x\,dx-\int\left\{\frac{d}{dx}(\log x)\times\int x\,dx\right\}dx$$

$$=(\log x)\cdot\frac{x^2}{2}-\int\frac{1}{x}\times\frac{x^2}{2}dx$$

$$=\frac{1}{2}x^2\log x-\frac{1}{2}\int x\,dx$$

$$=\frac{1}{2}x^2\log x-\frac{1}{2}\left(\frac{x^2}{2}\right)+C=\frac{1}{2}x^2\log x-\frac{x^2}{4}+C$$

Hence, Assertion and Reason both are correct and Reason is the correct explanation of Assertion.

33. (d) We have,

$$\int_0^1\frac{dx}{1+x^2}$$

We know that $\int_a^b f(x)=g(b)-g(a)$, $g(x)$ is anti-derivative of $f(x)$.

$$\therefore \int_0^1\frac{dx}{1+x^2}=[\tan^{-1}x]_0^1$$

$$=\tan^{-1}(1)-\tan^{-1}(0)$$

$$=\frac{\pi}{4}-0=\frac{\pi}{4}$$

Hence, Assertion is incorrect and Reason is correct.

34. (a) Let $I=\int_{-\pi}^{\pi}(1-x^2)\sin x\cos^2 x\,dx$

Again, let $f(x)=(1-x^2)\sin x\cos^2 x$

$$\therefore f(-x)=[1-(-x)^2]\sin(-x)\cos^2(-x)$$

$$=(1-x^2)(-\sin x)\cos^2 x$$

$$=-(1-x^2)\sin x\cos^2 x=-f(x)$$

$\therefore f(x)$ is an odd function.

$\therefore I=0$ $\quad\left[\because \int_{-a}^{a}f(x)\,dx=0, \text{ if } f(x) \text{ is an odd function}\right]$

35. (a) Let $I=\int_2^8\frac{\sqrt{10-x}}{\sqrt{x}+\sqrt{10-x}}dx$ ...(i)

$$=\int_2^8\frac{\sqrt{10-(10-x)}}{\sqrt{10-x}+\sqrt{10-(10-x)}}dx$$

$$\left[\because \int_a^b f(x)\,dx=\int_a^b f(a+b-x)\,dx\right]$$

$$=\int_2^8\frac{\sqrt{x}}{\sqrt{10-x}+\sqrt{x}}dx \quad \text{...(ii)}$$

On adding Eqs. (i) and (ii), we get

$$2I=\int_2^8\frac{\sqrt{10-x}+\sqrt{x}}{\sqrt{10-x}+\sqrt{x}}dx=\int_2^8 1dx$$

$\Rightarrow$ $2I=[x]_2^8=8-2=6$

$\Rightarrow$ $I=3$

Thus, Assertion and Reason both are correct and Reason is the correct explanation of Assertion.

36. (i) Given that constant velocity of a moving car is 15 m/s and acceleration $a(t)=-\frac{t}{3}$ m/s^2

Now, velocity function of the car,

$$v(t)=\int a(t)\,dt$$

$\Rightarrow$ $v(t)=\int-\frac{t}{3}dt$

$\Rightarrow$ $v(t)=-\frac{1}{3}\cdot\frac{t^2}{2}+C$

$\Rightarrow$ $v(t)=-\frac{t^2}{6}+C$ ...(i)

At $t=0$, $v(0)=15$

$\therefore$ $15=-\frac{0}{6}+C\Rightarrow C=15$

On putting the value of C in Eq. (i), we get

$$v(t)=-\frac{t^2}{6}+15 \quad \text{(ii)}$$

(ii) The velocity of the car will be zero, when the car stops i.e. $v(t)=0$.

From Eq. (ii), we get

$$v(t)=-\frac{t^2}{6}+15$$

$\Rightarrow$ $-\frac{t^2}{6}+15=0$

$\Rightarrow$ $-t^2=-90$

$\Rightarrow$ $t=\pm3\sqrt{10}$ s

$\therefore$ $t=3\sqrt{10}$ s $\quad$ [$\because$ time cannot be negative]

(iii) The displacement function of the car is

$$x(t)=\int v(t)\,dt$$

From Eq. (ii), we get

$$v(t)=-\frac{t^2}{6}+15$$

$$\therefore x(t)=\int\left(15-\frac{t^2}{6}\right)dt$$

$\Rightarrow \quad x(t) = 15t - \dfrac{t^3}{3\cdot 6} + C$

$\Rightarrow \quad x(t) = 15t - \dfrac{t^3}{18} + C, \quad$ ..(iii)

where C is an arbitrary constant.

At $t = 0$, the car starts decelerating till it stops and $x(0) = 0$, then

$x(0) = 0 \Rightarrow 15\cdot 0 - \dfrac{0}{18} + C = 0 \Rightarrow C = 0$

From Eq. (iii), we get

$$x(t) = 15t - \frac{t^3}{18}$$

On putting the value $t = 3\sqrt{10}$ from part (ii), we get

$$x(3\sqrt{10}) = 45\sqrt{10} - \frac{27(10)^{3/2}}{18}$$
$$= 45\sqrt{10} - \frac{3\cdot 10\cdot\sqrt{10}}{2} = 30\sqrt{10} \text{ m}$$

37. Given that $f(-x) = f(x)$

$\Rightarrow f(x)$ is an even function

and $\quad f(-x) = -f(x)$

$\Rightarrow f(x)$ is an odd function.

(i) $\quad f(x) = x^3 \sin^{40} x$

$\Rightarrow f(-x) = (-x)^3 \cdot \sin^{40}(-x) = -x^3 \sin^{40} x$

$\Rightarrow f(-x) = -f(x)$

Hence, $f(x)$ is an odd function.

(ii) $\quad f(x) = \sin|x| + \cos|x|$

$\Rightarrow f(-x) = \sin|-x| + \cos|-x|$

$= \sin|x| + \cos|x|$

$\Rightarrow f(-x) = f(x)$

Hence, $f(x)$ is an even function.

(iii) Let $\quad I = \int_{-\pi}^{\pi} x^{17} \cos^4 x\, dx$

Let $\quad f(x) = x^{17} \cos^4 x$

$\Rightarrow \quad f(-x) = (-x)^{17} \cos^4(-x) = -x^{17} \cos^4 x$

$\Rightarrow \quad f(-x) = -f(x)$

$f(x)$ is an odd function.

So, $\int_{-\pi}^{\pi} x^{17} \cos^4 x\, dx = 0$

(iv) Let $I = \int_{-2}^{2} (x^3 + x\cos x + \tan^5 x + 1)dx$

$\Rightarrow \quad I = \int_{-2}^{2} x^3 dx + \int_{-2}^{2} x\cos x\, dx + \int_{-2}^{2} \tan^5 x\, dx + \int_{-2}^{2} 1 dx$

Let $f(x) = x^3$

$\Rightarrow \quad f(-x) = (-x)^3 = -x^3 = -f(x)$

$f(x)$ is an odd function.

Let $\quad g(x) = x\cos x$

$\Rightarrow g(-x) = (-x)\cos(-x) = -x\cos x$ [$\because \cos(-x) = \cos x$]

$\Rightarrow g(-x) = -g(x)$

Hence, $g(x)$ is an odd function.

Let $\quad h(x) = \tan^5 x$

$\Rightarrow \quad h(-x) = \tan^5(-x) = -\tan^5 x$

$\Rightarrow \quad h(-x) = -h(x)$

$h(x)$ is an odd function.

Let $r(x) = 1$, which is a constant function, so it is an even function.

$\therefore \quad I = 0 + 0 + 0 + 2\int_0^2 dx = 2(x)_0^2 = 4$

38. (i) We have, $\int e^x\left(\dfrac{1}{x^2} - \dfrac{2}{x^3}\right)dx = e^x f(x) + C$

LHS $= \int e^x\left(\dfrac{1}{x^2} - \dfrac{2}{x^3}\right)dx$

Let $\quad f(x) = \dfrac{1}{x^2} \Rightarrow f'(x) = \dfrac{-2}{x^3}$

$\therefore \quad$ LHS $= e^x \cdot \dfrac{1}{x^2} + C$

[$\because \int e^x[f(x) + f'(x)]dx = e^x f(x) + C$]

On comparing with RHS, we get

$$f(x) = \frac{1}{x^2}$$

(ii) Let $I = \int e^x \sec x(1 + \tan x)dx$

$= \int e^x[\sec x + \sec x\tan x]dx$

Let $f(x) = \sec x$

$\Rightarrow f'(x) = \sec x\tan x$

$\therefore \quad I = e^x \sec x + C$

[$\because \int e^x[f(x) + f'(x)]dx = e^x f(x) + C$]

(iii) Let $I = \int \dfrac{e^x}{x}\{x(\log x)^2 + 2\log x\}dx$

$= \int e^x\left[(\log x)^2 + \dfrac{2\log x}{x}\right]dx$

Here, $f(x) = (\log x)^2 \Rightarrow \quad f'(x) = \dfrac{2\log x}{x}$

$\therefore \quad I = e^x(\log x)^2 + C$

[$\because \int e^x[f(x) + f'(x)]dx = e^x f(x) + C$]

Or

Let $I = \int[\tan(\log x) + \sec^2(\log x)]dx$

Put $\log x = t \Rightarrow x = e^t \Rightarrow dx = e^t\, dt$

Then, $I = \int(\tan t + \sec^2 t)e^t dt$

Here, $f(t) = \tan t \Rightarrow f'(t) = \sec^2 t$

We know that

$\int e^x\{f(x) + f'(x)\} = e^x f(x) + C$

Then, $I = e^t \cdot \tan t + C = x\cdot\tan(\log x) + C \quad$ [$\because x = e^t$]

39. We have, $\int_0^a f(x)\,dx = \int_0^a f(a-x)\,dx$

and $\quad \int_a^b f(x)\,dx = \int_a^b f(a+b-x)\,dx$

(i) Let $\quad I = \int_0^{\pi/2} \sin^2 x\, dx \quad$ ...(i)

$\Rightarrow \quad I = \int_0^{\pi/2} \sin^2\left(\dfrac{\pi}{2} - x\right)dx$

$\left[\because \int_0^a f(x)\,dx = \int_0^a f(a-x)\,dx\right]$

$\Rightarrow \quad I = \int_0^{\pi/2} \cos^2 x\, dx \quad$ ...(ii)

On adding Eqs. (i) and (ii), we get

$$2I=\int_0^{\pi/2}(\sin^2 x+\cos^2 x)\,dx$$

$$=\int_0^{\pi/2}dx=(x)_0^{\pi/2}=\frac{\pi}{2} \qquad [\because \sin^2 x+\cos^2 x=1]$$

$$\Rightarrow \quad I=\frac{\pi}{4}$$

(ii) Let $I=\int_0^{\pi/2}\frac{\sin x-\cos x}{1+\sin x\cos x}dx$ ...(i)

$$\Rightarrow \quad I=\int_0^{\pi/2}\frac{\sin\left(\frac{\pi}{2}-x\right)-\cos\left(\frac{\pi}{2}-x\right)}{1+\sin\left(\frac{\pi}{2}-x\right)\cos\left(\frac{\pi}{2}-x\right)}dx$$

$$\left[\because \int_0^a f(x)\,dx=\int_0^a f(a-x)\,dx\right]$$

$$=\int_0^{\pi/2}\frac{\cos x-\sin x}{1+\cos x\sin x}dx \qquad \text{...(ii)}$$

On adding Eqs. (i) and (ii), we get

$$2I=\int_0^{\pi/2}\frac{\sin x-\cos x+\cos x-\sin x}{1+\sin x\cos x}dx=0$$

$$\Rightarrow I=0$$

(iii) Let $I=\int_0^{\pi/4}\log(1+\tan x)\,dx$ ...(i)

$$\Rightarrow \quad I=\int_0^{\pi/4}\log\left(1+\tan\left(\frac{\pi}{4}-x\right)\right)dx$$

$$\left[\because \int_0^a f(x)\,dx=\int_0^a f(a-x)\,dx\right]$$

$$\Rightarrow \quad I=\int_0^{\pi/4}\log\left(1+\frac{1-\tan x}{1+\tan x}\right)dx$$

$$\left[\because \tan(x-y)=\frac{\tan x-\tan y}{1+\tan x\cdot\tan y}\right]$$

$$\Rightarrow \quad I=\int_0^{\pi/4}\log\left(\frac{1+\tan x+1-\tan x}{1+\tan x}\right)dx$$

$$\Rightarrow \quad I=\int_0^{\pi/4}\log\left(\frac{2}{1+\tan x}\right)dx$$

$$\Rightarrow \quad I=\int_0^{\pi/4}\log 2\,dx-\int_0^{\pi/4}\log(1+\tan x)\,dx$$

$$\Rightarrow \quad I=\log 2\int_0^{\pi/4}dx-I \qquad \text{[from Eq. (i)]}$$

$$\Rightarrow \quad 2I=\log 2\,(x)_0^{\pi/4}=\frac{\pi}{4}\log 2$$

$$\Rightarrow \quad I=\frac{\pi}{8}\log 2$$

(iv) Let $I=\int_{\pi/6}^{\pi/3}\log(\tan x)\,dx$ ...(i)

$$\Rightarrow I=\int_{\pi/6}^{\pi/3}\log\tan\left(\frac{\pi}{6}+\frac{\pi}{3}-x\right)dx$$

$$\left[\because \int_a^b f(x)\,dx=\int_a^b f(a+b-x)\,dx\right]$$

$$=\int_{\pi/6}^{\pi/3}\log\tan\left(\frac{\pi}{2}-x\right)dx$$

$$=\int_{\pi/6}^{\pi/3}\log\cot x\,dx \qquad \text{...(ii)}$$

On adding Eqs. (i) and (ii), we get

$$2I=\int_{\pi/6}^{\pi/3}(\log\tan x+\log\cot x)\,dx$$

$$=\int_{\pi/6}^{\pi/3}\log(\tan x\cdot\cot x)\,dx=\int_{\pi/6}^{\pi/3}\log 1\,dx$$

$$\Rightarrow \quad I=0$$

Subjective Questions

1. Let $I=\int\frac{2}{1-\cos 2x}dx=\int\frac{2}{1-(1-2\sin^2 x)}dx$

$$=\int\frac{2}{2\sin^2 x}dx=\int \text{cosec}^2 x\,dx=-\cot x+C$$

2. Let $I=\int\frac{\cos 2x+2\sin^2 x}{\sin^2 x}dx$

$$=\int\frac{1-2\sin^2 x+2\sin^2 x}{\sin^2 x}dx=\int\frac{1}{\sin^2 x}dx$$

$$=\int \text{cosec}^2 x\,dx=-\cot x+C$$

3. Let $I=\int\left(\frac{x^4+x^2+1}{x^2-x+1}\right)dx=\int\frac{(x^2-x+1)(x^2+x+1)}{x^2-x+1}dx$

$$=\int(x^2+x+1)\,dx=\int x^2dx+\int x\,dx+\int 1dx$$

$$=\frac{x^3}{3}+\frac{x^2}{2}+x+C$$

4. Let $I=\int\sin x\left(\cot x+\frac{1}{\sin^3 x}\right)dx$

$$=\int\left(\sin x\times\cot x+\frac{\sin x}{\sin^3 x}\right)dx$$

$$=\int\left(\sin x\times\frac{\cos x}{\sin x}\right)dx+\int\frac{1}{\sin^2 x}dx$$

$$=\int\cos x\,dx+\int\text{cosec}^2 x\,dx$$

$$=\sin x+(-\cot x)+C$$

$$=\sin x-\cot x+C$$

5. Let $I=\int\frac{x^4}{x^2+1}dx=\int\frac{x^4-1+1}{x^2+1}dx$

$$=\int\frac{x^4-1}{x^2+1}dx+\int\frac{1}{x^2+1}dx$$

$$=\int\frac{(x^2-1)(x^2+1)}{x^2+1}dx+\int\frac{1}{x^2+1}dx$$

$$[\because a^4-b^4=(a^2-b^2)(a^2+b^2)]$$

$$=\int(x^2-1)dx+\int\frac{1}{x^2+1}dx$$

$$=\int x^2dx-\int dx+\int\frac{dx}{x^2+1}$$

$$=\frac{x^3}{3}-x+\tan^{-1}x+C \qquad \left[\because \int\frac{dx}{x^2+1}=\tan^{-1}x+C\right]$$

6. Let $I=\int \frac{\cos 2x+2\sin^2 x}{\cos^2 x}dx$

$=\int \frac{1-2\sin^2 x+2\sin^2 x}{\cos^2 x}dx$

$=\int \frac{1}{\cos^2 x}dx=\int \sec^2 x\,dx=\tan x+C$

7. Let $I=\int \frac{1}{e^x+1}dx=\int \frac{e^{-x}}{1+e^{-x}}dx$

Put $1+e^{-x}=t$

$\Rightarrow\ -e^{-x}dx=dt \Rightarrow e^{-x}dx=-dt$

$\therefore\quad I=-\int \frac{dt}{t}=-\log|t|+C$

$=-\log|1+e^{-x}|+C$

8. Let $I=\int \sin^3 x\cos^5 x\,dx$

Here, the powers of both $\sin x$ and $\cos x$ are odd.

So, either put $\sin x=t$ or $\cos x=t$.

Now, put $\cos x=t \Rightarrow -\sin x dx=dt \Rightarrow dx=\frac{-dt}{\sin x}$

$\therefore\quad I=\int \sin^3 x\cdot t^5\left(\frac{-dt}{\sin x}\right)$

$=-\int \sin^2 x\, t^5\,dt$

$=-\int (1-\cos^2 x)\,t^5 dt$

$=-\int (1-t^2)\,t^5\,dt \qquad [\because \cos x=t]$

$=-\int (t^5-t^7)\,dt=\int (t^7-t^5)\,dt$

$=\frac{t^8}{8}-\frac{t^6}{6}+C$

$=\frac{\cos^8 x}{8}-\frac{\cos^6 x}{6}+C \qquad [\because \cos x=t]$

9. Let $I=\int \cos^3 x\, e^{\log \sin x}dx$

$=\int \cos^3 x\sin x\,dx \qquad [\because e^{\log x}=x]$

On putting $\cos x=t$

$\Rightarrow\quad -\sin x\,dx=dt$

$\Rightarrow\quad \sin x\,dx=-dt$

$\therefore\quad I=-\int t^3\cdot dt=-\frac{t^4}{4}+C=-\frac{\cos^4 x}{4}+C$

10. Let $I=\int \tan^{-1}\sqrt{\frac{1+\cos x}{1-\cos x}}\,dx=\int \tan^{-1}\sqrt{\frac{2\cos^2\frac{x}{2}}{2\sin^2\frac{x}{2}}}\,dx$

$[\because \cos 2\theta=2\cos^2\theta-1=1-2\sin^2\theta]$

$=\int \tan^{-1}\sqrt{\cot^2\frac{x}{2}}\,dx=\int \tan^{-1}\left(\cot\frac{x}{2}\right)dx$

$=\int \tan^{-1}\left[\tan\left(\frac{\pi}{2}-\frac{x}{2}\right)\right]dx \qquad \left[\because \tan\left(\frac{\pi}{2}-\theta\right)=\cot\theta\right]$

$=\int \left(\frac{\pi}{2}-\frac{x}{2}\right)dx \qquad [\because \tan^{-1}(\tan\theta)=\theta]$

$=\frac{\pi}{2}x-\frac{x^2}{2\cdot 2}+C=\frac{\pi}{2}x-\frac{x^2}{4}+C$

11. Let $I=\int \frac{dx}{\sqrt{9-25x^2}}=\int \frac{dx}{\sqrt{25\left(\frac{9}{25}-x^2\right)}}$

$=\frac{1}{5}\int \frac{dx}{\sqrt{\left(\frac{3}{5}\right)^2-x^2}}$

$=\frac{1}{5}\sin^{-1}\left(\frac{x}{(3/5)}\right)+C$

$=\frac{1}{5}\sin^{-1}\left(\frac{5x}{3}\right)+C$

12. Let $I=\int \frac{dx}{5-8x-x^2}$

$=\int \frac{dx}{5-2\cdot 4\cdot x-x^2-(4)^2+(4)^2}$

$=\int \frac{dx}{5+16-[x^2+(4)^2+2\cdot 4\cdot x]}$

$=\int \frac{dx}{21-(x+4)^2}=\int \frac{dx}{(\sqrt{21})^2-(x+4)^2}$

$=\frac{1}{2\sqrt{21}}\log\left|\frac{\sqrt{21}+x+4}{\sqrt{21}-x-4}\right|+C$

$\left[\because \int \frac{dx}{a^2-x^2}=\frac{1}{2a}\log\left|\frac{a+x}{a-x}\right|+C\right]$

13. Let $I=\int \frac{e^x}{\sqrt{9-e^{2x}}}dx=\int \frac{e^x}{\sqrt{(3)^2-(e^x)^2}}dx$

Now, put $e^x=t \Rightarrow e^x dx=dt$

$\therefore\quad I=\int \frac{dt}{\sqrt{(3)^2-t^2}}=\sin^{-1}\frac{t}{3}+C \qquad \left[\because \int \frac{dx}{\sqrt{a^2-x^2}}=\sin^{-1}\left(\frac{x}{a}\right)\right]$

$=\sin^{-1}\left(\frac{e^x}{3}\right)+C$

14. Let $I=\int \underset{\text{I}}{x}\,\underset{\text{II}}{\sin 3x}\,dx$

$=x\int \sin 3x\,dx-\int\left(\frac{d}{dx}(x)\times\int \sin 3x\,dx\right)dx$

$=x\left(-\frac{\cos 3x}{3}\right)-\int -\frac{1}{3}\cos 3x\,dx$

$=-\frac{1}{3}x\cos 3x+\frac{1}{3}\int \cos 3x\,dx$

$=-\frac{1}{3}x\cos 3x+\frac{1}{9}\sin 3x+C$

15. Let $I = \int \frac{\log x}{x^2} dx$

$= \int \underset{\text{I}}{\log x} \cdot \underset{\text{II}}{\frac{1}{x^2}} dx$

$= \log \int \frac{1}{x^2} dx - \int \left\{ \frac{d}{dx}(\log x) \int \frac{1}{x^2} dx \right\} dx$

$= \log x \left(-\frac{1}{x} \right) - \int \frac{1}{x}\left(-\frac{1}{x} \right) dx = -\frac{\log x}{x} + \int \frac{1}{x^2} dx$

$= \frac{-\log x}{x} - \frac{1}{x} + C = -\frac{1}{x}(1 + \log x) + C$

16. Let $I = \int \underset{\text{II}}{x} \underset{\text{I}}{\tan^{-1} x}\, dx$

$= \tan^{-1} x \int x\, dx - \int \left\{ \frac{d}{dx}(\tan^{-1} x) . \int x\, dx \right\} dx$

$= (\tan^{-1} x) \frac{x^2}{2} - \int \frac{1}{1+x^2} . \frac{x^2}{2} dx$

$= \frac{x^2}{2} \tan^{-1} x - \frac{1}{2} \int \frac{x^2 + 1 - 1}{x^2 + 1} dx$

$= \frac{x^2}{2} \tan^{-1} x - \frac{1}{2} \int \left(1 - \frac{1}{x^2 + 1} \right) dx$

$= \frac{x^2}{2} \tan^{-1} x - \frac{1}{2}(x - \tan^{-1} x) + C$

17. Let $I = \int e^x \left(\frac{2 + \sin 2x}{1 + \cos 2x} \right) dx$

$= \int e^x \left(\frac{2 + 2\sin x \cos x}{2\cos^2 x} \right) dx$

$= \int e^x (\sec^2 x + \tan x)\, dx$

$= \int e^x \sec^2 x\, dx + \int \underset{\text{II}}{e^x} \underset{\text{I}}{\tan x}\, dx$

$= \int e^x \sec^2 x\, dx + \tan x (e^x) - \int e^x \sec^2 x\, dx$

$= e^x \tan x + C$

18. Let $I = \int \sin^{-1} 2x\, dx$

$= \int \underset{\text{II}}{1} \cdot \underset{\text{I}}{\sin^{-1} 2x}\, dx$

$= \sin^{-1} 2x \cdot x - \int x \cdot \frac{1}{\sqrt{1 - 4x^2}} (2)\, dx$

$= x \sin^{-1} 2x - \int \frac{2x}{\sqrt{1 - 4x^2}} dx$

$= x \sin^{-1} 2x + \frac{1}{4} \int \frac{-8x}{\sqrt{1 - 4x^2}} dx$

Let $I_1 = \int \frac{-8x}{\sqrt{1 - 4x^2}} dx$

Let $1 - 4x^2 = t$

$\Rightarrow -8x\, dx = dt$

Then, $I_1 = \int \frac{dt}{\sqrt{t}} = 2\sqrt{t} = 2\sqrt{1 - 4x^2}$

$\therefore \quad I = x \sin^{-1} 2x + \frac{1}{4} (2\sqrt{1 - 4x^2}) + C$

$= x \sin^{-1} 2x + \frac{1}{2} \sqrt{1 - 4x^2} + C$

19. Let $I = \int_0^{\pi/2} \sin^2 x\, dx = \int_0^{\pi/2} \left(\frac{1 - \cos 2x}{2} \right) dx$

$= \left[\frac{1}{2} \{ \int 1 dx - \int \cos 2x\, dx \} \right]_0^{\pi/2}$

$= \left[\frac{1}{2} \left\{ x - \frac{\sin 2x}{2} \right\} \right]_0^{\pi/2} = \left[\frac{x}{2} - \frac{\sin 2x}{4} \right]_0^{\pi/2}$

$= \frac{\pi}{4} - \frac{\sin \pi}{4} - \{0 - \sin 0\} = \frac{\pi}{4} - 0 - 0 = \frac{\pi}{4}$

20. Let $I = \int_0^3 \frac{dx}{9 + x^2} \Rightarrow I = \int_0^3 \frac{dx}{x^2 + (3)^2}$

$\Rightarrow \quad I = \left[\frac{1}{3} \tan^{-1} \frac{x}{3} \right]_0^3 \qquad \left[\because \int \frac{dx}{x^2 + a^2} = \frac{1}{a} \tan^{-1} \frac{x}{a} \right]$

$\Rightarrow \quad I = \frac{1}{3} \left[\tan^{-1} \left(\frac{3}{3} \right) - \tan^{-1} (0) \right]$

$= \frac{1}{3} [\tan^{-1} (1) - 0] = \frac{1}{3} \left(\frac{\pi}{4} \right) = \frac{\pi}{12}$

21. Let $I = \int_0^1 x e^{x^2} dx$

Now, put $x^2 = t \Rightarrow 2x\, dx = dt$

Upper limit When $x = 1$, then $t = 1^2 = 1$

Lower limit When $x = 0$, then $t = 0$

$\therefore \quad I = \int_0^1 e^t \frac{dt}{2} = \frac{1}{2} [e^t]_0^1 = \frac{1}{2} [e^1 - e^0] = \frac{1}{2} (e - 1)$

22. Let $I = \int_{-1}^2 \frac{|x|}{x} dx$

$= \int_{-1}^0 \frac{|x|}{x} dx + \int_0^2 \frac{|x|}{x} dx$

$= \int_{-1}^0 -\frac{x}{x} dx + \int_0^2 \frac{x}{x} dx \qquad \left[\because |x| = \begin{cases} -x, & x < 0 \\ x, & x \geq 0 \end{cases} \right]$

$= -\int_{-1}^0 dx + \int_0^2 dx = -[x]_{-1}^0 + [x]_0^2$

$= -[0 - (-1)] + [2 - 0] = -1 + 2 = 1$

23. Let $I = \int \frac{x^3 - x^2 + x - 1}{x - 1} dx$

$= \int \frac{x^2 (x - 1) + 1(x - 1)}{(x - 1)} dx = \int \frac{(x - 1)(x^2 + 1)}{(x - 1)} dx$

$= \int (x^2 + 1)\, dx = \frac{x^3}{3} + x + C$

24. Let $I = \int \frac{3 - 5\sin x}{\cos^2 x} dx$

$= \int \left(\frac{3}{\cos^2 x} - \frac{5\sin x}{\cos^2 x} \right) dx$

$= 3\int \sec^2 x\, dx - 5\int \sec x \tan x\, dx$

$= 3\tan x - 5\sec x + C$

25. Let $I=\int \frac{dx}{\cos x\sqrt{\cos 2x}}$

$=\int \frac{dx}{\cos x\sqrt{1-2\sin^2 x}}$ $[\because \cos 2\theta=1-2\sin^2\theta]$

$=\int \frac{\sec^2 x\,dx}{\sqrt{\frac{1}{\cos^2 x}-\frac{2\sin^2 x}{\cos^2 x}}}$

[dividing numerator and denominator by $\cos^2 x$]

$=\int \frac{\sec^2 x dx}{\sqrt{\sec^2 x-2\tan^2 x}}$

$=\int \frac{\sec^2 x dx}{\sqrt{1+\tan^2 x-2\tan^2 x}}$ $[\because 1+\tan^2\theta=\sec^2\theta]$

$=\int \frac{\sec^2 x dx}{\sqrt{1-\tan^2 x}}$

Again, let $\tan x=t$

$\Rightarrow \quad \sec^2 x dx=dt$

$\therefore \quad I=\int \frac{dt}{\sqrt{1-t^2}}$

$=\sin^{-1}t+C$ $\left[\because \int \frac{dx}{\sqrt{1-x^2}}=\sin^{-1}x+C\right]$

$=\sin^{-1}(\tan x)+C$ $[\because t=\tan x]$

26. Let $I=\int \frac{x^3}{(x+2)^4}dx$

Put $x+2=t \Rightarrow dx=dt$ and $x=t-2$

$\therefore \quad I=\int \frac{(t-2)^3}{t^4}dt$

$=\int \frac{t^3-6t^2+12t-8}{t^4}dt$

$[\because (a-b)^3=a^3-b^3-3a^2b+3ab^2]$

$=\int\left(\frac{1}{t}-\frac{6}{t^2}+\frac{12}{t^3}-\frac{8}{t^4}\right)dt$

$=\log t+\frac{6}{t}-\frac{6}{t^2}+\frac{8}{3t^3}+C$

$=\log|x+2|+\frac{6}{x+2}-\frac{6}{(x+2)^2}+\frac{8}{3(x+2)^3}+C$

27. Let $I=\int \frac{3x+1}{(3x^2+2x+1)^3}dx$

Put $3x^2+2x+1=t$

$\Rightarrow \quad (6x+2)\,dx=dt$

$\Rightarrow \quad (3x+1)\,dx=\frac{1}{2}dt$

$\therefore \quad I=\frac{1}{2}\int\frac{dt}{t^3}=\frac{1}{2}\int t^{-3}dt$

$=\frac{1}{2}\frac{t^{-2}}{(-2)}+C=\frac{-1}{4t^2}+C$

$=\frac{-1}{4(3x^2+2x+1)^2}+C$

28. Let $I=\int \cos 6x\sqrt{1+\sin 6x}\,dx$

Put $1+\sin 6x=t \Rightarrow \quad 6\cos 6x\,dx=dt$

$\Rightarrow \cos 6x\,dx=\frac{dt}{6}$

$\therefore \quad I=\frac{1}{6}\int\sqrt{t}\,dt=\frac{1}{6}\frac{t^{1/2+1}}{\left(\frac{1}{2}+1\right)}+C$

$=\frac{1}{6}\cdot\frac{t^{3/2}}{\frac{3}{2}}+C$

$=\frac{1}{6}\times\frac{2}{3}t^{3/2}+C$

$=\frac{1}{9}(1+\sin 6x)^{3/2}+C$

29. Let $I=\int \sin 5x\cos 3x dx$

$=\frac{1}{2}\int 2\sin 5x\cos 3x dx$

[multiply numerator and denominator by 2]

$=\frac{1}{2}[\int(\sin(5x+3x)+\sin(5x-3x))dx]$

$=\frac{1}{2}[(\sin 8x+\sin 2x)dx]$

$=\frac{1}{2}\left[-\frac{1}{8}\cos 8x-\frac{1}{2}\cos 2x\right]+C$

30. Let $I=\int \frac{dx}{\sin^2 x\cos^2 x}$

On dividing the numerator and denominator by $\cos^4 x$, we get

$I=\int \frac{\sec^2 x\cdot\sec^2 x}{\tan^2 x}dx$

$\Rightarrow \quad I=\int \frac{(1+\tan^2 x)\cdot\sec^2 x}{\tan^2 x}dx$

Put $\tan x=t \Rightarrow \sec^2 x dx=dt$

$\therefore \quad I=\int \frac{1+t^2}{t^2}dt$

$=\int 1dt+\int\frac{1}{t^2}dt$

$\Rightarrow \quad I=t-\frac{1}{t}+C$

$\Rightarrow \quad I=\tan x-\cot x+C$ $[\because t=\tan x]$

31. Let $I=\int \cos^{-1}(\sin x)\,dx$

$=\int \cos^{-1}\left[\cos\left(\frac{\pi}{2}-x\right)\right]dx$

$=\int\left(\frac{\pi}{2}-x\right)dx$ $[\because \cos^{-1}(\cos\theta)=\theta]$

$=\frac{\pi}{2}\int dx-\int x\,dx$

$=\frac{\pi}{2}x-\frac{x^2}{2}+C$

32. Let $I=\int \frac{dx}{\sqrt{x^2-4x}}$

$$=\int \frac{dx}{\sqrt{x^2-2\cdot 2\cdot x+2^2-2^2}}=\int \frac{dx}{\sqrt{(x-2)^2-2^2}}$$

$$=\log|(x-2)+\sqrt{(x-2)^2-2^2}|+C$$

$$\left[\because \int \frac{dx}{\sqrt{x^2-a^2}}=\log|x+\sqrt{x^2-a^2}|+C\right]$$

$$=\log|(x-2)+\sqrt{x^2-4x}|+C$$

33. Let $I=\int \frac{\tan^2 x\cdot \sec^2 x}{1-\tan^6 x}dx$

Let $\tan^3 x=t$

$\Rightarrow 3\tan^2 x\sec^2 x\,dx=dt \Rightarrow \tan^2 x\sec^2 dx=\frac{1}{3}dt$

$$\therefore \quad I=\frac{1}{3}\int \frac{dt}{1-t^2}=\frac{1}{3}\left[\frac{1}{2}\log\left|\frac{1+t}{1-t}\right|+C\right]$$

$$\left[\because \int \frac{dx}{a^2-x^2}=\frac{1}{2a}\log\left|\frac{a+x}{a-x}\right|+C\right]$$

$$=\frac{1}{6}\log\left|\frac{1+t}{1-t}\right|+C$$

Now, put the value of t, we get

$$I=\frac{1}{6}\log\left|\frac{1+\tan^3 x}{1-\tan^3 x}\right|+C \qquad [\because \tan^3 x=t]$$

34. Let $I=\int \frac{\cos x}{(1+\sin x)(2+\sin x)}dx$

Put $\sin x=t \Rightarrow \cos x\,dx=dt$

$$\therefore\ I=\int \frac{dt}{(1+t)(2+t)}=\int\left[\frac{A}{1+t}+\frac{B}{2+t}\right]dt \qquad \text{...(i)}$$

$$\therefore \quad \frac{1}{(1+t)(2+t)}=\frac{A(2+t)+B(1+t)}{(1+t)(2+t)}$$

$\Rightarrow \quad 1=2A+tA+B+Bt \Rightarrow 1=1(2A+B)+t(A+B)$

On comparing the coefficients of t and constant terms from both sides, we get

$$2A+B=1 \text{ and } A+B=0$$

$$\Rightarrow \quad A=1 \text{ and } B=-1$$

$$\therefore\ I=\int\left(\frac{1}{1+t}-\frac{1}{2+t}\right)dt$$

$$=\int \frac{1}{(1+t)}dt-\int \frac{1}{(2+t)}dt$$

$$=\log|1+t|-\log|2+t|+C$$

$$=\log\left|\frac{1+t}{2+t}\right|+C=\log\left|\frac{1+\sin x}{2+\sin x}\right|+C \qquad [\because t=\sin x]$$

35. Let $I=\int \frac{4}{(x-2)(x^2+4)}dx$

Again, let $\frac{4}{(x-2)(x^2+4)}=\frac{A}{(x-2)}+\frac{Bx+C}{x^2+4}$

$\Rightarrow \quad 4=A(x^2+4)+(Bx+C)(x-2)$

$\Rightarrow \quad 4=x^2(A+B)+x(-2B+C)+4A-2C$

On equating the coefficients of x^2, x and constant terms from both sides, we get

$$A+B=0 \qquad \text{...(i)}$$

$$-2B+C=0 \qquad \text{...(ii)}$$

and $\quad 4A-2C=4 \qquad$ ...(iii)

On solving Eqs. (i), (ii) and (iii), we get

$$A=\frac{1}{2}, B=-\frac{1}{2} \text{ and } C=-1$$

$$\therefore \quad I=\int \frac{4}{(x-2)(x^2+4)}dx$$

$$=\int \frac{1/2}{(x-2)}dx+\int \frac{\frac{-1}{2}x-1}{x^2+4}dx$$

$$=\frac{1}{2}\int \frac{dx}{(x-2)}-\int \frac{x+2}{2(x^2+4)}dx$$

$$=\frac{1}{2}\log|x-2|-\frac{1}{4}\log|x^2+4|-\frac{1}{2}\tan^{-1}\left(\frac{x}{2}\right)+C$$

36. Let $I=\int \underset{\text{II}}{x^3}\ \underset{\text{I}}{\log 2x}\,dx$

$$=\log 2x\int x^3dx-\int\left\{\frac{d}{dx}(\log 2x)\int x^3dx\right\}dx$$

$$=\log 2x\cdot\frac{x^4}{4}-\int \frac{1}{2x}\cdot 2\cdot\frac{x^4}{4}dx$$

$$=\frac{1}{4}x^4\log 2x-\frac{1}{4}\int x^3dx$$

$$=\frac{1}{4}x^4\log 2x-\frac{1}{16}x^4+C$$

37. Let $I=\int_0^{\pi/2}\frac{x}{\cos x+\sin x}dx \qquad$ ...(i)

$$\Rightarrow\ I=\int_0^{\pi/2}\frac{\frac{\pi}{2}-x}{\cos\left(\frac{\pi}{2}-x\right)+\sin\left(\frac{\pi}{2}-x\right)}dx$$

$$\Rightarrow\ I=\int_0^{\pi/2}\frac{\frac{\pi}{2}-x}{\sin x+\cos x}dx \qquad \text{...(ii)}$$

On adding Eqs. (i) and (ii), we get

$$2I=\int_0^{\pi/2}\frac{\frac{\pi}{2}-x+x}{\sin x+\cos x}dx$$

$$\Rightarrow 2I=\frac{\pi}{2}\int_0^{\pi/2}\frac{1}{\sin x+\cos x}dx$$

$$\Rightarrow \quad I=\frac{\pi}{4}\int_0^{\pi/2}\frac{1}{\sin x+\cos x}dx$$

$$\Rightarrow \quad I=\frac{\pi}{4}\times\frac{1}{\sqrt{2}}\int_0^{\pi/2}\frac{1}{\sin x\cos\frac{\pi}{4}+\sin\frac{\pi}{4}\cos x}$$

$$\Rightarrow \quad I=\frac{\pi}{4\sqrt{2}}\int_0^{\pi/2}\frac{1}{\sin\left(x+\frac{\pi}{4}\right)}dx$$

$$\Rightarrow \quad I=\frac{\pi}{4\sqrt{2}}\int_0^{\pi/2}\operatorname{cosec}\left(x+\frac{\pi}{4}\right)dx$$

$$=\frac{\pi}{4\sqrt{2}}\left[\ln\left|\operatorname{cosec}\left(x+\frac{\pi}{4}\right)-\cot\left(x+\frac{\pi}{4}\right)\right|\right]_0^{\pi/2}$$

$$\Rightarrow \quad I=\frac{\pi}{4\sqrt{2}}[\ln(\sqrt{2}+1)-\ln(\sqrt{2}-1)]$$

$$\Rightarrow \quad I=\frac{\pi}{4\sqrt{2}}\ln\left(\frac{\sqrt{2}+1}{\sqrt{2}-1}\right)$$

38. Let $I=\int_0^2\frac{1}{\sqrt{x}+\sqrt{1+x}}dx$

$$=\int_0^2\frac{\sqrt{1+x}-\sqrt{x}}{(\sqrt{1+x}+\sqrt{x})(\sqrt{1+x}-\sqrt{x})}dx$$

$$=\int_0^2(\sqrt{1+x}-\sqrt{x})\,dx$$

$$=\left[\frac{2}{3}(1+x)^{3/2}-\frac{2}{3}x^{3/2}\right]_0^2$$

$$=\frac{2}{3}(3^{3/2}-1)-\frac{2}{3}(2)^{3/2}$$

$$=\frac{2}{3}\times 3\sqrt{3}-\frac{2}{3}-\frac{2}{3}\times 2\sqrt{2}$$

$$=2\sqrt{3}-\frac{2}{3}-\frac{4}{3}\sqrt{2}$$

39. Let $I=\int_1^4\frac{1}{\sqrt{2x+1}-\sqrt{2x-1}}dx$

$$I=\int_1^4\frac{\sqrt{2x+1}+\sqrt{2x-1}}{(\sqrt{2x+1}-\sqrt{2x-1})(\sqrt{2x+1}+\sqrt{2x-1})}dx$$

$$=\int_1^4\frac{\sqrt{2x+1}+\sqrt{2x-1}}{(2x+1)-(2x-1)}dx$$

$$=\frac{1}{2}\int_1^4\{(2x+1)^{1/2}+(2x-1)^{1/2}\}dx$$

$$=\frac{1}{2}[\int_1^4(2x+1)^{1/2}dx+\int_1^4(2x-1)^{1/2}dx]$$

$$=\frac{1}{2}\left[\frac{1}{2}\left(\frac{(2x+1)^{3/2}}{3/2}\right)_1^4+\frac{1}{2}\left(\frac{(2x-1)^{3/2}}{3/2}\right)_1^4\right]$$

$$=\frac{1}{2}\times\frac{1}{2}\times\frac{2}{3}[\{(2x+1)^{3/2}\}_1^4+\{(2x-1)^{3/2}\}_1^4]$$

$$=\frac{1}{6}[(9)^{3/2}-(3)^{3/2}+(7)^{3/2}-(1)^{3/2}]$$

$$=\frac{1}{6}[27-3^{3/2}+7^{3/2}-1]$$

$$=\frac{1}{6}(26-3^{3/2}+7^{3/2})$$

40. Let $I=\int_0^{\pi/4}\sqrt{1-\sin 2x}\,dx$

$$=\int_0^{\pi/4}\sqrt{\cos^2 x+\sin^2 x-2\sin x\cos x}\,dx$$

$$=\int_0^{\pi/4}\sqrt{(\cos x-\sin x)^2}\,dx=\int_0^{\pi/4}|\cos x-\sin x|\,dx$$

$$=\int_0^{\pi/4}(\cos x-\sin x)\,dx=[\sin x+\cos x]_0^{\pi/4}$$

$$=\left(\sin\frac{\pi}{4}+\cos\frac{\pi}{4}\right)-(\sin 0+\cos 0)$$

$$=\left(\frac{1}{\sqrt{2}}+\frac{1}{\sqrt{2}}\right)-(0+1)=\sqrt{2}-1$$

41. Let $I=\int_0^1\frac{2x+3}{5x^2+1}dx=\int_0^1\frac{2x}{5x^2+1}dx+\int_0^1\frac{3}{5x^2+1}dx$

$$=\frac{1}{5}\int_0^1\frac{10x}{5x^2+1}dx+\frac{3}{5}\int_0^1\frac{1}{x^2+\left(\frac{1}{\sqrt{5}}\right)^2}dx$$

$$=\frac{1}{5}[\log|5x^2+1|]_0^1+\frac{3}{5}\frac{1}{\left(\frac{1}{\sqrt{5}}\right)}\left[\tan^{-1}\frac{x}{\left(\frac{1}{\sqrt{5}}\right)}\right]_0^1$$

$$=\frac{1}{5}(\log 6-\log 1)+\frac{3}{\sqrt{5}}[\tan^{-1}\sqrt{5}-\tan^{-1}0]$$

$$=\frac{1}{5}\log 6+\frac{3}{\sqrt{5}}\tan^{-1}\sqrt{5}$$

42. Let $I=\int_0^1 \underset{\text{II}}{x}\,\underset{\text{I}}{\tan^{-1}x}\,dx$

$$=\left[\tan^{-1}x\cdot\frac{x^2}{2}\right]_0^1-\int_0^1\frac{1}{1+x^2}\cdot\frac{x^2}{2}dx$$

[using integration by parts]

$$=\left[\frac{x^2}{2}\cdot\tan^{-1}x\right]_0^1-\frac{1}{2}\int_0^1\frac{x^2+1-1}{1+x^2}dx$$

$$=\left[\frac{x^2}{2}\tan^{-1}x\right]_0^1-\frac{1}{2}\int_0^1dx+\frac{1}{2}\int_0^1\frac{dx}{1+x^2}$$

$$=\left[\frac{1}{2}\tan^{-1}(1)-0\right]-\frac{1}{2}(1-0)+\frac{1}{2}[\tan^{-1}x]_0^1$$

$$=\frac{1}{2}\cdot\frac{\pi}{4}-\frac{1}{2}+\frac{1}{2}[\tan^{-1}(1)-\tan^{-1}(0)]$$

$$=\frac{\pi}{8}-\frac{1}{2}+\frac{1}{2}\frac{\pi}{4}=\frac{\pi}{4}-\frac{1}{2}$$

43. Let $I=\int_{\pi/4}^{\pi/2}e^{2x}\left(\frac{1-\sin 2x}{1-\cos 2x}\right)dx$

Now, $\int e^{2x}\left(\frac{1-\sin 2x}{1-\cos 2x}\right)dx=\int e^{2x}\left(\frac{1-2\sin x\cos x}{2\sin^2 x}\right)dx$

$$=\frac{1}{2}\int e^{2x}\left(\frac{1}{\sin^2 x}-\frac{2\sin x\cos x}{\sin^2 x}\right)dx$$

$$=\frac{1}{2}\int e^{2x}(\operatorname{cosec}^2 x-2\cot x)\,dx$$

$$= \frac{1}{2}\int e^{2x}\text{cosec}^2 x\,dx - \int e^{2x}\cot x\,dx$$

$$= \frac{1}{2}\left[e^{2x}\int \text{cosec}^2 x\,dx - \int\left(\frac{d}{dx}(e^{2x})\int \text{cosec}^2 x\,dx\right)dx\right] - \int e^{2x}\cot x\,dx$$

$$= \frac{1}{2}[e^{2x}(-\cot x) - \int 2e^{2x}(-\cot x)\,dx] - \int e^{2x}\cot x\,dx$$

$$= \frac{1}{2}e^{2x}(-\cot x) + \int e^{2x}\cot x\,dx - \int e^{2x}\cot x\,dx$$

$$= -\frac{1}{2}e^{2x}\cot x$$

$$\therefore\ I = -\frac{1}{2}(e^{2x}\cot x)_{\pi/4}^{\pi/2}$$

$$= -\frac{1}{2}\left[e^{\pi}\cot\frac{\pi}{2} - e^{\pi/2}\cot\frac{\pi}{4}\right]$$

$$= -\frac{1}{2}(0 - e^{\pi/2}) = \frac{1}{2}e^{\pi/2}$$

44. Let $I = \int_0^1 \frac{\tan^{-1}x}{1+x^2}dx$

Again, let $\tan^{-1}x = t$

$$\Rightarrow \quad \frac{dx}{1+x^2} = dt$$

Upper limit When $x = 1$, then $t = \tan^{-1}(1) = \frac{\pi}{4}$

Lower limit When $x = 0$, then $t = \tan^{-1}(0) = 0$

Now, $I = \int_0^{\frac{\pi}{4}} t\,dt$

$$\Rightarrow \quad I = \left[\frac{t^2}{2}\right]_0^{\frac{\pi}{4}}$$

$$\Rightarrow \quad I = \frac{1}{2}\left[\frac{\pi}{4}\right]^2 - 0$$

$$\Rightarrow \quad I = \frac{\pi^2}{32}$$

45. Let $I = \int_{-4}^{0} |x+2|dx$

Again let $f(x) = |x+2| = \begin{cases} -(x+2), & x < -2 \\ (x+2), & x \geq -2 \end{cases}$

$$\therefore \quad I = \int_{-4}^{-2} -(x+2)\,dx + \int_{-2}^{0}(x+2)\,dx$$

$$= -\left[\frac{x^2}{2} + 2x\right]_{-4}^{-2} + \left[\frac{x^2}{2} + 2x\right]_{-2}^{0}$$

$$= -\left[\frac{4}{2} - 4 - \left(\frac{16}{2} - 8\right)\right] + \left[0 + 0 - \left(\frac{4}{2} - 4\right)\right]$$

$$= -[-2 - 0] + [2]$$

$$= 2 + 2 = 4$$

46. Let $I = \int_0^{\pi/4} \frac{\sin 2x}{\sin^4 x + \cos^4 x}dx$

$$= \int_0^{\pi/4} \frac{2\sin x\cos x}{\sin^4 x + \cos^4 x}dx$$

$$= \int_0^{\pi/4} \frac{2\tan x\sec^2 x}{\tan^4 x + 1}dx$$

Put $\tan^2 x = t \Rightarrow 2\tan x\sec^2 x\,dx = dt$

Lower limit When $x = 0 \Rightarrow t = \tan^2 0 = 0$

Upper limit When $x = \pi/4 \Rightarrow t = \tan^2 \pi/4 = 1$

Now, $I = \int_0^1 \frac{dt}{t^2+1} = [\tan^{-1}t]_0^1 = \tan^{-1}1 - \tan^{-1}0$

$$= \frac{\pi}{4} - 0 = \frac{\pi}{4}$$

47. Let $I = \int_{-1}^{2} |x^3 - x|dx$

$$= \int_{-1}^{2} |x(x-1)(x+1)|dx$$

The sign of $(x^3 - x)$ for different values of x are shown as below

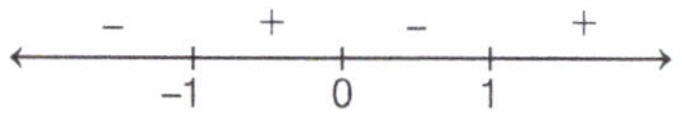

$$\therefore |x^3 - x| = \begin{cases} x^3 - x, & -1 < x \leq 0 \\ -(x^3 - x), & 0 < x \leq 1 \\ x^3 - x, & 1 < x \leq 2 \end{cases}$$

$$\therefore \quad I = \int_{-1}^{0} |x^3 - x|dx + \int_0^1 |x^3 - x|dx + \int_1^2 |x^3 - x|dx$$

$$= \int_{-1}^{0}(x^3 - x)\,dx - \int_0^1 (x^3 - x)\,dx + \int_1^2 (x^3 - x)\,dx$$

$$= \left[\frac{x^4}{4} - \frac{x^2}{2}\right]_{-1}^{0} - \left[\frac{x^4}{4} - \frac{x^2}{2}\right]_0^1 + \left[\frac{x^4}{4} - \frac{x^2}{2}\right]_1^2$$

$$= -\left(\frac{1}{4} - \frac{1}{2}\right) - \left(\frac{1}{4} - \frac{1}{2}\right) + \left(\frac{16}{4} - \frac{4}{2}\right) - \left(\frac{1}{4} - \frac{1}{2}\right)$$

$$= \frac{3}{4} + 4 - 2$$

$$= \frac{11}{4}$$

48. Let $I = \int_{-\pi/3}^{\pi/3} \frac{1}{1+e^{\sin x}}dx$ ...(i)

$$\Rightarrow \quad I = \int_{-\pi/3}^{\pi/3} \frac{1}{1+e^{\sin\left(\frac{\pi}{3} - \frac{\pi}{3} - x\right)}}dx$$

$$\left[\because \int_a^b f(x)\,dx = \int_a^b f(a+b-x)\,dx\right]$$

$$= \int_{-\pi/3}^{\pi/3} \frac{1}{1+e^{\sin(-x)}}dx$$

$$= \int_{-\pi/3}^{\pi/3} \frac{1}{1+e^{-\sin x}}dx$$

$$= \int_{-\pi/3}^{\pi/3} \frac{e^{\sin x}}{e^{\sin x}+1}dx \quad \text{...(ii)}$$

On adding Eqs. (i) and (ii), we get

$$2I=\int_{-\pi/3}^{\pi/3}\frac{e^{\sin x}+1}{e^{\sin x}+1}dx$$

$$=\int_{-\pi/3}^{\pi/3}1dx=[x]_{-\pi/3}^{\pi/3}$$

$$=\frac{\pi}{3}-\left(-\frac{\pi}{3}\right)=\frac{2\pi}{3}$$

$$\therefore\quad I=\frac{\pi}{3}$$

49. Let $I=\int_0^{\pi/2}\frac{\sin^3 x}{\sin^3 x+\cos^3 x}dx$ ...(i)

$$\Rightarrow I=\int_0^{\pi/2}\frac{\sin^3\left(\frac{\pi}{2}-x\right)}{\sin^3\left(\frac{\pi}{2}-x\right)+\cos^3\left(\frac{\pi}{2}-x\right)}dx$$

$$\left[\because \int_0^a f(x)\,dx=\int_0^a f(a-x)\,dx\right]$$

$$\Rightarrow I=\int_0^{\pi/2}\frac{\cos^3 x}{\cos^3 x+\sin^3 x}dx \quad \text{...(ii)}$$

On adding Eqs. (i) and (ii), we get

$$2I=\int_0^{\pi/2}\frac{\sin^3 x+\cos^3 x}{\cos^3 x+\sin^3 x}dx$$

$$\Rightarrow \quad 2I=\int_0^{\pi/2}1dx=[x]_0^{\pi/2}=\frac{\pi}{2}-0$$

$$\Rightarrow \quad I=\frac{\pi}{4}$$

50. Let $I=\int_0^{\pi/2}\frac{\tan^7 x}{\cot^7 x+\tan^7 x}dx$ ...(i)

$$\Rightarrow \quad I=\int_0^{\pi/2}\frac{\tan^7(\pi/2-x)}{\cot^7(\pi/2-x)+\tan^7(\pi/2-x)}dx$$

$$\left[\because \int_0^a f(x)\,dx=\int_0^a f(a-x)\,dx\right]$$

$$\Rightarrow \quad I=\int_0^{\pi/2}\frac{\cot^7 x}{\tan^7 x+\cot^7 x}dx \quad \text{...(ii)}$$

$$\left[\because \tan\left(\frac{\pi}{2}-x\right)=\cot x \text{ and } \cot\left(\frac{\pi}{2}-x\right)=\tan x\right]$$

On adding Eqs. (i) and (ii), we get

$$2I=\int_0^{\pi/2}\frac{\tan^7 x+\cot^7 x}{\tan^7 x+\cot^7 x}dx$$

$$=\int_0^{\pi/2}1\,dx=[x]_0^{\pi/2}=\frac{\pi}{2}-0=\frac{\pi}{2}$$

$$\Rightarrow \quad I=\frac{\pi}{4}$$

51. Let $I=\int \cos 2x\cos 4x\cos 6x\,dx$

$$=\frac{1}{2}\int(2\cos 4x\cos 2x)\cos 6x\,dx$$

$$=\frac{1}{2}\int[\cos(4x+2x)+\cos(4x-2x)]\cos 6x\,dx$$

$$[\because 2\cos A\cos B=\cos(A+B)+\cos(A-B)]$$

$$=\frac{1}{2}\int(\cos 6x+\cos 2x)\cos 6x\,dx$$

$$=\frac{1}{2}\int(\cos^2 6x+\cos 6x\cos 2x)dx$$

$$=\frac{1}{4}\int(2\cos^2 6x+2\cos 6x\cos 2x)dx$$

$$=\frac{1}{4}\int(1+\cos 12x+\cos 8x+\cos 4x)dx$$

$$\left[\because \cos^2\theta=\frac{1+\cos 2\theta}{2} \text{ and } 2\cos x\cos y=\cos(x+y)+\cos(x-y)\right]$$

$$=\frac{1}{4}\left(x+\frac{\sin 12x}{12}+\frac{\sin 8x}{8}+\frac{\sin 4x}{4}\right)+C$$

$$\left[\because \int\cos ax\,dx=\frac{1}{a}\sin ax\right]$$

$$=\frac{x}{4}+\frac{1}{48}\sin 12x+\frac{1}{32}\sin 8x+\frac{1}{16}\sin 4x+C$$

52. Let $I=\int\frac{\sin^6 x+\cos^6 x}{\sin^2 x\cos^2 x}dx$

$$\Rightarrow \quad I=\int\frac{(\sin^2 x)^3+(\cos^2 x)^3}{\sin^2 x\cos^2 x}dx$$

$$=\int\frac{(\sin^2 x+\cos^2 x)^3-3\sin^2 x\cos^2 x(\sin^2 x+\cos^2 x)}{\sin^2 x\cos^2 x}dx$$

$$[\because a^3+b^3=(a+b)^3-3ab(a+b)]$$

$$=\int\frac{(1)^3-3\sin^2 x\cos^2 x}{\sin^2 x\cos^2 x}dx \quad [\because \sin^2\theta+\cos^2\theta=1]$$

$$=\int\frac{1}{\sin^2 x\cos^2 x}dx-3\int\frac{\sin^2 x\cos^2 x}{\sin^2 x\cos^2 x}dx$$

$$=\int\frac{\sin^2 x+\cos^2 x}{\sin^2 x\cos^2 x}dx-3\int 1dx \quad [\because 1=\sin^2\theta+\cos^2\theta]$$

$$=\int\left[\frac{\sin^2 x}{\sin^2 x\cos^2 x}+\frac{\cos^2 x}{\sin^2 x\cos^2 x}\right]dx-3\int 1dx$$

$$=\int(\sec^2 x+\operatorname{cosec}^2 x)\,dx-3\int 1dx$$

$$=\int\sec^2 x\,dx+\int\operatorname{cosec}^2 x\,dx-3\int 1dx$$

$$=\tan x-\cot x-3x+C$$

53. Let $I=\int\frac{dx}{a^2\sin^2 x+b^2\cos^2 x}$

On dividing numerator and denominator by $\cos^2 x$, we get

$$I=\int\frac{\left(\frac{1}{\cos^2 x}\right)}{\left(\frac{a^2\sin^2 x}{\cos^2 x}+\frac{b^2\cos^2 x}{\cos^2 x}\right)}dx$$

$$=\int\frac{\sec^2 x}{a^2\tan^2 x+b^2}dx=\int\frac{\sec^2 x}{(a\tan x)^2+b^2}dx$$

Now, put $a\tan x = t$

$\Rightarrow \quad a\sec^2 x\,dx = dt$

$\Rightarrow \quad \sec^2 x\,dx = \dfrac{dt}{a}$

$\therefore \quad I = \dfrac{1}{a}\displaystyle\int \dfrac{dt}{t^2+b^2}$

$= \dfrac{1}{a}\cdot\dfrac{1}{b}\tan^{-1}\dfrac{t}{b} + C \qquad \left[\because \displaystyle\int \dfrac{dx}{x^2+a^2} = \dfrac{1}{a}\tan^{-1}\dfrac{x}{a} + C\right]$

$= \dfrac{1}{ab}\tan^{-1}\dfrac{t}{b} + C$

$= \dfrac{1}{ab}\tan^{-1}\left(\dfrac{a\tan x}{b}\right) + C \qquad [\because t = a\tan x]$

54. Let $I = \displaystyle\int \dfrac{x^2+x+1}{(x+2)(x^2+1)}dx$

By partial fraction,

$$\frac{x^2+x+1}{(x^2+1)(x+2)} = \frac{A}{(x+2)} + \frac{Bx+C}{x^2+1}$$

$\Rightarrow \quad x^2+x+1 = A(x^2+1) + (Bx+C)(x+2)$

On putting $x = -2$,

$4-2+1 = A(5)+0 \Rightarrow 5A = 3 \Rightarrow A = \dfrac{3}{5}$

On putting $x = 0$,

$0+0+1 = A(0+1) + (0+C)(0+2)$

$\Rightarrow 1 = A+2C \Rightarrow 1 = \dfrac{3}{5}+2C \Rightarrow 2C = \dfrac{2}{5} \Rightarrow C = \dfrac{1}{5}$

and on putting $x = 1$,

$1+1+1 = 2A + (B+C)(3)$

$\Rightarrow \quad 3 = 2A + 3(B+C)$

$\Rightarrow \quad 3 = 2\left(\dfrac{3}{5}\right) + 3\left(B+\dfrac{1}{5}\right)$

$\Rightarrow \quad 3 - \dfrac{6}{5} = 3\left(B+\dfrac{1}{5}\right)$

$\Rightarrow \quad \dfrac{9}{5} = 3\left(B+\dfrac{1}{5}\right) \Rightarrow \dfrac{3}{5} - \dfrac{1}{5} = B \Rightarrow B = \dfrac{2}{5}$

Thus, $\dfrac{x^2+x+1}{(x+2)(x^2+1)} = \dfrac{3}{5(x+2)} + \dfrac{\left(\frac{2}{5}x+\frac{1}{5}\right)}{(x^2+1)}$

Now, $\displaystyle\int \dfrac{x^2+x+1}{(x+2)(x^2+1)}dx$

$= \displaystyle\int \dfrac{3}{5(x+2)}dx + \dfrac{1}{5}\int \dfrac{2x}{x^2+1}dx + \dfrac{1}{5}\int \dfrac{dx}{x^2+1}$

$= \dfrac{3}{5}\log|x+2| + \dfrac{1}{5}\log|x^2+1| + \dfrac{1}{5}\tan^{-1}x + C$

55. Let $I = \displaystyle\int \dfrac{x}{(x^2+1)(x-1)}dx$

Here, integrand $= \dfrac{x}{(x^2+1)(x-1)} = \dfrac{P(x)}{Q(x)}$ (say)

where degree of $P(x)$ is less than degree of $Q(x)$, so it is a proper fraction.

Now, let $\dfrac{x}{(x^2+1)(x-1)} = \dfrac{A}{(x-1)} + \dfrac{Bx+C}{x^2+1}$ ...(i)

On multiplying both sides of Eq. (i) by $(x^2+1)(x-1)$, we get

$$x = A(x^2+1) + (Bx+C)(x-1) \quad \text{...(ii)}$$

On putting $x = 1$ in Eq. (ii), we get

$1 = A(1+1) + (B+C)(0) \Rightarrow 1 = 2A \Rightarrow A = \dfrac{1}{2}$

On equating the coefficients of x^2 and x from both sides of Eq. (ii), we get

$0 = A+B$ and $1 = -B+C$

$\Rightarrow \quad 0 = \dfrac{1}{2} + B \Rightarrow B = -\dfrac{1}{2} \qquad \left[\because A = \dfrac{1}{2}\right]$

and $\quad 1 = -\left(-\dfrac{1}{2}\right) + C \Rightarrow C = 1 - \dfrac{1}{2} = \dfrac{1}{2}$

From Eq. (i), we get

$$\frac{x}{(x^2+1)(x-1)} = \frac{1}{2(x-1)} + \frac{-\frac{1}{2}x+\frac{1}{2}}{x^2+1} \quad \text{...(iii)}$$

Now, on putting partial fraction form of integrand from Eq. (iii) in given integral, we get

$I = \displaystyle\int \dfrac{1}{2(x-1)}dx + \dfrac{1}{2}\int \dfrac{(-x+1)}{x^2+1}dx$

$= \dfrac{1}{2}\log|x-1| + \dfrac{1}{2}\left[-\displaystyle\int \dfrac{x}{x^2+1}\times\dfrac{2}{2}dx + \int \dfrac{1}{x^2+1}dx\right]$

$= \dfrac{1}{2}\log|x-1| - \dfrac{1}{4}\displaystyle\int \dfrac{2x}{x^2+1}dx + \dfrac{1}{2}\int \dfrac{1}{x^2+1}dx$

$= \dfrac{1}{2}\log|x-1| - \dfrac{1}{4}\log|x^2+1| + \dfrac{1}{2}\tan^{-1}x + C$

$\left[\begin{array}{l}\text{for evaluating } \displaystyle\int \dfrac{2x}{x^2+1}dx, \text{ put } x^2+1 = t \Rightarrow 2x\,dx = dt, \\ \text{then } \displaystyle\int \dfrac{2x}{x^2+1}dx = \int \dfrac{1}{t}dt = \log|t| = \log|x^2+1|\end{array}\right]$

56. Let $I = \displaystyle\int \dfrac{\sec x\,dx}{1+\operatorname{cosec} x} = \int \dfrac{\frac{1}{\cos x}}{1+\frac{1}{\sin x}}dx$

$= \displaystyle\int \dfrac{\sin x\,dx}{\cos x(1+\sin x)}$

$= \displaystyle\int \dfrac{\sin x\cos x\,dx}{\cos^2 x(1+\sin x)}$

$= \displaystyle\int \dfrac{\sin x\cos dx}{(1-\sin^2 x)(1+\sin x)}$

$= \displaystyle\int \dfrac{\sin x\cos x\,dx}{(1-\sin x)(1+\sin x)^2} \qquad [\because a^2-b^2 = (a+b)(a-b)]$

On putting $\sin x = t$

$\Rightarrow \quad \cos x\, dx = dt$, we get

$$I = \int \frac{t}{(1+t)^2(1-t)}dt$$

Now, $\dfrac{t}{(1+t)^2(1-t)} = \dfrac{A}{1+t} + \dfrac{B}{(1+t)^2} + \dfrac{C}{1-t}$

$\Rightarrow \quad t = A(1+t)(1-t) + B(1-t) + C(1+t)^2$

Put $t = -1 \Rightarrow -1 = 2B$

$\Rightarrow B = \dfrac{-1}{2}$

Put $t = 1$,

$1 = 4C$

$\Rightarrow \quad C = 1/4$

Put $t = 0$,

$0 = A + B + C$

$\Rightarrow \quad 0 = A + \left(\dfrac{-1}{2}\right) + \left(\dfrac{1}{4}\right)$

$\Rightarrow \quad A = \dfrac{1}{2} - \dfrac{1}{4} = \dfrac{2-1}{4} = \dfrac{1}{4}$

Hence, the required integral

$$= \frac{1}{4}\int \frac{1}{1+t}dt + \left(\frac{-1}{2}\right)\int \frac{1}{(1+t)^2}dt + \frac{1}{4}\int \frac{1}{(1-t)}dt$$

$$= \frac{1}{4}\log|1+t| + \frac{-1}{2} \times \frac{-1}{1+t} - \frac{1}{4}\log|1-t| + C$$

$$= \frac{1}{4}\log|1+\sin x| + \frac{1}{2(1+\sin x)} - \frac{1}{4}\log|1-\sin x| + C$$

$[\because t = \sin x]$

57. Let $I = \int \underset{\text{II}}{e^{ax}} \underset{\text{I}}{\sin bx}\, dx$

$\Rightarrow I = \sin bx\left(\dfrac{e^{ax}}{a}\right) - \int(\cos bx \cdot b)\dfrac{e^{ax}}{a}dx$

$\Rightarrow I = \dfrac{1}{a}e^{ax}\sin bx - \dfrac{b}{a}\int \underset{\text{II}}{e^{ax}} \underset{\text{I}}{\cos bx}\, dx$

$\Rightarrow I = \dfrac{1}{a}e^{ax}\sin bx - \dfrac{b}{a}\left[\cos bx \cdot \left(\dfrac{e^{ax}}{a}\right) - \int(-\sin bx \cdot b)\left(\dfrac{e^{ax}}{a}\right)dx\right]$

$\Rightarrow I = \dfrac{1}{a}e^{ax}\sin bx - \dfrac{b}{a^2}e^{ax}\cos bx - \dfrac{b^2}{a^2}\int e^{ax}\sin bx\, dx$

$\Rightarrow I = \dfrac{1}{a}e^{ax}\sin bx - \dfrac{b}{a^2}e^{ax}\cos bx - \dfrac{b^2}{a^2}I$

$\Rightarrow \quad I + \dfrac{b^2}{a^2}I = \dfrac{e^{ax}}{a^2}[a\sin bx - b\cos bx]$

$\Rightarrow \left(\dfrac{a^2+b^2}{a^2}\right)I = \dfrac{e^{ax}}{a^2}[a\sin bx - b\cos bx]$

$\Rightarrow \quad I = \dfrac{e^{ax}}{a^2+b^2}[a\sin bx - b\cos bx] + C$

58. Let $I = \int \dfrac{(2x-5)e^{2x}}{(2x-3)^3}dx = \int \dfrac{(2x-3-2)e^{2x}}{(2x-3)^3}dx$

$= \int \dfrac{e^{2x}}{(2x-3)^2}dx - 2\int \dfrac{e^{2x}}{(2x-3)^3}dx$

$= \int \underset{\text{II}}{e^{2x}} \underset{\text{I}}{(2x-3)^{-2}}\, dx - 2\int e^{2x}(2x-3)^{-3}dx$

$= \left[(2x-3)^{-2}\int e^{2x}dx - \int\left\{\dfrac{d}{dx}(2x-3)^{-2}\int e^{2x}dx\right\}dx\right]$

$-2\int e^{2x}(2x-3)^{-3}dx$

[using integration by parts]

$= (2x-3)^{-2}\dfrac{e^{2x}}{2} - \int -2(2x-3)^{-3} \times 2 \times \dfrac{e^{2x}}{2}dx$

$-2\int e^{2x}(2x-3)^{-3}dx$

$= \dfrac{e^{2x}(2x-3)^{-2}}{2} + 2\int e^{2x}(2x-3)^{-3}dx$

$-2\int e^{2x}(2x-3)^{-3}dx$

$= \dfrac{e^{2x}(2x-3)^{-2}}{2} + C$

59. Let $I = \int e^{2x}\sin(3x+1)dx$ ...(i)

$= \sin(3x+1)\int e^{2x}dx - \int\left\{\dfrac{d}{dx}\sin(3x+1)\int e^{2x}dx\right\}dx$

[using integration by parts]

$= \dfrac{\sin(3x+1)\cdot e^{2x}}{2} - \int 3\cos(3x+1)\cdot\dfrac{e^{2x}}{2}dx$

$= \dfrac{e^{2x}\sin(3x+1)}{2} - \dfrac{3}{2}\int e^{2x}\cos(3x+1)dx$

$= \dfrac{e^{2x}\sin(3x+1)}{2} - \dfrac{3}{2}[\cos(3x+1)\int e^{2x}dx$

$-\int\left\{\dfrac{d}{dx}\cos(3x+1)\int e^{2x}dx\right\}dx]$

[again, using integration by parts]

$= \dfrac{e^{2x}\sin(3x+1)}{2} - \dfrac{3}{2}\left[\cos(3x+1)\cdot\dfrac{e^{2x}}{2}\right.$

$\left.-\int -3\sin(3x+1)\cdot\dfrac{e^{2x}}{2}dx\right] + C_1$

$\Rightarrow I = \dfrac{e^{2x}\sin(3x+1)}{2} - \dfrac{3}{4}e^{2x}\cos(3x+1)$

$-\dfrac{9}{4}\int e^{2x}\sin(3x+1)dx + C_1$

$\Rightarrow I = \dfrac{e^{2x}\sin(3x+1)}{2} - \dfrac{3}{4}e^{2x}\cos(3x+1) - \dfrac{9}{4}I + C_1$

[from Eq. (i)]

$\Rightarrow \dfrac{13}{4}I = \dfrac{e^{2x}\sin(3x+1)}{2} - \dfrac{3e^{2x}\cos(3x+1)}{4} + C_1$

$\therefore \quad I = \dfrac{2e^{2x}\sin(3x+1)}{13} - \dfrac{3e^{2x}\cos(3x+1)}{13} + C,$

where $C = \dfrac{4C_1}{13}$.

60. Let $I=\int_0^{\pi/4}\frac{dx}{\cos^3 x\sqrt{2\sin 2x}}$

$=\int_0^{\pi/4}\frac{dx}{\cos^3 x\sqrt{2\,(2\sin x\cos x)}}$ $[\because \sin 2\theta=2\sin\theta\cos\theta]$

$=\frac{1}{2}\int_0^{\pi/4}\frac{dx}{\cos^3 x\cos^{1/2}x\sin^{1/2}x}$

$=\frac{1}{2}\int_0^{\pi/4}\frac{dx}{\cos^{7/2}x\sin^{1/2}x}$

$=\frac{1}{2}\int_0^{\pi/4}\frac{\sec^4 x}{\cos^{7/2-4}x\sin^{1/2}x}dx$

[dividing numerator and denominator by $\cos^4 x$]

$=\frac{1}{2}\int_0^{\pi/4}\frac{\sec^4 x}{\cos^{-1/2}x\sin^{1/2}x}dx$

$=\frac{1}{2}\int_0^{\pi/4}\frac{\sec^2 x(1+\tan^2 x)}{\tan^{1/2}x}dx$ $[\because \sec^2 x-\tan^2 x=1]$

Now, put $\tan x=t\Rightarrow \sec^2 x\,dx=dt$

Lower limit When $x=0$, then $t=\tan 0=0$

Upper limit When $x=\frac{\pi}{4}$, then $t=\tan\frac{\pi}{4}=1$

$\therefore I=\frac{1}{2}\int_0^1\left(\frac{1+t^2}{t^{1/2}}\right)dt$

$=\frac{1}{2}\int_0^1(t^{-1/2}+t^{3/2})\,dt$

$=\frac{1}{2}\left[2t^{1/2}+\frac{2}{5}t^{5/2}\right]_0^1$

$=(1)^{1/2}+\frac{1}{5}(1)^{5/2}-0$

$=1+\frac{1}{5}=\frac{6}{5}$

61. Let $I=\int_0^{\pi/4}\frac{\sin x+\cos x}{16+9\sin 2x}dx$

$=\int_0^{\pi/4}\frac{\sin x+\cos x}{9\,(2\sin x\cos x)+16}dx$

$=\int_0^{\pi/4}\frac{\sin x+\cos x}{-9(-2\sin x\cos x)+16}dx$

$=\int_0^{\pi/4}\frac{\sin x+\cos x}{-9(\sin^2 x+\cos^2 x-2\sin x\cos x-1)+16}dx$

$[\because \sin^2\theta+\cos^2\theta=1]$

$=\int_0^{\pi/4}\frac{\sin x+\cos x}{25-9(\sin x-\cos x)^2}dx$

$[\because a^2+b^2-2ab=(a-b)^2]$

Put $\sin x-\cos x=t\Rightarrow(\cos x+\sin x)dx=dt$

Lower limit When $x=0$, then $t=-1$

Upper limit When $x=\frac{\pi}{4}$, then $t=0$

$\therefore\quad I=\int_{-1}^0\frac{dt}{25-9t^2}=\frac{1}{9}\int_{-1}^0\frac{dt}{\left(\frac{5}{3}\right)^2-t^2}$

$=\frac{1}{9}\times\frac{1}{2\times\frac{5}{3}}\left[\log\left|\frac{\frac{5}{3}+t}{\frac{5}{3}-t}\right|\right]_{-1}^0$

$\left[\because \int\frac{dx}{a^2-x^2}=\frac{1}{2a}\log\left|\frac{a+x}{a-x}\right|+C\right]$

$=\frac{1}{30}\left[\log\left|\frac{5+3t}{5-3t}\right|\right]_{-1}^0=\frac{1}{30}\left[\log 1-\log\left(\frac{2}{8}\right)\right]$

$=\frac{1}{30}\left[0-\log\frac{1}{4}\right]$ $[\because \log 1=0]$

$=\frac{1}{30}[-\log 4^{-1}]=\frac{1}{30}\log 4$ $[\because \log m^n=n\log m]$

62. Let $I=\int_0^{\pi}x\log|\sin x|dx$ ...(i)

$\Rightarrow\quad I=\int_0^{\pi}(\pi-x)\log|\sin(\pi-x)|dx$

$=\int_0^{\pi}(\pi-x)\log|\sin x|dx$ ...(ii)

On adding Eqs. (i) and (ii), we get

$2I=\pi\int_0^{\pi}\log|\sin x|dx$ ...(iii)

$\Rightarrow\quad 2I=2\pi\int_0^{\pi/2}\log|\sin x|dx$

$\left[\because \int_0^{2a}f(x)dx=2\int_0^a f(x)dx,\text{ if } f(2a-x)=f(x)\right]$

$\Rightarrow\quad I=\pi\int_0^{\pi/2}\log|\sin x|dx$ ...(iv)

$\Rightarrow\quad I=\pi\int_0^{\pi/2}\log|\sin(\pi/2-x)|dx$

$\left[\because \int_0^a f(x)\,dx=\int_0^a f(a-x)\,dx\right]$

$=\pi\int_0^{\pi/2}\log|\cos x|dx$ ...(v)

On adding Eqs. (iv) and (v), we get

$2I=\pi\int_0^{\pi/2}(\log|\sin x|+\log|\cos x|)dx$

$\Rightarrow\quad 2I=\pi\int_0^{\pi/2}\log|\sin x\cos x|dx$

$\Rightarrow\quad 2I=\pi\int_0^{\pi/2}\log\left|\frac{2\sin x\cos x}{2}\right|dx$

[multiply by 2 in numerator and denominator]

$\Rightarrow\quad 2I=\pi\int_0^{\pi/2}(\log|\sin 2x|-\log 2)dx$

$2I=\pi\int_0^{\pi/2}\log|\sin 2x|dx-\pi\int_0^{\pi/2}\log 2\,dx$

$\Rightarrow\quad 2I=\pi\int_0^{\pi/2}\log|\sin 2x|dx-\pi\log 2[x]_0^{\pi/2}$

Now, put $2x=t\ \Rightarrow\ dx=\frac{1}{2}dt$

Lower limit When $x=0$, then $t=0$

Upper limit When $x=\frac{\pi}{2}$, then $t=\pi$

$\therefore\quad 2I=\frac{\pi}{2}\int_0^{\pi}\log|\sin t|dt-\frac{\pi^2}{2}\log 2$

$$\Rightarrow \quad 2I = \frac{\pi}{2}\int_0^{\pi} \log|\sin x|\,dx - \frac{\pi^2}{2}\log 2$$

$$\left[\because \int_a^b f(x)\,dx = \int_a^b f(t)\,dt\right]$$

$$\Rightarrow \quad 2I = I - \frac{\pi^2}{2}\log 2 \qquad \text{[from Eq. (iii)]}$$

$$\therefore \quad I = -\frac{\pi^2}{2}\log 2$$

$$= \frac{\pi^2}{2}\log\left(\frac{1}{2}\right)$$

63. Let $I = \int_0^{\pi/2} (2\log(\sin x) - \log(\sin 2x)\,dx$

$$= \int_0^{\pi/2} [\log(\sin^2 x) - \log(\sin 2x)]dx \quad [\because m\log n = \log n^m]$$

$$= \int_0^{\pi/2} \log\left(\frac{\sin^2 x}{\sin 2x}\right)dx \quad \left[\because \log m - \log n = \log\frac{m}{n}\right]$$

$$= \int_0^{\pi/2} \log\left(\frac{\sin^2 x}{2\sin x\cos x}\right)dx \quad [\because \sin 2x = 2\sin x\cos x]$$

$$= \int_0^{\pi/2} \log\left(\frac{\tan x}{2}\right)dx$$

$$= \int_0^{\pi/2} [\log(\tan x) - \log 2]\,dx$$

$$= \int_0^{\pi/2} \log(\tan x)\,dx - \int_0^{\pi/2} \log 2\,dx$$

$$= \int_0^{\pi/2} \log(\tan x)\,dx - \log 2\int_0^{\pi/2} 1\,dx$$

$$\Rightarrow I = I_1 - (\log 2)[x]_0^{\pi/2} = I_1 - \left(\frac{\pi}{2} - 0\right)\log 2, \qquad \text{...(i)}$$

where $I_1 = \int_0^{\pi/2} \log(\tan x)\,dx$ ...(ii)

Now, $I_1 = \int_0^{\pi/2} \log\left[\tan\left(\frac{\pi}{2} - x\right)\right]dx$

$$\left[\because \int_0^a f(x)\,dx = \int_0^a f(a-x)\,dx\right]$$

$$\Rightarrow \quad I_1 = \int_0^{\pi/2} \log(\cot x)\,dx \qquad \text{...(iii)}$$

On adding Eqs. (ii) and (iii), we get

$$2I_1 = \int_0^{\pi/2} [\log(\tan x) + \log(\cot x)]dx$$

$$= \int_0^{\pi/2} \log(\tan x\cot x)\,dx$$

$$[\because \log m + \log n = \log(mn)]$$

$$= \int_0^{\pi/2} \log 1\,dx = 0 \quad \left[\because \tan x = \frac{1}{\cot x}\right]$$

$$\Rightarrow \quad I_1 = 0$$

From Eq. (i), we get

$$I = 0 - \frac{\pi}{2}\log 2$$

$$\Rightarrow \quad I = -\frac{\pi}{2}\log 2$$

QR Code for Quick Test 1	QR Code for Quick Test 2	QR Code for Quick Test 3	QR Code for Quick Test 4	QR Code for Quick Test 5	QR Code for Quick Test 6

Mind Map

Integrals

Integration of some standard functions

	Functions	Intergration
1.	$\int x^n dx$	$\frac{x^{n+1}}{n+1} + C, n \neq -1$
2.	$\int dx$	$x + C$
3.	$\int \cos x\, dx$	$\sin x + C$
4.	$\int \sin x\, dx$	$-\cos x + C$
5.	$\int \sec^2 x\, dx$	$\tan x + C$
6.	$\int \operatorname{cosec}^2 x\, dx$	$-\cot x + C$
7.	$\int \sec x \tan x\, dx$	$\sec x + C$
8.	$\int \operatorname{cosec} x \cot x\, dx$	$-\operatorname{cosec} x + C$
9.	$\int \frac{dx}{\sqrt{1-x^2}}$	$\sin^{-1} x + C$
10.	$\int \frac{dx}{\sqrt{1-x^2}}$	$-\cos^{-1} x + C$
11.	$\int \frac{dx}{1+x^2}$	$\tan^{-1} x + C$
12.	$\int e^x\, dx$	$e^x + C$
13.	$\int dx \frac{1}{x}$	$\log \lvert x\rvert + C$
14.	$\int a^x\, dx$	$\frac{a^x}{\log a} + C, a > 0, a \neq 1$

Some Standard Formulae

(i) $\int \tan x\, dx = -\log \lvert\cos x\rvert + C$

$= \log \lvert\sec x\rvert + C$

(ii) $\int \cot x\, dx = \log \lvert\sin x\rvert + C$

(iii) $\int \sec x\, dx = \log \lvert\sec x + \tan x\rvert + C$

(iv) $\int \operatorname{cosec} x\, dx = \log \lvert\operatorname{cosec} x - \cot x\rvert + C$

Integration by Substitution

The method of reducing a given integral into one of the standard integrals by a proper substitution is called method of substitution.

Suppose, in the integral $I = \int f(x)dx$, $f(x)$ is not in any standard form.

Now, $\int f(x)dx$ can be transformed to another form by changing the independent variable x to other variable t by substituting $x = g(t)$.

$\therefore \frac{dx}{dt} = g'(t)$ or $dx = g'(t)dt$

Now, putting the value of dx in the above integral, we get

$$\int f(x)dx = \int f[g(t)]\, g'(t)\, dt$$

Integration

Integration is reverse process of differentiation. If the derivative of $f(x)$ is $f(x)$, then we say that the integral (anti-derivative) of $f(x)$ is $F(x)$ and we write

$$\int f(x)dx = F(x) + C$$

where C is an arbitrary constant known as constant of integration.

Some Special Integrals

(i) $\int \frac{dx}{x^2 - a^2} = \frac{1}{2a} \log \left|\frac{x-a}{x+a}\right| + C$

(ii) $\int \frac{dx}{a^2 - x^2} = \frac{1}{2a} \log \left|\frac{a+x}{a-x}\right| + C$

(iii) $\int \frac{dx}{x^2 + a^2} = \frac{1}{a} \tan^{-1} \frac{x}{a} + C$

(iv) $\int \frac{dx}{\sqrt{x^2 - a^2}} = \log \lvert x + \sqrt{x^2 - a^2}\rvert + C$

(v) $\int \frac{dx}{\sqrt{a^2 - x^2}} = \sin^{-1} \frac{x}{a} + C$

(vi) $\int \frac{dx}{\sqrt{x^2 + a^2}} = \log \lvert x + \sqrt{x^2 + a^2}\rvert + C$

Definite Integral

Let $f(x)$ be a continuous function defined on an interval $[a, b]$ and having anti-derivative $F(x)$.

Then, its definite integral over $[a, b]$ is denoted by $\int_a^b f(x)dx$, which is defined as

$$\int_a^b f(x)dx = [F(x)]_a^b = F(b) - F(a)$$

where, a and b are known as **lower limit** and **upper limit**, respectively.

Integration by Partial Fractions

A rational function is a ratio of two polynomials i.e. of the form $\frac{p(x)}{q(x)}$, where $p(x)$ and $q(x)$ are polynomials in x and $q(x) \neq 0$. If degree of $p(x) >$ degree of $q(x)$, then we may divide $p(x)$ by $q(x)$ so that $\frac{p(x)}{q(x)} = t(x) + \frac{p_1(x)}{q(x)}$, where $t(x)$ is a polynomial in x which can be integrated easily and degree of $p_1(x)$ is less than the degree of $q(x)$. Now, $\frac{p_1(x)}{q(x)}$ can be integrated by expressing $\frac{p_1(x)}{q(x)}$ as the sum of partial fractions of the following types :

S. No.	Form of the rational function	Form of the partial fraction
1.	$\frac{px+q}{(x-a)(x-b)}, a \neq b$	$\frac{A}{x-a} + \frac{B}{x-b}$
2.	$\frac{px+q}{(x-a)^2}$	$\frac{A}{(x-a)} + \frac{B}{(x-a)^2}$
3.	$\frac{px^2+qx+r}{(x-a)(x-b)(x-c)}$	$\frac{A}{(x-a)} + \frac{B}{(x-b)} + \frac{C}{(x-c)}$
4.	$\frac{px^2+qx+r}{(x-a)^2(x-b)}$	$\frac{A}{(x-a)} + \frac{B}{(x-a)^2} + \frac{C}{(x-b)}$
5.	$\frac{px^2+qx+r}{(x-a)(x^2+bx+c)}$	$\frac{A}{(x-a)} + \frac{Bx+C}{x^2+bx+c}$, where

$x^2 + bx + c$ cannot be factorised further.

Integration by Parts

Let u and v be two differentiable functions of x.

Then, $\int \underset{I}{u} \times \underset{II}{v} dx = u\int v dx - \int \left(\frac{d}{dx}(u) \int v dx\right) dx$

Here, we can choose first function according to its position in ILATE, where

- I Inverse trigonometric function. e.g. $\sin^{-1} x$
- L Logarithmic function. e.g. $\log x$
- A Algebraic function. e.g. $1, x, x^2$
- T Trigonometric function. e.g. $\sin x, \cos x$
- E Exponential function. e.g. e^x

The function which comes first in ILATE should taken as first function and other as second function.

Properties of Definite Integral

(i) $\int_a^b f(x)dx = \int_a^b f(t)dt$

(ii) $\int_a^a f(x)dx = 0$

(iii) $\int_a^b f(x)dx = -\int_b^a f(x)dx$

(iv) $\int_a^b f(x)dx = \int_a^c f(x)dx + \int_c^b f(x)dx$, where $a < c < b$

(v) $\int_a^b f(x)dx = \int_a^b f(a+b-x)dx$

(vi) $\int_0^a f(x)dx = \int_0^a f(a-x)dx$

(vii) $\int_0^{2a} f(x)dx = \int_0^a f(x)dx + \int_0^a f(2a-x)dx$

Properties of Indefinite Integrals

(i) $\int \{f(x) \pm g(x)\}dx = \int f(x)dx \pm \int g(x)dx$

(ii) $\int k \times f(x)\, dx = k \times \int f(x)dx$, where k is any non-zero real number.

(iii) In general, if $f_1, f_2 \ldots f_n$ are functions and $k_1, k_2, \ldots, k_n$ are non-zero real numbers, then $\int [k_1 f_1(x) + k_2 f_2(x) + \ldots + k_n f_n(x)]dx$
$= k_1 \int f_1(x)dx + k_2 \int f_2(x)dx + \ldots + k_n \int f_n(x)dx$

Some More Special Types of Integrals

(i) $\int \sqrt{x^2 - a^2}\, dx = \frac{x}{2}\sqrt{x^2 - a^2} - \frac{a^2}{2} \log \lvert x + \sqrt{x^2 - a^2}\rvert + C$

(ii) $\int \sqrt{x^2 + a^2}\, dx = \frac{x}{2}\sqrt{x^2 + a^2} + \frac{a^2}{2} \log \lvert x + \sqrt{x^2 + a^2}\rvert + C$

(iii) $\int \sqrt{a^2 - x^2}\, dx = \frac{x}{2}\sqrt{a^2 - x^2} + \frac{a^2}{2} \sin^{-1} \frac{x}{a} + C$

(iv) $\int e^x [f(x) + f'(x)]\, dx = e^x f(x) + C$

08

CHAPTER

God may not play dice with the universe , but something strange is going on with the prime numbers. — *Paul Erdos*

Application of Integrals

YOUR STUDY GOALS

8.1 Area of a Curve Between Two Ordinates

8.2 Area of a Curve Between Two Abscissae

YOUR PRACTICE GOALS

- Objective Type Questions (25 Qs ; 15 MCQs, 7 A-R, 3 Case Based)
- Subjective Type Questions (18 Qs; 14 SA, 4 LA)

8.1 Area of a Curve Between Two Ordinates

The area bounded by the curve $y = f(x)$, the X-axis and the ordinates $x = a$ and $x = b$ is calculated as

$$\text{Area} = \int_a^b y\, dx$$

$$= \int_a^b f(x)\, dx$$

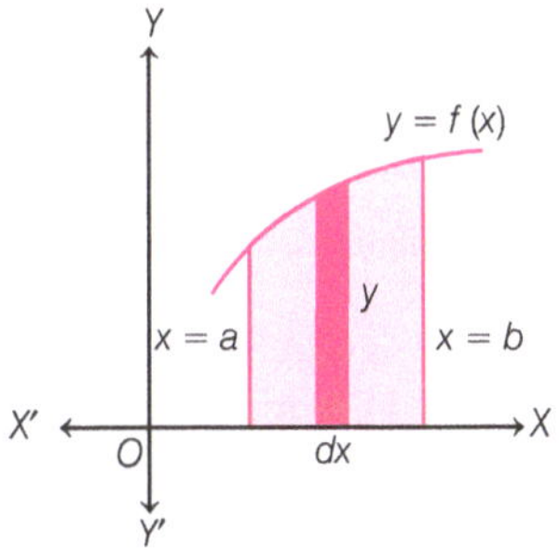

8.2 Area of a Curve Between Two Abscissae

The area bounded by the curve $x = f(y)$, the Y-axis and the lines $y = c$ and $y = d$ is calculated as

$$\text{Area} = \int_c^d x\, dy = \int_c^d f(y)\, dy$$

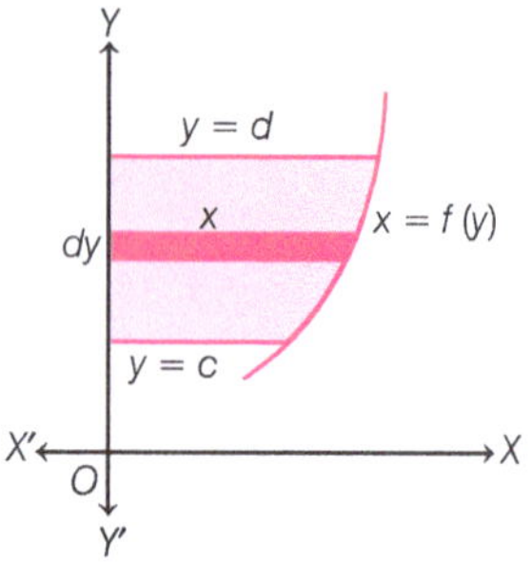

Some Important Points

(i) If area lies below X-axis or left of Y-axis, then it is negative and in such a case, we take its absolute value because the area of region is always positive,

i.e. $A = \left|\int_a^b f(x)dx\right|$ or $A = \left|\int_c^d f(y)dy\right|$

(ii) It may happen that some portion of the curve is above X-axis and some is below the X-axis, then the area bounded by the curve $y = f(x)$, X-axis and the ordinates $x = a$ and $x = b$ is given by Area $= |A_1| + A_2$.

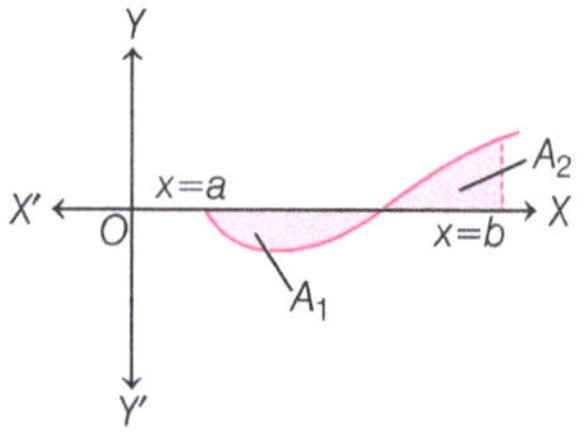

Example 1 **Find the area of the region bounded by the parabola $y^2 = 4ax$, its axis and two ordinates $x = 4$ and $x = 9$ in first quadrant.**

Sol. Given equation of parabola is $y^2 = 4ax$, its axis is $Y = 0$ and vertex is (0, 0).

Also, given ordinates $x = 4$ and $x = 9$.

The bounded region in I quadrant is $ABCDA$.

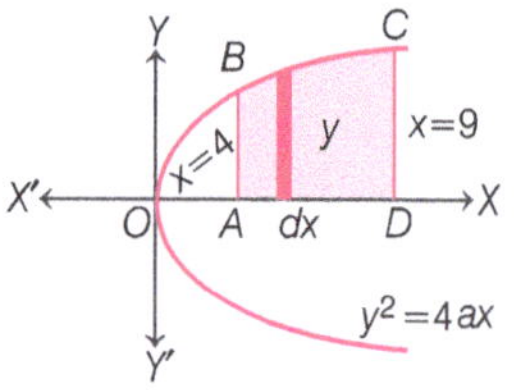

$\therefore$ Required area $= \int_4^9 y\, dx$

$= \int_4^9 \sqrt{4ax}\, dx$

$[\because y^2 = 4ax \Rightarrow y = \sqrt{4ax}$, as y is in I quadrant$]$

$= 2\sqrt{a} \int_4^9 \sqrt{x}\, dx$

$= 2\sqrt{a}\left[\frac{x^{3/2}}{3/2}\right]_4^9$

$= 2\sqrt{a} \times \frac{2}{3}[(9)^{3/2} - (4)^{3/2}]$

$= \frac{4}{3}\sqrt{a}\,[(3^2)^{3/2} - (2^2)^{3/2}]$

$= \frac{4}{3}\sqrt{a}\,[27 - 8]$

$= \frac{4}{3}\sqrt{a}\,(19)$

$= \frac{76}{3}\sqrt{a}$ sq units

Hence, the required area is $\frac{76\sqrt{a}}{3}$ sq units.

Example 2 **Find the area of the region bounded by the ellipse $\frac{x^2}{9} + \frac{y^2}{4} = 1$ in fourth quadrant.**

Sol. Given, equation of ellipse is $\frac{x^2}{9} + \frac{y^2}{4} = 1$ ...(i)

We know that the standard equation of ellipse is

$$\frac{x^2}{a^2} + \frac{y^2}{b^2} = 1 \quad \text{...(ii)}$$

On comparing Eqs. (i) and (ii), we get

$a^2 = 9$ and $b^2 = 4$

$\Rightarrow$ $a = 3$ and $b = 2$

Here, we see that $a > b$, so the horizontal ellipse will be formed.

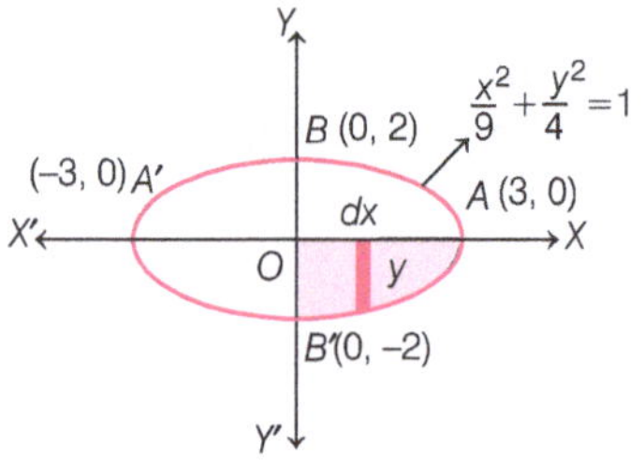

Now, required area = Area of region in IV quadrant

= Area of region $OAB'O$

$= \left|\int_0^3 y\, dx\right|$

$$= \left| \int_0^3 \frac{2\sqrt{9-x^2}}{3} dx \right|$$

$$\left[\because \frac{y^2}{4} = 1 - \frac{x^2}{9} \Rightarrow y = \frac{2\sqrt{9-x^2}}{3} \right]$$

$$= \frac{2}{3} \left| \left[\frac{x}{2}\sqrt{9-x^2} + \frac{9}{2}\sin^{-1}\left(\frac{x}{3}\right) \right]_0^3 \right|$$

$$\left[\because \int \sqrt{a^2-x^2}\, dx = \frac{x}{2}\sqrt{a^2-x^2} + \frac{a^2}{2}\sin^{-1}\left(\frac{x}{a}\right) \right]$$

$$= \frac{2}{3} \left| \left[\frac{3}{2}\sqrt{9-9} + \frac{9}{2}\sin^{-1}\frac{3}{3} - 0 - \frac{9}{2}\sin^{-1}(0) \right] \right|$$

$$= \frac{2}{3} \left| \left[0 + \frac{9}{2} \times \frac{\pi}{2} - 0 \right] \right|$$

$$= \frac{2}{3} \times \frac{9\pi}{4}$$

$$= \frac{3\pi}{2} \text{ sq units}$$

Hence, the required area is $\frac{3\pi}{2}$ sq units.

Example 3 **Sketch the region bounded by the lines $2x + y = 8$, $y = 2$, $y = 4$ and the Y-axis. Hence, obtain its area using integration.** *CBSE 2023*

Sol. Given lines $2x + y = 8$, $y = 2$, $y = 4$

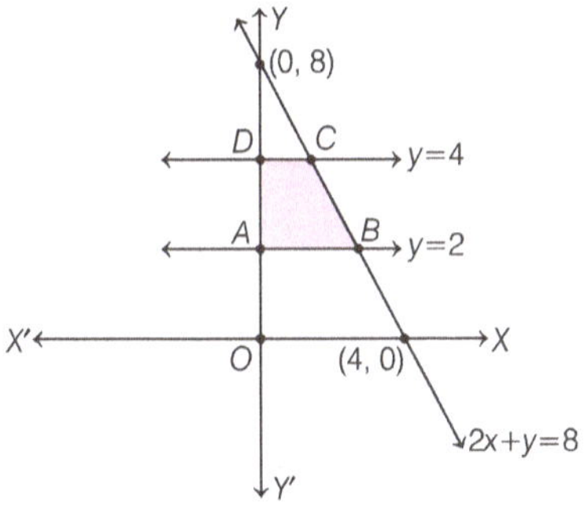

$\therefore$ Required area = Area of the region *ABCDA*

$$= \int_2^4 x\, dy = \int_2^4 \left(\frac{8-y}{2} \right) dy$$

$$= \frac{1}{2} \int_2^4 (8-y)\, dy$$

$$= \frac{1}{2} \left[8y - \frac{y^2}{2} \right]_2^4$$

$$= \frac{1}{2} \left[\left(8 \times 4 - \frac{16}{2} \right) - \left(8 \times 2 - \frac{2^2}{2} \right) \right]$$

$$= \frac{1}{2}[32 - 8 - 16 + 2] = \frac{1}{2}(10)$$

$$= 5 \text{ sq units}$$

Example 4 **Find the area bounded by the line $y = x$, the X-axis and the lines $x = -1$ and $x = 2$.**

Sol. We know that $y = x$ is the line passing through the origin and making angle of 45° with the X-axis as shown in the given figure.

Now, we have to find the area of the shaded region.

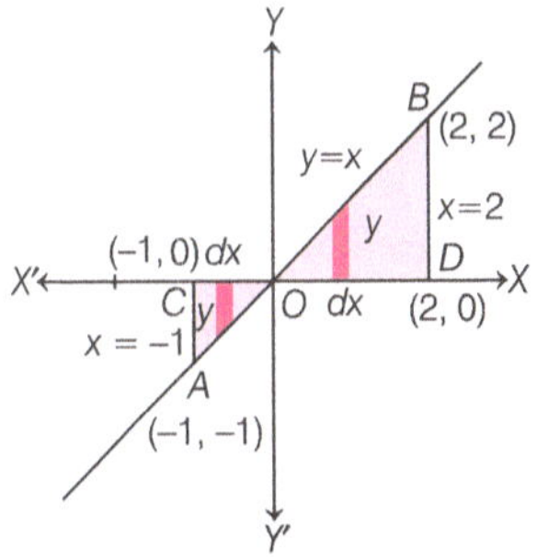

Required area = Area of *OACO* + Area of *OBDO*

$$= \left| \int_{-1}^0 y\, dx \right| + \int_0^2 y\, dx$$

[$\because$ area *OACO* is below the X-axis, so we take its absolute value]

$$= \left| \int_{-1}^0 x\, dx \right| + \int_0^2 x\, dx$$

$$= \left| \left[\frac{x^2}{2} \right]_{-1}^0 \right| + \left[\frac{x^2}{2} \right]_0^2 = \left| \left[0 - \frac{1}{2} \right] \right| + \left[\frac{4}{2} - 0 \right]$$

$$= \frac{1}{2} + \frac{4}{2} = \frac{5}{2} \text{ sq units}$$

Hence, the required area is $\frac{5}{2}$ sq units.

Example 5 **Find the area of the region bounded by the curve $x^2 + y^2 = 16$ and lines $y = 1$ and $y = 2$ in first quadrant.**

Sol. The area of the region bounded by the curve $x^2 + y^2 = 16$ and lines $y = 1$ and $y = 2$ in I quadrant is given by

$$A = \int_1^2 x\, dy = \int_1^2 \sqrt{4^2 - y^2}\, dy$$

[here, we take a horizontal strip]

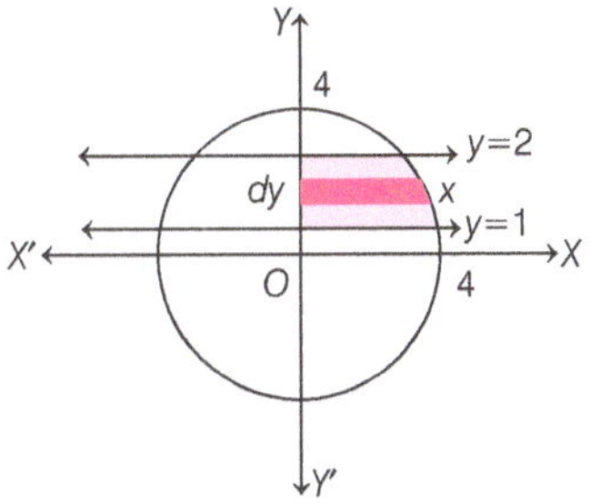

$$= \left[\frac{y}{2}\sqrt{16-y^2} + \frac{4^2}{2}\sin^{-1}\frac{y}{4}\right]_1^2$$

$$= \left[\frac{2}{2}\sqrt{16-4} + 8\sin^{-1}\frac{2}{4} - \left(\frac{1}{2}\sqrt{16-1} + 8\sin^{-1}\frac{1}{4}\right)\right]$$

$$= \left[2\sqrt{3} + 8 \times \frac{\pi}{6} - \left(\frac{1}{2}\sqrt{15} + 8\sin^{-1}\frac{1}{4}\right)\right]$$

$$= \left[2\sqrt{3} + \frac{4\pi}{3} - \left(\frac{\sqrt{15}}{2} + 8\sin^{-1}\frac{1}{4}\right)\right] \text{ sq units}$$

Example 6 **Find the area of the region bounded by the line $3x - y = 3$ and lines $x = \frac{1}{2}$ and $x = 2$.**

Sol. The area of the region bounded by the line $3x - y = 3$ and lines $x = \frac{1}{2}$ and $x = 2$ is given by

$$\text{Area} = \left|\int_{1/2}^{1} y\,dx\right| + \int_1^2 y\,dx$$

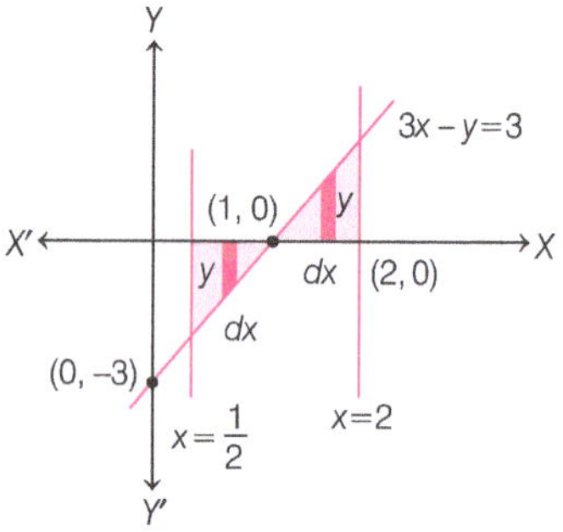

$$= \left|\int_{1/2}^{1} (3x-3)\,dx\right| + \int_1^2 (3x-3)\,dx$$

$$= \left|3\left[\frac{x^2}{2} - x\right]_{1/2}^{1}\right| + 3\left[\frac{x^2}{2} - x\right]_1^2$$

$$= 3\left|\left[\frac{1}{2} - 1 - \left(\frac{1}{8} - \frac{1}{2}\right)\right]\right| + 3\left[\frac{4}{2} - 2 - \left(\frac{1}{2} - 1\right)\right]$$

$$= 3\left|\left[-\frac{1}{2} + \frac{3}{8}\right]\right| + 3\left[0 + \frac{1}{2}\right]$$

$$= 3\left|-\frac{1}{8}\right| + \frac{3}{2}$$

$$= \frac{3}{8} + \frac{3}{2}$$

$$= \frac{3+12}{8}$$

$$= \frac{15}{8} \text{ sq units}$$

Example 7 **Find the area bounded by the curve $y = \sin x$ between $x = 0$ and $x = 2\pi$.** NCERT

Sol. The graph of $y = \sin x$ is shown in the figure below.

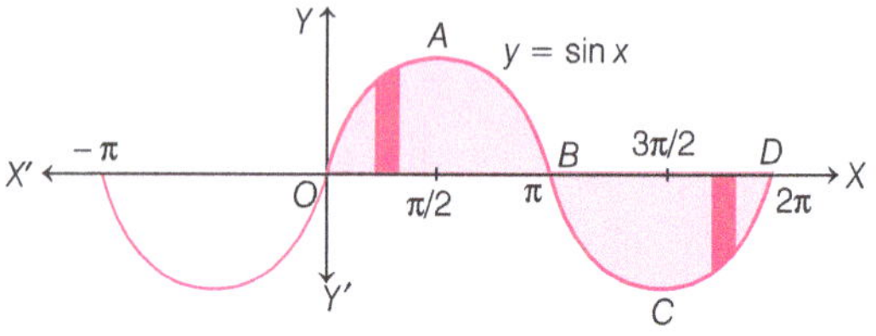

Clearly, required region is bounded by $y = \sin x$, X-axis and lines $x = 0$ and $x = 2\pi$, which is represented by shaded region.

$\therefore$ Required area = Area of region $OABO$
+ Area of region $BCDB$

$$= \int_0^{\pi} \sin x\,dx + \left|\int_{\pi}^{2\pi} \sin x\,dx\right|$$

[$\because$ in region $BCDB$, the graph is below the X-axis, so its area comes out to be negative, therefore we take the absolute value]

$$= [-\cos x]_0^{\pi} + \left|[-\cos x]_{\pi}^{2\pi}\right|$$

$$= (-\cos \pi + \cos 0) + |-\cos 2\pi + \cos \pi|$$

$$= (1+1) + |-1-1|$$

$$= 2 + |-2|$$

$$= 2 + 2$$

$$= 4 \text{ sq units}$$

Hence, the required area is 4 sq units.

Example 8 **Sketch the region $\{(x, y) : y = \sqrt{4 - x^2}\}$ and X-axis. Find the area of the region using integration.**
Competency Based Que, NCERT Exemplar

Sol. Given region is $\{(x, y) : y = \sqrt{4 - x^2}\}$ and X-axis.

We have, $y = \sqrt{4 - x^2}$

$\Rightarrow \quad y^2 = 4 - x^2$

$\Rightarrow x^2 + y^2 = 4$

This represent the equation of circle having centre (0, 0) and radius 2 units.

But, original equation is $y = \sqrt{4 - x^2}$, so y is positive.

It means that we have to take a curve above the X-axis.

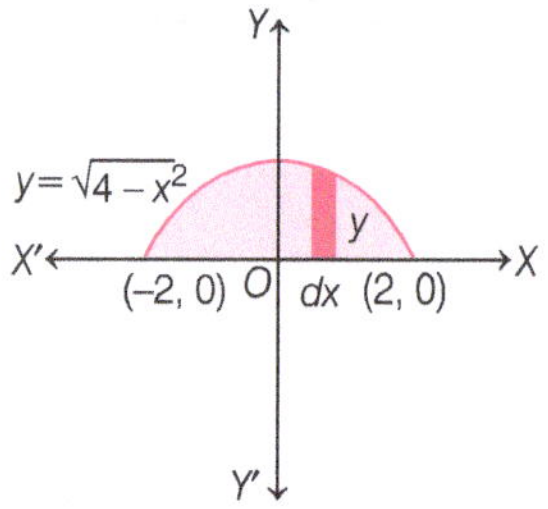

Thus, only semi-circle is formed above the X-axis.

Since, the region is symmetrical about Y-axis.

$\therefore$ Area of shaded region,

$$A = 2\int_0^2 y\,dx = 2\int_0^2 \sqrt{4 - x^2}\,dx$$

$$= 2\int_0^2 \sqrt{2^2 - x^2}\,dx$$

$$= 2\left[\frac{x}{2}\sqrt{2^2 - x^2} + \frac{2^2}{2}\cdot\sin^{-1}\frac{x}{2}\right]_0^2$$

$$= 2\left[\frac{2}{2}\cdot 0 + 2\cdot\frac{\pi}{2} - \frac{0}{2}\cdot 2 - 2\sin^{-1}0\right]$$

$$= 2\left[2\cdot\frac{\pi}{2} + 0\right] = 2\pi \text{ sq units}$$

Example 9 **Find the area bounded by the curve $x = 4 - y^2$ in the first quadrant.** *CBSE 2025*

Sol. We have, $x = 4 - y^2$

$\Rightarrow \quad y^2 = -x + 4$

Table for $y^2 = -x + 4$

x	0	4	1	2
y	2	0	1.73	1.4

The region bounded by the curve $y^2 = -x + 4$ in the first quadrant is represented by the shaded portion.

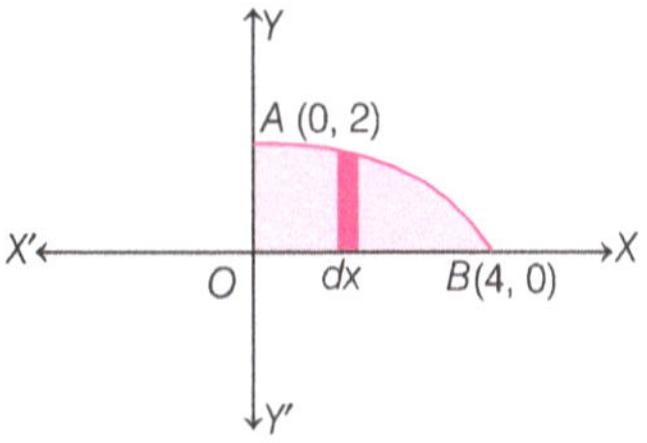

$\therefore$ Required area = Area of shaded region

= Area of region $OABO$

$$= \int_0^4 y\,dx = \int_0^4 \sqrt{4 - x}\,dx$$

$[\because x = 4 - y^2 \Rightarrow y = \sqrt{4 - x}$, as y is in I quadrant$]$

$$= \int_0^4 (4 - x)^{1/2}\,dx$$

$$= \left[\frac{-(4 - x)^{3/2}}{3/2}\right]_0^4 = -\frac{2}{3}[(4 - x)^{3/2}]_0^4$$

$$= -\frac{2}{3}[(4 - 4)^{3/2} - (4 - 0)^{3/2}]$$

$$= -\frac{2}{3}[0 - (4)^{3/2}] = \frac{2}{3}\times(4)^{3/2}$$

$$= \frac{2}{3}\times(2^2)^{3/2} = \frac{2}{3}\times 8 = \frac{16}{3} \text{ sq units}$$

Hence, the required area is $\frac{16}{3}$ sq units.

Example 10 **Find the area of the region bounded by the curves $y = |x - 2|$, $x = 1$, $x = 3$ and X-axis.** *Competency Based Que*

Sol. Given, $y = |x - 2|$

$$\therefore \quad y = \begin{cases} (x - 2), & x - 2 \ge 0 \\ -(x - 2), & x - 2 < 0 \end{cases} = \begin{cases} (x - 2), & x \ge 2 \\ (2 - x), & x < 2 \end{cases}$$

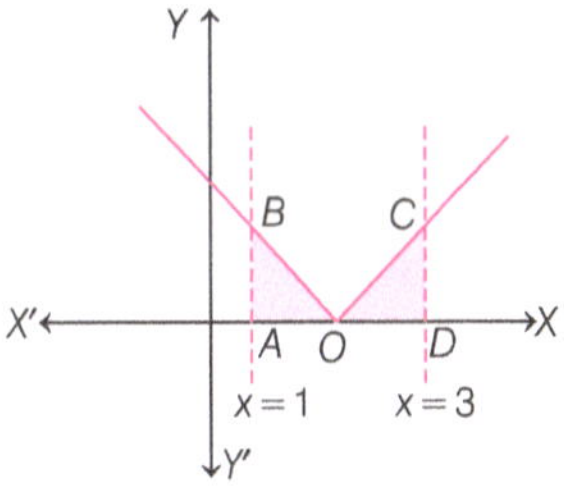

$$\therefore \text{ Required area} = \int_1^3 |x - 2|\,dx$$

$$= \int_1^2 (2 - x)\,dx + \int_2^3 (x - 2)\,dx$$

$$= \left[2x - \frac{x^2}{2}\right]_1^2 + \left[\frac{x^2}{2} - 2x\right]_2^3$$

$$= 2 - \frac{3}{2} - \frac{3}{2} + 2 = 1 \text{ sq unit}$$

Example 11 **Using integration, find the area enclosed by the circle $x^2 + y^2 = a^2$.**

Sol. Given equation of circle is $x^2 + y^2 = a^2$, its centre is (0, 0) and radius is a. It cuts the X-axis at $A(a, 0)$ and Y-axis at $B(0, a)$. Also, it is symmetrical about X and Y-axes both.

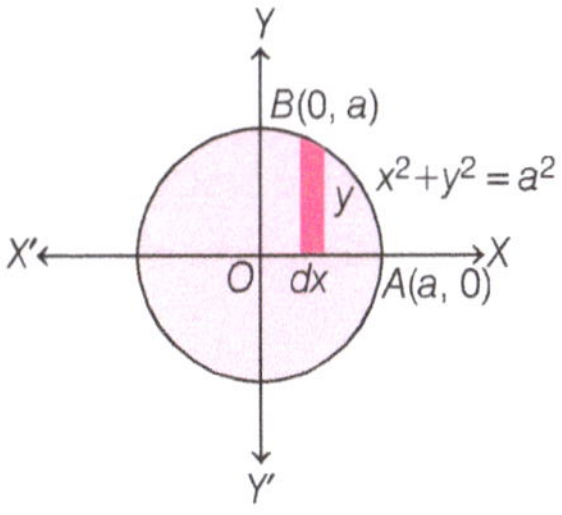

Clearly, area of region in I quadrant

$$= \int_0^a y\,dx = \int_0^a \sqrt{a^2 - x^2}\,dx \quad \text{[consider vertical strip]}$$

$[\because x^2 + y^2 = a^2 \Rightarrow y = \sqrt{a^2 - x^2}$, as y is in I quadrant$]$

$$= \left[\frac{x}{2}\sqrt{a^2 - x^2} + \frac{a^2}{2}\sin^{-1}\frac{x}{a}\right]_0^a$$

$$= \left[\left(\frac{a}{2}\times 0 + \frac{a^2}{2}\sin^{-1}1\right) - 0\right]$$

$$= \frac{a^2}{2}\cdot\frac{\pi}{2} = \frac{\pi a^2}{4} \quad \left[\because \sin^{-1}1 = \frac{\pi}{2}\right]$$

Now, required area = 4 × Area of region in I quadrant

[∵ region is symmetrical in all quadrants]

$$= 4 \times \frac{\pi a^2}{4}$$

$$= \pi a^2 \text{ sq units}$$

Example 12 **Find the area of region bounded by the curve $y^2 = 4x$ and the line $x = 4$.**

Sol. Given curve is a parabola, $y^2 = 4x$ ...(i)

which is of the form of $Y^2 = 4aX$ having vertex (0, 0)

and given line is $x = 4$. ...(ii)

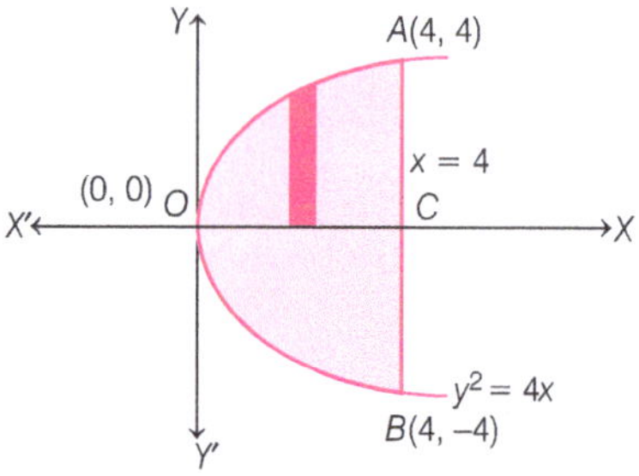

It is clear from the figure that, the region for which we have to find area is *OBCAO*. Also, the region *OCAO* is symmetrical about *X*-axis.

Now, let us find the intersection point of curve and line.

On putting the value of x from Eq. (ii) in Eq. (i), we get

$$y^2 = 4(4) = 16$$

$$\Rightarrow \quad y = \pm 4$$

Thus, line and curve intersect at two points (4, 4) and (4, –4). So, coordinates of point *A* are (4, 4), as it is in I quadrant.

Now, area of bounded region *OACBO*

= 2 (Area of region *OACO*)

[∵ parabola is symmetrical about the *X*-axis]

$$= 2\int_0^4 y\, dx$$

$$= 2\int_0^4 2\cdot x^{1/2}\, dx \quad [\because y^2 = 4x \Rightarrow y = \sqrt{4x} = 2\cdot x^{1/2}]$$

$$= 4\int_0^4 x^{1/2} dx$$

$$= 4\left[\frac{x^{3/2}}{3/2}\right]_0^4$$

$$= 4\cdot\frac{2}{3}[x^{3/2}]_0^4$$

$$= \frac{8}{3}[(4)^{3/2} - 0] = \frac{8}{3}\times(2^2)^{3/2}$$

$$= \frac{8}{3}\times 8 = \frac{64}{3} \text{ sq units}$$

Hence, the required area is $\frac{64}{3}$ sq units.

Example 13 **Find the area of the region bounded by the curve $4x^2 + y^2 = 36$ using integration.** *CBSE 2024*

Sol. Given curve is $4x^2 + y^2 = 36$

$$\Rightarrow \quad \frac{4x^2}{36} + \frac{y^2}{36} = 1$$

$$\Rightarrow \quad \frac{x^2}{9} + \frac{y^2}{36} = 1 \quad \text{...(i)}$$

We know that the standard equation of ellipse is

$$\frac{x^2}{a^2} + \frac{y^2}{b^2} = 1 \quad \text{..(ii)}$$

On comparing Eqs. (i) and (ii), we get

$$a^2 = 9 \text{ and } b^2 = 36$$

$$\Rightarrow \quad a = 3 \text{ and } b = 6$$

Here, we see that $a < b$, so the vertical ellipse will be formed.

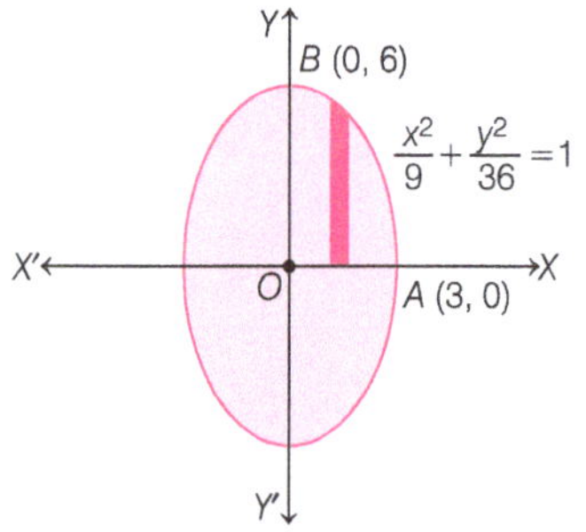

Now, required area = 4 (Area of region (*OABO*) in I quadrant)

$$= 4\int_0^3 y dx = 4\int_0^3 2\sqrt{9 - x^2} dx$$

$$\left[\because \frac{y^2}{36} = 1 - \frac{x^2}{9} \Rightarrow y = 2\sqrt{9 - x^2}\right]$$

$$= 8\int_0^3 \sqrt{9 - x^2} dx$$

$$= 8\left[\frac{x}{2}\sqrt{9 - x^2} + \frac{9}{2}\sin^{-1}\left(\frac{x}{3}\right)\right]_0^3$$

$$\left[\because \int\sqrt{a^2 - x^2} dx = \frac{x}{2}\sqrt{a^2 - x^2} + \frac{a^2}{2}\sin^{-1}\left(\frac{x}{a}\right)\right]$$

$$= 8\left[\frac{3}{2}\sqrt{9-9} + \frac{9}{2}\sin^{-1}\frac{3}{3} - 0 - \frac{9}{2}\sin^{-1}0\right]$$

$$= 8\left[0 + \frac{9}{2}\times\frac{\pi}{2} - 0\right]$$

$$= 8\times\frac{9\pi}{4} = 18\pi \text{ sq units}$$

Hence, the required area is 18π sq units.

EXAM PATTERN QUESTIONS

Objective Type Questions

Multiple Choice Questions

1. Area of the region bounded by the curve $y^2 = 4x$ and the X-axis between $x = 0$ and $x = 1$ is **CBSE 2024**

(a) $\frac{2}{3}$ (b) $\frac{8}{3}$ (c) 3 (d) $\frac{4}{3}$

2. The area bounded by the curve $y = \sqrt{x}$, Y-axis and between the lines $y = 0$ and $y = 3$ is **CBSE 2024**

(a) $2\sqrt{3}$ (b) 27 (c) 9 (d) 3

3. The area under the curve $y = x^2$ between the line $x = 0$ and $x = k$ is 9 sq units. Which of the following could be the value of k? **Competency Based Que, CBSE QB**

(a) 3 (b) 4.5 (c) 9 (d) 27

4. Shown below is the graph of $(-x = y^2 - 3)$,

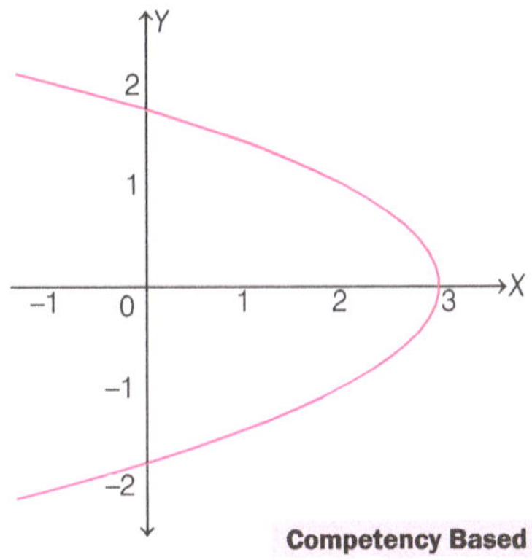

Competency Based Que, CBSE QB

Ravi says that the area under the curve in the first quadrant can be found as

$$\int_0^3 \sqrt{3-x}\, dx$$

Kanika says that the area under the curve in the first quadrant can be found as

$$\int_0^{\sqrt{3}} (3-y^2)\, dy$$

Who is correct?

(a) Only Ravi
(b) Only Kanika
(c) Both Ravi and Kanika
(d) Neither Ravi nor Kanika

5. The area of region bounded by the $y = x|x|$ and $x = -2$, $x = 2$ and X-axis is **Competency Based Que**

(a) $\frac{1}{3}$ sq units
(b) $\frac{16}{3}$ sq units
(c) $\frac{4}{3}$ sq units
(d) $\frac{7}{3}$ sq units

6. The area bounded by the curve $y = \cos x$ and X-axis and the ordinates $x = 0$ and $x = \pi$ is

(a) 4 sq units (b) 3 sq units
(c) 2 sq units (d) 1 sq unit

7. Shown below are partial graphs of two distinct functions, $f(y)$ and $g(y)$. The region between them is shaded.

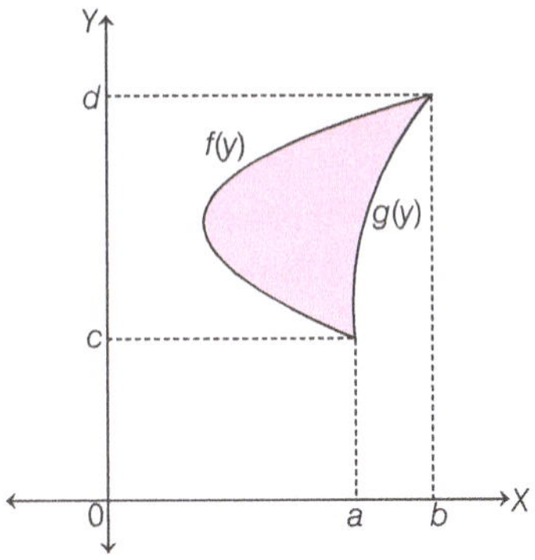

Which expression gives the area of this shaded region? **Competency Based Que, CBSE QB**

(a) $\int_a^b |f(y) - g(y)|\, dy$

(b) $\int_a^b |f(x) - g(x)|\, dx$

(c) $\int_c^d |f(y) - g(y)|\, dy$

(d) $\int_c^d |f(x) + g(x)|\, dx$

8. The area of the shaded region (figure) represented by the curves $y = x^2$, $0 \le x \le 2$ and Y-axis is given by **CBSE 2025**

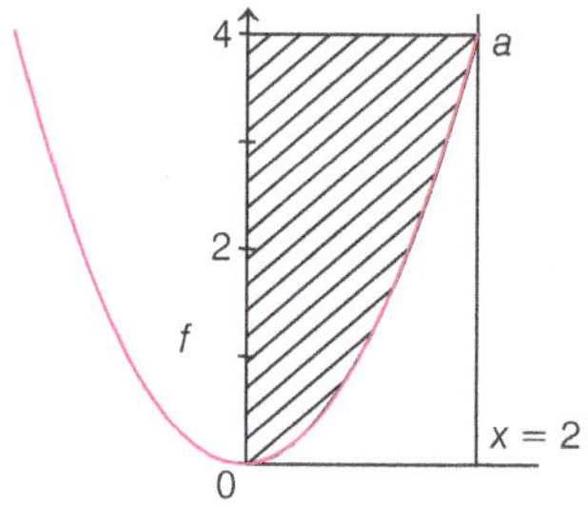

(a) $\int_0^2 x^2\,dx$ (b) $\int_0^2 \sqrt{y}\,dy$

(c) $\int_0^4 x^2\,dx$ (d) $\int_0^4 \sqrt{y}\,dy$

9. Area enclosed by the curve $x^2 + y^2 = 9$ is

(a) 9π sq units (b) 3π sq units

(c) 9 sq units (d) None of these

10. The area of the region bounded by the curve $y = \sqrt{16 - x^2}$ and X-axis is

(a) 8π sq units (b) 64π sq units

(c) 4π sq units (d) None of these

11. The area (in sq units) of the region bounded by the curve $y = x$, X-axis, $x = 0$ and $x = 2$ is **CBSE 2024C**

(a) $\frac{3}{2}$ (b) $\frac{1}{2}\log 2$ (c) 2 (d) 4

12. If a curve $y = a\sqrt{x} + bx$ passes through the point (1, 2) and the area bounded by the curve, line $x = 4$ and X-axis is 8 sq units, then **Competency Based Que**

(a) $a = 3, b = -1$ (b) $a = 3, b = 1$

(c) $a = -3, b = 1$ (d) $a = -3, b = -1$

13. The area bounded by the curve $y = x|x|$, X-axis and the coordinates $x = -1$ and $x = 1$ is given by **NCERT**

(a) 0 (b) $\frac{1}{3}$

(c) $\frac{2}{3}$ (d) $\frac{4}{3}$

14. Area lying in the first quadrant and bounded by the circle $x^2 + y^2 = 4$ and the lines $x = 0$ and $x = 2$ is **NCERT**

(a) π (b) $\frac{\pi}{2}$ (c) $\frac{\pi}{3}$ (d) $\frac{\pi}{4}$

15. Area of the region bounded by the curve $y^2 = 4x$, Y-axis and the line $y = 3$ is **NCERT**

(a) 2 (b) $\frac{9}{4}$ (c) $\frac{9}{3}$ (d) $\frac{9}{2}$

Assertion Reason Based Questions

Directions (Q. Nos. 16-23) *In the questions given below are two statements labelled as Assertion (A) and Reason (R). In the context of the two statements, which one of the following is correct?*

(a) Both A and R are correct; R is the correct explanation of A.
(b) Both A and R are correct; R is not the correct explanation of A.
(c) A is correct; R is incorrect.
(d) R is correct; A is incorrect.

16. **Assertion** (A) The area bounded by $y^2 = 4x$ and $y = x$ is $\frac{8}{3}$ sq units.

Reason (R) The area bounded by $y^2 = 4ax$ and $y = mx$ is $\frac{8a^2}{3m^3}$ sq units.

17. **Assertion** (A) The area bounded by the curve $y = \sin x$ between $x = 0$ and $x = 4\pi$ is 4 sq units.

Reason (R) $\int_0^{\pi/2} \sin x\,dx = 1$.

18. **Assertion** (A) Area enclosed by the circle $x^2 + y^2 = 64$ is equal to 64π sq units.

Reason (R) Area enclosed by the circle $x^2 + y^2 = r^2$ is πr^2.

19. **Assertion** (A) Area bounded between $x^2 + y^2 = 4$ and $x + y = 2$ is $(\pi - 2)$ sq units.

Reason (R) The area bounded by circle $x^2 + y^2 = a^2$ and line $x + y = a$ is represented by $\int_0^a \sqrt{a^2 - x^2}\,dx - \int_0^a (a - x)\,dx$.

20. **Assertion** (A) Area of the region given by $\{(x, y) : y^2 \le 6x, 2 \le x \le 5, x, y \ge 0\}$ is $\frac{21}{2}$ sq unit.

Reason (R) Area under a curve $x = f(y)$ lying to the right of Y-axis between $y = a$ and $y = b$ is given by $\int_a^b f(y)\,dy$. **Competency Based Que**

21. **Assertion** (A) Area bounded by the curve $y = |x - 1|$ and $y = 1$ is 1 sq unit.

Reason (R) The area bounded by the curve $y = |x|$, the X-axis and between $x = -2$ and $x = 1$ is $\frac{5}{2}$ sq units. **Competency Based Que**

22. **Assertion** (A) Area of the lines $y = \sqrt{3}x$ and $y = 0$ and $x = 4$ in first quadrant is $8\sqrt{3}$ sq units.

Reason (R) Area of the lines $y = \sqrt{3}x$ and $x = 0$ and $y = 4$ in first quadrant is $\frac{8}{\sqrt{3}}$ sq units.

Case Study Based Questions

23. A child cut a pizza with a knife. Pizza is circular in shape which is represented by $x^2 + y^2 = 4$ and sharp edge of knife represents a straight line given by $x = \sqrt{3}y$.

Based on the above information, answer the following questions.

(i) Find the point of intersection of the edge of knife and pizza.

(ii) Draw the graph of both circle and line and hence shade the smaller area bounded by edge of knife and pizza in the first quadrant.

(iii) Using integration find the area of that smallar part.

(iv) If child cut the pizza into four equal part. Find the area of each part.

(v) Find the area of whole pizza.

24. Location of three houses of a society is represented by the points $A(-1, 0)$, $B(1, 3)$ and $C(3, 2)$ as shown in figure.

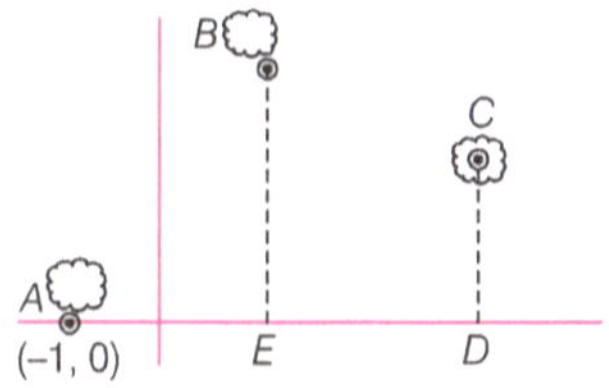

Based on the above information, answer the following questions.

(i) Find the equation of line AB.

(ii) Find the equation of BC.

(iii) Find the area of ΔABE.

(iv) Find the area of trapezium $EBCD$.

(v) Find the area of ΔACD.

(vi) Find the area of ΔABC.

25. A Lorenz curve is used to graphically represent income inequality in a society. It was developed by Max Lorenz in 1905.

In this curve, the percentile of the population according to their income is plotted on the X-axis and on the Y-axis, the percentage of cumulative income from that percentile of the population is plotted.

e.g. In the graph below, the point (20, 4) denotes that people with more income than that of 20% of the total population contribute 4% of the total income for the country.

Similarly, the point (64, 40) denotes that people with more income than that of 64% of the country's population contribute 40% of the total income for the country.

On the graph, there is also a line of equality, given by the function $g(x) = x$. The further away the Lorenz curve of a society is from the line of equality, the more unequal its income distribution is.

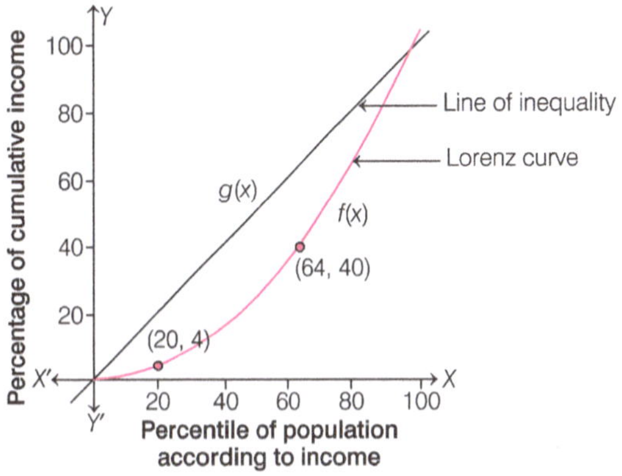

In order to compare this data for multiple countries, the area under the Lorenz Curve is used to find the Gini coefficient (G), whose value ranges between 0 and 1. The closer G's value is to 1, the more unequal the income distribution of the society is.

The Lorenz curve shown above can be approximated by the following function

$$f(x) = \frac{\sqrt{x}}{100} + \frac{(x-1)^2}{100}$$

Competency Based Que, CBSE QB

Based on the above information, answer the following questions.

(i) Find the area under the Lorenz curve from 0 to 100. Show your work.

(ii) The Gini coefficient is given by $G = \frac{A}{A+B}$, where A is the area between the Lorenz curve and the line of equality and B is the area under the Lorenz curve. Find the Gini coefficient for the given Lorenz curve, using integration. Show your work.

Subjective Questions

Short Answer Type Questions

1. Find the area of the region bounded by $y^2 = 9x$, $x = 2$, $x = 4$ and the X-axis in the first quadrant. **NCERT**

2. Using integration, evaluate the area of the region bounded by the curve $y = x^2$, the lines $y = 1$ and $y = 3$ and the Y-axis. **CBSE 2024C, Competency Based Que**

3. Using integration, find the area of the region bounded by $y = mx (m > 0)$, $x = 1$, $x = 2$ and the X-axis. **CBSE 2023**

4. Find the area of the smaller part of the circle $x^2 + y^2 = a^2$ cut-off by the line $x = \frac{a}{\sqrt{2}}$.
Competency Based Que, NCERT

5. Find the area of the region bounded by the curve $y = x^2$ and the line $y = 4$. **NCERT**

6. Find the area of the parabola $y^2 = 4ax$ bounded by its latusrectum. **Competency Based Que, CBSE 2023, NCERT**

7. Find the area of the region bounded by $y = -1$, $y = 2$, $x = y^3$ and $x = 0$.

8. Find the area bounded by the curve $y = x|x|$, X-axis and the ordinates $x = -3$ and $x = 3$. **Competency Based Que**

9. Find the area of the region bounded by the line $y = 5x + 2$, the X-axis and the ordinates $x = -2$ and $x = 2$. **CBSE 2025**

10. Draw the graph of the curve $y = |\sin x|$ and find the area bounded by the curve, X-axis and ordinates $x = -\pi$ to 2π. **Competency Based Que**

11. Draw a rough sketch of the curve $y = |x - 2|$. Find the area under the curve and line $x = 0$ and $x = 4$.

12. Find the area bounded $x^2 = 4y$ and $y = 4$ in the first quadrant. **Diksha App**

13. Find the area bounded by ellipse $9x^2 + 4y^2 = 36$.

14. Sketch the graph of $y = |x + 3|$ and evaluate the area under the curve $y = |x + 3|$ above X-axis and between $x = -6$ to $x = 0$. **Competency Based Que, CBSE 2011**

Long Answer Type Questions

15. Find the area bounded by the curve $y = \cos x$ between $x = 0$ and $x = 2\pi$. **NCERT Exemplar**

16. Find the area bounded by the curve $y = x^3$, the X-axis and the ordinates $x = -2$ and $x = 1$. **NCERT**

17. The area between $x = y^2$ and $x = 4$ is divided into two equal parts by the line $x = a$. Find the value of a. **Competency Based Que**

18. Find the area bounded by the ellipse $\frac{x^2}{a^2} + \frac{y^2}{b^2} = 1$ and the coordinates $x = 0$ and $x = ae$, where $b^2 = a^2(1 - e^2)$ and $e < 1$. **Competency Based Que**

Hints & Solutions

Objective Type Questions

1. (b) We draw the curve $y^2 = 4x$ and the line $x = 1$.

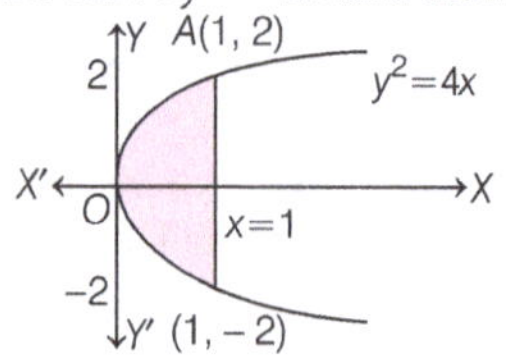

Thus, the area of required region $= 2\int_0^1 y\,dx$

$$= 2\int_0^1 \sqrt{4x}\,dx = 4\int_0^1 x^{\frac{1}{2}}\,dx$$

$$= 4\left[\frac{x^{\frac{3}{2}}}{\frac{3}{2}}\right]_0^1 = \frac{8}{3}\left[1^{\frac{3}{2}} - 0\right] = \frac{8}{3} \text{ sq units}$$

2. (c) Given curve is $y = \sqrt{x}$

Required area $= \int_0^3 x \cdot dy = \int_0^3 y^2 dy$

$$= \left(\frac{y^3}{3}\right)_0^3 = \left(\frac{27}{3} - 0\right) = 9 \text{ sq units}$$

3. (a) Given, the area under the curve $y = x^2$ between the line $x = 0$ and $x = k$ is 9 sq units.

$\therefore$ Area under a curve $= \int_a^b f(x)\,dx$

$$\Rightarrow \quad 9 = \int_0^k x^2 dx \Rightarrow 9 = \left[\frac{x^3}{3}\right]_0^k$$

$$\Rightarrow \quad \frac{k^3}{3} = 9$$

$$\Rightarrow \quad k^3 = 27 \Rightarrow k = 3$$

4. (c) We have, $-x = y^2 - 3 \Rightarrow y^2 = 3 - x \Rightarrow y^2 = -(x-3)$

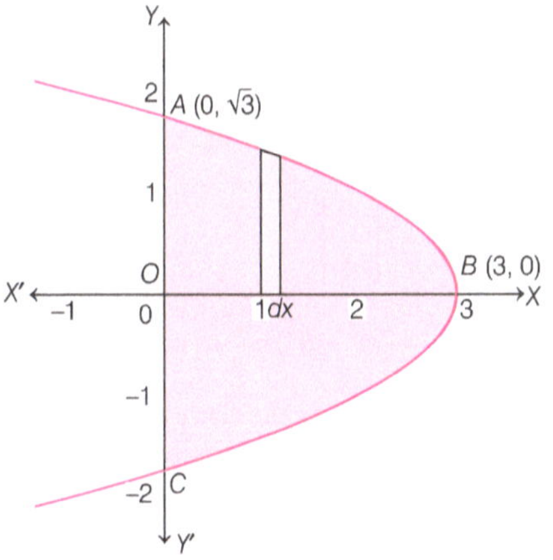

$\therefore$ Required area = Area under the curve in the I quadrant

$$= \int_0^3 \sqrt{3-x}\, dx$$

$[\because -x = y^2 - 3 \Rightarrow y = \sqrt{3-x},$ as y is in I quadrant$]$

Hence, Ravi says correct.

Now, area of the parabola along Y-axis

= Area under the curve in the first quadrant

$$= \int_0^{\sqrt{3}} (3 - y^2)\, dy$$

Hence, Kanika says also correct.

5. (b) Given, $y = x|x|, x = -2, x = 2$

$$y = \begin{cases} -x^2, & x < 0 \\ x^2, & > 0 \end{cases}$$

Shaded area is the required area.

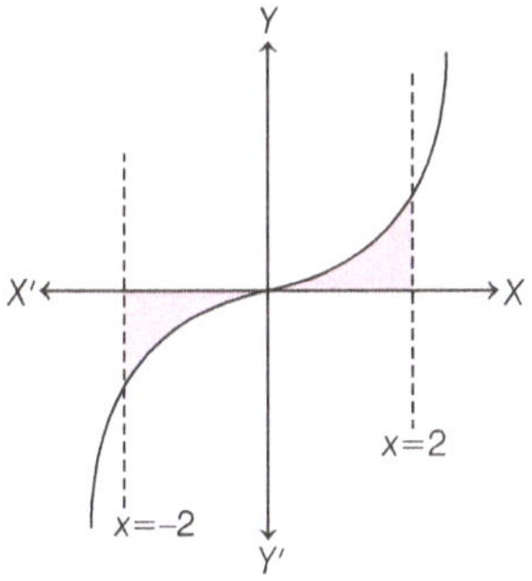

$$\therefore \text{ Required area} = \int_{-2}^{0} x|x|\, dx + \int_0^2 x|x|\, dx$$

$$= \int_{-2}^{0} -x^2\, dx + \int_0^2 x^2\, dx$$

$$= 2\int_0^2 x^2\, dx$$

$$= 2\left(\frac{x^3}{3}\right)_0^2 = 2\left(\frac{8}{3} - 0\right)$$

$$= \frac{16}{3} \text{ sq units}$$

6. (c) Given, $y = \cos x, x = 0, x = \pi$

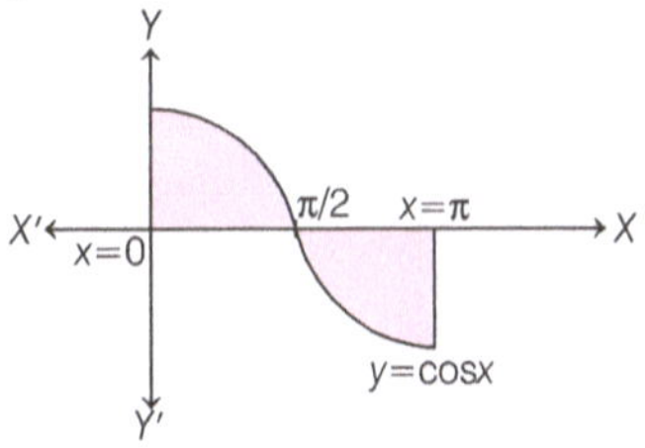

Shaded area is the required area.

$$\therefore \text{ Required area} = \int_0^{\pi/2} \cos x\, dx + \left| \int_{\pi/2}^{\pi} \cos x \cdot dx \right|$$

$$= [\sin x]_0^{\pi/2} + |[\sin x]_{\pi/2}^{\pi}|$$

$$= \sin\frac{\pi}{2} - \sin 0 + |\sin \pi - \sin \pi/2|$$

$$= 1 - 0 + |0 - 1| = 1 + 1 = 2 \text{ sq units}$$

7. (c) Area between any two curves $f(x)$ and $g(x)$, from x_1 to x_2.

$$= \int_{x_1}^{x_2} |f(x) - g(x)|\, dx$$

and area between $f(y)$ and $g(y)$ from y_1 to y_2

$$= \int_{y_1}^{y_2} |f(y) - g(y)|\, dy$$

$\therefore$ According to given question, Area $= \int_c^d |f(y) - g(y)|\, dy$

8. (d) Given function is

$$y = x^2, 0 \le x \le 2 \Rightarrow x = \sqrt{y} \quad \ldots\text{(i)}$$

$\therefore$ Required area as showing in the figure

$$= \int_0^4 x\, dy = \int_0^4 \sqrt{y}\, dy \quad \text{[using Eq. (i)]}$$

9. (a) Given, curve $x^2 + y^2 = 9$ is a circle with centre (0, 0) and radius = 3 units.

$$\therefore \text{ Required area} = 4\int_0^3 \sqrt{9 - x^2}\, dx$$

$$= 4\left[\frac{x}{2}\sqrt{9 - x^2} + \frac{9}{2}\sin^{-1}\frac{x}{3}\right]_0^3$$

$$= 4\left[\left(0 + \frac{9}{2}\sin^{-1} 1\right) - (0 + 0)\right]$$

$$= 4 \times \frac{9}{2} \times \frac{\pi}{2} = 9\pi \text{ sq units}$$

10. (a) **Hint** We have, $y = \sqrt{16 - x^2}$

$$\Rightarrow \quad y^2 = 16 - x^2 \Rightarrow x^2 + y^2 = 16$$

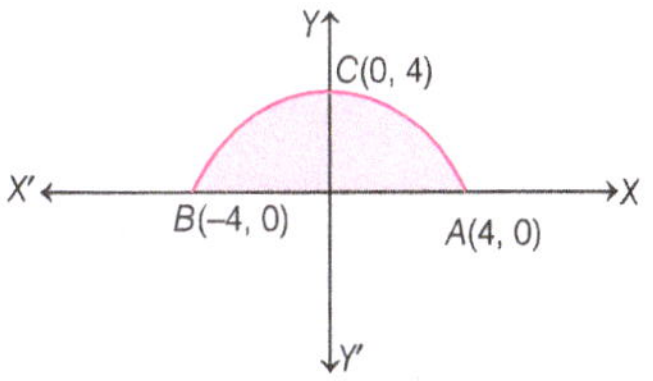

$$\therefore \text{ Required area} = \int_{-4}^{4} \sqrt{16 - x^2}\, dx = 2\int_0^4 \sqrt{16 - x^2}\, dx$$

11. (c) Given, curve $y = x$

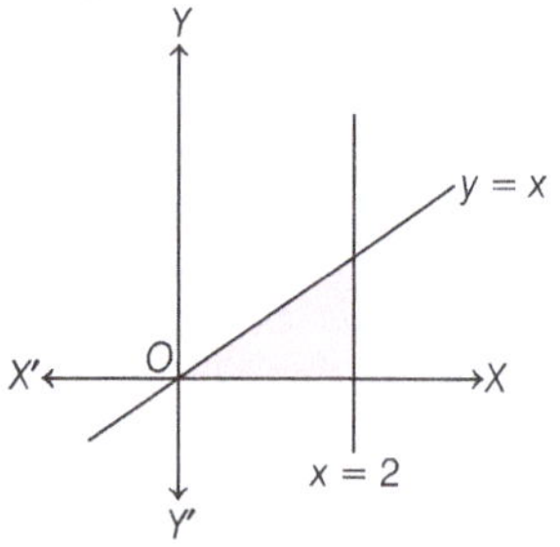

$\therefore$ Required area $= \int_0^2 y\,dx$

$= \int_0^2 x\,dx = \left[\frac{x^2}{2}\right]_0^2$

$= \frac{1}{2}[4 - 0]$

$= 2$ sq units

12. (a) Given, curve $y = a\sqrt{x} + bx$ passes through point (1, 2).

$\therefore \quad 2 = a\sqrt{1} + b(1)$

$\Rightarrow \quad 2 = a + b \quad$ ...(i)

Area bounded by this curve, line $x = 4$ and X-axis $= 8$ sq units

$\Rightarrow \quad \int_0^4 y\,dx = 8$

$\Rightarrow \quad 8 = \int_0^4 (a\sqrt{x} + bx)\,dx$

$\Rightarrow \quad 8 = \left[a \cdot \frac{2}{3}x^{3/2}\right]_0^4 + \left[\frac{bx^2}{2}\right]_0^4$

$\Rightarrow \quad 8 = \frac{2a}{3} \times 8 - 0 + \frac{b}{2} \times 16 - 0$

$\Rightarrow \quad 8 = \frac{16a}{3} + 8b$

$\Rightarrow \quad 3 = 2a + 3b \quad$ ...(ii)

On solving Eqs. (i) and (ii), we get

$a = 3$ and $b = -1$

13. (c) Given, $y = x|x| = \begin{cases} x^2, x \geq 0 \\ -x^2, x < 0 \end{cases}$

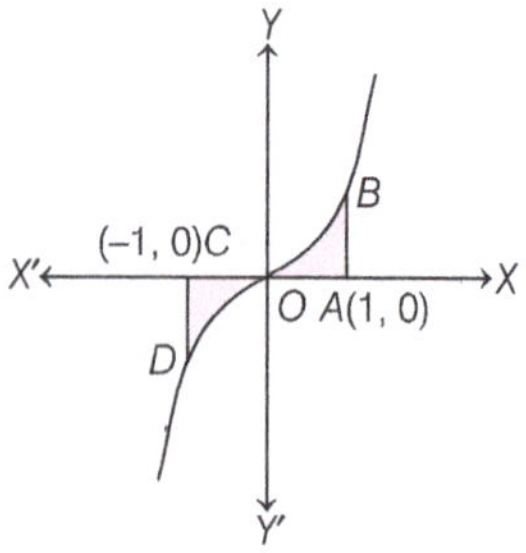

$\therefore$ Required area $= 2$ [Area under the curve $y = x^2$ and between $x = 0$ and $x = 1$]

[$\because$ the curve is symmetrical in opposite quadrant.]

$= 2\int_0^1 x|x| = 2\int_0^1 x^2 dx$

$= 2\left[\frac{x^3}{3}\right]_0^1$

$= \frac{2}{3}(1^3 - 0^3) = \frac{2}{3}$ sq units

14. (a) The area bounded by the circle and the lines $x = 0$ and $x = 2$, in the first quadrant is represented in the figure by shaded region

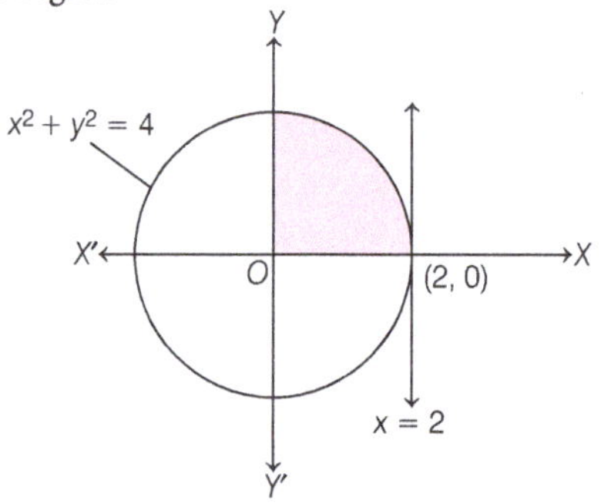

$\therefore$ Required area $= \int_0^2 y\,dx = \int_0^2 \sqrt{4 - x^2}\,dx$

$= \left[\frac{x}{2}\sqrt{4 - x^2} + \frac{4}{2}\sin^{-1}\left(\frac{x}{2}\right)\right]_0^2$

$= 0 + 2\sin^{-1}(1) - 0 = 2 \times \frac{\pi}{2} = \pi$ sq units

15. (b) The area bounded by the curve $y^2 = 4x$, Y-axis and $y = 3$ is represented in the figure by shaded region.

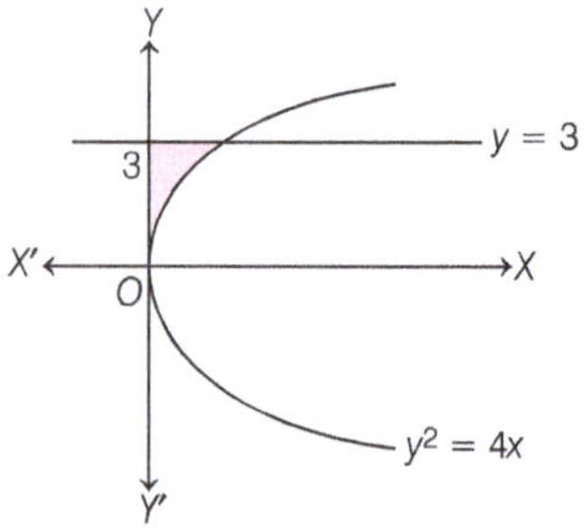

$\therefore$ Required area $= \int_0^3 x\,dy$

$= \int_0^3 \frac{y^2}{4}dy = \frac{1}{4}\left[\frac{y^3}{3}\right]_0^3$

$= \frac{1}{12}(3^3 - 0) = \frac{1}{12}(27) = \frac{9}{4}$ sq units.

16. (a) **Hint**

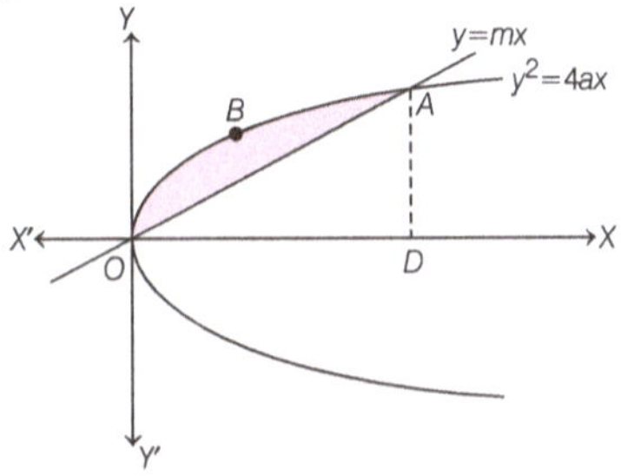

$\therefore$ Required area = Area of $OBADO$ – Area of $OADO$

$$= \int_0^{4a/m^2} y\,dx - \int_0^{4a/m^2} y\,dx$$

$$= \int_0^{4a/m^2} \sqrt{4ax}\,dx - \int_0^{4a/m^2} mx\,dx$$

17. (d) **Hint**

Assertion

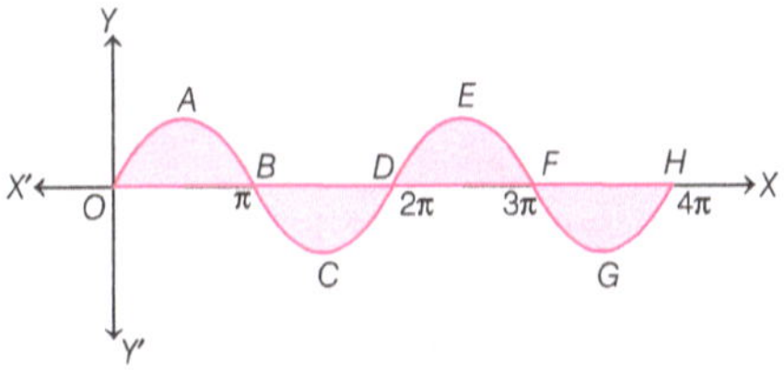

$\therefore$ Required area = Area of $OABO$ + Area of $BCDB$ + Area of $DEFD$ + Area of $FGHF$

$$= \int_0^{\pi} y\,dx + \left|\int_{\pi}^{2\pi} y\,dx\right| + \int_{2\pi}^{3\pi} y\,dx + \left|\int_{3\pi}^{4\pi} y\,dx\right|$$

$$= 4\int_0^{\pi} y\,dx = 8 \text{ sq units}$$

18. (a) **Hint**

Assertion

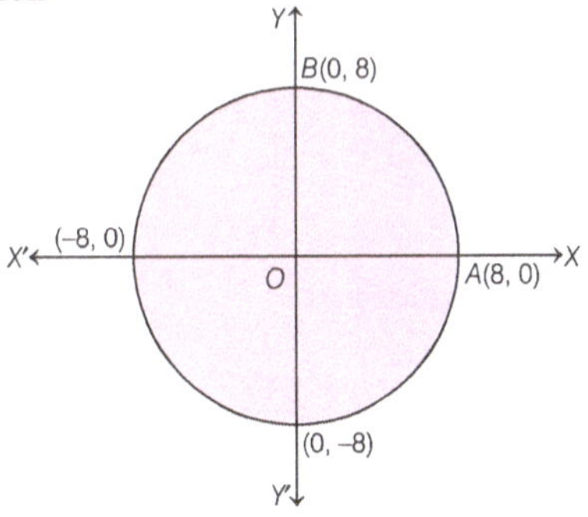

$\therefore$ Required area = 4 × Area of $OABO$

$$= 4 \times \int_0^8 \sqrt{8^2 - x^2}\,dx$$

$$= 4 \times \left[\frac{x}{2}\sqrt{8^2 - x^2} + \frac{64}{2}\sin^{-1}\left(\frac{x}{8}\right)\right]_0^8$$

$$= 4 \times [(0 + 32\sin^{-1}(1)) - (0 + 0)]$$

$$= 4 \times 32 \times \sin^{-1} 1 = 128 \times \frac{\pi}{2} = 64\pi \text{ sq units}$$

Hence, both Assertion and Reason are correct and Reason is the correct explanation of Assertion.

19. (a) Given, $x^2 + y^2 = 4$ and $x + y = 2$

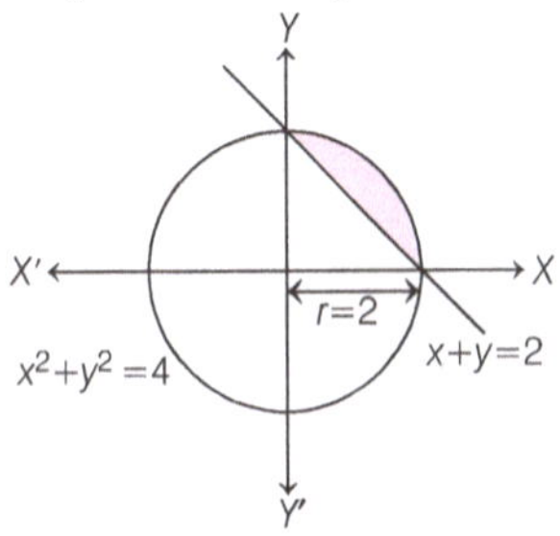

Shaded area is required area $= \int_0^2 y_{\text{circle}}\,dx - \int_0^2 y_{\text{line}}\,dx$

$$= \int_0^2 \sqrt{4 - x^2}\,dx - \int_0^2 (2 - x)\,dx$$

$$= \left(\frac{x}{2}\sqrt{4 - x^2} + \frac{4}{2}\sin^{-1}\frac{x}{2}\right)_0^2 - \left(2x - \frac{x^2}{2}\right)_0^2$$

$$= (0 + 2\sin^{-1} 1) - \left(4 - \frac{4}{2}\right) = 2 \cdot \frac{\pi}{2} - 2$$

$$= (\pi - 2) \text{ sq units}$$

Hence, both Assertion and Reason are correct and Reason is the correct explanation of Assertion.

20. (d) Given, $y^2 \le 6x, 2 \le x \le 5, x, y \ge 0$

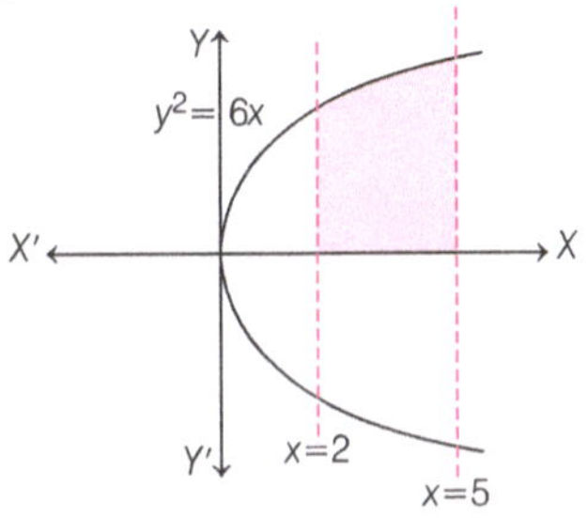

Shaded area is required area.

Now, area $= \int_2^5 y\,dx = \int_2^5 \sqrt{6x}\,dx$

$$= \sqrt{6} \cdot \left(\frac{x^{3/2}}{\frac{3}{2}}\right)_2^5 = \sqrt{6} \cdot \frac{2}{3}[5^{3/2} - 2^{3/2}]$$

Assertion is incorrect but Reason is correct.

21. (b) **Assertion** Given, $y = |x - 1|$ and $y = 1$

$$\Rightarrow \qquad y = \begin{cases} x - 1 & , x \ge 1 \\ 1 - x & , x < 1 \end{cases}$$

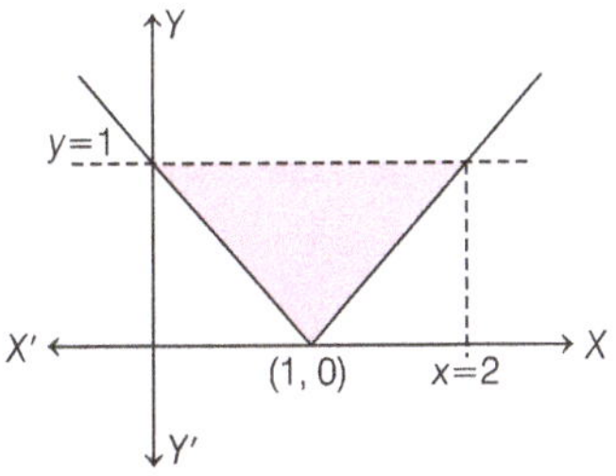

Area of shaded region

$$= \int_0^2 (y = 1)\, dx - \int_0^1 (1 - x)\, dx - \int_1^2 (x - 1)\, dx$$

$$= (x)_0^2 - \left(x - \frac{x^2}{2}\right)_0^1 - \left(\frac{x^2}{2} - x\right)_1^2$$

$$= 2 - \left[1 - \frac{1}{2}\right] - \left[\left(\frac{4}{2} - 2\right) - \left(\frac{1}{2} - 1\right)\right]$$

$$= 2 - \frac{1}{2} - \frac{1}{2} = 1 \text{ sq unit}$$

Assertion is correct.

Reason

$$y = |x|, x = -2, x = 1$$

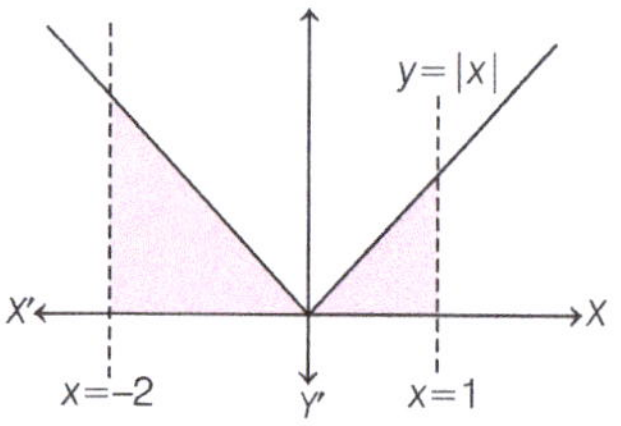

Area of shaded region $= \int_{-2}^{1} |x|\, dx$

$$= \int_{-2}^{0} -x\, dx + \int_0^1 x\, dx$$

$$\left[\because |x| = \begin{cases} x & x \geq 0 \\ -x & x < 0 \end{cases}\right]$$

$$= -\left(\frac{x^2}{2}\right)_{-2}^{0} + \left(\frac{x^2}{2}\right)_0^1$$

$$= -\left(0 - \frac{4}{2}\right) + \left(\frac{1}{2} - 0\right)$$

$$= 2 + \frac{1}{2} = \frac{5}{2} \text{ sq units}$$

Hence, Assertion and Reason both are correct but Reason is not correct explanation of Assertion.

22. (b) **Assertion** Given, $y = \sqrt{3}x, y = 0, x = 4$

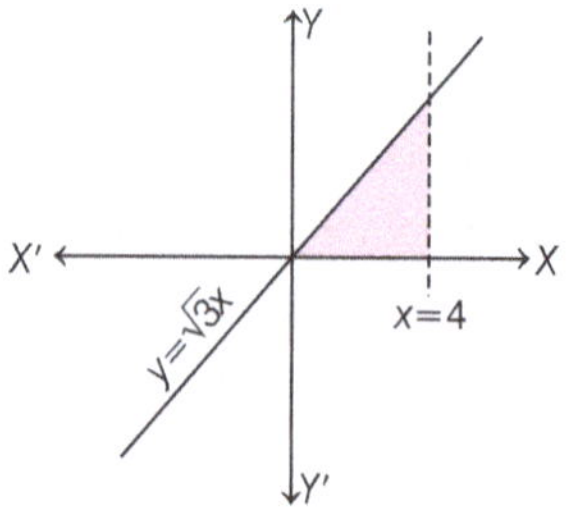

Shaded area $= \int_0^4 \sqrt{3}x\, dx = \sqrt{3}\left(\frac{x^2}{2}\right)_0^4$

$$= \sqrt{3} \cdot \frac{16}{2} = 8\sqrt{3} \text{ sq. units}$$

Assertion is correct.

Reason

Given line, $y = \sqrt{3}x, x = 0$ and $y = 4$

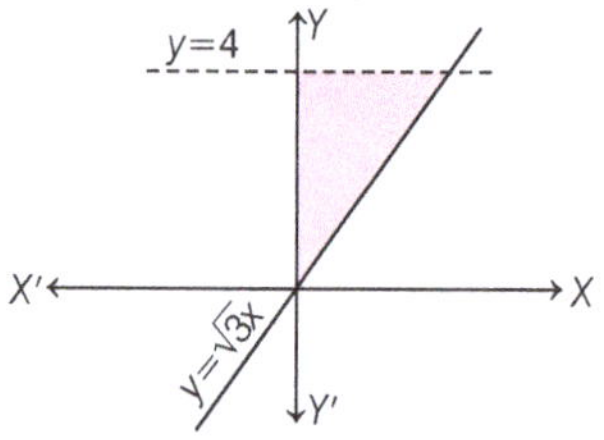

Area of shaded region $= \int_0^4 x\, dy$

$$= \int_0^4 \frac{y}{\sqrt{3}}\, dy = \frac{1}{\sqrt{3}}\left(\frac{y^2}{2}\right)_0^4 = \frac{8}{\sqrt{3}} \text{ sq units}$$

Hence, Assertion and Reason both are correct but Reason is not correct explanation of Assertion.

23. (i) For point of intersection, solve

$$x^2 + y^2 = 4 \quad \ldots(i)$$

and $\quad x = \sqrt{3}y \quad \ldots(ii)$

From Eqs. (i) and (ii), we get

$$(\sqrt{3}y)^2 + y^2 = 4 \Rightarrow 4y^2 = 4$$

So, $\quad y = \pm 1, x = \pm\sqrt{3}$

There are two points of intersection.

$$A = (\sqrt{3}, 1)$$
$$B = (-\sqrt{3}, -1)$$

(ii)

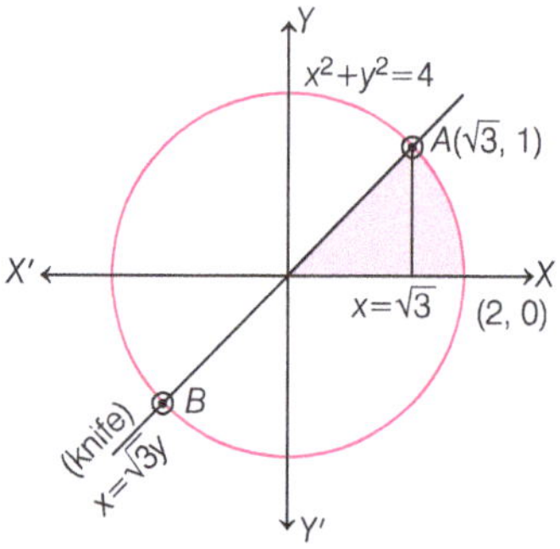

(iii) Area of shaded part

$$= \int_0^{\sqrt{3}} y_{\text{line}}\, dx + \int_{\sqrt{3}}^{2} y_{\text{circle}}\, dx$$

$$= \int_0^{\sqrt{3}} \frac{x}{\sqrt{3}}\, dx + \int_{\sqrt{3}}^{2} \sqrt{4 - x^2}\, dx$$

$$= \frac{1}{\sqrt{3}}\left(\frac{x^2}{2}\right)_0^{\sqrt{3}} + \left[\frac{x}{2}\sqrt{4 - x^2} + \frac{4}{2}\sin^{-1}\frac{x}{2}\right]_{\sqrt{3}}^{2}$$

$$= \frac{1}{\sqrt{3}}\left(\frac{3}{2} - 0\right) + \left[(0 + 2\sin^{-1} 1) - \left(\frac{\sqrt{3}}{2} + 2\sin^{-1}\frac{\sqrt{3}}{2}\right)\right]$$

$$= \frac{\sqrt{3}}{2} + 2 \cdot \frac{\pi}{2} - \frac{\sqrt{3}}{2} - 2 \cdot \frac{\pi}{3}$$

$$= \pi - \frac{2\pi}{3} = \frac{\pi}{3} \text{ sq units}$$

(iv) If child cut the pizza into four equal part than shaded part is the required part.

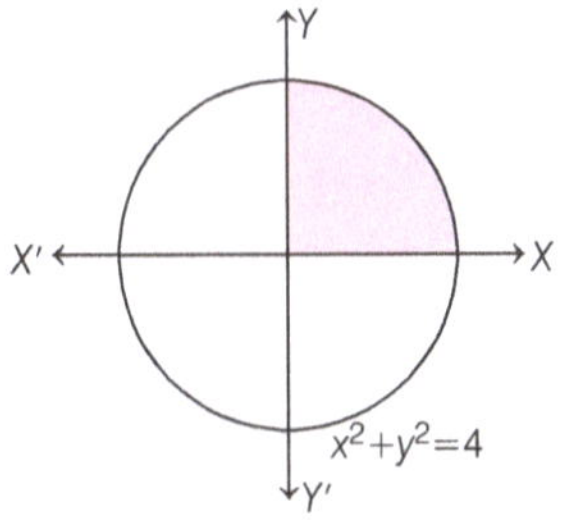

$$= \int_0^2 y_{\text{circle}}\, dx$$
$$= \int_0^2 \sqrt{4-x^2}\, dx$$
$$= \left[\frac{x}{2}\sqrt{4-x^2} + \frac{4}{2}\sin^{-1}\frac{x}{2}\right]_0^2$$
$$= (0 + 2\sin^{-1}1) - 0$$
$$= 2\cdot\pi/2 = \pi \text{ sq units}$$

(v) Area of whole pizza = 4 (shaded part) = 4π

24. (i) Given, points $A(-1, 0), B(1, 3)$ and $C(3, 2)$.

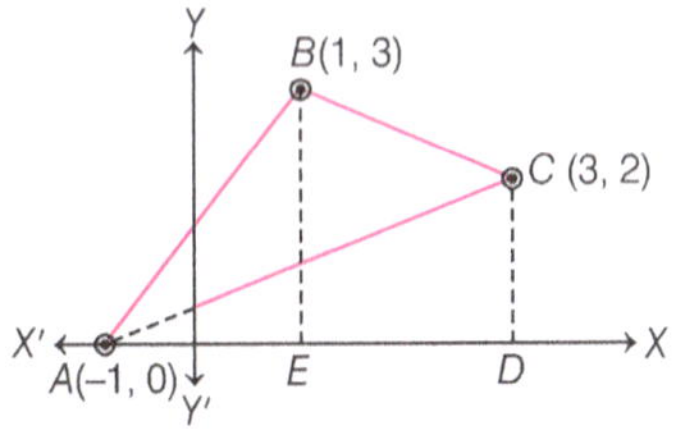

Equation of $AB, A = (-1, 0)\ B = (1, 3)$ is

$$y - 0 = \frac{3-0}{1-(-1)}(x-(-1))$$
$$\left[\because y - y_1 = \frac{y_2 - y_1}{x_2 - x_1}(x - x_1)\right]$$
$$\Rightarrow \quad y = \frac{3}{2}(x+1) \quad \ldots\text{(i)}$$

(ii) Equation of $BC, B = (1, 3), C = (3, 2)$ is

$$y - 3 = \frac{2-3}{3-1}(x-1) \Rightarrow y - 3 = \frac{-1}{2}(x-1)$$
$$\Rightarrow \quad y = \frac{-x}{2} + \frac{1}{2} + 3 \Rightarrow y = \frac{-x}{2} + \frac{7}{2}$$

(iii) Area of $\Delta ABE = \int_{-1}^{1} y_{AB}\, dx = \int_{-1}^{1}\frac{3}{2}(x+1)\, dx$

$$\Rightarrow \frac{3}{2}\int_{-1}^{1}(x+1)\, dx \Rightarrow \frac{3}{2}\left[\frac{x^2}{2} + x\right]_{-1}^{1}$$
$$\Rightarrow \frac{3}{2}\left[\frac{1}{2} + 1 - \left(\frac{1}{2} - 1\right)\right] \Rightarrow \frac{3}{2}\left[\frac{1}{2} + 1 - \frac{1}{2} + 1\right] = \frac{3}{2}\cdot 2$$
$$= 3 \text{ sq units}$$

(iv) Area of trapezium $EBCD$

$$= \int_1^3 y_{BC} dx = \int_1^3\left(\frac{-x}{2} + \frac{7}{2}\right) dx$$
$$= \left(\frac{-x^2}{4} + \frac{7x}{2}\right)_1^3 = \left(\frac{-9}{4} + \frac{21}{2}\right) - \left(\frac{-1}{4} + \frac{7}{2}\right)$$
$$= \frac{-9}{4} + \frac{1}{4} + \frac{21}{2} - \frac{7}{2}$$
$$= -2 + 7 = 5 \text{ sq units}$$

(v) For area of ΔACD

Equation of $AC, A = (-1, 0)\ C = (3, 2)$ is

$$y - 0 = \frac{2-0}{3-(-1)}(x-(-1))$$
$$\Rightarrow \quad y = \frac{2}{4}(x+1) = \frac{1}{2}(x+1)$$

$\therefore$ Required area $= \int_{-1}^{3} y_{AC} dx$

$$= \frac{1}{2}\int_{-1}^{3}(x+1)\, dx$$
$$= \frac{1}{2}\left[\frac{x^2}{2} + x\right]_{-1}^{3} = \frac{1}{2}\left[\frac{9}{2} + 3 - \left(\frac{1}{2} - 1\right)\right]$$
$$= \frac{1}{2}[4+4] = 4 \text{ sq units}$$

(vi) Area of ΔABC

= Area of ΔABE + Area of tripizium $EBCD$ – Area of ΔACD

$= 3 + 5 - 4$

$= 4$ sq units

25. (i) We have, $f(x) = \dfrac{\sqrt{x}}{100} + \dfrac{(x-1)^2}{100}$

$\therefore$ The area under the Lorenz curve from 0 to 100

$$= \int_0^{100} f(x)\, dx$$
$$= \int_0^{100}\left(\frac{\sqrt{x}}{100} + \frac{(x-1)^2}{100}\right) dx$$
$$= \int_0^{100}\frac{\sqrt{x}}{100} dx + \int_0^{100}\frac{(x-1)^2}{100} dx$$
$$= \int_0^{100}\frac{\sqrt{x}}{100} dx + \int_0^{100}\frac{x^2}{100} dx - \int_0^{100}\frac{2x}{100} dx + \int_0^{100}\frac{1}{100} dx$$
$$= \left[\frac{2x^{3/2}}{300}\right]_0^{100} + \left[\frac{x^3}{300}\right]_0^{100} - \left[\frac{2x^2}{200}\right]_0^{100} + \left[\frac{x}{100}\right]_0^{100}$$
$$= \frac{20}{3} + \frac{10000}{3} - 100 + 1$$
$$= \frac{10020}{3} - 99$$
$$= 3241 \text{ sq units}$$

(ii) Given, Gini coefficient $=\frac{A}{A+B}$

where, $A =$ The area between the Lorenz curve and the line of equality.

$B =$ The area under the Lorenz curve.

$\because \quad g(x)=x$

The area under $g(x)$

$$A+B=\int_0^{100} x\,dx$$

$$=\left[\frac{x^2}{2}\right]_0^{100}=5000$$

$\therefore \quad A =$ [area under $g(x)$] − [the area under the Lorenz curve from 0 to 100]

$$=5000-3241=1759 \text{ sq. units}$$

$\therefore$ Gini coefficient for given Lorenz curve

$$=\frac{1759}{5000}=0.3518$$

Subjective Questions

1. Hint Given equation of parabola is $y^2=9x$.

Also, given ordinates $x=2$ and $x=4$

The bounded region in I[st] quadrant is $BCFEB$.

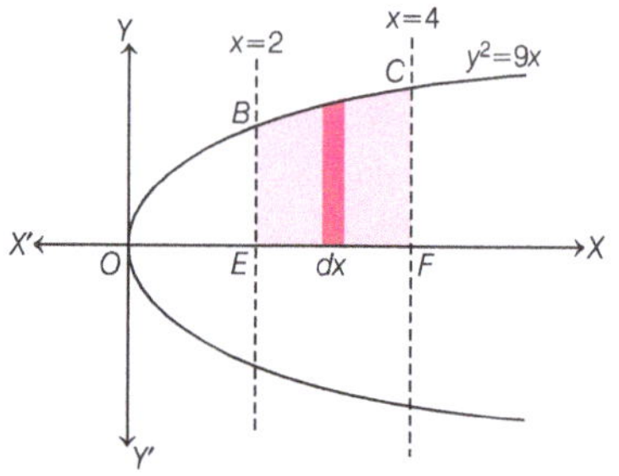

$\therefore$ Required area $=\int_2^4 y\,dx=3\int_2^4\sqrt{x}\,dx$

Ans. $4(4-\sqrt{2})$ sq units

2. Given, curve $y=x^2$

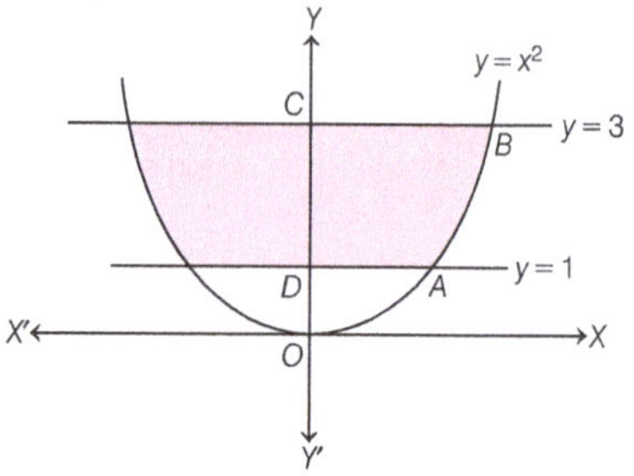

$\therefore$ Required area $=2$ (Area of shaded region $ABCDA$)

$$=2\int_1^3 x\,dy$$

$$=2\int_1^3\sqrt{y}\,dy=\frac{4}{3}[y^{3/2}]_1^3$$

$$=\frac{4}{3}[(3)^{3/2}-1^{3/2}]$$

$$=\frac{4}{3}[3\sqrt{3}-1]$$

$$=\left[4\sqrt{3}-\frac{4}{3}\right]\text{ sq units}$$

3. Given, equation of curve $y=mx\,(m>0)$, $x=1, 2$

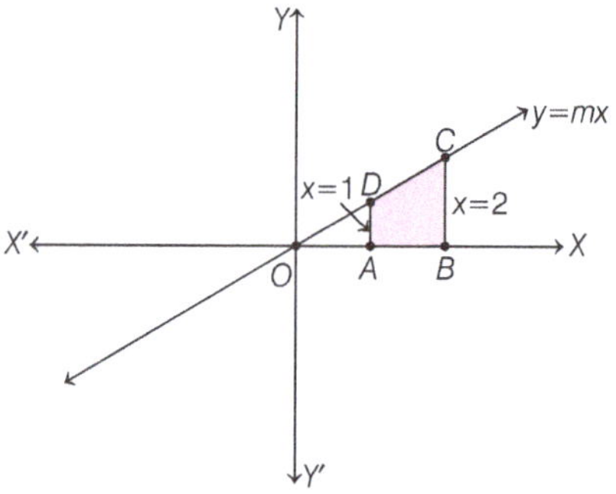

$\therefore$ Required area = Area of the region $ABCDA$

$$=\int_1^2 (mx)\,dx=m\left[\frac{x^2}{2}\right]_1^2=m\left(\frac{4}{2}-\frac{1}{2}\right)$$

$$=m\left(2-\frac{1}{2}\right)=\frac{3}{2}m\text{ sq units}$$

4. Hint Given equations of circle and line are

$$x^2+y^2=a^2 \quad \dots(i)$$

and $$x=\frac{a}{\sqrt{2}} \quad \dots(ii)$$

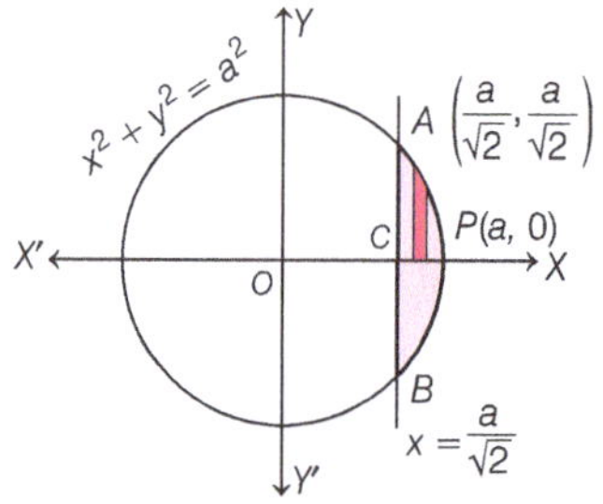

Clearly, required region is $APBCA$, which is symmetrical about X-axis and the x-coordinate of point of intersection of curve and line is $\frac{a}{\sqrt{2}}$.

Now, required area = Area of region $APBCA$

$$=2\text{ (Area of region } APCA)$$

$$=2\int_{a/\sqrt{2}}^{a} y\,dx$$

$$=2\int_{a/\sqrt{2}}^{a}\sqrt{a^2-x^2}\,dx$$

Ans. $\frac{a^2(\pi-2)}{4}$ sq units

5. Hint Required area = 2 (Area of region $OABO$)

$$= 2\int_0^4 x\,dy$$

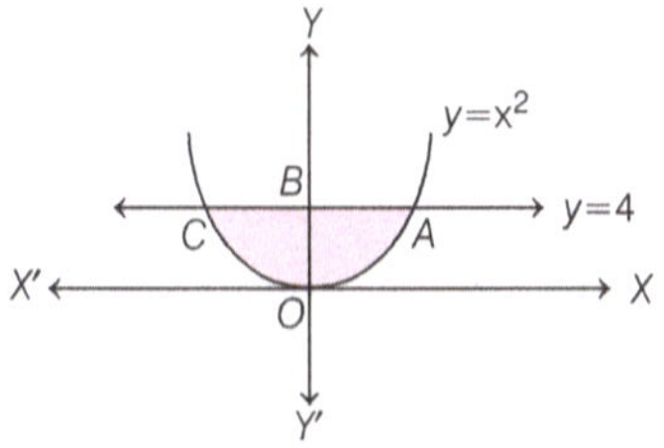

Ans. $\frac{32}{3}$ sq units

6. Hint For parabola, $y^2 = 4ax$

Latusrectum is line $x = a$

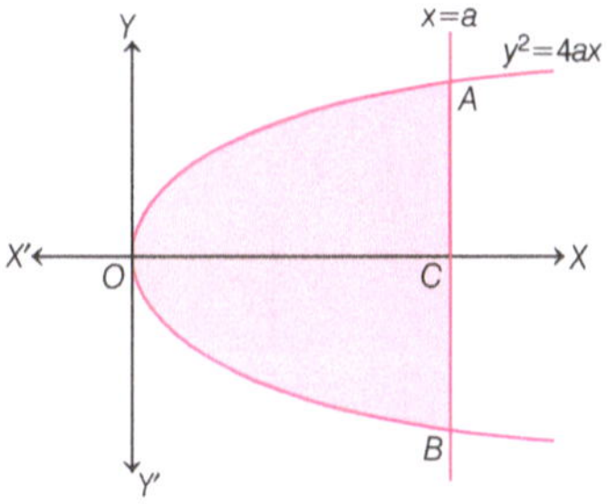

$\therefore$ Required area = Area of $OBCAO = 2 \times$ Area of $OCAO$

$$= 2 \times \int_0^a y\,dx = 2\int_0^a \sqrt{4ax}\,dx$$

Ans. $\frac{8}{3}a^2$ sq units

7. Hint Required area $= \int_0^2 y^3 dy + \left|\int_{-1}^0 y^3 dy\right|$

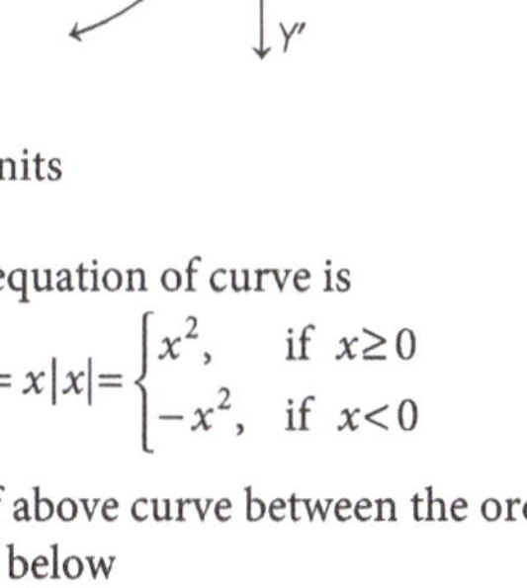

Ans. $\frac{17}{4}$ sq units

8. Hint Given equation of curve is

$$y = x|x| = \begin{cases} x^2, & \text{if } x \geq 0 \\ -x^2, & \text{if } x < 0 \end{cases}$$

The graph of above curve between the ordinates $x = -3$ and $x = 3$ is given below

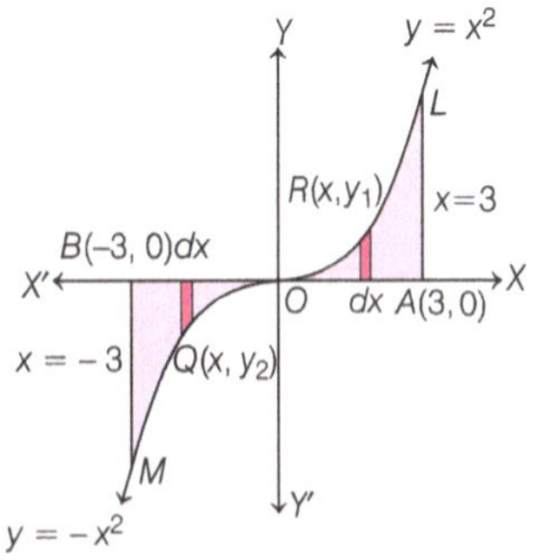

Clearly, shaded portion is the required region.

$\therefore$ Required area

= Area of region $OALO$ + Area of region $OBMO$

$$= \int_0^3 x^2\,dx + \left|\int_{-3}^0 -x^2\,dx\right|$$

Ans. 18 sq units

9. Hint Given lines are

$y = 5x + 2$ ...(i)

$y = 0$ (X-axis) ...(ii)

$x = -2$ ...(iii)

and $x = 2$ ...(iv)

Table for $y = 5x + 2$ is

x	0	$-2/5$
y	2	0

The region bounded by $y = 5x + 2$, X-axis and the ordinates $x = -2$ and $x = 2$ is represented by the shaded portion.

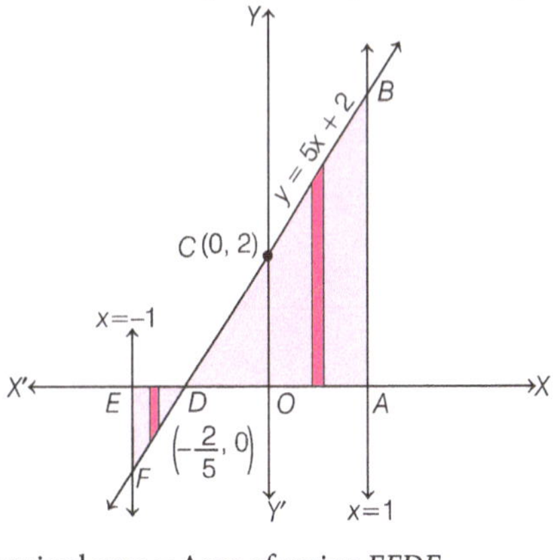

$\therefore$ Required area = Area of region $EFDE$

+ Area of region $ABDA$

$$= \left|\int_{-2}^{-2/5} y\,dx\right| + \int_{-2/5}^{2} y\,dx$$

Ans. $\frac{104}{5}$ sq units

10. **Hint** We have, $y=|\sin x|=\begin{cases}\sin x, & x\in(0,\pi),(2\pi,3\pi),\ldots\\ -\sin x, & x\in(-\pi,0),(\pi,2\pi),\ldots\end{cases}$

The graph of given curve is shown below

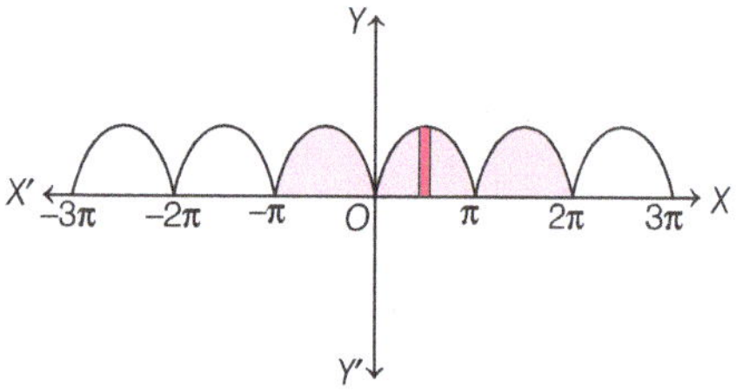

Now, required area = Area of shaded region

$= 3$ (Area of one shaded region)

[∵ all parts are of equal areas]

$=3\int_0^{\pi} y\,dx=3\int_0^{\pi}(\sin x)\,dx$

Ans. 6 sq units

11. **Hint** Required area $=\int_0^2(2-x)dx+\int_2^4(x-2)dx$

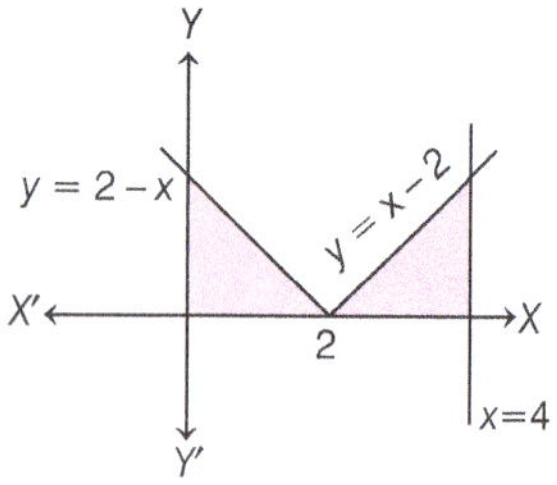

Ans. 4 sq units

12. Required area = Area of $OABO=\int_0^4 x\,dy$

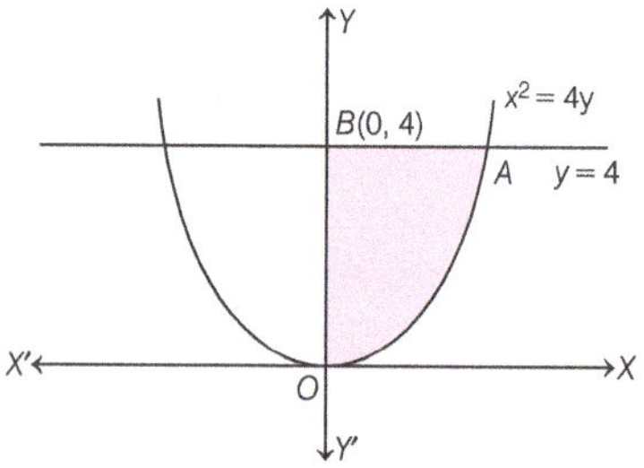

$$=\int_0^4 2\sqrt{y}\,dy=2\left[\frac{y^{\frac{1}{2}+1}}{\frac{1}{2}+1}\right]_0^4$$

$$=2\times\frac{2}{3}\left[y^{\frac{3}{2}}\right]_0^4=\frac{4}{3}[(4)^{3/2}-0]$$

$$=\frac{4}{3}[(2^2)^{3/2}]=\frac{4}{3}[2^3]=\frac{32}{3}\text{ sq units}$$

13. We have, $9x^2+4y^2=36$

$\Rightarrow \quad \dfrac{9x^2}{36}+\dfrac{4y^2}{36}=\dfrac{36}{36}$ [dividing by 36 both sides]

$\Rightarrow \quad \dfrac{x^2}{4}+\dfrac{y^2}{9}=1$

The given curve is an ellipse with centre at (0, 0) and symmetric about both axis.

$\because a^2<b^2$

∴ It is a vertical ellipse.

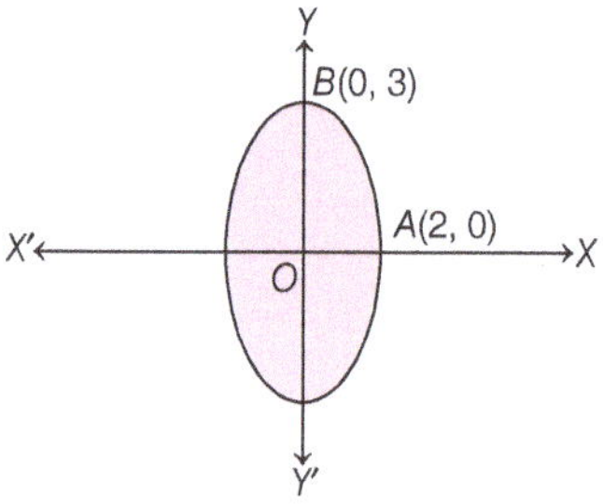

∴ Required area $=4\times$ ar $(OABO)$

$$=4\int_0^2\frac{3}{2}\sqrt{4-x^2}\,dx$$

$$\left[\because \frac{x^2}{4}+\frac{y^2}{9}=1\Rightarrow y=\frac{3}{2}\sqrt{4-x^2}\right]$$

$$=6\int_0^2\sqrt{(2)^2-x^2}\,dx$$

$$=6\left[\frac{x}{2}\sqrt{2^2-x^2}+\frac{2^2}{2}\sin^{-1}\frac{x}{2}\right]_0^2$$

$$\left[\because \int\sqrt{a^2-x^2}\,dx=\frac{x}{2}\sqrt{a^2-x^2}+\frac{a^2}{2}\sin^{-1}\frac{x}{a}\right]$$

$$=6\left[\frac{2}{2}\sqrt{2^2-2^2}+2\sin^{-1}\frac{2}{2}-(0+2\sin^{-1}0)\right]$$

$$=6[0+2\sin^{-1}(1)-0]$$

$$=6\left(2\sin^{-1}\left(\sin\frac{\pi}{2}\right)\right)=6\times2\times\frac{\pi}{2}$$

$$=6\pi\text{ sq units}$$

14. First, we sketch the graph of $y=|x+3|$.

$$\therefore \quad y=|x+3|=\begin{cases}x+3, & \text{if } x+3\ge 0\\ -(x+3), & \text{if } x+3<0\end{cases}$$

$$\Rightarrow \quad y=|x+3|=\begin{cases}x+3, & \text{if } x\ge -3\\ -x-3, & \text{if } x<-3\end{cases}$$

So, we have $y=x+3$ for $x\ge-3$ and $y=-x-3$ for $x<-3$.

A sketch of $y=|x+3|$ is shown below.

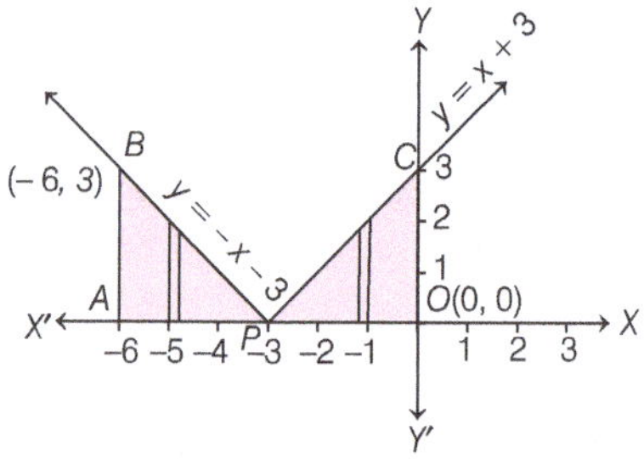

Here, $y = x+3$ is the straight line which cuts X and Y-axes at $(-3, 0)$ and $(0, 3)$, respectively.

Thus, $y = x+3$ for $x \geq -3$ represents the part of line which lies on the right side of $x = -3$.

Similarly, $y = -x-3$, $x < -3$ represents the part of line $y = -x-3$, which lies on left side of $x = -3$.

Clearly, required area = Area of region $ABPA$ + Area of region $PCOP$

$$= \int_{-6}^{-3} (-x-3)\,dx + \int_{-3}^{0} (x+3)\,dx$$

$$= \left[-\frac{x^2}{2} - 3x\right]_{-6}^{-3} + \left[\frac{x^2}{2} + 3x\right]_{-3}^{0}$$

$$= \left[\left(-\frac{9}{2}+9\right) - (-18+18)\right] + \left[0 - \left(\frac{9}{2}-9\right)\right]$$

$$= \frac{9}{2} + \frac{9}{2} = 9 \text{ sq units}$$

15. Hint

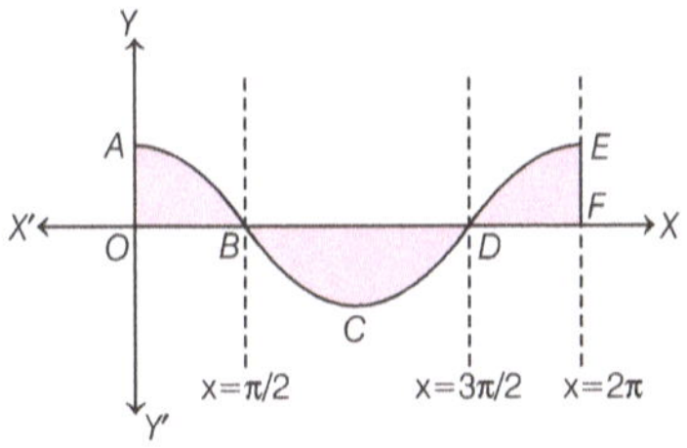

$\therefore$ Required area = Area of $OABO$ + Area of $BCDB$ + Area of $DEFD$

$$= \int_0^{\pi/2} y\,dx + \left|\int_{\pi/2}^{3\pi/2} y\,dx\right| + \int_{3\pi/2}^{2\pi} y\,dx$$

Ans. 4 sq units

16. Hint

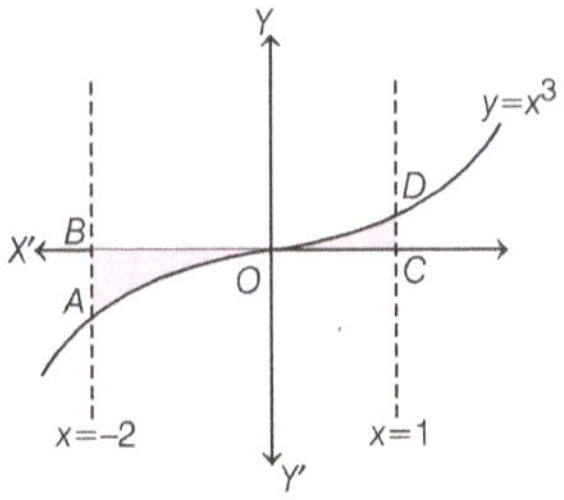

$\therefore$ Required area = Area of $ABOA$ + Area of $DCOD$

$$= \left|\int_{-2}^{0} y\,dx\right| + \int_0^1 y\,dx$$

Ans. $\frac{17}{4}$ sq. units

17. Hint

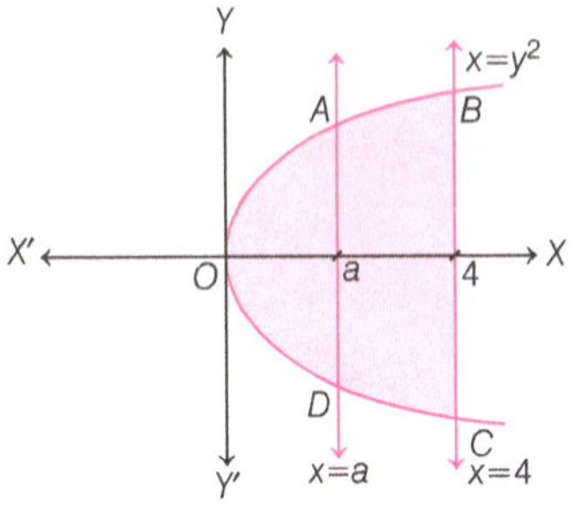

So, area $(OABCDO) = 2 \times$ Area $(OADO)$

$$= 2\int_0^4 \sqrt{x}\,dx$$

$$= 2\left(2\int_0^a \sqrt{x}\,dx\right)$$

$$\Rightarrow \quad \frac{32}{3} = \frac{8}{3}(a)^{3/2}$$

$$\Rightarrow \quad a = (4)^{2/3}$$

18. Hint

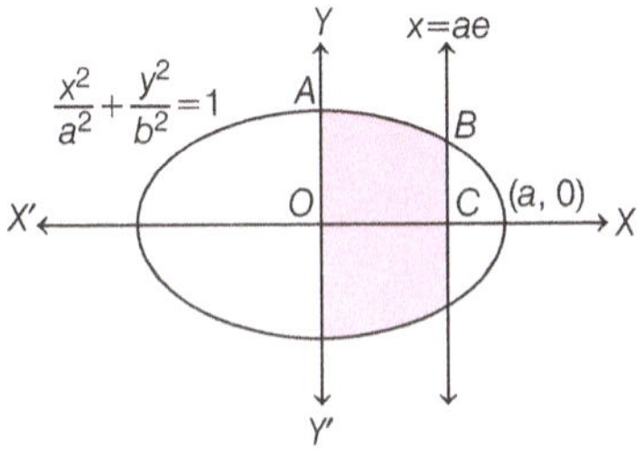

Therefore, shaded area $= 2 \times$ Area $(OABCO)$

$$= 2\int_0^{ae} \frac{b}{a}\sqrt{a^2 - x^2}\,dx$$

$$= ab[e\sqrt{1-e^2} + \sin^{-1} e] \text{ sq units}$$

Mind Map

Application of Integral

Area of a Curve Between Two Ordinates

The area bounded by the curve $y = f(x)$, the X-axis and the ordinates $x = a$ and $x = b$ is calculated as

$$\text{Area} = \int_a^b y\,dx$$
$$= \int_a^b f(x)\,dx$$

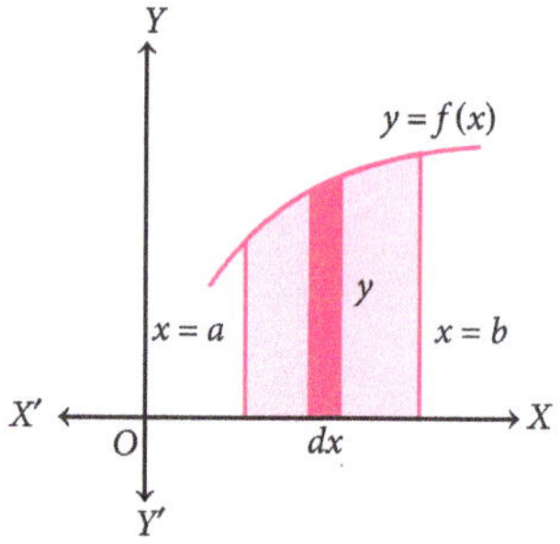

Area of a Curve Between Two Abscissae

The area bounded by the curve $x = f(y)$, the Y-axis and the lines $y = c$ and $y = d$ is calculated as

$$\text{Area} = \int_c^d x\,dy = \int_c^d f(y)\,dy$$

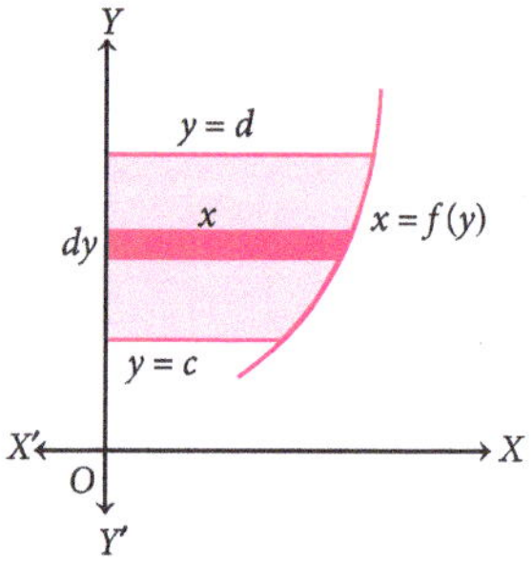

Some Important Points

- If area lies below X-axis or left of Y-axis, then it is negative and in such a case, we take its absolute value because the area of region is always positive, i.e. $A = \left|\int_a^b f(x)dx\right|$ or $A = \left|\int_c^d f(y)dy\right|$
- It may happen that some portion of the curve is above X-axis and some is below the X-axis, then the area bounded by the curve $y = f(x)$, X-axis and the ordinates $x = a$ and $x = b$ is given by

$$\text{Area} = |A_1| + A_2.$$

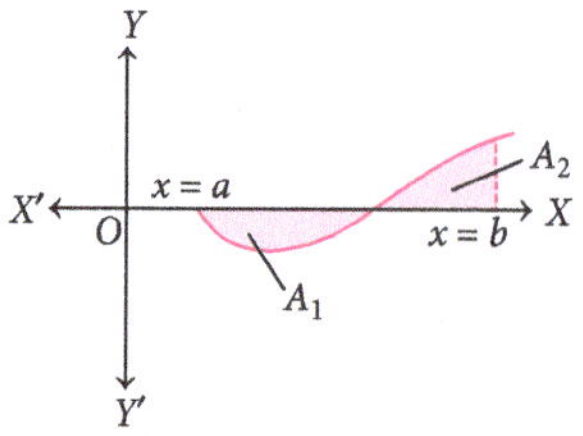

09

CHAPTER

Mathematics is a great motivator for all humans, because its career starts with zero and it never ends. — *Martin Gardner*

Differential Equations

YOUR STUDY GOALS

9.1 Differential Equations
9.2 Methods of Solving First Order and First Degree Differential Equations
9.3 Homogeneous Differential Equations
9.4 Linear Differential Equations

YOUR PRACTICE GOALS

- Objective Type Questions (33 Qs ; 19 MCQs, 10 A-R, 4 Case Based)
- Subjective Type Questions (44 Qs; 13 VSA, 20 SA, 11 LA)

9.1 Differential Equations

An equation involving independent variable, dependent variable, derivatives of dependent variable with respect to one (or more) independent variable and constant is called a differential equation.

e.g. $$x\frac{dy}{dx}+xy\frac{d^2y}{dx^2}+4=0$$

Order of a Differential Equation

The highest order derivative involved in a differential equation, is called order of differential equation.

e.g. (i) $\frac{dy}{dx}-\sin x=0$ (ii) $\frac{d^3y}{dx^3}+x^2\left(\frac{d^2y}{dx^2}\right)=0$

Here, in example (i), equation has the highest derivative of first order and in example (ii), equation has the highest derivative of third order.

Hence, orders of the differential equations in examples (i) and (ii) are 1 and 3, respectively.

Degree of a Differential Equation

The highest power (positive integral index) of the highest order derivative involved in a differential equation, when it is written as a polynomial in derivatives, is called the degree of a differential equation.

e.g. $$\left(\frac{d^3y}{dx^3}\right)^2 + x\left(\frac{d^3y}{dx^3}\right) + 3y\left(\frac{dy}{dx}\right) = 0$$

In above differential equation, highest order derivative is $\left(\frac{d^3y}{dx^3}\right)$, whose highest power is 2. So, degree of differential equation is 2.

Solution of a Differential Equation

A function of the form $y = \phi(x) + C$, which satisfies given differential equation, is called the solution of the differential equation.

General Solution of a Differential Equation

If the solution of a differential equation of order n, contains n arbitrary constants, then it is called a general solution.

Particular Solution of a Differential Equation

The solution of a differential equation obtained by giving particular values to the arbitrary constants in the general solution, is called the particular solution.

In other words, the solution free from arbitrary constant is called particular solution.

TEACHER TIPS

(i) Order and degree (if defined) of a differential equation are always positive integers.

(ii) If the given differential equation is not polynomial equation in its derivative, then its degree is not defined i.e. if the differential equations involving one or more terms of the form $e^{(dy/dx)}, \log\left(\frac{dy}{dx}\right), \sin\left(\frac{dy}{dx}\right), \cos\left(\frac{dy}{dx}\right)$, etc. the degree is not defined.

(iii) If the differential equation have radical (like $\sqrt{\ }, \sqrt[3]{\ }$ etc.) and fractions $\left(\text{like } \frac{1}{\frac{dy}{dx}}, \frac{1}{\sqrt{1+\frac{d^2y}{dx^2}}} \text{ etc.}\right)$, then to find degree, first made it free from radicals and fractions by simplifying it.

Example 1 **Find the order and degree (if defined) of the differential equation $\frac{dy}{dx} - \sec x = 0$.**

Sol. Given differential equation is $\frac{dy}{dx} - \sec x = 0$.

The highest order derivative occurring in the differential equation is $\frac{dy}{dx}$. So, its order is 1.

It is a polynomial in $\frac{dy}{dx}$ and highest power raised to $\frac{dy}{dx}$ is 1. So, its degree is 1.

Example 2 **Find the order and degree of the differential equation $\left(\frac{d^3y}{dx^3}\right)^3 + 2\frac{d^2y}{dx^2} = \log\frac{dy}{dx}$.**

Sol. Given differential equation is

$$\left(\frac{d^3y}{dx^3}\right)^3 + 2\frac{d^2y}{dx^2} = \log\left(\frac{dy}{dx}\right)$$

The highest order derivative which occurs in the given differential equation is $\frac{d^3y}{dx^3}$, so its order is 3.

The given differential equation is not a polynomial equation in derivatives of y, so its degree is not defined.

Example 3 **Find the order and degree of the differential equation $\frac{d^2y}{dx^2} = \sqrt{y + \left(\frac{dy}{dx}\right)^2}$.**

Sol. Given differential equation is $\frac{d^2y}{dx^2} = \sqrt{y + \left(\frac{dy}{dx}\right)^2}$.

On squaring both sides, we get

$$\left(\frac{d^2y}{dx^2}\right)^2 = y + \left(\frac{dy}{dx}\right)^2$$

$$\Rightarrow \left(\frac{d^2y}{dx^2}\right)^2 - y - \left(\frac{dy}{dx}\right)^2 = 0$$

Here, highest order derivative $= \frac{d^2y}{dx^2}$

$\therefore$ Order of differential equation = 2

and degree of differential equation

= Power of highest order derivative = 2

Example 4 **Find the sum of the order and the degree of the following differential equation.**

$$\frac{d^2y}{dx^2} + \sqrt[3]{\frac{dy}{dx}} + (1+x) = 0$$

CBSE Sample Paper 2017

Sol. Given differential equation is

$$\frac{d^2y}{dx^2}+\sqrt[3]{\frac{dy}{dx}}+(1+x)=0$$

$$\Rightarrow \quad \frac{d^2y}{dx^2}+(1+x)=-\sqrt[3]{\frac{dy}{dx}}$$

On cubing both sides, we get

$$\left\{\frac{d^2y}{dx^2}+(1+x)\right\}^3=-\frac{dy}{dx}$$

Hence, the order is 2 and degree is 3. So, the sum is 5.

Example 5 Verify that the function $y=e^{-3x}$ is a solution of the differential equation $\frac{d^2y}{dx^2}+\frac{dy}{dx}-6y=0.$

Sol. Given differential equation is

$$\frac{d^2y}{dx^2}+\frac{dy}{dx}-6y=0 \quad \text{...(i)}$$

and given function is

$$y=e^{-3x} \quad \text{...(ii)}$$

Here, order of the given differential equation is 2.

So, we differentiate Eq. (ii) two times.

On differentiating Eq. (ii) w.r.t. x, we get

$$\frac{dy}{dx}=-3e^{-3x} \quad \text{...(iii)}$$

Again, on differentiating Eq. (iii) w.r.t. x, we get

$$\frac{d^2y}{dx^2}=9e^{-3x}$$

On putting the values of y, $\frac{dy}{dx}$ and $\frac{d^2y}{dx^2}$ in LHS of Eq. (i), we get

$$\begin{aligned}\text{LHS}&=9e^{-3x}+(-3e^{-3x})-6e^{-3x}\\&=9e^{-3x}-3e^{-3x}-6e^{-3x}\\&=0=\text{RHS}\end{aligned}$$

Hence, the given function is a solution of given differential equation.

Example 6 Verify that $y=A\cos x-B\sin x$ is a solution of the differential equation $\frac{d^2y}{dx^2}+y=0.$

Sol. Given, $\quad y=A\cos x-B\sin x \quad$ ...(i)

Here, order of the given differential equation is 2.

So, we differentiate the Eq. (i) two times.

On differentiating both sides of Eq. (i) w.r.t. x, we get

$$\frac{dy}{dx}=-A\sin x-B\cos x \quad \text{...(ii)}$$

Again, on differentiating Eq. (ii) w.r.t. x, we get

$$\Rightarrow \quad \frac{d^2y}{dx^2}=-A\cos x+B\sin x$$

$$\Rightarrow \quad \frac{d^2y}{dx^2}=-(A\cos x-B\sin x)$$

$$\Rightarrow \quad \frac{d^2y}{dx^2}=-y \quad \text{[from Eq. (i)]}$$

$$\Rightarrow \quad \frac{d^2y}{dx^2}+y=0,$$

which is the given differential equation.

Hence, $y=A\cos x-B\sin x$ is a solution of given differential equation.

Example 7 Show that the function $y=ax+2a^2$ is a solution of the differential equation

$$2\left(\frac{dy}{dx}\right)^2+x\left(\frac{dy}{dx}\right)-y=0.$$

CBSE 2020

Sol. Here, order of differential equation is 1.

So, we differentiate given equation one time.

We have, $y=ax+2a^2$ ...(i)

On differentiating Eq. (i), w.r.t. x, we get

$$\frac{dy}{dx}=a$$

On substituting the value of a in Eq. (i), we get

$$y=x\left(\frac{dy}{dx}\right)+2\left(\frac{dy}{dx}\right)^2$$

$$\Rightarrow 2\left(\frac{dy}{dx}\right)^2+x\left(\frac{dy}{dx}\right)-y=0$$

Hence, $y=ax+2a^2$ is a solution of differential equation

$$2\left(\frac{dy}{dx}\right)^2+x\left(\frac{dy}{dx}\right)-y=0$$

Example 8 Show that the function $xy=\log y+C$ is a solution of the differential equation

$$y'=\frac{y^2}{1-xy},\ (xy\neq 1).$$

NCERT

Sol. Given, $xy=\log y+C$

On differentiating both sides w.r.t. x, we get

$$xy'+y\cdot 1=\frac{1}{y}\cdot y'+0$$

[using product rule of derivative]

$$\Rightarrow \quad xy'+y=\frac{y'}{y}$$

$$\Rightarrow \quad xy\cdot y'+y^2=y'$$

$$\Rightarrow \quad y^2=y'-xy\cdot y'$$

$$\Rightarrow \quad y^2=y'(1-xy)$$

$$\therefore \quad y'=\frac{y^2}{1-xy},\ (xy\neq 1)$$

Hence proved.

Example 9. **Show that $y = x^2 + 2x + 1$ is the solution of the initial value problem**

$$\frac{d^3y}{dx^3} = 0,\ y(0) = 1,\ y'(0) = 2,\ y''(0) = 2.$$

Competency Based Que

Sol. Given function is $y = x^2 + 2x + 1$. ...(i)

Here, order of the given differential equation is 3. So, we differentiate Eq. (i) three times.

On differentiating Eq. (i) three times w.r.t. x, we get

$$\frac{dy}{dx} = 2x + 2, \quad \text{...(ii)}$$

$$\frac{d^2y}{dx^2} = 2 \quad \text{...(iii)}$$

and $$\frac{d^3y}{dx^3} = 0,$$

which is the given differential equation.

So, $y = x^2 + 2x + 1$ is the solution of given differential equation.

Now, $y(0) = (0)^2 + 2(0) + 1$

$= 1$ [using Eq. (i)]

$$y'(0) = \left(\frac{dy}{dx}\right)_{\text{at } x=0}$$

$= 2(0) + 2$ [using Eq. (ii)]

$= 2$

and $$\left(\frac{d^2y}{dx^2}\right)_{\text{at } x=0}$$

$= 2$ [using Eq. (iii)]

Hence, $y = x^2 + 2x + 1$ is the solution of initial value problem.

Quick Test 1

1. Find the order and degree of the following differential equations.

(i) $x\left(\frac{d^3y}{dx^3}\right)^2 + \left(\frac{dy}{dx}\right)^4 + y^2 = e^{-x}$

(ii) $\left(\frac{ds}{dt}\right)^4 + 3s\frac{d^2s}{dt^2} = 0$ NCERT

(iii) $\left(\frac{d^2y}{dx^2}\right)^3 + \left(\frac{dy}{dx}\right)^2 + \sin\left(\frac{dy}{dx}\right) + 1 = 0$ NCERT

(iv) $\left(\frac{d^2y}{dx^2}\right) + \cos\left(\frac{dy}{dx}\right) = 0$ NCERT

(v) $x^3\left(\frac{d^2y}{dx^2}\right)^2 + x\left(\frac{dy}{dx}\right)^4 = 0$ CBSE 2019, 13

2. If the order and degree of the differential equation $\log\left(1 + \frac{d^2y}{dx^2}\right) = x$ are m and n, respectively. Find the value of $m + n$. Competency Based Que

3. If the order and degree of the differential equation $\left[1 + \left(\frac{dy}{dx}\right)^2\right]^{\frac{3}{2}} = \frac{d^2y}{dx^2}$ are m and n, respectively, then find the value of $m - n$. Competency Based Que

4. Write the sum of order and degree of differential equation $1 + \left(\frac{dy}{dx}\right)^4 = 7\left(\frac{d^2y}{dx^2}\right)^3$. CBSE 2015C

5. Verify that the function $y = 4\sin 3x$ is a solution of differential equation $\frac{d^2y}{dx^2} + 9y = 0$.

6. Verify that $y = e^{-x} + Ax + B$ is a solution of the differential equation $e^x\left(\frac{d^2y}{dx^2}\right) = 1$. NCERT

7. Verify that the function $y - \cos y = x$ is a solution of the differential equation $(y\sin y + \cos y + x)\,y' = y$. NCERT

8. Verify that $y = x\sin x$ is a solution of differential equation $xy' = y + x\sqrt{x^2 - y^2}$, $(x \neq 0$ and $x > y$ or $x < -y)$. NCERT

Answers

1. (i) Order = 3, Degree = 2
(ii) Order = 2, Degree = 1
(iii) Order = 2, Degree = not defined
(iv) Order = 2, Degree = not defined
(v) Order = 2 and Degree = 2

2. 3 **3.** Zero **4.** 5

For Solutions, See QR Code on Pg. 289

9.2 Methods of Solving First Order and First Degree Differential Equations

Differential Equation of the Type $\frac{dy}{dx} = f(x)$ or $\frac{dy}{dx} = f(y)$

In this type of differential equations, we integrate both sides to obtain general solutions.

e.g. For $\frac{dy}{dx} = f(x)$, general solution is $\int dy = \int f(x)\,dx + C$

and for $\frac{dy}{dx} = f(y)$, general solution is $\int \frac{1}{f(y)} dy = \int dx + C$.

Differential Equation in the Form of Variables Separable

A first order and first degree differential equation $\frac{dy}{dx} = F(x, y)$ is in the form of variable separable, if the function F can be expressed as the product of the functions of x and the functions of y.

i.e. $$\frac{dy}{dx} = h(y) \cdot g(x) \quad \text{...(i)}$$

If $h(y) \neq 0$, then separate the variables i.e. write Eq. (i) as

$$\frac{1}{h(y)} dy = g(x)dx$$

On integrating both sides, we get

$$\int \frac{1}{h(y)} dy = \int g(x)dx \text{ or } H(y) = G(x) + C$$

which is the required solution of given differential equation, where $H(y)$ and $G(x)$ are the anti-derivatives of $\frac{1}{h(y)}$ and $g(x)$, respectively and C is the arbitrary constant.

Example 1 Solve the differential equation

$$\frac{dy}{dx} = (1 + x^2)(1 + y^2).$$

NCERT

Sol. Given differential equation is $\frac{dy}{dx} = (1 + x^2)(1 + y^2)$

$$\left(\frac{1}{1+y^2}\right) dy = (1+x^2)dx \quad \text{[separating the variables]}$$

On integrating both sides, we get

$$\int \frac{1}{1+y^2} dy = \int (1 + x^2)\,dx$$

$$\Rightarrow \quad \tan^{-1} y = x + \frac{x^3}{3} + C,$$

where C is a constant of integration.

Example 2 Solve the differential equation $(e^x + e^{-x}) \frac{dy}{dx} = (e^x - e^{-x})$.

NCERT

Sol. We have, $(e^x + e^{-x}) \frac{dy}{dx} = (e^x - e^{-x})$

$$\Rightarrow \quad \frac{dy}{dx} = \frac{e^x - e^{-x}}{e^x + e^{-x}}$$

$$\Rightarrow \quad dy = \frac{e^x - e^{-x}}{e^x + e^{-x}} dx$$

On integrating both sides, we get

$$\int dy = \int \frac{e^x - e^{-x}}{e^x + e^{-x}} dx$$

Let $e^x + e^{-x} = t \Rightarrow (e^x - e^{-x})dx = dt$

$$\Rightarrow \quad \int dy = \int \frac{dt}{t}$$

$$\Rightarrow \quad y = \log|t| + C$$

$$\therefore \quad y = \log|e^x + e^{-x}| + C,$$

which is the required solution.

Example 3 Solve the differential equation $e^{dy/dx} = x + 1, y(0) = 5$.

CBSE 2023

Sol. We have, $e^{dy/dx} = x + 1$

On taking log both sides, we get

$$\Rightarrow \quad \frac{dy}{dx} = \log(x+1) \Rightarrow dy = \log(x+1)\,dx$$

On integrating both sides, we get

$$\int dy = \int \log(x+1)\,dx$$

$$\Rightarrow \quad y = \int \underset{\text{I}}{\log(x+1)} . \underset{\text{II}}{1}\,dx$$

$$\Rightarrow \quad y = x\log(x+1) - \int \frac{x}{x+1} dx$$

$$\Rightarrow \quad y = x\log(x+1) - \int \frac{x+1-1}{x+1} dx$$

$$\Rightarrow \quad y = x\log(x+1) - \int \left(1 - \frac{1}{x+1}\right) dx$$

$$\Rightarrow \quad y = x\log(x+1) - x + \log(x+1) + C \quad \text{...(i)}$$

Now, it is given that $y(0) = 5$ i.e. when $x = 0$, we have

$$y = 5$$

$$\therefore \quad 5 = \log 1 + C$$

$$\Rightarrow \quad C = 5 \quad \text{...(ii)}$$

From Eqs. (i) and (ii), we get

$$y = x\log(x+1) - x + \log(x+1) + 5$$

which is the required solution.

Example 4 **Find the general solution of the differential equation $\log\left(\dfrac{dy}{dx}\right) = ax+by$.** *CBSE 2022 (Term II)*

Sol. Given differential equation is

$$\log\left(\frac{dy}{dx}\right) = ax+by$$

$$\Rightarrow \frac{dy}{dx} = e^{ax+by} \qquad [\because \log m = n \Rightarrow e^n = m]$$

$$\Rightarrow \frac{dy}{dx} = e^{ax}\cdot e^{by}$$

On separating the variables, we get

$$\frac{1}{e^{by}}dy = e^{ax}\,dx$$

On integrating both sides, we get

$$\int \frac{1}{e^{by}}dy = \int e^{ax}\,dx$$

$$\Rightarrow \frac{e^{-by}}{-b} = \frac{e^{ax}}{a} + C$$

$\therefore$ General solution is $\dfrac{e^{-by}}{-b} = \dfrac{e^{ax}}{a} + C.$

Example 5 **Solve the differential equation $(1-x)\,dy - (3+y)\,dx = 0$.** *CBSE 2018*

Sol. Given differential equation is

$$(1-x)\,dy - (3+y)\,dx = 0$$

$$\Rightarrow (1-x)dy = (3+y)dx$$

On separating the variables, we get

$$\frac{dy}{3+y} = \frac{dx}{1-x}$$

On integrating both sides, we get

$$\int \frac{dy}{3+y} = \int \frac{dx}{1-x}$$

$$\Rightarrow \log|3+y| = -\log|1-x| + \log C$$

$$\Rightarrow \log|1-x| + \log|3+y| = \log C$$

$$\Rightarrow \log|(1-x)(3+y)| = \log C \qquad [\because \log m + \log n = \log mn]$$

$$\therefore (1-x)(3+y) = C,$$

which is the required solution of the given differential equation.

Example 6 **Find the particular solution of the differential equation $\dfrac{dy}{dx} = \dfrac{x(2\log x+1)}{\sin y + y\cos y}$, given that $y = \dfrac{\pi}{2}$, when $x=1$.** *CBSE 2023*

Sol. Given differential equation is

$$\frac{dy}{dx} = \frac{x(2\log x+1)}{\sin y + y\cos y}$$

On separating the variables, we get

$$(\sin y + y\cos y)\,dy = x(2\log x + 1)\,dx$$

$$\Rightarrow \sin y\,dy + y\cos y\,dy = 2x\log x\,dx + x\,dx$$

On integrating both sides, we get

$$\int \sin y\,dy + \int \underset{\text{I}}{y}\,\underset{\text{II}}{\cos y}\,dy = 2\int \underset{\text{II}}{x}\,\underset{\text{I}}{\log x}\,dx + \int x\,dx$$

$$\Rightarrow -\cos y + \left[y\int \cos y\,dy - \int\left\{\frac{d}{dy}(y)\int \cos y\,dy\right\}dy\right]$$

$$= 2\left[\log x\int x\,dx - \int\left\{\frac{d}{dx}(\log x)\int x\,dx\right\}dx\right] + \frac{x^2}{2}$$

$$\Rightarrow -\cos y + y\sin y - \int \sin y\,dy$$

$$= 2\left[\frac{x^2}{2}\log x - \int\left\{\frac{1}{x}\times\frac{x^2}{2}\right\}dx\right] + \frac{x^2}{2}$$

$$\Rightarrow -\cos y + y\sin y + \cos y = x^2\log x - \int x\,dx + \frac{x^2}{2}$$

$$\Rightarrow y\sin y = x^2\log x - \frac{x^2}{2} + \frac{x^2}{2} + C$$

$$\Rightarrow y\sin y = x^2\log x + C \qquad \text{...(i)}$$

On putting $y = \dfrac{\pi}{2}$ and $x=1$ in Eq. (i), we get

$$\frac{\pi}{2}\sin\left(\frac{\pi}{2}\right) = (1)^2\log(1) + C$$

$$\Rightarrow C = \frac{\pi}{2} \qquad \left[\because \sin\frac{\pi}{2} = 1, \log 1 = 0\right]$$

On substituting the value of C in Eq. (i), we get

$$y\sin y = x^2\log x + \frac{\pi}{2},$$

which is the required particular solution.

Example 7. **For the differential equation given below, find a particular solution satisfying the given condition $(x+1)\dfrac{dy}{dx} = 2e^{-y}+1$; $y=0$ when $x=0$.** *CBSE 2020*

Sol. Given differential equation is

$$(x+1)\frac{dy}{dx} = 2e^{-y}+1$$

$$\Rightarrow (x+1)\frac{dy}{dx} = \frac{2+e^y}{e^y}$$

$$\Rightarrow \frac{e^y}{e^y+2}dy = \frac{dx}{x+1}$$

On integrating both sides, we get

$$\int \frac{e^y}{e^y+2}dy = \int \frac{dx}{x+1}$$

$$\Rightarrow \log(e^y+2) = \log(x+1) + \log C$$

$$\Rightarrow \log(e^y+2) = \log C(x+1)$$

$$\Rightarrow e^y + 2 = C(x+1) \qquad \text{...(i)}$$

Also, given that $y = 0$, when $x = 0$

On putting $x = 0$ and $y = 0$ in Eq. (i), we get

$$e^0 + 2 = C(0+1)$$

$$\Rightarrow \quad C = 1 + 2 = 3$$

On putting C in Eq. (i), we get

$$e^y + 2 = 3(x+1) \Rightarrow e^y = 3x + 3 - 2$$

$$\Rightarrow \quad e^y = 3x + 1 \Rightarrow y = \log(3x+1)$$

Example 8 Find the particular solution of the differential equation $e^x \tan y\, dx + (2 - e^x) \sec^2 y\, dy = 0$, given that $y = \dfrac{\pi}{4}$ when $x = 0$. Competency Based Que, CBSE 2018

Sol. Given differential equation is

$$e^x \tan y\, dx + (2 - e^x)\sec^2 y\, dy = 0$$

$$\Rightarrow \quad e^x \tan y\, dx = (e^x - 2)\sec^2 y\, dy$$

On separating the variables, we get

$$\frac{\sec^2 y}{\tan y} dy = \frac{e^x}{e^x - 2} dx$$

On integrating both sides, we get

$$\int \frac{\sec^2 y}{\tan y} dy = \int \frac{e^x}{e^x - 2} dx$$

$$\Rightarrow \quad \log|\tan y| = \log|e^x - 2| + C$$

$$\left[\because \int \frac{f'(x)}{f(x)} dx = \log|f(x)| + C\right]$$

$$\Rightarrow \log|\tan y| - \log|e^x - 2| = C$$

$$\Rightarrow \quad \log\left|\frac{\tan y}{e^x - 2}\right| = C \quad \left[\because \log m - \log n = \log\left(\frac{m}{n}\right)\right]$$

$$\Rightarrow \quad \frac{\tan y}{e^x - 2} = e^C \quad [\because \log m = n \Rightarrow m = e^n]$$

$$\Rightarrow \quad \tan y = e^C (e^x - 2)$$

Now, it is given that $y = \dfrac{\pi}{4}$ when $x = 0$

$$\therefore \quad \tan\frac{\pi}{4} = e^C(e^0 - 2) \Rightarrow 1 = e^C(1-2) \Rightarrow e^C = -1$$

Thus, the particular solution of the given differential equation is $\tan y = 2 - e^x$.

Example 9 Find the particular solution of the differential equation $e^x \sqrt{1 - y^2}\, dx + \dfrac{y}{x} dy = 0$, given that $y = 1$, when $x = 0$. CBSE 2014

Sol. Given differential equation is

$$e^x \sqrt{1 - y^2}\, dx + \frac{y}{x} dy = 0$$

$$\Rightarrow \quad e^x \sqrt{1 - y^2}\, dx = \frac{-y}{x} dy$$

$$\Rightarrow \quad \frac{-y}{\sqrt{1 - y^2}} dy = x e^x dx$$

On integrating both sides, we get

$$\int \frac{-y}{\sqrt{1 - y^2}} dy = \int x e^x dx$$

On putting $1 - y^2 = t$, then $-y\,dy = \dfrac{dt}{2}$ in LHS, we get

$$\int \frac{1}{2\sqrt{t}} dt = \int x e^x dx$$

$$\Rightarrow \quad \frac{1}{2}[2\sqrt{t}] = x\int e^x dx - \int\left[\frac{d}{dx}(x)\int e^x dx\right]dx$$

$$\Rightarrow \quad \sqrt{1 - y^2} = xe^x - \int e^x dx \quad [\text{put } t = 1 - y^2]$$

$$\Rightarrow \quad \sqrt{1 - y^2} = xe^x - e^x + C \quad \text{...(i)}$$

On putting $y = 1$ and $x = 0$ in Eq. (i), we get

$$\sqrt{1 - 1} = 0 - e^0 + C$$

$$\Rightarrow \quad C = 1 \quad [\because e^0 = 1]$$

Now, on substituting the value of C in Eq. (i), we get

$$\sqrt{1 - y^2} = xe^x - e^x + 1,$$

which is the required particular solution of given differential equation.

Example 10 If $y(x)$ is a solution of $\left(\dfrac{2 + \sin x}{1 + y}\right)\dfrac{dy}{dx} = -\cos x$ and $y(0) = 1$, then find the value of $y\left(\dfrac{\pi}{2}\right)$. NCERT Exemplar, CBSE 2014

Sol. We have, differential equation

$$\left(\frac{2 + \sin x}{1 + y}\right)\frac{dy}{dx} = -\cos x \Rightarrow \frac{dy}{1 + y} = -\frac{\cos x}{2 + \sin x} dx$$

On integrating both sides, we get

$$\int \frac{1}{1 + y} dy = -\int \frac{\cos x}{2 + \sin x} dx$$

$$\Rightarrow \quad \log|1 + y| = -\log|2 + \sin x| + \log|C|$$

$$\Rightarrow \quad \log|1 + y| + \log|2 + \sin x| = \log|C|$$

$$\Rightarrow \quad \log|(1 + y)(2 + \sin x)| = \log|C|$$

$$\Rightarrow \quad (1 + y)(2 + \sin x) = C$$

$$\Rightarrow \quad 1 + y = \frac{C}{2 + \sin x} \Rightarrow y = \frac{C}{2 + \sin x} - 1 \quad \text{...(i)}$$

It is given that when $x = 0$, then $y = 1$.

$$\therefore \quad 1 = \frac{C}{2} - 1 \Rightarrow C = 4$$

On putting $C = 4$ in Eq. (i), we get

$$y = \frac{4}{2 + \sin x} - 1$$

Now, $$y\left(\frac{\pi}{2}\right) = \frac{4}{2 + \sin\frac{\pi}{2}} - 1 = \frac{1}{3}$$

Quick Test 2

1. Solve the following differential equations.
(i) $\frac{dy}{dx} = x\log x$ (ii) $\frac{dy}{dx} = \sin^2 y$
(iii) $\frac{dy}{dx} = \sqrt{4-y^2}, (-2<y<2)$ NCERT

2. Solve the differential equation $(1-e^x)\sec y\, dy = -e^x \sin y\, dx$.

3. Find the general solution of the differential equation $\log\left(\frac{dy}{dx}\right) = 3x + 4y$. CBSE 2017C

4. Given that $\frac{dy}{dx} = e^{-2y}$ and $y=0$, when $x=5$. Find the value of x, when $y=3$. NCERT Exemplar

5. Find the particular solution of the differential equation $\frac{dy}{dx} = 1+x+y+xy$, given that $y=0$, when $x=1$. Competency Based Que

6. Find the particular solution of the differential equation $(1-y^2)(1+\log|x|)\,dx + 2xy\,dy = 0$, given that $y=0$ when $x=1$. CBSE 2016

7. Find a particular solution of the differential equation $(x-y)(dx+dy) = dx - dy$, given that $y=-1$, when $x=0$. NCERT

8. Find the particular solution of the differential equation $x\cos y\, dy = (xe^x \log x + e^x)\, dx$ given that $y = \frac{\pi}{2}$ when $x=1$. CBSE 2024C

Answers

1. (i) $y = \frac{x^2}{2}\log x - \frac{1}{4}x^2 + C$
(ii) $x + \cot y + C = 0$
(iii) $y = 2\sin(x+C)$

2. $y = \tan^{-1}\left(\frac{e^x - 1}{C}\right)$

3. $4e^{3x} + 3e^{-4y} + 12C = 0$

4. $y = \frac{e^6+9}{2}$

5. $\log|1+y| = x + \frac{x^2}{2} - \frac{3}{2}$

6. $\log|x| + \frac{(\log|x|)^2}{2} - \log|1-y^2| = 0$

7. $\log|x-y| = x+y+1$

8. $\sin y = e^x \log x + 1$

For Solutions, See QR Code on Pg. 289

9.3 Homogeneous Differential Equations

A function $F(x, y)$ is called homogeneous function of degree n, if $F(\lambda x, \lambda y) = \lambda^n F(x, y)$, where λ is non-zero real number.

A differential equation $\frac{dy}{dx} = \frac{f(x, y)}{g(x, y)}$ is said to be **homogeneous**, if $f(x, y)$ and $g(x, y)$ are homogeneous functions of same degree i.e. it may be written as

$$\frac{dy}{dx} = \frac{x^n f\left(\frac{y}{x}\right)}{x^n g\left(\frac{y}{x}\right)} = \frac{f\left(\frac{y}{x}\right)}{g\left(\frac{y}{x}\right)} = F\left(\frac{y}{x}\right)$$

To check that given differential equation is homogeneous or not, we write differential equation as

$$\frac{dy}{dx} = F(x, y) \text{ or } \frac{dx}{dy} = F(x, y)$$

and replace x by λx, y by λy to get the function

$$F(\lambda x, \lambda y) = \lambda^n F(x, y)$$

Here, if power of λ is zero, then differential equation is homogeneous otherwise not.

Solution of Homogeneous Differential Equation

To solve homogeneous differential equation of the form

$$\frac{dy}{dx} = F(x, y) \quad \text{...(i)}$$

We put $y = vx \Rightarrow \frac{dy}{dx} = v + x\frac{dv}{dx}$ in Eq. (i) to reduce it into variable separable form. Then, solve it and in the final result put $v = \frac{y}{x}$ to get the required solution.

TEACHER TIPS

If the homogeneous differential equation is in the form of $\frac{dx}{dy} = F(x,y)$, where $F(x,y)$ is homogeneous function of degree zero, then we make substitution $x = vy$ and we proceed to find the general solution.

Example 1 **Show that the differential equation $x\cos\left(\frac{y}{x}\right)\frac{dy}{dx} = y\cos\left(\frac{y}{x}\right)+x$ is homogeneous.**

Sol. Given differential equation is

$$x\cos\left(\frac{y}{x}\right)\frac{dy}{dx} = y\cos\left(\frac{y}{x}\right)+x$$

$$\Rightarrow \quad \frac{dy}{dx} = \frac{y\cos(y/x)+x}{x\cos(y/x)}$$

Let $F(x, y) = \frac{y\cos(y/x)+x}{x\cos(y/x)}$ ...(i)

On replacing y by λy and x by λx in Eq. (i), we get

$$F(\lambda x, \lambda y) = \frac{\lambda y\cos\left(\frac{\lambda y}{\lambda x}\right)+\lambda x}{\lambda x\cos\left(\frac{\lambda y}{\lambda x}\right)}$$

$$= \frac{\lambda[y\cos(y/x)+x]}{\lambda x\cos(y/x)}$$

$$= \lambda^0 F(x, y) \quad \text{[from Eq. (i)]}$$

Since, power of λ is 0 (zero), so $F(x, y)$ is a homogeneous function of degree 0.

Hence, the given differential equation is a homogeneous differential equation.

Example 2 **Find the general solution of the differential equation $(xy - x^2)dy = y^2dx$.** CBSE 2023

Sol. Given differential equation is

$$\frac{dy}{dx} = \frac{y^2}{xy - x^2} \quad \text{...(i)}$$

This is a homogeneous differential equation.

On putting $y = vx \Rightarrow \frac{dy}{dx} = v + x\frac{dv}{dx}$ in Eq. (i), we get

$$v + x\frac{dv}{dx} = \frac{v^2x^2}{vx^2 - x^2} = \frac{v^2}{v-1}$$

$$\Rightarrow \quad \frac{x\,dv}{dx} = \frac{v^2}{v-1} - v = \frac{v^2 - v^2 + v}{v-1} = \frac{v}{v-1}$$

$$\Rightarrow \quad \frac{v-1}{v}dv = \frac{dx}{x}$$

On integrating both sides, we get

$$\int\frac{v-1}{v}dv = \int\frac{dx}{x} \Rightarrow \int\left(1-\frac{1}{v}\right)dv = \int\frac{dx}{x}$$

$$\Rightarrow \quad v - \log v = \log x + C$$

$$\Rightarrow \quad \frac{y}{x} - \log\frac{y}{x} = \log x + C$$

$$\Rightarrow \quad \frac{y}{x} - \log y + \log x = \log x + C$$

$$\Rightarrow \quad \frac{y}{x} - \log y = C,$$

which is the required general solution.

Example 3 **Solve the following differential equation $xe^{\frac{y}{x}} - y + x\frac{dy}{dx} = 0$.** CBSE 2023

Sol. Given differential equation is

$$xe^{y/x} - y + x\frac{dy}{dx} = 0$$

$$\Rightarrow \quad \frac{dy}{dx} = \frac{y}{x} - e^{y/x} \quad \text{...(i)}$$

This is a homogeneous differential equation.

On putting $y = vx \Rightarrow \frac{dy}{dx} = v + x\cdot\frac{dv}{dx}$ in Eq. (i), we get

$$v + x\frac{dv}{dx} = v - e^v \Rightarrow x\frac{dv}{dx} = -e^v$$

$$\Rightarrow \quad \frac{dv}{e^v} = -\frac{dx}{x}$$

On integrating both sides, we get

$$\int\frac{dv}{e^v} = -\int\frac{dx}{x}$$

$$\Rightarrow \quad \int e^{-v}dv = -\log x + C$$

$$\Rightarrow \quad -e^{-v} = -\log x + C$$

$$\Rightarrow \quad -e^{-y/x} = -\log x + C$$

$$\Rightarrow \quad e^{-y/x} = \log x - C,$$

which is the required solution.

Example 4 **Find the general solution of the following differential equation $x\frac{dy}{dx} = y - x\sin\left(\frac{y}{x}\right)$.**

CBSE Sample Paper 2022 (Term II)

Sol. Given differential equation is

$$x\frac{dy}{dx} = y - x\sin\frac{y}{x}$$

$$\text{or} \quad \frac{dy}{dx} = \frac{y}{x} - \sin\frac{y}{x} \quad \text{...(i)}$$

Eq. (i) is a homogeneous differential equation.

On putting $y = vx \Rightarrow \frac{dy}{dx} = v + x\frac{dv}{dx}$ in Eq. (i), we get

$$v + x\frac{dv}{dx} = v - \sin v$$

$$\Rightarrow \quad \frac{dv}{\sin v} = -\frac{dx}{x}$$

$$\Rightarrow \quad \operatorname{cosec} v\,dv = -\frac{dx}{x} \quad \text{...(ii)}$$

On integrating both sides of Eq. (ii), we get

$$\int\operatorname{cosec} v\,dv = -\int\frac{dx}{x}$$

$$\log|\operatorname{cosec} v - \cot v| = -\log|x| + \log K, K > 0$$

[here, $\log K$ is an arbitrary constant]

$$\Rightarrow \quad \log|(\operatorname{cosec} v - \cot v)x| = \log K$$

$$\Rightarrow \quad |(\text{cosec } v - \cot v)\, x| = K$$
$$\Rightarrow \quad (\text{cosec } v - \cot v)\, x = \pm K$$
$$\Rightarrow \quad \left(\text{cosec } \frac{y}{x} - \cot \frac{y}{x}\right) x = C, \text{ where } \pm K = C \quad \left[\because v = \frac{y}{x}\right]$$

which is the required general solution.

Example 5 **Solve the differential equation $xdy - ydx = \sqrt{x^2 + y^2}\, dx.$**

CBSE 2023; CBSE Sample Paper 2023, 20

Sol. Given, $xdy - ydx = \sqrt{x^2 + y^2}\, dx$

$$\Rightarrow \quad x\, dy = \sqrt{x^2 + y^2}\, dx + ydx$$
$$\Rightarrow \quad x\, dy = (\sqrt{x^2 + y^2} + y)\, dx$$
$$\Rightarrow \quad \frac{dy}{dx} = \frac{\sqrt{x^2 + y^2} + y}{x} \quad \ldots \text{(i)}$$

This is the homogeneous equation.

On putting $y = vx \Rightarrow \frac{dy}{dx} = v + x\frac{dv}{dx}$ in Eq. (i), we get

$$v + x\frac{dv}{dx} = \frac{\sqrt{x^2 + v^2x^2} + vx}{x}$$
$$\Rightarrow \quad v + x\frac{dv}{dx} = \frac{x\sqrt{1 + v^2} + vx}{x}$$
$$\Rightarrow \quad v + x\frac{dv}{dx} = \sqrt{1 + v^2} + v$$
$$\Rightarrow \quad x\frac{dv}{dx} = \sqrt{1 + v^2}$$
$$\Rightarrow \quad \frac{dv}{\sqrt{1 + v^2}} = \frac{dx}{x} \quad \ldots \text{(ii)}$$

On integrating both sides of Eq. (ii), we get

$$\int \frac{dv}{\sqrt{1 + v^2}} = \int \frac{dx}{x}$$
$$\Rightarrow \quad \log| v + \sqrt{1 + v^2} | = \log|x| + \log C, C > 0$$
$$\Rightarrow \quad \log\left|\frac{y}{x} + \sqrt{1 + \frac{y^2}{x^2}}\right| = \log|x| + \log C \quad \left[\because v = \frac{y}{x}\right]$$
$$\Rightarrow \log|y + \sqrt{x^2 + y^2}| - \log|x| = \log|x| + \log C$$
$$\Rightarrow \quad \log|y + \sqrt{x^2 + y^2}| = 2\log|x| + \log C = \log(x^2 C)$$
$$\Rightarrow \quad y + \sqrt{x^2 + y^2} = \pm Cx^2$$
$$\Rightarrow \quad y + \sqrt{x^2 + y^2} = Kx^2, \quad [\text{where, } K = \pm C]$$

which is the required general solution.

Example 6 **Solve the following differential equation $x^2 dy + y(x + y)dx = 0.$**

CBSE 2024

Sol. Given differential equation is

$$x^2 dy + y(x + y)dx = 0$$
$$\Rightarrow \quad x^2 dy + (xy + y^2)dx = 0$$
$$\Rightarrow \quad x^2 dy = -(xy + y^2)dx$$
$$\Rightarrow \quad \frac{dy}{dx} = -\left(\frac{yx + y^2}{x^2}\right)$$
$$\Rightarrow \quad \frac{dy}{dx} = -\left(\frac{y}{x}\right) - \left(\frac{y}{x}\right)^2 \quad \ldots \text{(i)}$$

which is a homogeneous,

$$\text{as } \frac{dy}{dx} = f\left(\frac{y}{x}\right)$$

On putting $y = vx$ and $\frac{dy}{dx} = v + x\frac{dv}{dx}$ in Eq. (i), we get

$$v + x\frac{dv}{dx} = -v - v^2$$
$$\Rightarrow \quad x\frac{dv}{dx} = -2v - v^2$$
$$\Rightarrow \quad \frac{1}{2v + v^2} \cdot dv = -\frac{1}{x}dx$$
$$\Rightarrow \quad \frac{1}{v(2 + v)}dv = -\frac{1}{x}dx$$
$$\Rightarrow \quad \frac{2}{2v(2 + v)}dv = -\frac{1}{x}dx$$
$$\Rightarrow \quad \frac{1}{2}\left(\frac{1}{v} - \frac{1}{v + 2}\right)dv = -\frac{1}{x}dx$$
$$\Rightarrow \quad \frac{1}{2}\int\frac{1}{v}dv - \frac{1}{2}\int\frac{1}{v + 2}dv = -\int\frac{1}{x}dx$$
$$\Rightarrow \frac{1}{2}\log|v| - \frac{1}{2}\log|v + 2| = -\log|x| + \log C$$
$$\Rightarrow \quad \frac{1}{2}\log\left|\frac{v}{v + 2}\right| = \log\left|\frac{C}{x}\right|$$
$$\Rightarrow \quad \log\left|\frac{v}{v + 2}\right| = 2\log\left|\frac{C}{x}\right|$$
$$\Rightarrow \quad \frac{v}{v + 2} = \left(\frac{C}{x}\right)^2$$
$$\Rightarrow \quad \frac{\frac{y}{x}}{\frac{y}{x} + 2} = \left(\frac{C}{x}\right)^2$$
$$\Rightarrow \quad \frac{y}{y + 2x} = \left(\frac{C}{x}\right)^2,$$

which is the required solution.

Example 7 **Show that the differential equation $2y \cdot e^{x/y}\, dx + (y - 2x e^{x/y})\, dy = 0$ is homogeneous and find its particular solution, given that $x = 0$, when $y = 1$.**

NCERT Solved Example

Sol. Given differential equation is

$$2y \cdot e^{x/y} dx + (y - 2x \cdot e^{x/y})\, dy = 0$$

$$\Rightarrow \quad 2y \cdot e^{x/y} \frac{dx}{dy} + (y - 2x \cdot e^{x/y}) = 0$$

$$\Rightarrow \quad 2y \cdot e^{x/y} \frac{dx}{dy} = 2x \cdot e^{x/y} - y$$

$$\Rightarrow \quad \frac{dx}{dy} = \frac{2x \cdot e^{x/y} - y}{2y \cdot e^{x/y}} \quad \text{...(i)}$$

Let $F(x, y) = \dfrac{2x \cdot e^{x/y} - y}{2y \cdot e^{x/y}}$

Then, $F(\lambda x, \lambda y) = \dfrac{2(\lambda x) e^{(\lambda x/\lambda y)} - \lambda y}{2(\lambda y) e^{(\lambda x/\lambda y)}} = \dfrac{\lambda(2x \cdot e^{x/y} - y)}{\lambda(2y \cdot e^{x/y})}$

$$= \lambda^0 [F(x, y)]$$

So, $F(x, y)$ is a homogeneous function of degree zero. Therefore, the given differential equation is a homogeneous differential equation.

Also, $\dfrac{dx}{dy} = \dfrac{2\left(\dfrac{x}{y}\right) e^{x/y} - 1}{2e^{x/y}} = f\left(\dfrac{x}{y}\right)$ ...(ii)

On putting $x = vy$ and $\dfrac{dx}{dy} = v + y\dfrac{dv}{dy}$ in Eq. (ii), we get

$$v + y\frac{dv}{dy} = \frac{2v\, e^{v} - 1}{2e^{v}}$$

$$\Rightarrow \quad y\frac{dv}{dy} = \frac{2v\, e^{v} - 1}{2e^{v}} - v$$

$$\Rightarrow \quad y\frac{dv}{dy} = \frac{2v\, e^{v} - 1 - 2v\, e^{v}}{2e^{v}} \Rightarrow y\frac{dv}{dy} = -\frac{1}{2e^{v}}$$

On separating the variables, we get

$$2e^{v}\, dv = -\frac{dy}{y}$$

On integrating both sides, we get

$$\int 2e^{v}\, dv = -\int \frac{dy}{y}$$

$$\Rightarrow \quad 2e^{v} = -\log|y| + C$$

$$\Rightarrow \quad 2e^{x/y} = -\log|y| + C \quad \left[\text{put } v = \frac{x}{y}\right] \text{...(iii)}$$

Also, given that $x = 0$, when $y = 1$.

Now, put $x = 0$ and $y = 1$ in Eq. (iii), we get

$$2\, e^{0/1} = -\log|1| + C$$

$$\Rightarrow \quad 2 = 0 + C \Rightarrow C = 2$$

On putting $C = 2$ in Eq. (iii), we get

$$2e^{x/y} = -\log|y| + 2$$

$$\Rightarrow \quad 2e^{x/y} + \log|y| = 2,$$

which is the particular solution.

Quick Test 3

1. Solve the following differential equation.

$$xy \log\left(\frac{y}{x}\right) dx + \left[y^2 - x^2 \log\left(\frac{y}{x}\right)\right] dy = 0.$$

CBSE 2010C

2. Solve the differential equation $y + x\dfrac{dy}{dx} = x - y\dfrac{dy}{dx}$.

3. Find the general solution of $y^2 dx + (x^2 - xy + y^2) dy = 0$.

NCERT Exemplar

4. Solve the differential equation $ye^{x/y}\, dx = (xe^{x/y} + y)\, dy$ $(y \neq 0)$.

5. Show that the following differential equation is homogeneous and then solve it.

$$y\, dx + x \log\left|\frac{y}{x}\right| dy - 2x\, dy = 0$$

NCERT, CBSE 2011C

6. Show that the differential equation $(x - y)\dfrac{dy}{dx} = x + 2y$ is homogeneous and solve it. *NCERT, CBSE 2014*

7. Show that the differential equation

$x\dfrac{dy}{dx} \sin\left(\dfrac{y}{x}\right) + x - y \sin\left(\dfrac{y}{x}\right) = 0$ is homogeneous. Find the particular solution of this differential equation, given that $x = 1$, when $y = \dfrac{\pi}{2}$.

CBSE 2013

8. Solve the differential equation

$\left[x \sin^2\left(\dfrac{y}{x}\right) - y\right] dx + x dy = 0$, given $y = \dfrac{\pi}{4}$, when $x = 1$.

CBSE 2015C, 14C, 13, 11C

9. Find the particular solution of the differential equation $\dfrac{dy}{dx} = \dfrac{x + y}{x}, y(1) = 0$

CBSE 2023

10. Find the particular solution of the differential equation $x^2 dy = (2xy + y^2)\, dx$, given that $y = 1$, when $x = 1$.

CBSE 2015

Answers

1. $x^2\left[2 \log\left|\dfrac{y}{x}\right| + 1\right] + 4y^2 \log|y| + 4y^2 C = 0$

2. $y^2 + 2xy - x^2 = C$

3. $\tan^{-1}\left(\dfrac{x}{y}\right) + \log|y| = C$

4. $e^{x/y} = \log|y| + C$

5. $\log \dfrac{y}{x} - 1 = Cy$

6. $\log|y^2 + xy + x^2| = 2\sqrt{3} \tan^{-1}\left(\dfrac{2y + x}{\sqrt{3}x}\right) + C$

7. $\cos \dfrac{y}{x} = \log|x|$

8. $1 + \log|x| - \cot\left(\dfrac{y}{x}\right) = 0$

9. $y = x \log|x|$

10. $x^2 + xy - 2y = 0$

For Solutions, See QR Code on Pg. 289

9.4 Linear Differential Equation

A first order differential equation in which the degree of dependent variable and its derivative is one and they do not get multiplied together, is called a **linear differential equation of first order.**

The general form of linear differential equation is

$$\frac{dy}{dx}+Py=Q \quad \ldots(i)$$

where, P and Q are functions of x or constants.

The solution of Eq. (i) is given by the equation

$$y\times \text{IF}=\int (Q\times \text{IF})\,dx+C$$

where, IF = Integrating Factor and IF $= e^{\int P\,dx}$.

If general form of linear differential equation is

$$\frac{dx}{dy}+P'x=Q' \quad \ldots(ii)$$

where, P' and Q' are functions of y or constants.

Then, solution of Eq. (ii) is given by the equation

$$x\times \text{IF}=\int (Q'\times \text{IF})\,dy+C$$

where, IF = Integrating Factor and IF $= e^{\int P'dy}$.

Example 1 **Find the integrating factor of the differential equation $x\frac{dy}{dx}=2x^2+y$.** CBSE 2020

Sol. Given differential equation is

$$x\frac{dy}{dx}=2x^2+y \Rightarrow \frac{dy}{dx}=2x+\frac{y}{x} \Rightarrow \frac{dy}{dx}-\frac{1}{x}y=2x,$$

which is of the form $\frac{dy}{dx}+Py=Q$

Here, $P=\frac{-1}{x}$ and $Q=2x$

$\therefore$ Integrating Factor, IF $= e^{\int P dx}=e^{\int \frac{-1}{x}dx}$

$$= e^{-\log x}=e^{\log(x)^{-1}}=(x)^{-1}=\frac{1}{x}$$

Example 2 **Find the general solution of the differential equation $(x^2+1)\frac{dy}{dx}+2xy=\sqrt{x^2+4}$.** CBSE 2023

Sol. Given differential equation is

$$(x^2+1)\frac{dy}{dx}+2xy=\sqrt{x^2+4}$$

$$\Rightarrow \quad \frac{dy}{dx}+\frac{2x}{x^2+1}\cdot y=\frac{\sqrt{x^2+4}}{x^2+1}$$

On comparing with the linear differential equation $\frac{dy}{dx}+Py=Q$, we get

$$P=\frac{2x}{x^2+1} \text{ and } Q=\frac{\sqrt{x^2+4}}{x^2+1}$$

$\therefore$ Integrating factor (IF) $= e^{\int P dx}=e^{\int \frac{2x}{x^2+1}dx}$

$$= e^{\log(x^2+1)}=x^2+1$$

Now, the solution of given differential equation is

$$y(\text{IF})=\int (Q\times \text{IF})dx+C$$

$$\Rightarrow \quad y(x^2+1)=\int \frac{\sqrt{x^2+4}}{x^2+1}\times (x^2+1)\,dx+C$$

$$\Rightarrow \quad (x^2+1)y=\int \sqrt{x^2+4}\,dx+C$$

$$\Rightarrow \quad (x^2+1)y=\frac{x}{2}\sqrt{x^2+4}+\frac{4}{2}\log\left|x+\sqrt{x^2+4}\right|+C$$

$$\Rightarrow \quad (x^2+1)y=\frac{x}{2}\sqrt{x^2+4}+2\log\left|x+\sqrt{x^2+4}\right|+C,$$

which is the required solution.

Example 3 **Find the general solution of the differential equation $\frac{d}{dx}(xy^2)=2y(1+x^2)$.** CBSE 2023

Sol. Given differential equation is

$$\frac{d}{dx}(xy^2)=2y(1+x^2)$$

$$\Rightarrow \quad x\cdot 2y\frac{dy}{dx}+y^2=2y(1+x^2) \Rightarrow \frac{dy}{dx}+\frac{1}{2x}\cdot y=\frac{1+x^2}{x}$$

On comparing with the linear differential equation $\frac{dy}{dx}+Py=Q$, we get

$$P=\frac{1}{2x} \text{ and } Q=\frac{1+x^2}{x}$$

$\therefore$ Integrating factor

$$(\text{IF})=e^{\int P dx}=e^{\int \frac{1}{2x}dx}=e^{\frac{1}{2}\log x}=\sqrt{x}$$

Now, the solution of given differential equation is

$$y(\text{IF})=\int (Q\times \text{IF})dx+C$$

$$\Rightarrow \quad \sqrt{x}\cdot y=\int \left(\frac{1+x^2}{x}\right)\sqrt{x}\,dx+C$$

$$=\int \left(\frac{1}{x}+x\right)\sqrt{x}dx+C$$

$$=\int \left(\frac{1}{\sqrt{x}}+x^{3/2}\right)dx+C$$

$$\Rightarrow \quad \sqrt{x}\cdot y=2\sqrt{x}+\frac{2}{5}x^{5/2}+C,$$

which is the required solution.

Example 4 **Find the general solution of the differential equation $(3y^2 - x)\,dy = y\,dx$.**

Sol. Given differential equation is

$$(3y^2 - x)\,dy = y\,dx$$

$$\Rightarrow \quad 3y^2 - x = y\frac{dx}{dy} \Rightarrow y\frac{dx}{dy} + x = 3y^2$$

$$\Rightarrow \quad \frac{dx}{dy} + x \times \frac{1}{y} = 3y \qquad \text{[dividing both sides by } y\text{]}$$

This is of the form $\frac{dx}{dy} + Px = Q$.

Here, $P = \frac{1}{y}$ and $Q = 3y$

Now, Integrating factor

$$\text{IF} = e^{\int P dy} = e^{\int \frac{1}{y} dy} = e^{\log y} = y \quad [\because e^{\log f(x)} = f(x)]$$

and the solution of differential equation is given by

$$x \times \text{IF} = \int (Q \times \text{IF})\,dy + C$$

$$\Rightarrow \quad x \times y = \int 3y \times y\,dy + C = 3\int y^2 dy + C$$

$$\Rightarrow \quad xy = \frac{3y^3}{3} + C \Rightarrow xy = y^3 + C,$$

which is the required solution.

Example 5 **Solve the following differential equation.**

$$(1+x^2)\frac{dy}{dx} + 2xy = 4x^2$$

CBSE 2025

Sol. Given differential equation is $(1+x^2)\frac{dy}{dx} + 2xy = 4x^2$

On dividing both sides by $(1+x^2)$, we get

$$\frac{dy}{dx} + \frac{2x}{1+x^2} \cdot y = \frac{4x^2}{1+x^2}$$

which is a linear differential equation of the form $\frac{dy}{dx} + Py = Q$.

Here, $P = \frac{2x}{1+x^2}$ and $Q = \frac{4x^2}{1+x^2}$

Now, $\text{IF} = e^{\int P dx} = e^{\int \frac{2x}{1+x^2} dx} = e^{\log|1+x^2|} = 1 + x^2$

$$\left[\begin{array}{l} \because \text{put } 1 + x^2 = t \Rightarrow 2x dx = dt \\ \therefore \int \frac{2x}{1+x^2} dx = \int \frac{1}{t} dt = \log|t| = \log|1+x^2| \end{array}\right]$$

$\therefore$ The solution of differential equation is given by

$$y \times \text{IF} = \int (Q \times \text{IF}) dx + C$$

$$\Rightarrow y(1+x^2) = \int \frac{4x^2}{(1+x^2)} \times (1+x^2) dx + C$$

$$\Rightarrow y(1+x^2) = \int 4x^2 dx + C$$

$$\Rightarrow y(1+x^2) = \frac{4x^3}{3} + C, \text{ which is the required solution.}$$

Example 6 **Find the particular solution of the differential equation $\frac{dy}{dx} + \sec^2 x \cdot y = \tan x \cdot \sec^2 x$, given that $y(0) = 0$.**

CBSE 2023

Sol. Given differential equation is

$$\frac{dy}{dx} + \sec^2 x \cdot y = \tan x \cdot \sec^2 x,$$

which is of the form $\frac{dy}{dx} + Py = Q$.

Here, $P = \sec^2 x$ and $Q = \tan x \cdot \sec^2 x$

$$\therefore \quad \text{IF} = e^{\int P dx} = e^{\int \sec^2 x\,dx} = e^{\tan x}$$

and the solution of differential equation is given by

$$y \times \text{IF} = \int (Q \times \text{IF}) dx + C$$

$$\Rightarrow \quad ye^{\tan x} = \int \tan x \cdot \sec^2 x \cdot e^{\tan x} dx + C$$

Put $\tan x = t \Rightarrow \sec^2 x\,dx = dt$

$$\Rightarrow ye^{\tan x} = \int t \cdot e^t dt + C = (te^t - e^t) + C = (t-1)e^t + C$$

$$\Rightarrow ye^{\tan x} = (\tan x - 1)e^{\tan x} + C$$

Now, when $x = 0$, $y = 0$

$$\Rightarrow \quad 0 = (0-1)e^0 + C \Rightarrow 0 = -1 + C \Rightarrow C = 1$$

$$\therefore \quad ye^{\tan x} = (\tan x - 1)e^{\tan x} + 1,$$

which is the required solution.

Example 7 **Find the particular solution of the differential equation $\frac{dy}{dx} - 2xy = 3x^2 e^{x^2}$; $y(0) = 5$.**

CBSE 2024

Sol. Given differential equation is $\frac{dy}{dx} - 2xy = 3x^2 e^{x^2}$,

which is of the form $\frac{dy}{dx} + Py = Q$.

Here, $P = -2x$ and $Q = 3x^2 e^{x^2}$

$$\therefore \text{IF} = e^{\int P dx} = e^{-2\int x\,dx} = e^{-2\left(\frac{x^2}{2}\right)} = e^{-x^2}$$

and the solution of differential equation is given by

$$y \times \text{IF} = \int (Q \times \text{IF})\,dx + C$$

$$\Rightarrow \quad y \times e^{-x^2} = \int (3x^2 \cdot e^{x^2}) \times e^{-x^2} dx + C = \int 3x^2 dx + C$$

$$= 3\left(\frac{x^3}{3}\right) + C$$

$$\Rightarrow \quad y \times e^{-x^2} = x^3 + C \qquad \text{...(i)}$$

Now, when $x = 0$, then $y = 5$

$$\Rightarrow \quad 5e^0 = 0 + C \Rightarrow C = 5$$

$$\therefore \quad ye^{-x^2} = x^3 + 5, \qquad \text{[put } C = 5 \text{ in Eq. (i)]}$$

which is the required solution.

Quick Test 4

1. Find the integrating factor of the following differential equation $(1+y^2)+(2xy-\cot y)\dfrac{dy}{dx}=0$. CBSE 2015

2. Solve the differential equation $\cos^2 x\dfrac{dy}{dx}+y=\tan x$.

3. Find the general solution of the differential equation $\dfrac{dy}{dx}+(\sec x)y=\tan x,\left(0\le x<\dfrac{\pi}{2}\right)$. NCERT, CBSE 2012

4. Find the particular solution of the differential equation $x\dfrac{dy}{dx}-y=x^2e^x$. [given, $y(1)=0$]. CBSE 2022 (Term II)

5. Find the particular solution of differential equation $\dfrac{dy}{dx}=-\dfrac{x+y\cos x}{1+\sin x}$, given that $y=1$, when $x=0$. CBSE 2016

6. Find the particular solution of the differential equation $\dfrac{dy}{dx}+2y\tan x=\sin x$, given that $y=0$ when $x=\dfrac{\pi}{3}$.

7. Solve the differential equation $dy=\cos x(2-y\ \text{cosec}\ x)dx$ given that $y=2$, when $x=\pi/2$.

8. Find the particular solution of the differential equation $x\dfrac{dy}{dx}+y-x+xy\cot x=0, x\neq 0$, given that when $x=\dfrac{\pi}{2}, y=0$. CBSE 2015C, 11C

9. Solve $\dfrac{dy}{dx}-3y\cot x=\sin 2x$, where $y=2$ and $x=\dfrac{\pi}{2}$. NCERT, CBSE 2015C

10. If $y(t)$ is a solution of $(1+t)\dfrac{dy}{dt}-ty=1$ and $y(0)=-1$, then show that $y(1)=\dfrac{-1}{2}$. NCERT Exemplar

Answers

1. $1+y^2$
2. $y\cdot e^{\tan x}=e^{\tan x}(\tan x-1)+C$
3. $y\cdot(\sec x+\tan x)=\sec x+\tan x-x+C$
4. $y=xe^x-xe$
5. $y(1+\sin x)=-\dfrac{x^2}{2}+1$
6. $y=\cos x-2\cos^2 x$
7. $y\sin x=-\dfrac{1}{2}\cos 2x+\dfrac{3}{2}$
8. $xy\sin x=-x\cos x+\sin x-1$
9. $y=4\sin^3 x-2\sin^2 x$

For Solutions, See QR Code on Pg. 289

EXAM PATTERN QUESTIONS

Objective Type Questions

Multiple Choice Questions

1. The order of the differential equation **CBSE 2024**

$\frac{d^4y}{dx^4} - \sin\left(\frac{d^2y}{dx^2}\right) = 5$ is

(a) 4 (b) 3
(c) 2 (d) Not defined

2. The order of the following differential equation

$\frac{d^3y}{dx^3} + x\left(\frac{dy}{dx}\right)^5 = 4\log\left(\frac{d^4y}{dx^4}\right)$ is **CBSE 2024**

(a) Not defined (b) 3
(c) 4 (d) 5

3. The order and degree (if defined) of the differential equation, $\left(\frac{d^2y}{dx^2}\right)^2 + \left(\frac{dy}{dx}\right)^3 = x\sin\left(\frac{dy}{dx}\right)$, respectively are

Competency Based Que

(a) 2, 2 (b) 1, 3
(c) 2, 3 (d) 2, degree not defined

4. The order and degree of the differential equation $\left(1+3\frac{dy}{dx}\right)^2 = 4\frac{d^3y}{dx^3}$ respectively are **CBSE 2023**

(a) $1, \frac{2}{3}$ (b) 3, 1 (c) 3, 3 (d) 1, 2

5. What is the product of the order and degree of the differential equation $\frac{d^2y}{dx^2}\sin y + \left(\frac{dy}{dx}\right)^3 \cos y = \sqrt{y}$?

CBSE 2023

(a) 3 (b) 2
(c) 6 (d) Not defined

6. Degree of the differential equation $\sin x + \cos\left(\frac{dy}{dx}\right) = y^2$ is **CBSE 2023**

(a) 2 (b) 1
(c) Not defined (d) 0

7. If p and q are respectively the order and degree of the differential equation $\frac{d}{dx}\left(\frac{dy}{dx}\right)^3 = 0$ then $(p-q)$ is

CBSE 2025

(a) 0 (b) 1 (c) 2 (d) 3

8. If m and n are the order and degree of the differential equation $\left(\frac{d^2y}{dx^2}\right)^5 + 4\frac{\left(\frac{d^2y}{dx^2}\right)^3}{\frac{d^3y}{dx^3}} + \frac{d^3y}{dx^3} = x^2 - 1$, then

Competency Based Que

(a) $m=3, n=3$ (b) $m=3, n=2$
(c) $m=3, n=5$ (d) $m=3, n=1$

9. The order of differential equation corresponding to family of curve $y = Ae^{2x} + Be^{-2x}$ is

(a) 1 (b) 2 (c) 3 (d) 4

10. The number of arbitrary constants in the general solution of the differential equation $\frac{dy}{dx} + y = 0$ is

CBSE 2024C

(a) 0 (b) 1 (c) 2 (d) 3

11. The general solution of the differential equation $\frac{dy}{dx} = e^{x+y}$ is **CBSE 2024**

(a) $e^x + e^{-y} = C$ (b) $e^{-x} + e^{-y} = C$
(c) $e^{x+y} = C$ (d) $2e^{x-y} = C$

12. The solution of the differential equation $\frac{dx}{x} + \frac{dy}{y} = 0$ is

CBSE 2023

(a) $\frac{1}{x} + \frac{1}{y} = C$ (b) $\log x - \log y = C$
(c) $xy = C$ (d) $x + y = C$

13. The number of solutions of the differential equation $\frac{dy}{dx} = \frac{y+1}{x-1}$, when $y(1) = 2$, is **CBSE 2023**

(a) zero (b) one
(c) two (d) infinite

14. The general solution of the differential equation $ydx - xdy = 0$ is **CBSE Sample Paper 2023**

(a) $xy = C$ (b) $x = Cy^2$
(c) $y = Cx$ (d) $y = Cx^2$

15. A particular solution of the differential equation $x\frac{dy}{dx} + y = 0$, when $x = 1$ and $y = 1$, is

CBSE 2024C

(a) $y = x$ (b) $y = e^x$ (c) $y = \frac{1}{x}$ (d) $y = \log x$

16. The solution of $\frac{dy}{dx}-y=1$, $y(0)=1$ is given by

(a) $xy=-e^{x}$ (b) $xy=-e^{-x}$
(c) $xy=-1$ (d) $y=2e^{x}-1$

17. The integrating factor of the differential equation $(1-y^2)\frac{dx}{dy}+yx=ay$ is **CBSE 2023**

(a) $\frac{1}{y^2-1}$ (b) $\frac{1}{\sqrt{y^2-1}}$ (c) $\frac{1}{1-y^2}$ (d) $\frac{1}{\sqrt{1-y^2}}$

18. The integrating factor of differential equation $\frac{dy}{dx}+y\tan x-\sec x=0$ is **Competency Based Que**

(a) $\cos x$ (b) $\sec x$ (c) $e^{\cos x}$ (d) $e^{\sec x}$

19. The integrating factor of differential equation $\frac{dy}{dx}+y=\frac{1+y}{x}$ is

(a) $\frac{x}{e^x}$ (b) $\frac{e^x}{x}$ (c) xe^x (d) e^x

Assertion-Reason Based Questions

Directions (Q. Nos. 20-29) *In the questions given below are two statements labelled as Assertion (A) and Reason (R). In the context of the two statements, which one of the following is correct?*

(a) Both A and R are correct; R is the correct explanation of A.
(b) Both A and R are correct; R is not the correct explanation of A.
(c) A is correct; R is incorrect.
(d) R is correct; A is incorrect.

20. **Assertion** (A) The order and degree of differential equation $y+\frac{dy}{dx}=\frac{1}{4}\int y\,dx$, respectively are 2 and 1.

Reason (R) Order of the differential equation is the order of the highest order derivative occurring in the differential equation and the degree of differential equation is the highest power of the highest order derivative.

21. **Assertion** (A) The order of the differential equation $\log_e\left(1+\frac{d^2y}{dx^2}\right)=x$ is not defined.

Reason (R) Order of the differential equation is the order of the highest order derivative occurring in the differential equation.

22. **Assertion** (A) The general solution of differential equation $\frac{y}{x}\frac{dy}{dx}=\frac{1+y^2}{1+x^2}$ is $1+x^2=C(1+y^2)$.

Reason (R) $\int\frac{x}{1+x^2}dx=\frac{1}{2}\log(1+x^2)+C$.

23. **Assertion** (A) The number of arbitrary constants in the solution of differential equation $\frac{d^2y}{dx^2}=0$ is 2.

Reason (R) The solution of a differential equation contains as many arbitrary constants as the order of differential equation.

24. **Assertion** (A) The equation of curve passing through (3, 9) which satisfies differential equation $\frac{dy}{dx}=x+\frac{1}{x^2}$ is $6xy=3x^3+29x-6$.

Reason (R) The solution of differential equation $\frac{dy}{dx}=\sqrt{4-y^2}$, $y\in(-2,2)$ is $y=2\sin(x+C)$.

25. **Assertion** (A) The differential equation $2ye^{x/y}dx+(y-2xe^{x/y})\,dy=0$ can be solved by making the substitution $y=vx$.

Reason (R) A homogeneous differential equation of the form $\frac{dx}{dy}=h\left(\frac{x}{y}\right)$ can be solved by making the substitution $x=vy$ and of the form $\frac{dy}{dx}=h\left(\frac{y}{x}\right)$ by substitution $y=vx$.

26. **Assertion** (A) The general solution of $\frac{dy}{dx}-\frac{2}{1+x}y=(1+x)^3$ is $\frac{2y}{(1+x)^2}=(1+x)^2+C$.

Reason (R) The general solution of linear differential equation is $y\cdot(\text{IF})=\int Q\cdot(\text{IF})\,dx$.

27. **Assertion** (A) Integrating factor of $\frac{dy}{dx}+\frac{y}{2x}=3x^2$ is $x^{1/2}$.

Reason (R) Integrating factor of $\frac{dy}{dx}+Py=Q$ is $e^{\int P\,dx}$.

28. **Assertion** (A) The general solution of the differential equation

$$x\frac{dy}{dx}+2y=x^2\ (x\neq 0)\text{ is }y=\frac{x^2}{4}+Cx^{-2}.$$

Reason (R) The number of arbitrary constant in the general solution is equal to the order of the differential equation.

29. **Assertion** (A) $\frac{dy}{dx}-y\cdot\cos x=5$ is a first order linear differential equation.

Reason (R) If P and Q are functions of x only or constant, then differential equation of the form $\frac{dy}{dx}+Py=Q$ is a first order linear differential equation.

Case Study Based Questions

30. **Order** The order of a differential equation is the highest order derivative appearing in the differential equation.

Degree The degree of differential equation is the power of the highest order derivative, when differential coefficients are made free from radicals and fractions.

Also, differential equation must be a polynomial equation in derivatives for the degree to be defined.

Based on the given information, answer the following questions.

(i) Find the sum of order and degree of differential equation $5\cdot\frac{d^2y}{dx^2}=\left[1+\frac{dy}{dx}\right]^{3/2}$.

(ii) Find the order and degree of differential equation $(y'')^2+5(y')^5+\sin x=0$.

(iii) Find the order and degree of differential equation $y\cdot\frac{dy}{dx}=\frac{x}{\frac{dy}{dx}+\left(\frac{dy}{dx}\right)^3}$.

(iv) Find the order and degree of differential equation $\sqrt{a+x}\left(\frac{dy}{dx}\right)=-x$.

(v) Find the order and degree of differential equation $y'''+y^2=e^{y'}$.

31. An equation involving derivatives of the dependent variable with respect to the independent variables is called a differential equation. A differential equation of the form $\frac{dy}{dx}=F(x,y)$ is said to be homogeneous if $F(x,y)$ is a homogeneous function of degree zero. Whereas a function $F(x,y)$ is a homogeneous function of degree n, if $F(\lambda x,\lambda y)=\lambda_0 F(x,y)$. To solve a homogeneous differential equation of the type $\frac{dy}{dx}=F(x,y)=g\left(\frac{y}{x}\right)$ we make the substitution $y=vx$ and then separate the variables.

Based on the above information, answer the following questions.

(i) Show that $(x^2-y^2)dx+2xy\,dy=0$ is a differential equation of the type $\frac{dy}{dx}=g\left(\frac{y}{x}\right)$.

(ii) Solve the above equation to find the general solution. **CBSE 2023**

32. The mixing tank shown below generates saline water (a mixture of salt and water) for the cooling of a thermoelectric power plant.

The tank initially holds 20000 L of water in which 2000 kg of salt has been dissolved. Then, pure water is poured into the tank at a rate of 5000 L per minute. The mixture in the tank, which is stirred continuously, flows out at a rate of 3000 L per minute.

The quantity of salt in the tank at time t is denoted by Q_t, where t is in minutes and Q_t is in kilograms.

The rate of flow of salt into the tank is measured as

$$\left(\frac{dQ_t}{dt}\right)_{in}=0\text{ kg/min}$$

The rate of flow of salt out of the tank is measured as

$$\left(\frac{dQ_t}{dt}\right)_{\text{out}}=\text{Rate of flow of water out of the tank}\times\frac{\text{Quantity of salt in the tank at time } t}{\text{Amount of water in the tank at time } t}$$

The rate of change of quantity of salt in the tank with respect to time is given by

$$\left[\left(\frac{dQ_t}{dt}\right)_{\text{in}}-\left(\frac{dQ_t}{dt}\right)_{\text{out}}\right]$$

Based on the given information, answer the following questions.

(i) Find the expression for the rate of change of quantity of salt in the tank with time t. Show your work.

(ii) Find the general solution of the differential equation corresponding to the rate of change of quantity of salt in the tank with time t. Show your work.

(iii) Use the initial conditions to determine the particular solution for the differential equation obtained. Show your work. **CBSE QB**

33. Reshma, a Mathematics teacher of Class XII, writes a differential equation $\frac{dy}{dx}+(\sec x)y=\tan x$ on the blackboard and asks some questions which are based on above differential equation to check the preparation of the topic, then answer the following questions.

(i) What is the form of given equation?

(ii) Write the differential equation in the form of $\frac{dy}{dx}+Py=Q$ and find the value of (P^2-Q^2).

(iii) Find the integration factor of equation $\frac{dy}{dx}+y\sec x=\tan x$.

Or

What is the solution of $\frac{dy}{dx}+Py=Q$?

Subjective Questions

Very Short Answer Type Questions

1. Find the order and degree of the following differential equation $x\sqrt{1-y^2}\,dx + y\sqrt{1-x^2}\,dy = 0$.

2. Find the order and degree of the differential equation $x - \sin\left(\frac{dy}{dx}\right) = 0$.

3. Find the degree of the differential equation $1+\left(\frac{dy}{dx}\right)^2 = x$. **CBSE 2020**

4. Find the order and the degree of the differential equation $x^2\frac{d^2y}{dx^2} = \left\{1+\left(\frac{dy}{dx}\right)^2\right\}^4$. **CBSE 2019**

5. Find the order and degree (if defined) of the differential equation $\frac{d^2y}{dx^2} + x\left(\frac{dy}{dx}\right)^2 = 2x^2\log\left(\frac{d^2y}{dx^2}\right)$. **Competency Based Que**

6. Write the degree of the differential equation $\left(\frac{dy}{dx}\right)^4 + 6x\frac{d^2y}{dx^2} = 0$.

7. Solve the differential equation $\frac{dy}{dx} = \frac{1+y^2}{y^3}$.

8. Solve the differential equation $\frac{dy}{dx} = x^3 e^{-2y}$. **Competency Based Que**

9. How many arbitrary constants are there in the particular solution of the differential equation $\frac{dy}{dx} = -4xy^2;\ y(0) = 1$? **CBSE Sample Paper 2021**

10. Write the solution of the differential equation $\frac{dy}{dx} = 2^{-y}$. **Competency Based Que**

11. For what value of n, the following is a homogeneous differential equation $\frac{dy}{dx} = \frac{x^3 - y^n}{x^2y + xy^2}$? **Competency Based Que**

12. Find the integrating factor of the differential equation $x\frac{dy}{dx} + 2y = x^2$. **CBSE 2020**

13. Write the integrating factor of the following differential equation $(1+y^2) + (4xy - \cot y)\frac{dy}{dx} = 0$.

Short Answer Type Questions

14. Find the order and degree of the differential equation $y = x\frac{dy}{dx} + \sqrt{1+\left(\frac{dy}{dx}\right)^2}$.

15. Solve the following differential equation $\frac{dy}{dx} = x^3 \operatorname{cosec} y$, given that $y(0) = 0$. **CBSE Sample paper 2021**

16. Verify that $ax^2 + by^2 = 1$ is a solution of the differential equation $x(yy_2 + y_1^2) = yy_1$. **CBSE Sample Paper 2018**

17. Verify that the function $x + y = \tan^{-1}y$ is a solution of the differential equation $y^2y' + y^2 + 1 = 0$.

18. Find the general solution of the differential equation $(x+2)\frac{dy}{dx} = x^2 + 5x - 3,\ x \neq -2$.

19. Find the general solution of the differential equation $e^x \tan y\,dx + (1-e^x)\sec^2 y\,dy = 0$.

20. Solve the differential equation $xy\frac{dy}{dx} = (x+2)(y+2)$. **CBSE 2017C**

21. Solve the differential equation $(x-1)\frac{dy}{dx} = 2x^3y$.

22. Solve the differential equation

$$x^2\frac{dy}{dx} = x^2 - 2y^2 + xy.$$

23. Find the particular solution of the differential equation $x\frac{dy}{dx} - y + x\operatorname{cosec}\left(\frac{y}{x}\right) = 0,\ y = \frac{\pi}{3}$ when $x = 1$.

24. Find the general solution of the differential equation $x\frac{dy}{dx} = y(\log y - \log x + 1)$. **CBSE 2022 (Term II)**

25. What will be the integrating factor of given differential equation $y\,dx + (x - y^2)\,dy = 0$?

26. Find integrating factor of the differential equation

$$\left(\frac{e^{-2\sqrt{x}}}{\sqrt{x}} - \frac{y}{\sqrt{x}}\right)\frac{dx}{dy} = 1.$$

27. Find the general solution of the differential equation $e^{2x}\frac{dy}{dx} + 3e^{2x}y = 1$.

28. Find the general solution of the differential equation

$$y\,dx - x\,dy + (x\log x)\,dx = 0.$$ **CBSE 2024C**

29. Find the general solution of the following differential equation $xdy-(y+2x^2)dx=0$. **CBSE Sample Paper 2021**

30. Solve the differential equation $\frac{dy}{dx}+2xy=y$.

31. Solve the differential equation

$$\cos x\cdot\frac{dy}{dx}+(2\sin x)\cdot y=\sin x\cdot\cos x.$$

32. Solve the differential equation

$$(1+x^2)\frac{dy}{dx}+y=e^{\tan^{-1}x}.$$

CBSE 2014

33. Solve the differential equation $x\frac{dy}{dx}+y=x\cos x+\sin x$, given that $y=1$ when $x=\frac{\pi}{2}$. **CBSE 2017**

Long Answer Type Questions

34. Prove that $(x^2-y^2)=c(x^2+y^2)^2$ is the general solution of the differential equation $(x^3-3xy^2)\,dx=(y^3-3x^2y)\,dy$, where c is a parameter. **NCERT, CBSE 2017**

35. Show that the general solution of the differential equation $\frac{dy}{dx}+\frac{y^2+y+1}{x^2+x+1}=0$ is given by $(x+y+1)=A(1-x-y-2xy)$, where A is a parameter. **NCERT**

36. Show that given differential equation $(x-y)\,dy=(x+y)\,dx$ is homogeneous and solve it. **NCERT**

37. Show that the differential equation $x\frac{dy}{dx}\sin\frac{y}{x}+x-y\sin\frac{y}{x}=0$ is homogeneous and find the particular solution, when $x=1$ and $y=\frac{\pi}{2}$. **Diksha App**

38. Find the solution of the differential equation

$$\left\{x\cos\left(\frac{y}{x}\right)+y\sin\left(\frac{y}{x}\right)\right\}y\,dx=\left\{y\sin\left(\frac{y}{x}\right)-x\cos\left(\frac{y}{x}\right)\right\}x\,dy.$$

NCERT, CBSE 2010C

39. Find the particular solution of the differential equation $(\tan^{-1}y-x)\,dy=(1+y^2)\,dx$, given that $x=1$ when $y=0$. **CBSE 2015**

40. Find the particular solution of the differential equation $(1+x^2)\frac{dy}{dx}+2xy=\frac{1}{1+x^2}$, given that $y=0$, when $x=1$. **CBSE 2018C, 11**

41. Solve the following differential equation $(\cot^{-1}y+x)dy=(1+y^2)dx$. **Competency Based Que**

42. Solve the differential equation $(x-\sin y)dy+(\tan y)dx=0$, given $y(0)=0$. **CBSE 2025**

43. Find the particular solution of differential equation $\frac{dy}{dx}+y\cot x=2x+x^2\cot x\;x\neq 0$, given that $y=0$, when $x=\frac{\pi}{2}$. **CBSE 2012C**

44. Find the particular solution of the differential equation $ye^y dx=(y^3+2xe^y)dy, y(0)=1$. **CBSE Sample Paper 2018**

Hints & Solutions

Objective Type Questions

1. (a) Given differential equation is

$$\frac{d^4y}{dx^4}-\sin\left(\frac{d^2y}{dx^2}\right)=5$$

The order of a differential equation is the highest order derivative it contains.

The highest order derivative in given equation is $\frac{d^4y}{dx^4}$.

$\therefore$ The order of differential equation is 4.

2. (c) Given differential equation is

$$\frac{d^3y}{dx^3}+x\left(\frac{dy}{dx}\right)^5=4\log\left(\frac{d^4y}{dx^4}\right)$$

The highest order derivative occurring in the differential equation is $\frac{d^4y}{dx^4}$, so its order is 4.

3. (d) Given differential equation is

$$\left(\frac{d^2y}{dx^2}\right)^2+\left(\frac{dy}{dx}\right)^3=x\sin\left(\frac{dy}{dx}\right)$$

The highest order derivative occurring in differential equation is $\frac{d^2y}{dx^2}$, so its order is 2.

The given differential equation is not a polynomial equation in derivatives of y, so its degree is not defined.

4. (b) Given differential equation is $\left(1+3\frac{dy}{dx}\right)^2=4\frac{d^3y}{dx^3}$.

The highest order derivative occurring in differential equation is $\frac{d^3y}{dx^3}$, so its order is 3.

Also, it is a polynomial equation in derivatives and highest power raised to $\frac{d^3y}{dx^3}$ is 1, so its degree is 1.

5. (b) Given differential equation is

$$\frac{d^2y}{dx^2}\sin y+\left(\frac{dy}{dx}\right)^3\cos y=\sqrt{y}$$

The highest order derivative occurring in differential equation is $\frac{d^2y}{dx^2}$, so its order is 2.

Also, it is a polynomial equation in derivatives and highest power raised to $\frac{d^2y}{dx^2}$ is 1, so its degree is 1.

Hence, the product of the order and degree of the above differential equation $2\times1=2$.

6. (c) The given differential equation is not a polynomial equation in $\frac{dy}{dx}$. Therefore, its degree is not defined.

7. (b) Given, $\frac{d}{dx}\left[\left(\frac{dy}{dx}\right)\right]^3=0$

$$\Rightarrow\quad 3\left(\frac{dy}{dx}\right)^2\frac{d}{dx}\left(\frac{dy}{dx}\right)=0$$

$$\Rightarrow\quad 3\left(\frac{dy}{dx}\right)^2\frac{d^2y}{dx^2}=0 \quad \ldots\text{(i)}$$

From Eq. (i), we get

order $p=2$ and degree $q=1$

$\therefore\ p-q=2-1=1$

8. (b) Given differential equation is

$$\left(\frac{d^2y}{dx^2}\right)^5+4\frac{\left(\frac{d^2y}{dx^2}\right)^3}{\frac{d^3y}{dx^3}}+\frac{d^3y}{dx^3}=x^2-1$$

Here, the highest order derivative occurring in the differential equation is $\frac{d^3y}{dx^3}$, so its order $m=3$.

It is a polynomial equation in derivatives and highest power raised to $\frac{d^3y}{dx^3}$ is 2.

So, its degree $n=2$.

9. (b) Given equation is $y=Ae^{2x}+Be^{-2x}$

Here, there are two arbitrary constants so, we have to differentiate twice.

Hence, the order of its is 2.

10. (b) If the order of differential equation is n, then it contains n arbitrary constants.

$\therefore$ Given differential equation contains 1 arbitrary constant.

11. (a) Given, $\frac{dy}{dx}=e^{x+y}$

$$\Rightarrow\quad \frac{dy}{dx}=e^x\cdot e^y$$

$$\Rightarrow\quad e^xdx=\frac{1}{e^y}dy$$

$$\Rightarrow\quad e^xdx=e^{-y}dy$$

$$\Rightarrow\quad \int e^xdx=\int e^{-y}dy$$

$$\Rightarrow\quad e^x=-e^{-y}+C$$

$$\Rightarrow\quad e^x+e^{-y}=C,$$

which is the required solution.

12. (c) Given differential equation is $\frac{dx}{x}+\frac{dy}{y}=0$

On integrating both sides, we get

$$\int\frac{dx}{x}+\int\frac{dy}{y}=0$$

$$\Rightarrow\quad \log x+\log y=k$$

$$\Rightarrow\quad \log(xy)=k \quad [\because \log(m\cdot n)=\log m+\log n]$$

$$\Rightarrow\quad xy=e^k \quad [\because \log_e A=B\Rightarrow A=e^B]$$

$$\Rightarrow\quad xy=C,\text{ where } C=e^k$$

13. (b) Given differential equation is

$$\frac{dy}{dx}=\frac{y+1}{x-1}\Rightarrow\frac{dy}{y+1}=\frac{dx}{x-1}$$

On integrating both sides, we get

$$\int\frac{dy}{y+1}=\int\frac{dx}{x-1}$$

$$\Rightarrow\quad \log(y+1)=\log(x-1)-\log C$$

$$\Rightarrow\quad C(y+1)=(x-1)$$

$$\Rightarrow\quad C=\frac{x-1}{y+1}$$

When $x=1$ and $y=2$, then $C=0$, so required solution is $x-1=0$.

Hence, only one solution exists.

14. (c) We have, $ydx-xdy=0$

$$\Rightarrow\quad xdy=ydx$$

$$\Rightarrow\quad \frac{dy}{y}=\frac{dx}{x} \quad \ldots\text{(i)}$$

On integrating both sides of Eq. (i), we get

$$\int\frac{dy}{y}=\int\frac{dx}{x}$$

$$\Rightarrow\quad \log|y|=\log|x|+\log C$$

$$\Rightarrow\quad \log|y|=\log|x|C$$

$$\Rightarrow\quad |y|=|x|C$$

$$\Rightarrow\quad y=\pm Cx$$

$$\Rightarrow\quad y=Cx$$

15. (c) Given, $x\frac{dy}{dx}+y=0,\ x=1$ and $y=1$

$$\Rightarrow \quad x\frac{dy}{dx}=-y$$
$$\Rightarrow \quad \frac{dy}{dx}=-\frac{y}{x}$$
$$\Rightarrow \quad \frac{dy}{y}=-\frac{dx}{x}$$

On integrating both sides, we get

$$\int\frac{dy}{y}=-\int\frac{dx}{x}$$
$$\Rightarrow \quad \log y=-\log x+\log C$$
$$\Rightarrow \quad \log(yx)=\log C$$
$$\Rightarrow \quad xy=C \quad \ldots(i)$$

On putting $x=1$ and $y=1$, we get

$$C=1$$

From Eq. (i), we get

$$xy=1 \Rightarrow \ y=\frac{1}{x}$$

16. (d) We have, $\frac{dy}{dx}-y=1,\ y(0)=1$

$$\Rightarrow \quad \frac{dy}{dx}=1+y \Rightarrow \frac{dy}{1+y}=dx$$

On integrating both sides, we get

$$\int\frac{1}{1+y}dy=\int dx$$
$$\Rightarrow \quad \log(1+y)=x+C \quad \ldots(i)$$

Now, it is given that $y(0)=1$ i.e. $x=0,\ y=1$

On putting $x=0,\ y=1$ in Eq. (i), we get

$$\log(1+1)=0+C \Rightarrow C=\log 2$$

Now, on putting $C=\log 2$ in Eq. (i), we get

$$\log(1+y)-\log 2=x$$
$$\Rightarrow \quad \log\frac{1+y}{2}=x \Rightarrow \ y=2e^x-1$$

17. (d) Given differential equation is

$$(1-y^2)\frac{dx}{dy}+yx=ay \ \Rightarrow \ \frac{dx}{dy}+\frac{y}{1-y^2}x=\frac{ay}{1-y^2}$$

On comparing with the linear differential equation $\frac{dx}{dy}+Px=Q$, we get

$$P=\frac{y}{1-y^2} \text{ and } Q=\frac{ay}{1-y^2}$$

$\therefore$ Integrating factor (IF) $=e^{\int P dy}=e^{\int\frac{y}{1-y^2}dy}$

On putting $1-y^2=t \Rightarrow -2y\,dy=dt \Rightarrow y\,dy=\frac{-dt}{2}$

$$\therefore \quad \text{IF}=e^{\int\frac{-1}{2t}dt}=e^{-\frac{1}{2}\log t}=\frac{1}{\sqrt{t}}=\frac{1}{\sqrt{1-y^2}}$$

18. (b) We have, $\frac{dy}{dx}+y\tan x-\sec x=0$

which is a linear differential equation.

On comparing it with $\frac{dy}{dx}+Py=Q$, we get

$$P=\tan x,\ Q=\sec x$$
$$\therefore \quad \text{IF}=e^{\int P dx}=e^{\int \tan x\, dx}$$
$$=e^{\log \sec x}$$
$$=\sec x$$

19. (b) Given differential equation is $\frac{dy}{dx}+y=\frac{1+y}{x}$.

$$\Rightarrow \quad \frac{dy}{dx}+\left(1-\frac{1}{x}\right)y=\frac{1}{x},$$

which is a linear differential equation.

On comparing it with $\frac{dy}{dx}+Py=Q$, we get

$$P=\left(1-\frac{1}{x}\right) \text{ and } Q=\frac{1}{x}$$
$$\therefore \quad \text{IF}=e^{\int P dx}=e^{\int\left(1-\frac{1}{x}\right)dx}$$
$$=e^{(x-\log x)}$$
$$=e^x\cdot e^{-\log x}=\frac{e^x}{x}$$

20. (a) Given differential equation is

$$y+\frac{dy}{dx}=\frac{1}{4}\int y\,dx \quad \ldots(i)$$

Let us first remove the integral sign by differentiate it w.r.t. x.

On differentiating Eq. (i) w.r.t. x, we get

$$\frac{dy}{dx}+\frac{d^2y}{dx^2}=\frac{1}{4}y$$

Since, the highest order derivative is $\frac{d^2y}{dx^2}$.

So, its order is 2.

Also, it is a polynomial equation in $\frac{d^2y}{dx^2}$ and $\frac{dy}{dx}$, where highest power of $\frac{d^2y}{dx^2}$ is 1. So, its degree is 1.

Hence, Assertion and Reason both are correct and Reason is the correct explanation of Assertion.

21. (d) Given differential equation is $\log_e\left(1+\frac{d^2y}{dx^2}\right)=x$,

which can be written as $1+\frac{d^2y}{dx^2}=e^x$

Clearly, the order of differential equation is 2.

Thus, Assertion is incorrect but Reason in correct.

22. (a) We have, differential equation

$$\frac{y}{x}\cdot\frac{dy}{dx}=\frac{1+y^2}{1+x^2}$$

$$\Rightarrow \int\frac{y\,dy}{1+y^2}=\int\frac{x\,dx}{1+x^2}$$

Let $1+y^2=u$ and $1+x^2=v$

$$\Rightarrow y\,dy=\frac{1}{2}du \text{ and } x\,dx=\frac{1}{2}dv$$

$$\therefore \frac{1}{2}\int\frac{du}{u}=\frac{1}{2}\int\frac{dv}{v}$$

$$\Rightarrow \log u=\log v+\log C$$

$$\Rightarrow \log u=\log(v\cdot C)\Rightarrow u=v\cdot C$$

$$\Rightarrow (1+y^2)=(1+x^2)C \text{ or } (1+y^2)C=(1+x^2)$$

Also, $\int\frac{x}{1+x^2}dx=\frac{1}{2}\log(1+x^2)+C$

Hence, both Assertion and Reason are correct and Reason is the correct explanation of Assertion.

23. (a) We have, $\frac{d^2y}{dx^2}=0$

$$\Rightarrow \frac{d}{dx}\left(\frac{dy}{dx}\right)=0$$

On integrating both sides, we get

$$\frac{dy}{dx}=C$$

Now, on integrating $\frac{dy}{dx}=C$, we get

$$\int dy=C\int dx\Rightarrow y=Cx+C'$$

There are two arbitrary constants in the solution of differential equation $\frac{d^2y}{dx^2}=0$.

We had a equation of order 2, so the Reason is also correct.

Both Assertion and Reason are correct and Reason is the correct explanation of Assertion.

24. (b) **Assertion** We have, $\frac{dy}{dx}=x+\frac{1}{x^2}$

$$\Rightarrow \int dy=\int\left(x+\frac{1}{x^2}\right)dx$$

$$\Rightarrow y=\frac{x^2}{2}-\frac{1}{x}+C \quad \text{...(i)}$$

It is passing through (3, 9), so

$$9=\frac{3^2}{2}-\frac{1}{3}+C\Rightarrow 9=\frac{9}{2}-\frac{1}{3}+C$$

$$\Rightarrow \frac{9}{2}+\frac{1}{3}=C\Rightarrow C=\frac{29}{6}$$

On putting in Eq. (i), we get

$$y=\frac{x^2}{2}-\frac{1}{x}+\frac{29}{6}\Rightarrow y=\frac{3x^3-6+29x}{6x}$$

$$\Rightarrow 6xy=3x^3+29x-6$$

$\therefore$ Assertion is correct.

Reason We have,

$$\frac{dy}{dx}=\sqrt{4-y^2}$$

$$\Rightarrow \int\frac{dy}{\sqrt{4-y^2}}=\int dx$$

$$\Rightarrow \sin^{-1}\frac{y}{2}=x+C$$

$$\Rightarrow \frac{y}{2}=\sin(x+C)$$

$$\Rightarrow y=2\sin(x+C)$$

Both Assertion and Reason are correct but Reason is not the correct explanation of Assertion.

25. (d) We have, $2y\,e^{x/y}dx+(y-2x\cdot e^{x/y})\,dy=0$

$$\Rightarrow 2y\,e^{x/y}dx=(2x\,e^{x/y}-y)\,dy$$

$$\Rightarrow \frac{dy}{dx}=\frac{2y\,e^{x/y}}{2x\,e^{x/y}-y}=\frac{2e^{x/y}}{2\frac{x}{y}e^{x/y}-1}$$

So, it is in the form of $\frac{dy}{dx}=h\left(\frac{x}{y}\right)$.

But if right hand side is a function in $\frac{x}{y}$, then LHS should be $\frac{dx}{dy}$ and we substituted $x=vy$.

So, Assertion is incorrect but Reason is correct.

26. (a) We have, $\frac{dy}{dx}-\frac{2}{1+x}y=(1+x)^3$

On comparing with $\frac{dy}{dx}+Py=Q$, we get

$$P=\frac{-2}{1+x}, Q=(1+x)^3$$

$$\therefore \text{IF}=e^{\int\frac{-2}{1+x}dx}=e^{-2\log(1+x)}=e^{\log(1+x)^{-2}}=(1+x)^{-2}$$

Now, solution is

$$y(\text{IF})=\int Q(\text{IF})\,dx+C$$

$$\Rightarrow y(1+x)^{-2}=\int(1+x)^{-2}(1+x)^3\,dx$$

$$\Rightarrow y\cdot(1+x)^{-2}=\int(1+x)\,dx$$

$$\Rightarrow \frac{y}{(1+x)^2}=\frac{(1+x)^2}{2}+C$$

$$\Rightarrow \frac{2y}{(1+x)^2}=(1+x)^2+C$$

Both Assertion and Reason are correct and Reason is the correct explanation of Assertion.

27. (a) We have, the differential equation $\frac{dy}{dx}+\frac{y}{2x}=3x^2$, which is linear differential equation of form $\frac{dy}{dx}+Py=Q$, where $P=\frac{1}{2x}$ and $Q=3x^2$.

$\therefore \quad \text{IF} = e^{\int P\,dx}$

$$= e^{\int \frac{1}{2x} dx} = e^{\left(\frac{1}{2}\log|x|\right)} = e^{\left(\log|x|^{\frac{1}{2}}\right)} = x^{\frac{1}{2}}$$

Hence, both Assertion and Reason are correct and Reason is the correct explanation of Assertion.

28. (b) We have, differential equation

$$x\frac{dy}{dx} + 2y = x^2 \Rightarrow \frac{dy}{dx} + y\frac{2}{x} = x,$$

which is linear differential equation of form $\frac{dy}{dx} + Py = Q$,

where $P = \frac{2}{x}$ and $Q = x$.

Now, $\text{IF} = e^{\int P dx}$

$$= e^{\int \frac{2}{x} dx} = e^{2\log x} \qquad \left[\because \int \frac{1}{x} dx = \log x\right]$$

$$= x^2$$

General solution, $y\,(\text{IF}) = \int Q\,(\text{IF})\,dx + C$

$$\Rightarrow \quad yx^2 = \int x.x^2 dx + C$$

$$\Rightarrow \quad yx^2 = \frac{x^4}{4} + C$$

$$\Rightarrow \quad y = \frac{x^2}{4} + Cx^{-2}$$

Hence, Assertion is correct. Reason is also correct but Reason is not the correct explanation of Assertion.

29. (a) Given, $\frac{dy}{dx} - y\cos x = 5$

Yes, it is in the form of $\frac{dy}{dx} + Py = Q$, so it is a first order linear differential equation.

Here, $P = -\cos x, Q = 5$ which are functions of x or constants. So, Reason is also correct.

30. (i) $5 \cdot \frac{d^2y}{dx^2} = \left[1 + \left(\frac{dy}{dx}\right)^2\right]^{3/2}$

On squaring both sides, we get

$$\left(5\frac{d^2y}{dx^2}\right)^2 = \left[1 + \left(\frac{dy}{dx}\right)^2\right]^3$$

Highest order derivative is $\frac{d^2y}{dx^2}$, so order is 2.

The highest power of highest order derivative is 2, so degree is 2.

$\therefore$ Required sum $= 2 + 2 = 4$

(ii) $(y'')^2 + 5(y')^5 + \sin x = 0$

Highest order derivative is of order 2 and the highest power of highest order derivative = 2

$\therefore$ Degree = 2

(iii) $y \cdot \frac{dy}{dx} = \frac{x}{\frac{dy}{dx} + \left(\frac{dy}{dx}\right)^3} \Rightarrow y\left(\frac{dy}{dx}\right)^2 + y\left(\frac{dy}{dx}\right)^4 = x$ [cross multiply]

Highest order derivative is of order 1.

The highest power of highest order derivative is 4.

$\therefore$ Degree = 4

(iv) $\sqrt{a + x}\left(\frac{dy}{dx}\right) = -x$

Highest order derivative is of order 1.

The highest power of highest order derivative is 1.

$\therefore$ Degree = 1

(v) $y''' + y^2 = e^{y'}$

Highest derivative is of order 3.

Exponent of highest derivative is 1.

But y' is in $e^{y'}$. It is not a polynomial equation, so degree is not defined.

31. (i) Given differential equation is

$(x^2 - y^2)dx + 2xy\,dy = 0$

$$\Rightarrow \frac{dy}{dx} = \frac{-(x^2 - y^2)}{2xy} = \frac{y^2 - x^2}{2xy}$$

$$= \frac{x^2\left(\frac{y^2}{x^2} - 1\right)}{2xy} = \frac{\left(\frac{y}{x}\right)^2 - 1}{2\left(\frac{y}{x}\right)}$$

$\therefore$ In RHS, degree of numerator and denominator is same.

$\therefore$ It is a homogeneous differential equation and can be written as

$$\frac{dy}{dx} = g\left(\frac{y}{x}\right).$$

(ii) Given differential equation is

$$(x^2 - y^2)dx + 2xy\,dy = 0$$

$$\Rightarrow \frac{dy}{dx} = -\frac{(x^2 - y^2)}{2xy} = \frac{y^2 - x^2}{2xy} \qquad \text{...(i)}$$

This is a homogeneous differential equation.

On putting $y = vx \Rightarrow \frac{dy}{dx} = v + x \cdot \frac{dv}{dx}$

$\therefore$ From Eq (i), we get

$$v + x \cdot \frac{dv}{dx} = \frac{v^2 - 1}{2v}$$

$$\Rightarrow x\frac{dv}{dx} = \frac{v^2 - 1}{2v} - v$$

$$= \frac{v^2 - 1 - 2v^2}{2v} = \frac{-v^2 - 1}{2v}$$

$$\Rightarrow \frac{2v}{v^2 + 1} dv = \frac{-dx}{x}$$

On integrating both sides, we get

$$\log|v^2+1| = -\log x + \log C$$

$$\Rightarrow \quad \log\left|\frac{y^2}{x^2}+1\right| = -\log x + \log C$$

$$\Rightarrow \quad \log\left|\frac{y^2+x^2}{x^2}\cdot x\right| = \log C$$

$$\Rightarrow \quad \frac{y^2+x^2}{x} = C$$

$$\Rightarrow \quad y^2+x^2 = Cx,$$

which is the required solution.

32. (i) According to the given condition, the rate of change of quantity of salt can be written as

$$\frac{dQ_t}{dt} = 0 - 3000 \times \frac{Q_t}{20000+5000t-3000t}$$

$$\Rightarrow \quad \frac{dQ_t}{dt} = \frac{-3Q_t}{20+2t},$$ which is the required expression.

(ii) Consider the differential equation

$$\frac{dQ_t}{dt} = \frac{-3Q_t}{20+2t}$$

On separating the variable of the above differential equation, we get

$$\Rightarrow \quad \frac{dQ_t}{-3Q_t} = \frac{dt}{20+2t}$$

On integrating both sides, we get

$$\int \frac{dQ_t}{-3Q_t} = \int \frac{dt}{20+2t}$$

$$\Rightarrow \quad -\frac{1}{3}\ln(Q_t) = \frac{1}{2}\ln(10+t) + C,$$

where C is an arbitrary constant.

This is the required solution corresponding to the rate of change of quantity of salt in the tank with time t.

(iii) Given, initial condition $Q_t(0) = 2000$

On substituting $Q_t(0) = 2000$ in the equation, we get

$$-\frac{1}{3}\ln(Q_t) = \frac{1}{2}\ln(10+t) + C$$

$$\Rightarrow \quad -\frac{1}{3}\ln(2000) = \frac{1}{2}\ln(10) + C$$

$$\Rightarrow \quad C = -\frac{1}{3}\ln(2\times 10^3) - \frac{1}{2}\ln(10)$$

$$\Rightarrow \quad C = -\frac{1}{3}[\ln 2 + 3\ln(10)] - \frac{1}{2}\ln(10)$$

$$\Rightarrow \quad C = -\frac{1}{3}\ln 2 - \frac{3}{2}\ln 10$$

$\therefore$ The particular solution for the differential equation obtained is $-\frac{1}{3}\ln Q_t = \frac{1}{2}\ln(10+t) - \frac{1}{3}\ln 2 - \frac{3}{2}\ln 10.$

33. (i) Given differential equation is

$$\frac{dy}{dx} + (\sec x)y = \tan x,$$

which is the form of linear differential equation i.e. the form of $\frac{dy}{dx} + Px = Q.$

(ii) We have, $\frac{dy}{dx} + (\sec x)\, y = \tan x$

On comparing with $\frac{dy}{dx} + Py = Q$, we get

$$P = \sec x \text{ and } Q = \tan x$$

$$\therefore \quad P^2 - Q^2 = \sec^2 x - \tan^2 x$$

$$= 1 + \tan^2 x - \tan^2 x = 1$$

Hence, the value of $P^2 - Q^2$ is 1.

(iii) From part (ii), we have

$$P = \sec x \text{ and } Q = \tan x$$

$$\therefore \quad \text{IF} = e^{\int P dx} = e^{\int \sec x\, dx}$$

$$= e^{\log|\sec x + \tan x| + C}$$

$$\therefore \quad \text{IF} = \sec x + \tan x + C$$

or

Required solution is

$$y\,(\text{IF}) = \int (Q \times \text{IF})\, dx + C$$

$$\Rightarrow y(\sec x + \tan x) = \int \tan x (\sec x + \tan x)\, dx + C$$

$$\Rightarrow y(\sec x + \tan x) = \int \tan x \sec x\, dx + \int \tan^2 x\, dx + C$$

$$\Rightarrow y(\sec x + \tan x) = \sec x + \int (\sec^2 x - 1)\, dx + C$$

$$[\because 1 + \tan^2\theta = \sec^2\theta]$$

$$\Rightarrow y(\sec x + \tan x) = \sec x + \tan x - x + C$$

Subjective Questions

1. The given equation can be written as

$$x\sqrt{1-y^2}\,dx = -y\sqrt{1-x^2}\,dy \Rightarrow \frac{dy}{dx} = \frac{-x\sqrt{1-y^2}}{y\sqrt{1-x^2}}$$

Since, the highest order derivative is $\frac{dy}{dx}$. So, its order is 1.

It is a polynomial equation in $\frac{dy}{dx}$ and highest power of $\frac{dy}{dx}$ is 1.

So, its degree is 1.

2. Given differential equation is $x - \sin\left(\frac{dy}{dx}\right) = 0.$

Since, the highest order derivative is $\frac{dy}{dx}$. So, its order is 1.

Now, if possible, then convert the given differential equation into polynomial equation of derivatives.

Consider, $x - \sin\left(\frac{dy}{dx}\right) = 0 \Rightarrow \sin\left(\frac{dy}{dx}\right) = x$

$$\Rightarrow \quad \frac{dy}{dx} = \sin^{-1} x,$$

which is a polynomial in $\frac{dy}{dx}$.

Also, highest power of $\frac{dy}{dx}$ is 1.

So, its degree is 1.

3. We have, $1+\left(\frac{dy}{dx}\right)^2 = x$

Since, the highest order derivative is $\frac{dy}{dx}$

and the highest power of $\frac{dy}{dx}$ is 2.

$\therefore$ Degree = 2

4. Given differential equation is $x^2\frac{d^2y}{dx^2} = \left\{1+\left(\frac{dy}{dx}\right)^2\right\}^4$.

Since, highest order derivative occurring in the differential equation is $\frac{d^2y}{dx^2}$, therefore order is 2 and as given equation can be expressed as a polynomial in derivatives, so its degree is 1, which is the power of $\frac{d^2y}{dx^2}$.

5. Since, highest order derivative occurring in the differential equation is $\frac{d^2y}{dx^2}$, therefore order is 2 and as the differential equation is not a polynomial in derivatives, therefore its degree is not defined.

6. Given differential equation is $\left(\frac{dy}{dx}\right)^4 + 6x\frac{d^2y}{dx^2} = 0$.

Here, highest order derivative is d^2y/dx^2, whose degree is one. So, the degree of differential equation is 1.

7. We have, $\frac{dy}{dx} = \frac{1+y^2}{y^3}$

$$\Rightarrow \quad \frac{dx}{dy} = \frac{y^3}{1+y^2}$$

$$\Rightarrow \quad dx = \frac{y^3}{1+y^2}dy$$

On integrating both sides, we get

$$\int dx = \int \frac{y^3}{1+y^2}dy$$

$$\Rightarrow \quad x = \int\left(y - \frac{y}{1+y^2}\right)dy$$

$$\Rightarrow \quad x = \frac{y^2}{2} - \frac{1}{2}\log(1+y^2) + C,$$

which is the required solution.

8. Given differential equation is

$$\frac{dy}{dx} = x^3e^{-2y} \Rightarrow e^{2y}\,dy = x^3\,dx$$

On integrating both sides, we get

$$\int e^{2y}\,dy = \int x^3\,dx$$

$$\Rightarrow \quad \frac{e^{2y}}{2} = \frac{x^4}{4} + C,$$

which is the required solution.

9. In the particular solution of a differential equation, the number of arbitrary constants are always zero.

10. Given differential equation is

$$\frac{dy}{dx} = 2^{-y}$$

On separating the variables, we get

$$2^y\,dy = dx$$

On integrating both sides, we get

$$\int 2^y\,dy = \int dx$$

$$\Rightarrow \quad \frac{2^y}{\log 2} = x + C_1$$

$$\Rightarrow \quad 2^y = x\log 2 + C_1\log 2$$

$$\therefore \quad 2^y = x\log 2 + C, \text{ where } C = C_1\log 2$$

11. For the given differential equation to be homogeneous, degree of $(x^3 - y^n)$ and $(x^2y + xy^2)$ must be same and also degree of x^3 and y^n must be same.

$$\therefore \quad n = 3$$

12. We have, $x\frac{dy}{dx} + 2y = x^2$

$$\Rightarrow \quad \frac{dy}{dx} + \frac{2}{x}y = x,$$

which is a linear differential equation of the form $\frac{dy}{dx} + Py = Q$.

Here, $P = \frac{2}{x}$ and $Q = x$.

$\therefore$ Integrating factor (IF) $= e^{\int\frac{2}{x}dx} = e^{2\log x} = e^{\log x^2} = x^2$

13. Given differential equation is

$$(1+y^2) + (4xy - \cot y)\frac{dy}{dx} = 0.$$

The above equation can be written as

$$(\cot y - 4xy)\frac{dy}{dx} = 1+y^2$$

$$\Rightarrow \quad \frac{\cot y - 4xy}{(1+y^2)} = \frac{dx}{dy}$$

$$\Rightarrow \quad \frac{dx}{dy} = \frac{\cot y}{1+y^2} - \frac{4xy}{1+y^2}$$

$$\Rightarrow \quad \frac{dx}{dy} + \frac{4y}{1+y^2}\cdot x = \frac{\cot y}{1+y^2},$$

which is a linear differential equation of the form $\frac{dx}{dy} + Px = Q$, here $P = \frac{4y}{1+y^2}$ and $Q = \frac{\cot y}{1+y^2}$.

Now, integrating factor $= e^{\int P\,dy} = e^{\int\frac{4y}{1+y^2}dy}$

On putting $1+y^2 = t \Rightarrow 2y\,dy = dt$

$$\therefore \quad \text{IF} = e^{\int\frac{2dt}{t}} = e^{2\log|t|} = t^2 = (1+y^2)^2$$

14. Given differential equation is $y = x\frac{dy}{dx} + \sqrt{1+\left(\frac{dy}{dx}\right)^2}$.

It has radical sign in power i.e. not have positive integer powers, so we first convert it into differential equation having positive integer powers.

We can rewrite the given differential equation as

$$y - x\frac{dy}{dx} = \sqrt{1+\left(\frac{dy}{dx}\right)^2}$$

$$\Rightarrow y^2 + x^2\left(\frac{dy}{dx}\right)^2 - 2xy\frac{dy}{dx} = 1+\left(\frac{dy}{dx}\right)^2 \quad \text{[squaring both sides]}$$

$$\Rightarrow (x^2-1)\left(\frac{dy}{dx}\right)^2 - 2xy\frac{dy}{dx} + y^2 - 1 = 0,$$

which represents a quadratic polynomial in $\frac{dy}{dx}$.

Since, the highest order derivative is $\frac{dy}{dx}$.

So, order of the differential equation is 1 and the highest power of $\frac{dy}{dx}$ is 2, so the degree of the differential equation is 2.

15. We have,

$$\frac{dy}{dx} = x^3 \operatorname{cosec} y$$

$$\Rightarrow \frac{1}{\operatorname{cosec} y}dy = x^3 dx$$

On integrating both sides, we get

$$\int \frac{1}{\operatorname{cosec} y}dy = \int x^3 dx$$

$$\Rightarrow \int \sin y\, dy = \int x^3 dx$$

$$\Rightarrow -\cos y = \frac{x^4}{4} + C$$

It is given that $y = 0$ when $x = 0$.

$$\therefore \quad -\cos 0 = 0 + C$$

$$\Rightarrow \quad C = -1$$

$$\therefore \quad -\cos y = \frac{x^4}{4} - 1$$

$$\Rightarrow \quad \cos y = 1 - \frac{x^4}{4}$$

16. We have, $ax^2 + by^2 = 1$

On differentiating both sides w.r.t. x, we get

$$2ax + 2by\, y_1 = 0 \quad [\because y_1 = dy/dx]$$

$$\Rightarrow 2(ax + by\, y_1) = 0$$

$$\Rightarrow ax + byy_1 = 0 \quad \ldots\text{(i)}$$

Again, on differentiating both sides w.r.t. x, we get

$$a + b(y_1y_1 + yy_2) = 0 \quad [\because y_2 = d^2y/dx^2]$$

$$\Rightarrow a + b(y_1^2 + yy_2) = 0$$

$$\Rightarrow a = -b(yy_2 + y_1^2) \quad \ldots\text{(ii)}$$

On putting $a = -b(yy_2 + y_1^2)$ in Eq. (i), we get

$$-b(yy_2 + y_1^2)x + byy_1 = 0$$

$$\Rightarrow b\{-(yy_2 + y_1^2)x + yy_1\} = 0$$

$$\Rightarrow x(yy_2 + y_1^2) = yy_1$$

Hence proved.

17. Given function is $x + y = \tan^{-1} y$ ...(i)

Here, order of differential equation is 1.

So, we differentiate Eq. (i) one time.

On differentiating Eq. (i), w.r.t. x, we get

$$1 + y' = \frac{1}{1+y^2}\cdot y'$$

$$\Rightarrow (1+y')(1+y^2) = y' \Rightarrow 1 + y' + y^2(1+y') = y'$$

$$\Rightarrow 1 + y^2 + y^2y' = 0,$$

which is the given differential equation.

18. Given differential equation is $(x+2)\frac{dy}{dx} = x^2 + 5x - 3$

$$\Rightarrow dy = \frac{x^2+5x-3}{(x+2)}dx \quad \text{[separating the variables]}$$

On integrating both sides, we get

$$\int dy = \int \frac{x^2+5x-3}{(x+2)}dx$$

$$\Rightarrow y = \int\left\{(x+3) - \frac{9}{(x+2)}\right\}dx$$

[dividing (x^2+5x-3) by $(x+2)$]

$$\Rightarrow y = \frac{x^2}{2} + 3x - 9\log|x+2| + C,$$

which is the required general solution.

19. Given differential equation is

$$e^x \tan y\, dx + (1-e^x)\sec^2 y\, dy = 0$$

$$\Rightarrow (1-e^x)\sec^2 y\, dy = -e^x \tan y\, dx$$

$$\Rightarrow \frac{\sec^2 y}{\tan y}dy = \frac{-e^x}{1-e^x}dx$$

On taking integration on both sides, we get

$$\int \frac{\sec^2 y}{\tan y}dy = \int \frac{-e^x}{1-e^x}dx$$

$$\Rightarrow \log(\tan y) = \log(1-e^x) + \log C$$

$$\Rightarrow \log(\tan y) = \log C\cdot(1-e^x)$$

$[\because \log mn = \log m + \log n]$

$$\Rightarrow \tan y = C(1-e^x) \Rightarrow y = \tan^{-1} C(1-e^x),$$

which is the required solution.

20. Hint $xy\frac{dy}{dx} = (x+2)(y+2)$ ...(i)

$$\Rightarrow \frac{y}{y+2}dy = \frac{x+2}{x}dx$$

$$\Rightarrow \int \frac{y}{y+2}dy = \int \frac{x+2}{2}dx$$

$$\Rightarrow \int\left(\frac{y+2-2}{y+2}\right)dy = \int \frac{x+2}{x}dx$$

$$\Rightarrow \int \frac{y+2}{y+2}dy - \int \frac{2}{y+2}dy = \int \frac{x}{x}dx + \int \frac{2}{x}dx$$

$$\Rightarrow \int dy - 2\int \frac{1}{y+2}dy = \int dx + 2\int \frac{1}{x}dx$$

Ans. $y - 2\log|y+2| = x + 2\log|x| + C$

21. Hint $(x-1)\frac{dy}{dx} = 2x^3 y$

$$\Rightarrow \frac{dy}{y} = \frac{2x^3}{(x-1)}dx$$

$$\Rightarrow \frac{dy}{y} = 2\left(\frac{x^3}{x-1}\right)dx$$

$$\Rightarrow \frac{dy}{y} = 2\left[\frac{(x^3-1)+1}{x-1}\right]dx$$

$$\Rightarrow \frac{dy}{y} = 2\left[\frac{(x-1)(x^2+x+1)}{(x-1)} + \frac{1}{(x-1)}\right]dx$$

$$[\because a^3 - b^3 = (a-b)(a^2+ab+b^2)]$$

$$\Rightarrow \frac{dy}{y} = 2\left(x^2+x+1+\frac{1}{x-1}\right)dx$$

$$\Rightarrow \int \frac{dy}{y} = 2\int\left(x^2+x+1+\frac{1}{x-1}\right)dx$$

Ans. $\log|y| = 2\left(\frac{x^3}{3}+\frac{x^2}{2}+x+\log|x-1|\right)+C$

22. Given differential equation is

$$x^2\frac{dy}{dx} = x^2 - 2y^2 + xy$$

$$\Rightarrow \frac{dy}{dx} = 1 - \frac{2y^2}{x^2} + \frac{y}{x} \quad \ldots(i)$$

which is homogeneous differential equation.

On putting $y = vx \Rightarrow \frac{dy}{dx} = x\frac{dv}{dx} + v$ in Eq (i), we get

$$x\frac{dv}{dx} + v = 1 - 2\frac{(vx)^2}{x^2} + \frac{vx}{x}$$

$$\Rightarrow x\frac{dv}{dx} + v = 1 - \frac{2v^2x^2}{x^2} + v \Rightarrow \frac{dv}{1-2v^2} = \frac{dx}{x}$$

On integrating both sides, we get

$$\int \frac{dv}{1-2v^2} = \int \frac{dx}{x}$$

$$\Rightarrow \frac{1}{2}\int \frac{dv}{\frac{1}{2}-v^2} = \int \frac{dx}{x}$$

$$\Rightarrow \frac{1}{2} \times \frac{1}{2\left(\frac{1}{\sqrt{2}}\right)}\log\left|\frac{\frac{1}{\sqrt{2}}+v}{\frac{1}{\sqrt{2}}-v}\right| = \log|x| + C$$

$$\left[\because \int \frac{1}{a^2-x^2} = \frac{1}{2a}\log\left|\frac{a+x}{a-x}\right|\right]$$

$$\Rightarrow \frac{\sqrt{2}}{4}\log\left|\frac{1+\sqrt{2}v}{1-\sqrt{2}v}\right| = \log|x| + C \quad \left[\because v = \frac{y}{x}\right]$$

$$\Rightarrow \frac{1}{2\sqrt{2}}\log\left|\frac{x+\sqrt{2}y}{x-\sqrt{2}y}\right| = \log|x| + C$$

23. Given differential equation can be written as

$$\frac{dy}{dx} - \frac{y}{x} + \operatorname{cosec}\left(\frac{y}{x}\right) = 0 \Rightarrow \frac{dy}{dx} = \frac{y}{x} - \operatorname{cosec}\left(\frac{y}{x}\right) \quad \ldots(i)$$

which is a homogeneous differential equation of the form $\frac{dy}{dx} = f\left(\frac{y}{x}\right)$.

On putting $y = vx$ and $\frac{dy}{dx} = v + x\frac{dv}{dx}$ in Eq. (i), we get

$$v + x\frac{dv}{dx} = v - \operatorname{cosec} v$$

$$\Rightarrow x\frac{dv}{dx} = -\operatorname{cosec} v \Rightarrow \sin v\, dv = -\frac{dx}{x}$$

On integrating both sides, we get

$$\int \sin v\, dv = -\int \frac{dx}{x}$$

$$\Rightarrow -\cos v = -\log|x| + C \Rightarrow \cos v = \log|x| - C$$

$$\Rightarrow \cos\left(\frac{y}{x}\right) = \log|x| - C \quad \left[\text{put } v = \frac{y}{x}\right] \ldots(ii)$$

Also, given that $y = \frac{\pi}{3}$, when $x = 1$.

Then, $\cos\frac{\pi}{3} = \log 1 - C \Rightarrow \frac{1}{2} = 0 - C \Rightarrow C = -\frac{1}{2}$

So, Eq. (ii) becomes $\cos\left(\frac{y}{x}\right) = \log|x| + \frac{1}{2}$,

which is the required equation.

24. Given differential equation is

$$x\frac{dy}{dx} = y(\log y - \log x + 1)$$

$$\Rightarrow \frac{dy}{dx} = \frac{y}{x}\left(\log\frac{y}{x} + 1\right) \quad \ldots(i)$$

On putting $y = vx$ and $\frac{dy}{dx} = v + x\frac{dv}{dx}$ in Eq. (i), we get

$$v + x\frac{dv}{dx} = v(\log v + 1)$$

$$\Rightarrow x\frac{dv}{dx} = v\log v \Rightarrow \frac{1}{v\log v}dv = \frac{1}{x}dx$$

On integrating both sides, we get

$$\int \frac{1}{v\log v}dv = \int \frac{1}{x}dx$$

$$\Rightarrow \log|\log v| = \log|x| + C$$

$\therefore$ Required solution is $\log\left|\log\left(\frac{y}{x}\right)\right| = \log|x| + C.$

25. Given differential equation is

$$y\,dx + (x - y^2)\,dy = 0$$

$$\Rightarrow y\frac{dx}{dy} + (x - y^2) = 0 \Rightarrow y\frac{dx}{dy} + x = y^2$$

$\Rightarrow \quad \dfrac{dx}{dy} + \dfrac{1}{y}x = y,$ [dividing both sides by y]

which is of the form $\dfrac{dx}{dy} + Px = Q.$

Here, $P = \dfrac{1}{y}$ and $Q = y$

$\therefore$ Integrating factor (IF) $= e^{\int P\,dy} = e^{\int \frac{1}{y} dy}$

$= e^{\log y} = y \quad [\because e^{\log f(x)} = f(x)]$

26. The given differential equation can be written as

$$\frac{dy}{dx} = \frac{e^{-2\sqrt{x}}}{\sqrt{x}} - \frac{y}{\sqrt{x}} \Rightarrow \frac{dy}{dx} + \frac{y}{\sqrt{x}} = \frac{e^{-2\sqrt{x}}}{\sqrt{x}},$$

which is a linear differential equation of the form $\dfrac{dy}{dx} + Py = Q.$

Here, $P = \dfrac{1}{\sqrt{x}}$ and $Q = \dfrac{e^{-2\sqrt{x}}}{\sqrt{x}}.$

Now, Integrating factor

$$\text{IF} = e^{\int P\,dx} = e^{\int \frac{1}{\sqrt{x}} dx} = e^{\int \frac{1}{\sqrt{x}} dx} = e^{2\sqrt{x}}$$

27. Given differential equation is $e^{2x}\dfrac{dy}{dx} + 3e^{2x}y = 1$

$\Rightarrow \quad e^{2x}\left(\dfrac{dy}{dx} + 3y\right) = 1 \Rightarrow \dfrac{dy}{dx} + 3y = e^{-2x}$

This is the form of $\dfrac{dy}{dx} + Py = Q.$

Here, $\quad P = 3$ and $Q = e^{-2x}$

Now, Integrating factor (IF) $= e^{\int 3\,dx} = e^{3x}$

and the solution of differential equation is given by

$$y \times \text{IF} = \int (Q \times \text{IF})\,dx + C$$

$\Rightarrow \quad y \times e^{3x} = \int (e^{-2x} \times e^{3x})\,dx + C$

$= \int e^{x} dx + C$

$\Rightarrow \quad ye^{3x} = e^{x} + C,$

which is the required solution.

28. Given, $y\,dx - x\,dy + (x\log x)\,dx = 0$

$\Rightarrow \quad (y + x\log x)\,dx - xdy = 0$

$\Rightarrow \quad \dfrac{dy}{dx} = \dfrac{y + x\log x}{x}$

$\Rightarrow \quad \dfrac{dy}{dx} = \dfrac{y}{x} + \log x \Rightarrow \dfrac{dy}{dx} - \dfrac{y}{x} = \log x$

On comparing with $\dfrac{dy}{dx} + Py = Q,$ we get

Here, $P = -\dfrac{1}{x}, Q = \log x$

$\therefore \quad \text{IF} = e^{\int P\,dx} = e^{\int -\frac{1}{x} dx}$

$= e^{-\log x} = \dfrac{1}{x}$

Now, the general solution of differential equation is given by

$$y \times \text{IF} = \int (\text{IF} \times \text{Q})\,dx + C$$

$\Rightarrow \quad y \cdot \dfrac{1}{x} = \int \dfrac{1}{x} \cdot \log x\,dx + C$

Let $\log x = t$

$\dfrac{1}{x}dx = dt$

$\therefore \quad y \cdot \dfrac{1}{x} = \int t\,dt + C$

$\Rightarrow \quad \dfrac{y}{x} = \dfrac{t^2}{2} + C \Rightarrow y = \dfrac{x}{2}(\log x)^2 + Cx$

29. We have, $\quad xdy - (y + 2x^2)dx = 0$

$\Rightarrow \quad x\dfrac{dy}{dx} - y - 2x^2 = 0$

$\Rightarrow \quad \dfrac{dy}{dx} - \dfrac{1}{x}y = 2x \quad \ldots\text{(i)}$

Eq. (i) is a linear differential equation.

On comparing Eq. (i) with $\dfrac{dy}{dx} + Py = Q,$ we get

$$P = -\frac{1}{x} \text{ and } Q = 2x$$

$\therefore \quad \text{IF} = e^{\int P\,dx} = e^{\int -\frac{1}{x} dx} = e^{-\log x} = e^{\log(x)^{-1}} = (x)^{-1} = \dfrac{1}{x}$

The solution is $y \cdot \text{IF} = \int Q \cdot (\text{IF})\,dx + C$

$\therefore \quad y \times \dfrac{1}{x} = \int \left(2x \times \dfrac{1}{x}\right)dx + C$

$\Rightarrow \quad \dfrac{y}{x} = \int 2dx + C$

$\Rightarrow \quad \dfrac{y}{x} = 2x + C$

$\Rightarrow \quad y = 2x^2 + Cx$

30. Given that $\dfrac{dy}{dx} + 2xy = y$

$\Rightarrow \quad \dfrac{dy}{dx} + 2xy - y = 0$

$\Rightarrow \quad \dfrac{dy}{dx} + (2x - 1)y = 0,$

which is a linear differential equation.

On comparing it with $\dfrac{dy}{dx} + Py = Q,$ we get

$$P = (2x - 1) \text{ and } Q = 0$$

Now, $\text{IF} = e^{\int P\,dx} = e^{\int (2x-1)\,dx} = e^{\left(\frac{2x^2}{2} - x\right)} = e^{x^2 - x}$

and the solution is given by

$$y \cdot \text{IF} = \int Q \cdot (\text{IF})\,dx + C$$

$\therefore \quad y \cdot e^{x^2 - x} = \int (0 \times e^{x^2 - x})\,dx + C$

$\Rightarrow \quad y \cdot e^{x^2 - x} = 0 + C$

$\Rightarrow \quad y = Ce^{x - x^2}$

31. Given differential equation is

$$\cos x \frac{dy}{dx} + (2\sin x)\, y = \sin x \cdot \cos x$$

$$\Rightarrow \quad \frac{dy}{dx} + \frac{2\sin x}{\cos x} \cdot y = \frac{\sin x \cdot \cos x}{\cos x}$$

$$\therefore \quad \frac{dy}{dx} + 2\tan x \cdot y = \sin x \qquad \ldots(\text{i})$$

which is a linear differential equation of the form $\frac{dy}{dx} + Py = Q$.

Here, $P = 2\tan x$ and $Q = \sin x$.

Now, $\text{IF} = e^{\int P dx} = e^{\int 2\tan x\, dx} = e^{2\log \sec x}$ $[\because \int \tan x\, dx = \log \sec x]$

$$= e^{\log \sec^2 x} = \sec^2 x$$

and the required solution is given by

$$y \times \text{IF} = \int (Q \times \text{IF})\, dx + C$$

$$\therefore \quad y \cdot \sec^2 x = \int \sin x \cdot \frac{1}{\cos^2 x} dx + C$$

$$\Rightarrow \quad y \cdot \sec^2 x = \int \sec x \cdot \tan x\, dx + C$$

$$\Rightarrow \quad y \cdot \sec^2 x = \sec x + C \qquad [\because \int \sec x \tan x\, dx = \sec x]$$

$$\Rightarrow \quad y = \cos x + C\cos^2 x, \qquad [\text{divide by } \sec^2 x]$$

which is the required solution.

32. Given differential equation is

$$(1+x^2)\frac{dy}{dx} + y = e^{\tan^{-1} x}$$

$$\Rightarrow \quad \frac{dy}{dx} + \frac{y}{1+x^2} = \frac{e^{\tan^{-1} x}}{(1+x^2)},$$

which is a linear differential equation of the form $\frac{dy}{dx} + Py = Q$.

Here, $P = \frac{1}{1+x^2}$ and $Q = \frac{e^{\tan^{-1} x}}{(1+x^2)}$

Now, $\text{IF} = e^{\int P\, dx} = e^{\int \frac{1}{1+x^2} dx} = e^{\tan^{-1} x}$

The solution of differential equation is given by

$$y \cdot e^{\tan^{-1} x} = \int \frac{e^{2\tan^{-1} x}}{1+x^2} dx$$

$$\Rightarrow \quad y e^{\tan^{-1} x} = \frac{e^{2\tan^{-1} x}}{2} + C$$

33. Given differential equation is

$$x\frac{dy}{dx} + y = x\cos x + \sin x$$

$$\Rightarrow \quad \frac{dy}{dx} + \frac{y}{x} = \cos x + \frac{\sin x}{x} \qquad \ldots(\text{i})$$

which is a linear differential equation of the form $\frac{dy}{dx} + Py = Q$.

Here, $P = \frac{1}{x}$ and $Q = \cos x + \frac{\sin x}{x}$

$$\therefore \quad \text{IF} = e^{\int P dx} = e^{\int \frac{1}{x} dx} = e^{\log x} = x$$

and the solution of differential equation is given by

$$y \cdot (\text{IF}) = \int Q \cdot (\text{IF})\, dx + C$$

$$\Rightarrow \quad yx = \int (x\cos x + \sin x)\, dx + C$$

$$\Rightarrow \quad xy = \int x\cos x\, dx + \int \sin x\, dx + C$$

$$\Rightarrow \quad xy = x\sin x - \int \sin x\, dx + \int \sin x\, dx + C$$

[integrating by parts]

$$\Rightarrow \quad xy = x\sin x + C \qquad \ldots(\text{ii})$$

On putting $x = \frac{\pi}{2}$ and $y = 1$ in Eq. (ii), we get

$$\frac{\pi}{2} \times 1 = \frac{\pi}{2}\sin\frac{\pi}{2} + C$$

$$\Rightarrow \quad \frac{\pi}{2} = \frac{\pi}{2} + C \Rightarrow C = 0$$

Now, on putting the value of C in Eq. (ii), we get

$$xy = x\sin x + 0$$

$$\Rightarrow \quad y = \sin x$$

34. The given differential equation is

$$(x^3 - 3xy^2)\, dx = (y^3 - 3x^2 y)\, dy \qquad \ldots(\text{i})$$

and the given function is

$$(x^2 - y^2) = c(x^2 + y^2)^2 \qquad \ldots(\text{ii})$$

On differentiating Eq. (ii) w.r.t. x, we get

$$2x - 2y\frac{dy}{dx} = 2c(x^2 + y^2)\left(2x + 2y\frac{dy}{dx}\right)$$

$$\Rightarrow \quad \left(x - y\frac{dy}{dx}\right) = 2c(x^2 + y^2)\left(x + y\frac{dy}{dx}\right) \qquad \ldots(\text{iii})$$

$$\Rightarrow \quad \left(x - y\frac{dy}{dx}\right) = \frac{2(x^2 - y^2)}{(x^2 + y^2)^2}(x^2 + y^2)\left(x + y\frac{dy}{dx}\right)$$

[using Eq. (ii)]

$$\Rightarrow \quad (x^2 + y^2)\left(x - y\frac{dy}{dx}\right) = 2(x^2 - y^2)\left(x + y\frac{dy}{dx}\right)$$

$$\Rightarrow (x^2 + y^2)\, x - (x^2 + y^2)\, y\frac{dy}{dx} = 2(x^2 - y^2)\, x + 2(x^2 - y^2)\, y\frac{dy}{dx}$$

$$\Rightarrow \{x(x^2 + y^2) - 2x(x^2 - y^2)\} = \{2y(x^2 - y^2) + y(x^2 + y^2)\}\frac{dy}{dx}$$

$$\Rightarrow \quad (3xy^2 - x^3) = (3x^2 y - y^3)\frac{dy}{dx}$$

$$\Rightarrow \quad (x^3 - 3xy^2)\, dx = (y^3 - 3x^2 y)\, dy,$$

which is the given differential equation.

Hence, the given function is the solution of the given differential equation.

35. Hint $\frac{dy}{dx}+\frac{y^2+y+1}{x^2+x+1}=0$

$$\Rightarrow \frac{dy}{y^2+y+1}+\frac{dx}{x^2+x+1}=0$$

$$\Rightarrow \int\frac{dy}{y^2+y+1}+\int\frac{dx}{x^2+x+1}=C$$

$$\Rightarrow \int\frac{dy}{y^2+y+1+\left(\frac{1}{2}\right)^2-\left(\frac{1}{2}\right)^2}+\int\frac{dx}{x^2+x+1+\left(\frac{1}{2}\right)^2-\left(\frac{1}{2}\right)^2}=C$$

$$\Rightarrow \int\frac{dy}{\left(y+\frac{1}{2}\right)^2+\left(1-\frac{1}{4}\right)}+\int\frac{dx}{\left(x+\frac{1}{2}\right)^2+\left(1-\frac{1}{4}\right)}=C$$

$$\Rightarrow \int\frac{dy}{\left(y+\frac{1}{2}\right)^2+\left(\frac{\sqrt{3}}{2}\right)^2}+\int\frac{dx}{\left(x+\frac{1}{2}\right)^2+\left(\frac{\sqrt{3}}{2}\right)^2}=C$$

$$\Rightarrow \frac{2}{\sqrt{3}}\tan^{-1}\left(\frac{y+\frac{1}{2}}{\frac{\sqrt{3}}{2}}\right)+\frac{2}{\sqrt{3}}\tan^{-1}\left(\frac{x+\frac{1}{2}}{\frac{\sqrt{3}}{2}}\right)=C$$

$$\Rightarrow \tan^{-1}\left(\frac{2y+1}{\sqrt{3}}\right)+\tan^{-1}\left(\frac{2x+1}{\sqrt{3}}\right)=\frac{\sqrt{3}C}{2}=k \text{ (say)}$$

$$\Rightarrow \tan^{-1}\left[\frac{\frac{2y+1}{\sqrt{3}}+\frac{2x+1}{\sqrt{3}}}{1-\left(\frac{2y+1}{\sqrt{3}}\right)\left(\frac{2x+1}{\sqrt{3}}\right)}\right]=k$$

$$\Rightarrow \tan^{-1}\left[\frac{\frac{2y+1+2x+1}{\sqrt{3}}}{1-\left(\frac{4xy+2x+2y+1}{3}\right)}\right]=k$$

$$\Rightarrow \frac{2\sqrt{3}(x+y+1)}{3-(4xy+2x+2y+1)}=\tan k$$

$$\Rightarrow \frac{2\sqrt{3}(x+y+1)}{2(1-x-y-2xy)}=\tan k$$

$$\Rightarrow x+y+1=\frac{1}{\sqrt{3}}\tan k(1-x-y-2xy)$$

Ans. $x+y+1=A(1-x-y-2xy)$,

where $A=\frac{1}{\sqrt{3}}\tan k$ is an arbitrary constant.

36. Given differential equation is

$$(x-y)\,dy=(x+y)\,dx$$

or $\frac{dy}{dx}=\frac{x+y}{x-y}$ ...(i)

Let $F(x,y)=\frac{x+y}{x-y}$ ...(ii)

On replacing x by λx and y by λy in Eq. (ii), we get

$$F(\lambda x,\lambda y)=\frac{\lambda x+\lambda y}{\lambda x-\lambda y}=\frac{\lambda(x+y)}{\lambda(x-y)}=\lambda^0 F(x,y)$$

Thus, $F(x,y)$ is a homogeneous function of degree zero.

Now, on putting $y=vx$ and $\frac{dy}{dx}=v+x\frac{dv}{dx}$ in Eq. (i), we get

$$v+x\frac{dv}{dx}=\frac{x+vx}{x-vx}$$

$$\Rightarrow v+x\frac{dv}{dx}=\frac{1+v}{1-v}$$

$$\Rightarrow x\frac{dv}{dx}=\frac{1+v}{1-v}-v$$

$$\Rightarrow x\frac{dv}{dx}=\frac{1+v-v+v^2}{1-v}$$

$$\Rightarrow x\frac{dv}{dx}=\frac{1+v^2}{1-v}$$

On separating the variables, we get

$$\frac{1-v}{1+v^2}dv=\frac{1}{x}dx$$

On integrating both sides, we get

$$\int\frac{1-v}{1+v^2}dv=\int\frac{1}{x}dx$$

$$\Rightarrow \int\frac{1}{1+v^2}dv-\frac{1}{2}\int\frac{2v}{1+v^2}dv=\int\frac{1}{x}dx$$

$$\Rightarrow \tan^{-1}v-\frac{1}{2}\log|(1+v^2)|=\log|x|+C$$

$$\Rightarrow \tan^{-1}\left(\frac{y}{x}\right)-\frac{1}{2}\log\left|\left(1+\frac{y^2}{x^2}\right)\right|=\log|x|+C \quad \left[\text{put } v=\frac{y}{x}\right]$$

$$\Rightarrow 2\tan^{-1}\left(\frac{y}{x}\right)-\log\left|\left(1+\frac{y^2}{x^2}\right)\right|=2(\log|x|+C)$$

$$\Rightarrow 2\tan^{-1}\left(\frac{y}{x}\right)=\log\left|\frac{(x^2+y^2)}{x^2}\right|+\log|x|^2+2C$$

$$\Rightarrow 2\tan^{-1}\left(\frac{y}{x}\right)=\log\left[\left|\frac{x^2+y^2}{x^2}\right||x|^2\right]+2C$$

$$[\because \log m+\log n=\log mn]$$

$$\Rightarrow 2\tan^{-1}\left(\frac{y}{x}\right)-\log|x^2+y^2|=2C$$

$$\Rightarrow \tan^{-1}\left(\frac{y}{x}\right)-\frac{1}{2}\log|x^2+y^2|=C,$$

which is the required solution.

37. We have,

$$x\frac{dy}{dx}\sin\frac{y}{x}+x-y\sin\frac{y}{x}=0$$

On dividing by $x\cdot\sin\frac{y}{x}$, we get

$$\frac{dy}{dx}+\frac{x}{x\sin\frac{y}{x}}-\frac{y}{x}=0$$

$$\Rightarrow \quad \frac{dy}{dx}=\frac{y}{x}-\frac{1}{\sin\frac{y}{x}} \quad \ldots(\text{i})$$

Let $f(x,y)=\frac{y}{x}-\operatorname{cosec}\frac{y}{x}$

and $f(\lambda x,\lambda y)=\frac{\lambda y}{\lambda x}-\operatorname{cosec}\frac{\lambda y}{\lambda x}=\lambda^0 f(xy)$

Therefore, $f(x,y)$ is a homogeneous function of degree zero, so the given differential equation is a homogeneous equation.

Let $y=vx$

On differentiating both sides w.r.t. x, we get

$$\frac{dy}{dx}=v+x\cdot\frac{dv}{dx} \quad \ldots(\text{ii})$$

On substituting the values of y and $\frac{dy}{dx}$ in Eq. (i), we get

$$v+x\frac{dv}{dx}=v-\operatorname{cosec}v$$

$$\Rightarrow \quad x\frac{dv}{dx}=-\operatorname{cosec}v$$

$$\Rightarrow \quad \frac{dv}{\operatorname{cosec}v}=-\frac{dx}{x}$$

$$\Rightarrow \quad \sin v\,dv=-\frac{dx}{x}$$

On integrating both sides, we get

$$\int\sin v\,dv=-\int\frac{dx}{x}$$

$$\Rightarrow \quad -\cos v=-\log x+C$$

$$\Rightarrow \quad \cos v=\log x+C$$

On putting $v=\frac{y}{x}$, we get

$$\cos\frac{y}{x}=\log x+C \quad \ldots(\text{iii})$$

On substituting $x=1$ and $y=\frac{\pi}{2}$ in Eq. (iii), we get

$$\cos\frac{\pi}{2}=\log 1+C$$

$$\Rightarrow \quad C=0$$

On substituting $C=0$ in Eq. (iii), we get

$$\cos\frac{y}{x}=\log x,$$

which is the particular solution of differential equation.

38. Given, $\left\{x\cos\left(\frac{y}{x}\right)+y\sin\left(\frac{y}{x}\right)\right\}y\,dx$

$$=\left\{y\sin\left(\frac{y}{x}\right)-x\cos\left(\frac{y}{x}\right)\right\}x\,dy$$

$$\Rightarrow \quad \frac{dy}{dx}=\frac{y\left\{x\cos\frac{y}{x}+y\sin\frac{y}{x}\right\}}{x\left\{y\sin\frac{y}{x}-x\cos\frac{y}{x}\right\}} \quad \ldots(\text{i})$$

Clearly, the given differential equation is homogeneous.

On putting $y=vx$ and $\frac{dy}{dx}=v+x\frac{dv}{dx}$ in Eq. (i), we get

$$v+x\frac{dv}{dx}=\frac{vx(x\cos v+vx\sin v)}{x(vx\sin v-x\cos v)}$$

$$\Rightarrow \quad v+x\frac{dv}{dx}=\frac{v(\cos v+v\sin v)}{v\sin v-\cos v}$$

$$\Rightarrow \quad x\frac{dv}{dx}=\frac{v\cos v+v^2\sin v}{v\sin v-\cos v}-v$$

$$\Rightarrow \quad x\frac{dv}{dx}=\frac{v\cos v+v^2\sin v-v^2\sin v+v\cos v}{v\sin v-\cos v}$$

$$\Rightarrow \quad x\frac{dv}{dx}=\frac{2v\cos v}{v\sin v-\cos v}$$

$$\Rightarrow \quad \left(\frac{v\sin v-\cos v}{v\cos v}\right)dv=\frac{2}{x}dx$$

$$\Rightarrow \quad \left(\tan v-\frac{1}{v}\right)dv=\frac{2}{x}dx$$

On integrating both sides, we get

$$\int\left(\tan v-\frac{1}{v}\right)dv=\int\frac{2\,dx}{x}$$

$$\Rightarrow \quad \int\tan v\,dv-\int\frac{1}{v}dv=2\int\frac{1}{x}dx$$

$$\Rightarrow \quad -\log|\cos v|-\log|v|=2\log|x|+C$$

$$\Rightarrow \quad \log|v\cos v|+2\log|x|=-C \quad [\because \log m+\log n=\log mn]$$

$$\Rightarrow \quad \log[(v\cos v)x^2]=-C$$

$$\Rightarrow \quad (v\cos v)x^2=e^{-C} \quad [\because \log_e x=m\Rightarrow x=e^m]$$

$$\Rightarrow \quad x^2v\cos v=A \quad [\text{consider } A=e^{-C}]$$

$$\Rightarrow \quad x^2\frac{y}{x}\cos\frac{y}{x}=A \quad \left[\text{put } v=\frac{y}{x}\right]$$

$$\Rightarrow \quad xy\cos\frac{y}{x}=A,$$

which is the required solution.

39. Given, $(\tan^{-1}y-x)dy=(1+y^2)dx$

$$\Rightarrow \quad (1+y^2)\frac{dx}{dy}+x=\tan^{-1}y$$

$$\Rightarrow \quad \frac{dx}{dy}+\frac{x}{1+y^2}=\frac{\tan^{-1}y}{1+y^2}$$

$\therefore \quad P=\dfrac{1}{1+y^2},\ Q=\dfrac{\tan^{-1}y}{1+y^2}$

Integrating factor (IF) $=e^{\int P\,dy}=e^{\int\frac{dy}{1+y^2}}=e^{\tan^{-1}y}$

Solution of equation is

$$x\times \text{IF}=\int Q\times \text{IF}\,dy+C$$

$$\Rightarrow \quad x\times e^{\tan^{-1}y}=\int\frac{\tan^{-1}y}{1+y^2}\times e^{\tan^{-1}y}\,dy$$

On putting $\tan^{-1}y=t$, we get

$$x\cdot e^{\tan^{-1}y}=\int t\cdot e^t dt \Rightarrow xe^{\tan^{-1}y}=te^t-e^t+C$$

$\therefore$ Solution of differential equation is

$$xe^{\tan^{-1}y}=e^{\tan^{-1}y}(\tan^{-1}y-1)+C$$

Also, it is given that $x=1$, when $y=0$.

Therefore, we have $1\cdot e^0=e^0(0-1)+C$

$\Rightarrow \quad 1=-1+C\Rightarrow C=2$

Hence, the required solution is

$$xe^{\tan^{-1}y}=e^{\tan^{-1}y}(\tan^{-1}y-1)+2.$$

40. Given differential equation is

$$(x^2+1)\frac{dy}{dx}+2xy=\frac{1}{x^2+1}$$

On dividing both sides by (x^2+1), we get

$$\frac{dy}{dx}+\frac{2x}{x^2+1}y=\frac{1}{(x^2+1)^2},$$

which is a linear differential equation of the form $\dfrac{dy}{dx}+Py=Q.$

Here, $P=\dfrac{2x}{x^2+1}$ and $Q=\dfrac{1}{(x^2+1)^2}$

Now, integrating factor (IF) $=e^{\int Pdx}=e^{\int\frac{2x}{x^2+1}dx}$

$$=e^{\log|x^2+1|}=x^2+1$$

$$\left[\begin{array}{l}\text{put } x^2+1=t\Rightarrow 2x\,dx=dt, \text{ then}\\ \int\frac{2x}{x^2+1}dx=\int\frac{1}{t}dt=\log|t|=\log|x^2+1|\end{array}\right]$$

So, the required general solution is

$$y\times \text{IF}=\int(Q\times\text{IF})\,dx+C$$

$$\Rightarrow \quad y(x^2+1)=\int\frac{1}{(x^2+1)^2}\times(x^2+1)\,dx+C$$

$$\Rightarrow \quad y(x^2+1)=\int\frac{1}{x^2+1}dx+C$$

$$\Rightarrow \quad y(x^2+1)=\tan^{-1}x+C \qquad \ldots(\text{i})$$

When $x=1$, then $y=0$

$\therefore\ 0=\tan^{-1}1+C\Rightarrow C=\dfrac{-\pi}{4}$

Now, $y(x^2+1)=\tan^{-1}x-\dfrac{\pi}{4}$, [from Eq. (i)]

which is the required differential equation.

41. We have, $(\cot^{-1}y+x)dy=(1+y^2)\,dx$

$$\Rightarrow \quad \frac{dx}{dy}=\frac{\cot^{-1}y+x}{1+y^2}\Rightarrow\frac{dx}{dy}+\left(-\frac{1}{1+y^2}\right)x=\frac{\cot^{-1}y}{1+y^2}$$

This is a linear differential equation of the form $\dfrac{dx}{dy}+Px=Q.$

Here, $P=\dfrac{-1}{1+y^2}$ and $Q=\dfrac{\cot^{-1}y}{1+y^2}.$

$$\therefore \quad \text{IF}=e^{-\int\frac{1}{1+y^2}dy}=e^{\cot^{-1}y}$$

Now, the solution of linear differential equation is given by $x\cdot\text{IF}=\int(Q\times\text{IF})\,dy+C.$

$$\therefore \quad xe^{\cot^{-1}y}=\int\frac{\cot^{-1}y}{(1+y^2)}e^{\cot^{-1}y}\,dy+C \qquad \ldots(\text{i})$$

On putting $\cot^{-1}y=t\Rightarrow\dfrac{1}{1+y^2}dy=-dt$ in Eq. (i), we get

$$xe^{\cot^{-1}y}=-\int te^t\,dt+C=-e^t(t-1)+C$$

$$\Rightarrow \quad xe^{\cot^{-1}y}=e^{\cot^{-1}y}(1-\cot^{-1}y)+C, \qquad [\because t=\cot^{-1}y]$$

which is the required solution.

42. Given differential equation is $(x-\sin y)dy+(\tan y)dx=0$

$$\Rightarrow \quad \frac{dx}{dy}=-\left(\frac{x-\sin y}{\tan y}\right)$$

$$\Rightarrow \quad \frac{dx}{dy}=\frac{\sin y}{\tan y}-\frac{x}{\tan y}$$

$$\Rightarrow \quad \frac{dx}{dy}=\cos y-\cot y\cdot x \qquad \left[\because\frac{1}{\tan\theta}=\cot\theta=\frac{\cos\theta}{\sin\theta}\right]$$

$$\Rightarrow \quad \frac{dx}{dy}+\cot y\cdot x=\cos y$$

It is a linear differential equation of the form $\dfrac{dx}{dy}+Px=Q.$

Here, $P=\cot y$ and $Q=\cos y$

$\therefore \text{IF}=e^{\int Pdy}=e^{\int\cot y\,dy}=e^{\log\sin y}=\sin y$

The general solution is given by

$$x\times\text{IF}=\int(\text{IF}\times Q)dy+C$$

$$\Rightarrow \quad x\cdot\sin y=\int\sin y\cdot\cos y\,dy+C$$

$$\Rightarrow \quad x\cdot\sin y=\frac{1}{2}\int 2\sin y\cdot\cos y\,dy+C$$

$$\Rightarrow \quad x\cdot\sin y=\frac{1}{2}\int\sin 2y\,dy+C \qquad [\because 2\sin\theta\cos\theta=\sin 2\theta]$$

$$\Rightarrow \quad x\cdot\sin y=-\frac{1}{4}\cos 2y+C \qquad \ldots(\text{i})$$

Also, given that $y=0$ when $x=0$

On putting $x=0$ and $y=0$ in Eq. (i), we get

$$0=-\frac{1}{4}\cos 0+C \qquad [\because \cos 0=1]$$

$$\Rightarrow \quad C=\frac{1}{4}$$

On putting the value of C in Eq (i), we get

$$x \cdot \sin y = -\frac{1}{4}\cos 2y + \frac{1}{4}$$

$$\Rightarrow \quad x \cdot \sin y = \frac{1}{4}(1 - \cos 2y) = \frac{1}{2}\sin^2 y \quad [\because \cos 2\theta = 1 - 2\sin^2\theta]$$

$\therefore$ $2x = \sin y$, which is the required solution.

43. We have, $\frac{dy}{dx} + y \cot x = 2x + x^2 \cot x, (x \neq 0)$

This is a linear differential equation of the form $\frac{dy}{dx} + Py = Q$.

Here, $P = \cot x$ and $Q = 2x + x^2 \cot x$.

$$\therefore \quad \text{IF} = e^{\int P dx} = e^{\int \cot x \, dx}$$

$$= e^{\log |\sin x|} = \sin x$$

The general solution is given by

$$y \cdot \text{IF} = \int (\text{IF} \times Q) dx + C$$

$$\Rightarrow y \cdot \sin x = \int (2x + x^2 \cdot \cot x) \sin x \, dx + C$$

$$= 2\int x \sin x \, dx + \int x^2 \cos x \, dx + C$$

$$= 2\int x \sin x \, dx + x^2 \sin x - \int 2x \sin x \, dx + C$$

$$\Rightarrow y \cdot \sin x = x^2 \sin x + C \quad \dots(\text{i})$$

On putting $x = \frac{\pi}{2}$ and $y = 0$ in Eq. (i), we get

$$(0) \sin\frac{\pi}{2} = \left(\frac{\pi}{2}\right)^2 \cdot \sin\frac{\pi}{2} + C$$

$$\Rightarrow \quad C = -\frac{\pi^2}{4}$$

On putting $C = \frac{-\pi^2}{4}$ in Eq. (i), we get

$$y \cdot \sin x = x^2 \sin x - \frac{\pi^2}{4}$$

$$\therefore \quad y = x^2 - \frac{\pi^2}{4} \operatorname{cosec} x$$

[dividing both sides by $\sin x$]

44. We have,

$$ye^y dx = (y^3 + 2xe^y) dy$$

$$\Rightarrow \quad \frac{dx}{dy} = y^2 e^{-y} + \frac{2x}{y}$$

$$\Rightarrow \quad \frac{dx}{dy} - \frac{2}{y}x = y^2 e^{-y} \quad \dots(\text{i})$$

This is a linear differential equation of the form $\frac{dy}{dx} + Py = Q$.

Here, $P = -\frac{2}{y}$ and $Q = y^2 e^{-y}$

$$\therefore \quad \text{IF} = e^{\int \frac{-2}{y} dy}$$

$$= e^{-2\log y}$$

$$= y^{-2} = \frac{1}{y^2}$$

$$\because \quad x \times \text{IF} = \int Q \times \text{IF} \, dy + C$$

$$\therefore \quad x\left(\frac{1}{y^2}\right) = \int y^2 e^{-y} \times \frac{1}{y^2} dy + C$$

$$\Rightarrow \quad x\left(\frac{1}{y^2}\right) = \int e^{-y} dy + C$$

$$\Rightarrow \quad \frac{x}{y^2} = -e^{-y} + C \quad \dots(\text{ii})$$

It is given that $y(0) = 1$ i.e. $y = 1$ when $x = 0$.

On putting $x = 0$ and $y = 1$ in Eq. (ii), we get

$$0 = -e^{-1} + C$$

$$\Rightarrow \quad C = \frac{1}{e}$$

On putting $C = \frac{1}{e}$ in Eq. (ii), we get

$$\frac{x}{y^2} = -e^{-y} + \frac{1}{e}$$

$$\Rightarrow \quad x = y^2(e^{-1} - e^{-y})$$

Hence, the required solution is $x = y^2 (e^{-1} - e^{-y})$.

QR Code for Quick Test 1	QR Code for Quick Test 2	QR Code for Quick Test 3	QR Code for Quick Test 4

Mind Map

Differential Equation

An equation involving independent variable, dependent variable, derivatives of dependent variable with respect to one (or more) independent variable and constant is called a differential equation.

e.g. $x\frac{dy}{dx} + xy\frac{d^2y}{dx^2} + 4 = 0$

Particular Solution of a Differential Equation

The solution of a differential equation obtained by giving particular values to the arbitrary constants in the general solution, is called the particular solution.

Degree of a Differential Equation

The highest power (positive integral index) of the highest order derivative involved in a differential equation, when it is written as a polynomial in derivatives, is called the degree of a differential equation.

e.g. $\left(\frac{d^3y}{dx^3}\right)^2 + x\left(\frac{d^3y}{dx^3}\right) + 3y\left(\frac{dy}{dx}\right) = 0$

Order of a Differential Equation

The highest order derivative involved in a differential equation, is called order of differential equation.

e.g. $\frac{d^3y}{dx^3} + x^2\left(\frac{d^2y}{dx^2}\right) = 0$

Hence, order of differential equation is 3.

Solution of a Differential Equation

A function of the form $y = \phi(x) + C$, which satisfies given differential equation, is called the solution of the differential equation.

General Solution of a Differential Equation

If the solution of a differential equation of order n, contains n arbitrary constants, then it is called a general solution.

Methods of Solving First Order and First Degree Differential Equations

Linear Differential Equation

A differential equation of the form

$$\frac{dy}{dx} + Py = Q \quad \text{...(i)}$$

where, P and Q are functions of x or constants is known as a first order linear differential equation.

The solution of Eq. (i) is given by the equation

$$y \times \text{IF} = \int (Q \times \text{IF})\, dx + C$$

where, IF = Integrating Factor and IF = $e^{\int P dx}$

If general form of linear differential equation is

$$\frac{dx}{dy} + P'x = Q' \quad \text{...(ii)}$$

where, P' and Q' are functions of y or constants.

Then, solution of Eq. (ii) is given by the equation

$$x \times \text{IF} = \int (Q' \times \text{IF})\, dx + C$$

where, IF = Integrating Factor and IF = $e^{\int P' dy}$.

Differential Equation of the Type $\frac{dy}{dx} = f(x)$ or $\frac{dy}{dx} = f(y)$

In this type of differential equations, we integrate both sides to obtain general solutions.

e.g. For $\frac{dy}{dx} = f(x)$, general solution is $\int dy = \int f(x)dx + C$

and for $\frac{dy}{dx} = f(y)$, general solution is $\int \frac{1}{f(y)} dy = \int dx + C$

Homogeneous Differential Equations

A function $F(x, y)$ is called homogeneous function of degree n, if $F(\lambda x, \lambda y) = \lambda^n F(x, y)$, where λ is non-zero real number.

A differential equation $\frac{dy}{dx} = \frac{f(x, y)}{g(x, y)}$ is said to be **homogeneous**, if $f(x, y)$ and $g(x, y)$ are homogeneous functions of same degree i.e. it may be written as

$$\frac{dy}{dx} = \frac{x^n f\left(\frac{y}{x}\right)}{x^n g\left(\frac{y}{x}\right)} = \frac{f\left(\frac{y}{x}\right)}{g\left(\frac{y}{x}\right)} = F\left(\frac{y}{x}\right)$$

Differential Equation in the Form of Variables Separable

A first order and first degree differential equation $\frac{dy}{dx} = F(x, y)$ is in the form of variable separable, if the function F can be expressed as the product of the functions of x and the functions of y.

i.e. $$\frac{dy}{dx} = h(y) \cdot g(x) \quad \text{...(i)}$$

If $h(y) \neq 0$, then separate the variables i.e. write Eq. (i) as

$$\frac{1}{h(y)} dy = g(x) dx$$

On integrating both sides, we get

$$\int \frac{1}{h(y)} dy = \int g(x) dx \text{ or } H(y) = G(x) + C$$

which is the required solution of given differential equation, where $H(y)$ and $G(x)$ are the anti-derivatives of $\frac{1}{h(y)}$ and $g(x)$, respectively and C is the arbitrary constant.

Solution of Homogeneous Differential Equation

To solve homogeneous differential equation of the form

$$\frac{dy}{dx} = F(x, y) \quad \text{...(i)}$$

We put $y = vx \Rightarrow \frac{dy}{dx} = v + x\frac{dv}{dx}$ in Eq. (i) to reduce it into variable separable form. Then, solve it and in the final result put $v = \frac{y}{x}$ to get the required solution.

CHAPTER 10

> Life is good for two things, discovering Mathematics and teaching Mathematics.
>
> — *Simeon Poisson*

▼ YOUR STUDY GOALS

10.1 Scalars and Vectors
10.2 Algebra of Vectors
10.3 Components of a Vector
10.4 Direction Cosines and Direction Ratios of a Vector
10.5 Vector Joining Two Points
10.6 Section Formula
10.7 Scalar (or Dot) Product of Two Vectors
10.8 Vector (or Cross) Product of Two Vectors

▼ YOUR PRACTICE GOALS

- Objective Type Questions (39 Qs ; 26 MCQs, 10 A-R, 3 Case Based)
- Subjective Type Questions (49 Qs ; 32 VSA, 8 SA, 9 LA)

Vector Algebra

10.1 Scalars and Vectors

Those quantities which have only magnitude but no direction, are called **scalar quantities** or **scalars**. e.g. area, volume, mass etc.

Those quantities which have magnitude as well as direction are called **vector quantities** or **vectors**. e.g. velocity, acceleration, force, etc.

Representation of a Vector

A vector is represented by a directed line segment having an initial and terminal point.

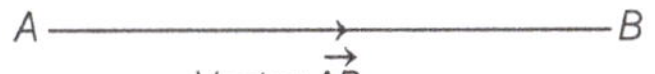

Vector $\vec{AB}$

Here, direction represents **direction of vector**. Generally, vectors are denoted by $\vec{a}$, $\vec{b}$, $\vec{c}$, etc.

Magnitude of a Vector

The length of the vector $\overrightarrow{AB}$ or $\vec{a}$ is called magnitude of $\overrightarrow{AB}$ or $\vec{a}$ and it is represented by $|\overrightarrow{AB}|$ or $|\vec{a}|$ or a.

Types of Vectors

(i) **Zero or Null Vector** A vector whose magnitude is zero is called a null vector or zero vector. It is denoted by $\vec{0}$.

(ii) **Unit Vector** A vector whose magnitude is one unit (i.e. unity) is called a unit vector. The unit vector in the direction of $\vec{a}$ is denoted by $\hat{a}$ and read as '*a* cap'.

(iii) **Coinitial Vectors** Two or more vectors having the same initial point are called coinitial vectors.

(iv) **Free Vector** If the value of a vector depends only on its magnitude and direction and is independent of its position in the space, it is called free vector.

(v) **Collinear or Parallel Vectors** Two or more vectors are said to be collinear, if they are parallel to same line, irrespective of their magnitudes and directions.

(vi) **Equal Vectors** Two vectors are said to be equal, if they have same magnitude and direction regardless of the positions of their initial points.

Symbolically if $\vec{a}$ and $\vec{b}$ are equal, then it is written as $\vec{a} = \vec{b}$.

(vii) **Negative of a Vector** A vector whose magnitude is same as that of a given vector but the direction is opposite to that of it, is called negative of the given vector.

e.g. Vector $\overrightarrow{BA}$ is negative of the vector $\overrightarrow{AB}$ and written as $\overrightarrow{BA} = -\overrightarrow{AB}$.

(viii) **Coplanar Vectors** Three or more vectors, which either lie in the same plane or are parallel to the same plane, are called coplanar vectors. Generally, two vectors are always coplanar.

(ix) **Position Vector** The vector joining a point in the space to the origin is called position vector of the point. Let $O(0, 0, 0)$ be the origin and P be a point in space having coordinates (x, y, z) with respect to the origin O.

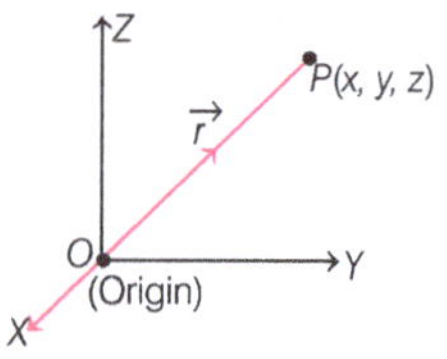

Then, the vector $\overrightarrow{OP}$ or $\vec{r}$ is called the position vector of the point P with respect to O.

10.2 Algebra of Vectors

Addition of Vectors

There are two laws of vector addition, which are given below.

Triangle Law of Vector Addition

If two vectors are represented along two sides of a triangle taken in order, then their resultant is represented by its third side taken in opposite order. By triangle law of vector addition in ΔABC, we have

$$\overrightarrow{BC} + \overrightarrow{CA} = \overrightarrow{BA}$$

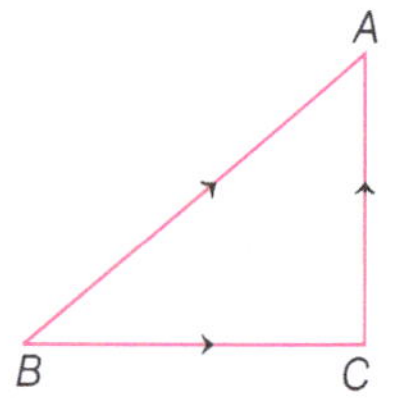

Parallelogram Law of Vector Addition

If two vectors are represented along the two adjacent sides of a parallelogram, then their resultant is represented by the diagonal of the parallelogram through the common point.

In the parallelogram $OABC$, we have

$$\overrightarrow{OA} + \overrightarrow{OC} = \overrightarrow{OB}.$$

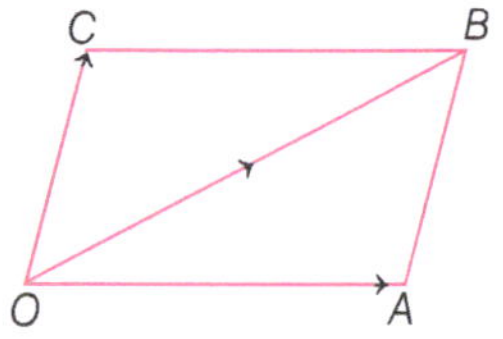

Properties of Vector Addition

- **Commutative** For vectors $\vec{a}$ and $\vec{b}$, we have $\vec{a} + \vec{b} = \vec{b} + \vec{a}$.
- **Associative** For vectors $\vec{a}$, $\vec{b}$ and $\vec{c}$, we have $\vec{a} + (\vec{b} + \vec{c}) = (\vec{a} + \vec{b}) + \vec{c}$.
- **Additive identity** For any vector $\vec{a}$, a zero vector $\vec{0}$ is its additive identity as $\vec{a} + \vec{0} = \vec{a}$.
- **Additive inverse** For a vector $\vec{a}$, a negative vector of $\vec{a}$ is its additive inverse as $\vec{a} + (-\vec{a}) = \vec{0}$.

Difference of Two Vectors

The subtraction of vector $\vec{B}$ from vector $\vec{A}$ is simply the vector sum of $\vec{A}$ and $-\vec{B}$.

$$\vec{A}-\vec{B}=\vec{A}+(-\vec{B})$$

Thus, to subtract the vector $\vec{B}$ from vector $\vec{A}$, we reverse the direction of $\vec{B}$ and add it to $\vec{A}$.

Multiplication of a Vector by a Scalar

Let λ be a scalar and $\vec{a}$ be a vector, then $\lambda\vec{a}$ (multiplication of vector by scalar) is defined as a vector whose magnitude is $|\lambda|$ times the magnitude of $\vec{a}$.

i.e. $|\lambda\vec{a}|=|\lambda||\vec{a}|$.

The direction of $\lambda\vec{a}$ is same or opposite to $\vec{a}$, depending on whether λ is positive or negative.

Properties of Multiplication of a Vector by a Scalar

- Let $\vec{a}$ and $\vec{b}$ be any two vectors and k and m be any two scalars, then
  (i) $k\vec{a}+m\vec{a}=(k+m)\vec{a}$
  (ii) $k(\vec{a}+\vec{b})=k\vec{a}+k\vec{b}$
  (iii) $k(m\vec{a})=km(\vec{a})$
- (a) For any value of λ, the vector $\lambda\vec{a}$ is always collinear to the vector $\vec{a}$.
  (b) The unit vector in the direction of $\vec{a}$ is written as $\hat{a}=\frac{1}{|\vec{a}|}\cdot\vec{a}$.

10.3 Components of a Vector

Let a point P in a space has coordinates (x, y, z) and $\hat{i}$, $\hat{j}$ and $\hat{k}$ are unit vectors along OX, OY and OZ-axes, respectively.

Then, the position vector of P with respect to O is given by

$$\overrightarrow{OP}\ (\text{or } \vec{r})=x\hat{i}+y\hat{j}+z\hat{k}$$

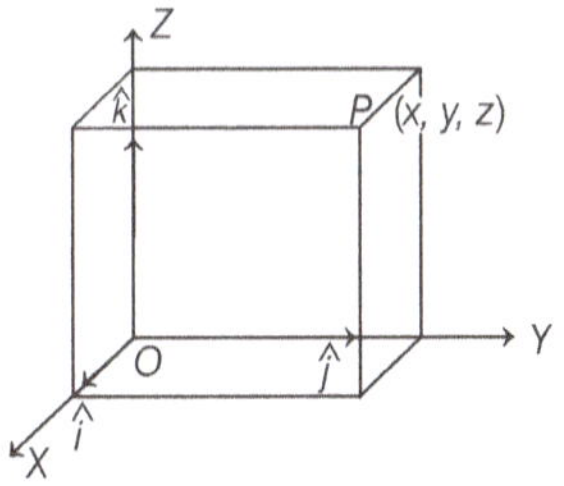

Here, x, y and z are called the **scalar (or rectangular) components** and $x\hat{i}$, $y\hat{j}$ and $z\hat{k}$ are called the **vector components** of $\overrightarrow{OP}$ (or $\vec{r}$) along the respective axes.

The length of any vector $\vec{r}=x\hat{i}+y\hat{j}+z\hat{k}$ is given by

$$\vec{r}=|x\hat{i}+y\hat{j}+z\hat{k}|=\sqrt{x^2+y^2+z^2}.$$

TEACHER TIPS

If we have two vectors $\vec{a}$ and $\vec{b}$, given in component form as $\vec{a}=a_1\hat{i}+a_2\hat{j}+a_3\hat{k}$ and $\vec{b}=b_1\hat{i}+b_2\hat{j}+b_3\hat{k}$ and λ be any scalar, then

(i) $\vec{a}+\vec{b}=(a_1+b_1)\hat{i}+(a_2+b_2)\hat{j}+(a_3+b_3)\hat{k}$

(ii) $\vec{a}-\vec{b}=(a_1-b_1)\hat{i}+(a_2-b_2)\hat{j}+(a_3-b_3)\hat{k}$

(iii) $\lambda\vec{a}=(\lambda a_1)\hat{i}+(\lambda a_2)\hat{j}+(\lambda a_3)\hat{k}$

(iv) $\vec{a}=\vec{b}$ iff $a_1=b_1$, $a_2=b_2$ and $a_3=b_3$

(v) $\vec{a}$ and $\vec{b}$ are collinear (or parallel), iff $\frac{a_1}{b_1}=\frac{a_2}{b_2}=\frac{a_3}{b_3}=\lambda$ (non-zero scalar).

10.4 Direction Cosines and Direction Ratios of a Vector

Suppose $\overrightarrow{OP}$ makes α, β and γ with the coordinate axes OX, OY and OZ, respectively, then direction cosines of a line OP are $l=\cos\alpha$, $m=\cos\beta$ and $n=\cos\gamma$.

The direction ratios of line OP are lr, mr and nr where $r = |\overrightarrow{OP}|$.

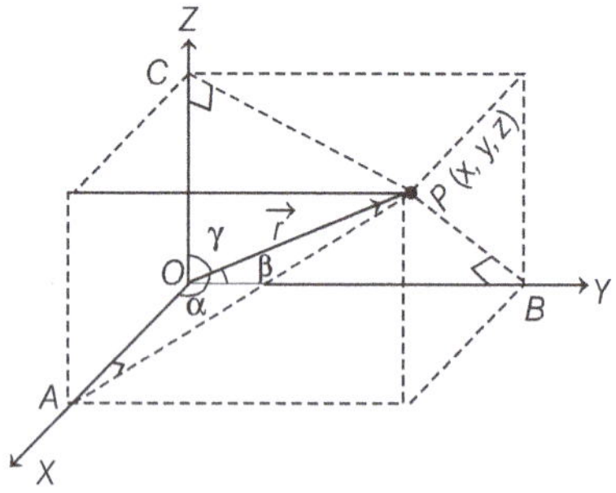

(i) In general, it may be noted that $l^2 + m^2 + n^2 = 1$ but $x^2 + y^2 + z^2 \neq 1$.

(ii) If $\vec{a} = a_1\hat{i} + a_2\hat{j} + a_3\hat{k}$, then a_1, a_2 and a_3 are also called **direction ratios** of $\vec{a}$.

The **direction cosines** of $\vec{a}$ is given by

$$\frac{a_1}{\sqrt{a_1^2 + a_2^2 + a_3^2}}, \frac{a_2}{\sqrt{a_1^2 + a_2^2 + a_3^2}}, \frac{a_3}{\sqrt{a_1^2 + a_2^2 + a_3^2}}.$$

10.5 Vector Joining Two Points

If $P_1(x_1, y_1, z_1)$ and $P_2(x_2, y_2, z_2)$ are any two points, then the vector joining P_1 and P_2 is the vector $\overrightarrow{P_1P_2}$.

$$\overrightarrow{P_1P_2} = \overrightarrow{OP_2} - \overrightarrow{OP_1}$$

$$= (x_2\hat{i} + y_2\hat{j} + z_2\hat{k}) - (x_1\hat{i} + y_1\hat{j} + z_1\hat{k})$$

i.e. $\overrightarrow{P_1P_2} = (x_2 - x_1)\hat{i} + (y_2 - y_1)\hat{j} + (z_2 - z_1)\hat{k}$

- The distance between two points, $|\overrightarrow{P_1P_2}| = \sqrt{(x_2 - x_1)^2 + (y_2 - y_1)^2 + (z_2 - z_1)^2}$
- The direction ratios and direction cosines of a line joining two vectors are $(x_2 - x_1)$, $(y_2 - y_1)$, $(z_2 - z_1)$ and $\frac{x_2 - x_1}{d}, \frac{y_2 - y_1}{d}, \frac{z_2 - z_1}{d}$.

10.6 Section Formula

Position vector $\overrightarrow{OR}$ of point R which divides the line segment joining the points A and B with position vectors $\vec{a}$ and $\vec{b}$ respectively, internally in the ratio $m : n$ is given by

$$\overrightarrow{OR} = \frac{m\vec{b} + n\vec{a}}{m + n}$$

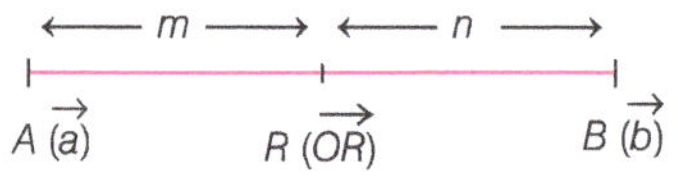

For external division,

$$\overrightarrow{OR} = \frac{m\vec{b} - n\vec{a}}{m - n}$$

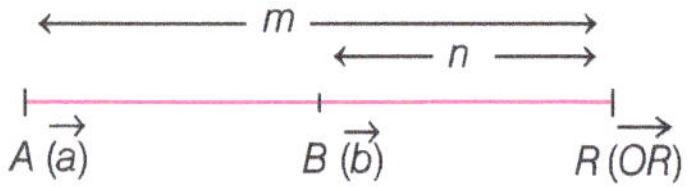

TEACHER TIPS

- If $\vec{a} = \vec{b}$, then $|\vec{a}| = |\vec{b}|$ but converse may not be true.
- The vector sum of three sides of a triangle taken in order is $\vec{0}$.
- Both laws of vector addition are equivalent to each other.
- Position vector $\overrightarrow{OR}$ of mid-point R of the line segment joining the points $A(\vec{a})$ and $B(\vec{b})$ is given by $\overrightarrow{OR} = \frac{\vec{a} + \vec{b}}{2}$.
- Three points $\vec{A}, \vec{B}$ and $\vec{C}$ are said to be collinear if $\overrightarrow{AB} = \lambda\, \overrightarrow{BC}$, where λ is a scalar quantity.

Example 1 **If A, B and C are the vertices of a ΔABC, then what is the value of $\overrightarrow{AB} + \overrightarrow{BC} + \overrightarrow{CA}$?** CBSE 2011C

Sol. We have, $\overrightarrow{AB} + \overrightarrow{BC} + \overrightarrow{CA} = \overrightarrow{CA} + \overrightarrow{AC}$

[by triangle law of vector addition $\overrightarrow{AB} + \overrightarrow{BC} = \overrightarrow{AC}$]

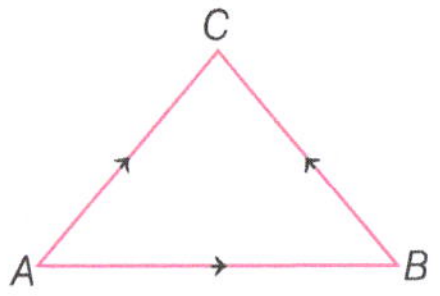

$\Rightarrow \overrightarrow{AB} + \overrightarrow{BC} + \overrightarrow{CA} = \overrightarrow{CA} - \overrightarrow{CA}$ $[\because \overrightarrow{AC} = -\overrightarrow{CA}]$

$\therefore \overrightarrow{AB} + \overrightarrow{BC} + \overrightarrow{CA} = \vec{0}$

Example 2 **In figure, $ABCD$ is a parallelogram, in which E and F are respectively the mid-points of AB and BC. If $\overrightarrow{AB} = \vec{a}$ and $\overrightarrow{AD} = \vec{b}$, then find the value of vector $\overrightarrow{EF}$.**

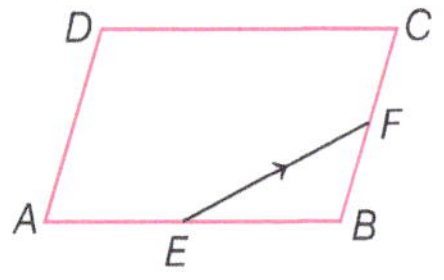

CBSE 2018

Sol. Given, $\overrightarrow{AB} = \vec{a}$ and $\overrightarrow{AD} = \vec{b}$

In ΔEBF, $\overrightarrow{EF} = \overrightarrow{EB} + \overrightarrow{BF}$

[triangle law of vector addition]

$$= \frac{1}{2}\overrightarrow{AB} + \frac{1}{2}\overrightarrow{BC}$$

[$\because$ E and F are the mid-points of AB and BC, respectively]

$$= \frac{1}{2}(\overrightarrow{AB} + \overrightarrow{BC}) = \frac{1}{2}(\overrightarrow{AB} + \overrightarrow{AD})$$

[$\because$ opposite sides of a parallelogram are equal, therefore $\overrightarrow{BC} = \overrightarrow{AD}$]

$$\Rightarrow \quad \overrightarrow{EF} = \frac{1}{2}(\vec{a} + \vec{b}) \qquad [\because \overrightarrow{AB} = \vec{a} \text{ and } \overrightarrow{AD} = \vec{b}]$$

Example 3 Find the sum of the vectors $\overrightarrow{AB}$, $\overrightarrow{BC}$, $\overrightarrow{CD}$, $\overrightarrow{DE}$ and $\overrightarrow{AE}$, where $ABCDE$ is a pentagon. CBSE 2018

Sol. Given, $ABCDE$ is a pentagon.

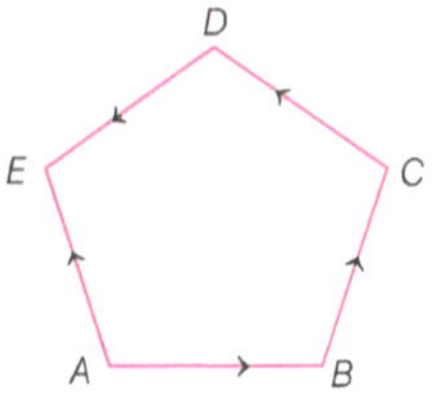

$\therefore$ Sum of $\overrightarrow{AB}$, $\overrightarrow{BC}$, $\overrightarrow{CD}$, $\overrightarrow{DE}$ and $\overrightarrow{AE}$

$$= \overrightarrow{AB} + \overrightarrow{BC} + \overrightarrow{CD} + \overrightarrow{DE} + \overrightarrow{AE}$$

$$= (\overrightarrow{AB} + \overrightarrow{BC}) + (\overrightarrow{CD} + \overrightarrow{DE}) + \overrightarrow{AE}$$

$$= \overrightarrow{AC} + \overrightarrow{CE} + \overrightarrow{AE}$$

[using triangle law of vector addition]

$$= \overrightarrow{AE} + \overrightarrow{AE} = 2\overrightarrow{AE}$$

Example 4 Find a unit vector in the direction opposite to $-\frac{3}{4}\hat{j}$. CBSE Sample Paper 2021

Sol. Let $\vec{a} = -\frac{3}{4}\hat{j}$.

So, any vector in the direction opposite to $\vec{a}$ is given by

$$\vec{b} = -\vec{a} = \frac{3}{4}\hat{j}$$

$$\therefore \quad \hat{b} = \frac{\vec{b}}{|\vec{b}|} = \frac{\frac{3}{4}\hat{j}}{\left(\frac{3}{4}\right)} = \hat{j}$$

So, the required unit vector is $\hat{j}$.

Example 5 Find a vector in the direction of vector $\vec{a} = \hat{i} - 2\hat{j}$ that has magnitude 7 units. NCERT Exemplar

Sol. We have, $\vec{a} = \hat{i} - 2\hat{j}$

$$\therefore \quad |\vec{a}| = \sqrt{(1)^2 + (-2)^2} = \sqrt{1+4} = \sqrt{5}$$

The unit vector in the direction of the given vector $\vec{a}$ is

$$\hat{a} = \frac{1}{|\vec{a}|}\cdot\vec{a} = \frac{1}{\sqrt{5}}(\hat{i} - 2\hat{j}) = \frac{1}{\sqrt{5}}\hat{i} - \frac{2}{\sqrt{5}}\hat{j}$$

Now, the vector having magnitude 7 units and in the direction of $\vec{a} = 7\hat{a} = 7\left(\frac{1}{\sqrt{5}}\hat{i} - \frac{2}{\sqrt{5}}\hat{j}\right) = \frac{7}{\sqrt{5}}\hat{i} - \frac{14}{\sqrt{5}}\hat{j}$

Example 6 Evaluate $|4\vec{a} - 3\vec{b}|$, if $\vec{a} = 7\hat{i} - \hat{j} - \hat{k}$ and $\vec{b} = 2\hat{i} + \hat{j}$. CBSE 2013, 12, 10

Sol. Given, $\vec{a} = 7\hat{i} - \hat{j} - \hat{k}$ and $\vec{b} = 2\hat{i} + \hat{j}$

Then, $4\vec{a} - 3\vec{b} = 4(7\hat{i} - \hat{j} - \hat{k}) - 3(2\hat{i} + \hat{j})$

$$= 28\hat{i} - 4\hat{j} - 4\hat{k} - 6\hat{i} - 3\hat{j}$$

$$= 22\hat{i} - 7\hat{j} - 4\hat{k}$$

$$\therefore \quad |4\vec{a} - 3\vec{b}| = \sqrt{(22)^2 + (-7)^2 + (-4)^2}$$

$$= \sqrt{484 + 49 + 16}$$

$$= \sqrt{549}$$

Example 7 For what values of a, the vectors $2\hat{i} - 3\hat{j} + 4\hat{k}$ and $a\hat{i} + 6\hat{j} - 8\hat{k}$ are collinear? Competency Based Que, CBSE 2011

Sol. Let given vectors are $\vec{a} = 2\hat{i} - 3\hat{j} + 4\hat{k}$ and $\vec{b} = a\hat{i} + 6\hat{j} - 8\hat{k}$.

We know that vectors $\vec{a} = a_1\hat{i} + a_2\hat{j} + a_3\hat{k}$ and $\vec{b} = b_1\hat{i} + b_2\hat{j} + b_3\hat{k}$ are collinear, iff

$$\frac{b_1}{a_1} = \frac{b_2}{a_2} = \frac{b_3}{a_3}.$$

$$\therefore \quad \frac{a}{2} = \frac{6}{-3} = \frac{-8}{4}$$

$$\Rightarrow \quad \frac{a}{2} = -2$$

$$\therefore \quad a = -4$$

Example 8 Position vectors of the points A, B and C as shown in the figure below are $\vec{a}$, $\vec{b}$ and $\vec{c}$, respectively.

If $\overrightarrow{AC} = \frac{5}{4}\overrightarrow{AB}$, then express $\vec{c}$ in terms of $\vec{a}$ and $\vec{b}$. CBSE 2023

Sol. Given, $\overrightarrow{OA}=\vec{a}$, $\overrightarrow{OB}=\vec{b}$, $\overrightarrow{OC}=\vec{c}$

$\therefore\quad \overrightarrow{AC}=\overrightarrow{OC}-\overrightarrow{OA}=\vec{c}-\vec{a}$

and $\quad \overrightarrow{AB}=\overrightarrow{OB}-\overrightarrow{OA}=\vec{b}-\vec{a}$

Also given, $\overrightarrow{AC}=\dfrac{5}{4}\overrightarrow{AB} \Rightarrow \vec{c}-\vec{a}=\dfrac{5}{4}(\vec{b}-\vec{a})$

$\Rightarrow\quad 4\vec{c}-4\vec{a}=5\vec{b}-5\vec{a} \Rightarrow 4\vec{c}=5\vec{b}-5\vec{a}+4\vec{a}$

$\therefore\quad \vec{c}=\dfrac{5\vec{b}-\vec{a}}{4}$

Example 9 Find all the vectors of magnitude $3\sqrt{3}$ which are collinear to vector $\hat{i}+\hat{j}+\hat{k}$. *CBSE 2023*

Sol. Vectors collinear to $\hat{i}+\hat{j}+\hat{k}$ can be written as

$\lambda(\hat{i}+\hat{j}+\hat{k})$

$\Rightarrow\quad \vec{A}=\lambda\hat{i}+\lambda\hat{j}+\lambda\hat{k}$ [let $\vec{A}$]

Also, it is given that $|\vec{A}|=3\sqrt{3}$

$\Rightarrow\quad \sqrt{\lambda^2+\lambda^2+\lambda^2}=3\sqrt{3}$

On squaring both sides, we get

$3\lambda^2=27 \Rightarrow \lambda^2=9 \Rightarrow \lambda=\pm 3$

Since, λ is a scalar. It can be positive or negative.

So, we have two possible values for λ,

$\lambda=3$ and $\lambda=-3$

$\therefore$ Vectors collinear to $\hat{i}+\hat{j}+\hat{k}$ having magnitude $3\sqrt{3}$ are $3\hat{i}+3\hat{j}+3\hat{k}$ and $-3\hat{i}-3\hat{j}-3\hat{k}$.

Example 10 If $\vec{a}=\hat{i}+2\hat{j}+3\hat{k}$ and $\vec{b}=2\hat{i}+4\hat{j}-5\hat{k}$ represent two adjacent sides of a parallelogram, then find unit vectors parallel to the diagonals of the parallelogram. *CBSE 2020*

Sol. We have, $\vec{a}=\hat{i}+2\hat{j}+3\hat{k}$ and $\vec{b}=2\hat{i}+4\hat{j}-5\hat{k}$

So, the diagonals of the parallelogram whose adjacent sides are $\vec{a}$ and $\vec{b}$ are given by

$\vec{p}=\vec{a}+\vec{b}$ and $\vec{q}=\vec{a}-\vec{b}$

Now, $\quad \vec{p}=(\hat{i}+2\hat{j}+3\hat{k})+(2\hat{i}+4\hat{j}-5\hat{k})=3\hat{i}+6\hat{k}-2\hat{k}$

and $\quad \vec{q}=(\hat{i}+2\hat{j}+3\hat{k})-(2\hat{i}+4\hat{j}-5\hat{k})=-\hat{i}-2\hat{j}+8\hat{k}$

$\therefore\quad \hat{p}=\dfrac{\vec{p}}{|\vec{p}|}=\dfrac{3\hat{i}+6\hat{j}-2\hat{k}}{\sqrt{9+36+4}}$

$=\dfrac{3\hat{i}+6\hat{j}-2\hat{k}}{7}=\dfrac{3}{7}\hat{i}+\dfrac{6}{7}\hat{j}-\dfrac{2}{7}\hat{k}$

and $\quad \hat{q}=\dfrac{\vec{q}}{|\vec{q}|}=\dfrac{-\hat{i}-2\hat{j}+8\hat{k}}{\sqrt{1+4+64}}=\dfrac{-\hat{i}-2\hat{j}+8\hat{k}}{\sqrt{69}}$

$=\dfrac{-1}{\sqrt{69}}\hat{i}-\dfrac{2}{\sqrt{69}}\hat{j}+\dfrac{8}{\sqrt{69}}\hat{k}$

Example 11 Find a vector $\vec{a}$ of magnitude $5\sqrt{2}$, making an angle of $\dfrac{\pi}{4}$ with X-axis, $\dfrac{\pi}{2}$ with Y-axis and an acute angle θ with Z-axis. *Competency Based Que, CBSE 2014*

Sol. Given, vector $\vec{a}$ makes an angle $\dfrac{\pi}{4}$ with X-axis and $\dfrac{\pi}{2}$ with Y-axis.

So, $l=\cos\dfrac{\pi}{4}$ and $m=\cos\dfrac{\pi}{2} \Rightarrow l=\dfrac{1}{\sqrt{2}}$ and $m=0$

We know that $l^2+m^2+n^2=1$

$\therefore\quad \left(\dfrac{1}{\sqrt{2}}\right)^2+(0)^2+n^2=1 \Rightarrow \dfrac{1}{2}+n^2=1$

$\Rightarrow\quad n^2=1-\dfrac{1}{2} \Rightarrow n=\pm\dfrac{1}{\sqrt{2}}$

$\Rightarrow\quad n=\dfrac{1}{\sqrt{2}}$ [$\because$ $\vec{a}$ makes acute angle with Z-axis, so we take a positive sign]

$\therefore\quad \cos\theta=\dfrac{1}{\sqrt{2}}$ [$\because$ θ is an acute angle with Z-axis]

Thus, the direction cosines of $\vec{a}$ are $\dfrac{1}{\sqrt{2}}, 0, \dfrac{1}{\sqrt{2}}$.

Now, vector $\vec{a}=|\vec{a}|\left(\cos\dfrac{\pi}{4}\hat{i}+\cos\dfrac{\pi}{2}\hat{j}+\cos\theta\hat{k}\right)$

$=5\sqrt{2}\left(\dfrac{1}{\sqrt{2}}\hat{i}+(0)\hat{j}+\dfrac{1}{\sqrt{2}}\hat{k}\right)=5\hat{i}+5\hat{k}$

Example 12 Write the direction ratios of the vector $\vec{a}=\hat{i}+\hat{j}-2\hat{k}$ and hence calculate its direction cosines. *NCERT*

Sol. We have, vector $\vec{a}=\hat{i}+\hat{j}-2\hat{k}$

We know that direction ratios of a vector $\vec{r}=x\hat{i}+y\hat{j}+z\hat{k}$ are the scalar components x, y and z of the vector.

So, required direction ratios are 1, 1 and -2.

Now, $|\vec{a}|=|\hat{i}+\hat{j}-2\hat{k}|$

$=\sqrt{(1)^2+(1)^2+(-2)^2}$

$=\sqrt{1+1+4}=\sqrt{6}$

Suppose l, m and n are the direction cosines of given vector $\vec{a}$.

Then, $l=\dfrac{x}{|\vec{a}|}$, $m=\dfrac{y}{|\vec{a}|}$ and $n=\dfrac{z}{|\vec{a}|}$

$\Rightarrow\quad l=\dfrac{1}{\sqrt{6}}$, $m=\dfrac{1}{\sqrt{6}}$ and $n=\dfrac{-2}{\sqrt{6}}$

Hence, the required direction cosines are $\left(\dfrac{1}{\sqrt{6}}, \dfrac{1}{\sqrt{6}}, \dfrac{-2}{\sqrt{6}}\right)$.

Example 13 **A vector $\vec{r}$ is inclined at equal angles to the three axes. If the magnitude of $\vec{r}$ is $2\sqrt{3}$ units, then find the value of $\vec{r}$.** CBSE 2023

Sol. We have, $|\vec{r}| = 2\sqrt{3}$

Since, $\vec{r}$ is equally inclined to the three axes. So, direction cosines of $\vec{r}$ will be same i.e. $l = m = n$

We know that $l^2 + m^2 + n^2 = 1$

$$\Rightarrow \quad l^2 + l^2 + l^2 = 1 \Rightarrow l^2 = \frac{1}{3} \Rightarrow l = \pm\left(\frac{1}{\sqrt{3}}\right)$$

So, $\hat{r} = \pm\left(\frac{1}{\sqrt{3}}\hat{i} + \frac{1}{\sqrt{3}}\hat{j} + \frac{1}{\sqrt{3}}\hat{k}\right)$

Now, $\vec{r} = \hat{r}\cdot|\vec{r}|$ $\quad \left[\because \hat{r} = \frac{\vec{r}}{|\vec{r}|}\right]$

$$= \pm\left[\frac{1}{\sqrt{3}}\hat{i} + \frac{1}{\sqrt{3}}\hat{j} + \frac{1}{\sqrt{3}}\hat{k}\right] 2\sqrt{3} \quad [\because |\vec{r}| = 2\sqrt{3}]$$

$$= \pm(2\hat{i} + 2\hat{j} + 2\hat{k})$$

$$= \pm 2(\hat{i} + \hat{j} + \hat{k})$$

Example 14 **Find the vector joining the points $P(2, 3, 0)$ and $Q(-1, -2, -4)$ directed from Q to P. Also, determine the direction ratios and direction cosines of joning two points.**

Sol. Given points are $P(2, 3, 0)$ and $Q(-1, -2, -4)$,

then the position vector of P, $\vec{OP} = 2\hat{i} + 3\hat{j} + 0\hat{k}$

and position vector of Q, $\vec{OQ} = -\hat{i} - 2\hat{j} - 4\hat{k}$.

Here, the vector is directed from Q to P. So, Q is the initial point and P is the terminal point.

$\therefore$ Required vector, $\vec{QP} = \vec{OP} - \vec{OQ}$

$$= (2\hat{i} + 3\hat{j} + 0\hat{k}) - (-\hat{i} - 2\hat{j} - 4\hat{k})$$

$$= (2+1)\hat{i} + (3+2)\hat{j} + (0+4)\hat{k}$$

$$= 3\hat{i} + 5\hat{j} + 4\hat{k}$$

Now, $|QP| = d = \sqrt{3^2 + 5^2 + 4^2}$

$$= \sqrt{9 + 25 + 16} = \sqrt{50} = 5\sqrt{2}$$

$\therefore$ The direction ratios of vector joining two points is $(x_2 - x_1, y_2 - y_1, z_2 - z_1)$ i.e. $(2+1, 3+2, 0+4)$ or $(3, 5, 4)$.

And direction cosines of vector joining two points is

$$\left(\frac{x_2 - x_1}{d}, \frac{y_2 - y_1}{d}, \frac{z_2 - z_1}{d}\right)$$

$$\left(\frac{3}{5\sqrt{2}}, \frac{5}{5\sqrt{2}}, \frac{4}{5\sqrt{2}}\right) \text{ or } \left(\frac{3}{5\sqrt{2}}, \frac{1}{\sqrt{2}}, \frac{4}{5\sqrt{2}}\right).$$

Example 15 **Find the position vector of a point which divides the join of points with position vectors $\vec{a} - 2\vec{b}$ and $2\vec{a} + \vec{b}$ externally in the ratio 2:1.** CBSE 2016

Sol. Let given position vectors are $\vec{OA} = \vec{a} - 2\vec{b}$ and $\vec{OB} = 2\vec{a} + \vec{b}$.

Let $\vec{OC}$ be the position vector of a point C which divides the join of points, with position vectors $\vec{OA}$ and $\vec{OB}$, externally in the ratio $2 : 1$.

$$\therefore \vec{OC} = \frac{2\,\vec{OB} - 1\,\vec{OA}}{2 - 1} \quad \text{[by external section formula]}$$

$$= \frac{2(2\vec{a} + \vec{b}) - 1(\vec{a} - 2\vec{b})}{1}$$

$$= 4\vec{a} + 2\vec{b} - \vec{a} + 2\vec{b}$$

$$= 3\vec{a} + 4\vec{b}$$

Example 16 **Show that the three points $A(2, 1, -1)$, $B(3, -2, 1)$ and $C(1, 4, -3)$ are collinear. Also, find the ratio in which B divides AC.**

Sol. Let position vector of points A, B and C are

$\vec{OA} = 2\hat{i} + \hat{j} - \hat{k}$, $\vec{OB} = 3\hat{i} - 2\hat{j} + \hat{k}$ and $\vec{OC} = \hat{i} + 4\hat{j} - 3\hat{k}$.

Now, $\vec{AB} = \vec{OB} - \vec{OA}$

$$= (3\hat{i} - 2\hat{j} + \hat{k}) - (2\hat{i} + \hat{j} - \hat{k})$$

$$= \hat{i} - 3\hat{j} + 2\hat{k}$$

$$\vec{BC} = \vec{OC} - \vec{OB}$$

$$= (\hat{i} + 4\hat{j} - 3\hat{k}) - (3\hat{i} - 2\hat{j} + \hat{k})$$

$$= -2\hat{i} + 6\hat{j} - 4\hat{k}$$

and $\vec{AC} = \vec{OC} - \vec{OA}$

$$= \hat{i} + 4\hat{j} - 3\hat{k} - (2\hat{i} + \hat{j} - \hat{k})$$

$$= -\hat{i} + 3\hat{j} - 2\hat{k}$$

Now, $\vec{BC} = -2\hat{i} + 6\hat{j} - 4\hat{k}$

$$= -2(\hat{i} - 3\hat{j} + 2\hat{k})$$

$$= -2\,\vec{AB}$$

or $\vec{AB} = -\frac{1}{2}\vec{BC}$ ...(i)

Hence, the points A, B and C are collinear.

From Eq. (i), it is clear that point B divides AC externally in the ratio $1 : 2$.

Quick Test 1

1. If A, B, P, Q and R be the five points in a plane, then show that the sum of the vectors $\overrightarrow{AP}$, $\overrightarrow{AQ}$, $\overrightarrow{AR}$, $\overrightarrow{PB}$, $\overrightarrow{QB}$ and $\overrightarrow{RB}$ is $3\,\overrightarrow{AB}$. *Competency Based Que*
2. If $\vec{a}\ \ x\hat{i}+2\hat{j}-z\hat{k}$ and $\vec{b}=3\hat{i}-y\hat{j}+\hat{k}$ are two equal vectors, then find the value of $x+y+z$. *Competency Based Que*
3. Find a vector, in the direction of the following vectors having the given magnitude.
   (i) $\vec{a}=\hat{i}-2\hat{j}+2\hat{k}$, magnitude 9 units. *CBSE 2014C*
   (ii) $\vec{a}=2\hat{i}-\hat{j}+2\hat{k}$, magnitude 6 units. *NCERT Exemplar*
   (iii) $\vec{a}=2\hat{i}-3\hat{j}+6\hat{k}$, magnitude 21 units.
4. Write unit vector in the direction of the sum of the following vectors.
   (i) $\vec{a}=2\hat{i}+3\hat{j}-\hat{k}$ and $\vec{b}=4\hat{i}-3\hat{j}+2\hat{k}$.
   (ii) $\vec{a}=2\hat{i}-\hat{j}+2\hat{k}$ and $\vec{b}=-\hat{i}+\hat{j}+3\hat{k}$. *NCERT Exemplar*
5. If $\vec{a}=\hat{i}+\hat{j}+2\hat{k}$ and $\vec{b}=2\hat{i}+\hat{j}-2\hat{k}$, then find the unit vector in the direction of $2\vec{a}-\vec{b}$. *NCERT Exemplar*
6. Check whether the following points are collinear.
   (i) $\vec{p}=\hat{i}+2\hat{j}-7\hat{k}$ and $\vec{q}=-3\hat{i}-6\hat{j}+21\hat{k}$
   (ii) $\vec{a}=4\hat{i}-6\hat{j}+8\hat{k}$ and $\vec{b}=2\hat{i}-3\hat{j}+4\hat{k}$
7. Find the direction ratios and direction cosines of the vector $3\hat{i}-2\hat{j}+5\hat{k}$.
8. If a unit vector $\vec{a}$ makes angle $\frac{\pi}{3}$ with $\hat{i}$, $\frac{\pi}{4}$ with $\hat{j}$ and an acute angle θ with $\hat{k}$, then find the value of θ. *Competency Based Que*
9. P and Q are two points with position vectors $3\vec{a}-2\vec{b}$ and $\vec{a}+\vec{b}$, respectively. Write the position vector of a point R which divides the line segment PQ in the ratio $2:1$ externally. *Competency Based Que*
10. Show that three points $A(1,-2,-8)$, $B(5,0,-2)$ and $C(11,3,7)$ are collinear and find the ratio in which B divides AC.

Answers

2. 0 3. (i) $3\hat{i}-6\hat{j}+6\hat{k}$ (ii) $4\hat{i}-2\hat{j}+4\hat{k}$ (iii) $6\hat{i}-9\hat{j}+18\hat{k}$
4. (i) $\frac{6}{\sqrt{37}}\hat{i}+\frac{\hat{k}}{\sqrt{37}}$ (ii) $\frac{1}{\sqrt{26}}\hat{i}+\frac{5}{\sqrt{26}}\hat{k}$ 5. $\frac{\hat{j}+6\hat{k}}{\sqrt{37}}$
6. (i) Collinear (ii) Collinear
7. $(3,-2,5)$, $\left(\frac{3}{\sqrt{38}},\frac{-2}{\sqrt{38}},\frac{5}{\sqrt{38}}\right)$
8. $\theta=\frac{\pi}{3}$ 9. $-\vec{a}+4\vec{b}$ 10. $2:3$

For Solutions, See QR Code on Pg. 325

10.7 Scalar (or Dot) Product of Two Vectors

If θ is the angle between two non-zero vectors $\vec{a}$ and $\vec{b}$, then the scalar or dot product, denoted by $\vec{a}\cdot\vec{b}$, is given by $\vec{a}\cdot\vec{b}=|\vec{a}||\vec{b}|\cos\theta$, where $0\le\theta\le\pi$.

Properties of Dot Product of Two Vectors

(i) $\vec{a}\cdot\vec{b}=\vec{b}\cdot\vec{a}$ [i.e. dot product is commutative]

(ii) $(\vec{a}\cdot\vec{0})=0$

(iii) $\vec{a}\cdot(\vec{b}+\vec{c})=\vec{a}\cdot\vec{b}+\vec{a}\cdot\vec{c}$ [distributive property]

(iv) $(\lambda\cdot\vec{a})\cdot\vec{b}=\lambda(\vec{a}\cdot\vec{b})=\vec{a}\cdot(\lambda\cdot\vec{b})$, where λ is any scalar.

(v) If $\vec{a}$ and $\vec{b}$ are perpendicular to each other, then $\vec{a}\cdot\vec{b}=0$, converse is also true.

Projection of a Vector on the other Vector

Projection of $\vec{a}$ on $\vec{b}=\frac{\vec{a}\cdot\vec{b}}{|\vec{b}|}$ and projection of $\vec{b}$ on $\vec{a}=\frac{\vec{a}\cdot\vec{b}}{|\vec{a}|}$.

Angle Between Two Non-zero Vectors

Angle between two non-zero vectors $\vec{a}$ and $\vec{b}$ is given by

$$\cos\theta=\frac{\vec{a}\cdot\vec{b}}{|\vec{a}|\cdot|\vec{b}|}\quad\text{or}\quad\theta=\cos^{-1}\left[\frac{\vec{a}\cdot\vec{b}}{|\vec{a}|\cdot|\vec{b}|}\right]$$

Relations Between Unit Vectors

(i) $\vec{a}\cdot\vec{a}=|\vec{a}|^2$

(ii) $\hat{i}\cdot\hat{i}=\hat{j}\cdot\hat{j}=\hat{k}\cdot\hat{k}=1$ or $|\hat{i}|^2=|\hat{j}|^2=|\hat{k}|^2=1$

(iii) $\hat{i}\cdot\hat{j}=\hat{j}\cdot\hat{k}=\hat{k}\cdot\hat{i}=0$

Scalar Product of Two Vectors Component Form

If $\vec{a}=a_1\hat{i}+a_2\hat{j}+a_3\hat{k}$ and $\vec{b}=b_1\hat{i}+b_2\hat{j}+b_3\hat{k}$, then

$$\vec{a}\cdot\vec{b}=a_1b_1+a_2b_2+a_3b_3.$$

TEACHER TIPS

(i) $\vec{a}\cdot\vec{b}$ is a real number.

(ii) If either $\vec{a}=\vec{0}$ or $\vec{b}=\vec{0}$, then θ is not defined and in this case, we define $\vec{a}\cdot\vec{b}=0$

(iii) If $\theta=0$, then $\vec{a}\cdot\vec{b}=|\vec{a}||\vec{b}|$; if $\theta=\pi$, then $\vec{a}\cdot\vec{b}=-|\vec{a}||\vec{b}|$.

(iv) For any two triangle $\vec{a}$ and $\vec{b}$, we always have $|\vec{a}+\vec{b}|\le|\vec{a}|+|\vec{b}|$. [triangle inequality]

(v) Any two vectors $\vec{a}$ and $\vec{b}$, $|\vec{a}\cdot\vec{b}|<|\vec{a}|\cdot|\vec{b}|$. [Cauchy-Schwarz inequality]

Example 1 Find $|\vec{a}|$ and $|\vec{b}|$, if $|\vec{a}|=2|\vec{b}|$ and $(\vec{a}+\vec{b})\cdot(\vec{a}-\vec{b})=12$. *Competency Based Que*

Sol. Given, $(\vec{a}+\vec{b})\cdot(\vec{a}-\vec{b})=12$

$$\vec{a}\cdot\vec{a}-\vec{a}\cdot\vec{b}+\vec{b}\cdot\vec{a}-|\vec{b}|^2=12$$

$$\Rightarrow |\vec{a}|^2-\vec{a}\cdot\vec{b}+\vec{a}\cdot\vec{b}-|\vec{b}|=12 \quad [\because \vec{a}\cdot\vec{b}=\vec{b}\cdot\vec{a}]$$

$$\Rightarrow |\vec{a}|^2-|\vec{b}|^2=12$$

$$\Rightarrow (2|\vec{b}|)^2-|\vec{b}|^2=12 \quad [\text{given}, |\vec{a}|=2|\vec{b}|]$$

$$\Rightarrow 4|\vec{b}|^2-|\vec{b}|^2=12$$

$$\Rightarrow 3|\vec{b}|^2=12$$

$$\Rightarrow |\vec{b}|^2=4$$

$$\Rightarrow |\vec{b}|=2$$

$$\therefore |\vec{a}|=2|\vec{b}| = 2(2)=4$$

Example 2 If $|\vec{a}|=3$, $|\vec{b}|=5$, $|\vec{c}|=4$ and $\vec{a}+\vec{b}+\vec{c}=\vec{0}$, then find the value of $(\vec{a}\cdot\vec{b}+\vec{b}\cdot\vec{c}+\vec{c}\cdot\vec{a})$. *CBSE 2022 (Term II)*

Sol. Given, $\vec{a}+\vec{b}+\vec{c}=0$

$$(\vec{a}+\vec{b}+\vec{c})^2=|\vec{a}|^2+|\vec{b}|^2+|\vec{c}|^2 + 2(\vec{a}\cdot\vec{b}+\vec{b}\cdot\vec{c}+\vec{c}\cdot\vec{a})$$

$$\Rightarrow 0=9+25+16+2(\vec{a}\cdot\vec{b}+\vec{b}\cdot\vec{c}+\vec{c}\cdot\vec{a})$$

$$\Rightarrow -\frac{50}{2}=(\vec{a}\cdot\vec{b}+\vec{b}\cdot\vec{c}+\vec{c}\cdot\vec{a})$$

$$\therefore (\vec{a}\cdot\vec{b}+\vec{b}\cdot\vec{c}+\vec{c}\cdot\vec{a})=-25$$

Example 3 If $\vec{a}$, $\vec{b}$ and $\vec{c}$ are three non-zero unequal vectors such that $\vec{a}\cdot\vec{b}=\vec{a}\cdot\vec{c}$, then find the angle between $\vec{a}$ and $\vec{b}-\vec{c}$. *CBSE 2023*

Sol. Given, $\vec{a}$, $\vec{b}$ and $\vec{c}$ are three non-zero unequal vectors

such that $\vec{a}\cdot\vec{b}=\vec{a}\cdot\vec{c}$

$$\Rightarrow \vec{a}\cdot\vec{b}-\vec{a}\cdot\vec{c}=0 \quad [\text{subtracting } \vec{a}\cdot\vec{c} \text{ from both sides}]$$

$$\Rightarrow \vec{a}\cdot(\vec{b}-\vec{c})=0 \quad \text{...(i)}$$

Now, let θ be the angle between $\vec{a}$ and $\vec{b}-\vec{c}$.

$$\therefore \cos\theta=\frac{\vec{a}\cdot(\vec{b}-\vec{c})}{|\vec{a}||\vec{b}-\vec{c}|}$$

$$\Rightarrow \cos\theta=\frac{0}{|\vec{a}||\vec{a}-\vec{c}|} \quad [\text{using Eq. (i)}]$$

$$\Rightarrow \cos\theta=0$$

$$\Rightarrow \cos\theta=\cos\frac{\pi}{2} \Rightarrow \theta=\frac{\pi}{2}$$

Example 4 If $\vec{a}=\hat{i}-\hat{j}+7\hat{k}$ and $\vec{b}=5\hat{i}-\hat{j}+\lambda\hat{k}$, then find the value of λ so that the vectors $\vec{a}+\vec{b}$ and $\vec{a}-\vec{b}$ are orthogonal. *CBSE Sample Paper 2023*

Sol. Given, $\vec{a}=\hat{i}-\hat{j}+7\hat{k}$ and $\vec{b}=5\hat{i}-\hat{j}+\lambda\hat{k}$

Now, $\vec{a}+\vec{b}=6\hat{i}-2\hat{j}+(7+\lambda)\hat{k}$

and $\vec{a}-\vec{b}=-4\hat{i}+(7-\lambda)\hat{k}$

$\because (\vec{a}+\vec{b})$ and $(\vec{a}-\vec{b})$ are orthogonal.

$$\therefore (\vec{a}+\vec{b})\cdot(\vec{a}-\vec{b})=0$$

$$\Rightarrow [6\hat{i}-2\hat{j}+(7+\lambda)\hat{k}]\cdot[-4\hat{i}+(7-\lambda)\hat{k}]=0$$

$$\Rightarrow -24+49-\lambda^2=0$$

$$\Rightarrow \lambda^2=25$$

$$\therefore \lambda=\pm 5$$

Example 5 If $\hat{a}$ and $\hat{b}$ are unit vectors, then prove that $|\hat{a}+\hat{b}|=2\cos\frac{\theta}{2}$, where θ is the angle between them. *CBSE Sample Paper 2022 (Term II)*

Sol. Given, $|\hat{a}|=|\hat{b}|=1$

Now, consider $|\hat{a}+\hat{b}|^2=(\hat{a}+\hat{b})\cdot(\hat{a}+\hat{b})$

$$\Rightarrow |\hat{a}+\hat{b}|^2=|\hat{a}|^2+|\hat{b}|^2+2(\hat{a}\cdot\hat{b})$$

$$\Rightarrow |\hat{a}+\hat{b}|^2=1+1+2|\hat{a}||\hat{b}|\cos\theta$$

$$=2+2\cos\theta \quad [\because |\hat{a}|=|\hat{b}|=1]$$

$$= 2(1 + \cos\theta)$$

$$\Rightarrow \quad |\hat{a} + \hat{b}|^2 = 2\left(2\cos^2\frac{\theta}{2}\right) = 4\cos^2\frac{\theta}{2}$$

$$\therefore \quad |\hat{a} + \hat{b}| = 2\cos\frac{\theta}{2}$$

Hence proved.

Example 6 **Find the projection of vector $(\vec{b} + \vec{c})$ on vector $\vec{a}$, where $\vec{a} = 2\hat{i} + 2\hat{j} + \hat{k}, \vec{b} = \hat{i} + 3\hat{j} + \hat{k}$ and $\vec{c} = \hat{i} + \hat{k}$.**

CBSE 2024

Sol. Given, $\vec{a} = 2\hat{i} + 2\hat{j} + \hat{k}, \vec{b} = \hat{i} + 3\hat{j} + \hat{k}$ and $\vec{c} = \hat{i} + \hat{k}$

$\therefore \vec{b} + \vec{c} = \hat{i} + 3\hat{j} + \hat{k} + \hat{i} + \hat{k} = 2\hat{i} + 3\hat{j} + 2\hat{k}$

Now, projection of $(\vec{b} + \vec{c})$ on $\vec{a}$

$$= \frac{(\vec{b} + \vec{c})\cdot\vec{a}}{|\vec{a}|} = \frac{(2\hat{i} + 3\hat{j} + 2\hat{k})\cdot(2\hat{i} + 2\hat{j} + \hat{k})}{\sqrt{4 + 4 + 1}}$$

$$= \frac{4 + 6 + 2}{3} = \frac{12}{3} = 4$$

Example 7 **If the projection of the vector $\hat{i} + \hat{j} + \hat{k}$ on the vector $p\hat{i} + \hat{j} - 2\hat{k}$ is $\frac{1}{3}$, then find the value of p.**

Competency Based Que, CBSE 2023

Sol. Let, the given vectors be $\vec{a} = \hat{i} + \hat{j} + \hat{k}$

and $\vec{b} = p\hat{i} + \hat{j} - 2\hat{k}$.

Also, given projection of $\vec{a}$ on $\vec{b} = \frac{1}{3}$

$\therefore$ Projection of $\vec{a}$ on $\vec{b} = \frac{\vec{a}\cdot\vec{b}}{|\vec{b}|}$

$$\Rightarrow \quad \frac{1}{3} = \frac{(\hat{i} + \hat{j} + \hat{k})\cdot(p\hat{i} + \hat{j} - 2\hat{k})}{\sqrt{p^2 + (1)^2 + (-2)^2}}$$

$$\Rightarrow \quad \frac{1}{3} = \frac{p + 1 - 2}{\sqrt{p^2 + 1 + 4}} = \frac{p - 1}{\sqrt{p^2 + 5}}$$

$$\Rightarrow \quad \sqrt{p^2 + 5} = 3p - 3$$

On squaring both sides, we get

$$p^2 + 5 = 9p^2 + 9 - 18p$$

$$\Rightarrow \quad 8p^2 - 18p + 4 = 0$$

$$\Rightarrow \quad 4p^2 - 9p + 2 = 0$$

$$\Rightarrow \quad 4p^2 - 8p - p + 2 = 0$$

$$\Rightarrow \quad (4p - 1)(p - 2) = 0$$

$$\Rightarrow \quad p = \frac{1}{4} \text{ or } p = 2$$

Example 8 **The scalar product of the vector $\vec{a} = \hat{i} + \hat{j} + \hat{k}$ with a unit vector along the sum of the vectors $\vec{b} = 2\hat{i} + 4\hat{j} - 5\hat{k}$ and $\vec{c} = \lambda\hat{i} + 2\hat{j} + 3\hat{k}$ is equal to 1. Find the value of λ and hence find the unit vector along $\vec{b} + \vec{c}$.**

CBSE 2019, 14

Sol. Given, $\vec{a} = \hat{i} + \hat{j} + \hat{k}, \vec{b} = 2\hat{i} + 4\hat{j} - 5\hat{k}$

and $\vec{c} = \lambda\hat{i} + 2\hat{j} + 3\hat{k}$

$\therefore \vec{b} + \vec{c} = (2 + \lambda)\hat{i} + 6\hat{j} - 2\hat{k}$

Let $\hat{r}$ denotes the unit vector along $\vec{b} + \vec{c}$.

Then, $$\hat{r} = \frac{\vec{b} + \vec{c}}{|\vec{b} + \vec{c}|} = \frac{(2 + \lambda)\hat{i} + 6\hat{j} - 2\hat{k}}{\sqrt{(2 + \lambda)^2 + 36 + 4}}$$

$$= \frac{(2 + \lambda)\hat{i} + 6\hat{j} - 2\hat{k}}{\sqrt{(2 + \lambda)^2 + 40}} \quad \text{...(i)}$$

Now, according to given condition, we have

$$(\hat{i} + \hat{j} + \hat{k})\cdot\hat{r} = 1$$

$$\Rightarrow \quad (\hat{i} + \hat{j} + \hat{k})\cdot\frac{(2 + \lambda)\hat{i} + 6\hat{j} - 2\hat{k}}{\sqrt{(2 + \lambda)^2 + 40}} = 1 \quad \text{[from Eq. (i)]}$$

$$\Rightarrow \quad (\hat{i} + \hat{j} + \hat{k})\cdot\{(2 + \lambda)\hat{i} + 6\hat{j} - 2\hat{k}\} = \sqrt{(2 + \lambda)^2 + 40}$$

$$\Rightarrow \quad 2 + \lambda + 6 - 2 = \sqrt{(2 + \lambda)^2 + 40}$$

$$\Rightarrow \quad (\lambda + 6)^2 = (2 + \lambda)^2 + 40$$

$$\Rightarrow \quad 8\lambda = 8$$

$$\Rightarrow \quad \lambda = 1$$

On putting $\lambda = 1$ in Eq. (i), we get

$$\hat{r} = \frac{1}{7}(3\hat{i} + 6\hat{j} - 2\hat{k})$$

Example 9 **If $\hat{i} + \hat{j} + \hat{k}, 2\hat{i} + 5\hat{j}, 3\hat{i} + 2\hat{j} - 3\hat{k}$ and $\hat{i} - 6\hat{j} - \hat{k}$ respectively, are the position vectors of points *A*, *B*, *C* and *D*, then find the angle between the straight lines *AB* and *CD*. Find whether $\overrightarrow{AB}$ and $\overrightarrow{CD}$ are collinear or not.**

CBSE 2019

Sol. Given $\overrightarrow{OA} = (\hat{i} + \hat{j} + \hat{k}), \overrightarrow{OB} = (2\hat{i} + 5\hat{j})$,

$\overrightarrow{OC} = (3\hat{i} + 2\hat{j} - 3\hat{k})$ and $\overrightarrow{OD} = (\hat{i} - 6\hat{j} - \hat{k})$

Angle between $\overrightarrow{AB}$ and $\overrightarrow{CD}$ is given by

$$\cos\theta = \frac{\overrightarrow{AB}\cdot\overrightarrow{CD}}{|\overrightarrow{AB}|\cdot|\overrightarrow{CD}|} \quad \text{...(i)}$$

Here, $\overrightarrow{AB} = (2 - 1)\hat{i} + (5 - 1)\hat{j} + (0 - 1)\hat{k}$

$= \hat{i} + 4\hat{j} - \hat{k}$,

$$\overrightarrow{CD} = (1-3)\hat{i} + (-6-2)\hat{j} + \{-1-(-3)\}\hat{k}$$
$$= -2\hat{i} - 8\hat{j} + 2\hat{k},$$
$$|\overrightarrow{AB}| = \sqrt{1^2 + 4^2 + (-1)^2} = \sqrt{18} = \sqrt{9 \times 2} = 3\sqrt{2}$$

and $|\overrightarrow{CD}| = \sqrt{(-2)^2 + (-8)^2 + 2^2}$
$$= \sqrt{72} = \sqrt{36 \times 2} = 6\sqrt{2}$$

Now, $\cos\theta = \dfrac{(\hat{i} + 4\hat{j} - \hat{k})\cdot(-2\hat{i} - 8\hat{j} + 2\hat{k})}{3\sqrt{2} \times 6\sqrt{2}}$ [from Eq. (i)]

$$= \frac{1(-2) + 4(-8) + (-1)(2)}{3 \times 6 \times 2} = -1$$

$\Rightarrow$ $\cos\theta = -1$

$\Rightarrow$ $\theta = 180° = \pi$

So, angle between $\overrightarrow{AB}$ and $\overrightarrow{CD}$ is π.

Since, angle between $\overrightarrow{AB}$ and $\overrightarrow{CD}$ is 180°, they are in opposite directions.

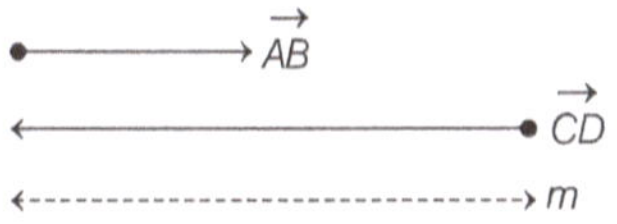

Since, $\overrightarrow{AB}$ and $\overrightarrow{CD}$ are parallel to the same line m, therefore they are collinear.

Example 10 **Three vectors $\vec{a} \cdot \vec{b}$ and $\vec{c}$ satisfy the condition $\vec{a} + \vec{b} + \vec{c} = \vec{0}$. Evaluate the quantity $\mu = \vec{a}\cdot\vec{b} + \vec{b}\cdot\vec{c} + \vec{c}\cdot\vec{a}$. If $|\vec{a}| = 3, |\vec{b}| = 4$ and $|\vec{c}| = 2$.**

CBSE 2023

Sol. Given, $|\vec{a}| = 3, |\vec{b}| = 4$ and $|\vec{c}| = 2$

Now, $\vec{a} + \vec{b} + \vec{c} = 0$

On squaring both sides, we get

$$(\vec{a} + \vec{b} + \vec{c})^2 = (\vec{0})^2$$

$\Rightarrow$ $|\vec{a}|^2 + |\vec{b}|^2 + |\vec{c}|^2 + 2(\vec{a}\cdot\vec{b} + \vec{b}\cdot\vec{c} + \vec{c}\cdot\vec{a}) = 0$

$\Rightarrow$ $(3)^2 + (4)^2 + (2)^2 + 2(\vec{a}\cdot\vec{b} + \vec{b}\cdot\vec{c} + \vec{c}\cdot\vec{a}) = 0$

$\Rightarrow$ $9 + 16 + 4 + 2(\vec{a}\cdot\vec{b} + \vec{b}\cdot\vec{c} + \vec{c}\cdot\vec{a}) = 0$

$\Rightarrow$ $29 + 2(\vec{a}\cdot\vec{b} + \vec{b}\cdot\vec{c} + \vec{c}\cdot\vec{a}) = 0$

$\Rightarrow$ $2(\vec{a}\cdot\vec{b} + \vec{b}\cdot\vec{c} + \vec{c}\cdot\vec{a}) = -29$

$\Rightarrow$ $\vec{a}\cdot\vec{b} + \vec{b}\cdot\vec{c} + \vec{c}\cdot\vec{a} = \dfrac{-29}{2}$

Hence, $\mu = \vec{a}\cdot\vec{b} + \vec{b}\cdot\vec{c} + \vec{c}\cdot\vec{a} = \dfrac{-29}{2}$

Example 11 **If $\vec{a} = \hat{i} + \hat{j} + \hat{k}$ and $\vec{b} = \hat{i} + 2\hat{j} + 3\hat{k}$, then find a unit vector perpendicular to both $\vec{a} + \vec{b}$ and $\vec{a} - \vec{b}$.**

CBSE 2023

Sol. Given, $\vec{a} = \hat{i} + \hat{j} + \hat{k}$

and $\vec{b} = \hat{i} + 2\hat{j} + 3\hat{k}$

Let the required unit vector be $\vec{r} = x\hat{i} + y\hat{j} + z\hat{k}$,

then $\sqrt{x^2 + y^2 + z^2} = 1$

$\Rightarrow$ $x^2 + y^2 + z^2 = 1$ ...(i)

Now, $\vec{a} + \vec{b} = (\hat{i} + \hat{j} + \hat{k}) + (\hat{i} + 2\hat{j} + 3\hat{k}) = 2\hat{i} + 3\hat{j} + 4\hat{k}$

and $\vec{a} - \vec{b} = (\hat{i} + \hat{j} + \hat{k}) - (\hat{i} + 2\hat{j} + 3\hat{k}) = -\hat{j} - 2\hat{k}$

Since, $\vec{r}$ is perpendicular to $\vec{a} + \vec{b}$ and $\vec{a} - \vec{b}$,

$\therefore$ $\vec{r}\cdot(\vec{a} + \vec{b}) = 0$ and $\vec{r}\cdot(\vec{a} - \vec{b}) = 0$

i.e. $(x\hat{i} + y\hat{j} + z\hat{k})\cdot(2\hat{i} + 3\hat{j} + 4\hat{k}) = 0$

$\Rightarrow$ $2x + 3y + 4z = 0$ ...(ii)

and $(x\hat{i} + y\hat{j} + z\hat{k})\cdot(-\hat{j} - 2\hat{k}) = 0$

$\Rightarrow$ $-y - 2z = 0$

$\Rightarrow$ $y = -2z$

On putting the value of y in Eq. (ii), we get

$$2x + 3(-2z) + 4z = 0$$

$\Rightarrow$ $x = z$

On substituting the value of x and y in Eq. (i), we get

$$z^2 + 4z^2 + z^2 = 1$$

$\Rightarrow$ $6z^2 = 1 \Rightarrow z = \pm\dfrac{1}{\sqrt{6}}$

then, $x = \pm\dfrac{1}{\sqrt{6}}$ and $y = \mp\dfrac{2}{\sqrt{6}}$

Hence, the required vectors are

$$\frac{1}{\sqrt{6}}\hat{i} - \frac{2}{\sqrt{6}}\hat{j} + \frac{1}{\sqrt{6}}\hat{k} \text{ and } \frac{-1}{\sqrt{6}}\hat{i} + \frac{2}{\sqrt{6}}\hat{j} - \frac{1}{\sqrt{6}}\hat{k}.$$

Example 12 **Given $\vec{a} = 2\hat{i} - \hat{j} + \hat{k}, \vec{b} = 3\hat{i} - \hat{k}$ and $\vec{c} = 2\hat{i} + \hat{j} - 2\hat{k}$. Find a vector $\vec{d}$ which is perpendicular to both $\vec{a}$ and $\vec{b}$ and $\vec{c}\cdot\vec{d} = 3$.**

CBSE 2024

Sol. Let $\vec{d} = x\hat{i} + y\hat{j} + z\hat{k}$ be a vector such that

$\vec{a}\cdot\vec{d} = 0$ and $\vec{b}\cdot\vec{d} = 0$.

Given, $\vec{a} = 2\hat{i} - \hat{j} + \hat{k}, \vec{b} = 3\hat{i} - \hat{k}, \vec{c} = 2\hat{i} + \hat{j} - 2\hat{k}$

and $\vec{c}\cdot\vec{d} = 3$

$\because$ $\vec{a}\cdot\vec{d} = 0$

$\Rightarrow \quad (2\hat{i} - \hat{j} + \hat{k}) \cdot (x\hat{i} + y\hat{j} + z\hat{k}) = 0$

$\Rightarrow \quad 2x - y + z = 0 \quad$ ...(i)

and $\quad \vec{b} \cdot \vec{d} = 0$

$\Rightarrow \quad (3\hat{i} - \hat{k}) \cdot (x\hat{i} + y\hat{j} + z\hat{k}) = 0$

$\Rightarrow \quad 3x - z = 0 \quad$ ...(ii)

and $\quad \vec{c} \cdot \vec{d} = 3$

$\Rightarrow \quad (2\hat{i} + \hat{j} - 2\hat{k}) \cdot (x\hat{i} + y\hat{j} + z\hat{k}) = 3$

$\Rightarrow \quad 2x + y - 2z = 3 \quad$ ...(iii)

From Eq. (ii), we get

$z = 3x$

On putting $z = 3x$ in Eq. (i), we get

$2x - y + 3x = 0$

$\Rightarrow \quad y = 5x$

On putting $y = 5x$ and $z = 3x$ in Eq. (iii), we get

$2x + 5x - 6x = 3$

$\Rightarrow \quad x = 3$

$\therefore \quad x = 3, y = 15$ and $z = 9$

Hence, $\vec{d} = 3\hat{i} + 15\hat{j} + 9\hat{k}$

Example 13 **If $\vec{a} = 2\hat{i} - \hat{j} - 2\hat{k}$ and $\vec{b} = 7\hat{i} + 2\hat{j} - 3\hat{k}$, then express $\vec{b}$ in the form of $\vec{b} = \vec{b_1} + \vec{b_2}$, where $\vec{b_1}$ is parallel to $\vec{a}$ and $\vec{b_2}$ is perpendicular to $\vec{a}$.** *Competency Based Que*

Sol. As $\vec{b_1}$ is parallel to $\vec{a}$.

$\therefore \quad \vec{b_1} = \lambda \vec{a}$

Then, $\vec{b} = \lambda \vec{a} + \vec{b_2}$, where $\vec{b_2} \perp \vec{a}$.

$\Rightarrow \quad \vec{b_2} = \vec{b} - \lambda \vec{a} \Rightarrow (\vec{b} - \lambda \vec{a}) \perp \vec{a}$

$\therefore \quad (\vec{b} - \lambda \vec{a}) \cdot \vec{a} = 0 \Rightarrow \vec{b} \cdot \vec{a} - \lambda \vec{a} \cdot \vec{a} = 0$

$\Rightarrow \quad (7\hat{i} + 2\hat{j} - 3\hat{k}) \cdot (2\hat{i} - \hat{j} - 2\hat{k})$

$\quad - \lambda(2\hat{i} - \hat{j} - 2\hat{k}) \cdot (2\hat{i} - \hat{j} - 2\hat{k}) = 0$

$\Rightarrow \quad 14 - 2 + 6 - \lambda[4 + 1 + 4] = 0$

$\Rightarrow \quad 18 - 9\lambda = 0$

$\Rightarrow \quad \lambda = 2$

$\therefore \quad \vec{b_1} = \lambda \vec{a} = 2(2\hat{i} - \hat{j} - 2\hat{k}) = 4\hat{i} - 2\hat{j} - 4\hat{k}$

and $\quad \vec{b_2} = (\vec{b} - \lambda \vec{a})$

$= (7\hat{i} + 2\hat{j} - 3\hat{k}) - (4\hat{i} - 2\hat{j} - 4\hat{k})$

$= 3\hat{i} + 4\hat{j} + \hat{k}$

Hence, we get the expression in the form

$\vec{b} = \vec{b_1} + \vec{b_2}$

or $\quad \vec{b} = (4\hat{i} - 2\hat{j} - 4\hat{k}) + (3\hat{i} + 4\hat{j} + \hat{k})$

Quick Test 2

1. If $\vec{a}$ and $\vec{b}$ are two vectors such that $|\vec{a}| = 2, |\vec{b}| = 1$ and $\vec{a} \cdot \vec{b} = 1$, then find $(3\vec{a} - 5\vec{b}) \cdot (2\vec{a} + 7\vec{b})$.

2. Find the magnitude of each of the two vectors $\vec{a}$ and $\vec{b}$, having the same magnitude such that the angle between them is 60° and their scalar product is $\frac{9}{2}$. *CBSE 2018*

3. Vectors $\vec{a}$ $\vec{b}$ and $\vec{c}$ are such that $\vec{a} + \vec{b} + \vec{c} = \vec{}$ and $|\vec{a}| = 3, |\vec{b}| = 5$ and $|\vec{c}| = 7$. Then, find the angle between $\vec{a}$ and $\vec{b}$. *CBSE 2025*

4. Let $\vec{a}, \vec{b}$ and $\vec{c}$ be three vectors of magnitudes 3, 4 and 5, respectively. If each one is perpendicular to the sum of the other two vectors, then prove that $|\vec{a} + \vec{b} + \vec{c}| = 5\sqrt{2}$. *Diksha App*

5. If $\vec{a}, \vec{b}$ and $\vec{c}$ are three mutually perpendicular vectors of the same magnitude, then prove that $\vec{a} + \vec{b} + \vec{c}$ is equally inclined with the vectors $\vec{a}, \vec{b}$ and $\vec{c}$. Also, find the angle which $\vec{a} + \vec{b} + \vec{c}$ makes with $\vec{a}$ or $\vec{b}$ or $\vec{c}$. *CBSE 2017, 13C, 11*

6. In the following question, find the value of constant, when they are perpendicular.

(i) $\vec{a} = 2\hat{i} + \lambda\hat{j} + \hat{k}$ and $\vec{b} = \hat{i} + 2\hat{j} + 3\hat{k}$ *NCERT Exemplar*

(ii) $\vec{a} = 3\hat{i} + \lambda\hat{j} + \hat{k}$ and $\vec{b} = \hat{i} - 4\hat{j} + 3\hat{k}$ *CBSE 2013C*

7. If $\vec{a} = (5\hat{i} - \hat{j} - 3\hat{k})$ and $\vec{b} = (\hat{i} + 3\hat{j} - 5\hat{k})$, then show that $(\vec{a} + \vec{b})$ and $(\vec{a} - \vec{b})$ are orthogonal.

8. If $\vec{a} = 2\hat{i} + 2\hat{j} + 3\hat{k}, \vec{b} = -\hat{i} + 2\hat{j} + \hat{k}$ and $\vec{c} = 3\hat{i} + \hat{j}$ such that $\vec{a} + \lambda\vec{b}$ is perpendicular to $\vec{c}$, then find the value of λ.

9. Find the value of x for which the angle between the vectors $\vec{a} = 2x^2\hat{i} + 4x\hat{j} + \hat{k}$ and $\vec{b} = 7\hat{i} - 2\hat{j} + x\hat{k}$ is obtuse. *CBSE 2025*

10. Find the projection of the vector $2\hat{i} - 3\hat{j} + 5\hat{k}$ on the line joining the points $P(1, 2, -3)$ and $Q(-1, 1, 2)$.

Answers

1. 0 **2.** $|\vec{a}| = |\vec{b}| = 3$ **3.** $\frac{\pi}{3}$

5. $\cos^{-1}\left(\pm\frac{1}{\sqrt{3}}\right)$ **6.** (i) $\lambda = \frac{5}{2}$ (ii) $\lambda = 3/2$

8. 8 **9.** $x \in \left(0, \frac{1}{2}\right)$ **10.** $\frac{24}{\sqrt{30}}$

For Solutions, See QR Code on Pg. 325

10.8 Vector (or Cross) Product of Two Vectors

If θ is the angle between two non-zero and non-parallel vectors $\vec{a}$ and $\vec{b}$, then the cross product of vectors, denoted by $\vec{a}\times\vec{b}$, is given by

$$\vec{a}\times\vec{b}=|\vec{a}||\vec{b}|\sin\theta\,\hat{n} \text{ such that } 0\le\theta\le\pi,$$

where $\hat{n}$ is a unit vector perpendicular to both $\vec{a}$ and $\vec{b}$ such that $\vec{a}$, $\vec{b}$ and $\hat{n}$ form a right handed system.

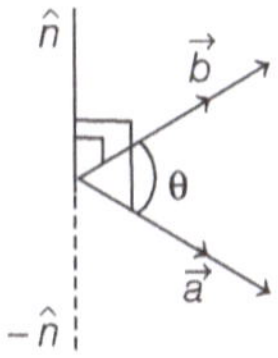

Important Results on Vector Product of Two Vectors

(i) Unit vector $\hat{n}$ which is perpendicular to both the vectors $\vec{a}$ and $\vec{b}$, is given by

$$\hat{n}=\pm\frac{\vec{a}\times\vec{b}}{|\vec{a}\times\vec{b}|}.$$

(ii) Relation between dot and cross-product is

$$(\vec{a}\cdot\vec{b})^2+|\vec{a}\times\vec{b}|^2=|\vec{a}|^2|\vec{b}|^2.$$

(iii) Angle between two non-zero vectors is given by

$$\sin\theta=\frac{|\vec{a}\times\vec{b}|}{|\vec{a}||\vec{b}|} \text{ or } \theta=\sin^{-1}\left[\frac{|\vec{a}\times\vec{b}|}{|\vec{a}||\vec{b}|}\right].$$

(iv) $\vec{a}\times\vec{a}=\vec{0}$

(v) If $\vec{a}$ is parallel to $\vec{b}$, then $\vec{a}\times\vec{b}=\vec{0}$ and converse is also true.

Or

Two non-zero vectors $\vec{a}$, $\vec{b}$ are collinear, iff

$$\vec{a}\times\vec{b}=\vec{0}.$$

(vi) If $\theta=\frac{\pi}{2}$, then $|\vec{a}\times\vec{b}|=|\vec{a}||\vec{b}|$.

Properties of Cross Product of Two Vectors

(i) $\vec{a}\times\vec{b}=-\vec{b}\times\vec{a}$ [not commutative]

(ii) $\vec{a}\times(\vec{b}+\vec{c})=\vec{a}\times\vec{b}+\vec{a}\times\vec{c}$ [distributive property]

(iii) $\lambda(\vec{a}\times\vec{b})=(\lambda\vec{a})\times\vec{b}=\vec{a}\times(\lambda\vec{b})$

Vector Product of an Orthonormal Vector Trial

- $\hat{i}\times\hat{i}=\hat{j}\times\hat{j}=\hat{k}\times\hat{k}=\vec{0}$ and $\hat{i}\times\hat{j}=\hat{k}, \hat{j}\times\hat{k}=\hat{i}, \hat{k}\times\hat{i}=\hat{j}$

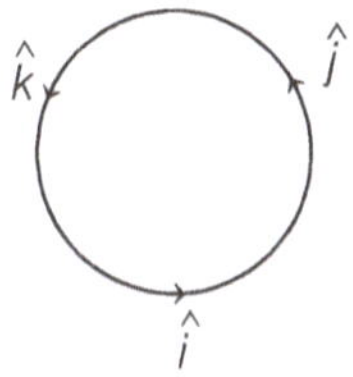

- $\hat{j}\times\hat{i}=-\hat{k},\ \hat{k}\times\hat{j}=-\hat{i}$ and $\hat{i}\times\hat{k}=-\hat{j}$

Application of Vector Product of Two Vectors

(i) If $\vec{a}$ and $\vec{b}$ represent the adjacent sides of a triangle, then its area is given by $=\frac{1}{2}|\vec{a}\times\vec{b}|$.

(ii) If $\vec{a}$ and $\vec{b}$ represent the adjacent sides of a parallelogram, then its area is given by $|\vec{a}\times\vec{b}|$.

(iii) If $\vec{d_1}$ and $\vec{d_2}$ represent the diagonals of a parallelogram, then its area is given by $\frac{1}{2}|\vec{d_1}\times\vec{d_2}|$.

Vector Product of Two Vectors in Component Form

If $\vec{a}=a_1\hat{i}+a_2\hat{j}+a_3\hat{k}$ and $\vec{b}=b_1\hat{i}+b_2\hat{j}+b_3\hat{k}$, then

$$\vec{a}\times\vec{b}=\begin{vmatrix}\hat{i} & \hat{j} & \hat{k}\\ a_1 & a_2 & a_3\\ b_1 & b_2 & b_3\end{vmatrix}$$

$$=(a_2b_3-a_3b_2)\hat{i}+(a_3b_1-a_1b_3)\hat{j}+(a_1b_2-a_2b_1)\hat{k}$$

TEACHER TIPS

- $\vec{a}\times\vec{b}$ is a vector quantity, whose magnitude is $|\vec{a}\times\vec{b}|=|\vec{a}||\vec{b}|\sin\theta$.
- If either $\vec{a}=\vec{0}$ or $\vec{b}=\vec{0}$, then θ is not defined and in this case, we define $\vec{a}\times\vec{b}=\vec{0}$.
- If A, B and C are the position vectors of plane ABC, then the unit vector perpendicular to the plane ABC is $\dfrac{\overrightarrow{AB}\times\overrightarrow{AC}}{|\overrightarrow{AB}\times\overrightarrow{AC}|}$.

Example 1 **Find $\vec{a}\times\vec{b}$, if $\vec{a}=2\hat{i}+\hat{j}+3\hat{k}$ and $\vec{b}=3\hat{i}+5\hat{j}-2\hat{k}$.** CBSE 2019

Sol. We have, $\vec{a}=2\hat{i}+\hat{j}+3\hat{k}$ and $\vec{b}=3\hat{i}+5\hat{j}-2\hat{k}$

$$\therefore \quad \vec{a}\times\vec{b}=\begin{vmatrix}\hat{i} & \hat{j} & \hat{k}\\ 2 & 1 & 3\\ 3 & 5 & -2\end{vmatrix}$$

$$=\hat{i}(-2-15)-\hat{j}(-4-9)+\hat{k}(10-3)$$

$$=-17\hat{i}+13\hat{j}+7\hat{k}$$

Example 2 **If $\vec{r}=3\hat{i}-2\hat{j}+6\hat{k}$, then find the value of $(\vec{r}\times\hat{j})\cdot(\vec{r}\times\hat{k})-12$.** CBSE 2023

Sol. Given, $\vec{r}=3\hat{i}-2\hat{j}+6\hat{k}$

Then, $\vec{r}\times\hat{j}=(3\hat{i}-2\hat{j}+6\hat{k})\times\hat{j}=3\hat{k}-6\hat{i}$

$[\because \hat{i}\times\hat{j}=\hat{k},\ \hat{j}\times\hat{j}=0,\ \hat{k}\times\hat{j}=-\hat{i}]$

Also, $\vec{r}\times\hat{k}=(3\hat{i}-2\hat{j}+6\hat{k})\times\hat{k}=-3\hat{j}-2\hat{i}$

$[\because \hat{i}\times\hat{k}=-\hat{j},\ \hat{j}\times\hat{k}=\hat{i},\ \hat{k}\times\hat{k}=0]$

Now, $(\vec{r}\times\hat{j})\cdot(\vec{r}\times\hat{k})-12=(3\hat{k}-6\hat{i})\cdot(-3\hat{j}-2\hat{i})-12$

$=12-12$

$[\because \hat{k}\cdot\hat{j}=0,\ \hat{k}\cdot\hat{i}=0,\ \hat{i}\cdot\hat{j}=0,\ \hat{i}\cdot\hat{i}=1]$

$\Rightarrow (\vec{r}\times\hat{j})\cdot(\vec{r}\times\hat{k})-12=0$

Example 3 **If the vectors $\vec{a}$ and $\vec{b}$ are such that $|\vec{a}|=3$, $|\vec{b}|=\frac{2}{3}$ and $\vec{a}\times\vec{b}$ is a unit vector, then find the angle between $\vec{a}$ and $\vec{b}$.** CBSE 2023, 14, 10

Sol. Given, $|\vec{a}|=3$ and $|\vec{b}|=\frac{2}{3}$

Let θ be the angle between $\vec{a}$ and $\vec{b}$.

Also given, $|\vec{a}\times\vec{b}|=1$

$\Rightarrow \quad |\vec{a}||\vec{b}|\sin\theta=1$

$\Rightarrow \quad 3\times\frac{2}{3}\sin\theta=1$

$\Rightarrow \quad 2\sin\theta=1$

$\Rightarrow \quad \sin\theta=\frac{1}{2}$

$\therefore \quad \theta=\frac{\pi}{6}$

Example 4 **If $\vec{a}=4\hat{i}-\hat{j}+\hat{k}$ and $\vec{b}=2\hat{i}-2\hat{j}+\hat{k}$, then find a unit vector along the vector $\vec{a}\times\vec{b}$.** CBSE 2023

Sol. Given, $\vec{a}=4\hat{i}-\hat{j}+\hat{k}$ and $\vec{b}=2\hat{i}-2\hat{j}+\hat{k}$

$$\text{Now, } \vec{a}\times\vec{b}=\begin{vmatrix}\hat{i} & \hat{j} & \hat{k}\\ 4 & -1 & 1\\ 2 & -2 & 1\end{vmatrix}$$

$$=\hat{i}(-1+2)-\hat{j}(4-2)+\hat{k}(-8+2)$$

$$=\hat{i}-2\hat{j}-6\hat{k}$$

$\therefore$ Required unit vector along the vector $\vec{a}\times\vec{b}$

$$=\frac{\vec{a}\times\vec{b}}{|\vec{a}\times\vec{b}|}$$

$$=\frac{\hat{i}-2\hat{j}-6\hat{k}}{\sqrt{1^2+(-2)^2+(-6)^2}}=\frac{\hat{i}-2\hat{j}-6\hat{k}}{\sqrt{1+4+36}}$$

$$=\frac{\hat{i}-2\hat{j}-6\hat{k}}{\sqrt{41}}=\frac{1}{\sqrt{41}}\hat{i}-\frac{2}{\sqrt{41}}\hat{j}-\frac{6}{\sqrt{41}}\hat{k}$$

Example 5 **Find a vector of magnitude 4 units perpendicular to each of the vectors $2\hat{i}-\hat{j}+\hat{k}$ and $\hat{i}+\hat{j}-\hat{k}$ and hence verify your answer.** CBSE 2024

Sol. Let $\vec{a}=2\hat{i}-\hat{j}+\hat{k}$ and $\vec{b}=\hat{i}+\hat{j}-\hat{k}$

So, any vector perpendicular to both the vector.

$\vec{a}$ and $\vec{b}$ is given by $\dfrac{\vec{a}\times\vec{b}}{|\vec{a}\times\vec{b}|}$.

$$\text{Calculate, } \vec{a}\times\vec{b}=\begin{vmatrix}\hat{i} & \hat{j} & \hat{k}\\ 2 & -1 & 1\\ 1 & 1 & -1\end{vmatrix}$$

$$=\hat{i}(1-1)-\hat{j}(-2-1)+\hat{k}(2+1)$$

$$=3\hat{j}+3\hat{k}=\vec{r}\ \text{(say)}$$

A vector of magnitude 4 in direction of $\vec{r}$

$$4\frac{\vec{r}}{|\vec{r}|} = 4\cdot\frac{3\hat{j}+3\hat{k}}{\sqrt{9+9}} = 4\cdot\frac{3\hat{j}+3\hat{k}}{\sqrt{18}}$$

$$= \frac{4}{3\sqrt{2}}(3\hat{j}+3\hat{k})$$

$$= \frac{4}{\sqrt{2}}(\hat{j}+\hat{k})$$

Example 6 **If $\vec{a} \neq \vec{0}$, $\vec{a}\cdot\vec{b} = \vec{a}\cdot\vec{c}$, $\vec{a}\times\vec{b} = \vec{a}\times\vec{c}$, then show that $\vec{b} = \vec{c}$.**

CBSE 2025, 22 Term II; CBSE Sample Paper 2022 (Term II)

Sol. Given, $\vec{a}\cdot\vec{b} = \vec{a}\cdot\vec{c}$

$\Rightarrow$ $\vec{a}\cdot\vec{b} - \vec{a}\cdot\vec{c} = 0 \Rightarrow \vec{a}\cdot(\vec{b}-\vec{c}) = 0$

$\Rightarrow$ $\vec{b}-\vec{c} = \vec{0}$ or $\vec{a} \perp (\vec{b}-\vec{c})$ $[\because \vec{a} \neq 0]$

Also, $\vec{a}\times\vec{b} = \vec{a}\times\vec{c}$

$\Rightarrow$ $\vec{a}\times\vec{b} - \vec{a}\times\vec{c} = \vec{0} \Rightarrow \vec{a}\times(\vec{b}-\vec{c}) = 0$

$\Rightarrow$ $\vec{b}-\vec{c} = \vec{0}$ or $\vec{a} \parallel (\vec{b}-\vec{c})$

$\Rightarrow$ $\vec{b} = \vec{c}$ or $\vec{a} \parallel (\vec{b}-\vec{c})$

$\because$ $\vec{a}$ cannot be both perpendicular to $(\vec{b}-\vec{c})$ and parallel to $(\vec{b}-\vec{c})$.

Hence, $\vec{b} = \vec{c}$

Example 7 **If $|\vec{a}| = 2$, $|\vec{b}| = 7$ and $\vec{a}\times\vec{b} = 3\hat{i}+2\hat{j}+6\hat{k}$, then find the angle between $\vec{a}$ and $\vec{b}$.** Competency Based Que

Sol. Let θ be the angle between $\vec{a}$ and $\vec{b}$.

We have, $\vec{a}\times\vec{b} = 3\hat{i}+2\hat{j}+6\hat{k}$

Now, $|\vec{a}\times\vec{b}| = \sqrt{3^2+2^2+6^2}$

$= \sqrt{49} = 7$

$\Rightarrow$ $|\vec{a}||\vec{b}|\sin\theta = 7$ $[\because |\vec{a}\times\vec{b}| = |\vec{a}||\vec{b}|\sin\theta]$

$\Rightarrow$ $\sin\theta = \dfrac{7}{|\vec{a}||\vec{b}|}$

$= \dfrac{7}{2\times 7} = \dfrac{1}{2}$

$\Rightarrow$ $\sin\theta = \sin\left(\dfrac{\pi}{6}\right)$

$\Rightarrow$ $\theta = \dfrac{\pi}{6}$

Hence, the required angle between $\vec{a}$ and $\vec{b}$ is $\dfrac{\pi}{6}$.

Example 8 **If θ is the angle between two vectors $\hat{i}-2\hat{j}+3\hat{k}$ and $3\hat{i}-2\hat{j}+\hat{k}$, then find sin θ.** CBSE 2018

Sol. Let $\vec{a} = \hat{i}-2\hat{j}+3\hat{k}$ and $\vec{b} = 3\hat{i}-2\hat{j}+\hat{k}$

Then, $\sin\theta = \dfrac{|\vec{a}\times\vec{b}|}{|\vec{a}|\,|\vec{b}|}$ $\left[\because |\vec{a}\times\vec{b}| = |\vec{a}||\vec{b}|\sin\theta\right]$ ...(i)

Here, $|\vec{a}| = \sqrt{1^2+(-2)^2+3^2} = \sqrt{1+4+9} = \sqrt{14}$,

$|\vec{b}| = \sqrt{3^2+(-2)^2+1^2} = \sqrt{9+4+1} = \sqrt{14}$

and $\vec{a}\times\vec{b} = \begin{vmatrix}\hat{i} & \hat{j} & \hat{k}\\ 1 & -2 & 3\\ 3 & -2 & 1\end{vmatrix}$

$= \hat{i}(-2+6) - \hat{j}(1-9) + \hat{k}(-2+6)$

$= 4\hat{i}+8\hat{j}+4\hat{k} = 4(\hat{i}+2\hat{j}+\hat{k})$

$\Rightarrow$ $|\vec{a}\times\vec{b}| = 4\sqrt{1^2+2^2+1^2}$

$= 4\sqrt{1+4+1} = 4\sqrt{6}$

Now, from Eq. (i), we get

$$\sin\theta = \frac{4\sqrt{6}}{\sqrt{14}\cdot\sqrt{14}} = \frac{4\sqrt{6}}{14} = \frac{2\sqrt{6}}{7}$$

Example 9 **Let $\vec{a} = 4\hat{i}+5\hat{j}-\hat{k}$, $\vec{b} = \hat{i}-4\hat{j}+5\hat{k}$ and $\vec{c} = 3\hat{i}+\hat{j}-\hat{k}$. Find a vector $\vec{d}$ which is perpendicular to both $\vec{c}$ and $\vec{b}$ and $\vec{d}\cdot\vec{a} = 21$.** CBSE 2018

Sol. We have, $\vec{a} = 4\hat{i}+5\hat{j}-\hat{k}$, $\vec{b} = \hat{i}-4\hat{j}+5\hat{k}$

and $\vec{c} = 3\hat{i}+\hat{j}-\hat{k}$

Since, $\vec{d}$ is perpendicular to both $\vec{c}$ and $\vec{b}$.

$\therefore$ $\vec{d} = \lambda(\vec{c}\times\vec{b}) = \lambda\begin{vmatrix}\hat{i} & \hat{j} & \hat{k}\\ 3 & 1 & -1\\ 1 & -4 & 5\end{vmatrix}$

$= \lambda\,[\hat{i}(5-4) - \hat{j}(15+1) + \hat{k}(-12-1)]$

$= \lambda(\hat{i}-16\hat{j}-13\hat{k})$ ...(i)

Also, it is given that $\vec{d}\cdot\vec{a} = 21$

$\therefore$ $\lambda(\hat{i}-16\hat{j}-13\hat{k})\cdot(4\hat{i}+5\hat{j}-\hat{k}) = 21$

$\Rightarrow$ $\lambda(4-80+13) = 21$

$\Rightarrow$ $\lambda(-63) = 21$

$\Rightarrow$ $\lambda = \dfrac{-1}{3}$

Now from Eq. (i), we get

$$\vec{d} = -\frac{1}{3}(\hat{i}-16\hat{j}-13\hat{k})$$

Example 10 **Using vectors, find the area of the triangle ABC with vertices $A(1, 2, 3)$, $B(2, -1, 4)$ and $C(4, 5, -1)$.** CBSE 2020

Sol. Let $\vec{a}$, $\vec{b}$ and $\vec{c}$ be the position vectors of points A, B and C, respectively.

Then, $\vec{a} = \hat{i} + 2\hat{j} + 3\hat{k}$, $\vec{b} = 2\hat{i} - \hat{j} + 4\hat{k}$

and $\vec{c} = 4\hat{i} + 5\hat{j} - \hat{k}$.

Clearly, the area of $\Delta ABC = \frac{1}{2}|\vec{AB} \times \vec{AC}|$

Now, $\vec{AB}$ = Position vector of B – Position vector of A

$$= \vec{b} - \vec{a} = 2\hat{i} - \hat{j} + 4\hat{k} - (\hat{i} + 2\hat{j} + 3\hat{k})$$
$$= \hat{i} - 3\hat{j} + \hat{k}$$

and $\vec{AC}$ = Position vector of C – Position vector of A

$$= \vec{c} - \vec{a} = 4\hat{i} + 5\hat{j} - \hat{k} - (\hat{i} + 2\hat{j} + 3\hat{k})$$
$$= 3\hat{i} + 3\hat{j} - 4\hat{k}$$

$$\therefore \quad \vec{AB} \times \vec{AC} = \begin{vmatrix} \hat{i} & \hat{j} & \hat{k} \\ 1 & -3 & 1 \\ 3 & 3 & -4 \end{vmatrix}$$

$$= (12 - 3)\hat{i} - (-4 - 3)\hat{j} + (3 + 9)\hat{k}$$
$$= 9\hat{i} + 7\hat{j} + 12\hat{k}$$

and $|\vec{AB} \times \vec{AC}| = \sqrt{(9)^2 + (7)^2 + (12)^2}$

$$= \sqrt{81 + 49 + 144} = \sqrt{274}$$

So, area of $\Delta ABC = \frac{1}{2}|\vec{AB} \times \vec{AC}| = \frac{\sqrt{274}}{2}$ sq units

Example 11 **Find the area of a parallelogram whose adjacent sides are determined by the vectors $\vec{a} = \hat{i} - \hat{j} + 3\hat{k}$ and $\vec{b} = 2\hat{i} - 7\hat{j} + \hat{k}$.** CBSE 2023

Sol. Given, adjacent sides of a parallelogram are

$\vec{a} = \hat{i} - \hat{j} + 3\hat{k}$ and $\vec{b} = 2\hat{i} - 7\hat{j} + \hat{k}$.

$\therefore$ Area of parallelogram $= |\vec{a} \times \vec{b}|$

$$\text{Now, } \vec{a} \times \vec{b} = \begin{vmatrix} \hat{i} & \hat{j} & \hat{k} \\ 1 & -1 & 3 \\ 2 & -7 & 1 \end{vmatrix}$$

$$= \hat{i}(-1 + 21) - \hat{j}(1 - 6) + \hat{k}(-7 + 2)$$
$$= 20\hat{i} + 5\hat{j} - 5\hat{k}$$

$$\therefore \quad |\vec{a} \times \vec{b}| = \sqrt{(20)^2 + (5)^2 + (-5)^2}$$
$$= \sqrt{400 + 25 + 25} = \sqrt{450} = 15\sqrt{2}$$

Hence, the area of parallelogram is $15\sqrt{2}$ sq units.

Example 12 **Find the area of the parallelogram whose diagonals are represented by the vectors $\vec{d_1} = \hat{i} - 3\hat{j} + 2\hat{k}$ and $\vec{d_2} = -\hat{i} + \hat{j}$.** CBSE 2023

Sol. Given diagonals of a parallelogram are

$$\vec{d_1} = \hat{i} - 3\hat{j} + 2\hat{k} \text{ and } \vec{d_2} = -\hat{i} + \hat{j}$$

$$\text{Now, } \vec{d_1} \times \vec{d_2} = \begin{vmatrix} \hat{i} & \hat{j} & \hat{k} \\ 1 & -3 & 2 \\ -1 & 1 & 0 \end{vmatrix}$$

$$= \hat{i}(0 - 2) - \hat{j}(0 + 2) + \hat{k}(1 - 3)$$
$$= -2\hat{i} - 2\hat{j} - 2\hat{k}$$

$$\therefore \text{ Area of parallelogram} = \frac{1}{2}|\vec{d_1} \times \vec{d_2}|$$
$$= \frac{1}{2}|-2\hat{i} - 2\hat{j} - 2\hat{k}|$$
$$= \frac{2}{2}|\hat{i} + \hat{j} + \hat{k}|$$
$$= \sqrt{1^2 + 1^2 + 1^2}$$
$$= \sqrt{3} \text{ sq units}$$

Example 13 **Find the area of the parallelogram whose one side and a diagonal are represented by coinitial vectors $\hat{i} - \hat{j} + \hat{k}$ and $4\hat{i} + 5\hat{k}$, respectively.** Competency Based Que

Sol. Let the sides of the parallelogram be $\vec{a} = \hat{i} - \hat{j} + \hat{k}$ and $\vec{b}$, and diagonal $\vec{d} = 4\hat{i} + 5\hat{k}$.

We know that

$$\vec{a} + \vec{b} = \vec{d} \Rightarrow \vec{b} = \vec{d} - \vec{a}$$
$$= (4\hat{i} + 5\hat{k}) - (\hat{i} - \hat{j} + \hat{k})$$
$$= 3\hat{i} + \hat{j} + 4\hat{k}$$

$$\text{Now, } \vec{a} \times \vec{b} = \begin{vmatrix} \hat{i} & \hat{j} & \hat{k} \\ 1 & -1 & 1 \\ 3 & 1 & 4 \end{vmatrix}$$

$$= \hat{i}(-4 - 1) - \hat{j}(4 - 3) + \hat{k}(1 + 3)$$
$$= -5\hat{i} - \hat{j} + 4\hat{k}$$

$$\therefore \text{ Area of parallelogram} = |\vec{a} \times \vec{b}|$$
$$= |-5\hat{i} - \hat{j} + 4\hat{k}|$$
$$= \sqrt{(-5)^2 + (-1)^2 + (4)^2}$$
$$= \sqrt{25 + 1 + 16}$$
$$= \sqrt{42} \text{ sq units}$$

Quick Test 3

1. If the angle between two vectors $\vec{a}$ and $\vec{b}$ is $\frac{\pi}{3}$ and the magnitude of these vectors are 3 and 7. Find the magnitude of cross product of these vectors.

2. If $|\vec{a}|=8, |\vec{b}|=3$ and $|\vec{a}\times\vec{b}|=12$, then find the angle between $\vec{a}$ and $\vec{b}$. CBSE 2014C

3. Find the value of λ for which the vectors $3\hat{i}-6\hat{j}+\hat{k}$ and $2\hat{i}-4\hat{j}+\lambda\hat{k}$ are parallel. NCERT Exemplar, Competency Based Que

4. If $|\vec{a}|=3, |\vec{b}|=5$ and $\vec{a}\times\vec{b}=6\hat{i}+3\hat{j}+2\hat{k}$, then find the angle between $\vec{a}$ and $\vec{b}$.

5. Find the unit vector perpendicular to each of the vector $\vec{a}=\hat{i}-2\hat{j}+3\hat{k}$ and $\vec{b}=\hat{i}+2\hat{j}-\hat{k}$. Competency Based Que

6. Let $\vec{a}=4\hat{i}+5\hat{j}-\hat{k}, \vec{b}=\hat{i}-4\hat{j}+5\hat{k}$ and $\vec{c}=3\hat{i}+\hat{j}-\hat{k}$. Find a vector $\vec{d}$ which is perpendicular to both $\vec{a}$ and $\vec{b}$ and satisfying $\vec{d}\cdot\vec{c}=21$. CBSE 2016C

7. If the three vectors $\vec{a}, \vec{b}$ and $\vec{c}$ are given as $a_1\hat{i}+a_2\hat{j}+a_3\hat{k}$, $b_1\hat{i}+b_2\hat{j}+b_3\hat{k}$ and $c_1\hat{i}+c_2\hat{j}+c_3\hat{k}$. Then, show that $\vec{a}\times(\vec{b}+\vec{c})=(\vec{a}\times\vec{b})+(\vec{a}\times\vec{c})$.

Competency Based Que, NCERT Exemplar

8. Find the area of the triangle whose adjacent sides are represented by the vector $\vec{a}=\hat{i}+2\hat{j}+3\hat{k}$ and $\vec{b}=-3\hat{i}-2\hat{j}+\hat{k}$.

9. Find the area of the parallelogram whose adjacent sides are $\vec{a}=2\hat{i}-\hat{j}+\hat{k}$ and $\vec{b}=3\hat{i}+4\hat{j}-\hat{k}$.

10. Find the area of the parallelogram whose diagonals are $\vec{d_1}=2\hat{i}+\hat{j}+\hat{k}$ and $\vec{d_2}=3\hat{i}+4\hat{j}-\hat{k}$.

Answers

1. $\frac{21}{2}\sqrt{3}$
2. $\frac{\pi}{6}$
3. $\frac{2}{3}$
4. $\sin^{-1}\left(\frac{7}{15}\right)$
5. $\pm\frac{1}{\sqrt{3}}(-\hat{i}+\hat{j}+\hat{k})$
6. $7\hat{i}-7\hat{j}-7\hat{k}$
8. $3\sqrt{5}$ sq units
9. $\sqrt{155}$ sq units
10. $\frac{5}{2}\sqrt{3}$ sq units

For Solutions, See QR Code on Pg. 325

EXAM PATTERN QUESTIONS

Objective Type Questions

Multiple Choice Questions

1. The magnitude of the vector $6\hat{i} - 2\hat{j} + 3\hat{k}$ is **CBSE 2023**

(a) 1 (b) 5 (c) 7 (d) 12

2. If $\vec{a} + \vec{b} = \hat{i}$ and $\vec{a} = 2\hat{i} - 2\hat{j} + 2\hat{k}$, then $|\vec{b}|$ is equal to **CBSE 2023**

(a) $\sqrt{14}$ (b) 3 (c) $\sqrt{12}$ (d) $\sqrt{17}$

3. In ΔABC, $\overrightarrow{AB} = \hat{i} + \hat{j} + 2\hat{k}$ and $\overrightarrow{AC} = 3\hat{i} - \hat{j} + 4\hat{k}$. If D is mid-point of BC, then vector $\overrightarrow{AD}$ is equal to **CBSE 2023**

(a) $4\hat{i} + 6\hat{k}$ (b) $2\hat{i} - 2\hat{j} + 2\hat{k}$
(c) $\hat{i} - \hat{j} + \hat{k}$ (d) $2\hat{i} + 3\hat{k}$

4. $ABCD$ is a rhombus whose diagonals intersect at E. Then, $\overrightarrow{EA} + \overrightarrow{EB} + \overrightarrow{EC} + \overrightarrow{ED}$ is equal to **CBSE Sample paper 2023**

(a) $\vec{0}$ (b) $\overrightarrow{AD}$
(c) $2\overrightarrow{BD}$ (d) $2\overrightarrow{AD}$

5. Two vectors $\vec{a} = a_1\hat{i} + a_2\hat{j} + a_3\hat{k}$ and $\vec{b} = b_1\hat{i} + b_2\hat{j} + b_3\hat{k}$ are collinear, if **CBSE 2023**

(a) $a_1b_1 + a_2b_2 + a_3b_3 = 0$ (b) $\frac{a_1}{b_1} = \frac{a_2}{b_2} = \frac{a_3}{b_3}$
(c) $a_1 = b_1, a_2 = b_2, a_3 = b_3$ (d) $a_1 + a_2 + a_3 = b_1 + b_2 + b_3$

6. A unit vector along the vector $4\hat{i} - 3\hat{k}$ is **CBSE 2023**

(a) $\frac{1}{7}(4\hat{i} - 3\hat{k})$ (b) $\frac{1}{5}(4\hat{i} - 3\hat{k})$
(c) $\frac{1}{\sqrt{7}}(4\hat{i} - 3\hat{k})$ (d) $\frac{1}{\sqrt{5}}(4\hat{i} - 3\hat{k})$

7. Unit vector along $\overrightarrow{PQ}$, where coordinates of P and Q, respectively are (2, 1, – 1) and (4, 4 – 7) is **CBSE 2023**

(a) $2\hat{i} + 3\hat{j} - 6\hat{k}$ (b) $-2\hat{i} - 3\hat{j} + 6\hat{k}$
(c) $-\frac{2\hat{i}}{7} - \frac{3\hat{j}}{7} + \frac{6\hat{k}}{7}$ (d) $\frac{2\hat{i}}{7} + \frac{3\hat{i}}{7} - \frac{6\hat{k}}{7}$

8. If a vector makes an angle of $\frac{\pi}{4}$ with the positive directions of both X-axis and Y-axis, then the angle which it makes with positive Z-axis is **CBSE 2023**

(a) $\frac{\pi}{4}$ (b) $\frac{3\pi}{4}$ (c) $\frac{\pi}{2}$ (d) 0

9. The position vectors of points P and Q are $\vec{p}$ and $\vec{q}$, respectively. The point R divides line segment PQ in the ratio 3 : 1 and S is the mid-point of line segment PR. The position vector of S is **CBSE 2024**

(a) $\frac{\vec{p} + 3\vec{q}}{4}$ (b) $\frac{\vec{p} + 3\vec{q}}{8}$ (c) $\frac{5\vec{p} + 3\vec{q}}{4}$ (d) $\frac{5\vec{p} + 3\vec{q}}{8}$

10. Position vector of the mid-point of line segment AB is $3\hat{i} + 2\hat{j} - 3\hat{k}$. If position vector of the point A is $2\hat{i} + 3\hat{j} - 4\hat{k}$, then position vector of the point B is **CBSE 2023**

(a) $\frac{5}{2}\hat{i} + \frac{5}{2}\hat{j} - \frac{7}{2}\hat{k}$ (b) $4\hat{i} + \hat{j} - 2\hat{k}$
(c) $5\hat{i} + 5\hat{j} - 7\hat{k}$ (d) $\frac{\hat{i}}{2} - \frac{\hat{j}}{2} + \frac{\hat{k}}{2}$

11. If two vectors $\vec{a}$ and $\vec{b}$ are such that $|\vec{a}| = 2$, $|\vec{b}| = 3$ and $\vec{a} \cdot \vec{b} = 4$, then $|\vec{a} - 2\vec{b}|$ is equal to **CBSE Sample paper 2023**

(a) $\sqrt{2}$ (b) $2\sqrt{6}$ (c) 24 (d) $2\sqrt{2}$

12. The value of p for which the vectors $2\hat{i} + p\hat{j} + \hat{k}$ and $-4\hat{i} - 6\hat{j} + 26\hat{k}$ are perpendicular to each other is **CBSE 2023**

(a) 3 (b) –3 (c) $-\frac{17}{3}$ (d) $\frac{17}{3}$

13. If $\vec{a} = 4\hat{i} + 6\hat{j}$ and $\vec{b} = 3\hat{j} + 4\hat{k}$, then the vector form of the component of $\vec{a}$ along $\vec{b}$ is **CBSE Sample Paper 2023**

(a) $\frac{18}{5}(3\hat{i} + 4\hat{k})$ (b) $\frac{18}{25}(3\hat{j} + 4\hat{k})$
(c) $\frac{18}{5}(3\hat{i} + 4\hat{k})$ (d) $\frac{18}{25}(2\hat{i} + 4\hat{j})$

14. The value of λ, for which two vectors $2\hat{i} - \hat{j} + 2\hat{k}$ and $3\hat{i} + \lambda\hat{j} + \hat{k}$ are perpendicular is **CBSE Sample Paper 2023**

(a) 2 (b) 4 (c) 6 (d) 8

15. If $\vec{a} \cdot \hat{i} = \vec{a} \cdot (\hat{i} + \hat{j}) = \vec{a}(\hat{i} + \hat{j} + \hat{k}) = 1$, then $\vec{a}$ is **CBSE 2023**

(a) $\hat{k}$ (b) $\hat{i}$ (c) $\hat{j}$ (d) $\hat{i} + \hat{j} + \hat{k}$

16. Let $\vec{a} = \hat{i} - 2\hat{j} + 3\hat{k}$. If $\vec{b}$ is a vector such that $\vec{a} \cdot \vec{b} = |\vec{b}|^2$ and $|\vec{a} - \vec{b}| = \sqrt{7}$, then $|\vec{b}|$ is equal to

(a) 7 (b) 14 (c) $\sqrt{7}$ (d) 21

17. $\vec{a}$ and $\vec{b}$ are two non-zero vectors such that the projection of $\vec{a}$ on $\vec{b}$ is 0. The angle between $\vec{a}$ and $\vec{b}$ is **CBSE 2023**

(a) $\frac{\pi}{2}$ (b) π (c) $\frac{\pi}{4}$ (d) 0

18. If θ is the angle between two vectors $\vec{a}$ and $\vec{b}$, then $\vec{a}\cdot\vec{b}\geq 0$ only when **CBSE 2023**

(a) $0<\theta<\frac{\pi}{2}$ (b) $0\leq\theta\leq\frac{\pi}{2}$

(c) $0<\theta<\pi$ (d) $0\leq\theta\leq\pi$

19. What is the value of $\frac{\text{projection of } \vec{a} \text{ on } \vec{b}}{\text{projection of } \vec{b} \text{ on } \vec{a}}$ for vectors $\vec{a}=2\hat{i}-3\hat{j}-6\hat{k}$ and $\vec{b}=2\hat{i}-2\hat{j}+\hat{k}$? **CBSE 2024C**

(a) $\frac{3}{7}$ (b) $\frac{7}{3}$ (c) $\frac{4}{3}$ (d) $\frac{4}{7}$

20. If $\hat{i},\hat{j},\hat{k}$ are unit vectors along three mutually perpendicular directions, then

(a) $\hat{i}\cdot\hat{j}=1$ (b) $\hat{i}\times\hat{j}=1$ (c) $\hat{i}\cdot\hat{k}=0$ (d) $\hat{i}\times\hat{k}=0$

21. The sine of the angle between the vectors $\vec{a}=3\hat{i}+\hat{j}+2\hat{k}$ and $\vec{b}=\hat{i}+\hat{j}+2\hat{k}$ is **CBSE 2023**

(a) $\sqrt{\frac{5}{21}}$ (b) $\frac{5}{\sqrt{21}}$ (c) $\sqrt{\frac{3}{21}}$ (d) $\frac{4}{\sqrt{21}}$

22. If the angle between the vectors $\vec{a}$ and $\vec{b}$ is $\frac{\pi}{4}$ and $|\vec{a}\times\vec{b}|=1$, then $\vec{a}\cdot\vec{b}$ is equal to **CBSE 2023**

(a) -1 (b) 1 (c) $\frac{1}{\sqrt{2}}$ (d) $\sqrt{2}$

23. If $\vec{a}$ and $\vec{b}$ are two vectors such that $\vec{a}\cdot\vec{b}>0$ and $|\vec{a}\cdot\vec{b}|=|\vec{a}\times\vec{b}|$, then the angle between $\vec{a}$ and $\vec{b}$ is **CBSE 2024C**

(a) $\frac{\pi}{4}$ (b) $\frac{\pi}{3}$ (c) $\frac{2\pi}{3}$ (d) $\frac{3\pi}{4}$

24. The value of $(\hat{i}\times\hat{j})\cdot\hat{j}+(\hat{j}\times\hat{i})\cdot\hat{k}$ is **CBSE 2023**

(a) 2 (b) 0 (c) 1 (d) -1

25. For any vector $\vec{a}$, the value of $(\vec{a}\times\hat{i})^2+(\vec{a}\times\hat{j})^2+(\vec{a}\times\hat{k})^2$ is **NCERT Exemplar**

(a) $\vec{a}^2$ (b) $3\vec{a}^2$ (c) $4\vec{a}^2$ (d) $2\vec{a}^2$

26. The area of a triangle with vertices A, B and C is given by **CBSE Sample Paper 2023**

(a) $|\overrightarrow{AB}\times\overrightarrow{AC}|$ (b) $\frac{1}{2}|\overrightarrow{AB}\times\overrightarrow{AC}|$

(c) $\frac{1}{4}|\overrightarrow{AC}\times\overrightarrow{AB}|$ (d) $\frac{1}{8}|\overrightarrow{AC}\times\overrightarrow{AB}|$

Assertion-Reason Based Questions

Directions (Q. Nos. 27-36) *In the questions given below are two statements labelled as Assertion (A) and Reason (R). In the context of the two statements, which one of the following is correct?*

(a) Both A and R are correct; R is the correct explanation of A.
(b) Both A and R are correct; R is not the correct explanation of A.
(c) A is correct; R is incorrect.
(d) R is correct; A is incorrect.

27. Assertion (A) The sum of two vectors can be zero.

Reason (R) The vector cancels each other when they are equal and opposite.

28. Assertion (A) If $\vec{a}=\hat{i}-2\hat{j}+3\hat{k}$, then its direction cosines are $\frac{1}{\sqrt{14}},\frac{-2}{\sqrt{14}},\frac{3}{\sqrt{14}}$.

Reason (R) If $\vec{a}=a_1\hat{i}+a_2\hat{j}+a_3\hat{k}$, then its direction cosines are $\frac{a_1}{|\vec{a}|},\frac{a_2}{|\vec{a}|},\frac{a_3}{|\vec{a}|}$, where $|\vec{a}|=\sqrt{a_1^2+a_2^2+a_3^2}$.

29. Assertion (A) If a vector makes α,β and γ with X, Y and Z-axes respectively, then

$$\cos 2\alpha+\cos 2\beta+\cos 2\gamma+1=0.$$

Reason (R) Sum of the square of the direction cosines of a vector is equal to 1.

30. Assertion (A) The vectors $\vec{a}=6\hat{i}+2\hat{j}-8\hat{k}$, $\vec{b}=10\hat{i}-2\hat{j}-6\hat{k}$ and $\vec{c}=4\hat{i}-4\hat{j}+2\hat{k}$ represent the sides of a right angled triangle.

Reason (R) Three non-zero vectors of which none of two are collinear forms a triangle, if their resultant is zero vector or sum of any two vectors is equal to the third. **CBSE 2024**

31. Assertion (A) If $\vec{a}$ and $\vec{b}$ are unit vectors such that $|\vec{a}+\vec{b}|=\sqrt{3}$, then the angle between $\vec{a}$ and $\vec{b}$ is $\frac{\pi}{3}$.

Reason (R) Angle between vectors $\vec{a}$ and $\vec{b}$ is given by $\cos\theta=\frac{\vec{a}\cdot\vec{b}}{|\vec{a}||\vec{b}|}$.

32. Assertion (A) If $|2\vec{a}+\vec{b}|=|2\vec{a}-\vec{b}|$, then $\vec{a}$ parallel to $\vec{b}$.

Reason (R) Two non-zero vectors $\vec{a}$ and $\vec{b}$ are perpendicular, if $\vec{a}\cdot\vec{b}=0$.

33. Assertion (A) If $\vec{a} = 2\hat{i} - 2\hat{j} + 3\hat{k}$ and $\vec{b} = \hat{i} - \hat{j} + 2\hat{k}$, then $\vec{a} \cdot \vec{b} = 10$.

Reason (R) If $\vec{a} = a_1\hat{i} + a_2\hat{j} + a_3\hat{k}$, then $|\vec{a}| = a_1^2 + a_2^2 + a_3^2$.

34. Assertion (A) The projection of the vector $\vec{a} = 2\hat{i} + 3\hat{j} + 2\hat{k}$ on the vector $\vec{b} = \hat{i} + 2\hat{j} + \hat{k}$ is $\frac{5}{3}\sqrt{6}$.

Reason (R) The projection of vector $\vec{a}$ on vector $\vec{b}$ is $\frac{1}{|\vec{a}|}(\vec{a} \cdot \vec{b})$.

35. Assertion (A) Unit vector perpendicular to $\hat{i} - 2\hat{j} + 3\hat{k}$ and $\hat{i} + 2\hat{j} - \hat{k}$ is $\frac{1}{\sqrt{3}}(-\hat{i} + \hat{j} - \hat{k})$.

Reason (R) For two vectors $\vec{a}$ and $\vec{b}$, vector $\vec{a} \times \vec{b}$ is perpendicular to both $\vec{a}$ and $\vec{b}$ and unit vector along a vector $\vec{a}$ is $\frac{\vec{a}}{|\vec{a}|}$.

36. Assertion (A) Two adjacent sides of a triangle are represented by $\vec{a} = 3\hat{i} + 4\hat{j}$ and $\vec{b} = -5\hat{i} + 7\hat{j}$, then the area of the triangle is $\frac{41}{2}$ sq units.

Reason (R) Area of the triangle whose two adjacent sides are $\vec{a}$ and $\vec{b}$ is $\frac{1}{2}|\vec{a} \times \vec{b}|$.

Case Study Based Questions

37. Ram's house is situated at Shalimar Bagh at point O, for going to Anant's house he first travels 8 km by bus in the East. Here, at point A, a hospital is situated.

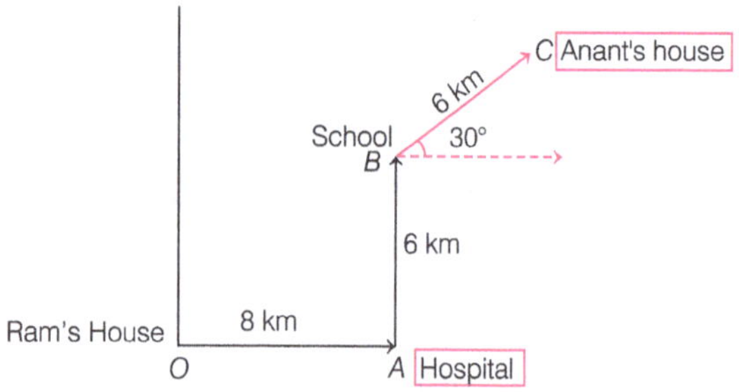

From hospital, Ram takes an auto and goes 6 km in the North, here at point B, school is situated.

From school, he travels by bus to reach Anant's house which is at 30° East, 6 km from point B.

Based on the above information, answer the following questions.

(i) What is the vector distance between Ram's house and school?

(ii) How much distance Ram travelled to reach school?

(iii) What is the vector distance from school to Anant's house?

(iv) What is the vector distance from Ram's house to Anant's house?

(v) Find the distance between Ram's house to Anant's house.

38. On a certain night, Ziad was observing stars using his telescope. **CBSE QB**

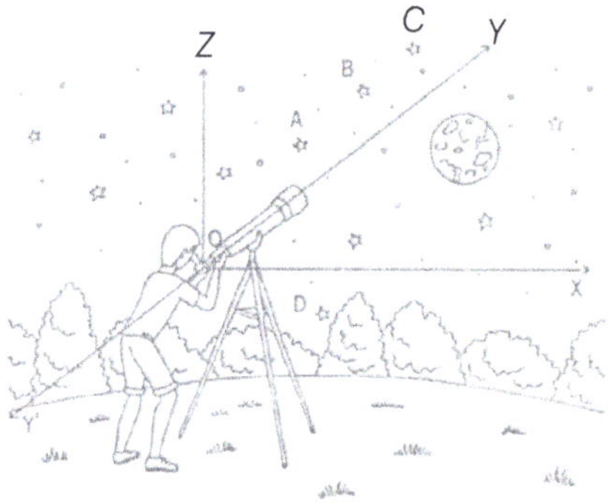

(**Note** image is purely for representation purposes).

Considering the eyepiece of the telescope as the origin, the position vectors of some of the stars are given below.

$A(2\hat{i} + 3\hat{j} + 4\hat{k})$, $B(5\hat{i} + 6\hat{j} + 8\hat{k})$,
$C(8\hat{i} + 9\hat{j} + 12\hat{k})$ and $D(2\hat{i} + 3\hat{j} - 6\hat{k})$

Based on the above information, answer the following questions.

(i) Show that the stars with position vectors A, B and C are collinear.

(ii) Express the vector $\vec{AD}$ in terms of its components and find the distance between the stars A and D.

(**Note** 1 unit = 1 light year)

(iii) A star at a certain position is inclined at angles of 45° and 60° with the positive direction of the X-axis and Y-axis, respectively.

If the star is 2 light years away from O, find its position vector. (**Note** 1 unit = 1 light year)

39. Read the following passage and answer the questions given below. **CBSE Sample Paper 2023**

Teams A, B and C went for playing a tug of war game. Teams A, B and C have attached a rope to a metal ring and is trying to pull the ring into their own area.

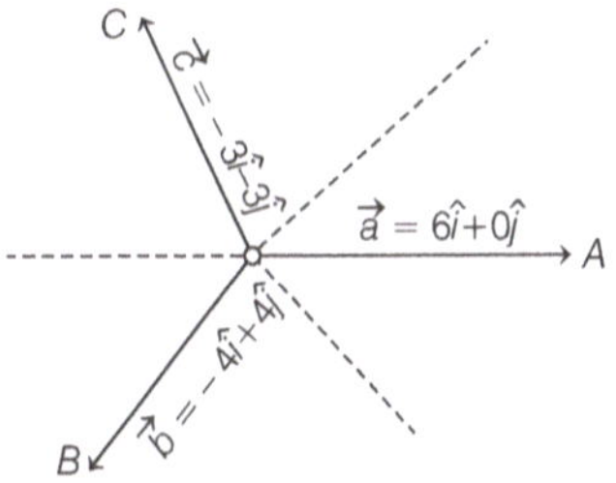

Team A pulls with force $\vec{F_1} = 6\hat{i} + 0\hat{j}\ kN$,

Team B pulls with force $\vec{F_2} = -4\hat{i} + 4\hat{j}kN$,

Team C pulls with force $\vec{F_3} = -3\hat{i} - 3\hat{j}kN$,

(i) What is the magnitude of the force of team A?

(ii) Which team will win the game?

(iii) Find the magnitude of the resultant force exerted by the teams.

Or

In what direction is the ring getting pulled?

Subjective Questions

Very Short Answer Type Questions

1. If $\vec{a} = 4\hat{i} - \hat{j} + \hat{k}$ and $\vec{b} = 2\hat{i} - 2\hat{j} + \hat{k}$, then find a unit vector parallel to the vector $\vec{a} + \vec{b}$. **CBSE 2016**

2. Two vectors $\hat{j} + \hat{k}$ and $3\hat{i} - \hat{j} + 4\hat{k}$ represent the two sides AB and AC, respectively of ΔABC. Find the length of the median through A. **Competency Based Que**

3. Find the value of p for which the vectors $3\hat{i} + 2\hat{j} + 9\hat{k}$ and $\hat{i} - 2p\hat{j} + 3\hat{k}$ are parallel. **CBSE 2014**

4. Find the angle between X-axis and the vector $\hat{i} + \hat{j} + \hat{k}$. **CBSE 2014C**

5. Write the direction ratios of the vector $3\vec{a} + 2\vec{b}$, where $\vec{a} = \hat{i} + \hat{j} - 2\hat{k}$ and $\vec{b} = 2\hat{i} - 4\hat{j} + 5\hat{k}$. **CBSE 2015C**

6. Write the value of cosine of the angle which the vector $\vec{a} = \hat{i} + \hat{j} + \hat{k}$ makes with Y-axis. **CBSE 2014C**

7. Let $l_i, m_i, n_i; i = 1, 2, 3$ be the direction cosines of three mutually perpendicular vectors in space. Show that $AA' = I_3$, where $A = \begin{bmatrix} l_1 & m_1 & n_1 \\ l_2 & m_2 & n_2 \\ l_3 & m_3 & n_3 \end{bmatrix}$. **CBSE Sample Paper 2017**

8. Write a unit vector in the direction of vector $\overrightarrow{PQ}$, where P and Q are the points (1, 3, 0) and (4, 5, 6), respectively. **Competency Based Que**

9. L and M are two points with position vectors $2\vec{a} - \vec{b}$ and $\vec{a} + 2\vec{b}$, respectively. Write the position vector of a point N, which divides the line segment LM in the ratio 2 : 1 externally. **Competency Based Que**

10. Find $|\vec{x}|$, if for a unit vector $\hat{a}$, $(\vec{x} - \hat{a}) \cdot (\vec{x} + \hat{a}) = 15$. **CBSE 2013**

11. For what value of λ, the vectors $\hat{i} + 2\lambda\hat{j} + \hat{k}$ and $2\hat{i} + \hat{j} - 3\hat{k}$ are perpendicular? **CBSE 2011C**

12. Find λ, when projection of $\vec{a} = \lambda\hat{i} + \hat{j} + 4\hat{k}$ on $\vec{b} = 2\hat{i} + 6\hat{j} + 3\hat{k}$ is 4 units. **CBSE 2012**

13. If $\vec{a}$ and $\vec{b}$ are two vectors such that $|\vec{a} + \vec{b}| = |\vec{a}|$, then prove that vector $2\vec{a} + \vec{b}$ is perpendicular to vector $\vec{b}$. **CBSE 2013**

14. If $\vec{a}$ and $\vec{b}$ are unit vectors, then what is the angle between $\vec{a}$ and $\vec{b}$ so that $\sqrt{2}\vec{a} - \vec{b}$ is a unit vector? **CBSE 2015C**

15. Find the angle between the unit vectors $\hat{a}$ and $\hat{b}$, given that $|\hat{a} + \hat{b}| = 1$. **CBSE Sample Paper 2021**

16. Find the projection of the vector $\hat{i} - \hat{j}$ on the vector $\hat{i} + \hat{j}$. **CBSE 2020**

17. If $\vec{a}$ is a non-zero vector, then find the value of $(\vec{a} \cdot \hat{i})\hat{i} + (\vec{a} \cdot \hat{j})\hat{j} + (\vec{a} \cdot \hat{k})\hat{k}$. **CBSE 2020**

18. Find the magnitude of projection of $(2\hat{i} + \hat{j} + \hat{k})$ on $(\hat{i} - 2\hat{j} + 2\hat{k})$. **CBSE Sample Paper 2020**

19. Find $|\vec{x}|$, if $(\vec{x} - \vec{a}) \cdot (\vec{x} + \vec{a}) = 12$, where $\vec{a}$ is a unit vector. **CBSE Sample Paper 2023**

20. If $\vec{a} + \vec{b} + \vec{c} = 0$ and $|\vec{a}| = 3, |\vec{b}| = 5, |\vec{c}| = 7$, then find the value of $\vec{a} \cdot \vec{b} + \vec{b} \cdot \vec{c} + \vec{c} \cdot \vec{a}$. **Competency Based Que**

21. If the sum of two unit vectors $\hat{a}$ and $\hat{b}$ is a unit vector, then show that the magnitude of their difference is $\sqrt{3}$. **CBSE 2019, 12C**

22. If $\vec{a} + \vec{b} + \vec{c} = 0$ and $|\vec{a}| = 5, |\vec{b}| = 6$ and $|\vec{c}| = 9$, then find the angle between $\vec{a}$ and $\vec{b}$. **CBSE 2018C**

23. Find the projection (vector) of $2\hat{i}-\hat{j}+\hat{k}$ on $\hat{i}-2\hat{j}+\hat{k}$. **CBSE Sample Paper 2018**

24. Find the vector product of the vectors $3\hat{i}-\hat{k}$ and $-\hat{i}-\hat{j}+5\hat{k}$.

25. Write the value of $(\hat{k}\times\hat{j})\cdot\hat{i}+\hat{j}\cdot\hat{k}$. **CBSE 2012**

26. Write the angle between the vectors $\vec{a}\times\vec{b}$ and $\vec{b}\times\vec{a}$. **CBSE 2017C**

27. Let $\vec{a}$, $\vec{b}$ and $\vec{c}$ be three vectors such taht $\vec{a}\neq 0$ and $\vec{a}\times\vec{b}=2\vec{a}\times\vec{c}, |\vec{a}|=|\vec{c}|=1, |\vec{b}|=4$ and $|\vec{b}\times\vec{c}|=\sqrt{15}$ $\vec{b}-2\vec{c}=\lambda\vec{a}$. Then, find the value of λ. **Diksha App**

28. If $(\vec{a}\times\vec{b})^2+(\vec{a}\cdot\vec{b})^2=225$ and $|\vec{a}|=5$, then find the value of $|\vec{b}|$. **Competency Based Que**

29. If $\vec{a}\cdot\vec{b}=\vec{0}$ and $\vec{a}\times\vec{b}=\vec{0}$, then prove that $\vec{a}=\vec{0}$ or $\vec{b}=\vec{0}$.

30. Find the area of the triangle whose two sides are represented by the vectors $2\hat{i}$ and $-3\hat{j}$. **CBSE Sample Paper 2021**

31. Find λ and μ, if $(\hat{i}+3\hat{j}+9\hat{k})\times(3\hat{i}-\lambda\hat{j}+\mu\hat{k})=\vec{0}$. **CBSE 2016**

32. Write the number of vectors of unit length perpendicular to both the vectors $\vec{a}=2\hat{i}+\hat{j}+2\hat{k}$ and $\vec{b}=\hat{j}+\hat{k}$. **Competency Based Que**

Short Answer Type Questions

33. If the points with position vectors $10\hat{i}+3\hat{j}, 12\hat{i}-5\hat{j}$ and $\lambda\hat{i}+11\hat{j}$ are collinear, then find the value of λ. **CBSE 2017C**

34. The position vectors of points A, B and C are $\lambda\hat{i}+3\hat{j}$, $12\hat{i}+\mu\hat{j}$ and $11\hat{i}-3\hat{j}$, respectively. If C divides the line segment joining A and B in the ratio 3 : 1, then find the value of λ and μ. **CBSE 2017C**

35. If a unit vector $\vec{a}$ makes angle $\frac{\pi}{4}$ with $\hat{i}$, $\frac{\pi}{3}$ with $\hat{j}$ and an acute angle θ with $\hat{k}$, then find the components of $\vec{a}$ and the angle θ.

36. Find the projection of $\vec{b}+\vec{c}$ on $\vec{a}$, where $\vec{a}=2\hat{i}-2\hat{j}+\hat{k}$, $\vec{b}=\hat{i}+2\hat{j}-2\hat{k}$ and $\vec{c}=2\hat{i}-\hat{j}+4\hat{k}$.

37. Find $|\vec{a}-\vec{b}|$, if two vectors $\vec{a}$ and $\vec{b}$ are such that $|\vec{a}|=2, |\vec{b}|=3$ and $\vec{a}\cdot\vec{b}=5$.

38. If $\vec{a}=3\hat{i}-\hat{j}$ and $\vec{b}=2\hat{i}+\hat{j}-3\hat{k}$, then express $\vec{b}$ in the form $\vec{b}=\vec{b}_1+\vec{b}_2$, where $\vec{b}_1 \parallel \vec{a}$ and $\vec{b}_2\perp\vec{a}$. **CBSE 2013C**

39. If $\vec{a}=\hat{i}-\hat{j}+7\hat{k}$ and $\vec{b}=5\hat{i}-\hat{j}+\lambda\hat{k}$, then find the value of λ, so that $\vec{a}+\vec{b}$ and $\vec{a}-\vec{b}$ are perpendicular vectors. **CBSE 2013**

40. Let $\vec{a}, \vec{b}$ and $\vec{c}$ be three vectors such that $\vec{a}+\vec{b}+\vec{c}=0$ $|\vec{a}|=1, |\vec{c}|=3, |\vec{b}|=2$ then find $\vec{a}\cdot\vec{b}+\vec{b}\cdot\vec{c}+\vec{c}\cdot\vec{a}$ **Diksha App**

Long Answer Type Questions

41. If $\vec{a}=\hat{i}+2\hat{j}+3\hat{k}$ and $\vec{b}=2\hat{i}+4\hat{j}-5\hat{k}$ represent two adjacent sides of a parallelogram, find unit vectors parallel to the diagonals of the parallelogram. **Competency Based Que**

42. Show that the points A, B and C with position vectors $2\hat{i}-\hat{j}+\hat{k}$, $\hat{i}-3\hat{j}-5\hat{k}$ and $3\hat{i}-4\hat{j}-4\hat{k}$ respectively, are the vertices of a right angled triangle. Hence, find the area of the triangle. **CBSE 2017**

43. The two adjacent sides of a parallelogram are $2\hat{i}-4\hat{j}-5\hat{k}$ and $2\hat{i}+2\hat{j}+3\hat{k}$. Find the two unit vectors parallel to its diagonals. Using the diagonal vectors, find the area of the parallelogram. **Competency Based Que**

44. If $\vec{r}=x\hat{i}+y\hat{j}+z\hat{k}$, then find $(\vec{r}\times\hat{i})\cdot(\vec{r}\times\hat{j})+xy$. **CBSE 2015**

45. If $\vec{a}=\hat{i}+2\hat{j}+\hat{k}, \vec{b}=2\hat{i}+\hat{j}$ and $\vec{c}=3\hat{i}-4\hat{j}-5\hat{k}$, then find a unit vector perpendicular to both of the vectors $(\vec{a}-\vec{b})$ and $(\vec{c}-\vec{b})$. **CBSE 2015**

46. If $\vec{a}=2\hat{i}-3\hat{j}+\hat{k}, \vec{b}=-\hat{i}+\hat{k}$ and $\vec{c}=2\hat{j}-\hat{k}$ are three vectors, then find the area of the parallelogram having diagonals $(\vec{a}+\vec{b})$ and $(\vec{b}+\vec{c})$. **Competency Based Que**

47. Find the vector $\vec{p}$, which is perpendicular to both $\vec{\alpha}=4\hat{i}+5\hat{j}-\hat{k}$ and $\vec{\beta}=\hat{i}-4\hat{j}+5\hat{k}$ and $\vec{p}\cdot\vec{q}=21$, where $\vec{q}=3\hat{i}+\hat{j}-\hat{k}$. **CBSE 2014C**

48. Find the unit vector perpendicular to the plane ABC, where the position vectors of A, B and C are $2\hat{i}-\hat{j}+\hat{k}$, $\hat{i}+\hat{j}+2\hat{k}$ and $2\hat{i}+3\hat{k}$, respectively. **CBSE 2014C**

49. If $\vec{a}=\hat{i}+\hat{j}+\hat{k}$ and $\vec{b}=\hat{j}-\hat{k}$, then find a vector $\vec{c}$, such that $\vec{a}\times\vec{c}=\vec{b}$ and $\vec{a}\cdot\vec{c}=3$. **CBSE 2013, 08**

Hints & Solutions

Objective Type Questions

1. (c) Let $\vec{a} = 6\hat{i} - 2\hat{j} + 3\hat{k}$

Magnitude of $\vec{a} = |\vec{a}| = \sqrt{(6)^2 + (-2)^2 + (3)^2}$

$= \sqrt{36 + 4 + 9} = \sqrt{49} = 7$

2. (b) Given, $\vec{a} + \vec{b} = \hat{i}$ and $\vec{a} = 2\hat{i} - 2\hat{j} + 2\hat{k}$

Let $\vec{b} = b_1\hat{i} + b_2\hat{j} + b_3\hat{k}$

Now, $\vec{a} + \vec{b} = \hat{i}$

$\Rightarrow (2\hat{i} - 2\hat{j} + 2\hat{k}) + (b_1\hat{i} + b_2\hat{j} + b_3\hat{k}) = \hat{i} + 0\hat{j} + 0\hat{k}$

$\Rightarrow (2 + b_1)\hat{i} + (-2 + b_2)\hat{j} + (2 + b_3)\hat{k} = \hat{i} + 0\hat{j} + 0\hat{k}$

On comparing the coefficients of $\hat{i}, \hat{j}$ and $\hat{k}$, we get

$2 + b_1 = 1 \Rightarrow b_1 = -1,$

$-2 + b_2 = 0 \Rightarrow b_2 = 2$

and $2 + b_3 = 0 \Rightarrow b_3 = -2$

$\therefore \vec{b} = b_1\hat{i} + b_2\hat{j} + b_3\hat{k} = -\hat{i} + 2\hat{j} - 2\hat{k}$

$|\vec{b}| = \sqrt{(-1)^2 + (2)^2 + (-2)^2} = \sqrt{1 + 4 + 4} = \sqrt{9} = 3$

3. (d) Using the triangle law of vector addition, we have

$\overrightarrow{BC} = \overrightarrow{AC} - \overrightarrow{AB} = (3\hat{i} - \hat{j} + 4\hat{k}) - (\hat{i} + \hat{j} + 2\hat{k}) = 2\hat{i} - 2\hat{j} + 2\hat{k}$

$\therefore \overrightarrow{BD} = \frac{1}{2}\overrightarrow{BC}$ [given]

$= \hat{i} - \hat{j} + \hat{k}$

In ΔABD, using triangle law of vector addition, we have

$\overrightarrow{AD} = \overrightarrow{AB} + \overrightarrow{BD} = (\hat{i} + \hat{j} + 2\hat{k}) + (\hat{i} - \hat{j} + \hat{k}) = 2\hat{i} + 3\hat{k}$

4. (a) We know that diagonals of a rhombus bisect each other.

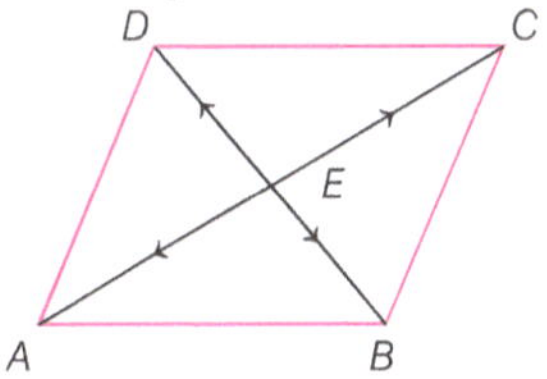

$\therefore |\overrightarrow{EA}| = |\overrightarrow{EC}|$ and $|\overrightarrow{ED}| = |\overrightarrow{EB}|$

$\Rightarrow \overrightarrow{EA} = -\overrightarrow{EC}$ and $\overrightarrow{ED} = -\overrightarrow{EB}$

[$\because$ they are opposite to each other]

$\Rightarrow \overrightarrow{EA} + \overrightarrow{EC} = \vec{0}$ and $\overrightarrow{ED} + \overrightarrow{EB} = \vec{0}$

On adding both the equations, we get

$\overrightarrow{EA} + \overrightarrow{EB} + \overrightarrow{EC} + \overrightarrow{ED} = \vec{0}$

5. (b) We know that two vectors $\vec{a} = a_1\hat{i} + a_2\hat{j} + a_3\hat{k}$ and $\vec{b} = b_1\hat{i} + b_2\hat{j} + b_3\hat{k}$ are collinear, iff $\frac{a_1}{b_1} = \frac{a_2}{b_2} = \frac{a_3}{b_3}$.

6. (b) Let $\vec{a} = 4\hat{i} - 3\hat{k}$

Now, unit vector along $\vec{a}$ is

$\hat{a} = \frac{\vec{a}}{|\vec{a}|} = \frac{4\hat{i} - 3\hat{k}}{\sqrt{(4)^2 + (0)^2 + (-3)^2}} = \frac{4\hat{i} - 3\hat{k}}{\sqrt{16 + 9}}$

$= \frac{4\hat{i} - 3\hat{k}}{\sqrt{25}} = \frac{1}{5}(4\hat{i} - 3\hat{k})$

7. (d) Given points are $P(2, 1, -1)$ and $Q(4, 4, -7)$.

Here, $x_1 = 2, y_1 = 1, z_1 = -1$ and $x_2 = 4, y_2 = 4, z_2 = -7$

So, vector $\overrightarrow{PQ} = (x_2 - x_1)\hat{i} + (y_2 - y_1)\hat{j} + (z_2 - z_1)\hat{k}$

$= (4 - 2)\hat{i} + (4 - 1)\hat{j} + (-7 + 1)\hat{k} = 2\hat{i} + 3\hat{j} - 6\hat{k}$

$\therefore$ Magnitude of given vector

$|\overrightarrow{PQ}| = \sqrt{2^2 + 3^2 + (-6)^2}$

$= \sqrt{4 + 9 + 36} = \sqrt{49} = 7$ units

Hence, the unit vector in the direction of $\overrightarrow{PQ}$ is

$\frac{\overrightarrow{PQ}}{|\overrightarrow{PQ}|} = \frac{2\hat{i} + 3\hat{j} - 6\hat{k}}{7} = \frac{2}{7}\hat{i} + \frac{3}{7}\hat{j} - \frac{6}{7}\hat{k}$

8. (c) Let the required angle be θ.

$\because l = \cos\frac{\pi}{4}, m = \cos\frac{\pi}{4}$ and $n = \cos\theta$

We know that $l^2 + m^2 + n^2 = 1$

$\Rightarrow \cos^2\frac{\pi}{4} + \cos^2\frac{\pi}{4} + \cos^2\theta = 1$

$\Rightarrow \frac{1}{2} + \frac{1}{2} + \cos^2\theta = 1$

$\Rightarrow \cos^2\theta = 0$

$\therefore \theta = \frac{\pi}{2}$

9. (d) Position vector of P, $\overrightarrow{OP} = \vec{p}$

Position vector of Q, $\overrightarrow{OQ} = \vec{q}$

Since, point R divides line segment PQ in the ratio 3 : 1.

$\therefore$ Position vector of point R is

$\overrightarrow{OR} = \frac{3 \cdot \overrightarrow{OQ} + 1 \cdot \overrightarrow{OP}}{3 + 1} = \frac{3\vec{q} + \vec{p}}{4}$

Also, S is the mid-point of line segment PR.

$\therefore$ Position vector of point S is

$\overrightarrow{OS} = \frac{\overrightarrow{OP} + \overrightarrow{OR}}{1 + 1} = \frac{\vec{p} + \frac{3\vec{q} + \vec{p}}{4}}{2}$

$= \frac{4\vec{p} + 3\vec{q} + \vec{p}}{8} = \frac{5\vec{p} + 3\vec{q}}{8}$

10. (b) Given, position vector of the mid-point of line segment $AB = 3\hat{i} + 2\hat{j} - 3\hat{k}$

and position vector of point $A = 2\hat{i} + 3\hat{j} - 4\hat{k}$.

Let M be the mid-point of line segment AB and position vector of B is $(x\hat{i} + y\hat{j} + z\hat{k})$.

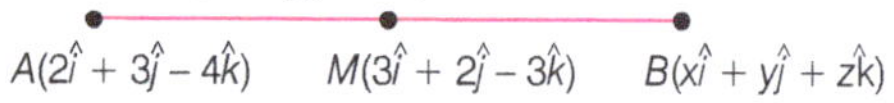

∴ By mid-point of line segment, we have

$$\frac{x+2}{2} = 3 \Rightarrow x + 2 = 6 \Rightarrow x = 4,$$

$$\frac{y+3}{2} = 2 \Rightarrow y + 3 = 4 \Rightarrow y = 1$$

and $$\frac{z-4}{2} = -3 \Rightarrow z - 4 = -6 \Rightarrow z = -2$$

Hence, the position vector of point $B = 4\hat{i} + \hat{j} - 2\hat{k}$.

11. (b) Given, $|\vec{a}| = 2, |\vec{b}| = 3$ and $\vec{a} \cdot \vec{b} = 4$

Now, $|\vec{a} - 2\vec{b}|^2 = (\vec{a} - 2\vec{b}) \cdot (\vec{a} - 2\vec{b})$

$\Rightarrow \quad |\vec{a} - 2\vec{b}|^2 = \vec{a} \cdot \vec{a} - 2\vec{a} \cdot \vec{b} - 2\vec{b} \cdot \vec{a} + 4\vec{b} \cdot \vec{b}$

$= |\vec{a}|^2 - 4\vec{a} \cdot \vec{b} + 4|\vec{b}|^2$

$= (2)^2 - 4(4) + 4(3)^2$

$= 4 - 16 + 36 = 24$

$\Rightarrow \quad |\vec{a} - 2\vec{b}|^2 = 24$

$\therefore \quad |\vec{a} - 2\vec{b}| = \sqrt{24} = 2\sqrt{6}$

12. (a) Let $\vec{a} = 2\hat{i} + p\hat{j} + \hat{k}$ and $\vec{b} = -4\hat{i} - 6\hat{j} + 26\hat{k}$

Given, $\vec{a}$ and $\vec{b}$ are perpendicular.

$\therefore \quad \vec{a} \cdot \vec{b} = 0$

$\Rightarrow (2\hat{i} + p\hat{j} + \hat{k}) \cdot (-4\hat{i} - 6\hat{j} + 26\hat{k}) = 0$

$\Rightarrow \quad (2)(-4) + (p)(-6) + (1)(26) = 0$

$\Rightarrow \quad -8 - 6p + 26 = 0$

$\Rightarrow \quad 6p = 18$

$\therefore \quad p = 3$

13. (b) Vector component of $\vec{a}$ along $\vec{b}$ is $\dfrac{(\vec{a} \cdot \vec{b})}{|b|}\hat{b}$

$$\Rightarrow \quad (4\hat{i} + 6\hat{j}) \cdot (3\hat{j} + 4\hat{k}) \frac{(3\hat{j} + 4\hat{k})}{|\sqrt{3^2 + 4^2}|^2} = \frac{18}{25}(3\hat{j} + 4\hat{k})$$

14. (d) Let $\vec{a} = 2\hat{i} - \hat{j} + 2\hat{k}$ and $\vec{b} = 3\hat{i} + \lambda\hat{j} + \hat{k}$

Now, $\vec{a} \perp \vec{b}$, then

$\Rightarrow \quad \vec{a} \cdot \vec{b} = 0$

$\Rightarrow \quad (2\hat{i} - \hat{j} + 2\hat{k}) \cdot (3\hat{i} + \lambda\hat{j} + \hat{k}) = 0$

$\Rightarrow \quad 6 - \lambda + 2 = 0$

$\therefore \quad \lambda = 8$

15. (b) We have, $\vec{a} \cdot \hat{i} = \vec{a} \cdot (\hat{i} + \hat{j}) = \vec{a} \cdot (\hat{i} + \hat{j} + \hat{k}) = 1$

Let $\vec{a} = a_1\hat{i} + a_2\hat{j} + a_3\hat{k}$ ...(i)

Now, $\quad \vec{a} \cdot \hat{i} = 1$

$\Rightarrow \quad (a_1\hat{i} + a_2\hat{j} + a_3\hat{k}) \cdot \hat{i} = 1 \Rightarrow a_1 = 1$ ...(ii)

$\vec{a} \cdot (\hat{i} + \hat{j}) = 1$

$\Rightarrow \quad (a_1\hat{i} + a_2\hat{j} + a_3\hat{k}) \cdot (\hat{i} + \hat{j}) = 1 \Rightarrow a_1 + a_2 = 1$

$\Rightarrow \quad 1 + a_2 = 1$ [∵ from Eq. (ii)]

$\Rightarrow \quad a_2 = 0$ ...(iii)

and $\quad \vec{a} \cdot (\hat{i} + \hat{j} + \hat{k}) = 1$

$\Rightarrow \quad (a_1\hat{i} + a_2\hat{j} + a_3\hat{k}) \cdot (\hat{i} + \hat{j} + \hat{k}) = 1$

$\Rightarrow \quad a_1 + a_2 + a_3 = 1$

$\Rightarrow \quad 1 + 0 + a_3 = 1$ [from Eqs. (ii) and (iii)]

$\Rightarrow \quad a_3 = 0$

Now, on putting the values of a_1, a_2 and a_3 from Eqs. (ii), (iii) and (iv) in Eq. (i), we get

$$\vec{a} = (1)\hat{i} + 0\hat{j} + 0\hat{k} = \hat{i}$$

16. (c) Given, $\vec{a} = \hat{i} - 2\hat{j} + 3\hat{k}, \vec{a} \cdot \vec{b} = |\vec{b}|^2$ and $|\vec{a} - \vec{b}| = \sqrt{7}$

Now, $\quad |\vec{a} - \vec{b}| = \sqrt{7}$

$\Rightarrow \quad |\vec{a} - \vec{b}|^2 = (\sqrt{7})^2$

$\Rightarrow \quad (\vec{a} - \vec{b})(\vec{a} - \vec{b}) = 7$

$\Rightarrow \quad \vec{a} \cdot \vec{a} - \vec{a} \cdot \vec{b} - \vec{a} \cdot \vec{b} + \vec{b} \cdot \vec{b} = 7$

$\Rightarrow \quad |\vec{a}|^2 - 2\vec{a} \cdot \vec{b} + |\vec{b}|^2 = 7$

$\Rightarrow \quad |\vec{a}|^2 - 2|\vec{b}|^2 + |\vec{b}|^2 = 7$

$\Rightarrow \quad |\vec{a}|^2 - |\vec{b}|^2 = 7$

$\Rightarrow \quad |\vec{b}|^2 = |\vec{a}|^2 - 7$

$\Rightarrow \quad |\vec{b}|^2 = (\sqrt{(1)^2 + (-2)^2 + (3)^2})^2 - 7$

$= (\sqrt{14})^2 - 7 = 14 - 7$

$\Rightarrow \quad |\vec{b}|^2 = 7$

$\therefore \quad |\vec{b}| = \sqrt{7}$

17. (a) Given, projection of $\vec{a}$ on $\vec{b}$ is 0.

$$\therefore \quad \frac{\vec{a} \cdot \vec{b}}{|\vec{b}|} = 0 \Rightarrow \vec{a} \cdot \vec{b} = 0$$

Now, let θ be the angle between the two vectors.

Then, $\quad \cos\theta = \dfrac{\vec{a} \cdot \vec{b}}{|\vec{a}| \cdot |\vec{b}|} = 0$

$\Rightarrow \quad \cos\theta = \cos\dfrac{\pi}{2} \Rightarrow \theta = \dfrac{\pi}{2}$

18. (b) We have, $\vec{a}\cdot\vec{b}\geq 0$

$\Rightarrow \quad |\vec{a}||\vec{b}|\cos\theta \geq 0 \Rightarrow \cos\theta \geq 0$

$\therefore \quad 0 \leq \theta \leq \frac{\pi}{2}$

19. (b) Given, $\vec{a} = 2\hat{i} - 3\hat{j} - 6\hat{k}$ and $\vec{b} = 2\hat{i} + 2\hat{j} + \hat{k}$

We know, projection of $\vec{a}$ on $\vec{b} = \frac{\vec{a}\cdot\vec{b}}{|\vec{b}|}$

$$= \frac{(2\hat{i} - 3\hat{j} - 6\hat{k})\cdot(2\hat{i} + 2\hat{j} + \hat{k})}{\sqrt{2^2 + 2^2 + (-1)^2}}$$

$$= \frac{4 - 6 - 6}{\sqrt{4 + 4 + 1}} = \frac{-8}{3}$$

and projection of $\vec{b}$ on $\vec{a} = \frac{\vec{b}\cdot\vec{a}}{|\vec{a}|}$

$$= \frac{(2\hat{i} + 2\hat{j} + \hat{k})\cdot(2\hat{i} - 3\hat{j} - 6\hat{k})}{\sqrt{2^2 + (-3)^2 + (-6)^2}}$$

$$= \frac{4 - 6 - 6}{\sqrt{4 + 9 + 36}} = \frac{-8}{\sqrt{49}} = \frac{-8}{7}$$

Now, $\frac{\text{Projection of } \vec{a} \text{ on } \vec{b}}{\text{Projection of } \vec{b} \text{ on } \vec{a}} = \frac{\frac{-8}{3}}{\frac{-8}{7}} = \frac{7}{3}$

20. (c) Given, $\hat{i}, \hat{j}$ and $\hat{k}$ are unit vectors.

$\therefore \quad \hat{i}\cdot\hat{j} = 1 \times 1 \times \cos 90° = 0$

$\hat{i} \times \hat{j} = 1 \times 1 \times \sin 90° \hat{k} = \hat{k}$

$\hat{i}\cdot\hat{k} = 1 \times 1 \times \cos 90° = 0$

$\hat{i} \times \hat{k} = 1 \times 1 \times \sin 90° \hat{j} = \hat{j}$

21. (a) Given vectors are $\vec{a} = 3\hat{i} + \hat{j} + 2\hat{k}$ and $\vec{b} = \hat{i} + \hat{j} + 2\hat{k}$.

Let θ be the angle between the vectors $\vec{a}$ and $\vec{b}$, then

$\sin\theta = \frac{|\vec{a}\times\vec{b}|}{|\vec{a}||\vec{b}|}$.

$$\vec{a}\times\vec{b} = \begin{vmatrix} \hat{i} & \hat{j} & \hat{k} \\ 3 & 1 & 2 \\ 1 & 1 & 2 \end{vmatrix}$$

$$= \hat{i}(2-2) - \hat{j}(6-2) + \hat{k}(3-1) = -4\hat{j} + 2\hat{k}$$

$|\vec{a}\times\vec{b}| = \sqrt{(-4)^2 + (2)^2} = \sqrt{20}$

$\therefore \quad \sin\theta = \frac{\sqrt{20}}{\sqrt{14}\sqrt{6}}$

$$= \frac{(2\times\sqrt{5})}{(\sqrt{2}\times\sqrt{7})\times(\sqrt{2}\times\sqrt{3})}$$

$$= \frac{\sqrt{5}}{\sqrt{21}} = \sqrt{\frac{5}{21}}$$

22. (b) Given, the angle between the vectors $\vec{a}$ and $\vec{b}$ is $\frac{\pi}{4}$ and $|\vec{a}\times\vec{b}| = 1$.

We know that $\sin\theta = \frac{|\vec{a}\times\vec{b}|}{|\vec{a}||\vec{b}|}$

$\Rightarrow \quad \sin\frac{\pi}{4} = \frac{1}{|\vec{a}||\vec{b}|} \Rightarrow |\vec{a}|\cdot|\vec{b}| = \sqrt{2} \quad \ldots(i)$

and $\quad \cos\theta = \frac{\vec{a}\cdot\vec{b}}{|\vec{a}||\vec{b}|}$

$\Rightarrow \quad \vec{a}\cdot\vec{b} = |\vec{a}||\vec{b}|\cos\frac{\pi}{4} = \sqrt{2}\cdot\frac{1}{\sqrt{2}}$ [using Eq. (i)]

$= 1$

23. (a) We have, $|\vec{a}\cdot\vec{b}| = |\vec{a}\times\vec{b}|$

$|\vec{a}|\cdot|\vec{b}|\cos\theta = |\vec{a}|\cdot|\vec{b}|\sin\theta$

$\Rightarrow \quad \cos\theta = \sin\theta$

$\Rightarrow \quad \tan\theta = 1$

$\therefore \quad \theta = \frac{\pi}{4}$

24. (d) We have, $(\hat{i}\times\hat{j})\cdot\hat{j} + (\hat{j}\times\hat{i})\cdot\hat{k} = (\hat{k}\cdot\hat{j}) + (-\hat{k})\cdot(\hat{k})$

$\Rightarrow \quad = 0 - 1 = -1$

25. (d) Let $\vec{a} = a_1\hat{i} + a_2\hat{j} + a_3\hat{k}$

$|\vec{a}| = \sqrt{a_1^2 + a_2^2 + a_3^2}$

$\Rightarrow \quad |\vec{a}|^2 = a_1^2 + a_2^2 + a_3^2 \quad \ldots(i)$

Now, $(\vec{a}\times\hat{i})^2 + (\vec{a}\times\hat{j})^2 + (\vec{a}\times\hat{k})^2$

$$= [(a_1\hat{i} + a_2\hat{j} + a_3\hat{k})\times\hat{i}]^2 + [(a_1\hat{i} + a_2\hat{j} + a_3\hat{k})\times\hat{j}]^2 + [(a_1\hat{i} + a_2\hat{j} + a_3\hat{k})\times\hat{k}]^2$$

$$= (-a_2\hat{k} + a_3\hat{j})^2 + (a_1\hat{k} - a_3\hat{i})^2 + (-a_1\hat{j} + a_2\hat{i})^2$$

$$= a_2^2 + a_3^2 + a_1^2 + a_3^2 + a_1^2 + a_2^2$$

$$= 2a_1^2 + 2a_2^2 + 2a_3^2$$

$$= 2(a_1^2 + a_2^2 + a_3^2)$$

$$= 2|\vec{a}|^2 = 2\vec{a}^2$$

26. (b) $\because$ The area of the parallelogram with adjacent sides AB and AC is given by $|\overrightarrow{AB}\times\overrightarrow{AC}|$.

Hence, the area of the triangle with vertices A, B and C is given by $\frac{1}{2}|\overrightarrow{AB}\times\overrightarrow{AC}|$.

27. (a) Yes, sum of two vectors can be zero,

$$\vec{b} + (-\vec{b}) = 0$$

Assertion and Reason both are correct and Reason is the correct explanation of Assertion.

28. (a) We have, $\vec{a} = \hat{i} - 2\hat{j} + 3\hat{k}$

$$\therefore \quad |\vec{a}| = \sqrt{(1)^2 + (-2)^2 + (3)^2} = \sqrt{1+4+9} = \sqrt{14}$$

Thus, direction cosines are $\frac{1}{\sqrt{14}}, \frac{-2}{\sqrt{14}}, \frac{3}{\sqrt{14}}$.

Hence, Assertion and Reason both are correct and Reason is the correct explanation of Assertion.

29. (a) $\cos^2\alpha + \cos^2\beta + \cos^2\gamma = 1$

$$\frac{1+\cos 2\alpha}{2} + \frac{1+\cos 2\beta}{2} + \frac{1+\cos 2\gamma}{2} = 1$$

$$\Rightarrow \quad \cos 2\alpha + \cos 2\beta + \cos 2\gamma = -1$$

Hence, Assertion and Reason both are correct and Reason is the correct explanation of Assertion.

30. (a) Given vectors are $\vec{a} = 6\hat{i} + 2\hat{j} - 8\hat{k}$,

$$\vec{b} = 10\hat{i} - 2\hat{j} - 6\hat{k} \text{ and } \vec{c} = 4\hat{i} - 4\hat{j} + 2\hat{k}$$

If these three vectors forms right angled triangle, then they satisfy the Pythagoras theorem.

i.e. $\vec{c}^2 = \vec{a}^2 + \vec{b}^2$ or $\vec{a}^2 = \vec{c}^2 + \vec{b}^2$ or $\vec{b}^2 = \vec{a}^2 + \vec{c}^2$

Now, $|\vec{a}| = \sqrt{6^2 + 2^2 + (-8)^2}$

$$= \sqrt{36+4+64} = \sqrt{104} = 2\sqrt{26}$$

$$|\vec{b}| = \sqrt{10^2 + (-2)^2 + (-6)^2}$$

$$= \sqrt{100+4+36} = \sqrt{140} = 2\sqrt{35}$$

$$|\vec{c}| = \sqrt{4^2 + (-4)^2 + 2^2}$$

$$= \sqrt{16+16+4} = \sqrt{36} = 6$$

Here, $\vec{a} + \vec{c} = \vec{b}$

Thus, they represent the sides of triangle.

Also, $|\vec{a}|^2 + |\vec{c}|^2 = |\vec{b}|^2$

Hence, the given vectors form a right angled triangle.

$\therefore$ Assertion and Reason both are correct and Reason is the correct explanation of Assertion.

31. (a) Given, $\vec{a}$ and $\vec{b}$ are unit vectors.

$$\therefore \quad |\vec{a}| = 1 \text{ and } |\vec{b}| = 1$$

Also given, $|\vec{a} + \vec{b}| = \sqrt{3}$

$$\Rightarrow \quad |\vec{a} + \vec{b}|^2 = 3$$

$$\Rightarrow \quad |\vec{a}|^2 + |\vec{b}|^2 + 2(\vec{a}\cdot\vec{b}) = 3$$

$$\Rightarrow \quad 1 + 1 + 2\vec{a}\cdot\vec{b} = 3$$

$$\Rightarrow \quad 2(a\cdot\vec{b}) = 1$$

$$\Rightarrow \quad \vec{a}\cdot\vec{b} = \frac{1}{2} \Rightarrow |\vec{a}||\vec{b}|\cos\theta = \frac{1}{2}$$

$$\Rightarrow \quad \cos\theta = \frac{1}{2} \Rightarrow \theta = \pi/3$$

Hence, Assertion and Reason both are correct and Reason is the correct explanation of Assertion.

32. (d) We have, $|2\vec{a} + \vec{b}| = |2\vec{a} - \vec{b}|$

$$\Rightarrow \quad |2\vec{a} + \vec{b}|^2 = |2\vec{a} - \vec{b}|^2$$

$$\Rightarrow \quad 4|\vec{a}|^2 + |\vec{b}|^2 + 4\vec{a}\cdot\vec{b} = 4|\vec{a}|^2 + |\vec{b}|^2 - 4\vec{a}\cdot\vec{b}$$

$$\Rightarrow \quad 8\vec{a}\cdot\vec{b} = 0 \Rightarrow \vec{a}\cdot\vec{b} = 0$$

$\Rightarrow$ $\vec{a}$ is perpendicular to $\vec{b}$.

Thus, Assertion is incorrect but Reason is correct.

33. (b) Given, $\vec{a} = 2\hat{i} - 2\hat{j} + 3\hat{k}$ and $\vec{b} = \hat{i} - \hat{j} + 2\hat{k}$

$$\therefore \quad \vec{a}\cdot\vec{b} = (2\hat{i} - 2\hat{j} + 3\hat{k})\cdot(\hat{i} - \hat{j} + 2\hat{k})$$

$$= (2)(1) + (-2)(-1) + (3)(2) = 2 + 2 + 6 = 10$$

Thus, Assertion and Reason both are correct but Reason is not the correct explanation of Assertion.

34. (c) Given, $\vec{a} = 2\hat{i} + 3\hat{j} + 2\hat{k}$ and $\vec{b} = \hat{i} + 2\hat{j} + \hat{k}$

Now, $|\vec{b}| = \sqrt{(1)^2 + (2)^2 + (1)^2} = \sqrt{1+4+1} = \sqrt{6}$

and $\vec{a}\cdot\vec{b} = (2\hat{i} + 3\hat{j} + 2\hat{k})\cdot(\hat{i} + 2\hat{j} + \hat{k})$

$$= (2)(1) + (3)(2) + (2)(1)$$

$$= 2 + 6 + 2 = 10$$

$$\therefore \text{Projection of } \vec{a} \text{ on } \vec{b} = \frac{\vec{a}\cdot\vec{b}}{|\vec{b}|} = \frac{10}{\sqrt{6}} = \frac{10}{\sqrt{6}} \times \frac{\sqrt{6}}{\sqrt{6}} = \frac{5}{3}\sqrt{6}$$

Thus, Assertion is correct but Reason is incorrect.

35. (d) Let $\vec{a} = \hat{i} - 2\hat{j} + 3\hat{k}$ and $\vec{b} = \hat{i} + 2\hat{j} - \hat{k}$

$$\vec{a} \times \vec{b} = \begin{vmatrix} \hat{i} & \hat{j} & \hat{k} \\ 1 & -2 & 3 \\ 1 & 2 & -1 \end{vmatrix}$$

$$= \hat{i}(2-6) - \hat{j}(-1-3) + \hat{k}(2+2)$$

$$= -4\hat{i} + 4\hat{j} + 4\hat{k}$$

Unit vector perpendicular to the given vector

$$= \frac{\vec{a}\times\vec{b}}{|\vec{a}\times\vec{b}|} = \frac{-4\hat{i} + 4\hat{j} + 4\hat{k}}{\sqrt{16+16+16}} = \frac{1}{\sqrt{3}}(-\hat{i} + \hat{j} + \hat{k})$$

Thus, Assertion is incorrect but Reason is correct.

36. (a) Given, $\vec{a} = 3\hat{i} + 4\hat{j}$ and $\vec{b} = -5\hat{i} + 7\hat{j}$

We know that if $\vec{a}$ and $\vec{b}$ are any two adjacent sides.

Then, area of triangle $= \frac{1}{2}|\vec{a} \times \vec{b}|$

$$\text{Now,} \quad \vec{a} \times \vec{b} = \begin{vmatrix} \hat{i} & \hat{j} & \hat{k} \\ 3 & 4 & 0 \\ -5 & 7 & 0 \end{vmatrix}$$

$$= 0\hat{i} - \hat{j}(0) + \hat{k}(21+20) = 41\hat{k}$$

$$\therefore \quad \text{Area} = \frac{1}{2}|\vec{a} \times \vec{b}| = \frac{41}{2} \text{ sq units}$$

Hence, Assertion and Reason both are correct and Reason is the correct explanation of Assertion.

37. (i) Let $\overrightarrow{OA} = 8\hat{i}$ and $\overrightarrow{AB} = 6\hat{j}$

$\therefore \quad \overrightarrow{OB} = \overrightarrow{OA} + \overrightarrow{AB} = 8\hat{i} + 6\hat{j}$

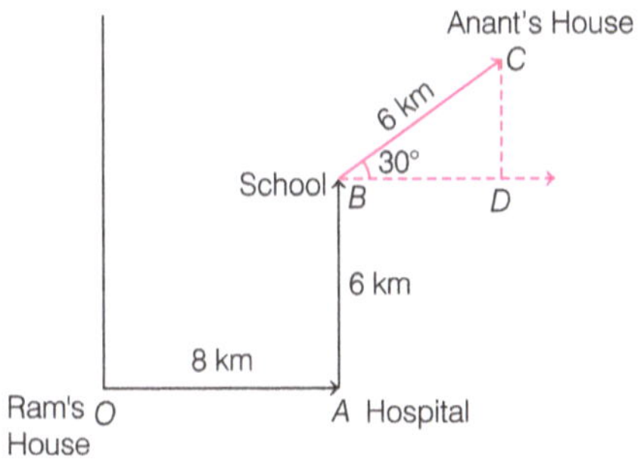

(ii) Distance from Ram's house to school = 8 + 6 = 14 km

(iii) Let a point D such that $\overrightarrow{CD} \perp \overrightarrow{BD}$

$$\overrightarrow{BD} = 6\cos 30° \text{ and } \overrightarrow{DC} = 6\sin 30°$$

Vector distance from school to Anant's house

$$\overrightarrow{BC} = \overrightarrow{BD} + \overrightarrow{DC} = 6\cos 30°\,\hat{i} + 6\sin 30°\,\hat{j}$$
$$= \frac{6\sqrt{3}}{2}\hat{i} + \frac{6}{2}\hat{j}$$
$$= 3\sqrt{3}\,\hat{i} + 3\hat{j}$$

(iv) Vector distance from Ram's house to Anant's house

$$\overrightarrow{OC} = \overrightarrow{OB} + \overrightarrow{BC} = (8\hat{i} + 6\hat{j}) + (3\sqrt{3}\hat{i} + 3\hat{j})$$
$$= (8 + 3\sqrt{3})\,\hat{i} + 9\hat{j}$$

(v) Distance between Ram's house to Anant's house

$$= OA + AB + BC = 8 + 6 + 6 = 20 \text{ km}$$

38. (i) Given position vectors of some stars

$A(2\hat{i} + 3\hat{j} + 4\hat{k}), B(5\hat{i} + 6\hat{j} + 8\hat{k}), C(8\hat{i} + 9\hat{j} + 12\hat{k})$ and $D(2\hat{i} + 3\hat{j} - 6\hat{k})$

Now, $\quad \overrightarrow{AB} = \overrightarrow{OB} - \overrightarrow{OA} = 3\hat{i} + 3\hat{j} + 4\hat{k}$

$\qquad \overrightarrow{AC} = \overrightarrow{OC} - \overrightarrow{OA} = 6\hat{i} + 6\hat{j} + 8\hat{k}$

We know that vectors $\vec{a} = a_1\hat{i} + a_2\hat{j} + a_3\hat{k}$ and $\vec{b} = b_1\hat{i} + b_2\hat{j} + b_3\hat{k}$ are collinear, if $\frac{b_1}{a_1} = \frac{b_2}{a_2} = \frac{b_3}{a_3}$

$\therefore \quad \frac{3}{6} = \frac{3}{6} = \frac{4}{8} = \frac{1}{2}$

Hence, $\overrightarrow{AC} = 2\,\overrightarrow{AB}$

Therefore, position vectors A, B and C are collinear.

(ii) The vector $\overrightarrow{AD}$ in component form as

$$\overrightarrow{AD} = \overrightarrow{OD} - \overrightarrow{OA} = 0\hat{i} - 0\hat{j} - 10\hat{k}$$

Now, distance between A and D

$$= \sqrt{0^2 + 0^2 + (-10)^2} = \sqrt{100} = 10 \text{ light years}$$

(iii) Let a star at a certain position P be inclined at angles of 45° and 60° with positive direction of X-axis and Y-axis, respectively.

Let l, m and n be the direction cosines of the stars with respect to X-axis, Y-axis and Z-axis, respectively.

Then, $l = \cos 45° = \frac{1}{\sqrt{2}}$

$\qquad m = \cos 60° = \frac{1}{2}$

We know that $\quad l^2 + m^2 + n^2 = 1$

$$\Rightarrow \quad \left(\frac{1}{\sqrt{2}}\right)^2 + \left(\frac{1}{2}\right)^2 + n^2 = 1$$
$$\Rightarrow \quad \frac{1}{2} + \frac{1}{4} + n^2 = 1 \Rightarrow \frac{3}{4} + n^2 = 1$$
$$\Rightarrow \quad n^2 = \frac{1}{4} \Rightarrow n = \pm\frac{1}{2}$$

Now, the position vector of the star is

$$\overrightarrow{OP} = |\overrightarrow{OP}|(l\hat{i} + m\hat{j} + n\hat{k}) = 2\left(\frac{1}{\sqrt{2}}\hat{i} + \frac{1}{2}\hat{j} \pm \frac{1}{2}\hat{k}\right)$$

$\overrightarrow{OP} = (\sqrt{2}\,\hat{i} + \hat{j} \pm \hat{k}) \qquad [\because |\overrightarrow{OP}| = 2 \text{ (given)}]$

39. Given, $\vec{F_1} = 6\hat{i} + 0\hat{j}\,kN$

$\therefore \quad |\vec{F_1}| = \sqrt{6^2 + 0^2} = 6\,kN$

$\qquad \vec{F_2} = -4\hat{i} + 4\hat{j}\,kN$

$\therefore \quad |\vec{F_2}| = \sqrt{(-4)^2 + 4^2} = 4\sqrt{2}\,kN$

$\qquad \vec{F_3} = -3\hat{i} - 3\hat{j}\,kN$

$\Rightarrow \quad |\vec{F_3}| = \sqrt{(-3)^2 + (-3)^2} = 3\sqrt{2}\,kN$

(i) Magnitude of force of team $A = |\vec{F_1}| = 6\,kN$

(ii) Since, magnitude of force of team A is greater than other teams, therefore team A will win the game.

(iii) Resultant force,

$$\vec{F} = \vec{F_1} + \vec{F_2} + \vec{F_3} = (6\hat{i} + 0\hat{j}) + (-4\hat{i} + 4\hat{j}) + (-3\hat{i} - 3\hat{j})$$
$$\vec{F} = (-\hat{i} + \hat{j})\,kN$$
$$\Rightarrow |\vec{F}| = \sqrt{(-1)^2 + (1)^2} = \sqrt{2}\,kN$$

Or

Resultant force, $\vec{F} = -\hat{i} + \hat{j}$

Let $\vec{F}$ makes an angle θ with the X-axis, then its direction cosine along X-axis is $\cos\theta$.

$\therefore \cos\theta = \frac{f_x}{\sqrt{f_x^2 + f_y^2}}$ (where f_x and f_y are direction ratios along X-axis and Y-axis, respectively)

$$\cos\theta = \frac{-1}{\sqrt{(-1)^2 + (1)^2}} = \frac{-1}{\sqrt{2}}$$

$$\Rightarrow \quad \theta = \cos^{-1}\left(\frac{-1}{\sqrt{2}}\right) \Rightarrow \theta = \pi - \frac{\pi}{4} = \frac{3\pi}{4},$$

where θ is the angle made by the resultant force with the '+ ve' direction of the X-axis.

Subjective Questions

1. Given vectors,

$$\vec{a} = 4\hat{i} - \hat{j} + \hat{k} \text{ and } \vec{b} = 2\hat{i} - 2\hat{j} + \hat{k}$$

Now, $\vec{a} + \vec{b} = (4\hat{i} - \hat{j} + \hat{k}) + (2\hat{i} - 2\hat{j} + \hat{k}) = 6\hat{i} - 3\hat{j} + 2\hat{k}$

and $|\vec{a} + \vec{b}| = \sqrt{(6)^2 + (-3)^2 + (2)^2}$

$= \sqrt{36 + 9 + 4}$

$= \sqrt{49} = 7$ units

$\therefore$ The unit vector parallel to the vector $\vec{a} + \vec{b}$ is

$$\frac{\vec{a} + \vec{b}}{|\vec{a} + \vec{b}|} = \frac{6\hat{i} - 3\hat{j} + 2\hat{k}}{7}$$

2. Given, $\overrightarrow{AB} = \hat{j} + \hat{k}$ and $\overrightarrow{AC} = 3\hat{i} - \hat{j} + 4\hat{k}$

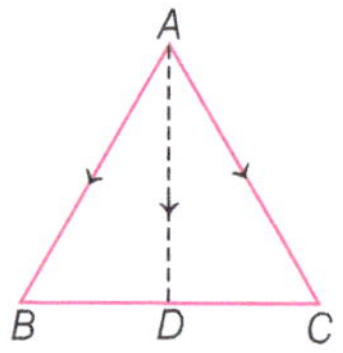

Clearly, median vector, $\overrightarrow{AD} = \dfrac{\overrightarrow{AB} + \overrightarrow{AC}}{2}$

$= \dfrac{(\hat{j} + \hat{k}) + (3\hat{i} - \hat{j} + 4\hat{k})}{2}$

$= \dfrac{3\hat{i} + 5\hat{k}}{2}$

Now, length of median $= |\overrightarrow{AD}|$

$= \sqrt{\left(\dfrac{3}{2}\right)^2 + \left(\dfrac{5}{2}\right)^2} = \dfrac{1}{2}\sqrt{9 + 25} = \dfrac{\sqrt{34}}{2}$

$= \dfrac{\sqrt{17} \times \sqrt{2}}{2} = \sqrt{\dfrac{17}{2}}$ units

3. Given, $3\hat{i} + 2\hat{j} + 9\hat{k}$ and $\hat{i} - 2p\hat{j} + 3\hat{k}$ are two parallel vectors, so their direction ratios will be proportional.

$\therefore \quad \dfrac{3}{1} = \dfrac{2}{-2p} = \dfrac{9}{3} \Rightarrow \dfrac{2}{-2p} = \dfrac{3}{1}$

$\Rightarrow -6p = 2 \Rightarrow p = \dfrac{2}{-6} \Rightarrow p = -\dfrac{1}{3}$

4. Let $\vec{a} = \hat{i} + \hat{j} + \hat{k}$

Now, unit vector in the direction of $\vec{a}$ is

$$\hat{a} = \frac{\vec{a}}{|\vec{a}|} = \frac{\hat{i} + \hat{j} + \hat{k}}{\sqrt{1^2 + 1^2 + 1^2}}$$

$\Rightarrow \quad \hat{a} = \dfrac{\hat{i} + \hat{j} + \hat{k}}{\sqrt{3}}$

$\Rightarrow \quad \hat{a} = \dfrac{1}{\sqrt{3}}\hat{i} + \dfrac{1}{\sqrt{3}}\hat{j} + \dfrac{1}{\sqrt{3}}\hat{k}$

So, angle between X-axis and the vector

$\hat{i} + \hat{j} + \hat{k}$ is $\cos\alpha = \dfrac{1}{\sqrt{3}} \Rightarrow \alpha = \cos^{-1}\left(\dfrac{1}{\sqrt{3}}\right)$

[$\because \hat{a} = l\hat{i} + m\hat{j} + n\hat{k}$ and $\cos\alpha = l \Rightarrow \alpha = \cos^{-1} l$]

5. Given, $\vec{a} = \hat{i} + \hat{j} - 2\hat{k}$ and $\vec{b} = 2\hat{i} - 4\hat{j} + 5\hat{k}$

Now, $3\vec{a} + 2\vec{b} = 3(\hat{i} + \hat{j} - 2\hat{k}) + 2(2\hat{i} - 4\hat{j} + 5\hat{k})$

$= 3\hat{i} + 3\hat{j} - 6\hat{k} + 4\hat{i} - 8\hat{j} + 10\hat{k}$

$= 7\hat{i} - 5\hat{j} + 4\hat{k}$

Therefore, direction ratios of $3\vec{a} + 2\vec{b}$ are $7, -5, 4$.

6. Given, $\vec{a} = \hat{i} + \hat{j} + \hat{k}$

Now, unit vector in the direction of $\vec{a}$ is

$$\hat{a} = \frac{\vec{a}}{|\vec{a}|} = \frac{\hat{i} + \hat{j} + \hat{k}}{\sqrt{(1)^2 + (1)^2 + (1)^2}}$$

$= \dfrac{\hat{i} + \hat{j} + \hat{k}}{\sqrt{3}} = \dfrac{1}{\sqrt{3}}\hat{i} + \dfrac{1}{\sqrt{3}}\hat{j} + \dfrac{1}{\sqrt{3}}\hat{k}$

$\therefore$ Cosine of the angle which given vector makes with Y-axis is $\dfrac{1}{\sqrt{3}}$.

7. Given, $A = \begin{bmatrix} l_1 & m_1 & n_1 \\ l_2 & m_2 & n_2 \\ l_3 & m_3 & n_3 \end{bmatrix}$, then $A' = \begin{bmatrix} l_1 & l_2 & l_3 \\ m_1 & m_2 & m_3 \\ n_1 & n_2 & n_3 \end{bmatrix}$

Also given, l_i, m_i, n_i; $(i = 1, 2, 3)$ are direction cosines of mutually perpendicular vectors, so

$l_i^2 + m_i^2 + n_i^2 = \Sigma l_i^2 = 1$, for each $i = 1, 2, 3$ ...(i)

and $l_i l_j + m_i m_j + n_i n_j = \Sigma l_i l_j = 0 \, (i \neq j)$ for each $i, j = 1, 2, 3$ ...(ii)

Now, $AA' = \begin{bmatrix} l_1 & m_1 & n_1 \\ l_2 & m_2 & n_2 \\ l_3 & m_3 & n_3 \end{bmatrix} \begin{bmatrix} l_1 & l_2 & l_3 \\ m_1 & m_2 & m_3 \\ n_1 & n_2 & n_3 \end{bmatrix}$

$= \begin{bmatrix} \Sigma l_i^2 & \Sigma l_i l_j & \Sigma l_i l_j \\ \Sigma l_i l_j & \Sigma l_i^2 & \Sigma l_i l_j \\ \Sigma l_i l_j & \Sigma l_i l_j & \Sigma l_i^2 \end{bmatrix}$

$= \begin{bmatrix} 1 & 0 & 0 \\ 0 & 1 & 0 \\ 0 & 0 & 1 \end{bmatrix}$ [using Eqs. (i) and (ii)]

$= I_3$

8. Given points are $P(1, 3, 0)$ and $Q(4, 5, 6)$.

Here, $x_1 = 1, y_1 = 3, z_1 = 0$ and $x_2 = 4, y_2 = 5, z_2 = 6$

So, vector $\overrightarrow{PQ} = (x_2 - x_1)\hat{i} + (y_2 - y_1)\hat{j} + (z_2 - z_1)\hat{k}$

$= (4 - 1)\hat{i} + (5 - 3)\hat{j} + (6 - 0)\hat{k}$

$= 3\hat{i} + 2\hat{j} + 6\hat{k}$

$\therefore$ Magnitude of given vector

$|\overrightarrow{PQ}| = \sqrt{3^2 + 2^2 + 6^2} = \sqrt{9 + 4 + 36} = \sqrt{49} = 7$ units

Hence, the unit vector in the direction of $\overrightarrow{PQ}$ is

$$\frac{\overrightarrow{PQ}}{|\overrightarrow{PQ}|}=\frac{3\hat{i}+2\hat{j}+6\hat{k}}{7}=\frac{3}{7}\hat{i}+\frac{2}{7}\hat{j}+\frac{6}{7}\hat{k}$$

9. Given position vectors are $\overrightarrow{OL}=2\vec{a}-\vec{b}$ and $\overrightarrow{OM}=\vec{a}+2\vec{b}$.

Now, $\overrightarrow{ON}$ is the position vector of point N, which divides the join of points, with position vectors $\overrightarrow{OL}$ and $\overrightarrow{OM}$, externally in the ratio 2 : 1.

$$\therefore \quad \overrightarrow{ON}=\frac{2\overrightarrow{OM}-1\overrightarrow{OL}}{2-1} \quad \text{[by external section formula]}$$

$$=\frac{2(\vec{a}+2\vec{b})-(2\vec{a}-\vec{b})}{1}$$

$$=2\vec{a}+4\vec{b}-2\vec{a}+\vec{b}=5\vec{b}$$

10. Given, $\vec{a}$ is a unit vector.

$$\therefore \quad |\vec{a}|=1$$

Now, $(\vec{x}-\vec{a})\cdot(\vec{x}+\vec{a})=15$

$$\Rightarrow \quad |\vec{x}|^2-\vec{a}\cdot\vec{x}+\vec{a}\cdot\vec{x}-|\vec{a}|^2=15$$

$$\Rightarrow \quad |\vec{x}|^2-1=15$$

$$\Rightarrow \quad |\vec{x}|^2=16$$

$$\therefore \quad |\vec{x}|=4$$

11. Let $\vec{a}=\hat{i}+2\lambda\hat{j}+\hat{k}$ and $\vec{b}=2\hat{i}+\hat{j}-3\hat{k}$

Given, $\vec{a}$ and $\vec{b}$ are perpendicular.

$$\therefore \quad \vec{a}\cdot\vec{b}=0$$

$$\Rightarrow \quad (\hat{i}+2\lambda\hat{j}+\hat{k})\cdot(2\hat{i}+\hat{j}-3\hat{k})=0$$

$$\Rightarrow \quad (1)(2)+(2\lambda)(1)+(1)(-3)=0$$

$$\Rightarrow \quad 2+2\lambda-3=0$$

$$\Rightarrow \quad 2\lambda=1$$

$$\therefore \quad \lambda=\frac{1}{2}$$

12. Given, $\vec{a}=\lambda\hat{i}+\hat{j}+4\hat{k}$ and $\vec{b}=2\hat{i}+6\hat{j}+3\hat{k}$

Also given, projection of $\vec{a}$ on $\vec{b}=4$

$$\Rightarrow \quad \frac{\vec{a}\cdot\vec{b}}{|\vec{b}|}=4$$

$$\Rightarrow \quad \frac{(\lambda\hat{i}+\hat{j}+4\hat{k})\cdot(2\hat{i}+6\hat{j}+3\hat{k})}{\sqrt{4+36+9}}=4$$

$$\Rightarrow \quad \frac{2\lambda+6+12}{7}=4$$

$$\Rightarrow \quad 2\lambda+18=28$$

$$\Rightarrow \quad 2\lambda=10$$

$$\therefore \quad \lambda=5$$

13. Given, $\quad |\vec{a}+\vec{b}|=|\vec{a}|$

$$\Rightarrow \quad |\vec{a}+\vec{b}|^2=|\vec{a}|^2$$

$$\Rightarrow \quad |\vec{a}|^2+|\vec{b}|^2+2\vec{a}\cdot\vec{b}=|\vec{a}|^2$$

$$\Rightarrow \quad |\vec{b}|^2+2\vec{a}\cdot\vec{b}=0 \quad \ldots(\text{i})$$

Now, $\quad (2\vec{a}+\vec{b})\cdot(\vec{b})=2\vec{a}\cdot\vec{b}+|\vec{b}|^2=0 \quad$ [using Eq. (i)]

Hence, $2\vec{a}+\vec{b}$ is perpendicular to $\vec{b}$.

14. Given, $\vec{a}$ and $\vec{b}$ are unit vectors.

$$\therefore \quad |\vec{a}|=1 \text{ and } |\vec{b}|=1$$

Also given, $\sqrt{2}\vec{a}-\vec{b}$ is a unit vector.

$$\therefore \quad |\sqrt{2}\vec{a}-\vec{b}|=1$$

$$\Rightarrow \quad |\sqrt{2}\vec{a}-\vec{b}|^2=1$$

$$\Rightarrow \quad 2|\vec{a}|^2+|\vec{b}|^2-2\sqrt{2}\vec{a}\cdot\vec{b}=1$$

$$\Rightarrow \quad 2+1-2\sqrt{2}\vec{a}\cdot\vec{b}=1$$

$$\Rightarrow \quad 2\sqrt{2}\vec{a}\cdot\vec{b}=2$$

$$\Rightarrow \quad \vec{a}\cdot\vec{b}=\frac{1}{\sqrt{2}}$$

$$\Rightarrow \quad |\vec{a}||\vec{b}|\cos\theta=\frac{1}{\sqrt{2}}$$

$$\Rightarrow \quad (1)(1)\cos\theta=\frac{1}{\sqrt{2}} \Rightarrow \cos\theta=\frac{1}{\sqrt{2}}$$

$$\therefore \quad \theta=\frac{\pi}{4}$$

15. We have, $|\hat{a}+\hat{b}|=1$

Let θ be the angle between $\hat{a}$ and $\hat{b}$.

Now, $\quad |\hat{a}+\hat{b}|=1$

$$\Rightarrow \quad |\hat{a}+\hat{b}|^2=1$$

$$\Rightarrow \quad (\hat{a}+\hat{b})\cdot(\hat{a}+\hat{b})=1$$

$$\Rightarrow \quad |\hat{a}|^2+|\hat{b}|^2+2\hat{a}\cdot\hat{b}=1$$

$$\Rightarrow \quad 1+1+2|\hat{a}||\hat{b}|\cos\theta=1 \quad [\because |\hat{a}|=|\hat{b}|=1]$$

$$\Rightarrow \quad 2\cos\theta=-1$$

$$\Rightarrow \quad \cos\theta=-\frac{1}{2}$$

$$\Rightarrow \quad \theta=\pi-\frac{\pi}{3}=\frac{2\pi}{3}$$

16. Let $\vec{a}=\hat{i}-\hat{j}$ and $\vec{b}=\hat{i}+\hat{j}$

We know that projection of $\vec{a}$ on $\vec{b}=\dfrac{\vec{a}\cdot\vec{b}}{|\vec{b}|}$.

$$=\frac{(\hat{i}-\hat{j})\cdot(\hat{i}+\hat{j})}{|\hat{i}+\hat{j}|}=\frac{1-1}{\sqrt{2}}=0$$

17. Let $\vec{a} = x\hat{i} + y\hat{j} + z\hat{k}$

$\therefore \quad (\vec{a}\cdot\hat{i}) = (x\hat{i} + y\hat{j} + z\hat{k})\cdot\hat{i} = x$

Similarly, $(\vec{a}\cdot\hat{j}) = y$ and $(\vec{a}\cdot\hat{k}) = z$

Now, $(\vec{a}\cdot\hat{i})\hat{i} + (\vec{a}\cdot\hat{j})\hat{j} + (\vec{a}\cdot\hat{k})\hat{k} = x\hat{i} + y\hat{j} + z\hat{k} = \vec{a}$

18. Projection of $(2\hat{i} + \hat{j} + \hat{k})$ on $(\hat{i} - 2\hat{j} + 2\hat{k})$ is

$$\frac{(2\hat{i} + \hat{j} + \hat{k})\cdot(\hat{i} - 2\hat{j} + 2\hat{k})}{|\hat{i} - 2\hat{j} + 2\hat{k}|} = \frac{2-2+2}{\sqrt{1+(-2)^2+(2)^2}}$$

$$= \frac{2}{\sqrt{9}} = \frac{2}{3}$$

$\therefore$ Required magnitude is $\frac{2}{3}$ unit.

19. Given, $\vec{a}$ is a unit vector.

$\therefore \quad |\vec{a}| = 1$

Now, we have

$$(\vec{x} - \vec{a})\cdot(\vec{x} + \vec{a}) = 12$$

$\Rightarrow \vec{x}\cdot\vec{x} + \vec{x}\cdot\vec{a} - \vec{a}\cdot\vec{x} - \vec{a}\cdot\vec{a} = 12$

$\Rightarrow \quad |\vec{x}|^2 - |\vec{a}|^2 = 12 \quad [\because \vec{x}\cdot\vec{a} = \vec{a}\cdot\vec{x}]$

$\Rightarrow \quad |\vec{x}|^2 - 1 = 12 \quad [\because |\vec{a}| = 1 \text{(given)}]$

$\Rightarrow \quad |\vec{x}|^2 = 13$

$\therefore \quad |\vec{x}| = \sqrt{13}$

20. We have, $\vec{a} + \vec{b} + \vec{c} = 0$ and $|\vec{a}| = 3, |\vec{b}| = 5, |\vec{c}| = 7$

Now, consider $\quad (\vec{a} + \vec{b} + \vec{c})\cdot(\vec{a} + \vec{b} + \vec{c}) = 0$

$\Rightarrow \vec{a}\cdot\vec{a} + \vec{a}\cdot\vec{b} + \vec{a}\cdot\vec{c} + \vec{b}\cdot\vec{a} + \vec{b}\cdot\vec{b} + \vec{b}\cdot\vec{c}$

$\qquad + \vec{c}\cdot\vec{a} + \vec{c}\cdot\vec{b} + \vec{c}\cdot\vec{c} = 0$

$\Rightarrow |\vec{a}|^2 + |\vec{b}|^2 + |\vec{c}|^2 + 2(\vec{a}\cdot\vec{b} + \vec{b}\cdot\vec{c} + \vec{c}\cdot\vec{a}) = 0$

$\Rightarrow \quad 3^2 + 5^2 + 7^2 + 2(\vec{a}\cdot\vec{b} + \vec{b}\cdot\vec{c} + \vec{c}\cdot\vec{a}) = 0$

$\Rightarrow \quad 2(\vec{a}\cdot\vec{b} + \vec{b}\cdot\vec{c} + \vec{c}\cdot\vec{a}) = -(9 + 25 + 49)$

$\therefore \quad (\vec{a}\cdot\vec{b} + \vec{b}\cdot\vec{c} + \vec{c}\cdot\vec{a}) = -\frac{83}{2}$

21. Let $\vec{c} = \hat{a} + \hat{b}$. Then, according to given condition $\vec{c}$ is a unit vector i.e. $|\vec{c}| = 1$.

To show $|\hat{a} - \hat{b}| = \sqrt{3}$

Consider, $\vec{c} = \hat{a} + \hat{b} \Rightarrow |\vec{c}| = |\hat{a} + \hat{b}|$

$\Rightarrow \quad 1 = |\hat{a} + \hat{b}| \Rightarrow |\hat{a} + \hat{b}|^2 = 1$

$\Rightarrow \quad (\hat{a} + \hat{b})\cdot(\hat{a} + \hat{b}) = 1$

$\Rightarrow \quad |\hat{a}|^2 + 2\hat{a}\cdot\hat{b} + |\hat{b}|^2 = 1$

$\Rightarrow \quad 1 + 2\hat{a}\cdot\hat{b} + 1 = 1$

$\Rightarrow \quad 2\hat{a}\cdot\hat{b} = -1 \quad \ldots\text{(i)}$

Now, consider $|\hat{a} - \hat{b}|^2 = (\hat{a} - \hat{b})\cdot(\hat{a} - \hat{b})$

$\qquad = |\hat{a}|^2 - 2\hat{a}\cdot\hat{b} + |\hat{b}|^2$

$\qquad = 1 - (-1) + 1 \quad$ [using Eq. (i)]

$\Rightarrow \quad |\hat{a} - \hat{b}|^2 = 3$

$\therefore \quad |\hat{a} - \hat{b}| = \sqrt{3}$ [taking positive square root, as magnitude cannot be negative]

Hence proved.

22. Given, $\quad \vec{a} + \vec{b} + \vec{c} = 0$

$\Rightarrow \quad \vec{a} + \vec{b} = -\vec{c}$

$\Rightarrow \quad (\vec{a} + \vec{b})^2 = (-\vec{c})^2 \quad$ [squaring both sides]

$\Rightarrow \quad (\vec{a} + \vec{b})(\vec{a} + \vec{b}) = (-\vec{c})\cdot(-\vec{c})$

$\Rightarrow \quad \vec{a}\cdot\vec{a} + \vec{a}\cdot\vec{b} + \vec{b}\cdot\vec{a} + \vec{b}\cdot\vec{b} = \vec{c}\cdot\vec{c}$

$\Rightarrow \quad |\vec{a}|^2 + 2\vec{a}\cdot\vec{b} + |\vec{b}|^2 = |\vec{c}|^2 \quad [\because \vec{a}\cdot\vec{b} = \vec{b}\cdot\vec{a}]$

$\Rightarrow |\vec{a}|^2 + 2|\vec{a}||\vec{b}|\cos\theta + |\vec{b}|^2 = |\vec{c}|^2 \quad \ldots\text{(i)}$

$[\because \vec{a}\cdot\vec{b} = |\vec{a}||\vec{b}|\cos\theta]$

On putting the values of $|\vec{a}| = 5$, $|\vec{b}| = 6$ and $|\vec{c}| = 9$ in Eq. (i), we get

$$(5)^2 + 2\times5\times6\times\cos\theta + (6)^2 = (9)^2$$

$\Rightarrow \quad 25 + 60\cos\theta + 36 = 81$

$\Rightarrow \quad 60\cos\theta = 81 - 61 = 20$

$\Rightarrow \quad \cos\theta = \frac{20}{60} = \frac{1}{3}$

$\therefore \quad \theta = \cos^{-1}\left(\frac{1}{3}\right)$

23. Let $\vec{a} = 2\hat{i} - \hat{j} + \hat{k}$ and $\vec{b} = \hat{i} - 2\hat{j} + \hat{k}$

Now, projection vector of $\vec{a}$ on $\vec{b} = \frac{\vec{a}\cdot\vec{b}}{|\vec{b}|^2}\vec{b}$

Here, $\quad \vec{a}\cdot\vec{b} = (2\hat{i} - \hat{j} + \hat{k})\cdot(\hat{i} - 2\hat{j} + \hat{k})$

$\qquad = 2\times1 + (-1)\times(-2) + 1\times1$

$\qquad = 2 + 2 + 1 = 5$

and $\quad |\vec{b}| = \sqrt{(1)^2 + (-2)^2 + (1)^2}$

$\qquad = \sqrt{1+4+1} = \sqrt{6}$

$\therefore$ Projection vector of $\vec{a}$ on $\vec{b} = \frac{5}{6}(\hat{i} - 2\hat{j} + \hat{k})$

24. Let $\vec{a} = 3\hat{i} - \hat{k}$ and $\vec{b} = -\hat{i} - \hat{j} + 5\hat{k}$

Now, $\quad \vec{a}\times\vec{b} = \begin{vmatrix} \hat{i} & \hat{j} & \hat{k} \\ 3 & 0 & -1 \\ -1 & -1 & 5 \end{vmatrix}$

$\qquad = \hat{i}(0 - 1) - \hat{j}(15 - 1) + \hat{k}(-3 - 0)$

$\qquad = -\hat{i} - 14\hat{j} - 3\hat{k}$

25. We have, $(\hat{k}\times\hat{j})\cdot\hat{i} + \hat{j}\cdot\hat{k} = (-\hat{i})\cdot(\hat{i}) + 0$

$\qquad = -1$

26. We know that $\vec{a}\times\vec{b}=-(\vec{b}\times\vec{a})$

So, $\vec{a}\times\vec{b}$ and $\vec{b}\times\vec{a}$ are vectors of same magnitude but opposite in sign.

Thus, the angle between $\vec{a}\times\vec{b}$ and $\vec{b}\times\vec{a}$ is π.

27. Given, $|\vec{a}|=|\vec{c}|=1$ and $|\vec{b}|=4$

Let angle between $\vec{b}$ and $\vec{c}$ be α.

Then, $|\vec{b}\times\vec{c}|=\sqrt{15}$

$\Rightarrow\quad |\vec{b}||\vec{c}|\sin\alpha=\sqrt{15}$

$\Rightarrow\quad \sin\alpha=\dfrac{\sqrt{15}}{4\times 1}=\dfrac{\sqrt{15}}{4}$

$\therefore\quad \cos\alpha=\dfrac{1}{4}\qquad [\because \cos\theta=\sqrt{1-\sin^2\theta}]$

We have, $\vec{b}-2\vec{c}=\lambda\vec{a}$

$\Rightarrow\quad (\vec{b}-2\vec{c})^2=(\lambda\vec{a})^2\qquad$ [squaring both sides]

$\Rightarrow\quad \vec{b}^2+4\vec{c}^2-4\vec{b}\cdot\vec{c}=\lambda^2\vec{a}^2$

$\Rightarrow\quad 16+4-4|\vec{b}||\vec{c}|\cos\alpha=\lambda^2$

$\Rightarrow\quad 20-16\cos\alpha=\lambda^2$

$\Rightarrow\quad 20-16\times\dfrac{1}{4}=\lambda^2$

$\Rightarrow\quad 16=\lambda^2$

$\therefore\quad \lambda=\pm 4$

28. We have, $(\vec{a}\times\vec{b})^2+(\vec{a}\cdot\vec{b})^2=225$

$\Rightarrow (|\vec{a}||\vec{b}|\sin\theta)^2+(|\vec{a}||\vec{b}|\cos\theta)^2=225$

$\Rightarrow |\vec{a}|^2|\vec{b}|^2\sin^2\theta+|\vec{a}|^2|\vec{b}|^2\cos^2\theta=225$

$\Rightarrow\quad |\vec{a}|^2|\vec{b}|^2(\sin^2\theta+\cos^2\theta)=225$

$\Rightarrow\quad |\vec{a}|^2|\vec{b}|^2=225$

$[\because \sin^2 A+\cos^2 A=1]$

$\Rightarrow\quad |\vec{b}|^2=\dfrac{225}{25}\qquad [\because |\vec{a}|=5 \text{ (given)}]$

$\Rightarrow\quad |\vec{b}|^2=9$

$\therefore\quad |\vec{b}|=3$

29. We have, $\vec{a}\cdot\vec{b}=\vec{0}$ and $\vec{a}\times\vec{b}=\vec{0}$

$\Rightarrow (\vec{a}=\vec{0}$ or $\vec{b}=\vec{0}$ or $a\perp b)$ and $(\vec{a}=\vec{0}$ or $\vec{b}=\vec{0}$ or $\vec{a}\,||\,\vec{b})$

Hence, $\vec{a}=\vec{0}$ and $\vec{b}=\vec{0}$

[$\because \vec{a}\perp\vec{b}$ and $\vec{a}\,||\,\vec{b}$ cannot occur simultaneously]

30. Let $\vec{a}=2\hat{i}$ and $\vec{b}=-3\hat{j}$

$\therefore$ Area of triangle $=\dfrac{1}{2}|\vec{a}\times\vec{b}|$

$=\dfrac{1}{2}|(2\hat{i})\times(-3\hat{j})|$

$=\dfrac{1}{2}|-6\hat{k}|\qquad [\because \hat{i}\times\hat{j}=\hat{k}]$

$=\dfrac{1}{2}\times 6=3$ sq units

31. Given, $(\hat{i}+3\hat{j}+9\hat{k})\times(3\hat{i}-\lambda\hat{j}+\mu\hat{k})=\vec{0}$

$$\therefore\quad \begin{vmatrix}\hat{i} & \hat{j} & \hat{k}\\ 1 & 3 & 9\\ 3 & -\lambda & \mu\end{vmatrix}=\vec{0}$$

$\Rightarrow \hat{i}(3\mu+9\lambda)-\hat{j}(\mu-27)+\hat{k}(-\lambda-9)=0\hat{i}+0\hat{j}+0\hat{k}$

On comparing the coefficients of $\hat{i}$, $\hat{j}$ and $\hat{k}$, we get

$3\mu+9\lambda=0,\ -\mu+27=0$ and $-\lambda-9=0$

$\Rightarrow\quad \mu=27$ and $-\lambda=9$

$\Rightarrow\quad \mu=27$ and $\lambda=-9$

Also, the values of μ and λ satisfy the equation $3\mu+9\lambda=0$.

Hence, $\mu=27$ and $\lambda=-9$.

32. We know that unit vectors perpendicular to $\vec{a}$ and $\vec{b}$ are $\pm\left(\dfrac{\vec{a}\times\vec{b}}{|\vec{a}\times\vec{b}|}\right)$.

So, there are two unit vectors perpendicular to the given vectors.

33. Let A, B and C be the points with position vectors $10\hat{i}+3\hat{j}$, $12\hat{i}-5\hat{j}$ and $\lambda\hat{i}+11\hat{j}$, respectively.

Then, $\overrightarrow{AB}=$ Position vector of $B-$ Position vector of A

$=12\hat{i}-5\hat{j}-10\hat{i}-3\hat{j}$

$=2\hat{i}-8\hat{j}$

and $\overrightarrow{BC}=$ Position vector of $C-$ Position vector of B

$=\lambda\hat{i}+11\hat{j}-12\hat{i}+5\hat{j}$

$=(\lambda-12)\hat{i}+16\hat{j}$

Since, A, B and C are collinear.

$\therefore\quad \overrightarrow{AB}=\mu\overrightarrow{BC}$

$\Rightarrow\quad 2\hat{i}-8\hat{j}=\mu(\lambda-12)\hat{i}+\mu 16\hat{j}$

On comparing the coefficients of $\hat{i}$ and $\hat{j}$, we get

$2=\mu(\lambda-12)$ and $-8=\mu 16$

$\Rightarrow\quad 2=\mu(\lambda-12)$ and $\mu=\dfrac{-1}{2}$

$\Rightarrow\quad 2=\dfrac{-1}{2}(\lambda-12)$

$\Rightarrow\quad -\lambda+12=4\Rightarrow\ \lambda=8$

34. The position vectors of points A, B and C are $\lambda\hat{i}+3\hat{j}, 12\hat{i}+\mu\hat{j}$ and $11\hat{i}-3\hat{j}$, respectively.

Given that C divides the line segment joining A and B in the ratio 3 : 1.

$$\therefore \quad 11\hat{i}-3\hat{j}=\frac{3\times(12\hat{i}+\mu\hat{j})+1\times(\lambda\hat{i}+3\hat{j})}{3+1}$$

$$\Rightarrow \quad 11\hat{i}-3\hat{j}=\frac{(36+\lambda)\hat{i}+(3\mu+3)\hat{j}}{4}$$

$$\Rightarrow 44\hat{i}-12\hat{j}=(36+\lambda)\hat{i}+(3\mu+3)\hat{j}$$

On equating the corresponding coefficients of $\hat{i}$ and $\hat{j}$, we get

$$36+\lambda=44 \text{ and } 3\mu+3=-12$$

$$\Rightarrow \quad \lambda=44-36 \text{ and } 3\mu=-15$$

$$\therefore \quad \lambda=8 \text{ and } \mu=-5$$

35. We know that if a vector $\vec{a}$ makes angles α, β and γ with $\hat{i}, \hat{j}$ and $\hat{k}$ respectively, then

$$\cos^2\alpha+\cos^2\beta+\cos^2\gamma=1$$

It is given that $\alpha=\frac{\pi}{4}, \beta=\frac{\pi}{3}$ and $\gamma=\theta$ an acute angle.

$$\therefore \cos^2\alpha+\cos^2\beta+\cos^2\gamma=1$$

$$\Rightarrow \cos^2\frac{\pi}{4}+\cos^2\frac{\pi}{3}+\cos^2\theta=1$$

$$\Rightarrow \quad \frac{1}{2}+\frac{1}{4}+\cos^2\theta=1 \Rightarrow \cos^2\theta=\frac{1}{4}$$

$$\Rightarrow \quad \cos\theta=\frac{1}{2}$$

[$\because \theta$ is an acute angle, therefore $\cos\theta>0$]

$$\Rightarrow \quad \theta=\frac{\pi}{3}$$

$$\Rightarrow \quad \gamma=\frac{\pi}{3}$$

Now, $\vec{a}=|\vec{a}|\{(\cos\alpha)\hat{i}+(\cos\beta)\hat{j}+(\cos\gamma)\hat{k}\}$

$$\Rightarrow \quad \vec{a}=\left(\cos\frac{\pi}{4}\right)\hat{i}+\left(\cos\frac{\pi}{3}\right)\hat{j}+\left(\cos\frac{\pi}{3}\right)\hat{k}$$

$$\left[\because |\vec{a}|=1, \alpha=\frac{\pi}{4}, \beta=\frac{\pi}{3} \text{ and } \gamma=\frac{\pi}{3}\right]$$

$$\Rightarrow \quad \vec{a}=\frac{1}{\sqrt{2}}\hat{i}+\frac{1}{2}\hat{j}+\frac{1}{2}\hat{k}$$

Thus, the components of $\vec{a}$ are $\left(\frac{1}{\sqrt{2}}\hat{i}, \frac{1}{2}\hat{j}, \frac{1}{2}\hat{k}\right)$.

36. Given, $\vec{a}=2\hat{i}-2\hat{j}+\hat{k}, \vec{b}=\hat{i}+2\hat{j}-2\hat{k}$ and $\vec{c}=2\hat{i}-\hat{j}+4\hat{k}$

Now, $(\vec{b}+\vec{c})=(\hat{i}+2\hat{j}-2\hat{k})+(2\hat{i}-\hat{j}+4\hat{k})=3\hat{i}+\hat{j}+2\hat{k}$

$$\therefore \text{Projection of } (\vec{b}+\vec{c}) \text{ on } \vec{a}=\frac{(\vec{b}+\vec{c})\cdot\vec{a}}{|\vec{a}|}$$

$$=\frac{(3\hat{i}+\hat{j}+2\hat{k})\cdot(2\hat{i}-2\hat{j}+\hat{k})}{\sqrt{4+4+1}}$$

$$=\frac{3(2)+1(-2)+2(1)}{\sqrt{9}}=\frac{6-2+2}{3}=2$$

37. Given, $|\vec{a}|=2, |\vec{b}|=3$ and $\vec{a}\cdot\vec{b}=5$

Now, $|\vec{a}-\vec{b}|^2=|\vec{a}|^2+|\vec{b}|^2-2\vec{a}\cdot\vec{b}$

$$=4+9-2\times5=13-10$$

$$\Rightarrow \quad |\vec{a}-\vec{b}|^2=3$$

$$\therefore \quad |\vec{a}-\vec{b}|=\sqrt{3}$$

38. Given, $\vec{a}=3\hat{i}-\hat{j}$ and $\vec{b}=2\hat{i}+\hat{j}-3\hat{k}$

Let $\vec{b_1}=x_1\hat{i}+y_1\hat{j}+z_1\hat{k}$ and $\vec{b_2}=x_2\hat{i}+y_2\hat{j}+z_2\hat{k}$ are two vectors such that $\vec{b_1}+\vec{b_2}=\vec{b}$, where $\vec{b_1}\parallel\vec{a}$ and $\vec{b_2}\perp\vec{a}$.

Consider, $\vec{b_1}+\vec{b_2}=\vec{b}$

$$\Rightarrow \quad (x_1+x_2)\hat{i}+(y_1+y_2)\hat{j}+(z_1+z_2)\hat{k}=2\hat{i}+\hat{j}-3\hat{k}$$

On comparing the coefficients of $\hat{i}, \hat{j}$ and $\hat{k}$ both sides, we get

$$\Rightarrow \quad x_1+x_2=2 \quad \text{...(i)}$$

$$y_1+y_2=1 \quad \text{...(ii)}$$

and $$z_1+z_2=-3 \quad \text{...(iii)}$$

Now, consider, $\vec{b_1}\parallel\vec{a}$

$$\Rightarrow \quad \frac{x_1}{3}=\frac{y_1}{-1}=\frac{z_1}{0}=\lambda \text{ (say)}$$

$$\Rightarrow \quad x_1=3\lambda, y_1=-\lambda \text{ and } z_1=0 \quad \text{...(iv)}$$

On substituting the values of x_1, y_1 and z_1, from Eq. (iv) to Eq. (i), (ii) and (iii), respectively, we get

$$x_2=2-3\lambda, y_2=1+\lambda \text{ and } z_2=-3 \quad \text{...(v)}$$

Since, $\vec{b_2}\perp\vec{a}$, therefore $\vec{b_2}\cdot\vec{a}=0$

$$\Rightarrow \quad 3x_2-y_2=0$$

$$\Rightarrow \quad 3(2-3\lambda)-(1+\lambda)=0 \quad \text{[from Eq. (v)]}$$

$$\Rightarrow \quad 6-9\lambda-1-\lambda=0$$

$$\Rightarrow \quad 5-10\lambda=0$$

$$\Rightarrow \quad \lambda=\frac{1}{2}$$

On substituting $\lambda=\frac{1}{2}$ in Eqs. (iv) and (v), we get

$$x_1=\frac{3}{2}, y_1=\frac{-1}{2}, z_1=0$$

and $$x_2=\frac{1}{2}, y_2=\frac{3}{2} \text{ and } z_2=-3$$

Hence, $$\vec{b_1}+\vec{b_2}=\left(\frac{3}{2}\hat{i}-\frac{1}{2}\hat{j}\right)+\left(\frac{1}{2}\hat{i}+\frac{3}{2}\hat{j}-3\hat{k}\right)$$

$$=2\hat{i}+\hat{j}-3\hat{k}=\vec{b},$$

where $\vec{b_1}\parallel\vec{a}$ and $\vec{b_2}\perp\vec{a}$.

39. Given, $\vec{a}=\hat{i}-\hat{j}+7\hat{k}$ and $\vec{b}=5\hat{i}-\hat{j}+\lambda\hat{k}$

Then, $\vec{a}+\vec{b}=(\hat{i}-\hat{j}+7\hat{k})+(5\hat{i}-\hat{j}+\lambda\hat{k})=6\hat{i}-2\hat{j}+(7+\lambda)\hat{k}$

and $\vec{a}-\vec{b}=(\hat{i}-\hat{j}+7\hat{k})-(5\hat{i}-\hat{j}+\lambda\hat{k})=-4\hat{i}+(7-\lambda)\hat{k}$

Since, $(\vec{a}+\vec{b})$ and $(\vec{a}-\vec{b})$ are perpendicular vectors, then

$(\vec{a}+\vec{b})\cdot(\vec{a}-\vec{b})=0$

$\Rightarrow [6\hat{i}-2\hat{j}+(7+\lambda)\hat{k}]\cdot[-4\hat{i}+(7-\lambda)\hat{k}]=0$

$\Rightarrow -24+(7+\lambda)(7-\lambda)=0$

$\Rightarrow 49-\lambda^2=24$

$\Rightarrow \lambda^2=25$

$\therefore \lambda=\pm 5$

40. We have, $|\vec{a}|=1, |\vec{b}|=2$ and $|\vec{c}|=3$

Now, $\vec{a}+\vec{b}+\vec{c}=\vec{0}$

On squaring both sides, we get

$$(\vec{a}+\vec{b}+\vec{c})^2=(\vec{0})^2$$

$\Rightarrow |\vec{a}|^2+|\vec{b}|^2+|\vec{c}|^2+2(\vec{a}\cdot\vec{b}+\vec{b}\cdot\vec{c}+\vec{c}\cdot\vec{a})=0$

$\Rightarrow (1)^2+(2)^2+(3)^2+2(\vec{a}\cdot\vec{b}+\vec{b}\cdot\vec{c}+\vec{c}\cdot\vec{a})=0$

$\Rightarrow 2(\vec{a}\cdot\vec{b}+\vec{b}\cdot\vec{c}+\vec{c}\cdot\vec{a})=-(1+4+9)$

$\Rightarrow \vec{a}\cdot\vec{b}+\vec{b}\cdot\vec{c}+\vec{c}\cdot\vec{a}=-\frac{1}{2}(14)$

$\Rightarrow \vec{a}\cdot\vec{b}+\vec{b}\cdot\vec{c}+\vec{c}\cdot\vec{a}=-7$

41. We have, $\vec{a}=\hat{i}+2\hat{j}+3\hat{k}$ and $\vec{b}=2\hat{i}+4\hat{j}-5\hat{k}$

So, the diagonals of the parallelogram whose adjacent sides are $\vec{a}$ and $\vec{b}$ are given by

$$\vec{p}=\vec{a}+\vec{b} \text{ and } \vec{q}=\vec{b}-\vec{a}$$

Now, $\vec{p}=(\hat{i}+2\hat{j}+3\hat{k})+(2\hat{i}+4\hat{j}-5\hat{k})$

$=3\hat{i}+6\hat{j}-2\hat{k}$

and $\vec{q}=(2\hat{i}+4\hat{j}-5\hat{k})-(\hat{i}+2\hat{j}+3\hat{k})$

$=\hat{i}+2\hat{j}-8\hat{k}$

$\therefore \hat{p}=\frac{\vec{p}}{|\vec{p}|}=\frac{3\hat{i}+6\hat{j}-2\hat{k}}{\sqrt{9+36+4}}$

$=\frac{3\hat{i}+6\hat{j}-2\hat{k}}{7}$

$=\frac{3}{7}\hat{i}+\frac{6}{7}\hat{j}-\frac{2}{7}\hat{k}$

and $\hat{q}=\frac{\vec{q}}{|\vec{q}|}=\frac{\hat{i}+2\hat{j}-8\hat{k}}{\sqrt{1+4+64}}$

$=\frac{\hat{i}+2\hat{j}-8\hat{k}}{\sqrt{69}}$

$=\frac{1}{\sqrt{69}}\hat{i}+\frac{2}{\sqrt{69}}\hat{j}-\frac{8}{\sqrt{69}}\hat{k}$

42. We have, $\overrightarrow{AB}=$ Position vector of B – Position vector of A

$=(\hat{i}-3\hat{j}-5\hat{k})-(2\hat{i}-\hat{j}+\hat{k})=-\hat{i}-2\hat{j}-6\hat{k}$

$\overrightarrow{BC}=(3\hat{i}-4\hat{j}-4\hat{k})-(\hat{i}-3\hat{j}-5\hat{k})=2\hat{i}-\hat{j}+\hat{k}$

and $\overrightarrow{CA}=(2\hat{i}-\hat{j}+\hat{k})-(3\hat{i}-4\hat{j}-4\hat{k})$

$=-\hat{i}+3\hat{j}+5\hat{k}$

Here, $\overrightarrow{AB}+\overrightarrow{BC}+\overrightarrow{CA}=0$

$\Rightarrow$ *A, B* and *C* are the vertices of a triangle.

Now, $\overrightarrow{BC}\cdot\overrightarrow{CA}=(2\hat{i}-\hat{j}+\hat{k})\cdot(-\hat{i}+3\hat{j}+5\hat{k})$

$=-2-3+5=0$

$\Rightarrow \overrightarrow{BC}\perp\overrightarrow{CA} \Rightarrow \angle C=90°$

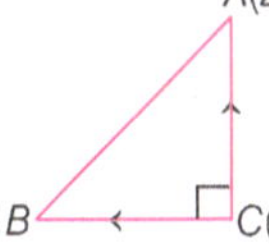

Now, area of $\Delta ABC=\frac{1}{2}|\overrightarrow{CA}\times\overrightarrow{BC}|$

$=\frac{1}{2}\begin{vmatrix}\hat{i} & \hat{j} & \hat{k}\\ -1 & 3 & 5\\ 2 & -1 & 1\end{vmatrix}$

$=\frac{1}{2}|(8\hat{i}-11\hat{j}-5\hat{k})|$

$=\frac{1}{2}\sqrt{64+121+25}$

$=\frac{1}{2}\sqrt{210}$ sq units

43. Let *ABCD* be the given parallelogram with $\overrightarrow{AB}=2\hat{i}-4\hat{j}-5\hat{k}$ and $\overrightarrow{AD}=2\hat{i}+2\hat{j}+3\hat{k}$.

Clearly, the diagonal $\overrightarrow{AC}$ is given by $\overrightarrow{AB}+\overrightarrow{AD}$

$=4\hat{i}-2\hat{j}-2\hat{k}$

and the diagonal $\overrightarrow{BD}$ is given by $\overrightarrow{BC}+\overrightarrow{BA}$

$=\overrightarrow{AD}-\overrightarrow{AB}=6\hat{j}+8\hat{k}$

[using parallelogram law of addition]

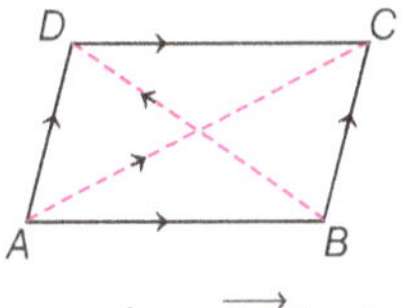

Since, the unit vector along $\overrightarrow{AC}$ is given by

$\frac{\overrightarrow{AC}}{|\overrightarrow{AC}|}=\frac{4\hat{i}-2\hat{j}-2\hat{k}}{\sqrt{16+4+4}}=\frac{4\hat{i}-2\hat{j}-2\hat{k}}{\sqrt{24}}$

$=\frac{4\hat{i}-2\hat{j}-2\hat{k}}{2\sqrt{6}}=\frac{1}{\sqrt{6}}(2\hat{i}-\hat{j}-\hat{k})$

and the unit vector along $\overrightarrow{BD}$ is given by

$\frac{\overrightarrow{BD}}{|\overrightarrow{BD}|}=\frac{6\hat{j}+8\hat{k}}{\sqrt{36+64}}$

$=\frac{6\hat{j}+8\hat{k}}{10}=\frac{1}{5}(3\hat{j}+4\hat{k})$

Since, area of parallelogram $ABCD = \frac{1}{2}|\overrightarrow{AC} \times \overrightarrow{BD}|$

Here, $\overrightarrow{AC} \times \overrightarrow{BD} = \begin{vmatrix} \hat{i} & \hat{j} & \hat{k} \\ 4 & -2 & -2 \\ 0 & 6 & 8 \end{vmatrix}$

$= \hat{i}(-16+12) - \hat{j}(32-0) + \hat{k}(24-0)$

$= -4\hat{i} - 32\hat{j} + 24\hat{k}$

and $|\overrightarrow{AC} \times \overrightarrow{BD}| = \sqrt{(-4)^2 + (-32)^2 + (24)^2}$

$= \sqrt{4^2(1 + 8^2 + 6^2)}$

$= 4\sqrt{1+64+36}$

$= 4\sqrt{101}$

$\therefore$ Area of parallelogram $ABCD = \frac{1}{2} \times 4\sqrt{101} = 2\sqrt{101}$ sq units

44. Given, $\vec{r} = x\hat{i} + y\hat{j} + z\hat{k}$

Now, $\vec{r} \times \hat{i} = (x\hat{i} + y\hat{j} + z\hat{k}) \times \hat{i}$

$= x(\hat{i} \times \hat{i}) + y(\hat{j} \times \hat{i}) + z(\hat{k} \times \hat{i})$

$= x \cdot 0 + y(-\hat{k}) + z(\hat{j})$

$[\because \hat{i} \times \hat{i} = 0, \hat{j} \times \hat{i} = -\hat{k} \text{ and } \hat{k} \times \hat{i} = \hat{j}]$

$= -y\hat{k} + z\hat{j}$

and $(\vec{r} \times \hat{j}) = (x\hat{i} + y\hat{j} + z\hat{k}) \times \hat{j}$

$= x(\hat{i} \times \hat{j}) + y(\hat{j} \times \hat{j}) + z(\hat{k} \times \hat{j})$

$= x\hat{k} + y \cdot 0 + z(-\hat{i})$

$= x\hat{k} - z\hat{i}$ $[\because \hat{j} \times \hat{j} = 0, \hat{i} \times \hat{j} = \hat{k} \text{ and } \hat{k} \times \hat{j} = -\hat{i}]$

$\therefore (\vec{r} \times \hat{i}) \cdot (\vec{r} \times \hat{j}) = (-y\hat{k} + z\hat{j}) \cdot (x\hat{k} - z\hat{i})$

$= -yx + yz \cdot 0 + 0 \cdot zx - z^2 \cdot 0$

$[\because \hat{k} \cdot \hat{k} = 1, \hat{k} \cdot \hat{i} = 0, \hat{j} \cdot \hat{k} = 0 \text{ and } \hat{j} \cdot \hat{i} = 0]$

$= -xy$

$\therefore (\vec{r} \times \hat{i}) \cdot (\vec{r} \times \hat{j}) + xy = -xy + xy = 0$

45. Given, vectors are $\vec{a} = \hat{i} + 2\hat{j} + \hat{k}$, $\vec{b} = 2\hat{i} + \hat{j}$

and $\vec{c} = 3\hat{i} - 4\hat{j} - 5\hat{k}$

Now, $\vec{a} - \vec{b} = (\hat{i} + 2\hat{j} + \hat{k}) - (2\hat{i} + \hat{j}) = -\hat{i} + \hat{j} + \hat{k}$

and $\vec{c} - \vec{b} = (3\hat{i} - 4\hat{j} - 5\hat{k}) - (2\hat{i} + \hat{j})$

$= \hat{i} - 5\hat{j} - 5\hat{k}$

Now, a vector perpendicular to $(\vec{a} - \vec{b})$ and $(\vec{c} - \vec{b})$ is given by

$(\vec{a} - \vec{b}) \times (\vec{c} - \vec{b}) = \begin{vmatrix} \hat{i} & \hat{j} & \hat{k} \\ -1 & 1 & 1 \\ 1 & -5 & -5 \end{vmatrix}$

$= \hat{i}(-5+5) - \hat{j}(5-1) + \hat{k}(5-1)$

$= \hat{i}(0) - \hat{j}(4) + \hat{k}(4) = -4\hat{j} + 4\hat{k}$

and unit vector along $(\vec{a} - \vec{b}) \times (\vec{c} - \vec{b})$ is given by

$\frac{-4\hat{j} + 4\hat{k}}{|-4\hat{j} + 4\hat{k}|} = \frac{-4\hat{j} + 4\hat{k}}{\sqrt{(-4)^2 + 4^2}} = \frac{-4\hat{j} + 4\hat{k}}{\sqrt{32}}$

$= \frac{-4\hat{j} + 4\hat{k}}{4\sqrt{2}} = -\frac{\hat{j}}{\sqrt{2}} + \frac{\hat{k}}{\sqrt{2}}$

46. Given, $\vec{a} = 2\hat{i} - 3\hat{j} + \hat{k}$, $\vec{b} = -\hat{i} + \hat{k}$ and $\vec{c} = 2\hat{j} - \hat{k}$.

Let $\vec{d_1} = \vec{a} + \vec{b}$ and $\vec{d_2} = \vec{b} + \vec{c}$.

Then, $\vec{d_1} = (2\hat{i} - 3\hat{j} + \hat{k}) + (-\hat{i} + \hat{k}) = \hat{i} - 3\hat{j} + 2\hat{k}$

and $\vec{d_2} = (-\hat{i} + \hat{k}) + (2\hat{j} - \hat{k}) = -\hat{i} + 2\hat{j}$

Clearly, area of given parallelogram with diagonals $\vec{d_1}$ and $\vec{d_2}$ is given by $\frac{1}{2}|\vec{d_1} \times \vec{d_2}|$.

Here, $\vec{d_1} \times \vec{d_2} = \begin{vmatrix} \hat{i} & \hat{j} & \hat{k} \\ 1 & -3 & 2 \\ -1 & 2 & 0 \end{vmatrix}$

$= \hat{i}(-4) - \hat{j}(0+2) + \hat{k}(2-3) = -4\hat{i} - 2\hat{j} - \hat{k}$

So, area of parallelogram $= \frac{1}{2}|-4\hat{i} - 2\hat{j} - \hat{k}|$

$= \frac{1}{2}\sqrt{(-4)^2 + (-2)^2 + (-1)^2}$

$= \frac{1}{2}\sqrt{16+4+1} = \frac{1}{2}\sqrt{21}$ sq units

47. Given, $\vec{\alpha} = 4\hat{i} + 5\hat{j} - \hat{k}$, $\vec{\beta} = \hat{i} - 4\hat{j} + 5\hat{k}$ and $\vec{q} = 3\hat{i} + \hat{j} - \hat{k}$

Also, vector $\vec{p}$ is perpendicular to α and β.

Then, $\vec{p} = \lambda(\vec{\alpha} \times \vec{\beta})$ ...(i)

Now, $\vec{\alpha} \times \vec{\beta} = \begin{vmatrix} \hat{i} & \hat{j} & \hat{k} \\ 4 & 5 & -1 \\ 1 & -4 & 5 \end{vmatrix}$

$= \hat{i}(25-4) - \hat{j}(20+1) + \hat{k}(-16-5)$

$= \hat{i}(21) - \hat{j}(21) + \hat{k}(-21)$

$\Rightarrow \vec{\alpha} \times \vec{\beta} = 21\hat{i} - 21\hat{j} - 21\hat{k}$

So, $\vec{p} = 21\lambda\hat{i} - 21\lambda\hat{j} - 21\lambda\hat{k}$ [from Eq. (i)] ...(ii)

Also, given that $\vec{p} \cdot \vec{q} = 21$

$\therefore (21\lambda\hat{i} - 21\lambda\hat{j} - 21\lambda\hat{k}) \cdot (3\hat{i} + \hat{j} - \hat{k}) = 21$

$\Rightarrow 63\lambda - 21\lambda + 21\lambda = 21$

$\Rightarrow 63\lambda = 21 \Rightarrow \lambda = \frac{1}{3}$

On putting $\lambda = \frac{1}{3}$ in Eq. (ii), we get

$\vec{p} = 21 \times \frac{1}{3}\hat{i} - 21 \times \frac{1}{3}\hat{j} - 21 \times \frac{1}{3}\hat{k}$

$\therefore \vec{p} = 7\hat{i} - 7\hat{j} - 7\hat{k}$, which is the required vector.

48. Let O be the origin of reference.

Then, $\overrightarrow{OA} = 2\hat{i} - \hat{j} + \hat{k}$, $\overrightarrow{OB} = \hat{i} + \hat{j} + 2\hat{k}$

and $\overrightarrow{OC} = 2\hat{i} + 3\hat{k}$

Now, $\overrightarrow{AB} = \overrightarrow{OB} - \overrightarrow{OA}$

$= \hat{i} + \hat{j} + 2\hat{k} - 2\hat{i} + \hat{j} - \hat{k}$

$= -\hat{i} + 2\hat{j} + \hat{k}$

and $\overrightarrow{AC} = \overrightarrow{OC} - \overrightarrow{OA}$

$= 2\hat{i} + 3\hat{k} - 2\hat{i} + \hat{j} - \hat{k} = \hat{j} + 2\hat{k}$

Now, $\overrightarrow{AB} \times \overrightarrow{AC} = \begin{vmatrix} \hat{i} & \hat{j} & \hat{k} \\ -1 & 2 & 1 \\ 0 & 1 & 2 \end{vmatrix}$

$= \hat{i}(4-1) - \hat{j}(-2-0) + \hat{k}(-1-0)$

$= 3\hat{i} + 2\hat{j} - \hat{k}$

and $|\overrightarrow{AB} \times \overrightarrow{AC}| = \sqrt{(3)^2 + (2)^2 + (-1)^2}$

$= \sqrt{9+4+1} = \sqrt{14}$

$\therefore$ Unit vector perpendicular to the plane ABC

$= \dfrac{\overrightarrow{AB} \times \overrightarrow{AC}}{|\overrightarrow{AB} \times \overrightarrow{AC}|}$

$= \dfrac{3\hat{i} + 2\hat{j} - \hat{k}}{\sqrt{14}}$

$= \dfrac{3}{\sqrt{14}}\hat{i} + \dfrac{2}{\sqrt{14}}\hat{j} - \dfrac{1}{\sqrt{14}}\hat{k}$

49. Given, $\vec{a} = \hat{i} + \hat{j} + \hat{k}$ and $\vec{b} = \hat{j} - \hat{k}$

Let $\vec{c} = x\hat{i} + y\hat{j} + z\hat{k}$ ...(i)

Now, $\vec{a} \times \vec{c} = \begin{vmatrix} \hat{i} & \hat{j} & \hat{k} \\ 1 & 1 & 1 \\ x & y & z \end{vmatrix} = \hat{i}(z-y) - \hat{j}(z-x) + \hat{k}(y-x)$

Now, $\vec{a} \times \vec{c} = \vec{b}$ [given]

$\Rightarrow \hat{i}(z-y) + \hat{j}(x-z) + \hat{k}(y-x) = 0\hat{i} + 1\hat{j} + (-1)\hat{k}$

$[\because \vec{b} = \hat{j} - \hat{k}]$

On comparing the coefficients from both sides, we get

$z - y = 0, x - z = 1, y - x = -1$

$\Rightarrow$ $y = z$ and $x - y = 1$ ...(ii)

Also given, $\vec{a} \cdot \vec{c} = 3$

$\Rightarrow (\hat{i} + \hat{j} + \hat{k}) \cdot (x\hat{i} + y\hat{j} + z\hat{k}) = 3$

$\Rightarrow x + y + z = 3$

$\Rightarrow x + 2y = 3$ $[\because y = z]$ ...(iii)

On subtracting Eq. (ii) from Eq. (iii), we get

$3y = 2$

$\Rightarrow y = \dfrac{2}{3} = z$ $[\because y = z]$

From Eq. (ii),

$x = 1 + y = 1 + \dfrac{2}{3} = \dfrac{5}{3}$

Hence, $\vec{c} = \dfrac{5}{3}\hat{i} + \dfrac{2}{3}\hat{j} + \dfrac{2}{3}\hat{k}$ [from Eq. (i)]

QR Code for Quick Test 1

QR Code for Quick Test 2

QR Code for Quick Test 3

Mind Map

Vector Algebra

Vector Joining Two Points

If $P_1(x_1, y_1, z_1)$ and $P_2(x_2, y_2, z_2)$ are any two points, then the vector joining P_1 and P_2 is the vector P_1P_2.

$P_1P_2 = OP_2 - OP_1 = (x_2 - x_1)\hat{i} + (y_2 - y_1)\hat{j} + (z_2 - z_1)\hat{k}$

- The distance between two points,

$|\overrightarrow{P_1P_2}| = \sqrt{(x_2 - x_1)^2 + (y_2 - y_1)^2 + (z_2 - z_1)^2}$

- The direction ratios and direction cosines of a line joining two vectors are $(x_2 - x_1), (y_2 - y_1), (z_2 - z_1)$ and $\frac{x_2 - x_1}{d}, \frac{y_2 - y_1}{d}, \frac{z_2 - z_1}{d}$.

Direction Cosines and Direction Ratios of a Vector

Suppose $\overrightarrow{OP}$ makes α, β and γ with the coordinate axes OX, OY and OZ respectively, then direction cosines of a line OP are $l = \cos\alpha$, $m = \cos\beta$ and $n = \cos\gamma$.

(i) In general, it may be noted that $l^2 + m^2 + n^2 = 1$ but $x^2 + y^2 + z^2 \neq 1$.

(ii) If $\vec{a} = a_1\hat{i} + a_2\hat{j} + a_3\hat{k}$, then a_1, a_2 and a_3 are also called **direction ratios** of $\vec{a}$.

The **direction cosines** of $\vec{a}$ is given by

$$\frac{a_1}{\sqrt{a_1^2 + a_2^2 + a_3^2}}, \frac{a_2}{\sqrt{a_1^2 + a_2^2 + a_3^2}}, \frac{a_3}{\sqrt{a_1^2 + a_2^2 + a_3^2}}.$$

Section Formula

Position vector OR of point R which divides the line segment joining the points A and B with position vectors $\vec{a}$ and $\vec{b}$ respectively, in the ratio $m : n$.

(i) Internally, is given by $\frac{m\vec{b} + n\vec{a}}{m + n}$

(ii) Externally, is given by $\frac{m\vec{b} - n\vec{a}}{m - n}$

The position vector of middle point of AB is given by $\frac{1}{2}(\vec{a} + \vec{b})$.

Algebra of Vectors

Addition of Vectors

Triangle Law of Vector Addition

$\overrightarrow{BC} + \overrightarrow{CA} = \overrightarrow{BA}$

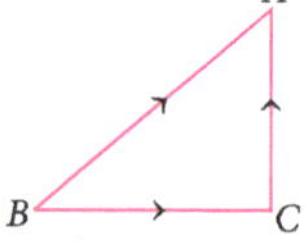

Parallelogram Law of Vector Addition

$\overrightarrow{OA} + \overrightarrow{OC} = \overrightarrow{OB}$

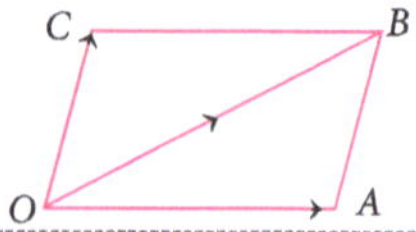

Difference of Two Vectors

The subtraction of vector B from vector A is simply the vector sum of $\vec{A}$ and $-\vec{B}$.

$\vec{A} - \vec{B} = \vec{A} + (-\vec{B})$

Multiplication of a Vector by a Scalar

Let λ be a scalar and $\vec{a}$ be a vector, then $\lambda\vec{a}$ (multiplication of vector by scalar) is defined as a vector whose magnitude is $|\lambda|$ times the magnitude of $\vec{a}$. i.e. $|\lambda\vec{a}| = |\lambda||\vec{a}|$

Scalar (or Dot) Product of Two Vectors

If θ is the angle between two non-zero vectors $\vec{a}$ and $\vec{b}$, then the scalar or dot product, denoted by $\vec{a} \cdot \vec{b}$, is given by $\vec{a} \cdot \vec{b} = |\vec{a}||\vec{b}|\cos\theta$, where $0 \leq \theta \leq \pi$.

Projection of a Vector on the other Vector

Projection of $\vec{a}$ on $\vec{b} = \frac{\vec{a} \cdot \vec{b}}{|\vec{b}|}$ and

projection of $\vec{b}$ on $\vec{a} = \frac{\vec{a} \cdot \vec{b}}{|\vec{a}|}$

Angle Between Two Non-zero Vectors

Angle between two non-zero vectors $\vec{a}$ and $\vec{b}$ is given by

$$\cos\theta = \frac{\vec{a} \cdot \vec{b}}{|\vec{a}| \cdot |\vec{b}|}$$

$$\text{or } \theta = \cos^{-1}\left[\frac{\vec{a} \cdot \vec{b}}{|\vec{a}| \cdot |\vec{b}|}\right]$$

Relations Between Unit Vectors

(i) $\vec{a} \cdot \vec{a} = |\vec{a}|^2$

(ii) $\hat{i} \cdot \hat{i} = \hat{j} \cdot \hat{j} = \hat{k} \cdot \hat{k} = 1$ or $|\hat{i}|^2 = |\hat{j}|^2 = |\hat{k}|^2 = 1$

(iii) $\hat{i} \cdot \hat{j} = \hat{j} \cdot \hat{k} = \hat{k} \cdot \hat{i} = 0$

Scalar Product of Two Vectors Component Form

If $\vec{a} = a_1\hat{i} + a_2\hat{j} + a_3\hat{k}$ and

$\vec{b} = b_1\hat{i} + b_2\hat{j} + b_3\hat{k}$

$\vec{a} \cdot \vec{b} = a_1b_1 + a_2b_2 + a_3b_3$

Components of a Vector

Let a point P in a space has coordinates (x, y, z) and $\hat{i}, \hat{j}$ and $\hat{k}$ are unit vectors along OX, OY and OZ-axes, respectively. Then, the position vector of P with respect to O is given by

$\overrightarrow{OP}$ (or $\vec{r}$) $= x\hat{i} + y\hat{j} + z\hat{k}$

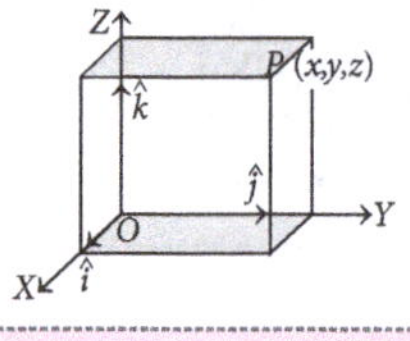

Here, x, y and z are called the **scalar (or rectangular) components** and $x\hat{i}$, $y\hat{j}$ and $z\hat{k}$ are called the **vector components** of $\overrightarrow{OP}$ (or $\vec{r}$) along the respective axes.

The length of any vector $\vec{r} = x\hat{i} + y\hat{j} + z\hat{k}$ is given by

$|\vec{r}| = |x\hat{i} + y\hat{j} + z\hat{k}| = \sqrt{x^2 + y^2 + z^2}$

Vector (or Cross) Product of Two Vectors

If θ is the angle between two non-zero and non-parallel vectors $\vec{a}$ and $\vec{b}$, then the cross product of vectors, denoted by $\vec{a} \times \vec{b}$, is given by $\vec{a} \times \vec{b} = |\vec{a}||\vec{b}|\sin\theta\, n$ such that $0 \leq \theta \leq \pi$.

Important Results on Vector Product of Two Vectors

(i) Unit vector $\hat{n}$ which is perpendicular to both the vectors $\vec{a}$ and $\vec{b}$, is given by

$$\hat{n} = \pm \frac{\vec{a} \times \vec{b}}{|\vec{a} \times \vec{b}|}$$

(ii) Relation between dot and cross product is

$$(\vec{a} \cdot \vec{b})^2 + |\vec{a} \times \vec{b}|^2 = |\vec{a}|^2|\vec{b}|^2$$

(iii) Angle between two non-zero vectors is given by

$$\sin\theta = \frac{|\vec{a} \times \vec{b}|}{|\vec{a}|\,|\vec{b}|} \text{ or } \theta = \sin^{-1}\left[\frac{|\vec{a} \times \vec{b}|}{|\vec{a}|\,|\vec{b}|}\right]$$

(iv) $\vec{a} \times \vec{a} = \vec{0}$

(v) If $\vec{a}$ is parallel to b, then $\vec{a} \times \vec{b} = \vec{0}$ and converse is also true.

Or Two non-zero vectors $\vec{a}, \vec{b}$ are collinear, iff $\vec{a} \times \vec{b} = \vec{0}$

(vi) If $\theta = \frac{\pi}{2}$, then $|\vec{a} \times \vec{b}| = |\vec{a}||\vec{b}|$

Vector Product of an Orthonormal Vector Trial

- $\hat{i} \times \hat{i} = \hat{j} \times \hat{j} = \hat{k} \times \hat{k} = \vec{0}$

and $\hat{i} \times \hat{j} = \hat{k}$, $\hat{j} \times \hat{k} = \hat{i}$, $\hat{k} \times \hat{i} = \hat{j}$

- $\hat{j} \times \hat{i} = -\hat{k}$, $\hat{k} \times \hat{j} = -\hat{i}$ and $\hat{i} \times \hat{k} = -\hat{j}$

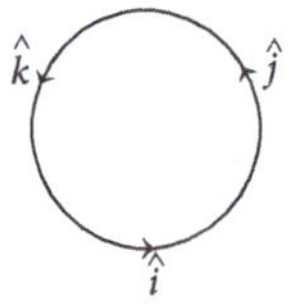

Vector Product of Two Vectors in Component Form

If $\vec{a} = a_1\hat{i} + a_2\hat{j} + a_3\hat{k}$ and $\vec{b} = b_1\hat{i} + b_2\hat{j} + b_3\hat{k}$, then

$$\vec{a} \times \vec{b} = \begin{vmatrix} \hat{i} & \hat{j} & \hat{k} \\ a_1 & a_2 & a_3 \\ b_1 & b_2 & b_3 \end{vmatrix}$$

11

CHAPTER

A mathematician is a blind man in a dark room looking for a black cat which is not there. — *Charles Darwin*

Three-Dimensional Geometry

YOUR STUDY GOALS

11.1 Direction Cosines of a Line
11.2 Direction Ratios of a Line
11.3 Lines in Space
11.4 Shortest Distance between Two Lines

YOUR PRACTICE GOALS

- Objective Type Questions (29 Qs ; 17 MCQs, 9 A-R, 3 Case Based)
- Subjective Type Questions (42 Qs ; 15 VSA, 16 SA, 11 LA)

11.1 Direction Cosines of a Line

If a line makes angles α, β and γ with the X, Y and Z-axes, then direction cosines (or DC's) of a line are given by

$$l = \cos\alpha, m = \cos\beta, n = \cos\gamma$$

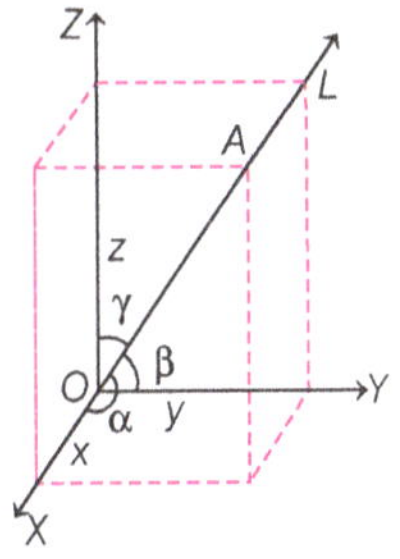

If we consider the angles of a line is reverse (or opposite), then the angles becomes $\pi - \alpha$, $\pi - \beta$ and $\pi - \gamma$, respectively. Also, the signs of direction cosines are reversed i.e. $(-l, -m, -n)$.

Let l, m and n be the direction cosines of a line. Then, the relation between direction cosines of a line is given by

$$l^2 + m^2 + n^2 = 1$$

Direction Cosines of a Line Passing Through Two Points

The direction cosines of a line passing through the points $A(x_1, y_1, z_1)$ and $B(x_2, y_2, z_2)$ are given by

$$\frac{x_2 - x_1}{AB}, \frac{y_2 - y_1}{AB} \text{ and } \frac{z_2 - z_1}{AB}$$

Where, $AB = \sqrt{(x_2 - x_1)^2 + (y_2 - y_1)^2 + (z_2 - z_1)^2}$

11.2 Direction Ratios of a Line

Any three numbers a, b and c proportional to the direction cosines l, m and n respectively, are called the direction ratios or direction numbers of the line.

$\therefore$ We have, $\frac{l}{a} = \frac{m}{b} = \frac{n}{c}$

Hence, if a, b and c are the direction ratios of a line, then its direction cosines are given by

$$l = \frac{a}{\sqrt{a^2 + b^2 + c^2}}, m = \frac{b}{\sqrt{a^2 + b^2 + c^2}}$$

and $n = \frac{c}{\sqrt{a^2 + b^2 + c^2}}$

The direction ratios of a line passing through two points $P(x_1, y_1, z_1)$ and $Q(x_2, y_2, z_2)$ are given by $(x_2 - x_1)$, $(y_2 - y_1)$ and $(z_2 - z_1)$.

Condition for Collinearity of Three Points

Suppose, $A(x_1, y_1, z_1)$, $B(x_2, y_2, z_2)$ and $C(x_3, y_3, z_3)$ are three points in a space.

Then, direction ratios of line joining A and B and B and C are $(x_2 - x_1, y_2 - y_1, z_2 - z_1)$ and $(x_3 - x_2, y_3 - y_2, z_3 - z_2)$, respectively.

If direction ratios of AB and BC are proportional, then these points are collinear, otherwise not.

TEACHER TIPS

(i) Direction cosines of a directed line are unique.

(ii) Direction cosines of X, Y and Z-axes are (1, 0, 0), (0, 1, 0) and (0, 0, 1), respectively.

(iii) The direction ratios of two parallel lines are proportional as two parallel lines have same set of direction cosines.

Example 1 **If a line makes angles 90°, 135°, 45° with the X, Y and Z-axes, respectively. Find its direction cosines.** NCERT, CBSE 2019

Sol. Let direction cosines of the line be l, m and n.

Given, $\alpha = 90°$, $\beta = 135°$ and $\gamma = 45°$

Then, $l = \cos\alpha = \cos 90° = 0$,

$m = \cos\beta = \cos 135° = \frac{-1}{\sqrt{2}}$

and $n = \cos\gamma = \cos 45° = \frac{1}{\sqrt{2}}$

Hence, the direction cosines of a line are $0, \frac{-1}{\sqrt{2}}, \frac{1}{\sqrt{2}}$.

Example 2 **If a line makes angles 90°, 60° and θ with X, Y and Z-axes respectively, where θ is acute, then find θ.** Competency Based Que, CBSE 2015

Sol. Given, $\alpha = 90°$, $\beta = 60°$ and $\gamma = \theta$.

Then, $\cos^2 90° + \cos^2 60° + \cos^2\theta = 1$

$[\because \cos^2\alpha + \cos^2\beta + \cos^2\gamma = 1]$

$\Rightarrow 0 + \frac{1}{4} + \cos^2\theta = 1$

$\Rightarrow \cos^2\theta = \frac{3}{4}$

$\Rightarrow \cos\theta = \pm\frac{\sqrt{3}}{2}$

$\Rightarrow \cos\theta = \frac{\sqrt{3}}{2}$ or $\cos\theta = -\frac{\sqrt{3}}{2}$

$\Rightarrow \theta = 30°$ or $\theta = 150°$

$\therefore \theta = 30°$

$[\because \theta$ is an acute angle$]$

Example 3 **If a line makes angles α, β and γ with the positive direction of coordinate axes, then write the value of $\sin^2\alpha + \sin^2\beta + \sin^2\gamma$.** Competency Based Que, CBSE 2015C

Sol. Since, the line makes angles α, β and γ with positive direction of coordinate axes, therefore $\cos\alpha$, $\cos\beta$ and $\cos\gamma$ are the direction cosines of the line.

So, we have, $\cos^2\alpha + \cos^2\beta + \cos^2\gamma = 1$

$\Rightarrow 1 - \sin^2\alpha + 1 - \sin^2\beta + 1 - \sin^2\gamma = 1$

$[\because \sin^2 x + \cos^2 x = 1]$

$\Rightarrow 3 - 1 = \sin^2\alpha + \sin^2\beta + \sin^2\gamma$

Hence, $\sin^2\alpha + \sin^2\beta + \sin^2\gamma = 2$

Example 4 **If a line has direction ratios 2, –1, 2, then determine its direction cosines.**

Sol. Given, direction ratios are (2, –1, 2) i.e. $a = 2$, $b = -1$ and $c = 2$.

Then, $\sqrt{a^2 + b^2 + c^2} = \sqrt{(2)^2 + (-1)^2 + (2)^2} = \sqrt{9} = 3$

Now, direction cosines are

$$l=\frac{a}{\sqrt{a^2+b^2+c^2}}=\frac{2}{3},\ m=\frac{b}{\sqrt{a^2+b^2+c^2}}=\frac{-1}{3}$$

and $n=\frac{c}{\sqrt{a^2+b^2+c^2}}=\frac{2}{3}$.

Example 5 **Find the direction ratios and direction cosines of the line passing through two points (2, –4, 5) and (0, 1, –1).**

Sol. Let $A(x_1, y_1, z_1)=(2,-4,5)$ and $B(x_2, y_2, z_2)=(0,1,-1)$.

Then, direction ratios of line AB are $(0-2, 1+4, -1-5)$, i.e. $(-2, 5, -6)$.

Now, direction cosines of AB are

$$\left(\frac{-2}{\sqrt{(-2)^2+5^2+(-6)^2}}, \frac{5}{\sqrt{(-2)^2+5^2+(-6)^2}}, \frac{-6}{\sqrt{(-2)^2+5^2+(-6)^2}}\right)$$

Hence, direction cosines of line AB are $\left(\frac{-2}{\sqrt{65}}, \frac{5}{\sqrt{65}}, \frac{-6}{\sqrt{65}}\right)$.

Example 6 **Find the direction cosines of the sides of the triangle whose vertices are (3, 5, –4), (–1, 1, 2) and (–5, –5, –2).** *NCERT*

Sol. Let the vertices of ΔABC be $A(3,5,-4)$, $B(-1,1,2)$ and $C(-5,-5,-2)$.

Then, the direction ratios of side AB are $(-1-3, 1-5, 2-(-4))$, i.e. $(-4,-4,6)$.

[$\because$ if the given points are $A(x_1, y_1, z_1)$ and $B(x_2, y_2, z_2)$, then direction ratios of $AB=(x_2-x_1, y_2-y_1, z_2-z_1)$]

and the direction cosines of AB are

$$\left(\frac{-4}{2\sqrt{17}}, \frac{-4}{2\sqrt{17}}, \frac{6}{2\sqrt{17}}\right) \text{ or } \left(\frac{-2}{\sqrt{17}}, \frac{-2}{\sqrt{17}}, \frac{3}{\sqrt{17}}\right)$$

$\left[\because \text{if } a, b \text{ and } c \text{ are direction ratios, then direction cosines are } \left(\frac{a}{\sqrt{a^2+b^2+c^2}}, \frac{b}{\sqrt{a^2+b^2+c^2}}, \frac{c}{\sqrt{a^2+b^2+c^2}}\right)\right]$

Similarly, the direction ratios of side BC are $((-5-(-1)), (-5-1), (-2-2))$ i.e. $(-4,-6,-4)$

and the direction cosines of BC are

$$\left(\frac{-4}{2\sqrt{17}}, \frac{-6}{2\sqrt{17}}, \frac{-4}{2\sqrt{17}}\right) \text{ or } \left(\frac{-2}{\sqrt{17}}, \frac{-3}{\sqrt{17}}, \frac{-2}{\sqrt{17}}\right).$$

The direction ratios of side AC are

$((-5-3), (-5-5), ((-2-(-4)))$ i.e. $(-8, -10, 2)$

and the direction cosines of AC are

$$\left(\frac{-8}{2\sqrt{42}}, \frac{-10}{2\sqrt{42}}, \frac{2}{2\sqrt{42}}\right) \text{ or } \left(\frac{-4}{\sqrt{42}}, \frac{-5}{\sqrt{42}}, \frac{1}{\sqrt{42}}\right).$$

Example 7 **Show that the points $A(2, 3, -4)$, $B(1, -2, 3)$ and $C(3, 8, -11)$ are collinear.** *NCERT*

Sol. Given points are $A(2,3,-4)$, $B(1,-2,3)$ and $C(3,8,-11)$.

Direction ratios of line joining A and B are

$(1-2, -2-3, 3-(-4))$ i.e. $(-1, -5, 7)$.

Direction ratios of line joining B and C are

$(3-1, 8+2, -11-3)$ i.e. $(2, 10, -14)$.

Now, ratios of direction ratios of AB and BC are

$$\frac{-1}{2}, \frac{-5}{10}, \frac{7}{-14} \text{ i.e. } -\frac{1}{2}, -\frac{1}{2}, -\frac{1}{2}.$$

Thus, the direction ratios of AB and BC are proportional. So, AB is parallel to BC but B is common to both AB and BC.

Hence, A, B and C are collinear points.

Quick Test 1

1. If a line makes angles 90°, 60° and 30° with the positive direction of X, Y and Z-axes respectively, then find its direction cosines.
2. If a line makes angles 90° and 60° with the positive directions of X and Y-axes respectively, then find the angle which it makes with the positive direction of Z-axis. *CBSE 2017*
3. Find the direction cosines of a line whose direction ratios are $(2,-6,3)$.
4. Find the direction ratios of a line whose direction cosines are $\frac{1}{2}, \frac{1}{\sqrt{2}}, \frac{1}{2}$. *Competency Based Que*
5. Find the direction ratios and direction cosines of a line passing through the points $(7,-5,9)$ and $(5,-3,8)$.
6. Show that the line segment joining the point $A(-4,3,-6)$ and $B(2,9,2)$ is parallel to the line joining the points $P(1,2,3)$ and $Q(4,5,7)$. *Competency Based Que*
7. Find the value of λ for which the points $P(-1,3,2)$, $Q(-4,2,-2)$ and $R(5,5,\lambda)$ are collinear. *Competency Based Que*

Answers

1. $\left(0, \frac{1}{2}, \frac{\sqrt{3}}{2}\right)$ **2.** 30° or 150° **3.** $\left[\frac{2}{7}, \frac{-6}{7}, \frac{3}{7}\right]$

4. $(1, \sqrt{2}, 1)$ **5.** $(-2, 2, -1)$, $\left(-\frac{2}{3}, \frac{2}{3}, -\frac{1}{3}\right)$ **7.** 10

For Solutions, See QR Code on Pg. 357

11.3 Lines in Space

A line (or straight line) is a curve such that all the points on the line segment joining any two points of it lies on it.

Equation of a Line through a Given Point and Parallel to a Given Vector

Vector Equation

The vector equation of a line l passing through a point A with position vector $\vec{a}$ and parallel to a given vector $\vec{b}$ is

$$\vec{r} = \vec{a} + \lambda \vec{b},$$

where $\vec{r} = x\hat{i} + y\hat{j} + z\hat{k}$ is the position vector of an arbitrary point P on the line and λ is a real number.

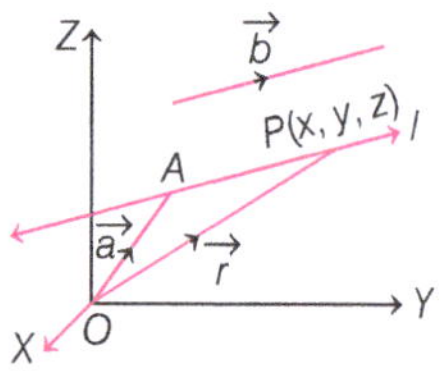

The vector equation of a straight line passing through the origin and parallel to given vector $\vec{b}$ is

$$\vec{r} = \lambda \vec{b}$$

Cartesian Equation

The cartesian equation of a line passing through a point $A(x_1, y_1, z_1)$ and having direction ratios a, b and c is

$$\frac{x - x_1}{a} = \frac{y - y_1}{b} = \frac{z - z_1}{c},$$

where (x, y, z) are coordinates of any point on the line.

If l, m and n are the direction cosines of the line, then equation of the line is

$$\frac{x - x_1}{l} = \frac{y - y_1}{m} = \frac{z - z_1}{n}$$

The cartesian equation of a line passing through origin and having direction ratios (a, b, c) is

$$\frac{x}{a} = \frac{y}{b} = \frac{z}{c}$$

> **TEACHER TIPS**
>
> The cartesian equation of line $\frac{x - x_1}{a} = \frac{y - y_1}{b} = \frac{z - z_1}{c} = \lambda$ is written in vector form as $\vec{r} = (x_1 + y_1 + z_1) + \lambda(a\hat{i} + b\hat{j} + c\hat{k})$ and *vice-versa*.

Angle between Two Lines

Vector Form

Angle between the lines $\vec{r} = \vec{a_1} + \lambda \vec{b_1}$ and $\vec{r} = \vec{a_2} + \mu \vec{b_2}$ is given as

$$\cos\theta = \left| \frac{\vec{b_1} \cdot \vec{b_2}}{|\vec{b_1}||\vec{b_2}|} \right|,$$

where θ is an acute angle between the lines.

Cartesian Form

Angle between the lines $\frac{x - x_1}{a_1} = \frac{y - y_1}{b_1} = \frac{z - z_1}{c_1}$ and $\frac{x - x_2}{a_2} = \frac{y - y_2}{b_2} = \frac{z - z_2}{c_2}$ is given as

$$\cos\theta = \left| \frac{a_1a_2 + b_1b_2 + c_1c_2}{\sqrt{a_1^2 + b_1^2 + c_1^2} \cdot \sqrt{a_2^2 + b_2^2 + c_2^2}} \right|$$

$$\text{or } \sin\theta = \frac{\sqrt{(a_1b_2 - a_2b_1)^2 + (b_1c_2 - b_2c_1)^2 + (c_1a_2 - c_2a_1)^2}}{\sqrt{a_1^2 + b_1^2 + c_1^2} \cdot \sqrt{a_2^2 + b_2^2 + c_2^2}}.$$

Also, angle (θ) between two lines with direction cosines, l_1, m_1, n_1 and l_2, m_2, n_2 is given by

$$\cos\theta = |l_1l_2 + m_1m_2 + n_1n_2|$$

$$\text{or } \sin\theta = \sqrt{(m_1n_2 - m_2n_1)^2 + (n_1l_2 - n_2l_1)^2 + (l_1m_2 - l_2m_1)^2}.$$

Condition of Perpendicularity

Two lines are said to be perpendicular,

in **vector form** if $\vec{b_1} \cdot \vec{b_2} = 0$,

in **cartesian form** if $a_1a_2 + b_1b_2 + c_1c_2 = 0$ [direction ratio form]

or $l_1l_2 + m_1m_2 + n_1n_2 = 0$. [direction cosine form]

Condition that Two Lines are Parallel

Two lines are said to be parallel, in **vector form** if $\vec{b_1} = \lambda \vec{b_2}$;

in **cartesian form** if $\frac{a_1}{a_2} = \frac{b_1}{b_2} = \frac{c_1}{c_2}$ [direction ratio form]

or $\frac{l_1}{l_2} = \frac{m_1}{m_2} = \frac{n_1}{n_2}$ [direction cosine form]

Point of Intersection of Lines

Vector Form

Suppose, two lines be

$$\vec{r} = (a_1\hat{i} + a_2\hat{j} + a_3\hat{k}) + \lambda(b_1\hat{i} + b_2\hat{j} + b_3\hat{k}) \quad \text{...(i)}$$

and $\vec{r} = (a_1'\hat{i} + a_2'\hat{j} + a_3'\hat{k}) + \mu(b_1'\hat{i} + b_2'\hat{j} + b_3'\hat{k})$ ...(ii)

If Eqs. (i) and (ii) intersect, then

$$a_1 + \lambda b_1 = a_1' + \mu b_1', a_2 + \lambda b_2 = a_2' + \mu b_2'$$

and $a_3 + \lambda b_3 = a_3' + \mu b_3'$

Now, find the value of λ and μ by solving any two of above equations.

- If the values of λ and μ satisfy the third equation, then the two lines intersect, otherwise not.
- If intersect, then the point of intersection can be obtain by substituting the value of λ (or μ) in Eq. (i) [or Eq. (ii)].

Cartesian Form

Let two lines be

$$L_1 : \frac{x - x_1}{a_1} = \frac{y - y_1}{b_1} = \frac{z - z_1}{c_1} = \lambda \text{ (say)} \quad \text{...(i)}$$

and $$L_2 : \frac{x - x_2}{a_2} = \frac{y - y_2}{b_2} = \frac{z - z_2}{c_2} = \mu \text{ (say)} \quad \text{...(ii)}$$

If the lines L_1 and L_2 intersect, then

$$x_1 + a_1\lambda = x_2 + a_2\mu,$$

$$y_1 + b_1\lambda = y_2 + b_2\mu$$

and $$z_1 + c_1\lambda = z_2 + c_2\mu$$

Now, find the values of λ and μ by solving any two of above equations.

- If the values of λ and μ satisfy the third equation, then the two lines intersect, otherwise not.
- If intersect, then the point of intersection can be obtain by substituting the value of λ(or μ) in Eq. (i) [or Eq. (ii)].

11.4 Angle between Two Lines

Let L_1 and L_2 be two lines and θ be the acute angle between them

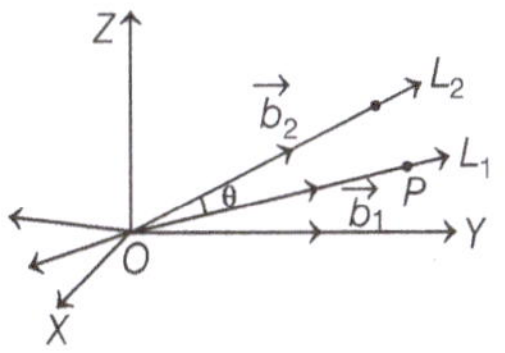

Vector Form

Let the vector equations of lines L_1 and L_2 be $\vec{r} = \vec{a_1} + \lambda\vec{b_1}$ and $\vec{r} = \vec{a_2} + \mu\vec{b_2}$, then angle between these two lines is given by

$$\cos\theta = \left|\frac{\vec{b_1}\cdot\vec{b_2}}{|\vec{b_1}||\vec{b_2}|}\right|$$

where λ and μ are scalars.

Important Results

If two lines are perpendicular, then $\vec{b_1}\cdot\vec{b_2} = 0$

and if two lines are parallel, then $\vec{b_1} = \lambda\vec{b_2}$.

Cartesian Form

Let the cartesian equations of lines L_1 and L_2 be

$$\frac{x - x_1}{a_1} = \frac{y - y_1}{b_1} = \frac{z - z_1}{c_1}$$

and $$\frac{x - x_2}{a_2} = \frac{y - y_2}{b_2} = \frac{z - z_2}{c_2}$$

Then, angle between the lines L_1 and L_2 is given by

$$\cos\theta = \frac{|a_1a_2 + b_1b_2 + c_1c_2|}{\sqrt{a_1^2 + b_1^2 + c_1^2}\sqrt{a_2^2 + b_2^2 + c_2^2}}$$

The angle between the lines in terms of $\sin\theta$ is given by

$$\sin\theta = \frac{\sqrt{(a_1b_2 - a_2b_1)^2 + (b_1c_2 - b_2c_1)^2 + (c_1a_2 - c_2a_1)^2}}{\sqrt{a_1^2 + b_1^2 + c_1^2}\sqrt{a_2^2 + b_2^2 + c_2^2}}$$

where a_1, b_1, c_1 and a_2, b_2, c_2 are direction ratios of lines L_1 and L_2, respectively. If l_1, m_1, n_1 and l_2, m_2, n_2 are direction cosines of lines L_1 and L_2, then angle between the lines is given by $\cos\theta = |l_1l_2 + m_1m_2 + n_1n_2|$

$$[\because l_1^2 + m_1^2 + n_1^2 = 1 = l_2^2 + m_2^2 + n_2^2]$$

and $$\sin\theta = \sqrt{(l_1m_2 - l_2m_1)^2 + (m_1n_2 - m_2n_1)^2 + (n_1l_2 - n_2l_1)^2}$$

TEACHER TIPS

If two lines are perpendicular, then $a_1a_2 + b_1b_2 + c_1c_2 = 0$ and if two lines are parallel, then $\frac{a_1}{a_2} = \frac{b_1}{b_2} = \frac{c_1}{c_2}$.

11.5 Shortest Distance between Two Lines

There are various conditions to find the shortest distance are as follow.

- If two lines in space intersect at a point, then the shortest distance between them is zero.
- If two lines in space are parallel, then the shortest distance between them will be the perpendicular distance.
- If two lines are neither intersecting nor parallel, then such pair of lines are **non-coplanar** and are called **skew-lines**.

TEACHER TIPS

Coplanar lines Two lines lying in the same plane are called coplanar lines. Coplanar lines are either parallel or intersecting.

Shortest Distance between Two Skew-lines

For skew-lines, the line of the shortest distance will be perpendicular to both the lines and it is unique also.

In figure, the shortest distance (SD) between two skew-lines L_1 and L_2 is the length of the line segment PQ.

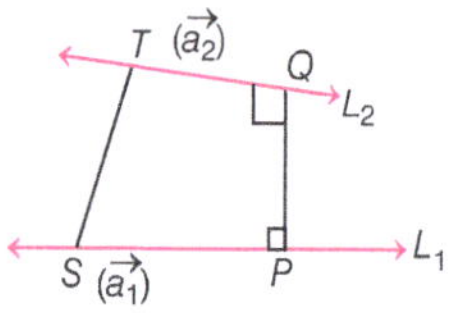

Vector Form

Let the equations of L_1 and L_2 be

$$\vec{r} = \vec{a_1} + \lambda \vec{b_1}$$

and $$\vec{r} = \vec{a_2} + \mu \vec{b_2}$$

Then, shortest distance PQ between these two skew-lines is

$$SD = \frac{|(\vec{a_2} - \vec{a_1}) \cdot (\vec{b_1} \times \vec{b_2})|}{|\vec{b_1} \times \vec{b_2}|}$$

Condition for Two Given Lines to be Intersect

The lines L_1 and L_2 will intersect, if the shortest distance between them is zero.

i.e. $$\frac{\left|(\vec{a_2} - \vec{a_1}) \cdot (\vec{b_1} \times \vec{b_2})\right|}{|\vec{b_1} \times \vec{b_2}|} = 0 \Rightarrow (\vec{a_2} - \vec{a_1}) \cdot (\vec{b_1} \times \vec{b_2}) = 0$$

Cartesian Form

Let L_1 and L_2 be two skew-lines with equations

$$L_1: \frac{x - x_1}{a_1} = \frac{y - y_1}{b_1} = \frac{z - z_1}{c_1}$$

and $$L_2: \frac{x - x_2}{a_2} = \frac{y - y_2}{b_2} = \frac{z - z_2}{c_2}$$

Then, the shortest distance between these lines is

$$\left| \frac{\begin{vmatrix} x_2 - x_1 & y_2 - y_1 & z_2 - z_1 \\ a_1 & b_1 & c_1 \\ a_2 & b_2 & c_2 \end{vmatrix}}{\sqrt{(b_1c_2 - b_2c_1)^2 + (c_1a_2 - c_2a_1)^2 + (a_1b_2 - a_2b_1)^2}} \right|$$

Condition for Two Given Lines to be Intersect

The lines L_1 and L_2 will intersect, if the shortest distance between them is zero

i.e. $$\begin{vmatrix} x_2 - x_1 & y_2 - y_1 & z_2 - z_1 \\ a_1 & b_1 & c_1 \\ a_2 & b_2 & c_2 \end{vmatrix} = 0$$

Shortest Distance between Parallel Lines

If two lines L_1 and L_2 are parallel, then they are coplanar.

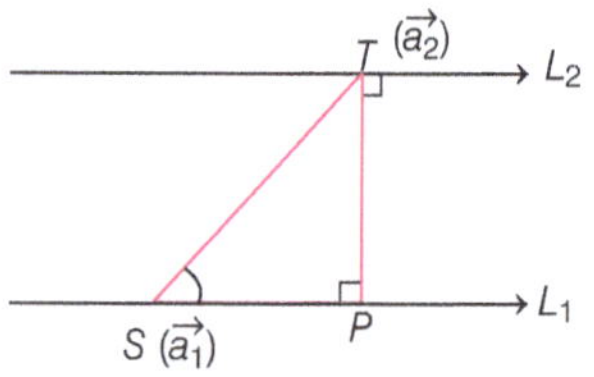

The shortest distance TP between parallel lines

$$L_1: \vec{r} = \vec{a_1} + \lambda \vec{b} \text{ and } L_2: \vec{r} = \vec{a_2} + \mu \vec{b} \text{ is}$$

$$\text{SD or } d = |\overrightarrow{PT}| = \left| \frac{\vec{b} \times (\vec{a_2} - \vec{a_1})}{|\vec{b}|} \right|$$

Perpendicular Distance of a Line from a Given Point

Vector Form

Let L be the foot of perpendicular drawn from the point $P(\vec{\alpha})$ on the given line and the position vector of L be

$\vec{a}+\lambda\vec{b}$, where $\lambda = -\dfrac{(\vec{a}-\vec{\alpha})\cdot\vec{b}}{|\vec{b}|^2}$.

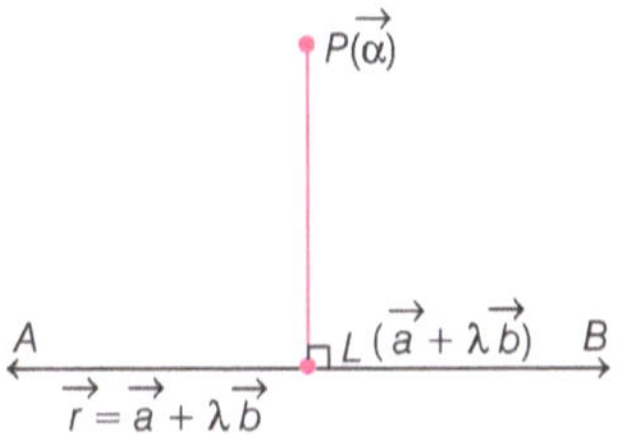

Cartesian Form

Let L be the foot of the perpendicular drawn from $P(\alpha, \beta, \gamma)$ on the line

$$\frac{x-x_1}{a} = \frac{y-y_1}{b} = \frac{z-z_1}{c} = \lambda \text{ (say)}$$

and the coordinates of L can be determined by

$$(x_1 + a\lambda,\ y_1 + b\lambda,\ z_1 + c\lambda),$$

where $\lambda = \dfrac{[a(\alpha - x_1) + b(\beta - y_1) + c(\gamma - z_1)]}{a^2 + b^2 + c^2}$

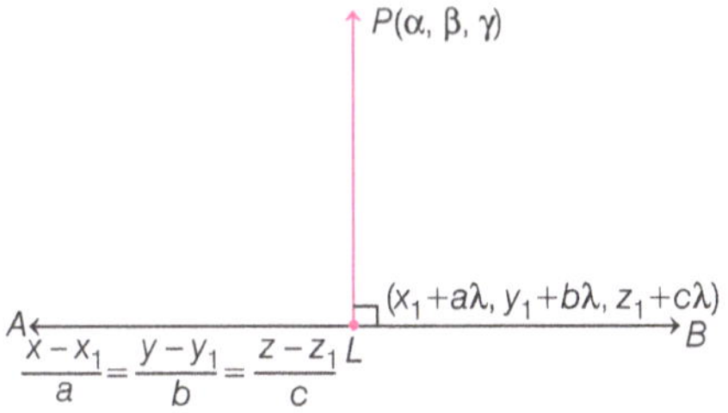

Example 1 **Find the vector equation of the line which passes through the point (3, 4, 5) and is parallel to the vector $2\hat{i} + 2\hat{j} - 3\hat{k}$.** *CBSE 2019*

Sol. Equation of a line passing through a point with position vector $\vec{a}$ and parallel to a vector $\vec{b}$ is

$$\vec{r} = \vec{a} + \lambda\vec{b}$$

Since, line passes through the point (3, 4, 5).

$\therefore \quad \vec{a} = 3\hat{i} + 4\hat{j} + 5\hat{k}$

Since, line is parallel to $2\hat{i} + 2\hat{j} - 3\hat{k}$.

$\therefore \quad \vec{b} = 2\hat{i} + 2\hat{j} - 3\hat{k}$

Equation of line is $\vec{r} = \vec{a} + \lambda\vec{b}$

i.e. $\quad \vec{r} = (3\hat{i} + 4\hat{j} + 5\hat{k}) + \lambda(2\hat{i} + 2\hat{j} - 3\hat{k})$,

which is the required vector equation.

Example 2 **Find the vector equation of the line passing through the point (2, 3, – 5) and making equal angles with the coordinate axes.** *Competency Based Que, CBSE 2024*

Sol. Given, $\alpha = \beta = \gamma$

$\because \cos^2\alpha + \cos^2\beta + \cos^2\gamma = 1$

$\therefore \quad 3\cos^2\alpha = 1$

$\Rightarrow \quad \cos^2\alpha = \dfrac{1}{3}$

$\Rightarrow \quad \cos\alpha = \pm\dfrac{1}{\sqrt{3}}$

$\therefore \quad \cos\alpha = \cos\beta = \cos\gamma = \pm\dfrac{1}{\sqrt{3}}$

So, the required vector equation is

$$\vec{r} = (2\hat{i} + 3\hat{j} - 5\hat{k}) \pm \frac{\lambda}{\sqrt{3}}(\hat{i} + \hat{j} + \hat{k})$$

Example 3 **A line passes through the point with position vector $2\hat{i} - \hat{j} + 4\hat{k}$ and is in the direction of the vector $\hat{i} + \hat{j} - 2\hat{k}$. Find the equation of the line in cartesian form.** *CBSE 2019*

Sol. The given line passes through the point A having position vector $\vec{a} = 2\hat{i} - \hat{j} + 4\hat{k}$ and is parallel to the vector $\vec{b} = (\hat{i} + \hat{j} - 2\hat{k})$

$\therefore$ The equation of the given line is

$$\vec{r} = \vec{a} + \lambda\vec{b}$$

$\Rightarrow \quad \vec{r} = (2\hat{i} - \hat{j} + 4\hat{k}) + \lambda(\hat{i} + \hat{j} - 2\hat{k}) \quad$ ...(i)

For cartesian equation,

On putting $\vec{r} = x\hat{i} + y\hat{j} + z\hat{k}$ in Eq. (i), we get

$\Rightarrow \quad (x\hat{i} + y\hat{j} + z\hat{k}) = (2\hat{i} - \hat{j} + 4\hat{k}) + \lambda(\hat{i} + \hat{j} - 2\hat{k})$

$\Rightarrow \quad x\hat{i} + y\hat{j} + z\hat{k} = (2 + \lambda)\hat{i} + (\lambda - 1)\hat{j} + (4 - 2\lambda)\hat{k}$

$\Rightarrow \quad x = 2 + \lambda,\ y = \lambda - 1$ and $z = 4 - 2\lambda$

$\Rightarrow \quad \dfrac{x-2}{1} = \dfrac{y+1}{1} = \dfrac{z-4}{-2} = \lambda$

Hence, $\dfrac{x-2}{1} = \dfrac{y+1}{1} = \dfrac{z-4}{-2}$ is the required equation of the given line in cartesian form.

Example 4 **Find the vector equation of the line passing through the point (2, 1, 3) and perpendicular to both the lines**

$$\frac{x-1}{1}=\frac{y-2}{2}=\frac{z-3}{3} \text{ and } \frac{x}{-3}=\frac{y}{2}=\frac{z}{5}$$

Competency Based Que, CBSE 2023

Sol. Let $\vec{b_1}=\hat{i}+2\hat{j}+3\hat{k}$ and $\vec{b_2}=-3\hat{i}+2\hat{j}+5\hat{k}$

Since, the required line is perpendicular to the lines parallel to the vectors.

Now, $\vec{b}=\vec{b_1}\times\vec{b_2}$

$$=\begin{vmatrix}\hat{i} & \hat{j} & \hat{k}\\ 1 & 2 & 3\\ -3 & 2 & 5\end{vmatrix}=\hat{i}(10-6)-\hat{j}(5+9)+\hat{k}(2+6)$$

$$=4\hat{i}-14\hat{j}+8\hat{k}$$

$$=2(2\hat{i}-7\hat{j}+4\hat{k})$$

Thus, the direction ratios of the required line are proportional to $(2, -7, 4)$.

Hence, the vector equation of the required line passing through the points (2, 1, 3) and having direction ratios are proportional to $2, -7, 4$ is

$(2\hat{i}+\hat{j}+3\hat{k})+\lambda(2\hat{i}-7\hat{j}+4\hat{k})$.

Example 5 **In vector as well as cartesian method, find the angle between the lines with direction ratios proportional to $(4\hat{i}-3\hat{j}+5\hat{k})$ or (4, – 3, 5) and $(3\hat{i}+4\hat{j}+5\hat{k})$ or (3, 4, 5), respectively.**

Sol. Let θ be the acute angle between the given lines.

Vector Method

Here, $\vec{b_1}=4\hat{i}-3\hat{j}+5\hat{k}$ and $\vec{b_2}=3\hat{i}+4\hat{j}+5\hat{k}$

$$\because \cos\theta=\left|\frac{\vec{b_1}\cdot\vec{b_2}}{|\vec{b_1}||\vec{b_2}|}\right|=\left|\frac{(4\hat{i}-3\hat{j}+5\hat{k})\cdot(3\hat{i}+4\hat{j}+5\hat{k})}{|4\hat{i}-3\hat{j}+5\hat{k}|\,|3\hat{i}+4\hat{j}+5\hat{k}|}\right|$$

$$=\left|\frac{12-12+25}{\sqrt{16+9+25}\sqrt{9+16+25}}\right|=\left|\frac{25}{\sqrt{50}\sqrt{50}}\right|=\frac{25}{50}$$

$$\Rightarrow \cos\theta=\frac{1}{2}$$

$$\therefore \quad \theta=\frac{\pi}{3}$$

Cartesian Method

Here, $a_1=4, b_1=-3, c_1=5$ and $a_2=3, b_2=4, c_2=5$

$$\because \cos\theta=\frac{|a_1a_2+b_1b_2+c_1c_2|}{\sqrt{a_1^2+b_1^2+c_1^2}\sqrt{a_2^2+b_2^2+c_2^2}}$$

$$\therefore \cos\theta=\frac{|4\times3+(-3)\times4+5\times5|}{\sqrt{4^2+(-3)^2+5^2}\sqrt{3^2+4^2+5^2}}$$

$$=\frac{|12-12+25|}{\sqrt{16+9+25}\sqrt{9+16+25}}$$

$$=\frac{25}{\sqrt{50}\sqrt{50}}=\frac{25}{50}=\frac{1}{2}$$

$$\Rightarrow \cos\theta=\cos\left(\frac{\pi}{3}\right)$$

$$\therefore \quad \theta=\frac{\pi}{3}$$

Example 6 **If the angle between the lines**

$$\frac{x-5}{\alpha}=\frac{y+2}{-5}=\frac{z+\frac{24}{5}}{\beta} \text{ and } \frac{x}{1}=\frac{y}{0}=\frac{z}{1} \text{ is } \frac{\pi}{4}, \text{ then find the}$$

relation between α and β. *CBSE 2023*

Sol. Given equations of lines are

$$\frac{x-5}{\alpha}=\frac{y+2}{-5}=\frac{z+\frac{24}{5}}{\beta} \text{ and } \frac{x}{1}=\frac{y}{0}=\frac{z}{1}$$

Here, direction ratios of two lines are $(\alpha, -5, \beta)$ and $(1, 0, 1)$.

We know that for the angle between two lines,

$$\cos\theta=\frac{|a_1a_2+b_1b_2+c_1c_2|}{\sqrt{a_1^2+b_1^2+c_1^2}\sqrt{a_2^2+b_2^2+c_2^2}}$$

Also, given that the angle between the lines is $\frac{\pi}{4}$.

$$\therefore \quad \cos\frac{\pi}{4}=\frac{|\alpha\times1+(-5)\times(0)+\beta\times1|}{\sqrt{\alpha^2+(-5)^2+\beta^2}\sqrt{1^2+0^2+1^2}}$$

$$\Rightarrow \quad \frac{1}{\sqrt{2}}=\frac{|\alpha+\beta|}{\sqrt{\alpha^2+25+\beta^2}\sqrt{2}}$$

$$\Rightarrow \quad \alpha+\beta=\sqrt{\alpha^2+\beta^2+25}$$

On squaring both sides, we get

$$(\alpha+\beta)^2=\alpha^2+\beta^2+25$$

$$\Rightarrow \quad \alpha^2+\beta^2+2\alpha\beta=\alpha^2+\beta^2+25$$

$$\Rightarrow \quad 2\alpha\beta=25 \Rightarrow \alpha\beta=\frac{25}{2}$$

Example 7 **Find the value of λ for which the angle between the lines $\vec{r}=\hat{i}+\hat{j}+\hat{k}+p(2\hat{i}+\hat{j}+2\hat{k})$ and $\vec{r}=(1+q)\hat{i}+(1+q\lambda)\hat{j}+(1+q)\hat{k}$ is $\frac{\pi}{2}$.** *CBSE 2023*

Sol. Given, vector equations of lines are written as

$$\vec{r}=\hat{i}+\hat{j}+\hat{k}+p(2\hat{i}+\hat{j}+2\hat{k})$$

and $$\vec{r}=(\hat{i}+\hat{j}+\hat{k})+q(\hat{i}+\lambda\hat{j}+\hat{k})$$

On comparing both Eqs. with $\vec{r} = \vec{a} + \lambda\vec{b}$, we get

$$\vec{b_1} = (2\hat{i} + \hat{j} + 2\hat{k}) \text{ and } \vec{b_2} = (\hat{i} + \lambda\hat{j} + \hat{k})$$

Since, the angle between the lines is $\frac{\pi}{2}$.

∴ The given lines are perpendicular to each other.

The condition for perpendicular lines is $\vec{b_1}\cdot\vec{b_2} = 0$

$\Rightarrow \quad (2\hat{i} + \hat{j} + 2\hat{k})\cdot(\hat{i} + \lambda\hat{j} + \hat{k}) = 0$

$\Rightarrow \quad 2\cdot1 + 1\cdot\lambda + 2\cdot1 = 0 \Rightarrow 2 + \lambda + 2 = 0$

$\Rightarrow \quad \lambda = -4$

Hence, the value of λ is -4.

Example 8 **Show that lines $\vec{r} = (\hat{i} + \hat{j} - \hat{k}) + \lambda(3\hat{i} - \hat{j})$ and $\vec{r} = (4\hat{i} - \hat{k}) + \mu(2\hat{i} + 3\hat{k})$ intersect each other. Find their point of intersection.** CBSE 2014

Sol. Given lines are $\vec{r} = (\hat{i} + \hat{j} - \hat{k}) + \lambda(3\hat{i} - \hat{j})$ ...(i)

and $\vec{r} = (4\hat{i} - \hat{k}) + \mu(2\hat{i} + 3\hat{k})$ ...(ii)

Clearly, these lines will intersect, if like terms of lines $(\hat{i} + \hat{j} - \hat{k}) + \lambda(3\hat{i} - \hat{j})$ and $(4\hat{i} - \hat{k}) + \mu(2\hat{i} + 3\hat{k})$ are equal for some particular values of λ and μ.

Collecting the like terms, we get

$$(1 + 3\lambda)\hat{i} + (1 - \lambda)\hat{j} - \hat{k} \text{ and } (4 + 2\mu)\hat{i} + (-1 + 3\mu)\hat{k}$$

On equating the coefficients of $\hat{i}$, we get

$$1 + 3\lambda = 4 + 2\mu$$

$\Rightarrow \quad 3\lambda - 2\mu = 3$

On equating the coefficients of $\hat{j}$, we get

$$1 - \lambda = 0$$

$\Rightarrow \quad \lambda = 1$

On equating the coefficients of $\hat{k}$, we get

$$-1 = -1 + 3\mu$$

$\Rightarrow \quad \mu = 0$

$\therefore \quad \mu = 0$ and $\lambda = 1$

Also, these values satisfy $3\lambda - 2\mu = 3$, therefore the given lines intersect.

On putting $\lambda = 1$ in Eq. (i), we get

$$\vec{r} = (\hat{i} + \hat{j} - \hat{k}) + 1(3\hat{i} - \hat{j})$$
$$= 4\hat{i} + 0\hat{j} - \hat{k}$$

Hence, the point of intersection of given lines is $(4, 0, -1)$.

Example 9 **Find the value of b, if the lines $\frac{x-1}{2} = \frac{y-b}{3} = \frac{z-3}{4}$ and $\frac{x-4}{5} = \frac{y-1}{2} = z$ are intersecting lines. Also, find the point of intersection of these given lines.** CBSE 2023

Sol. Given equations of lines are

$$\frac{x-1}{2} = \frac{y-b}{3} = \frac{z-3}{4} = \lambda \text{ (say)} \quad \text{...(i)}$$

and $$\frac{x-4}{5} = \frac{y-1}{2} = \frac{z-0}{1} = \mu \text{ (say)} \quad \text{...(ii)}$$

The coordinates of points on lines (i) and (ii) will be $(2\lambda + 1, 3\lambda + b, 4\lambda + 3)$ and $(5\mu + 4, 2\mu + 1, \mu)$.

If the lines intersect, then point will be equal.

So, $\quad 2\lambda + 1 = 5\mu + 4 \Rightarrow 2\lambda - 5\mu = 3$ ...(iii)

$\quad 3\lambda + b = 2\mu + 1 \Rightarrow 3\lambda - 2\mu = 1 - b$ ...(iv)

and $\quad 4\lambda + 3 = \mu \Rightarrow 4\lambda - \mu = -3$ ...(v)

On solving Eqs. (iii) and (v), we get

$$\lambda = -1 \text{ and } \mu = -1$$

Since, given lines are intersect to each other.

∴ The value of λ and μ satisfy the Eq. (iv), we get

$$3(-1) - 2(-1) = 1 - b$$

$\Rightarrow \quad -3 + 2 = 1 - b$

$\Rightarrow \quad b = 1 + 1 \Rightarrow b = 2$

Now, on putting $\lambda = -1$ and $b = 2$ in coordinates of points on line (i), we get

$$= [2(-1) + 1, 3(-1) + 2, 4(-1) + 3]$$
$$= (-2 + 1, -3 + 2, -4 + 3) = (-1, -1, -1)$$

Hence, the intersection point is $(-1, -1, -1)$.

Example 10 **Find the angle between the lines**

(i) $\vec{r} = 2\hat{i} - 5\hat{j} + \hat{k} + \lambda(3\hat{i} + 2\hat{j} + 6\hat{k})$ and $\vec{r} = 7\hat{i} - 6\hat{k} + \mu(\hat{i} + 2\hat{j} + 2\hat{k})$.

(ii) $\frac{x}{2} = \frac{y}{2} = \frac{z}{1}$ and $\frac{x-5}{4} = \frac{y-2}{1} = \frac{z-3}{8}$. Foreign 2014

Sol.

(i) Given lines are $\vec{r} = 2\hat{i} - 5\hat{j} + \hat{k} + \lambda(3\hat{i} + 2\hat{j} + 6\hat{k})$

and $\vec{r} = 7\hat{i} - 6\hat{k} + \mu(\hat{i} + 2\hat{j} + 2\hat{k})$

On comparing with $\vec{r} = \vec{a_1} + \lambda\vec{b_1}$ and $\vec{r} = \vec{a_2} + \mu\,\vec{b_2}$,

we get $\vec{b_1} = 3\hat{i} + 2\hat{j} + 6\hat{k}$ and $\vec{b_2} = \hat{i} + 2\hat{j} + 2\hat{k}$

∴ The angle between the lines is given by

$$\cos\theta = \left|\frac{\vec{b_1}\cdot\vec{b_2}}{|\vec{b_1}||\vec{b_2}|}\right| = \left|\frac{(3\hat{i} + 2\hat{j} + 6\hat{k})\cdot(\hat{i} + 2\hat{j} + 2\hat{k})}{\sqrt{3^2 + 2^2 + 6^2}\sqrt{1^2 + 2^2 + 2^2}}\right|$$

$$= \left|\frac{3 + 4 + 12}{\sqrt{9 + 4 + 36}\sqrt{1 + 4 + 4}}\right| = \frac{19}{\sqrt{49}\sqrt{9}}$$

$$= \frac{19}{7 \times 3} = \frac{19}{21} \Rightarrow \theta = \cos^{-1}\left(\frac{19}{21}\right)$$

(ii) Given equations of lines are $\frac{x}{2} = \frac{y}{2} = \frac{z}{1}$

and $\frac{x-5}{4} = \frac{y-2}{1} = \frac{z-3}{8}$

Here, direction ratios of two lines are (2, 2, 1) and (4, 1, 8).

Let θ be the acute angle between the given lines, then

$$\cos\theta = \frac{|a_1a_2 + b_1b_2 + c_1c_2|}{\sqrt{a_1^2 + b_1^2 + c_1^2}\sqrt{a_2^2 + b_2^2 + c_2^2}}$$

$$\Rightarrow \cos\theta = \frac{|2 \times 4 + 2 \times 1 + 1 \times 8|}{\sqrt{2^2 + 2^2 + 1^2}\sqrt{4^2 + 1^2 + 8^2}}$$

$$= \frac{|8 + 2 + 8|}{\sqrt{4 + 4 + 1}\sqrt{16 + 1 + 64}}$$

$$= \frac{18}{\sqrt{9}\sqrt{81}} = \frac{18}{3 \times 9} = \frac{2}{3} \Rightarrow \theta = \cos^{-1}\left(\frac{2}{3}\right)$$

Example 11 **Find the angle between the lines with direction ratios proportional to 4, – 3, 5 and 3, 4, 5, respectively.**

Sol. Let θ be the acute angle between the given lines.

Here, $a_1 = 4, b_1 = -3, c_1 = 5$ and $a_2 = 3, b_2 = 4, c_2 = 5$

$$\because \cos\theta = \frac{a_1a_2 + b_1b_2 + c_1c_2}{\sqrt{a_1^2 + b_1^2 + c_1^2}\sqrt{a_2^2 + b_2^2 + c_2^2}}$$

$$\therefore \cos\theta = \frac{4 \times 3 + (-3) \times 4 + 5 \times 5}{\sqrt{4^2 + (-3)^2 + 5^2}\sqrt{3^2 + 4^2 + 5^2}}$$

$$= \frac{12 - 12 + 25}{\sqrt{16 + 9 + 25}\sqrt{9 + 16 + 25}}$$

$$= \frac{25}{\sqrt{50}\sqrt{50}} = \frac{25}{50} = \frac{1}{2}$$

$$\Rightarrow \cos\theta = \cos\left(\frac{\pi}{3}\right) \Rightarrow \theta = \frac{\pi}{3}$$

Example 12 **Find the shortest distance between the lines $\vec{r} = (\hat{i} + 2\hat{j} + 3\hat{k}) + \lambda(\hat{i} - 3\hat{j} + 2\hat{k})$ and $\vec{r} = (4\hat{i} + 5\hat{j} + 6\hat{k}) + \mu(2\hat{i} + 3\hat{j} + \hat{k})$.** *NCERT*

Sol. Given lines are

$$\vec{r} = (\hat{i} + 2\hat{j} + 3\hat{k}) + \lambda(\hat{i} - 3\hat{j} + 2\hat{k}) \quad ...(i)$$

and $$\vec{r} = (4\hat{i} + 5\hat{j} + 6\hat{k}) + \mu(2\hat{i} + 3\hat{j} + \hat{k}). \quad ...(ii)$$

On comparing Eqs. (i) and (ii) with $\vec{r} = a_1 + \lambda b_1$ and $\vec{r} = a_2 + \lambda b_2$ respectively, we get

$$\vec{a_1} = \hat{i} + 2\hat{j} + 3\hat{k}, \ \vec{b_1} = \hat{i} - 3\hat{j} + 2\hat{k}$$

and $\vec{a_2} = 4\hat{i} + 5\hat{j} + 6\hat{k}, \ \vec{b_2} = 2\hat{i} + 3\hat{j} + \hat{k}$

Clearly, $$\vec{b_1} \times \vec{b_2} = \begin{vmatrix} \hat{i} & \hat{j} & \hat{k} \\ 1 & -3 & 2 \\ 2 & 3 & 1 \end{vmatrix}$$

$$= \hat{i}(-3 - 6) - \hat{j}(1 - 4) + \hat{k}(3 + 6)$$

$$= -9\hat{i} + 3\hat{j} + 9\hat{k}$$

$$\Rightarrow |\vec{b_1} \times \vec{b_2}| = |-9\hat{i} + 3\hat{j} + 9\hat{k}|$$

$$= \sqrt{(-9)^2 + (3)^2 + (9)^2}$$

$$= \sqrt{81 + 9 + 81} = \sqrt{171} = 3\sqrt{19}$$

Now, $\vec{a_2} - \vec{a_1} = (4\hat{i} + 5\hat{j} + 6\hat{k}) - (\hat{i} + 2\hat{j} + 3\hat{k})$

$$= 3\hat{i} + 3\hat{j} + 3\hat{k}$$

$$\therefore \text{Required SD} = \frac{|(\vec{a_2} - \vec{a_1}) \cdot (\vec{b_1} \times \vec{b_2})|}{|\vec{b_1} \times \vec{b_2}|}$$

$$= \frac{|(3\hat{i} + 3\hat{j} + 3\hat{k}) \cdot (-9\hat{i} + 3\hat{j} + 9\hat{k})|}{3\sqrt{19}}$$

$$= \frac{|-27 + 9 + 27|}{3\sqrt{19}} = \frac{9}{3\sqrt{19}} = \frac{3}{\sqrt{19}} \text{ unit,}$$

which is the required shortest distance.

Example 13 **Find the shortest distance between the lines $\frac{1-x}{-2} = \frac{2-y}{-3} = \frac{z-3}{4}$ and $\frac{x-2}{3} = \frac{y-4}{4} = \frac{z-5}{5}$.**

Competency Based Que

Sol. Given lines are $\frac{1-x}{-2} = \frac{2-y}{-3} = \frac{z-3}{4}$

and $\frac{x-2}{3} = \frac{y-4}{4} = \frac{z-5}{5}$ which are not in standard form.

Given equations of lines can be written in standard form as

$$\frac{x-1}{2} = \frac{y-2}{3} = \frac{z-3}{4}$$

and $$\frac{x-2}{3} = \frac{y-4}{4} = \frac{z-5}{5}$$

On comparing the given equations of lines with

$$\frac{x - x_1}{a_1} = \frac{y - y_1}{b_1} = \frac{z - z_1}{c_1}$$

and $\frac{x - x_2}{a_2} = \frac{y - y_2}{b_2} = \frac{z - z_2}{c_2}$, we get

$$x_1 = 1, y_1 = 2, z_1 = 3; a_1 = 2, b_1 = 3, c_1 = 4$$

and $x_2 = 2, y_2 = 4, z_2 = 5; a_2 = 3, b_2 = 4, c_2 = 5$

On putting these values in $\begin{vmatrix} x_2 - x_1 & y_2 - y_1 & z_2 - z_1 \\ a_1 & b_1 & c_1 \\ a_2 & b_2 & c_2 \end{vmatrix}$,

we get

$$\begin{vmatrix} 2-1 & 4-2 & 5-3 \\ 2 & 3 & 4 \\ 3 & 4 & 5 \end{vmatrix} = \begin{vmatrix} 1 & 2 & 2 \\ 2 & 3 & 4 \\ 3 & 4 & 5 \end{vmatrix}$$

$$= 1(15-16) - 2(10-12) + 2(8-9)$$

$$= -1 + 4 - 2 = 1$$

Now, $\sqrt{(b_1c_2 - b_2c_1)^2 + (c_1a_2 - c_2a_1)^2 + (a_1b_2 - a_2b_1)^2}$

$$= \sqrt{(3\times 5 - 4\times 4)^2 + (4\times 3 - 5\times 2)^2 + (2\times 4 - 3\times 3)^2}$$

$$= \sqrt{(15-16)^2 + (12-10)^2 + (8-9)^2}$$

$$= \sqrt{(-1)^2 + (2)^2 + (-1)^2}$$

$$= \sqrt{1+4+1} = \sqrt{6}$$

$$\therefore \text{SD} = \frac{\begin{vmatrix} x_2 - x_1 & y_2 - y_1 & z_2 - z_1 \\ a_1 & b_1 & c_1 \\ a_2 & b_2 & c_2 \end{vmatrix}}{\sqrt{(b_1c_2 - b_2c_1)^2 + (c_1a_2 - c_2a_1)^2 + (a_1b_2 - a_2b_1)^2}}$$

$$= \frac{1}{\sqrt{6}} \text{ unit,}$$

which is the required shortest distance.

Example 14 **Find the distance between the lines**

$$\vec{r} = (\hat{i} + 2\hat{j} - 4\hat{k}) + \lambda(2\hat{i} + 3\hat{j} + 6\hat{k})$$

and $\vec{r} = (3\hat{i} + 3\hat{j} - 5\hat{k}) + \mu(4\hat{i} + 6\hat{j} + 12\hat{k})$ CBSE 2023, 14

Sol. Given equations of lines are

$$\vec{r} = (\hat{i} + 2\hat{j} - 4\hat{k}) + \lambda(2\hat{i} + 3\hat{j} + 6\hat{k})$$

and $\vec{r} = (3\hat{i} + 3\hat{j} - 5\hat{k}) + \mu(4\hat{i} + 6\hat{j} + 12\hat{k})$

On comparing with $\vec{r} = a + \lambda\vec{b}$, we get

$$\vec{a_1} = (\hat{i} + 2\hat{j} - 4\hat{k}), \vec{b_1} = (2\hat{i} + 3\hat{j} + 6\hat{k})$$

and $\vec{a_2} = (3\hat{i} + 3\hat{j} - 5\hat{k}), \vec{b_2} = (4\hat{i} + 6\hat{j} + 12\hat{k})$

Now, $\vec{a_2} - \vec{a_1} = (3\hat{i} + 3\hat{j} - 5\hat{k}) - (\hat{i} + 2\hat{j} - 4\hat{k})$

$$= 2\hat{i} + \hat{j} - \hat{k}$$

and $\vec{b_1} \times \vec{b_2} = \begin{vmatrix} \hat{i} & \hat{j} & \hat{k} \\ 2 & 3 & 6 \\ 4 & 6 & 12 \end{vmatrix}$

$$= \hat{i}(36-36) - \hat{j}(24-24) + \hat{k}(12-12) = \vec{0}$$

So, both given lines are parallel and $\vec{b} = 2\hat{i} + 3\hat{j} + 6\hat{k}$.

Then, $\vec{b} \times |\vec{a_2} - \vec{a_1}| = \begin{vmatrix} \hat{i} & \hat{j} & \hat{k} \\ 2 & 3 & 6 \\ 2 & 1 & -1 \end{vmatrix}$

$$= \hat{i}(-3-6) - \hat{j}(-2-12) + \hat{k}(2-6)$$

$$= -9\hat{i} + 14\hat{j} - 4\hat{k}$$

Now, required distance between given lines is

$$d = \left|\frac{\vec{b} \times (\vec{a_2} - \vec{a_1})}{|\vec{b}|}\right| = \left|\frac{-9\hat{i} + 14\hat{j} - 4\hat{k}}{2^2 + 3^2 + 6^2}\right|$$

$$= \frac{\sqrt{81+196+16}}{\sqrt{4+9+36}} = \frac{\sqrt{293}}{\sqrt{49}} = \frac{\sqrt{293}}{7} \text{ units}$$

Example 15 **Find the coordinates of the foot of the perpendicular drawn from the point (2, 3, – 8) to the line** $\frac{4-x}{2} = \frac{y}{6} = \frac{1-z}{3}$**. Also, find the perpendicular distance of the given point from the line.** CBSE 2024

Sol. Given equation of line is $\frac{4-x}{2} = \frac{y}{6} = \frac{1-z}{3}$

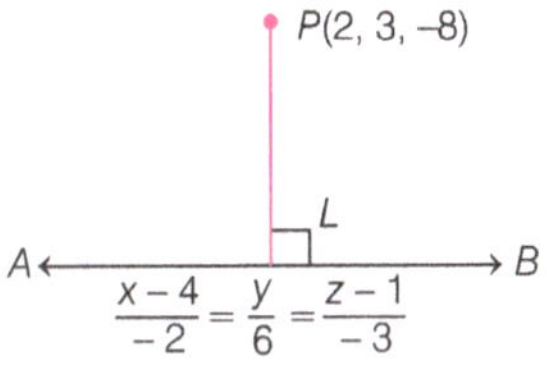

Let $\frac{x-4}{-2} = \frac{y}{6} = \frac{z-1}{-3} = \lambda$

$\Rightarrow \frac{x-4}{-2} = \lambda, \frac{y}{6} = \lambda$

and $\frac{z-1}{-3} = \lambda$

$\Rightarrow \quad x = -2\lambda + 4, y = 6\lambda$ and $z = -3\lambda + 1$

$\therefore$ Coordinates of point L are $(-2\lambda + 4, 6\lambda, -3\lambda + 1)$

Now, direction ratios of line PL

$$= (-2\lambda + 4 - 2, 6\lambda - 3, -3\lambda + 1 + 8)$$

$$= (-2\lambda + 2, 6\lambda - 3, -3\lambda + 9)$$

and direction ratios of line AB are $-2, 6, -3$.

$\because \quad PL \perp AB$

The condition for perpendicular lines is

$$a_1a_2 + b_1b_2 + c_1c_2 = 0, \quad \text{...(i)}$$

where $a_1 = -2\lambda + 2, b_1 = 6\lambda - 3, c_1 = -3\lambda + 9$

and $a_2 = -2, b_2 = 6$ and $c_2 = -3$

From Eq. (i), we get

$$(-2\lambda + 2)(-2) + (6\lambda - 3)(6) + (-3\lambda + 9)(-3) = 0$$

$\Rightarrow \quad 4\lambda - 4 + 36\lambda - 18 + 9\lambda - 27 = 0$

$\Rightarrow \quad 49\lambda = 49 \Rightarrow \lambda = 1$

$\therefore$ Foot of perpendicular $L = (-2\lambda + 4, 6\lambda, -3\lambda + 1)$

$$= (2, 6, -2)$$

Also, length of perpendicular,

PL = Distance between points P and L

$$= \sqrt{(2-2)^2 + (6-3)^2 + (-2+8)^2}$$

$$= \sqrt{9+36} = \sqrt{45} = 3\sqrt{5} \text{ units}$$

Quick Test 2

1. Find the vector equation of the line passing through the point $(1, -2, 3)$ and parallel to the vector $3\hat{i} - 2\hat{j} + 6\hat{k}$.
2. Find the cartesian equation of the line which passes through the point $(-2, 4, -5)$ and is parallel to the line $\frac{x+3}{3} = \frac{4-y}{5} = \frac{z+8}{6}$. CBSE 2013
3. Find the vector and the cartesian equation of the line passing through the point $A(1, 2, -1)$ and parallel to the line $5x - 25 = 14 - 7y = 35z$. CBSE 2023
4. Find the angle between the pair of lines

$$\vec{r} = 3\hat{i} + 2\hat{j} - 4\hat{k} + \lambda(\hat{i} + 2\hat{j} + 2\hat{k})$$

and $\vec{r} = 5\hat{i} - 2\hat{j} + \mu(3\hat{i} + 2\hat{j} + 6\hat{k})$. Competency Based Que

5. Find the value of p so that the following lines are perpendicular.

(i) $\frac{1-x}{3} = \frac{7y-14}{2p} = \frac{z-3}{1}$ and $\frac{7-7x}{3p} = \frac{5-y}{1} = \frac{11-z}{7}$

(ii) $\frac{x-1}{-3} = \frac{y-2}{2p} = \frac{z-3}{2}$ and $\frac{x-1}{3p} = \frac{y-1}{1} = \frac{z-6}{-5}$

6. Check whether the lines given by equations $x = 2\lambda + 2, y = 7\lambda + 1, z = -3\lambda - 3$ and $x = -\mu - 2, y = 2\mu + 8, z = 4\mu + 5$ are perpendicular to each other or not. CBSE 2023
7. Find the shortest distance between the lines

$$\vec{r} = (t+1)\hat{i} + (2-t)\hat{j} + (1+t)3\hat{k}$$

and $\vec{r} = (2s+2)\hat{i} - (1-s)\hat{j} + (2s-1)3\hat{k}$.

Competency Based Que, CBSE 2016C

8. Find the shortest distance between the lines $\frac{x-1}{2} = \frac{y-2}{3} = \frac{z-3}{4}$ and $\frac{x-2}{3} = \frac{y-4}{4} = \frac{z-5}{5}$. CBSE 2018C
9. Find the shortest distance between the following pair of lines

$$\vec{r} = (1+2\lambda)\hat{i} + (1-\lambda)\hat{j} + \lambda\hat{k}$$

and $\vec{r} = (2+4\mu)\hat{i} + (1-2\mu)\hat{j} + (-1+2\mu)\hat{k}$.

10. Find the coordinates of the foot of the perpendicular drawn from the point $P(0, 2, 3)$ to the line

$$\frac{x+3}{5} = \frac{y-1}{2} = \frac{z+4}{3}.$$

Competency Based Que, CBSE 2023

Answers

1. $\vec{r} = \hat{i} - 2\hat{j} + 3\hat{k} + \lambda(3\hat{i} - 2\hat{j} + 6\hat{k})$
2. $\frac{x+2}{3} = \frac{y-4}{-5} = \frac{z+5}{6}$
3. $\vec{r} = \hat{i} + 2\hat{j} - \hat{k} + \lambda\left(\frac{1}{5}\hat{i} - \frac{1}{7}\hat{j} + \frac{1}{35}\hat{k}\right)$ and $5x - 5 = 14 - 7y = 35z + 35$
4. $\cos^{-1}\left(\frac{19}{21}\right)$
5. (i) $p = 7$ (ii) $p = \frac{-10}{7}$
6. The given lines are perpendicular to each other.
7. $\frac{9\sqrt{10}}{10}$ units
8. $\frac{1}{\sqrt{6}}$ unit
9. $\sqrt{\frac{11}{6}}$ unit
10. $(2, 3, -1)$

For Solutions, See QR Code on Pg. 357

EXAM PATTERN QUESTIONS

Objective Type Questions

Multiple Choice Questions

1. The angle which the line $\frac{x}{1}=\frac{y}{-1}=\frac{z}{0}$ makes with the positive direction of Y-axis is

Competency Based Que, CBSE 2024

(a) $\frac{5\pi}{6}$ (b) $\frac{3\pi}{4}$ (c) $\frac{5\pi}{4}$ (d) $\frac{7\pi}{4}$

2. If $\frac{1}{2}, \frac{1}{3}, n$ are the direction cosines of a line, then n is

Competency Based Que, Diksha App

(a) $\frac{\sqrt{23}}{6}$ (b) $\frac{23}{6}$ (c) $\frac{2}{3}$ (d) $\frac{1}{6}$

3. The direction cosines of vector $\overrightarrow{BA}$, where coordinates of A and B are $(1, 2, -1)$ and $(3, 4, 0)$ respectively, are

Competency Based Que, CBSE 2023

(a) $-2, -2, -1$ (b) $-\frac{2}{3}, -\frac{2}{3}, -\frac{1}{3}$

(c) $2, 2, 1$ (d) $\frac{2}{3}, \frac{2}{3}, \frac{1}{3}$

4. Direction cosines of the line $\frac{x-1}{2}=\frac{1-y}{3}=\frac{2z-1}{12}$ are

CBSE 2023

(a) $\frac{2}{7}, \frac{3}{7}, \frac{6}{7}$ (b) $\frac{2}{\sqrt{157}}, -\frac{3}{\sqrt{157}}, \frac{12}{\sqrt{157}}$

(c) $\frac{2}{7}, -\frac{3}{7}, -\frac{6}{7}$ (d) $\frac{2}{7}, -\frac{3}{7}, \frac{6}{7}$

5. A vector makes equal angles with positive directions of X, Y and Z-axes. The direction cosines of the vector are

CBSE 2024C

(a) $\frac{1}{\sqrt{3}}, \frac{1}{\sqrt{3}}, \frac{1}{\sqrt{3}}$ (b) $\frac{-1}{\sqrt{3}}, \frac{-1}{\sqrt{3}}, \frac{1}{\sqrt{3}}$

(c) $\frac{-1}{2}, \frac{1}{2}, \frac{-1}{2}$ (d) $\frac{1}{\sqrt{6}}, \frac{1}{\sqrt{6}}, \frac{-2}{\sqrt{6}}$

6. If O is the origin and $OP = 3$ with direction ratios $-1, 2$ and -2, then coordinates of P are

(a) $(-1, 2, -2)$ (b) $\left(-\frac{1}{3}, \frac{2}{3}, \frac{-2}{3}\right)$

(c) $(-3, 6, 9)$ (d) $(1, 2, 2)$

7. The cartesian equation of the line $\vec{r}=(\hat{i}+2\hat{j}-4\hat{k})+\lambda(2\hat{i}+3\hat{j}+6\hat{k})$ is

(a) $\frac{x-2}{1}=\frac{y-3}{2}=\frac{z-6}{-4}$ (b) $\frac{x+1}{2}=\frac{y+2}{3}=\frac{z-4}{6}$

(c) $\frac{x-1}{2}=\frac{y-2}{3}=\frac{z+4}{5}$ (d) None of these

8. The lines $\vec{r}=\hat{i}+\hat{j}-\hat{k}+\lambda(2\hat{i}+3\hat{j}-6\hat{k})$ and $\vec{r}=2\hat{i}-\hat{j}-\hat{k}+\mu(6\hat{i}+9\hat{j}-18\hat{k})$, (where λ and μ are scalars) are **Competency Based Que, CBSE Sample Paper 2023**

(a) coincident (b) skew

(c) intersecting (d) parallel

9. The cartesian equation of the line passing through the point $(1, -3, 2)$ and parallel to the line $\vec{r}=(2+\lambda)\hat{i}+\lambda\hat{j}+(2\lambda-1)\hat{k}$ is

CBSE 2024

(a) $\frac{x-1}{2}=\frac{y+3}{0}=\frac{z-2}{-1}$ (b) $\frac{x+1}{1}=\frac{y-3}{1}=\frac{z+2}{2}$

(c) $\frac{x+1}{2}=\frac{y-3}{0}=\frac{z+2}{-1}$ (d) $\frac{x-1}{1}=\frac{y+3}{1}=\frac{z-2}{2}$

10. The equation of the line in vector form passing through the point $(-1, 3, 5)$ and parallel to line $\frac{x-3}{2}=\frac{y-4}{3}, z=2$ is

CBSE Sample Paper 2020

(a) $\vec{r}=(-\hat{i}+3\hat{j}+5\hat{k})+\lambda(2\hat{i}+3\hat{j}+\hat{k})$

(b) $\vec{r}=(-\hat{i}+3\hat{j}+5\hat{k})+\lambda(2\hat{i}+3\hat{j})$

(c) $\vec{r}=(2\hat{i}+3\hat{j}-2\hat{k})+\lambda(-\hat{i}+3\hat{j}+5\hat{k})$

(d) $\vec{r}=(2\hat{i}+3\hat{j})+\lambda(-\hat{i}+3\hat{j}+5\hat{k})$

11. The angle between the lines $2x = 3y = -z$ and $6x = -y = -4z$ is **Competency Based Que, CBSE 2023**

(a) $0°$ (b) $30°$ (c) $45°$ (d) $90°$

12. Direction ratios of the line which is perpendicular to the lines with direction ratios $-1, 2, 2$ and $0, 2, 1$ are

Competency Based Que, Diksha App

(a) $1, 1, 2$ (b) $2, -1, 2$ (c) $-2, 1, -2$ (d) $2, 1, -2$

13. The value of λ for which the angle between the lines $\vec{r}=\hat{i}+\hat{j}+\hat{k}+p(2\hat{i}+\hat{j}+2\hat{k})$ and $\vec{r}=(1+q)\hat{i}+(1+q\lambda)\hat{j}+(1+q)\hat{k}$ is $\frac{\pi}{2}$, is

CBSE 2023

(a) -4 (b) 4 (c) 2 (d) -2

14. The lines $\frac{x-2}{1}=\frac{y-3}{1}=\frac{4-z}{k}$ and $\frac{x-1}{k}=\frac{y-4}{2}=\frac{z-5}{-2}$ are mutually perpendicular, if the value of k is

CBSE 2020

(a) $-\frac{2}{3}$ (b) $\frac{2}{3}$ (c) -2 (d) 2

15. Find the angle between the lines $\frac{x-3}{3}=\frac{y-1}{5}=\frac{z+3}{4}$ and $\frac{x+1}{1}=\frac{y-4}{1}=\frac{z-5}{2}$.

(a) $\cos^{-1}\left(\frac{8\sqrt{3}}{15}\right)$ (b) $\cos^{-1}\left(\frac{16}{10\sqrt{2}}\right)$

(c) $\cos^{-1}\left(\frac{16}{15\sqrt{3}}\right)$ (d) None of these

16. The angle between any two diagonals of a cube is

Competency Based Que

(a) 60° (b) $\cos^{-1}\left(\frac{1}{3}\right)$ (c) $\sin^{-1}\left(\frac{1}{3}\right)$ (d) $\frac{\pi}{2}$

17. Find the distance between the lines l_1 and l_2 given by

$$\vec{r}=(\hat{i}+2\hat{j}-4\hat{k})+\lambda(2\hat{i}+3\hat{j}+6\hat{k})$$

and $\vec{r}=(3\hat{i}+3\hat{j}-5\hat{k})+\lambda(2\hat{i}+3\hat{j}+6\hat{k})$

(a) $\frac{15}{7}$ (b) $\frac{\sqrt{293}}{7}$ (c) $\frac{17}{7}$ (d) $\frac{\sqrt{296}}{7}$

Assertion-Reason Based Questions

Directions (Q. Nos. 18-27) *In the questions given below are two statements labelled as Assertion (A) and Reason (R). In the context of the two statements, which one of the following is correct?*

(a) Both A and R are correct; R is the correct explanation of A.
(b) Both A and R are correct; R is not the correct explanation of A.
(c) A is correct; R is incorrect.
(d) R is correct; A is incorrect.

18. Assertion (A) If a line has direction ratios 2, – 1, – 2, then its direction cosines are $\frac{2}{3},\frac{-1}{3},\frac{-2}{3}$.

Reason (R) If a, b and c are the direction ratios of a line, then the direction cosines are

$$\left[\frac{a}{\sqrt{a^2+b^2+c^2}},\frac{b}{\sqrt{a^2+b^2+c^2}},\frac{c}{\sqrt{a^2+b^2+c^2}}\right].$$

19. Assertion (A) The direction cosines of a line passing through the points (1, 3, 5) and (2, 4, 6) are $\left(\frac{1}{\sqrt{3}},\frac{1}{\sqrt{3}},\frac{1}{\sqrt{3}}\right)$.

Reason (R) The direction ratios of a line passing through two points (x_1,y_1,z_1) and (x_2,y_2,z_2) are $[(x_2-x_1),(y_2-y_1),(z_2-z_1)]$.

20. Assertion (A) If a line makes α,β and γ with X, Y and Z-axes respectively, then $\cos 2\alpha+\cos 2\beta+\cos 2\gamma=-1$.

Reason (R) Sum of the square of the direction cosines of a line is equal to 1.

Competency Based Que

21. Assertion (A) The points (1, 2, 3), (–2, 3, 4) and (7, 0, 1) are collinear.

Reason (R) If a line makes angles $\frac{\pi}{2},\frac{3\pi}{4}$ and $\frac{\pi}{4}$ with X, Y and Z-axes respectively, then its direction cosines are $0,\frac{-1}{\sqrt{2}}$ and $\frac{1}{\sqrt{2}}$.

22. Assertion (A) Equation of the line passing through the point (1, – 2, 3) and parallel to the vector $(3\hat{i}+2\hat{j}+6\hat{k})$ is $\vec{r}=(\hat{i}-2\hat{j}+3\hat{k})+\lambda(3\hat{i}+2\hat{j}+6\hat{k})$.

Reason (R) The vector equation of a straight line passing through a given point with a position vector $\vec{r_1}$ and parallel to a given vector $\vec{m}$ is $\vec{r}=\vec{r_1}+\lambda\vec{m}$ (where λ is a scalar).

23. Assertion (A) The equation of a line which passes through the point (1, 2, 3) and is parallel to the vector $3\hat{i}+2\hat{j}-2\hat{k}$ is $\vec{r}=(\hat{i}+2\hat{j}+3\hat{k})+\lambda(2\hat{i}+3\hat{j}-2\hat{k})$.

Reason (R) The vector equation of a line passing through a point with position vector $\vec{a}$ and parallel to a given vector $\vec{b}$ is $\vec{r}=\vec{a}+\lambda\vec{b}$.

24. Assertion (A) Line $\frac{-x+2}{-2}=\frac{y-1}{7}=\frac{z+3}{-3}$ and $\frac{x+2}{-1}=\frac{2y-8}{4}=\frac{z-5}{4}$ are perpendicular to each other.

Reason (R) If dot product of the direction ratios of two lines is zero, then lines are perpendicular.

25. Assertion (A) The lines $\vec{r}=\vec{a_1}+\lambda\vec{b_1}$ and $\vec{r}=\vec{a_1}+\mu\vec{b_2}$ are perpendicular, when $\vec{b_1}\cdot\vec{b_2}=0$.

Reason (R) The angle θ between the lines $\vec{r}=\vec{a_1}+\lambda\vec{b_1}$ and $\vec{r}=\vec{b_2}+\mu\vec{b_2}$ is given by $\cos\theta=\left|\frac{\vec{b_1}\cdot\vec{b_2}}{|\vec{b_1}||\vec{b_2}|}\right|$.

Competency Based Que

26. Assertion (A) Angle between $\frac{x+2}{2}=\frac{y-1}{3}=\frac{z-2}{1}$ and $\frac{x-3}{-3}=\frac{y}{-2}=\frac{z+1}{2}$ is $\frac{\pi}{6}$.

Reason (R) If direction ratios of two lines are in same ratio, then lines are parallel.

Case Study Based Questions

27. A cricket match is organized between two clubs A and B for which a team from each club is chosen. Remaining of club A and club B, respectively sitting on the lines, represented by the equation $\frac{x-1}{2}=\frac{y-2}{3}=\frac{z-3}{4}$ and $\frac{x-4}{3}=\frac{y+2}{2}=\frac{z}{6}$ and to cheer the team of their club.

Based on the above information, answer the following questions.

(i) Find the vector equation of the line on which players of club A are seated.

(ii) Find the direction cosines of the line on which players of club B are seated.

(iii) If the line on which players of club A are seated is perpendicular to the line $\frac{x-3}{7}=\frac{7-y}{4}=\frac{kz-7}{1}$, then find the value of k.

(iv) Find the angle between the lines on which players of club A and club B are seated.

(v) Find the shortest distance between the lines on which players of club A and club B are seated.

28. A new railway line is to be created in the direction whose cartesian equation is $6x-2=3y+1=2z-2$.

Based on the above information, answer the following questions.

(i) Find the direction cosines of the line.

(ii) Find the equation of the line parallel to this line and passing through (1, 2, 3).

(iii) If a city with coordinate $\left(\frac{2}{3},\frac{1}{3},2\right)$, then find whether it lie in the path or not.

(iv) If the path with equation $\frac{x-1}{2}=\frac{y-2}{3}=\frac{z}{\lambda}$ is perpendicular to the original path find the value of λ.

(v) Find the angle between the original path and $\frac{x}{-1}=\frac{y+2}{2}=\frac{3-6z}{5}$.

29. A supply ship left a port to replenish food and equipment for the Indian navy. Enemies used a submarine to track the ship and scout the port.

Assuming the port to be at the origin, the position of the ship is (5 km, 0 km, 9 km) and the position of the submarine is (11 km, –0.9 km, –10 km). **CBSE QB**

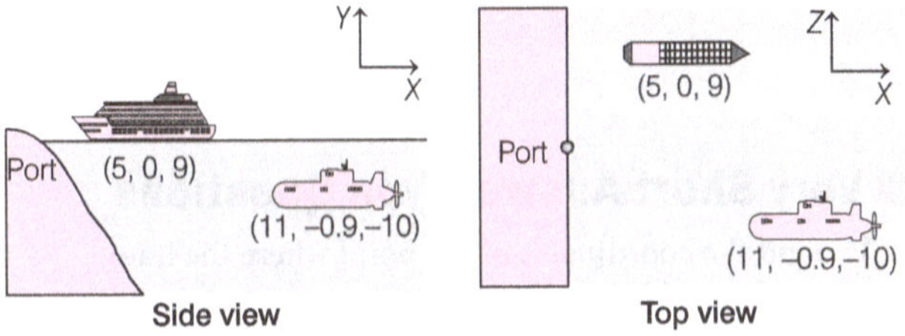

(**Note** the figure is not to scale.)

Based on the above information, answer the following questions.

(i) What angle does the line joining the ship and the port make with the Z-axis?

(a) $\cos^{-1}0$ (b) $\cos^{-1}\pm 1$

(c) $\cos^{-1}\pm\left(\frac{9}{\sqrt{106}}\right)$ (d) $\cos^{-1}\pm\left(\frac{10}{\sqrt{302}}\right)$

(ii) The submarine squad wants to find the direction cosines of the line joining the submarine to the port. The captain of the submarine says that the direction cosines are $\frac{-11}{\sqrt{221.81}},\frac{0.9}{\sqrt{221.81}},\frac{10}{\sqrt{221.81}}$ and his sub-ordinate says that the direction cosines are $\frac{11}{\sqrt{221.81}},\frac{-0.9}{\sqrt{221.81}},\frac{-10}{\sqrt{221.81}}$.

Who is correct?

(a) The captain (b) The sub-ordinate

(c) Both of them (d) Neither of them

(iii) The distance between the port and the ship is $\sqrt{106}$ km, the distance between submarine and the port is $\sqrt{221.81}$ km and the distance between the ship and the submarine is $\sqrt{397.81}$ km.

Which of the following represents the angle between the lines joining the submarine to the ship and the line joining the submarine to the port?

(a) $\cos^{-1}\left|\frac{-35}{\sqrt{106}\times\sqrt{221.81}}\right|$ (b) $\cos^{-1}\left|\frac{201}{\sqrt{397.81}\times\sqrt{106}}\right|$

(c) $\cos^{-1}\left|\frac{256.81}{\sqrt{397.81}\times\sqrt{221.81}}\right|$

(d) $\cos^{-1}\left|\frac{2040}{\sqrt{397.81}\times\sqrt{106}\times\sqrt{221.81}}\right|$

(iv) Which of the following is the equation of the line joining the submarine and the port?

Equation I $11\hat{i}-0.9\hat{j}-10\hat{k}+\lambda(-11\hat{i}+0.9\hat{j}+10\hat{k})$

Equation II $\lambda(-11\hat{i}-0.9\hat{j}-10\hat{k})$

(a) Equation I

(b) Equation II

(c) Both equation I and equation II

(d) Neither equation I nor equation II

Subjective Questions

Very Short Answer Type Questions

1. Find the coordinates of the point where the line $\frac{x+3}{3}=\frac{y-1}{-1}=\frac{z-5}{-5}$ cuts the XY-plane.
Competency Based Que, CBSE Sample Paper 2021

2. If a line makes angle 60°, 135° and 45° with the X, Y and Z-axes, respectively. Find its direction cosines.

3. If a line makes angles 60°, 45° and θ with X, Y and Z-axes respectively, then find the angle θ, where θ is acute angle.

4. If a line has direction ratios 1, -2, 1, then determine its direction cosines.

5. Find the direction ratios of the line segment joining the points $A(1, 5, 4)$ and $B(4, 1, -2)$.

6. Check the following points are collinear or not.
$A(5, 7, 8)$, $B(-1, -2, 1)$ and $C(2, 3, 4)$

7. If the cartesian equation of a line is $\frac{3-x}{5}=\frac{y+4}{7}=\frac{2z-6}{4}$, then write the vector equation of the line. **Competency Based Que, CBSE 2014**

8. Write the equation of the straight line through the point (α, β, γ) and parallel to Z-axis.
Competency Based Que, CBSE 2014

9. Find the direction cosines of the line
$$\frac{4-x}{2}=\frac{y}{6}=\frac{1-z}{3}.$$
CBSE 2013

10. Write the vector equation of a line passing through the point $(1, -1, 2)$ and parallel to the line whose equation is $\frac{x-3}{1}=\frac{y-1}{2}=\frac{z+1}{-2}$. **CBSE 2013**

11. Find the cartesian equation of the line which passes through the point $(-2, 4, -5)$ and is parallel to the line $\frac{x+3}{3}=\frac{4-y}{5}=\frac{z+8}{6}$. **CBSE 2013**

12. Find the equation of the line which passes through the point (2, 4, 6) and is parallel to the vector $3\hat{i}+2\hat{j}-2\hat{k}$.

13. Find the equation of a line passing through the point $(-3, 2, -4)$ and equally inclined to the axes.
Competency Based Que

14. Find the angle between two lines whose direction ratios are (2, 1, 2) and (4, 8, 1).

15. Show that the equations of line $\frac{x-2}{2}=\frac{y-1}{7}=\frac{z+3}{-3}$ and $\frac{x+2}{-1}=\frac{y-8}{2}=\frac{z-5}{4}$ are perpendicular to each other.
Competency Based Que

Short Answer Type Questions

16. A line makes the same angle θ with each of the X and Z-axes. If the angle β, which it makes with Y-axis, is such that $\sin^2\beta = 3\sin^2\theta$, then find the value of $\cos^2\theta$.
Competency Based Que

17. The equations of a line is $5x-3=15y+7=3-10z$. Write the direction cosines of the line.
Competency Based Que, CBSE 2015

18. Show that the following points are collinear $P(1, -2, -2)$, $Q(3, -6, -8)$, $R(-2, 4, 7)$.

19. A line passes through the point with position vector $2\hat{i}-3\hat{j}+4\hat{k}$ and makes angles 60°, 120° and 45° with X, Y and Z-axes, respectively. Find the equation of the line in the cartesian form. **Competency Based Que, CBSE 2016C**

20. Find the vector equation of the line which is parallel to vector $5\hat{i}+\hat{j}-7\hat{k}$ and passing through the point $(5, 2, -4)$.

21. Find the equation of a line in cartesian form, which is parallel to vector $2\hat{i}-\hat{j}+3\hat{k}$ and passing through a point with position vector $5\hat{i}-2\hat{j}+4\hat{k}$. **Competency Based Que**

22. Find the vector equation for the line which passes through the point (1, 2, 3) and is parallel to the line $\frac{x-1}{-2}=\frac{1-y}{3}=\frac{3-z}{-4}$.
CBSE 2016C

23. If the cartesian equation of a line is $\frac{3-x}{5}=\frac{y+4}{9}=\frac{2z-6}{4}$, then write the vector equation for the line.

24. Find the angle between the lines
$$\vec{r}=2\hat{i}-5\hat{j}+\hat{k}+\lambda(3\hat{i}+2\hat{j}+6\hat{k})$$
and $$\vec{r}=7\hat{i}-6\hat{k}+\mu(\hat{i}+2\hat{j}+2\hat{k}).$$

25. Find the angle between the lines
$$\frac{x}{2}=\frac{y}{2}=\frac{z}{1} \text{ and } \frac{x-5}{4}=\frac{y-2}{1}=\frac{z-3}{8}.$$
CBSE 2014

26. Find the value of μ, so that lines

$$\vec{r} = (3\hat{i} - \hat{j} + 2\hat{k}) + \lambda(2\hat{i} - 3\mu\hat{j} + 4\hat{k})$$

and $\vec{r} = -2\hat{i} + 4\hat{j} - 5\hat{k} + \lambda(2\mu\hat{i} + 4\hat{j} + 4\hat{k})$ are perpendicular to each other.

27. Find the value of k so that the lines joining the points $(1, -1, 2)$ and $(3, 4, k)$ is perpendicular to the line joining the points $(0, 3, 2)$ and $(3, 5, 6)$. **CBSE 2024C**

28. Show that the shortest distance between the lines

$\vec{r} = -\hat{i} + 4\hat{j} + 3\hat{k} + \lambda(4\hat{i} + \hat{j})$ and

$\vec{r} = -4\hat{i} + \hat{j} + \mu(5\hat{i} + 2\hat{j} + \hat{k})$ is zero.

29. Find the shortest distance between the lines

$\vec{r} = (2\hat{i} - \hat{j} + 3\hat{k}) + \lambda(\hat{i} - 2\hat{j} + 3\hat{k})$

and $\vec{r} = (\hat{i} + 4\hat{k}) + \mu(3\hat{i} - 6\hat{j} + 9\hat{k})$ **CBSE 2025**

30. Find the shortest distance between the lines $\frac{x+1}{2} = \frac{y-1}{1} = \frac{z-9}{-3}$ and $\frac{x-3}{2} = \frac{y+15}{-7} = \frac{z-9}{5}$ **CBSE 2025**

31. Find the coordinates of the foot of the perpendicular drawn from point $P(5, 7, 3)$ to the line

$$\frac{x-15}{3} = \frac{y-29}{8} = \frac{z-5}{-5}.$$

Competency Based Que, CBSE 2023

Long Answer Type Questions

32. Find the vector and cartesian equations of the line through the point $(1, 2, -4)$ and perpendicular to the two lines $\vec{r} = (8\hat{i} - 19\hat{j} + 10\hat{k}) + \lambda(3\hat{i} - 16\hat{j} + 7\hat{k})$ and

$\vec{r} = (15\hat{i} + 29\hat{j} + 5\hat{k}) + \mu(3\hat{i} + 8\hat{j} - 5\hat{k})$. **CBSE 2016**

33. A line passes through the point $(2, -1, 3)$ and is perpendicular to the lines $\vec{r} = (\hat{i} + \hat{j} - \hat{k}) + \lambda(2\hat{i} - 2\hat{j} + \hat{k})$ and $\vec{r} = (2\hat{i} - \hat{j} - 3\hat{k}) + \mu(\hat{i} + 2\hat{j} + 2\hat{k})$. Obtain its equation in vector and cartesian form. **Competency Based Que, CBSE 2014**

34. Find the vector and cartesian equations of the line which is perpendicular to the lines with equations $\frac{x+2}{1} = \frac{y-3}{2} = \frac{z+1}{4}$ and $\frac{x-1}{2} = \frac{y-2}{3} = \frac{z-3}{4}$ and passes through the point $(1, 1, 1)$. Also, find the angle between the given lines. **CBSE 2020**

35. Show that the lines $\frac{x+1}{3} = \frac{y+3}{5} = \frac{z+5}{7}$ and $\frac{x-2}{1} = \frac{y-4}{3} = \frac{z-6}{5}$ intersect. Also, find their points of intersection. **CBSE 2014**

36. Find the value of λ so that the lines

$$\frac{1-x}{3} = \frac{7y-14}{\lambda} = \frac{z-3}{2}$$

and $\frac{7-7x}{3\lambda} = \frac{y-5}{1} = \frac{6-z}{5}$

are at right angles. Also, find whether the lines are intersecting or not. **Competency Based Que, CBSE 2019**

37. Find the shortest distance between the lines $\frac{x-8}{3} = \frac{y+9}{-16} = \frac{z-10}{7}$ and $\frac{x-15}{3} = \frac{y-29}{8} = \frac{z-5}{-5}$.

Competency Based Que, CBSE 2024C

38. Find the shortest distance between the lines L_1 and L_2 given below.

L_1 : The line passing through $(2, -1, 1)$ and parallel to $\frac{x}{1} = \frac{y}{1} = \frac{z}{3}$.

$L_2 : \vec{r} = \hat{i} + (2\mu + 1)\hat{j} - (\mu + 2)\hat{k}$.

Competency Based Que, CBSE 2024

39. Vertices B and C of ΔABC lie on the line $\frac{x+2}{2} = \frac{y-1}{1} = \frac{z}{4}$. Find the area of ΔABC given that point A has coordinates $(1, -1, 2)$ and the line segment BC has length of 5 units.

Competency Based Que, CBSE 2023

40. Find the image of the point $(2, -1, 5)$ in the line $\frac{x-11}{10} = \frac{y+2}{-4} = \frac{z+8}{-11}$. **Competency Based Que, CBSE 2023**

41. Find the foot of the perpendicular drawn from the point $(\hat{i} + 6\hat{j} + 3\hat{k})$ to the line $\vec{r} = \hat{j} + 2\hat{k} + \lambda(\hat{i} + 2\hat{j} + 3\hat{k})$. Also, find the length of the perpendicular.

42. Find the image of the point $(-1, 5, 2)$ in the line $\frac{2x-4}{2} = \frac{y}{2} = \frac{2-z}{3}$. Find the length of the line segment joining the points (given point and the image **CBSE 2025**

Hints & Solutions

Objective Type Questions

1. (b) For the line, $\frac{x}{1}=\frac{y}{-1}=\frac{z}{0}$

Direction ratios of the given line are 1, − 1, 0.

$\therefore$ Direction cosines of the given line are

$$\frac{1}{\sqrt{1^2+(-1)^2+0^2}},\frac{-1}{\sqrt{1^2+(-1)^2+0^2}},\frac{0}{\sqrt{1^2+(-1)^2+0^2}}$$

$$=\frac{1}{\sqrt{2}},\frac{-1}{\sqrt{2}},0$$

Since, we need to find the angle which the line $\frac{x}{1}=\frac{y}{-1}=\frac{z}{0}$ makes with the positive direction of Y-axis.

$\therefore\ \cos\beta=-\frac{1}{\sqrt{2}}$

$\Rightarrow\quad \beta=\cos^{-1}\left(\frac{-1}{\sqrt{2}}\right)=\frac{3\pi}{4}$

2. (a) If $\frac{1}{2},\frac{1}{3}$ and n are direction cosines of a line then we know that the sum of square of direction cosine is 1.

$\Rightarrow\quad \left(\frac{1}{2}\right)^2+\left(\frac{1}{3}\right)^2+n^2=1$

$\Rightarrow\quad n^2=1-\frac{1}{4}-\frac{1}{9}$

$=\frac{36-9-4}{36}$

$\Rightarrow\quad n^2=\frac{23}{36}$

$\therefore\quad n=\pm\frac{\sqrt{23}}{6}$

3. (b) The given points are $A(1,2,-1)$ and $B(3,4,0)$.

$\therefore\ \overrightarrow{BA}=(1-3)\hat{i}+(2-4)\hat{j}+(-1-0)\hat{k}=-2\hat{i}-2\hat{j}-\hat{k}$

$|\overrightarrow{BA}|=\sqrt{(-2)^2+(-2)^2+(-1)^2}$

$=\sqrt{4+4+1}=\sqrt{9}=3$

Hence, the direction cosines of $\overrightarrow{BA}$ are $-\frac{2}{3},-\frac{2}{3},-\frac{1}{3}$.

4. (d) Given equation of line is

$$\frac{x-1}{2}=\frac{1-y}{3}=\frac{2z-1}{12}$$

$$\Rightarrow\quad \frac{x-1}{2}=\frac{y-1}{-3}=\frac{z-\frac{1}{2}}{6}$$

Its direction cosines are

$$\frac{2}{\sqrt{(2)^2+(-3)^2+(6)^2}},\frac{-3}{\sqrt{(2)^2+(-3)^2+(6)^2}},$$

$$\frac{6}{\sqrt{(2)^2+(-3)^2+(6)^2}}\text{ i.e. }\frac{2}{7},\frac{-3}{7},\frac{6}{7}.$$

5. (a) Let the vector makes angle α with each of the axis.

Then, its direction cosines are $\cos\alpha,\cos\alpha,\cos\alpha$.

Since, $\cos^2\alpha+\cos^2\alpha+\cos^2\alpha=1$

$\therefore\quad \cos\alpha=\pm\frac{1}{\sqrt{3}}$

Since, angle makes with positive directions of the axes.

Hence, direction cosines are $\left(\frac{1}{\sqrt{3}},\frac{1}{\sqrt{3}},\frac{1}{\sqrt{3}}\right)$.

6. (a) Given, O is the origin and $OP=3$ with direction ratios $-1,2,-2$.

Let $P=(x,y,z)$ and $O=(0,0,0)$

As we know that direction ratios of a line joining the points $A(x_1,y_1,z_1)$ and $B(x_2,y_2,z_2)$ are $(x_2-x_1,y_2-y_1,z_2-z_1)$.

$\therefore$ Direction ratios of OP are $(x-0,y-0,z-0)=(x,y,z)$

Thus, $(x,y,z)=(-1,2,-2)$

Hence, coordinates of point P are $(-1,2,-2)$.

7. (d) Given vector equation of a line is

$$\vec{r}=(\hat{i}+2\hat{j}-4\hat{k})+\lambda(2\hat{i}+3\hat{j}+6\hat{k})$$

Here, $\vec{a}=(\hat{i}+2\hat{j}-4\hat{k})=(1,2,-4)$

and $\quad \vec{b}=2\hat{i}+3\hat{j}+6\hat{k}$

$=(2,3,6)$

$\therefore\quad \frac{x-1}{2}=\frac{y-2}{3}=\frac{z+4}{6}$

8. (d) Given lines are

$\vec{r}=\hat{i}+\hat{j}-\hat{k}+\lambda(2\hat{i}+3\hat{j}-6\hat{k})$ ...(i)

and $\quad \vec{r}=2\hat{i}-\hat{j}-\hat{k}+\mu(6\hat{i}+9\hat{j}-18\hat{k})$

$\Rightarrow\quad \vec{r}=2\hat{i}-\hat{j}-\hat{k}+3\mu(2\hat{i}+3\hat{j}-6\hat{k})$

$=2\hat{i}-\hat{j}-\hat{k}+\mu'(2\hat{i}+3\hat{j}-6\hat{k})$ ...(ii)

Where, $\mu'=3\mu$

Here, direction ratios of both the lines are same.

$\therefore$ The lines are parallel to each other.

9. (d) For the given line, $\vec{r}=(2+\lambda)\hat{i}+\lambda\hat{j}+(2\lambda-1)\hat{k}$

$$=(2\hat{i}+0\hat{j}-\hat{k})+\lambda(\hat{i}+\hat{j}+2\hat{k})$$

So, parallel vector to the given line is $(\hat{i}+\hat{j}+2\hat{k})$.

The direction ratios are (1, 1, 2) and position vector of the given point on the required line is $(\hat{i}-3\hat{j}+2\hat{k})$.

Thus, the vector equation of line is

$$\vec{r}=(\hat{i}-3\hat{j}+2\hat{k})+\lambda(\hat{i}+\hat{j}+2\hat{k})$$

In cartesian form, the required equation is

$$\frac{x-1}{1}=\frac{y+3}{1}=\frac{z-2}{2}.$$

10. (b) The given line is $\frac{x-3}{2}=\frac{y-4}{3}, z=2$.

These equations can be written as $\frac{x-3}{2}=\frac{y-4}{3}=\frac{z-2}{0}$

Direction ratios of the given line are 2, 3, 0.

$\Rightarrow$ Direction ratios of a line parallel to the given line are proportional to 2, 3, 0.

$\therefore$ The required equation of line which is passing through (−1, 3, 5) and having direction ratios 2, 3, 0 is

$\vec{r}=(-\hat{i}+3\hat{j}+5\hat{k})+\lambda(2\hat{i}+3\hat{j})$.

11. (d) The given equations of lines can be rewritten as

$\frac{x-0}{3}=\frac{y-0}{2}=\frac{z-0}{-6}$ and $\frac{x-0}{2}=\frac{y-0}{-12}=\frac{z-0}{-3}$

Here, direction ratios of first line are (3, 2, − 6) and direction ratios of second line are (2, − 12, − 3).

Let θ be the angle between the lines.

$$\text{Then, } \cos\theta=\left|\frac{3\times2+2\times(-12)+(-6)\times(-3)}{\sqrt{3^2+2^2+(-6)^2}\,\sqrt{2^2+(-12)^2+(-3)^2}}\right|$$

$$=\left|\frac{6-24+18}{\sqrt{49}\,\sqrt{157}}\right|=0\Rightarrow\theta=\frac{\pi}{2}=90^\circ$$

Hence, the angle between the given lines is 90°.

12. (c) We have direction ratios of two lines.

So, $l_1=-1,2,2$ and $l_2=0,2,1$

Direction ratio of a line which is perpendicular to l_1 and l_2 can be find by cross product of direction ratios of given line.

Then, direction ratio of required line

$$=\begin{vmatrix}\hat{i} & \hat{j} & \hat{k}\\ -1 & 2 & 2\\ 0 & 2 & 1\end{vmatrix}$$

$$=\hat{i}(2-4)-\hat{j}(-1-0)+\hat{k}(-2-0)$$

$$=-2\hat{i}+\hat{j}-2\hat{k}$$

Hence, direction ratios are − 2, 1, − 2.

13. (a) The given lines can be rewritten as

$$\vec{r}=\hat{i}+\hat{j}+\hat{k}+p(2\hat{i}+\hat{j}+2\hat{k})$$

and $$\vec{r}=(\hat{i}+\hat{j}+\hat{k})+q(\hat{i}+\lambda\hat{j}+\hat{k})$$

Let θ be the angle between these lines.

$$\text{Then, } \cos\theta=\left|\frac{(2\hat{i}+\hat{j}+2\hat{k}).(\hat{i}+\lambda\hat{j}+\hat{k})}{\sqrt{2^2+1^2+2^2}\,\sqrt{1^2+\lambda^2+1^2}}\right|$$

$$\Rightarrow \cos\frac{\pi}{2}=\left|\frac{2+\lambda+2}{3\sqrt{\lambda^2+2}}\right| \qquad \left[\because \text{given angle}=\frac{\pi}{2}\right]$$

$$\Rightarrow 0=\frac{|4+\lambda|}{3\sqrt{\lambda^2+2}}$$

$$\Rightarrow 4+\lambda=0\Rightarrow\lambda=-4$$

14. (a) We have, $\frac{x-2}{1}=\frac{y-3}{1}=\frac{4-z}{k}$

and $\frac{x-1}{k}=\frac{y-4}{2}=\frac{z-5}{-2}$

$\Rightarrow$ $\frac{x-2}{1}=\frac{y-3}{1}=\frac{z-4}{-k}$

and $\frac{x-1}{k}=\frac{y-4}{2}=\frac{z-5}{-2}$

Since, the given lines are perpendicular.

$\therefore$ $(1)(k)+(1)(2)+(-k)(-2)=0$

$\Rightarrow$ $k+2+2k=0\Rightarrow 3k+2=0$

$\therefore$ $k=-\frac{2}{3}$

15. (a) Lines are $\frac{x-3}{3}=\frac{y-1}{5}=\frac{z+3}{4}$

and $\frac{x+1}{1}=\frac{y-4}{1}=\frac{z-5}{2}$

$\therefore$ $\vec{b}_1=3\hat{i}+5\hat{j}+4\hat{k}$ and $\vec{b}_2=\hat{i}+\hat{j}+2\hat{k}$

$$\Rightarrow \cos\theta=\left|\frac{\vec{b}_1\cdot\vec{b}_2}{|\vec{b}_1|\cdot|\vec{b}_2|}\right|=\left|\frac{(3\hat{i}+5\hat{j}+4\hat{k})\cdot(\hat{i}+\hat{j}+2\hat{k})}{\sqrt{9+25+16}\,\sqrt{1+1+4}}\right|$$

$$=\left|\frac{3+5+8}{\sqrt{50}\cdot\sqrt{6}}\right|=\left|\frac{16}{5\sqrt{2}\cdot\sqrt{2}\cdot\sqrt{3}}\right|$$

$$=\left|\frac{16}{5\times2\times\sqrt{3}}\times\frac{\sqrt{3}}{\sqrt{3}}\right|=\frac{8\sqrt{3}}{15}$$

$$\therefore \theta=\cos^{-1}\left(\frac{8\sqrt{3}}{15}\right)$$

16. (b) Let each side of cube be a.

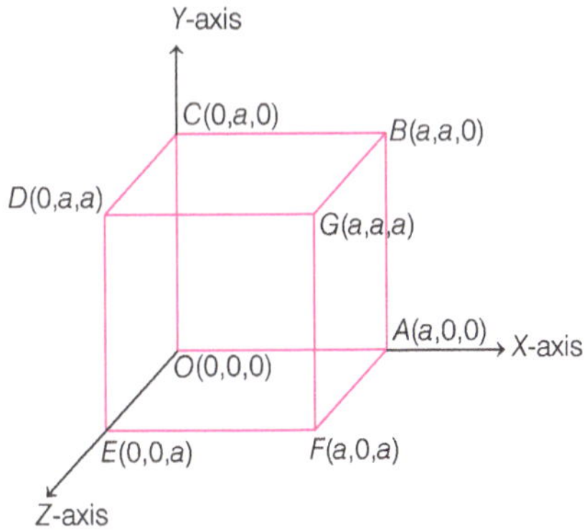

Let us take two diagonals

$$\overrightarrow{OG}=a\hat{i}+a\hat{j}+a\hat{k}$$

and $$\overrightarrow{DA}=\overrightarrow{OA}-\overrightarrow{OD}=a\hat{i}-a\hat{j}-a\hat{k}$$

Let the angle between $\overrightarrow{OG}$ and $\overrightarrow{DA}$ be θ.

$$\text{Given, } \cos\theta=\left|\frac{\overrightarrow{OG}\cdot\overrightarrow{DA}}{|\overrightarrow{OG}||\overrightarrow{DA}|}\right|$$

$$\Rightarrow \quad \cos\theta = \left|\frac{(a\hat{i} + a\hat{j} + a\hat{k})(a\hat{i} - a\hat{j} - a\hat{k})}{\sqrt{a^2+a^2+a^2}\sqrt{a^2+a^2+a^2}}\right|$$

$$= \left|\frac{a^2 - a^2 - a^2}{\sqrt{3a^2}\cdot\sqrt{3a^2}}\right| = \frac{1}{3}$$

$$\Rightarrow \quad \theta = \cos^{-1}\frac{1}{3}$$

17. (b) **Hint** Lines are parallel.

$$\vec{a_1} = \hat{i} + 2\hat{j} - 4\hat{k}$$

$$\vec{a_2} = 3\hat{i} + 3\hat{j} - 5\hat{k}$$

$$\vec{b} = 2\hat{i} + 3\hat{j} + 6\hat{k}$$

Shortest distance between two parallel lines

$$= \frac{|(\vec{a_2} - \vec{a_1}) \times \vec{b}|}{|\vec{b}|}$$

Now, $\vec{a_2} - \vec{a_1} = 2\hat{i} + \hat{j} - \hat{k}$

and $(\vec{a_2} - \vec{a_1}) \times \vec{b} = \begin{vmatrix} \hat{i} & \hat{j} & \hat{k} \\ 2 & 1 & -1 \\ 2 & 3 & 6 \end{vmatrix}$

$$= 9\hat{i} - 14\hat{j} + 4\hat{k}$$

$$\Rightarrow \quad |(\vec{a_2} - \vec{a_1}) \times \vec{b}| = \sqrt{81+196+16} = \sqrt{293}$$

and $|\vec{b}| = \sqrt{4+9+36} = 7$

$$\therefore \quad SD = \frac{\sqrt{293}}{7}$$

18. (a) $\because$ Direction ratios of line are $2, -1, -2$.

$\therefore$ Direction cosines of line are

$$\frac{2}{\sqrt{2^2+(-1)^2+(-2)^2}}, \frac{-1}{\sqrt{2^2+(-1)^2+(-2)^2}}, \frac{-2}{\sqrt{2^2+(-1)^2+(-2)^2}}$$

i.e. $\frac{2}{3}, \frac{-1}{3}, \frac{-2}{3}$

Hence, Assertion and Reason both are correct and Reason is the correct explanation of Assertion.

19. (b) Let the given points be $P(1,3,5)$ and $Q(2,4,6)$.

So, the direction ratios of the line through P and Q are $[(2-1), (4-3), (6-5)]$ i.e. $(1, 1, 1)$.

$\therefore$ Direction cosines of the line are

$$\frac{1}{\sqrt{1^2+1^2+1^2}}, \frac{1}{\sqrt{1^2+1^2+1^2}}, \frac{1}{\sqrt{1^2+1^2+1^2}}$$

i.e. $\frac{1}{\sqrt{3}}, \frac{1}{\sqrt{3}}, \frac{1}{\sqrt{3}}$

Hence, Assertion and Reason both are correct but Reason is not the correct explanation of Assertion.

20. (a) If α, β and γ are angles with X, Y and Z-axes, respectively.

Then, $\cos^2\alpha + \cos^2\beta + \cos^2\gamma = 1$

$$\frac{1+\cos 2\alpha}{2} + \frac{1+\cos 2\beta}{2} + \frac{1+\cos 2\gamma}{2} = 1$$

$$\Rightarrow \quad 3 + \cos 2\alpha + \cos 2\beta + \cos 2\gamma = 2$$

$$\Rightarrow \quad \cos 2\alpha + \cos 2\beta + \cos 2\gamma = -1$$

Hence, Assertion and Reason both are correct and Reason is the correct explanation of Assertion.

21. (b) **Assertion** Let the given points be $A(1,2,3)$, $B(-2,3,4)$ and $C(7,0,1)$.

Direction ratios of line joining A and B are $(-2-1, 3-2, 4-3)$ i.e. $(-3,1,1)$.

Direction ratios of line joining B and C are $(7+2, 0-3, 1-4)$ i.e. $(9,-3,-3)$.

Now, ratios of direction ratios of AB and BC are $\frac{-3}{9}, \frac{1}{-3}, \frac{1}{-3}$ i.e. $\frac{-1}{3}, \frac{-1}{3}, \frac{-1}{3}$.

$\because$ The direction ratios of AB and BC are proportional.

So, AB is parallel to BC but B is common to both AB and BC.

So, A, B and C are collinear.

Hence, Assertion is correct.

Reason Direction cosines $l = \cos\alpha, m = \cos\beta, n = \cos\gamma$

$\because$ α, β, γ are $\frac{\pi}{2}, \frac{3\pi}{4}$ and $\frac{\pi}{4}$, respectively.

So, $l = \cos\frac{\pi}{2} = 0, m = \cos\frac{3\pi}{4} = -\frac{1}{\sqrt{2}}$ and $n = \cos\frac{\pi}{4} = \frac{1}{\sqrt{2}}$

Hence, Assertion and Reason both are correct but Reason is not the correct explanation of Assertion.

22. (a) **Hint** Position vector and given vector are

$$\vec{a} = \hat{i} - 2\hat{j} + 3\hat{k} \text{ and } \vec{b} = 3\hat{i} + 2\hat{j} + 6\hat{k}$$

$\because$ Equation of line passes through point having position vector $\vec{a}$ and parallel to $\vec{b}$ is $\vec{r} = \vec{a} + \lambda\vec{b}$.

$$\therefore \quad \vec{r} = (\hat{i} - 2\hat{j} + 3\hat{k}) + \lambda(3\hat{i} + 2\hat{j} + 6\hat{k})$$

So, Assertion and Reason both are correct and Reason is the correct explanation of Assertion.

23. (d) Let $\vec{a}$ be the position vector of the point $(1, 2, 3)$.

Then, $\vec{a} = \hat{i} + 2\hat{j} + 3\hat{k}$

and $\vec{b} = 3\hat{i} + 2\hat{j} - 2\hat{k}$

Now, the equation of the line passing through the point having position vector $\vec{a}$ and parallel to vector $\vec{b}$ is $\vec{r} = \vec{a} + \lambda\vec{b}$.

$\therefore \vec{r} = (\hat{i} + 2\hat{j} + 3\hat{k}) + \lambda(3\hat{i} + 2\hat{j} - 2\hat{k})$

Hence, Assertion is incorrect but Reason is correct.

24. (a) Let $l_1 = \dfrac{-x+2}{-2} = \dfrac{y-1}{7} = \dfrac{z+3}{-3}$

$\Rightarrow \quad \dfrac{x-2}{2} = \dfrac{y-1}{7} = \dfrac{z+3}{-3}$

and $\quad l_2 = \dfrac{x+2}{-1} = \dfrac{2y-8}{4} = \dfrac{z-5}{4}$

$\Rightarrow \quad \dfrac{x+2}{-1} = \dfrac{y-4}{2} = \dfrac{z-5}{4}$

If $l_1 \perp l_2$, then $= -2+14-12=0 \qquad [\because a_1a_2+b_1b_2+c_1c_2=0]$

Hence, Assertion and Reason both are correct and Reason is the correct explanation of Assertion.

25. (a) **Assertion** The given lines are

$$\vec{r} = \vec{a_1} + \lambda \vec{b_1} \text{ and } \vec{r} = \vec{a_2} + \mu \vec{b_2}.$$

Let θ be the angle between these lines

$$\therefore \quad \cos\theta = \left|\frac{\vec{b_1}\cdot\vec{b_2}}{|\vec{b_1}||\vec{b_2}|}\right|$$

When $\vec{b_1}\cdot\vec{b_2} = 0$, then

$$\cos\theta = \left|\frac{0}{|\vec{b_1}||\vec{b_2}|}\right| = 0$$

$$\Rightarrow \quad \cos\theta = \cos\frac{\pi}{2} \Rightarrow \theta = \frac{\pi}{2}$$

Hence, the given lines are perpendicular.

Hence, Assertion and Reason both are correct and Reason is the correct explanation of Assertion.

26. (d) Angle between two lines

$$\cos\theta = \left|\frac{a_1a_2+b_1b_2+c_1c_2}{\sqrt{a_1^2+b_1^2+c_1^2}\cdot\sqrt{a_2^2+b_2^2+c_2^2}}\right|$$

$$= \left|\frac{2\times -3+3\times -2+1\times 2}{\sqrt{4+9+1}\sqrt{9+4+4}}\right|$$

$$\cos\theta = \left|\frac{-6-6+2}{\sqrt{14}\sqrt{17}}\right|$$

$$\cos\theta = \left|\frac{-10}{\sqrt{238}}\right|$$

$$\theta = \cos^{-1}\left(\frac{10}{\sqrt{238}}\right)$$

Hence, Assertion is incorrect but Reason is correct.

27. We have, equation of

$$\text{club } A = \frac{x-1}{2} = \frac{y-2}{3} = \frac{z-3}{4} \qquad \ldots\text{(i)}$$

$$\text{and club } B = \frac{x-4}{3} = \frac{y+2}{2} = \frac{z}{6} \qquad \ldots\text{(ii)}$$

(i) Vector equation of club A,

$$\vec{r} = (\hat{i} + 2\hat{j} + 3\hat{k}) + \lambda(2\hat{i} + 3\hat{j} + 4\hat{k})$$

(ii) Direction ratios of club $B = 3, 2, 6$

∴ Direction cosines

$$= \frac{3}{\sqrt{9+4+36}}, \frac{2}{\sqrt{9+4+36}}, \frac{6}{\sqrt{9+4+36}}$$

$$= \frac{3}{7}, \frac{2}{7}, \frac{6}{7}$$

(iii) Given line

$$\frac{x-3}{7} = \frac{7-y}{4} = \frac{kz-7}{1}$$

$$\Rightarrow \quad \frac{x-3}{7} = \frac{-(y-7)}{4} = \frac{k\left(z-\frac{7}{k}\right)}{1}$$

$$\Rightarrow \quad \frac{x-3}{7} = \frac{y-7}{-4} = \frac{z-\frac{7}{k}}{\frac{1}{k}}$$

∴ Direction ratios $= 7, -4, \dfrac{1}{k}$

∵ Direction ratios of club $A = 2, 3, 4$

If they are perpendicular, then

$$7\times 2 + (-4\times 3) + \frac{1}{k}\times 4 = 0$$

$$\Rightarrow \quad 14 - 12 + \frac{4}{k} = 0$$

$$\Rightarrow \quad \frac{4}{k} = -2$$

$$\Rightarrow \quad k = -2$$

(iv) For angle between A and B,

$$\cos\theta = \left|\frac{2\times 3+3\times 2+4\times 6}{\sqrt{2^2+3^2+4^2}\sqrt{3^2+2^2+6^2}}\right|$$

$$= \frac{|6+6+24|}{|\sqrt{29}\cdot\sqrt{49}|}$$

$$\Rightarrow \quad \cos\theta = \left|\frac{36}{7\sqrt{29}}\right|$$

$$\Rightarrow \quad \theta = \cos^{-1}\left(\frac{36}{7\sqrt{29}}\right)$$

(v) We have, lines of club A and club B are

$$\frac{x-1}{2} = \frac{y-2}{3} = \frac{z-3}{4}$$

$$\text{and} \quad \frac{x-4}{3} = \frac{y+2}{2} = \frac{z}{6}$$

On comparing the given equations of line with

$$\frac{x-x_1}{a_1} = \frac{y-y_1}{b_1} = \frac{z-z_1}{c_1}$$

and $\dfrac{x-x_2}{a_2} = \dfrac{y-y_2}{b_2} = \dfrac{z-z_2}{c_2}$, we get

$$x_1 = 1, y_1 = 2, z_1 = 3; a_1 = 2, b_1 = 3, c_1 = 4$$

and $\quad x_2 = 4, y_2 = -2, z_2 = 0; a_2 = 3, b_2 = 2, c_2 = 6$

On putting these values in $\begin{vmatrix} x_2-x_1 & y_2-y_1 & z_2-z_1 \\ a_1 & b_1 & c_1 \\ a_2 & b_2 & c_2 \end{vmatrix}$,

we get

$$\begin{vmatrix} 4-1 & -2-2 & 0-3 \\ 2 & 3 & 4 \\ 3 & 2 & 6 \end{vmatrix} = \begin{vmatrix} 3 & -4 & -3 \\ 2 & 3 & 4 \\ 3 & 2 & 6 \end{vmatrix}$$

$$= 3(18-8)+4(12-12)-3(4-9)$$
$$= 30+0+15 = 45$$

Now, $\sqrt{(b_1c_2-b_2c_1)^2+(c_1a_2-c_2a_1)^2+(a_1b_2-a_2b_1)^2}$

$$= \sqrt{(3\times6-2\times4)^2+(4\times3-6\times2)^2+(2\times2-3\times3)^2}$$
$$= \sqrt{(18-8)^2+(12-12)^2+(4-9)^2}$$
$$= \sqrt{(10)^2+(0)^2+(-5)^2} = \sqrt{100+25} = \sqrt{125} = 5\sqrt{5}$$

$$\therefore \text{SD} = \frac{\begin{vmatrix} x_2-x_1 & y_2-y_1 & z_2-z_1 \\ a_1 & b_1 & c_1 \\ a_2 & b_2 & c_2 \end{vmatrix}}{\sqrt{(b_1c_2-b_2c_1)^2+(c_1a_2-c_2a_1)^2+(a_1b_2-a_2b_1)^2}}$$

$$= \frac{45}{5\sqrt{5}} = \frac{45}{5\sqrt{5}}\times\frac{\sqrt{5}}{\sqrt{5}} = \frac{45\sqrt{5}}{25} = \frac{9\sqrt{5}}{5} \text{ units}$$

28. Given equation is $6x-2=3y+1=2z-2$

$$\Rightarrow \quad 6\left(x-\frac{1}{3}\right)=3\left(y+\frac{1}{3}\right)=2(z-1)$$

$$\Rightarrow \quad \frac{x-\frac{1}{3}}{\frac{1}{6}\times6}=\frac{y+\frac{1}{3}}{\frac{1}{3}\times6}=\frac{z-1}{\frac{1}{2}\times6}$$

$$\Rightarrow \quad \frac{x-\frac{1}{3}}{1}=\frac{y+\frac{1}{3}}{2}=\frac{z-1}{3}$$

(i) Direction ratios of line = 1, 2, 3

$\therefore$ Direction cosines

$$= \frac{1}{\sqrt{1^2+2^2+3^2}}, \frac{2}{\sqrt{1^2+2^2+3^2}}, \frac{3}{\sqrt{1^2+2^2+3^2}}$$
$$= \frac{1}{\sqrt{14}}, \frac{2}{\sqrt{14}}, \frac{3}{\sqrt{14}}$$

(ii) If lines are parallel, then direction ratio will be same and passing through (1, 2, 3).

So, equation $= \dfrac{x-1}{1}=\dfrac{y-2}{2}=\dfrac{z-3}{3}$

(iii) If line $\dfrac{x-\frac{1}{3}}{1}=\dfrac{y+\frac{1}{3}}{2}=\dfrac{z-1}{3}$ satisfies the point $\left(\frac{2}{3},\frac{1}{3},2\right)$, then it will lie on the path.

$$\Rightarrow \quad \frac{\frac{2}{3}-\frac{1}{3}}{1}=\frac{\frac{1}{3}+\frac{1}{3}}{2}=\frac{2-1}{3} \Rightarrow \frac{1}{3}=\frac{1}{3}=\frac{1}{3}$$

Hence, it is satisfying.

Therefore, the city is lying on the railway line.

(iv) If $\dfrac{x-1}{2}=\dfrac{y-2}{3}=\dfrac{z}{\lambda}$ is perpendicular to $\dfrac{x-\frac{1}{3}}{1}=\dfrac{y+\frac{1}{3}}{2}=\dfrac{z-1}{3}$, then

$$2\times1+3\times2+\lambda\times3=0 \Rightarrow 3\lambda=-8$$
$$\therefore \quad \lambda=-\frac{8}{3}$$

(v) Original line, $\dfrac{x-\frac{1}{3}}{1}=\dfrac{y+\frac{1}{3}}{2}=\dfrac{z-1}{3}$

Given line, $\dfrac{x}{-1}=\dfrac{y+2}{2}=\dfrac{3-6z}{5}$

$$\Rightarrow \quad \frac{x}{-1}=\frac{y+2}{2}=\frac{z-\frac{1}{2}}{-\frac{5}{6}}$$

For angle, $\cos\theta = \left|\dfrac{1\times(-1)+2\times2+3\times\left(\frac{-5}{6}\right)}{\sqrt{1+4+9}\sqrt{1+4+\frac{25}{36}}}\right|$

$$\Rightarrow \quad \cos\theta = \left|\frac{-1+4-\frac{5}{2}}{\sqrt{14}\sqrt{\frac{205}{36}}}\right|$$

$$\Rightarrow \quad \cos\theta = \frac{3}{\sqrt{2870}}$$

$$\Rightarrow \quad \theta = \cos^{-1}\left(\frac{3}{\sqrt{2870}}\right)$$

29. (i) (c) Given, port is at origin (0, 0, 0), position of ship is (5 km, 0 km, 9 km) and the position of the submarine is (11 km, – 0.9 km, –10 km).

The direction cosine n is given by

$$n = \pm\frac{c}{\sqrt{a^2+b^2+c^2}}$$

Here, $a=5$, $b=0$ and $c=9$

So, $\quad n=\pm\dfrac{9}{\sqrt{5^2+0^2+9^2}}=\pm\dfrac{9}{\sqrt{106}}$

We know that angle between the line at Z-axis is given by $\cos\gamma=n$, where γ is the angle formed with Z-axis.

So, $\quad \cos\gamma=n \Rightarrow \cos\gamma=\pm\dfrac{9}{\sqrt{106}}$

$$\Rightarrow \quad \gamma=\cos^{-1}\pm\left(\frac{9}{\sqrt{106}}\right)$$

Hence, the required angle is $\cos^{-1}\pm\left(\dfrac{9}{\sqrt{106}}\right)$.

(ii) (c) Given coordinates of submarine and port is (11, – 0.9, – 10) and (0, 0, 0), respectively. We know that the direction cosines of a line passing through the points $A(x_1,y_1,z_1)$ and $B(x_2,y_2,z_2)$ is given by

$$\frac{x_2-x_1}{AB}, \frac{y_2-y_1}{AB}, \frac{z_2-z_1}{AB},$$

where $AB=\sqrt{(x_2-x_1)^2+(y_2-y_1)^2+(z_2-z_1)^2}$

Here, $x_1=11, x_2=0, y_1=-0.9, y_2=0, z_1=-10$ and $z_2=0$

Now, $AB=\sqrt{(0-11)^2+(0+0.9)^2+(0+10)^2}$

$=\sqrt{121+0.81+100}$

$=\sqrt{221.81}$

So, $\dfrac{0-11}{\sqrt{221.81}},\dfrac{0-(-0.9)}{\sqrt{221.81}},\dfrac{0-(-10)}{\sqrt{221.81}}$

Or $\dfrac{11-0}{\sqrt{221.81}},\dfrac{-0.9-0}{\sqrt{221.81}},\dfrac{-10-0}{\sqrt{221.81}}$

$\Rightarrow \dfrac{-11}{\sqrt{221.81}},\dfrac{0.9}{\sqrt{221.81}},\dfrac{10}{\sqrt{221.81}}$

Or $\dfrac{11}{\sqrt{221.81}},\dfrac{-0.9}{\sqrt{221.81}},\dfrac{-10}{\sqrt{221.81}}$

Hence, the captain and sub-ordinate are correct.

(iii) (c) Given distance between the port and ship is $\sqrt{106}$ km, distance between the submarine and the port is $\sqrt{221.81}$ km and distance between the ship and the submarine is $\sqrt{397.81}$ km.

Now, the direction ratios of the line joining the submarine $(11,-0.9,-10)$ and ship $(5, 0, 9)$ is given by $(11-5,-0.9-0,-10-9)$ i.e. $(6,-0.9,-19)$.

Also, the direction ratio of the line joining the submarine $(11,-0.9,-10)$ and port $(0, 0, 0)$ is given by $[0-11, 0-(-0.9), 0-(-10)]$ i.e. $(-11, 0.9, 10)$.

We know that the angle between the lines having direction ratios (a_1, b_1, c_1) and (a_2, b_2, c_2) is given by

$$\cos\theta=\left|\frac{a_1a_2+b_1b_2+c_1c_2}{\sqrt{a_1^2+b_1^2+c_1^2}\sqrt{a_2^2+b_2^2+c_2^2}}\right|$$

$$\text{So,}\quad \cos\theta=\left|\frac{6(-11)+(-0.9)(0.9)+(-19)(10)}{\sqrt{(6)^2+(-0.9)^2+(-19)^2}\times\sqrt{(-11)^2+(0.9)^2+(10)^2}}\right|$$

$$\Rightarrow \quad \cos\theta=\left|\frac{-66-0.81-190}{\sqrt{397.81}\sqrt{221.81}}\right|$$

$$\Rightarrow \quad \cos\theta=\frac{256.81}{\sqrt{397.81}\sqrt{221.81}}$$

$$\Rightarrow \quad \theta=\cos^{-1}\left(\frac{256.81}{\sqrt{397.81}\sqrt{221.81}}\right)$$

(iv) (a) Given coordinates of submarine and port is $(11,-0.9,-10)$ and $(0, 0, 0)$, respectively.

We know that the equation of line joining two points $A(x_1,y_1,z_1)$ and $B(x_2,y_2,z_2)$ is given by

$$\vec{r}=\vec{a}+\lambda(\vec{b}-\vec{a}),$$

where $a=x_1\hat{i}+y_1\hat{j}+z_1\hat{k}$

and $b=x_2\hat{i}+y_2\hat{j}+z_2\hat{k}$

Here, $x_1=11, x_2=0, y_1=-0.9, y_2=0, z_1=-10$ and $z_2=0$.

So, $\vec{r}=11\hat{i}-0.9\hat{j}-10\hat{k}$

$+\lambda[(0-11)\hat{i}+[0-(-0.9)]\hat{j}+[0-(-10)]\hat{k}]$

$\Rightarrow \vec{r}=11\hat{i}-0.9\hat{j}-10\hat{k}+\lambda(-11\hat{i}+0.9\hat{j}+10\hat{k})$

$\therefore$ Equation I is correct.

Subjective Questions

1. The coordinates of any point on the line $\dfrac{x+3}{3}=\dfrac{y-1}{-1}=\dfrac{z-5}{-5}$ are given by $(3\lambda-3,-\lambda+1,-5\lambda+5)$.

   If $(3\lambda-3,-\lambda+1,-5\lambda+5)$ lies on XY-plane i.e. $z=0$, then $-5\lambda+5=0\Rightarrow\lambda=1$

   Hence, the coordinates of the points are $(3\times1-3,-1+1,-5\times1+5)=(0,0,0)$.

2. Let direction cosines of the line be l, m and n.

   Given, $\alpha=60^\circ, \beta=135^\circ$ and $\gamma=45^\circ$

   Then, $l=\cos\alpha=\cos 60^\circ=\dfrac{1}{2}$

   $m=\cos\beta=\cos 135^\circ=-\dfrac{1}{\sqrt{2}}$

   and $n=\cos\gamma=\cos 45^\circ=\dfrac{1}{\sqrt{2}}$

   Hence, the direction cosines of the line are $\dfrac{1}{2},\dfrac{-1}{\sqrt{2}}$ and $\dfrac{1}{\sqrt{2}}$.

3. Given, $\alpha=60^\circ, \beta=45^\circ$ and $\gamma=\theta$

   We know that $l^2+m^2+n^2=1$

   $\Rightarrow \cos^2\alpha+\cos^2\beta+\cos^2\gamma=1$

   $\Rightarrow \cos^2 60^\circ+\cos^2 45^\circ+\cos^2\theta=1$

   $\Rightarrow \dfrac{1}{4}+\dfrac{1}{2}+\cos^2\theta=1 \Rightarrow \cos^2\theta=1-\dfrac{3}{4}$

   $\Rightarrow \cos^2\theta=\dfrac{1}{4}\Rightarrow \cos\theta=\pm\dfrac{1}{2}$

   $\Rightarrow \cos\theta=\dfrac{1}{2}=\cos 60^\circ$

   or $\cos\theta=\dfrac{-1}{2}=\cos 120^\circ$

   $\Rightarrow \theta=60^\circ$ or 120°

   $\therefore \theta=60^\circ$ [$\because\theta$ is an acute angle]

4. Given direction ratios are $(1,-2,1)$.

   i.e. $a=1, b=-2$ and $c=1$.

   Then, $\sqrt{a^2+b^2+c^2}=\sqrt{(1)^2+(-2)^2+(1)^2}=\sqrt{6}$

   Now, direction cosines are

   $l=\dfrac{a}{\sqrt{a^2+b^2+c^2}}=\dfrac{1}{\sqrt{6}},$

   $m=\dfrac{b}{\sqrt{a^2+b^2+c^2}}=\dfrac{-2}{\sqrt{6}}$

   and $n=\dfrac{c}{\sqrt{a^2+b^2+c^2}}=\dfrac{1}{\sqrt{6}}$

   Hence, the direction cosines are $\dfrac{1}{\sqrt{6}},\dfrac{-2}{\sqrt{6}},\dfrac{1}{\sqrt{6}}$.

5. Let $A(x_1, y_1, z_1) = (1, 5, 4)$ and $B(x_2, y_2, z_2) = (4, 1, -2)$

Then, direction ratios of line AB are $(4-1, 1-5, -2-4)$ i.e. $(3, -4, -6)$.

6. Given points are $A(5, 7, 8)$, $B(-1, -2, 1)$ and $C(2, 3, 4)$.

Direction ratios of line joining A and B are $(-1-5, -2-7, 1-8)$ i.e. $(-6, -9, -7)$.

Direction ratios of line joining B and C are $(2-(-1), 3-(-2), 4-1)$ i.e. $(3, 5, 3)$.

Now, ratios of direction ratios of AB and BC are $\frac{-6}{3}, \frac{-9}{5}, \frac{-7}{3}$.

Thus, the direction ratios of AB and BC are not proportional.

Hence, A, B and C are not collinear points.

7. Given, cartesian equation of a line is

$$\frac{3-x}{5} = \frac{y+4}{7} = \frac{2z-6}{4}$$

On rewriting the given equation in standard form, we get

$$\frac{x-3}{-5} = \frac{y+4}{7} = \frac{z-3}{2} = \lambda \text{ (let)}$$

$\Rightarrow \quad x = -5\lambda + 3, y = 7\lambda - 4$ and $z = 2\lambda + 3$

Now, $x\hat{i} + y\hat{j} + z\hat{k} = (-5\lambda + 3)\hat{i} + (7\lambda - 4)\hat{j} + (2\lambda + 3)\hat{k}$

$\therefore \quad \vec{r} = (3\hat{i} - 4\hat{j} + 3\hat{k}) + \lambda(-5\hat{i} + 7\hat{j} + 2\hat{k})$,

which is the required equation of line in vector form.

8. The vector equation of a line parallel to Z-axis is $\vec{m} = 0\hat{i} + 0\hat{j} + \hat{k}$.

Then, the required line passes through the point $A(\alpha, \beta, \gamma)$, whose position vector is $\vec{r_1} = \alpha\hat{i} + \beta\hat{j} + \gamma\hat{k}$ and is parallel to the vector $\vec{m} = (0\hat{i} + 0\hat{j} + \hat{k})$.

$\therefore$ The equation is $\vec{r} = \vec{r_1} + \lambda\vec{m}$

$$= (\alpha\hat{i} + \beta\hat{j} + \gamma\hat{k}) + \lambda(0\hat{i} + 0\hat{j} + \hat{k})$$
$$= (\alpha\hat{i} + \beta\hat{j} + \gamma\hat{k}) + \lambda(\hat{k})$$

9. Given equation of line is

$$\frac{4-x}{2} = \frac{y}{6} = \frac{1-z}{3}.$$

It can be rewritten in standard form as

$$\frac{x-4}{-2} = \frac{y}{6} = \frac{z-1}{-3}$$

Here, direction ratios of the line are $(-2, 6, -3)$.

$\therefore$ Direction cosines of the line are

$$\frac{-2}{\sqrt{(-2)^2 + (6)^2 + (-3)^2}}, \frac{6}{\sqrt{(-2)^2 + (6)^2 + (-3)^2}}$$

and $\frac{-3}{\sqrt{(-2)^2 + (6)^2 + (-3)^2}}$ i.e. $\frac{-2}{\sqrt{49}}, \frac{6}{\sqrt{49}}$ and $\frac{-3}{\sqrt{49}}$

Thus, direction cosines of line are $\left(-\frac{2}{7}, \frac{6}{7}, -\frac{3}{7}\right)$.

10. We know that the vector equation of a line passing through a point with position vector $\vec{a}$ and parallel to a given vector $\vec{b}$ is $\vec{r} = \vec{a} + \lambda\vec{b}$, where $\lambda \in R$.

Here, $\vec{a} = \hat{i} - \hat{j} + 2\hat{k}$ and $\vec{b} = \hat{i} + 2\hat{j} - 2\hat{k}$.

[$\because$ direction ratios of given line are 1, 2 and -2]

$\therefore$ Required vector equation of line is

$\vec{r} = (\hat{i} - \hat{j} + 2\hat{k}) + \lambda(\hat{i} + 2\hat{j} - 2\hat{k})$, where $\lambda \in R$.

11. Given, the required line is parallel to the line

$$\frac{x+3}{3} = \frac{4-y}{5} = \frac{z+8}{6} \text{ or } \frac{x+3}{3} = \frac{y-4}{-5} = \frac{z+8}{6}$$

$\therefore$ Direction ratios of both lines are proportional to each other.

The required equation of the line passing through $(-2, 4, -5)$ having direction ratios $(3, -5, 6)$ is $\frac{x+2}{3} = \frac{y-4}{-5} = \frac{z+5}{6}$.

12. Let $\vec{a}$ be the position vector of the point (2, 4, 6).

Then, $\vec{a} = 2\hat{i} + 4\hat{j} + 6\hat{k}$

Now, the equation of the line passing through the point having position vector $\vec{a}$ and parallel to $\vec{b} = 3\hat{i} + 2\hat{j} - 2\hat{k}$ is

$$\vec{r} = \vec{a} + \lambda\vec{b}$$

$\Rightarrow \quad \vec{r} = (2\hat{i} + 4\hat{j} + 6\hat{k}) + \lambda(3\hat{i} + 2\hat{j} - 2\hat{k})$

13. We have, point $A(-3, 2, -4)$.

According to the question, $l = m = n$

Therefore, required equation of line is

$$\frac{x+3}{l} = \frac{y-2}{l} = \frac{z+4}{l} \Rightarrow x+3 = y-2 = z+4$$

14. Let θ be the angle between the given lines.

Here, $\vec{b_1} = 2\hat{i} + \hat{j} + 2\hat{k}$ and $\vec{b_2} = 4\hat{i} + 8\hat{j} + \hat{k}$

$$\therefore \cos\theta = \left|\frac{\vec{b_1} \cdot \vec{b_2}}{|\vec{b_1}||\vec{b_2}|}\right| = \left|\frac{(2\hat{i} + \hat{j} + 2\hat{k}) \cdot (4\hat{i} + 8\hat{j} + \hat{k})}{|2\hat{i} + \hat{j} + 2\hat{k}||4\hat{i} + 8\hat{j} + \hat{k}|}\right|$$

$$= \left|\frac{8+8+2}{\sqrt{4+1+4} \cdot \sqrt{16+64+1}}\right| = \frac{18}{3 \times 9} = \frac{2}{3}$$

$\Rightarrow \quad \theta = \cos^{-1}\left(\frac{2}{3}\right)$

15. Given lines are

$$\frac{x-2}{2} = \frac{y-1}{7} = \frac{z+3}{-3} \text{ and } \frac{x+2}{-1} = \frac{y-8}{2} = \frac{z-5}{4}$$

We know that if two lines are perpendicular, then

$$a_1a_2 + b_1b_2 + c_1c_2 = 0$$

$\therefore \quad a_1a_2 + b_1b_2 + c_1c_2 = 2 \times (-1) + 7 \times 2 + (-3) \times 4$

$$= -2 + 14 - 12 = 0$$

Hence, the given lines are perpendicular to each other.

16. Clearly, $\cos^2\theta + \cos^2\beta + \cos^2\theta = 1$

$\Rightarrow \quad 2\cos^2\theta + 1 - \sin^2\beta = 1$

$\Rightarrow \quad 2\cos^2\theta - \sin^2\beta = 0$

$\Rightarrow \quad 2\cos^2\theta - 3\sin^2\theta = 0$

$[\because \sin^2\beta = 3\sin^2\theta \text{ (given)}]$

$\Rightarrow \quad \tan^2\theta = \frac{2}{3}$

$\therefore \quad \cos^2\theta = \frac{1}{1+\tan^2\theta} = \frac{1}{1+\frac{2}{3}} = \frac{3}{5}$

17. Given equation of a line is

$$5x - 3 = 15y + 7 = 3 - 10z \quad \ldots\text{(i)}$$

Let us first convert the equation in standard form

$$\frac{x - x_1}{a} = \frac{y - y_1}{b} = \frac{z - z_1}{c} \quad \ldots\text{(ii)}$$

Let us divide Eq. (i) by LCM (coefficients of x, y and z) i.e. LCM (5, 15, 10) = 30

Now, the Eq. (i) becomes $\frac{5x-3}{30} = \frac{15y+7}{30} = \frac{3-10z}{30}$

$$\Rightarrow \quad \frac{5\left(x - \frac{3}{5}\right)}{30} = \frac{15\left(y + \frac{7}{15}\right)}{30} = \frac{-10\left(z - \frac{3}{10}\right)}{30}$$

$$\Rightarrow \quad \frac{x - \frac{3}{5}}{6} = \frac{y + \frac{7}{15}}{2} = \frac{z - \frac{3}{10}}{-3}$$

On comparing the above equation with Eq.(ii), we get

$$a = 6, b = 2 \text{ and } c = -3$$

which are the direction ratios of the given line.

Now, the direction cosines of given line are

$$\frac{6}{\sqrt{6^2+2^2+(-3)^2}}, \frac{2}{\sqrt{6^2+2^2+(-3)^2}}$$

and $\frac{-3}{\sqrt{6^2+2^2+(-3)^2}}$ i.e. $\frac{6}{7}, \frac{2}{7}, \frac{-3}{7}$.

18. Given points are $P(1, -2, -2)$, $Q(3, -6, -8)$ and $R(-2, 4, 7)$.

Direction ratios of line joining P and Q are $[3 - 1, -6 - (-2), -8 - (-2)]$ i.e. $(2, -4, -6)$.

Direction ratios of line joining Q and R are $[-2 - 3, 4 + 6, 7 + 8]$ i.e. $(-5, 10, 15)$.

Now, ratios of direction ratios of PQ and QR are

$\frac{2}{-5}, \frac{-4}{10}, \frac{-6}{15}$ i.e. $-\frac{2}{5}, -\frac{2}{5}, -\frac{2}{5}$.

Thus, the direction ratios of PQ and QR are proportional.

So, PQ is parallel to QR but Q is common to both PQ and QR.

Hence, P, Q and R are collinear.

19. The coordinates of the position vector $2\hat{i} - 3\hat{j} + 4\hat{k}$ is $(2, -3, 4)$.

Also, it is given, $l = \cos 60°$, $m = \cos 120°$ and $n = \cos 45°$

i.e. $\quad l = \frac{1}{2}, m = -\frac{1}{2}$ and $n = \frac{1}{\sqrt{2}}$

$\because$ The cartesian equation of line passes through point (x_1, y_1, z_1) and having direction cosines (l, m, n) is

$$\frac{x - x_1}{l} = \frac{y - y_1}{m} = \frac{z - z_1}{n}$$

Here, $(x_1, y_1, z_1) = (2, -3, 4)$ and $(l, m, n) = \left(\frac{1}{2}, -\frac{1}{2}, \frac{1}{\sqrt{2}}\right)$

$\therefore$ The required equation of line is

$$\frac{x-2}{\frac{1}{2}} = \frac{y+3}{-\frac{1}{2}} = \frac{z-4}{\frac{1}{\sqrt{2}}}.$$

20. Equation of a line passing through a point with position vector $\vec{a}$ and parallel to a vector $\vec{b}$ is $\vec{r} = \vec{a} + \lambda\vec{b}$.

Since, line passes through the point $(5, 2, -4)$ and parallel to $5\hat{i} + \hat{j} - 7\hat{k}$.

$\therefore \quad \vec{a} = 5\hat{i} + 2\hat{j} - 4\hat{k}$ and $\vec{b} = 5\hat{i} + \hat{j} - 7\hat{k}$

$\therefore$ Equation of line is $\vec{r} = (5\hat{i} + 2\hat{j} - 4\hat{k}) + \lambda(5\hat{i} + \hat{j} - 7\hat{k})$.

21. The given line passes through the point having position vector $\vec{a} = 5\hat{i} - 2\hat{j} + 4\hat{k}$ and is parallel to the vector $\vec{b} = 2\hat{i} - \hat{j} + 3\hat{k}$.

$\therefore$ The equation of given line is

$$\vec{r} = \vec{a} + \lambda\vec{b}$$

$$\Rightarrow \quad \vec{r} = (5\hat{i} - 2\hat{j} + 4\hat{k}) + \lambda(2\hat{i} - \hat{j} + 3\hat{k}) \quad \ldots\text{(i)}$$

For cartesian equation, put $\vec{r} = x\hat{i} + y\hat{j} + z\hat{k}$ in Eq. (i), we get

$$(x\hat{i} + y\hat{j} + z\hat{k}) = (5\hat{i} - 2\hat{j} + 4\hat{k}) + \lambda(2\hat{i} - \hat{j} + 3\hat{k})$$

$$\Rightarrow \quad x\hat{i} + y\hat{j} + z\hat{k} = (5 + 2\lambda)\hat{i} + (-2 - \lambda)\hat{j} + (4 + 3\lambda)\hat{k}$$

On equating the coefficients of $\hat{i}, \hat{j}$ and $\hat{k}$ both sides, we get

$$x = 5 + 2\lambda, y = -2 - \lambda, z = 4 + 3\lambda$$

$$\Rightarrow \quad \frac{x-5}{2} = \lambda, \frac{y+2}{-1} = \lambda, \frac{z-4}{3} = \lambda$$

$$\Rightarrow \quad \frac{x-5}{2} = \frac{y+2}{-1} = \frac{z-4}{3},$$

which is the required equation of the given line in cartesian form.

22. Given line is passing through the point (1, 2, 3).

$\therefore \quad \vec{a} = \hat{i} + 2\hat{j} + 3\hat{k}$

and parallel to the line $\frac{x-1}{-2} = \frac{1-y}{3} = \frac{3-z}{-4}$

or $\quad \frac{x-1}{-2} = \frac{y-1}{-3} = \frac{z-3}{4}$

Direction ratios of the above line are $(-2, -3, 4)$.

So, required line is parallel to the vector

$$\vec{b} = -2\hat{i} - 3\hat{j} + 4\hat{k}$$

$\because$ Equation of a line passing through the point having position vector $\vec{a}$ and parallel to $\vec{b}$ is $\vec{r} = \vec{a} + \lambda\vec{b}$

Thus, required equation is

$$\vec{r} = (\hat{i} + 2\hat{j} + 3\hat{k}) + \lambda(-2\hat{i} - 3\hat{j} + 4\hat{k}).$$

23. Given cartesian equation of a line is

$$\frac{3-x}{5} = \frac{y+4}{9} = \frac{2z-6}{4}$$

On rewriting the given equation in standard form, we get

$$\frac{x-3}{-5} = \frac{y+4}{9} = \frac{z-3}{2} = \lambda \text{ (say)}$$

$\Rightarrow \quad x = -5\lambda + 3, y = 9\lambda - 4$ and $z = 2\lambda + 3$

Now, $x\hat{i} + y\hat{j} + z\hat{k} = (-5\lambda + 3)\hat{i} + (9\lambda - 4)\hat{j} + (2\lambda + 3)\hat{k}$

$\Rightarrow \quad \vec{r} = (3\hat{i} - 4\hat{j} + 3\hat{k}) + \lambda(-5\hat{i} + 9\hat{j} + 2\hat{k}),$

which is the required equation of a line in vector form.

24. Given lines are $\vec{r} = 2\hat{i} - 5\hat{j} + \hat{k} + \lambda(3\hat{i} + 2\hat{j} + 6\hat{k})$

and $\quad \vec{r} = 7\hat{i} - 6\hat{k} + \mu(\hat{i} + 2\hat{j} + 2\hat{k})$

On comparing with $\vec{r} = \vec{a_1} + \lambda\vec{b_1}$ and $\vec{r} = \vec{a_2} + \mu\vec{b_2}$, we get

$$\vec{b_1} = 3\hat{i} + 2\hat{j} + 6\hat{k} \text{ and } \vec{b_2} = \hat{i} + 2\hat{j} + 2\hat{k}$$

$\therefore$ The angle between the lines is given by

$$\cos\theta = \left|\frac{\vec{b_1}\cdot\vec{b_2}}{|\vec{b_1}||\vec{b_2}|}\right| = \left|\frac{(3\hat{i} + 2\hat{j} + 6\hat{k})\cdot(\hat{i} + 2\hat{j} + 2\hat{k})}{\sqrt{3^2 + 2^2 + 6^2}\sqrt{1^2 + 2^2 + 2^2}}\right|$$

$$= \left|\frac{3+4+12}{\sqrt{9+4+36}\sqrt{1+4+4}}\right|$$

$$= \frac{19}{\sqrt{49}\sqrt{9}} = \frac{19}{7\times 3} = \frac{19}{21}$$

$$\therefore \quad \theta = \cos^{-1}\left(\frac{19}{21}\right)$$

25. Given equations of lines are $\frac{x}{2} = \frac{y}{2} = \frac{z}{1}$

and $\frac{x-5}{4} = \frac{y-2}{1} = \frac{z-3}{8}$.

Here, direction ratios of two lines are $(2, 2, 1)$ and $(4, 1, 8)$.

Let θ be the acute angle between the given lines, then

$$\cos\theta = \frac{|a_1a_2 + b_1b_2 + c_1c_2|}{\sqrt{a_1^2 + b_1^2 + c_1^2}\sqrt{a_2^2 + b_2^2 + c_2^2}}$$

$$\Rightarrow \quad \cos\theta = \frac{|2\times 4 + 2\times 1 + 1\times 8|}{\sqrt{2^2 + 2^2 + 1^2}\sqrt{4^2 + 1^2 + 8^2}}$$

$$= \frac{|8+2+8|}{\sqrt{4+4+1}\sqrt{16+1+64}}$$

$$= \frac{18}{\sqrt{9}\sqrt{81}} = \frac{18}{3\times 9} = \frac{2}{3}$$

$$\therefore \quad \theta = \cos^{-1}\left(\frac{2}{3}\right)$$

26. Given vector equations are

$$\vec{r} = (3\hat{i} - \hat{j} + 2\hat{k}) + \lambda(2\hat{i} - 3\mu\hat{j} + 4\hat{k})$$

and $\vec{r} = (-2\hat{i} + 4\hat{j} - 5\hat{k}) + \lambda(2\mu\hat{i} + 4\hat{j} + 4\hat{k})$.

Here, direction ratios of given lines are

$$\vec{b_1} = 2\hat{i} - 3\mu\hat{j} + 4\hat{k} \text{ and } \vec{b_2} = 2\mu\hat{i} + 4\hat{j} + 4\hat{k}$$

The condition for perpendicular lines is $\vec{b_1}\cdot\vec{b_2} = 0$

$\Rightarrow \quad (2\hat{i} - 3\mu\hat{j} + 4\hat{k})\cdot(2\mu\hat{i} + 4\hat{j} + 4\hat{k}) = 0$

$\Rightarrow \quad 4\mu - 12\mu + 16 = 0$

$\Rightarrow \quad -8\mu + 16 = 0$

$\therefore \quad \mu = 2$

27. Hint Let $A(1, -1, 2)$ and $B(3, 4, k)$

Then, direction ratios of line AB are

$$(3-1, 4+1, k-2) \text{ i.e. } (2, 5, k-2)$$

Again let $C(0, 3, 2)$ and $D(3, 5, 6)$

Then, direction ratios of line CD are

$$(3-0, 5-3, 6-2) \text{ i.e. } (3, 2, 4)$$

$\because AB \perp CD$

$\therefore a_1a_2 + b_1b_2 + c_1c_2 = 0$ [direction ratio form]

$\Rightarrow \quad 2\times 3 + 5\times 2 + 4(k-2) = 0$

$\Rightarrow \quad 6 + 10 + 4k - 8 = 0$

$\Rightarrow \quad k = -\frac{8}{4}$

$\therefore \quad k = -2$

28. Given equation of lines are

$$\vec{r} = -\hat{i} + 4\hat{j} + 3\hat{k} + \lambda(4\hat{i} + \hat{j})$$

and $\quad \vec{r} = (-4\hat{i} + \hat{j}) + \mu(5\hat{i} + 2\hat{j} + \hat{k})$

On comparing with standard equation $\vec{r} = a + \lambda b$, we get

$$\vec{a_1} = -\hat{i} + 4\hat{j} + 3\hat{k}, \vec{b_1} = 4\hat{i} + \hat{j}$$

and $\quad \vec{a_2} = (-4\hat{i} + \hat{j}), \vec{b_2} = 5\hat{i} + 2\hat{j} + \hat{k}$

The condition, for the shortest distance between given lines is zero, is

$$(\vec{a_2} - \vec{a_1})\cdot(\vec{b_1}\times\vec{b_2}) = 0 \quad \ldots\text{(i)}$$

Now, $\quad \vec{a_2} - \vec{a_1} = (-4\hat{i} + \hat{j}) - (-\hat{i} + 4\hat{j} + 3\hat{k})$

$$= -3\hat{i} - 3\hat{j} - 3\hat{k}$$

and $\quad \vec{b_1}\times\vec{b_2} = \begin{vmatrix} \hat{i} & \hat{j} & \hat{k} \\ 4 & 1 & 0 \\ 5 & 2 & 1 \end{vmatrix} = \hat{i}(1-0) - \hat{j}(4-0) + \hat{k}(8-5)$

$$= \hat{i} - 4\hat{j} + 3\hat{k}$$

From Eq. (i), $\quad (-3\hat{i} - 3\hat{j} - 3\hat{k})\cdot(\hat{i} - 4\hat{j} + 3\hat{k}) = 0$

$\Rightarrow \quad -3 + 12 - 9 = 0$

$\Rightarrow \quad 0 = 0,$

which is true. **Hence proved.**

29. Given lines are

$$\vec{r} = (2\hat{i} - \hat{j} + 3\hat{k}) + \lambda(\hat{i} - 2\hat{j} + 3\hat{k}) \quad \ldots(i)$$

and $\vec{r} = (\hat{i} + 4\hat{k}) + \mu(3\hat{i} - 6\hat{j} + 9\hat{k})$

$$= (\hat{i} + 4\hat{k}) + 3\mu(\hat{i} - 2\hat{j} + 3\hat{k}) \quad \ldots(ii)$$

On comparing Eqs. (i) and (ii) with $\vec{r} = \vec{a_1} + \lambda\vec{b}$ and $\vec{r} = \vec{a_2} + \lambda'\vec{b}$, we get

$$\vec{a_1} = 2\hat{i} - \hat{j} + 3\hat{k}, \vec{b} = \hat{i} - 2\hat{j} + 3\hat{k}$$

$$\vec{a_2} = \hat{i} + 4\hat{k}, \vec{b} = \hat{i} - 2\hat{j} + 3\hat{k}$$

Here, the lines are parallel.

$\therefore$ The shortest distance $= \dfrac{|(\vec{a_2} - \vec{a_1}) \times \vec{b}|}{|\vec{b}|}$

$$= \frac{|(-\hat{i} + \hat{j} + \hat{k}) \times (\hat{i} - 2\hat{j} + 3\hat{k})|}{\sqrt{1+4+9}}$$

Here, $(-\hat{i} + \hat{j} + \hat{k}) \times (\hat{i} - 2\hat{j} + 3\hat{k}) = \begin{vmatrix} \hat{i} & \hat{j} & \hat{k} \\ -1 & 1 & 1 \\ 1 & -2 & 3 \end{vmatrix}$

$$= \hat{i}(3+2) - \hat{j}(-3-1) + \hat{k}(2-1)$$
$$= 5\hat{i} + 4\hat{j} + \hat{k}$$

Hence, the required shortest distance $= \dfrac{|5\hat{i} + 4\hat{j} + \hat{k}|}{\sqrt{14}}$

$$= \frac{\sqrt{25+16+1}}{\sqrt{14}}$$

$$= \frac{\sqrt{42}}{\sqrt{14}} = \sqrt{3} \text{ units}$$

30. The given lines are

$$\frac{x+1}{2} = \frac{y-1}{1} = \frac{z-9}{-3} \text{ and } \frac{x-3}{2} = \frac{y+15}{-7} = \frac{z-9}{5}$$

$\therefore$ The equations of given lines in vector form are

$$\vec{r} = (-\hat{i} + \hat{j} + 9\hat{k}) + \lambda(2\hat{i} + \hat{j} - 3\hat{k})$$

and $\vec{r} = (3\hat{i} - 15\hat{j} + 9\hat{k}) + \mu(2\hat{i} - 7\hat{j} + 5\hat{k})$

Here, $\vec{a_1} = -\hat{i} + \hat{j} + 9\hat{k}, \vec{b_1} = 2\hat{i} + \hat{j} - 3\hat{k}$

and $\vec{a_2} = 3\hat{i} - 15\hat{j} + 9\hat{k}, \vec{b_2} = 2\hat{i} - 7\hat{j} + 5\hat{k}$

Now, $\vec{a_2} - \vec{a_1} = 4\hat{i} - 16\hat{j}$

and $\vec{b_1} \times \vec{b_2} = \begin{vmatrix} \hat{i} & \hat{j} & \hat{k} \\ 2 & 1 & -3 \\ 2 & -7 & 5 \end{vmatrix}$

$$= \hat{i}(5-21) - \hat{j}(10+6) + \hat{k}(-14-2)$$
$$= -16\hat{i} - 16\hat{j} - 16\hat{k}$$

Here, $|\vec{b_1} \times \vec{b_2}| = \sqrt{256+256+256} = 16\sqrt{3}$

$\therefore$ $\text{SD} = \left| \dfrac{(\vec{b_1} \times \vec{b_2}) \cdot (\vec{a_2} - \vec{a_1})}{|\vec{b_1} \times \vec{b_2}|} \right|$

$$= \left| \frac{(-16\hat{i} - 16\hat{j} - 16\hat{k}) \cdot (4\hat{i} - 16\hat{j})}{16\sqrt{3}} \right|$$

$$= \frac{-64 + 256}{16\sqrt{3}} = \frac{192}{16\sqrt{3}}$$

$$= \frac{12}{\sqrt{3}} = 4\sqrt{3} \text{ units}$$

31. Given line is $\dfrac{x-15}{3} = \dfrac{y-29}{8} = \dfrac{z-5}{-5} = \lambda$ (say)

$\Rightarrow \quad \dfrac{x-15}{3} = \lambda, \dfrac{y-29}{8} = \lambda$ and $\dfrac{z-5}{-5} = \lambda$

$\Rightarrow \quad x = 3\lambda + 15, y = 8\lambda + 29$ and $z = -5\lambda + 5$

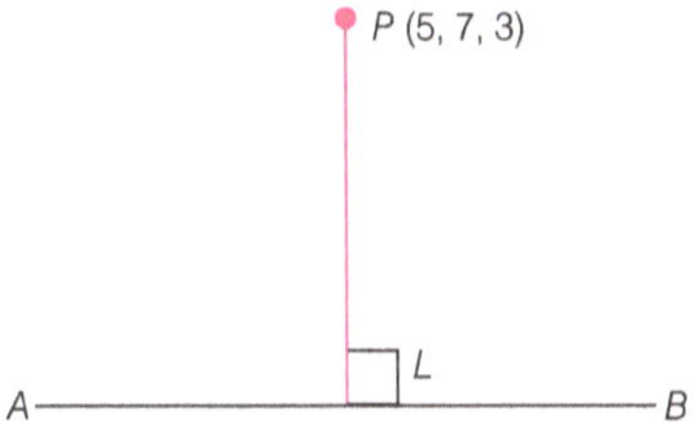

$\therefore$ Coordinate of point L are $\{(3\lambda + 15), (8\lambda + 29), (-5\lambda + 5)\}$

Direction ratios of line PL

$$= (3\lambda + 15 - 5, 8\lambda + 29 - 7, -5\lambda + 5 - 3)$$
$$= (3\lambda + 10, 8\lambda + 22, -5\lambda + 2)$$

Direction ratios of line AB are $(3, 8, -5)$.

$\because \quad PL \perp AB$

$\therefore \quad a_1a_2 + b_1b_2 + c_1c_2 = 0$

$\Rightarrow \quad 3(3\lambda + 10) + 8(8\lambda + 22) - 5(-5\lambda + 2) = 0$

$\Rightarrow \quad 98\lambda + 196 = 0$

$\Rightarrow \quad \lambda = \dfrac{-196}{98} = -2$

$\therefore$ Foot of perpendicular, $L = (3\lambda + 15, 8\lambda + 29, -5\lambda + 5)$

$$= (9, 13, 15)$$

32. Given equations of lines are

$$\vec{r} = (8\hat{i} - 19\hat{j} + 10\hat{k}) + \lambda(3\hat{i} - 16\hat{j} + 7\hat{k})$$

and $\vec{r} = (15\hat{i} + 29\hat{j} + 5\hat{k}) + \mu(3\hat{i} + 8\hat{j} - 5\hat{k})$

On comparing with $\vec{r} = \vec{a_1} + \lambda\vec{b_1}$ and $\vec{r} = \vec{a_2} + \mu\vec{b_2}$, we get

$$\vec{b_1} = 3\hat{i} - 16\hat{j} + 7\hat{k} \text{ and } \vec{b_2} = 3\hat{i} + 8\hat{j} - 5\hat{k}$$

Now, we determine

$$\vec{b} = \vec{b_1} \times \vec{b_2} = \begin{vmatrix} \hat{i} & \hat{j} & \hat{k} \\ 3 & -16 & 7 \\ 3 & 8 & -5 \end{vmatrix}$$

$$= \hat{i}(80 - 56) - \hat{j}(-15 - 21) + \hat{k}(24 + 48)$$
$$= 24\hat{i} + 36\hat{j} + 72\hat{k} = 12(2\hat{i} + 3\hat{j} + 6\hat{k})$$

Since, the required line is perpendicular to the given lines. So, it is parallel to $\vec{b_1} \times \vec{b_2}$.

Now, equation of a line passing through the point (1, 2, – 4) and parallel to $24\hat{i} + 36\hat{j} + 72\hat{k}$ or $(2\hat{i} + 3\hat{j} + 6\hat{k})$ is

$\vec{r} = (\hat{i} + 2\hat{j} - 4\hat{k}) + \lambda(2\hat{i} + 3\hat{j} + 6\hat{k})$,

which is required vector equation of the line.

For cartesian equation,

On putting $\vec{r} = x\hat{i} + y\hat{j} + z\hat{k}$, we get

$$x\hat{i} + y\hat{j} + z\hat{k} = (1 + 2\lambda)\hat{i} + (2 + 3\lambda)\hat{j} + (-4 + 6\lambda)\hat{k}$$

On comparing the coefficients of $\hat{i}$, $\hat{j}$ and $\hat{k}$, we get

$$x = 1 + 2\lambda,\ y = 2 + 3\lambda$$

and $z = -4 + 6\lambda$

$\Rightarrow \quad \dfrac{x-1}{2} = \lambda,\ \dfrac{y-2}{3} = \lambda$ and $\dfrac{z+4}{6} = \lambda$

$\therefore \quad \dfrac{x-1}{2} = \dfrac{y-2}{3} = \dfrac{z+4}{6}$,

which is the required cartesian equation of the line.

33. Let the required equation of line passing through the point (2, – 1, 3) and having direction ratios $\vec{b} = b_1\hat{i} + b_2\hat{j} + b_3\hat{k}$ is

$$\vec{r} = (2\hat{i} - \hat{j} + 3\hat{k}) + \lambda\vec{b} \quad \ldots(i)$$

The direction ratios of given lines are

$$\vec{b_1} = 2\hat{i} - 2\hat{j} + \hat{k} \text{ and } \vec{b_2} = \hat{i} + 2\hat{j} + 2\hat{k}$$

Since, line (i) is perpendicular to both the given lines.

$\therefore \quad \vec{b} \cdot \vec{b_1} = 0$ and $\vec{b} \cdot \vec{b_2} = 0$

$\Rightarrow \quad (b_1\hat{i} + b_2\hat{j} + b_3\hat{k}) \cdot (2\hat{i} - 2\hat{j} + \hat{k}) = 0$

and $\quad (b_1\hat{i} + b_2\hat{j} + b_3\hat{k}) \cdot (\hat{i} + 2\hat{j} + 2\hat{k}) = 0$

$\Rightarrow \quad 2b_1 - 2b_2 + b_3 = 0 \quad \ldots(ii)$

and $\quad b_1 + 2b_2 + 2b_3 = 0 \quad \ldots(iii)$

By cross-multiplication method, solve Eqs. (ii) and (iii), we get

$$\frac{b_1}{-4-2} = \frac{b_2}{-(4-1)} = \frac{b_3}{(4+2)}$$

$\Rightarrow \quad \dfrac{b_1}{-6} = \dfrac{b_2}{-3} = \dfrac{b_3}{6}$

$\Rightarrow \quad \dfrac{b_1}{-2} = \dfrac{b_2}{-1} = \dfrac{b_3}{2}$

$\therefore \quad \vec{b} = -2\hat{i} - \hat{j} + 2\hat{k}$

On putting the value of $\vec{b}$ in Eq. (i), we get

$$\vec{r} = 2\hat{i} - \hat{j} + 3\hat{k} + \lambda(-2\hat{i} - \hat{j} + 2\hat{k})$$

The cartesian equation of a line passing through (2, – 1, 3) and having direction ratios (– 2, – 1, 2) is

$$\frac{x-2}{-2} = \frac{y+1}{-1} = \frac{z-3}{2}.$$

34. Any line through the point (1, 1, 1) is given by

$$\frac{x-1}{a} = \frac{y-1}{b} = \frac{z-1}{c} \quad \ldots(i)$$

Where a, b and c are the direction ratios of line (i).

Now, the line (i) is perpendicular to the lines

$$\frac{x+2}{1} = \frac{y-3}{2} = \frac{z+1}{4} \text{ and } \frac{x-1}{2} = \frac{y-2}{3} = \frac{z-3}{4},$$

where direction ratios of these two lines are (1, 2, 4) and (2, 3, 4), respectively.

$\therefore \quad a + 2b + 4c = 0 \quad \ldots(ii)$

and $\quad 2a + 3b + 4c = 0 \quad \ldots(iii)$

[$\because$ if two lines having direction ratios (a_1, b_1, c_1) and (a_2, b_2, c_2) are perpendicular, then $a_1a_2 + b_1b_2 + c_1c_2 = 0$]

By cross-multiplication method, we get

$$\frac{a}{8-12} = \frac{b}{8-4} = \frac{c}{3-4} \Rightarrow \frac{a}{-4} = \frac{b}{4} = \frac{c}{-1}$$

$\therefore$ Direction ratios of line (i) are – 4, 4, – 1

$\therefore$ The required cartesian equation of line (i) is

$$\frac{x-1}{-4} = \frac{y-1}{4} = \frac{z-1}{-1}$$

and vector equation is $\vec{r} = \hat{i} + \hat{j} + \hat{k} + \lambda(-4\hat{i} + 4\hat{j} - \hat{k})$

Again, let θ be the angle between the given lines.

$\therefore \quad \cos\theta = \dfrac{1 \times 2 + 2 \times 3 + 4 \times 4}{\sqrt{1+4+16}\sqrt{4+9+16}} = \dfrac{24}{\sqrt{21}\sqrt{29}} = \dfrac{24}{\sqrt{609}}$

$\therefore \quad \theta = \cos^{-1}\left(\dfrac{24}{\sqrt{609}}\right)$

35. The given lines are

$$\frac{x+1}{3} = \frac{y+3}{5} = \frac{z+5}{7} = \lambda \text{ (let)} \quad \ldots(i)$$

and $\quad \dfrac{x-2}{1} = \dfrac{y-4}{3} = \dfrac{z-6}{5} = \mu \text{ (let)} \quad \ldots(ii)$

Then, any point on line (i) is

$$P(3\lambda - 1, 5\lambda - 3, 7\lambda - 5) \quad \ldots(iii)$$

and any point on line (ii) is

$$Q(\mu + 2, 3\mu + 4, 5\mu + 6) \quad \ldots(iv)$$

Clearly, the lines (i) and (ii) will intersect, if

$$(3\lambda - 1, 5\lambda - 3, 7\lambda - 5) = (\mu + 2, 3\mu + 4, 5\mu + 6),$$

for some particular value of λ and μ.

$\Rightarrow 3\lambda - 1 = \mu + 2,\ 5\lambda - 3 = 3\mu + 4$ and $7\lambda - 5 = 5\mu + 6$

$\Rightarrow \quad 3\lambda - \mu = 3, \quad \ldots(v)$

$\quad 5\lambda - 3\mu = 7 \quad \ldots(vi)$

and $\quad 7\lambda - 5\mu = 11 \quad \ldots(vii)$

On multiplying Eq. (v) by 3 and then subtracting Eq. (vi) from it, we get

$$9\lambda - 3\mu - 5\lambda + 3\mu = 9 - 7$$

$\Rightarrow \quad 4\lambda = 2 \Rightarrow \lambda = \dfrac{1}{2}$

On putting the value of λ in Eq. (v), we get

$$3\times\frac{1}{2}-\mu=3\Rightarrow\frac{3}{2}-\mu=3\Rightarrow\mu=-\frac{3}{2}$$

On putting the values of λ and μ in Eq. (vii), we get

$$7\times\frac{1}{2}-5\left(-\frac{3}{2}\right)=11\Rightarrow\frac{7}{2}+\frac{15}{2}=11$$

$$\Rightarrow\quad\frac{22}{2}=11\Rightarrow 11=11, \text{ which is true.}$$

Hence, lines (i) and (ii) intersect and their points of intersection is

$$P\left(3\times\frac{1}{2}-1, 5\times\frac{1}{2}-3, 7\times\frac{1}{2}-5\right)\quad\left[\text{put } \lambda=\frac{1}{2} \text{ in Eq.(iii)}\right]$$

i.e. $P\left(\frac{1}{2},-\frac{1}{2},-\frac{3}{2}\right)$.

36. Given equation of lines can be written in standard form as

$$\frac{x-1}{-3}=\frac{y-2}{\lambda/7}=\frac{z-3}{2}=r_1 \text{ (let)} \quad ...(i)$$

and $$\frac{x-1}{\frac{-3\lambda}{7}}=\frac{y-5}{1}=\frac{z-6}{-5}=r_2 \text{ (let)} \quad ...(ii)$$

These lines will intersect at right angle, if

$$-3\left(\frac{-3\lambda}{7}\right)+\frac{\lambda}{7}(1)+2(-5)=0$$

[$\because$ two lines with direction ratios a_1,b_1,c_1 and a_2,b_2,c_2 are perpendicular, if $a_1a_2+b_1b_2+c_1c_2=0$]

$$\Rightarrow\quad\frac{9\lambda}{7}+\frac{\lambda}{7}=10\Rightarrow\frac{10\lambda}{7}=10\Rightarrow\lambda=7,$$

which is the required value of λ.

Now, let us check whether the lines are intersecting or not.

Coordinates of any point on line (i) are $(-3r_1+1, r_1+2, 2r_1+3)$

and coordinates of any point on line (ii) are

$$(-3r_2+1, r_2+5, -5r_2+6)$$

Clearly, the line will intersect if

$$(-3r_1+1, r_1+2, 2r_1+3)=(-3r_2+1, r_2+5, -5r_2+6)$$

For some $r_1, r_2 \in R$

$\Rightarrow -3r_1+1=-3r_2+1, r_1+2=r_2+5$ and $2r_1+3=-5r_2+6$

$\Rightarrow \quad r_1=r_2, r_1-r_2=3$ and $2r_1+5r_2=3$,

which is not possible simultaneously for any $r_1, r_2 \in R$.

Hence, the lines are not intersecting.

37. The given lines are,

$$\frac{x-8}{3}=\frac{y+9}{-16}=\frac{z-10}{7} \text{ and } \frac{x-15}{3}=\frac{y-29}{8}=\frac{z-5}{-5}$$

$\therefore$ The equation of given lines in vector form are

$$\vec{r}=8\hat{i}-9\hat{j}+10\hat{k}+\lambda(3\hat{i}-16\hat{j}+7\hat{k})$$

and $$\vec{r}=15\hat{i}+29\hat{j}+5\hat{k}+\mu(3\hat{i}+8\hat{j}-5\hat{k})$$

Here, $\vec{a_1}=8\hat{i}-9\hat{j}+10\hat{k},\ \vec{b_1}=3\hat{i}-16\hat{j}+7\hat{k}$

$\vec{a_2}=15\hat{i}+29\hat{j}+5\hat{k}$ and $\vec{b_2}=3\hat{i}+8\hat{j}-5\hat{k}$

Now, $\vec{a_2}-\vec{a_1}=7\hat{i}+38\hat{j}-5\hat{k}$

and $$\vec{b_1}\times\vec{b_2}=\begin{vmatrix}\hat{i}&\hat{j}&\hat{k}\\3&-16&7\\3&8&-5\end{vmatrix}$$

$$=\hat{i}(80-56)-\hat{j}(-15-21)+\hat{k}(24+48)$$

$$=24\hat{i}+36\hat{j}+72\hat{k}$$

Here, $|\vec{b_1}\times\vec{b_2}|=\sqrt{576+1296+5184}=\sqrt{7056}=84$

$$\therefore\quad SD=\left|\frac{(|\vec{b_1}\times\vec{b_2}|)\cdot(|\vec{a_2}-\vec{a_1}|)}{|\vec{b_1}\times\vec{b_2}|}\right|$$

$$=\left|\frac{(24\hat{i}+36\hat{j}+72\hat{k})\cdot(7\hat{i}+38\hat{j}-5\hat{k})}{84}\right|$$

$$=\left|\frac{168+1368-360}{84}\right|=\left|\frac{1176}{84}\right|=14 \text{ units}$$

38. Given, L_1: The line passing through $(2,-1,1)$ and parallel to $\frac{x}{1}=\frac{y}{1}=\frac{z}{3}$

$$L_2:\vec{r}=\hat{i}+(2\mu+1)\hat{j}-(\mu+2)\hat{k}$$

Write the given equations of line in standard form

$$L_1:\vec{r}=(2\hat{i}-\hat{j}+\hat{k})+\lambda(\hat{i}+\hat{j}+3\hat{k}) \quad ...(i)$$

$$L_2:\vec{r}=(\hat{i}+\hat{j}-2\hat{k})+\mu(2\hat{j}-\hat{k}) \quad ...(ii)$$

On comparing Eqs. (i) and (ii) with $\vec{r}=a_1+\lambda b_1$ and $\vec{r}=a_2+\lambda b_2$ respectively, we get

$$\vec{a_1}=2\hat{i}-\hat{j}+\hat{k}, \vec{b_1}=\hat{i}+\hat{j}+3\hat{k}$$

and $$\vec{a_2}=(\hat{i}+\hat{j}-2\hat{k}), \vec{b_2}=2\hat{j}-\hat{k}$$

Clearly, $$\vec{b_1}\times\vec{b_2}=\begin{vmatrix}\hat{i}&\hat{j}&\hat{k}\\1&1&3\\0&2&-1\end{vmatrix}$$

$$=\hat{i}(-1-6)-\hat{j}(-1-0)+\hat{k}(2-0)$$

$$=-7\hat{i}+\hat{j}+2\hat{k}$$

$$\Rightarrow\quad|\vec{b_1}\times\vec{b_2}|=|-7\hat{i}+\hat{j}+2\hat{k}|=\sqrt{(-7)^2+(1)^2+(2)^2}$$

$$=\sqrt{49+1+4}=\sqrt{54}=3\sqrt{6}$$

Now, $\vec{a_2}-\vec{a_1}=(\hat{i}+\hat{j}-2\hat{k})-(2\hat{i}-\hat{j}+\hat{k})=-\hat{i}+2\hat{j}-3\hat{k}$

$$\therefore\text{ Required SD}=\frac{|(\vec{a_2}-\vec{a_1})\cdot(\vec{b_1}\times\vec{b_2})|}{|\vec{b_1}\times\vec{b_2}|}$$

$$=\frac{|(-\hat{i}+2\hat{j}-3\hat{k})\cdot(-7\hat{i}+\hat{j}+2\hat{k})|}{3\sqrt{6}}$$

$$=\frac{|7+2-6|}{3\sqrt{6}}$$

$$=\frac{3}{3\sqrt{6}}=\frac{1}{\sqrt{6}} \text{ unit}$$

39. Let h be the height of ΔABC. Then, h is the length of perpendicular from $A(1,-1,2)$ to the line $\frac{x+2}{2}=\frac{y-1}{1}=\frac{z-0}{4}$.

Clearly, line $\frac{x+2}{2}=\frac{y-1}{1}=\frac{z-0}{4}$ passes through the point say $P(-2,1,0)$ and parallel to the vector $\vec{b}=2\hat{i}+\hat{j}+4\hat{k}$.

Let $\frac{x+2}{2}=\frac{y-1}{1}=\frac{z-0}{4}=\lambda$.

Then, coordinates of M are $(2\lambda-2, \lambda+1, 4\lambda)$.

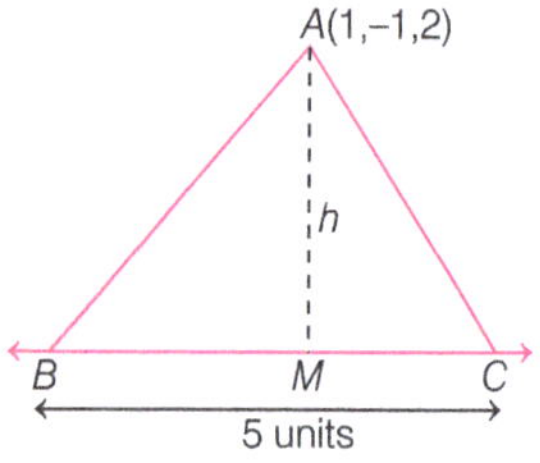

Now, direction ratios of $AM = 2\lambda-2-1, \lambda+1+1, 4\lambda-2$
$= 2\lambda-3, \lambda+2, 4\lambda-2$

Since, $AM \perp BC$.

$\therefore\quad 2(2\lambda-3)+1(\lambda+2)+4(4\lambda-2)=0$

$\Rightarrow\quad 4\lambda-6+\lambda+2+16\lambda-8=0$

$\Rightarrow\quad 21\lambda=12$

$\Rightarrow\quad \lambda=\frac{4}{7}$

Thus, the coordinates of M are $\left(2\times\frac{4}{7}-2, \frac{4}{7}+1, 4\times\frac{4}{7}\right)$

i.e. $\left(-\frac{6}{7},\frac{11}{7},\frac{16}{7}\right)$.

Now, $h=|AM|=\sqrt{\left(-\frac{6}{7}-1\right)^2+\left(\frac{11}{7}+1\right)^2+\left(\frac{16}{7}-2\right)^2}$

$=\sqrt{\left(-\frac{13}{7}\right)^2+\left(\frac{18}{7}\right)^2+\left(\frac{2}{7}\right)^2}$

$=\sqrt{\left(\frac{169}{7^2}+\frac{324}{7^2}+\frac{4}{7^2}\right)}$

$=\sqrt{\frac{497}{7^2}}=\sqrt{\frac{71}{7}}$

It is given that the length of BC is 5 units.

$\therefore$ Area of $\Delta ABC=\frac{1}{2}(BC\times h)=\frac{1}{2}\times 5\times\sqrt{\frac{71}{7}}$

$=\sqrt{\frac{1775}{28}}$ sq units

40. Let T be the image of the point $P(2,-1,5)$. Q is the foot of perpendicular drawn from point P on the line AB.

Given equation of line AB is

$$\frac{x-11}{10}=\frac{y+2}{-4}=\frac{z+8}{-11} \quad \text{...(i)}$$

Let $\frac{x-11}{10}=\frac{y+2}{-4}=\frac{z+8}{-11}=\lambda$ (say)

$\Rightarrow\quad x=10\lambda+11, y=-4\lambda-2$ and $z=-11\lambda-8$

Then, coordinates of Q are

$$(10\lambda+11, -4\lambda-2, -11\lambda-8) \quad \text{...(ii)}$$

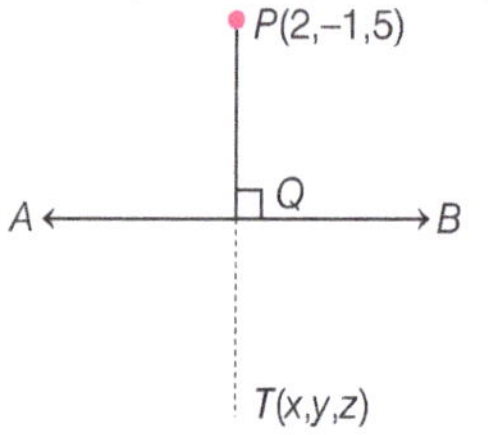

Now, direction ratios of line PQ
$=10\lambda+11-2, -4\lambda-2+1, -11\lambda-8-5$
$=10\lambda+9, -4\lambda-1, -11\lambda-13$

Since, line $PQ \perp AB$.

$\therefore\quad a_1a_2+b_1b_2+c_1c_2=0$

where $a_1=10\lambda+9, b_1=-4\lambda-1, c_1=-11\lambda-13$

and $a_2=10, b_2=-4, c_2=-11$

$\therefore (10\lambda+9)(10)+(-4\lambda-1)(-4)+(-11\lambda-13)(-11)=0$

$\Rightarrow\quad 100\lambda+90+16\lambda+4+121\lambda+143=0$

$\Rightarrow\quad 237\lambda+237=0$

$\Rightarrow\quad \lambda=-1$

On putting $\lambda=-1$ in Eq. (ii), we get

$Q=(10(-1)+11, -4(-1)-2, -11(-1)-8)$
$=(-10+11, 4-2, 11-8)=(1, 2, 3)$

Let image of a point P be $T(x,y,z)$.

Then, Q will be the mid-point of PT.

By mid-point formula, we get

$Q=$ Mid-point of $P(2,-1,5)$ and $T(x,y,z)$.
$=\left(\frac{x+2}{2},\frac{y-1}{2},\frac{z+5}{2}\right)$

But $Q=(1,2,3)$

$\therefore\left(\frac{x+2}{2},\frac{y-1}{2},\frac{z+5}{2}\right)=(1,2,3)$

On equating corresponding coordinates, we get

$\frac{x+2}{2}=1, \frac{y-1}{2}=2, \frac{z+5}{2}=3$

$\Rightarrow\quad x=2-2, y=4+1, z=6-5$

$\therefore\quad x=0, y=5, z=1$

$\therefore$ Coordinates of $T=(x,y,z)=(0,5,1)$

Hence, the image of point $P(2,-1,5)$ is $T(0,5,1)$.

41. Let L be the foot of the perpendicular drawn from $P(\hat{i}+6\hat{j}+3\hat{k})$ on the line.

$$\vec{r}=\hat{j}+2\hat{k}+\lambda(\hat{i}+2\hat{j}+3\hat{k}) \quad \text{... (i)}$$

Then, $\overrightarrow{PL}=$ Position vector of $L-$ Position vector of P

$=\lambda\hat{i}+(1+2\lambda)\hat{j}+(2+3\lambda)\hat{k}-(\hat{i}+6\hat{j}+3\hat{k})$
$=(\lambda-1)\hat{i}+(-5+2\lambda)\hat{j}+(-1+3\lambda)\hat{k}$

Since, $\overrightarrow{PL}$ is perpendicular to the given line which is parallel to $\vec{b} = \hat{i} + 2\hat{j} + 3\hat{k}$.

$\therefore \quad \overrightarrow{PL} \perp \vec{b}$

$\Rightarrow [(\lambda - 1)\hat{i} + (-5 + 2\lambda)\hat{j} + (-1 + 3\lambda)\hat{k}] \cdot [\hat{i} + 2\hat{j} + 3\hat{k}] = 0$

$\Rightarrow \quad (\lambda - 1) \times 1 + (-5 + 2\lambda) \times 2 + (-1 + 3\lambda) \times 3 = 0$

$\Rightarrow \quad \lambda - 1 - 10 + 4\lambda - 3 + 9\lambda = 0$

$\Rightarrow \quad 14\lambda - 14 = 0$

$\Rightarrow \quad \lambda = 1$

On putting $\lambda = 1$ in Eq. (i), we get the position vector of L is $\hat{j} + 2\hat{k} + 1(\hat{i} + 2\hat{j} + 3\hat{k})$) or $(\hat{i} + 3\hat{j} + 5\hat{k})$.

Now, $\overrightarrow{PL} = (\hat{i} + 3\hat{j} + 5\hat{k}) - (\hat{i} + 6\hat{j} + 3\hat{k}) = -3\hat{j} + 2\hat{k}$

$\therefore$ The length of perpendicular drawn from P to the line

$$= |\overrightarrow{PL}|$$
$$= \sqrt{(-3)^2 + (2)^2}$$
$$= \sqrt{9 + 4} = \sqrt{13}$$

42. Let T be the image of the point $P(-1, 5, 2)$. Q is the foat of perpendicular drawn from point P on the line AB.

Given equation of line AB is

$$\frac{2x - 4}{2} = \frac{y}{2} = \frac{2 - z}{3}$$

$$\Rightarrow \quad \frac{x - 2}{1} = \frac{y}{2} = \frac{z - 2}{-3} \quad \ldots(i)$$

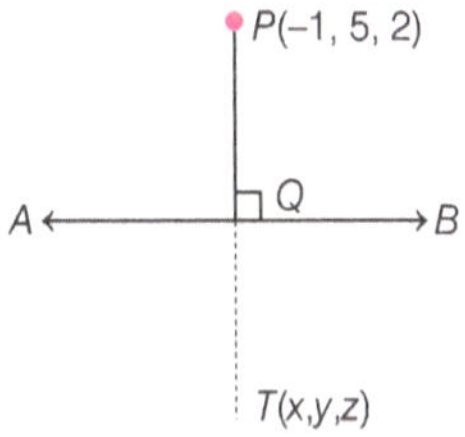

Let $\frac{x - 2}{1} = \frac{y}{2} = \frac{z - 2}{-3} = \lambda$

$\Rightarrow \quad x = \lambda + 2, y = 2\lambda, z = -3\lambda + 2$

Then, $Q = (\lambda + 2, 2\lambda, -3\lambda + 2)$ $\quad \ldots$(ii)

Now, direction ratios of line PQ

$$= (\lambda + 2 + 1, 2\lambda - 5, -3\lambda + 2 - 2)$$
$$= (\lambda + 3, 2\lambda - 5, -3\lambda)$$

Since, line $PQ \perp AB$.

$\therefore \quad a_1a_2 + b_1b_2 + c_1c_2 = 0,$

where $a_1 = \lambda + 3, b_1 = 2\lambda - 5, c_1 = -3\lambda$

and $a_2 = 1, b_2 = 2, c_3 = -3$

$\therefore \quad 1(\lambda + 3) + 2(2\lambda - 5) - 3(-3\lambda) = 0$

$\Rightarrow \quad 14\lambda - 7 = 0$

$\Rightarrow \quad \lambda = \frac{1}{2}$

On putting $\lambda = \frac{1}{2}$ in Eq. (ii), we get

$$Q = \left(\frac{1}{2} + 2, 2 \times \frac{1}{2}, -3 \times \frac{1}{2} + 2\right) = \left(\frac{5}{2}, 1, \frac{1}{2}\right)$$

Let image of a point P be $T\,(x, y, z)$.

Then, $Q\left(\frac{5}{2}, 1, \frac{1}{2}\right)$ will be the mid-point of $P(-1, 5, 2)$ and $T(x, y, z)$.

$$\therefore \left(\frac{5}{2}, 1, \frac{1}{2}\right) = \left(\frac{x - 1}{2}, \frac{y + 5}{2}, \frac{z + 2}{2}\right)$$

On equating corresponding coordinates, we get

$$\frac{x - 1}{2} = \frac{5}{2}, \frac{y + 5}{2} = 1, \frac{z + 2}{2} = \frac{1}{2}$$

$\Rightarrow \quad x = 6, y = -3, z = -1$

$\therefore$ Coordinates of $T = (x, y, z) = (6, -3, -1)$

Hence, the image of point $P(-1, 5, 2)$ is $T(6, -3, -1)$

Now, distance of $PT = \sqrt{\{6 - (-1)\}^2 + (-3 - 5)^2 + (-1 - 2)^2}$

[$\because$ by distance formula]

$$= \sqrt{7^2 + (-8)^2 + (-3)^2}$$
$$= \sqrt{49 + 64 + 9}$$
$$= \sqrt{122}$$

So, the length of line segment joining the points is $\sqrt{122}$ units.

QR Code for Quick Test 1

QR Code for Quick Test 2

Mind Map

Three-Dimensional Geometry

Direction Cosines of a Line

If a line makes angles α, β and γ with the X, Y and Z-axes, then direction cosines (or DC's) of a line are given by $l = \cos\alpha$, $m = \cos\beta$, $n = \cos\gamma$

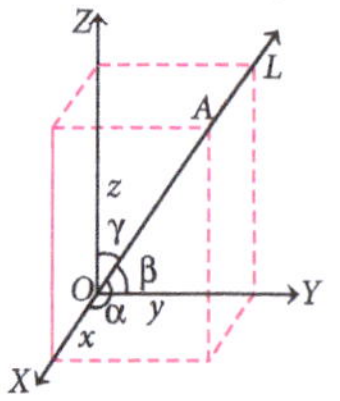

Direction Cosines of a Line Passing Through Two Points

The direction cosines of a line passing through the points $A(x_1, y_1, z_1)$ and $B(x_2, y_2, z_2)$ are given by

$$\frac{x_2 - x_1}{AB}, \frac{y_2 - y_1}{AB} \text{ and } \frac{z_2 - z_1}{AB}$$

where, $AB = \sqrt{(x_2 - x_1)^2 + (y_2 - y_1)^2 + (z_2 - z_1)^2}$

Cartesian Equation

The cartesian equation of a line passing through a point $A(x_1, y_1, z_1)$ and having direction ratios a, b and c is $\dfrac{x - x_1}{a} = \dfrac{y - y_1}{b} = \dfrac{z - z_1}{c}$

where, (x, y, z) are coordinates of any point on the line.

Condition of Perpendicularity

Two lines are said to be perpendicular,

in **vector form** if $\vec{b_1} \cdot \vec{b_2} = 0$,

in **cartesian form** if $a_1a_2 + b_1b_2 + c_1c_2 = 0$ [direction ratio form]

or $l_1l_2 + m_1m_2 + n_1n_2 = 0$ [direction cosine form]

Shortest Distance between Parallel Lines

$$\text{SD or } d = |\overrightarrow{PT}| = \left|\frac{\vec{b} \times (\vec{a_2} - \vec{a_1})}{|\vec{b}|}\right|$$

Condition that Two Lines are Parallel

Two lines are said to be parallel,

in **vector form** $\vec{b_1} = \lambda\vec{b_2}$;

in **certesian form** if $\dfrac{a_1}{a_2} = \dfrac{b_1}{b_2} = \dfrac{c_1}{c_2}$ [direction ratio form]

or $\dfrac{l_1}{l_2} = \dfrac{m_1}{m_2} = \dfrac{n_1}{n_2}$ [direction cosine form]

Condition for Two Given Lines to be Intersect

Vector Form

The lines L_1 and L_2 will intersect, if the shortest distance between them is zero.

i.e. $\dfrac{|(\vec{a_2} - \vec{a_1}) \cdot (\vec{b_1} \times \vec{b_2})|}{|(\vec{b_1} \times \vec{b_2})|} = 0$

$\Rightarrow (\vec{a_2} - \vec{a_1}) \cdot (\vec{b_1} \times \vec{b_2}) = 0$

Cartesian Form

The lines L_1 and L_2 will intersect, if the shortest distance between them is zero.

i.e. $\begin{vmatrix} x_2 - x_1 & y_2 - y_1 & z_2 - z_1 \\ a_1 & b_1 & c_1 \\ a_2 & b_2 & c_2 \end{vmatrix} = 0$

Lines in Space

A line (or straight line) is a curve such that all the points on the line segment joining any two points of it lies on it.

Equation of a Line through a Given Point and Parallel to a Given Vector

Vector Equation

The vector equation of a line l passing through a point A with position vector $\vec{a}$ and parallel to a given vector $\vec{b}$ is $\vec{r} = \vec{a} + \lambda\vec{b}$

The vector equation of a straight line passing through the origin and parallel to given vector $\vec{b}$ is

$$\vec{r} = \lambda\vec{b}$$

Angle between Two Lines

Vector Form Angle between the lines $\vec{r} = \vec{a_1} + \lambda\vec{b_1}$ and $\vec{r} = \vec{a_2} + \mu\,\vec{b_2}$ is given as

$$\cos\theta = \left|\frac{\vec{b_1} \cdot \vec{b_2}}{|\vec{b_1}||\vec{b_2}|}\right|$$

where, θ is an acute angle between the lines.

Cartesian Form

Angle between the lines $\dfrac{x - x_1}{a_1} = \dfrac{y - y_1}{b_1} = \dfrac{z - z_1}{c_1}$

and $\dfrac{x - x_2}{a_2} = \dfrac{y - y_2}{b_2} = \dfrac{z - z_2}{c_2}$ is given as

$$\cos\theta = \left|\frac{a_1a_2 + b_1b_2 + c_1c_2}{\sqrt{a_1^2 + b_1^2 + c_1^2} \cdot \sqrt{a_2^2 + b_2^2 + c_2^2}}\right|$$

$$\text{or } \sin\theta = \frac{\sqrt{(a_1b_2 - a_2b_1)^2 + (b_1c_2 - b_2c_1)^2 + (c_1a_2 - c_2a_1)^2}}{\sqrt{a_1^2 + b_1^2 + c_1^2} \cdot \sqrt{a_2^2 + b_2^2 + c_2^2}}$$

Direction Ratios of a Line

Any three numbers a, b and c proportional to the direction cosines l, m and n respectively, are called the direction ratios or direction numbers of the line.

$\therefore$ We have, $\dfrac{l}{a} = \dfrac{m}{b} = \dfrac{n}{c}$

Hence, if a, b and c are the direction ratios of a line, then its direction cosines are given by

$$l = \frac{a}{\sqrt{a^2 + b^2 + c^2}}, \quad m = \frac{b}{\sqrt{a^2 + b^2 + c^2}}$$

and $n = \dfrac{c}{\sqrt{a^2 + b^2 + c^2}}$

The direction ratios of a line passing through two points and are given by $P(x_1, y_1, z_1))$ and $Q(x_2, y_2, z_2)$ are given by $(x_2 - x_1)$, $(y_2 - y_1)$ and $(z_2 - z_1)$

Condition for Collinearity of Three Points

Suppose $A(x_1, y_1, z_1)$, $B(x_2, y_2, z_2)$ and $C(x_3, y_3, z_3)$ are three points in a space.

In direction ratios of AB and BC are proportional, then these points are collinear, otherwise not.

Perpendicular Distance of a Line from a Given Point

Vector Form

Let L be the foot of perpendicular drawn from the point $P(\alpha)$ on the given line and the position vector of L be $\vec{a} + \lambda\vec{b}$, where $\lambda = -\dfrac{(\vec{a} - \alpha) \cdot \vec{b}}{|\vec{b}|^2}$

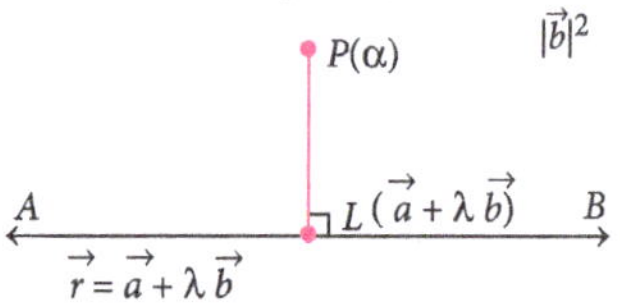

Cartesian Form

Let L be the foot of the perpendicular drawn from $P(\alpha, \beta, \gamma)$ on the line

$$\frac{x - x_1}{a} = \frac{y - y_1}{b} = \frac{z - z_1}{c} = \lambda \text{ (say)}$$

and the coordinates of L can be determined by $(x_1 + a\lambda, y_1 + b\lambda, z_1 + c\lambda)$.

Where, $\lambda = \dfrac{[a(\alpha - x_1) + b(\beta - y_1) + c(\gamma - z_1)]}{a^2 + b^2 + c^2}$

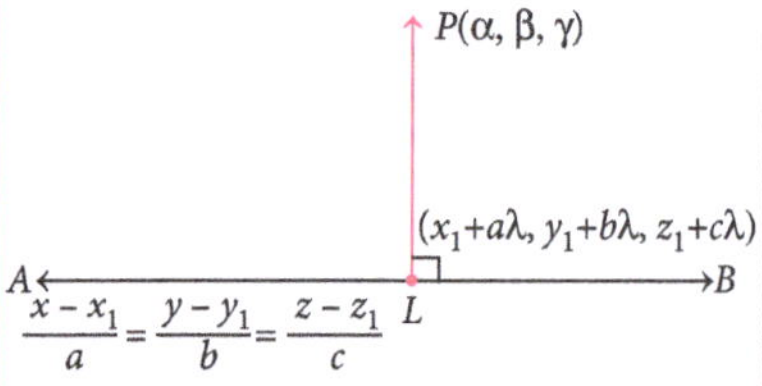

12 CHAPTER

Young man, in Mathematics, you don't understand things. You just get used to them. — *John Von Neumann*

Linear Programming

▼ YOUR STUDY GOALS

12.1 Mathematical Form of LPP

12.2 Graphical Method for Solving Linear Programming Problem

▼ YOUR PRACTICE GOALS

- Objective Type Questions (28 Qs ; 15 MCQs, 10 A-R, 3 Case Based)
- Subjective Type Questions (19 Qs ; 14 SA, 5 LA)

Linear programming is a mathematical method for maximising and minimising a linear function of several variables subject to the constraints on the variables that satisfy the linear inequation.

Here, linear function is known as objective function and constraints are linear inequalities.

12.1 Mathematical Form of LPP

The mathematical form of a linear programming problem is as follows

Objective function, $Z = c_1x + c_2y$

Subject to constraints are $a_1x + b_1y \le d_1, a_2x + b_2y \le d_2$, etc.

and $x \ge 0,\ y \ge 0$.

Important Terms Related to LPP

- **Constraints** The linear inequations or inequalities or restrictions on the variables of a linear programming problem are called constraints. The conditions $x \ge 0,\ y \ge 0$ are called **non-negative restrictions.**

- **Optimisation Problem** A problem which need to maximise or minimise a linear function subject to certain constraints as determined by a set of linear inequalities is called an optimisation problem. Linear programming problems are special type of optimisation problems.
- **Objective Function** A linear function of two or more variables which has to be maximised or minimised under the given restrictions is called an objective function.
- **Optimal Value** The maximum or minimum value of an objective function is known as the optimal value of LPP.
- **Feasible and Infeasible Region** The common region determined by all the constraints including non-negative constraints $x, y \geq 0$ of a linear programming problem is called the feasible region or solution region. The region other than feasible region is called an infeasible region.
- **Bounded and Unbounded Region** A feasible region of a system of linear inequalities is said to be bounded, if it can be enclosed within lines.

  Otherwise, it is said to be unbounded region, i.e. the feasible region does extend infinitely in any direction.
- **Feasible and Infeasible Solution** Points within and on the boundary of the feasible region, represents feasible solution of the constraints.
  Any point outside the feasible region is called an infeasible solution.
- **Optimal Feasible Solution** A feasible solution at which the objective function has optimal value (maximum or minimum), is called the optimal solution or optimal feasible solution of the linear programming problem.
- **Optimisation Technique** The process of obtaining the optimal solution of the linear programming problem is called optimisation technique.
- **Corner Point** A corner point of a feasible region is a point of intersection of two boundary lines in the region.

Some Important Theorems

Theorem 1 Let R be the feasible region (convex polygon) for a linear programming problem and $Z = ax + by$ be the objective function. When Z has an optimal value (maximum or minimum), where the variables x and y are subject to constraints described by linear inequalities, this optimal value must occur at a corner point (vertex) of the feasible region.

Theorem 2 Let R be the feasible region for a linear programming problem and $Z = ax + by$ be the objective function.

If R is **bounded**, then the objective function Z has both a maximum and minimum values on R and each of these occurs at a corner point (vertex) of R. If R is **unbounded**, then a maximum or minimum value of the objective function may not exist. However, if it exists, it must occur at a corner point of R.

12.2 Graphical Method for Solving Linear Programming Problem

This method of solving linear programming problem is referred as **corner point method**. The process of this method is as follows.

I. Draw the graph of each linear equation.

II. Find the feasible region of the LPP and determine its corner points (vertices).

III. Determine the value of objective function, $Z = ax + by$ at each corner point.

(a) When the feasible region is **bounded**, then find maximum (M) and minimum (m) values of Z.

(b) When the feasible region is **unbounded**, then

(i) The maximum (M) value of Z exist, if the open half plane determined by $ax + by > M$ has no point in common with the feasible region. Otherwise, Z has no maximum value.

(ii) The minimum (m) value of Z exists, if the open half plane determined by $ax + by < m$ has no point in common with the feasible region. Otherwise, Z has no minimum value.

(c) If two corner points of the feasible region are both optimal solution of the same type

i.e. both produce the same maximum or minimum, then any point on the line segment joining these two points is also an optimal solution of the same type.

Example 1 **In the LPP, find the point/points giving maximum value for $Z = 5x + 10y$.**
Subject to constraints,

$$x + 2y \le 120$$
$$x + y \ge 60$$
$$x - 2y \ge 0$$
$$x, y \ge 0$$

CBSE 2025

Sol. Our problem is maximise,

$$Z = 5x + 10y \quad \text{...(i)}$$

Subject to constraints,

$$x + 2y \le 120 \quad \text{...(ii)}$$
$$x + y \ge 60 \quad \text{...(iii)}$$
$$x - 2y \ge 0 \quad \text{...(iv)}$$

and $x \ge 0,\ y \ge 0$

Firstly, draw the graph of the line $x + 2y = 120$.

x	0	120
y	60	0

On putting (0, 0) in the inequality $x + 2y \le 120$, we get

$0 + 2 \times 0 \le 120 \Rightarrow 0 \le 120$, which is true.

So, the half plane is towards the origin.

Secondly, draw the graph of the line $x + y = 60$.

x	0	60
y	60	0

On putting (0, 0) in the inequality $x + y \ge 60$, we get

$0 + 0 \ge 60 \Rightarrow 0 \ge 60$, which is false.

So, the half plane is away from the origin.

Thirdly, draw the graph of the line $x - 2y = 0$.

x	0	10
y	0	5

On putting (5, 0) in the inequality $x - 2y \ge 0$, we get

$5 - 2 \times 0 \ge 0 = 5 \ge 0$, which is true.

So, the half plane is towards the X-axis.

Since, $x, y \ge 0$, so the feasible region lies in the I quadrant.

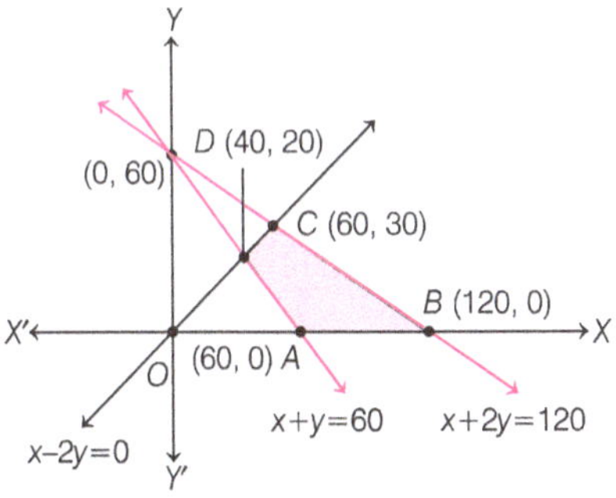

On solving equations $x - 2y = 0$ and $x + y = 60$, we get $D(40, 20)$ and on solving equations $x - 2y = 0$ and $x + 2y = 120$, we get C (60, 30).

So, the feasible region is $ABCDA$. The corner points of the feasible region are A (60, 0), B (120, 0), C (60, 30) and D (40, 20).

The values of Z at these points are as follows

Corner points	$Z = 5x + 10y$
A (60, 0)	300
B (120, 0)	600 (Maximum)
C (60, 30)	600 (Maximum)
D (40, 20)	400

So, the maximum value of Z is 600 at the points (120, 0) and (60, 30).

Example 2 **Minimise $Z = x + 2y$, subject to constraints $2x + y \ge 3$, $x + 2y \ge 6$ and $x, y \ge 0$.**

(i) Show that the minimum of Z occurs at more than two points.

(ii) Also, check whether the point $P(5, 2)$ lies inside the shaded portion, if it lies inside the shaded region, then find the distance between the origin and point.

NCERT

Sol. Our problem is to minimise,

$$Z = x + 2y \quad \text{...(i)}$$

Subject to constraints,

$$2x + y \ge 3 \quad \text{...(ii)}$$
$$x + 2y \ge 6 \quad \text{...(iii)}$$

and $x \ge 0,\ y \ge 0$ ...(iv)

Table for line $2x + y = 3$ is

x	0	3/2
y	3	0

So, line passes through the points (0, 3) and $\left(\frac{3}{2}, 0\right)$.

On putting (0, 0) in the inequality $2x + y \ge 3$, we get

$2 \times 0 + 0 \ge 3 \Rightarrow 0 \ge 3$, which is not true.

So, the half plane is away from the origin.

Table for line $x + 2y = 6$ is

x	0	6
y	3	0

So, line passes through the points (0, 3) and (6, 0).

On putting (0, 0) in the inequality $x + 2y \ge 6$, we get

$0 + 2 \times 0 \ge 6 \Rightarrow 0 \ge 6$, which is not true.

So, the half plane is away from the origin.

Also, $x \ge 0$ and $y \ge 0$, so the region lies in the I quadrant.

The intersection point of the lines $x + 2y = 6$ and $2x + y = 3$ is $B(0, 3)$.

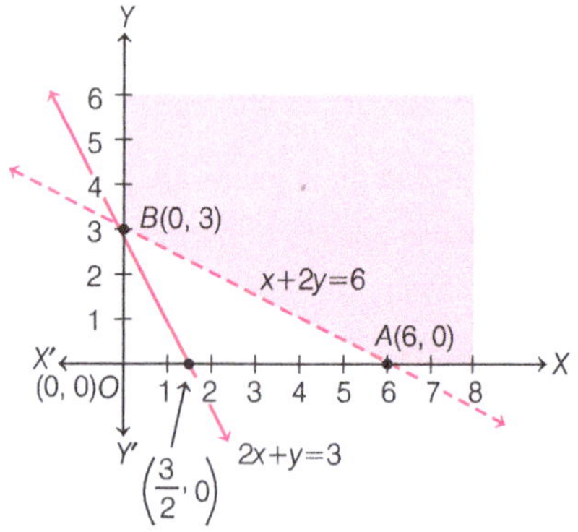

The corner points of the feasible region are $A(6, 0)$ and $B(0, 3)$.

The values of Z at the corner points are given below.

Corner points	$Z = x + 2y$
$A(6, 0)$	$Z = 6 + 2 \times 0 = 6$
$B(0, 3)$	$Z = 0 + 2 \times 3 = 6$

As the feasible region is unbounded, therefore 6 may or may not be the minimum value of Z. For this, we draw a dotted graph of the inequality $x + 2y < 6$ and check whether the resulting half plane has points in common with the feasible region or not. It can be seen that the feasible region has no common point with $x + 2y < 6$.

Therefore, the minimum value of Z is 6.

Thus, the minimum value of Z occurs at more than 2 points. [the value of Z is minimum at every point on the line segment AB]

Let $f(x, y) = x + 2y - 6$

At point $P(5, 2)$, $f(5, 2) = 5 + 2 \times 2 - 6 = 3 > 0$

Hence, point lies inside the shaded region.

Now, distance between O and P

$$= \sqrt{(5-0)^2 + (2-0)^2}$$

$$= \sqrt{25+4} = \sqrt{29} = 5.39$$

Example 3 **Find the maximum value of the objective function, $Z = 3x + 4y$.**

Subject to constraints, $x + y \leq 4$; $x \geq 0$ and $y \geq 0$.

CBSE Sample Paper 2017

Sol. Our problem is to maximise

$$Z = 3x + 4y \quad \text{...(i)}$$

Subject to the constraints are

$$x + y \leq 4 \quad \text{...(ii)}$$

and $$x \geq 0, y \geq 0 \quad \text{...(iii)}$$

Table for the line $x + y = 4$ is

x	0	4
y	4	0

On putting (0, 0) in the inequality $x + y \leq 4$, we get

$$0 + 0 \leq 4$$

$\Rightarrow$ $$0 \leq 4 \quad \text{(which is true)}$$

So, the half plane is towards the origin.

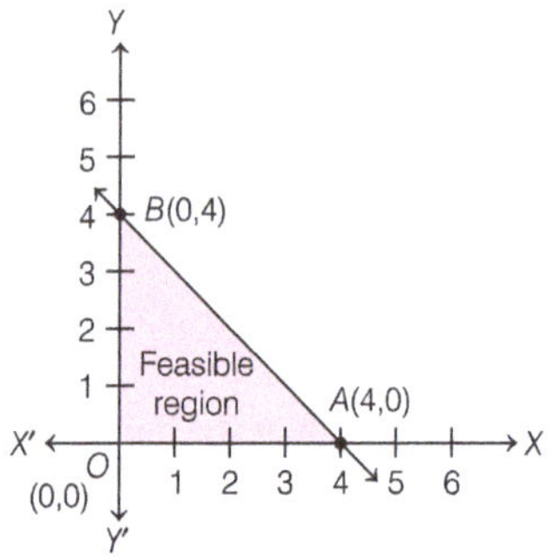

Since, $x, y \geq 0$.

So, the feasible region lies in the I quadrant.

$\therefore$ Feasible region is $OABO$.

The corner points of the feasible region are $O(0, 0)$, $A(4,0)$ and $B(0, 4)$. The values of Z at these points are as follow.

Corner points	$Z = 3x + 4y$
$O(0, 0)$	0
$A(4, 0)$	12
$B(0, 4)$	16 (Maximum)

Therefore, the maximum value of Z is 16 at the point $B(0, 4)$.

Example 4 **Solve the following linear programming problem graphically : Maximise $Z = 5x + 3y$.**

Subject to the constraints are

$3x + 5y \leq 15$, $5x + 2y \leq 10$ and $x, y \geq 0$ *CBSE 2023*

Sol. We have the following LPP.

Maximise $Z = 5x + 3y$

Subject to the constraints,

$$3x + 5y \leq 15 \quad \text{...(i)}$$

$$5x + 2y \leq 10 \quad \text{...(ii)}$$

and $$x, y \geq 0 \quad \text{...(iii)}$$

Table for line $3x + 5y = 15$ is

x	5	0
y	0	3

So, the line passes through the points (5, 0) and (0, 3).

On putting (0, 0) in the inequality $3x+5y\le 15$, we get

$$0+0\le 15, \text{ which is true.}$$

So, the half plane is towards the origin.

Table for line $5x+2y=10$ is

x	2	0
y	0	5

So, the line passes through the points (2, 0) and (0, 5).

On putting (0, 0) in the inequality $5x+2y\le 10$, we get

$$0+0\le 10, \text{ which is true.}$$

So, the half plane is towards the origin.

Also, $x\ge 0$ and $y\ge 0$, so the region lies in the I quadrant.

The above inequations (i), (ii) and (iii) can be represented in the graph as shown below.

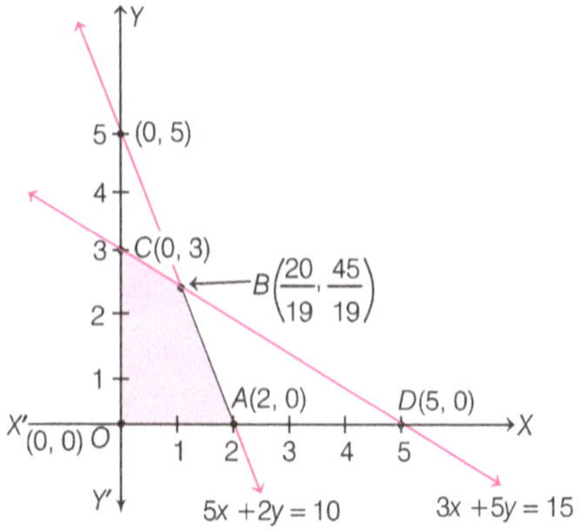

The intersection point of lines corresponding to Eqs. (i) and (ii) is $B\left(\frac{20}{19}, \frac{45}{19}\right)$.

Clearly, the feasible region is $OABCO$, where corner points are $O(0, 0)$, $A(2, 0)$, $B\left(\frac{20}{19}, \frac{45}{19}\right)$ and $C(0, 3)$.

The values of Z at corner points are given below.

Corner points	$Z=5x+3y$
$O(0,0)$	$Z=5\times 0+3\times 0=0$
$A(2,0)$	$Z=5\times 2+3\times 0=10$
$B\left(\frac{20}{19}, \frac{45}{19}\right)$	$Z=5\times\frac{20}{19}+3\times\frac{45}{19}=\frac{235}{19}$ $=12.36$ (Maximum)
$C(0,3)$	$Z=5\times 0+3\times 3=9$

Hence, the maximum value of Z is 12.36 at $B\left(\frac{20}{19}, \frac{45}{19}\right)$.

Example 5 **Find graphically the maximum value of $Z=2x+5y$, subject to constraints are $2x+4y\le 8$, $3x+y\le 6$, $x+y\le 4$ and $x\ge 0$, $y\ge 0$.** CBSE 2015

Sol. We have the following LPP.

Maximise $Z=2x+5y$

Subject to constraints,

$$2x+4y\le 8 \text{ or } x+2y\le 4 \quad \text{...(i)}$$
$$3x+y\le 6 \quad \text{...(ii)}$$
$$x+y\le 4 \quad \text{...(iii)}$$
and $$x\ge 0,\ y\ge 0 \quad \text{...(iv)}$$

Table for line $x+2y=4$ is

x	4	0
y	0	2

So, the line passes through the points (4, 0) and (0, 2).

On putting (0, 0) in the inequality $x+2y\le 4$, we get

$0+0\le 4$, which is true.

So, the half plane is towards the origin.

Table for line $3x+y=6$ is

x	2	0
y	0	6

So, the line passes through the points (2, 0) and (0, 6).

On putting (0, 0) in the inequality $3x+y\le 6$, we get

$0+0\le 6$, which is true.

So, the half plane is towards the origin.

Table for line $x+y=4$ is

x	4	0
y	0	4

So, the line passes through the points (4, 0) and (0, 4).

On putting (0, 0) in the inequality $x+y\le 4$, we get

$0+0\le 4$, which is true.

So, the half plane is towards the origin.

Also, $x\ge 0$ and $y\ge 0$, so the region lies in the I quadrant.

The intersection point of lines corresponding to Eqs. (i) and (ii) is $B\left(\frac{8}{5}, \frac{6}{5}\right)$.

The above inequations (i), (ii), (iii) and (iv) can be represented in the graph as shown below.

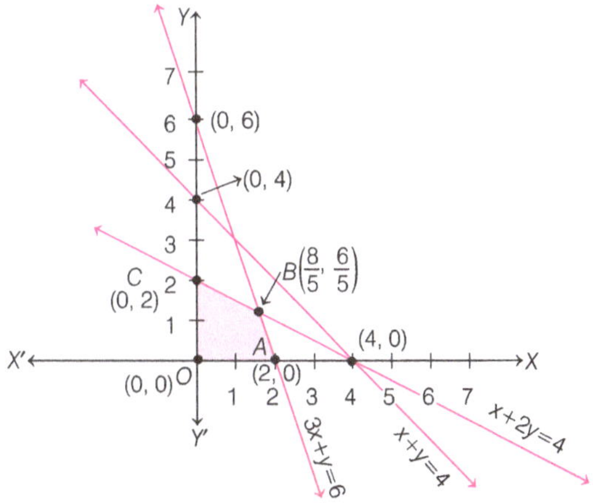

Clearly, the feasible region is $OABCO$, where corner points are $O(0, 0)$, $A(2, 0)$, $B\left(\frac{8}{5}, \frac{6}{5}\right)$ and $C(0, 2)$.

The values of Z at corner points are given below.

Corner points	$Z=2x+5y$
$O(0,0)$	$Z=2\times0+5\times0=0$
$A(2,0)$	$Z=2\times2+5\times0=4$
$B\left(\frac{8}{5},\frac{6}{5}\right)$	$Z=2\times\frac{8}{5}+5\times\frac{6}{5}=\frac{46}{5}=9.2$
$C(0,2)$	$Z=2\times0+5\times2=10$ (Maximum)

Hence, the maximum value of Z is 10 at $C(0, 2)$.

Example 6 **The corner points of the feasible region determined by the system of linear constraints are (0, 3), (1, 1) and (3, 0). Let $Z = px+qy$, where $p, q > 0$. Find the condition in p and q so that the minimum of Z occurs at (3, 0) and (1, 1).** *NCERT Exemplar*

Sol. Given, corner points of feasible region are (0,3), (1,1) and (3,0). The value of objective function at these corner points are given below.

Corner points	$Z=px+qy$
(0, 3)	$Z=p\times0+q\times3=3q$
(1, 1)	$Z=p\times1+q\times1=p+q$
(3, 0)	$Z=p\times3+q\times0=3p$

Also, given that the minimum of Z occurs at (3, 0) and (1, 1).

$\therefore \quad 3p = p+q \Rightarrow 2p = q$

Example 7 **Solve the following problem graphically. Minimise and maximise $Z = 3x+9y$, subject to constraints $x+3y \le 60$, $x+y \ge 10$, $x \le y$ and $x \ge 0$, $y \ge 0$.** *CBSE 2023, NCERT*

Sol. Given, objective function is maximise and minimise $Z = 3x+9y$.

Subject to constraints,

$x+3y \le 60$ ...(i)

$x+y \ge 10$ ...(ii)

$x \le y$ ...(iii)

and $x \ge 0, y \ge 0$ ...(iv)

Table for line $x+3y=60$ is

x	60	0
y	0	20

So, the line $x+3y=60$ is passing through (60, 0) and (0, 20).

On putting (0, 0) in the inequality $x+3y \le 60$, we get $0+0 \le 60$, which is true.

So, the half plane is towards the origin.

Table for line $x+y=10$ is

x	10	0
y	0	10

So, the line $x+y=10$ is passing through (10, 0) and (0, 10).

On putting (0, 0) in the inequality $x+y \ge 10$, we get $0+0 \ge 10$, which is not true.

So, the half plane is away from the origin.

Table for line $x = y$ is

x	0	5
y	0	5

So, the line $x = y$ is passing through (0, 0) and (5, 5).

On putting (0, 4) is the inequality $x \le y$, we get $0 \le 4$, which is true.

So, the half plane is towards the Y-axis.

Also, $x \ge 0$ and $y \ge 0$, so the region lies in the I quadrant.

On drawing these lines on graph paper, we get the following graph.

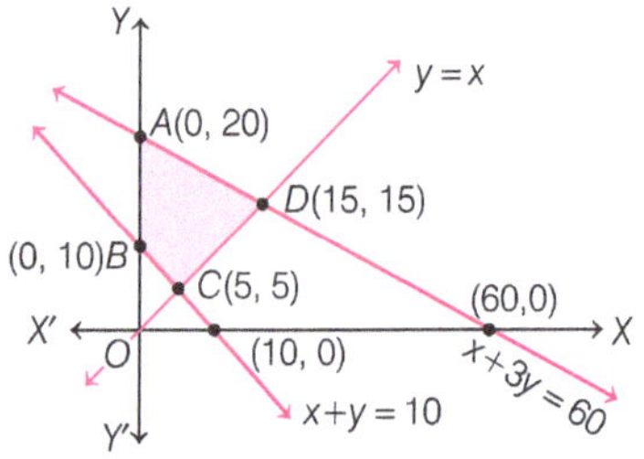

The intersection point of lines corresponding to Eqs. (i) and (iii) is D (15, 15) and corresponding to Eqs. (ii) and (iii) is C(5, 5).

Now, shading the common region, we get the feasible region $ABCDA$.

Hence, the region is bounded and corner points of feasible region are A(0, 20), B(0, 10), C(5, 5) and D(15, 15).

The values of Z at corner points are given below.

Corner points	$Z=3x+9y$
$A(0,20)$	$Z=3(0)+9(20)=180$ (Maximum)
$B(0,10)$	$Z=3(0)+9(10)=90$
$C(5,5)$	$Z=3(5)+9(5)=60$ (Minimum)
$D(15,15)$	$Z=3(15)+9(15)=180$ (Maximum)

Here, minimum value of Z is 60, which occurs at point C(5, 5) and maximum value of Z is 180, which occurs at two points A(0, 20) and D(15, 15). So, each point on the line segment AD will give the maximum value of Z.

Example 8 **Maximise and minimise $Z = x+2y$, subject to the constraints are $x+2y \ge 100$, $2x-y \le 0$, $2x+y \le 200$ and $x, y \ge 0$. Solve the above LPP graphically.** *CBSE 2023, 17, CBSE Sample Paper 2021*

Sol. Our problem is to minimise and maximise,

$Z = x+2y$ ...(i)

Subject to constraints, $x+2y \ge 100$ ...(ii)

$2x-y \le 0$ ...(iii)

$$2x + y \leq 200 \quad ...(iv)$$

and $$x \geq 0, y \geq 0 \quad ...(v)$$

Table for line $x + 2y = 100$ is

x	0	100
y	50	0

So, the line $x + 2y = 100$ is passing through the points (0, 50) and (100, 0).

On putting (0, 0) in the inequality $x + 2y \geq 100$, we get

$$0 + 2 \times 0 \geq 100$$

$\Rightarrow$ $0 \geq 100$, which is not true.

So, the half plane is away from the origin.

Table for line $2x - y = 0$ is

x	0	10
y	0	20

So, the line $2x - y = 0$ is passing through the points (0, 0) and (10, 20).

On putting (5, 0) in the inequality $2x - y \leq 0$, we get

$2 \times 5 - 0 \leq 0 \Rightarrow 10 \leq 0$, which is not true.

So, the half plane is towards Y-axis.

Table for line $2x + y = 200$ is

x	0	100
y	200	0

So, the line $2x + y = 200$ is passing through the points (0, 200) and (100, 0).

On putting (0, 0) in the inequality $2x + y \leq 200$, we get

$2 \times 0 + 0 \leq 200 \Rightarrow 0 \leq 200$, which is true.

So, the half plane is towards the origin.

Also, $x, y \geq 0$.

So, the region lies in the I quadrant.

On solving equations $2x - y = 0$ and $x + 2y = 100$, we get $B(20, 40)$.

Again, on solving the equations $2x - y = 0$ and $2x + y = 200$, we get $C(50, 100)$.

Clearly, the feasible region is $ABCDA$.

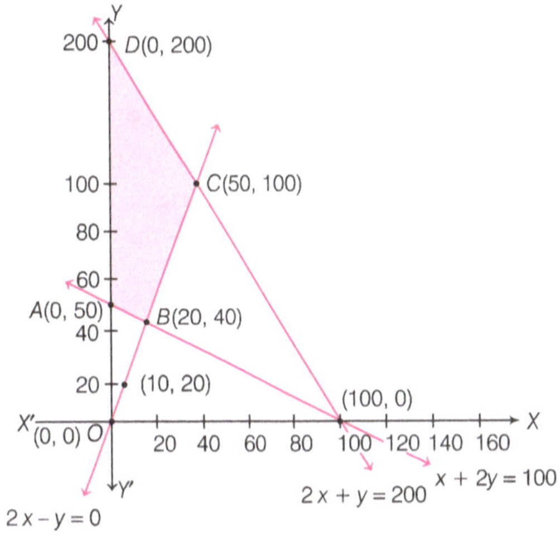

The corner points of the feasible region are $A(0, 50)$, $B(20, 40)$, $C(50, 100)$ and $D(0, 200)$.

The values of Z at corner points are given below.

Corner points	$Z = x + 2y$
$A(0, 50)$	$Z = 0 + 2 \times 50 = 100$ (Minimum)
$B(20, 40)$	$Z = 20 + 2 \times 40 = 100$ (Minimum)
$C(50, 100)$	$Z = 50 + 2 \times 100 = 250$
$D(0, 200)$	$Z = 0 + 2 \times 200 = 400$ (Maximum)

The maximum value of Z is 400 at $D(0, 200)$ and the minimum value of Z is 100 at the points on the line segment joining $A(0, 50)$ and $B(20, 40)$.

EXAM PATTERN QUESTIONS

Objective Type Questions

Multiple Choice Questions

1. The graph of the inequality $2x+3y>6$ is **CBSE 2020**

(a) half plane that contains the origin.

(b) half plane that neither contains the origin nor the points of the line $2x+3y=6$.

(c) whole XOY-plane excluding the points on the line $2x+3y=6$.

(d) entire XOY-plane.

2. **In LPP, if the objective function $Z=ax+by$ has the same maximum value on two corner points of the feasible region, then the number of points at which Z_{max} occurs is**

(a) 0 (b) 2 (c) finite (d) infinite

3. **The corner points of the feasible region determined by the system of linear constraints are (0, 10), (5, 5), (15, 15), (0, 20). Let $Z=px+qy$, where $p, q>0$. Then, the condition on p and q, so that the maximum of Z occurs at both the points (15, 15) and (0, 20) is** **NCERT Exemplar**

(a) $p=q$ (b) $p=2q$ (c) $q=2p$ (d) $q=3p$

4. **The corner points of the feasible region in the graphical representation of a linear programming problem are (2, 72), (15, 20) and (40,15). If $Z=18x+9y$ be the objective function, then** **CBSE 2023**

(a) Z is maximum at (2, 72) and minimum at (15, 20).

(b) Z is maximum at (15, 20) and minimum at (40, 15).

(c) Z is maximum at (40, 15) and minimum at (15, 20).

(d) Z is maximum at (40,15) and minimum at (2, 72).

5. **The number of corner points of the feasible region determined by the constraints $x-y\geq 0$, $2y\leq x+2$ and $x\geq 0$, $y\geq 0$ is** **CBSE 2023**

(a) 2 (b) 3 (c) 4 (d) 5

6. **The objective function $Z=ax+by$ of LPP, if its maximum value 42 at (4, 6) and minimum value 19 at (3,2). Which of the following is true?** **CBSE 2023**

(a) $a=9$ and $b=1$ (b) $a=5$ and $b=2$

(c) $a=3$ and $b=5$ (d) $a=5$ and $b=3$

7. **The corner points of the feasible region of linear programming problem are (0, 4), (8,0) and $\left(\frac{20}{4}, \frac{4}{3}\right)$.**

If $Z=30x+24y$ is the objective function, then (Maximum value of Z – Minimum value of Z) is equal to **CBSE 2023**

(a) 144 (b) 96 (c) 120 (d) 136

8. The feasible region of a linear programming problem is shown in the figure below. **CBSE 2023**

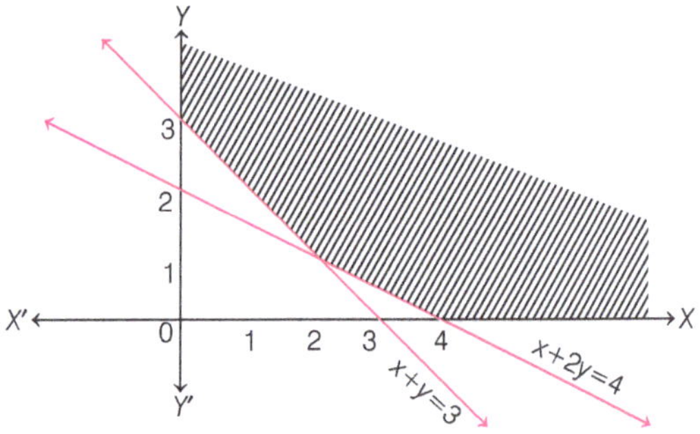

Which of the following are the possible constraints?

(a) $x+2y\geq 4$, $x+y\leq 3$ and $x\geq 0, y\geq 0$

(b) $x+2y\leq 4$, $x+y\leq 3$ and $x\geq 0, y\geq 0$

(c) $x+2y\geq 4$, $x+y\geq 3$ and $x\geq 0, y\geq 0$

(d) $x+2y\geq 4$, $x+y\geq 3$ and $x\leq 0, y\leq 0$

9. **The solution set of the inequality $3x+5y<4$ is** **CBSE Sample Paper 2023**

(a) an open half plane not containing the origin.

(b) an open half plane containing the origin.

(c) the whole XY-plane not containing the line $3x+5y=4$.

(d) a closed half plane containing the origin.

10. **The corner points of the shaded unbounded feasible region of an LPP are (0, 4), (0.6, 1.6) and (3, 0) as shown in the figure. The minimum value of the objective function $Z=4x+6y$ occurs at** **CBSE Sample Paper 2023**

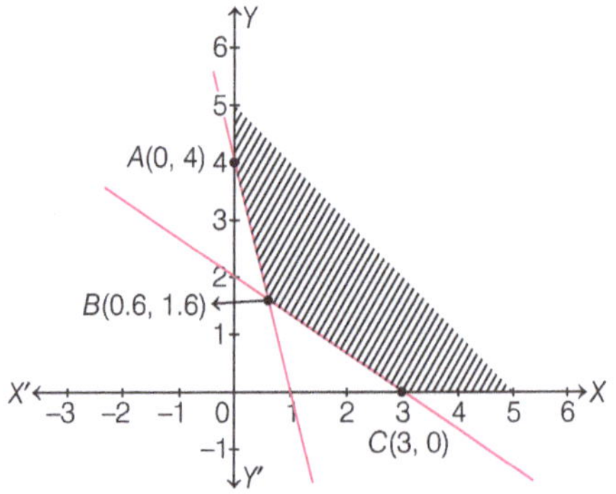

(a) (0.6, 1.6) only.

(b) (3, 0) only.

(c) (0.6, 1.6) and (3, 0) only.

(d) at every point of the line segment joining the points (0.6, 1.6) and (3, 0).

11. A linear programming problem is as follows

Minimise $Z = 30x + 50y$

Subject to the constraints,

$3x + 5y \geq 15,\ 2x + 3y \leq 18$ and $x \geq 0,\ y \geq 0.$

In the feasible region, the minimum value of Z occurs at **CBSE Sample Paper 2022 (Term II)**

(a) a unique point
(b) no point
(c) infinitely many points
(d) two points only

12. In a linear programming problem, the constraints on the decision variables x and y are $x - 3y \geq 0,\ y \geq 0,$ $0 \leq x \leq 3$. The feasible region **CBSE Sample Paper 2022 (Term II)**

(a) is not in the first quadrant.
(b) is bounded in the first quadrant.
(c) is unbounded in the first quadrant.
(d) Does not exist.

13. In the given graph, the feasible region for a LPP is shaded. The objective function $Z = 2x - 3y$ will be minimum at **CBSE Sample Paper 2022 (Term II)**

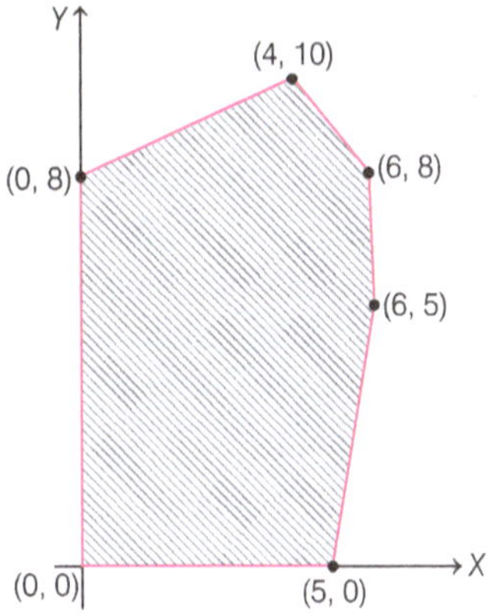

(a) (4, 10) (b) (6, 8) (c) (0, 8) (d) (6, 5)

14. The value of objective function is maximum under linear constraints **Diksha App**

(a) At the centre feasible region
(b) At (0, 0)
(c) At any vertex of feasible region
(d) The vertex which is maximum distance from (0, 0).

15. The point which does not lie in the half plane $2x + 3y - 12 \leq 0$ is **CBSE Sample Paper 2021**

(a) (1, 2) (b) (2, 1) (c) (2, 3) (d) (−3, 2)

Assertion-Reason Based Questions

Directions (Q.Nos. 16-25) *In the questions given below are two statements labelled as Assertion (A) and Reason (R). In the context of the two statements, which one of the following is correct?*

(a) Both A and R are correct; R is the correct explanation of A.
(b) Both A and R are correct; R is not the correct explanation of A.
(c) A is correct; R is incorrect.
(d) R is correct; A is incorrect.

16. Consider the graph of constraints stated as linear inequalities as below.

$$5x + y \leq 100 \quad \text{...(i)}$$
$$x + y \leq 60 \quad \text{...(ii)}$$
$$x \geq 0 \quad \text{...(iii)}$$
$$y \geq 0 \quad \text{...(iv)}$$

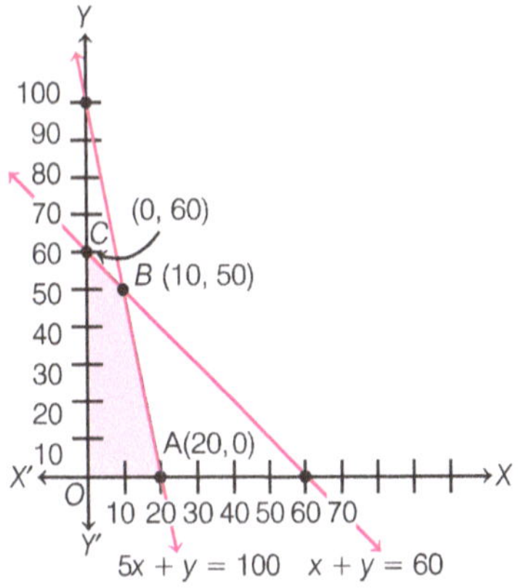

Assertion (A) The points (10, 50), (0, 60) or (20, 0) are feasible solutions.

Reason (R) Points within and on the boundary of the feasible region represent feasible solutions of the constraints.

17. Assertion (A) The objective function,

$$Z = -50x + 20y$$

Subject to the constraints,

$$2x - y \geq -5,$$
$$3x + y \geq 3,$$
$$2x - 3y \leq 12$$
and $$x \geq 0,\ y \geq 0.$$

In the feasible region has no minimum value.

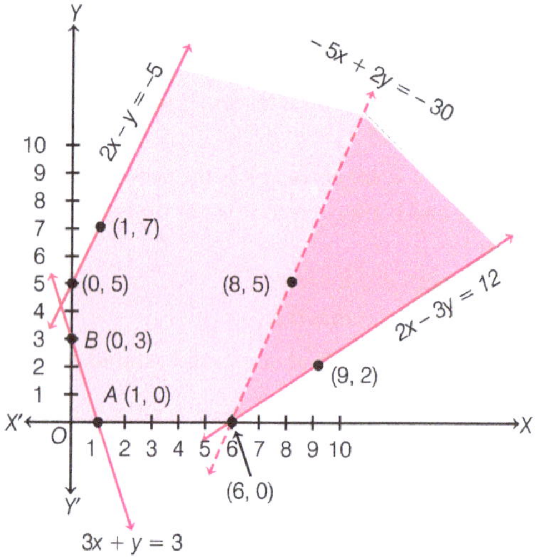

Reason (R) If the open half plane determined by $ax + by < m$, where m is the minimum value of Z, has a point in common with feasible region, then Z has no minimum value.

18. **Assertion** (A) The maximum value of $Z = 11x + 7y$

Subject to the constraints,

$$2x + y \leq 6,$$
$$x \leq 2$$
and $$x \geq 0, y \geq 0.$$

In the feasible region occurs at the corner point (0, 6).

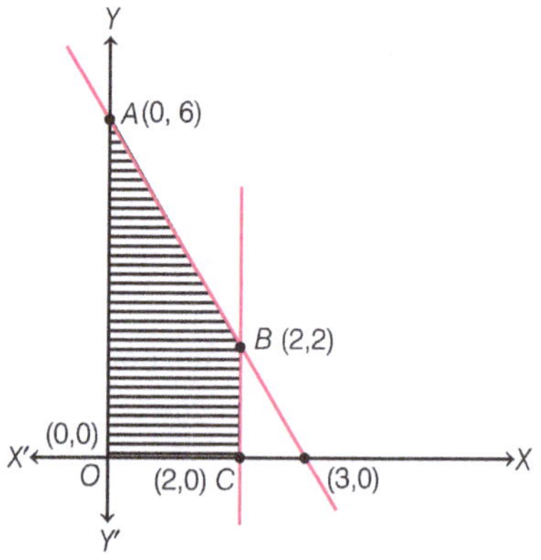

Reason (R) If the feasible region of the given LPP is bounded, then the maximum and minimum value of the objective function occurs at corner points.

19. **Assertion** (A) If LPP attains its maximum value at two corner points of the feasible region, then it attains maximum value at infinitely many points.

Reason (R) If the value of the objective function of a LPP is same at two corners, then it is same at every point on the line joining two corner points.

20. Let the feasible region of a LPP with objective function $Z = ax + by$. M and m are maximum and minimum value of Z.

Assertion (A) M is the maximum value of Z, if the open half plane determined by $ax + by > M$ has no point in common in the feasible region. Otherwise Z has no maximum value.

Reason (R) m is the minimum value of Z, if the open half plane determined by $ax + by < m$ has no point in common in the feasible region. Otherwise Z has no minimum value.

21. **Assertion** (A) Every point of the feasible region of a LPP is an optimal solution.

Reason (R) The optimal solution for a LPP exists only at one or more corner point(s) of the feasible region.

CBSE 2025

22. **Assertion** (A) If a LPP admits two optional solutions, then it has infinitely many optimal solutions.

Reason (R) If the value of the objective function of a LPP is same at two corners, then it is same at every point on the line segment joining the two corner points.

23. **Assertion** (A) The maximum value of $Z = 3x + 4y$, subject to the constraints $x \geq 0, y \geq 0$ and $x + y \leq 1$, is 4.

Reason (R) A feasible region may be bounded or unbounded.

24. **Assertion** (A) If the corner points of the feasible region of LPP are $A(0, 3), B(3, 2)$ and $C(0, 5)$, then the minimum value of $Z = 11x + 7y$ is 21.

Reason (R) A feasible region is always bounded.

25. **Assertion** (A) The corner points of the feasible region determined by the set of constraints are $A(0, 5), B(3, 5), C(5, 0)$ and $D(4, 1)$ and the objective function $Z = ax + 2by$, where $a, b > 0$. The condition on a and b such that the maximum Z occurs at B and D is $a - 8b = 0$.

Reason (R) A feasible region is always unbounded.

Case Study Based Questions

26. In the figure given below, O is the origin and shaded area is the feasible region.

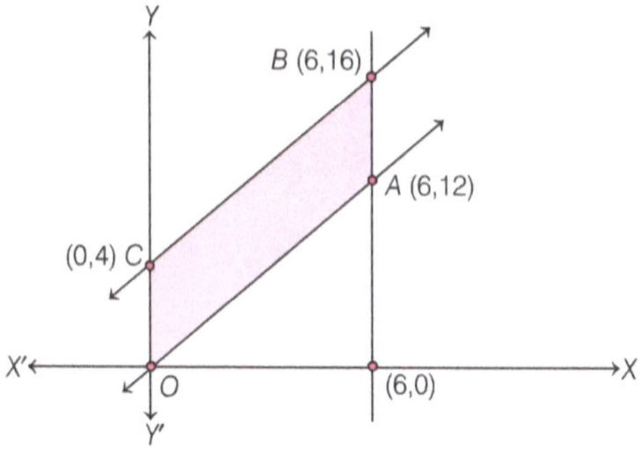

Based on the given figure, answer the following questions.

(i) Write the equation of OA and BC.

(ii) Write all the inequalities.

(iii) If $Z = 5x + 3y$, then find the maximum value of Z.

(iv) If $Z = 5x - 2y$, then find the minimum value of Z.

27. A dietician wishes to mix together two kinds of food X and Y in such a way that the mixture contains atleast 10 units of vitamin A, 12 units of vitamin B and 8 units of vitamin C. The vitamin contents of one kg food is given below.

Food	Vitamin A	Vitamin B	Vitamin C
X	1	2	3
Y	2	2	1

One kg of food X costs ₹ 16 and one kg of food Y costs ₹ 20.

Based on the above information, answer the following questions.

(i) Write all the constraints of above LPP problem.

(ii) Draw the feasible region.

(iii) Find the objective function of LPP.

(iv) Find all the corner points of the feasible region.

(v) Find the least value of Z.

28. Star Auto Private Limited (SAPL), an automobile company, manufactures and supplies precision machine components. Among other products, two products manufactured by SAPL are Roller Bush and Hydraulic Valve shown below. These products are manufactured and packed in boxes of 25.

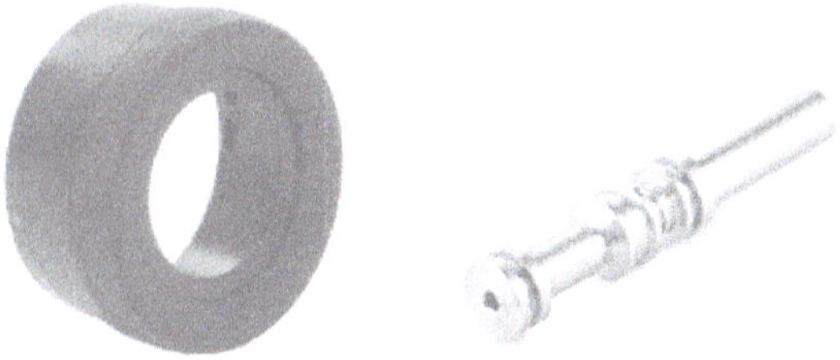

ROLLER BUSH HYDRAULIC VALVE

Each box of Roller Bush required 2 kg of aluminium and 1 kg of steel. Each box of Hydraulic Valve requires 14 kg of aluminium and 2 kg of steel. SAPL has an available supply of 70 kg of aluminium and 20 kg of steel per day to manufacture these two products.

The plant makes a profit of ₹ 20 on each box of Roller Bush and ₹ 50 on each box of Hydraulic Valve. **CBSE QB**

Based on the above information, answer the following questions.

(i) Write the mathematical formulation of the given scenario that given the number of units of Roller Bush and Hydraulic Valve that SAPL must manufacture in order to maximise its profit.

(ii) Determine the feasible region of the linear programming problem defined by the above scenario graphically.

(iii) Determine the number of units of Roller Bush and Hydraulic Valve that SAPL must manufacture in order to maximise its profit. Show your work.

Subjective Questions

Short Answer Type Questions

1. For a LPP, find min $Z = 5x + 3y$ (where Z is the objective function) for the feasible region shaded in the given figure. **CBSE 2025**

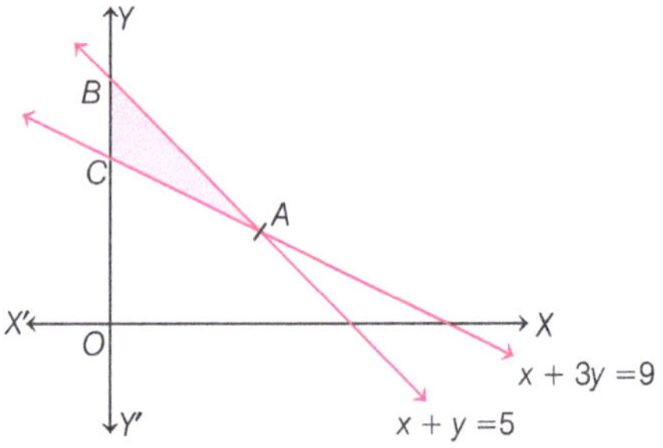

(**Note** The figure is not to scale)

Direction (Q. Nos. 2-6) *Maximise the following linear programming problems graphically.*

2. $Z = 2x + 3y$

Subject to the constraints are

$x + 2y \le 10, 2x + y \le 14$ and $x \ge 0, \ y \ge 0.$

3. $Z = 8000x + 12000y$

Subject to the constraints are

$3x + 4y \le 60, x + 3y \le 30$ and $x \ge 0, y \ge 0.$ **CBSE 2017C**

4. $Z = x + y$

Subject to the constraints are

$x - y \le -1, -x + y \le 0$ and $x, y \ge 0.$

5. $Z = -x + 2y$

Subject to the constraints are

$x \ge 3, x + y \ge 5, x + 2y \ge 6$ and $x, y \ge 0.$ **NCERT**

6. $Z = 105x + 90y$

Subject to the constraints are

$x + y \le 50, 2x + y \le 80, \ x \ge 20$ and $x \ge 0, y \ge 0.$

CBSE 2017C

Direction (Q. Nos. 7-8) *Minimise the following linear programming problems graphically.*

7. $Z = 2x + 3y$

Subject to the constraints are

$2x + 5y \ge 100, 8x + 5y \le 200$ and $x, y \ge 0.$

8. $Z = x + y$

Subject to the constraints are

$3x + 2y \ge 12, x + 3y \ge 11$ and $x \ge 0, y \ge 0.$

9. Solve the following LPP graphically.

Maximise $Z = 3x + 2y$

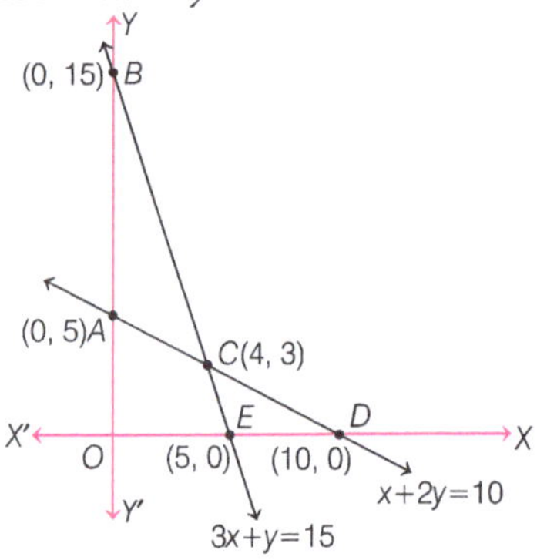

Subject to constraints are $x + 2y \le 10, 3x + y \le 15$ and $x \ge 0, y \ge 0.$

Also, determine the area of the feasible region.

10. A linear programming problem (LPP) along with the graph of its constraints is shown below.

The shaded portion represents the feasible region.

Maximise $Z = 10x + 20y$

Subject to constraints,

$2x + 3y \ge 6, 4x + y \ge 4$ and $x \ge 0, y \ge 0$

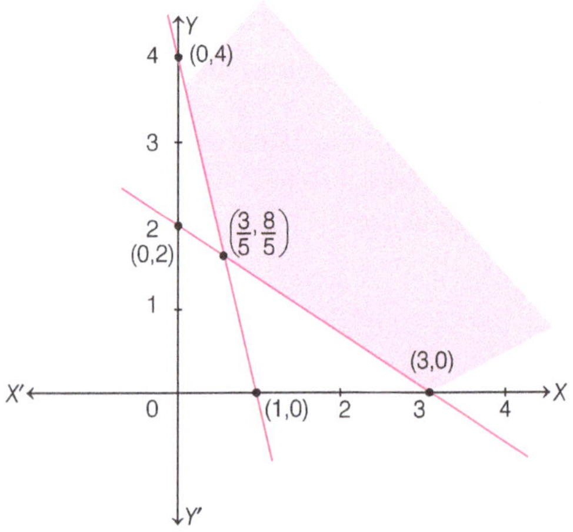

What can you conclude about the existence of optimal solution for the above LPP? Justify your answer. **CBSE QB**

11. Feasible region (shaded) for LPP is shown in the following figure, Maximise $Z = 5x + 7y$. **NCERT Exemplar**

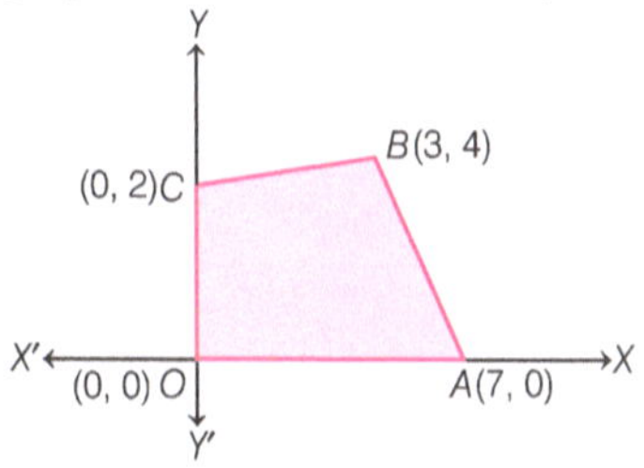

12. Solve the following linear programming problem graphically. **CBSE 2023**

Minimise $Z = -3x + 4y$

Subject to constraints,

$$x + 2y \leq 8, 3x + 2y \leq 12 \text{ and } x, y \geq 0.$$

13. Solve the following linear programming problem graphically. **CBSE 2023**

Maximise $Z = -3x - 5y$

Subject to the constraints

$$-2x + y \leq 4, \; x + y \geq 3,$$
$$x - 2y \leq 2 \text{ and } x \geq 0, y \geq 0.$$

14. Solve the following linear programming problem graphically. **CBSE 2023, 17C**

Maximise $Z = 6x + 3y$

Subject to the constraints,

$$4x + y \geq 80, 3x + 2y \leq 150,$$
$$x + 5y \geq 115 \text{ and } x \geq 0, y \geq 0.$$

Long Answer Type Questions

15. Solve the following LPP graphically.

Maximise $Z = 60x + 40y$

Subject to the constraints,

$$x + 2y \leq 12, 2x + y \leq 12,$$
$$4x + 5y \geq 20 \text{ and } x, y \geq 0.$$ **CBSE 2024**

16. Solve the following linear programming problem graphically.

Maximise $Z = 300x + 600y$

Subject to the constraints,

$$x + 2y \leq 12,$$
$$2x + y \leq 12,$$
$$x + \frac{5}{4}y \geq 5 \text{ and } x \geq 0, y \geq 0.$$ **CBSE 2024**

17. Solve the following linear programming problem graphically. **CBSE 2023**

Maximise $Z = 70x + 40y$

Subject to constraints,

$$3x + 2y \leq 9,$$
$$3x + y \leq 9$$
and $\quad x \geq 0, y \geq 0.$

18. The corner points of the feasible region determined by the system of linear constraints are as shown below

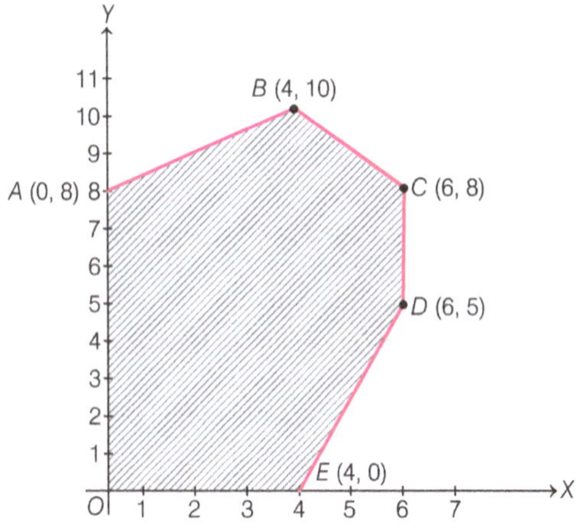

CBSE Sample Paper 2021

Answer each of the following.

(i) Let $Z = 3x - 4y$ be the objective function. Find the maximum and minimum value of Z and also the corresponding points at which the maximum and minimum value occurs.

(ii) Let $Z = px + qy$, where $p, q > 0$ be the objective function. Find the condition on p and q so that the maximum value of Z occurs at $B(4, 10)$ and $C(6, 8)$. Also, mention the number of optimal solutions in this case.

19. Solve the following linear programming problem graphically.

Minimise $Z = 6x + 7y$

Subject to constraints,

$$x + 2y \geq 240,$$
$$3x + 4y \leq 620,$$
$$2x + y \geq 180$$
and $\quad x, y \geq 0$

Hints & Solutions

Objective Type Questions

1. (b) The inequality $2x + 3y > 6$ represents half plane that neither contains the origin nor the points of the line $2x + 3y = 6$

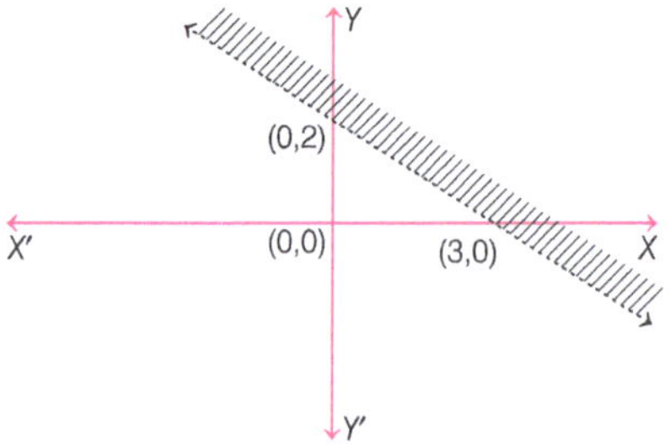

2. (d) An objective function has the same maximum value at two corner points. Therefore, the maximum value occurs on the line joining two points.

3. (d) Let the given corner points of feasible region are $A(0,10)$, $B(5,5)$, $C(15,15)$ and $D(0,20)$. The values of objective function at these corner points are given below.

Corner points	$Z = px + qy$
$A(0,10)$	$Z = p\times 0 + q\times 10 = 10q$
$B(5,5)$	$Z = p\times 5 + q\times 5 = 5p + 5q$
$C(15,15)$	$Z = p\times 15 + q\times 15 = 15p + 15q$
$D(0,20)$	$Z = p\times 0 + q\times 20 = 20q$

Also, given that the maximum of Z occurs at $C(15,15)$ and $D(0,20)$.

$\therefore\ 15p + 15q = 20q$

$\Rightarrow\quad 5q = 15p$

$\Rightarrow\quad q = 3p$

4. (c) Given, $Z = 18x + 9y$

At (2, 72), $Z = 18\times 2 + 9\times 72 = 684$

At (15, 20), $Z = 18\times 15 + 9\times 20 = 450$

At (40, 15), $Z = 18\times 40 + 9\times 15 = 855$

Thus, Z is maximum at (40, 15) and minimum at (15, 20).

5. (a) Given, subject to constraints

$$x - y \ge 0,\ 2y \le x + 2 \text{ and } x \ge 0,\ y \ge 0$$

Now, considering the inequations as equations, we get

$$x - y = 0 \quad \ldots\text{(i)}$$

and $$2y = x + 2$$

$$2y - x = 2 \quad \ldots\text{(ii)}$$

Table for line $x - y = 0$ is

x	0	2
y	0	2

Table for line $2y - x = 2$ is

x	0	2
y	1	2

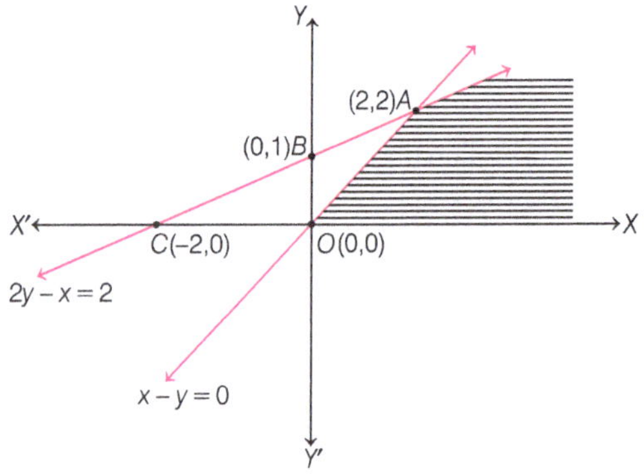

$\therefore$ The corner points are $O(0, 0)$ and $A(2, 2)$.

6. (c) Given, $Z = ax + by$

At (4, 6), $Z = ax + by$

$\Rightarrow\quad 42 = a\times 4 + b\times 6$

$\Rightarrow\quad 42 = 4a + 6b$

$\Rightarrow\quad 21 = 2a + 3b \quad \ldots\text{(i)}$

At (3, 2), $19 = 3a + 2b \quad \ldots\text{(ii)}$

On multiplying Eq. (i) by 2 and Eq. (ii) by 3 and on solving, we get

$$4a + 6b = 42$$
$$9a + 6b = 57$$
$$-\quad -\quad -$$
$$-5a = -15$$
$$a = 3$$

On substituting $a = 3$, in Eq. (i), we get

$$2\times 3 + 3b = 21$$

$\Rightarrow\quad b = 5$

7. (a) $Z = 30x + 24y$ [given]

At (0, 4), $Z = 30\times 0 + 24\times 4 = 96$ (minimum)

At (8, 0), $Z = 30\times 8 + 24\times 0 = 240$ (maximum)

At $\left(\frac{20}{3}, \frac{4}{3}\right)$, $Z = 30\times\frac{20}{3} + 24\times\frac{4}{3} = 232$

Now, (Maximum value of Z – Minimum value of Z)

$$= 240 - 96 = 144$$

8. (c) If we put $O(0, 0)$ in $x + 2y \ge 4$ inequality, then it will be false and it will be away from origin.

So, $x + 2y \ge 4$ is possible.

Similarly, the inequality $x + y \ge 3$ will also be away from origin, which means it is false when $O(0, 0)$ is put in the inequality.

So, $x+y\geq 3$ is possible.

$\therefore$ It is clear that feasible region lies in Ist quadrant, so $x\geq 0, y\geq 0$.

9. (b) Given inequality, $3x+5y<4$ ...(i)

On putting (0, 0) in inequality (i), we get

$$3(0)+5(0)<4$$

$\Rightarrow$ $0<4$ (which is true)

Hence, the given strict inequality represents an open half plane and it contains the origin as (0, 0) satisfies it.

10. (d)

Corner points	$Z=4x+6y$
$A(0, 4)$	24
$B(0.6, 1.6)$	12 (Minimum)
$C(3, 0)$	12 (Minimum)

The minimum value of the objective function occurs at two adjacent corner points (0.6, 1.6) and (3, 0).

Now, on plotting $4x+6y<12$, we found there is no point in the half plane $4x+6y<12$ in common with the feasible region.

So, the minimum value occurs at every point on the line segment joining the points (0.6, 1.6) and (3, 0).

11. (c) Minimise $Z=30x+50y$
Subject to constraints,

$$3x+5y\geq 15,$$
$$2x+3y\leq 18$$

and $x\geq 0, y\geq 0$

Graph of inequalities are

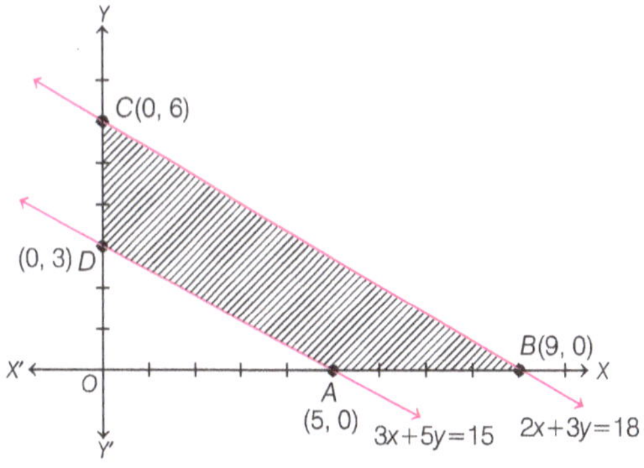

Corner points	$Z=30x+50y$
A (5, 0)	$Z=30(5)+0=150$ (Minimum)
B (9, 0)	$Z=30(9)+0=270$
C (0, 6)	$Z=0+50\times 6=300$
D (0, 3)	$Z=0+50\times 3=150$ (Minimum)

The minimum value of Z lies on line segment AD.

$\therefore$ Minimum value of Z occurs at infinitely many points.

12. (b) Given, $x-3y\geq 0, y\geq 0$ and $0\leq x\leq 3$

The graph of inequalities is shown below.

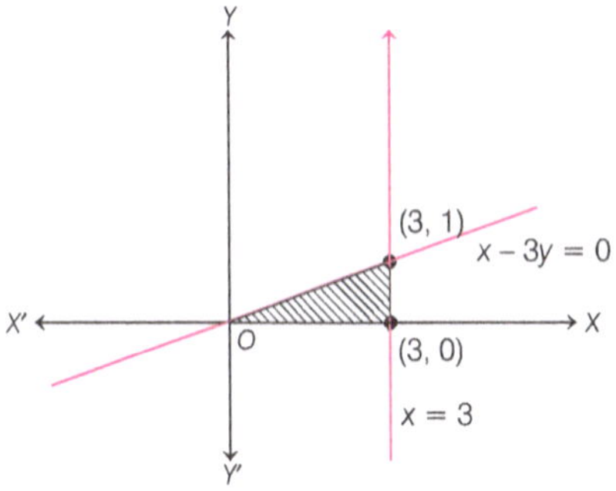

Clearly, the feasible region is bounded in the I quadrant.

13. (c) Construct the following table of values of the objective function.

Corner points	$Z=2x-3y$
(0, 0)	$2\times 0-3\times 0=0$
(5, 0)	$2\times 5-3\times 0=10$ (Maximum)
(6, 5)	$2\times 6-3\times 5=-3$
(6, 8)	$2\times 6-3\times 8=-12$
(4, 10)	$2\times 4-3\times 10=-22$
(0, 8)	$2\times 0-3\times 8=-24$ (Minimum)

$\therefore$ Minimum value of Z is -24 at (0, 8).

14. (c) The value of objective function is maximum under linear constraints at any vertex of feasible region.

15. (c) On putting (2, 3) in the half plane $2x+3y-12\leq 0$, we get

$$2\times 2+3\times 3-12\leq 0$$

$\Rightarrow$ $1\leq 0$ (which is false)

So, (2, 3) does not lie in the half plane.

16. (a) **Feasible solutions** Points within and on the boundary of the feasible region represent feasible solutions of the constraints. In the given figure, every point within and on the boundary of the feasible region $OABC$ represents feasible solution to the problem. For example, the point (10, 50) is a feasible solution of the problem and the points (0, 60), (20, 0) etc.

17. (a)

Corner points	$Z=-50x+20y$
(0, 5)	100
(0, 3)	60
(1, 0)	-50
(6, 0)	-300 (Minimum)

From this table, we find that -300 is the minimum value of Z at the corner point (6, 0). Can we say that minimum value of Z is -300?

As the feasible region is unbounded.

Therefore, –300 may or may not be the minimum value of Z. So, we consider the inequality

$$-50x+20y<-300$$

i.e. $$-5x+2y<-30$$

As shown in the figure, it has common points with feasible region.

Therefore, $Z=-50x+20y$ has no minimum value subject to the given constraints.

18. (a) The given LPP is maximise $Z=11x+7y$

Subject to the constraints are

$$2x+y\le 6,$$
$$x\le 2$$

and $$x\ge 0, y\ge 0$$

In graph, we see that the shaded region is the feasible region $OABC$ which is bounded.

The corner points are O (0, 0), A (0, 6), B (2, 2), C (2, 0).

The values of Z at these corner points are given by

Corner points	$Z=11x+7y$
(0, 0)	0
(0, 6)	42 (Maximum)
(2, 2)	36
(2, 0)	22

Thus, the maximum value of Z is 42 which occurs at the point (0, 6).

19. (a) If maximum value of Z occurs at two points, then Z will be maximum at all points between those points means infinity many points.

∴ Assertion is correct.

The values of Z will be same at every point between those points. So, Reason is also correct and Reason is the correct explanation of Assertion.

20. (b) We have, $Z=ax+by$

$m=$ Minimum value of Z

$M=$ Maximum value of Z

Yes, it is true that if $ax+by>M$ has a common point with feasible region, then M is not maximum value of Z and if $ax+by<m$ has a common point with feasible region, then m is not minimum value of Z.

Assertion and Reason both are correct but Reason is not the correct explanation of Assertion.

21. (d) We know that any point in the feasible region that gives the optimal value (maximum or minimum) of the objective function is called an optimal solution.

Therefore, all the points in the feasible region of a linear programming problem cannot be optimal solution to the problem.

∴ Assertion is incorrect.

Clearly, Reason is true.

22. (a) In LPP, if there is more than one optimal solution, then there are infinitely many optimal solutions.

Hence, Assertion and Reason both are correct and Reason is the correct explanation of Assertion.

23. (b) We have, $Z=3x+4y$

Subject to constraints, $x+y\le 1$ and $x\ge 0, y\ge 0$.

The graph of inequalities is shown below.

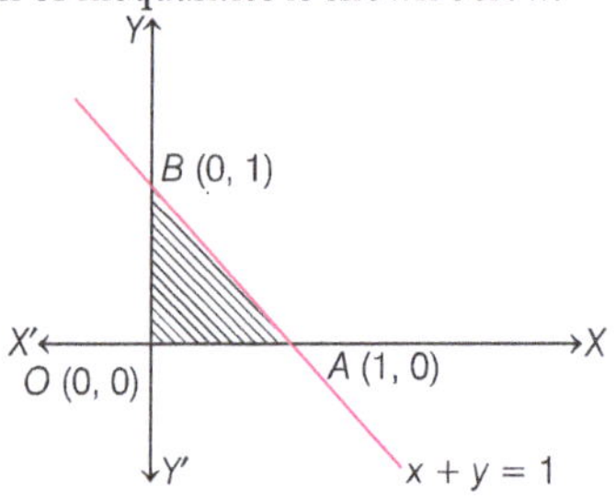

From graph, we get

Corner points	$Z=3x+4y$
$O(0,0)$	0
$A(1,0)$	3
$B(0,1)$	4 (Maximum)

Here, maximum value of Z is 4.

Hence, Assertion and Reason both are correct and Reason is not the correct explanation of Assertion.

24. (c) Given corner points are $A(0,3), B(3,2)$ and $C(0,5)$.

At $A(0,3)$, $Z=11\times 0+7\times 3=21$ (Minimum)

At $B(3,2)$, $Z=11\times 3+7\times 2=47$

At $C(0,5)$, $Z=11\times 0+7\times 5=35$

∴ $Z_{min}=21$

Thus, Assertion is correct.

Reason is incorrect as a feasible region may be bounded or unbounded.

25. (c) Given, $Z=ax+2by$ has maximum value at $B(3,5)$ and $D(4,1)$.

∴ $Z(3,5)=Z(4,1)$

⇒ $3a+10b=4a+2b$

⇒ $a=8b\Rightarrow a-8b=0$

Thus, Assertion is correct.

But Reason is incorrect because feasible reason may be bounded or unbounded.

26. (i) Equation of OA, $y=2x$

Points are $B=(6,16)$ and $C=(0,4)$

For equation of BC, $y-2x=4$

(ii) Area of BC is towards the origin.

So, constraint $BC\Rightarrow y-2x\le 4$

Area of OA is towards, Y-axis.

So, constraints $OA\Rightarrow y\ge 2x$

Area of AB is towards the origin.

So constraints AB, $x\le 6$ and $x\ge 0, y\ge 0$.

(iii) We have four corner points, $O(0,0), A(6,12), B(6,16)$ and $C(0,4)$.

Corner Points	$Z=5x+3y$
(0, 0)	0
(6, 12)	66
(6, 16)	78
(0, 4)	12 (Maximum)

(iv) We have four corner points $O(0,0), A(6,12), B(6,16)$ and $C(0,4)$.

Corner Points	$Z=5x-2y$
(0, 0)	0
(6, 12)	6
(6, 16)	−2
(0, 4)	−8 (Minimum)

27.

Food	Vitamin A	Vitamin B	Vitamin C
x	x	$2x$	$3x$
y	$2y$	$2y$	y

(i) Total Vitamin A, $x+2y$

It is given that Vitamin A must be atleast 10 units

$\Rightarrow \quad x+2y \geq 10 \quad$ ...(i)

Total Vitamin B, $2x+2y$

It is given that Vitamin B must be atleast 12 units

$\Rightarrow \quad 2x+2y \geq 12 \quad$ ...(ii)

Total Vitamin C, $3x+y$

It is given that Vitamin C must be atleast 8 units

$\Rightarrow \quad 3x+y \geq 8 \quad$ ...(iii)

(ii) We have, $x+2y \geq 10$

$\Rightarrow \quad \frac{x}{10}+\frac{y}{5} \geq 1 \quad$ [divide both sides by 10] ...(i)

$2x+2y \geq 12$

$\Rightarrow \quad \frac{x}{6}+\frac{y}{6} \geq 1 \quad$ [divide both sides by 12] ...(ii)

$3x+y \geq 8 \quad$ [divide both sides by 8]

$\Rightarrow \quad \frac{x}{8/3}+\frac{y}{8} \geq 1 \quad$ ...(iii)

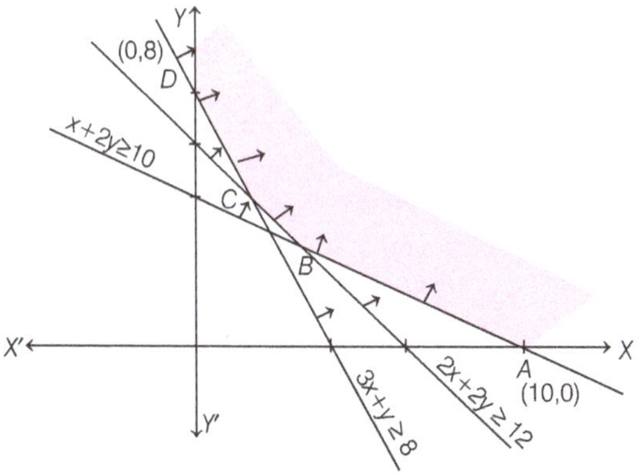

(iii) Cost of food $x=16$ kg

$y=20$ kg

$\therefore$ Objective function of LPP is

$$Z=16x+20y$$

(iv) We have four corner points

On solving $x+2y=10$ and $2x+2y=12$, we get point B (2, 4)

On solving $2x+2y=12$ and $3x+y=8$, we get point $C(1, 5)$

Four corner points are

$$A=(10,0)$$
$$B=(2,4)$$
$$C=(1,5)$$
$$D=(0,8)$$

(v) $Z_{(10,\,0)}=160+0=160$

$Z_{(2,\,4)}=32+80=112$

$Z_{(1,\,5)}=16+100=116$

$Z_{(0,\,8)}=0+160=160$

Hence, minimum value of Z is 112 occurs at point B (2, 4).

28. (i) Let x be the number of units of Roller Bush to be manufactured and y be the number of units of Hydraulic Valve to be manufactured.

$\therefore$ The objective function to maximise profit

$$Z=20x+50y$$

Subject to the following constraints.

1. Aluminium constraint

$$2x+14y \leq 70$$

2. Steel constraint

$$x+2y \leq 20$$

3. Non-negative constraints

$$x, y \geq 0$$

$\therefore$ Complete Linear programming

Maximise $Z=20x+50y$

Subject to the constraints,

$$2x+14y \leq 70,\ x+2y \leq 20$$

and $\quad x \geq 0, y \geq 0$

(ii) Here, aluminium constraint

$2x+14y=70 \quad$ ...(i)

and steel constraint $x+2y=20 \quad$ ...(ii)

From Eq. (i), we get

x	0	35
y	5	0

From Eq. (ii), we get

x	0	20
y	10	0

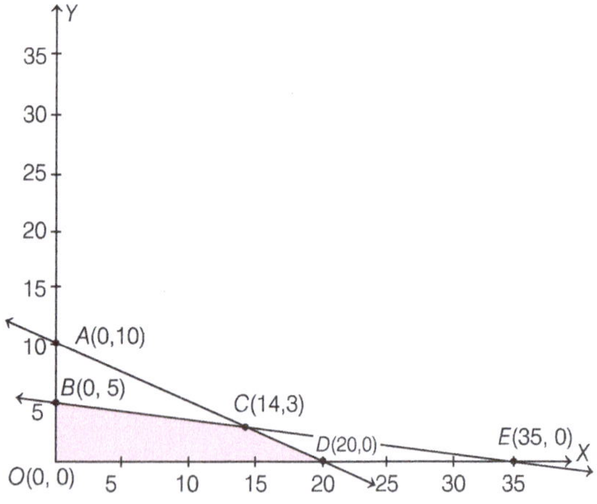

(iii) From the graph, the corner points of feasible region are

Corner points	$Z = 20x + 50y$
$O(0,0)$	$Z = 0$
$B(0,5)$	$Z = 250$
$C(14,3)$	$Z = 430$ (Maximum)
$D(20,0)$	$Z = 400$

Hence, the number of units of Roller Bush and Hydraulic Valve that SAPL must manufacture to maximise its profit are 14 and 3, respectively.

Subjective Questions

1. **Hint** The corner points of the feasible region are $A(3,2), B(0,5)$ and $C(0,3)$.

   The values of objective function at corner points are given below.

Corner points	$Z = 5x + 3y$
$A(3,2)$	$Z = 5\times3+3\times2 = 21$
$B(0,5)$	$Z = 5\times0+3\times5 = 15$
$C(0,3)$	$Z = 5\times0+3\times3 = 9$ (Minimum)

Ans. 9

2. **Hint**

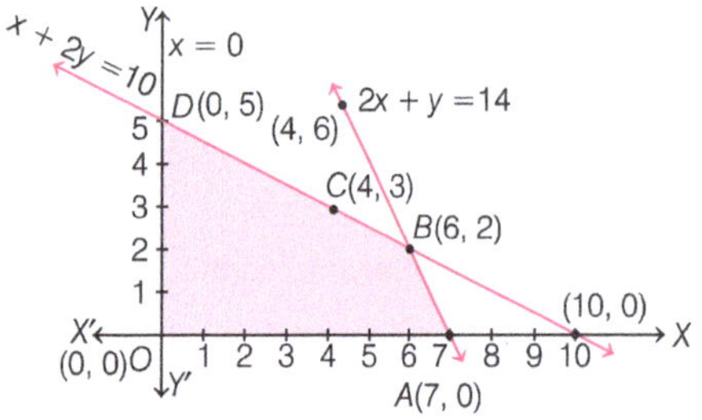

The values of Z at corner points are given below.

Corner points	$Z = 2x + 3y$
$O(0, 0)$	$Z = 2\times0+3\times0 = 0$
$A(7, 0)$	$Z = 2\times7+3\times0 = 14$
$B(6, 2)$	$Z = 2\times6+3\times2 = 18$
$D(0, 5)$	$Z = 2\times0+3\times5 = 15$

Ans. The maximum value of Z is 18 at the point $B(6, 2)$.

3. **Hint**

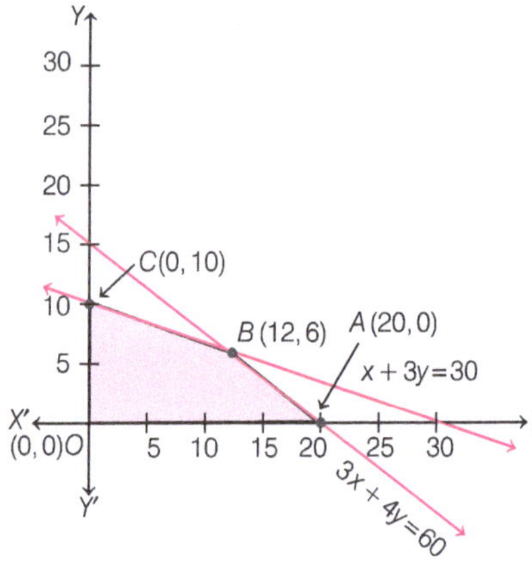

Corner points	$Z = 8000x + 12000y$
$O(0, 0)$	0
$A(20, 0)$	160000
$B(12, 6)$	168000 (Maximum)
$C(0,10)$	120000

Ans. Maximum $Z = 168000$, when $x = 12, y = 6$.

4. **Hint**

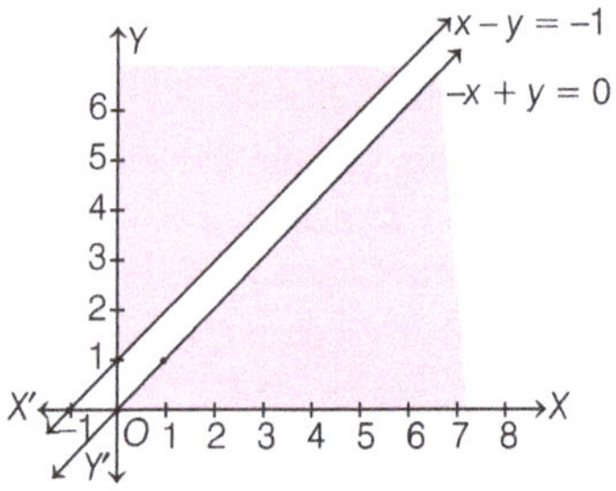

Ans. Hence, there is no feasible region, thus Z has no maximum value.

5. **Hint**

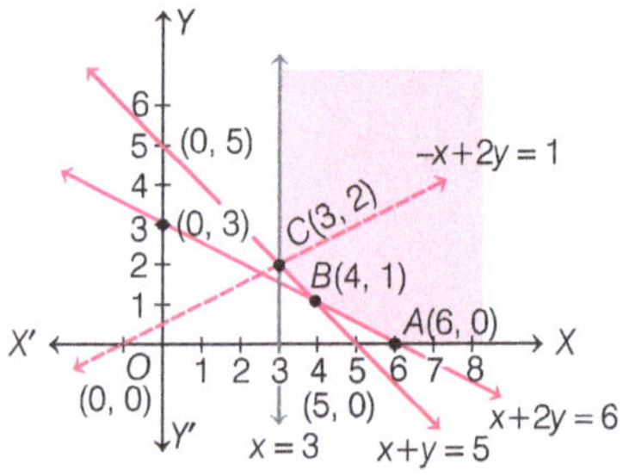

Corner points	$Z = -x + 2y$
$A(6, 0)$	$Z = -6+2\times0 = -6$
$B(4,1)$	$Z = -4+2\times1 = -2$
$C(3,2)$	$Z = -3+2\times2 = 1$ (Maximum)

As the feasible region is unbounded, therefore $Z = 1$ may or may not be the maximum value.

For this, we draw the graph of the inequality $-x+2y>1$ and check whether the resulting half plane has points in common with the feasible region or not.

The feasible region has points in common with the $-x+2y>1$. Therefore, $Z=1$ is not the maximum value.

Hence, Z has no maximum value.

6. Hint

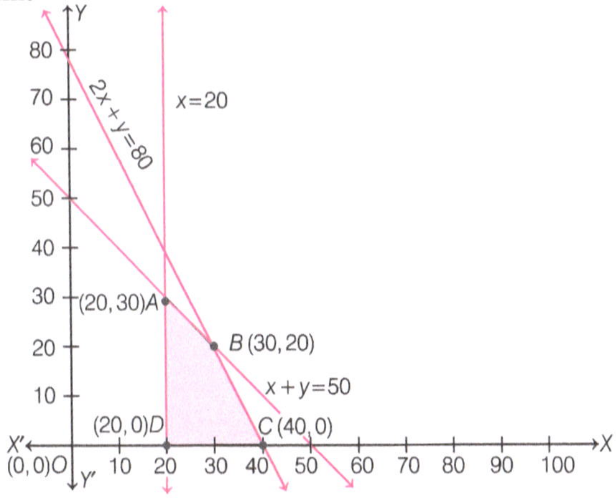

Corner points	$Z=105x+90y$
$A(20,30)$	4800
$B(30,20)$	4950 (Max.)
$C(40,0)$	4200
$D(20,0)$	2100

Ans. Maximum value of Z is 4950, when $x=30$ and $y=20$.

7. Hint

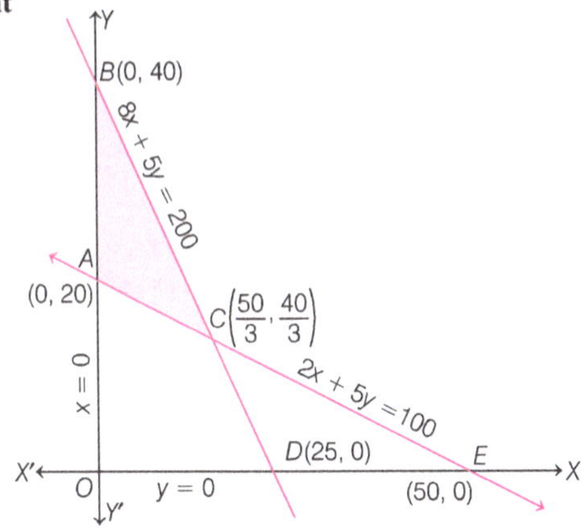

Corner points	$Z=2x+3y$
$A(0,20)$	$Z=2\times0+3\times20=60$ (Minimum)
$B(0,40)$	$Z=2\times0+3\times40=120$
$C\left(\frac{50}{3},\frac{40}{3}\right)$	$Z=2\times\frac{50}{3}+3\times\frac{40}{3}=73.33$

The minimum value of Z is 60 at the point $A(0,20)$.

8.

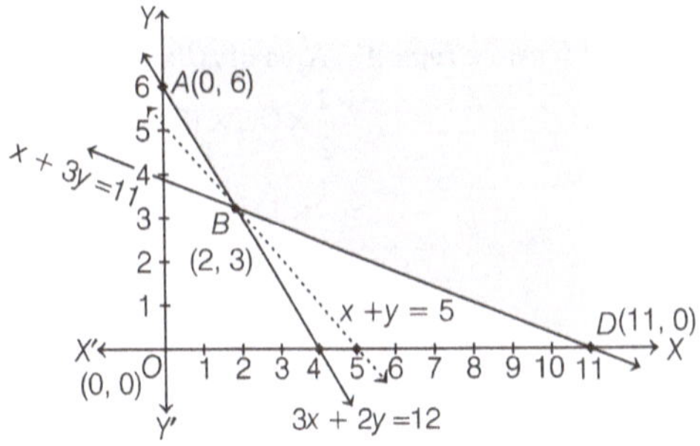

The values of Z at corner points are given below.

Corner points	$Z=x+y$
$A(0,6)$	$Z=0+6=6$
$B(2,3)$	$Z=2+3=5$ (Minimum)
$D(11,0)$	$Z=11+0=11$

Thus, the minimum value of Z is 5 at the point $B(2,3)$.

As the feasible region is unbounded, therefore 5 may or may not be the minimum value of Z.

For this, we draw a dotted graph of the inequality $x+y<5$ and check whether the resulting half plane has points in common with a feasible region or not. It can be seen that the feasible region has no common point with $x+y<5$.

Hence, the minimum value of Z is 5 at the point $B(2,3)$.

9. Hint

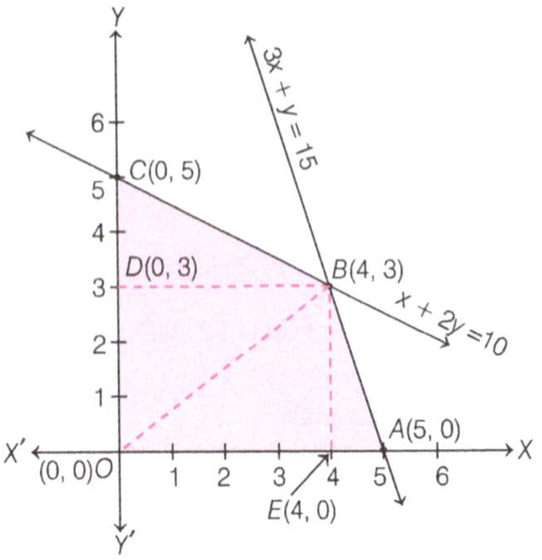

The corner points of the feasible region are

$O(0,0), A(5,0), B(4,3)$ and $C(0,5)$.

The values of Z at the corner points are given below.

Corner points	$Z=3x+2y$
$O(0,0)$	$Z=3\times0+2\times0=0$
$A(5,0)$	$Z=3\times5+2\times0=15$
$B(4,3)$	$Z=3\times4+2\times3=18$ (Maximum)
$C(0,5)$	$Z=3\times0+2\times5=10$

Hence, the maximum value of Z is 18 at the point $B(4,3)$.

$\therefore$ Area of feasible region = Area of ΔBOC + Area of ΔOAB

$$= \frac{1}{2} \times OC \times BD + \frac{1}{2} \times OA \times BE$$

$$= \frac{1}{2} \times 5 \times 4 + \frac{1}{2} \times 5 \times 3$$

$$= 10 + \frac{15}{2} = 10 + 7.5 = 17.5 \text{ sq units}$$

10. **Hint** From the given graph, there are three corner points, which are (0, 4), $\left(\frac{3}{5}, \frac{8}{5}\right)$ and (3, 0).

$\because \quad Z = 10x + 20y$

$\therefore$ At (0,4), $Z_{(0,4)} = 10 \times 0 + 20 \times 4 = 80$

At (3, 0), $Z_{(3,0)} = 10 \times 3 + 0 \times 20 = 30$

At $\left(\frac{3}{5}, \frac{8}{5}\right)$, $Z_{\left(\frac{3}{5}, \frac{8}{5}\right)} = 10 \times \frac{3}{5} + 20 \times \frac{8}{5} = 38$

We get the maximum value at (0, 4) is 80.

But this graph has no maximum value. As the open balance determined $10x + 20y > 80$ has points in common with the feasible region and hence the given graph has no maximum value. This is my conclusion for this graph.

11. Given, Maximise $Z = 5x + 7y$

and feasible region is $OABC$.

The corner points of the feasible region are $O(0,0), A(7,0), B(3,4)$ and $C(0,2)$.

Corner points	$Z = 5x + 7y$
$O(0,0)$	$Z = 5 \times 0 + 7 \times 0 = 0$
$A(7,0)$	$Z = 5 \times 7 + 7 \times 0 = 35$
$B(3,4)$	$Z = 5 \times 3 + 7 \times 4 = 43$ (Maximum)
$C(0,2)$	$Z = 5 \times 0 + 7 \times 2 = 14$

Hence, the maximum value of Z is 43 at the point $B(3,4)$.

12. Given, $Z = -3x + 4y$

Subject to the constraints,

$x + 2y \le 8, 3x + 2y \le 12$ and $x \ge 0, y \ge 0$

Now, considering the inequations as equations, we get

$$x + 2y = 8 \quad \dots(i)$$

$$3x + 2y = 12 \quad \dots(ii)$$

Table for line $x + 2y = 8$ is

x	8	0
y	0	4

On putting (0, 0) in the inequality $x + 2y \le 8$

$0 \le 8$ (which is true)

So, half plane is towards the origin.

Table for line $3x + 2y = 12$ is

x	4	0
y	0	6

On putting (0, 0) in the inequality $3x + 2y \le 12$

$0 \le 12$ (which is true)

So, half plane is towards the origin. Also, $x \ge 0$ and $y \ge 0$, so the feasible region lies in the I quadrant.

The point of intersection of Eqs. (i) and (ii) is (2, 3).

The graphical representation of the above system of inequations is given below.

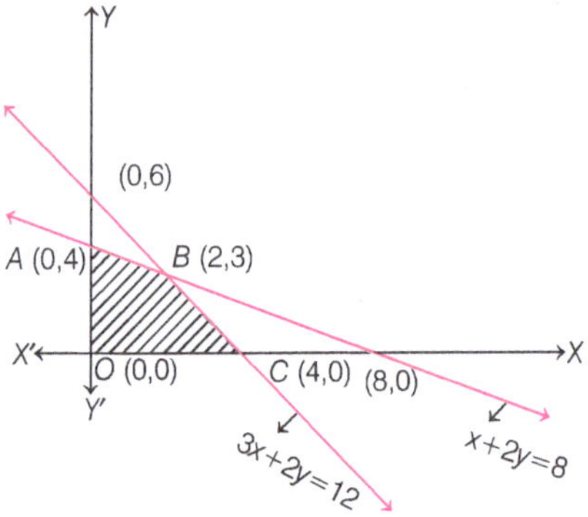

Corner points	$Z = -3x + 4y$
$A(0,4)$	16
$B(2,3)$	6
$C(4,0)$	-12 (Minimum)
$O(0,0)$	0

Hence, $Z = -12$ is minimum at the point $C(4,0)$.

13. Maximise $Z = -3x - 5y$

Subject to the constraints,

$-2x + y \le 4, x + y \ge 3,$

$x - 2y \le 2$ and $x \ge 0, y \ge 0$

Now, considering the inequations as equations, we get

$$-2x + y = 4 \quad \dots(i)$$

$$x + y = 3 \quad \dots(ii)$$

and $$x - 2y = 2 \quad \dots(iii)$$

Table for line $-2x + y = 4$ is

x	-2	0
y	0	4

So, it passes through the points $(-2, 0)$ and (0, 4).

On putting (0, 0) in the inequality $-2x + y \le 4$, we get

$0 \le 4$ (which is true)

So, the half plane is towards the origin.

Table for line $x+y=3$ is

x	3	0
y	0	3

So, it passes through the points (3, 0) and (0, 3).

$0 \geq 3$ (which is false)

So, the half plane is away from the origin.

Table for line $x-2y=2$ is

x	2	0
y	0	–1

So, it passes through the points (2, 0) and (0, – 1).

On putting (0, 0) in the inequality $x-2y \leq 2$.

$0 \leq 2$ (which is true)

So, the half plane is towards the origin. Also, $x \geq 0$, $y \geq 0$, so the feasible region lies in the I quadrant.

The point of intersection of Eqs. (i) and (ii) is $\left(-\frac{1}{3}, \frac{10}{3}\right)$, Eqs. (ii) and (iii) is $\left(\frac{8}{3}, \frac{1}{3}\right)$ and Eqs. (i) and (iii) is $\left(\frac{-10}{3}, \frac{-8}{3}\right)$. The graphical representation of the above system of inequations is given below.

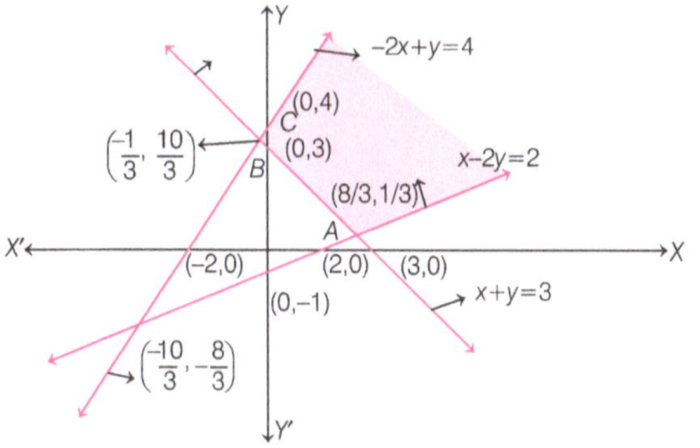

∴ Clearly, feasible region is shaded.

The values of Z at corner points are as follow.

Corner points	Value of $Z=-3x-5y$
$A\left(\frac{8}{3}, \frac{1}{3}\right)$	$-3 \times \frac{8}{3} - 5 \times \frac{1}{3} = -8 - \frac{5}{3} = \frac{-29}{3}$ (Max.)
$B(0,3)$	$-3 \times 0 - 5 \times 3 = -15$
$C(0,4)$	$-3 \times 0 - 5 \times 4 = -20$

Here, the feasible region is unbounded and the open half plane determined by $-3x-5y > \frac{-29}{3}$ has no point in common with the feasible region.

Hence, $Z = -\frac{29}{3}$ is maximum at $A\left(\frac{8}{3}, \frac{1}{3}\right)$.

14. We have the following LPP, maximise $Z = 6x + 3y$

Subject to the constraints,

$$4x + y \geq 80,$$
$$3x + 2y \leq 150,$$
$$x + 5y \geq 115$$
and $$x \geq 0, y \geq 0.$$

Now, considering the inequations as equations, we get

$$4x + y = 80 \quad \text{...(i)}$$
$$3x + 2y = 150 \quad \text{...(ii)}$$
and $$x + 5y = 115 \quad \text{...(iii)}$$

Table for line $4x + y = 80$ is

x	20	0
y	0	80

So, it passes through the points (20, 0) and (0, 80).

On putting (0, 0) in the inequality $4x + y \geq 80$, we get $0 \geq 80$ (which is false).

So, the half plane is away from the origin.

Table for line $3x + 2y = 150$ is

x	50	0
y	0	75

So, it passes through the points (50, 0) and (0, 75).

On putting (0, 0) in the inequality $3x + 2y \leq 150$, we get

$0 \leq 150$ (which is true).

So, the half plane is towards the origin.

Table for line $x + 5y = 115$ is

x	115	0
y	0	23

So, it passes through the points (115, 0) and (0, 23).

On putting (0,0) in the inequality $x + 5y \geq 115$, we get

$0 \geq 115$ (which is false).

So, the half plane is away from the origin. Also, $x \geq 0$, $y \geq 0$, so the feasible region lies in the I quadrant.

The point of intersection of Eqs. (i) and (ii) is (2, 72), Eqs. (ii) and (iii) is (40, 15) and Eqs. (i) and (iii) is (15, 20).

The graphical representation of the above system of inequations is given below.

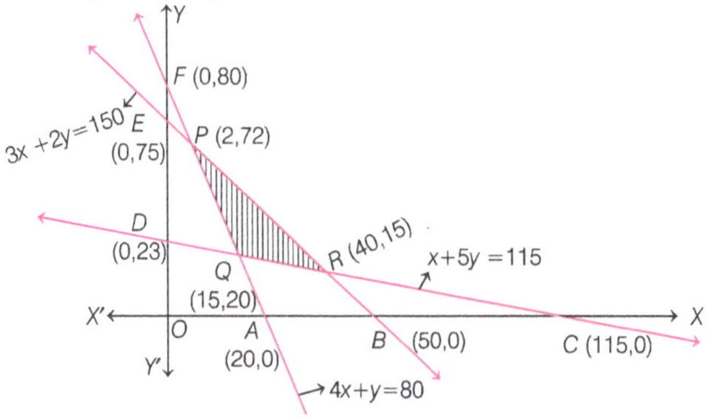

Clearly, feasible region is PQR, whose corner points are $P(2,72)$, $Q(15,20)$ and $R(40,15)$.

The values of Z at corner points are as follow.

Corner points	$Z = 6x + 3y$
$P(2, 72)$	$6\times2+3\times72=228$
$Q(15, 20)$	$6\times15+3\times20=150$
$R(40, 15)$	$6\times40+3\times15=285$ (Maximum)

In the table, we find that maximum value of Z is 285 at $R(40,15)$.

15. We have,

maximise $Z = 60x + 40y$ ...(i)

Subject to the constraints,

$x + 2y \le 12$ ...(ii)

$2x + y \le 12$ ...(iii)

$4x + 5y \ge 20$ ...(iv)

and $x, y \ge 0$ ...(v)

Table for line $x + 2y = 12$ is

x	0	12
y	6	0

So, the line $x + 2y = 12$ is passing through the points (0, 6) and (12, 0).

On putting (0, 0) in the inequality $x + 2y \le 12$, we get $0 + 2(0) \le 12 \Rightarrow 0 \le 12$, which is true

So, the half plane is towards the origin.

Table for line $2x + y = 12$ is

x	0	6
y	12	0

So, the line $2x + y = 12$ is passing through the points (0, 12) and (6, 0).

On putting (0, 0) in the inequality $2x + y \le 12$, we get $2(0) + 0 \le 12 \Rightarrow 0 \le 12$, which is true.

So, the half plane is towards the origin.

Table for line $4x + 5y = 20$ is

x	0	5
y	4	0

So, the line $4x + 5y = 20$ is passing through the points (0,4) and (5, 0).

On putting (0, 0) in the inequality $4x + 5y \ge 20$, we get $4(0) + 5(0) \ge 20 \Rightarrow 0 \ge 20$, which is not true.

So, the half plane is away from the origin.

Also, $x, y \ge 0$

So, the region lies in I quadrant.

On solving equations $x + 2y = 12$ and $2x + y = 12$, we get $D(4, 4)$.

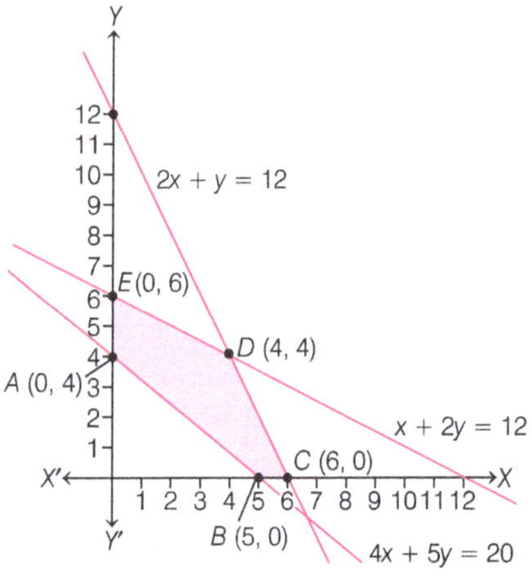

Clearly, the feasible region is $ABCDEA$.

The corner points of the feasible region are $A(0, 4)$, $B(5, 0)$, $C(6, 0)$, $D(4, 4)$ and $E(0, 6)$.

The values of Z at corner points are given below.

Corner points	$Z = 60x + 40y$
$A(0, 4)$	$Z = 60\times0 + 40\times4 = 160$
$B(5, 0)$	$Z = 60\times5 + 40\times0 = 300$
$C(6, 0)$	$Z = 60\times6 + 40\times0 = 360$
$D(4, 4)$	$Z = 60\times4 + 40\times4 = 400$ (Max.)
$E(0, 6)$	$Z = 60\times0 + 40\times6 = 240$

The maximum value of Z is 400 at $D(4, 4)$.

16. **Hint** By solving same as Q. 15, we get the values of Z at corner points are given below.

Corner points	$Z = 300x + 600y$
$A(0, 4)$	$Z = 300\times0 + 600\times4 = 2400$
$B(5, 0)$	$Z = 300\times5 + 600\times0 = 1500$
$C(6, 0)$	$Z = 300\times6 + 600\times0 = 1800$
$D(4, 4)$	$Z = 300\times4 + 600\times4 = 3600$ (Max.)
$E(0, 6)$	$Z = 300\times0 + 600\times6 = 3600$ (Max.)

Ans. The maximum value of Z is 3600 at $D(4, 4)$ and $E(0, 6)$.

17. Maximise $Z = 70x + 40y$

Subject to the constraints,

$3x + 2y \le 9$, $3x + y \le 9$ and $x \ge 0, y \ge 0$

Now, considering the inequations as equations, we get

$$3x + 2y = 9 \quad \text{...(i)}$$

and $$3x + y = 9 \quad \text{...(ii)}$$

Table for line $3x + 2y = 9$ is

x	3	0
y	0	9/2

So, it passes through the points (3, 0) and (0, 9/2).

On putting (0, 0) in the inequality $3x + 2y \le 9$, we get $0 \le 9$ (which is true)

So, the half plane is towards the origin.

Table for line $3x + y = 9$ is

x	3	0
y	0	9

On putting (0, 0) in the inequality $3x + y \le 9$, we get $0 \le 9$ (which is true)

So, the half plane is towards the origin.

Also, $x \ge 0$, $y \ge 0$, so the feasible region lies in the I quadrant.

The point of intersection of Eqs. (i) and (ii) is (3, 0).

The graphical representation of the above system of inequations is given below.

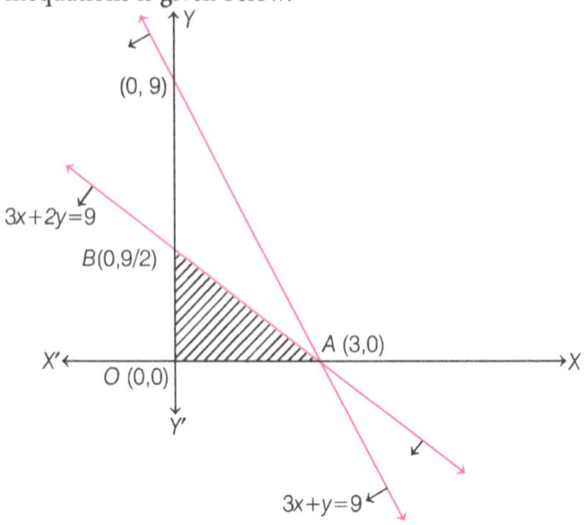

Clearly, feasible region is $OABO$, whose corner points are $O(0, 0)$, $A(3, 0)$ and $B(0, 9/2)$.

Corner points	$Z = 70x + 40y$
$O(0, 0)$	0
$A(3, 0)$	210 (Maximum)
$B(0, 9/2)$	180

In the table, we find that maximum value of Z is 210 at the point $A(3, 0)$.

18. (i)

Corner points	$Z = 3x - 4y$
$O(0, 0)$	0
$A(0, 8)$	-32 (Minimum)
$B(4, 10)$	-28
$C(6, 8)$	-14
$D(6, 5)$	-2
$E(4, 0)$	12 (Maximum)

$\therefore$ Z is maximum at $(4, 0)$ and minimum at $(0, 8)$.

Also, $Z_{max} = 12$ and $Z_{min} = -32$

(ii) Since, maximum value of Z occurs at $B(4, 10)$ and $C(6, 8)$.

$\therefore \quad 4p + 10q = 6p + 8q$

$\Rightarrow \quad 2q = 2p \Rightarrow p = q$

Number of optimal solutions is infinite.

19. Given, objective function is minimise,

$$Z = 6x + 7y \quad \text{...(i)}$$

Subject to constraints,

$$x + 2y \ge 240 \quad \text{...(ii)}$$

$$3x + 4y \le 620 \quad \text{...(iii)}$$

$$2x + y \ge 180 \quad \text{...(iv)}$$

and $$x, y \ge 0 \quad \text{...(v)}$$

Firstly, draw the graph of the line $x + 2y = 240$.

x	0	240
y	120	0

On putting (0, 0) in the inequality $x + 2y \ge 240$, we get $0 + 2 \times 0 \ge 240 \Rightarrow 0 \ge 240$, which is not true.

So, the half plane is away from the origin.

Secondly, draw the graph of the line $3x + 4y \le 620$.

x	0	$\frac{620}{3}$
y	155	0

So, the line passes through the points $(0, 155)$ and $\left(\frac{620}{3}, 0\right)$.

On putting (0, 0) in the inequality $3x + 4y \le 620$, we get

$$3 \times 0 + 4 \times 0 \le 620$$

$\Rightarrow \quad 0 \le 620$, which is true.

So, the half plane is towards the origin.

Thirdly, draw the graph of the line $2x + y = 180$.

x	90	0
y	0	180

So, the line passes through the points $(90, 0)$ and $(0, 180)$.

On putting (0, 0) in the inequality $2x+y \geq 180$, we get

$$2 \times 0 + 0 \geq 180$$

$\Rightarrow$ $0 \geq 180$, which is not true.

So, the half plane is away from the origin.

Also, $x \geq 0$ and $y \geq 0$, so the region lies in the I quadrant.

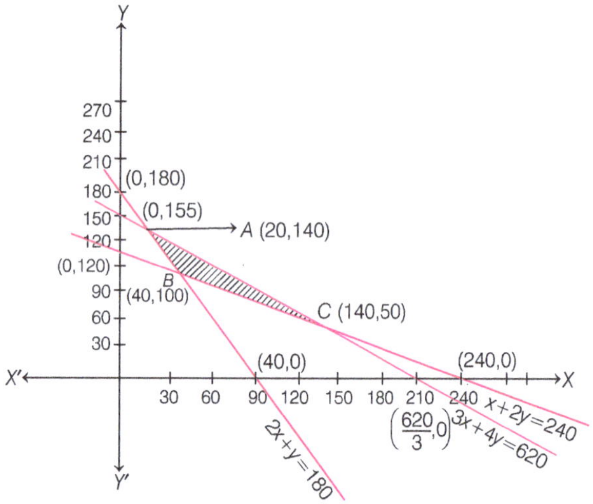

The above inequations (i), (ii), (iii), (iv) and (v) can be represented in the graph as shown below.

The intersection point of lines corresponding to Eqs. (iii) and (iv) is $A(20, 140)$, corresponding to Eqs. (ii) and (iv) is $B(40, 100)$ and corresponding to Eqs. (ii) and (iii) is $C(140, 50)$.

Clearly, the feasible region is $ABCA$, where corner points are $A(20, 140)$, $B(40, 100)$ and $C(140, 50)$.

The values of Z at corner points are given below.

Corner points	$Z = 6x + 7y$
$A(20,140)$	$Z = 6 \times 20 + 7 \times 140 = 1100$
$B(40,100)$	$Z = 6 \times 40 + 7 \times 100 = 940$ (Min.)
$C(140, 50)$	$Z = 6 \times 140 + 7 \times 50 = 1190$

Hence, the minimum value of Z is 940 at $B(40, 100)$.

Mind Map

Linear Programming

Mathematical Form of LPP

The mathematical form of a linear programming problem is as follows

Objective function,

$$Z = c_1x + c_2y$$

Subject to constraints are

$$a_1x + b_1y \le d_1, a_2x + b_2y \le d_2 \text{ etc.}$$

and $\quad x \ge 0, y \ge 0$

Graphical Method for Solving Linear Programming Problem

This method of solving linear programming problem is referred as corner point method. The process of this method is as follows.

I. Draw the graph of each linear equation.

II. Find the feasible region of the LPP and determine its corner points (vertices).

III. Determine the value of objective function, $Z = ax + by$ at each corner point.

(a) When the feasible region is **bounded**, then find maximum (M) and minimum (m) values of Z.

(b) When the feasible region is **unbounded**, then

(i) The maximum (M) value of Z exist, if the open half plane determined by $ax + by > M$ has no point in common with the feasible region. Otherwise, Z has no maximum value.

(ii) The minimum (m) value of Z exists, if the open half plane determined by $ax + by < m$ has no point in common with the feasible region. Otherwise, Z has no minimum value.

(c) If two corner points of the feasible region are both optimal solution of the same type i.e. both produce the same maximum or minimum, then any point on the line segment joining these two points is also an optimal solution of the same type.

Linear programming is a mathematical method for maximising and minimising a linear function of several variables subject to the constraints on the variables that satisfy the linear inequation.

Here, linear function is known as objective function and constraints are linear inequalities.

Some Important Theorems

Theorem 1 Let R be the feasible region (convex polygon) for a linear programming problem and $Z = ax + by$ be the objective function. When Z has an optimal value (maximum or minimum), where the variables x and Y are subject to constraints described by linear inequalities, this optimal value must occur at a corner point (vertex) of the feasible region.

Theorem 2 Let R be the feasible region for a linear programming problem and $Z = ax + by$ be the objective function.

If R is **bounded**, then the objective function Z has both a maximum and minimum values on R and each of these occurs at a corner point (vertex) of R. If R is **unbounded**, then a maximum or minimum value of the objective function may not exist. However, if it exists, it must occur at a corner point of R.

Important Terms Related to LPP

- **Constraints** The linear inequations or inequalities or restrictions on the variables of a linear programming problem are called constraints. The conditions $x \ge 0$, $y \ge 0$ are called **non-negative restrictions**.
- **Optimisation Problem** A problem which need to maximise or minimise a linear function subject to certain constraints as determined by a set of linear inequalities is called an optimisation problem. Linear programming problems are special type of optimisation problems.
- **Objective Function** A linear function of two or more variables which has to be maximised or minimised under the given restrictions is called an objective function.
- **Optimal Value** The maximum or minimum value of an objective function is known as the optimal value of LPP.
- **Feasible and Infeasible Region** The common region determined by all the constraints including non-negative constraints $x, y \ge 0$ of a linear programming problem is called the feasible region or solution region. The region other than feasible region is called an infeasible region.
- **Bounded and Unbounded Region** A feasible region of a system of linear inequalities is said to be bounded, if it can be enclosed within lines. Otherwise, it is said to be unbounded region, i.e. the feasible region does extend infinitely in any direction.
- **Feasible and Infeasible Solution** Points within and on the boundary of the feasible region, represents feasible solution of the constraints. Any point outside the feasible region is called an infeasible solution.
- **Optimal Feasible Solution** A feasible solution at which the objective function has optimal value (maximum or minimum), is called the optimal solution or optimal feasible solution of the linear programming problem.
- **Optimisation Technique** The process of obtaining the optimal solution of the linear programming problem is called optimisation technique.
- **Corner Point** A corner point of a feasible region is a point of intersection of two boundary lines in the region.

13 CHAPTER

It is not enough to have a good mind, the main thing is to use it well.

— *Rene Descartes*

Probability

▼ **YOUR STUDY GOALS**

13.1 Recapitulations of Basic Concept
13.2 Conditional Probability
13.3 Multiplication Theorem
13.4 Theorem of Total Probability
13.5 Baye's Theorem
13.6 Random Variable

▼ **YOUR PRACTICE GOALS**

- Objective Type Questions (41 Qs ; 25 MCQs, 10 A-R, 6 Case Based)
- Subjective Type Questions (47 Qs; 11 VSA, 21 SA, 15 LA)

13.1 Recapitulations of Basic Concept

- **Experiment** An operation which can produce some well-defined outcomes is called an experiment.
- **Random Experiment** An experiment is called random experiment, if it satisfies the following two conditions.
  (i) It has more than one possible outcomes.
  (ii) It is not possible to predict the outcome in advance.
- **Outcomes and Sample Space** A possible result of a random experiment is called its outcome. The set of all possible outcomes of a random experiment is called its sample space. Each element of a sample space is called a sample point or an event point.
- **Trial** When a random experiment is repeated under identical conditions and the outcomes in each time may be different or same, then each such action is called a trial.
- **Event** A subset of the sample space associated with a random experiment is called an event.
- **Impossible and Sure Events** The empty set ϕ and the sample space S describe events (as S and ϕ are also subset of S). The empty set ϕ is called an impossible event and whole sample space S is called the sure event.

- **Simple Event** If an event has only one sample point of a sample space, then it is called a simple or elementary event.
- **Compound Event** If an event has more than one sample point, then it is called a compound event.
- **Equally Likely Events** The given events are said to be equally likely, if none of them is expected to occur in preference to the other.
- **Mutually Exclusive Events** Two or more events are said to be mutually exclusive, if the happening of one excludes the happening of the other i.e. if no two of them can occur together. If A and B are mutually exclusive events, then $(A \cap B) = \phi$.
- **Exhaustive Events** A set of events are said to be exhaustive, if one of them necessarily occurs whenever the experiment is performed.
  Let $E_1, E_2, \ldots, E_n$ be subsets of sample space S.
  Then, events $E_1, E_2, \ldots, E_n$ are exhaustive events, if $E_1 \cup E_2 \cup \ldots \cup E_n = S$.
- **Complement of an Event** Let A be an event in a sample space S, then complement of A is the set of all sample points, which are not in A and it is denoted by A' or $\bar{A}$.
  i.e. $A' = \{n : n \in S, n \notin A\}$

Probability of an Event

If there are n elementary equally likely events associated with a random experiment and m of them are favourable to an event A, then the probability of happening or occurrence of A is denoted by $P(A)$ and defined as

$$P(A) = \frac{m}{n} = \frac{\left[\begin{array}{l}\text{Number of elementary events}\\ \text{favourable to event } A\end{array}\right]}{\left[\begin{array}{l}\text{Total number of elementary}\\ \text{events to the experiment}\end{array}\right]}$$

Here,

- $0 \le P(A) \le 1$
- Probability of impossible event is zero.
- Probability of sure event is 1.
- $P(A \cup A') = 1$
- $P(A \cap A') = 0$
- $P(A')' = P(A)$
- Sometimes, we have to select r objects from n distinct objects, then we use the formula,

$$^nC_r = \frac{n!}{r!(n-r)!}, \quad 0 \le r \le n.$$

Important Results on Probability

1. **Addition Theorem of Probability**
   (i) For two events A and B,
   $$P(A \cup B) = P(A) + P(B) - P(A \cap B)$$
   If A and B are mutually exclusive events, then
   $$P(A \cap B) = 0$$
   $$\therefore \quad P(A \cup B) = P(A) + P(B)$$
   (ii) For three events A, B and C,
   $$P(A \cup B \cup C) = P(A) + P(B) + P(C) - P(A \cap B) - P(B \cap C) - P(A \cap C) + P(A \cap B \cap C)$$
   If A, B and C are mutually exclusive events, then
   $$P(A \cup B \cup C) = P(A) + P(B) + P(C)$$
   [for mutually exclusive events, $P(A \cap B) = P(B \cap C) = P(C \cap A) = P(A \cap B \cap C) = 0$]
2. If A and B are two events associated with a random experiment, then
   (i) $P(\bar{A} \cap B) = P(B) - P(A \cap B)$
   (ii) $P(A \cap \bar{B}) = P(A) - P(A \cap B)$
   (iii) $P(\bar{A} \cap \bar{B}) = 1 - P(A \cup B)$
   (iv) $P(\bar{A} \cup \bar{B}) = 1 - P(A \cap B)$
   (v) $P(A) = P(A \cap B) + P(A \cap \bar{B})$
   (vi) $P(B) = P(A \cap B) + P(B \cap \bar{A})$
   (vii) P(exactly one of A, B occurs)
   $$= P[(A \cap \bar{B}) \cup (\bar{A} \cap B)]$$
   $$= P(A) + P(B) - 2P(A \cap B)$$
   $$= P(A \cup B) - P(A \cap B)$$
3. If A, B and C are three events, then
   P(exactly one of A, B, C occurs)
   $$= P(A) + P(B) + P(C) - 2P(A \cap B) - 2P(B \cap C) - 2P(A \cap C) + 3P(A \cap B \cap C)$$
4. $P(\bar{A}) = 1 - P(A)$

13.2 Conditional Probability

If A and B are two events associated with the same sample space of a random experiment, then conditional probability of the event A under the condition B has already occurred.

i.e. $P(A/B)$ is given by

$$P\left(\frac{A}{B}\right) = \frac{P(A \cap B)}{P(B)}, \text{ provided } P(B) \ne 0$$

Also, we can determine

$$P\left(\frac{B}{A}\right)=\frac{P(B\cap A)}{P(A)}, \text{ provided } P(A)\neq 0$$

If A and B are mutually exclusive events, then

$$P\left(\frac{A}{B}\right)=P\left(\frac{B}{A}\right)=0$$

Properties of Conditional Probability

Let A and B be the events of a sample space S of an experiment, then

(i) $P(S/A)=P(A/A)=1$

(ii) If A and B are any two events of a sample space S and C is an event of S, such that $P(C)\neq 0$, then

$P\{(A\cup B)/C\}=P(A/C)+P(B/C)-P\{(A\cap B)/C\}$

In particular, if A and B are disjoint events, then

$$P\left(\frac{A\cup B}{C}\right)=P\left(\frac{A}{C}\right)+P\left(\frac{B}{C}\right)$$

(iii) $P(A'/B)=1-P(A/B)$, where A' is complement of A.

Example 1 **4 cards are drawn from a well-shuffled deck of 52 cards. What is the probability of obtaining 3 diamond cards?**

Sol. Total number of cards in a deck = 52 [given]

Total number of ways of selecting 4 cards out of 52 cards,

$$n(S)={}^{52}C_4$$

Let E = Event of getting 3 diamond and one another card

Then, $n(E)={}^{13}C_3\times{}^{39}C_1$

$\therefore$ Required probability, $P(E)=\frac{n(E)}{n(S)}=\frac{{}^{13}C_3\times{}^{39}C_1}{{}^{52}C_4}$

Example 2 **Three distinct numbers are chosen randomly from the first 50 natural numbers. Find the probability that all the three numbers are divisible by both 2 and 3.** CBSE 2020

Sol. Three distinct number are chosen from first 50 natural number is ${}^{50}C_3$.

The numbers which are divisible by both 2 and 3 from first 50 natural number are

{6, 12, 18, 24, 30, 36, 42, 48} i.e. 8 in number

$\therefore$ Required probability $=\frac{{}^{8}C_3}{{}^{50}C_3}$

$$=\frac{8\times 7\times 6}{50\times 49\times 48}=\frac{1}{350}$$

Example 3 **Two cards are drawn at random from a pack of 52 cards one-by-one without replacement. What is the probability of getting first card red and second card jack?** CBSE Sample Paper 2022 (Term II)

Sol. $\because$ Two cards are drawn at random from a pack of 52 cards one-by-one without replacement.

$\therefore$ The required probability

= P {(the first is a red jack card and the second is a jack card) or (the first is a red non-jack card and the second is a jack card)}

$$=\frac{2}{52}\times\frac{3}{51}+\frac{24}{52}\times\frac{4}{51}=\frac{1}{26}$$

Example 4 **A and B throw a die alternately till one of them gets a 6 and wins the game. Find their respective probabilities of wining, if A starts the game first.** CBSE 2023

Sol. Let A be the event that player A gets 6 and B be the event that player B get 6. When a die is thrown, then the probability of getting 6 is $\frac{1}{6}$.

$\therefore P(A)=\frac{1}{6}, P(A')=1-P(A)=\frac{5}{6}$

Similarly, $P(B)=\frac{1}{6}, P(B')=\frac{5}{6}$

It is given that A starts the game and he will win in the following mutually exclusive ways.

(i) Player A wins at the first throw.

(ii) Player A wins in the third throw when A and B fail in the first and second throw and so on.

$$\therefore P(A \text{ wins})=P(A)+P(A')P(B')P(A)+P(A')P(B')P(A')P(B')P(A)+\ldots..$$

$$=\frac{1}{6}+\frac{5}{6}\times\frac{5}{6}\times\frac{1}{6}+\frac{5}{6}\times\frac{5}{6}\times\frac{5}{6}\times\frac{5}{6}\times\frac{1}{6}+\ldots$$

$$=\frac{1}{6}\left[1+\left(\frac{5}{6}\right)^2+\left(\frac{5}{6}\right)^4+\ldots.\right]$$

$$=\frac{1}{6}\left[\frac{1}{1-\left(\frac{5}{6}\right)^2}\right]$$

$$\left[\because \text{it is an infinite GP with } a=1, r=\frac{25}{36}\right]$$

$$=\frac{1}{6}\left[\frac{1}{\frac{11}{36}}\right]=\frac{6}{11}$$

$$\therefore P(B \text{ wins})=1-P(A \text{ wins})=1-\frac{6}{11}=\frac{5}{11}$$

Example 5 **Three friends go for coffee. They decide who will pay the bill, by each tossing a coin and then letting the 'odd person' pay. There is no odd person, if all three tosses produce the same result. If there is no odd person in the first round, they make a second round of tosses and they continue to do so until there is an odd person. What is the probability that exactly three rounds of tosses are made?** *CBSE Sample Paper 2023*

Sol. P(not obtaining an odd person in a single round)

= P(all three of them throw tails or all three of them throw heads)

= P(all three of them throw tails) + P(all three of them throw heads)

$$= \left(\frac{1}{2}\times\frac{1}{2}\times\frac{1}{2}\right)+\left(\frac{1}{2}\times\frac{1}{2}\times\frac{1}{2}\right)$$

$$\left[\because P(\text{Head}) = P(\text{Tails}) = \frac{1}{2}\right]$$

$$= 2\times\frac{1}{2}\times\frac{1}{2}\times\frac{1}{2}=\frac{1}{4}$$

Now, P (obtaining an odd person in a single round)

= 1 − P (not obtaining an odd person in a single round)

$$= 1-\frac{1}{4}=\frac{3}{4}$$

Now, the required probability is given by P('in first round there is no odd person' and 'in second round there is no odd person' and 'in third round there is an odd person')

= P(in first round there is no odd person) × P(in second round there is no odd person) × P(in third round there is an odd person)

$$= \frac{1}{4}\times\frac{1}{4}\times\frac{3}{4}=\frac{3}{64}$$

Example 6 **If A and B are two events such that $P(A) = 0.42$, $P(B) = 0.48$ and $P(A\cap B) = 0.16$, then find $P(A\cup B)$.**

Sol. Given, $P(A) = 0.42$, $P(B) = 0.48$ and $P(A\cap B) = 0.16$

$$\therefore\ P(A\cup B) = P(A) + P(B) - P(A\cap B)$$
$$= 0.42 + 0.48 - 0.16$$
$$= 0.90 - 0.16 = 0.74$$

Example 7 **There are 25 tickets bearing numbers from 1 to 25. One ticket is drawn at random. Find the probability that the number on it is a multiple of 5 or 6.**

Sol. Let E = Event of getting a multiple of 5

F = Event of getting a multiple of 6

and $E\cap F$ = Event of getting a multiple of 5 and 6 i.e. 30.

$$\therefore\quad P(E) = \frac{5}{25}\qquad [\because E = \{5, 10, 15, 20, 25\}]$$

$$P(F) = \frac{4}{25}\qquad [\because F = \{6, 12, 18, 24\}]$$

and $$P(E\cap F) = \frac{0}{25} = 0\qquad [\because E\cap F = \phi]$$

∴ Required probability,

$$P(E\cup F) = P(E) + P(F) - P(E\cap F)$$
$$= \frac{5}{25}+\frac{4}{25}-0=\frac{9}{25}$$

Example 8 **If $P(\text{not } A) = 0.7$, $P(B) = 0.7$ and $P(B/A) = 0.5$, then find $P(A/B)$.** *Competency Based Que*

Sol. Given, $P(A') = 0.7$, $P(B) = 0.7$ and $P\left(\frac{B}{A}\right) = 0.5$

Clearly, $P(A) = 1 - P(A') = 1 - 0.7 = 0.3$

Now, $$P\left(\frac{B}{A}\right) = \frac{P(A\cap B)}{P(A)}$$

$$\Rightarrow\quad 0.5 = \frac{P(A\cap B)}{0.3}$$

$$\Rightarrow\quad P(A\cap B) = 0.15$$

$$\therefore\quad P\left(\frac{A}{B}\right) = \frac{P(A\cap B)}{P(B)} = \frac{0.15}{0.7}\ \Rightarrow\ P\left(\frac{A}{B}\right) = \frac{3}{14}$$

Example 9 **Find $[P(B/A) + P(A/B)]$, if $P(A) = \frac{3}{10}$, $P(B) = \frac{2}{5}$ and $P(A\cup B) = \frac{3}{5}$.** *CBSE 2020*

Sol. We have, $P(A) = \frac{3}{10}$, $P(B) = \frac{2}{5}$ and $P(A\cup B) = \frac{3}{5}$

We know that $P(A\cup B) = P(A) + P(B) - P(A\cap B)$

$$\Rightarrow\quad \frac{3}{5} = \frac{3}{10}+\frac{2}{5}-P(A\cap B)$$

$$\Rightarrow\quad P(A\cap B) = \frac{3}{10}+\frac{2}{5}-\frac{3}{5}=\frac{1}{10}$$

Now, $$[P(B/A) + P(A/B)] = \frac{P(A\cap B)}{P(A)}+\frac{P(A\cap B)}{P(B)}$$

$$= \frac{\frac{1}{10}}{3/10}+\frac{\frac{1}{10}}{2/5}=\frac{1}{3}+\frac{1}{4}=\frac{7}{12}$$

Example 10 **Given that E and F are events such that $P(E) = 0.8$, $P(F) = 0.7$, $P(E\cap F) = 0.6$. Find $P(\bar{E}/\bar{F})$.** *CBSE Sample Paper 2021*

Sol. We have, $P(E) = 0.8$, $P(F) = 0.7$, $P(E\cap F) = 0.6$

We know that $P(E\cup F) = P(E) + P(F) - P(E\cap F)$

$$= 0.8 + 0.7 - 0.6 = 0.9$$

Now, $$P(\bar{E}/\bar{F}) = \frac{P(\bar{E}\cap\bar{F})}{P(\bar{F})} = \frac{P(\overline{E\cup F})}{P(\bar{F})}$$

$$= \frac{1-P(E\cup F)}{1-P(F)} = \frac{1-0.9}{1-0.7} = \frac{0.1}{0.3} = \frac{1}{3}$$

Example 11 **A pair of dice is thrown and the sum of the numbers appearing on the dice is observed to be 7. Find the probability that the number 5 has appeared on atleast one die.** CBSE 2022 (Term II)

Sol. We know that when a pair of dice is thrown, total possible outcomes $= 6 \times 6 = 36$

Let A be the event of getting sum as 7.

Possible outcomes = (1, 6), (2, 5), (3, 4), (4, 3), (5, 2), (6, 1)

Therefore, $P(A) = \frac{6}{36} = \frac{1}{6}$

Let B be the event of getting number 5 on atleast one dice.

Possible outcomes = (1, 5), (2, 5), (3, 5), (4, 5), (5, 1), (5, 2), (5, 3), (5, 4), (5, 5), (5, 6), (6, 5)

$(A \cap B)$ = Getting sum as 7 with atleast one die showing 5 = (2, 5), (5, 2)

Hence, $P(A \cap B) = \frac{2}{36}$

$\therefore P\left(\frac{B}{A}\right) = \frac{P(A \cap B)}{P(A)} = \frac{2/36}{1/6} = \frac{1}{3}$

Example 12 **A couple has 2 children. Find the probability that both are boys, if it is known that**

(i) one of them is a boy.

(ii) the older child is a boy. CBSE 2014C

Sol. Let B_1 represents older child is a boy, B_2 represents younger child is a boy, G_1 represents older child is a girl and G_2 represents younger child is girl.

If a family has two children, then all possible cases are

$$S = \{B_1B_2, B_1G_2, G_1B_2, G_1G_2\}$$

Let us define event A that both children are boys, then

$$A = \{B_1B_2\} \Rightarrow n(A) = 1$$

(i) Let E_1 be the event that one of them is a boy

Then, $P\left(\frac{A}{E_1}\right) = \frac{P(A \cap E_1)}{P(E_1)}$

Here, $E_1 = \{B_1 G_2, G_1 B_1, B_1 B_2\}$

and $A \cap E_1 = \{B_1 B_2\}$

$\therefore P(A \cap E_1) = \frac{1}{4}, P(E_1) = \frac{3}{4}$

$\therefore P\left(\frac{A}{E_1}\right) = \frac{1/4}{3/4} = \frac{1}{3}$

(ii) Let E_2 be the event that older child is a boy.

Then, $P\left(\frac{A}{E_2}\right) = \frac{P(A \cap E_2)}{P(E)}$

Here, $E_2 = \{B_1 G_2, B_1 B_2\}$ and $A \cap E_2 = \{B_1B_2\}$

$\therefore P(A \cap E_2) = \frac{1}{4}$ and $P(E_2) = \frac{2}{4}$

$\therefore P\left(\frac{A}{E_2}\right) = \frac{1/4}{2/4} = \frac{1}{2}$

Example 13 **Given that the two numbers appearing on throwing two dice are different. Find the probability of the events**

(i) the sum of numbers on the dice is 4.

(ii) the sum of numbers on the dice is not 4. NCERT

Sol. Here, two dice are thrown, so number of outcomes in the sample space, $S = 6 \times 6 = 36$ (equally likely sample events) i.e. $n(S) = 36$.

Let E be the event of getting sum of the numbers on the dice is 4 and F be the event that numbers appearing on the two dice are different.

Then, $E = \{(1, 3), (2, 2), (3, 1)\} \Rightarrow n(E) = 3$

and $F = \left\{\begin{matrix}(1, 2), (1, 3), (1, 4), (1, 5), (1, 6), \\ (2, 1), (2, 3), (2, 4), (2, 5), (2, 6), \\ (3, 1), (3, 2), (3, 4), (3, 5), (3, 6), \\ (4, 1), (4, 2), (4, 3), (4, 5), (4, 6), \\ (5, 1), (5, 2), (5, 3), (5, 4), (5, 6), \\ (6, 1), (6, 2), (6, 3), (6, 4), (6, 5)\end{matrix}\right\}$

$\Rightarrow n(F) = 30$

Here, $E \cap F = \{(1, 3), (3, 1)\} \Rightarrow n(E \cap F) = 2$

$\therefore P(F) = \frac{\text{Number of favourable outcomes}}{\text{Total number of outcomes}}$

$= \frac{30}{36} = \frac{5}{6}$

and $P(E \cap F) = \frac{2}{36} = \frac{1}{18}$

(i) The probability that the sum of numbers on the dice showing different number is 4,

$P\left(\frac{E}{F}\right) = \frac{P(E \cap F)}{P(F)}$

$= \frac{1/18}{5/6} = \frac{1}{15}$

(ii) The probability that the sum of numbers on the dice showing different numbers is not 4,

$P\left(\frac{E'}{F}\right) = 1 - P\left(\frac{E}{F}\right) = 1 - \frac{1}{15} = \frac{14}{15}$

Example 14 **Consider the experiment of tossing a coin. If the coin shows head, toss it again but if it shows tail, then throw a die. Find the conditional probability of the event that 'the die shows a number greater than 4' given that there is atleast one tail.** NCERT, CBSE 2014C

Sol. The outcomes of the experiment can be represented in the following tree diagram.

The sample space S of the experiment is given as

$S = \{(H, H), (H, T), (T, 1), (T, 2), (T, 3), (T, 4), (T, 5), (T, 6)\}$

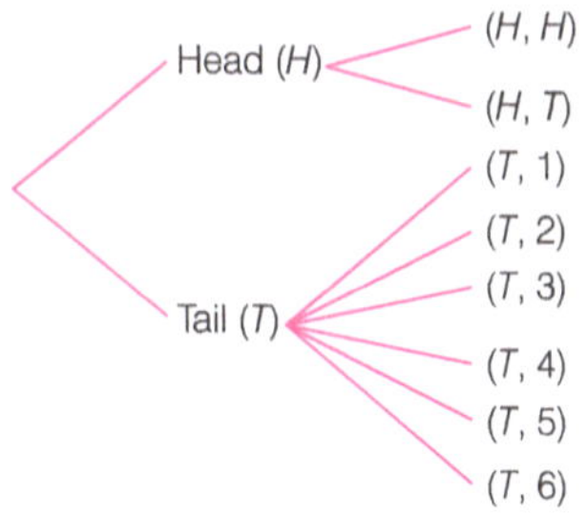

The probabilities of these elementary events are

$P\{(H, H)\} = \frac{1}{2} \times \frac{1}{2} = \frac{1}{4}$, $P\{(H, T)\} = \frac{1}{2} \times \frac{1}{2} = \frac{1}{4}$,

$P\{(T, 1)\} = \frac{1}{2} \times \frac{1}{6} = \frac{1}{12}$, $P\{(T, 2)\} = \frac{1}{2} \times \frac{1}{6} = \frac{1}{12}$,

$P\{(T, 3)\} = \frac{1}{2} \times \frac{1}{6} = \frac{1}{12}$, $P\{(T, 4)\} = \frac{1}{2} \times \frac{1}{6} = \frac{1}{12}$,

$P\{(T, 5)\} = \frac{1}{2} \times \frac{1}{6} = \frac{1}{12}$ and $P\{(T, 6)\} = \frac{1}{2} \times \frac{1}{6} = \frac{1}{12}$

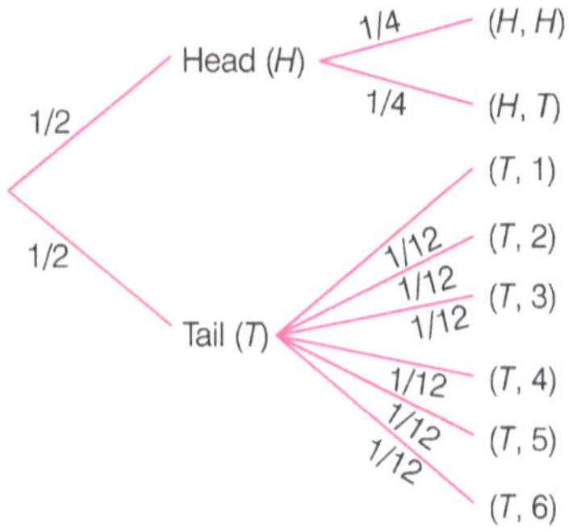

Consider the following events

A = The die shows a number greater than 4

and B = There is atleast one tail.

We have,

$A = \{(T, 5), (T, 6)\}$,

$B = \{(H, T), (T, 1), (T, 2), (T, 3), (T, 4), (T, 5), (T, 6)\}$

and $A \cap B = \{(T, 5), (T, 6)\}$

$\therefore \quad P(B) = P\{(H, T)\} + P\{(T, 1)\} + P\{(T, 2)\} + P\{(T, 3)\} + P\{(T, 4)\} + P\{(T, 5)\} + P\{(T, 6)\}$

$\Rightarrow \quad P(B) = \frac{1}{4} + \frac{1}{12} + \frac{1}{12} + \frac{1}{12} + \frac{1}{12} + \frac{1}{12} + \frac{1}{12} = \frac{3}{4}$

and $P(A \cap B) = P\{(T, 5)\} + P\{(T, 6)\} = \frac{1}{12} + \frac{1}{12} = \frac{1}{6}$

$\therefore$ Required probability $= P\left(\frac{A}{B}\right) = \frac{P(A \cap B)}{P(B)} = \frac{1/6}{3/4} = \frac{4}{18} = \frac{2}{9}$

Quick Test 1

1. The probability that atleast one of the two events A and B occurs is 0.6. If A and B occur simultaneously with probability 0.3, then evaluate $P(\overline{A}) + P(\overline{B})$. *NCERT Exemplar*
2. If $P(B) = \frac{3}{5}, P(A/B) = \frac{1}{2}$ and $P(A \cup B) = \frac{4}{5}$, then find $P(A \cup B)'$.
3. If $P(A) = \frac{2}{5}, P(B) = \frac{3}{10}$ and $P(A \cap B) = \frac{1}{5}$, then find $P(A'/B') \cdot P(B'/A')$. *Competency Based Que, NCERT Exemplar*
4. A fair die is rolled. Consider the following events $A = \{2, 4, 6\}, B = \{4, 5\}$ and $C = \{3, 4, 5, 6\}$
   Find (i) $P(A \cup B / C)$ (ii) $P(A \cap B / C)$
5. Three events A, B and C have probabilities $\frac{2}{5}, \frac{1}{3}$ and $\frac{1}{2}$, respectively. If $P(A \cap C) = \frac{1}{5}$ and $P(B \cap C) = \frac{1}{4}$, then find the values of $P(C / B)$ and $P(A' \cap C')$. *NCERT Exemplar*
6. A black and a red die are rolled together. Find the conditional probability of obtaining the sum 8, given that the red die resulted in a number less than 4. *CBSE 2018*
7. A couple has two children. Find the probability that both children are males, if it is known that atleast one of the children is male. *Competency Based Que*
8. An instructor has a question bank consisting of 300 easy true/false questions, 200 difficult true/false questions, 500 easy multiple choice questions and 400 difficult multiple choice questions. If a question is selected at random from the question bank, then what is the probability that it will be an easy question, given that it is a multiple choice questions? *NCERT*
9. In a hostel, 60% of the students read Hindi newspaper, 40% read English newspaper and 20% read both Hindi and English newspapers. A student is selected at random,
   (i) find the probability that he/she reads neither Hindi nor English newspaper.
   (ii) if he/she reads Hindi newspaper, then find the probability that she reads English newspaper.
   (iii) if he/she reads English newspaper, then find the probability he/she reads Hindi newspaper.
   NCERT, CBSE 2011

Answers

1. 1.1 **2.** $\frac{1}{5}$ **3.** $\frac{25}{42}$ **4.** (i) $\frac{3}{4}$ (ii) $\frac{1}{4}$

5. $\frac{3}{4}$ and $\frac{3}{10}$ **6.** $\frac{1}{9}$ **7.** $\frac{1}{3}$ **8.** $\frac{5}{9}$

9. (i) $\frac{1}{5}$ (ii) $\frac{1}{3}$ (iii) $\frac{1}{2}$

For Solutions, See QR Code on Pg. 418

13.3 Multiplication Theorem

Let A and B be two events associated with a random experiment, then multiplication rule is defined as

$$P(A \cap B) = \begin{cases} P(A) \cdot P(B/A), \text{ where } P(A) \neq 0 \\ P(B) \cdot P(A/B), \text{ where } P(B) \neq 0 \end{cases}$$

where, $A \cap B$ (or AB) denotes the simultaneous occurrence of the events A and B.

Multiplication Rule for More than Two Events

Let E, F, G and H be four events of sample space S. Then,

(i) $P(E \cap F \cap G) = P(E) \cdot P\left(\frac{F}{E}\right) \cdot P\left(\frac{G}{E \cap F}\right)$

(ii) $P(E \cap F \cap G \cap H)$

$$= P(E) \cdot P\left(\frac{F}{E}\right) \cdot P\left(\frac{G}{E \cap F}\right) \cdot P\left(\frac{H}{E \cap F \cap G}\right)$$

Independent Events

Two events A and B are said to be independent, if the occurrence or non-occurrence of one event does not affect the occurrence or non-occurrence of another event.

For two independent events E and F,

$$P\left(\frac{F}{E}\right) = P(F), \text{ provided } P(E) \neq 0$$

and $$P\left(\frac{E}{F}\right) = P(E), \text{ provided } P(F) \neq 0.$$

For two events E and F to be independent the necessary condition is $P(E \cap F) = P(E) \cdot P(F)$.

Some Important Results

1. Two events E and F are said to be dependent, if they are not independent
   i.e. $P(E \cap F) \neq P(E) \cdot P(F)$
2. If A and B are independent events, then
   (i) A and B' are also independent events.
   (ii) A' and B are also independent events.
   (iii) A' and B' are also independent events.
3. Three events A, B and C are said to be mutually independent, if $P(A \cap B) = P(A) \cdot P(B)$
   $P(A \cap C) = P(A) \cdot P(C)$
   $P(B \cap C) = P(B) \cdot P(C)$
   and $P(A \cap B \cap C) = P(A) \cdot P(B) \cdot P(C)$
   If atleast one of the above is not true for three given events, then events are not independent i.e. dependent.

Example 1 If $P(A) = \frac{1}{5}$, $P(B) = \frac{1}{7}$ and $P\left(\frac{A}{B}\right) = \frac{5}{8}$, then find $P(A \cap B)$ and $P\left(\frac{\bar{A}}{B}\right)$.

Competency Based Que

Sol. We have, $P(A) = \frac{1}{5}$, $P(B) = \frac{1}{7}$ and $P\left(\frac{A}{B}\right) = \frac{5}{8}$.

By multiplication theorem,

$$P(A \cap B) = P(B) \times P\left(\frac{A}{B}\right) = \frac{1}{7} \times \frac{5}{8} = \frac{5}{56}$$

and $$P\left(\frac{\bar{A}}{B}\right) = \frac{P(\bar{A} \cap B)}{P(B)} = \frac{P(B) - P(A \cap B)}{P(B)}$$

$$= \frac{\frac{1}{7} - \frac{5}{56}}{\frac{1}{7}} = \frac{8-5}{56 \times \frac{1}{7}} = \frac{3}{8}$$

Example 2 Given two independent events A and B such that $P(A) = 0.3$ and $P(B) = 0.6$, find $P(A' \cap B')$.

Competency Based Que

Sol. Given, $P(A) = 0.3$ and $P(B) = 0.6$

Now, $P(A' \cap B') = P(A \cup B)'$

$= 1 - P[A \cup B]$

$= 1 - [P(A) + P(B) - P(A \cap B)]$

$= 1 - (0.3 + 0.6 - 0.3 \times 0.6)$

[$\because$ A and B are independent events $\therefore P(A \cap B) = P(A)P(B)$]

$= 1 - (0.9 - 0.18) = 1 - (0.72) = 0.28$

Example 3 Suppose E_1 and E_2 are events defined as $P(E_1) = 0.4$, $P(E_2) = y$ and $P(E_1 \cup E_2) = 0.6$. Find the value of y, if

(i) events E_1 and E_2 are independent events.

(ii) events E_1 and E_2 are mutually exclusive.

Sol. We have, $P(E_1) = 0.4$, $P(E_2) = y$ and $P(E_1 \cup E_2) = 0.6$.

(i) Since, E_1 and E_2 are independent events.

$\therefore$ $P(E_1 \cap E_2) = P(E_1) \times (E_2)$

$\Rightarrow P(E_1 \cap E_2) = 0.4 \times y = 0.4y$

$\because$ $P(E_1 \cup E_2) = P(E_1) + P(E_2) - P(E_1 \cap E_2)$

$\therefore$ $0.6 = 0.4 + y - 0.4y \Rightarrow 0.2 = 0.6y$

$\Rightarrow$ $y = \frac{0.2}{0.6} = \frac{1}{3}$

(ii) Since, events E_1 and E_2 are mutually exclusive.

$\therefore$ $E_1 \cap E_2 = \phi$

$\therefore$ $P(E_1 \cup E_2) = P(E_1) + P(E_2) - P(E_1 \cap E_2)$

$\Rightarrow$ $0.6 = 0.4 + y - 0$

$\Rightarrow$ $y = 0.6 - 0.4 = 0.2 = \frac{1}{5}$

Example 4 **A die marked 1, 2, 3 in red and 4, 5, 6 in green is tossed. Let A be the event 'number is even' and B be the event 'number is marked red'. Find whether the events A and B are independent or not.** CBSE 2019

Sol. When a die is thrown, then the sample space is

$$S = \{1, 2, 3, 4, 5, 6\}$$

$\Rightarrow \quad n(S) = 6$

Also, A : number is even and B : number is red.

$\therefore \quad A = \{2, 4, 6\}$ and $B = \{1, 2, 3\}$ and $A \cap B = \{2\}$

$\Rightarrow n(A) = 3, n(B) = 3$ and $n(A \cap B) = 1$

Now, $$P(A) = \frac{n(A)}{n(S)} = \frac{3}{6} = \frac{1}{2},$$

$$P(B) = \frac{n(B)}{n(S)} = \frac{3}{6} = \frac{1}{2}$$

and $$P(A \cap B) = \frac{n(A \cap B)}{n(S)} = \frac{1}{6}$$

Now, $$P(A) \times P(B) = \frac{1}{2} \times \frac{1}{2}$$

$$= \frac{1}{4} \neq \frac{1}{6} = P(A \cap B)$$

$\therefore \quad P(A \cap B) \neq P(A) \times P(B)$

Thus, A and B are not independent events.

Example 5 **Three groups of children contains 2 boys and 2 girls; 1 boy and 3 girls and 3 boys and 1 girl. If one child is selected from each group, then find the chance that the selected children are 1 boy and 2 girls.** CBSE 2023

Sol. Let B_1, B_2, B_3 be the events of selecting a boy from the first, second and third group, respectively. And let G_1, G_2, G_3 be the events of selecting a girl from each group respectively.

Then, $P(B_1) = \frac{2}{4} = \frac{1}{2}$, $P(B_2) = \frac{1}{4}$, $P(B_3) = \frac{3}{4}$, $P(G_1) = \frac{2}{4} = \frac{1}{2}$,

$$P(G_2) = \frac{3}{4}, P(G_3) = \frac{1}{4}$$

$\therefore P(1 \text{ boy and } 2 \text{ girls})$

$$= P[(B_1\, G_2\, G_3) \text{ or } (G_1\, B_2\, G_3) \text{ or } (G_1\, G_2\, B_3)]$$

$$= P(B_1\, G_2\, G_3) + P(G_1\, B_2\, G_3) + P(G_1\, G_2\, B_3)$$

$$= P(B_1)\, P(G_2)\, P(G_3) + P(G_1)\, P(B_2)\, P(G_3) + P(G_1)\, P(G_2)\, P(B_3)$$

[$\because$ events are independent]

$$= \frac{1}{2} \times \frac{3}{4} \times \frac{1}{4} + \frac{1}{2} \times \frac{1}{4} \times \frac{1}{4} + \frac{1}{2} \times \frac{3}{4} \times \frac{3}{4}$$

$$= \frac{3}{32} + \frac{1}{32} + \frac{9}{32} = \frac{13}{32}$$

Example 6 **A and B throw a pair of dice alternately. A wins the game, if he gets a total of 7 and B wins the game, if he gets a total of 10. If A starts the game, then find the probability that B wins.** CBSE 2016

Sol. Here, $n(S) = 6 \times 6 = 36$

Let A = Event of getting a sum of 7 in pair of dice

$= \{(1, 6), (2, 5), (3, 4), (6, 1), (5, 2), (4, 3)\}$

$\Rightarrow \quad n(A) = 6$

and B = Event of getting a sum of 10 in pair of dice

$= \{(4, 6), (5, 5), (6, 4)\}$

$\Rightarrow \quad n(B) = 3$

$$\therefore \quad P(A) = \frac{n(A)}{n(S)} = \frac{6}{36} = \frac{1}{6}$$

and $$P(B) = \frac{n(B)}{n(S)} = \frac{3}{36} = \frac{1}{12}$$

$$\Rightarrow \quad P(\bar{A}) = 1 - \frac{1}{6} = \frac{5}{6}$$

and $$P(\bar{B}) = 1 - \frac{1}{12} = \frac{11}{12}$$

Now, the probability that if A starts the game, then B wins,

$$P(B \quad) = P(\bar{A} \cap B) + P(\bar{A} \cap \bar{B} \cap \bar{A} \cap B) + P(\bar{A} \cap \bar{B} \cap \bar{A} \cap \bar{B} \cap \bar{A} \cap B) + \dots$$

$$= P(\bar{A})\, P(B) + P(\bar{A}) P(\bar{B}) P(\bar{A}) P(B) + P(\bar{A}) P(\bar{B}) P(\bar{A}) P(\bar{B}) P(\bar{A})\, P(B) + \dots$$

[$\because$ events are independent]

$$= \frac{5}{6} \times \frac{1}{12} + \frac{5}{6} \times \frac{11}{12} \times \frac{5}{6} \times \frac{1}{12} + \frac{5}{6} \times \frac{11}{12} \times \frac{5}{6} \times \frac{11}{12} \times \frac{5}{6} \times \frac{1}{12} + \dots$$

$$= \frac{5}{72} + \frac{5}{72} \times \frac{55}{72} + \frac{5}{72} \times \left(\frac{55}{72}\right)^2 + \dots$$

$$= \frac{5}{72}\left[1 + \frac{55}{72} + \left(\frac{55}{72}\right)^2 + \dots\right]$$

$$= \frac{5}{72}\left(\frac{1}{1 - \frac{55}{72}}\right)$$

$\left[\because \text{sum of infinite GP series is } \frac{a}{1-r}\right]$

$$= \frac{5}{72}\left(\frac{1}{17/72}\right)$$

$$= \frac{5}{17}$$

Example 7 *A* and *B* are independent events such that $P(A \cap \overline{B}) = \frac{1}{4}$ and $P(\overline{A} \cap B) = \frac{1}{6}$. Find $P(A)$ and $P(B)$. CBSE 2023

Sol. Given, A and B are two independent events such that

$$P(A \cap \overline{B}) = \frac{1}{4} \text{ and } P(\overline{A} \cap B) = \frac{1}{6}$$

Now, $P(A \cap \overline{B}) = \frac{1}{4}$

$\Rightarrow P(A) \cdot P(\overline{B}) = \frac{1}{4}$

$\Rightarrow P(A)[1 - P(B)] = \frac{1}{4}$ $[\because P(B) + P(\overline{B}) = 1]$

$\Rightarrow P(A) - P(A)\, P \cdot (B) = \frac{1}{4}$ ...(i)

and $P(\overline{A} \cap B) = \frac{1}{6} \Rightarrow P(\overline{A}) \cdot P(B) = \frac{1}{6}$

$\Rightarrow [1 - P(A)]\, P(B) = \frac{1}{6}$

$\Rightarrow P(B) - P(A)\, P(B) = \frac{1}{6}$ ...(ii)

On subtracting Eq. (ii) from Eq. (i), we get

$$P(A) - P(B) = \frac{1}{4} - \frac{1}{6}$$

$\Rightarrow P(A) = \frac{1}{12} + P(B)$

Now, on substituting this value in Eq. (ii), we get

$$P(B) - \left(\frac{1}{12} + P(B)\right) P(B) = \frac{1}{6}$$

Let $P(B) = x$, then $x - \left(\frac{1 + 12x}{12}\right) x = \frac{1}{6}$

$\Rightarrow 12x - x - 12x^2 = 2$

$\Rightarrow 12x^2 - 11x + 2 = 0$

$\Rightarrow 12x^2 - 8x - 3x + 2 = 0$

$\Rightarrow (4x - 1)(3x - 2) = 0$

$\Rightarrow x = \frac{1}{4} \text{ or } x = \frac{2}{3}$

$\Rightarrow P(B) = \frac{1}{4} \text{ or } P(B) = \frac{2}{3}$ [put $x = P(B)$]

Now, if $P(B) = \frac{1}{4}$, then $P(A) = \frac{1}{12} + \frac{1}{4} = \frac{1+3}{12} = \frac{4}{12} = \frac{1}{3}$

and if $P(B) = \frac{2}{3}$, then

$$P(A) = \frac{1}{12} + \frac{2}{3} = \frac{1+8}{12} = \frac{9}{12} = \frac{3}{4}$$

Example 8 Probabilities of solving a specific problem independently by *A* and *B* are $\frac{1}{2}$ and $\frac{1}{3}$, respectively. If both try to solve problem independently, then find the probability that

(i) problem is solved.

(ii) exactly one of them solves the problem.

CBSE 2015C, 11

Sol. Let $P(A)$ = Probability that A solves the problem

$P(B)$ = Probability that B solves the problem

$P(\overline{A})$ = Probability that A does not solve the problem

and $P(\overline{B})$ = Probability that B does not solve the problem

According to the question,

$$P(A) = \frac{1}{2}$$

Then, $P(\overline{A}) = 1 - P(A)$ $[\because P(A) + P(\overline{A}) = 1]$

$= 1 - \frac{1}{2} = \frac{1}{2}$

and $P(B) = \frac{1}{3}$, then

$P(\overline{B}) = 1 - P(B)$

$= 1 - \frac{1}{3} = \frac{2}{3}$

(i) P (problem is solved)

$= P(A \cap \overline{B}) + P(\overline{A} \cap B) + P(A \cap B)$

$= P(A) \cdot P(\overline{B}) + P(\overline{A}) \cdot P(B) + P(A) \cdot P(B)$

[$\because$ A and B are independent events]

$= \left(\frac{1}{2} \times \frac{2}{3}\right) + \left(\frac{1}{2} \times \frac{1}{3}\right) + \left(\frac{1}{2} \times \frac{1}{3}\right)$

$= \frac{2}{6} + \frac{1}{6} + \frac{1}{6} = \frac{4}{6} = \frac{2}{3}$

Hence, probability that the problem is solved, is $\frac{2}{3}$.

(ii) P (exactly one of them solves the problem)

$= P$ (A solves but B does not solve) + P (A does not solve but B solves)

$= P(A \cap \overline{B}) + P(\overline{A} \cap B)$

$= P(A) \cdot P(\overline{B}) + P(\overline{A}) \cdot P(B)$

$= \left(\frac{1}{2} \times \frac{2}{3}\right) + \left(\frac{1}{2} \times \frac{1}{3}\right)$

$= \frac{2}{6} + \frac{1}{6} = \frac{3}{6} = \frac{1}{2}$

Quick Test 2

1. If $P(A)=0.8, P(B)=0.5$ and $P\left(\frac{B}{A}\right)=0.4$, then find $P(A\cap B)$ and also determine the value of $P(A\cup B)$.

2. Two cards are drawn at random and without replacement from a pack of 52 playing cards. Find the probability that both the cards are black. *NCERT*

3. An urn contains 8 white and 4 red balls. Two balls are drawn from the urn one after the other without replacement. What is the probability that both drawn balls are white?

4. Events A and B are such that $P(A)=\frac{1}{2}, P(B)=\frac{7}{12}$ and $P(\text{not } A \text{ or not } B)=\frac{1}{4}$. State whether A and B are independent. *NCERT*

5. If A and B are two independent events, then prove that the probability of occurrence of at least one of A and B is given by $1-P(A')\cdot P(B')$. *Competency Based Que*

6. If A and B are two independent events such that $P(\bar{A}\cap B)=\frac{2}{15}$ and $P(A\cap\bar{B})=\frac{1}{6}$, then find $P(A)$ and $P(B)$. *Competency Based Que*

7. Prove that if E and F are independent events, then the events E and F' are also independent. *CBSE 2017*

8. A fair coin and an unbiased die are tossed together. Let A be the event 'head appears on the coin' and B be the event '3 on the die'. Check whether A and B are independent events or not. *NCERT*

9. A and B throw a pair of dice alternately, till one of them gets a total of 10 and wins the game. Find their respective probabilities of winning, if A starts first. *Competency Based Que*

10. Two dice are thrown together and the total score is noted. The events E, F and G are 'a total of 4', 'a total of 9 or more' and 'a total divisible by 5', respectively. Calculate $P(E), P(F)$ and $P(G)$ and decide which pairs of events, if any are independent? *NCERT Exemplar*

Answers

1. $P(A\cap B)=0.32$ and $P(A\cup B)=0.98$
2. $\frac{25}{102}$
3. $\frac{14}{33}$
4. A and B are not independent events.
6. $P(A)=\frac{1}{5}, P(B)=\frac{1}{6}$ or $P(A)=\frac{5}{6}, P(B)=\frac{4}{5}$
8. A and B are independent events.
9. $P(A)=\frac{12}{13}$ and $P(B)=\frac{11}{23}$
10. $P(E)=\frac{1}{12}, P(F)=\frac{5}{18}, P(G)=\frac{7}{36}$; No pair which is independent.

For Solutions, See QR Code on Pg. 418

13.4 Theorem of Total Probability

A set of events $E_1, E_2, \dots, E_n$ is said to represent a **partition of the sample space** S, if it satisfies the following conditions

- $E_i \cap E_j = \phi, i \neq j; i, j = 1, 2, \dots, n$
- $E_1 \cup E_2 \cup \dots \cup E_n = S$
- $P(E_i) > 0, \forall i = 1, 2, \dots, n$

Let $\{E_1, E_2, \dots, E_n\}$ be a partition of the sample space S and each having non-zero probability of occurrence.

Again, let A be any event associated with S, then

$$P(A) = P(E_1)\cdot P(A/E_1) + P(E_2)\cdot P(A/E_2) + \dots + P(E_n)\cdot P(A/E_n)$$
$$= \sum_{j=1}^{n} P(E_j)\cdot P(A/E_j)$$

13.5 Bayes' Theorem

If $E_1, E_2, \dots, E_n$ are n non-empty events, which constitute a partition of sample space S (or E_i's are mutually exclusive and exhaustive events) i.e. $E_1, E_2, \dots, E_n$ are pairwise disjoint, $E_1 \cup E_2 \cup \dots \cup E_n = S$ and $P(E_i) > 0$, $\forall i = 1, 2, 3, \dots, n$.

Also, let A be any event of non-zero probability, then

$$P(E_i/A) = \frac{P(E_i)\cdot P(A/E_i)}{\sum_{j=1}^{n} P(E_j)\cdot P(A/E_j)}, \text{ for any } i = 1, 2, 3, \dots, n$$

Example 1 **Suppose that 5 men out of 100 and 25 women out of 1000 are good orators. Assuming that there are equal number of men and women, find the probability of choosing a good orator.** *CBSE 2020*

Sol. Let E_1 be the event that selected person is men and E_2 be the event that selected person is women, E_1 and E_2 are mutually exclusive and exhaustive event moreover.

$P(E_1) = P(E_2) = \frac{1}{2}$.

Let E be the event that selected person is good orator.

$\therefore P(E/E_1) = \frac{5}{100} = \frac{1}{20}$ and $P(E/E_2) = \frac{25}{1000} = \frac{1}{40}$

The probability of choosing a good orator,

$$P(E) = P(E_1)\times P(E/E_1) + P(E_2)\times P(E/E_2)$$
$$= \frac{1}{2}\times\frac{1}{20} + \frac{1}{2}\times\frac{1}{40} = \frac{2+1}{2\times 40} = \frac{3}{80}$$

Example 2 There are two coins. One of them is a biased coin such that P (head) : P (tail) is 1 : 3 and the other coin is a fair coin. A coin is selected at random and tossed once. If the coin showed head, then find the probability that it is biased coin. *CBSE 2023*

Sol. Let E_1 = Event of selecting biased coin,

E_2 = Event of selecting fair coin

and A = Event of getting head

Then, $P(E_1) = P(E_2) = \frac{1}{2}; P\left(\frac{A}{E_1}\right) = \frac{1}{4}, P\left(\frac{A}{E_2}\right) = \frac{1}{2}$

By Bayes' theorem,

$$P\left(\frac{E_1}{A}\right) = \frac{P(E_1)\cdot P\left(\frac{A}{E_1}\right)}{P(E_1)\cdot P\left(\frac{A}{E_1}\right) + P(E_2)\cdot P\left(\frac{A}{E_2}\right)}$$

$$= \frac{\frac{1}{2}\cdot\frac{1}{4}}{\frac{1}{2}\cdot\frac{1}{4}+\frac{1}{2}\cdot\frac{1}{2}} = \frac{\frac{1}{8}}{\frac{1}{8}+\frac{1}{4}} = \frac{1}{8}\times\frac{8}{3} = \frac{1}{3}$$

Example 3 A bag contains $(2n+1)$ coins. It is known that $(n-1)$ of these coins have a head on both sides, whereas the rest of the coins are fair. A coin is picked up at random from the bag and is tossed. If the probability that the toss results in a head is 31/42, determine the value of n. *Competency Based Que*

Sol. Number of coins with head on both sides = $(n-1)$

Number of fair coins = $(n+2)$

Let E_1 = Picking a coin with head on both sides,

E_2 = Picking a fair coin

and A = Getting a head on tossing the coin

Then, $P(E_1) = \frac{n-1}{2n+1}$ and $P(E_2) = \frac{n+2}{2n+1}$

$\Rightarrow \quad P\left(\frac{A}{E_1}\right) = 1$ and $P\left(\frac{A}{E_2}\right) = \frac{1}{2}$

$\therefore \quad P(A) = P(E_1)P(A/E_1) + P(E_2)P(A/E_2)$

$$= \frac{n-1}{2n+1}\cdot 1 + \frac{n+2}{2n+1}\cdot\frac{1}{2} = \frac{3n}{2(2n+1)}$$

According to question,

$$\frac{3n}{2(2n+1)} = \frac{31}{42} \Rightarrow 126n = 62\,(2n+1)$$

$\Rightarrow \quad 126n = 124n + 62$

$\therefore \quad n = 31$

EXAMPLE 4 In a Shop X, 30 tins of ghee of Type A and 40 tins of ghee of Type B which look alike, are kept for sale. While in Shop Y, similar 50 tins of ghee of Type A and 60 tins of ghee of Type B are there. One tin of ghee is purchased from one of the randomly selected shop and is found to be of Type B. Find the probability that it is purchased from Shop Y. *CBSE 2020*

Sol. Let E_1 = Getting ghee from Shop X,

E_2 = Getting ghee from Shop Y

and A = Getting Type B ghee

$\therefore \quad P(E_1) = P(E_2) = \frac{1}{2}$ [$\because$ both shops have equal chances]

$P(A/E_1)$ = Probability that Type B ghee is purchased from Shop X

$$= \frac{40}{70} = \frac{4}{7}$$

$P(A/E_2)$ = Probability that Type B ghee is purchased from Shop Y

$$= \frac{60}{110} = \frac{6}{11}$$

Now, by Bayes' theorem, we get

$$P(E_2/A) = \frac{P(E_2)\,P(A/E_2)}{P(E_1)\,P(A/E_1) + P(E_2)\,P(A/E_2)}$$

$$= \frac{\frac{1}{2}\times\frac{6}{11}}{\frac{1}{2}\times\frac{4}{7}+\frac{1}{2}\times\frac{6}{11}} = \frac{\frac{6}{11}}{\frac{4}{7}+\frac{6}{11}}$$

$$= \frac{\frac{6}{11}}{\frac{44+42}{77}} = \frac{42}{86} = \frac{21}{43}$$

Example 5 A letter is known to have come either from TATANAGAR or from CALCUTTA. On the envelope, just two consecutive letter TA are visible. What is the probability that the letter came from TATANAGAR? *NCERT Exemplar*

Sol. Let E_1 = Letter has come from CALCUTTA,

E_2 = Letter has come from TATANAGAR

and E = Two consecutive letters (i.e. alphabets) TA are visible on envelope

$\therefore \quad P(E_1) = \frac{1}{2}, P(E_2) = \frac{1}{2}, P\left(\frac{E}{E_1}\right) = \frac{1}{7}$

[$\because$ 7 pairs of consecutive letters are CA, AL, LC, CU, UT, TT, TA]

and $P\left(\frac{E}{E_2}\right) = \frac{2}{8}$

[$\because$ 8 pairs of consecutive letters are TA, AT, TA, AN, NA, AG, GA, AR]

$$\therefore \quad P\left(\frac{E_2}{E}\right) = \frac{P(E_2)\cdot P\left(\frac{E}{E_2}\right)}{P(E_1)\cdot P\left(\frac{E}{E_1}\right) + P(E_2)\cdot P\left(\frac{E}{E_2}\right)}$$

[using Bayes' theorem]

$$= \frac{\frac{1}{2} \times \frac{2}{8}}{\frac{1}{2} \times \frac{1}{7} + \frac{1}{2} \times \frac{2}{8}} = \frac{\frac{2}{16}}{\frac{8+14}{2 \times 7 \times 8}} = \frac{2 \times 7}{22} = \frac{7}{11}$$

Hence, the probability that the letter TA came from TATANAGAR is $\frac{7}{11}$.

Example 6 **Bag I contains 3 red and 4 black balls, Bag II contains 5 red and 2 black balls. Two balls are transferred at random from Bag I to Bag II and then a ball is drawn at random from Bag II. Find the probability that the drawn ball is red in colour.** CBSE 2024

Sol. Let E_1, E_2, E_3 and A be events such that

E_1 = Two red balls are transferred from Bag I to Bag II,

E_2 = Two black balls are transferred from Bag I to Bag II,

E_3 = Out of two transferred ball one is red and other is black

and A = Drawing a red ball from Bag II

Here, $P\left(\frac{E_1}{A}\right) + P\left(\frac{E_3}{A}\right)$ is required.

Now, $P(E_1) = \frac{{}^3C_2}{{}^7C_2} = \frac{3!}{2!1!} \times \frac{2!5!}{7!} = 3 \times \frac{2}{7 \times 6} = \frac{1}{7}$

$$P(E_2) = \frac{{}^4C_2}{{}^7C_2} = \frac{4!}{2!2!} \times \frac{2!5!}{7!} = \frac{4 \times 3}{2} \times \frac{2}{7 \times 6} = \frac{2}{7}$$

$$P(E_3) = \frac{{}^3C_1 \times {}^4C_1}{{}^7C_2} = \frac{3 \times 4}{1} \times \frac{2!5!}{7!} = \frac{4}{7}$$

$$P\left(\frac{A}{E_1}\right) = \frac{7}{9}, P\left(\frac{A}{E_2}\right) = \frac{5}{9}, P\left(\frac{A}{E_3}\right) = \frac{6}{9}$$

$\therefore P\left(\frac{E_1}{A}\right) + P\left(\frac{E_3}{A}\right)$

$$= \frac{P(E_1) \cdot P\left(\frac{A}{E_1}\right) + P(E_3) \cdot P\left(\frac{A}{E_3}\right)}{P(E_1) \cdot P\left(\frac{A}{E_1}\right) + P(E_2) \cdot P\left(\frac{A}{E_2}\right) + P(E_3) \cdot P\left(\frac{A}{E_3}\right)}$$

$$= \frac{\frac{1}{7} \times \frac{7}{9} + \frac{4}{7} \times \frac{6}{9}}{\frac{1}{7} \times \frac{7}{9} + \frac{2}{7} \times \frac{5}{9} + \frac{4}{7} \times \frac{6}{9}}$$

$$= \frac{\frac{7}{63} + \frac{24}{63}}{\frac{7}{63} + \frac{10}{63} + \frac{24}{63}} = \frac{\frac{31}{63}}{\frac{41}{63}} = \frac{31}{41} = 0.76$$

Example 7 **There are three coins. One is a two headed coin, another is a biased coin that comes up heads 75% of the time and third is an unbiased coin. One of the three coins is chosen at random and tossed. If it shows head, then what is the probability that it is two headed coin?** NCERT, CBSE 2019, 14

Sol. Let us define the events as

E_1 = Selecting a two headed coin,

E_2 = Selecting a biased coin,

E_3 = Selecting an unbiased coin,

A = Head comes up

Here, $P(E_1) = P(E_2) = P(E_3) = 1/3$

[∵ all coins have equal chances]

$P(A/E_1)$ = Probability that head comes up on a two headed coin

$= 1$

$P(A/E_2)$ = Probability that head comes up on a biased coin

$= 75\% = 75/100$

and $P(A/E_3)$ = Probability that head comes up on an unbiased coin

$= 1/2$

Now, by Bayes' theorem, we get

$$P(E_1/A) = \frac{P(E_1) \cdot P(A/E_1)}{\left[P(E_1) \cdot P(A/E_1) + P(E_2) \cdot P(A/E_2) + P(E_3) \cdot P(A/E_3)\right]}$$

$$\therefore \quad P(E_1/A) = \frac{\frac{1}{3} \times 1}{\left(\frac{1}{3} \times 1\right) + \left(\frac{1}{3} \times \frac{75}{100}\right) + \left(\frac{1}{3} \times \frac{1}{2}\right)}$$

$$= \frac{1}{1 + \frac{75}{100} + \frac{1}{2}} = \frac{1}{\frac{100 + 75 + 50}{100}}$$

$$= \frac{100}{225} = \frac{4}{9}$$

Hence, the required probability is $\frac{4}{9}$.

Example 8 **In a factory which manufactures bolts, machines *A*, *B* and *C* manufacture respectively 30%, 50% and 20% of the bolts. Of their outputs, 3%, 4% and 1% respectively are defective bolts. A bolt is drawn at random from the product and is found to be defective. Find the probability that this is not manufactured by Machine *B*.** CBSE 2015

Sol. Let E_1 = Bolt is manufactured by Machine A,

E_2 = Bolt is manufactured by Machine B,

E_3 = Bolt is manufactured by Machine C

and E = Bolt is defective.

Then, we have $P(E_1) = 30\% = \frac{30}{100}$, $P(E_2) = 50\% = \frac{50}{100}$

and $P(E_3) = 20\% = \frac{20}{100}$

Also, given that 3%, 4% and 1% bolts manufactured by machines A, B and C respectively, are defective. So,

$$P\left(\frac{E}{E_1}\right) = 3\% = \frac{3}{100}, P\left(\frac{E}{E_2}\right) = 4\% = \frac{4}{100}, P\left(\frac{E}{E_3}\right) = 1\% = \frac{1}{100}$$

Now, firstly find the probability that selected bolt which is defective is manufactured by Machine B, is

$$P\left(\frac{E_2}{E}\right)=\frac{P(E_2)\cdot P\left(\frac{E}{E_2}\right)}{P(E_1)\cdot P\left(\frac{E}{E_1}\right)+P(E_2)\cdot P\left(\frac{E}{E_2}\right)+P(E_3)\cdot P\left(\frac{E}{E_3}\right)}$$

$$=\frac{\frac{50}{100}\times\frac{4}{100}}{\frac{30}{100}\times\frac{3}{100}+\frac{50}{100}\times\frac{4}{100}+\frac{20}{100}\times\frac{1}{100}}$$

$$=\frac{200}{90+200+20}=\frac{200}{310}$$

$\therefore$ The probability that selected bolt which is defective is not manufactured by Machine B, is

$$1-P\left(\frac{E_2}{E}\right)=1-\frac{200}{310}=\frac{110}{310}=\frac{11}{31}$$

Example 9 **Three persons A, B and C apply for a job of Manager in a private company. Chances of their selection (A, B and C) are in the ratio 1 : 2 : 4. The probabilities that A, B and C can introduce changes to improve profits of the company are 0.8, 0.5 and 0.3, respectively. If the change does not take place, then find the probability that it is due to the appointment of C.** *CBSE 2016*

Sol. Let us define the following events

A = Selecting person A, B = Selecting person B

and C = Selecting person C

$$P(A)=\frac{1}{1+2+4},\ P(B)=\frac{2}{1+2+4}\text{ and }P(C)=\frac{4}{1+2+4}$$

$$\Rightarrow P(A)=\frac{1}{7},\ P(B)=\frac{2}{7}\text{ and }P(C)=\frac{4}{7}$$

Let E = Person introduce the changes in their profit.

Also, given $P\left(\frac{E}{A}\right)=0.8$, $P\left(\frac{E}{B}\right)=0.5$ and $P\left(\frac{E}{C}\right)=0.3$

$$\Rightarrow\quad P\left(\frac{\overline{E}}{A}\right)=1-0.8=0.2,\ P\left(\frac{\overline{E}}{B}\right)=1-0.5=0.5$$

and $$P\left(\frac{\overline{E}}{C}\right)=1-0.3=0.7$$

The probability that change does not take place by the appointment of C,

$$P\left(\frac{C}{\overline{E}}\right)=\frac{P(C)\cdot P\left(\frac{\overline{E}}{C}\right)}{P(A)\times P\left(\frac{\overline{E}}{A}\right)+P(B)\times P\left(\frac{\overline{E}}{B}\right)+P(C)\times P\left(\frac{\overline{E}}{C}\right)}$$

$$=\frac{\frac{4}{7}\times0.7}{\frac{1}{7}\times0.2+\frac{2}{7}\times0.5+\frac{4}{7}\times0.7}=\frac{2.8}{0.2+1.0+2.8}=\frac{2.8}{4}=0.7$$

Hence, the required probability is 0.7.

Quick Test 3

1. Bag I contains 3 black and 2 white balls, Bag II contains 2 black and 4 white balls. A bag and a ball is selected at random. Determine the probability of selecting a black ball. *NCERT Exemplar*

2. There are two bags, one of which contains 3 black and 4 white balls, while the other contains 4 black and 3 white balls. A die is thrown. It shows up 1 or 3, a ball is taken from the first bag, but it shows up any other number, a ball is chosen from the second bag. Find the probability of choosing a black ball.

3. In answering a question on a multiple choice test, a student either knows the answer or guesses. Let 3/5 be the probability that he knows the answers and 2/5 be the probability that he guesses. Assuming that a student who guesses the answer will be correct with probability 1/3. What is the probability that the student knows the answer, given that he answered it correctly?

4. A bag contains 3 red and 7 black balls. Two balls are selected at random one-by-one without replacement. If the second selected ball happens to be red, then what is the probability that the first selected ball is also red? *CBSE 2014C*

5. An insurance company insured 2000 scooter drivers, 4000 car drivers and 6000 truck drivers. The probabilities of an accident for them are 0.01, 0.03 and 0.15, respectively. One of the insured person meets with an accident. What is the probability that he is a scooter driver or a car driver? *Competency Based Que*

6. A doctor is visit to a patient. From the past experience, it is known that the probabilities that he will come by train, bus, scooter or by other means of transport, are respectively $\frac{3}{10},\frac{1}{5},\frac{1}{10}$ and $\frac{2}{5}$. The probabilities that he will be late are $\frac{1}{4},\frac{1}{3}$ and $\frac{1}{12}$, if he comes by train, bus and scooter respectively, but if he comes by other means of transport, then he will not be late. When he arrives, he is late. What is the probability that he comes by train? *NCERT*

7. An urn contains 4 balls. Two balls are drawn at random from the urn (without replacement) and are found to be white. What is the probability that all the balls in the urn are white? *CBSE 2014C*

For Solutions, See QR Code on Pg. 418

Answers

1. $\frac{7}{15}$ 2. $\frac{11}{21}$ 3. $\frac{9}{11}$ 4. $\frac{2}{9}$ 5. $\frac{7}{52}$ 6. $\frac{1}{2}$ 7. $\frac{3}{5}$

EXAM PATTERN QUESTIONS

Objective Type Questions

Multiple Choice Questions

1. The probability that A speaks the truth is $\frac{4}{5}$ and that of B speaking the truth is $\frac{3}{4}$. The probability that they contradict each other in stating the same fact is **CBSE 2023**

(a) $\frac{7}{20}$ (b) $\frac{1}{5}$ (c) $\frac{3}{20}$ (d) $\frac{4}{5}$

2. Five fair coins are tossed simultaneously. The probability of the events that atleast one head comes up is **CBSE 2023**

(a) $\frac{27}{32}$ (b) $\frac{5}{32}$ (c) $\frac{31}{32}$ (d) $\frac{1}{32}$

3. A problem in Mathematics is given to three students whose chances of solving it are $\frac{1}{2}, \frac{1}{3}, \frac{1}{4}$, respectively.

If the events of their solving the problem are independent, then the probability that the problem will be solved, is **CBSE Sample Paper 2023**

(a) $\frac{1}{4}$ (b) $\frac{1}{3}$ (c) $\frac{1}{2}$ (d) $\frac{3}{4}$

4. A bag contains 3 white, 4 black and 2 red balls. If 2 balls are drawn at random (without replacement), then the probability that both the balls are white, is **CBSE 2020**

(a) $\frac{1}{18}$ (b) $\frac{1}{36}$ (c) $\frac{1}{12}$ (d) $\frac{1}{24}$

5. From the set $\{1, 2, 3, 4, 5\}$, two numbers a and $b (a \neq b)$ are chosen at random. The probability that $\frac{a}{b}$ is an integer, is **CBSE 2020**

(a) $\frac{1}{3}$ (b) $\frac{1}{4}$ (c) $\frac{1}{2}$ (d) $\frac{3}{5}$

6. An urn contains 6 balls of which two are red and four are black. Two balls are drawn at random. Probability that they are of the different colours is **CBSE Sample Paper 2020**

(a) $\frac{2}{5}$ (b) $\frac{1}{15}$ (c) $\frac{8}{15}$ (d) $\frac{4}{15}$

7. Three dice are thrown simultaneously. The probability of obtaining a total score of 5 is **CBSE 2020**

(a) $\frac{5}{216}$ (b) $\frac{1}{6}$ (c) $\frac{1}{36}$ (d) $\frac{1}{49}$

8. A die is thrown once. Let A be the event that the number obtained is greater than 3. Let B be the event that the number obtained is less than 5. Then, $P(A \cup B)$ is **CBSE 2020**

(a) $\frac{2}{5}$ (b) $\frac{3}{5}$ (c) 0 (d) 1

9. If A and B are events such that $P\left(\frac{A}{B}\right) = P\left(\frac{B}{A}\right) \neq 0$, then **CBSE 2024**

(a) $A \subset B$, but $A \neq B$ (b) $A = B$
(c) $A \cap B = \phi$ (d) $P(A) = P(B)$

10. If $P(A \cap B) = \frac{1}{8}$ and $P(\overline{A}) = \frac{3}{4}$, then $P\left(\frac{B}{A}\right)$ is equal to **CBSE 2023**

(a) $\frac{1}{2}$ (b) $\frac{1}{3}$ (c) $\frac{1}{6}$ (d) $\frac{2}{3}$

11. For two events A and B, if $P(A) = 0.4$, $P(B) = 0.8$ and $P(B / A) = 0.6$, then $P(A \cup B)$ is equal to **CBSE 2023**

(a) 0.24 (b) 0.3
(c) 0.48 (d) 0.96

12. If the sum of numbers obtained on throwing a pair of dice is 9, then the probability that number obtained on one of the dice is 4, is **CBSE 2023**

(a) $\frac{1}{9}$ (b) $\frac{4}{9}$ (c) $\frac{1}{18}$ (d) $\frac{1}{2}$

13. For any two events A and B, if $P(\overline{A}) = \frac{1}{2}$, $P(\overline{B}) = \frac{2}{3}$ and $P(A \cap B) = \frac{1}{4}$, then $P\left(\frac{\overline{A}}{\overline{B}}\right)$ is equal to **CBSE 2023**

(a) $\frac{3}{8}$ (b) $\frac{5}{8}$ (c) $\frac{1}{8}$ (d) $\frac{1}{4}$

14. A and B are two events such that $P(A \cup B) = \frac{3}{4}$, $P(A \cap B) = \frac{1}{4}$, $P(\overline{A}) = \frac{2}{3}$, then $P(\overline{A} \cap B)$ is equal to **Diksha App**

(a) $\frac{5}{12}$ (b) $\frac{3}{8}$ (c) $\frac{5}{8}$ (d) $\frac{7}{4}$

15. A coin is tossed and a card is selected at random from a well shuffled pack of 52 playing cards. The probability of getting head on the coin and a face card from the pack is **CBSE 2025**

(a) $\frac{3}{12}$ (b) $\frac{3}{26}$ (c) $\frac{19}{26}$ (d) $\frac{3}{13}$

16. If A and B are two events such that $P(A) = 0.2$, $P(B) = 0.4$ and $P(A \cup B) = 0.5$, then value of $P(A/B)$ is **CBSE Sample Paper 2020**

(a) 0.1 (b) 0.25 (c) 0.5 (d) 0.08

17. If A and B are two events such that $P(B) = \frac{1}{5}$, $P\left(\frac{A}{B}\right) = \frac{2}{3}$ and $P(A \cup B) = \frac{3}{5}$, then $P(A)$ is **CBSE 2025**

(a) $\frac{10}{15}$ (b) $\frac{2}{15}$ (c) $\frac{1}{5}$ (d) $\frac{8}{15}$

18. If $P\left(\frac{A}{B}\right) = 0.3$, $P(A) = 0.4$ and $P(B) = 0.8$, then $P\left(\frac{B}{A}\right)$ is equal to **CBSE 2023**

(a) 0.6 (b) 0.3 (c) 0.06 (d) 0.4

19. The events E and F are independent. If $P(E) = 0.3$ and $P(E \cup F) = 0.5$, then $P(E/F) - P(F/E)$ is equal to **CBSE 2023**

(a) $\frac{1}{7}$ (b) $\frac{2}{7}$ (c) $\frac{3}{35}$ (d) $\frac{1}{70}$

20. The probability that A speaks truth is $\frac{3}{5}$ and for B is $\frac{3}{4}$, then probability that they contradict each other when asked to speak on a fact.

(a) $\frac{4}{5}$ (b) $\frac{1}{5}$ (c) $\frac{9}{20}$ (d) $\frac{3}{20}$

21. It is given that events A and B are such that $P(A) = \frac{1}{4}$, $P\left(\frac{A}{B}\right) = \frac{1}{2}$ and $P\left(\frac{B}{A}\right) = \frac{2}{3}$, then $P(B)$ is equal to **Diksha App**

(a) $\frac{2}{3}$ (b) $\frac{1}{2}$ (c) $\frac{1}{6}$ (d) $\frac{1}{3}$

22. A mapping is selected at random from set $A = \{1, 2, ..., 20\}$ into itself. The probability that mapping selected is an injective, is **Competency Based Que**

(a) $\frac{20}{20^{20}}$ (b) $\frac{19!}{20^{19}}$

(c) $\frac{19}{20}$ (d) None of these

23. If A and B are two events such that $P(A) = \frac{1}{3}$, $P(B) = \frac{1}{4}$ and $P\left(\frac{A}{B}\right) = \frac{1}{5}$, then $P(A' \cap B')$ is equal to

(a) $\frac{1}{12}$ (b) $\frac{3}{4}$ (c) $\frac{7}{15}$ (d) $\frac{3}{16}$

24. The chances that doctor A will diagnose a disease X correctly is 60%. The chances that a patient will die by his treatment after correct diagnose is 40% and the chance of death by wrong diagnose is 70%. A patient of doctor A, who had disease X, died. What is the chance that his disease was diagnosed correctly? **CBSE QB**

(a) $\frac{7}{13}$ (b) $\frac{3}{10}$ (c) $\frac{6}{13}$ (d) $\frac{7}{10}$

Assertion-Reason Based Questions

Directions (Q. Nos. 25-33) *In the questions given below are two statements labelled as Assertion (A) and Reason (R). In the context of the two statements, which one of the following is correct?*

(a) Both A and R are correct; R is the correct explanation of A.
(b) Both A and R are correct; R is not the correct explanation of A.
(c) A is correct; R is incorrect.
(d) R is correct; A is incorrect.

25. Two coins are tossed once.

Assertion (A) If E : tail appears on one coin and F : one coin shows head, then $P(E/F)$ is 1.

Reason (R) If E : no tail appears and F : no head appears, then $P(E/F)$ is 0.

26. **Assertion** (A) Two coins are tossed simultaneously. The probability getting two heads, if it is known that atleast one head comes up, is $\frac{1}{3}$.

Reason (R) Let E and F be two events with a random experiment, $P\left(\frac{F}{E}\right) = \frac{P(E \cap F)}{P(E)}$. **CBSE 2023**

27. **Assertion** (A) If A and B are two events such that $0 < P(A), P(B) < 1$, then $P(A/\overline{B}) + P(\overline{A}/\overline{B}) = 3/2$.

Reason (R) If A and B are two events such that $0 < P(A)$, $P(B) < 1$, then $P(A/B) = \frac{P(A \cap B)}{P(B)}$ and $P(\overline{B}) = P(A \cap \overline{B}) + P(\overline{A} \cap \overline{B})$.

28. **Assertion** (A) Three cards are drawn from a well shuffled deck of 52 cards without replacement, then the probability that first two cards are black and third card is red is $\frac{13}{102}$.

Reason (R) For three events,

$P(A \cap B \cap C) = P(A) \cdot P\left(\frac{B}{A}\right) \cdot P\left(\frac{C}{A \cap B}\right)$.

29. **Assertion** (A) Consider the experiment of drawing a card from a deck of 52 playing cards, in which the elementary events are assumed to be equally likely. If E and F denote the events the card drawn is a spade and the card drawn is an ace respectively, then $P(E/F) = \frac{1}{4}$ and $P(F/E) = \frac{1}{13}$.

Reason (R) E and F are two events such that the probability of occurrence of one of them is not affected by occurrence of the other. Such events are called independent events.

30. **Assertion** (A) If A and B are independent events such that $P(A) = \frac{3}{5}$ and $P(B) = \frac{1}{5}$, then $P(A \cap B)$ is $\frac{3}{25}$.

Reason (R) Two cards are drawn at random and without replacement from a pack of 52 playing cards. Then, the probability that both the cards are red, is $\frac{25}{102}$. **CBSE 2025**

31. **Assertion** (A) In rolling a dice, event $A = \{1, 3, 5\}$ and event $B = \{2, 4\}$ are mutually exclusive events.

Reason (R) In a sample space, two events are mutually exclusive if they do not occur at the same time.

32. **Assertion** (A) Let A and B be two independent events and $P(A) = 0.3$, $P(A \cup \overline{B}) = 0.8$, then $P(B) = \frac{2}{7}$.

Reason (R) $P(\overline{E}) = 1 - P(E)$, where E be any event.

33. **Assertion** (A) Three coins are tossed, consider the event E 'three heads or three tails' and F 'atmost two heads'. Events E and F are independent.

Reason (R) Two events are independents if $P(A \cap B) = P(A) \cdot P(B)$.

Case Study Based Questions

34. There are different types of Yoga which involve the usage of different poses of Yoga Asanas, Meditation and Pranayam as shown in the figure below.

Types of Yoga

The Venn diagram below represents the probabilities of three different types of Yoga, A, B and C performed by the people of a society. Further, it is given that probability of a member performing type C Yoga is 0.44.

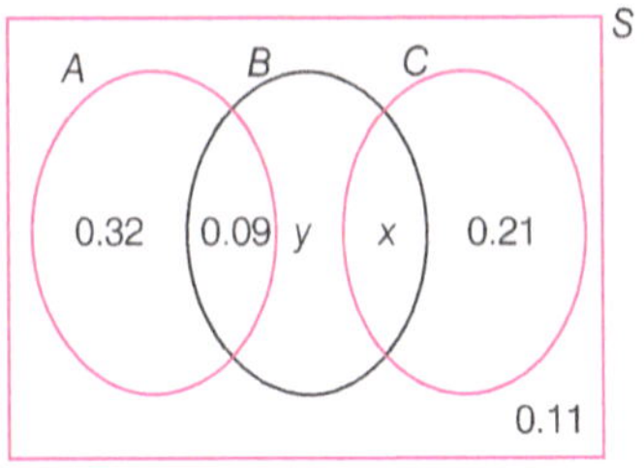

On the basis of the above information, answer the following questions.

(i) Find the value of x.

(ii) Find the value of y.

(iii) (a) Find $P\left(\frac{C}{B}\right)$.

Or

(b) Find the probability that a randomly selected person of the society does yoga of type A or B but not C. **CBSE 2023**

35. Read the following passage and answer the questions given below.

There are two anti-aircraft guns, named as A and B. The probabilities that the shell fired from them hits an airplane are 0.3 and 0.2, respectively. Both of them fired one shell at an airplane at the same time.

(i) What is the probability that the shell fired from exactly one of them hit the plane?

(ii) If it is known that the shell fired from exactly one of them hit the plane, then what is the probability that it was fired from B? **CBSE Sample Paper 2023**

36. In a clinic, out of 40 patients who are waiting to see the doctor.

- 24 have cold
- 18 have fever
- 9 have migraine
- 4 have both cold and fever
- 6 have both fever and migraine
- 3 have both migraine and cold
- 2 have all the three

(**Note** Assume that each of the 40 patients present is suffering from one or more of the 3 ailment - cold, fever or migraine only.)

Based on the above information, answer the following questions.

(i) If a patient is selected at random, find the probability that he/she does not have migraine given that he/she has fever. Show your work.

(ii) If a patient is selected at random, what is the probability that he/she has cold or fever or both, given that he/she has migraine? Show your work. **CBSE QB**

37. A departmental store sends bills to charge its customers once a month. Past experience shows that 70% of its customers pay their first month bill in time. The store also found that the customer who pays the bill in time has the probability of 0.8 of paying in time next month and the customer who does not pay in time has the probability of 0.4 of paying in time the next month. **CBSE 2024**

Based on the above information, answer the following questions.

(i) Let E_1 and E_2 respectively denote the event of customer paying or not paying the first month bill in time.

Find $P(E_1)$ and $P(E_2)$.

(ii) Let A denotes the event of customer paying second month's bill in time, then find $P\left(\frac{A}{E_1}\right)$ and $P\left(\frac{A}{E_2}\right)$.

(iii) (a) Find the probability of customer paying second month's bill in time.

Or

(b) Find the probability of customer paying first month's bill in time, if it is found that customer has paid the second month's bill in time.

38. A building contractor undertakes a job to construct 4 flats on a plot along with parking area. Due to strike, the probability of many construction workers not being present for the job is 0.65. The probability that many are not present and still the work gets completed on time is 0.35. The probability that work will be completed on time when all workers are present is 0.80.

Let E_1 : represents the event when many workers were not present for the job; E_2 : represents the event when all workers were present; and E : represents completing the construction work on time.

Based on the above information, answer the following questions.

(i) What is the probability that all the workers are present for the job?

(ii) What is the probability that construction will be completed on time?

(iii) (a) What is the probability that many workers are not present given that the construction work is completed on time?

Or (b) What is the probability that all workers were present given that the construction job was completed on time? **CBSE 2023**

39. Recent studies suggest that roughly 12% of the world population is left handed.

Roughly 12% of the world is Left Handed

Depending upon the parents, the chances of having a left handed child are as follows :

A: When both father and mother are left handed : Chances of left handed child is 24%.

B: When father is right handed and mother is left handed : Chances of left handed child is 22%.

C: When father is left handed and mother is right handed : Chances of left handed child is 17%.

D: When both father and mothers are right handed : Chances of left handed child is 9%.

Assuming that $P(A) = P(B) = P(C) = P(D) = \frac{1}{4}$ and

L denotes the event that child is left handed.

Based on the above information, answer the following questions.

(i) Find $P(L / C)$. (ii) Find $P(\bar{L} / A)$.

(iii) (a) Find $P(A / L)$.

Or (b) Find the probability that a randomly selected child is left handed given that exactly one of the parents is left handed. **CBSE 2023**

Subjective Questions

Very Short Answer Type Questions

1. Four distinct numbers are chosen randomly from the first 60 natural numbers. Find the probability that all the four numbers are divisible by both 3 and 4.

2. There are 40 tickets bearing numbers from 1 to 40. One ticket is drawn at random. Find the probability that the number on it is a multiple of 3 or 5.

3. The probability that A hits the target is $\frac{1}{3}$ and the probability that B hits it is $\frac{2}{5}$. If both try to hit the target independently, find the probability that the target is hit. **CBSE 2022 (Term II)**

4. The probabilities of A and B solving a problem independently are $\frac{1}{3}$ and $\frac{1}{4}$, respectively. If both of them try to solve the problem independently, then what is the probability that the problem is solved? **CBSE Sample paper 2021**

5. The probability that it will rain on any particular day is 50%. Find the probability that it rains only on first 4 days of the week. **CBSE Sample paper 2021**

6. If A and B are two events such that $P(A) = 0.4, P(B) = 0.8$ and $P(B/A) = 0.6$, then find $P(A/B)$. **CBSE Sample Paper 2018**

7. Evaluate $P(A \cup B)$, if $2P(A) = P(B) = \frac{5}{13}$ and $P(A/B) = \frac{2}{5}$. **CBSE 2018C**

8. Given that E and F are events such that $P(E) = 0.6, P(F) = 0.3$ and $P(E \cap F) = 0.2$.
Find $P\left(\frac{E}{F}\right)$ and $P\left(\frac{F}{E}\right)$. **NCERT**

9. A speaks truth in 80% cases and B speaks truth in 90% cases. In what percentage of cases are they likely to agree with each other in stating the same fact? **CBSE Sample Paper 2020**

10. If $P(A) = \frac{4}{5}$ and $P(A \cap B) = \frac{7}{10}$, then find $P(B/A)$. **NCERT Exemplar**

Short Answer Type Questions

11. If A and B are two events such that
$P(A) = \frac{1}{4},\ P(B) = \frac{1}{6}$ and $P(A \cap B) = \frac{1}{7}$,
then find (i) $P(A \cup B)$ (ii) $P\left(\frac{\overline{B}}{\overline{A}}\right)$.

12. Two dice are thrown. Find the probability of getting an even number on first die, if the outcomes on the two dice always exhibits a sum of 8.

13. An anti-aircraft gun can take a maximum of 4 shots at an enemy plane moving away from it. The probabilities of hitting the plane at the first, second, third and fourth shots are 0.4, 0.3, 0.2 and 0.1, respectively. What is the probability that atleast one shot hits the plane?

14. A speaks truth in 75% of the cases, while B in 90% of the cases. In what percent of cases are they likely to contradict each other in stating the same fact? Do you think that statement of B is true? **CBSE 2013**

15. P speaks truth in 70% of the cases and Q in 80% of the cases. In what percent of cases are they likely to agree in stating the same fact? Do you think, when they agree, means both are speaking truth? **CBSE 2013**

16. A speaks truth in 60% of the cases, while B in 90% of the cases. In what percent of cases are they likely to contradict each other in stating the same fact? In the cases of contradiction do you think, the statement of B will carry more weight as he speaks truth in more number of cases than A? **CBSE 2013**

17. An unbiased die is thrown twice. Let the event A be 'odd number on the first throw' and B be the event 'odd number on the second throw'. Check the independent of the events A and B.

18. A die marked 1, 2, 3 in red and 4, 5, 6 in green is tossed. Let A be the event, 'number is odd' and B be the event, 'number is green'. Are A and B independent? **NCERT**

19. Assume that each born child is equally likely to be a boy or a girl. If a family has two children, then what is the conditional probability that both are girls? Given that
(i) the youngest is a girl?
(ii) atleast one is a girl? **CBSE 2014**

20. Let bag A contains 4 black and 6 red balls and bag B contains 7 black and 3 red balls. A die is thrown. If 1 or 2 appears on it, then bag A is chosen, otherwise bag B. If two balls are drawn at random (without replacement) from the selected bag, then find the probability of one of them being red and another black. **CBSE 2015**

21. A bag contains $(2n + 1)$ coins. It is known that n of these coins have a head on both its sides whereas the rest of the coins are fair. A coin is picked up at random from the bag and is tossed. If the probability that the toss results in a head is $\frac{31}{42}$, then find the value of n. **CBSE Sample Paper 2017**

22. Bag I contains 3 red and 4 black balls and Bag II contains 4 red and 5 black balls. One ball is transferred from Bag I to Bag II and then ball is drawn from Bag II. The ball so drawn is found to be red in colour. Find the probability that the transferred ball is black. **NCERT**

23. Suppose a girl throws a die. If she gets 1 or 2, she tosses a coin three times and notes the number of tails. If she gets 3, 4, 5 or 6, she tosses a coin once and notes whether a 'head' or 'tail' is obtained. If she obtained exactly one 'tail', what is the probability that she threw 3, 4, 5 or 6 with the die? **CBSE 2018**

24. Suppose a girl throws a die. If she gets a 5 or 6, she tosses a coin three times and notes the number of heads. If she gets 1, 2, 3 or 4, she tosses a coin once and notes whether a head or tail is obtained. If she obtained exactly one head, then what is the probability that she threw 1, 2, 3 or 4 with the die? **NCERT**

25. Two groups are competing for the positions of the Board of Directors of a corporation. The probabilities that the first and second group will win are 0.6 and 0.4, respectively. Further, if the first group wins, the probability of introducing a new product is 0.7 and the corresponding probability is 0.3 if the second group wins. Find the probability that the new product introduced way by the second group. **CBSE 2018C**

26. Bag I contains 1 white, 2 black and 3 red balls; Bag II contains 2 white, 1 black and 1 red balls; Bag III contains 4 white, 3 black and 2 red balls. A bag is chosen at random and two balls are drawn from it with replacement. They happen to be one white and one red. What is the probability that they came from Bag III? **CBSE Sample Paper 2018**

27. A bag X contains 4 white balls and 2 black balls, while another bag Y contains 3 white balls and 3 black balls. Two balls are drawn (without replacement) at random from one of the bags and were found to be one white and one black. Find the probability that the balls were drawn from bag Y. **CBSE 2016**

28. Three machines E_1, E_2 and E_3 in a certain factory producing electric bulbs, produce 50%, 25% and 25% respectively, of the total daily output of electric bulbs. It is known that 4% of the bulbs produced by each of machines E_1 and E_2 are defective and that 5% of those produced by machine E_3 are defective. If one bulb is picked up at random from a day's production, calculate the probability that it is defective. **CBSE 2015**

Long Answer Type Questions

29. The odds against a man who is 45 yr old, living till he is 70 are 7 : 5 and the odds against his wife who is now 36, living till she is 61 are 5 : 3. Find the probability that

(i) the couple will be alive 25 yr hence.

(ii) atleast one of them will be alive 25 yr hence.

30. A manufacturer has three machine operators A, B and C. The first operator A produces 1% of defective items, whereas the other two operators B and C produces 5% and 7% defective items, respectively. A is on the job for 50% of the time, B on the job 30% of the time and C on the job for 20% of the time.

All the items are put into one stockpile and then one items is chosen at random from this and is found to be defective. What is the probability that it was produced by A? **CBSE 2019**

31. A man is known to speak the truth 3 out of 5 times. He throws a die and reports that it is 1. Find the probability that it is actually 1. **CBSE 2014C**

32. A card from a pack of 52 playing cards is lost. From the remaining cards of the pack three cards are drawn at random (without replacement) and are found to be all spades. Find the probability of the lost card being a spade. **CBSE 2014**

33. An insurance company insured 2000 scooter drivers, 4000 car drivers and 6000 truck drivers, the probability of their meeting an accident respectively are 0.01, 0.03 and 0.15. One of the insured persons meets with an accident. What is the probability that he is a car driver? **CBSE 2012C**

34. There are three coins. One is a two headed coin (having head on both faces), another is a biased coin that comes up heads 75% of the times and third is also a biased coin that comes up tails 40% of the times. One of the three coins is chosen at random and tossed and it shows head. What is the probability that it was the two headed coin? **CBSE 2014**

35. A bag contains 5 red and 4 black balls, a second bag contains 3 red and 6 black balls. One of the two bags is selected at random and two balls are drawn at random (without replacement) both of which are found to be red. Find the probability that the balls are drawn from the second bag. **CBSE 2019**

36. Bag A contains 3 red and 5 black balls, while bag B contains 4 red and 4 black balls. Two balls are transferred at random from bag A to bag B and then a ball is drawn from bag B at random. If the ball drawn from bag B is found to be red, find the probability that two red balls were transferred from A to B. **CBSE 2016**

37. A bag contains 4 red and 4 black balls, another bag contains 2 red and 6 black balls. One of the two bags is selected at random and a ball is drawn at random from the bag and is found to be red. Find the probability that the balls are drawn from the first bag.

38. By examining the chest X-ray, the probability that TB is detected when a person is actually suffering is 0.99. The probability of an healthy person diagnosed to have TB is 0.001. In a certain city, 1 in 1000 people suffers from TB. A person is selected at random and is diagnosed to have TB. What is the probability that he actually has TB? **NCERT Exemplar**

39. A laboratory blood test is 99% effective in detecting a certain disease,when it is infact present. However, the test also yields a false positive result for 0.5% of the healthy person tested (i.e. if a healthy person is tested, then with probability 0.005, the test will imply he has the disease). If 0.1% of the population actually has the disease, then what is the probability that a person has disease, given that his test result is positive? **NCERT**

40. There are four boxes, *A*, *B*, *C* and *D*, contaning marbles. *A* contains 1 red, 6 white and 3 black marbles; *B* contains 6 red, 2 white and 2 black marbles; *C* contains 8 red, 1 white and 1 black marbles; and *D* contains 6 white and 4 black marbles. One of the boxes is selected at random and a single marble is drawn from it. If the marble is red, then what is the probability that it was drawn from the Box *A*?

41. Among the students in a college, it is known that 60% reside in hostel and 40% are day scholars (not residing in hostel). Previous year results report that 30% of all students who reside in hostel attain *A* grade and 20% of day scholars attain *A* grade in their annual exams. At the end of year, one student is chosen at random from the college and he has *A* grade, what is the probability that the student is a hosteler? **CBSE 2012, 11C**

42. It is known that 20% of the students in a school have above 90% attendance and 80% of the students are irregular. Past year results show that 80% of students who have above 90% attendance and 20% of irregular students get *A* grade in their annual examination. At the end of a year, a student is chosen at random from the school and is found to have an '*A*' grade. What is the probability that the student is irregular? **CBSE 2024C**

43. Assume that the chances of a patient having a heart attack is 40%. Assuming that a meditation and yoga course reduces the risk of heart attack by 30% and prescription of certain drug reduces its chance by 25%. At a time, a patient can choose anyone of the two options with equal probabilities. It is given that after going through one of the two options, the patient selected at random suffers a heart attack. Find the probability that the patient followed a course of meditation and yoga. Interpret the result and state which of the above stated methods, is more beneficial for the patient? **CBSE 2013**

Hints & Solutions

Objective Type Questions

1. (a) The probability that *A* speaks the truth, $P(A)=\frac{4}{5}$

The probability that *A* does not speak the truth,

$$P(\overline{A})=1-\frac{4}{5}=\frac{1}{5}$$

The probability that *B* speaks the truth, $P(B)=\frac{3}{4}$

The probability that *B* does not speak truth,

$$P(\overline{B})=1-\frac{3}{4}=\frac{1}{4}$$

Now, the probability of they contradict each other

$$=P(A)\cdot P(\overline{B})+P(\overline{A})\cdot P(B)$$

$$=\frac{4}{5}\times\frac{1}{4}+\frac{1}{5}\times\frac{3}{4}=\frac{1}{5}+\frac{3}{20}=\frac{7}{20}$$

2. (c) Total number of outcomes $=2^5=32$

Probability of getting all tails $=\frac{1}{32}$

$\therefore$ Probability of getting atleast one head

$=1-$ Probability of getting all tails

$$=1-\frac{1}{32}=\frac{31}{32}$$

3. (d) Let *A*, *B* and *C* be the respective events of solving the problem by first, second and third students.

Then, $P(A)=\frac{1}{2}$, $P(B)=\frac{1}{3}$ and $P(C)=\frac{1}{4}$

The problem will be solved if one or more of them can solve the problem.

The probability is

$$P(A)\cdot P(\overline{B})\,P(\overline{C})+P(\overline{A})\,P(B)\,P(\overline{C})+P(\overline{A})\,P(\overline{B})\,P(C)+P(A)\,P(B)\,P(\overline{C})+P(A)\,P(\overline{B})\,P(C)+P(\overline{A})\,P(B)\,P(C)+P(A)\,P(B)\,P(C)$$

$$=\frac{1}{2}\cdot\frac{2}{3}\cdot\frac{3}{4}+\frac{1}{2}\cdot\frac{1}{3}\cdot\frac{3}{4}+\frac{1}{2}\cdot\frac{2}{3}\cdot\frac{1}{4}+\frac{1}{2}\cdot\frac{1}{3}\cdot\frac{3}{4}+\frac{1}{2}\cdot\frac{2}{3}\cdot\frac{1}{4}+\frac{1}{2}\cdot\frac{1}{3}\cdot\frac{1}{4}+\frac{1}{2}\cdot\frac{1}{3}\cdot\frac{1}{4}$$

[$\because$ *A*, *B* and *C* are independent events]

$$=\frac{1}{4}+\frac{1}{8}+\frac{1}{12}+\frac{1}{8}+\frac{1}{12}+\frac{1}{24}+\frac{1}{24}=\frac{3}{4}$$

4. (c) We have, 3 white, 4 black and 2 red balls.

Total number of balls $= 3 + 4 + 2 = 9$

Two balls are drawn at random (without replacement).

Then, the probability that both the balls are white $= \frac{3}{9} \times \frac{2}{8}$

$= \frac{6}{72} = \frac{1}{12}$

5. (c) We have set of numbers {1, 2, 3, 4, 5}.

Sample space of choosing two numbers $= {}^5C_2 = \frac{5 \times 4}{1 \times 2} = 10$

Favourable outcomes are $\left(\frac{2}{1}, \frac{3}{1}, \frac{4}{1}, \frac{5}{1}, \frac{4}{2}\right)$ i.e. 5 in number

$\therefore$ Required probability $= \frac{5}{10} = \frac{1}{2}$

6. (c) Let E be the event of getting two balls of different colours.

Then, $n(E) = {}^2C_1 \times {}^4C_1 = 8$

and $n(S) = {}^6C_2 = 15$

$\therefore$ Required probability, $P(E) = \frac{n(E)}{n(S)} = \frac{8}{15}$

7. (c) Three dice are thrown simultaneously.

Then, favourable outcomes of total score of 5

$= \{(1, 1, 3), (1, 3, 1), (3, 1, 1), (1, 2, 2)\ (2, 1, 2)\ (2, 2, 1)\}$

i.e. 6 in number

Total number of outcomes $= 6^3 = 216$

$\therefore$ Required probability $= \frac{6}{216} = \frac{1}{36}$

8. (d) We have, $A = \{4, 5, 6\}$ and $B = \{1, 2, 3, 4\}$

Now, $A \cap B = \{4\}$

Now, $P(A \cup B) = P(A) + P(B) - P(A \cap B)$

$= \frac{3}{6} + \frac{4}{6} - \frac{1}{6}$

$= \frac{6}{6} = 1$

9. (d) Given, $P\left(\frac{A}{B}\right) = P\left(\frac{B}{A}\right) \neq 0$

Then, $\frac{P(A \cap B)}{P(B)} = \frac{P(B \cap A)}{P(A)}$

$\Rightarrow \frac{1}{P(B)} = \frac{1}{P(A)}$ $[\because P(A \cap B) \neq 0]$

$\Rightarrow P(A) = P(B)$

10. (a) Given, $P(A \cap B) = \frac{1}{8}$ and $P(\bar{A}) = \frac{3}{4}$

Now, $P\left(\frac{B}{A}\right) = \frac{P(A \cap B)}{P(A)} = \frac{P(A \cap B)}{1 - P(\bar{A})}$

$= \frac{1/8}{1 - \frac{3}{4}} = \frac{1/8}{1/4} = \frac{4}{8} = \frac{1}{2}$

11. (d) Given, $P(A) = 0.4$, $P(B) = 0.8$ and $P(B / A) = 0.6$

We know that $P\left(\frac{B}{A}\right) = \frac{P(B \cap A)}{P(A)} = \frac{P(A \cap B)}{P(A)}$

$\Rightarrow 0.6 = \frac{P(A \cap B)}{0.4} \Rightarrow P(A \cap B) = 0.24$

Now, $P(A \cup B) = P(A) + P(B) - P(A \cap B)$

$= 0.4 + 0.8 - 0.24 = 0.96$

12. (d) **Hint** In two throw of a dice the sample space S is given by,

$n(S) = 6 \times 6 = 36$

Let E = Event of getting a sum of 9

$E = \{(3, 6)\ (4, 5)\ (5, 4)\ (6, 3)\}$

$\Rightarrow n(E) = 4$

Let F = Event of getting a 4 on one of the dice

$F = \{(4, 1), (4, 2), (4, 3), (4, 4), (4, 5), (4, 6), (1, 4), (2, 4), (3, 4), (5, 4), (6, 4)\}$

$\therefore E \cap F = \{(4, 5), (5, 4)\}$

$\therefore n(E \cap F) = 2$

Required probability $= P\left(\frac{F}{E}\right) = \frac{P(F \cap E)}{P(E)} = \frac{2/36}{4/36} = \frac{1}{2}$

13. (b) Given, $P(\bar{A}) = \frac{1}{2}$, $P(\bar{B}) = \frac{2}{3}$ and $P(A \cap B) = \frac{1}{4}$

$\therefore P(A) = 1 - \frac{1}{2} = \frac{1}{2}$ and $P(B) = 1 - \frac{2}{3} = \frac{1}{3}$

Now, $P(A \cup B) = P(A) + P(B) - P(A \cap B)$

$= \frac{1}{2} + \frac{1}{3} - \frac{1}{4} = \frac{6 + 4 - 3}{12} = \frac{7}{12}$

We have to find,

$$P\left(\frac{\bar{A}}{\bar{B}}\right) = \frac{P(\bar{A} \cap \bar{B})}{P(\bar{B})} = \frac{P(\overline{A \cup B})}{P(\bar{B})} = \frac{1 - P(A \cup B)}{P(\bar{B})}$$

$$= \frac{1 - \frac{7}{12}}{2/3} = \frac{5/12}{2/3} = \frac{5}{12} \times \frac{3}{2} = \frac{5}{8}$$

14. (a) We have,

$P(A \cup B) = \frac{3}{4}$, $P(A \cap B) = \frac{1}{4}$ and $P(\bar{A}) = \frac{2}{3}$

$\therefore P(A) = 1 - P(\bar{A})$

$\Rightarrow P(A) = 1 - \frac{2}{3} = \frac{1}{3}$

We know that

$P(A \cup B) = P(A) + P(B) - P(A \cap B)$

$\Rightarrow \frac{3}{4} = \frac{1}{3} + P(B) - \frac{1}{4}$

$\Rightarrow P(B) = \frac{3}{4} + \frac{1}{4} - \frac{1}{3} = 1 - \frac{1}{3} = \frac{2}{3}$

Now, $P(\bar{A} \cap B) = P(B) - P(A \cap B)$

$= \frac{2}{3} - \frac{1}{4} = \frac{8 - 3}{12} = \frac{5}{12}$

15. (b) Let A be the event of getting head on the coin and B be the event of getting face card.

$$\therefore \quad P(A) = \frac{1}{2}, P(B) = \frac{12}{52} = \frac{3}{13}$$

$$\therefore P(A \cap B) = P(A) \cdot P(B)$$

$$= \frac{1}{2} \times \frac{3}{13} = \frac{3}{26}$$

16. (b) We know that

$$P(A \cup B) = P(A) + P(B) - P(A \cap B)$$

$$\Rightarrow \quad 0.5 = 0.2 + 0.4 - P(A \cap B)$$

$$\Rightarrow \quad 0.5 = 0.6 - P(A \cap B)$$

$$\Rightarrow \quad P(A \cap B) = 0.6 - 0.5 = 0.1$$

$$\therefore \quad P\left(\frac{A}{B}\right) = \frac{P(A \cap B)}{P(B)}$$

$$= \frac{0.1}{0.4} = \frac{1}{4} = 0.25$$

17. (d) Given, $P(B) = \frac{1}{5}, P\left(\frac{A}{B}\right) = \frac{2}{3}$ and $P(A \cup B) = \frac{3}{5}$

We know that $P\left(\frac{A}{B}\right) = \frac{P(A \cap B)}{P(B)}$

$$\Rightarrow \quad \frac{2}{3} = \frac{P(A \cap B)}{1/5}$$

$$\Rightarrow \quad P(A \cap B) = \frac{2}{15}$$

Now, $\quad P(A \cup B) = P(A) + P(B) - P(A \cap B)$

$$\Rightarrow \quad \frac{3}{5} = P(A) + \frac{1}{5} - \frac{2}{15}$$

$$\Rightarrow \quad \frac{3}{5} = P(A) + \frac{1}{15}$$

$$\Rightarrow \quad P(A) = \frac{3}{5} - \frac{1}{15} = \frac{8}{15}$$

$$\therefore \quad P(A) = \frac{8}{15}$$

18. (a) Given, $P\left(\frac{A}{B}\right) = 0.3, P(A) = 0.4$ and $P(B) = 0.8$

We know that $\quad P\left(\frac{A}{B}\right) = \frac{P(A \cap B)}{P(B)}$

$$\Rightarrow \quad 0.3 = \frac{P(A \cap B)}{0.8}$$

$$\Rightarrow \quad P(A \cap B) = 0.24$$

Now, $\quad P\left(\frac{B}{A}\right) = \frac{P(B \cap A)}{P(A)} = \frac{P(A \cap B)}{P(A)}$

$$\Rightarrow \quad P\left(\frac{B}{A}\right) = \frac{0.24}{0.4} = 0.6$$

19. (d) Given, $P(E) = 0.3$ and $P(E \cup F) = 0.5$

$\because$ Events E and F are independent.

$$\therefore \quad P(E \cap F) = P(E) \cdot P(F) \quad \ldots\text{(i)}$$

Let $P(F) = x$

We know that

$$P(E \cup F) = P(E) + P(F) - P(E \cap F)$$

$$= P(E) + P(F) - P(E) \cdot P(F) \quad \text{[from Eq. (i)]}$$

$$\Rightarrow \quad 0.5 = 0.3 + x - 0.3x$$

$$\Rightarrow \quad 0.7x = 0.5 - 0.3$$

$$\Rightarrow \quad x = \frac{0.2}{0.7} = \frac{2}{7}$$

$$\therefore \quad P(F) = \frac{2}{7}$$

Now, $P(E / F) - P(F / E) = \frac{P(E \cap F)}{P(F)} - \frac{P(F \cap E)}{P(E)}$

$$= \frac{P(E \cap F)\, P(E) - P(F \cap E) \cdot P(F)}{P(E) \cdot P(F)}$$

$$= \frac{P(E \cap F)\,[P(E) - P(F)]}{P(E \cap F)} \quad \text{[from Eq. (i)]}$$

$$= P(E) - P(F)$$

$$= \frac{3}{10} - \frac{2}{7} = \frac{21 - 20}{70} = \frac{1}{70}$$

20. (c) Given, probability of A speaks truth $= \frac{3}{5} \Rightarrow P(A) = \frac{3}{5}$

and probability of B speaks truth $= \frac{3}{4} \Rightarrow P(B) = \frac{3}{4}$

If they are contradicting for the same fact, then either A speaks truth and B speaks lie or A speaks lie and B speaks truth.

i.e. $\quad = P(A) \cdot P(\overline{B}) + P(B) \cdot P(\overline{A})$

$$= P(A)\,(1 - P(B)) + P(B)\,(1 - P(A)) \quad [\because P(\overline{A}) = 1 - P(A)]$$

$$= \frac{3}{5}\left(1 - \frac{3}{4}\right) + \frac{3}{4}\left(1 - \frac{3}{5}\right)$$

$$= \frac{3}{5} \times \frac{1}{4} + \frac{3}{4} \times \frac{2}{5} = \frac{9}{20}$$

21. (d) We have, $P(A) = \frac{1}{4}, P\left(\frac{A}{B}\right) = \frac{1}{2}$ and $P\left(\frac{B}{A}\right) = \frac{2}{3}$

Now, $P\left(\frac{B}{A}\right) = \frac{P(A \cap B)}{P(A)} = \frac{2}{3} \quad \left[\because P\left(\frac{B}{A}\right) = \frac{P(A \cap B)}{P(A)}\right]$

$$\Rightarrow P(A \cap B) = \frac{2}{3} \cdot P(A)$$

$$= \frac{2}{3} \times \frac{1}{4} = \frac{1}{6}$$

and $\quad P\left(\frac{A}{B}\right) = \frac{P(A \cap B)}{P(B)} = \frac{1}{2} \quad$ [given]

On putting $P(A \cap B) = \frac{1}{6}$, we get

$$\frac{\frac{1}{6}}{P(B)} = \frac{1}{2} \Rightarrow \frac{1}{6} = \frac{1}{2} \cdot P(B)$$

$$\therefore \quad P(B) = \frac{1}{3}$$

22. (b) Given, $n(A)=20$

$\therefore$ Number of mapping (function) from A to $A=20^{20}$

Out of 20^{20}, number of injective functions is $20!$.

$$\therefore\ P(A)=\frac{20!}{20^{20}}=\frac{20\times 19!}{20^{20}}=\frac{19!}{20^{19}}$$

23. (c) Given, $P(A)=\frac{1}{3}, P(B)=\frac{1}{4}$ and $P\left(\frac{A}{B}\right)=\frac{1}{5}$

Now, $P\left(\frac{A}{B}\right)=\frac{P(A\cap B)}{P(B)}$

$$\Rightarrow \quad \frac{1}{5}=\frac{P(A\cap B)}{\frac{1}{4}}$$

$$\Rightarrow \quad P(A\cap B)=\frac{1}{20}$$

We know,

$$P(A\cup B)=P(A)+P(B)-P(A\cap B)$$
$$=\frac{1}{3}+\frac{1}{4}-\frac{1}{20}=\frac{32}{60}$$

Now, $P(A'\cap B')=P(A\cup B)'=1-P(A\cup B)$

$$=1-\frac{32}{60}=\frac{60-32}{60}=\frac{28}{60}=\frac{7}{15}$$

24. (c) Let event E_1 = Doctor diagnose correctly

Event E_2 = Doctor diagnose wrongly

Event E = Patient die

$$P(E_1)=\frac{60}{100},\ P(E_2)=1-P(E_1)=\frac{40}{100}$$

$$P\left(\frac{E}{E_1}\right)=\frac{40}{100}, P\left(\frac{E}{E_2}\right)=\frac{70}{100}$$

Probability that patient of disease X died when his disease was diagnosed correctly.

$$P\left(\frac{E_1}{E}\right)=\frac{P(E_1)\cdot P\left(\frac{E}{E_1}\right)}{P(E_1)\cdot P\left(\frac{E}{E_1}\right)+P(E_2)\cdot P\left(\frac{E}{E_2}\right)}$$

$$=\frac{\frac{60}{100}\times\frac{40}{100}}{\frac{60}{100}\times\frac{40}{100}+\frac{40}{100}\times\frac{70}{100}}$$

$$=\frac{2400}{2400+2800}=\frac{24}{52}=\frac{6}{13}$$

25. (b) **Assertion** Here, $S=\{(H,H),(H,T),(T,H),(T,T)\}$

$$E=\{(H,T),(T,H)\} \text{ and } F=\{(H,T),(T,H)\}$$

$$\Rightarrow \quad P(E)=\frac{2}{4}=\frac{1}{2} \text{ and } P(F)=\frac{2}{4}=\frac{1}{2}$$

Now, $E\cap F=\{(H,T),(T,H)\} \Rightarrow P(E\cap F)=\frac{2}{4}=\frac{1}{2}$

$$\therefore \quad P(E/F)=\frac{P(E\cap F)}{P(F)}=\frac{1/2}{1/2}=1$$

Reason Here, $E=\{H,H\}$ and $F=\{T,T\}$

$\Rightarrow \quad P(E)=1/4$ and $P(F)=1/4$

Now, $\quad E\cap F=\phi \Rightarrow P(E\cap F)=0$

$$\therefore \quad P(E/F)=\frac{P(E\cap F)}{P(F)}=\frac{0}{1/4}=0$$

26. (a) If two coins are tossed simultaneously, then sample space is given by $S=\{(H,H),(H,T),(T,H),(T,T)\}$.

Now, let A be the event of getting two heads.

$\therefore \quad P(A)=\frac{1}{4}$

and B be the event of getting atleast one head.

$\therefore \quad P(B)=\frac{3}{4}$

Thus, $P\left(\frac{A}{B}\right)=\frac{P(A\cap B)}{P(B)}$

$$=\frac{1/4}{3/4}=\frac{1}{4}\times\frac{4}{3}=\frac{1}{3}$$

Hence, Assertion is correct.

Reason is also correct.

27. (d) Given, $P(A)>0$ and $P(B)<1$

$$P\left(\frac{A}{\overline{B}}\right)+P\left(\frac{\overline{A}}{\overline{B}}\right)=\frac{P(A\cap\overline{B})}{P(\overline{B})}+\frac{P(\overline{A}\cap\overline{B})}{P(\overline{B})}$$

$$=\frac{[P(A)-P(A\cap B)]+1-P(A\cup B)}{P(\overline{B})}$$

$$=\frac{[P(A\cup B)-P(B)]+1-P(A\cup B)}{1-P(B)}$$

$[\because P(A\cup B)=P(A)+P(B)-P(A\cap B)]$

$$=\frac{1-P(B)}{1-P(B)}=1$$

Hence, Assertion is incorrect but Reason is correct.

28. (a) Probability that first two cards are black and third card is red when three cards are drawn from a deck of 52 cards

$$=P(A\cap B\cap C)=P(A)\cdot P\left(\frac{B}{A}\right)\cdot P\left(\frac{C}{A\cap B}\right)$$

$$=\frac{26}{52}\times\frac{25}{51}\times\frac{26}{50}=\frac{13}{102}$$

$\therefore$ Both Assertion and Reason are correct and Reason is the correct explanation of Assertion.

29. (b) **Assertion** Here, $P(E)=\frac{13}{52}=\frac{1}{4}$ and $P(F)=\frac{4}{52}=\frac{1}{13}$

Now, $\quad P(E\cap F)=\frac{1}{52}$ $\quad [\because$ ace of spades $=1]$

$$\therefore \quad P(E/F)=\frac{P(E\cap F)}{P(F)}=\frac{1/52}{1/13}=\frac{1}{4}$$

and $$P(F/E)=\frac{P(F\cap E)}{P(E)}=\frac{P(E\cap F)}{P(E)}=\frac{1/52}{1/4}=\frac{1}{13}$$

Hence, Assertion and Reason both are correct and Reason is not the correct explanation of Assertion.

30. (b) **Assertion** Given, $P(A) = \frac{3}{5}$ and $P(B) = \frac{1}{5}$

$\therefore \quad P(A \cap B) = P(A) \times P(B)$ [$\because$ A and B are independent events]

$= \frac{3}{5} \times \frac{1}{5} = \frac{3}{25}$

Reason Let E be the event that both the cards are red.

$\therefore \quad n(E) = {}^{26}C_2$

and $\quad n(S) = {}^{52}C_2$

Now, $\quad P(E) = \frac{n(E)}{n(S)} = \frac{{}^{26}C_2}{{}^{52}C_2}$

$= \frac{25}{102}$

Hence, Assertion and Reason both are correct but Reason is not the correct explanation of Assertion.

31. (a) Given, $A = \{1, 3, 5\}$, $B = \{2, 4\}$

$\because \quad A \cap B = \phi$

Therefore, A and B are mutually exclusive.

Hence, Assertion and Reason both are correct and Reason is the correct explanation of Assertion.

32. (b) Given, $P(A) = 0.3$ and $P(A \cup \overline{B}) = 0.8$

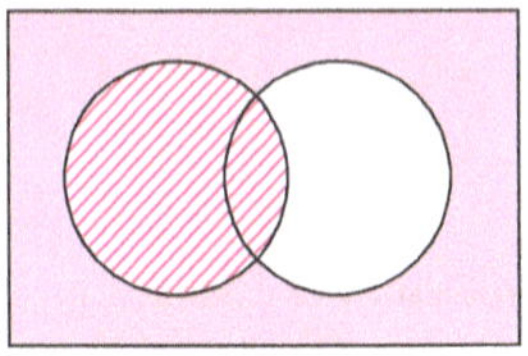

Blue = *A*
Red = not *B*

$\Rightarrow \quad 1 - P(B - A) = 0.8$

$\Rightarrow \quad 1 - [P(B) - P(A \cap B)] = 0.8$

$\Rightarrow \quad 1 - P(B) + P(A) \cdot P(B) = 0.8$

$\Rightarrow \quad 1 - P(B) + 0.3P(B) = 0.8$

$\Rightarrow \quad 1 - 0.8 = 0.7P(B)$

$\Rightarrow \quad P(B) = \frac{0.2}{0.7} = \frac{2}{7}$

Hence, Assertion and Reason both are correct but Reason is not the correct explanation of Assertion.

33. (d) Sample space for tossing three coins.

$S = \{HHH, HHT, HTH, THH, TTH, THT, HTT, TTT\}$

$\therefore \quad n(S) = 8$

Now, $\quad E = \{HHH, TTT\}$

$\therefore \quad P(E) = \frac{2}{8} = \frac{1}{4}$

and $\quad F = \{HHT, HTH, THH, TTH, THT, HTT, TTT\}$

$\Rightarrow \quad n(F) = 7$

$\therefore \quad P(F) = \frac{7}{8}$ and $E \cap F = \{TTT\}$

$\therefore \quad P(E \cap F) = \frac{1}{8}$

We know that for independent events

$P(A \cap B) = P(A) \cdot P(B)$

$\because \quad P(E \cap F) \neq P(E) \cdot P(F)$

So, Assertion is incorrect but Reason is correct.

34. From Venn diagram, we have

$P(A) = 0.32 + 0.09 = 0.41,$

$P(B) = 0.09 + x + y$

and $\quad P(C) = x + 0.21$

(i) Given, $P(C) = 0.44$

$\Rightarrow \quad x + 0.21 = 0.44 \Rightarrow x = 0.23$

(ii) From diagram, we have

$0.32 + 0.09 + y + x + 0.21 = 1 - 0.11$

$\Rightarrow \quad 0.85 + y = 0.89 \Rightarrow y = 0.04$

(iii) (a) We have, $P\left(\frac{C}{B}\right) = \frac{P(C \cap B)}{P(B)}$

$= \frac{x}{0.09 + y + x}$

$= \frac{0.23}{0.09 + 0.04 + 0.23} = \frac{23}{36}$

Or

(b) Probability of person does yoga of type A or B but not $C = 0.32 + 0.09 + y$

$= 0.32 + 0.09 + 0.04 = 0.45$

35. We have,

P(Shell from A hits the plane) = 0.3

$\therefore$ P(Shell from A does not hit the plane) = 1 − 0.3 = 0.7

and P(Shell from B hits the plane) = 0.2

$\therefore$ P(Shell from B does not hit the plane) = 1 − 0.2 = 0.8

(i) P(Shell fired from exactly one of them hits the plane)

= P(Shell from A hits the plane and Shell from B does not hit the plane) or P(Shell from A does not hit the plane and shell from B hits the plane)

$= 0.3 \times 0.8 + 0.7 \times 0.2 = 0.38$

(ii) P(Shell fired from B hit the plane/Exactly one of them hit the plane)

$= \frac{P(\text{Shell fired from } B \text{ hit the plane} \cap \text{Exactly one of them hit the plane})}{P(\text{Exactly one of them hit the plane})}$

$= \frac{P(\text{Shell fired from only } B \text{ hit the plane})}{P(\text{Exactly one of them hit the plane})} = \frac{0.14}{0.38} = \frac{7}{19}$

36. (i) Let the set of patients having fever F and set of patients having migraine be M.

Probability that patient having fever $= \frac{18}{40} \Rightarrow P(F) = \frac{18}{40}$

Probability that patient having both fever and migraine

$P(M \cap F) = \frac{6}{40}$

Probability that patient does not have migraine and having fever

$$P\left(\frac{M'}{F}\right)=1-P\left(\frac{M}{F}\right)$$

$$=1-\frac{P(M\cap F)}{P(F)}$$

$$=1-\frac{\frac{6}{40}}{\frac{18}{40}}=1-\frac{6}{18}=1-\frac{1}{3}=\frac{2}{3}$$

Hence, the probability that patient does not have migraine given that he/she having fever is $\frac{2}{3}$.

(ii) Let the set of patients having cold, fever and migraine to be C, F and M respectively.

Probability that patient having both migraine and cold

$$=P(C\cap M)=\frac{3}{40}$$

Probability that patient having migraine

$$=P(M)=\frac{9}{40}$$

Probability that patient having cold given that he/she has migraine $=P\left(\frac{C}{M}\right)=\frac{P(C\cap M)}{P(M)}=\frac{\frac{3}{40}}{\frac{9}{40}}=\frac{1}{3}$

Probability that patient having both fever and migraine

$$=P(F\cap M)=\frac{6}{40}$$

Probability that patient having fever given that he/she has migraine $=P\left(\frac{F}{M}\right)=\frac{P(F\cap M)}{P(M)}=\frac{\frac{6}{40}}{\frac{9}{40}}=\frac{2}{3}$

Probability that patient having all 3 of cold, fever and migraine

$$=P(C\cap F\cap M)=\frac{2}{40}=\frac{1}{20}$$

Probability that patient having both cold and fever given that he/she has migraine

$$=P\left(\frac{C\cap F}{M}\right)=\frac{P(C\cap F\cap M)}{P(M)}=\frac{\frac{1}{20}}{\frac{9}{40}}=\frac{2}{9}$$

Probability that a patient selected at random has cold or fever or both, provided that he/she has migraine

$$=P\left(\frac{C}{M}\right)+P\left(\frac{F}{M}\right)-P\left(\frac{C\cap F}{M}\right)$$

$$=\frac{1}{3}+\frac{2}{3}-\frac{2}{9}=\frac{3+6-2}{9}=\frac{7}{9}$$

Hence, the probability that a patient selected at random has cold or fever or both provided that he/she has migraine is $\frac{7}{9}$.

37. Given, 70% customers pay their first month bill in time, therefore the customers who do not pay bill in time is 30%.

(i) Let E_1 and E_2 denote the event of customer paying or not paying the first month bill in time, respectively.

Then, $P(E_1)=70\%=0.7$ and $P(E_2)=30\%=0.3$

(ii) Given that the probability of customers who pays the bill in time next month is 0.8 and who does not pay in time is 0.4.

Let A denotes the event of customer paying second month's bill in time.

$\therefore P\left(\frac{A}{E_1}\right)=P$ (customer paying second month bill in time when they pay first month bill)

$=0.8$

and $P\left(\frac{A}{E_2}\right)=P$ (customer paying second month bill in time when they do not pay first month bill in time)

$=0.4$

(iii) (a) The probability of customer paying second month's bill in time $=P(A)=P(E_1)P\left(\frac{A}{E_1}\right)+P(E_2)P\left(\frac{A}{E_2}\right)$

$$=0.7\times 0.8+0.3\times 0.4$$

$$=0.56+0.12=0.68$$

Or

(b) The probability of customer paying first month's bill in time, if it is found that customer has paid the second month's bill in time is $P\left(\frac{E_1}{A}\right)$.

$$P\left(\frac{E_1}{A}\right)=\frac{P(E_1)\cdot P\left(\frac{A}{E_1}\right)}{P(E_1)\cdot P\left(\frac{A}{E_1}\right)+P(E_2)\cdot P\left(\frac{A}{E_2}\right)}$$

$$=\frac{0.7\times 0.8}{0.7\times 0.8+0.3\times 0.4}=\frac{0.56}{0.56+0.12}=\frac{0.56}{0.68}$$

$$=0.824$$

38. Given, $P(E_1)=0.65$, $P(E/E_1)=0.35$ and $P\left(\frac{E}{E_2}\right)=0.80$

(i) $P(E_2)=1-P(E_1)=1-0.65=0.35$

(ii) $P(E)=P(E_1)\cdot P\left(\frac{E}{E_1}\right)+P(E_2)\cdot P\left(\frac{E}{E_2}\right)$

$$=0.65\times 0.35+0.35\times 0.80$$

$$=0.2275+0.28\approx 0.51$$

(iii) (a) $P\left(\frac{E_1}{E}\right)=\frac{P(E_1)\cdot P(E/E_1)}{P(E_1)\cdot P(E/E_1)+P(E_2)P(E/E_2)}$

$$=\frac{0.65\times 0.35}{0.65\times 0.35+0.35\times 0.80}=0.45$$

or (b) $P\left(\frac{E_2}{E}\right) = \frac{P(E_2)P(E/E_2)}{P(E_1)\cdot P(E/E_1) + P(E_2)P(E/E_2)}$

$= \frac{0.35 \times 0.80}{0.65 \times 0.35 + 0.35 \times 0.80}$

$= 0.55$

39. Given, $P(A) = P(B) = P(C) = P(D) = \frac{1}{4}$

and $P\left(\frac{L}{A}\right) = \frac{24}{100}, P\left(\frac{L}{B}\right) = \frac{22}{100}, P\left(\frac{L}{C}\right) = \frac{17}{100}, P\left(\frac{L}{D}\right) = \frac{9}{100}$

(i) $P(L/C) = \frac{17}{100}$

(ii) $P(\bar{L}/A) = \frac{76}{100} = \frac{19}{25}$

(iii) By Bayes' theorem,

(a) $P(A/L) = \frac{P(A)\cdot P(L/A)}{P(A)P(L/A) + P(B)P(L/B) + P(C)P\left(\frac{L}{C}\right) + P(D)P\left(\frac{L}{D}\right)}$

$= \frac{\frac{1}{4}\times\frac{24}{100}}{\frac{1}{4}\times\frac{24}{100} + \frac{1}{4}\times\frac{22}{100} + \frac{1}{4}\times\frac{17}{100} + \frac{1}{4}\times\frac{9}{100}}$

$= \frac{24}{24+22+17+9}$

$= \frac{24}{72} = \frac{1}{3}$

Or

(b) $P\left(\frac{L}{B \text{ or } C}\right) = P\left(\frac{L}{B}\right) + P\left(\frac{L}{C}\right)$

$= \frac{22}{100} + \frac{17}{100}$

$= \frac{39}{100}$

Subjective Questions

1. **Hint** Total numbers which is divisible by 3 and 4 is {12, 24, 36, 48, 60} **Ans.** $\frac{^5C_4}{^{60}C_4}$

2. Let E = Event of getting a multiple of 3.

F = Event of getting a multiple of 5.

and $E \cap F$ = Event of getting a multiple of 3 and 5 i.e. 15

$\therefore \quad P(E) = \frac{13}{40}$

$[\because E = \{3, 6, 9, 12, 15, 18, 21, 24, 27, 30, 33, 36, 39\}]$

$P(F) = \frac{8}{40}$ $\quad [\because E = \{5, 10, 15, 20, 25, 30, 35, 40\}]$

and $P(E \cap F) = \frac{2}{40}$ $\quad [\because E \cap F = \{15, 30\}]$

$\therefore$ Required probability,

$P(E \cup F) = P(E) + P(F) - P(E \cap F)$

$= \frac{13}{40} + \frac{8}{40} - \frac{2}{40}$

$= \frac{13+8-2}{40} = \frac{19}{40}$

3. Let E and F be the events defined as follows

E : A hits the target

and F : B hits the target

$P(E) = \frac{1}{3}, \; P(\bar{E}) = 1 - P(E) = \frac{2}{3}$

$P(F) = \frac{2}{5}, \; P(\bar{F}) = 1 - P(F) = \frac{3}{5}$

P (the target is hit) $= 1 - P$ (the target is not hit)

$= 1 - \left(\frac{2}{3} \times \frac{3}{5}\right) = 1 - \frac{6}{15}$

$= \frac{9}{15} = \frac{3}{5}$

4. Let A and B be the respective events of solving the problem by A and B, respectively.

Then, $P(A) = \frac{1}{3}$ and $P(B) = \frac{1}{4}$

$\therefore$ Required probability $= 1 - P(\bar{A})\,P(\bar{B})$

$= 1 - \left(1 - \frac{1}{3}\right)\left(1 - \frac{1}{4}\right)$

$= 1 - \frac{2}{3} \times \frac{3}{4}$

$= 1 - \frac{1}{2} = \frac{1}{2}$

5. Let E be the event that it will rain on any particular day.

$\therefore \; P(E) = 50\% = \frac{1}{2} \Rightarrow P(\bar{E}) = 1 - P(E) = 1 - \frac{1}{2} = \frac{1}{2}$

$\therefore$ Required probability

$= P(E)\cdot P(E)\cdot P(E)\cdot P(E)\cdot P(\bar{E})\cdot P(\bar{E})\cdot P(\bar{E})$

$= (P(E))^4 (P(\bar{E}))^3$

$= \left(\frac{1}{2}\right)^4 \left(\frac{1}{2}\right)^3 = \left(\frac{1}{2}\right)^7$

6. We have, $P(A) = 0.4, P(B) = 0.8$ and $P\left(\frac{B}{A}\right) = 0.6$

We know that

$P\left(\frac{B}{A}\right) = \frac{P(A \cap B)}{P(A)}$

$\Rightarrow \quad 0.6 = \frac{P(A \cap B)}{0.4}$

$\therefore \quad P(A \cap B) = 0.6 \times 0.4 = 0.24$

Now, $\quad P\left(\frac{A}{B}\right) = \frac{P(A \cap B)}{P(B)} = \frac{0.24}{0.8} = 0.3$

7. We have, $2P(A) = P(B) = \frac{5}{13}$

$\Rightarrow \quad P(A) = \frac{5}{26}, P(B) = \frac{5}{13}$

and $\quad P(A/B) = \frac{2}{5}$

$\because \quad P\left(\frac{A}{B}\right) = \frac{P(A \cap B)}{P(B)}$

$\therefore \quad \frac{2}{5} = \frac{P(A \cap B)}{5/13}$

$\Rightarrow \quad P(A \cap B) = \frac{2}{5} \times \frac{5}{13} = \frac{2}{13}$

$\because \quad P(A \cup B) = P(A) + P(B) - P(A \cap B)$

$= \frac{5}{26} + \frac{5}{13} - \frac{2}{13}$

$= \frac{5 + 10 - 4}{26} = \frac{11}{26}$

8. Given, $P(E) = 0.6, P(F) = 0.3$ and $P(E \cap F) = 0.2$

We know that $P\left(\frac{A}{B}\right) = \frac{P(A \cap B)}{P(B)}$

and $\quad P\left(\frac{B}{A}\right) = \frac{P(A \cap B)}{P(A)}$

Now, $P\left(\frac{E}{F}\right) = \frac{P(E \cap F)}{P(F)} = \frac{0.2}{0.3} = \frac{2}{3}$

and $\quad P\left(\frac{F}{E}\right) = \frac{P(E \cap F)}{P(E)} = \frac{0.2}{0.6} = \frac{1}{3}$

9. Let A_T : Event that A speaks truth

and B_T : Event that B speaks truth.

Given, $P(A_T) = \frac{80}{100} = \frac{4}{5}, \quad P(B_T) = \frac{90}{100} = \frac{9}{10}$

$P(\text{agree}) = P(\text{both speaking truth or both telling lie})$

$= P(A_T B_T \text{ or } \bar{A}_T \bar{B}_T)$

$= P(A_T)P(B_T) \text{ or } P(\bar{A}_T)P(\bar{B}_T)$

$= \left(\frac{4}{5}\right)\left(\frac{9}{10}\right) + \left(\frac{1}{5}\right)\left(\frac{1}{10}\right)$

$= \frac{36+1}{50} = \frac{37}{50}$

$= \frac{74}{100} = 74\%$

10. Given, $P(A) = \frac{4}{5}$ and $P(A \cap B) = \frac{7}{10}$

We know that $P\left(\frac{B}{A}\right) = \frac{P(A \cap B)}{P(A)}$

$\Rightarrow \quad P\left(\frac{B}{A}\right) = \frac{\frac{7}{10}}{\frac{4}{5}} = \frac{7}{10} \times \frac{5}{4}$

$= \frac{7}{8}$

11. Given, $P(A) = \frac{1}{4}, P(B) = \frac{1}{6}$ and $P(A \cap B) = \frac{1}{7}$

(i) $P(A \cup B) = P(A) + P(B) - P(A \cap B)$

$= \frac{1}{4} + \frac{1}{6} - \frac{1}{7}$

$= \frac{21 + 14 - 12}{84} = \frac{23}{84}$

(ii) $\quad P\left(\frac{\bar{B}}{\bar{A}}\right) = \frac{P(\bar{B} \cap \bar{A})}{P(\bar{A})}$

$= \frac{P(\overline{A \cup B})}{P(\bar{A})} = \frac{1 - P(A \cup B)}{1 - P(A)}$

$= \frac{1 - \frac{23}{84}}{1 - \frac{1}{4}} = \frac{\frac{84-23}{84}}{\frac{4-1}{4}}$

$= \frac{61}{84} \times \frac{4}{3} = \frac{61}{63}$

12. Here, two dice are thrown. So, sample space is

$$S = \left\{ \begin{array}{l} (1,1),(1,2),(1,3),(1,4),(1,5),(1,6), \\ (2,1),(2,2),(2,3),(2,4),(2,5),(2,6), \\ (3,1),(3,2),(3,3),(3,4),(3,5),(3,6), \\ (4,1),(4,2),(4,3),(4,4),(4,5),(4,6), \\ (5,1),(5,2),(5,3),(5,4),(5,5),(5,6), \\ (6,1),(6,2),(6,3),(6,4),(6,5),(6,6) \end{array} \right\}$$

$\therefore \quad n(S) = 36$

Let A = Event of getting an even number on first die

i.e. $\quad A = \left\{ \begin{array}{l} (2,1),(2,2),(2,3),(2,4),(2,5),(2,6), \\ (4,1),(4,2),(4,3),(4,4),(4,5),(4,6), \\ (6,1),(6,2),(6,3),(6,4),(6,5),(6,6) \end{array} \right\}$

$\therefore \quad n(A) = 18$

and $\quad B$ = Event of getting a sum of 8

$= \{(2, 6), (3, 5), (4, 4), (5, 3), (6, 2)\}$

$\therefore \quad n(B) = 5$

Here, $(A \cap B) = \{(2,6),(4,4),(6,2)\}$

$\therefore \quad n(A \cap B) = 3$

Now, $P(A \cap B) = \frac{n(A \cap B)}{n(S)} = \frac{3}{36}$ and $P(B) = \frac{n(B)}{n(S)} = \frac{5}{36}$

Since, we have to find the conditional probability of getting an even number on first die, when the dice always exhibits a sum of 8.

$\therefore$ Required probability $= P\left(\frac{A}{B}\right) = \frac{P(A \cap B)}{P(B)} = \frac{3/36}{5/36} = \frac{3}{5}$

13. Let E_1, E_2, E_3, E_4 be the respective events that the plane is hit in the 1st, 2nd, 3rd and 4th shot. Then,

$$P(E_1) = 0.4, P(E_2) = 0.3, P(E_3) = 0.2 \text{ and } P(E_4) = 0.1$$

$$\therefore\ P(\bar{E}_1) = (1-0.4) = 0.6, P(\bar{E}_2) = (1-0.3) = 0.7,$$
$$P(\bar{E}_3) = (1-0.2) = 0.8, P(\bar{E}_4) = (1-0.1) = 0.9.$$

$\therefore$ P(atleast one shot hits the plane)

$$= 1 - P(\bar{E}_1 \text{ and } \bar{E}_2 \text{ and } \bar{E}_3 \text{ and } \bar{E}_4)$$
$$= 1 - \{P(\bar{E}_1) \times P(\bar{E}_2) \times P(\bar{E}_3) \times P(\bar{E}_4)\}$$
$$= 1 - \{0.6 \times 0.7 \times 0.8 \times 0.9\} = 1 - \{0.3024\} = 0.6976$$

Hence, the probability that atleast one shot hits the plane is 0.6976.

14. Let A_T : Event that A speaks truth
and B_T : Event that B speaks truth.

Given, $P(A_T) = \frac{75}{100}$,

then $P(\bar{A}_T) = 1 - \frac{75}{100} = \frac{25}{100}$ $[\because P(\bar{A}) = 1 - P(A)]$

and $P(B_T) = \frac{90}{100}$,

then $P(\bar{B}_T) = 1 - \frac{90}{100} = \frac{10}{100}$

Now, P (A and B are contradict to each other)

$$= P(A_T \cap \bar{B}_T) + P(\bar{A}_T \cap B_T)$$
$$= P(A_T) \cdot P(\bar{B}_T) + P(\bar{A}_T) \cdot P(B_T)$$

[$\because A_T$ and B_T are independent events]

$$= \frac{75}{100} \times \frac{10}{100} + \frac{25}{100} \times \frac{90}{100}$$
$$= \frac{750 + 2250}{10000} = \frac{3000}{10000} = \frac{3}{10}$$

$\therefore$ Percentage of P (A and B are contradict to each other)

$$= \frac{3}{10} \times 100 = 30\%$$

Since, B speaks truth in only 90% (i.e. not 100%) of the cases, therefore we think, the statement of B may be false.

15. Let P_T : Event that P speaks truth
and Q_T : Event that Q speaks truth.

Given, $P(P_T) = \frac{70}{100}$, then $P(\bar{P}_T) = 1 - \frac{70}{100} = \frac{30}{100}$

and $P(Q_T) = \frac{80}{100}$, then $P(\bar{Q}_T) = 1 - \frac{80}{100} = \frac{20}{100}$

P (A and B are agree to each other)

$$= P(P_T \cap Q_T) + P(\bar{P}_T \cap \bar{Q}_T)$$
$$= P(P_T) \cdot P(Q_T) + P(\bar{P}_T) \cdot P(\bar{Q}_T)$$

[$\because P_T$ and Q_T are independent events]

$$= \frac{70}{100} \times \frac{80}{100} + \frac{30}{100} \times \frac{20}{100}$$
$$= \frac{5600}{10000} + \frac{600}{10000} = \frac{6200}{10000} = \frac{62}{100}$$

$\therefore$ Percentage of P(A and B are agree to each other)

$$= \frac{62}{100} \times 100 = 62\%$$

No, agree does not mean that they are speaking truth.

16. Let A and B denote the events A speaks the truth and B speaks the truth, respectively.

We have, $P(A) = \frac{60}{100}$

$\Rightarrow$ $P(\bar{A}) = 1 - P(A)$
$$= 1 - \frac{60}{100} = \frac{40}{100}$$

and $P(B) = \frac{90}{100}$

$\Rightarrow$ $P(\bar{B}) = 1 - P(B) = 1 - \frac{90}{100} = \frac{10}{100}$

So, required probability $= P(A)\,P(\bar{B}) + P(\bar{A})\,P(B)$

$$= \frac{60}{100} \times \frac{10}{100} + \frac{40}{100} \times \frac{90}{100}$$
$$= \frac{42}{100} = 42\%$$

Hence, they are likely to contradict each other in 42% of cases in stating the same fact.

Since, no one trusts a liar, so two statement of B will carry more weight as he speaks the truth in more number of cases than A.

17. On throwing a die twice, we get 36 elementary events of the experiment which are to be considered to be equally likely. Odd numbers are 1, 3 and 5.

$P(A) = P$ (odd number on the first throw) $= \frac{18}{36} = \frac{1}{2}$

[$\because$ possible outcomes (1, 1), (1, 2), (1, 3), (1, 4), (1, 5), (1, 6), (3, 1), (3, 2), (3, 3), (3, 4), (3, 5), (3, 6), (5, 1), (5, 2), (5, 3), (5, 4), (5, 5) and (5, 6) i.e. 18 outcomes]

Similarly, $P(B) = P$ (odd number on the second throw)

$$= \frac{18}{36} = \frac{1}{2}$$

Also, $P(A \cap B) = P$(odd number on both throws)

$$= \frac{9}{36} = \frac{1}{4}$$

[$\because$ events are (1, 1), (1, 3), (1, 5), (3, 1), (3, 3), (3, 5), (5, 1), (5, 3) and (5, 5) i.e. 9 outcomes]

Now, $P(A) \cdot P(B) = \frac{1}{2} \times \frac{1}{2} = \frac{1}{4}$

Thus, $P(A \cap B) = P(A) \cdot P(B)$

Hence, A and B are independent events.

18. When a die is thrown, then sample space is

$$S = \{1, 2, 3, 4, 5, 6\} \Rightarrow n(S) = 6$$

Also, A: number is odd and B: number is green.

$\therefore$ $A = \{1, 3, 5\}$ and $B = \{4, 5, 6\}$

So, $A \cap B = \{5\}$

$\Rightarrow$ $n(A) = 3$, $n(B) = 3$ and $n(A \cap B) = 1$

Now, $P(A) = \frac{n(A)}{n(S)} = \frac{3}{6} = \frac{1}{2}$, $n(B) = \frac{n(B)}{n(S)} = \frac{3}{6} = \frac{1}{2}$

and $P(A \cap B) = \frac{n(A \cap B)}{n(S)} = \frac{1}{6}$

Now, $P(A)\times P(B)=\frac{1}{2}\times\frac{1}{2}=\frac{1}{4}\neq\frac{1}{6}=P(A\cap B)$

$\therefore \quad P(A\cap B)\neq P(A)\times P(B)$

Thus, A and B are not independent events.

19. Let B and b represent elder and younger boy child, respectively. Also, G and g represent elder and younger girl child, respectively. If a family has two children, then all possible cases are

$$S=\{Bb, Bg, Gg, Gb\}$$

$\therefore \quad n(S)=4$

Let us define event A: Both children are girls, then

$$A=\{Gg\}\Rightarrow n(A)=1$$

(i) Let E_1 : The event that youngest child is a girl.

Then, $E_1=\{Bg, Gg\}\Rightarrow n(E_1)=2$

So, $P(E_1)=\frac{n(E_1)}{n(S)}=\frac{2}{4}=\frac{1}{2}$

and $A\cap E_1=\{Gg\}$

$\Rightarrow n(A\cap E_1)=1$

So, $P(A\cap E_1)=\frac{n(A\cap E_1)}{n(S)}=\frac{1}{4}$

Now, $P\left(\frac{A}{E_1}\right)=\frac{P(A\cap E_1)}{P(E_1)}=\frac{1/4}{1/2}=\frac{1}{2}$

$\therefore$ Required probability $=\frac{1}{2}$

(ii) Let E_2 : The event that atleast one is girl.

Then, $E_2=\{Bg, Gg, Gb\}\Rightarrow n(E_2)=3$

So, $P(E_2)=\frac{n(E_2)}{n(S)}=\frac{3}{4}$

and $(A\cap E_2)=\{Gg\}$

$\Rightarrow n(A\cap E_2)=1$

So, $P(A\cap E_2)=\frac{n(A\cap E_2)}{n(S)}=\frac{1}{4}$

Now, $P\left(\frac{A}{E_2}\right)=\frac{P(A\cap E_2)}{P(E_2)}=\frac{1/4}{3/4}=\frac{1}{3}$

$\therefore$ Required probability $=\frac{1}{3}$

20. Given, bag $A=4$ black and 6 red balls

and bag $B=7$ black and 3 red balls.

Let $E_1=$ The event that die show 1 or 2

$E_2=$ The event that die show 3, 4, 5 or 6

and $E=$ The event that among two drawn balls, one of them is red and other is black

Now, $P(E_1)=\frac{2}{6}, P(E_2)=\frac{4}{6}$ [$\because$ total number in a die is six]

$P\left(\frac{E}{E_1}\right)=P$(getting one red and one black from bag A)

$$=\frac{{}^4C_1\times{}^6C_1}{{}^{10}C_2}=\frac{4\times6\times2}{10\times9}$$

and $P\left(\frac{E}{E_2}\right)=P$ (getting one red and one black from bag B)

$$=\frac{{}^7C_1\times{}^3C_1}{{}^{10}C_2}=\frac{7\times3\times2}{10\times9}$$

$\therefore$ Total probability,

$$P(E)=P(E_1)\cdot P\left(\frac{E}{E_1}\right)+P(E_2)\cdot P\left(\frac{E}{E_2}\right)$$

$$=\frac{2}{6}\cdot\left(\frac{4\times6\times2}{10\times9}\right)+\frac{4}{6}\cdot\left(\frac{7\times3\times2}{10\times9}\right)$$

$$=\frac{4\times6}{6\times10\times9}(4+7)=\frac{4\times6\times11}{6\times10\times9}=\frac{22}{45}$$

21. Given, total number of coins $=2n+1$

Number of coins having head on both sides $=n$

Number of fair coins $=(2n+1)-n=n+1$

Let E_1 : Event of a coin having head on both sides is selected,

E_2 : Event of a fair coin is selected

and A: Event of head comes up in tossing a selected coin.

Then, $P(E_1)=\frac{n}{2n+1}; P(E_2)=\frac{n+1}{2n+1};$

$$P(A/E_1)=1; P(A/E_2)=\frac{1}{2}$$

It is given that $P(A)=\frac{31}{42}$.

So, $P(E_1)P(A/E_1)+P(E_2)P(A/E_2)=\frac{31}{42}$

$\Rightarrow \quad \frac{n}{2n+1}\times1+\frac{n+1}{2n+1}\times\frac{1}{2}=\frac{31}{42}$

$\Rightarrow \quad \frac{1}{2n+1}\left[n+\frac{n+1}{2}\right]=\frac{31}{42}$

$\Rightarrow \quad 42(3n+1)=62(2n+1)$

$\Rightarrow \quad 126n+42=124n+62$

$\Rightarrow \quad 2n=20$

$\therefore \quad n=10$

22. Hint Let $E_1=$ Red ball is transferred from Bag I to Bag II

and $E_2=$ Black ball is transferred from Bag I to Bag II

$\therefore \quad P(E_1)=\frac{3}{3+4}=\frac{3}{7}$ and $P(E_2)=\frac{4}{3+4}=\frac{4}{7}$

$$P\left(\frac{E}{E_1}\right)=\frac{4+1}{(4+1)+5}=\frac{5}{10}=\frac{1}{2}$$

and $P\left(\frac{E}{E_2}\right)=\frac{4}{4+(5+1)}=\frac{4}{10}=\frac{2}{5}$

$$\therefore \quad P\left(\frac{E_2}{E}\right)=\frac{P\left(\frac{E}{E_2}\right)\cdot P(E_2)}{P\left(\frac{E}{E_1}\right)\cdot P(E_1)+P\left(\frac{E}{E_2}\right)\cdot P(E_2)}$$ **Ans.** $\frac{16}{31}$

23. Let E_1 be the event that the girl gets 1 or 2, E_2 be the event that the girl gets 3, 4, 5 or 6 and A be the event that the girl gets exactly a 'tail'.

Then, $P(E_1)=\frac{2}{6}=\frac{1}{3}$ and $P(E_2)=\frac{4}{6}=\frac{2}{3}$

$P\left(\frac{A}{E_1}\right)=P$ (getting exactly one tail when a coin is tossed three times)

$=\frac{3}{8}$

$P\left(\frac{A}{E_2}\right)=P$ (getting exactly a tail when a coin is tossed once)

$=\frac{1}{2}$

Now, required probability

$$P\left(\frac{E_2}{A}\right)=\frac{P(E_2)\cdot P\left(\frac{A}{E_2}\right)}{P(E_1)\cdot P\left(\frac{A}{E_1}\right)+P(E_2)\cdot P\left(\frac{A}{E_2}\right)}$$

$$=\frac{\frac{2}{3}\cdot\frac{1}{2}}{\frac{1}{3}\cdot\frac{3}{8}+\frac{2}{3}\cdot\frac{1}{2}}=\frac{\frac{1}{3}}{\frac{1}{8}+\frac{1}{3}}=\frac{8}{11}$$

24. Hint Let E_1 = Event that 5 or 6 is shown on die

and E_2 = Event that 1, 2, 3 or 4 is shown on die.

Here, $n(E_1)=2$ and $n(E_2)=4$

Also, $n(S)=6$

$\therefore\quad P(E_1)=\frac{2}{6}=\frac{1}{3}$ and $P(E_2)=\frac{4}{6}=\frac{2}{3}$

Let E = The event that exactly one head show up.

$\therefore P\left(\frac{E}{E_1}\right)=P$ (exactly one head show up when coin is tossed thrice)

$=P\{HTT, THT, TTH\}=\frac{3}{8}$

[$\because$ total number of outcomes $=2^3=8$]

$P\left(\frac{E}{E_2}\right)=P$ (head shows up when coin is tossed once)

$=\frac{1}{2}$

The probability that the girl threw 1, 2, 3 or 4 with the die, if she obtained exactly one head, is given by

$$P\left(\frac{E_2}{E}\right)=\frac{P(E_2)\cdot P\left(\frac{E}{E_2}\right)}{P(E_1)\cdot P\left(\frac{E}{E_1}\right)+P(E_2)\cdot P\left(\frac{E}{E_2}\right)}$$

$$=\frac{\frac{2}{3}\times\frac{1}{2}}{\frac{1}{3}\times\frac{3}{8}+\frac{2}{3}\times\frac{1}{2}}\quad \textbf{Ans. } \frac{8}{11}$$

25. Let E_1 and E_2 denote the events that first and second group will win. Then,

$$P(E_1)=0.6 \text{ and } P(E_2)=0.4$$

Let E be the event of introducing the new product.

Then, $P\left(\frac{E}{E_1}\right)=0.7$ and $P\left(\frac{E}{E_2}\right)=0.3$

Now, we have to find the probability that new product is introduced by second event.

$$\therefore\quad P\left(\frac{E_2}{E}\right)=\frac{P(E_2)P\left(\frac{E}{E_2}\right)}{P(E_1)P\left(\frac{E}{E_1}\right)+P(E_2)P\left(\frac{E}{E_2}\right)}$$

$$=\frac{0.4\times 0.3}{0.6\times 0.7+0.4\times 0.3}$$

$$=\frac{0.12}{0.42+0.12}=\frac{0.12}{0.54}$$

$$=0.22$$

26. Let E_1, E_2, E_3 and A denote the following events.

E_1 = Bag I is chosen, E_2 = Bag II is chosen, E_3 = Bag III is chosen, A = The balls drawn from the chosen bag are white and red.

Since, one of the bags is chosen at random.

$$\therefore\quad P(E_1)=\frac{1}{3}=P(E_2)=P(E_3)$$

If one white and red balls are chosen from bag I with replacement.

Then, $P\left(\frac{A}{E_1}\right)=\frac{1}{6}\times\frac{3}{6}\times 2$

Similarly, $P\left(\frac{A}{E_2}\right)=\frac{2}{4}\times\frac{1}{4}\times 2$ and $P\left(\frac{A}{E_3}\right)=\frac{4}{9}\times\frac{2}{9}\times 2$

By Bayes' theorem,

$$\text{Required probability}=P\left(\frac{E_3}{A}\right)=\frac{P(E_3)\times P\left(\frac{A}{E_3}\right)}{\sum_{i=1}^{3}P(E_i)\times P\left(\frac{A}{E_i}\right)}$$

$$=\frac{\frac{1}{3}\times\frac{4}{9}\times\frac{2}{9}\times 2}{\frac{1}{3}\times\frac{1}{6}\times\frac{3}{6}\times 2+\frac{1}{3}\times\frac{2}{4}\times\frac{1}{4}\times 2+\frac{1}{3}\times\frac{4}{9}\times\frac{2}{9}\times 2}=\frac{64}{199}$$

27. Let us define the following events

E_1 : Bag X is selected

E_2 : Bag Y is selected

and E : Getting one white and one black ball in a draw of two balls.

Here, $P(E_1)=P(E_2)=\frac{1}{2}$

[$\because$ probability of selecting each bag is equal]

Now, $P\left(\frac{E}{E_1}\right)$ = Probability of drawing one white and one black ball from bag X

$$= \frac{{}^4C_1 \times {}^2C_1}{{}^6C_2} = \frac{4\times 2}{\frac{6\times 5}{2\times 1}} = \frac{16}{6\times 5} = \frac{8}{15}$$

and $P\left(\frac{E}{E_2}\right)$ = Probability of drawing one white and one black ball from bag Y

$$= \frac{{}^3C_1 \times {}^3C_1}{{}^6C_2} = \frac{3\times 3}{\frac{6\times 5}{2\times 1}} = \frac{3}{5}$$

∴ The probability that the one white and one black balls are drawn from bag Y,

$$P\left(\frac{E_2}{E}\right) = \frac{P(E_2)\cdot P\left(\frac{E}{E_2}\right)}{P(E_1)\cdot P\left(\frac{E}{E_1}\right) + P(E_2)\cdot P\left(\frac{E}{E_2}\right)}$$

[using Baye's theorem]

$$= \frac{\frac{1}{2}\times\frac{3}{5}}{\frac{1}{2}\times\frac{8}{15}+\frac{1}{2}\times\frac{3}{5}} = \frac{\frac{3}{5}}{\frac{8}{15}+\frac{3}{5}} = \frac{\frac{3}{5}}{\frac{8+9}{15}} = \frac{3\times 15}{5\times 17} = \frac{9}{17}$$

28. Let A_1 : Event that the bulb is produced by machine E_1

A_2 : Event that the bulb is produced by machine E_2

A_3 : Event that the bulb is produced by machine E_3

A: Event that the picked up bulb is defective

Here, $P(A_1) = 50\% = \frac{50}{100} = \frac{1}{2}$,

$P(A_2) = 25\% = \frac{25}{100} = \frac{1}{4}$,

and $P(A_3) = 25\% = \frac{25}{100} = \frac{1}{4}$

Also, $P\left(\frac{A}{A_1}\right) = 4\% = \frac{4}{100} = \frac{1}{25}$,

$P\left(\frac{A}{A_2}\right) = 4\% = \frac{4}{100} = \frac{1}{25}$

and $P\left(\frac{A}{A_3}\right) = 5\% = \frac{5}{100} = \frac{1}{20}$

∴ The probability that the picked bulb is defective,

$$P(A) = P(A_1)\times P\left(\frac{A}{A_1}\right) + P(A_2)\times P\left(\frac{A}{A_2}\right) + P(A_3)\times P\left(\frac{A}{A_3}\right)$$

$$= \frac{1}{2}\times\frac{1}{25} + \frac{1}{4}\times\frac{1}{25} + \frac{1}{4}\times\frac{1}{20}$$

$$= \frac{1}{50} + \frac{1}{100} + \frac{1}{80}$$

$$= \frac{8+4+5}{400} = \frac{17}{400} = 0.0425$$

29. Let E_1 = Event that the husband will be alive 25 yr hence and E_2 = Event that the wife will be alive 25 yr hence

Then, $P(E_1) = \frac{5}{12}$ and $P(E_2) = \frac{3}{8}$

∴ $P(\bar{E}_1) = \left(1 - \frac{5}{12}\right) = \frac{7}{12}$ and $P(\bar{E}_2) = \left(1 - \frac{3}{8}\right) = \frac{5}{8}$

Clearly, E_1 and E_2 are independent events.

(i) P(the couple will be alive 25 yr hence)

$$= P(E_1 \text{ and } E_2) = P(E_1 \cap E_2)$$

$$= P(E_1)\cdot P(E_2) = \left(\frac{5}{12}\times\frac{3}{8}\right) = \frac{5}{32}$$

(ii) P(atleast one of them will be alive 25 yr hence)

$$= 1 - P(\text{none will be alive 25 yr hence})$$

$$= 1 - P[(\text{not } E_1) \text{ and } (\text{not } E_2)]$$

$$= 1 - P[\bar{E}_1 \cap \bar{E}_2]$$

$$= 1 - [P(\bar{E}_1)\cdot P(\bar{E}_2)$$

[∵ $\bar{E}_1$ and $\bar{E}_2$ are independent events]

$$= 1 - \left(\frac{7}{12}\times\frac{5}{8}\right) = \left(1 - \frac{35}{96}\right) = \frac{61}{96}$$

30. Let A: Event that item produced by Operator A

B: Event that item produced by Operator B

C: Event that item produced by Operator C

D: Event that item produced is defective

We need to find out the probability that item is produced by Operator A if it is defective i.e. $P(A/D)$.

So, $$P(A/D) = \frac{P(A)\cdot P(D/A)}{P(A)\cdot P(D/A) + P(B)\cdot P(D/B) + P(C)\cdot P(D/C)}$$

...(i) [by Bayes' theorem]

$P(A)$ = Probability of item is produced by Operator A

$= 50\% = \frac{50}{100} = 0.5$

$P(B)$ = Probability of item is produced by Operator B

$= 30\% = \frac{30}{100} = 0.3$

$P(C)$ = Probability of item is produced by Operator C

$= 20\% = \frac{20}{100} = 0.2$

$P(D/A)$ = Probability of a defective item produced by Operator A

$= 1\% = \frac{1}{100} = 0.01$

$P(D/B)$ = Probability of a defective item produced by Operator B

$= 5\% = \frac{5}{100} = 0.05$

$P(D/C)$ = Probability of a defective item produced by Operator C

$= 7\% = \frac{7}{100} = 0.07$

On putting these values in the Eq. (i), we get

$$P(A/D)=\frac{0.5\times 0.01}{0.5\times 0.01+0.3\times 0.05+0.2\times 0.07}$$

$$=\frac{0.005}{0.005+0.015+0.014}$$

$$=\frac{0.005}{0.034}=\frac{5}{34}$$

Therefore, required probability is $\frac{5}{34}$.

31. Let E_1 = Event that 1 occurs in a die

E_2 = Event that 1 does not occur in a die

A = Event that the man reports that 1 occurs in a die

Then, $P(E_1)=\frac{1}{6}$ and $P(E_2)=\frac{5}{6}$

$\therefore$ P (man reports that 1 occurs when 1 occur) $=P\left(\frac{A}{E_1}\right)=\frac{3}{5}$

and P (man reports that 1 occurs but 1 does not occur)

$$=P\left(\frac{A}{E_2}\right)=\frac{2}{5}$$

Thus, by Bayes' theorem, we get

P(get actually 1 when he reports that 1 occur)

$$=P\left(\frac{E_1}{A}\right)=\frac{P(E_1)\cdot P\left(\frac{A}{E_1}\right)}{P(E_1)\cdot P\left(\frac{A}{E_1}\right)+P(E_2)\cdot P\left(\frac{A}{E_2}\right)}$$

$$=\frac{\frac{1}{6}\times\frac{3}{5}}{\frac{1}{6}\times\frac{3}{5}+\frac{5}{6}\times\frac{2}{5}}=\frac{3}{13}$$

32. Let us define the following events :

E_1 = Lost card is a spade card,

E_2 = Lost card is not a spade card

and A = Drawn cards are spade cards

Then, $P(E_1)=\frac{13}{52}=\frac{1}{4}$, $P(E_2)=\frac{39}{52}=\frac{3}{4}$,

$$P(A/E_1)=\frac{^{12}C_3}{^{51}C_3}=\frac{220}{20825}$$

and $P(A/E_2)=\frac{^{13}C_3}{^{51}C_3}=\frac{286}{20825}$

Now, required probability, $P(E_1/A)$

$$=\frac{P(E_1)\cdot P(A/E_1)}{P(E_1)\cdot P(A/E_1)+P(E_2)\cdot P(A/E_2)}$$

$$=\frac{\frac{1}{4}\cdot\frac{220}{20825}}{\frac{1}{4}\cdot\frac{220}{20825}+\frac{3}{4}\cdot\frac{286}{20825}}$$

$$=\frac{220}{220+858}=\frac{220}{1078}=\frac{20}{98}=\frac{10}{49}$$

33. Given, number of scooter drivers = 2000

Number of car drivers = 4000

Number of truck drivers = 6000

Let A: Insured person is a scooter driver.

B: Insured person is a car driver.

C: Insured person is a truck driver.

D: The insured person meets with an accident.

$\therefore$ $P(A)=\frac{2000}{2000+4000+6000}=\frac{1}{6}$

$\therefore$ Probability the scooter driver meets with an accident.

$$P\left(\frac{D}{A}\right)=0.01$$

$$P(B)=\frac{4000}{2000+4000+6000}=\frac{1}{3}$$

Also, $P\left(\frac{D}{B}\right)=0.03$

and $P(C)=\frac{6000}{2000+4000+6000}=\frac{1}{2}$

Also, $P\left(\frac{D}{C}\right)=0.15$

By Bayes' theorem,

$$P\left(\frac{B}{D}\right)=\frac{P(B)\times P\left(\frac{D}{B}\right)}{P(A)\times P\left(\frac{D}{A}\right)+P(B)+P\left(\frac{D}{B}\right)+P(C)\times P\left(\frac{D}{C}\right)}$$

$$=\frac{\frac{1}{3}\times 0.03}{\frac{1}{6}\times 0.01+\frac{1}{3}\times 0.03+\frac{1}{2}\times 0.15}$$

$$=\frac{\frac{3}{300}}{\frac{1}{600}+\frac{3}{300}+\frac{15}{200}}$$

$$=\frac{3}{300}\times\frac{600}{52}=\frac{6}{52}=\frac{3}{26}$$

Hence, the probability that he is a car driver is $\frac{3}{26}$.

34. Given that there are 3 coins.

Let these are A, B and C, respectively.

$\therefore$ $P(A)=\frac{1}{3}$, $P(B)=\frac{1}{3}$ and $P(C)=\frac{1}{3}$

Let H be the event that the coin shows heads.

For coin A, probability of getting head $=P\left(\frac{H}{A}\right)=1$

For coin B, probability of getting head $=P\left(\frac{H}{B}\right)=\frac{3}{4}$

For coin C, probability of getting head $=P\left(\frac{H}{C}\right)=0.6$

We have to find $P\left(\frac{A}{H}\right)$ = Probability of getting H by coin A.

By Bayes' theorem,

$$P\left(\frac{A}{H}\right)=\frac{P\left(\frac{H}{A}\right)\cdot P(A)}{P\left(\frac{H}{A}\right)\cdot P(A)+P\left(\frac{H}{B}\right)\cdot P(B)+P\left(\frac{H}{C}\right)\cdot P(C)}$$

$$=\frac{1\times\frac{1}{3}}{1\times\frac{1}{3}+\frac{3}{4}\times\frac{1}{3}+0.6\times\frac{1}{3}}$$

$$=\frac{1}{1+0.75+0.6}=\frac{100}{235}=\frac{20}{47}$$

Hence, the required probability that it was the two headed coin is $\frac{20}{47}$.

35. Let E_1, E_2 and A denote the following events.

E_1 = First bag is chosen, E_2 = Second bag is chosen

and A = Two balls drawn at random are red.

Since, one of the bag is chosen at random.

$\therefore \quad P(E_1)=P(E_2)=\frac{1}{2}$

If E_1 has already occurred i.e. first bag is chosen. Therefore, the probability of drawing two red balls in this case $=P\left(\frac{A}{E_1}\right)=\frac{{}^5C_2}{{}^9C_2}=\frac{10}{36}$

Similarly, $P\left(\frac{A}{E_2}\right)=\frac{{}^3C_2}{{}^9C_2}=\frac{3}{36}$

We are required to find $P\left(\frac{E_2}{A}\right)$.

By Bayes' theorem, $P\left(\frac{E_2}{A}\right)=\frac{P(E_2)\cdot P\left(\frac{A}{E_2}\right)}{P(E_1)\cdot P\left(\frac{A}{E_1}\right)+P(E_2)\cdot P\left(\frac{A}{E_2}\right)}$

$$=\frac{\frac{1}{2}\times\frac{3}{36}}{\frac{1}{2}\times\frac{10}{36}+\frac{1}{2}\times\frac{3}{36}}=\frac{\frac{3}{72}}{\frac{10}{72}+\frac{3}{72}}=\frac{\frac{3}{72}}{\frac{13}{72}}=\frac{3}{13}$$

Therefore, required probability is $\frac{3}{13}$.

36.

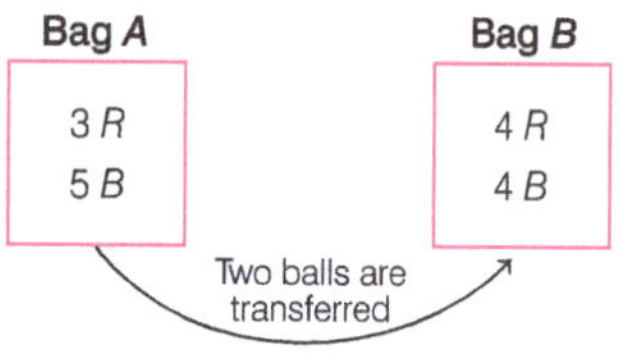

Let us define the following events :

E_1 = One red and one black ball is transferred,

E_2 = Two red balls are transferred,

E_3 = Two black balls are transferred

and E = Drawn ball is red.

Then, $P(E_1)=\frac{{}^3C_1\times{}^5C_1}{{}^8C_2}=\frac{3\times5}{28}=\frac{15}{28}$

$P(E_2)=\frac{{}^3C_2}{{}^8C_2}=\frac{3}{28},\ P(E_3)=\frac{{}^5C_2}{{}^8C_2}=\frac{10}{28}$

$P(E/E_1)=\frac{5}{10},\ P(E/E_2)=\frac{6}{10},\ P(E/E_3)=\frac{4}{10}$

Now, required probability,

$$P(E_2/E)=\frac{P(E_2)\cdot P(E/E_2)}{P(E_1)\cdot P(E/E_1)+P(E_2)\cdot P(E/E_2)+P(E_3)\cdot P(E/E_3)}$$

$$=\frac{\frac{3}{28}\cdot\frac{6}{10}}{\frac{15}{28}\cdot\frac{5}{10}+\frac{3}{28}\cdot\frac{6}{10}+\frac{10}{28}\cdot\frac{4}{10}}$$

$$=\frac{18}{75+18+40}=\frac{18}{133}$$

37. Given,

Bag I	Bag II
4 Red and 4 Black balls	2 Red and 6 Black balls

Let E_1 = Event that bag I is chosen

E_2 = Event that bag II is chosen

and A = Event that ball is drawn red

Since, one of the bag is chosen at random.

$\therefore \quad P(E_1)=\frac{1}{2}=P(E_2)$

Probability that ball is red and drawn from bag I

$$P\left(\frac{A}{E_1}\right)=\frac{4}{4+4}=\frac{1}{2}$$

Probability that ball is red and drawn from bag II

$$P\left(\frac{A}{E_2}\right)=\frac{2}{2+6}=\frac{1}{4}$$

By Bayes' theorem,

$$P\left(\frac{E_1}{A}\right)=\left[\frac{P(E_1)\times P\left(\frac{A}{E_1}\right)}{P(E_1)\times P\left(\frac{A}{E_1}\right)+P(E_2)\times P\left(\frac{A}{E_2}\right)}\right]$$

$$=\frac{\frac{1}{2}\times\frac{1}{2}}{\frac{1}{2}\times\frac{1}{2}+\frac{1}{2}\times\frac{1}{4}}=\frac{\frac{1}{4}}{\frac{1}{4}+\frac{1}{8}}$$

$$\Rightarrow\quad P\left(\frac{E_1}{A}\right)=\frac{1}{4}\times\frac{8}{3}=\frac{2}{3}$$

Hence, the probability that the ball is drawn from bag I, and the drawn ball is red $=\frac{2}{3}$

38. Let E_1 be the event that person is suffering from TB and E_2 be the event that person is not suffering from TB.

Let E be the event that the doctor diagnoses that person has TB.

Then, $P(E_1) = \frac{1}{1000}$

$$P(E_2) = 1 - \frac{1}{1000} = \frac{999}{1000}$$

$P\left(\frac{E}{E_1}\right) = P$ (TB is detected when a person is actually suffering)

$$= 0.99 = \frac{990}{1000}$$

and $P\left(\frac{E}{E_2}\right) = P$ (TB is detected when a person is not actually suffering)

$$= 0.001 = \frac{1}{1000}$$

P (A selected person has actually TB), is given by

$$P\left(\frac{E_1}{E}\right) = \frac{P(E_1)\cdot P\left(\frac{E}{E_1}\right)}{\left[P(E_1)\cdot P\left(\frac{E}{E_1}\right) + P(E_2)\cdot P\left(\frac{E}{E_2}\right)\right]}$$

$$= \frac{\left(\frac{1}{1000}\right)\left(\frac{990}{1000}\right)}{\left(\frac{1}{1000}\right)\left(\frac{990}{1000}\right) + \left(\frac{999}{1000}\right)\left(\frac{1}{1000}\right)}$$

$$= \frac{\frac{990}{1000000}}{\frac{990+999}{1000000}} = \frac{990}{1000000} \times \frac{1000000}{1989} = \frac{990}{1989} = \frac{110}{221}$$

39. Let E_1 = Event that the person has disease and E_2 = Event that the person is healthy

Then, E_1 and E_2 are mutually exclusive and exhaustive events.

$\therefore$ $P(E_1) = 0.1\% = \frac{0.1}{100} = 0.001$

and $P(E_2) = 1 - 0.001 = 0.999$

Let E: Event that test is positive.

$P\left(\frac{E}{E_1}\right) = P$ (result is positive, given that person has disease)

$$= 99\% = \frac{99}{100} = 0.99$$

$P\left(\frac{E}{E_2}\right) = P$ (result is positive, given that person does not have disease)

$$= 0.5\% = \frac{0.5}{100} = 0.005$$

$\therefore$ Probability that a person has disease, given that test result is positive, is given by

$$\therefore \quad P\left(\frac{E_1}{E}\right) = \frac{P(E_1)\cdot P\left(\frac{E}{E_1}\right)}{P(E_1)\cdot P\left(\frac{E}{E_1}\right) + P(E_2)\cdot P\left(\frac{E}{E_2}\right)}$$

$$= \frac{0.001 \times 0.99}{0.001 \times 0.99 + 0.999 \times 0.005}$$

$$= \frac{0.00099}{0.00099 + 0.004995} = \frac{0.00099}{0.005985} = \frac{22}{133}$$

40. Hint Let E_1, E_2, E_3 and E_4 be the events of selecting boxes, A, B, C and D, respectively.

Then, $P(E_1) = P(E_2) = P(E_3) = P(E_4) = \frac{1}{4}$.

Let E = Event that the marble drawn is red. Then,

$$P(E/E_1) = \frac{1}{10}, P(E/E_2) = \frac{6}{10} = \frac{3}{5}, P(E/E_3) = \frac{8}{10} = \frac{4}{5}, P(E/E_4) = 0.$$

$$\therefore P(E_1/E) = \frac{P(E/E_1)\cdot P(E_1)}{P(E/E_1)\cdot P(E_1) + P(E/E_2)\cdot P(E_2) + P(E/E_3)\cdot P(E_3) + P(E/E_4)\cdot P(E_4)}$$

Ans. $\frac{1}{15}$

41. Let us define the events as

E_1 : Students reside in a hostel,

E_2 : Students are day scholars

and A: Students get A grade

Then, $P(E_1)$ = Probability that student reside in a hostel

$$= 60\% = \frac{60}{100}$$

and $P(E_2)$ = Probability that students are day scholars

$$= 1 - \frac{60}{100} = \frac{40}{100}$$

Also, $P(A/E_1)$ = Probability that hostelers get A grade

$$= 30\% = \frac{30}{100}$$

and $P(A/E_2)$ = Probability that students having day scholars get A grade

$$= 20\% = \frac{20}{100}$$

$\therefore$ The probability that the selecting student is a hosteler having A grade,

$$P(E_1/A) = \frac{P(E_1)\cdot P(A/E_1)}{P(E_1)\cdot P(A/E_1) + P(E_2)\cdot P(A/E_2)}$$

[by Bayes' theorem]

$$= \frac{\frac{60}{100} \times \frac{30}{100}}{\left(\frac{60}{100} \times \frac{30}{100}\right) + \left(\frac{40}{100} \times \frac{20}{100}\right)}$$

$$= \frac{1800}{1800 + 800} = \frac{1800}{2600} = \frac{18}{26} = \frac{9}{13}$$

Hence, required probability is $\frac{9}{13}$.

42. Let us define the events as

E_1 = Event of students which have 90% attendance.

E_2 = Event of students which are irregular

and A = Event of students which attendance A grade.

Then, $P(E_1) = 0.2$ and $P(E_2) = 0.8$

Also, $P\left(\frac{A}{E_1}\right) = 0.8$ and $P\left(\frac{A}{E_2}\right) = 0.2$

Using the law of total probability, we compute $P(A)$.

$$P(A) = P\left(\frac{A}{E_1}\right)P(E_1) + P\left(\frac{A}{E_2}\right)P(E_2)$$

$$\Rightarrow \quad P(A) = (0.8)\,(0.2) + (0.2) + (0.8)$$

$$\Rightarrow \quad P(A) = 0.16 + 0.16 \Rightarrow P(A) = 0.32$$

Now, using Bayes' theorem,

$$P\left(\frac{E_2}{A}\right) = \frac{P\left(\frac{A}{E_2}\right)P(E_2)}{P(A)}$$

$$= \frac{(0.2)(0.8)}{0.32} = 0.5$$

The probability that the student is irregular given they have an A grade is 0.5 or 50%.

43. Let E_1 : The patient follows meditation and yoga.

E_2 : The patient uses drug.

Then, E_1 and E_2 are mutually exclusive

and $\quad P(E_1) = P(E_2) = 1/2$

Also, let E : The selected patient suffers a heart attack.

Then, $P(E/E_1) = \frac{40}{100}\left(1-\frac{30}{100}\right) = \frac{40}{100} \times \frac{70}{100} = \frac{28}{100}$

and $P(E/E_2) = \frac{40}{100}\left(1-\frac{25}{100}\right) = \frac{40}{100} \times \frac{75}{100} = \frac{30}{100}$

$\therefore$ P (patient who suffers heart attack follows meditation and yoga)

$$= P(E_1/E) = \frac{P(E/E_1)\cdot P(E_1)}{P(E/E_1)\cdot P(E_1) + P(E/E_2)\cdot P(E_2)}$$

[using Bayes' theorem]

$$= \frac{\frac{28}{100} \times \frac{1}{2}}{\frac{28}{100} \times \frac{1}{2} + \frac{30}{100} \times \frac{1}{2}} = \frac{28}{58} = \frac{14}{29}$$

Hence, Yoga course and meditation are more beneficial for the heart patient.

QR Code for Quick Test 1

QR Code for Quick Test 2

QR Code for Quick Test 3

Mind Map

Probability

Probability of an Event

If there are n elementary equally likely events associated with a random experiment and m of them are favourable to an event A, then the probability of happening or occurrence of A is denoted by $P(A)$ and defined as

$$P(A) = \frac{m}{n} = \frac{\left[\text{Number of elementary events favourable to event } A\right]}{\left[\text{Total number of elementary events to the experiment}\right]}$$

Here,

- $0 \le P(A) \le 1$
- Probability of impossible event is zero.
- Probability of sure event is 1.
- $P(A \cup A') = 1$
- $P(A \cap A') = 0$
- $P(A')' = P(A)$
- Sometimes, we have to select r objects from n distinct objects, then we use the formula,

$$^nC_r = \frac{n!}{r!(n-r)!}, \ 0 \le r \le n$$

Important Results on Probability

1. **Addition Theorem of Probability**

   (i) For two events A and B,

   $$P(A \cup B) = P(A) + P(B) - P(A \cap B)$$

   If A and B are mutually exclusive events, then

   $$P(A \cap B) = 0$$

   $$\therefore \quad P(A \cup B) = P(A) + P(B)$$

   (ii) For three events A, B and C,

   $$P(A \cup B \cup C) = P(A) + P(B) + P(C) - P(A \cap B) - P(B \cap C) - P(A \cap C) + P(A \cap B \cap C)$$

   If A, B and C are mutually exclusive events, then

   $$P(A \cup B \cup C) = P(A) + P(B) + P(C)$$

   [for mutually exclusive events, $P(A \cap B) = P(B \cap C) = P(C \cap A) = P(A \cap B \cap C) = 0$]

2. If A and B are two events associated with a random experiment, then

   (i) $P(\bar{A} \cap B) = P(B) - P(A \cap B)$

   (ii) $P(A \cap \bar{B}) = P(A) - P(A \cap B)$

   (iii) $P(\bar{A} \cap \bar{B}) = 1 - P(A \cup B)$

   (iv) $P(\bar{A} \cup \bar{B}) = 1 - P(A \cap B)$

   (v) $P(A) = P(A \cap B) + P(A \cap \bar{B})$

   (vi) $P(B) = P(A \cap B) + P(B \cap \bar{A})$

   (vii) $P(\text{exactly one of } A, B \text{ occurs})$

   $$= P[(A \cap \bar{B}) \cup (\bar{A} \cap B)]$$
   $$= P(A) + P(B) - 2P(A \cap B)$$
   $$= P(A \cup B) - P(A \cap B)$$

3. If A, B and C are three events, then $P(\text{exactly one of } A, B, C \text{ occurs})$

   $$= P(A) + P(B) + P(C) - 2P(A \cap B) - 2P(B \cap C) - 2P(A \cap C) + 3P(A \cap B \cap C)$$

4. $P(\bar{A}) = 1 - P(A)$

Multiplication Theorem

Let A and B be two events associated with a random experiment, then multiplication rule is defined as

$$P(A \cap B) = \begin{cases} P(A) \cdot P(B/A), \text{ where } P(A) \neq 0 \\ P(B) \cdot P(A/B), \text{ where } P(B) \neq 0 \end{cases}$$

where, $A \cap B$ (or AB) denotes the simultaneous occurrence of the events A and B.

Multiplication Rule for More than Two Events

Let E, F, G and H be form events of sample space S. Then,

(i) $P(E \cap F \cap G) = P(E) \cdot P\left(\frac{F}{E}\right) \cdot P\left(\frac{G}{E \cap F}\right)$

(ii) $P(E \cap F \cap G \cap H)$

$$= P(E) \cdot P\left(\frac{F}{E}\right) \cdot P\left(\frac{G}{E \cap F}\right) \cdot P\left(\frac{H}{E \cap F \cap G}\right)$$

Theorem of Total Probability

A set of events $E_1, E_2, \ldots, E_n$ is said to represent a **partition of the sample space** S, if it satisfies the following conditions

- $E_1 \cap E_j = \phi, \ i \neq j; \ i, j = 1, 2, \ldots n$
- $E_1 \cup E_2 \cup \ldots \cup E_n = S$
- $P(E_i) > 0, \ \forall \ i = 1, 2, \ldots, n$

Let $\{E_1, E_2, \ldots, E_n\}$ be a partition of the sample space S and each having non-zero probability of occurrence.

Again, let A be any event associated with S, then

$$P(A) = P(E_1) \cdot P(A/E_1) + P(E_2) \cdot P(A/E_2) + \ldots + P(E_n) \cdot P(A/E_n) = \sum_{j=1}^{n} P(E_j) \cdot P(A/E_j)$$

Baye's Theorem

If $E_1, E_2, \ldots E_n$ are n non-empty events, which constitute a partition of sample space S (or E_i's are mutually exclusive and exhaustive events) i.e. $E_1, E_2, \ldots E_n$ are pairwise disjoint, $E_1 \cup E_2 \cup \ldots \cup E_n = S$ and $P(E_i) > 0, \forall i = 1, 2, 3, \ldots n$.

Also, let A be any event of non-zero probability, then

$$P(E_i/A) = \frac{P(E_i) \cdot P(A/E_i)}{\sum_{j=1}^{n} P(E_j) \cdot P(A/E_j)}, \text{ for any } i = 1, 2, 3, \ldots n$$

Conditional Probability

If A and B are two events associated with the same sample space of a random experiment, then conditional probability of the event A under the condition B has already occurred. i.e. $P(A/B)$ is given by

$$P\left(\frac{A}{B}\right) = \frac{P(A \cap B)}{P(B)}, \text{ provided } P(B) \neq 0$$

Also, we can determine

$$P\left(\frac{B}{A}\right) = \frac{P(B \cap A)}{P(A)}, \text{ provided } P(A) \neq 0$$

If A and B are mutually exclusive events, then $P\left(\frac{A}{B}\right) = P\left(\frac{B}{A}\right) = 0$

Properties of Conditional Probability

Let A and B be the events of a sample space S of an experiment, then

(i) $P(S/A) = P(A/A) = 1$

(ii) If A and B are any two events of a sample space S and C is an event of S such that $P(C) \neq 0$, then

$$P\{(A \cup B)/C\} = P(A/C) + P(B/C) - P\{(A \cap B)/C\}$$

In particular, if A and B are disjoint events, then

$$P\left(\frac{A \cup B}{C}\right) = P\left(\frac{A}{C}\right) + P\left(\frac{B}{C}\right)$$

(iii) $P(A'/B) = 1 - P(A/B)$, where A' is complement of A.

Pre-Mid Term Tests

[Chapters Covered — 1-4] **10 Marks**

TEST 1

1. Find the value of $\tan^{-1}(-1)$ in the interval $\left(\frac{\pi}{2}, \frac{3\pi}{2}\right)$. [1]

   (a) $\frac{3\pi}{4}$ (b) $\frac{2\pi}{3}$ (c) π (d) 2π

2. Let R be the equivalence relation in the set $A = \{0, 1, 2, 3, 4, 5\}$ given by $R = \{(a, b) : 2$ divides $(a - b)\}$. Then, the equivalence class [0] is [1]

   (a) $\{0, 2, 4\}$ (b) $\{1, 2, 3\}$

   (c) $\{0, 1, 3\}$ (d) $\{2, 3, 5\}$

3. For what values of k, the system of linear equations $x + y + z = 2$, $2x + y - z = 3$ and $3x + 2y + kz = 4$ has a unique solution? [1]

   (a) $k = 0$ (b) $k \neq 0$

   (c) $k = 1$ (d) $k \neq 1$

4. If $x\begin{bmatrix}2\\3\end{bmatrix} + y\begin{bmatrix}-1\\1\end{bmatrix} = \begin{bmatrix}10\\5\end{bmatrix}$, then find the value of $x + y$. [1]

5. Find the transpose of matrix $\begin{bmatrix}-1 & 5 & 6\\ \sqrt{3} & 5 & 6\\ 2 & 3 & -1\end{bmatrix}$. [1]

6. If $A' = \begin{bmatrix}-2 & 3\\ 1 & 2\end{bmatrix}$ and $B = \begin{bmatrix}-1 & 0\\ 1 & 2\end{bmatrix}$, then find $(A + 2B)'$. [1]

7. Find the domain of $\cos^{-1}(2x - 1)$. [2]

8. Let a relation R on the set N of natural number be define as $R = \{(x, y) : 3x^2 - 7xy + 4y^2 = 0; x, y \in N\}$.

   Then, show that relation R is reflexive but neither symmetric nor transitive. [2]

TEST 2

1. If $2\begin{bmatrix}3 & 4\\ 5 & x\end{bmatrix} + \begin{bmatrix}1 & y\\ 0 & 1\end{bmatrix} = \begin{bmatrix}7 & 0\\ 10 & 5\end{bmatrix}$, then the value of $(x - y)$ is [1]

   (a) 5 (b) 10

   (c) 15 (d) 20

2. The value of $2\ {}^{-1}2 + \sin^{-1}\left(\frac{1}{2}\right)$ is [1]

   (a) $\frac{\pi}{2}$ (b) $\frac{2\pi}{5}$

   (c) $\frac{5\pi}{6}$ (d) $\frac{3\pi}{4}$

3. If the function $f : R \to A$ given by $f(x) = \frac{x^2}{1 + x^2}$ is a surjection, then A is equal to [1]

   (a) R (b) $[0, 1]$ (c) $(0, 1]$ (d) $[0, 1)$

4. Evaluate : $\sin\left\{\frac{\pi}{2} - \sin^{-1}\left(\frac{-\sqrt{3}}{2}\right)\right\}$. [1]

5. Find the value of $\begin{vmatrix}1 & 2 & 4\\ -1 & 3 & 0\\ 4 & 1 & 0\end{vmatrix}$. [1]

6. If a matrix has 14 elements, then what are the possible orders it can have? What it has 17 elements? [1]

7. If $A = \begin{bmatrix}\cos\alpha & -\sin\alpha\\ \sin\alpha & \cos\alpha\end{bmatrix}$ is identity matrix, then write the value of α. [2]

8. Find the value of $\cos^{-1}\left(\frac{1}{2}\right) + 2\sin^{-1}\left(\frac{1}{2}\right)$. [2]

TEST 3

1. If $A = \text{diag}[2, -1, 3]$ and $B = \text{diag}[3, 0, -1]$, then the value of $(4A + 2B)$ is [1]
(a) diag $[7, -1, 5]$
(b) diag $[1, 5, -10]$
(c) diag $[14, -4, 10]$
(d) None of the above

2. If area of a triangle is 35 sq units with vertices $(2, -6)$, $(5, 4)$ and $(k, 4)$, then the value of k is [1]
(a) 2 and 4
(b) −2 and 6
(c) 2 and 12
(d) 12 and −2

3. The relation R in the set $\{1, 2, 3, \ldots, 13, 14\}$ defined as $R = \{(x, y) : 3x - y = 0\}$ is [1]
(a) reflexive (b) transitive
(c) symmetric (d) None of these

4. If the points (a_1, b_1), (a_2, b_2) and $(a_1 + a_2, b_1 + b_2)$ are collinear, then show that $a_1 b_2 = a_2 b_1$. [1]

5. Find the value of $\sin^{-1}\left(\frac{-\sqrt{3}}{2}\right) + \cos^{-1}\left(\frac{\sqrt{3}}{2}\right)$. [1]

6. Find the values of $\sec^{-1}\left(\frac{1}{2}\right)$. [1]

7. If $\begin{bmatrix} x+3 & z+4 & 2y-7 \\ -6 & a-1 & 0 \\ b-3 & -21 & 0 \end{bmatrix} = \begin{bmatrix} 0 & 6 & 3y-2 \\ -6 & -3 & 2c+2 \\ 2b+4 & -21 & 0 \end{bmatrix}$

then find the value of a, b, c and z. [2]

8. Find the value of
$\tan^{-1}\left(\frac{1}{\sqrt{3}}\right) + \cot^{-1}\left(\frac{1}{\sqrt{3}}\right) + \tan^{-1}\left(\sin\left(\frac{\pi}{2}\right)\right)$. [2]

Answers

TEST 1

1. (a) 2. (a) 3. (b) 4. −1 5. $\begin{bmatrix} -1 & \sqrt{3} & 2 \\ 5 & 5 & 3 \\ 6 & 6 & -1 \end{bmatrix}$

6. $\begin{bmatrix} -4 & 5 \\ 1 & 6 \end{bmatrix}$ 7. $[0, 1]$

TEST 2

1. (b) 2. (c) 3. (d) 4. $\frac{1}{2}$

5. −52 6. $[1 \times 14, 14 \times 1, 2 \times 7, 7 \times 2]$, $[1 \times 17, 17 \times 1]$

7. 0 8. $\frac{2\pi}{3}$

TEST 3

1. (c) 2. (d) 3. (d) 5. $\frac{-\pi}{6}$

6. ϕ 7. $a = -2$, $b = -7$, $c = -1$ and $z = 2$. 8. $\frac{3\pi}{4}$

Mid Term Tests

[Chapters Covered — 1-8] **10 Marks**

TEST 1

1. The domain of the function defined by $f(x) = \sin^{-1}\sqrt{x-1}$ is [1]
   (a) [1, 2] (b) [2, 1]
   (c) [−1, 1] (d) [0, 1]

2. The value of $\begin{vmatrix} \log_3 256 & \log_4 3 \\ \log_3 8 & \log_4 9 \end{vmatrix}$, is [1]
   (a) $\frac{7}{2}$ (b) $\frac{13}{2}$
   (c) $\frac{11}{2}$ (d) 2

3. If $3A - B = \begin{bmatrix} 5 & 0 \\ 1 & 1 \end{bmatrix}$ and $B = \begin{bmatrix} 4 & 3 \\ 2 & 5 \end{bmatrix}$, then the value of matrix A, is [1]
   (a) $\begin{bmatrix} 3 & 1 \\ 1 & 2 \end{bmatrix}$ (b) $\begin{bmatrix} 1 & 3 \\ 2 & 1 \end{bmatrix}$ (c) $\begin{bmatrix} 2 & 3 \\ 1 & 1 \end{bmatrix}$ (d) $\begin{bmatrix} 1 & 1 \\ 2 & 1 \end{bmatrix}$

4. If $f(x) = x \cos x + e^x$, then find $f'(0)$. [1]

5. Determine whether the function $f : A \to B$ defined by $f(x) = 4x + 7$, $x \in A$ is one-one. [1]

6. Show that the function $f(x) = 4x^3 - 18x^2 + 27x - 7$ is always increasing on R. [1]

7. Evaluate $\int_0^{\pi/2} \frac{\sin^{3/2} x}{\sin^{3/2} x + \cos^{3/2} x} dx$ [2]

8. Solve, $\int \sin^{-1}\sqrt{\frac{a}{a+x}}\, dx$ [2]

TEST 2

1. The value of $\operatorname{cosec}^{-1}\sqrt{2}$ is [1]
   (a) does not exist (b) $\frac{\pi}{3}$
   (c) $\frac{\pi}{4}$ (d) $\frac{\pi}{6}$

2. If $y = \tan(x + y)$, then $\frac{dy}{dx}$ is [1]
   (a) $\operatorname{cosec}^2 (x + y)$
   (b) $-\operatorname{cosec}^2 (x + y)$
   (c) $\sec^2 (x + y)$
   (d) $-\sec^2 (x + y)$

3. Which of the following function from z to itself are bijections? [1]
   (a) $f(x) = x^3$
   (b) $f(x) = x^2 + x$
   (c) $f(x) = 2x + 1$
   (d) $f(x) = x + 2$

4. Evaluate $\int \tan^2 x \quad {}^4 x\, dx$ [1]

5. Find the maximum and minimum values of $f(x) = \sin x$ in the interval $[\pi, 2\pi]$. [1]

6. If $P = \begin{bmatrix} x & 0 \\ 1 & 1 \end{bmatrix}$ and $Q = \begin{bmatrix} 1 & 0 \\ 5 & 1 \end{bmatrix}$, find the values of x for which $P^2 = Q$. [1]

7. Find the value of a, so that the function $f(x)$ is defined by
   $f(x) = \begin{cases} \frac{\sin^2 ax}{x^2}, & x \neq 0 \\ 1, & x = 0 \end{cases}$ may be continuous at $x = 0$. [2]

8. Find the maximum and minimum values of the function $2x^3 - 15x^2 + 36x + 11$. [2]

TEST 3

1. Let A and B be two non-empty sets and let $f:(A \times B) \to (B \times A): f(a, b) = (b, a)$. Then, f is [1]
   (a) many-one and onto (b) many-one and into
   (c) one-one and onto (d) one-one and into

2. The domain of the function defined by $f(x) = \sin^{-1}\sqrt{x-1}$, is [1]
   (a) $x \in [0, 2]$ (b) $x \in [1, 2]$
   (c) $x \in [1, 3]$ (d) $x \in (1, 2)$

3. If matrix $\begin{bmatrix} 0 & a & 3 \\ 2 & b & -1 \\ c & 1 & 0 \end{bmatrix}$ is a skew symmetric matrix, then the value of a, b and c is, [1]
   (a) $-2, 0, -3$ (b) $1, 0, 2$
   (c) $2, 1, -1$ (d) $-2, 1, -4$

4. If $x = at^2$ and $y = 2at$, then find $\frac{dy}{dx}$. [1]

5. Differentiate $(\sin x)^{\log x}$ w.r.t $\sin x$. [1]

6. Evaluate $\int \frac{\cos x}{\sqrt{1+\sin x}}\,dx$ [1]

7. If A is a square matrix such that $|A| \neq 0$ and $A^2 - A + 2I = 0$, then find A^{-1}. [2]

8. Show that the function $f(x) = |x-5|$ is continuous but not differentiable at $x = 5$. [2]

Answers

TEST 1

1. (a) 2. (b) 3. (a) 4. (2) 5. Yes $f(x)$ is one-one

7. $\frac{\pi}{4}$ 8. $a\left[\tan^{-1}\sqrt{\frac{x}{a}} \cdot \frac{a+x}{a} - \sqrt{\frac{x}{a}}\right] + C$

TEST 2

1. (c) 2. (b) 3. (b) 4. $\frac{\tan^5 x}{5} + \frac{\tan^3 x}{3} + C$

5. $0, -1$ 6. No value of x for which $P^2 = Q$ is true 7. ± 1

8. Maximum value = 39 and minimum value = 38

TEST 3

1. (c) 2. (b) 3. (a) 4. $\frac{1}{t}$

5. $(\sin x)^{\log x}\left[\cot x \log x + \frac{\log \sin x}{x}\right]$ 6. $2\sqrt{1+\sin x} + C$ 7. $\frac{1}{2}(I - A)$

PERIODIC TESTS

Post-Mid Term Tests

[Chapters Covered — 1-13] **10 Marks**

TEST 1

1. If $A = \{1, 2, 3\}$, then a relation $R = \{\{2, 3\}\}$ on A is [1]
   (a) symmetric and transitive only
   (b) symmetric only
   (c) transitive only
   (d) none of these

2. If $y = \sec^{-1} x$, then [1]
   (a) $\frac{-\pi}{2} < y < \frac{\pi}{2}$ (b) $0 \le y < \frac{\pi}{2}$ or $\frac{\pi}{2} < y \le \pi$
   (c) $0 \le y \le \pi$ (d) $\pi \le y \le 2\pi$

3. If A is 3×4 matrix and B is a matrix such that $A^T B$ and BA^T are both defined. Then, B is on f the type. [1]
   (a) 3×4 (b) 3×3
   (c) 4×4 (d) 4×3

4. If $\int_a^b x^3\, dx = 0$ and if $\int_a^b x^2\, dx = \frac{2}{3}$, find a and b. [1]

5. If $\vec{a}$ and $\vec{b}$ are two vectors such that $|\vec{a} \times \vec{b}| = \sqrt{3}$ and $\vec{a} \cdot \vec{b} = 1$, find the angle between $\vec{a}$ and $\vec{b}$. [1]

6. A die is rolled twice and the sum of the numbers appearing on them is observed to be 7. What is the conditional probability that the number 2 has appeared at least once? [1]

7. Solve the following linear programming problem graphically.
   Maximize $Z = 50x + 15y$
   Subject to constraints are
   $5x + y \le 100$
   $x + y \le 60$
   $x, y \ge 0$ [2]

8. If $y = x^x$, prove that $\frac{d^2y}{dx^2} - \frac{1}{y}\left(\frac{dy}{dx}\right)^2 - \frac{y}{x} = 0$. [2]

TEST 2

1. If $AA^T = 4I$, then $|A|$ is equal to [1]
   (a) ± 1 (b) ± 2
   (c) 0 (d) None of these

2. Differential coefficient of $(\tan^{-1} x)$ is [1]
   (a) $\frac{x}{1 + x^2}$ (b) $x\sqrt{1 + x^2}$ (c) $\frac{1}{\sqrt{1 + x^2}}$ (d) $\frac{x}{\sqrt{1 + x^2}}$

3. $\int \frac{x}{4 + x^4}\, dx$ is equal to [1]
   (a) $\frac{1}{4}\tan^{-1} x^2 + c$ (b) $\frac{1}{4}\tan^{-1}\left(\frac{x^2}{2}\right) + C$
   (c) $\frac{1}{2}\tan^{-1}\left(\frac{x^2}{2}\right) + C$ (d) None of these

4. If $n(A) = 4$ and $n(B) = 6$. Then, find the number of one-one function from A to B. [1]

5. If $\vec{a}$ and $\vec{b}$ are two unit vectors such that $\vec{a} + \vec{b}$ is also a unit vector, then find the angle between $\vec{a}$ and $\vec{b}$. [1]

6. A sphere increases its volume at the rate of π cm^3/s. Find the rate at which its surface area increases, when the radius is 1 cm. [1]

7. Evaluate,
   $P(A \cup B)$, if $2P(A) = P(B) = \frac{6}{13}$ and $P\left(\frac{A}{B}\right) = \frac{1}{3}$ [2]

8. Solve the given initial value problem :
   $(x^2 + 1)\frac{dy}{dx} - 2xy = (x^4 + 2x^2 + 1)\cos x,\ y(0) = 0$ [2]

TEST 3

1. The function $f:[0, \infty) \to [0, \infty)$ defined by

$$f(x) = \frac{2x}{1+2x} \text{ is}$$ [1]

(a) one-one and onto
(b) one-one but not onto
(c) not one-one but onto
(d) neither one-one nor onto

2. The number of all possible matrices of order 3×3 with each entry 0 or 1 is [1]

(a) 27 (b) 18
(c) 81 (d) 512

3. A unit vector perpendicular to both $i + j$ and $j + k$ is [1]

(a) $i - j + k$ (b) $i + j + k$
(c) $\frac{1}{\sqrt{3}}(i + j + k)$ (d) $\frac{1}{\sqrt{3}}(i - j + k)$

4. If $\sin^{-1} x + \sin^{-1} y + \sin^{-1} z = \frac{3\pi}{2}$, then find the value of $x^9 + y^9 + z^9 - \frac{1}{x^9 y^9 z^9}$. [1]

5. If $y = \tan^{-1}\left(\frac{1-x}{1+x}\right)$, find $\frac{dy}{dx}$. [1]

6. Evaluate : $\int e^x \left(\frac{\sqrt{1-x^2}\sin^{-1} x + 1}{\sqrt{1-x^2}}\right) dx$ [1]

7. Find the shortest distance between the lines whose vector equations are

$$\vec{r} = 3i + 8j + 3k + \lambda(3i - j + k)$$

and $\vec{r} = -3i - 7j + 6k + \mu(-3i + 2j + 4k)$ [2]

8. Find the maximum value of $Z = 4x + 2y$ subject to constraints $4x + 2y \geq 46$, $x + 3y \leq 24$ and $x, y \geq 0$. [2]

Answers

TEST 1

1. (c) 2. (b) 3. (a) 4. $a = -1, b = 1$ 5. $\frac{\pi}{3}$
6. $\frac{1}{3}$ 7. 1250

TEST 2

1. (b) 2. (d) 3. (b) 4. 360 5. $\frac{2\pi}{3}$
6. $2\pi\ cm^2/s$ 7. $\frac{7}{13}$ 8. $y = (x^2 + 1)\sin x$

Test 3

1. (b) 2. (d) 3. (c) 4. 2 5. $\frac{-1}{1+x^2}$
6. $e^x \sin^{-1} x + c$ 7. $\sqrt{270}$ 8. 96

ACTIVITY 1

To verify that the relation R in the set L of all lines in a plane, defined by $R = \{(l, m): l \perp m\}$ is symmetric but neither reflexive nor transitive.

Material Required

A piece of plywood, 8 pieces of wires, some nails, white paper, gum etc.

Method of Construction

Take a piece of plywood and paste a white paper on it. Fix all the 8 wires randomly on the plywood with the help of nails such that some of them are parallel, some are perpendicular to each other and some are inclined as shown in figure given below.

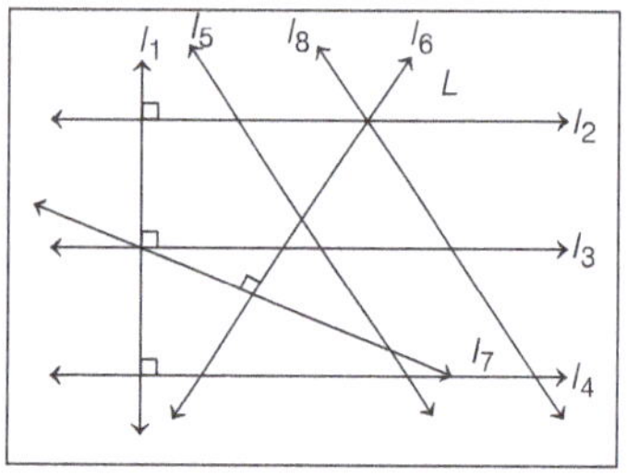

Figure 1.1

Demonstration

1. Let the wires represent the lines $l_1, l_2, \ldots l_8$.
2. l_1 is perpendicular to each of the lines l_2, l_3, l_4 [see above figure]
3. l_6 is perpendicular to l_7.
4. l_2 is parallel to l_3, l_3 is parallel to l_4 and l_5 is parallel to l_8.
5. $(l_1, l_2), (l_1, l_3), (l_1, l_4), (l_6, l_7) \in R$

Observation

1. In the above figure, no line is perpendicular to itself, so the relation $R = \{(l, m): l \perp m\}$ ...... reflexive (is/is not).
2. In Fig, $l_1 \perp l_2$. Is $l_2 \perp l_1$? .... (Yes/No)
   $\therefore (l_1, l_2) \in R \Rightarrow (l_2, l_1)$........... $R(\notin / \in)$
   Similarly, $l_3 \perp l_1$. Is $l_1 \perp l_3$? .... (Yes/No)
   $\therefore (l_3, l_1) \in R \Rightarrow (l_1, l_3)$........... $R(\notin / \in)$
   Also, $l_6 \perp l_7$. Is $l_7 \perp l_6$? .... (Yes/No)
   $\therefore (l_6, l_7) \in R \Rightarrow (l_7, l_6)$........... $R(\notin / \in)$
   $\therefore$ The relation R.... symmetric (is/is not).
3. In Fig $l_2 \perp l_1$ and $l_1 \perp l_3$. Is $l_2 \perp l_3$? .... (Yes/No)
   i.e., $(l_2, l_1) \in R$ and $(l_1, l_3) \in R$
   $\Rightarrow (l_2, l_3)$........ $R(\notin / \in)$
   $\therefore$ The relation R... transitive (is/is not).

Application

On the basis of this activity we can check whether a given relation is an equivalence relation or not.

Note

1. In this case, the relation is not an equivalence relation.
2. The activity can be repeated by taking some more wire in different positions.

VIVA-VOCE

1 What is the neccessary condition for a relation to be reflexive?

Ans A relation R on a set A is said to be reflexive if every element of A is related to itself. Thus, R is reflexive $\Leftrightarrow (a, a) \in R \ \forall \ a \in A$.

2 Define a relation.

Ans Let A and B be two sets. Then, a relation R from set A to set B is a subset of $A \times A$. Thus, R is a relation from A to $B \Leftrightarrow R \leq A \times B$.

3 Write the smallest reflexive relation on set $A = \{1, 2, 3\}$

Ans $\{(1, 1), (2, 2), (3, 3)\}$

4 State the reason for the relation R on the set $\{1, 2, 3\}$ given by $R = \{(1, 2), (2, 1)\}$ not to be transitive.

Ans We observe that $(1, 2) \in R$ and $(2, 1) \in R$ but $(1, 1) \notin R$. Hence, R is not transitive.

5 Let $A = \{a, b, c\}$ and R be a set on A define as $R = \{(a, a), (b, b)\}$. State whether it is reflexive or identity relation.

Ans Since, $(c, c) \notin R$, hence it is reflexive but not identity relation on A.

6 Give a practical example of a equivalence relation.

Ans R be a relation on the set B of all books in a library, defined by $R = \{(a, b) : a$ and b both have same page$\}$.

7 The union of two equivalence relation on a set is not neccessarily on equivalence, relation on the set. True or false?

Ans True. Let $A = \{a, b, c\}$ and set R and S be two relations on A, given by $R = \{(a, a), (b, b), (c, c), (a, b), (b, a)\}$ and $S = \{(a, a), (b, b), (c, c), (b, c), (c, b)\}$
Both R and S are equivalence. But $R \cup S$ is not transitive, because $(a, b) \in R \cup S$ and $(b, c) \in R \cup S$ but $(a, c) \in R \cup S$.

8 Let $A = \{0, 1, 2, 3\}$ and R be a relation on A defined as $R = \{(0, 0), (0, 1), (0, 3), (1, 0), (1, 1), (2, 2), (3, 0), (3, 3)\}$
Is R is reflexive? Symmetric ? Transitive ?

Ans Reflexive and symmetric.

ACTIVITY 2

To verify that the relation R in the set L of all lines in a plane, defined by $R = \{(l, m) : l \parallel m\}$ is an equivalence relation.

Material Required

A piece of plywood, 8 pieces of wire, plywood, some nails, white paper, gum etc.

Method of Construction

Take a piece of plywood and paste a white paper on it. Fix all the 8 wires randomly on the plywood with the help of nails such that some of them are parallel, some are perpendicular to each other and some are inclined as shown in figure given below.

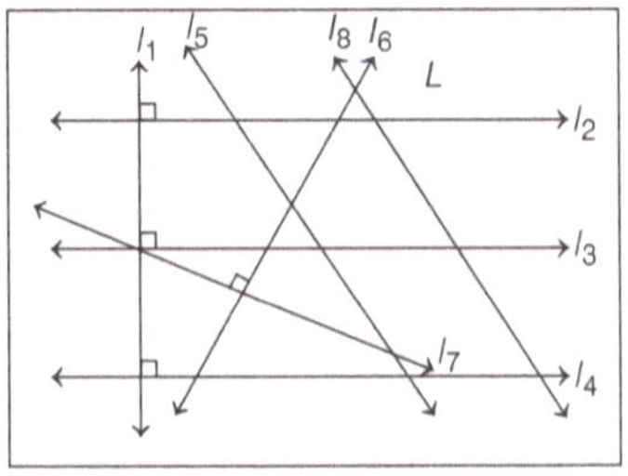

Figure 2.1

Demonstration

1. Let the wires represent the lines $l_1, l_2, \ldots l_8$.
2. l_1 is perpendicular to each of the lines l_2, l_3, l_4 [see figure].
3. l_6 is perpendicular to l_7.
4. l_2 is parallel to l_3, l_3 is parallel to l_4 and l_5 is parallel to l_8.
5. $(l_2, l_3), (l_3, l_4), (l_5, l_8) \in R$

Observation

1. In fig., every line is parallel to itself. So the relation $R = \{(l, m) : l \| m\}$ .... reflexive relation (is/is not)
2. In fig., observe that $l_2 \| l_3$. $l_3 \ldots\ldots l_2$? (II/II)
   So, $(l_2, l_3) \in R \Rightarrow (l_3, l_2) \ldots . R (\notin / \in)$
   Similarly, $l_3 \| l_4$. Is $l_4 \ldots . l_3$? (II/II)
   So, $(l_3, l_4) \in R \Rightarrow (l_4, l_3) \ldots . R (\notin / \in)$
   and $(l_5, l_8) \in R \Rightarrow (l_8, l_5) \ldots . R (\notin / \in)$
   $\therefore$ The relation R .... symmetric relation (is/is not)
3. In fig., observe that $l_2 \| l_3$ and $l_3 \| l_4$. Is $l_2 \ldots . l_4$? (II/II)
   So, $(l_2, l_3) \in R$ and $(l_3, l_4) \in R \Rightarrow (l_2, l_4) \ldots . R (\notin / \in)$
   Similarly, $l_3 \| l_4$ and $l_4 \| l_2$. Is $l_3 \ldots . l_2$? (II/II)
   So, $(l_3, l_4) \in R$,
   $(l_4, l_2) \in R \Rightarrow (l_3, l_2) \ldots . R (\notin / \in)$
   Thus, the relation R... transitive relation (is/is not)
   Hence, the relation R is reflexive, symmetric and transitive. So, R is an equivalence relation.

Application

From this activity we can easily understand start the concept of an equivalence relation.

Note

1. This activity can be repeated by taking fixing some more wires in different positions.
2. In this case, the relation is an equivalence relation.

VIVA-VOCE

1 Define a symmetric relation.

Ans A relation R on a set A is said to be a symmetric relation iff

$$(a, b) \in R \Rightarrow (b, a) \in R \; \forall \; a, b \in A$$

2 Define a transitive relation.

Ans Let A be any set A relation R on A is said to be transitive relation iff.

$$(a, b) \in R \text{ and } (b, c) \in R$$
$$\Rightarrow \quad (a, c) \in R \; \forall \; a, b, c \in A$$

3 Define an equivalence relation.

Ans A relation R on a set A is said to be an equivalence relation on A iff it is reflexive, symmetric and transitive.

4 For the set $A = \{1, 2, 3\}$ define a relation R on the set A as follow: $R = \{(1, 1), (2, 2), (3, 3), (1, 3)\}$

Write the ordered pairs to be added to R to make the smallest equivalence relation.

Ans (3, 1)

5 Write the smallest equivalence relation on the set $A = \{1, 2, 3\}$

Ans $\{(1, 1), (2, 2), (3, 3)\}$

6 If R is a symmetric relation on a set A then write a relation between R and R^{-1}.

Ans $R = R^{-1}$

7 Let R be the equivalence relation in the set $A = \{0, 1, 2, 3, 4, 5\}$ given by $R = \{(a, b) : 2 \text{ divides } (a - b)\}$. write the equivalence class of [0].

Ans Clearly 2-0 and 4-0 are divisible by 2. Therefore, $(2, 0) \in R$ and $(4, 0) \in R$.

$\therefore \quad [0] = [2, 4]$

8 Is it true, the inverse of an equivalence relation is an equivalence relation.

Ans Yes.

ACTIVITY 3

To demonstrate a function which is not one-one but is onto.

Material Required

A piece of cardboard, some nails, some strings of 5-6 cm length, gum and some plastic strips.

Method of Construction

1. Paste a plastic strip on the left hand side of the cardboard and fix three nails on it as shown in the fig (a). Name them as 1, 2 and 3.
2. Paste another strip on the right hand side of the cardboard and fix two nails in the plastic strip as shown in fig (b). Name them as a and b.
3. Join nails on the left strip to the nails on the right strip as shown in fig (c).

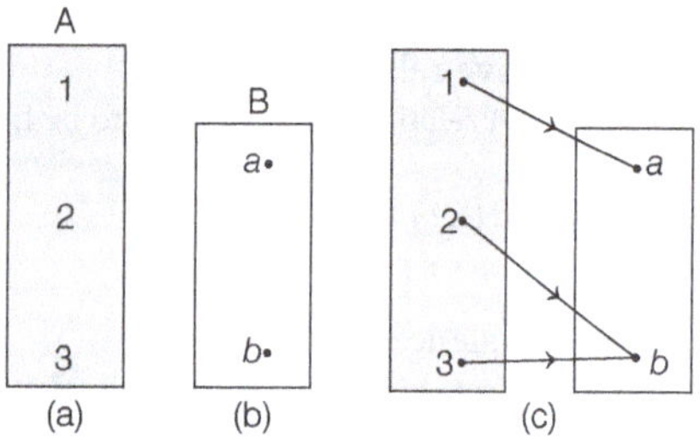

Figure 3.1

Demonstration

1. Take the set $A = \{1, 2, 3\}$.
2. Take the set $B = \{a, b\}$.
3. Join (correspondence) elements of A to the elements of B as shown in fig (c).

Observation

1. The image of the element 1 of A in B is ....
   The image of the element 2 of A in B is
   The image of the element 3 of A in B is
   So, fig (c) represents a ......
2. Every element in A has a .... image in B.
   So, the function is ...... (one - one/not one-one).
3. The pre-image of each element of B in A .... (exists / does not exist). So, the function is .... (onto/ not onto).

Application

This activity is very helpful to understand the concept of a function to be one - one and onto.

Note Demonstrate the same activity by increasing the number of the elements (nails) of the sets A and B.

VIVA-VOCE

1 Write the condition for a function $f(x)$ to be one-one

Ans A function $f(x)$ is said to be one-one, if for x_1 and x_2.

iff $f(x_1) = f(x_2) \Rightarrow x_1 = x_2$

2 What do you mean by injective mapping

Ans If a function is one-one than it is known as injective mapping.

3 Let A be the set of all 50 students of class XII in a school. Let $F : A \to N$ be a function defined by $f(x) =$ Roll number of student y state weflur it is one-one or not.

Ans Since, no two different students of the class can have the same roll number. Therefore, f is one-one.

4 Is $\cos x$ is one-one or not?

Ans We know that, $\cos 0 = \cos 2\pi = 1$.

Hence, $\cos x$ is not one-one.

5 Let $A = \{-1, 0, 1\}$ and $f(x) = x^2$, $x \in A$. Find whether $f(x)$ is one-one or not on A.

Ans We have, $f(-1) = (-1)^2 = 1$ and $f(1) = (1)^2 = 1$

$\therefore\ f(-1) = f(1)$

But $-1 \neq 1$

Hence, $f(x)$ is not one-one.

ACTIVITY 4

To demonstrate a function which is one-one but not onto.

Material Required

A piece of cardboard, some nails, some strings of 5-6 cm length, gum and some plastic strips.

Method of Construction

1. Paste a plastic strip on the left hand side of the cardboard and fix two nails in it as shown in the fig (a). Name them as a and b.
2. Paste another strip on the right hand side of the cardboard and fix three nails on it as shown in fig (b). Name them as 1, 2 and 3.
3. Join nails on the left strip to the nails on the right strip as shown in the fig (c).

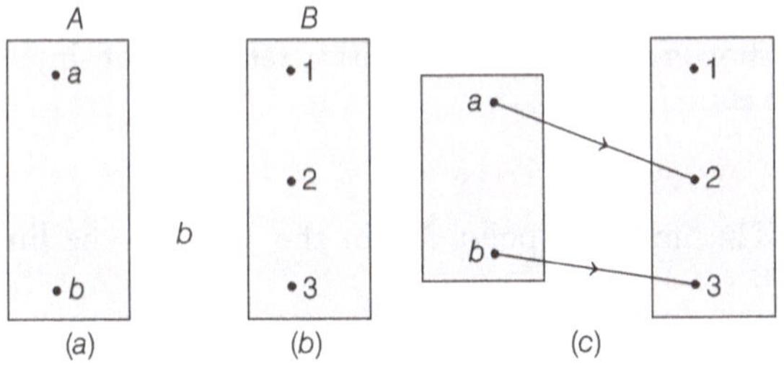

Figure 4.1

Demonstration

1. Take the set $A = \{a, b\}$.
2. Take the set $B = \{1, 2, 3\}$.
3. Join elements of A to the elements of B as shown in fig (c).

Observation

1. The image of the element a of A in B is ....
   The image of the element b of A in B is
   So, the fig (c) represents a ......
2. Every element in A has a .... image in B. So, the function is ...... (one - one/not one-one).
3. The pre-image of the element 1 of B in A of B in A .... (exists / does not exist). So, the function is .... (onto/ not onto).
   Thus fig (c) represents a function which is .... but not onto.

Application

This activity is very useful to understand the concept of a function to be one - one and onto.

Note Demonstrate the same activity by increasing the number of the elements (nails) of the set A and B.

VIVA-VOCE

1 Define onto function.

Ans A function $f : A \to B$ is said to be an onto function if every element of B is the f - image of same element of A.

2 Give another name of onto function.

Ans Another name of onto function is surjection.

3 Give condition to r a function to be bijective.

Ans For a function to be bijective it must be injective (one-one) and surjective (onto) both.

4 For a function $f(x) = \sin x$ on R to be onto, what must be its co-domain.

Ans For a function to be onto, co-domain must be equal to range of the function

$\therefore$ For $f(x) = \sin x$, to be onto

Co-domain = Range of $\sin x = [-1, 1]$

5 Let $A = \{1, 2\}$, $B = \{a, b, c\}$. A function is defined from A to B. What is number of possible onto function?

Ans Since, $n(A) < n(B)$, so there is no onto function is possible from A to B.

6 Let $f : R \to R$ defined by $f(x) = \text{sgn}(x)$. Check whether $f(x)$ is one-one and onto.

Ans We know that,

$$\text{sgn}(x) = \begin{cases} -1, & x < 0 \\ 0, & x = 0 \\ 1, & x > 1 \end{cases}$$

So, $f(x)$ is neither one-one nor onto.

7 Given an example of a bijective function.

Ans $f : R \to R$ defined by $f(x) = x$

8 State why $f(x) = e^x$ on R is not onto

Ans We know that, Range of $f(x) = (0, \infty) \neq R$

So, $f(x)$ is not onto.

ACTIVITY 5

To draw the graph of $\sin^{-1} x$*, using the graph of* $\sin x$ *and demonstrate the concept of mirror reflection (about the line* $y = x$*).*

Material Required

Cardboard, white chart paper, scale, coloured pens, gum, pencil, eraser, cutter, some nails and some thin wires.

Method of Construction

1. Take a cardboard of suitable dimensions, say, 40 $\times$40 .
2. On the cardboard, fix a white chart paper of size 30 $\times$30 (say) using gum.
3. On the paper, draw two lines, perpendicular to each other and name them $X'OX$ and YOY' as rectangular axes [see given Fig.].
4. Graduate the axes approximately as shown in figure by taking unit on X - axis = 1.25 times the unit of Y-axis.
5. Mark the points (approximately) $\left(\frac{\pi}{6}, \sin\frac{\pi}{6}\right), \left(\frac{\pi}{4}, \sin\frac{\pi}{4}\right), \ldots, \left(\frac{\pi}{2}, \sin\frac{\pi}{2}\right)$ in the coordinate plane.
   Also, fix nail at each point and name them N_1, N_2, N_3, N_4.
6. Repeat the above process on the other side of the X - axis, marking the points $\left(\frac{-\pi}{6}, \sin\frac{-\pi}{6}\right), \left(\frac{-\pi}{4}, \sin\frac{-\pi}{4}\right), \ldots, \left(\frac{-\pi}{2}, \sin\frac{-\pi}{2}\right)$ approximately and fix nails on these points as N_1', N_2', N_3', N_4'. At O, also fix a nail.

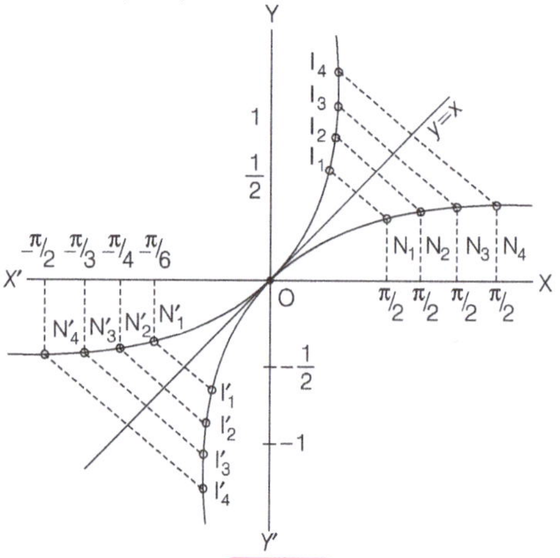

Figure 5.1

7. With the help of wire join the nail on both sides of X-axis to get the graph of $\sin x$ from $\frac{-\pi}{2}$ to $\frac{\pi}{2}$.
8. Draw the graph of the line $y = x$ by plotting the points (1, 1), (2, 2), (3, 3), ... etc. At these points fix a wire.
9. From the nails N_1, N_2, N_3, N_4, draw perpendicular on the line $y = x$ and produce these lines such that length of perpendicular on both sides of the line $y = x$ are equal. Name them I_1, I_2, I_3, I_3 and fix nails at these points.
10. Similarly, repeat the above activity on the other side of X - axis and fix nails at I_1', I_2', I_3', I_4'.
11. Join the nails on both sides of the line $y = x$ by a tight wire. The curve so obtain shows the graph of $y = \sin^{-1} x$.

Demonstration

Put a mirror on the line $y = x$. The image of the graph of $\sin x$ in the mirror will represent the graph of $\sin^{-1} x$ showing that $\sin^{-1} x$ is mirror reflection of $\sin x$ and vice versa.

Observation

The image of point N_1 in the mirror (the line $y = x$) is ....

The image of point N_2 in the mirror (the line $y = x$) is ....

The image of point N_3 in the mirror (the line $y = x$) is ....

The image of point N_4 in the mirror (the line $y = x$) is ....

The image of point N_1' in the mirror (the line $y = x$) is ....

The image of point N_2' in the mirror (the line $y = x$) is ....

The image of point N_3' in the mirror (the line $y = x$) is ....

The image of point N_4' in the mirror (the line $y = x$) is ....

The image of the graph of $\sin x$ in $y = x$ is the graph of ...., and the image of the graph of $\sin^{-1} x$ in $y = x$ is the graph of ....

Application

In the same way we can draw the graph of other inverse trigonometric functions i.e. $\cos^{-1} x$, $\tan^{-1} x$ etc.

VIVA-VOCE

1 What is the domain of $\sin^{-1} x$?

Ans Domain of $\sin^{-1} x$ is $\left[\frac{-\pi}{2}, \frac{\pi}{2}\right]$

2 What is the range of $\sin^{-1} x$?

Ans Range of $\sin^{-1} x$ is $[-1, 1]$.

3 What is the relation between the graphs of a function and its inverse.

Ans The graphs of a function and its inverse are mirror images of each other in the line $y = x$.

4 Evaluate : $\sin^{-1}\left(\frac{\sqrt{3}}{2}\right)$

Ans Let $\theta = \sin^{-1}\left(-\frac{\sqrt{3}}{2}\right) \Rightarrow \sin\theta = -\frac{\sqrt{3}}{2}$

$\Rightarrow \sin\theta = \sin\left(\frac{-\pi}{3}\right) \Rightarrow \theta = \frac{-\pi}{3}$

5 Write the difference between maximum and minimum value of $\sin^{-1} x$ for $x \in [-1, 1]$.

Ans The minimum and maximum values of $\sin^{-1} x$ are $\frac{-\pi}{2}$ and $\frac{\pi}{2}$, respectively.

$\therefore$ Required difference $= \frac{\pi}{2} - \left(\frac{-\pi}{2}\right) = \pi$

6 If $\sin^{-1} x + \sin^{-1} y + \sin^{-1} z = \frac{3\pi}{2}$, then write the value of $x + y + z$.

Ans We know that, the maximum value of $\sin^{-1} x$ for $x \in [-1, 1]$ is $\frac{\pi}{2}$.

$\therefore \sin^{-1} x \le \frac{\pi}{2}, \sin^{-1} y \le \frac{\pi}{2}, \sin^{-1} z \le \frac{\pi}{2}$ for all

$\therefore x, y, z \in [-1, 1]$

$\therefore \sin^{-1} x + \sin^{-1} y + \sin^{-1} z \le \frac{3\pi}{2}$

$\therefore \sin^{-1} x + \sin^{-1} y + \sin^{-1} z = \frac{3\pi}{2}$

$\Rightarrow \sin^{-1} x = \sin^{-1} y = \sin^{-1} z = \frac{\pi}{2}$

$\Rightarrow x + y + z = 1 + 1 + 1 = 3$

7 Find the domain of $f(x) = \sin^{-1} x + \sin x$.

Ans The domain of $\sin^{-1} x$ is $[-1, 1]$ and that of $\sin x$ is R.

Therefore, domain of $f(x) = \sin^{-1} x + \sin x$ is $[-1,1] \cap R = [-1, 1]$.

ACTIVITY 6

To find analytically the limit of a function $f(x)$ at $x = c$ and also to check the continuity of the function at that point.

Material Required

Paper, pencil, calculator.

Method of Construction

1. Consider the function given by

$$f(x) = \begin{cases} \frac{x^2 - 9}{x - 3}, & x \ne 3 \\ 7, & x = 3 \end{cases}$$

2. Take some points on the left side and some points on the right side of $c (= 3)$ which are very near to c.
3. Calculate the corresponding values of $f(x)$ for each of the points considered in above step.
4. Record the values of points on the left side and right side of c as x and the corresponding values of $f(x)$ in a form of a table.

Demonstration

1. The values of x and $f(x)$ are recorded as follows:

Table 1: For points on the left of $c (= 3)$

x	2.9	2.99	2.999	2.9999	2.99999	2.999999	2.9999999
$f(x)$	5.9	5.99	5.999	5.9999	5.99999	5.99999	5.9999999

2. **Table 2:** For points on the right of $c (= 3)$

x	3.1	3.01	3.001	3.0001	3.00001	3.000001	3.0000001
$f(x)$	6.1	6.01	6.001	6.0001	6.00001	6.000001	6.0000001

Observation

1. The value of $f(x)$ is approaching to ...., as $x \to 3$ from the left.
2. The value of $f(x)$ is approaching to ...., as $x \to 3$ from the right.
3. So, $\lim_{x \to 3} f(x) =$ .... and $\lim_{x \to 3^+} f(x) =$ ....
4. Therefore, $\lim_{x \to 3} f(x) =$ ...., $f(3) =$......
5. Is $\lim_{x \to 3} f(x) = f(3)$ ...... ? (Yes/No)
6. Since $f(c) \ne \lim_{x \to c} f(x)$, so, the function is .... at $x = 3$ (continuous/not continuous).

Application

From the above activity we can easily understand the basic concept of limit and continuity of a function at a given point.

VIVA-VOCE

1 What is the neccessary condition for limit to be exist?

Ans For a function at $x = a$, limit will exist if left hand limit is equal to right hand limit i.e. LHL = RHL

2 What is the value of $\lim\limits_{x \to c^-} [x]$?

Ans $\lim\limits_{x \to c^-} [x] = \lim\limits_{h \to 0} [c - h] = c - 1$

3 What is the value $\lim\limits_{x \to c^+} [x]$?

Ans $\lim\limits_{x \to c^+} [x] = \lim\limits_{h \to 0} [c + h] = c$

4 Check whether $\lim\limits_{x \to 0} \dfrac{|x|}{x}$ exists or not.

Ans. LHL $= \lim\limits_{x \to 0^-} \dfrac{|x|}{x} = \lim\limits_{h \to 0} \dfrac{|0-h|}{0-h} = \lim\limits_{h \to 0} \dfrac{h}{-h} = -1$

and RHL $= \lim\limits_{x \to 0^+} \dfrac{|x|}{x} = \lim\limits_{h \to 0} \dfrac{|0+h|}{0+h} = \lim\limits_{h \to 0} \dfrac{h}{h} = 1$

Since, $\neq$, so limit does not exist.

5 What $x \to a^-$ is equivalent to?

Ans $x \to a^-$ is equivalent to $x = a - h$, where $h \to 0$

6 What $x \to a^+$ is equivalent to ?

Ans $x \to a^+$ is equivalent to $x = a + h$ where $h \to 0$

7 What is the neccessary condition for a function to be continuous at a given point?

Ans A function $f(x)$ is said to be continuous at a point $x = a$ of its domain, iff $\lim\limits_{x \to a} f(x) = f(a)$.

8 State whether, if $f(x)$ and $g(x)$ are continuous at $x = a$, then $(f + g)(x)$ is also continuous at $x = a$ or not.

Ans Yes. Since, f and g are continuous at $x = a$.

Then $\lim\limits_{x \to a} f(x) = f(a)$ and $\lim\limits_{x \to a} g(x) = g(a)$.

$$\therefore \lim_{x \to a} (f + g)(x) = \lim_{x \to a} [f(x) + g(x)]$$
$$= \lim_{x \to a} f(x) + \lim_{x \to a} g(x)$$
$$= f(a) + g(a)$$
$$= (f + g)(a).$$

ACTIVITY 7

To verify that for a function f to be continuous at given point x_0, $\Delta y = |f(x_0 + \Delta x) - f(x_0)|$ is arbitrarily small, provided Δx is sufficiently small.

Material Required

Hardboard, some white sheets, pencil, scale, calculator, gum.

Method of Construction

1. Paste a white sheet on the hardboard.
2. Draw the curve of the given continuous function as represented in the given Fig.
3. Take any point $P(x_0, 0)$ on the positive side of X-axis and corresponding to this point, mark the point $Q(x_0, y_0)$ on the curve.

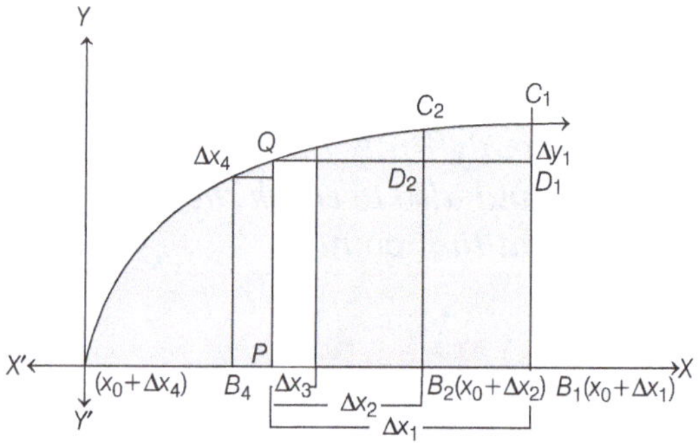

Figure 7.1

Demonstration

1. Take one more point $B_1(x_0 + \Delta x_1, 0)$ to the right of P, where Δx_1 is an increment in x.
2. Draw the perpendicular from B_1 to meet the curve at C_1. Let the coordinates of C_1 be $(x_0 + \Delta x_1, y_0 + \Delta y_1)$.
3. Draw a perpendicular from the point $Q(x_0, y_0)$ to meet C_1B_1 at D_1.

4. Now measure $AB_1 = \Delta x_1$ (say) and record it and also measure $C_1D_1 = \Delta y_1$ and record it.
5. Reduce the increment in x to Δx_2 (i.e., $\Delta x_2 < \Delta x_1$) to get another point $B_2 (x_0 + \Delta x_2, 0)$.
   Get the corresponding point C_2 on the curve.
6. Let the perpendicular QD_1 intersects C_2B_2 at D_2.
7. Again, measure $PB_2 = \Delta x_2$ and record it.
   Measure $C_2D_2 = \Delta y_2$ and record it.
8. Repeat the above steps for some more points so that Δx becomes smaller and smaller.

Observation

S. No	Value of increment in x_0	Corresponding increment in y
1.	$\lvert\Delta x_1\rvert =$	$\lvert\Delta y_1\rvert =$ ....
2.	$\lvert\Delta x_2\rvert =$	$\lvert\Delta y_2\rvert =$ ....
3.	$\lvert\Delta x_3\rvert =$	$\lvert\Delta y_3\rvert =$ ....
4.	$\lvert\Delta x_4\rvert =$	$\lvert\Delta y_4\rvert =$ ....
5.	$\lvert\Delta x_5\rvert =$	$\lvert\Delta y_5\rvert =$ ....
6.	$\lvert\Delta x_6\rvert =$	$\lvert\Delta y_6\rvert =$ ....
7.	$\lvert\Delta x_7\rvert =$	$\lvert\Delta y_7\rvert =$ ....
8.	$\lvert\Delta x_8\rvert =$	$\lvert\Delta y_8\rvert =$ ....
9.	$\lvert\Delta x_9\rvert =$	$\lvert\Delta y_9\rvert =$ ....
10.		

2. So, Δy becomes .... when Δx becomes smaller.
3. Thus, $\lim_{\Delta x \to 0} \Delta y = 0$ for a continuous function.

Application

This activity is helpful in explaining the concept of derivative (left hand or right hand) at any point on the curve corresponding to a function.

VIVA-VOCE

1 Define diferentiability of a function at a point.

Ans A function is differentiable at a given point if it has a unique tangent at the given point.

2 Is every differentiable function is continuous?

Ans Yes.

3 Is every continuous function is differentiable?

Ans It is not neccessary that every continuous function is differentiable.

4 Given an example of a function which is continuous but not differentiable at a point.

Ans $f(x) = |x|$ at $x = 0$ is continuous but not differentiable.

5 What LHD and RHD stands for?

Ans LHD stands for left hand derivative and RHD stands for right hand derivative.

6 If $f(x)$ is differentiable at $x = c$, then write the value of $\lim_{x \to c} f(x)$.

Ans Since, $f(x)$ is differentiable at $x = c$, then it must be continuous at $x = c$.

$\therefore \lim_{x \to c} f(x) = f(c)$

ACTIVITY 8

To understand the concepts of decreasing and increasing functions.

Material Required

Some pieces of wire of different lengths, piece of plywood, white paper, gum, geometry box, trigonometric tables.

Method of Construction

1. Take a piece of plywood of a convenient size and using gum paste a white paper on it.
2. Take two pieces of wires of length say 25 cm each and fix them on the white paper to represent coordinate axes, X-axis and Y-axis.
3. Take two more pieces of wire each of suitable length and bend them in the shape of curves representing two functions and with the help of gum paste them on the paper as shown in the given Fig.

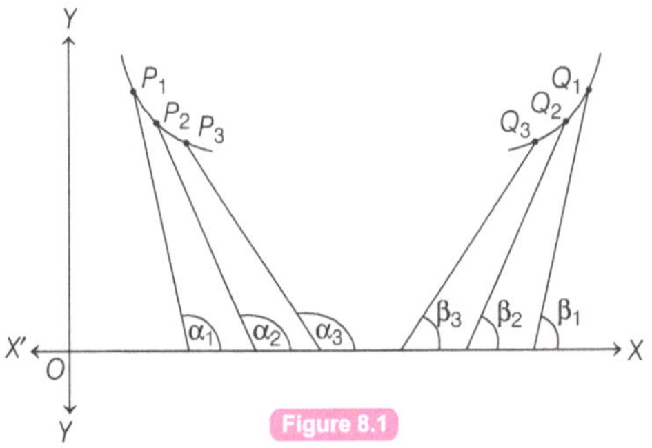

Figure 8.1

4. Take two straight wires each of suitable length for the purpose of showing tangents to the curves at different points on them.

Demonstration

1. Take one straight wire and place it on the left curve such that it is tangent to the curve at the point say A_1 and making an angle α_1 with the positive direction of X-axis.
2. α_1 is an obtuse angle, so $\tan\alpha_1$ is negative, i.e. the slope of the tangent at A_1 (derivative of the function at A_1 is negative.
3. Take another two points say A_2 and A_3 on the same curve, and make tangents, using the same wire, at A_2 and A_3 making angles α_2 and α_3, respectively with the positive direction of X-axis.
4. Here again α_2 and α_3 are obtuse angles and therefore slopes of the tangents $\tan\alpha_2$ and $\tan\alpha_3$ are both negative, i.e., derivatives of the function at A_2 and A_3 are negative.
5. The function given by the left curve is a decreasing function.
6. On the right curve take three point B_1, B_2, B_3 and using the other straight wires, form tangents at each of these points making angle $\beta_1, \beta_2, \beta_3$, respectively with the positive direction of X-axis, as shown in the figure. $\beta_1, \beta_2, \beta_3$ are all acute angles. So, the derivatives of the function at these points are positive. Thus, the function given by this right curve is an increasing function.

Observation

1. α_1 = ———, $>90°$
   α_2 = ——— > ———,
   α_3 = ——— > ——— ,
   $\tan\alpha_1$ = ——— , (negative)
   $\tan\alpha_2$ = ——— ,(———),
   $\tan\alpha_3$ = ——— ,(———). Thus, the function is ——— .
2. β_1 = ——— , $<90°$,
   β_2 = ——— , < ———,
   β_3 = ——— , < ——— ,
   $\tan\beta_1$ = ——— ,(positive),
   $\tan\beta_2$ = ——— , (———),
   $\tan\beta_3$ = ——— ,(———). Thus, the function is ——— .

Application

This activity helps us in explaining the basic concepts of decreasing and increasing functions.

VIVA-VOCE

1 Write the neccessary condition for a function to be strictly increasing.

Ans A function $f(x)$ is said to be strictly increasing on (a, b), if

$$x_1 < x_2 \Rightarrow f(x_1) < f(x_2) \ \forall x_1, x_2 \in (a, b).$$

2 Write the neccessary condition for a function to be strictly decreasing.

Ans A function $f(x)$ is said to be strictly decreasing on (a, b), if

$$x_1 < x_2 \Rightarrow f(x_1) > f(x_2) \ \forall x_1, x_2 \in (a, b)$$

3 Define monotonic function.

Ans A function $f(x)$ is said to be monotonic on an interval (a, b), if it is either increasing or decreasing on (a, b).

4 State whether $f(x) = \tan x - x$ is increasing or decreasing in its domain.

Ans We have, $f(x) = \tan x - x$

$\therefore \quad f'(x) = \sec^2 x - 1 > 0 \ \forall x \in R$

Therefore, $f(x)$ is increasing function.

5 State whether $f(x) = \sin x$ on the interval $\left[\frac{-\pi}{2}, \frac{\pi}{2}\right]$ is increasing or decreasing

Ans We have, $f(x) = \sin x$

$\therefore \quad f'(x) = \cos x \geq 0, \forall x \in \left[\frac{-\pi}{2}, \frac{\pi}{2}\right]$

Hence, $f(x)$ is increasing function

6 What can you say whether $f(x) = x^3 - 3x^2 + 4x$ is increasing or decreasing on R?

Ans We have, $f(x) = x^3 - 3x^2 + 4x$

$$\therefore \quad f'(x) = 3x^2 - 6x + 4 = 3x^2 - 6x + 3 + 1$$
$$= 3(x^2 - 2x + 1) + 1 = 3(x-1)^2 + 1$$

$\therefore \ f'(x) > 0 \ \forall \ x \in R.$

Hence, $f(x)$ is increasing function.

7 If $f'(x) = 0$ for each $x \in (a, b)$ then f is a constant function in $[a, b]$ is it true or false?

Ans True.

ACTIVITY 9

To construct an open box of maximum volume from a given rectangular sheet by cutting equal squares from each corner.

Material Required

Chart papers, scissors, cellotape, calculator.

Method of Construction

1. Take a rectangular chart paper of size 20 $\times$10 and name it as *PQRS*.
2. Cut four equal squares each of side x cm from each corner P, Q, R and S.

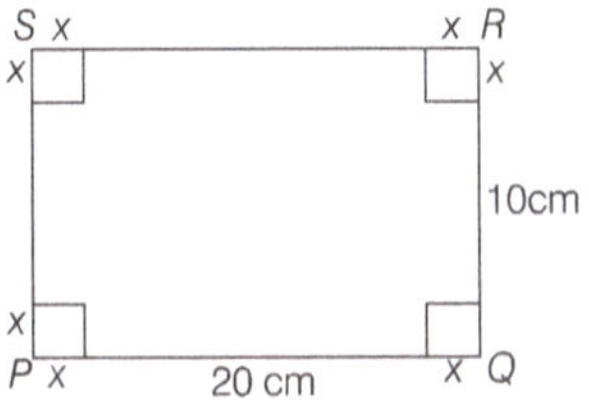

Figure 9.1

3. Repeat this process by taking the same size of chart papers for different values of x.
4. Make an open box by folding its flaps using cellotape/gum.

Demonstration

1. When, $x=1$, Volume of the box = 144 ^{3}.
2. When $x=1.5$, Volume of the box = 178.5 ^{3}.
3. When $x=1.8$, Volume of the box = 188.9 ^{3}.
4. When $x=2$, Volume of the box = 192 ^{3}.
5. When $x=2.1$, Volume of the box = 192.4 ^{3}.
6. When $x=2.2$, Volume of the box = 192.2 ^{3}.
7. When $x=2.5$, Volume of the box = 187.5 ^{3}.
8. When $x=3$, Volume of the box = 168 ^{3}.

Clearly, volume of the box is maximum when $x = 2.1$.

Observation

1. V_1 = Volume of the open box (when $x = 1.6$) = ...
2. V_2 = Volume of the open box (when $x = 1.9$) = ...
3. V = Volume of the open box (when $x = 2.1$) = ...
4. V_3 = Volume of the open box (when $x = 2.2$) = ...
5. V_4 = Volume of the open box (when $x = 2.4$) = ...
6. V_5 = Volume of the open box (when $x = 3.2$) = ...
7. Volume V_1 is .... than volume V.
8. Volume V_2 is .... than volume V.
9. Volume V_3 is .... than volume V.
10. Volume V_4 is .... than volume V.
11. Volume V_5 is .... than volume V.

    So, volume of the open box is maximum when $x =$ ....

Application

This activity is very useful in understanding the concepts of maxima / minima of functions. By using this concept we can make packages of maximum volume with minimum cost.

Note Now, $V = (20-2x)(10-2x)x$

Or $V = 200x - 60x^2 + 4x^3$

$$\frac{dV}{dx} = 200 - 120x + 12x^2.$$

For maxima or minima, we have,

$$\frac{dV}{dx} = 0, \text{ i.e. } 3x^2 - 30x + 50 = 0$$

i.e. $$x = \frac{30 \pm \sqrt{900-600}}{6} = 7.9 \text{ or } 2.1$$

Reject $x = 7.9$

$$\frac{d^2V}{dx^2} = -120 + 24x$$

When $x = 2.1$, $\frac{d^2V}{dx^2}$ is negative.

Hence, V should be maximum at $x = 2.1$.

VIVA-VOCE

1 What do you mean by local maxima?

Ans A function $f(x)$ is said to attain a local maximum at $x = a$ if there exists a heigh bourhood $(a-\delta, a+\delta)$ of a such that $f(x) < f(a)$ for all $x \in (a-\delta, a+\delta)$, $x \neq a$

2 What do you mean by local minima?

Ans A function $f(x)$ is said to attain a local minimum at $x = a$ if there exists a heighbourhood $(a-\delta, a+\delta)$ of a such that $f(x) > f(a)$ for all $x \in (a-\delta, a+\delta)$, $x \neq a$

3 What is necessary condition for a point $x = c$ to be an extreme point of the function $f(x)$?

Ans $f'(c) = 0$.

4 Write the sufficient conditions for a point $x = c$ to be a point of local maximum.

Ans $f'(c) = 0$ and $f''(c) < 0$

5 If $f(x)$ attains a local minimum at $x = c$, then what are the values of $f'(c)$ and $f''(c)$?

Ans $f'(c) = 0$ and $f''(c) > 0$

6 What do you mean by point of inflexion?

Ans A point of inflexion is a point at which a curve is changing concave upward to concave downward, or vice-versa.

7 If $f(x)$ is continuous function in its domain, then how many maximum or minimum must lie between two equal values of $f(x)$?

Ans At least one maximum or minimum must lie between two equal values of a continuous function.

8 Write the condition for $f(x)$ at $x = a$ to be maximum according to first derivative test.

Ans For $x = a$ to be local maximum of $f(x)$, if $f'(a) = 0$ and $f'(x)$ changes sign from positive to negative as x increases through a.

9 Write the condition for $f(x)$ at $x = a$ to be minimum according to the first derivative test.

Ans For $x = a$ to be local minimum of $f(x)$, if $f'(a) = 0$ and $f'(x)$ changes sign from negative to positive as x increases through a.

ACTIVITY 10

To verify geometrically that
$\vec{c} \times (\vec{a} + \vec{b}) = \vec{c} \times \vec{a} + \vec{c} \times \vec{b}$

Material Required

Geometry box, cardboard, white paper, cutter, sketch pen, cellotape.

Method of Construction

1. Fix a white paper on the cardboard of suitable size.
2. Draw a line segment OA (= 8 cm, say) and let it represent $\vec{c}$.
3. Draw another line segment OB (= 6 cm, say) at an angle (say 60°) with OA.

   Let $\overrightarrow{OB} = \vec{a}$

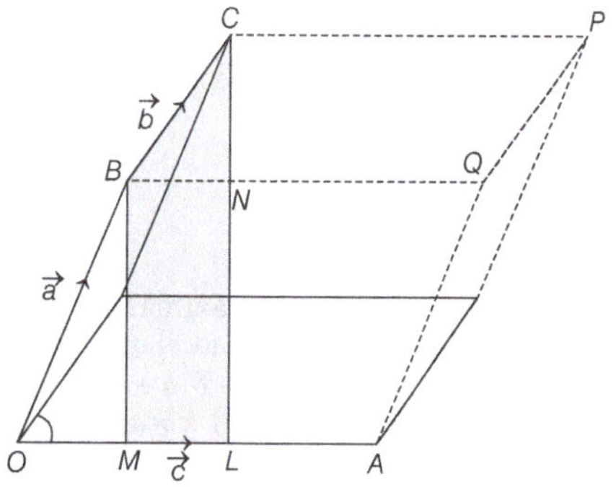

Figure 10.1

4. Draw BC (= 5 cm, say) making an angle (say 30°) with $\overrightarrow{OA}$. Let $\overrightarrow{BC} = \vec{b}$
5. Draw perpendiculars BM, CL and BN.
6. Complete parallelograms $OAPC$, $OAQB$ and $BQPC$.

Demonstration

1. $\overrightarrow{OC} = \overrightarrow{OB} + \overrightarrow{BC} = \vec{a} + \vec{b}$
2. Let $\angle COA = \alpha$
3. We know that $|\vec{c} \times (\vec{a} + \vec{b})| = |\vec{c}||\vec{a} + \vec{b}|\sin\alpha$
   = Area of parallelogram $OAPC$.
4. Again, $|\vec{c} \times \vec{a}|$ = Area of parallelogram $OAQB$.
5. Also, $|\vec{c} \times \vec{b}|$ = Area of parallelogram $BQPC$.
6. Therefore, Area of parallelogram $OAPC = (OA)(CL)$
   $= (OA)(LN + NC) = (OA)(BM + NC)$
   $= (OA)(BM) + (OA)(NC)$
   = Area of parallelogram $OAQB$ + Area of parallelogram $BQPC$
   $= |\vec{c} \times \vec{a}| + |\vec{c} \times \vec{b}|$

   So, $|\vec{c} \times (\vec{a} + \vec{b})| = |\vec{c} \times \vec{a}| + |\vec{c} \times \vec{b}|$

   Direction of each of these vectors $\vec{c} \times (\vec{a} + \vec{b})$, $\vec{c} \times \vec{a}$ and $\vec{c} \times \vec{b}$ is perpendicular to the same plane.

   So, $\vec{c} \times (\vec{a} + \vec{b}) = \vec{c} \times \vec{a} + \vec{c} \times \vec{b}$

Observation

$|\vec{c}| = |\overrightarrow{OA}| = OA =$ ______

$|\vec{a} + \vec{b}| = |\overrightarrow{OC}| = OC =$ ______

$CL =$ ______

$|\vec{c} \times (\vec{a} + \vec{b})|$ = Area of parallelogram $OAPC = (OA)(CL)$

= ________ sq units ...(i)

$|\vec{c} \times \vec{a}|$ = Area of parallelogram $OAQB = (OA)(BM)$

$= \_\_\_\_\_\_ \times \_\_\_\_\_\_ = \_\_\_\_\_\_$ ...(ii)

$|\vec{c} \times \vec{b}|$ = Area of parallelogram $BQPC = (OA)(CN)$

$= \_\_\_\_\_\_ \times \_\_\_\_\_\_ = \_\_\_\_\_\_$ ...(iii)

From Eqs. (i), (ii) and (iii), we get

Area of parallelogram $OAPC$

= Area of parallelogram $OAQB$ + Area of parallelogram ______

Thus, $|\vec{c} \times (\vec{a} + \vec{b})| = |\vec{c} \times \vec{a}| + |\vec{c} \times \vec{b}|$

$\vec{c} \times \vec{a}$, $\vec{c} \times \vec{b}$ and $\vec{c} \times (\vec{a} + \vec{b})$ are all in the direction of .... to the plane of paper.

Therefore, $\vec{c} \times (\vec{a} + \vec{b}) = \vec{c} \times \vec{a} +$ ______

Application

This activity explains the distributive property of vector multiplication over addition can be explained.

Note This activity can also be performed by taking rectangles instead of parallelograms.

VIVA-VOCE

1 Whether the vector product of two vectors is vector or scalar.

Ans The vector product of two vectors is always a vector.

2 Write the value of $\hat{i} \times (\hat{j} + \hat{k}) + \hat{j} \times (\hat{k} + \hat{i}) + \hat{k} \times (\hat{i} + \hat{j})$.

Ans We have, $\hat{i} \times (\hat{j} + \hat{k}) + \hat{j} \times (\hat{k} + \hat{i}) + \hat{k} \times (\hat{i} + \hat{j})$

$= \hat{i} \times \hat{j} + \hat{i} \times \hat{k} + \hat{j} \times \hat{k} + \hat{j} \times \hat{i} + \hat{k} \times \hat{i} + \hat{k} \times \hat{j}$

$= \hat{k} - \hat{j} + \hat{i} - \hat{k} + \hat{j} - \hat{i} = 0$

3 Is cross product of two vectors is commutative?

Ans No. For any two vectors $\vec{a}$ and $\vec{b}$ | $\vec{a} \times \vec{b} = -\vec{b} \times \vec{a}$.

4 Write the formula for the area of a parallelogram with adjacent sides $\vec{a}$ and $\vec{b}$.

Ans Area of a parallelogram whose adjacent sides are $\vec{a}$ and $\vec{b} = |\vec{a} \times \vec{b}|$.

5 What do you mean by right distributivity properly of vector product?

Ans For any three vector $\vec{a}, \vec{b}, \vec{c}$, right distributivity property is given as below.

$$(\vec{b} + \vec{c}) \times \vec{a} = \vec{b} \times \vec{a} + \vec{c} \times \vec{a}$$

6 If for any three vectors, we have $\vec{a} \times \vec{b} = \vec{c}$, then what is relation between them?

Ans $\vec{c}$ will be perpendicular to both $\vec{a}$ and $\vec{b}$

i.e. $\vec{a} \perp \vec{c}$ and $\vec{b} \perp \vec{c}$.

7 Write a unit vector which is perpendicular to both $\vec{a}$ and $\vec{b}$.

Ans Let $\hat{c}$ is required vector.

Then, $\hat{c} = \pm \dfrac{\vec{a} \times \vec{b}}{|\vec{a} \times \vec{b}|}$

8 Evaluate $(\vec{a} - \vec{b}) \times (\vec{a} + \vec{b})$.

Ans We have, $(\vec{a} - \vec{b}) \times (\vec{a} + \vec{b}) = \vec{a} \times \vec{a} + \vec{a} \times \vec{b} - \vec{b} \times \vec{a} - \vec{b} \times \vec{b}$

$= \vec{a} \times \vec{b} + \vec{a} \times \vec{b}$ $[\vec{x} \times \vec{x} = 0$ and $\vec{x} \times \vec{y} = -\vec{y} \times \vec{x}]$

$= 2(\vec{a} \times \vec{b})$

ACTIVITY 11

To measure the shortest distance between two skew lines and verify it analytically.

Material Required

A piece of cardboard of size 40 cm × 30 cm, a squared paper, three wooden block of size 2 cm × 2 cm × 2 cm each and one wooden blocks of size 2 cm × 2 cm × 4 cm, some wires of different lengths, set squares, gum, pen/pencil, etc.

Method of Construction

1. Paste a squared paper on a piece of cardboard.
2. On the squared paper, draw two lines OA and OB to represent X-axis and Y-axis, respectively.
3. Name the three blocks of size × × as I, II and III. Name the other wooden block of size × × as IV.
4. Place blocks I, II, III such that their base centres are at the points (2, 2), (1, 6) and (7, 6), respectively, and block IV with its base centre at (6, 2). Other wooden block of size × × as IV.
5. Place a wire joining the points C and D, the centres of the bases of the blocks I and III and another wire joining the centres E and F of the tops of blocks II and IV as shown in given below fig.
6. The lines represented by these two lines and skew lines.

7. Take a wire and join it perpendicularly with the skew lines and calculate the actual distance.

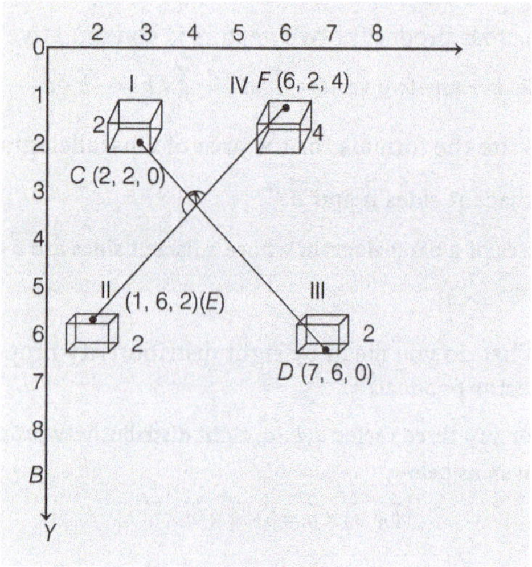

Figure 12.1

Demonstration

1. A set-square is placed in such a way that its one perpendicular side is along the wire CD
2. Move the set-square along CD till its other perpendicular side touches the other wire.
3. Using set-squares, measure the distance between the two lines in this position. This is known as the shortest distance between two skew lines.
4. Analytically, find the equation of line joining $C(2,2,0)$ and $D(7,6,0)$ and other line joining $E(1,6,2)$ and $F(6,2,4)$ and find S.D. using $\left|\frac{(\vec{a}_2-\vec{a}_1).(\vec{b}_1\times\vec{b}_2)}{|\vec{b}_1\times\vec{b}_2|}\right|$. The two distances obtained will be equal.

Observation

1. Coordinates of point C are ....
2. Coordinates of point D are ....
3. Coordinates of point E are ....
4. Coordinates of point F are ....
5. Equation of line CD is ....
6. Equation of line EF is ....

Shortest distance between CD and EF analytically = ...

Shortest distance by actual measurement = ...

The results so obtained are ....

Application

This activity can be used to explain the concept of skew lines and of shortest distance between two lines in space.

The activity explains the concept of skew lines and describe how to measure shortest distance between two lines in space.

VIVA-VOCE

1 Define skew lines.

Ans Two straight line in space which are neither parallel nor intersecting are called skew lines.

2 Explain line of shortest distance between two lines.

Ans If l_1 and l_2 are two skew lines, then there is one and only one line perpendicular to each of lines l_1 and l_2 which is known as the line of shortest distance.

3 Write the condition for two given lines to intersect.

Ans If the lines $\vec{r}=\vec{a}_1+\lambda\vec{b}_1$ and $\vec{r}=\vec{a}_2+\mu\vec{b}_2$ intersect, then the shortest distance between them is zero

$$\therefore \quad \left|\frac{(\vec{b}_1\times\vec{b}_2)\cdot(\vec{a}_2-\vec{a}_1)}{|\vec{b}_1\times\vec{b}_2|}\right|=0$$

$$\Rightarrow \quad (\vec{b}_1\times\vec{b}_2)\cdot(\vec{a}_2-\vec{a}_1)=0$$

4 Write the formula for shortest distance between the lines $\vec{r}=\vec{a}_1+\lambda\vec{b}$ and $\vec{r}_2=\vec{a}_2+\mu\vec{b}$

Ans Since, the given lines are parallel, therefore,

$$SD=\left|\frac{|(\vec{a}_2-\vec{a}_1)\times\vec{b}|}{|\vec{b}|}\right|$$

5 Write the equation of a line in cartesian form which passing through two points $A(x_1, y_1, z_1)$ and $B(x_2, y_2, z_2)$.

Ans $\frac{x-x_1}{x_2-x_1}=\frac{y-y_1}{y_2-y_1}=\frac{z-z_1}{z_2-z_1}$

6 Write the formula for angle between lines,

$$\vec{r}=\vec{a}_1+\lambda\vec{b}_1 \text{ and } \vec{r}=\vec{a}_2+\mu\vec{b}_2$$

Ans $\cos\theta=\left|\frac{\vec{b}_1\cdot\vec{b}_2}{|\vec{b}_1|\cdot|\vec{b}_2|}\right|$

SAMPLE QUESTION PAPER 1

A Highly Simulated Sample Question Paper for CBSE Class XII Examination

MATHEMATICS (Unsolved)

Time : 3 Hours **Max. Marks : 80**

General Instructions

(i) This question paper contains 38 questions. All questions are compulsory.
(ii) Question paper is divided into FIVE sections - Section A, B, C, D and E.
(iii) In Section A, Question number 1 to 18 are Multiple Choice Questions (MCQ) type and Question number 19 and 20 are Assertion-Reason based questions carrying 1 mark each.
(iv) In Section B, Question number 21 to 25 are Very Short Answer (VSA) type questions carrying 2 marks each.
(v) In Section C, Question number 26 to 31 are Short Answer (SA) type questions carrying 3 marks each.
(vi) In Section D, Question number 32 to 35 are Long Answer (LA) type questions carrying 5 marks each.
(vii) In Section E, Question number 36 to 38 are Case Study Based question carrying 4 marks each.
(viii) There is no overall choice. However, an internal choice has been provided in 2 questions in Section B, 3 questions in Section C, 2 questions in Section D and 2 questions in Section E.
(ix) Use of calculator is NOT allowed.

SECTION A

Multiple Choice Questions

Each question carries 1 mark

1. If $A'=\begin{bmatrix}-2 & 3\\ 1 & 2\end{bmatrix}$ and $B=\begin{bmatrix}-1 & 0\\ 1 & 2\end{bmatrix}$, then the value of $[A+2B]'$ is

(a) $\begin{bmatrix}-4 & 1\\ 5 & 6\end{bmatrix}$ (b) $\begin{bmatrix}-4 & 5\\ 1 & 6\end{bmatrix}$ (c) $\begin{bmatrix}-4 & 5\\ 6 & 1\end{bmatrix}$ (d) $\begin{bmatrix}-4 & 1\\ 2 & 4\end{bmatrix}$

2. The interval in which $y=x^2e^{-x}$ is increasing with respect to x is

(a) [0, 2] (b) (0, 2) (c) [0, 2) (d) (0, 2]

3. If the direction cosines of a line are $\left(\frac{1}{c},\frac{1}{c},\frac{1}{c}\right)$, then the value of c is

(a) $\pm\sqrt{3}$ (b) ± 1 (c) $\pm\frac{1}{\sqrt{3}}$ (d) ± 3

4. $\cos^{-1}\left(\frac{-\sqrt{3}}{2}\right)$ is equal to

(a) $\frac{\pi}{6}$ (b) $\frac{5\pi}{6}$ (c) $\frac{3\pi}{2}$ (d) $\frac{\pi}{3}$

5. If A and B are symmetric matrices of same order, then $(AB'-BA')$ is a

(a) symmetric matrix
(b) skew-symmetric matrix
(c) identify matrix
(d) null matrix

6. If $[2\ 1\ 3]\begin{bmatrix}-1 & 0 & -1\\ -1 & 1 & 0\\ 0 & 1 & 1\end{bmatrix}\begin{bmatrix}1\\ 0\\ -1\end{bmatrix}=A$, then the order of matrix A is

(a) 2×2 (b) 2×1
(c) 1×2 (d) 1×1

7. If A is a 3×3 non-singular matrix such that $AA^T=A^TA$ and $B=A^{-1}A^T$, then BB^T is

(a) B (b) B^{-1} (c) I (d) A

8. The non-zero values of x satisfying the matrix equation $x\begin{bmatrix}2x & 2\\ 3 & x\end{bmatrix}+2\begin{bmatrix}8 & 5x\\ 4 & 4x\end{bmatrix}=2\begin{bmatrix}x^2+8 & 24\\ 10 & 6x\end{bmatrix}$ is

(a) 1 (b) 2 (c) 3 (d) 4

9. The function $f(x) = \sin x + \cos x, x \in \left[0, \frac{\pi}{4}\right]$ is
(a) increasing function
(b) strictly increasing function
(c) decreasing function
(d) strictly decreasing function

10. $\int x^x (1 + \log x) dx$ is equal to
(a) $-x^x + C$ (b) $x^x + C$
(c) -1 (d) None of these

11. The maximum value of function $h(x) = \sin(2x) + 5$ is
(a) 4 (b) 6 (c) 2 (d) 1

12. The minimum value of function $f(x) = |x + 2| - 1$ is
(a) 1 (b) 0 (c) –1 (d) –2

13. If $\begin{bmatrix} 3y - x & -2x \\ 3 & 7 \end{bmatrix} = \begin{bmatrix} 5 & -2 \\ 3 & 7 \end{bmatrix}$, then the value of $x + y$ is
(a) 1 (b) 2 (c) 5 (d) 3

14. The direction cosines of a line which makes equal angles with the coordinate axes are
(a) $\pm\left(\frac{1}{\sqrt{2}}, \frac{1}{\sqrt{2}}, \frac{1}{\sqrt{2}}\right)$ (b) $\pm\left(\frac{1}{\sqrt{3}}, \frac{1}{\sqrt{3}}, \frac{1}{\sqrt{3}}\right)$
(c) $\pm\left(\frac{1}{\sqrt{5}}, \frac{1}{\sqrt{5}}, \frac{1}{\sqrt{5}}\right)$ (d) $\pm(1, 1, 1)$

15. If two line $\vec{r} = \vec{a}_1 + \lambda \vec{b}_1$ and $\vec{r} = \vec{a}_2 + \mu \vec{b}_2$ are coplanar then the value of $(\vec{a}_2 - \vec{a}_1) \cdot (\vec{b}_1 \times \vec{b}_2)$ is
(a) 1 (b) 2 (c) 0 (d) –1

16. For what value of a the vectors $2\hat{i} - 3\hat{j} + 4\hat{k}$ and $a\hat{i} + 6\hat{j} - 8\hat{k}$ are collinear?
(a) 1 (b) 2 (c) –3 (d) –4

17. If $|\vec{a}| = 4$ and $-3 \le \lambda \le 2$, then the range of $|\lambda \vec{a}|$ is
(a) [2, 8] (b) [–12, 8] (c) [–12, 8) (d) (–12, 8)

18. If A is a square matrix of order 3 such that $|\text{adj } A| = 64$. Then, the value of $|A|$ is
(a) ± 8 (b) ± 4 (c) ± 64 (d) 2

Assertion- Reason Based Questions

Directions (Q. Nos. 19-20) *In the following questions, a statement of Assertion (A) is followed by a statement of Reason (R). Choose the correct answer out of the following choices.*

(a) Both (A) and (R) are true and (R) is the correct explanation of (A).
(b) Both (A) and (R) are true, but (R) is not the correct explanation of (A).
(c) (A) is true and (R) is false.
(d) (A) is false, but (R) is true.

19. **Assertion** (A) The function $f: R \to R$ given by $f(x) = x^3$ is injective.

Reason (R) The function $f: X \to Y$ is injective, if $f(x) = f(y) \Rightarrow x = y, \forall x, y \in X$.

20. **Assertion** (A) If $\begin{vmatrix} 2x & 5 \\ 8 & x \end{vmatrix} = \begin{vmatrix} 6 & -2 \\ 7 & 3 \end{vmatrix}$, then $x = \pm 6$.

Reason (R) If A and B are matrices of order 3 and $|A| = 4, |B| = 6$, then $|2AB| = 192$.

SECTION B

[This section comprises of very short answer type questions (VSA) of 2 marks each]

21. If A and B are two symmetric matrices of same order. Then, find whether the matrix $AB - BA$ is symmetric or skew-symmetric.

Or $\begin{bmatrix} 2x + y & 4x \\ 5x - 7 & 4x \end{bmatrix} = \begin{bmatrix} 7 & 7y - 13 \\ y & x + 6 \end{bmatrix}$, then find the value of $x + y$.

22. If $y = \log[\sin(x^2)], 0 < x < \frac{\pi}{2}$, then find $\frac{dy}{dx}$ at $x = \frac{\sqrt{\pi}}{2}$.

23. If $\vec{a}$ and $\vec{b}$ are unit vectors, then find the angle between $\vec{a}$ and $\vec{b}$, given that $(\sqrt{3}\vec{a} - \vec{b})$ is a unit vector.

Or The x-coordinate of a point on the line joining the points $P(2, 2, 1)$ and $Q(5, 1, -2)$ is 4. Find its z-coordinate.

24. Find the angle between the pair of lines
$$\frac{x + 3}{3} = \frac{y - 1}{5} = \frac{z + 3}{4} \text{ and } \frac{x + 1}{1} = \frac{y - 4}{1} = \frac{z - 5}{2}.$$

25. Find the solution of equation
$$(2y - 1)dx - (2x + 3)dy = 0.$$

SECTION C

[This section comprises of short answer type questions (SA) of 3 marks each]

26. Evaluate $\int \frac{2x^2 + 1}{x^2(x^2 + 4)} dx$.

Or Find $\int \frac{(2x - 5)e^{2x}}{(2x - 3)^3} dx$.

27. Find the area bounded by the curve $y^2 = 4ax$ and the line $y = 2a$ and Y-axis.

28. If $f: R - \{2\} \to R - \{3\}$ is defined by $f(x) = \frac{3x + 1}{x - 2}$, where R is the set of real numbers, show that f is bijective.

29. Solve the differential equation

$$(x\,dy - y\,dx)\,y \sin\left(\frac{y}{x}\right) - (y\,dx + x\,dy)\,x \cos\left(\frac{y}{x}\right) = 0.$$

Or Solve the differential equation
$(x^2 - yx^2)dy + (y^2 + x^2y^2)dx = 0$, given that $y = 1$, when $x = 1$.

30. Find the domain of the function
$f(x) = \cos^{-1} x + \sin^{-1} 2x$.

31. If $y = x^{1/x}$, find $\frac{dy}{dx}$

Or If $x = a(\theta + \sin\theta)$, $y = a(1 - \cos\theta)$, find $\frac{dy}{dx}$.

SECTION D

[This section comprises of long answer type questions (LA) of 5 marks each]

32. Solve the given LPP graphically
Minimise $Z = 5x + 8y$, subject to constraints
$2x + y \ge 140$, $3x + 5y \ge 350$, $x, y \ge 0$

Or Solve the given LPP graphically
Maximise $Z = 22x + 18y$, subject to constraints
$x + y \le 20$, $x + y \le 20$, $360x + 240y \le 5760$, $x, y \ge 0$.

33. Evaluate $\int_0^{\pi/2} \log(\sin x)dx$.

34. Find the point on the curve $y^2 = 2x$, which is at a minimum distance from the point (1, 4).

35. Find the foot of the perpendicular drawn from the point $2\hat{i} - \hat{j} + 5\hat{k}$ to the line
$\vec{r} = (11\hat{i} - 2\hat{j} - 8\hat{k}) + \lambda(10\hat{i} - 4\hat{j} - 11\hat{k})$. Also, find the length of the perpendicular.

Or Show that area of the parallelogram whose diagonals are given by $\vec{a}$ and $\vec{b}$ is $\frac{|\vec{a} \times \vec{b}|}{2}$.

Also, find the area of the parallelogram whose diagonals are $2\hat{i} - \hat{j} + \hat{k}$ and $\hat{i} + 3\hat{j} - \hat{k}$.

SECTION E

[This section comprises 3 case-study/passage based questions of 4 marks each with sub parts. The first two case study questions have three sub parts (i), (ii), (iii) of marks 1, 1, 2 respectively. The third case study question has two sub parts (i), (ii) of 2 marks each]

36. A departmental store sends bills to charge its customers once a month. Past experience shows that 70% of its customers pay their first month bill in time. The store also found that the customer who pays the bill in time has the probability of 0.8 of paying in time next month and the customer who does not pay in time has the probability of 0.4 of paying in time the next month.

Based on the above information, answer the following questions.

(i) Let E_1 and E_2 respectively denote the event of customer paying or not paying the first month bill in time. Find $P(E_1)$ and $P(E_2)$.

(ii) Let A denotes the event of customer paying second month's bill in time, then find $P\left(\frac{A}{E_1}\right)$ and $P\left(\frac{A}{E_2}\right)$.

(iii) (a) Find the probability of customer paying second month's bill in time.

Or (b) Find the probability of customer paying first month's bill in time, if it is found that customer has paid the second month's bill in time.

37. The sum of the surface area of a rectangular parallelopiped with sides x, $2x$ and $\frac{x}{3}$ and a sphere of radius y is given to be constant.

On the basis of above information, answer the following questions.

(i) If S is the constant, then find the relation between S, x and y.

(ii) If the combined volume is denoted by V, then find the relation between V, x and y.

(iii) Find the relation between x and y when the volume V is minimum.

Or If at $x = 3y$, volume V is minimum, then find the value of minimum volume and the value of S.

38. An insurance company believes that people can be divided into two classes: those who are accident prone and those who are not. The company's statistics show that an accident-prone person will have an accident at sometime within a fixed one-year period with probability 0.6, whereas this probability is 0.2 for a person who is not accident prone. The company knows that 20% of the population is accident prone.

On the basis of above information, answer the following questions.

(i) What is the probability that a new policyholder will have an accident within a year of purchasing a policy?

(ii) Suppose that a new policy holder has an accident within a year of purchasing a policy. What is the probability that he or she is accident prone?

SAMPLE QUESTION PAPER 2

A Highly Simulated Sample Question Paper for CBSE Class XII Examination

MATHEMATICS (Unsolved)

Time : 3 Hours **Max. Marks : 80**

General Instructions

(i) This question paper contains 38 questions. All questions are compulsory.
(ii) Question paper is divided into FIVE sections - Section A, B, C, D and E.
(iii) In Section A, Question number 1 to 18 are Multiple Choice Questions (MCQ) type and Question number 19 and 20 are Assertion-Reason based questions carrying 1 mark each.
(iv) In Section B, Question number 21 to 25 are Very Short Answer (VSA) type questions carrying 2 marks each.
(v) In Section C, Question number 26 to 31 are Short Answer (SA) type questions carrying 3 marks each.
(vi) In Section D, Question number 32 to 35 are Long Answer (LA) type questions carrying 5 marks each.
(vii) In Section E, Question number 36 to 38 are Case Study Based question carrying 4 marks each.
(viii) There is no overall choice. However, an internal choice has been provided in 2 questions in Section B, 3 questions in Section C, 2 questions in Section D and 2 questions in Section E.
(ix) Use of calculator is NOT allowed.

SECTION A

Multiple Choice Questions

Each question carries 1 mark

1. If $\int_0^1 (3x^2 + 2x + k)\,dx = 0$, then the value of k is

(a) 2 (b) 0 (c) 1 (d) −2

2. The value of λ, if the vector $2\hat{i} + \lambda\hat{j} - 4\hat{k}$ and $2\hat{i} - \hat{j} + \hat{k}$ are perpendicular is

(a) 0 (b) 1 (c) 2 (d) −1

3. If a relation R on the set $\{1, 2, 3, 4\}$ be defined by $R = \{(x, y) : y = 2x\}$, then R is

(a) reflexive (b) symmetric
(c) transitive
(d) neither reflexive nor symmetric nor transitive

4. Set A has 4 elements and the set B has 5 elements. Then, the number of injective mappings that can be defined from A to B is

(a) 24 (b) 60 (c) 120 (d) 210

5. The domain of the function defined by $f(x) = \sin^{-1}\sqrt{x-1}$ is

(a) [1, 2] (b) (1, 2) (c) [1, 2) (d) (1, 2]

6. An equivalence relation R in A divides it into equivalence classes A_1, A_2, A_3. Then, the value of $A_1 \cup A_2 \cup A_3$ and, $A_1 \cap A_2 \cap A_3$ is respectively

(a) A, ϕ (b) ϕ, A
(c) A, A (d) ϕ, ϕ

7. The principal values of $\tan^{-1}(-\sqrt{3})$ and $\cos^{-1}\left(-\frac{1}{2}\right)$ are

(a) $-\frac{\pi}{3}$ and $-\frac{\pi}{3}$ (b) $\frac{2\pi}{3}$ and $\frac{2\pi}{3}$
(c) $-\frac{\pi}{3}$ and $\frac{2\pi}{3}$ (d) $\frac{2\pi}{3}$ and $-\frac{4\pi}{3}$

8. Let $f : R \to R$ be defined as $f(x) = x^4$. Then, f is

(a) One-one onto
(b) Many-one onto
(c) One-one but not onto
(d) Neither one-one nor onto

9. How many reflexive relations are possible in a set A whose $n(A) = 3$?

(a) 64 (b) 32
(c) 128 (d) 1024

10. Let $A=\begin{bmatrix}200 & 50\\ 10 & 2\end{bmatrix}$ and $B=\begin{bmatrix}50 & 40\\ 2 & 3\end{bmatrix}$, then $|AB|$ is equal to

(a) 460 (b) 2000 (c) 3000 (d) –7000

11. If $A=\begin{bmatrix}1 & 0\\ 1 & 1\end{bmatrix}$, then A^3 is

(a) $\begin{bmatrix}1 & 0\\ 3 & 1\end{bmatrix}$ (b) $\begin{bmatrix}1 & 3\\ 0 & 1\end{bmatrix}$ (c) $\begin{bmatrix}1 & 3\\ 0 & 0\end{bmatrix}$ (d) $\begin{bmatrix}3 & 0\\ 1 & 1\end{bmatrix}$

12. If $x=t^2$ and $y=t^3$, then $\frac{d^2y}{dx^2}$ is

(a) $\frac{3t}{4}$ (b) $\frac{3}{t}$ (c) $\frac{3}{4t}$ (d) $\frac{4}{3t}$

13. $\int e^x(1-\cot x+\operatorname{cosec}^2 x)\,dx$ is equal to

(a) $e^x(1-\cot x)+C$ (b) $e^x(1+\cot x)+C$

(c) $e^x(\operatorname{cosec} x)+C$ (d) $e^x\cot x+C$

14. $\int_{-\pi/2}^{\pi/2} x^2\sin x\,dx$ is equal to

(a) 1 (b) 0 (c) –1 (d) 2

15. The area bounded by $y=x^2$, the X-axis and the lines $x=-1$ and $x=1$ is

(a) $\frac{1}{3}$ sq unit (b) $\frac{2}{3}$ sq unit

(c) 3 sq units (d) 1 sq unit

16. How many arbitrary constants are there in the particular solution of the differential equation $\frac{dy}{dx}=-4xy^2$; $y(0)=1$?

(a) 1 (b) 2 (c) 0 (d) 3

17. For what value of n is the following differential equation homogeneous $\frac{dy}{dx}=\frac{x^3-y^n}{x^2y+xy^2}$?

(a) 1 (b) 2 (c) 3 (d) 4

18. $\int_0^2 [x]\,dx$ is equal to

(a) 0 (b) 1 (c) –1 (d) 2

Assertion- Reason Based Questions

Directions (Q. Nos. 19-20) *In the following questions, a statement of Assertion (A) is followed by a statement of Reason (R). Choose the correct answer out of the following choices.*

(a) Both (A) and (R) are true and (R) is the correct explanation of (A).

(b) Both (A) and (R) are true, but (R) is not the correct explanation of (A).

(c) (A) is true and (R) is false.

(d) (A) is false, but (R) is true.

19. **Assertion (A)** The function $f:R^*\to R^*$ defined by $f(x)=\frac{1}{x}$ is one-one and onto, where R^* is the set of all non-zero real numbers.

Reason (R) The function $g:N\to R^*$ defined by $g(x)=\frac{1}{x}$ is one-one and onto.

20. **Assertion (A)** If $\begin{bmatrix}xy & 4\\ z+5 & x+y\end{bmatrix}=\begin{bmatrix}4 & w\\ 0 & 4\end{bmatrix}$, then $x=2$, $y=2$, $z=-5$ and $w=4$.

Reason (R) Two matrices are equal, if their orders are same and their corresponding elements are equal.

SECTION B

[This section comprises of very short answer type questions (VSA) of 2 marks each]

21. If $f(x)=\begin{cases}\dfrac{\cos^2 x-\sin^2 x-1}{\sqrt{x^2+1}-1}, & x\neq 0\\ a & x=0\end{cases}$ is continuous at $x=0$, find the value of a.

22. Evaluate $\int \frac{x}{4+x^4}dx$.

Or Evaluate $\int_0^2 e^{[x]}\,dx$.

23. If A and B are matrix of order 3×3 and $|A|=2$, $|B|=4$, find $|AB|$.

Or If A is a matrix of order 3×3 such that $|A|=5$, find $|A(\operatorname{adj} A)|$.

24. Find the area of the region bounded by $y=9x^2$, $x=0$, $y=1$ and $y=4$ in first quadrant.

25. Evaluate $\sin^{-1}\left(-\frac{\sqrt{3}}{2}\right)-2\sec^{-1}\left(2\tan\frac{\pi}{6}\right)$.

SECTION C

[This section comprises of short answer type questions (SA) of 3 marks each]

26. Consider the function $f:R^+\to[4,\infty)$ defined by $f(x)=x^2+4$, where R^+ is the set of all non-negative real numbers. Show that f is bijective.

27. Show that the differential equation $\left[x\sin^2\left(\frac{y}{x}\right)-y\right]dx+x\,dy=0$ is homogeneous. Find the particular solution of this differential equation, given that $y=\frac{\pi}{4}$, when $x=1$.

Or Find the solution of differential equation $x^2dy+y(x+y)dx=0$, if $x=1$ and $y=1$.

28. Find the value of $\int \frac{\tan^2 x \sec^2 x}{1-\tan^6 x} dx$.

Or

Find the value of $\int \sin x \cdot \log \cos x \, dx$.

29. Let $\vec{a}, \vec{b}$ and $\vec{c}$ be three vectors such that $|\vec{a}|=1, |\vec{b}|=2$ and $|\vec{c}|=3$. If the projection of $\vec{b}$ along $\vec{a}$ is equal to the projection of $\vec{c}$ along $\vec{a}$ and $\vec{b}$ and $\vec{c}$ are perpendicular to each other, find $|3\vec{a}-2\vec{b}+2\vec{c}|$.

30. Show that $y=\log(1+x)-\frac{2x}{2+x}, x>-1$ is an increasing function of x, throughout its domain.

Or

Find the intervals in which the function given by $f(x)=\sin x+\cos x, 0 \le x \le 2\pi$ is

(i) increasing. (ii) decreasing.

31. Evaluate $\int \frac{x^2-1}{x^2+4} dx$.

SECTION D

[This section comprises of long answer type questions (LA) of 5 marks each]

32. If $A=\begin{bmatrix} 1 & 3 & 2 \\ 2 & 0 & -1 \\ 1 & 2 & 3 \end{bmatrix}$, then show that A satisfies the following equation.

$$A^3-4A^2+11I-3A=O.$$

Or

Solve the given system of linear equations using matrix method.

$$x+3y+4z=8,\ 2x+y+2z=5,\ 5x+y+z=7$$

33. Find the shortest distance between the lines

$$\frac{x-8}{3}=\frac{y+9}{-16}=\frac{z-10}{7}$$

and $$\frac{x-15}{3}=\frac{y-29}{8}=\frac{z-5}{-5}.$$

34. Solve the given graphically

Maximise $Z=1500(7x+6y)$, subject to constraints

$$x+y \le 50, 2x+y \le 80, x, y \ge 0$$

35. Evaluate $\int \frac{\cos x}{(1-\sin x)(2-\sin x)} dx$.

Or

Prove that $\int_0^{\pi} \frac{x}{(1+\sin x)} dx=\pi$.

SECTION E

[This section comprises 3 case-study/passage based questions of 4 marks each with sub parts. The first two case study questions have three sub parts (i), (ii), (iii) of marks 1, 1, 2 respectively. The third case study question has two sub parts (i), (ii) of 2 marks each]

36. A building contractor undertakes a job to construct

4 flats on a plot along with parking area. Due to strike, the probability of many construction workers not being present for the job is 0.65. The probability that many are not present and still the work gets completed on time is 0.35. The probability that work will be completed on time when all workers are present is 0.80.

Let E_1 : represents the event when many workers were not present for the job; E_2 : represents the event when all workers were present; and E : represents completing the construction work on time.

Based on the above information, answer the following questions.

(i) What is the probability that all the workers are present for the job?

(ii) What is the probability that construction will be completed on time?

(iii) (a) What is the probability that many workers are not present given that the construction work is completed on time?

Or

(b) What is the probability that all workers were present given that the construction job was completed on time?

37. A toy making company made a toy in which a cylinder is inscribed in a sphere. The height and radius of cylinder is H and R, respectively, while the radius of sphere is a.

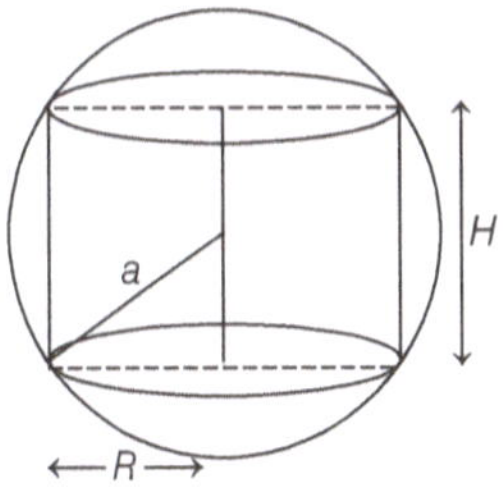

On the basis of above information, answer the following questions.

(i) Find the relation between R and H.

(ii) Find the value of volume of cylinder V in terms of H.

(iii) Find the value of H when V is maximum.

Or If V is maximum at $H = \frac{2}{\sqrt{3}}a$, then find the maximum value of V.

38. A doctor is to visit a patient. From the past experience, it is known that the probabilities that he will come by train, bus, scooter or by other means of transport are respectively $\frac{3}{10}, \frac{1}{5}, \frac{1}{10}$ and $\frac{2}{5}$. The probability that he will be late are $\frac{1}{4}, \frac{1}{3}$ and $\frac{1}{12}$, if he comes by train, bus and scooter respectively, but if he comes by other means of transport, then he will not be late.

On the basis of above information, answer the following questions.

(i) Find the probability that doctor comes by train and he is late.

(ii) When doctor arrives, he is late. What is the probability that he comes by scooter.

SAMPLE QUESTION PAPER 3

A Highly Simulated Sample Question Paper for CBSE Class XII Examination

MATHEMATICS (Unsolved)

Time : 3 Hours **Max. Marks : 80**

General Instructions

(i) This question paper contains 38 questions. All questions are compulsory.
(ii) Question paper is divided into FIVE sections - Section A, B, C, D and E.
(iii) In Section A, Question number 1 to 18 are Multiple Choice Questions (MCQ) type and Question number 19 and 20 are Assertion-Reason based questions carrying 1 mark each.
(iv) In Section B, Question number 21 to 25 are Very Short Answer (VSA) type questions carrying 2 marks each.
(v) In Section C, Question number 26 to 31 are Short Answer (SA) type questions carrying 3 marks each.
(vi) In Section D, Question number 32 to 35 are Long Answer (LA) type questions carrying 5 marks each.
(vii) In Section E, Question number 36 to 38 are Case Study Based question carrying 4 marks each.
(viii) There is no overall choice. However, an internal choice has been provided in 2 questions in Section B, 3 questions in Section C, 2 questions in Section D and 2 questions in Section E.
(ix) Use of calculator is NOT allowed.

SECTION A

Multiple Choice Questions

Each question carries 1 mark

1. $\cot^{-1}(-\sqrt{3})+\tan^{-1}(1)$ is equal to

(a) $\frac{\pi}{12}$ (b) $\frac{13\pi}{12}$ (c) $\frac{13\pi}{2}$ (d) $\frac{\pi}{2}$

2. Let R be the relation in the set {1, 2, 3, 4} given by $R=\{(1, 2), (2, 2), (1, 1), (4, 4), (1, 3), (3, 3), (3, 2)\}$. Then, R is

(a) reflexive but not transitive
(b) reflexive and transitive
(c) neither reflexive nor symmetric
(d) symmetric but not transitive

3. $\tan^{-1}\left(\sqrt{2}\sin\frac{3\pi}{4}\right)$ is equal to

(a) $\frac{\pi}{2}$ (b) $\frac{\pi}{6}$
(c) $\frac{\pi}{3}$ (d) $\frac{\pi}{4}$

4. Matrix X, if $X+\begin{bmatrix}4 & 6\\ -3 & 7\end{bmatrix}=\begin{bmatrix}3 & -6\\ 5 & -8\end{bmatrix}$ is

(a) $\begin{bmatrix}-1 & -12\\ 8 & -15\end{bmatrix}$ (b) $\begin{bmatrix}1 & -12\\ -8 & 15\end{bmatrix}$
(c) $\begin{bmatrix}-1 & 8\\ -12 & -15\end{bmatrix}$ (d) $\begin{bmatrix}1 & 1\\ 0 & 0\end{bmatrix}$

5. If $\cos^{-1}\alpha+\cos^{-1}\beta+\cos^{-1}\gamma=3\pi$, then evaluate $(\alpha^3+\beta^3+\gamma^3)-\left(\frac{1}{\alpha}+\frac{1}{\beta}+\frac{1}{\gamma}\right)$

(a) 1 (b) 0
(c) –1 (d) 2

6. If $A=\begin{bmatrix}\cos\theta & -\sin\theta\\ \sin\theta & \cos\theta\end{bmatrix}$, then find the value of θ $\left(\text{where}, \theta\in\left(0,\frac{\pi}{2}\right)\right)$ satisfying the equation $A^T+A=I_2$.

(a) $\frac{\pi}{2}$ (b) $\frac{\pi}{6}$
(c) $\frac{\pi}{3}$ (d) π

7. If $f(x)=ax^2+bx+c$, then $f'(1)+f'(4)-f'(5)$ is equal to

(a) a (b) b

(c) –1 (d) c

8. Find the point where, $f(x)=xe^x$ is minimum.

(a) 1 (b) –1

(c) 0 (d) 2

9. $\int_0^{\pi/2} x\sin x\, dx$ is equal to

(a) –1 (b) 1

(c) 2 (d) –3

10. If $y=1-x+\frac{x^2}{2!}-\frac{x^3}{3!}+\frac{x^4}{4!}\ldots\infty$, then $\frac{d^2y}{dx^2}-y$ is equal to

(a) 0 (b) –1

(c) x (d) x^2

11. $\int \frac{x^3}{x+1} dx$ is equal to

(a) $x+\frac{x^2}{2}-\frac{x^3}{3}-\log|1+x|+C$

(b) $x-\frac{x^2}{2}+\frac{x^3}{3}-\log|1+x|+C$

(c) $x+\log x+C$

(d) $x-\frac{x^3}{3}+\frac{x^4}{2}+\log|1+x|+C$

12. If $\{x\}$ is fractional part function, then $\int_0^2 \{x\}\, dx$ is equal to

(a) 1 (b) 2

(c) –1 (d) 3

13. If the angle between the vectors $\hat{i}+\hat{k}$ and $\hat{i}-\hat{j}+\alpha\hat{k}$ is $\frac{\pi}{2}$, then the value of α is

(a) 1 (b) –1

(c) 0 (d) 2

14. If $\vec{a}=(\hat{i}+3\hat{j}-2\hat{k})\times(-\hat{i}+3\hat{k})$, then the value of $|\vec{a}|$ is

(a) 91 (b) $\sqrt{91}$

(c) 31 (d) $\sqrt{31}$

15. $\int_0^1 3^{x-[x]}dx$ is equal to

(a) $\frac{1}{\log 3}$ (b) $\frac{2}{\log 3}$

(c) $\frac{3}{\log 3}$ (d) $\frac{\log 3}{2}$

16. If $|\vec{a}|=2, |\vec{b}|=3$ and $\vec{a}\cdot\vec{b}=3$, then the projection of $\vec{b}$ on $\vec{a}$ is

(a) $\frac{2}{3}$ (b) $\frac{3}{2}$ (c) $\frac{4}{5}$ (d) $\frac{5}{4}$

17. If the lines $\frac{x-1}{2}=\frac{2-y}{1}=\frac{z}{3}$ and $\frac{x+1}{5}=\frac{-y-2}{-3}=\frac{1-z}{\alpha}$ are perpendicular, then α is equal to

(a) 2 (b) $\frac{7}{3}$ (c) $\frac{1}{3}$ (d) $\frac{1}{7}$

18. If $|\vec{a}\times\vec{b}|^2+(\vec{a}\cdot\vec{b})^2=144$ and $|\vec{a}|=4$, then the value of $|\vec{b}|$ is

(a) 2 (b) 1 (c) 3 (d) 5

Assertion- Reason Based Questions

Directions (Q. Nos. 19-20) *In the following questions, a statement of Assertion (A) is followed by a statement of Reason (R). Choose the correct answer out of the following choices.*

(a) Both (A) and (R) are true and (R) is the correct explanation of (A).

(b) Both (A) and (R) are true, but (R) is not the correct explanation of (A).

(c) (A) is true and (R) is false.

(d) (A) is false, but (R) is true.

19. **Assertion (A)** Let A and B be sets. Then, the function $f: A\times B \rightarrow B\times A$ such that $f(a,b)=(b,a)$ is bijective.

Reason (R) A function f is said to be bijective, if it is both one-one and onto.

20. **Assertion (A)** If $A=\begin{bmatrix}1 & 1 & -2\\ 2 & 1 & -3\\ 5 & 4 & -9\end{bmatrix}$, then $|A|=0$.

Reason (R) $|\text{adj}\, A|=|A|^{n-1}$, where n is order of matrix.

SECTION B

[This section comprises of very short answer type questions (VSA) of 2 marks each]

21. Find the values of 'a', so that the function $f(x)$ defined by $f(x)=\begin{cases}\frac{\sin^2 ax}{x^2}, & x\neq 0\\ 1, & x=0\end{cases}$ may be continuous at $x=0$.

Or

If $\sec\left(\frac{x+y}{x-y}\right)=a$, prove that $\frac{dy}{dx}=\frac{y}{x}$.

22. Find the equation of the line joining $A(1,3)$ and $B(0,0)$ using determinant and find k, if $D(k,0)$ is a point such that area of ΔABD is 3 sq units.

Or

Find X and Y, if $X+Y=\begin{bmatrix}7 & 0\\ 2 & 5\end{bmatrix}$ and $X-Y=\begin{bmatrix}3 & 0\\ 0 & 3\end{bmatrix}$.

23. Evaluate $\int_3^4 \frac{\sqrt{x}}{\sqrt{x}+\sqrt{7-x}}dx$.

24. If $\vec{a}\times\vec{b}=\vec{a}\times\vec{c}, \vec{a}\neq 0$ and $\vec{b}\neq\vec{c}$, show that $\vec{b}=\vec{c}+t\vec{a}$ for some scalar t.

25. Find the area of the region bounded by the line $y=3x+2$, the X-axis and the ordinates $x=-1$ and $x=1$.

SECTION C

[This section comprises of short answer type questions (SA) of 3 marks each]

26. Show that the relation R in the S at $A=\{x : x\in W, 0\le x\le 12\}$ given by $R=\{(a,b):|a-b|$ is multiple of 4} is an equivalence relation.

Or

Show that the function $f:R\to\{x\in R:-1<x<1\}$ defined by $f(x)=\frac{x}{1+|x|}, x\in R$ is one-one and onto function.

27. A man is moving away from a tower 41.6 m high at the rate of 2 m/sec. Find the rate at which the angle of elevation of the top of tower is changing, when he is at a distance of 30 m from the foot of the tower. Assume that the eye level of the man is 1.6 m from the ground.

28. If $x=a\left\{\cos\theta+\log\tan\frac{\theta}{2}\right\}$ and $y=a\sin\theta$, find $\frac{d^2y}{dx^2}$.

Or

If $y=\frac{x\cos^{-1}x}{\sqrt{1-x^2}}-\log\sqrt{1-x^2}$, then prove that $\frac{dy}{dx}=\frac{\cos^{-1}x}{(1-x^2)^{3/2}}$.

29. Find the value of c for which the vectors $\vec{a}=(c\log_2 x)\hat{i}-6\hat{j}+3\hat{k}$ and $\vec{b}=(\log_2 x)\hat{i}+2\hat{j}+(2c\log_2 x)\hat{k}$ make an obtuse angle for any $x\in(0,\infty)$.

30. Find the particular solution of the differential equation $e^x\tan y\,dx+(2-e^x)\sec^2 y\,dy=0$, given that $y=\frac{\pi}{4}$ when $x=0$.

Or

Find the particular solution of the differential equation $(3xy+y^2)dx+(x^2+xy)dy=0$, for $x=1, y=1$.

31. Find the area bounded by the curve $x^2+y^2=a^2$ using integration.

SECTION D

[This section comprises of long answer type questions (LA) of 5 marks each]

32. Find the value of $\int\frac{x^2+1}{(x^2+2)(x^2+3)}dx$.

Or

Evaluate $\int\frac{x^2}{(x\sin x+\cos x)^2}dx$.

33. Find the shortest distance between the following lines

$\vec{r}=(\hat{i}+\hat{j}-\hat{k})+s(2\hat{i}+\hat{j}+\hat{k})$

and $\vec{r}=(\hat{i}+\hat{j}+2\hat{k})+t(4\hat{i}+2\hat{j}+2\hat{k})$

Or

For any two vectors $\vec{a}$ and $\vec{b}$, show that

$(1+|\vec{a}|^2)(1+|\vec{b}|^2)=\{(1-\vec{a}\cdot\vec{b})\}^2+|\vec{a}+\vec{b}+(\vec{a}\times\vec{b})|^2$.

34. Evaluate the product AB, where

$$A=\begin{bmatrix}1 & -1 & 1\\ 1 & -2 & -2\\ 2 & 1 & 3\end{bmatrix} \text{ and } B=\begin{bmatrix}-4 & 4 & 4\\ -7 & 1 & 3\\ 5 & -3 & -1\end{bmatrix}$$

Hence, solve the system of linear equations

$x-y+z=4,\ x-2y-2z=9$ and $2x+y+3z=1$

35. Solve the LPP graphically
Minimise $Z=30x-30y+1800$ subject to constraints $x+y\le 30, x\le 15, y\le 20, x+y\ge 15; x, y\ge 0$

SECTION E

[This section comprises 3 case-study/passage based questions of 4 marks each with sub parts. The first two case study questions have three sub parts (i), (ii), (iii) of marks 1, 1, 2 respectively. The third case study question has two sub parts (i), (ii) of 2 marks each]

36. Given three identical boxes I, II and III, each containing two coins. In box I both coins are gold coins, in box II both are silver coins and in box III there is one gold and one silver coin. A person chooses a box at random and takes out a coin.

On the basis of above information, answer the following questions.

(i) Find the probability of choosing one box and the probability of getting gold coin from III box.

(ii) Find the probability of getting gold coin from II box.

(iii) Find total probability of drawing gold coin.

Or If drawn coin is of gold, then find the probability that other coin in I box is also of gold.

37. A building has front gate of the shape as shown below.

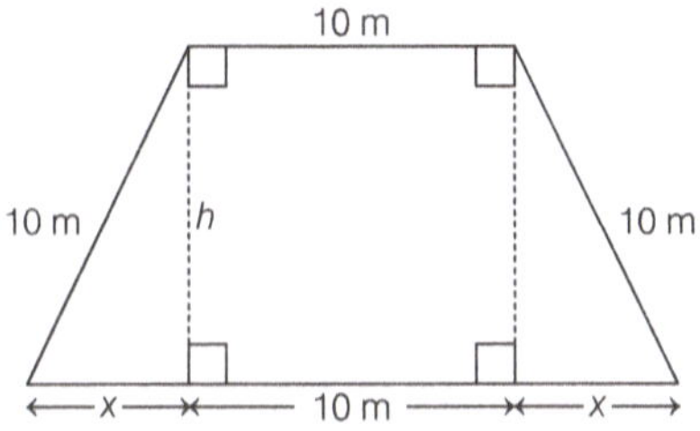

It is in the shape of trapezium whose three sides other than base is 10 m. Height of the gate is h m.

On the basis of above information, answer the following questions.

(i) Find the relation between x and h.

(ii) Express the area of gate A in terms of x.

(iii) Find the value of x when the area A is maximum.

Or If at $x = 5$ the area A is maximum, then find the value of h and the maximum value of A.

38. Recent studies suggest that roughly 12% of the world population is left handed.

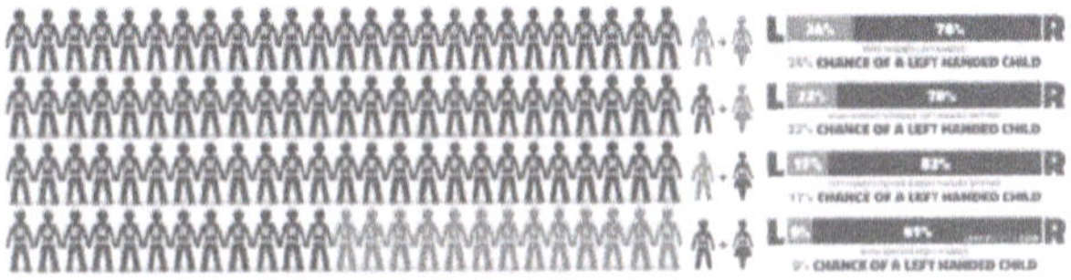

Roughly 12% of the world is Left Handed

Depending upon the parents, the chances of having a left handed child are as follows :

A : When both father and mother are left handed : Chances of left handed child is 24%.

B : When father is right handed and mother is left handed : Chances of left handed child is 22%.

C : When father is left handed and mother is right handed : Chances of left handed child is 17%.

D : When both father and mothers are right handed : Chances of left handed child is 9%.

Assuming that $P(A) = P(B) = P(C) = P(D) = \frac{1}{4}$ and L denotes the event that child is left handed.

Based on the above information, answer the following questions.

(i) Find $P(L / C)$. (ii) Find $P(\bar{L} / A)$.

(iii) (a) Find $P(A / L)$.

Or

(b) Find the probability that a randomly selected child is left handed given that exactly one of the parents is left handed.

Answers

Sample Paper 1

1. (b) 2. (b) 3. (a) 4. (b)
5. (b) 6. (d) 7. (c) 8. (d)
9. (a) 10. (b) 11. (b) 12. (c)
13. (d) 14. (b) 15. (c) 16. (d)
17. (b) 18. (a) 19. (a) 20. (b)

21. Skew-symmetric *Or* $x + y = 5$

22. $\sqrt{\pi}$

23. $\theta = \frac{\pi}{6}$ *Or* $z = -1$

24. $\cos^{-1}\left(\frac{8}{5\sqrt{3}}\right)$

25. $\frac{2x+3}{2y-1} = C$

26. $-\frac{1}{4x} + \frac{7}{8}\tan^{-1}\left(\frac{x}{2}\right) + C$ *Or* $\frac{e^{2x}(2x-3)^{-2}}{2} + C$

27. $\frac{2a^2}{3}$ sq units

29. $\sec\left(\frac{y}{x}\right) = Cxy$ *Or* $\log|y| + \frac{1}{y} = \frac{-1}{x} + x + 1$

30. $\left[-\frac{1}{2}, \frac{1}{2}\right]$

31. $x^{1/x}\left[\frac{1-\log x}{x^2}\right]$ *Or* $\tan\frac{\theta}{2}$

32. Minimum value of Z is 570 at (50, 40).
Or Maximum value of Z is 392 at (8, 12).

33. $-\frac{\pi}{2}\log 2$

34. (2, 2)

35. $\hat{i} + 2\hat{j} + 3\hat{k}, \sqrt{14}$ unit *Or* $\frac{\sqrt{62}}{2}$ sq units

36. (i) 03 (ii) 0.4 (iii) 0.68 *or* 0.824

37. (i) $S = 6x^2 + 4\pi y^2$ (ii) $V = \frac{4}{3}\pi y^3 + \frac{2}{3}x^3$
(iii) $x = 3y$ *Or* $V = \frac{2}{3}x^3\left(1 + \frac{2\pi}{27}\right)$, $S = 2x^2\left[3 + \frac{2}{9}\pi\right]$

38. (i) $\frac{7}{25}$ (ii) $\frac{3}{7}$

Sample Paper 2

1. (d) 2. (a) 3. (d) 4. (c)
5. (a) 6. (a) 7. (c) 8. (d)
9. (a) 10. (d) 11. (a) 12. (c)
13. (a) 14. (b) 15. (b) 16. (c)
17. (c) 18. (b) 19. (c) 20. (a)

21. $a = -4$

22. $\frac{1}{4}\tan^{-1}\frac{x^2}{2}$ *Or* $e + 1$

23. 8 *Or* 125

24. $\frac{14}{9}$ sq units

25. $-\frac{2\pi}{3}$

27. $1 + \log(x) - \cot\left(\frac{y}{x}\right) = 0$ *Or* $3x^2y = y + 2x$

28. $\frac{1}{6}\log\left|\frac{1+\tan^3 x}{1-\tan^3 x}\right| + C$ Or $-\cos x \log\cos x + \cos x + C$

29. $\sqrt{61}$

30. *Or* (i) $\left[0, \frac{\pi}{4}\right] \cup \left[\frac{5\pi}{4}, 2\pi\right]$ (ii) $\left[\frac{\pi}{4}, \frac{5\pi}{4}\right]$

31. $x - \frac{5}{2}\tan^{-1}\left(\frac{x}{2}\right) + C$

32. *Or* $x = 1$, $y = 1$ and $z = 1$

33. 14 units

34. $Z = 49500$ at (30, 20)

35. $\log\left|\frac{2-\sin x}{1-\sin x}\right| + C$

36. (i) 0.35 (ii) 0.51 (iii) (a) 0.45 *or* (b) 0.55

37. (i) $\frac{5}{32}$ (iii) $\frac{61}{96}$

38. (i) $\frac{3}{40}$ (ii) $\frac{1}{18}$

Sample Paper 3

1. (b) 2. (b) 3. (d) 4. (a)
5. (b) 6. (c) 7. (b) 8. (b)
9. (b) 10. (a) 11. (b) 12. (a)
13. (b) 14. (b) 15. (b) 16. (b)
17. (b) 18. (c) 19. (a) 20. (b)

21. ± 1

22. $3x - y = 0, k = \pm 2$ *Or* $X = \begin{bmatrix} 5 & 0 \\ 1 & 4 \end{bmatrix}$ and $Y = \begin{bmatrix} 2 & 0 \\ 1 & 1 \end{bmatrix}$

23. $\frac{1}{2}$

25. $\frac{13}{3}$ sq units

27. $\frac{4}{125}$ rad/sec

28. $\frac{1}{a}\sec^3\theta\tan\theta$

29. $c \in \left(-\frac{4}{3}, 0\right)$

30. $\tan y = 2 - e^x$ *Or* $y^2x^2 + 2yx^3 = 3$

31. πa^2

32. $-\frac{1}{\sqrt{2}}\tan^{-1}\left(\frac{x}{\sqrt{2}}\right) + \frac{2}{\sqrt{3}}\tan^{-1}\left(\frac{x}{\sqrt{3}}\right) + C$

Or $\frac{-x\sec x}{x\sin x + \cos x} + \tan x + C$

33. $\sqrt{\frac{15}{2}}$ units

34. $AB = 8I$; $x = 3$, $y = -2$ and $z = -1$

35. $Z_{\min} = 1200$ at $(0, 20)$

36. (i) $\frac{1}{3}$ and $\frac{1}{2}$ (ii) 0 (iii) $\frac{1}{2}$ *Or* $\frac{2}{3}$

37. (i) $x^2 + h^2 = 100$ (ii) $A = (10 + x)\sqrt{100 - x^2}$

(iii) $x = 5$ *Or* $h = 5\sqrt{3}$ m and $A = 75\sqrt{3}$ m^2

38. (i) $\frac{17}{100}$ (ii) $\frac{19}{25}$ (iii) (a) $\frac{1}{3}$ (b) $\frac{39}{100}$

CBSE
Examination Paper 2025

CBSE EXAMINATION PAPER 2025

MATHEMATICS

Time 3 Hours **Max. Marks 80**

General Instructions

(i) This question paper contains 38 questions. All questions are compulsory.

(ii) Question paper is divided into FIVE sections - Section A, B, C, D and E.

(iii) In Section A, Question number 1 to 18 are Multiple Choice Questions (MCQ) and Question number 19 and 20 are Assertion-Reason based questions carrying 1 mark each.

(iv) In Section B, Question number 21 to 25 are Very Short Answer (VSA) type questions carrying 2 marks each.

(v) In Section C, Question number 26 to 31 are Short Answer (SA) type questions carrying 3 marks each.

(vi) In Section D, Question number 32 to 35 are Long Answer (LA) type questions carrying 5 marks each.

(vii) In Section E, Question number 36 to 38 are Case Study Based questions carrying 4 marks each.

(viii) There is no overall choice. However, an internal choice has been provided in 2 questions in Section B, 3 questions in Section C, 2 questions in Section D and 2 questions in Section E.

(ix) Use of calculator is NOT allowed.

SECTION A

Multiple Choice Questions

Each question carries 1 mark

1. The principal value of $\cot^{-1}\left(-\frac{1}{\sqrt{3}}\right)$ is

(a) $-\frac{\pi}{3}$ (b) $-\frac{2\pi}{3}$ (c) $\frac{\pi}{3}$ (d) $\frac{2\pi}{3}$

2. If $A=[a_{ij}]$ is a 3×3 diagonal matrix such that $a_{11}=1$, $a_{22}=5$ and $a_{33}=-2$ then $|A|$ is

(a) 0 (b) -10 (c) 10 (d) 1

3. If $A=kB$, where A and B are two square matrices of order n and k is scalar, then

(a) $|A|=k|B|$ (b) $|A|=k^n|B|$

(c) $|A|=k+|B|$ (d) $|A|=|B|^k$

4. If $f(x)=\begin{cases}\frac{\sin^2 ax}{x^2}, & x\neq 0\\ 1, & x=0\end{cases}$ is continuous at $x=0$, then the value of a is

(a) 1 (b) -1 (c) ± 1 (d) 0

5. If $\begin{vmatrix}2x & 5\\ 12 & x\end{vmatrix}=\begin{vmatrix}6 & -5\\ 4 & 3\end{vmatrix}$ then the value of x is

(a) 3 (b) 7 (c) ± 7 (d) ± 3

6. If $P(A\cup B)=0.9$ and $P(A\cap B)=0.4$ then $P(\bar{A})+P(\bar{B})$ is

(a) 0.3 (b) 1 (c) 1.3 (d) 0.7

7. If $A=\begin{bmatrix}5&0&0\\0&5&0\\0&0&5\end{bmatrix}$ then A^3 is

(a) $3\begin{bmatrix}5&0&0\\0&5&0\\0&0&5\end{bmatrix}$ (b) $\begin{bmatrix}125&0&0\\0&125&0\\0&0&125\end{bmatrix}$

(c) $\begin{bmatrix}15&0&0\\0&15&0\\0&0&15\end{bmatrix}$ (d) $\begin{bmatrix}5^3&0&0\\0&5&0\\0&0&5\end{bmatrix}$

8. Let A and B be two matrices of suitable orders. Then, which of the following is not correct?

(a) $(A')'=A$

(b) $(kA)'=kA'$, k is a scalar.

(c) $(A'+B')'=A+B$

(d) $(AB)'=A'B'$

9. The area of the region enclosed between the curve $y=x|x|$, X-axis, $x=-2$ and $x=2$ is

(a) $\frac{8}{3}$ (b) $\frac{16}{3}$

(c) 0 (d) 8

* *Out of Syllabus*

10. If $f(x)=\{[x], x \in R\}$ is the greatest integer function then the correct statement is

(a) f is continuous but not differentiable at $x=2$.
(b) f is neither continuous not differentiable at $x=2$.
(c) f is continuous as well as differentiable at $x=2$.
(d) f is not continuous but differentiable at $x=2$.

11. $\int \frac{\cos 2x - \cos 2\theta}{\cos x - \cos \theta} dx$ is equal to

(a) $2(\sin x + x \sin \theta) + C$
(b) $2(\sin x - x \cos \theta) + C$
(c) $2(\sin x + \sin \theta) + C$
(d) $2(\sin x - x \sin \theta) + C$

12. $\int_0^1 \frac{2x}{5x^2+1} dx$ is equal to

(a) $\frac{1}{5}\log 6$ (b) $\frac{1}{5}\log 5$
(c) $\frac{1}{2}\log 6$ (d) $\frac{1}{2}\log 5$

13. The slope of the curve $y=-x^3+3x^2+8x-20$ is maximum at

(a) $(1, -10)$ (b) $(1, 10)$
(c) $(10, 1)$ (d) $(-10, 1)$

14. The integrating factors of the differential equation $\frac{dx}{dy} = \frac{-(1+\sin x)}{x + y\cos x}$ is

(a) $\log \cos x$ (b) $1+\sin x$
(c) $e^{(1+\sin x)}$ (d) $e^{\log \cos x}$

15. For a Linear Programming Problem (LPP), the given objective function $Z=3x+2y$ is subject to constraints

$$x+2y \le 10, 3x+y \le 15, x, y \ge 0$$

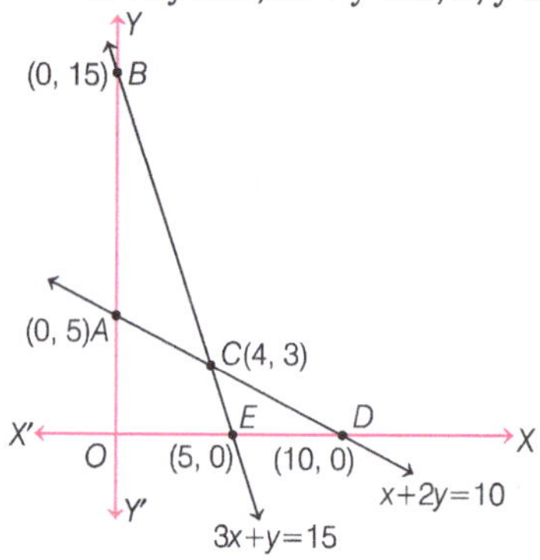

The correct feasible region is

(a) ABC
(b) $AOEC$
(c) CED
(d) Open unbounded region BCD

16. The sum of the order and degree of the differential equation $\left[1+\left(\frac{dy}{dx}\right)^2\right]^3 = \frac{d^2y}{dx^2}$ is

(a) 2 (b) $\frac{5}{2}$ (c) 3 (d) 4

17. The respective values of $|\vec{a}|$ and $|\vec{b}|$, if given $(\vec{a}-\vec{b})\cdot(\vec{a}+\vec{b})=512$ and $|\vec{a}|=3|\vec{b}|$ are

(a) 48 and 16 (b) 3 and 1
(c) 24 and 8 (d) 6 and 2

18. Let $\vec{a}$ be a position vector whose tip is the point $(2, -3)$. If $\overrightarrow{AB}=\vec{a}$, where coordinates of A are $(-4, 5)$, then the coordinates of B are

(a) $(-2, -2)$ (b) $(2, -2)$
(c) $(-2, 2)$ (d) $(2, 2)$

Assertion- Reason Based Questions

Directions (Q. Nos. 19 and 20) *are Assertion and Reason based questions. Two statements are given, one labelled Assertion (A) and the other labelled Reason (R). Select the correct answer from the codes (a), (b), (c) and (d) as given below.*

(a) Both A and R are true and R is the correct explanation of A.
(b) Both A and R are true but R is not the correct explanation of A.
(c) A is true, but R is false.
(d) A is false, but R is true.

19. **Assertion** (A) The shaded portion of the graph represents the feasible region for the given Linear Programming Problem (LPP).

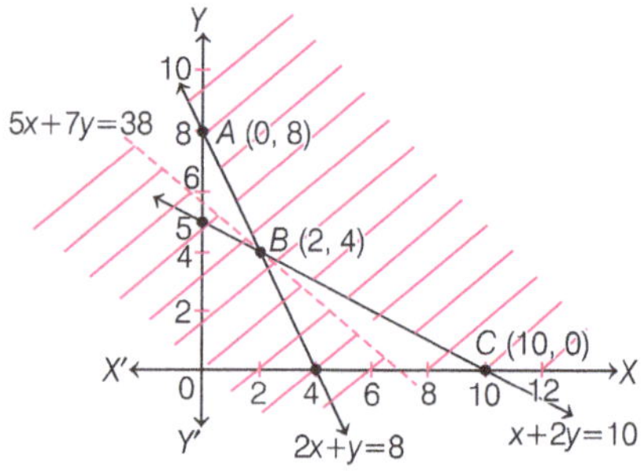

Min $Z=50x+70y$
Subject to constraints
$2x+y \ge 8, x+2y \ge 10, x, y \ge 0$
$Z=50x+70y$ has a minimum value $=380$ at $B(2, 4)$.

Reason (R) The region representing $50x + 70y < 380$ does not have any point common with the feasible region.

20. **Assertion** (A) Let $A = \{x \in R : -1 \le x \le 1\}$. If $f : A \to A$ be defined as $f(x) = x^2$ then f is not an onto function.

Reason (R) If $y = -1 \in A$ then $x = \pm\sqrt{-1} \notin A$.

SECTION B

[This section comprises of very short answer type questions (VSA) of 2 marks each]

21. Find the domain of $\sin^{-1}(x^2 - 3)$.

22. Let the volume of a metallic hollow sphere be constant. If the inner radius increases at the rate of 2 cm/s, find the rate of increase of the outer radius when the radii are 2 cm and 4 cm, respectively.

23. A man needs to hang two lanterns on a straight wire whose end points have coordinates $A(4, 1, -2)$ and $B(6, 2, -3)$. Find the coordinates of the points where he hangs the lanterns such that these points trisect the wire AB.

24. (a) Differentiate $\frac{\sin x}{\sqrt{\cos x}}$ with respect to x.

Or (b) If $y = 5\cos x - 3\sin x$ prove that $\frac{d^2y}{dx^2} + y = 0$.

25. (a) Find a vector of magnitude 5 which is perpendicular to both the vectors $3\hat{i} - 2\hat{j} + \hat{k}$ and $4\hat{i} + 3\hat{j} - 2\hat{k}$.

Or (b) Let $\vec{a}, \vec{b}$ and $\vec{c}$ be three vectors such that $\vec{a} \cdot \vec{b} = \vec{a} \cdot \vec{c}$ and $\vec{a} \times \vec{b} = \vec{a} \times \vec{c}, \vec{a} \ne 0$. Show that $\vec{b} = \vec{c}$.

SECTION C

[This section comprises of short answer type questions (SA) of 3 marks each]

26. Find the interval/intervals in which the function $f(x) = \sin 3x - \cos 3x, 0 < x < \frac{\pi}{2}$ is strictly increasing.

27. (a) If $\vec{a} + \vec{b} + \vec{c} = \vec{0}$ such that $|\vec{a}| = 3, |\vec{b}| = 5, |\vec{c}| = 7$ then find the angle between $\vec{a}$ and $\vec{b}$.

Or (b) If $\vec{a}$ and $\vec{b}$ are unit vectors inclined with each other at an angle θ, then prove that $\frac{1}{2}|\vec{a} - \vec{b}| = \sin\frac{\theta}{2}$.

28. Solve the differential equation $x\cos\left(\frac{y}{x}\right)\frac{dy}{dx} = y\cos\left(\frac{y}{x}\right) + x$.

29. (a) The probability that a student buys a colouring book is 0.7 and that she buys a box of colours is 0.2. The probability that she buys a colouring book, given that she buys a box of colours, is 0.3. Find the probability that the student:

(i) Buys both the colouring book and the box of colours.

(ii) Buys a box of colours given that she buys the colouring book.

Or

*(b) A person has a fruit box that contains 6 apples and 4 oranges. He picks out a fruit three times, one after the other, after replacing the previous one in the box. Find

(i) The probability distribution of the number of oranges he draws.

(ii) The expectation of the random variable (number of oranges).

30. (a) Find $\int \frac{2x}{(x^2 + 3)(x^2 - 5)} dx$

Or

(b) Evaluate $\int_1^4 (|x - 2| + |x - 4|)\, dx$

31. In the Linear Programming Problem (LPP), find the point/points giving maximum value for $Z = 5x + 10y$

Subject to constraints

$$x + 2y \le 120,$$
$$x + y \ge 60,$$
$$x - 2y \ge 0,$$
$$x, y \ge 0$$

SECTION D

[This section comprises 4 Long Answer (LA) type questions of 5 marks each]

32. In a rough sketch, mark the region bounded by $y = 1 + |x + 1|, x = -2, x = 2$ and $y = 0$. Using integration, find the area of the marked region.

33. Three students run on a racing track such that their speeds add up to 6 km/h. However, double the speed of the third runner added to the speed of the first results in 7 km/h. If thrice the speed of the first runner is added to the original speeds of the other two, the result is 12 km/h. Using matrix method, find the original speed of each runner.

34. (a) For a positive constant a, differentiate $a^{t+\frac{1}{t}}$ with respect to $\left(t+\frac{1}{t}\right)^a$, where t is a non-zero real number.

Or

(b) Find $\frac{dy}{dx}$ if $y^x + x^y + x^x = a^b$, where a and b are constants.

35. (a) Find the foot of the perpendicular drawn from the point (1, 1, 4) on the line $\frac{x+2}{5}=\frac{y+1}{2}=\frac{-z+4}{-3}$.

Or

(b) Find the point on the line $\frac{x-1}{3}=\frac{y+1}{2}=\frac{z-4}{3}$ at a distance of $2\sqrt{2}$ units from the point $(-1,-1,2)$.

SECTION E

[This section comprises 3 case-study/passage based questions of 4 marks each with sub parts. The first two case study questions have three sub parts (i), (ii), (iii) of marks 1, 1, 2 respectively. The third case study question has two sub parts (i), (ii) of 2 marks each]

36. Let A be the set of 30 students of class XII in a school. Let $f: A \to N$, N is a set of natural numbers such that function $f(x)$ = Roll Number of student x. On the basis of the given information, answer the following

(i) Is f a bijective function?

(ii) Give reasons to support your answer to (i).

(iii) (a) Let R be a relation defined by the teacher to plan the seating arrangement of students in pairs, where $R = \{(x, y): x, y$ are roll numbers of students such that $y = 3x\}$. List the elements of R. Is the relation R reflexive, symmetric and transitive? Justify your answer.

Or

(iii) (b) Let R be a relation defined by $R = \{(x, y): x, y$ are roll numbers of students such that $y = x^3\}$. List the elements of R. Is R a function? Justify your answer.

37. A gardener wanted to plant vegetables in his garden. Hence, he bought 10 seeds of brinjal plant, 12 seeds of cabbage plant and 8 seeds of radish plant. The shopkeeper assured him of germination probabilities of brinjal, cabbage and radish to be 25%, 35% and 40%, respectively. But before he could plant the seeds, they got mixed up in the bag and he had to sow them randomly.

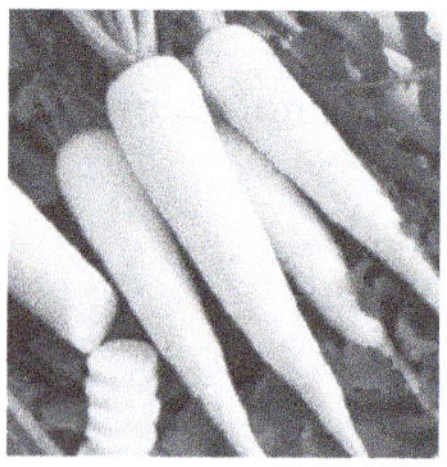

Radish

Cabbage

Brinjal

Based on the above information, answer the following questions

(i) Calculate the probability of a randomly chosen seed to germinate.

(ii) What is the probability that it is a cabbage seed, given that the chosen seed germinates?

38. A carpenter needs to make a wooden cuboidal box, closed from all sides, which has a square base and fixed volume. Since, he is short of the paint required to paint the box on completion, he wants the surface area to be minimum.

On the basis of the above information, answer the following questions

(i) Taking length = breadth = x m and height = y m, express the surface area (S) of the box in terms of x and its volume (V), which is constant.

(ii) Find $\frac{dS}{dx}$.

(iii) (a) Find a relation between x and y such that the surface area (S) is minimum.

Or

(iii) (b) If surface area (S) is constant, the volume $(V)=\frac{1}{4}(Sx-2x^3)$, x being the edge of base.

Show that volume (V) is maximum for $x=\sqrt{\frac{S}{6}}$.

Solutions

1. (d) Let $y = \cot^{-1}\left(-\frac{1}{\sqrt{3}}\right)$

$\Rightarrow \cot y = -\frac{1}{\sqrt{3}}$

$\Rightarrow \cot y = -\cot\frac{\pi}{3} = \cot\left(\pi - \frac{\pi}{3}\right)$ $[\because \cot(\pi - \theta) = -\cot\theta]$

$\Rightarrow \cot y = \cot\left(\frac{2\pi}{3}\right)$

$\therefore \quad y = \frac{2\pi}{3} \in (0, \pi)$

[$\because$ principal value branch of $\cot^{-1}$ is $(0, \pi)$]

2. (b) Given, $A = [a_{ij}]$ is a 3×3 diagonal matrix and $a_{11} = 1$, $a_{22} = 5$, $a_{33} = -2$.

If A is a diagonal matrix, then

$|A| = a_{11} \cdot a_{22} \cdot a_{33}$

$= 1 \times 5 \times (-2) = -10$

Hence, the value of $|A|$ is -10.

3. (b) If $A = kB$, then determinant of matrix A is equal to k raised to the power of n times the determinant of matrix B.

$\therefore \quad |A| = k^n |B|$

4. (c) Given, $f(x) = \begin{cases} \frac{\sin^2 ax}{x^2}, & x \neq 0 \\ 1, & x = 0 \end{cases}$

At $x = 0$,

$\lim_{x \to 0} f(x) = f(0)$

$\Rightarrow \quad \lim_{x \to 0} \frac{\sin^2 ax}{x^2} = 1$

$\Rightarrow a^2 \lim_{x \to 0}\left(\frac{\sin ax}{ax}\right)^2 = 1$

$\Rightarrow \quad a^2 = 1 \Rightarrow a = \pm 1$

Hence, the value of a is ± 1.

5. (c) We have, $\begin{vmatrix} 2x & 5 \\ 12 & x \end{vmatrix} = \begin{vmatrix} 6 & -5 \\ 4 & 3 \end{vmatrix}$

On expanding both the determinants, we get

$2x^2 - 60 = 18 + 20 \Rightarrow \quad 2x^2 = 98$

$\Rightarrow \quad x^2 = \frac{98}{2} = 49 \Rightarrow \quad x = \pm 7$

Hence, the value of x is ± 7.

6. (d) Given, $P(A \cup B) = 0.9$ and $P(A \cap B) = 0.4$

We know that

$P(A \cup B) = P(A) + P(B) - P(A \cap B)$

$\Rightarrow \quad 0.9 = P(A) + P(B) - 0.4$

$\Rightarrow \quad P(A) + P(B) = 0.9 + 0.4 = 1.3$

Now, $\quad P(\bar{A}) + P(\bar{B}) = 2 - [P(A) + P(B)]$

$\left[\because P(\bar{A}) = 1 - P(A) \text{ and } P(\bar{B}) = 1 - P(B)\right]$

$= 2 - 1.3 = 0.7$

7. (b) Given, $A = \begin{bmatrix} 5 & 0 & 0 \\ 0 & 5 & 0 \\ 0 & 0 & 5 \end{bmatrix}$

Now, $\quad A^2 = A \cdot A = \begin{bmatrix} 5 & 0 & 0 \\ 0 & 5 & 0 \\ 0 & 0 & 5 \end{bmatrix}\begin{bmatrix} 5 & 0 & 0 \\ 0 & 5 & 0 \\ 0 & 0 & 5 \end{bmatrix}$

$= \begin{bmatrix} 5 \times 5 & 0 & 0 \\ 0 & 5 \times 5 & 0 \\ 0 & 0 & 5 \times 5 \end{bmatrix} = \begin{bmatrix} 25 & 0 & 0 \\ 0 & 25 & 0 \\ 0 & 0 & 25 \end{bmatrix}$

and $\quad A^3 = A^2 \cdot A = \begin{bmatrix} 25 & 0 & 0 \\ 0 & 25 & 0 \\ 0 & 0 & 25 \end{bmatrix}\begin{bmatrix} 5 & 0 & 0 \\ 0 & 5 & 0 \\ 0 & 0 & 5 \end{bmatrix}$

$= \begin{bmatrix} 125 & 0 & 0 \\ 0 & 125 & 0 \\ 0 & 0 & 125 \end{bmatrix}$

8. (d) $\because (AB)' = B'A'$

$\therefore \quad (AB)' \neq A'B'$

9. (b) Given equation of curve is

$y = x|x| = \begin{cases} x^2, & \text{if } x \geq 0 \\ -x^2, & \text{if } x < 0 \end{cases}$

The graph of above curve between the ordinates $x = -2$ and $x = 2$ is given below.

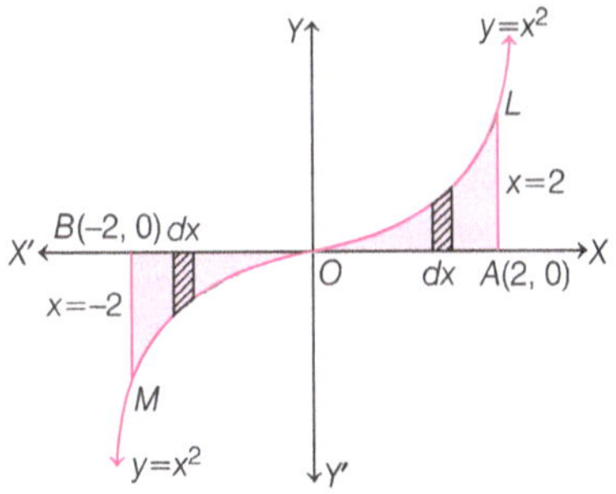

Clearly, shaded portion is the required region.

$\therefore$ Required area = Area of region $OBMO$ + Area of region $OALO$

$= \left|\int_{-2}^{0} x^2 dx\right| + \int_0^2 x^2 dx$

$= \left|\left[\frac{x^3}{3}\right]_{-2}^{0}\right| + \left[\frac{x^3}{3}\right]_0^2 = \left|\frac{-8}{3}\right| + \frac{8}{3} = \frac{8}{3} + \frac{8}{3} = \frac{16}{3}$ sq. units

10. (b) Given, $f(x) = \{[x], x \in R\}$

For continuous at $x = 2$,

LHL $= \lim_{x \to 2^-} f(x) = \lim_{h \to 0} f(2-h) = \lim_{h \to 0}[2-h] = 1$

RHL $= \lim_{x \to 2^+} f(x) = \lim_{h \to 0} f(2+h) = \lim_{h \to 0}[2+h] = 2$

$\because$ LHL $\neq$ RHL

$\therefore$ The function is not continuous at $x = 2$.

Since, the function is not continuous at $x = 2$, so it cannot be differentiable at $x = 2$.

11. (a) See example 5 on page no. 190.

12. (a) Let $I = \int_0^1 \frac{2x}{5x^2+1} dx = \frac{1}{5}\int_0^1 \frac{10x}{5x^2+1} dx$

Let $5x^2 + 1 = t \Rightarrow 10x\, dx = dt = \frac{1}{5}\int_0^1 \frac{dt}{t} = \frac{1}{5}[\log|t|]_0^1$

$= \frac{1}{5}[\log|5x^2+1|]_0^1$ $\quad [\because t = 5x^2+1]$

$= \frac{1}{5}(\log 6 - \log 1) = \frac{1}{5}\log 6$ $\quad [\because \log 1 = 0]$

13. (a) We have, $y = -x^3 + 3x^2 + 8x - 20$ ...(i)

On differentiating both sides w.r.t. x, we get

$\frac{dy}{dx} = -3x^2 + 6x + 8 =$ Slope of curve $= m$ (say) ...(ii)

Now, on differentiating Eq. (ii) w.r.t. x, we get

$$\frac{dm}{dx} = -6x + 6$$

Again, on differentiating w.r.t. x, we get

$$\frac{d^2m}{dx^2} = -6$$

For maximum, put $\frac{dm}{dx} = 0 \Rightarrow -6x + 6 = 0$

$\Rightarrow \quad 6x = 6 \Rightarrow x = 1$

Now, $\left[\frac{d^2m}{dx^2}\right]_{x=1} = -6 < 0$

So, the slope of the curve is maximum, when $x = 1$

On putting the value of x in Eq. (i), we get

$y = -1 + 3 + 8 - 20 = -10$

So, the slope of the curve is maximum at $(1, -10)$.

14. (b) Given differential equation is

$$\frac{dx}{dy} = \frac{-(1+\sin x)}{x + y\cos x} \Rightarrow \frac{dy}{dx} = \frac{x + y\cos x}{-(1+\sin x)}$$

$\Rightarrow \quad \frac{dy}{dx} = \frac{-x}{1+\sin x} - \frac{y\cos x}{1+\sin x}$

$\Rightarrow \quad \frac{dy}{dx} + \frac{\cos x}{1+\sin x} y = \frac{-x}{1+\sin x}$,

which is a linear differential equation of the form $\frac{dy}{dx} + Py = Q$.

Here, $P = \frac{\cos x}{1+\sin x}$ and $Q = \frac{-x}{1+\sin x}$

Now, integrating factor (IF) $= e^{\int P dx} = e^{\int \frac{\cos x}{1+\sin x} dx}$

Put $1 + \sin x = t \Rightarrow \cos\, dx = dt$

$\therefore$ IF $= e^{\int \frac{dt}{t}} = e^{\log|t|} = t = 1 + \sin x$ $\quad [\because t = 1 + \sin x]$

15. (b) See question 9 on page no. 369.

16. (c) Given differential equation is $\left[1 + \left(\frac{dy}{dx}\right)^2\right]^3 = \frac{d^2y}{dx^2}$.

Here, highest order derivative is $\frac{d^2y}{dx^2}$, whose highest power is 1.

So, order of differential equation is 2 and degree is 1.

Hence, the sum of order and degree $= 2 + 1 = 3$.

17. (c) Given, $(\vec{a} - \vec{b})\cdot(\vec{a} + \vec{b}) = 512$ and $|\vec{a}| = 3|\vec{b}|$

Now, $(\vec{a} - \vec{b})\cdot(\vec{a} + \vec{b}) = 512$

$\Rightarrow \quad |\vec{a}|^2 - |\vec{b}|^2 = 512$

$[\because (\vec{a} - \vec{b})\cdot(\vec{a} + \vec{b}) = |\vec{a}|^2 - |\vec{b}|^2]$

$\Rightarrow \quad (3|\vec{b}|)^2 - |\vec{b}|^2 = 512$ $\quad [\because |\vec{a}| = 3|\vec{b}|]$

$\Rightarrow \quad 9|\vec{b}|^2 - |\vec{b}|^2 = 512 \Rightarrow 8|\vec{b}|^2 = 512$

$\Rightarrow \quad |\vec{b}|^2 = \frac{512}{8} = 64 \Rightarrow |\vec{b}| = 8$

and $\quad |\vec{a}| = 3|\vec{b}| = 3 \times 8 = 24$

Hence, the respective values of $|\vec{a}|$ and $|\vec{b}|$ are 24 and 8.

18. (c) Given, the coordinates of A are $(-4, 5)$.

Let $\vec{a}$ be a position vector whose tip is the point $(2, -3)$.

$\therefore \quad \vec{a} = 2\hat{i} - 3\hat{j} = \overrightarrow{AB}$ and $\overrightarrow{OA} = -4\hat{i} + 5\hat{j}$

We know that

$$\overrightarrow{AB} = \overrightarrow{OB} - \overrightarrow{OA}$$

$\Rightarrow \quad 2\hat{i} - 3\hat{j} = \overrightarrow{OB} - (-4\hat{i} + 5\hat{j})$

$\Rightarrow \quad \overrightarrow{OB} = 2\hat{i} - 3\hat{j} - 4\hat{i} + 5\hat{j} = -2\hat{i} + 2\hat{j}$

Hence, the coordinates of point B are $(-2, 2)$.

19. (a) The corner points of feasible region are $A(0, 8)$, $B(2, 4)$ and $C(10, 0)$.

The values of Z at corner points are given below.

Corner points	$Z = 50x + 70y$
$A(0, 8)$	$Z = 50 \times 0 + 70 \times 8 = 560$
$B(2, 4)$	$Z = 50 \times 2 + 70 \times 4 = 380$ (Minimum)
$C(10, 0)$	$Z = 50 \times 10 + 70 \times 0 = 500$

As the feasible region is unbounded, therefore 380 may or may not be the minimum value of Z. From graph, we can see that the feasible region has no common point with $5x + 7y < 38$.

Therefore, the minimum value of Z is 380.

So, both A and R are true and R is the correct explanation of A.

20. (a) **Assertion** (A) Given, $A = \{x \in R : -1 \le x \le 1\}$

Let $y = -1$

$\because y \in A$, for the function to be onto, there must exist $x \in A$ such that $f(x) = y$

Then, $x^2 = -1$

$\because x^2$ is always positive for real.

$\therefore f$ is not onto.

So, A is true.

Reason (R) If $y = -1 \in A$, then x must satisfy $x^2 = -1$.

Thus, $x = \pm\sqrt{-1} = \pm i$

$\because i$ is not a real number, $x \notin A$.

So, R is true.

21. We have, $f(x) = \sin^{-1}(x^2 - 3)$

$\because$ Domain of $\sin^{-1} x$ is $[-1, 1]$.

$$\therefore \quad -1 \le x^2 - 3 \le 1$$

$$\Rightarrow \quad -1 + 3 \le x^2 - 3 + 3 \le 1 + 3$$

$$\Rightarrow \quad 2 \le x^2 \le 4$$

$$\sqrt{2} \le |x| \le 2$$

$\therefore$ Domain $= [\sqrt{2}, 2] \cup [-2, -\sqrt{2}]$

22. Given, the radii of a metallic hollow sphere are 2 cm and 4 cm.

Let R be the outer radius and r be the inner radius of the hollow sphere.

$\therefore R = 4$ cm, $r = 2$ cm and $\dfrac{dr}{dt} = 2$ cm/s

Let V be the volume of a metallic hollow sphere.

$$\therefore V = \frac{4}{3}\pi R^3 - \frac{4}{3}\pi r^3$$

$\because$ The volume of a metallic hollow sphere is constant.

$$\therefore \quad \frac{dV}{dt} = 0 \Rightarrow 4\pi R^2 \frac{dR}{dt} - 4\pi r^2 \frac{dr}{dt} = 0$$

$$\Rightarrow \quad R^2 \frac{dR}{dt} - r^2 \frac{dr}{dt} = 0 \quad \text{[dividing by } 4\pi \text{ both sides]}$$

$$\Rightarrow (4)^2 \frac{dR}{dt} - (2)^2 (2) = 0$$

$$\left[\because R = 4 \text{ cm}, r = 2 \text{ cm and } \frac{dr}{dt} = 2 \text{ cm/s}\right]$$

$$\Rightarrow \quad 16\frac{dR}{dt} - 4 \times 2 = 0$$

$$\therefore \quad \frac{dR}{dt} = \frac{8}{16} = \frac{1}{2} = 0.5 \text{ cm/s.}$$

23. Given, the coordinates of points A and B are $(4, 1, -2)$ and $(6, 2, -3)$, respectively.

We know that trisection points divide the line segment in the ratio 1 : 2 and 2 : 1.

Let position vectors of points A and B are respectively $\overrightarrow{OA} = 4\hat{i} + \hat{j} - 2\hat{k}$ and $\overrightarrow{OB} = 6\hat{i} + 2\hat{j} - 3\hat{k}$.

Let the points P and Q divide the line AB in the ratio 1 : 2 and 2 : 1, respectively.

By section formula,

$$\overrightarrow{OP} = \frac{m\overrightarrow{OB} + n\overrightarrow{OA}}{m+n}$$

$$= \frac{1(6\hat{i} + 2\hat{j} - 3\hat{k}) + 2(4\hat{i} + \hat{j} - 2\hat{k})}{1+2} \quad [\because m = 1, n = 2]$$

$$= \frac{6\hat{i} + 2\hat{j} - 3\hat{k} + 8\hat{i} + 2\hat{j} - 4\hat{k}}{3}$$

$$= \frac{14\hat{i} + 4\hat{j} - 7\hat{k}}{3} = \frac{14}{3}\hat{i} + \frac{4}{3}\hat{j} - \frac{7}{3}\hat{k}$$

Hence, the coordinates of P are $\left(\frac{14}{3}, \frac{4}{3}, \frac{-7}{3}\right)$.

$$\text{Now, } \overrightarrow{OQ} = \frac{2(6\hat{i} + 2\hat{j} - 3\hat{k}) + 1(4\hat{i} + \hat{j} - 2\hat{k})}{2+1}$$

$$= \frac{12\hat{i} + 4\hat{j} - 6\hat{k} + 4\hat{i} + \hat{j} - 2\hat{k}}{3}$$

$$= \frac{16\hat{i} + 5\hat{j} - 8\hat{k}}{3} = \frac{16}{3}\hat{i} + \frac{5}{3}\hat{j} - \frac{8}{3}\hat{k}$$

Hence, the coordinates of Q are $\left(\frac{16}{3}, \frac{5}{3}, \frac{-8}{3}\right)$.

So, the coordinates of the points where the man hangs the lanterns are $\left(\frac{14}{3}, \frac{4}{3}, \frac{-7}{3}\right)$ and $\left(\frac{16}{3}, \frac{5}{3}, \frac{-8}{3}\right)$.

24. (a) Let $y = \dfrac{\sin x}{\sqrt{\cos x}}$

On differentiating both sides w.r.t. x, we get

$$\frac{dy}{dx} = \frac{(\sqrt{\cos x}) \cdot \frac{d}{dx}(\sin x) - \sin x \frac{d}{dx}(\sqrt{\cos x})}{(\sqrt{\cos x})^2}$$

[by quotient rule]

$$= \frac{\sqrt{\cos x} \cdot \cos x - \sin x \cdot \frac{1}{2}(\cos x)^{-1/2}(-\sin x)}{\cos x}$$

$$= \frac{\cos x \cdot \sqrt{\cos x} + \sin^2 x \cdot \frac{1}{2\sqrt{\cos x}}}{\cos x}$$

$$= \frac{2\sqrt{\cos x}\,(\cos x)^{3/2} + \sin^2 x}{2\sqrt{\cos x} \cdot \cos x} = \frac{2\cos^2 x + \sin^2 x}{2(\cos x)^{3/2}}$$

Or

(b) We have, $y = 5\cos x - 3\sin x$

On differentiating both sides w.r.t. x, we get

$$\frac{dy}{dx} = -5\sin x - 3\cos x$$

Again, on differentiating both sides w.r.t. x, we get

$$\frac{d^2y}{dx^2} = -5\cos x + 3\sin x$$
$$= -(5\cos x - 3\sin x)$$
$$= -y$$

$$\therefore \frac{d^2y}{dx^2} + y = 0$$ **Hence proved.**

25. (a) Let $\vec{a} = 3\hat{i} - 2\hat{j} + \hat{k}$

and $\vec{b} = 4\hat{i} + 3\hat{j} - 2\hat{k}$

Let $\vec{c}$ be a vector which is perpendicular to both vectors $\vec{a}$ and $\vec{b}$.

Now, we have, $\vec{c} = \vec{a} \times \vec{b}$

$$\therefore \quad \vec{a} \times \vec{b} = \begin{vmatrix} \hat{i} & \hat{j} & \hat{k} \\ 3 & -2 & 1 \\ 4 & 3 & -2 \end{vmatrix}$$
$$= \hat{i} + 10\hat{j} + 17\hat{k}$$

Now, $|\vec{a} \times \vec{b}| = \sqrt{1^2 + (10)^2 + (17)^2}$
$$= \sqrt{1 + 100 + 289} = \sqrt{390}$$

Unit vector along $\vec{c} = \frac{1}{\sqrt{390}}(\hat{i} + 10\hat{j} + 17\hat{k})$

$\therefore$ Required vector of magnitude 5 is

$$\frac{5}{\sqrt{390}}(\hat{i} + 10\hat{j} + 17\hat{k}).$$

Or

(b) See example 6 on page no. 305.

26. Given, $f(x) = \sin 3x - \cos 3x, 0 < x < \frac{\pi}{2}$

On differentiating both sides w.r.t. x, we get

$f'(x) = 3\cos 3x + 3\sin 3x$

On putting $f'(x) = 0$, we get

$$\sin 3x = -\cos 3x$$
$$\Rightarrow \tan 3x = -1$$
$$\Rightarrow \tan 3x = -\tan\frac{\pi}{4}$$
$$\Rightarrow \tan 3x = \tan\left(\pi - \frac{\pi}{4}\right)$$
$$\Rightarrow 3x = \frac{3\pi}{4}$$
$$\Rightarrow x = \frac{\pi}{4} \in \left(0, \frac{\pi}{2}\right)$$

Now, $\frac{\pi}{4}$ divides the interval $\left(0, \frac{\pi}{2}\right)$ into two sub intervals $\left(0, \frac{\pi}{4}\right)$ and $\left(\frac{\pi}{4}, \frac{\pi}{2}\right)$.

Interval	Test value	$f'(x) = 3(\cos 3x + \sin 3x)$	sign of $f'(x)$
$0 < x < \frac{\pi}{4}$	At $x = \frac{\pi}{6}$	$3\left(\cos\frac{\pi}{2} + \sin\frac{\pi}{2}\right) = 3(0+1) = 3$	+ve
$\frac{\pi}{4} < x < \frac{\pi}{2}$	At $x = \frac{\pi}{3}$	$3(\cos\pi + \sin\pi) = 3(-1+0) = -3$	−ve

Here, we see that $f'(x) > 0$, for $0 < x < \frac{\pi}{4}$

So, $f(x)$ is strictly increasing in $\left(0, \frac{\pi}{4}\right)$.

27. (a) See quick test-2, question 3 on page 302.

Or

(b) Given, $|\vec{a}| = |\vec{b}| = 1$

We know that $\vec{x} \cdot \vec{x} = |\vec{x}|^2$

$$\therefore |\vec{a} - \vec{b}|^2 = (\vec{a} - \vec{b}) \cdot (\vec{a} - \vec{b})$$
$$= \vec{a} \cdot \vec{a} - \vec{a} \cdot \vec{b} - \vec{b} \cdot \vec{a} + \vec{b} \cdot \vec{b}$$
$$= |\vec{a}|^2 - 2\vec{a} \cdot \vec{b} + |\vec{b}|^2 \quad [\because \vec{a} \cdot \vec{b} = \vec{b} \cdot \vec{a}]$$
$$= |\vec{a}|^2 - 2|\vec{a}||\vec{b}|\cos\theta + |\vec{b}|^2 \quad \left[\because \cos\theta = \frac{\vec{a} \cdot \vec{b}}{|\vec{a}||\vec{b}|}\right]$$
$$= 1 - 2 \cdot 1 \cdot 1\cos\theta + 1 \quad [\text{given, } |\vec{a}| = |\vec{b}| = 1]$$
$$= 2 - 2\cos\theta = 2(1 - \cos\theta)$$
$$= 2\left[2\sin^2\left(\frac{\theta}{2}\right)\right] \quad [\because \cos 2x = 1 - 2\sin^2 x]$$

$$\Rightarrow |\vec{a} - \vec{b}|^2 = 4\sin^2\frac{\theta}{2} \Rightarrow \sin^2\frac{\theta}{2} = \frac{1}{4}|\vec{a} - \vec{b}|^2$$

$$\therefore \quad \sin\frac{\theta}{2} = \frac{1}{2}|\vec{a} - \vec{b}|$$ **Hence proved.**

28. Given differential equation is

$$x\cos\left(\frac{y}{x}\right)\frac{dy}{dx} = y\cos\left(\frac{y}{x}\right) + x$$

$$\Rightarrow \frac{dy}{dx} = \frac{y\cos\left(\frac{y}{x}\right) + x}{x\cos\left(\frac{y}{x}\right)} \quad \text{...(i)}$$

which is a homogeneous differential equation.

On putting $y = vx$ and $\frac{dy}{dx} = v + x\frac{dv}{dx}$ in Eq. (i), we get

$$v + x\frac{dv}{dx} = \frac{vx\cos\left(\frac{vx}{x}\right) + x}{x\cos\left(\frac{vx}{x}\right)}$$

$$\Rightarrow \quad v + x\frac{dv}{dx} = \frac{v\cos v + 1}{\cos v}$$

$$\Rightarrow \quad x\frac{dv}{dx} = \frac{v\cos v + 1}{\cos v} - v = \frac{v\cos v + 1 - v\cos v}{\cos v}$$

$$\Rightarrow \quad x\frac{dv}{dx} = \frac{1}{\cos v}$$

$$\Rightarrow \quad \cos v\, dv = \frac{dx}{x}$$

On integrating both sides, we get

$$\int \cos v\, dv = \int \frac{1}{x} dx$$

$$\Rightarrow \quad \sin v = \log x + C$$

$$\Rightarrow \quad \sin\left(\frac{y}{x}\right) = \log x + C \qquad \left[\because v = \frac{y}{x}\right]$$

which is the required solution.

29. (a) Given, the probability of buying a colouring book, $P(A) = 0.7$, the probability of buying a box of colours, $P(B) = 0.2$ and the probability of buying a colouring book given a box of colours is bought,

$$P\left(\frac{A}{B}\right) = 0.3$$

(i) Now, by conditional probability,

$$P\left(\frac{A}{B}\right) = \frac{P(A \cap B)}{P(B)}$$

$$\Rightarrow \quad 0.3 = \frac{P(A \cap B)}{0.2}$$

$$\Rightarrow P(A \cap B) = 0.3 \times 0.2 = 0.06$$

(ii) Now, $P\left(\frac{B}{A}\right) = \frac{P(B \cap A)}{P(A)} = \frac{0.06}{0.7} = \frac{3}{35}$

Hence, the probability of buying a box of colours given a colouring book is bought is $\frac{3}{35}$.

Or

(b) This question is out of Syllabus.

30. (a) Let $I = \int \frac{2x}{(x^2+3)(x^2-5)} dx$

On putting $x^2 = t$ and $2xdx = dt$, we get

$$I = \int \frac{dt}{(t+3)(t-5)}$$

Let $\frac{1}{(t+3)(t-5)} = \frac{A}{t+3} + \frac{B}{t-5}$ ...(i)

$$\Rightarrow \quad 1 = A(t-5) + B(t+3)$$

$$\Rightarrow \quad 1 = (A+B)t + (-5A+3B) \qquad \text{...(ii)}$$

On comparing the coefficients of t and constant term both sides of Eq. (ii), we get

$$A + B = 0, \; -5A + 3B = 1$$

On solving these equations, we get

$$A = -\frac{1}{8} \text{ and } B = \frac{1}{8}$$

On substituting the values of A and B in Eq. (i), we get

$$\frac{1}{(t+3)(t-5)} = -\frac{1}{8(t+3)} + \frac{1}{8(t-5)}$$

$$\therefore \; I = \int \frac{1}{(t+3)(t-5)} dt = \int \left(-\frac{1}{8(t+3)} + \frac{1}{8(t-5)}\right) dt$$

$$= -\frac{1}{8}\log(t+3) + \frac{1}{8}\log(t-5) + C$$

$$= \frac{1}{8}\log\left|\frac{t-5}{t+3}\right| + C = \frac{1}{8}\log\left|\frac{x^2-5}{x^2+3}\right| + C$$

Or

(b) Let $I = \int_1^4 (|x-2| + |x-4|)\, dx$

Let $f(x) = |x-2| + |x-4|$

$$= \begin{cases} -(x-2)-(x-4) & \text{if } 1 \le x \le 2 \\ (x-2)-(x-4) & \text{if } 2 \le x \le 4 \end{cases}$$

$$= \begin{cases} -2x+6 & \text{if } 1 \le x \le 2 \\ 2 & \text{if } 2 \le x \le 4 \end{cases}$$

Now, $I = \int_1^4 f(x)\, dx = \int_1^2 (-2x+6)\, dx + \int_2^4 2\, dx$

$$= [-x^2 + 6x]_1^2 + [2x]_2^4$$

$$= -4 + 12 - (-1+6) + 8 - 4 = 8 - 5 + 4 = 7$$

31. See Example 1 on page no. 360.

32. Given, $y = 1 + |x+1|$

$$= \begin{cases} 1 - (x+1), & x < -1 \\ 1 + (x+1), & x \ge 1 \end{cases}$$

$$= \begin{cases} -x, & x < -1 \\ x+2, & x \ge 1 \end{cases}$$

The area of the region bounded by $y = 1 + |x+1|$, $x = -2$, $x = 2$ and $y = 0$ is given by

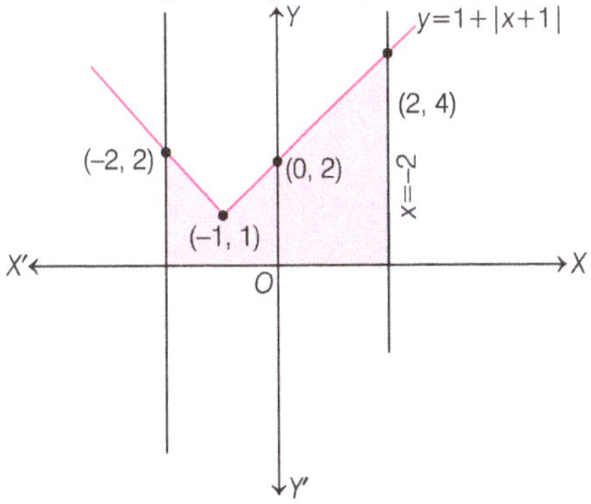

Required area $= \int_{-2}^{-1} - x\,dx + \int_{-1}^{2} (x+2)\,dx$

$$= -\left[\frac{x^2}{2}\right]_{-2}^{-1} + \left[\frac{x^2}{2} + 2x\right]_{-1}^{2}$$

$$= -\frac{1}{2}[1-4] + \frac{1}{2}[4+8-(1-4)]$$

$$= \frac{3}{2} + \frac{1}{2}[12+3] = \frac{3}{2} + \frac{15}{2} = \frac{18}{2} = 9 \text{ sq units}$$

Hence, the required area is 9 sq units.

33. Let x, y and z represent the speeds of the first, second and third runners, respectively.

According to the question, we have the following equations

$x + y + z = 6$, $x + 0y + 2z = 7$, $3x + y + z = 12$

Now, represent the system of equations in matrix form as $AX = B$.

Here, $A = \begin{bmatrix} 1 & 1 & 1 \\ 1 & 0 & 2 \\ 3 & 1 & 1 \end{bmatrix}$, $X = \begin{bmatrix} x \\ y \\ z \end{bmatrix}$ and $B = \begin{bmatrix} 6 \\ 7 \\ 12 \end{bmatrix}$

Now, $|A| = 1\begin{vmatrix} 0 & 2 \\ 1 & 1 \end{vmatrix} - 1\begin{vmatrix} 1 & 2 \\ 3 & 1 \end{vmatrix} + 1\begin{vmatrix} 1 & 0 \\ 3 & 1 \end{vmatrix}$

$$= 1(0-2) - 1(1-6) + 1(1-0)$$

$$= -2 + 5 + 1 = 4$$

Let C_{ij} be the cofactor of the element a_{ij} of $|A|$.

Now, cofactors of $|A|$ are

$$C_{11} = (-1)^{1+1}\begin{vmatrix} 0 & 2 \\ 1 & 1 \end{vmatrix} = 1(0-2) = -2$$

$$C_{12} = (-1)^{1+2}\begin{vmatrix} 1 & 2 \\ 3 & 1 \end{vmatrix} = -1(1-6) = 5$$

$$C_{13} = (-1)^{1+3}\begin{vmatrix} 1 & 0 \\ 3 & 1 \end{vmatrix} = 1(1-0) = 1$$

$$C_{21} = (-1)^{2+1}\begin{vmatrix} 1 & 1 \\ 1 & 1 \end{vmatrix} = -1(1-1) = 0$$

$$C_{22} = (-1)^{2+2}\begin{vmatrix} 1 & 1 \\ 3 & 1 \end{vmatrix} = 1(1-3) = -2$$

$$C_{23} = (-1)^{2+3}\begin{vmatrix} 1 & 1 \\ 3 & 1 \end{vmatrix} = -1(1-3) = 2$$

$$C_{31} = (-1)^{3+1}\begin{vmatrix} 1 & 1 \\ 0 & 2 \end{vmatrix} = 1(2-0) = 2$$

$$C_{32} = (-1)^{3+2}\begin{vmatrix} 1 & 1 \\ 1 & 2 \end{vmatrix} = -1(2-1) = -1$$

$$C_{33} = (-1)^{3+3}\begin{vmatrix} 1 & 1 \\ 1 & 0 \end{vmatrix} = 1(0-1) = -1$$

Now, the adjoint of the matrix A is given by

$$\text{adj}A = \begin{bmatrix} -2 & 5 & 1 \\ 0 & -2 & 2 \\ 2 & -1 & -1 \end{bmatrix}^T = \begin{bmatrix} -2 & 0 & 2 \\ 5 & -2 & -1 \\ 1 & 2 & -1 \end{bmatrix}$$

Now, $A^{-1} = \dfrac{1}{|A|}\cdot\text{adj}(A)$

$$= \frac{1}{4}\begin{bmatrix} -2 & 0 & 2 \\ 5 & -2 & -1 \\ 1 & 2 & -1 \end{bmatrix} = \begin{bmatrix} -\frac{1}{2} & 0 & \frac{1}{2} \\ \frac{5}{4} & -\frac{1}{2} & -\frac{1}{4} \\ \frac{1}{4} & \frac{1}{2} & -\frac{1}{4} \end{bmatrix}$$

Now, $X = A^{-1}B$

$$\Rightarrow \quad X = \begin{bmatrix} -\frac{1}{2} & 0 & \frac{1}{2} \\ \frac{5}{4} & -\frac{1}{2} & -\frac{1}{4} \\ \frac{1}{4} & \frac{1}{2} & -\frac{1}{4} \end{bmatrix}\begin{bmatrix} 6 \\ 7 \\ 12 \end{bmatrix} = \begin{bmatrix} -3+0+6 \\ \frac{15}{2} - \frac{7}{2} - 3 \\ \frac{3}{2} + \frac{7}{2} - 3 \end{bmatrix}$$

$$\Rightarrow \begin{bmatrix} x \\ y \\ z \end{bmatrix} = \begin{bmatrix} 3 \\ 1 \\ 2 \end{bmatrix}$$

On comparing both sides, we get

$x = 3$, $y = 1$ and $z = 2$

Hence, the speeds of the runners are 3 km/h, 1 km/h and 2 km/h, respectively.

34. (a) Let $y = a^{t+\frac{1}{t}}$ and $x = \left(t + \frac{1}{t}\right)^a$

Now, $y = a^{t+\frac{1}{t}}$

On taking log both sides, we get

$$\log y = \log a^{t+\frac{1}{t}} = \left(t + \frac{1}{t}\right)\log a$$

On differentiating both sides w.r.t. t, we get

$$\frac{1}{y}\cdot\frac{dy}{dt} = \left(1 - \frac{1}{t^2}\right)\log a$$

$$\Rightarrow \quad \frac{dy}{dt} = y\left[\left(1 - \frac{1}{t^2}\right)\log a\right] = a^{\left(t+\frac{1}{t}\right)}\left[\left(1 - \frac{1}{t^2}\right)\log a\right]$$

...(i) $\left[\because y = a^{t+\frac{1}{t}}\right]$

Now, $x = \left(t + \frac{1}{t}\right)^a$

On taking log both sides, we get

$$\log x = \log\left(t + \frac{1}{t}\right)^a = a\log\left(t + \frac{1}{t}\right)$$

On differentiating both sides w.r.t. t, we get

$$\frac{1}{x}\cdot\frac{dx}{dt} = a\cdot\frac{1}{\left(t+\frac{1}{t}\right)}\cdot\left(1-\frac{1}{t^2}\right)$$

$$\Rightarrow \frac{dx}{dt} = x\left[a\cdot\frac{1}{\left(t+\frac{1}{t}\right)}\cdot\left(1-\frac{1}{t^2}\right)\right]$$

$$= \left(t+\frac{1}{t}\right)^a\left[a\cdot\frac{1}{\left(t+\frac{1}{t}\right)}\cdot\left(1-\frac{1}{t^2}\right)\right] \quad \text{...(ii)}$$

$$\left[\because x = \left(t+\frac{1}{t}\right)^a\right]$$

Now, $$\frac{dy}{dx} = \frac{a^{\left(t+\frac{1}{t}\right)} \times \left(1-\frac{1}{t^2}\right)\log a}{\left(t+\frac{1}{t}\right)^a \times a\cdot\frac{1}{\left(t+\frac{1}{t}\right)} \times \left(1-\frac{1}{t^2}\right)}$$

[from Eqs. (i) and (ii)]

$$= \frac{a^{\left(t+\frac{1}{t}\right)}\log a}{a\left(t+\frac{1}{t}\right)^{a-1}}$$

Or

(b) We have, $y^x + x^y + x^x = a^b$

On taking log both sides, we get

$\log y^x + \log x^y + \log x^x = \log a^b$

$\Rightarrow x\log y + y\log x + x\log x = b\log a$

On differentiating both sides w.r.t. x, we get

$$x\cdot\frac{1}{y}\frac{dy}{dx} + \log y + y\cdot\frac{1}{x} + \log x\cdot\frac{dy}{dx} + x\cdot\frac{1}{x} + \log x = 0$$

$$\Rightarrow \frac{x}{y}\frac{dy}{dx} + \log y + \frac{y}{x} + \log x\cdot\frac{dy}{dx} + 1 + \log x = 0$$

$$\Rightarrow \frac{dy}{dx}\left[\frac{x}{y} + \log x\right] = -1 - \log x - \log y - \frac{y}{x}$$

$$\Rightarrow \frac{dy}{dx} = \frac{-\left[1+\frac{y}{x}+\log xy\right]}{\left[\frac{x}{y}+\log x\right]}$$

35. (a) Given equation of the line is

$$\frac{x+2}{5} = \frac{y+1}{2} = \frac{-z+4}{-3}$$

Let $$\frac{x+2}{5} = \frac{y+1}{2} = \frac{-z+4}{-3} = \lambda$$

$$\Rightarrow \frac{x+2}{5} = \lambda,\ \frac{y+1}{2} = \lambda \text{ and } \frac{-z+4}{-3} = \lambda$$

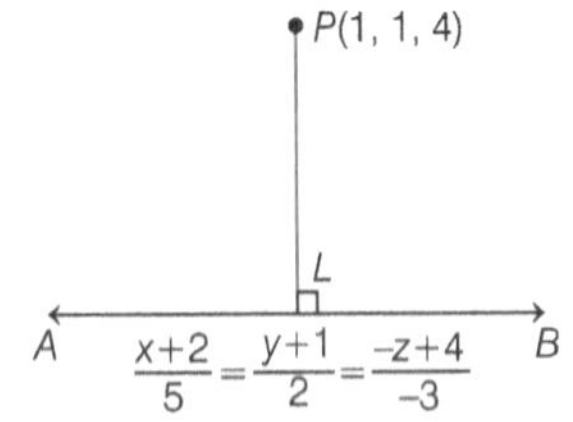

$\Rightarrow x = 5\lambda - 2,\ y = 2\lambda - 1$ and $z = 3\lambda + 4$

$\therefore$ Coordinates of point L are $(5\lambda - 2, 2\lambda - 1, 3\lambda + 4)$.

Now, DR's of line PL

$= (5\lambda - 2 - 1, 2\lambda - 1 - 1, 3\lambda + 4 - 4)$

$= (5\lambda - 3, 2\lambda - 2, 3\lambda)$

DR's of line AB are (5, 2, 3).

$\because \quad PL \perp AB$

$\therefore$ The condition for perpendicular lines is

$$a_1a_2 + b_1b_2 + c_1c_2 = 0 \quad \text{...(i)}$$

where, $a_1 = 5\lambda - 3,\ b_1 = 2\lambda - 2,\ c_1 = 3\lambda$

and $\quad a_2 = 5,\ b_2 = 2,\ c_2 = 3$

From Eq. (i), we get

$$5(5\lambda - 3) + 2(2\lambda - 2) + 3(3\lambda) = 0$$

$$\Rightarrow 25\lambda - 15 + 4\lambda - 4 + 9\lambda = 0$$

$$\Rightarrow 38\lambda - 19 = 0$$

$$\Rightarrow \lambda = \frac{19}{38} = \frac{1}{2}$$

$\therefore$ Foot of perpendicular L

$$= (5\lambda - 3, 2\lambda - 2, 3\lambda) = \left(-\frac{1}{2}, -1, \frac{3}{2}\right)$$

Or

(b) Given equation of the line is

$$\frac{x-1}{3} = \frac{y+1}{2} = \frac{z-4}{3}$$

Let $$\frac{x-1}{3} = \frac{y+1}{2} = \frac{z-4}{3} = \lambda \text{ (say)}$$

$$\Rightarrow \frac{x-1}{3} = \lambda,\ \frac{y+1}{2} = \lambda \text{ and } \frac{z-4}{3} = \lambda$$

$$\Rightarrow \quad x = 3\lambda + 1,\ y = 2\lambda - 1 \text{ and } z = 3\lambda + 4 \quad \text{...(i)}$$

Now, we have the distance between the point $(-1, -1, 2)$ and the point (x, y, z) on the line is $2\sqrt{2}$ units.

$$\therefore\ 2\sqrt{2} = \sqrt{(x+1)^2 + (y+1)^2 + (z-2)^2}$$

On squaring both sides, we get

$$(x+1)^2 + (y+1)^2 + (z-2)^2 = (2\sqrt{2})^2 = 8 \quad \text{...(ii)}$$

On putting the values of x, y and z in Eq. (ii), we get

$$(3\lambda+1+1)^2+(2\lambda-1+1)^2+(3\lambda+4-2)^2=8$$

$$\Rightarrow \quad (3\lambda+2)^2+(2\lambda)^2+(3\lambda+2)^2=8$$

$$\Rightarrow \quad 2[9\lambda^2+4+12\lambda]+4\lambda^2=8$$

$$\Rightarrow \quad 18\lambda^2+8+24\lambda+4\lambda^2=8$$

$$\Rightarrow \quad 22\lambda^2+24\lambda=0$$

$$\Rightarrow \quad 2\lambda(11\lambda+12)=0$$

$$\Rightarrow 2\lambda=0 \text{ or } 11\lambda+12=0$$

$$\Rightarrow \quad \lambda=0 \text{ or } \lambda=-\frac{12}{11}$$

On putting $\lambda=0$ in Eq. (i), we get

$x=3\times 0+1$, $y=2\times 0-1$ and $z=3\times 0+4$

$\Rightarrow x=1$, $y=-1$ and $z=4$

On putting $\lambda=-\frac{12}{11}$ in Eq. (i), we get

$$x=3\times\left(\frac{-12}{11}\right)+1,\ y=2\times\left(\frac{-12}{11}\right)-1$$

and $z=3\times\left(\frac{-12}{11}\right)+4$

$$\Rightarrow \quad x=\frac{-25}{11},\ y=\frac{-35}{11} \text{ and } z=\frac{8}{11}$$

Hence, the points on the line at a distance of $2\sqrt{2}$ from the point $(-1,-1,2)$ are $(1,-1,4)$ and $\left(\frac{-25}{11},\frac{-35}{11},\frac{8}{11}\right)$.

36. Given, $f(x)=$ Roll number of student x.

(i) **For one-one**

$f(x_1)=$ Roll number of student x_1

and $f(x_2)=$ Roll number of student x_2

such that $f(x_1)=f(x_2)$

$\because$ No two students of a class can have same roll number.

$\therefore \quad x_1=x_2$

So, f is one-one.

For onto

$$f:A\to N$$

$f(x)=$ Roll number of student x.

$\because$ There are 30 students.

$\therefore$ Roll number of students are from 1-30.

So, 31 is not a roll number of any student of the class.

Thus, there is no pre-image of 31.

So, f is not onto.

Hence, f is not bijective function.

(ii) A function $f:A\to B$ is said to be bijective function, if f is both one-one and onto.

(iii) (a) Given, $R=\{(x,y):x,y$ are roll numbers of students such that $y=3x\}$

$\because$ x and y are roll numbers, they must be positive integers.

If $x=1$, then $y=3(1)=3$, so $(1,3)\in R$

If $x=2$, then $y=3(2)=6$, so $(2,6)\in R$

If $x=3$, then $y=3(3)=9$, so $(3,9)\in R$

So, the elements of $R=\{(1,3),(2,6),(3,9),\ldots\}$

Reflexive

For any student x, (x,x) must be in R.

However, $(1,1),(2,2),\ldots.(30,30)$ are not in R, since $y=3x$ is not satisfied for $x=y$.

So, R is not reflexive.

Symmetric

For R to be symmetric, if $(x,y)\in R$, then (y,x) must also be in R.

Here, $(1,3)\in R$ but $(3,1)\notin R$

So, R is not symmetric.

Transitive

Here, $(1,3)\in R$ and $(3,9)\in R$ but $(1,9)\notin R$.

So, R is not transitive.

Hence, R is not reflexive, symmetric, or transitive.

Or

(iii) (b) Given, $R=\{(x,y):x,y$ are roll numbers of students such that $y=x^3\}$

$\because$ x and y are roll numbers, they must be positive integers.

If $x=1$ then $y=(1)^3=1$, so $(1,1)\in R$

If $x=2$, then $y=(2)^3=8$, so $(1,8)\in R$

If $x=3$, then $y=(3)^3=27$, so $(1,27)\in R$

So, the elements of $R=\{(1,1),(2,8),(3,27)\ldots\}$

For each x in the domain (roll numbers of students), there is a unique y such that $y=x^3$. Since, each roll number x will produce only one value for y, so R is a function.

37. Let Event $A=$ Number of brinjal seeds

Event $B=$ Number of cabbage seeds

Event $C=$ Number of radish seeds

The total number of seeds $=10+12+8=30$

Here, Probability of brinjal seeds germinating $P(A)=0.25$

Probability of cabbage seed germinating $P(B)=0.35$

Probability of radish seed germinating $P(C)=0.40$

(i) $\therefore$ Probability of a randomly chosen seed germinating

$$=\frac{10}{30}\times P(A)+\frac{12}{30}\times P(B)+\frac{8}{30}\times P(C)$$

$$=\frac{10}{30}\times 0.25+\frac{12}{30}\times 0.35+\frac{8}{30}\times 0.40$$

$$=0.083+0.14+0.1067=0.33$$

(ii) Let E be the event of seed germinates

$\therefore \quad P(B \cap E) = \frac{12}{30} \times 0.35 = 0.14$

Now, $P(B/E) = \frac{P(B \cap E)}{P(E)} = \frac{0.14}{0.33}$ [from (i) part]

$= 0.42$

Hence, the probability that it is a cabbage seed, given that the chosen seed germinates is 0.42 or 42.42%.

38. (i) Given, length = breadth = x m and height = y m

$\because$ Box is a shape of cuboid.

$\therefore$ The surface area of cuboidal box,

$$S = 2[x \times x + x \times y + y \times x]$$

$[\because S = 2(lb + bh + hl)]$

$$= 2[x^2 + 2xy]$$

$$\Rightarrow \quad S = 2x^2 + 4xy$$

and volume, $V = x \times x \times y = x^2 y$ $[\because V = lbh]$

(ii) $\because$ Volume $= x^2 y$ = constant = C (say)

$$\therefore \quad S = 2x^2 + 4xy$$

$$= 2x^2 + 4x \times \frac{C}{x^2} \qquad [\because C = x^2 y]$$

$$= 2x^2 + \frac{4C}{x}$$

On differentiating both sides w.r.t. x, we get

$$\frac{dS}{dx} = 4x + \left(-\frac{4C}{x^2}\right)$$

(iii) (a) For minimum, put $\frac{dS}{dx} = 0$

$$\therefore \quad 4x - \frac{4C}{x^2} = 0$$

$$\Rightarrow \quad -\frac{4C}{x^2} = -4x$$

$$\Rightarrow \quad C = x^3$$

$$\Rightarrow \quad x^2 y = x^3 \qquad [\because C = x^2 y]$$

$$\Rightarrow \quad x = y$$

Hence, the surface area is minimum, when $x = y$.

Or

(iii) (b) Given, volume $(V) = \frac{1}{4}(Sx - 2x^3)$

On differentiating both sides w.r.t. x, we get

$$\frac{dV}{dx} = \frac{1}{4}(S - 6x^2) \qquad [\because S \text{ is constant}]$$

Again, differentiating both sides w.r.t. x, we get

$$\frac{d^2V}{dx^2} = \frac{1}{4}(0 - 12x) = -3x \qquad \text{...(i)}$$

For maximum, put $\frac{dV}{dx} = 0$

$$\therefore \quad \frac{1}{4}(S - 6x^2) = 0$$

$$\Rightarrow \quad S - 6x^2 = 0$$

$$\Rightarrow \quad x^2 = \frac{S}{6} \Rightarrow x = \sqrt{\frac{S}{6}}$$

On putting the value of x in Eq. (i), we get

$$\left(\frac{d^2V}{dx^2}\right)_{x=\sqrt{\frac{S}{6}}} = -3 \times \sqrt{\frac{S}{6}}$$

$$\because \quad \frac{d^2V}{dx^2} < 0 \text{ at } x = \sqrt{\frac{S}{6}}$$

$\therefore$ The volume (V) is maximum for $x = \sqrt{\frac{S}{6}}$.